Women's Studies

A BIBLIOGRAPHY OF
DISSERTATIONS 1870-1982

Women's Studies

A BIBLIOGRAPHY OF DISSERTATIONS 1870-1982

Compiled by
V. F. Gilbert and D. S. Tatla

Blackwell Reference

First published 1985

Basil Blackwell Publisher Limited
108 Cowley Road, Oxford OX4 1JF, England

Basil Blackwell Inc.
432 Park Avenue South, Suite 1505
New York, NY 10016, USA

British Library Cataloguing in Publication Data

Gilbert, Victor F.
Women's studies: a bibliography of dissertations
1870–1982.—(Blackwell Reference)
1. Women—Bibliography
I. Title II. Tatla, Darshan Singh
016.3054 Z7961

ISBN 0–631–13714–9

Library of Congress Cataloging in Publication Data

Gilbert, Victor Francis.
Women's studies.

(Blackwell Reference)
1. Women's studies—Bibliography. 2. Dissertations, Academic—Bibliography. I. Tatla, Darshan Singh.
II. Title.
Z7961.G5S 1985 [HQ1180] 016.3054 85–6192
ISBN 0–631–13714–9

Typeset by Katerprint Co. Ltd, Cowley
Printed in Great Britain by
Page Bros, Norwich

Contents

Acknowledgements vii
Note on coverage and method of preparation viii
Subject guide xii
BIBLIOGRAPHY OF DISSERTATIONS 1
Checklist of bibliographical and reference sources 461
Index 467

Acknowledgements

It has been presumptuous of two males to venture into the field of women's studies. However, we have been greatly guided and steered away from potential traps by the diligent editorial work of Janet Godden and Gillian Forrester from Basil Blackwell, and the thoughtful guidance of Helen Corr and Diana Richardson from the University of Sheffield. We are grateful to Sally Graves for generously allowing us to incorporate into our introduction material from her unpublished MA dissertation 'Library provision resources for Women's Studies courses in the UK' presented to the Department of Information Studies, University of Sheffield in 1984.

We appreciate the patience of university library staff who have helped us to define more clearly the subject matter of elusive titles of some theses. Mrs. Eileen Nixon's efficient typing greatly helped to put the British material into coherent order.

Finally, given the subject of this bibliography, it behoves us to dedicate this work to our wives and daughters who had to bear the brunt of any domestic disorders caused by the avalanche of index cards and proof pages.

V. F. Gilbert, Sheffield
D. S. Tatla, Birmingham

Note On Coverage and Method of Preparation

Coverage

The aim of this bibliography is to provide as comprehensive as possible a classified list of theses and dissertations presented at British, Canadian, Irish and North American universities up to and including 1982 in the field of Women's Studies. There are a few scattered references to 1983 theses which caught our eye in passing.

We have deliberately limited the North American coverage to doctoral dissertations as the amount of material would otherwise have been quite unmanageable. North American masters' theses can be traced through *Masters' abstracts*. The British coverage includes theses submitted in partial fulfilment of the regulations for the award of a higher degree. These are indicated by an asterisk (MA*). Coverage of this category is inevitably patchy since these dissertations are not always officially deposited in university libraries and hence may evade detection.

We have attempted to include all theses relating to women. We have not limited ourselves to studies of the women's movement and feminism but have included such important topics as women's rights and position under the law, opportunities and discrimination in employment, wages and trade unions, health and welfare. Given the scale of the undertaking it is inevitable that we shall have omitted or mislocated theses and we shall be grateful for details. The size of the publication made it necessary to exclude related fields such as gender differences, and studies in areas of implicit relevance to women (e.g. in particular marriage and motherhood) unless the title indicated that the woman's angle was the focal point.

The entries have been divided into 23 chapters according to broad subject divisions (see Subject Guide, pp. xii–xiv). Entries within each chapter or subsection are arranged alphabetically by author's surname. Each entry contains the following information: author, thesis title, degree awarded, university (see list below), date. Notes to clarify the subject field have been added where necessary but this practice has been resorted to sparingly. It was intended at the outset that there should be some indication of which dissertations had subsequently appeared in published form, but the search for this would have been an enormously time-consuming operation and would have greatly delayed publication of the book. The idea was therefore reluctantly abandoned. Here again we would welcome details. The classified entries are followed by an extensive checklist of additional reference material and by a detailed index. The provision of an author index was, given the infrequency of author's name being the means of access to this kind of bibliography, a luxury beyond the means of the space and time at our disposal.

Universities and institutions

To avoid repetition abbreviated titles of colleges, universities and other institutions are given in the entry details. A list of those most frequently cited is given below. (Readers should note in particular that U. of York refers throughout to the English university, York U. to the Canadian.)

England

U. of Bath
U. of Birmingham
U. of Bristol
U. of Cambridge
U. of Durham
U. of Essex
U. of Exeter
U. of Hull
U. of Leeds
U. of Leicester
U. of Liverpool
U. of London (several individual colleges)
U. of Loughborough
U. of Manchester
U. of Newcastle upon Tyne
U. of Nottingham
U. of Oxford
U. of Reading
U. of Sheffield
U. of Surrey
U. of Sussex
U. of Warwick
U. of York
Open U., Milton Keynes
Leeds Polytechnic

Ireland

National U. of Ireland
Queen's U. of Belfast
Trinity College Dublin
University College Cork

Scotland

U. of Aberdeen
U. of Dundee
U. of Edinburgh
U. of Glasgow
U. of St Andrews
U. of Stirling
U. of Strathclyde

Wales

U. of Wales: Aberystwyth
Bangor
Cardiff
Swansea

United States (Excluding those incorporating the names of states or capital cities in their title, e.g. U. of Florida)

Adelphi School of Social Work, Garden City, NY
U. of Akron, Ohio
Albany State Coll., Georgia
American Conservatory of Music
American U., Washington DC
Andrews U.
Auburn U., Alabama

Ball State U., Muncie Indiana
Baylor U., Waco, Texas
Bowling Green State U., Ohio
Brandeis U., Waltham Massachusetts
Brigham Young U., Provo, Utah
Bryn Mawr Coll. Pennsylvania

Caribbean Center for Advanced Studies
Carnegie-Mellon U. Pittsburgh, Pennsylvania
Case Western Reserve U. Cleveland, Ohio
Catholic U. of America, Washington DC
Claremont Graduate School, California
Clark U., Worcester, Massachusetts
Colgate Rochester Divinity School
Columbia Theological Seminary, Decatur, Georgia
Columbia U., New York City
Cornell U., Ithaca, NY

U. of Denver, Colorado
DePaul U., Chicago, Illinois
U. of Detroit, Michigan
Drake U., Des Moines, Iowa
Drew U., Madison, New Jersey
Dropsie U. Philadelphia, Pennsylvania
Duke U., Durham, North Carolina
Duquesne U., Pittsburgh, Pennsylvania

Eden Theological Seminary
Emory U., Atlanta, Georgia

Fairleigh Dickinson, Rutherford, New Jersey
Fielding Institute
Fordham U., Bronx, NY
Fuller Theological Seminary, Pasadena, California

George Peabody Coll. for Teachers, Nashville, Tennessee
George Washington U., Washington DC
Georgetown U., Washington DC
Golden Gate U., San Francisco, California
Grace Theological Seminary and College

Howard U., Washington DC
Humanistic Psych Institute

Johns Hopkins U., Baltimore, Maryland

Kent State U., Ohio
La Verne U., California
Lehigh U., Bethlehem, Pennsylvania
Long Island U., NY
U. of Louisville, Kentucky

McNeese State U., Lake Charles, Louisiana
Marquette U., Milwaukee, Wisconsin
Maynooth U.
Middlebury Coll., Vermont

New School of Social Research, New York City
Niagara U., NY
U. of Notre Dame Indiana
Northwestern U., Evanston, Ill.
Nova U.

Pacific Graduate Sch. of Psychology
Peppardine U., Malibu, California
U. of Pittsburgh, Pennsylvania
U. of Portland, Oregon
Princeton Theological Seminary, NJ
Princeton U., NJ
Purdue U., West Lafayette, Indiana

Radcliffe Coll., Cambridge, Massachusetts
U. of Redlands
Rensselaer Polytechnic Institute, Troy, NY
Rice U., Houston, Texas
U. of Rochester, NY
Rosemead Sch. of Professional Psychology
Rush U.
Rutgers U., New Brunswick, NJ

School of Theology at Claremont
St John's U., Jamaica, NY
Sam Houston State U., Huntsville, Texas
Smith Coll., Northampton, Massachusetts
Southern Baptist Theological Seminary
Southern Methodist U., Dallas, Texas
Southwestern Baptist Theological Seminary, Fort Worth, Texas
Springfield Coll., Massachusetts
Stanfield U., California

Graduate Theological Union

Hartford Seminary Foundation
Harvard U., Cambridge, Mass.
Hebrew Union Coll., Cincinnati, Ohio
Hofstra U., Long Island, NY

Stevens Institute of Technology, Hoboken, New Jersey
Syracuse U., NY

Temple U., Philadelphia, Pennsylvania
U. of Toledo, Ohio
Trinity Evangelical School
Tufts U., Medford, Massachusetts
Tuland U., New Orleans, Louisiana
U. of Tulsa, Oklahoma

Union for Experimenting Colleges and Universities
Union Graduate Sch., Ohio
Union Theological Seminary, New York City
United States International U., San Diego, California

Vanderbilt U., Nashville, Tennessee

Coll. of William and Mary, Williamsburg, Virginia
Wayne State U., Detroit, Michigan
Wesleyan Theological Seminary
Wesleyan U., Middletown, Connecticut
Wright Institute, Berkeley, California

Yale U., New Haven, Connecticut
Yeshiva U., New York City

Canada

U. of Alberta
U. of British Columbia
U. of Calgary, Alberta
Carleton U., Ottowa, Ontario
Concordia U.
Dalhousie U., Halifax, Nova Scotia
Laval U., Quebec, Ontario
McGill U., Montreal, Quebec
McMaster U., Hamilton, Ontario
U. of Manitoba
U. of Montreal
Queen's U., Kingston, Ontario
U. of Western Ontario
U. of Regina, Saskatchewan
Simon Fraser U.
U. of Toronto
U. of Windsor, Ontario
York U., Downsview, Ontario

Method of preparation

The entries were collected in various ways. The chief source of information was *Comprehensive Dissertations Index* published by UM. From 1978 it is published annually and lists all US and Canadian dissertations (doctoral only) in various subjects. For the earlier period two cumulative index volumes are available for the years 1861–1977. A set of key-words (List 1) formed a data base for computer searching

Each key-word (with its derivatives and in its plural form) was searched for each subject on List 2. For literature a list of women authors and selected major book titles was searched through the literature volumes of the *Comprehensive Dissertations Index*.

In addition a short list of widely influential women was prepared (mainly from J. S. Uglow's *Dictionary of women's biography* (Macmillan 1982) and checked against the key-word list.

Computer search at the Central Information Service of the University of London was also carried out for some of the main key-words such as abortion, feminism, rape, puberty, etc. though the entries proved to be so many that the time-period on this data base had to be restricted to five years.

Although the overall search was comprehensive, there are bound to be some omissions, particularly in the field of arts, fine arts, cinema, etc. where individual names were not so comprehensively prepared or searched.

List 1: Key-words searched for

abortion
adultery
birth
bride
brothel
chastity
child
co-education
conception
consent
contraceptive
daughter
divorce
dowry
extra-
familial
family
female
feminine
feminism
fertility
gender
girl
housewife
marital
marriage
macho
masculinity
masturbation
maternity
mating
menopause
menstrual/ation
moral
mother
neo-natal
nurse
parent
paternal
pregnancy
pre-marital
pornography
prostitute
puberty
rape
rite
sex
single
husband
illegitimate
illicit
incest
infidelity
inheritance
intimation
kinship
lesbian
sister
suffrage
virgin
whore
widow
witch
wife
woman

List 2: Subject areas searched

anthropology
economics and business administration
education
fine arts
folklore
geology and geography
health sciences
history
home economics
law
literature
mass communications
music
philosophy
political science
psychology
religion
social work
sociology
speech communication
theatre

Subject Guide

1 The Arts 1

Film **1–30**
Music **31–82**
The performing arts **83–196**
The visual arts **197–257**

2 Criminology 11

General **1–75**
Delinquency and juvenile crime **76–172**
Offences against women and girls **173–299**
Battering **173–214**; Incest **215–228**; Rape and sexual assault **229–299**

3 Demography 23

4 Education 28

History of education **1–167**
Schools **168–203**
Higher education **204–323**
Roman Catholic schools and colleges **324–403**
Continuing education **404–431**
Physical education **432–562**
The women's studies curriculum **563–588**
The educational professions **589–1011**
General **589–607**; Administration **608–883**; Teachers and teacher training **884–1011**
Educational psychology **1012–1686**
General **1012–1304**; Counselling in schools and colleges **1305–1348**; Mature and re-entry students **1349–1432**; Vocational choice and commitment **1433–1686**

5 Employment 94

General **1–121**
The employment of married women and mothers **122–206**
Labour law, labour reform and trade unions **207–243**
Specific occupations **244–322**
Vocational and occupational psychology **323–625**

6 Family Dynamics 118

General **1–27**
Daughter-parent relationships **28–130**
Marriage **131–276**
General **131–201**; Divorce and separation **202–229**; Widowhood **230–276**
Motherhood **277–806**
General **277–783**; Child battering and neglect **784–806**
Other family relationships **807–815**
Women's employment and the family **816–955**

7 Feminism 154

8 Health 160

Alcohol, drugs and tobacco **1–89**
Alcohol **1–61**; Drugs **62–83**; Tobacco **84–89**
General health care and knowledge **90–121**
Mental health **122–293**
General **122–152**; Counselling and therapy **153–208**; Depression **209–245**; Phobias **246–253**; Schizophrenia **254–273**; Mental retardation **274–293**
Nutrition **294–390**
General **294–310**; Anorexia and bulimia **311–327**; Obesity and overweight **328–390**
Physical illness **391–476**
General **391–425**; Cancer **426–476**
The Medical Professions **477–558**
General **477–492**; Nursing **493–558**

9 History 182

Africa **1–8**
The Ancient World **9–41**
Asia **42–65**
The British Isles **66–219**
Up to *c.*1700 **66–110**; After *c.*1700 **111–219**
Continental Europe
General **220–222**; France **223–272**; Germany and Central Europe **274–302**;

Italy **303–305**
Russia and Eastern Europe **306–330**; Scandinavia **332–336**; Spain and Portugal **337–341**
Latin America and the Caribbean **342–349**
North America **350–723**
Up to *c.*1800 **350–366**; After *c.*1800 **367–723**

10 Language 208

11 Law 210

12 Literature 212

Comparative and general studies **1–105**
Up to *c.*1600 **1–21**; After *c.*1600 **22–105**
Feminist criticism **106–146**
African literature **147–196**
General studies **147–158**; Individual writers **159–96**
American literature **197–1245**
General studies **197–480**; Individual writers **481–1245**
Asian literature **1246–1267**
Chinese literature **1246–1252**; Indian and Persian literature **1253–1261**; Japanese literature **1262–1265**; Vietnamese literature **1266–1267**
Australasian literature **1268–1269**
Canadian literature
General studies **1270–1279**; Individual writers **1280–1295**
Classical literature **1296–1330**
English, Irish and Welsh literature **1331–2836**
Up to 1500 **1331–1398**
1500–1800: General studies **1399–1519**; Individual writers **1520–1541**; The eighteenth century: General studies **1542–1602**, Individual writers **1603–1676**; The nineteenth century: General studies **1677–1823**, Individual writers **1824–2470**; The twentieth century: General studies **2471–2539**, individual writers **2540–2836**
French literature **2837–3266**
General studies **2837–2983**; Individual writers **2984–3266**
German literature **3267–3423**
General studies **3267–3357**; Individual writers **3358–3423**
Hebrew literature **3424**
Islamic and Arabic literature **3425–3428**
Italian literature **3429–3441**
Latin American and Caribbean literature **3442–3498**
General studies **3442–3458**; Individual writers **3459–3498**
Russian, Turkish and East European literature **3499–3529**
Scandinavian and Icelandic literature **3530–3539**
General **3530–3533**; Individual **3534–3539**
Spanish and Portuguese literature **3540–3679**
General **3540–3618**; Individual writers **3619–3679**

13 Media 339

14 Philosophy 341

15 Physiology 343

16 Politics 350

17 Psychology 353

General psychology **1–44**
History, philosophy and theories **1–11**; Psychometrics **12–31**; Experimental psychology **32–44**
Behaviour therapy and modification **45–174**
Developmental psychology **175–760**
Childhood **175–199**; Adolescence **200–302**; Adult development **303–678** Midlife **679–734**; Old Age **735–760**
Social psychology **761–883**
Group interpersonal processes **761–828**; Social perception and attitudes **829–883**

18 Religion 387

Ancient and primitive religions **1–19**
Buddhism **20–21**
Christianity **22–284**
The New Testament period and the early Church **23–49**; The Middle Ages **50–74**; Protestantism **75–132**; Catholicism **133–155**; Women religious **156–239**; Feminist Christianity **240–241**; The ordination of women **242–261**; Overseas missions **262–268**; Pastoral care **269–284**
Hinduism and Indian religion **285–297**
Islam **298–301**
Judaism **302–315**

19 Reproduction 400

Abortion, contraception and family planning **1–132**

Infertility **133–141**
Menstruation **142–250**
General **142–234**; The menopause **235–250**
Pregnancy and childbirth **251–587**
General **251–494**; Teenage pregnancy **495–570**; Motivation for parenthood **571–587**

20 Sexuality 422

General **1–137**
Androgyny **138–153**
Lesbian sexuality **154–167**

21 Sociology 430

Domestic and household organization **1–56**
General **1–40**; Women as consumers **41–56**
Dress **57–102**
Ethnic, migrant and minority communities **103–181**
Leisure **182–191**
Social class role and status **192–240**
Voluntary work; voluntary organizations and clubs **241–265**
Welfare and social work **266–309**

22 Sport 442

General **1–69**
Athletics **70–124**
Specific sports and games **125–192**

23 Women in the Third World 450

1 The Arts

Film

See also **9** 536, 1043, 1087; **12** 3060, 3484.

BAKER,M.J. *1*
Images of women: the war years, 1941–1945; a study of the public perceptions of women's roles as revealed in top-grossing war films. PhD U. of California, Santa Barbara, 1978.

BATHRICK,S.K. *2*
The true woman and the family-film: the industrial production of memory. PhD U. of Wisconsin-Madison, 1981.

BELL-METERAU,R.L. *3*
Cross-dressing and sex-role reversals in American film. [Inc. studies of Marlene Dietrich and Doris Day] PhD U. of Indiana, 1981.

BYG,B.B. *4*
History, narrative and film form: Jean-Marie Straub and Danièle Huillet. [Screen writer and Straub's wife] PhD U. of Washington, 1982.

DONALSON,M.B. *5*
The representation of Afro-American women in the Hollywood feature film, 1915–1949. PhD Brown U. 1981.

DOWD,J.T. *6*
An investigation of the image of American women in selected American motion pictures, 1930–1971. PhD New York U. 1975.

DOYEN,M.L. *7*
Women in film: a study of aspects of feminist film theory and of images of women in the Hollywood cinema, with particular reference to three films of Howard Hawks. MA U. of Warwick, 1979.

DOZORETZ,W.H. *8*
Germaine Dulac; film-maker, polemicist, theoretician. PhD New York U. 1982.

FLITTERMAN,S. *9*
Women, representation, and cinematic discourse: the example of French cinema. [Work of Germaine Dulac, Marie Epstein and Agnès Varda] PhD U. of California, Berkeley, 1982.

GAINES,J. M. *10*
The popular icon as commodity and sign: the circulation of Betty Grable, 1941–1945. PhD Northwestern U. 1982.

HIGASHI,S. *11*
The silent screen heroine: a study of the popular image of women, 1914–1929. PhD U. of California, Los Angeles, 1974.

HIRSCH,V.A. *12*
Edith Head, film costume designer. PhD U. of Kansas, 1973.

HOUSEMAN,J.P. *13*
A study of selected Walt Disney screenplays and films and the stereotyping of the role of the female. EdD U. of the Pacific, 1973.

KOWALSKI,R.A.R. *14*
A vision of one's own: four women film directors. PhD U. of Michigan, 1980.

MCLANE,B.A. *15*
The woman's film: a rhetorical analysis from the work of John M. Stahl. PhD U. of Southern California, 1982.

PETERS,A.K. *16*
Acting and aspiring actresses in Hollywood: a sociological analysis. PhD U. of California, Los Angeles, 1971.

PORTUGES,C.E. *17*
Cinema and psyche: a psychoanalytic view of the representation of women in three French film directors of the 1960s. PhD U. of California, Los Angeles, 1982.

RABINOVITZ,L.H. *18*
Radical cinema: the films and film practice of Maya Deren, Shirley Clarke and Joyce Wieland. PhD U. of Texas at Austin, 1982.

RENOV,M. *19*
Hollywood's wartime women: a study of historical/ideological determinism. [A World War II study] PhD U. of California, Los Angeles, 1982.

ROSENBERG,J. *20*
Feminism into film: social bases of an artistic movement. PhD U. of Massachusetts, 1979.

SCHENKEL,T. *21*
Exploring the cinema of figurative animation with special consideration of the work of John and Faith Habley and Jan Levison. PhD, New York U. 1977.

STEWART,L.A.L. 22
Ida Lupino as film director, 1949–1953: an *auteur* approach. PhD U. of Michigan, 1979.

STODDARD,K.M. 23
The image of the aging woman in American popular film, 1930–1980. PhD U. of Maryland, 1980.

SWENSON-DAVIS,A.M. 24
From sex queen to cultural symbol: an interpretation of the image of Marilyn Monroe. PhD U. of Michigan, 1980.

TIESSEN,P.G. 25
Cinema: the medium as a metaphor in the work of Wyndham Lewis and Dorothy Richardson. PhD U. of Alberta, 1973.

WALSH,A.S. 26
'The weeds grow long near the shore': the 'women's film' and the American female experience, 1940–1950. PhD State U. of New York at Binghamton, 1982.

WEST,A. A. 27
Comédie noire thrillers of Alfred Hitchcock: genres, psychoanalysis, and woman's image. PhD U. of California, Berkeley, 1982.

WINKLE,S. 28
The male eye and the female image: the interruption of the visual encounter by abstraction in four movies by Lisa Wertmüller. PhD U. of Florida, 1982.

YECK,J.L. 29
The woman's film at Warner Brothers, 1935–1950. PhD U. of Southern California, 1982.

ZUCKER,C.P. 30
The idea of the image: Josef van Sternberg's Dietrich films (1929–1935). PhD U. of New York, 1982.

Music

See also **4** 139.

ANDERSON,J.S. 31
Music for women's chorus and harp: a study of the repertory and an analysis and performance of selected compositions. EdD Columbia U. Teachers Coll. 1977.

ARMENT,H.E. 32
A study by means of spectographic analysis of the brightness and darkness qualities of vowel tones in women's voices. EdD U. of Indiana, 1960.

ARMSTRONG,D.J. 33
A study of some important twentieth-century secular compositions for women's chorus, with a preliminary discussion of secular choral music from a historical and philosophical viewpoint. DMA U. of Texas at Austin, 1968.

BOUGHTON,H.C. 34
Katherine K. Davis: life and work. DMA U. of Missouri at Kansas City, 1974.

BRAND,M.F. 35
Poldowski (Lady Dean Paul): her life and her song settings of French and English poetry. DMA U. of Oregon, 1979.

BRINK,L. 36
Women characters in Richard Wagner: a study of *The Ring of the Nibelung*. PhD Columbia U. 1924.

BURNSWORTH,C.C. 37
Choral music for women's voices: an annotated bibliography of recommended works. DMA Boston U. 1965.

CARRUTHERS-CLEMENT,C.A. 38
(Part I) The madrigals and motets of Vittoria Raphaela Aleotti. PhD Kent State U. 1982.

CLARKE,D.E. 39
Transvestism in eighteenth- and nineteenth-century opera. DMS U. of Wisconsin-Madison, 1979.

CORNELL,H.L. 40
An evaluation of vocal music by American women composers as to its appropriateness in the elementary school. PhD Ohio State U. 1973.

CUNEO-LAURENT,L. 41
The performer as catalyst: the role of the singer Jane Bathori (1877–1970) in the careers of Debussy, Ravel, *les six* and their contemporaries in Paris, 1904–1926. PhD New York U. 1982.

DAUGHERTY,R.M. 42
(Part I) An analysis of Aaron Copland's *Twelve Poems of Emily Dickinson*. DMA Ohio State U. 1980.

DAUGHTRY,W.E. 43
Sissieretta Jones: a study of the negro's contribution to nineteenth- century American concert and theatrical life. PhD Syracuse U. 1968.

ELLIS,W.C. 44
The sentimental mother song in American country music 1923–45. PhD Ohio State U. 1978.

ESTILL,A.H.M. 45
The contributions of selected Afro-American women classical singers, 1850–1955. DA New York U. 1982.

FRANZONE,M.S. 46
The revival of *Bel canto* and its relevance to contemporary teaching and performance. [Inc. studies of Maria Callas and Joan Sutherland] EdD Columbia U. 1969.

GAUME,M.M. 47
Ruth Crawford Seeger: her life and works. PhD Indiana U. 1973.

GREEN,M.D. *48*
A study of the lives and works of five black women composers in America. DMus. U. of Oklahoma, 1975.

HARRIS,R.L. *49*
Music for women's chorus from the Venetian *opsedali* by Nicola Porpora: the British Museum manuscripts. DMA U. of Washington, 1979.

HOWE,A.W. *50*
Lily Strickland: her contribution to American music in the early twentieth century. PhD Catholic U. of America, 1968.

HYDE,D.E. *51*
Part-music for female voices, with particular reference to the twentieth century. MPhil U. of Reading, 1973.

HYDE,D.E. *52*
Women and music of nineteenth-century England. PhD U. of Reading, 1979.

JACKSON,M.Q. *53*
Sex and role differences in the use of the female register. PhD Yeshiva U. 1982.

JARRETT,J.C . *54*
The song of lament: an artistic women's heritage. [The modern Greek lamenting tradition and its ancient west Asian and Mediterranean prototypes] PhD Wesleyan U. 1977.

JENKINS-HALL,C. *55*
Comparative study of voice-role types and sex-role typing in female singers. PhD US International U. 1981.

JONES,J.E. *56*
Maria Jane Williams an cherddoriaeth werin Gymrieg. MA U. of Wales, Aberystwyth, 1981.

KIRK,B. *57*
The role of Zerline in Auber's *Fra Diavola*: a mirror of her age. DMA American Conservatory of Music, 1982.

KOLN,E.M. *58*
A tapestry of voices: the medieval women's song. PhD Indiana U. 1979.

LARGE ,J.W. *59*
Some spectral correlates of perceived differences in female chest and middle registers in singing. PhD Stanford U. 1971.

LIEB,S.R. *60*
The message of Ma Rainey's blues: a biographical and critical study of America's first women blues singer. PhD Stanford U. 1976.

McGREGOR,R.E. *61*
An analysis of Thea Musgrave's composition style from 1958 to 1967. PhD U. of Liverpool, 1980.

MASSMANN,R.L. *62*
Lillian Baldwin and the Cleveland plan for educational concerts. PhD U. of Michigan, 1972.

MUELLER,S.C. *63*
Motivation and reactions to the work role among female performers and music teachers. PhD U. of Michigan, 1975.

QUIN,C.L. *64*
Fanny Mendelssohn Hensel: her contributions to nineteenth-century musical life. PhD U. of Kentucky, 1981.

QUINN,J.P. *65*
Marathi- and Konkani-speaking women in Hindustani music, 1880–1940. PhD U. of Minnesota, 1982.

RANEY,C. *66*
Francesca Caccini, musician to the Medici, and her *primo libro* (1618). PhD New York U. 1971.

ROWLEY,V.W. *67*
The solo piano music of the Canadian composer Jean Coulthard. MusAD Boston U. Sch. of Fine and Applied Arts, 1973.

SARGENT,G.S. 68
An edition of Elizabeth Rogers' Virginal Book (British Museum Add. MS 10337). PhD Indiana U. 1965.

SCOTT,D.W. *69*
A study of the effect of changes in vocal intensity upon the harmonic structure of selected singing tones produced by female singers. MusD Indiana U. 1960.

SIROTA,V.R. *70*
The life and works of Fanny Mendelssohn Hensel. MusAD Boston U. Sch. of Fine and Applied Arts, 1981.

SQUIRE,R.N. *71*
The philosophy of music of George Santayana, Helen Huss Pankhurst and Theodore Meyer. PhD New York U. 1943.

STEVENS,E.M. *72*
The influence of Nadia Boulanger on composition in the United States: a study of piano solo writers by her American students. MusAD Boston U. Sch. of Fine and Applied Arts, 1975.

STODDARD,E.M. *73*
Frances Elliott Clark: her life and contributions to music education. PhD Brigham Young U. 1968.

TACKA,P.V. *74*
Denise Bacon, musician and educator: contributions to the adaptation of the Kodály concept in the United States. DMA Catholic U. of America, 1982.

TICK,J. *75*
Towards a history of American women composers before 1870. PhD City U. of New York.

TROLLINGER,L.W. *76*
Study of the biographical and personality factors of creative women in music. DMA Temple U. 1979.

TROMBLE,W.W. *77*
The American intellectual and music: an analysis of the writings of Susanne K. Langer, Paul Henry Lang, Jacques Barzun, John Dewey and Leonard Bernstein - with implications for music education at the college level. PhD U. of Michigan, 1968.

VAN ALAN,J.K. *78*
Stylistic and interpretive analysis and performance of selected choral compositions for women's voices by three American composers. EdD Columbia U. 1973.

WATKINS,B.K. *79*
The Devil to Pay, or *The Wives Metamorphosed*: an introduction to the opera with an edition of the text and music. MA U. of Exeter, 1982.

WEINER,J.R. *80*
The family of women: a mythological analysis of the rhetoric of contemporary feminist song. PhD State U. of New York at Buffalo, 1979.

WOODLEY,P. *81*
Nineteen settings of five Emily Dickinson poems by thirteen composers. DMA U. of Missouri at Kansas City, 1982.

ZURFLUH, J.D. *82*
An analysis of *Ballade fantastique* by Mary Carlisle Howe. DMA Catholic U. of America, 1981.

The performing arts

For drama see also **9** 229, 539; **10** 19; **12** *passim, esp.* 260, 315, 363, 383, 405, 424, 430, 441, 442, 444, 448, 450, 468, 480, 1087, 1095, 1130, 1417, 1486, 1551, 1612, 2916, 2492.

ANDREW,R.H. *83*
Augustine Daly's Big Four: John Drew, Ada Rehan, James Lewis and Mrs G.H. Gilbert. PhD U. of Illinois at Urbana-Champaign, 1971.

AUSTER,A. *84*
Chamber of diamonds and delight: actresses, suffragists and feminists in the American theatre, 1890–1920. PhD State U. of New York at Stony Brook, 1981.

BADAL,R.S. *85*
Kate and Ellen Bateman: a study in precocity. [Girl actresses] PhD Northwestern U. 1971.

BARKER,B.M. *86*
The American careers of Rita Sangalli, Giuseppina Morlachi and Maria Bonfanti: nineteenth-century ballerinas. PhD New York U. 1981.

BARTHOLOMEUSZ,D.S. *87*
Macbeth and the actors: a critical study of players' interpretation of the roles of Macbeth and Lady Macbeth on the English stage, 1611 to the present. PhD U. of London, King's Coll. 1966.

BARTLEY,M.M. *88*
A preliminary study of the Scottish royal entries of Mary Stuart, James VI and Anne of Denmark, 1558–1603. [Pageantry] PhD U. of Michigan, 1981.

BARTON,M.A. *89*
Aline Bernstein, theatrical designer: a history and evaluation. PhD Indiana U. 1971.

BEDARD,R.L. *90*
The life and work of Charlotte B. Chorpenning. [Children's theatre, US] PhD U. of Kansas, 1979.

BONGAS,P.J. *91*
The woman's woman on the American stage in the 1930s. PhD U. of Missouri- Columbia, 1980.

BOUSLIMAN,C.W. *92*
The Mabel Tainter Memorial Theatre: a pictorial case study of a late nineteenth-century American playhouse. PhD Ohio State U. 1969.

BUZECKY,R.C. *93*
The Bancrofts (Squire and Marie) at the Prince of Wales and Haymarket theatres, 1865–1885. PhD U. of Wisconsin, 1970.

CAMPANA DE WATTS,L.A. *94*
La Pericholi; mito literario nacional peruano. [Micaela Villegas, eighteenth-century Peruvian actress]. PhD U. of Southern California, 1969.

CASEY,L.S. *95*
Madame Vestris in America. PhD U. of Michigan, 1976.

CIMA,M.G.G. *96*
Elizabeth Robins: Ibsen actress-manageress. PhD Cornell U. 1978.

CLARK,P.F. *97*
A reconstruction of John Philip Kemble's Covent Garden production of *Romeo and Juliet* with Charles Kemble and Eliza O'Neill, 1815–1819. PhD U. of Nebraska, 1972.

COMER,I.F. *98*
Little Nell and the Marchioness: milestone in the development of American musical comedy. [Vehicle for the acting of Lotta Crabtree] PhD Tufts U. 1979.

COOPER,P.R. *99*
Eva Le Gallienne's Civic Repertory Theatre. PhD U. of Illinois at Urbana-Champaign, 1967.

CORTEZ,J.V. *100*
Fanny Janauschek: America's last queen of tragedy. PhD U. of Illinois at Urbana-Champaign, 1973.

COSTA,B.J. *101*
'Motley': an analysis of the costume designs of Elizabeth Montgomery, Margaret Harris and Sophie Devine. PhD Florida State U. 1980.

COURTOY,A.D. *102*
'A little, dirty kind of war': the life of Charlotte Cibber Charke. [Daughter of Colley Cibber] PhD Florida State U. 1982.

CREAN,P.J. *103*
A study of the life and times of Kitty Clive. PhD U. of London (External), 1933.

DIXON-STOWELL,B.M. *104*
Dancing in the dark: the life and times of Margot Webb in Aframerican vaudeville of the Swing era. PhD New York U. 1981.

DODGE,C.J. *105*
Rosamond Gilder and the theatre. PhD U. of Illinois at Urbana-Champaign, 1974.

DONKIN,E. *106*
Mrs Fiske's 1897 *Tess of the D'Urbervilles:* a structural analysis of the 1897–98 production. PhD U. of Washington, 1982.

DOTY,G.A. *107*
The career of Mrs Anne Brunton Merry in the American theatre. PhD Indiana U. 1967.

DRIVER,L.S. *108*
Fanny Kemble: Shakespeare's ambassadress to America. PhD Vanderbilt U. 1932.

DUMAIS,A.J. *109*
An analysis of the dramaturgical use of history in the writing of two full-length plays about Mary Todd Lincoln. PhD New York U. 1978.

ELLIS,O.C. de C. *110*
Cleopatra on the English stage. MA U. of Sheffield, 1946.

ELSBREE,L. *111*
The breaking chain: a study of the dance in the novels of Jane Austen, George Eliot, Thomas Hardy and D.H. Lawrence. PhD Claremont Grad. Sch. 1963.

GAMBLE,M.W. *112*
Clare Tree Major: children's theatre, 1927–1954. PhD New York U. 1976.

GOODMAN,J.L. *113*
Joan Littlewood and her theatre workshop. PhD New York U. 1975.

GRAY,J.A. *114*
To want to dance: a biography of Margarette H'Doubler. PhD U. of Arizona, 1978.

HALPERN,R.H. *115*
Female occupational exhibitionism: an exploratory study of topless and bottomless dancers. PhD U.S. International U. 1981.

HARPER,C.N. *116*
Mrs Leslie Carter: her life and acting career. PhD U. of Nebraska-Lincoln, 1978.

HARVEY,J. *117*
American burlesque as reflected through the career of Kitty Madison, 1916–1931. PhD Florida State U. 1980.

HEADRICK.C.J. *118*
Elizabeth Tudor: the historic character in four centuries of dramatic literature. PhD U. of Georgia, 1982.

HEARN,H.L. *119*
The student actress: a case study in the process of professionalization. PhD U. of Missouri-Columbia, 1966.

HELPERN,A.J. *120*
The evolution of Martha Graham's dance technique. PhD New York U. 1981.

HOOK,L. *121*
Mrs Elizabeth Barry and Mrs Anne Bracegirdle, actresses, their careers from 1672–1695: a study in influences. PhD New York U. 1945.

HUMBLE,A.L. *122*
Matilda Heron, American actress. PhD U. of Illinois at Urbana-Champaign, 1959.

IRVINE,J.D. *123*
Mary Shaw, actress, suffragist, activist (1854–1929). PhD Columbia U. 1978.

JOHNSON,E.A. *124*
The Greek productions of Margaret Anglin. PhD Case Western Reserve U. 1971.

KAEHLER,W.H. *125*
The operatic repertoire of Madame de Pompadour's *théâtre des petits cabinets*, 1741–1753. PhD U. of Michigan, 1971.

KLEIN,A. *126*
A study of Elisabeth Rachel Felix (1821–1858). PhD U. of Michigan, 1948.

KLEIN,E.S.S. *127*
The development of the leading feminine character in selected librettos of American musicals from 1900 to 1960. PhD Columbia U. 1962.

KNEPLER,H.W. *128*
Mary Stuart on the stage in England and America. PhD U. of Chicago, 1950.

KOENGETER,L.W. *129*
Mrs Mary Robinson: a biographical and critical appraisal. (English actress known as 'Perdita') PhD Harvard U. 1975.

KRAUS,J.H. *130*
A history of the Children's Theatre Association of Baltimore, Maryland, from 1943–1966. [Work of founder, Isabel B. Burger] EdD Columbia U. 1972.

LANDAU,P.M. *131*
The career of Mary Ann Duff: the American Siddons, 1810–1839. PhD Bowling Green State U. 1979.

LANG,W.A. *132*
The career of Alice Brady, stage and screen actress. PhD U. of Illinois at Urbana-Champaign, 1971.

LARSEN,J.B. *133*
Margo Jones: a life in the theatre. [American theatre director] PhD City U. of New York, 1982.

LEACH,W. 134
Gertrude Stein and the modern theatre. PhD U. of Illinois at Urbana-Champaign, 1956.

LEAVITT,D.L. 135
Feminist theatre groups in America: four case studies. PhD U. of Colorado at Boulder, 1978.

LINTNER,M.D.L. 136
The height of fashion: the construction (for the stage) of ladies' fashion headwear 1830–1914. PhD U. of Michigan, 1979.

LITTLE,R.D. 137
Toby and Susie: the show-business success story of Neil and Caroline Schaffner, 1925–1962. PhD Ohio State U. 1969.

LONG,L.S. 138
The art of Beatrice Herford, Cissie Loftus and Dorothy Sands within the tradition of solo performance. PhD U. of Texas at Austin, 1982.

MCKERROW,M. 139
A descriptive study of the acting of Alla Nazimova. PhD U. of Michigan, 1974.

MCLELLAN,E.J.H. 140
Sarah Siddons and natural acting in the eighteenth century. PhD U. of Nebraska-Lincoln, 1974.

MCMAHON, P.M. 141
The tragical art of Sarah Siddons: an analysis of her acting style. PhD Yale U. 1972.

MANSER,R.B. 142
The influence of the American actress on the development of the American theatre from 1835–1935. PhD New York U. 1938.

MARGARIDA,A.A. 143
Shakespeare's Rosalind: a survey and checklist of the role in performance, 1740–1980. PhD New York U. 1982.

MASON,S.V. 144
Ibsen's women: the acting in early Norwegian productions. PhD U. of Oregon, 1980.

MENDELSON,A.D. 145
The rise of melodrama and the schematization of women in England, 1780–1940: the relationship between theatrical stereotype, social mythology and social change during the Industrial Revolution. PhD Stanford U. 1977.

MENDOZA,B.M. 146
Hallie Flanagan: her role in American theatre 1924–1935. PhD New York U. 1976.

MESSANO-CIESLA,M.A.A. 147
Minnie Maddern Fiske: her battle with the theatrical syndicate. PhD New York U. 1982.

MILLSTONE,A.B. 148
Feminist theatre in France, 1870–1914. PhD U. of Wisconsin-Madison, 1977.

MITCHELL, S. 149
The early career of Julia Marlowe: the making of a star. PhD U. of Illinois at Urbana-Champaign, 1976.

MOSES,M.A.S. 150
Lydia Thompson and the 'British Blondes' in the United States. PhD U. of Oregon, 1978.

MOSS,L.T. 151
A historical study of Katharine Cornell as an actress-producer 1931–1960. PhD U. of Southern California, 1974.

MURPHY,R.A. 152
Ibsen's *Hedda Gabler* on the New York stage. PhD U. of Illinois, 1967.

MURRAY,V. 153
An analysis of the plays and operas of Gertrude Stein. PhD Kent State U. 1979.

NEILL,E.L. 154
The art of Minnie Maddern Fiske: a study of her realistic acting. PhD Tufts U. 1970.

OLSEN,J.A. 155
The stage history of Portia in England, 1900–1978. MA U. of Birmingham, 1980.

PAM,D.S. 156
Exploitation, independence and solidarity: the changing role of American working women as reflected in the working-girl melodrama 1870–1910. PhD New York U. 1980.

PLOTNICKI,R.M. 157
The evolution of a star: the career of Viola Allen, 1882–1918. PhD City U. of New York, 1979.

RAIDER,R.A. 158
A descriptive study of the acting of Marie Dressler. PhD U. of Michigan, 1980.

RECKLIES,K.A. 159
Fashion behind the footlights: the influence of stage costume on women's fashions in England from 1878–1914. PhD Ohio State U. 1982.

REID,A.M.C. 160
An analysis of the acting styles of Garrick, [Sarah] Siddons, and Edmund Keen in relation to the dominant trends in art and literature of the eighteenth century. PhD Yale U. 1944.

REIFF,R. 161
Male attitudes to females as expressed in the longest-running Broadway play of each decade from the 1920s through the 1960s. PhD U. of Maryland, 1972.

RICHTMAN,J. 162
Adrienne Lecouvreur: actress and woman under the *ancien régime*. PhD Columbia U. 1969.

RIDGE,P.L. 163
The contributions of Hallie Flanagan to the American theatre. PhD Columbia U. 1971.

RODMAN,E.R. 164
Edith King and Dorothy Coit and the King-Coit School and Children's Theatre. PhD New York U. 1980.

RUBIN,J.E. 165
The literary and theatrical contributions of Charlotte B. Chorpenning to children's theatre. PhD Ohio State U. 1978.

RUDISILL,A.S. 166
The contributions of Eva Le Gallienne, Margaret Webster, Margo Jones and Joan Littlewood to the establishment of repertory theatre in the United States and Great Britain. PhD Northwestern U. 1972.

RYAN,B.A. 167
Gertrude Stein's theatre of the absolute. PhD U. of Illinois at Urbana-Champaign, 1980.

SAWYER,R.C. 168
The Shakespearian acting of Mary Anderson, 1884–1889. PhD U. of Illinois at Urbana-Champaign, 1976.

SCHANKE,R.A. 169
Eva Le Gallienne: first lady of repertory. PhD U. of Nebraska-Lincoln, 1975.

SCHLUNDT,C.L. 170
The role of Ruth St Denis in the history of American dance 1906–1922. PhD Claremont Grad. Sch. 1959.

SCHOENHERR,D.E. 171
The pageant of the people: a study of Queen Elizabeth's royal entries. PhD Yale U. 1973.

SCUDDER,J.P. 172
The dramatic potential in the adaptations of the short stories of Flannery O'Connor for readers' theatre: a case study. PhD Kent State U. 1982.

SILVERMAN,E. 173
Margaret Webster's theory and practice of Shakespearean production in the United States (1937–1953). PhD New York U. 1964.

SIMON,B.A. 174
Twentieth-century American performing arts as viewed through the career of Peggy Wood. PhD New York U. 1981.

SIMON,N.L. 175
Henry Irving and Ellen Terry in Macbeth: Lyceum Theatre, 29 December 1888. PhD U. of Washington, 1975.

SMITH,G.L. 176
The International Ladies Garment Workers' Union 'Labor Stage': a propagandistic venture. PhD Kent State U. 1975.

SMITH,R.G. 177
Sarah Bernhardt in America: the factors in her success. PhD U. of Illinois at Urbana-Champaign, 1971.

SNYDER,D.M. 178
Theatre as a verb: the theatre art of Martha Graham 1923–1958. PhD U. of Illinois at Urbana-Champaign, 1980.

SOGLIUZZO,A.R. 179
Edward H. Sothern and Julia Marlowe, Shakespearean producers. PhD Indiana U. 1967.

SOMMER,S.R. 180
Loie Fuller: from the theatre of popular entertainment to the Parisian avant-garde. PhD New York U. 1979.

SONG,Q. 181
A promptbook study of Margaret Webster's production of *Macbeth*. PhD U. of Oregon, 1982.

SPECTOR,S.J. 182
Uta Hagen: the early years, 1919–1951. PhD New York U. 1982.

SULLIVAN,G.E. 183
Claudia Cassidy and American theatre criticism. PhD U. of Minnesota, 1968.

SWAIN,J.W. 184.
Mrs Alexander Drake: a biographical study. [Frances Ann Denny, American actress] PhD Tulane U. 1970.

SWISS,C.D. 185
Hallie Flanagan and the Federal Theater Project: an experiment in form. PhD U. of Wisconsin-Madison, 1982.

TACKEL,M.S. 186
Women and American pageantry: 1908 to 1918. PhD City U. of New York, 1982.

TARANOW,G. 187
The art of Sarah Bernhardt. PhD Yale U. 1961.

TAYLOR,D.J. 188
Laura Keene in America, 1852–1873. PhD Tulane U. 1966.

TUMBLESON,T.R. 189
Three female Hamlets: Charlotte Cushman, Sarah Bernhardt and Eva Le Gallienne. PhD U. of Oregon, 1981.

TURNER,B. 190
Sarah Bernhardt dans les grandes tragédies de Shakespeare. MA U. of Birmingham, 1954.

VAN DER YACHT,D.R. 191
Queen Victoria's patronage of Charles Kean, actor-manager. PhD Ohio State U. 1970.

WHITLATCH,R.C. 192
Fanny Davenport, actress and manager. PhD U. of Illinois at Urbana-Champaign, 1962.

WILLS,J.R. 193
The riddle of Olive Logan: a biographical profile. PhD Case Western Reserve U. 1971.

WILMETH,D.B. *194*
A history of the Margo Jones Theatre. PhD U. of Illinois at Urbana-Champaign, 1964.

WOODY,P.D. *195*
A comparison of Dorothy Heathcote's informal drama methodology and a formal drama approach in influencing self-esteem of preadolescents in a Christian education program. PhD Florida State U. 1974.

WORSLEY,R.C. *196*
Margaret Webster: a study of her contributions to the American theatre. PhD Wayne State U. 1972.

The visual arts

See also **4** 25, 139, 186, 930; **9** 27; **12** 995, 1731, 2842, 2978, 2982; **14** *passim.*

ALEXANDER,J.M. *197*
The theme of the wise and foolish virgins as part of the Last Judgement iconography in Flanders and Italy in the late fifteenth and the sixteenth centuries. MPhil U. of St Andrews, 1982.

ALLEN,V.M. *198*
The *femme fatale*: a study of the early development of the concept in mid-nineteenth-century (English) poetry and painting. PhD Boston U. Grad. Sch. 1979.

BODDY,J.M. *199*
The Farm Security Administration photographs of Marion Post Wolcott: a cultural history. PhD State U. of New York at Buffalo, 1982.

CARRERA,M.M. *200*
The representation of women in Aztec-Mexican sculpture. PhD Columbia U. 1979.

CILETTI,E. *201*
The patronage of the last Medici: the projects of the Electress Palatine Anna Maria Luisa de' Medici in the Basilica of S. Lorenzo. PhD U. of Chicago, 1981.

COHN,S.F. *202*
An analysis of selected works by Georgia O'Keeffe and a production of drawings by the researcher relating to the work of the artist studied. PhD New York U. 1974.

COLLINS,G.C. *203*
The sex-appropriateness of art activity for the female. PhD Ohio State U. 1978.

CORDRAY,R. *204*
A study guide to assist the female art student. EdD Columbia U. Teachers Coll. 1978.

DAVIS,G.R. *205*
The cooperative galleries of the Women's Art Movement 1969–1980. PhD Michigan State U. 1981.

DINNERSTEIN,L. *206*
Opulence and ocular delight, splendor and squalor: critical writings in art and architecture by Mariana Griswold van Rensselaer. PhD City U. of New York, 1979.

EDEN,M.G. *207*
Anna Hyatt Huntington, sculptor, and Mrs H.H.A. Bench, composer: a comparative study of two women representatives of the American cultivated tradition in the arts. PhD U. of Syracuse, 1977.

ELDREDGE,C.C. *208*
Georgia O'Keeffe: the development of an American modern. PhD U. of Minnesota, 1971.

FRATTO,T.F. *209*
Samplers: the historical ethnography of an American popular art. PhD U. of Pennsylvania, 1971.

FREID,C.G. *210*
Personality comparisons between outstanding creative craftswomen, women artists and women in the general population. PhD U. of Tennessee, 1979.

GAIETTO,M.M. *211*
An investigation of Marian symbols found in the courtly art of the late Gothic period. PhD U. of Ohio, 1969.

GASTON,A.M. *212*
The Dancing Siva and other dancing images in sculpture: an iconographic study, with reference to some of the living dance traditions of India. BLitt U. of Oxford, 1977.

GOVAN,S.J. *213*
Gwendolyn Bennett: portrait of an artist lost. PhD Emory U. 1980.

HALES,R.M. *214*
The symbolism and iconography of Mary Magdalene as the soul redeemed. MPhil U. of Reading, 1974.

HARPER,J.G. *215*
Product and response: the painting of Bridget Riley. MPhil U. of London, Courtauld Inst. of Art, 1982.

HENDERSON,A.L. *216*
Adelaide Johnson: issues of professionalism for a woman artist. PhD George Washington U. 1981.

HUMPHREY,J.M. *217*
The unconventional beauty: a study of the pre-Raphaelite and aesthetic woman in painting and life. MPhil U. of Nottingham, 1977.

KAHR,M.M. *218*
The Book of Esther in seventeenth-century Dutch art. PhD New York U. 1966.

KERR, J. *219*
Art and community: a sociological study of contemporary feminist art. PhD U. of California, Irvine, 1980.

KINNARD,C.D. *220*
The life and works of Mariana Griswold van Rensselaer, American art critic. PhD Johns Hopkins U. 1977.

KNILL-CATTANEO,M. *221*
Expression and self-awareness: the emergence of a feminist artist. PhD Union for Experimenting Colleges and Universities, 1982.

KRUCKMAN,L.D. *222*
Women in clay: the potters of La Chamba. PhD U. of Southern Illinois at Carbondale, 1977.

LADER,M.P. *223*
Peggy Guggenheim's art of this century: the surrealist milieu and the American avant-garde, 1942–47. PhD U. of Delaware, 1981.

LANDAU,E.G. *224*
Lee Krasner: a study of her early career (1926–1949). PhD U. of Delaware, 1981.

LAROW,M. *225*
The iconography of Mary Magdalene; the evolution of a Western tradition until 1300. PhD U. of New York, 1982.

LEADER,B.K. *226*
The Boston lady as a work of art: paintings by the Boston School at the turn of the century. PhD Columbia U. 1980.

LEDOGAR,J.W. *227*
Dress and nudity in the iconography of the Florentine Renaissance woman. PhD U. of North Carolina at Greensboro, 1932.

LOMBARDI,M. *228*
Women in the modern art movement in Brazil: salon leaders, artists and musicians. PhD U. of California, Los Angeles, 1977.

MCCALL,M.M. *229*
The sociology of female artists: a study of female painters, sculptors, and print-makers in St Louis. PhD U. of Illinois at Urbana-Champaign, 1975.

MCKENZIE,A.D. *230*
The Virgin Mary as the Throne of Solomon in medieval art. PhD New York U. 1965.

MCMILLAN,S.H. *231*
Gertrude Stein, the cubists and the futurists. PhD U. of Texas at Austin, 1964.

MCNIFF,K.K. *232*
Sex differences in children's art. EdD Boston U. Sch. of Educ. 1981.

MATHEWS, N.M. *233*
Mary Cassatt and the 'modern madonna' of the nineteenth century. PhD New York U. 1980.

MINC,J.B. *234*
An interdisciplinary study of the early works of Gertrude Stein in the context of cubism, 1904–1913. PhD State of New York at Binghamton, 1979.

NIGHTLINGER,E.B. *235*
The iconography of St Margaret of Cortona. PhD George Washington U. 1982.

NOEL,N.L. *236*
The creative process as experienced by women artists. PhD California Sch. of Prof. Psych. San Diego, 1981.

NUNN,P.G. *237*
The mid-Victorian women artist, 1850–1879. PhD U. of London, University Coll. 1982.

O'NEILL,J.N. *238*
Queen Elizabeth I as a patron of the arts: the relationship between royal patronage, society and culture in Renaissance England. PhD Vanderbilt U. 1961.

ORAM,K.A. *239*
Stylistic ornament in three fifteenth-century English legends of Mary Magdalene: a study in flamboyant styles. PhD Catholic U. of America, 1981.

PRICE,S. *240*
Women and art in an Afro-American society. PhD Johns Hopkins U. 1981.

REUTER,B.A. *241*
The career development of the professional female artist compared with that of the male. PhD Columbia U. 1974.

ROBERTS,A.M. *242*
The Master of the Legend of Lucy: a catalogue and critical essay. PhD U. of Pennsylvania, 1982.

ROBERTS,P.R. *243*
An experimental study of selected effects upon drawings produced by college age women using poetry as motivation. EdD Illinois State U. 1968.

RODEIRO,J.M. *244*
A comparative study of English Pre-Raphaelitism and Italian Pre-Raphaelitism's influence on the 'modernismo' art of Don Julio Romeo de Torres and the literature of Don Ramón del Valle-Inclán in their use of the feminine mystique. PhD U. of Ohio, 1976.

ROSS,D. *245*
Conflict between autonomy and affiliation in women artists: a case study approach. PhD California Sch. of Prof. Psych., Berkeley, 1980.

ROUGH,R.H. *246*
The gospels of Matilda, Countess of Tuscany. PhD Columbia U. 1969.

SANDELL,R.K. *247*
Feminist art education: definition, assessment and application to contemporary art education. PhD Ohio State U. 1978.

SANDERS,P.E.B *248*
The image of women in Rodin's sculpture, with a catalogue of relevant works in the California

Palace of the Legion of Honor, San Francisco. PhD U. of California, Berkeley, 1974.

SMITH,D.R. *249*
The Dutch double and pair portrait: studies in the imagery of marriage in the seventeenth century. PhD Columbia U. 1978.

SMITH,S.L. *250*
'To women's wiles I fell': the power of women 'topos' and the development of medieval secular art. PhD U. of Pennsylvania, 1978.

SPRINGER, A.M. *251*
Women in French *fin de siècle* posters. PhD Indiana U. 1971.

TROYEN,C.L. *252*
Dürer's *Life of the Virgin*. PhD Yale U. 1979.

WALCH,P.S. *253*
Angelica Kauffman. PhD Princeton U. 1968.

WARFORD,P.N. *254*
The social origins of female iconography: selected images of women in American popular culture, 1890–1945. PhD Saint Louis U. 1979.

WILTON,N.C. *255*
The antecedents of artistic success: a study of the early lives of women visual artists. EdD Boston U. Sch. of Educ. 1978.

WOODWARD,H.L. *256*
In bold and fearless connection: a study of the fiction of Flannery O'Connor and the photography of Diane Arbus. PhD U. of Minnesota, 1978.

YELDHAM,C.E. *257*
Woman artists in nineteenth-century France and England: their art education, exhibition opportunities and membership of exhibiting societies and academies. PhD U. of London, Courtauld Inst. of Art 1980.

2 Criminology

General

See also **8** 67, 69, 74, 75, 76; **9** 357, 464, 467, 544; **12** 1455; **20** 169, 181; **21** 60.

ADLER,F.S. *1*
The female offender in Philadelphia. PhD U. of Pennsylvania, 1971.

ALKEN,O.V. *2*
The process of socialization of adult female offenders by inmates into the inmate social system. DSW Catholic U. of America, 1972.

ARNOLD,R.A. *3*
Socio-structural determinants of self-esteem and the relationship between self-esteem and criminal behavior patterns of imprisoned minority women. PhD Bryn Mawr Coll. 1979.

ATESHZAR,D. *4*
The effect of prison confinement in changing the self-concept of criminal women. PhD United States International U. 1977.

BIRG,L.D. *5*
Support systems of female felons. PhD U. of Illinois at Chicago Circle, 1981.

BULARZIK,M.J. *6*
Sex, crime and justice: women in the criminal justice system of Massachusetts, 1900–1950. PhD Brandeis U. 1982.

CHASE,D.L.C. *7*
Empathy and trustworthiness in female prisoners. PhD Boston U. Grad. Sch. 1977.

CHESTER,B. *8*
Personality and life history of female offenders and their sibs: a taxonomic and genetic analysis. PhD U. of Minnesota, 1976.

CLARK,R.T. *9*
Inmate mothers: their perceptions of their mothering functions. PhD Oklahoma State U. 1979.

EARNEST,M.R. *10*
Criminal self-conceptions in the penal community of female offenders: an empirical study. PhD U. of Iowa, 1971.

ECKERT,J.L. *11*
Recidivism among females as a function of sociodemographic, state mental hospital, and aftercare treatment variables. PhD Kent State U. 1981.

FEINMAN,C. *12*
Imprisoned women: a history of the treatment of women incarcerated in New York City, 1932–1975. PhD New York U. 1976.

FISHER,K.L. *13*
The determination of some personality characteristics of women who escape from prison. PhD U. of Washington, 1977.

FONDREN,D.L. *14*
A comparison of institutionalized female offenders with non-offender females according to vocational self-concept, acquiescent response style, and vocational anxiety. PhD U. of Southern Mississippi, 1976.

FOX,J.G. *15*
Self-imposed stigmata: a study of tattooing among female inmates. PhD State U. of New York at Albany, 1976.

FREI,I.M. *16*
Relationship between experience in a specialized therapeutic program and behavior of women prisoners after release from jail. PhD United States International U. 1977.

FULLER,W.C. *17*
Life scripts of female offenders at the Kentucky Correctional Institution for Women. DMin Louisville Presbyterian Theological Seminary, 1977.

FURLONG,V.J. *18*
Anti-social behavior in youthful female offenders. EdD U. of Northern Colorado, 1971.

GATES,D.L. *19*
Theft and the status of women: the question of chivalry and equal treatment of men and women in the criminal justice system of Riverside County, California, from 1960 through 1971. PhD U. of Hawaii, 1975.

GROSS,D. *20*
A participant observation study of communication during activity of short-term imprisoned women. PhD State U. of New York at Buffalo, 1979.

HAGENAU,H.R. *21*
Parental attitudes, perceptions of parents, and

some personality characteristics of child-abusing women. PhD Catholic U. of America, 1977.

HENRIQUES,Z.W. [22
Incarcerated mothers' perceptions of their children's situation: a descriptive and analytical study. EdD Columbia U. Teachers Coll. 1979.

HERBIG,J.M. 23
Disparity in sentences recommended for women convicted of felonies: multivariate analysis programs. PhD Claremont Grad. Sch. 1977.

HOFFMAN,K.S. 24
Variables relating to program outcomes in a community-based program for women offenders. PhD Wayne State U. 1979.

JURIK,N.C. 25
Women ex-offenders: their work and rearrest patterns. PhD U. of California, 1980.

KAY,B.A. 26
Differential self-perceptions of female offenders. PhD Ohio State U. 1961.

KENEL,M.E. 27
A study of the cognitive dimension of impulsivity-reflectivity and aggression in female child-abusers. PhD Catholic U. of America, 1976.

KETTERLING,M.E. 28
Rehabilitation of women in the Milwaukee county jail: an exploratory experiment. EdD U. of Northern Colorado, 1964.

KNUDSON,B. 29
Career patterns of female misdemeanant offenders. PhD U. of Minnesota, 1968.

KOPROWSKI,E.C.G. 30
Women who kill: a study of violent behavior. PhD George Washington U. 1977.

KRUTTSCHNITT,C.M. 31
The social control of women offenders: a study of sentencing in a criminal court. PhD Yale U. 1979.

LACY,A.B. 32
Staff interactions in a woman's prison: a sociological drama. PhD U. of Maryland, 1973.

LIPPERT,M.C. 33
The effects of violent films upon aggressive institutionalized females. PhD California Sch. of Prof. Psych., Los Angeles, 1975.

LOMBARDI,N.J. 34
The absence of suicide in New York City's Women's House of Detention. PsyD Rutgers U. 1979.

MABB,V. 35
Marxism, patriarchy and the criminalization of women. MA* U. of Sheffield, 1976.

MAHAN,S.G. 36
The women's honor unit: case study of a women's prison. PhD U. of Missouri-Columbia, 1979.

MANE,K.V. 37
Volunteering behavior and personality characteristics of women prisoners. PhD Loyola U. Chicago, 1972.

MASLOVSKY,B. 38
Women in prison: the radicalization of women's deviance. MA* U. of Sheffield, 1979.

MITCHELL,A.E. 39
Informal inmate social structure in prisons for women: a comparative study. PhD U. of Washington, 1969.

MITCHELL,M.P. 40
A study of children of women prisoners. PhD Emory U. 1982.

MORALES,R. 41
History of the California Institution for Women, 1927–1960: a woman's regime. PhD U. of California, Riverside, 1980.

MOYSES,C.D. 42
The effects of three treatment approaches on locus of control of incarcerated females. PhD Auburn U. 1982.

MUSK,H.A. 43
Programs for incarcerated women and their children: psychodynamic considerations and implications. PhD U. of Maryland, 1981.

PANAGOPOULOS,J.A. 44
Korydullo: a study of a Greek prison for women offenders. PhD U. of New Hampshire, 1979.

PEARSON,V.L. 45
A study of relationships between the Porteus maze test and recidivism rates of female correctional institution inmates. PhD Texas Woman's U. 1972.

PETRAGLIA,G.G. 46
Female parole violators: an analysis of the situational aspects of their failure. PhD Fordham U. 1965.

POLLAK,O. 47
The criminology of women. PhD U. of Pennsylvania, 1947.

PORTER,H.K. 48
Prison homosexuality, locus of control and femininity. PhD Michigan State U. 1969.

PUNG,L.J. 49
The effects of a stressful transition experience on dreams: an analysis of dreams of women undergoing release from prison. PhD California Sch. of Prof. Psych., Los Angeles, 1977.

QUARLES,M.A.S. 50
Organizational analysis of the New Jersey Reformatory for Women in relation to stated principles of corrections, 1913–1963: a case study in institutional change. PhD Boston U. 1966.

RAMOS,M.O. *51*
Prisonization as an inhibitor of Puerto Rican female inmates' effective resocialization. PhD U. of Missouri-Columbia, 1982.

RASCHE,C.E. *52*
Problems, expectations and the post-release adjustment of the female felon. PhD U. of Washington, 1972.

RICKARDS-EKEH,K.A. *53*
Voluntary association membership of female inmates: a case study. PhD U. of Nebraska-Lincoln, 1981.

ROBINSON,E.B. *54*
Women on parole: reintegration of the female offender. PhD Ohio State U. 1971.

RODGERS,B.E. *55*
Inmate response to the home furlough program: the reactions of female offenders to temporary release from incarceration. PhD State U. of New York at Albany, 1978.

RUBINSTEIN,E.S. *56*
Body buffer zones in female prisoners. PhD Long Island U. Brooklyn Center, 1975.

SCHULTZ,C.G. *57*
Sociopathic and non-sociopathic female felons. PhD Ohio State U. 1973.

SCHWEBER,C. *58*
Sexual integration and prison education: a study of the educational opportunities for women inmates in the single sex, partially integrated and fully integrated federal prisons, 1975–76. PhD State U. of New York at Buffalo, 1977.

SELDIN,B.E. *59*
A comparison of selected personality variables among assaultive and non-assaultive female offenders with varying sex-role orientations. PhD Catholic U. of America, 1980.

SHORT,W. *60*
Sisterhoods: women and crime. MA U. of Sussex, 1976.

SILVA,S.S.H. *61*
A study of female offenders in Sri Lanka and England. MPhil U. of London, King's Coll. 1981.

SIMMONS,I.L. *62*
Interaction and leadership among female prisoners. PhD U. of Missouri-Columbia, 1975.

SMART,C. *63*
Women and crime: a feminist perspective. MA* U. of Sheffield, 1974.

SPENCER,E.J. *64*
The social system of a medium security women's prison. PhD U. of Kansas, 1977.

STANTON,A.M. *65*
Female offenders and their children: the effects of maternal incarceration on children. PhD Stanford U. 1978.

STRICKLAND,K.G. *66*
Correctional institutions for women in the United States. DSS Syracuse U. 1967.

TAITT,A.L. *67*
Counseling and recidivism: a study of women participants in the Teachers College, Columbia University, Rikers Island Correctional Institution for Women project. EdD Columbia U. 1974.

VAN HORNE,B.A. *68*
A study of selected variables, including the MMPI, as predicators of adult female recidivism. PhD U. of Wisconsin, 1979.

VANKATWYK,P.L. *69*
The re-entry process of women parolees: a case study in a socialization counseling model in pastoral care. PhD Sch. of Theology at Claremont, 1978.

VAN WORMER,K.S. *70*
Sex-role behavior in a women's prison: an ethnological analysis. PhD U. of Georgia, 1976.

WARD,J. *71*
A study of the social organization and work patterns in a women's prison. PhD U. of Manchester, 1977.

WHITSON,K.S. *72*
A comparison of the adult performance level of women offenders in the Texas Department of Corrections and Free-World Women in Texas. PhD Texas A&M U. 1977.

WILLIAMS,L.R. *73*
An analysis of recreational programs in state women's correctional institutions of the United States with suggested guidelines for recreation services. PhD U. of Maryland, 1978.

WILLIAMS,Y.C. *74*
Structural aspects of female criminality in the United States: aggregate analysis and policy implications. PhD Case Western Reserve U. 1982.

YOUNG,V.D. *75*
Patterns of female criminality. PhD State U. of New York at Albany, 1981.

Delinquency and juvenile crime

See also **9** 399; **17** 200–302; **19** 508.

ACKLAND,J.W. *76*
The community home setting: a comparison of staff and girl perceptions. MPhil U. of Sussex, 1982.

ALLEMANG,D.T. *77*
An intitial evaluation of the occupational preparation program: a work/study program for

institutionalized delinquent females. PhD U. of Wisconsin-Madison, 1974.

ANDERSON,A.J. *78*
Power in prison: houseparents and residents in a correctional institution for delinquent girls. PhD U. of Maine, 1975.

ANSTEY,S.C.F. *79*
A comparative evaluative study of List D schools for girls: modes of treatment and some effects upon girls. PhD U. of Edinburgh, 1978.

AUGUSTINE,E.A. *80*
Female adolescent status offenders: an investigation into demographic and familial factors, offense pattern and intellectual and personality functioning in a rural setting. PhD U. of Tennessee, 1979.

AURICCHIO,E.W. *81*
A comparison of the sociological and psychological backgrounds of unwed mothers and aggressively delinquent girls at various ages. PhD Fordham U. 1972.

BADEN,M.A. *81*
Becoming a female delinquent. PhD Indiana U. 1971.

BARRY,M.E. *82*
Differential disposition of female offenders appearing before five selected New Jersey juvenile courts. PhD Fordham U. 1969.

BARTON,N.J. *83*
Disregarded delinquency: a study of self-reported middle-class female delinquency in a suburb. PhD Indiana U. 1965.

BATDORF,R.L. *84*
An investigation of the applicability of Holland's theory to adjudicated female adolescent delinquents. EdD Washington State U. 1969.

BEATTY,E.B.S. *85*
A field study in juvenile delinquency reality and its perception by institutionalized inmates of a state training school for girls. PhD U. of Oklahoma, 1964.

BENKA,P.B. *86*
Value differences and value system changes in incorrigible girls. PhD Washington State U. 1979.

BERLAGE,G.I. *87*
The study of the relationship between girls' social class, values, self-reported and official delinquency in one urban community. PhD New York U. 1979.

BRONNER,A.F. *88*
A comparative study of the intelligence of delinquent girls. PhD Columbia U. 1914.

BROWN,E.J. *89*
Some psychological differences between neglected and delinquent adolescent girls. PhD U. of Oklahoma, 1968.

BROWN,M.B. *90*
Locus of control, self-concept, and level of aspiration in situation-specific institutionalized delinquent girls. EdD U. of Southern California, 1978.

BROWN,R.L.S. *91*
Changes in views of self and parents among a group of first-time incarcerated delinquent girls. PhD U. of Oklahoma, 1970.

CAMPBELL,A.C. *92*
The role of the peer group in female delinquency. DPhil U. of Oxford, 1976.

CAMPBELL,B.L. *93*
Systematic desensitization: an approach to the treatment of black female delinquent adolescents. PhD California Sch. of Prof. Psych., Berkeley, 1978.

CARMICHAEL,C.M. *94*
Borstal girls – as a focus for studying anti-social deviance in women. MSc U. of Edinburgh, 1972.

CARTER,B.L. *95*
On the grounds: informal culture in a girls' reform school. PhD Brandeis U. 1972.

CLAYTON,R.B. *96*
Personality traits of delinquent girls. PhD Case Western Reserve U. 1943.

COHN,R.R. *97*
The Tennessee self-concept scale as a differentiator of delinquent female sub-groups. PhD U. of Oklahoma, 1970.

COURTHIAL,A. *98*
Emotional differences of delinquent and non-delinquent girls of normal intelligence: a study of two groups paired by chronological age, intelligence and environment. PhD Columbia U. 1932.

CROWLEY,J.E. *99*
The relationships of delinquents with their mothers: attachment, labels, and interactions. PhD U. of Michigan, 1978.

D'ANGELO,R.Y. *100*
An evaluation of group psychotherapy with institutionalized delinquent girls. PhD Fordham U. 1961.

DAVENPORT,C.M. *101*
A study of the feasibility of developing a delinquent girl scale for the school interest inventory. PhD Boston Coll. 1969.

DILL,J.S. *102*
An experimental comparison of single therapist and multiple therapist group counseling with incarcerated female delinquents. EdD Ball State U. 1970.

DREDGE,E.D. *103*
Development of a model for the prediction of recidivism of female juvenile delinquents. PhD U. of Nebraska-Lincoln, 1973.

EDWARDS,A.R. *104*
Adolescence and delinquency: a sociological analysis of sex and area differences. PhD U. of London (External), 1975.

EISEN,V.W. *105*
An evaluation of several psychological tests for differentiating female delinquents from female nondelinquents. PhD Fordham U. 1956.

FARLEY,N.B. *106*
The temporal orientation of the female juvenile delinquent. EdD U. of Oklahoma, 1958.

FIORE,B.A. *107*
Female delinquency and the double standard of justice in the juvenile justice system. PhD Rutgers U. 1982.

GALLOWAY,J.R. *108*
A comparative study of the inhibition process in delinquent and non-dilenquent females. PhD U. of Oklahoma, 1958.

GIBBS,J.T. *109*
Personality patterns of delinquent females: ethnic and sociocultural variations. PhD U. of California, Berkeley, 1980.

GILBERT,M.J. *110*
A comparative study of delinquent and non-delinquent girls. MPhil U. of Southampton, 1970.

GILLAN,P.W. *110*
The measures of impulsiveness in female delinquents. MA U. of London, Inst. of Psych. 1965.

GOTTUSO,J.B. *111*
An interpersonal approach to female adolescent delinquency. PhD California Sch. of Prof. Psych. Los Angeles, 1973.

GRAIN,M.C. *112*
Recent trends in the delinquency of girls: a study of cases recorded by the City of Oxford Education Authority, Nov. 1933–Dec. 1946. BLitt U. of Oxford, 1949.

GRANT,R.B. *113*
An investigation of the self-image of institutionalized delinquent girls. PhD U. of Michigan, 1962.

HAYMOND,P.J. *114*
A new look at an old team: a correlational study of the Rorschach and MMPI with adolescent female delinquents. EdD Indiana U. 1982.

HOLSOPPLE,F.Q. *115*
Social non-conformity: an analysis of 420 cases of delinquent girls and women. PhD U. of Pennsylvania, 1919.

HULKOWER,B. *116*
Parental self-perceptions and perceptions of their delinquent children: an interpersonal approach to the study of female adolescent delinquency. PhD United States International U. 1977.

JANCHILL,M.P. *117*
Differential perception of the behavior characteristics of adolescent girls in residential treatment centers by caseworkers, child care workers, and teachers. DSW Columbia U. 1975.

KAGAN,H. *118*
Prostitution and sexual promiscuity among adolescent female offenders. PhD U. of Arizona, 1969.

KEEFE,J.B. *119*
The relation of locus of control, sex-role self-concept and sex-role attitudes to female delinquent behavior. PhD New York U. 1976.

KENNEDY,J.P. *120*
Identified common elements of scripts of adolescent girls in a delinquent institution. PhD Louisville Presbyterian Theological Seminary, 1975.

KOH,E.W.K. *121*
Seasonal distribution of girl delinquents in Detroit. PhD U. of Michigan, 1937.

KOPP,M.A. *122*
A study of anomia and homosexuality in delinquent adolescent girls. PhD Saint Louis U. 1960.

LEECH,K.R. *123*
A study of the adjustment of delinquent girls to an institutional setting. PhD U. of Tennessee, 1971.

LEVE,H.N. *124*
Prediction of parolee behavior utilizing the semantic differential and inmate and staff judgments for delinquent girls in a state correctional institution. EdD Indiana U. 1972.

LEWIS,J.W. *125*
Susceptibility to influence of two types of institutionalized female delinquents. PhD U. of Wisconsin, 1965.

LIGHT,H.K. *126*
Highly competent girls and delinquent girls: a comparative study of value-needs and self-concept profiles. PhD Michigan State U. 1976.

LUMPKIN,K.D.P. *127*
Factors in the commitment of correctional school girls in Wisconsin. PhD U. of Wisconsin, 1928.

MCCABE,S.F. *128*
A study of the treatment of delinquent girls. BLitt U. of Oxford, 1964.

MCDANIEL,J.S. *129*
A comparative study of extroversion, neuroticism, and self-concept of delinquent and non-delinquent girls. EdD Ball State U. 1976.

MACVICAR,J.A. *130*
Homosexual delinquent girls' identification with mother and perception of parents. PhD Boston U. 1967.

MANN,C. *131*
The juvenile female in the judicial process. PhD U. of Illinois at Chicago Circle, 1972.

MELLOR,V.G. *132*
Becoming a Borstal girl: assimilation, adjustment and reaction to the environment in two Borstal institutions for girls. PhD U. of London, LSE, 1975.

MORTOLA,D.S. *133*
Aspects of the self-concept in delinquent girls' maternal identification and body concept. PhD Fordham U. 1970.

NOLLENBERGER,H.A. *134*
A study of attitudes of female delinquents toward the functional and dysfunctional aspects of the school as compared to male juvenile delinquents. EdD U. of Toledo, 1981.

NORCROSS,B.N. *135*
A comparison of sex-role orientation, family ideology, and heterosexual relationships for delinquent and non-delinquent girls. PhD Rosemead Grad. Sch. 1977.

NOVAK,D.F. *136*
A comparison of vocational interests and aptitudes of delinquent and non-delinquent girls. PhD Loyola U. of Chicago, 1956.

O'CONNELL,M.A. *137*
Residential care: a study of the residential care of damaged and delinquent adolescent girls in Scotland. MEd U. of Dundee, 1977.

PATTERSON,E.J. *138*
Changes in perceptual field occurring among delinquent adolescent females. PhD U. of Pittsburgh, 1966.

POSTLEWAITE,M.M. *139*
The effects of human relations workshops upon the behavior of delinquent adolescent girls. PhD Columbia U. 1975.

PURCELL,J.F. *140*
Expressed self-concept and adjustment in sexually delinquent and non-delinquent adolscent girls. PhD Fordham U. 1961.

REARDON,J.P. *141*
The effects of rational stage directed therapy on self-concept and reduction of psychological stress in adolescent delinquent females. PhD Ohio State U 1976.

ROCHELLE,P.A. *142*
A study of the social system of an institution for adolescent delinquent girls. DSW U. of California, Berkeley, 1965.

ROSENTHAL,L. *143*
A comparison of social skills in delinquent and nondelinquent adolescent girls using a behavioral role-playing inventory. PhD U. of Wisconsin, 1978.

RUMNEY,L. *144*
Care and control: female delinquency and the welfare state. MA* U. of Sheffield, 1978.

SEPSI,V.J. *145*
Archival factors for predicting recidivism of female juvenile delinquents. PhD Kent State U. 1971.

SHACKLADY,L.A. *146*
Female delinquency and sex-role theory. MSc U. of Bath, 1973.

SHAPIRO,D.J. *147*
The factorial invariance of the Behavioral Research and Evaluation Corporation's self-report delinquency scale across age and sex. PhD Hofstra U. 1980.

SHEPHERD,J.G. *148*
Female delinquency: a control perspective. DSW U. of California, Berkeley, 1980.

SINGLETON,M.H. *149*
Personality factors in delinquent adolescent females. PhD U. of Tennessee, 1976.

SMITH,A.D. *150*
The treatment and rehabitation of delinquent women. PhD U. of Edinburgh, 1961.

SMITH,E.S. *151*
Psychoeducational factors for differentiating female juvenile recidivists and non-recidivists on probation. PhD Case Western Reserve U. 1977.

SMITH,R.E.Jr. *152*
Self-concept in female delinquents. PhD Ohio State U. 1972.

SPINKS,N.J. *153*
The effects of male and female models in vicarious therapy pretraining on the change in self-concept of institutionalized female juvenile delinquents in group counseling. PhD Florida State U. 1960.

STIEL,A. *154*
An investigation of the test characteristics associated with acceptable institutional adjustment in delinquent girls. PhD Loyola U. of Chicago, 1955.

SUDDICK,D.E. *155*
Female juvenile runaways from home. PhD U. of Northern Colorado, 1969.

SUKONECK,B. *156*
The relationship between hypnotic suggestibility and personality in delinquent and non-delinquent adolescent females. EdD Ball State U. 1973.

TAPPAN,P.W. *157*
Delinquent girls in court: a study of the Wayward Minor Court, New York. PhD Columbia U. 1947.

TEMMER,H.W. *158*
An investigation into the effects of psychotherapy upon habitual avoidance and escape patterns displayed by delinquent adolescent girls. PhD New York U. 1957.

TEMPLETON,G.J. *159*
The impact of the culture of a cottage in a residential treatment center on the implementation of a bibliotherapy program for delinquent girls. PhD U. of North Carolina at Chapel Hill, 1979.

TIMBERS,G.D.. *160*
Achievement place for girls: token reinforcement, social reinforcement and instructional procedures in a family style treatment setting for 'predelinquent' girls. PhD U. of Kansas, 1974.

TIMON,E.M. *161*
An assessment of the general knowledge and interests of adolescent delinquent girls committed to an approved school. MA U. of London, University Coll. 1955.

TRESE,L.J. *162*
Personality of the delinquent girl. EdD Wayne State U. 1957.

VANE,J.R. *163*
A study of frustration, aggression and level of aspiration in delinquent girls. PhD New York U. 1951.

VELDHUIZEN,J.F. *164*
The effect of institutional placement on delinquent adolescent girls: an MMPI and CPI sequence testing approach. ThD Grad. Theological Union, 1971.

VIAR,J.S. *165*
Differences between obese and non-obese female adolescent delinquents in terms of developmental patterns and psychological variables. PhD United States International U. 1976.

WALKER,J. *166*
Factors contributing to the delinquency of defective girls. PhD U. of California, Berkeley, 1922.

WARD-HULL,C.I. *167*
Correlates of female juvenile delinquency. PhD Indiana U. 1981.

WIDSETH,J.C. *168*
Reported dependent behaviors toward mother and use of alcohol in delinquent girls. PhD Boston U. 1972.

WILKINSON,K.R. *169*
Juvenile delinquency and femininity. PhD U. of Arizona, 1978.

WILLIAMSON,G.L. *170*
Commitment decisions in the juvenile justice systems: results and implications for the female delinquent. PhD U. of Georgia, 1982.

WILLOUGHBY,A. *171*
The effects of repeated success and failure evaluations upon the performances of female juvenile delinquents and non-delinquents. PhD U. of Connecticut, 1959.

YOUNGSON,S.C. *172*
Adolescent girls in a List D setting: academic achievement and personality. MPhil U. of Edinburgh, 1981.

Offences against women and girls

Battering

See also **11** 10.

ANAPOL,D.M. *173*
Women in battering relationships: the parameters of abuse. PhD U. of Washington, 1981.

ARNDT,N.Y. *174*
Domestic violence: an investigation of the psychological aspects of the battered woman. PhD Fielding Inst. 1981.

BERNARD,C.A. *175*
Unmarried battered women: demographic data, attitudes toward women, and locus of control. PhD U. of Maryland, 1981.

BIRNBAUM,L.F. *176*
Female submissiveness, assertiveness and aggressiveness and situational provocation in relation to wife abuse. PhD Hofstra U. 1980.

CRISTALL,L.M. *177*
A comparison of androgyny and self-actualization in battered women. PhD United States International U. 1978.

DUNCAN,D.C. *178*
Cognitive perceptions of battered women. PhD U. of Southern California, 1982.

DVOSKIN,J.A. *179*
Battered women – an epidemiological study of spousal violence. PhD U. of Arizona, 1981.

DYE,M.R.W. *180*
Identification of potential wife abusers and abusees in a college population. PhD Atlanta U. 1981.

ELLIS,R.M. *181*
Battered women: a case study of social control. MscEcon U. Coll. Cardiff, 1982.

FELDMAN,L.S. *182*
Conjugal violence: a psychological and symbolic interactionist analysis. PhD United States International U. 1979.

FERRARO,K.J. *183*
Battered women and the shelter movement. PhD Arizona State U. 1981.

GAYFORD,J.J. *184*
Battered wives: a study of the aetiology and psychological effects among one hundred women. MD U. of London, St George's Hospital Medical Sch. 1978.

GILES-SIMS,J.G. *185*
Stability and change in patterns of wife beating: a systems theory approach. PhD U. of New Hampshire, 1979.

GRAFF,T.T. *186*
Personality characteristics of battered women. PhD Brigham Young U. 1979.

GRAVDAL,B.W. *187*
A study of locus of control and sex-role typology in two groups of battered women. PhD Washington State U. 1982.

HARTIK,L.M. *188*
Identification of personality characteristics and self-concept factors of battered wives. PhD United States International U. 1978.

HEINTZELMAN,C.A. *189*
Differential utilization of selected community resources by abused women. DSW Catholic U. of America, 1980.

HOFELLER,K.H. *190*
Social, psychological and situational factors in wife abuse. PhD Claremont Grad. Sch. 1980.

JACQUES,K.N. *191*
Perceptions and coping behaviors of Anglo-American and Mexican immigrant battered women: a comparative study. PhD United States International U. 1981.

KUHL,A.F. *192*
The relationship of severity of abuse experienced and personality needs of abused women. PhD Washington State U. 1981.

LESSER,B.Z. *193*
Factors influencing battered women's return to their mates following a shelter program-attachment and situational variables. PhD California Sch. of Prof. Psych., Los Angeles, 1981.

LOMBARDI,J. *194*
Growing up with violence: an analysis of retrospective accounts of female offspring. PhD U. of Maryland, 1982.

LOPEZ,S. *195*
Marital satisfaction and wife abuse as functions of sex-role identity, self- esteem and interpersonal style. PhD Georgia State U. Coll. of Arts and Sciences, 1981.

LOSEKE,D.R. *196*
Social movement theory in practice: a shelter for battered women. PhD U. of California, Santa Barbara, 1982.

MCCANN,K.E. *197*
The legal response to wife abuse: a study of sex bias. MPhil U. of Sheffield, 1983.

MILLER,J.C. *198*
An application of learned helplessness theory to battered women. PhD California Sch. of Prof. Psych. San Diego, 1981.

MILLS,T.L. *199*
Violence and the self: a multi-method study. PhD U. of North Carolina at Chapel Hill, 1982.

MOORE,J.H. *200*
Sex-role stereotyping in battered women: responses to the BEM sex-role inventory. PhD Virginia Commonwealth U. 1983.

MORGAN,S.M. *201*
Conjugal terrorism: a psychological and community treatment model of wife abuse. PhD California Sch. of Prof. Psych., Fresno, 1979.

NOVAK,D.G. *202*
Life styles and social interest ratings of battered women. PhD U. of Texas at Austin, 1979.

PAGELOW,M.D. *203*
Woman battering, victims of spouse abuse and their perceptions of violent relationships. PhD U. of California, Riverside, 1980.

POLLACK,M. *204*
Battering husbands: a personality profile as perceived by their wives. PhD United States International U. 1980.

REYNOLDS,L. *205*
Power and inequality: a case study of abused women. PhD Fordham U. 1981.

ROGOVIN,S.A. *206*
The violent marriage: investigation of the battered woman, her parent-child relationship and family background. PhD America U. 1979.

ROSENBAUM,A. *207*
Wife abuse: characteristics of the participants and etiological considerations. PhD State U. of New York at Stony Brook, 1979.

RYAN,D.M. *208*
Patterns of antecedents to husbands' battering behavior as detected by the use of the critical incident technique. PhD United States International U. 1982.

SAUNDERS,D.G. *209*
The police response to battered women: predictors of officers' use of arrest, counseling or minimal action. PhD U. of Wisconsin-Madison, 1979.

THOENNES,N.A. *210*
Social network functioning among battered women: the consequences of geographic mobility. PhD U. of Denver, 1981.

TIERNEY,K.J. *211*
Social movement organization, resource mobilization, and the creation of a social problem: a case study of a movement for battered women. PhD Ohio State U. 1979.

WHARTON,C.S. *212*
Redefining woman battering: the construction of a social problem. PhD Michigan State U. 1982.

WOODS,F.B. *213*
A community approach to working with battered women. PhD U. of Arkansas, 1979.

YLLO,K.A. *214*
The status of women and wife beating in the US: a multi-level analysis. PhD U. of New Hampshire, 1980.

Incest

BENNETT,M.H. *215*
Father-daughter incest: a psychological study of the mother from an attachment theory perspective. PhD California Sch. of Prof. Psych., Los Angeles, 1980.

COURTOIS,C.A. *216*
Characteristics of a volunteer sample of adult women who experienced incest in childhood or adolescence. PhD U. of Maryland, 1979.

FREDRICKSON,R.M. *217*
Family sexual abuse and its relationship to pathology, sex-role orientation, attitudes toward women, and authoritariansim. PhD U. of Minnesota, 1981.

GIARRETTO,H. *218*
Integral psychology in the treatment of father-daughter incest. PhD California Inst. of Integral Studies, 1978.

GLIGOR,A.M. *219*
Incest and sexual delinquency: a comparative analysis of two forms of sexual behavior in minor females. PhD Case Western Reserve U. 1966.

HARRER,M.N. *220*
Father-daughter incest: a study of the mother. PhD Indiana U. 1980.

HUGHES,K.A. *221*
The reported incidence of incest among runaway female adolescents. PhD California Sch. of Prof. Psych., Berkeley, 1980.

KEGAN,K.A. *222*
Attachment and family sexual abuse: an investigation of the families of origin and social histories of mothers from present incest families. PhD U. of Minnesota, 1981.

KNUDSON,D.G. *223*
Interpersonal dynamics and mother involvement in father-daughter incest in Puerto Rico. PhD Ohio State U. 1981.

OWENS,T.H. *224*
Personality characteristics of female psychotherapy patients with a history of incest. PsyD Rosemead Grad. Sch. of Prof. Psych. 1982.

REISINGER,M.C. *225*
Psychological test profiles of latency-aged female incest victims: a comparative study. PhD Brigham Young U. 1981.

ROFSKY,M. *226*
Effects of father-daughter incest on the personality of daughters. PhD United States International U. 1979.

STRAUS,P.L. *227*
A study of the recurrence of father-daughter incest across generations. PhD California Sch. of Prof. Psych., Berkeley, 1981.

WILLIAMS,B.G. *228*
Sexual abuse of children: the maternal adult female's collusive role. PhD U. of Akron, 1982.

Rape and sexual assault

See also **11** 1, 13.

ABBEY,A.D. *229*
The effects of rape victims' attributions of responsibility on their long- term adjustment. PhD Northwestern U. 1982.

AMIR,M. *230*
Patterns in forcible rape: with special reference to Philadelphia, Pennsylvania, 1958 and 1960. PhD U. of Pennsylvania, 1965.

ANDREWS,F.M. *231*
The influence of evidenciary and extra evidenciary factors on decisions in a simulated rape trial. PhD Colorado State U. 1981.

BLEY,J.W. *232*
Effects of prior sex history and physical resistance evidence on verdicts of individuals and simulated juries in rape trials. PhD U. of Cincinnati, 1980.

BOND,S.B. *233*
Affective and sexual reactions to guided imagery of rape: implications for counseling. PhD U. of Connecticut, 1979.

BRAKENSEK,L.S. *234*
The effect of an educational program in reducing 'rape myth acceptance'. PhD Fuller Theological Seminary Sch. of Psych. 1982.

BROTHERS,D. *235*
Trust disturbances among rape and incest victims. PhD Yeshiva U. 1982.

CARSON,R. *236*
The effects of respectability, severity of consequences and probability of a similar fate on peers' perceptions of a rape victim. PhD U. of Alabama, 1981.

COHEN,P.B. *237*
The sexually assaulted woman: the relationship of sex-role style to resistance during the assault and adjustment. PhD U. of Pittsburgh, 1981.

CRYER,L.G. *238*
Life change measurement: an outcome evaluation study of a public health nursing program to assist rape victims. DrPH U. of Texas, Houston Sch. of Public Health, 1979.

DODSWORTH,J.A. *239*
The social ideology of rape. MA* U. of Sheffield, 1975.

DOWNING,N.E. *240*
An evaluation of the effectiveness of a training program for paraprofessional rape crisis hotline volunteers. PhD U. of Florida, 1980.

FISHER,W.S. *241*
Predictability of victim injury in incidents of rape. PhD City U. of New York, 1979.

FOLEY,T.S. *242*
The development and evaluation of an instructor's manual on nursing care of victims of rape (3 vols). PhD U. of Pittsburgh, 1979.

FORREST,L.M. *243*
Rape victim characteristics and crime circumstances: their relationship to the victim's perception of the treatment received from criminal justice personnel. PhD U. of Washington, 1979.

FRANK,E. *244*
Psychological response to rape: an analysis of response patterns. PhD U. of Pittsburgh, 1979.

GRIFFIN,B.S. *245*
Rape: risk, confrontation and normalization. PhD U. of Illinois at Urbana-Champaign, 1977.

GRIFFIN-STEEINK,K.M. *246*
Causal attribution in rape vs. aggravated robbery. PhD U. of Toledo, 1982.

GUSS,G.H. *247*
The woman's role in the victim-offender relationship in forcible rape. PhD California Sch. of Prof. Psych., Los Angeles, 1975.

HALL,R.L. *248*
Empathetic behavior in a simulated rape interview by police applicants. PhD Boston U. Grad. Sch. 1979.

HARRIS,S.P. *249*
Three psychological determinants of a woman's response to a sexual assault. PhD California Sch. of Prof. Psych., Los Angeles, 1977.

HEATH,L. *250*
A multi-methodological examination of the effects of perceptions of control on women's attitudes toward and behaviors concerning rape. PhD Northwestern U. 1980.

HOLMES,K.A. *251*
Rape-as-crisis: an empirical assessment. PhD U. of Texas at Austin, 1979.

JAMES,D.A. *252*
The crime of rape: towards a fully social theory of rape. MA* U. of Sheffield, 1979.

KELLY,D.P. *253*
Rape victims' perceptions of criminal justice. PhD Johns Hopkins U. 1983.

KENYON,K.J. *254*
The after-effects experienced by victims of rape and victims of attempted rape. EdD U. of California, San Francisco, 1982.

KIRKENDALL,A.R. *255*
Victim selection processes involved in rape. PhD Fuller Theological Seminary, Sch. of Psych. 1979.

KLEIN,R.A. *256*
An analysis of demographic and selected other factors related to the frequency of rape in the city of Long Beach, California, 1976–1980. EdD Pepperdine U. 1981.

KOZMA,C.L. *257*
An investigation of some hypotheses concerning rape and murder. PhD U. of Delaware, 1978.

LAFREE,G.D. *258*
Determinants of police, prosecution and court decisions in forcible rape cases. PhD U. of Indiana, 1979.

LAVES,R.G. *259*
Self-report correlates of crisis response to rape. PhD New York U. 1978.

LAZARUS,R.H. *260*
Attribution of fault to a rape victim as a function of moral development, sex of respondent, sex of victim and type of crime. PhD Temple U. 1982.

LEBEAU,J.L. *261*
The spatial dynamics of rape: the San Diego example. PhD Michigan State U. 1978.

LEVINE,J. *262*
Rape avoidance: a discriminant function analysis of non-victims, avoiders and victims. PhD Kent State U. 1982.

LIBOW,J.A. *263*
Self-attributed responsibility and self-derogation by rape victims from a social psychological perspective. PhD State U. of New York at Albany, 1978.

MASTRIA,M.A. *264*
A study of assertiveness as a function of training in rape prevention and assertive training. PhD U. of Mississippi, 1975.

MEYER,L.C. *265*
Rape cases in Philadelphia: court outcome and victim response. PhD U. of Pennsylvania, 1979.

MORGAN,J.B. *266*
Relationship between rape and physical damage during rape and phase of sexual cycle during which rape occurred. PhD U. of Texas at Austin, 1981.

MORGAN,W.K. *267*
The effect of a guided fantasy and information about rape on attitudes toward rape and victims of rape. PhD U. of Missouri-Columbia, 1979.

NELSON,S.H. 268
Jurors' verdicts in a mock rape trial experiment: a social learning approach. PhD Carleton U. 1979.

REMPELLY,J.P. 269
Attribution of responsibility by police officers and mental health professionals to victims and assailants in four paradigmatic episodes of rape and battery. PhD Columbia U. 1979.

RICHARDSON,D.D.A 270
The influence of socioeconomic status and reciprocity on mock jurors' verdicts in a hypothetical rape case. PhD Ohio State U. 1979.

RINEAR,C.E. 271
An epidemiological and attitudinal analysis of rape and other sexual assault among urban female hospital personnel. DEd Pennsylvania State U. 1977.

ROGEL,M.J. 272
Biosocial aspects of rape. PhD U. of Chicago, 1976.

SALISBURY,K.M. 273
Creating multi-cultural organizational responsiveness to rape victims: a study of organizational change. PhD U. of Massachusetts, 1981.

SATURANSKY,C.H. 274
A clinical study of rape victims: an analysis of the effects of rape experiences on personality dynamics and life styles. PhD Michigan State U. 1976.

SCHELL,D.W. 275
Pastoral care to sexually molested girls and their families. EdD New Orleans Baptist Theological Seminary, 1973.

SCHWENDINGER,J.R. 276
The rape victim and the criminal justice system. PhD U. of California, Berkeley, 1975.

SIMON,B.L. 277
Social movements and institutionalization: rape as a case study. PhD Bryn Mawr Coll. 1981.

SMITH,J.A. 278
Psychological features of rape victims: trauma, counseling and recovery. PhD Michigan State U. 1982.

SPARKS,C.H. 279
Program evaluation of a community rape prevention program. PhD Ohio State U. 1979.

STENZEL,E.J. 280
The violence of rape from a theological perspective. PhD Notre Dame U. 1981.

STOKES,F.G. 281
Assessing urban public space environments for danger of violent crime - especially rape. PhD U. of Washington, 1982.

STORY,M. 282
Social reactions towards rape. MPhil U. of Leicester, 1981.

STOWE,K. 283
The second victims: altruism and the affective reactions of affiliated males to their partner's rape. EdD Boston U. Sch. of Educ. 1980.

THOMPSON,G.E. 284
Attitudes of police officers and rape service volunteers toward rape and rape victims. PhD United States International U. 1980.

TYRA,P.A. 285
Volunteer rape counselors: selected characteristics – empathy, attribution of responsibility, and rape counselor syndrome. EdD Boston U. Sch. of Educ. 1979.

VAN DEN BERGH,N.J. 286
Predicting a feminist analysis of sexual assault: the differential effects of attitudes toward women, sex role, demographic life status variables, religiosity and interest in feminist issues. PhD U. of Pittsburgh, 1981.

VANDERMEER,J.M. 287
Psychological aspects and family dynamics of adolescent rape victims. PhD U. of New Mexico, 1976.

VERONEN,L.J. 288
Fear response of rape victims. PhD North Texas State U. 1977.

VOGELMANN-SINE,S. 289
Implicit consent and rape: an integration theory analysis of female responses in a dating context. PhD U. of Hawaii, 1980.

WALKER,C.G. 290
Psycho-legal aspects of rape. PhD Oklahoma State U. 1978.

WARD,M.A. 291
Attribution of blame in rape. PhD U. of South Dakota, 1980.

WEBB,C.L. 292
Social support and the psychological outcome of rape. PhD U. of Delaware, 1981.

WEBSTER,B.D. 293
An exploration of factors affecting women's predictions about sexual assault reporting and the prosecution of assailants. PhD California Sch. of Prof. Psych., San Diego, 1980.

WELSH,D.K. 294
Derogation of rape victims: a just world and defensive attribution analysis. PhD U. of Alabama, 1977.

WOJCIECHOWSKI-KIBBLE,N.T.C. 295
Rape and the victim: a socio-legal study. LLM U. of Warwick, 1976.

WOOTEN,J.N. 296
The effects of victim/assailant familiarity and victim resistance on attitudes toward rape among law enforcement personnel and college students. PhD Texas A&M U. 1980.

WRIGHT,R.T. *297*
Patterns of rape in England: an analysis of offences known to the police. PhD U. of Cambridge, 1980.

YANCHAR,N.V. *298*
Subject-juror decision-making in rape cases: effects of status of complainant, and gender of the defense attorney, the prosecuting attorney, and the subject-juror. PhD Bowling Green State U. 1982.

YATES,E.P. *299*
'Anger' evoked by insult and disinhibition of sexual arousal to rape cues. PhD Queen's U. at Kingston, 1980.

3 Demography

See also **9** 9, 108, 272, 383, 394; **19**, 6, 34; **19** 6, 34; **23** *passim. Related studies may also be found in ch.* **23**.

AANSTAD,J.A. *1*
Women in transition: a study of demographic and personality factors related to life-style choices. PhD U. of Florida, 1978.

ACHMAD,S.I. *2*
A study of the relationship between educational attainment and fertility behavior of women in Java and Bali. PhD Florida State U. 1980.

AKSORNKOOL,K. *3*
Desired and expected family size of rural Thai women in 1975: a study of fertility preferences in two rural villages. PhD Utah State U. 1980.

ANDERSON,J.L. *4*
Work plans and fertility expectations of teenage women: some tests of possible interpretations. PhD Columbia U. 1977.

ARTHUR,G.M. *5*
Employment and fertility among women in the United States. PhD U. of Kentucky, 1975.

BABATUNDE,D.E. *6*
Some aspects of Yoruba girls' fertility. MLitt U. of Oxford, 1980.

BEDWANY,T.L. *7*
The status of women and population control: the relationship of gross reproduction rate and selected indicators of the status of women in developed and developing countries. PhD Michigan State U. 1974.

BHATNAGAR,K.M. *8*
Education of rural women and fertility decline in India: an education policy analysis. EdD U. of South Dakota, 1980.

BOOTH,E.D. *9*
Female employment opportunity and fertility: an aggregate longitudinal analysis, US, 1969–1970. PhD U. of Washington, 1979.

BOUVIER,L.F. *10*
The effect of Catholicism on the fertility of Rhode Island women, 1968–1969. PhD Brown U. 1971.

BURLEIGH,J.D. *11*
A descriptive study of the demographic, ideological and environmental factors of the mature female undergraduate student attending Oklahoma State University during the spring semester of 1972. EdD Oklahoma State U. 1973.

CASTANEDA,T. *12*
Fertility, child schooling, and the labor force participation of mothers in Colombia. PhD U. of Chicago, 1977.

CASTERLINE,J.B. *13*
The determinants of rising female age at marriage: Taiwan, 1905–1976. PhD U. of Michigan, 1980.

CHAMIE,M.J.W. *14*
Middle Eastern marriages and contraceptive decisions: toward a sociopsychological understanding of fertility behavior. PhD U. of Michigan, 1978.

CHEN,P.C. *15*
The politics of population in Communist China: a case study of birth control policy, 1949–1965. PhD Princeton U. 1966.

CONCEPCION,M.B. *16*
Fertility differences among married women in the Philippines. PhD U. of Chicago, 1963.

COOK,C.C. *17*
Determinants of residential location of female householders. PhD Ohio State U. 1982.

COOK,M.J. *18*
Female labor force participation, modernity and fertility in rural Thailand. PhD Brown U. 1977.

COOKINGHAM,M.E. *19*
The demographic and labor force behavior of women college graduates, 1865 to 1965. PhD U. of California, Berkeley, 1980.

CORNWELL,G.T. *20*
The influence of premarital employment and education on the fertility of rural Philippine farm women. PhD Pennsylvania State U. 1981.

DA SILVA,L.M. *21*
Family size and female labor force participation in Brazil. PhD Duke U. 1976.

DAVIS,C.A. *22*
Social and economic correlates of ideal and desired family sizes of senior females in public high schools in the state of Utah. PhD Utah State U. 1972.

DAVIS,N.J. *23*
The political economy of reproduction: an analysis

of childlessness and single-child fertility among US women. PhD U. of Wisconsin-Madison, 1978.

DAY,L.H. 24
The age of women at completion of childbearing: demographic factors and possible social consequences, United States, 1919–1950. PhD Columbia U. 1957.

DEBAVALYA,N. 25
A study of female labor force participation and fertility in Thailand. PhD U. of Pennsylvania, 1975.

DEFRONZO,J.V. 26
Areal analyses of economic factors affecting the birth rate of young women: the United States, 1950–1970. PhD Indiana U. 1975.

DEIMLING,G.T. 27
Female labor force participation as related to fertility values among husbands and wives. PhD Bowling Green State U. 1976.

DELANCEY,V.H. 28
The relationship between female wage employment and fertility in Africa: an example from Cameroon. PhD U. of South Carolina, 1980.

DOESCHER,T.A. 29
Fertility and female occupational choice. PhD U. of North Carolina at Chapel Hill, 1980.

DOOLEY,M.D. 30
An analysis of the labor supply and fertility of married women with grouped data from the 1970 United States census. PhD U. of Wisconsin-Madison, 1977.

DUINELL,P.L. 31
The effects of selected demographic variables on the career development of women age 35 and over enrolled in higher education. PhD U. of Georgia, 1980.

EDWARDS,K.S. 32
The interrelationship between fertility patterns and type of occupation of working wives. PhD Michigan State U. 1977.

ENGRACIA,L.T. 33
Female labor force participation and fertility in the Philippines. PhD Utah State U. 1981.

FALLO-MITCHELL,L. 34
Changes in the timing of female/family life-cycle events: on-time vs. off-time? PhD Fordham U. 1980.

FIELD,P.L. 35
A comparative study of demographic and background characteristics of never-married and married women. PhD California Sch. of Prof. Psych., San Diego, 1979.

FLOGE,L.P. 36
The importance of child care for mothers' employment and fertility. PhD Columbia U. 1981.

FOLTZ,D. 37
Postponement of the first birth: patterns of childbearing in an educated group of women. PhD U. of Michigan, 1982.

FONTE,V.H. 38
Demographic variables and self-actualization for divorced and married women. PhD California Sch. of Prof. Psych., San Diego, 1976.

FRIED,E.S. 39
Female labor force participation and fertility: a life-cycle model. PhD U. of Chicago, 1975.

GARFINKLE,S.H. 40
Tables of working life for women. PhD American U. 1958.

GINN,H.L. 41
Women's market work and fertility: the influence of race. PhD U. of Maryland, 1982.

GOKGOL-KLINE,A.T. 42
A multivariate analysis of the effects of family structure, personal value system and status of women variables on the fertility behavior of urban migrant and rural populations in Turkey: a policy analysis. DSc Harvard U. 1979.

GORDON,L.W. 43
Women's work, role-conflict and fertility: a comparison of the Soviet Union and the United States. PhD Ohio State U. 1974.

GRAY,M.C. 44
Reproductive variability among Papago women born 1891–1930. PhD U. of Colorado at Boulder, 1977.

HAGOOD,M.J. 45
Mothers of the South: a population study of native white women of childbearing age of the southeast. PhD U. of North Carolina at Chapel Hill, 1938.

HAMZAWI,R.A. 46
The relationship between female employment and fertility. PhD Case Western Reserve U. 1982.

HASS,P.H. 47
Maternal employment and fertility in metropolitan Latin America. PhD Duke U. 1971.

HAVENS,E.G.M. 48
Female labor force participation and fertility. PhD U. of Texas at Austin, 1973.

HENDERSON,P.M. 49
Population policy, social structure and the health system in Puerto Rico: the case of female sterilization. PhD U. of Connecticut, 1976.

HEROLD,J.M. 50
Socioeconomic and demographic aspects of female labor force participation in urban Chile. PhD U. of Pennsylvania, 1982.

HILL,H.M. 51
The politics of fertility control: family planning

policy in the Philippines. PhD Northern Illinois U. 1982.

HOTZ,V.J. 52
A theoretical and empirical model of fertility and married women's allocation of time over the life-cycle. PhD U. of Wisconsin-Madison, 1980.

JONES,E.F. 53
The interrelations between childbearing and women's employment in the United States, 1970–1975. PhD U. of Pennsylvania, 1979.

KARIM,M.S. 54
Female nuptiality and fertility in Pakistan. PhD Cornell U. 1982.

KARPINOS,B.D. 55
The future growth of Iowa female population. PhD U. of Iowa, 1935.

KASSELMAN,M.J. 56
A comparative study of delivery patterns and reproductive efficiency in groups of negro and Caucasian women. PhD U. of Kansas, 1971.

KELLY,W.R. 57
A time-series analysis of the illegitimacy rate, marriage rate to pregnant women and sexual activity: Sweden and Australia, 1911–1974. PhD Indiana U. 1979.

KHAN,M.M. 58
Sequential analysis of fertility orientations and behavior of teenage mothers. PhD Catholic U. of America, 1981.

KIRIBANDA,B.M. 59
Education, female labor force status, and fertility interrelationships: a study of dynamics and differentials in Sri Lanka, 1971. PhD U. of Pennsylvania, 1981.

KOO,S.Y. 60
A study of fertility and labor force participation of married women in Korea. PhD U. of Hawaii, 1979.

KRAMER,M.J. 61
Abortion and fertility in economic perspective: a theoretical and empirical analysis with special reference to New York City, 1969–1972. PhD Harvard U. 1982.

LAMOUREAUX,J.W. 62
Receptivity of specific subaudiences to family planning communications in Iran: a typological approach. PhD Syracuse U. 1976.

LARRICK,D.V. 63
Having children: a study of white American wives' fertility in the early 1970s. PhD Ohio State U. 1981.

LECOCO,J.M. 64
Contemporary American values and women's fertility behavior. PhD Stanford U. 1980.

LEHRER,E.L. 65
Women's allocation of time over the life cycle: an econometric study. PhD Northwestern U. 1978.

MAANI-ENTESSARI,S.A. 66
A study of female labor force participation and fertility: a cross-cultural approach. PhD U. of Illinois at Urbana-Champaign, 1978.

MCCLAIN,M.K. 67
Indicators of economic well-being of female heads of families in relation to family structure and selected situational and demographic characteristics. PhD Ohio State U. 1980.

MCINTYRE,R.J. 68
Nature and causes of the fertility decline in Eastern Europe: structural change and abortion reform from 1955 to 1968. PhD U. of North Carolina at Chapel Hill, 1972.

MARSHALL,K.P. 69
Female participation in the labor force and fertility: cross-sectional and longitudinal perspectives. PhD U. of Florida, 1975.

MAZANY,R.L. 70
A model of the joint determination of labor force participation and fertility decisions of married women. PhD U. of British Columbia, 1982.

MAZUR,D.P. 71
Empirical tests of a demographic model with reference to fertility of women in the State of Washington 1920–1959. PhD U. of Washington, 1960.

MIRALAD,V.A. 72
Female employment and fertility in the Philippines. PhD Cornell U. 1981.

MOROFKA,V.J. 73
Perspectives on fertility control, social influence and fertility practices among selected low-income women. PhD Case Western Reserve U. 1973.

MOTT,F.L. 74
Labor force participation and fertility for women with small children in Rhode Island: an analysis of their interactions and antecedents. PhD Brown U. 1972.

NAMFUA,P.P. 75
Polygyny in Tanzania: its determinants and effect on fertility. PhD Johns Hopkins U. 1982.

NIZAMUDDIN,M. 76
The impact of community and program factors on the fertility behavior of rural Pakistani women. PhD U. of Michigan, 1979.

O'HARA,C.J. 77
The impact of serial marriage on the fertility of white, serially married American women, 1955–1970. PhD Emory U. 1978.

OLMSTEAD,J.V. 78
Female fertility, social structure and the economy:

a controlled comparison of two Southern Ethiopian communities. PhD Columbia U. 1974.

PALMER,S.J. *79*
Patterns of maternity in the Gambia. MD U. of Bristol, 1964.

POCS,O. *80*
Feminine social equality orientation and fertility expectations of college females. PhD Purdue U. 1978.

POTTER,J.E. *81*
The validity of measuring change in fertility by analysing birth histories obtained in surveys. PhD Princeton U. 1975.

PRAGER,L.K. *82*
A study of the effectivenes of inundation for initiating contraceptive use among noncontracepting women in Taiwan. DSc Johns Hopkins U. 1979.

REED,F.W. *83*
An analysis of the relationship between female employment and family contraception. PhD U. of North Carolina at Chapel Hill, 1972.

RENS,M.C. *84*
Breastfeeding and female employment in rural Java. PhD U. of California, Davis, 1980.

RIZK,I.A. *85*
The influence of infant and child mortality on the reproductive behavior of women in rural Egypt: combining individual and community-level data. PhD Pennsylvania State U. 1979.

ROSENBERG,H.M. *86*
The influence of fertility strategies on the labor force status of American wives. PhD Ohio State U. 1972.

ROSS,P.A. *87*
An investigation of the relationship among occupational opportunities for women, marriage and fertility. PhD North Texas State U. 1977.

ROSS,S.G. *88*
The timing and spacing of births and women's labor force participation: an economic analysis. PhD Columbia U. 1973.

SAMARAKKODY,A. *89*
Woman's status and fertility rates in Sri Lanka. PhD State U. of New York at Buffalo, 1976.

SANDERSON,W.C. *90*
Towards understanding the fertility of American women, 1920–1966. PhD Stanford U. 1974.

SANGADASA,A. *91*
Married female labor force participation and fertility in Canada. PhD U. of Alberta, 1981.

SASTRY,K.R. *92*
Female work participation and work-motivated contraception. PhD U. of North Carolina at Chapel Hill, 1973.

SCHMELZ,J.J. *93*
The fertility swing: an investigation of US fertiity trends in relation to income, housing, socio-economic aspirations, and female labor force activity. PhD U. of Minnesota, 1975.

SCHWARTZ-BARCOTT,D. *94*
National family planning programs in developing nations: a theoretical and empirical examination of the adoption process. PhD U. of North Carolina at Chapel Hill, 1978.

SHEDLIN,M.G. *95*
Anthropology and family planning: culturally appropriate intervention in a Mexican community. PhD Columbia U. 1982.

SIMPSON-HERBERT,M. *96*
Breastfeeding in Iran and its relation to fertility. PhD U. of North Carolina at Chapel Hill, 1977.

SINCLAIR,S.A. *97*
Socio-biological perspectives of female reproduction in Jamaica. PhD U. of Surrey, 1981.

SLAVIN,S.L. *98*
An evaluation of the economic cost and effectiveness of the Barbados Family Planning Association. PhD New York U. 1973.

SMITH,C.Y. *99*
Age at first birth and fertility decline in Costa Rica: an examination of the demographic context of the first birth and the related pattern of subsequent fertility. PhD Princeton U. 1982.

SMITH,S.K. *100*
Women's work and fertility in Mexico City. PhD U. of Michigan, 1976.

SNYDER,W.D. *101*
A life history approach to the study of social mobility in minority females in Job Corps. PhD U. of Oregon, 1973.

SPENCER,G.K. *102*
Childlessness and one-child fertility: a comparative and historical analysis of international data. PhD U. of California, Berkeley, 1983.

SPITZE,G.D. *103*
Work commitment among young women: its relation to labor force participation, marriage, and childbearing. PhD U. of Illinois at Urbana-Champaign, 1979.

STEIN,L.K. *104*
Fertility, health and life conditions of Polish women: a comparison between samples from rural and town populations. PhD State U. of New York at Buffalo, 1980.

STOKES,K.D. *105*
An analysis of the labor force behavior and fertility of remarried women, spouses present, United States, 1970. PhD Columbia U. 1979.

SUEBSONTHI,K. 106
The influences of Buddhism and Islam on family planning in Thailand: communication implication. PhD U. of Minnesota, 1980.

SUPADHILORE,B. 107
Mass communication and knowledge and attitude gaps about population and family planning in a developing urban society. PhD U. of Wisconsin-Madison, 1976.

SWEET,J.A. 108
Family composition and the labor force activity of married women in the United States. PhD U. of Michigan, 1968.

TAJ,K. 109
A comparative study of the attitudes of married women and college students toward family planning in a selected community of Hyderabad, West Pakistan. PhD Southern Illinois U. 1969.

TALBERT,C.S. 110
Ethnography of poor women: family design and natality. PhD U. of Washington, 1976.

TAN,J.P. 111
A comparative study of the marital fertility of older women in Nepal, Bangladesh and Sri Lanka. PhD Princeton U. 1981.

TERRY,G.B. 112
The interrelationship between female employment and fertility: a secondary analysis of the Growth of American Families Study, 1960. PhD Florida State U. 1973.

THOMPSON,E.D.B. 113
Marriage, childbirth and early childhood in a Gambian village: a socio-medical study. PhD U. of Aberdeen, 1966.

UHLMANN,J.M.Z. 114
The impact of urbanization on the fertility behavior of Papago Indian women. PhD U. of Colorado at Boulder, 1973.

UKPO,E.J. 115
Communication technology and strategies for rural development: the case for family planning and health care in Nigeria. PhD Wayne State U. 1974.

URDANETA,M.L. 116
Fertility regulation among Mexican-American women in an urban setting: a comparison of indigent vs. non-indigent Chicanas in a southwest city in the United States. PhD Southern Methodist U. 1976.

VANCE,C.S. 117
Female employment and fertility in Barbados. PhD Columbia U. 1979.

VAN HORN,S.H. 118
Women's roles: work and fertility for American women between 1900 and 1980. DA Carnegie-Mellon U. 1980.

VENTI,G. 119
The link between female employment and fertility: role ideals and values as explanatory variables in a study of a Danish commune. PhD U. of California, Berkeley, 1978.

VIJVERBERG,W.P.M. 120
Labor supply and fertility decisions: a dynamic model of the economic behavior of married women. PhD U. of Pittsburgh, 1981.

VOSS,B.M.B. 121
A demography of women students over forty years of age and five colleges in metropolitan Grand Rapids. PhD U. of Michigan, 1978.

WAITE,L.J. 122
Working wives and the life cycle. PhD U. of Michigan, 1976.

WARD,K.B. 123
The influence of the world economic system on the status of women and their fertility behavior. PhD U. of Iowa, 1982.

WEINSTEIN,M.A. 124
Childbearing and marital separation: evidence from the 1970 national fertility study. PhD Princeton U. 1981.

WELLES,B.L. 125
Maternal age and first birth in Sweden: a life course study. EdD Harvard U. 1982.

WHITE,P.E. 126
Patterns of marriage among the black population: a preliminary analysis of the black female. PhD Ohio State U. 1980.

WHITTAKER,L.V. 127
The impact of female education and other selected variables on fertility in Jamaica. PhD Pennsylvania State U. 1980.

WILLIAMS,J.S.Jr. 128
The single female population in the United States: a demographic analysis with primary emphasis on the white population. PhD Princeton U. 1967.

ZELMAN,E.A.C. 129
Women's rights and women's rites: a cross-cultural study of womanpower and reproductive ritual. PhD U. of Michigan, 1974.

4 Education

For psychological studies on all aspects of education see below 1012 ff.

History of education

See also 205, 300, 305, 314, 319, 902, 1110, 1225; **9** 3, 39, 48, 59, 62, 79, 116, 193, 520, 526, 631, 648; **12** 1552, 1704, 1760, 1767, 1883, 2430

ADIX,S.M. *1*
Differential treatment of women at the University of Utah from 1850 to 1915. PhD U. of Utah, 1976.

AHMED,N.S. *2*
The secondary education of girls in Belgium, France, and Germany in the nineteenth and twentieth centuries. PhD U. of Reading, 1963.

ALCOTT,P.M. *3*
Women at the Ohio State University in the first four decades, 1873–1912. PhD Ohio State U. 1979.

ALLEN,M.M. *4*
An historical study of Moravian education in North Carolina: the evolution and practice of the Moravian concept of education as it applied to women. PhD Florida State U. 1971.

APPELBAUM,P. *5*
The growth of the Montessori movement in the United States, 1900–1970. PhD New York U. 1971.

ARNFIELD,N.J. *6*
Gertrude Johnson, interpreter. [Speech education] PhD Wayne State U. 1971.

ATTWOOD,G.M. *7*
An eighteenth-century charity school: a history of Alderman Cogan's Girls' School, Hull, 1753–1950. MEd U. of Hull, 1961.

AUBUCHON,A. *8*
Feminism and women's education in England, 1860–1890. PhD Harvard U. 1976.

BAKER,C.E. *9*
Superintendent Mildred E. Doyle: educational leader, politician, woman. EdD U. of Tennessee, 1977.

BARKER,L.F. *10*
Les idées de Madame de Maintenon sur l'éducation des filles comparées à celles qui ont occurées à notre époque. MA U. of Liverpool, 1912.

BARNARD,H.C. *11*
Madame de Maintenon et Saint Cyr. MA U. of London, 1928.

BELHAM, P. *12*
The origins of elementary education in Somerset with particular reference to the work of Hannah More in the Mendips. MA U. of Bristol, 1957.

BERLS,J.W. *13*
The elementary school reforms of Maria Theresa and Joseph II in Bohemia. PhD Columbia U. 1970.

BERMAN,J.S.W. *14*
A sense of achievement: the significance of higher education for English college women, 1890–1930. PhD State U. of New York at Buffalo, 1980.

BIER,E.S. *15*
The education of women in England, 1603–1715. BLitt U. of Oxford 1928.

BIRCHENALL,M.S.S. *16*
A comparative historical and philosophical study of the educational theories of John Amos Comenius (1592–1670), Friedrich Froebel (1782–1852) and Maria Montessori (1870–1939). PhD U. of Denver, 1970.

BLUNDEN,M.A. *17*
The educational and political work of the Countess of Warwick. MA U. of Exeter, 1966.

BODDINGTON,M.E. *18*
The part played by Anglican women's religious communities in the education of children in England. MEd U. of Hull, 1975.

BRANDSTADTER,D.P. *19*
Developing the Coordinate College for Women at Duke University: the career of Alice Mary Baldwin, 1924–1947. PhD Duke U. 1977.

BREATHNACH, E. *20*
A history of the movement for women's higher education in Dublin, 1860–1912. MA University Coll. Dublin, 1981.

BRENNAN,E.J.T. *21*
The influence of Sidney and Beatrice Webb in English education, 1892–1903. MA U. of Sheffield, 1959.

BRUN, N. de *22*
Fénélon et l'éducation des filles. MA National U. of Ireland, Cork, 1967.

BURSTYN,J.N. 23
Higher education for women: the opposition in England during the nineteenth century. PhD U. of London (External), 1968.

CAMERON,F. 24
Some aspects of feminine education in England during the seventeenth century. MA U. of Liverpool, 1949.

CAMPBELL,A.D. 25
Marion Richardson: a misunderstood figure in art education. MPhil CNAA, 1981.

CANNON,M.A. 26
The education of women during the Renaissance. PhD Catholic U. of America, 1916.

CARR,L.M. 27
The intellectual woman's search for identity and education in late nineteenth-century England. MA U. of Sheffield, 1983.

COHEN,E.G. 28
An investigation into the early development of the training of schoolmistresses in the late nineteenth and early twentieth centuries, with special reference to the Faculty of Education in University College, Cardiff. MEd U. of Wales, Cardiff, 1977.

COLLINS,G.C. 29
Anna Freud, an educational biography with implications for teaching. PhD Claremont Grad. Sch. 1980.

COLUCCI,N.D. 30
Connecticut academies for females, 1800–1865. PhD U. of Connecticut, 1969.

CONWAY,J.K. 31
The first generation of American women graduates. PhD Harvard U. 1969.

CORCORAN,C.T. 32
Vida Dutton Scudden: the progressive years. [Professor of English Literature at Wellesley College; Christian Socialist and American religious thinker] PhD Georgetown U. 1973.

CROYLE-LANGHORAE,D.A. 33
Men will brand it an experiment: a study of undergraduate women at Michigan State College, 1870–1940. PhD State U. of New York at Binghamton, 1983.

CRUTCHELEY,A. 34
Madame de Maintenon. MA U. of Birmingham, 1912.

CULLEN,M.M. 35
The growth of the Roman Catholic training colleges for women in England during the nineteenth and twentieth centuries. MEd U. of Durham, 1964.

DAVIES,R.F.C. 36
The education of women in France from 1700 to 1789 as shown in the literature of the period. PhD U. of London, Birkbeck Coll. 1934.

DAVIS,H.H. 37
Hannah More as bluestocking. BLitt U. of Oxford, 1927.

DAWKINS,S. 38
Perspectives on childhood: Marianne Mason, inspector of boarded-out children (1885–1910). MEd* U. of Bristol, 1980.

DELANEY,C.J. 39
The contribution of Marion Flagg to music and education. DMA U. of Texas at Austin, 1974.

DEUTSCH,L.S. 40
The Giles sisters' contributions toward the higher education of women in the South 1874–1904. PhD U. of Pittsburgh, 1978.

DODGE,N.B. 41
Democracy and the education of women: the Colorado Woman's College story. PhD Columbia U. 1960.

DONOVAN,H. 42
History of women's higher education during the nineteenth century. MA National U. of Ireland, 1919.

DORGAN,J.N. 43
Eighteenth-century voices of educational change: Mary Wollstonecraft and Judith Sargent Murray. EdD Rutgers U. 1976.

DUDGEON,R.A.F. 44
Women and higher education in Russia, 1855–1905. PhD George Washington U. 1975.

DUFFY,L. 45
Education of women in the early nineteenth century: some French points of view. MA National U. of Ireland, 1916.

DYER,R. 46
Anna Freud and education: studies in the history, philosophy, science, and application of child psychoanalysis. PhD U. of Sheffield, 1980.

EDWARDS,P. 47
The contribution of British women to educational thought in the late eighteenth and early nineteenth centuries (with special reference to ideas on the teaching of English). MEd U. of Leeds, 1955.

ELIAS,L. 48
A story of Gulf Park College for Women 1917–1971. EdD U. of Mississippi, 1981.

ELMS,L.A. 49
Aspects of women's education in the nineteenth century. MEd* U. of Bristol, 1981.

ENTHOVEN,M.L.T. 50
Sixteenth-century ideas on the education of women in France. BLitt U. of Oxford, 1959.

ESHLEMAN,D.H. 51
Elizabeth Griffith: a biographical and critical

study. [Founder of Denver Opportunity School] PhD U. of Pennsylvania, 1947.

EVANS,S. *52*
Educational trends between 1775 and 1850 as revealed in the novels of Jane Austen and George Eliot. MEd* Univ. Coll. Swansea, 1980.

FISHER,L.J. *53*
The role of women in education: antecedents, current status and change strategies. PhD U. of North Dakota, 1981.

FLETCHER,M.M. *54*
Women writers on education, 1750–1800. MA U. of London, King's College, 1952.

FLETCHER,S.M. *55*
The part played by civil servants in promoting girls' secondary education, 1869–1902: some aspects of the administration of the Endowed Schools Acts. PhD U. of London, Birkbeck Coll. 1976.

FRERICHS,S.C. *56*
Elizabeth Missing Sewell: a minor novelist's search for the *via media* in the education of women in the Victorian era. PhD Brown U. 1974.

FRIEDMAN,B.B. *57*
Orie Latham Hatcher and the Southern Women's Educational Alliance. PhD Duke U. 1981.

FYNNE,R.J. *58*
Montessori and her inspirers. MA U. of London, 1921.

GIRARD,K.L. *59*
How schools fail women: a study of feminists' perceptions of their schooling experiences and women's schooling needs. EdD U. of Massachusetts, 1974.

GODFREY,M. *60*
Literature and the education of women: a study of attitudes reflected in the English literature of the nineteenth and early twentieth centuries. MEd U. of Wales, Aberystwyth, 1978.

GOMERSALL,M.C. *61*
Popular education for girls in Suffolk, 1800–1870. MA* U. of London, Inst. of Educ. 1981.

GORDON,S.C. *62*
Demands for the education of girls between 1790 and 1865. MA U. of London, Inst. of Educ. 1950.

HADDAD,G.M. *63*
Social roles and advanced education for women in nineteenth-century America: a study of three Western Reserve institutions. PhD Case Western Reserve U. 1980.

HANDLER,B.S. *64*
The schooling of 'unmarried sisters': Linden Hall and the Moravian educational tradition, 1863–1940. DEd Pennsylvania State U. 1980.

HANSON,A.R. *65*
The nineteenth-century movement to secure secondary education for girls, with special reference to the West Riding of Yorkshire. MEd U. of Leeds, 1958.

HEALY,F.P. *66*
A history of Evelyn College for Women, Princeton, New Jersey, 1887 to 1897. PhD Ohio State U. 1967.

HERMAN,D. *67*
College and after: the Vassar experiment in women's education, 1861–1924. PhD Stanford U. 1979.

HIGGINSON,J.H. *68*
The dame schools in Great Britain. MA U. of Leeds, 1939.

HILL,D.A. *69*
The development of girls' education from 1850 to 1939 with special reference to Doncaster. MEd U. of Sheffield, 1977.

HORN,M.A. *70*
Ideas of the founders of the early colleges for women on the role of women's education in American society. EdD Rutgers U. 1977.

HUFFMAN,M. *71*
The advancement of American women's education in relation to the Kondratieff theory of business cycles. PhD U. of Southern Illinois at Carbondale, 1976.

HUGHES,A.W. *72*
A study of the Abbé of Fénélon's treatise *De l'éducation des filles*, considered in relation to the educational ideas of his contemporaries. MA U. of Wales, 1944.

HUGHES,J. *73*
Mrs Senior, first woman local government board inspector. MEd U. of Bristol, 1981.

ILLING,M.T. *74*
Pupil teachers and the emancipation of women, 1870–1905. MPhil U. of London, King's Coll. 1979.

INGRAM,M.H. *75*
Development of higher education for white women in North Carolina prior to 1875 (Parts I-IV). EdD U. of North Carolina at Chapel Hill, 1961.

JACKSON,B.H. *76*
Susanna and Catherine Winkworth, 1830–1860. MA U. of Manchester, 1969.

JESSOP,C.E. *77*
Some perspectives on the curriculum for girls, 1880–1930. MEd* U. of Bristol, 1979.

JOHNSON,H.M. *78*
The education of girls in Derby and selected districts of Derbyshire from 1800–1930. MEd U. of Nottingham, 1967.

JONES,R.C. 79
The education of girls in post-war Germany. PhD U. of Bradford, 1974.

KASBEKAR,V.P. 80
Power over themselves: the controversy about female education in England, 1660–1820. PhD U. of Cincinnati, 1980.

KAUPMAN,P.A.W. 81
Boston women and city school politics, 1872–1905: nurturers and protectors in public education. EdD Boston U. Sch. of Educ. 1978.

KEANE,C.M. 82
A history of the foundation of the Presentation Convents in the Diocese of Kerry and their contribution to education in the nineteenth-century. MEd U. of Dublin, Trinity Coll. 1976.

KERBY,W.M. 83
The French thinkers of the seventeenth century on the subject of the education of women – Molière and Fénélon. DipEd U. of Cambridge, 1928.

KERR,M.P.G. 84
The work and influence of Dorothea Beale in the light of developments in the education of girls and women since 1850. MA U. of London, Inst. of Educ. 1952.

KLABIK-LOZOVSKY,N.N. 85
The education of Russian women: evolution or revolution, a comparative analysis. EdD U. of British Columbia, 1972.

LAGEMANN,E.C. 86
A generation of women: studies in educational biography. PhD Columbia U. 1978.

LAU,E.P.O. 87
Ellen C. Sabin, president of Milwaukee-Downer College, 1895–1921: proponent of higher education for women. PhD Marquette U. 1976.

LEMOINE,S.C. 88
The North of England Council for Promoting the Higher Education of Women, 1867–1875. MEd U. of Manchester, 1968.

LE SURE,L.L.F. 89
Willa A. Strong: an historical study of black education in southeastern Oklahoma. EdD U. of Oklahoma, 1982.

LEWIS,W.G. 90
The Edgeworths and their place in education. MEd U. of Newcastle upon Tyne, 1968.

LEIBELL,J.F. 91
Anglo-Saxon education of women: from Hilda to Hildegarde. PhD Georgetown U. 1922.

LINSCOTT,M.P. 92
The educational work of the Sisters of Notre Dame in Lancashire since 1850. MA U. of Liverpool, 1959.

LINSCOTT,M.P. 93
The educational experience of the Sisters of Notre Dame de Namur, 1804–1964. PhD U. of Liverpool, 1965.

LUCAS,F.J. 94
The educational writings of Mary Wollstonecraft. MEd* U. of Wales, Aberystwyth, 1980.

MCALLISTER,M.A. 95
Cultural and intellectual development in contemporary society: the relevance of Matthew Arnold's educational ideas, with special reference to an empirical study of Belfast schoolgirls and female university students. MA Queen's U. of Belfast, 1973.

MCCARTHY,J. 96
The contribution of the Sisters of Mercy to West Cork schools, 1844–1922, in the context of Irish elementary education development. MEd National U. of Ireland, Cork, 1979.

MCCAULEY,B.K. 97
A study of beliefs of leaders in education about the status of women. PhD U. of Southern California, 1949.

MACKENZIE,M. 98
Hegel's theory and practice of education, and problems of girls' education in elementary schools. MA U. of Wales, 1908.

MCLOUGHLIN,D. 99
'Birds of passage': women teachers in England; unions and equal pay, 1930–1960. MA U. of Essex, 1979.

MCPHERSON,L.M.G. 100
A historical perspective of career patterns of women in the teaching profession: 1900–1940. PhD Illinois State U. 1981.

MADDEN,A.M. 101
Edith Stein and the education of women: Augustinian themes. PhD Saint Louis U. 1962.

MARSH,J.P. 102
A study of selected stated objectives of American higher education of women to 1940. PhD Harvard U. 1959.

MAY,J. 103
The contribution of Madame Osterberg to the development of British education. MEd U. of Leicester, 1967.

MAYO-CHAMBERLAIN,J. 104
Women's experience of power: a theory for educational development. PhD Ohio State U. 1980.

MEADS,D.M. 105
An account of the education of women and girls in England in the time of the Tudors. PhD U. of London, 1929.

MILBURN,J. 106
The secondary schoolmistress: a study of her pro-

fessional views and their significance in the educational developments of the period, 1895–1914. PhD U. of London, Inst. of Educ. 1969.

MISENHEMER,H.E. *107*
Rousseau on the education of women. EdD U. of North Carolina at Greensboro, 1979.

MORRIS,E.M.D. *108*
The education of girls in England from 1600 to 1800. MA U. of London, 1926.

MOSLEY,M.J.C. *109*
Alaska native women's changing roles and the implications for education. EdD Seattle U. 1981.

MOUL,W.J.E. *110*
The life, works, and letters of Hannah More, with special reference to her influence in the social and educational movements of the eighteenth and early nineteenth centuries. MA U. of London, King's Coll. 1933.

MURPHY,M.B. *111*
Pioneer Roman Catholic girls' academies: their growth, character, and contribution to American education: a study of Roman Catholic education for girls from colonial times to the first Plenary Council of 1852. PhD Columbia U. 1958.

NASH,C.S. *112*
The education of women in Russia, 1762–1796. PhD New York U. 1978.

NAVARRE,J.P. *113*
The female teacher: the beginnings of teaching as a 'woman's profession'. PhD Bowling Green State U. 1977.

NUNLEY,J.E. *114*
A history of the Cumberland Female College, McMinnville, Tennessee. EdD U. of Tennessee, 1965.

O'CONNOR,A. *115*
Influences affecting girls' secondary education in Ireland, 1860–1910. MA Univ. Coll., Dublin, 1981.

O'DRISCOLL,J.F. *116*
Dominican convents in the diocese of Dublin and their contribution to the higher education of women, 1882–1924. MEd U. of Dublin, Trinity Coll. 1983.

O'KEEFE,C. *117*
Les idées pédagogiques de Madame de Maintenon. MA National U. of Ireland, Cork, 1959.

O'LEARY,M.P.M. *118*
Education with a tradition: an account of the educational work of the Society of the Sacred Heart, 1800–1935. PhD U. of London (External), 1935.

PALMER,B.H. *119*
Lace bonnets and academic gowns: faculty development in four women's colleges, 1875–1915. PhD Boston Coll. 1980.

PARRY,R.P. *120*
Astudineth o addysg bywyd a gwaith Sarah Winifred Parry ('Winnie Parry') 1870–1953, gan gynnwys llyfryddineh (the life and work of Sarah W. Parry). MEd U. of Wales, Aberystwyth, 1980.

PAUWELS,J.R.M. *121*
Women and university studies in the Third Reich, 1933–1945. PhD York U. Ontario, 1976.

PEDERSEN,J.B.S. *122*
The reform of women's secondary and higher education in nineteenth-century England: a study in elite groups. PhD U. of California, Berkeley, 1974.

PERKINS,L.M. *123*
Fanny Jackson Coppin and the Institute for Colored Youth: a model of nineteenth-century black female educational and community leadership, 1837–1902. PhD U. of Illinois at Urbana-Champaign, 1978.

PIZZANO,J.M. *124*
The education of women in the New Orleans area. EdD George Peabody Coll. for Teachers, 1978.

POPE,R.D. *125*
The development of formal higher education for women in England, 1862–1914. PhD U. of Pennsylvania, 1972.

PRESTON,J.A. *126*
Feminization of an occupation: teaching becomes women's work in nineteenth-century New England. PhD Brandeis U. 1982.

PRICE,D.D. *127*
Doctrines de l'éducation féminine de Fénélon à la Révolution. MA U. of Birmingham, 1975.

QUARTARARO,A.T. *128*
The *Écoles normales primaires d'institutrices*: a social history of women primary school teachers in France, 1879–1905. PhD U. of California, Los Angeles, 1982.

RENNER,M. *129*
Who will teach? Changing job opportunity and roles for women in Pittsburgh public schools. PhD U. of Pittsburgh, 1981.

ROBERTSON,D. *130*
Aspects of the development of secondary and higher education for girls in Northumberland and Durham from 1850 to 1910. MEd U. of Newcastle upon Tyne, 1967.

ROBSON,W.F. *131*
L'éducation des filles d'après les idées de Fénélon. MA U. of Liverpool, 1924.

ROCHE,C.M. *132*
Founded for the future: the educational legacy of Mary Ward. MEd Maynooth U. Coll. 1982.

ROE,A.M. *133*
The educational thought of Madeleine Sophie Barat. MEd U. of Dublin, Trinity Coll. 1974.

ROSENHAN,M.S. *134*
Women's place and cultural values in Soviet children's readers: an historical analysis of the maintenance of role and division by gender, 1920s and 1970s. PhD U. of Pennsylvania, 1981.

RUECKEL,P. *135*
The contributions of women in the progressive movement in education 1890–1919. EdD U. of Pittsburgh, 1964.

RURY,J.L. *136*
Women, cities and schools: education and the development of an urban female labor force, 1890–1930. PhD U.of Wisconsin-Madison, 1982.

RUSSELL,R. *137*
From Enlightenment philosophy to Utilitarian pedagogy: a study of Elizabeth Hamilton's philosophical ideas and an appraisal of her contribution to nineteenth-century educational theory. MEd* U. of Glasgow, 1982.

RUTHERFORD,M.A. *138*
Feminism and the secondary school curriculum, 1890–1920. PhD Stanford U. 1977.

SARAP,M.M. *139*
Marion Richardson and the new art: a biographical study of a pioneer. DipArtEd* U. of London, Inst. of Educ. 1969.

SAYRE,M.B. *140*
Half a century: an historical analysis of the National Association of Deans of Women 1900–1950. PhD Columbia U. 1951.

SCHNEIDER,J.F. **141**
An historical examination of women's education in Bavaria: *Mädchenschulen* and contemporary attitudes about them, 1799–1848. PhD Brown U., 1977.

SCHWAGER,S. *142*
'Harvard Women': a history of the founding of Radcliffe College (Boston, Massachusetts). EdD Harvard U. 1982.

SHAPIRO,M.S. *143*
A rhetorical critical analysis of lecturing of Maria Louise Sanford (1836–1920). PhD U. of Minnesota, 1959.

SHAW,M.E. *144*
Sarah Trimmer: a study of her life and works. DipEd U. of Hull, 1969.

SHAW,M.E. *145*
Ideas of women writers on the education of young children in the late eighteenth and early nineteenth centuries. MEd U. of Hull, 1971.

SMITH,P.W. *146*
The education of Englishwomen in the seventeenth century. MA U. of London, 1921.

STRAUSS,C.M. *147*
A pedagogy for independence in an age of constraints: the educational thought of Mary Wollstonecraft. EdD Columbia U. Teachers Coll. 1979.

STROBEL,M.E. *148*
Ideology and women's higher education, 1945–1960. PhD Duke U. 1976.

STUBBS,J.K. *149*
Miss Jemima Clough (1820–1892): a reconsideration of her work in the field of women's education. MEd* U. of Liverpool, 1982.

TEMPLE,A. *150*
The development of higher education for women in Ontario, 1867–1914. PhD Wayne State U. 1981.

TEMPLIN,L. de L. *151*
Some defects and merits in the education of women in Missouri: an analysis of past and present educational methods and a proposal for the future. PhD U. of Missouri-Columbia, 1926.

THOMAS,E.N. *152*
Mary Mills Patrick and the American College for Girls at Istanbul in Turkey. EdD Rutgers U. 1979.

THOMPSON,E.W. *153*
Education for ladies, 1830–1860: ideas on education in magazines for women. PhD Columbia U. 1947.

THUM,G.E. *154*
Bias against women in American educational history – a propaganda analysis. PhD Saint Louis U. 1975.

TILLETT,M.G. *155*
Madame Campan and her work at Écouen. MA U. of Reading, 1941.

TOBIN,R.B. *156*
Vincent of Beauvais's *De eruditione filiarum nobilium*: the education of women. PhD Boston Coll. 1972.

TURNER,E.M. *157*
Education of women for engineering in the United States, 1885–1952. PhD New York U. 1954.

VART,S.V. *158*
The development of intermediate education for girls in Wales, 1886–1920. MEd U. of Wales, Cardiff, 1981.

VERYARD,L. *159*
Aspects of early nineteenth-century education as reflected in the lives of the Brontë sisters. MEd* U. of Wales, Cardiff, 1979.

WALSH,M.J. *160*
A contribution made to the education of women by Catherine Esther Beecher in the nineteenth century. PhD U. of London, Inst. of Educ. 1980.

WARD,P.J. *161*
Madame de Genlis, educationalist. PhD U. of Cambridge, 1934.

WIDDOWSON,F. *162*
Elementary teacher training and the middle-class girl, 1846–1914. MA U. of Essex, 1976.

WILLS,S.R. *163*
The social and economic aspects of higher education for women between 1844 and 1870, with special reference to the North of England Council. MA U. of London, Inst. of Educ. 1952.

WILSON,A.N. *164*
Aporti, Agazzi, Montessori: a study of three Italian infant educators. MEd U. of Newcastle, 1967.

WOLFE,A. *165*
Women who dared: Northern teachers of the Southern freedmen, 1862–1872. PhD City U. of New York, 1982.

WOOLLEY,D.G.H. *166*
A study of the emphases of Mildred Agnes Dawson in the education of children in the American English language arts. EdD U. of the Pacific, 1978.

YOUNG,H.P. *167*
Origin and early history of Monticello Female Seminary, 1834–1865. PhD U. of Washington, 1951.

Schools

See also **1** 40; **17** 186; **19** 493–568.

ALLAN,J.R.F. *168*
An examination of the purpose of the municipal high school for girls in the light of changes in the social structure of Britain since the war. MA U. of Liverpool, 1939.

CHAMPREUX,A.B. *169*
Characteristics of students released from Utah State Industrial School, 1961: Part 1, white girls. PhD U. of Utah, 1963.

COOKE,S.P. *170*
A study of an experiment in extended education with groups of secondary modern school girls. MA U. of London, Inst. of Educ. 1953.

EAGLESON,D.E. *171*
Employment and training of girls leaving Belfast primary, secondary, intermediate, and grammar schools in relation to the educational system and the employment services. PhD Queen's U. of Belfast, 1959.

ELDRIDGE,G.J. *172*
Discussion work in a secondary girls' school: a study of two groups. MEd U. of Leicester, 1966.

EL-SHARANI,Z. *173*
The curriculum in girls' secondary schools, with special reference to England and Egypt. MA U. of Bristol, 1939.

GORDON,M.J. *173a*
A study of the provision for vocational training in the advanced courses of girls' secondary schools, with special reference to electricity. MA U. of London, King's Coll. 1941.

GRUNSPAN,J.M. *174*
An investigation into the reading interests of a group of girls in their first and second years at a city grammar school. MA U. of London, Inst. of Educ. 1956.

HAINSWORTH,M.D. *175*
An investigation into certain aspects of the study of biology and related science subjects in a girls' grammar school. MA U. of Liverpool, 1957.

HALL,S.M. *176*
An investigation of factors involved in girls' choices of science courses in the sixth form, and of scientific careers. BLitt U. of Oxford, 1966.

JONES,N. *177*
An investigation into the curriculum of girls' secondary schools. MA U. of London, 1927.

LAMBART,A.M. *178*
The sociology of an unstreamed grammar school for girls. MA(Econ) U. of Manchester, 1971.

LAVIGUEUR,J.M.L. *179*
Equality of educational opportunity for girls and its relation to co-education. MEd U. of Sheffield, 1977.

LERAND,L.W. *180*
Intelligence and reading level of girls. EdD U. of Northern Colorado, 1966.

LILLIS,H.I. *181*
A survey of some activities of a girls' secondary school from academic, religious, cultural, and recreational points of view. MA National U. of Ireland, Maynooth, 1972.

MAXWELL,M.P. *182*
Social structure: socialization and social class in a Canadian private school for girls. PhD Cornell U. 1970.

MOBERLY,A.W. *183*
The Grier School. [Private secondary school for girls] EdD Pennsylvania State U. 1971.

PANNETT,D.A. *184*
A comparison of girls' junior technical schools in London and Paris. MA U. of London, King's Coll. 1939.

POWELL,B.J. *185*
An analysis of the dominant themes in selected literature by Afro-American women with recommendations for inclusion in the high school curriculum. PhD U. of Pittsburgh, 1974.

REPTON,J. *186*
A comparative study of the development of art education in two London girls' schools – one

secondary modern and one comprehensive – reflecting one hundred years of public education and social change. DipArt Ed* U. of London, Inst. of Educ. 1968.

RIDDELL,J. *187*
The reading habits of adolescent girls in a grammar school. MA U. of Sheffield, 1968.

SANDERSON,L.M. *188*
A history of education in the Sudan with special reference to the development of girls' schools. MA U. of London (External), 1962.

SARA,R.J. *189*
The development of science education for girls, placing the Girls' Public Day School Trust in perspective, and a small-scale survey in a girls' school about attitudes towards chemistry. MSc U. of Reading, 1979.

SHIFFERRAN,M. *190*
Educational policy and practice affecting females in Zambian secondary schools. PhD U. of Wisconsin-Milwaukee, 1982.

SHURDEN,K.W. *191*
An analysis of adolescent responses to female characters in literature widely read by students in secondary schools. EdD U. of Tennesee, 1975.

SMITH,J.W. *192*
An appraisal of the treatment of females in selected United States high school history textbooks from 1959 until 1975. PhD U. of Indiana, 1977.

SMYTH,A.M. *193*
An investigation into the interest of children in school geography with special reference to the development of interest in girls between the ages of 11 and 16 years. MA U. of London, Inst. of Educ. 1946.

STORCH,S. *194*
Response of high school juniors to leading women characters in selected dramatic works. PhD New York U. 1975.

TANSEY,J. *195*
Selective perspectives on girls' secondary school education in the Republic of Ireland, 1925–1975. MEd Trinity Coll., Dublin, 1978.

TIMBERLAKE,C.H. *196*
A study of black female persisters compared with black female dropouts on the secondary school level. EdD Syracuse U. 1979.

TINSON,M.L. *197*
Female sex-stereotyping in primary reading textbooks. EdD Pepperdine U. 1981.

TODD,H. *198*
The technical high school, with special reference to girls. MEd U. of Leeds, 1941.

TULLOS,T. *199*
The role of women in children's literature: what do books recommended by public elementary school librarians reflect? PhD Texas A&M U. 1979.

TURNER,S.V. *200*
Encouraging women's participation in high school mathematics: an intervention study. PhD U. of South Florida, 1982.

WALKER,B. *201*
The design, implementation and evaluation of a course of social education with 14 to 15 year old girls of average and less than average ability. MEd U. of Newcastle upon Tyne, 1970.

WINTER,P.E. *202*
An investigation into the attitude towards Latin of girls at secondary grammar schools at the end of two years' study of Latin. MA U. of London, Inst. of Educ. 1950.

WORTLEY,M.A.B. *203*
A reappraisal of Enid Blyton's contribution to progressive education and children's reading. MPhil, CNAA, 1982.

Higher education

ADAIR,A.J.L.M. *204*
A study of women at the University of Utah from 1953 to 1964. PhD U. of Utah, 1980.

AIKEN,W.P. *205*
A survey of the social and philosophical factors which have affected the higher education of white women in Texas, 1825 to 1945. PhD U. of Texas at Austin, 1946.

AJGAONKAR,V.A. *206*
The problem of the higher education of girls in the Bombay Residency. MEd U. of Leeds, 1940.

ANDREWS,M.K. *207*
Preferential treatment for women in academia. PhD U. of Wisconsin, 1982.

ANGUS,E.Y. *208*
The higher education and employment of women in the twentieth century. MA U. of London, LSE, 1931.

ARANHA-SHENDY.M.A. *209*
The higher education of women in India, 1963. PhD Catholic U. of America, 1964.

BAKKEN,M.P. *210*
An examination of the factors which aid and impede women in completing an Associate of Science degree program. EdD Boston U. Sch. of Educ. 1981.

BARON,G.T. *211*
A study of women in industrial arts education. EdD Arizona State U. 1974.

BRISCOE,V.W. *213*
Bryn Mawr College traditions: women's rituals and expressive behavior. PhD U. of Pennsylvania, 1981.

BROMLEY,A. *214*
A study of women matriculants of the Chicago Undergraduate Division of the University of Illinois. PhD Northwestern U. 1954.

BROWN,L.E. *215*
Housing of women students at the normal schools and teachers' colleges in New York State. PhD New York U. 1934.

BURDETT,R.A. *216*
A comparative study of women granted doctoral degrees from the New York Philosophy and Doctor of Education degrees. PhD New York U. 1956.

BURTON,B. *217*
A study of opinions of college freshman women about home economics and related professional fields. EdD Pennsylvania State U. 1954.

CATO,W.H. *218*
The development of higher education for women in Virginia. PhD U. of Virginia, 1941.

CLARK,S.J. *219*
An exploratory analaysis of Educational Opportunity Program (EOP) women students in a UCLA residence hall. EdD U. of California, Los Angeles, 1969.

CONNOLLY,C.L. *220*
Effectiveness of an agricultural instructional model of basic vegetable production at Ahfad University College for Women in Omdurman, Sudan. PhD Iowa State U. 1980.

COOKE,R.L. *221*
Trade and industrial education for girls and women in California. EdD U. of California, Berkeley, 1932.

COOMBS,J.A. 222
A nationwide study of women in United States dental schools. DrPH Harvard U. 1975.

CORNELIUS,M. 223
Some trends in selected aspects of personnel service in American higher education with implications for women's colleges in India. PhD U. of Michigan, 1946.

CUNNINGHAM,S.M. *224*
The entry of girls to higher education. PhD U. of Aberdeen, 1978.

CUTHBERT,M.V. *225*
Education and marginality: a study of the negro woman college graduate. PhD Columbia U. 1943.

DAVIDSON,D.D. *226*
A survey of women studying science in the Los Angeles Community College district. EdD U. of California, Los Angeles, 1982.

DAVIS,S.L.O. *227*
Factors related to the persistence of women in a four-year institute of technology. PhD U. of Minnesota, 1973.

DAVIS,T. *228*
Characteristics of women choosing traditional and nontraditional college majors. EdD East Texas State U. 1981.

DEALEY,H.L. *229*
Student interests in relation to curricula of women's colleges. PhD Brown U. 1918.

DONNALLEY,M.J.M. **230**
A study of the factors which influence women college students to withdraw before completing their degree requirements. EdD U. of Virgina, 1966.

DORSEY,R.J. *231*
The effects of black students' protests on higher education as perceived by a select group of black females. PhD U. of Iowa, 1981.

DOWNING,B.M. *232*
The election of home economics by college-bound girls. EdD Columbia U. 1963.

EUSTACE,F.R. *233*
Freshman English in selected liberal arts colleges for women. PhD Catholic U. of America, 1963.

FELDMAN,R.C. *234*
The institutionalization of the women's movement in American higher education. PhD U. of Connecticut, 1982.

FELDMAN,S.D. *235*
Escape from the Doll's House: women in graduate and professional school education. PhD U. of Washington, 1972.

FOSTER,G.R. *236*
Social change in relation to curricular development in collegiate education for women. PhD Columbia U. 1934.

FREEMAN,K.H. *237*
An examination of the general education program of young women in a private junior college. PhD U. of Missouri-Columbia, 1947.

FRITSCHNER,L.M. *238*
The rise and fall of home economics: a study with implications for women, education, and change. PhD U. of California, Davis, 1973.

FUJIMURA-FANSELOW,K. *239*
Women and higher education in Japan: tradition and change. PhD Columbia U. 1981.

GIRSHEFSKI,M.J. *240*
Circumstances affecting curricular change as exemplified in selected women's colleges. PhD Saint Louis U. 1968.

GOODWIN,G.C. *241*
The women doctoral recipient: a study of the difficulties encountered in pursuing graduate degrees. EdD Oklahoma State U. 1966.

GRAY,D.E. 242
Social determinants of college entry for American black women. PhD U. of California, Berkeley, 1974.

GRAY,L.A. 243
A sociological study via participant observation of a two-year private liberal arts college for women. PhD Syracuse U. 1970.

GREENLEAF,E.A. 244
A comparison of women at Indiana University majoring in three different colleges. PhD Indiana U. 1953.

GREENWOOD,B.F.B. 245
Academic women in home economics at land-grant institutions. PhD Florida State U. 1968.

GREGORY,H.E. 246
Minorities and females at the United States Coast Guard Academy. EdD Indiana U. 1980.

GROTE,C. 247
Housing and living conditions of women students in the Western Illinois State Teachers College at Macomb – schools years 1926–1927, 1927–1928 and 1928–29. PhD Columbia U. 1932.

HANANIA,E.A.S. 248
Higher education for women in the Arab coun tries of the Near East. MA U. of London, Inst. of Educ. 1957.

HANSEN,M.L. 249
Barriers to women's completion of post-secondary vocational trade and technical programs. PhD Colorado State U. 1981.

HARRINGTON,J.C. 250
The status of women with doctoral degrees in collegiate business education. EdD Arizona State U. 1971.

HERKENHOFF,L.H. 251
A comparison of older and younger women students at San Jose City College with implications for curriculum and student personnel services. EdD U. of California, Berkeley, 1966.

HICKEY,B.G. 252
Wasted womanpower: factors affecting the plans of gifted girls to go or not to go to college. PhD Columbia U. 1959.

HILL,B. 253
Women and business education. MEd* U. of Sheffield, 1981.

HIROSE,H. 254
A guide for curriculum development for the religious education department of Seiwa Women's College in Nishinomiya, Japan. PhD Columbia U. 1951.

HOPWOOD,K.L. 255
Expectations of university freshman women. PhD Ohio State U. 1953.

HOROWITZ,S.A. 256
Rationale for colleges for women. EdD Indiana U. 1982.

IBRAHIM,M.H. 257
A study of the function of literature in higher education, with special reference to women's higher education in Egypt. PhD U. of Wales, Cardiff, 1980.

JAMES,E.A. 258
The role of women's private junior colleges. EdD Columbia U. 1962.

JENKINS,E.K. 259
The perceived institutional barriers of undergraduate women who discontinued their education at a southern urban university. PhD Georgia State U. Coll. of Educ. 1975.

KAMIYAMA,T. 260
Ideology and patterns in women's education in Japan. PhD Saint Louis U. 1977.

KIM,C.H. 261
Changing functions of women's higher education in the Republic of Korea: a study of educational equality between men and women. PhD George Peabody Coll. for Teachers, 1975.

KIRKPATRICK,W.J. 262
The emerging role of women in institutions of higher education in the United States. EdD U. of Arkansas, 1965.

KLOTZBURGER,K.M. 263
Politics in higher education: the issue of the status of women at the City University of New York, 1971–1973. PhD New York U. 1976.

KUELER,J.E. 264
The impact of a new women's college on its first graduating class. PhD Claremont Grad. Sch. 1970.

KYLE,S.A.P. 265
Curriculum resources: women in science, medicine and technology. EdD Wayne State U. 1980.

LALANE,M. de la M.B. 266
Conditions associated with women student withdrawals at the University of Southern California. PhD U. of Southern California, 1953.

LANE,W.C. 267
The lower-class girl in college: a study of Stanford freshman women. PhD Stanford U. 1961.

LARSON,L.W. 268
Liberal arts colleges for women, 1980–2000: is anyone listening? DBA Golden Gate U. 1979.

LATULIPPE,J.A. 269
Current status of women in industrial technology programs in Southern California community colleges. EdD Northern Arizona U. 1979.

LEE,A.M. 270
A study of married women students at Indiana

State Teachers College 1958–1959. EdD Indiana U. 1960.

LEE,S.D. *271*
An analysis of institutional goals perceived and preferred by students, assistants, faculty, and adminstrators at Seoul Woman's College in Korea. PhD George Peabody Coll. for Teachers, 1977.

LIPP,D.J. *272*
A survey of women graduates of the College of Liberal Arts of Northwestern University. PhD Northwestern U. 1952.

LUETH,C.A. *273*
Selected aspects in the attainment and use of the Doctor of Medicine, Doctor of Dental Surgery and Bachelor of Law degrees by women graduates of Tulane University and Loyola University of the South. EdD U. of Mississippi, 1973.

MCARDLE,E.E.H. *274*
Women in higher education: a case study at one large university in the Northeastern portion of the United States. PhD Syracuse U. 1980.

MCCUE,B. *275*
The significance of adult education in the biographies of six women. MEd U. of Liverpool, 1979.

MASKIELL,M.G. *276*
Women's higher education and family networks in South Asia: Kinnaird College, Lahore, 1913–60. PhD U. of Pennsylvania, 1979.

MICHII,T. *277*
The chosen few: women academics in Japan. PhD State U. of New York at Buffalo, 1982.

MILLER,E.L. *278*
The value of the doctorate for women in business education and business. PhD New York U. 1957.

MITCHELL,S.B. *279*
Women and the doctorate: a study of the enabling or impeding factors operative among Oklahoma's women doctoral recipients in the attainment and use of the degree. EdD Oklahoma State U. 1969.

MOORE,H.A. *280*
Female minority students: patterns of social conformity and schooling commitments. PhD U. of California, Riverside, 1979.

MORRIS,T.A. *281*
The measurement of continuity and variation in the curricula of the Southern Baptist Missionary education program for adult and young women. PhD New Orleans Baptist Theological Seminary, 1967.

MOURITSEN,R.H. *282*
A study of women at the University of Utah between 1941 and 1953. PhD U. of Utah, 1980.

NELSON,M.R. *283*
Possible contributions of home economics to the general education of women enrolled in one- and two-year post high school, occupational programs in Wisconsin schools of vocational and adult education. PhD U. of Wisconsin, 1965.

NOBLE,J.L. *284*
The negro woman looks at her college education. PhD Columbia U. 1955.

ODOM,K.P. *285*
Comparative study of older and younger women enrolled in an undergraduate degree program at the Ohio State University. PhD Ohio State U. 1974.

ORR,M.L. *286*
The state supported colleges for women. PhD George Peabody Coll. for Teachers, 1930.

PAGE,J.V. *287*
Women and the doctorate at Teachers College, Columbia University. PhD Columbia U. 1959.

PERREAULT,G.E. *288*
Contemporary feminist perspectives on women and higher education: a comparative analysis. PhD U. of Minnesota, 1981.

PHILLIPS,F.L. *289*
A socio-economic study of college women. EdD Indiana U. 1958.

POPE,R.V. *290*
Factors affecting the elimination of women students from selected coeducational colleges of liberal arts. PhD Columbia U. 1931.

POWELL,J. *291*
An analysis of factors relating to decisions to transfer from Northwestern University by freshman women. PhD Northwestern U. 1970.

PRESEREN,H. *292*
General education at the woman's college of the University of North Carolina as revealed through group interviews of the senior class of 1953. PhD U. of North Carolina at Chapel Hill, 1955.

RALSTON,Y.L. *293*
An analysis of attitudes as barriers to the selection of women as college presidents in Florida. EdD U. of Mississippi, 1974.

RANDOLPH,K.S. *294*
The mature woman in doctoral programs. EdD Indiana U. 1965.

REA,K. *295*
A follow-up study of women graduates from the state colleges in Mississippi, class of 1956. PhD Ohio State U. 1956.

RICE,L.T. *296*
A profile of the female doctoral student who persisted to the completion of the doctoral degree. EdD Auburn U. 1981.

ROBINSON,M.L. *297*
The curriculum of the woman's college. PhD Columbia U. 1916.

ROBINSON,O.T. 298
Contributions of black American academic women to American higher education. PhD Wayne State U. 1978.

ROGERS,N.L.D. 299
The development of federal policy for the elimination of discrimination in the post-secondary education of women. PhD U. of Michigan, 1979.

RUSS,A.J. 300
Higher education for women: intent, reality, and outcomes, Wells College, 1868–1913. PhD Cornell U. 1980.

SABRI,M.A. 301
Beirut College for Women and ten of its distinguished pioneering alumnae. EdD Columbia U. 1965.

SACK,D.G. 302
Institutional influences on women's undergraduate majors. PhD Johns Hopkins U. 1981.

SALIE,R.D. 303
The Harvard Annex experiment in the higher education of women: separate but equal? PhD Emory U. 1976.

SCHRIVER,A. 304
A plan of organization for the establishment of a major for health personnel at the Woman's College, University of North Carolina, with implications for state universities in the southern region of the United States. PhD Columbia U. 1952.

SEN,A. 305
Education of girls and women in Bengal (1800–1899), with special reference to the founding and development of the Bethune College. MA U. of London, Inst. of Educ. 1959.

SENDERACK,M.G. 306
Private colleges for women and junior college graduates in New Jersey. EdD Columbia U. 1971.

SEWARD,D.M. 307
A historical study of the women's residence program at Syracuse University. PhD Syracuse U. 1953.

SHANNON,A.R. 308
A Delphi Study of the future of women's colleges in the United States. EdD Lehigh U. 1971.

SHRIDEVI,S. 309
The development of women's higher education in India. PhD Columbia U. 1954.

SPAULDING,B.G. 311
Factors related to the choice of home economics as a college major by women. PhD Purdue U. 1972.

SPROUL,C. 312
The American College for Girls, Cairo, Egypt: its history and influence on Egyptian women – a study of selected graduates. PhD U. of Utah, 1982.

SPRING,C.V. 313
Women students of the Florida State University: a report of their characteristics and their perceptions of the Carnegie Commission recommendations for women in higher education. PhD Florida State U. 1978.

STAVELY,M.R. 314
A history of Stanford's program in education for women during the last fifty years. PhD Stanford U. 1945.

THOMPSON,D.E. 315
Concerns of black community college women. PhD North Texas State U. 1981.

WALLACE,J.A. 316
The organization, operation, and evaluation of a European field trip in international economics for 23 women college students. PhD U. of Pennsylvania, 1949.

WALLACE,J.E.S. 317
Afro-American studies in a suburban women's college: a case study. PhD Northwestern U. 1973.

WATSON,G.B. 318
A study of the curricula in selected colleges for women. PhD George Peabody Coll. for Teachers, 1950.

WILCOX,R.A. 319
A study of the education of women at the University of Utah, 1915–1916 to 1924–1925. PhD U. of Utah, 1979.

WILLIAMS,G. 320
An analysis of the effects of legislation and litigation on the enrolment of women and minority students in public institutions of higher education between 1945 and 1976. PhD U. of Oregon, 1980.

WILLIAMS,O.M. 321
Twenty years after college: a follow-up study of women of the entering class of 1949 at selected institutions of higher learning in Mississippi. EdD U. of Mississippi, 1975.

WILLS,L.A.H. 322
Peabody women doctorates, 1961–1975. PhD George Peabody Coll. for Teachers, 1978.

YOUNG,E.B. 323
A study of the curricula of seven selected women's colleges of the Southern states. PhD Columbia U. 1932.

Roman Catholic schools and colleges

See also 35, 82, 92, 93, 96, 111, 116; **9** 266.

BARRETT,M.M. 324
A study of the influences of Catholic high school experiences on vocational decisions to the sisterhoods. PhD Catholic U. of America, 1961.

BECKER,A.J. 325
A study of personality traits of successful religious women of teaching orders. PhD Loyola U. Chicago, 1962.

BOUEY,M.C. 326
The Sisters of Mercy in American higher education: 1962. PhD Catholic U. of America, 1963.

BOURGEOIS,M.A. 327
A study of the preparation for the role of parent as educator in selected Catholic women's colleges. PhD Catholic U. of America, 1961.

BOWLER,M.M. 328
Catholic higher education for women in the United States. PhD Catholic U. of America, 1934.

BUTTELL,M.F. 329
A history of Catholic colleges for women in the United States of America. PhD Catholic U. of America, 1934.

CAMERON,M.F. 330
A script and teacher's guide for a motion picture on the life and work of the Dominican Sisters of the Congregation of St Catharine of Siena. EdD Columbia U. 1963.

CASEY,C.E. 331
A descriptive study of the isolate sister-teacher and the quality of community life among Roman Catholic teaching sisters. PhD U. of Texas at Austin, 1976.

CONNOLLY,M.K. 332
The anomaly of Catholic higher education for women. EdD Columbia U. Teachers Coll. 1976.

COYLE,M.B. 333
Vocational guidance in the Catholic liberal arts colleges for women in the middle states. PhD St John's U. 1958.

DONOVAN,M.C. 334
Personnel work in Catholic colleges for women: a study of conditions and needs in selected colleges. PhD Fordham U. 1937.

DOYLE,M.M. 335
The curriculum of the Catholic Woman's College. PhD U. of Notre Dame, 1932.

DWYER,M.B. 336
Homemaking education in the Catholic four-year college for women. PhD U. of Nebraska, 1941.

ELY,A. 337
The youth problem and the education of the Catholic girl. PhD Catholic U. of America, 1941.

ENGELHARDT,M.V. 338
The role of the Franciscan sisters in American higher education. PhD Catholic U. of America, 1962.

FALLON,M. 339
An exploratory study to determine attitudes of young women at St Joseph College, West Hartford, Connecticut, towards their future role in the Church. PhD New York U. 1973.

FRIETSCH,M.O. 340
History of the educational activities of the Sisters of Saint Francis, Oldenburg, Indiana. PhD U. of Cincinnati, 1943.

GARVEY,I. 341
A curriculum in speech for the Catholic Women's Art College in the light of contemporary needs. EdD Columbia U. 1969.

GOLDEN,M.C. 342
An investigation of the teaching interests of sisters: their personality characteristics, and the ratings of their supervisors. PhD Fordham U. 1966.

GOOD,M.C. 343
Missiology in the curricula of elementary schools conducted by the Maryknoll sisters. PhD Fordham U. 1952.

GORMAN,M.J.T. 344
Tertiary Franciscan Missionary Sisters of the Sacred Heart and Catholic education in the United States. PhD Fordham U. 1946.

HARKLEROAD,M.A. 345
Selective effect of higher education on Catholic women's career orientations. PhD Catholic U. of America, 1973.

HAUSMANN,M.D.S. 346
The role of the president in American four-year liberal arts colleges conducted by the Benedictine sisters. PhD Catholic U. of America, 1963.

HEALY,M.M.I. 347
Assessment of academic aptitude, personality characteristics, and religious orientation of Catholic sister teacher-trainees. PhD U. of Minnesota, 1966.

HEAVERN,P.A. 348
Attitudes of the Sisters of Charity of Nazareth toward physical education and their relationship to leisure-time activities. PhD U. of Iowa, 1970.

HENNING,G. 349
A history of changing patterns of objectives in Catholic higher education for women in Michigan. PhD Michigan State U. 1969.

HERBERT,R.A. 350
A study of the problems of beginning sister-teachers of reading with implications for pre-service sister-teacher education. PhD Columbia U. 1959.

HIGHBAUGH,M.A. 351
An analysis of the teacher education programs of the Benedictine sisters in the United States. PhD Catholic U. of America, 1961.

HOERNER,M.W. 352
An analysis of student expenditures in high

schools for girls staffed by the Sisters of Providence of St Mary-of-the-Woods, Indiana. PhD Indiana U. 1961.

HOEY,A.F. 353
A comparative study of the problems and guidance resources of Catholic college women. PhD Catholic U. of America, 1957.

HUGHES,M.J. 354
The relationship among value preference dogmatism and cultural background to attitudes towards the rights and roles of women in two groups of Catholic high school girls in senior year. PhD St John's U. 1979.

HUTCHINSON,M.K. 355
A comparative study of the intelligence, achievement, cultural background, socio-economic status, and personality of teacher training and non-teacher training sophomores in five Catholic liberal arts colleges for women. PhD Fordham U. 1959.

KEALEY,R.J. 356
Attitudes of female Catholic black and Hispanic parish leaders and female Catholic white school personnel concerning the utilization of Catholic schools. EdD Fordham U. 1975.

KUZNICKI,E.M. 357
An ethnic school in American education: a study of the origin, development and merits of the educational system of the Felician sisters in the Polish American Catholic schools of western New York. PhD Kansas State U. 1973.

LAWLOR,S.M. 358
The attitudes of teaching sisters in the Archdiocese of Boston on Catholic education and Catholic schools. PhD Boston Coll. 1981.

LAWRY,J.D. 359
Student change on selected nonintellective variables in a Catholic college for women. PhD Fordham U. 1972.

LEMBO,J.M. 360
Altruistic attitudes among Catholic lay and religious female college students. EdD Case Western Reserve U. 1966.

LUFT,L.A. 361
Degree of authoritarianism of teaching sisters and lay teachers in Catholic schools. PhD U. of Wisconsin, 1971.

MCCREAL,M.N. 362
The role of a teaching sisterhood in American society. PhD Catholic U. of America, 1951.

MCDERMOTT,M.C. 363
A history of teacher education in a congregation of religious women, 1843–1964: Sisters of the Holy Cross. PhD U. of Notre Dame, 1964.

MCMURRAY,H.B. 364
Personnel services in Catholic four-year colleges for women. PhD Catholic U. of America, 1958.

MADDEN,M.L.A. 365
Role definitions of Catholic sister-educators and expectations of students, their parents, and teaching sisters in selected areas of the United States. PhD Catholic U. of America, 1960.

MAHER,M.G. 366
The organization of religious instruction in Catholic colleges for women. PhD Catholic U. of America, 1951.

MAKOVIC,M.V. 367
The relationships between nun-teachers' manifest psychogenic needs and attitudes toward students and student behavior. PhD Case Western Reserve U. 1968.

MANGINI,R. 368
Professional problems of sister teachers in the United States. PhD Fordham U. 1958.

MARTINEZ,R.A. 369
The administrative leadership of the Catholic secondary school sister principal in selected personnel relationships. PhD Fordham U. 1967.

MATTHEWS,M.A. 370
A design for inservice programs for the 24 high schools in New Jersey administered by the Sisters of Charity. EdD Columbia U. 1973.

MINNER,J.F. 371
A critical analysis of the introductory college biology program in Catholic women's junior colleges in the United States. PhD U. of Texas at Austin, 1965.

MURPHY,M.I. 372
The chaplain in Catholic colleges for women in the United States. PhD Catholic U. of America, 1965.

MURPHY,M.T. 373
The relationship of psychological needs to occupational satisfaction in religious women teachers. PhD Fordham U. 1965.

NASH,M.L. 374
A study of adjustment problems of sister students from Kerala, India, attending liberal arts colleges in the United States. PhD Catholic U. of America, 1963.

NOACK,J.A. 375
Catholic secondary education and fertility values: a study of Catholic girls in selected schools in the Washington metropolitan area. PhD Catholic U. of America, 1969.

O'CONNELL,M.M. 376
The educational contributions of the school Sisters of Notre Dame in America for the century 1847–1947. PhD Johns Hopkins U. 1950.

O'DONNELL,M. 377
An analysis of the leader behavior dimensions of women Catholic elementary school teachers. EdD St John's U. 1982.

OLHEISER,M.D. 378
Development of a sister-teacher interest scale for the Strong vocational interest blank for women. PhD Boston Coll. 1962.

O'NEILL,M.B. 379
An evaluation of the curricula of a selected group of Catholic women's colleges. PhD Saint Louis U. 1937.

O'NEILL,M.C. 380
Analysis of the instructional problems of beginning sister-teachers of English in Catholic secondary schools. PhD Catholic U. of America, 1966.

POWERS,M.B. 381
The changing patterns of enrolment in schools staffed by the religious Sisters of Mercy in the province of St Louis: causes and implications. PhD U. of Kansas, 1981.

PROSE,M.R. 382
The liberal arts ideal in Catholic colleges for women in the United States. PhD Catholic U. of America, 1943.

RANCOUR,L.E. 383
An analysis of master's degree programs for teachers in Roman Catholic women's colleges. EdD U. of Northern Colorado, 1961.

READY,M.C. 384
A survey of the training and function of counselors in Catholic colleges for women. PhD Fordham U. 1958.

RILEY,M.E. 385
Female non-stereotyping in parochial and public high schools: an analysis of Catholic students' attitudes and their literary preferences. EdD Boston U. Sch. of Educ. 1978.

ROONEY,M.C. 386
A survey and analysis of the preparation for teachers of elementary education in the sister formation program. PhD Fordham U. 1968.

ROY,E.L. 387
The four-year American Catholic colleges for women in 1965. PhD Saint Louis U. 1967.

RYAN,M.L. 388
General education in Catholic colleges for women. PhD Fordham U. 1950.

SAKAC,J.M.S. 389
An assessment of the place of Catholic four-year colleges for women within the framework of higher education in New York State. PhD Catholic U. of America, 1969.

SALAZAR,R.C. 390
Changes in the education of Roman Catholic religious sisters in the United States from 1952 to 1967. PhD U. of Southern California, 1971.

SCANLON,K.I. 391
Student government in Catholic colleges for women in the United States. PhD Fordham U. 1956.

SCHIRMER,M.A. 392
An evaluation of teacher education programs in selected Catholic liberal arts colleges for women. PhD Catholic U. of America, 1959.

SCHUH,M.J.S. 393
The status of freshmen English in selected Catholic women's colleges. PhD Catholic U. of America, 1954.

SEATON,J.R. 394
The impact of changing sex roles on higher education for women: the case of Ursuline College. PhD Case Western Reserve U. 1982.

SEAVER,A.M. 395
A study of professional laboratory experiences provided for prospective elementary school sister-teachers. EdD U. of Oregon, 1960.

SHINN,A.H. 396
Social living in Catholic four-year colleges for women. PhD Catholic U. of America, 1959.

SOLWAY,P.H. 397
An investigation of social-interactional variables related to level of moral development among Catholic high school girls. EdD U. of Houston, 1982.

SPEERSTRA,B.T. 398
A CUES environmental study at a small Catholic liberal arts college for women. EdD Indiana U. 1968.

SPURGEON,M.A. 399
Implications of teacher-pupil relations in the supervision of sister-teachers. PhD Fordham U. 1959.

THOMAS,M.A. 400
Terminal values, personal values, and locus of control in female Catholic high school students: a study of Rokeach's theory. PhD Kent State U. 1980.

THOMPSON,M.S.G. 401
Modifications in identity: a study of the socialization process during a sister formation program. PhD U. of Chicago, 1963.

VERLARDI,A. 402
Aspects of the preparation of sister-teachers for teaching in secondary schools. PhD Fordham U. 1959.

ZIMMER,M.K. 403
Role of American Benedictine institutions of higher education for women. PhD Catholic U. of America, 1962.

Continuing education

See also **5** 94; **6** 820, 829; **15** 111; **17** 575

BELLAMY,S.M. *404*
The origins and development of the educational role of Women's Institutes in England and Wales with particular reference to Essex. MA(Ed) U. of Southampton, 1979.

BERNSTEIN,R.K. *405*
A pilot study of the educational needs of non-urban women (Missouri) and a proposal for an extension division program to meet these needs. EdD Wayne State U. 1971.

CARLSEN,M.L.B. *406*
A four-year retrospective view of the educational experience of a group of mature women undergraduate students. PhD U. of Washington, 1973.

CORBIN,C. *407*
A comparative study of the adult education activities of women's business and professional groups in New York City. PhD New York U. 1956.

DINESS,P.A. *408*
Reschooling for careers: a sociological analysis of the education and career attainment of older re-entry women students. PhD American U. 1981.

ESPARZA,M.O. *409*
The impact of adult education on Mexican-American women. EdD Texas A&M U. 1981.

ESPERSSON,M.A. *410*
The mature women student returning to higher education in a liberal arts college for adults. EdD Columbia U. Teachers Coll. 1975.

FAST,B. *411*
A comparison of the continuing education needs of civilian women and active duty Air Force women. EdD U. of Southern California, 1982.

FOUGHT,C.A. *412*
The historical development of continuing education for women in the United States: economic, social, and psychological implications. PhD Ohio State U. 1966.

FREDERICKSON,M.E. *413*
A place to speak our minds: the Southern School for Women Workers. PhD U. of North Carolina at Chapel Hill, 1981.

GONSKI,M.E. []414
A directory of educational opportunities for adult women at degree-granting institutions in the New York metropolitan area. EdD Columbia U. 1968.

HAVEMEYER,E.A. *415*
Who returns to higher education? The timing of work, marriage and children among women's college alumnae. PhD Columbia U. 1981.

HENSHAW,D.M. *416*
An analysis of barriers to post-secondary educational participation by mature women. EdD North Carolina State U. Raleigh, 1980.

KAUFMAN,C.W.. *417*
Educational retraining requirements of the older female labor pool returnee. EdD U. of Arizona, 1967.

LORD,M.E.M. *418*
Mature women and the degree of Doctor of Philosophy. PhD U. of Wisconsin, 1968.

MCCLAIN,R.S. *419*
An assessment of the needs of adult women returning to higher education at Springfield Technical Community College, Springfield, Massachusetts. EdD U. of Massachusetts, 1979.

MAYHEW,H.C.. *420*
An analysis of comprehensive continuing education programs and services for women at selected Midwestern universities. EdD Ball State U. 1970.

MERRILL,D.P. *421*
Women's clubs in adult education. PhD Yale U. 1936.

O'NEILL,B.L. *422*
Continuing education for women in a California community college: a study of re-entry women (1969–1976). EdD U. of Southern California, 1977.

SCHNEIDER,F.H. *423*
The Bryn Mawr summer school for women workers in industry: a resident school in the Workers' Education Movement. PhD Bryn Mawr Coll. 1939.

SLOWEY,M. *424*
The structure and meaning of women's involvement in adult education. MLitt Trinity Coll. Dublin, 1980.

SPICER,J.L.M. *425*
Adult and continuing education needs of employed women aspiring to administrative assistant positions. EdD Montana State U. 1980.

SULLIVAN,K.M. *426*
Meeting educational needs of women in mid-life through postsecondary institutional planning. PhD U. of Mississippi, 1981.

VAN PEBOREH,M.J. *427*
A re-entry paradigm for educationally disadvantaged women at a community college. EdD U. of Southern California, 1975.

WARTENBERG,A.D. *428*
The design and implementation of a model program to meet the needs of returning undergraduate women. EdD U. of Pennsylvania, 1982.

WITHYCOMBE-BROCATO,C.J. *429*
The mature graduate woman student: who is she? PhD United States International U. 1969.

WOLFE,J.R. *430*
The educational needs of mature women in a western community. PhD Michigan State U. 1975.

WOLFF,L.C. *431*
An analysis of five institutional barriers to higher education as perceived by adult women students at SIU-C. PhD Southern Illinois U. at Carbondale, 1982.

Physical education

See also **22** *passim.*

AINSWORTH,D.S. *432*
The history of physical education in colleges for women as illustrated by Barnard, Bryn Mawr, Elmira, Goucher, Mills, Mount Holyoke, Radcliffe, Rockford, Smith, Vassar, Wellesley, and Wells. PhD Columbia U. 1930.

AITKEN,M.H. *433*
A study of physical education facilities for college women, with implications for Western Washington College of Education. PhD Columbia U. 1958.

ALLEN,P. *434*
An investigation of administrative leadership and group interaction in departments of physical education for women of selected colleges and universities. PhD U. of Oregon, 1972.

ARNSDORFF,D. *435*
Perceptions of critical behaviors for women physical education teachers at the secondary school level. EdD Stanford U. 1959.

BACON,L.S. *436*
A professional education program in physical education for Catholic teacher education institutions for women. EdD New York U. 1950.

BAKER,B.A. *437*
Analysis of girl student attitudes towards the physical education program of Arlington, Virginia. EdD George Peabody Coll. for Teachers, 1968.

BECK,B.A. *438*
Lifestyles of never married women: physical educators in institutions of higher education in the United States. EdD U. of North Carolina at Greensboro, 1976.

BEHLING,M.A. *439*
The development of a screening program for the selection and retention of women physical education major students. PhD Florida State U. 1969.

BELL,P.C. *440*
A history of physical education in girls' public schools, 1870–1920, with particular reference to the influence of Christianity. MEd U. of Manchester, 1978.

BILES,F.R. *441*
Self-concept changes in college freshmen women in a basic physical education course using two methods of instruction. PhD Ohio State U. 1968.

BLOCKLEY,G.E. *442*
A study of undergraduate professional preparation in physical education for women in selected colleges with implications for Central Connecticut State College. PhD Columbia U. 1961.

BRITTAIN,P.E. *443*
A study of the supply of and demand for certified women teachers of health and/or physical education in the State of New York. EdD State U. of New York, 1959.

BUIE,G.E. *444*
An evaluation of the women's non-major physical education program in selected American colleges and universities. EdD U. of Florida, 1956.

BUSWELL,M.M. *445*
A manual of girls' physical education for small high schools. PhD New York U. 1943.

CALDWELL,S.F. *446*
Conceptions of physical education in twentieth-century America: Rosalind Cassidy. PhD U. of Southern California, 1966.

CAMPBELL,S.C. *447*
Factors influencing the participation of female students in sports. MEd U. of Leicester, 1975.

CARTY,H.M.C.S. *448*
Six selected factors and their relationship to the expressed attitude of the high school girl towards physical education. PhD U. of Michigan, 1968.

CLARK,M.L. *449*
An assessment of characteristics of successful women intercollegiate athletic coaches. PED Indiana U. 1974.

CLARKE,J.A. *450*
Survey of the graduates of professional programs in physical education for women at the University of Iowa. PhD U. of Iowa, 1971.

COFFEY,M.A. *451*
The development of professional preparation in physical education for women in the colleges and universities of the Northwest. PhD U. of Iowa, 1963.

COLE,E.M. *452*
An investigation of the frequency, variety and intensity of problems reported by selected women physical education majors at the University of California at Los Angeles. PhD U. of California, Los Angeles, 1956.

CRAWFORD,E.A. *453*
The development of skill test batteries for evaluating the ability of women physical education major students in soccer and speedball. PhD U. of Oregon, 1958.

DOBSON,M.J. *454*
An evaluation of the Portland State College women's physical education classification test. PhD U. of Oregon, 1966.

DREISER,M.V. *455*
A study of health, physical education, and recreation programs for women in municipally owned colleges and universities in the USA. PhD New York U. 1944.

DUGGAN,A.S. *456*
A comparative study of undergraduate women majors and nonmajors in physical education with respect to certain personal traits. PhD Columbia U. 1937.

DUSEK,P.P. *457*
Marie Provaznik: her life and contributions to physical education. PhD U. of Utah, 1981.

FINGER,B. *458*
An administrative guide for the program of physical education for college women. PhD Columbia U. 1957.

FORKEY,H.B. *459*
Issues and concerns of the female physical education teacher. PhD Union Grad. Sch., Ohio, 1975.

FOSS,J.L. *460*
A history of professional preparation in physical education for women in the teachers' colleges of Wisconsin, Illinois and Iowa. PhD U. of Iowa, 1966.

FREY,B.G. *461*
A study of teaching procedures in selected physical education activities for college women of low motor ability. PhD U. of Iowa, 1948.

GALLOWAY,J.P. *462*
A conceptual approach for determining patterns of professional preparation for women in health and physical education. EdD U. of North Carolina at Greensboro, 1970.

GAZETTE,C.P. *463*
Self-perception and peer-perception of a group of women majoring in physical education. PhD Ohio State U. 1963.

GILCOYNE,K. *464*
The professional preparation of women for physical education in the first half of the twentieth century. PhD Columbia U. 1959.

GILL,B.J. *465*
A comparative review of physical education for women in England and Germany with special emphasis upon the period from 1933–1940. PhD U. of Iowa, 1951.

GRAYBEAL,S. *466*
Measurement in physical education for women, University of Minnesota. PhD U. of Minnesota, 1935.

GREENE,M.D. *467*
The growth of physical education for women in the United States in the early nineteenth century. PhD U. of California, Los Angeles, 1950.

GROVES,L. *468*
Physical education for slow learning girls in North East schools with special reference to the effect of creative dance on behaviour and friendship patterns amongst adolescent educationally subnormal (mild) girls. MEd U. of Durham, 1975.

HAGGERTY,H.R. *469*
Certain factors in the professional education of women teachers of physical education. PhD Columbia U. 1938.

HALL,B.C. *470*
A historical study of the early development of teacher education for women in physical education. PhD Columbia U. 1952.

HALL,M.A. *471*
Women and physical education: a causal analysis. PhD U. of Birmingham, 1973.

HARRISTHAL,J.W. *472*
A student reaction inventory for rating teachers in the college women's physical education service program. PhD U. of Oregon, 1962.

HAYES,J.O. *473*
The development of a psychographic profile of the female health physical education and recreational major. DA Middle Tennessee State U. 1973.

HENNIS,G.M. *474*
The construction of knowledge tests in selected physical education activities for college women. PhD U. of Iowa, 1955.

HETHERINGTON,E.L. *475*
Personality characteristics of college women students majoring in physical education with a concentrated study in contemporary dance (Research Study No. 1). EdD U. of Northern Colorado, 1961.

HOLEBROOK,V.R.F. *476*
A study of attitude and performance in gymnastics of college women physical education majors. EdD U. of New Mexico, 1970.

HOPKINS,M.J. *477*
Motor abilitiy performance of college freshman women in relation to previous experiences in physical education at selected liberal arts institutions. EdD U. of Idaho, 1971.

HUNTER,S.R. *479*
Attitudes of women students toward college physical education. EdD U. of Florida, 1956.

ISENBERGER,W.E. *480*
Self-attitudes of women physical education majors as related to measures of interest and success. PhD U. of Iowa, 1957.

JACOBS,M.G. 481
An evaluation of the physical education service program for women in certain selected colleges. EdD New York U. 1957.

JACOBSON,P.A. 482
Knowledge and practice of women physical education teachers in Indiana regarding negligence. PED Indiana U. 1974.

JOHANSON,A.J. 483
Factors related to career choice by women physical education majors and implications for early recruitment. PhD U. of Southern California, 1967.

JOHNSON,G.B. 484
Organization of the required physical education for women in state universities. PhD Columbia U. 1927.

JONES,M.G. 485
Perception, personality and movement characteristics of women students of physical education. MEd U. of Leicester, 1970.

JORGENSEN,L.M. 486
A survey of recruitment and selection practices and procedures of women physical educators in colleges and universities. PED Indiana U. 1960.

JUTTEN,J.B. 487
A job analysis of women physical education teachers in selected senior high schools in Missouri with implications for teacher education. PED Indiana U. 1961.

KAPPES,E.E. 488
An attitude inventory to determine the attitudes of college women toward physical education and the services offered students by a physical education department. PhD U. of Oklahoma, 1954.

KEMP,J. 489
Perceptions of leader behavior of selected women physical education administrators. EdD U. of North Carolina at Greensboro, 1977.

KINZIG,E.S. 490
A survey of women faculty members in the departments of physical education in colleges and universities offering a major physical education curriculum for women. PhD Ohio State U. 1950.

KORRI,L.J. 491
Instructional problems encountered by women physical education teachers and their relation to teaching competency as expressed by physical education majors in Minnesota. PhD U. of Minnesota, 1970.

KRUGER,L.M. 492
An analysis of aquatic competencies necessary for women secondary (four-year and senior high) school physical education teachers in the State of Illinois with implications for professional development. EdD Columbia U. 1962.

LANDERS,D.M. 493
Sibling sex status and ordinal position of female physical education majors and their sport participation and interests. PhD U. of Illinois at Urbana-Champaign, 1969.

LEWIS,C.G. 494
Expressed values of college women at the University of Georgia concerning selected social factors related to acceptance and participation in physical education. PhD Columbia U. 1961.

LEWIS,M.S. 495
A philosophy of Finnish women's physical education as represented in selected writings of Elin Kallio, Elli Bjorksten, and Hilma Jalkanen. PhD U. of Southern California, 1970.

LEYMAN,L. 496
Prediction of freshman grade point averages for women physical education majors. PED Indiana U. 1966.

LIPKOVICH,M.K. 497
A comparison of personality variables of achievement, aggression and dominance among female physical education teachers at the elementary, secondary and collegiate levels. EdD West Virginia U. 1977.

LOCKHART,B.D. 498
Personality factors of university women in relation to their attitudes toward physical education and physical activity. EdD Brigham Young U. 1971.

MACK,B.I. 499
Criteria for studying democratic practices in the preparation of women teachers of physical education. PhD U. of California, Los Angeles, 1951.

MANCHESTER,G.B. 500
The woman high school teacher of physical education in Ohio: a personnel study. PhD New York U. 1935.

MARKEL,M.R. 501
The relationship of selected measures of competence in the physical education basic instruction program for women at the University of Missouri-Columbia. EdD U. of Missouri-Columbia, 1969.

MARSHALL,M.E. 502
The position of women in the administration of physical education units in selected four-year public colleges and universities. EdD U. of North Carolina at Greensboro, 1975.

MCDONALD,A. 503
A study of the influence of physical characteristics and bodily functions upon the physical education of girls and women. MA Queen's U. of Belfast, 1959.

MCILROY,J.S. 504
An evaluation of the physical education programs for women in selected institutions of higher learn-

ing in three Northwest states. PED Indiana U. 1961.

MCKEMIE,K. 505
Perception of actual and ideal role concepts of women heads of departments of physical education by immediate superiors, department heads, and instructional staff. EdD U. of Tennessee, 1970.

MCKINNEY,P.R. 506
The construction of a motor fitness test battery for undergraduate female physical education majors. EdD Northwestern State U. of Louisiana, 1972.

MILLER,M.E. 507
Physical education teacher preparation for women in selected California state universities and English physical education specialist colleges: a comparative analysis. EdD U. of Southern California, 1973.

MISTA,N.J. 508
Attitudes of college women toward their high school physical education programs. PhD U. of Iowa, 1966.

MOHR,D.R. 509
Measured effects on physical education activities on certain aspects of the physical fitness of college women. PhD U. of Iowa, 1944.

NELSON,F.B. 510
Philosophical approach to the development of physical education programs for women in India. EdD New York U. 1950.

NESSLER,J. 511
An experimental study of methods adapted to teaching low skilled freshman women in physical education. PhD Pennsylvania State U. 1961.

PALMER,I. 512
Personal qualities of women teachers of physical education. PhD Yale U. 1933.

PATRI,V.C. 513
Womanpower and physical education. PhD Columbia U. 1959.

PAYNE,E.M. 514
Development of a film evaluation scale and application of the scale to physical education films for girls and women. PhD Indiana U. 1952.

PERSINGER,S. 515
A study of the suitability of selected New Jersey colleges to offer a physical education major for women. EdD New York U. 1964.

PHILLIPS,M.M. 516
Biographies of selected women leaders in physical education in the United States. PhD U. of Iowa, 1960.

PLUMMER,T.C. 517
Factors influencing the attitudes and interests of college women in physical education. PhD U. of Iowa, 1952.

QUISENBERRY,D.J. 518
A use of the semantic differential to determine the perceptions of students toward women high school physical education teachers. PhD Ohio State U. 1970.

REID,A.R. 519
The contribution of the freshman year of physical education in a liberal arts college for women to certain personality variables. PhD U. of Iowa, 1955.

RIDDLE,L. 520
Relationships between physical education activity preference, socioeconomic status, and personality needs of freshman and sophomore college women. EdD Syracuse U. 1968.

RIEFF,J.E. 521
A role perception study of chairmen of departments of physical education for women in institutions of higher education in the Midwest. EdD Illinois State U. 1972.

ROGERS,M.E. 522
An evaluation of selected physical education activities for college women: a comparative analysis of physical education activities to determine their educational potentials. PhD New York U. 1960.

ROSEWARNE-JENKINS,M.A. 523
Aims and objectives in a women's college of physical education. MEd U. of Leicester, 1970.

RUGGIERI,M.J. 524
A study to investigate the relationship of women in physical education to the total faculty workforce population in physical education at the Ohio State University, 1970–1975. EdD U. of Cincinnati, 1977.

RUSSELL,H.L. 525
Teacher education in physical education with special reference to the major programs for women in selected state teachers' colleges. PhD U. of Illinois at Urbana-Champaign, 1944.

SCHALK,I. 526
Service programs standards for physical education in women's Catholic liberal arts colleges. EdD New York U. 1950.

SCHLEEDE,J. 527
Comparative effects of isometric and isotonic training methods on selected physical performance tests with women physical education majors. EdD New York U. 1964.

SCHMID,A.B. 528
An evaluation of professional preparation in women's physical education departments in the state college system of California. EdD U. of California, Berkeley, 1968.

SERVIS,M.A. 529
Qualities related to success in women's physical

education professional preparation program. PhD Springfield Coll. 1965.

SKEPPER,J.D. *530*
Attitudes of specialist women teachers of physical education towards aspects of their initial training and the teaching of physical education. MPhil U. of Leeds, 1979.

SMITH,G.K. *531*
A kinesiological analysis of selected phases of the physical education program for college women. PhD U. of Iowa, 1947.

SMITH,N.A. *532*
Social and cultural factors in the backgrounds of women physical education majors. PhD U. of Iowa, 1967.

SPEARS,B.M. *533*
Philosophical bases for physical education experiences consistent with the goals of general education for college women. PhD New York U. 1956.

STANALAND,P. *534*
A study of selected cultural/social changes and their influence on physical education service programs for women in higher education with implications for changes in women's programs. PED Indiana U. 1968.

STERLE,M.J.R. *535*
The relative effectiveness of four activity courses on the development and maintenance of physical fitness in college freshmen women. PED Indiana U. 1963.

STERLING,V.D. *536*
An integrated program in audio-visual education for professional undergraduate women in physical education. PhD U. of Iowa, 1952.

STRATHAIRN,P.E. *537*
Elective and required aspects of women's physical education at Stanford University. EdD Stanford U. 1962.

TALBOT,B.J. *538*
Case studies of the participation of women students in physical education. MEd U. of Manchester, 1950.

THOMPSON,D.K. *539*
Self-concept and sex-role orientation of women physical education majors as perceived by themselves and the university community. EdD U. of Arkansas, 1982.

THORNBURG,M.L. *540*
Measurement of professional attitude held by women physical education major students in selected institutions. PhD U. of Iowa, 1967.

TRIPLETT,M. *541*
A survey of the professional qualifications, responsibilities, inadequacies, and needs of women physical education teachers in Kansas secondary schools with implications for teacher education. EdD U. of Oklahoma, 1958.

TURNER,M.J. *542*
An evaluation of the physical education program for its educative potential for democratic leadership development in college women. EdD New York U. 1957.

VERDA,M.M. *543*
A comparison of certain characteristics of undergraduate women at Eastern Michigan University who remain in or voluntarily withdraw from the physical education curriculum. PhD U. of Michigan, 1964.

WADDINGTON,H.M. *544*
Developments in physical education in the schools of Wales, with special reference to the teaching of girls. MA U. of Wales, 1951.

WAGGONER,B.E. *545*
A comparison of the profiles of temperament traits of women undergraduate students and full-time teachers in physical education departments in selected colleges and universities in the United States, with implications for the guidance of young women seeking careers in this field. PhD Texas Woman's U. 1966.

WARD,E. *546*
The use of tests of physical ability in the selection of students for specialist physical education colleges for women. MEd U. of Manchester, 1969.

WARDWELL,N.W. *547*
Rachel E. Bryant: contributions to physical education and girls' and women's sports. EdD U. of Toledo, 1979.

WATERMAN,E.F. *548*
The ability of the physical educator to make judgements on the items of a physical examination for women students in colleges and universities. PhD New York U. 1935.

WATKINS,E.L. *549*
A comparison of fundamentals of physical education, intermediate swimming, and progressive weight training within and between groups relative to selected elements of fitness in females. EdD East Texas State U. 1972.

WATSON,H.B. *550*
The comparative relationship of high school physical education programs in Tennessee to the development of strength and motor ability of college women. PhD U. of Michigan, 1955.

WAY,E.E. *551*
An investigation of the relationships of laterality to success in certain physical education activities among University of Washington women students. PhD U. of Washington, 1956.

WEBB,I.M. *552*
Women's physical education in Great Britain,

1800–1906, with special reference to teacher training. MEd U. of Leicester, 1967.

WEBER,M.L. *553*
The role of the woman high school physical education teacher as viewed by selected university and public school personnel in Wisconsin. PhD U. of Wisconsin-Madison, 1974.

WEINMANN,C.A. *554*
The effect of two types of augmented feedback on self-reinforcement of high school physical education female students at two levels of self-esteem. EdD U. of North Carolina at Greensboro, 1977.

WEST,B.G.H. *555*
Tests for use in assigning college women to physical education classes. EdD U. of Utah, 1964.

WEST,E.L. *556*
The role of women in American society with implications for the professional preparation of women for teaching physical education in college. PhD New York U. 1961.

WILSON,B.D. *557*
Self-perception and peer perception of a group of college women physical educators. PhD Ohio State U. 1970.

WOHLFORD,M.B. *558*
Certain personality traits of high school girls classified according to individual patterns of participation in physical education activities. PhD New York U. 1945.

WONG,J.C. *559*
The effect of instruction in health occupations and of vocational interest appraisal on the preference of health occupations among female college freshmen and sophomores. EdD U. of Missouri-Columbia, 1971.

WOOD,G.K. *560*
Academic achievement and athletic participation among college women. PhD U. of Maryland, 1975.

WOOD,S.J. *561*
Reciprocal role expectations of women physical education teachers and chairmen. PhD U. of Illinois at Urbana-Champaign, 1971.

YAGAR,B. *562*
Some characteristics of women who have chosen college teaching in physical education. EdD U. of Southern California, 1964.

The women's studies curriculum

See also 1422; **7** 61, 65; **9** 624.

AMIS,V.D. *563*
Selected women authors of Britain and America: a curriculum guide for teachers of college English courses. EdD U. of Arkansas, 1978.

BELL,M.P. *564*
Using the black female autobiography to teach freshman college English. AD U. of Michigan, 1977.

BOROD,J.C. *565*
The impact of a women's studies course on perceived sex differences, real and ideal self-perceptions, and attitudes towards women's rights and roles. PhD Case Western Reserve U. 1975.

CALLIN,D.T. *566*
A three-hour credit course in Women in Literature: toward a prototype. PhD U. of Illinois at Urbana-Champaign, 1976.

COFFMAN,S.J. *567*
The effect of introductory women's studies classes on sex-role stereotypes. PhD U. of Washington, 1978.

DEUTSCH,A. *568*
Women's studies as institutional policy: an analysis of the program coordinator's role. PhD U. of Miami, 1978.

DUNCAN,W.L. *569*
The educational implications for institutions of higher adult education of a study of twenty women creatives in the field of literature. PhD U. of Oklahoma, 1976.

FALLON,C.D. *570*
Women's studies in the social studies curricula of secondary schools. EdD U. of Rochester, 1980.

FLASHMAN,S.L. *571*
The Women's Learning Institute: a case study in alternative feminist education. EdD U. of Massachusetts, 1979.

FUTAS,E. *572*
Communication and information patterns in the emerging, interdisciplinary area of women's studies. PhD Rutgers U. 1980.

GOLTRA,R.D. *573*
Women's studies: a new program for the community college. PhD Oregon State U. 1974.

HENEK,T. *574*
The impact of a women's studies course on female ego development and attitudes toward women. PhD U. of Illinois at Chicago Circle, 1980.

JOHNSTON,J.C. *575*
A multicultural women's studies curriculum in American literature. DA Drake U. 1978.

LAFONTAINE,P.W. *576*
Non-sexist education: toward the emergence of an alternative curriculum paradigm for women's studies programs. PhD Ohio State U. 1981.

LEVINE,A.S. *577*
The effects of women's studies on the fear of success and locus of control of female college students. EdD Coll. of William and Mary in Virginia, 1981.

PHILLIPS,J.C. *578*
A proposed survey course of women's studies for students at the University of Mississippi. EdD U. of Mississippi, 1973.

RAPIN,L.S. *579*
The effects of a women's studies course on women students' attitudes toward self and other women. PhD U. of Illinois at Urbana-Champaign, 1973.

RICHARDSON,J.M. *580*
Women, society and change: a study of support for ameliorative and reconstructionist objectives among women's programs in higher education. PhD U. of Washington, 1975.

SPEIZER,J.J. *581*
An evaluation of the changes in attitudes toward women which occur as a result of participation in a women's studies course. EdD Boston U. Sch. of Educ. 1975.

SPAULDING,J.E. *582*
Women's studies at California Community College: a comprehensive model. EdD U. of Southern California, 1973.

STILES,D.A. *583*
Women's studies versus beauty culture programs as a therapeutic educational approach for adolescent girls who have emotional and adjustment problems. PhD Boston Coll. 1980.

STRAIN,S.M. *584*
An exploratory investigation of women's studies in selected institutions of higher education with emphasis upon the historical background of the status of women and the special needs of women in higher education. PhD U. of Southern California, 1977.

THAMES,A.M. *585*
Women's studies in three institutions of higher education in California. PhD U. of California, Los Angeles, 1975.

TUCKER,B.J. *586*
Woman in crisis: an integrated approach to women's studies. EdD U. of Northern Colorado, 1972.

WILSON,Y.A. *587*
Curricular materials for teaching post-secondary students about notable American women, 1920–1970. EdD U. of Arkansas, 1977.

WOOD,D.J. *588*
Women's studies programs in American colleges and universities: a case of organizational innovation. PhD Vanderbilt U. 1979.

The educational professions

See also **9** 243; **11** 7.

General

BARTER,A.K.S. *589*
A study of elementary school teachers' attitudes toward the women principal and toward the elementary principalship as a career. PhD U. of Michigan, 1957.

BAUGHMAN,M.K. *590*
Attitudes and perceptions of a selected sample of women senior high teachers toward becoming school administrators in Detroit public schools. PhD U. of Michigan, 1977.

BECK,B.D. *591*
Perceptions of female vocational faculty and administrators in Nebraska community colleges. PhD Colorado State U. 1978.

BRAYFIELD,C.H. *592*
Social literacy education for women educators: will it facilitate their entry into public school administration? EdD U. of Massachusetts, 1978.

BROOKS,H.L. *593*
Similarities and differences among secondary school women administrators and selected other educators. PhD U. of Connecticut, 1981.

BURLEIGHSAVAGE,I.C. *594*
A study of the relationship between the scarcity of women in higher educational administrative positions and the multiple factors which influence the career aspirations of women professors. PhD Michigan State U. 1979.

ERINAKES,D.M. *595*
An analysis of women elementary school principals and long-term women teachers in relation to selected psychological and situational variables. PhD U. of Connecticut, 1980.

KRAUSE,J.L. *596*
A study of teacher attitudes towards their women secondary school principals in New Jersey. EdD Temple U. 1964.

LANDON,G.L. *597*
Perceptions of sex-role stereotyping and women teachers' administrative career aspirations. PhD U. of Wisconsin-Madison, 1975.

LIPTON,L.K.P. *598*
Factors influencing female teachers seeking administrative positions. EdD Northern Arizona U. 1980.

NIXON,M.T. *599*
Women administrators and women teachers: a comparative study. PhD U. of Alberta, 1975.

PARKS,D.S. 600
The relationship between self-concept and management aspirations in female prospective teachers. EdD East Texas State U. 1974.

SCAFELLA,J.S. 601
Women in support of a university: the locus of women employees at West Virginia University and how they feel about their work. EdD West Virginia U. 1980.

SIMPSON,L.A. 602
A study of employing agents' attitudes towards academic women in higher education. EdD Pennsylvania State U. 1968.

SITES,P.T. 603
The role of professional women in area vocational schools. DEd Pennsylvania State U. 1975.

TOBIN,M. 604
A profile of black women doctorate holders in black public colleges and universities: 1973–1974. PhD Kansas State U. 1975.

WAIN,J.A. 605
Attitudes of teachers toward women school administrators and the aspirations of teachers for administrative positions in the State of Minnesota. PhD U. of Minnesota, 1975.

WHITTEN,J.E. 606
Women teachers' perceptions concerning career aspirations of the elementary principalship in selected schools in Texas. EdD U. of Houston, 1975.

WILLIAMS,P.J. 607
Career aspirations of selected women teachers as related to their perceptions of the chances of success in becoming a school administrator. EdD U. of Northern Colorado, 1977.

Administration

ACHESON,E.M. 608
The personal and professional characteristics of a selected group of deans of women. PhD Columbia U. 1932.

ADDIS,M.E. 609
Problems of administrative change in selected programs for the re-education of women. EdD Harvard U. 1967.

AIELLO,K.H. 610
A study of male principals' attitudes toward women aspiring to school-based administrative positions. EdD Florida Atlantic U. 1980.

ANDERSON,E.B. 611
The life-history correlates, work-related motivational characteristics and role-identification factors of on-site women administrators in Hawaiian public schools. EdD U. of Southern California, 1977.

ANDREASEN,V.K. 612
Housemothers and head residents: a sociological study of their work. PhD U. of Missouri, 1965.

APOSTOLON,S.F. 613
Training women for educational leadership: an impact assessment of an extra- institutional workshop. EdD Boston U. Sch. of Educ. 1980.

ARTER,M.H. 614
The role of women in administration in state universities and land-grant colleges. PhD Arizona State U. 1972.

AUGUSTINE,C.M. 615
Some aspects of management of college residence halls for women. PhD Columbia U. 1935.

AVILA,L.D. 616
Attitudes towards the employment of women administrators in Arizona public schools. EdD Arizona State U. 1981.

AYORA,R.H. 617
Career sponsorship of women school administrators. PhD U. of Oregon, 1981.

BARGNEGI,M.L. 618
Attitudes of superintendents and board members in Connecticut toward the employment and effectiveness of women as public school administrators: a replication study. PhD U. of Connecticut, 1981.

BARON,E.B. 619
The status of women senior high school principals in the United States. PhD U. of Pittsburgh, 1976.

BARRY,C.S. 620
The role of women in higher education administration in New York State in the 1980s. PhD Fordham U. 1975.

BAUER,L.M. 621
An investigation of determinants of levels of professional achievement attained by a group of women administrators employed in selected divisions of continuing education in Michigan during the years 1960–1976. PhD Michigan State U. 1978.

BAUR,B.M. 622
Admission and employment patterns of women matriculating in educational administration at selected Midwestern universities. EdD Ball State U. 1975.

BECK,H.N. 623
Attitudes toward women held by California School District Board members, superintendents, and personnel directors including a review of the historical, psychological and sociological foundations. EdD U. of the Pacific, 1978.

BELL,J.M. 624
An assessment of leadership behaviors of female administrators in an urban school district. PhD U. of Pittsburgh, 1977.

BELSON,B.A. *625*
Journal of the National Association for Women Deans, Administrators, and Counselors: an historical analysis, 1938–1974. PhD Michigan State U. 1974.

BENEDETTI,C.R. *626*
Similarities and differences in the leadership styles and personal characteristics of women in educational administration and women in business administration. EdD Western Michigan U. 1975.

BENTON,S.K.Y. *627*
Reported factors influencing the selection of women to top-level administrative positions in public community colleges. EdD U. of Tennessee, 1979.

BERMAN,J.S. *628*
The managerial behavior of female high school principals. EdD Columbia U. Teachers Coll. 1982.

BOCK,D.J. *629*
Women in instructional middle management in California community colleges: a study of mobility. EdD U. of Southern California, 1976.

BOWLING,R.P. *630*
Factors that limit the entry of women into the elementary principalship. EdD U. of Alabama, 1981.

BOWMAN,J.S. *631*
Women in educational administration as role models: toward empirical understanding. PhD U. of Colorado at Boulder, 1981.

BRANCH,E.G. *632*
A study of self-perceived leadership styles of female administrators compared to those of their superordinates of five major Texas junior/community college districts. EdD North Texas State U. 1979.

BRECK,A.R.W. *633*
Professional concerns of women in positions of administration in public schools. PhD U. of Denver, 1960.

BROOKS,B.J.R. *634*
A profile of black females in selected administrative positions in the public school systems in Florida. PhD U. of Michigan, 1975.

BROWN,A.V. *635*
Black female administrators in higher education – a survey of demographic data, previous work experiences, characteristics of present positions, and characteristics of employment institutions. PhD Bowling Green State U. 1980.

BROWN,E.M. *636*
A Delphi Study to determine factors which relate to decisions of women to seek positions in educational administration in selected cities in Texas. EdD East Texas State U. 1977.

BROWN,N.B. *637*
The National Association of Women Deans and Counselors, 1951–1961. EdD U. of Denver, 1963.

BURNS,D.M. *638*
Women in educational administration: a study of leadership in California public schools. EdD U. of Oregon, 1964.

BURTON,J.M.H. *639*
An exploratory study of racially different female administrators in selected colleges and universities. PhD U. of Michigan, 1976.

CABOTAJE,A.A. *640*
A comparative study of the qualifications for deans of women in institutions of higher education in the United States and in the Republic of the Philippines. EdD American U. 1962.

CHAMBERS,R.C. *641*
An identification and comparison of problems encountered by black and women superintendents. PhD U. of Iowa, 1979.

CHRISTENSEN,A.A. *642*
Attitudes toward women as leaders in community education. EdD Arizona State U. 1975.

CHRISTENSEN,J. *643*
Feminine sex-role conflict: a study of Colorado women public school administrators. PhD U. of Colorado at Boulder, 1980.

CHRISTENSEN-LIGGETT,T.M. *644*
An analysis of the attitudes that superintendents, board members, and female administrators in selected Nebraska school districts hold toward Title IX employment provisions and toward employing female administrators. PhD U. of Nebraska, 1977.

CIBIK,R.S. *645*
The personal, social, and professional backgrounds and the duties and responsibilities of women high school principals in the United States. EdD U. of Pittsburgh, 1957.

COATNEY,K.B. *646*
Women superintendents in the United States, 1981–1982 school year. EdD U. of Mississippi, 1982.

COBBLEY,L. *647*
A study of attitudes and opportunities for women in six western states to become elementary school principals. EdD Brigham Young U. 1970.

COGHLAN,P.C. *648*
The status of the female administrator in Texas senior colleges and universities. EdD Texas A&M U. 1979.

COLLIER,R.D. *649*
A study to identify and evaluate the attitudes of superintendents and boards of education in Wisconsin toward the employment of women as

public school administrators. EdD Marquette U. 1975.

COSTA,M.E. *650*
A descriptive study of women superintendents of public schools in the United States. EdD Columbia U. Teachers Coll. 1981.

COTTON,J.V. *651*
Role perception and characteristics of black female administrators in institutions of higher education in Tennessee. PhD U. of Pittsburgh, 1979.

COUGH,A.S. *652*
A study of employer attitudes regarding the employment of women administrators in vocational education in Kentucky. EdD U. of Kentucky, 1978.

COX,J. *653*
Comparison of leadership styles and personal characteristics of middle and upper-level women administrators in higher education and corporate business. PhD Georgia State U. Coll. of Educ. 1982.

CRISTO,M.G. *654*
Factors influencing career mobility and career attainment of women in the field of education. PhD U. of Virginia, 1975.

CROCHET,C.M. *655*
An exploratory study of characteristics of women administrators in vocational education in Georgia. PhD Florida State U. 1980.

CROSBY,J.W. *656*
An exploratory study of women superintendents. EdD U. of Massachusetts, 1973.

CURBY,V.M. *657*
Geographic mobility of women administrators in higher education. PhD U. of Missouri-Columbia, 1978.

DAVIS,M.C. *658*
Women administrators in southeastern institutions of higher education. PhD U. of Alabama, 1978.

DENNISON,J.A. *659*
Administrators' attitude toward the role of women. EdD U. of Missouri-Columbia, 1978.

DOLAN,F.A. *660*
Personal qualities and characteristics important in the selection of undergraduate staff members for women's residence halls. PhD Northwestern U. 1965.

DONOHUE, W.G. *661*
The life cycles and career stages of senior-level administrative women in higher education. EdD Memphis State U. 1981.

DOOLEY,E.P. *662*
An exploratory study of the educational values inherent in various patterns of housing for freshmen women. PhD Columbia U. 1957.

DORNER,S.A. *663*
Career paths of women school superintendents. EdD Rutgers U. 1982.

DOUGLAS,P.D. *664*
An analysis of demographic characteristics and career patterns of women administrators in higher education. PhD U. of Connecticut, 1976.

DRESSLER,F. *665*
A descriptive study of women administrators in higher education in San Diego county. PhD United States International U. 1981.

DRUST,B. *666*
Factors related to the employment of women as junior high school and high school principals, assistant superintendents, and superintendents in California public schools. EdD Brigham Young U. 1976.

DUBLON,F.J. *667*
Life-style aspirations, multiple role commitments, and role-conflict strategies of women doctoral students in comprehensive programs of higher education administration within the State of Florida. PhD Florida State U. 1982.

DUNN,C.J. *668*
The dean of women in Texas state-supported senior colleges and universities, 1965–1966. EdD U. of Houston, 1966.

DURAN,I.S. *669*
Grounded theory study: Chicana administrators in Colorado and New Mexico. [Mexican-American women in educational administration] EdD U. of Wyoming, 1982.

EAGER,J.C.S. *670*
A comparative study of women in administration positions and women seeking administration positions in the field of elementary education in the State of Pennsylvania. PhD U. of Pittsburgh, 1979.

EDSON,S.K. *671*
Female aspirants in public school administration: why do they continue to aspire to principalships? PhD U. of Oregon, 1980.

ELLIS,M.H. *672*
Upward mobility patterns of black and white women in higher education administration. EdD U. of Alabama, 1982.

ENGER,N.R. *673*
Priority-performance perceptions of the women public secondary school principals in Minnesota in eight key areas of responsibility. PhD U. of Minnesota, 1982.

FANSHER,T.R. *674*
Job satisfaction and dissatisfaction of female public secondary school principals in the United States. PhD U. of South Carolina, 1977.

FARMER,N.J. *675*
Characteristics of women principals in North Carolina. EdD U. of North Carolina at Chapel Hill, 1982.

FEATHER,C.A. *676*
Women band directors in higher education. PhD U. of Mississippi, 1980.

FECHER,A.A.R. *677*
Career patterns of women in college and university administration. EdD Indiana U. 1972.

FERGUSON,H.R. *678*
California women school board members: concerns, priorities, and self-perceived effectiveness. EdD U. of Southern California, 1977.

FISHER,F.P. *679*
A study of the relationship between the scarcity of women in educational administrative positions and the multiple factors which influence the career aspirations of women teachers. PhD Michigan State U. 1978.

FITZPATRICK,M.M. *680*
The advisory board in four-year Catholic women's colleges in the United States, 1964. PhD Catholic U. of America, 1965.

FLAHERTY,M.R. *681*
Patterns of administration in Catholic colleges for women in the United States. PhD Catholic U. of America, 1960.

FLEMING,J.T. *682*
Assessment of employment practices toward women administrators in institutions of higher education. EdD Arizona State U. 1974.

FORLINES,C.L. *683*
Superintendents' perceptions of public opinions toward women administrators and superintendents' opinions toward women administrators. PhD George Peabody Coll. for Teachers, 1981.

FOSTER,A.M. *684*
A study of the impact of co-educational residence halls at a large metropolitan university. EdD Boston U. Sch. of Educ. 1974.

FOX,F.J. *685*
Black women administrators in the Denver public schools. EdD U. of Colorado at Boulder, 1975.

GARDNER,H.R. *686*
Women administrators in higher education in Illinois: a study of current career patterns. EdD Indiana U. 1966.

GARDNER,L.C. *687*
Employment status of female administrators and attitudes toward employment of female administrators in the community college system of North Carolina. EdD East Tennessee State U. 1977.

GASSER,M.H. *688*
Career patterns of women administrators in higher education: barriers and constraints. PhD Southern Illinois U. at Carbondale, 1975.

GENERETT,M.N. *689*
The role of women trustees in private independent colleges and universities of Pennsylvania as defined by their characteristics, functions, and perceptions. PhD U. of Pittsburgh, 1978.

GIBSON,H.E. *690*
Public relations practices in institutions of higher education for women. PhD U. of Missouri-Columbia, 1946.

GIBSON,I.A. *691*
The dean of women's office at work. PhD U. of Colorado, 1949.

GIBSON,V.O.S. *692*
A normative survey of the status of women in administrative positions in the tri-county area of Wayne, Oakland, and Macomb counties. EdD Wayne State U. 1979.

GIGGLEMAN,L.J.C. *693*
A comparison of the personality characteristics of women administrators and women teachers in selected community colleges. EdD East Texas State U. 1978.

GLANCY,F. *694*
The present status and role of the registrar in a selected number of Catholic four-year liberal arts colleges for women. PhD Catholic U. of America, 1962.

GODFREY,H.R. *695*
A profile of female trustees of four-year public colleges and universities and a comparison of female and male trustee perceptions of selected trustee functions and university issues. PhD Michigan State U. 1971.

GOERSS,K.V.W. *696*
A study of personality factors of selected women administrators in higher education. PhD U. of Southern Mississippi, 1975.

GORDON,R.L.H. *697*
Differential value patterns of black and white women in higher education. PhD United States International U. 1974.

GORDON,S.E. *698*
Career patterns of female chief student affairs administrators. PhD Florida State U. 1979.

GORGONE,K. *699*
A comparison of perceptions held by superintendents, school board members, and teacher representatives regarding the role of women school board members in the State of Indiana. PhD Southern Illinois U. at Carbondale, 1976.

GORMAN,H.T. *700*
The relationship between gender, sex-role description, attitudes toward women, and the perceived leadership behavior of male and female

elementary school principals. EdD New York U. 1980.

GOSS,S.M.C. *701*
A study of attitudes toward women in public school administration in Tennessee. PhD George Peabody Coll. for Teachers, 1978.

GREER,C.B. *702*
The perceptions and status of the black administrative woman in selected two-year and four-year coeducational colleges and universities. PhD Florida State U. 1981.

GROSE,M.B. *703*
Factors contributing to the paucity of women elementary school principals in the State of Pennsylvania. EdD U. of Pennsylvania, 1979.

HADDOCK,R. *704*
A study of five deans of women. PhD Syracuse U. 1952.

HALLER,L.M. *705*
The future role of the highest ranking woman student personnel administrator in the college or university and a suggested training program. EdD Michigan State U. 1967.

HALLQUIST,M.W. *706*
Sex-role attitudes and deterrents for women in education administration. PhD U. of Wisconsin-Madison, 1981.

HANKIN,C.G. *707*
The female elementary school principal (4 vols). EdD Columbia U. Teachers Coll. 1978.

HANSON,T.F. *708*
A study of assumptions about female administrators in higher education as perceived by faculty and administrators of colleges and universities in Utah. PhD U. of Utah, 1975.

HARD,J.S. *709*
The effective woman home economics administrator. EdD Virginia Polytechnic Inst. and State U. 1980.

HARLBUT,J.A.A. *710*
Attitudes and other concerns related to women being employed as public school administrators in Texas. EdD North Texas State U., 1978.

HARRIS,E.S. *711*
California women school superintendents' characteristics and trends, 1874–1974. EdD U. of California, Los Angeles, 1976.

HAUN,H.T. *712*
A study of work satisfaction and dissatisfaction among selected women leaders in higher education. EdD U. of Tennessee, 1975.

HEMMING,R.M. *713*
Administrative women and affirmative action: a study of women administrators in California community colleges and their perceptions of sex discrimination and affirmative action. EdD U. of La Verne, 1981.

HENSCHEL,B.J.S. *714*
A comparison of the personality variables of women administrators and women teachers in education. EdD U. of Utah, 1964.

HILL,H.T. *715*
Characteristics of head residents and a proposed course of study for head residents of women's residence halls. EdD Oklahoma State U. 1970.

HILTON,M.E. *716*
The dean of women in the public junior college. PhD Syracuse U. 1934.

HINKLE,B.R. *717*
Superintendent and school board members' attitudes toward women in educational administration. EdD U. of Northern Colorado, 1979.

HOLMES,L.H. *718*
A history of the position of dean of women in a selected group of coeducational colleges and universities in the US. PhD Columbia U. 1939.

HOLT,Y.P. *719*
Female elementary principals of northern California: twelve profiles. PhD United States International U. 1979.

HOPKINS,S.M. *720*
Policies affecting the employment of women in the California public schools. PhD U. of California, Los Angeles, 1976.

HOWELL,S.E. *721*
The functions of the head resident in a women's residence hall in accredited colleges and universities in Mississippi. EdD U. of Mississippi, 1971.

HUFFTY,J.E. *722*
The relationship of personality types, leadership styles, and effectiveness with attitudes toward women in a selected group of public school superintendents. EdD East Texas State U. 1979.

HUGGINS,M.A. *723*
Educational needs of women administrative assistants and executive secretaries with implications for collegiate programs designed to meet these needs through continuing education or evening divisions. EdD U. of Southern Mississippi, 1977.

HUGHES,D.L. *724*
Aspirations and goals of 1976 Utah women educators for public school administration. EdD Brigham Young U. 1976.

HULETT,S.A. *725*
Selected vertical mobility determiners of women educators in Missouri. EdD U. of Missouri-Columbia, 1976.

HUNNICUTT,T.M. *726*
Defining and projecting the office of the dean of women at the University of Houston. EdD U. of Houston, 1956.

HUSERIK,M.C. *727*
Career aspirations and promotional opportunity for women administrators in California school districts. EdD U. of Southern California, 1975.

IRONSIDE,E.M. *728*
Career paths of women administrators in higher education institutions: perceptions of motivation and opportunity. PhD U. of North Carolina at Chapel Hill, 1982.

JACKSON,C.B. *729*
Career development for women in public school administration: a study of women school superintendents in the United States. PhD U. of Colorado at Boulder, 1980.

JOHANNINGMEIER,L.L.L. *730*
The attitudes of Iowa teachers toward women in educational administrative positions. PhD U. of Iowa, 1978.

JOHNSON,J.L.E. *731*
Women in academic administrative positions in higher education. EdD George Peabody Coll. for Teachers, 1981.

JONES,J.L. *732*
A personnel study of women deans in colleges and universities. PhD Columbia U. 1928.

KAUFMAN,H.M. *733*
The status of women in administration in selected institutions of higher education in the United States. EdD New York U. 1961.

KEOUGH,S.D. *734*
Sponsorship of the careers of women administrators at public institutions of higher education. PhD U. of Mississippi, 1982.

KILBOURN,D.W. *735*
A study of the status and roles of head residents in college and university residence halls for women. PhD Michigan State U. 1959.

KOENIG,W.L. *736*
The dean of women: ideal and actual perceptions of role. PhD U. of Michigan, 1964.

KONICK,E.J.R. *737*
Politics, recruitment patterns, and women: an analysis of school board membership in selected New Jersey school districts. EdD Rutgers U. 1978.

LA BARTHE,E.R. *738*
A study of the motivation of women in administrative and supervisory positions in selected unified school districts in Southern California. EdD U. of Southern California, 1973.

LA PUMA,B.A.D. *739*
A study of attitudes toward the employment of women in higher education as revealed in the literature of higher education. [Women as faculty members and administrators] PhD New York U. 1972.

LARSON,H.H. *740*
Some theoretical considerations: a guide for research on women administrators. EdD Columbia U. Teachers Coll. 1982.

LEE,C.F. *741*
Attitudes and perceptions of administrators and faculty members concerning the implementation of affirmative action goals for women in selected two-year colleges in New Jersey and the southeastern counties of Pennsylvania. EdD Temple U. 1979.

LENNY,M.R. *742*
Determination of the opportunities for upward mobility of women to positions of authority in three Illinois public community colleges. PhD Saint Louis U. 1980.

LIPFORD,M.A. *743*
A profile of the woman administrator in educational technology in higher education. EdD East Texas State U. 1978.

LITTLE,S.H. *745*
Sponsorship and other selected factors associated with the mobility of women to public school administrative positions. PhD U. of Texas at Austin, 1980.

LIVINGSTON,I.B. *746*
Social, economic and political influences on the development of residence halls for women in colleges and universities in the United States. PhD Ohio State U. 1966.

LOWE,M.E.B. *747*
The role, position, and perception of women school board members in Texas. EdD North Texas State U. 1976.

MCADA,B.D. *748*
Perceived characteristics and administrative skills of women administrators in vocational education in the United States. PhD North Texas State U. 1980.

MCBEE,M.L. *749*
The role of the dean of women in selected institutions of higher learning. PhD Ohio State U. 1961.

MCCAMEY,D.S. *750*
The status of black and white women in central administrative positions in Michigan public schools. PhD U. of Michigan, 1976.

MCCARTHY,M.S.M. *751*
A regional study of superintendents' and Title IX coordinators' feminist/political perspectives and the status of Title IX implementation in their districts. EdD U. of Massachusetts, 1981.

MCCORKLE,E.M. *752*
Top-level women administrators in higher education: a study of women presidents, chief academic officers, and academic deans in federal regions I, VI and X. EdD Oklahoma State U. 1974.

MCDADE,T.E. *753*
Career path models for women superintendents. EdD Arizona State U. 1981.

MCGINNISS,A.G. *754*
A study of the social regulations governing women students in American colleges and universities. PhD Northwestern U. 1953.

MACK,M.H. *755*
A study of attitude toward women as school administrators. EdD Auburn U. 1981.

MCNEER,E.J. *756*
The role of mentoring in the career development of women administrators in higher education. PhD Ohio State U. 1981.

MCNUTT,A.S. *757*
A study of the role models of top-echelon women administrators in southern public institutions of higher education. PhD George Peabody Coll. for Teachers, 1979.

MCSHEA,A.B. *758*
An analysis of the perceptions of women superintendents regarding selected career factors affecting their career tracks leading to the superintendency. PhD U. of Nebraska-Lincoln, 1979.

MAKULSKI,M.J.D. *759*
Case studies of the attitudes of superintendents and school board members of selected school districts in the State of Michigan toward the employment of women as school administrators. PhD U. of Michigan, 1976.

MALONEY,F.C. *760*
A study of the relationship between leadership behavior and particular personality characteristics of women elementary principals in public and Roman Catholic schools. EdD St John's U. 1978.

MANN,B.A. *761*
Career sponsorship of women senior-level administrators in higher education. PhD Florida State U. 1980.

MARABLE,J.M. *762*
The role of women in public school administration as perceived by black women administrators in the field. PhD U. of Miami, 1974.

MARSHALL,C. *763*
The career socialization of women in school administration. PhD U. of California, Santa Barbara, 1979.

MARTIN,E.B. *764*
A profile of women as secondary school vice-principals. PhD Columbia U. 1956.

MARTIN,K.J.L. *765*
Directors of continuing education for women: a study of the personnel and their position in general extension and continuing education. EdD U. of California, Los Angeles, 1976.

MARTIN,R.V.R. *766*
Minority women administrators' perceptions of barriers in higher education. PhD U. of Connecticut, 1980.

MATHENY,P.H.P. *767*
A study of the attitudes of selected male and female teachers, administrators and board of education presidents toward women in educational administrative positions. PhD Northwestern U. 1973.

MATTES,L.A. *768*
The status of women in schools of education and educational administration in higher education. EdD Auburn U. 1973.

MAUTER,M.A. *769*
Female administrators in Ohio public schools. PhD Ohio State U. 1980.

MEARS,F.L. *770*
A study of the attitudes of male and female superintendents concerning female superintendents. EdD Mississippi State U. 1982.

MESKIN,J.D. *771*
Career patterns and choice processes of women elementary principals. PhD U. of Chicago, 1981.

MEYER,M.A. *772*
Position analysis and attitudes of women in higher education administration in Illinois. PhD Southern Illinois U. at Carbondale, 1982.

MICAS,S.S. *773*
Commonalities among women district superintendents in public school education in the United States. EdD U. of Virginia, 1981.

MILLS-NOVOA,B.A. *774*
A study of selected variables affecting the career progression of women in higher education administration. PhD U. of Minnesota, 1980.

MITCHELL,B.A. *775*
An investigation into personality factors of administrators of women's centers. PhD Arizona State U. 1976.

MOOK,A.W. *776*
Attitudes toward women administrators by Minnesota secondary principals, boards of education, and superintendents. PhD U. of Iowa, 1981.

MOORE,S.E. *777*
Opportunities for women in the field of public school administration in the New Jersey counties of Cumberland, Hunterdon, and Passaic. EdD Rutgers U. 1977.

MORRIS,E.B. *778*
Women in educational leader positions: an investigation of some common factors in socialization, educational background and career commitment. EdD Western Michigan U. 1982.

MORRIS,M.P. *779*
Critical characteristics of top level women administrators in the overseas American sponsored schools. EdD U. of Denver, 1979.

MORRISSEY,W.M. *780*
The status and perceptions of women school board members in Indiana. EdD Indiana U. 1972.

MOTAMEDI,I. *781*
Women administrators in higher and secondary education in Iran. PhD Southern Illinois U. at Carbondale, 1978.

NAJIB,J.G. *782*
Professional preparation and perception of Indiana senior high school women teachers relative to the perceived opportunity to pursue an administrative career at the senior high school and/or central office level. EdD Ball State U. 1981.

NAPIER,S.R. *783*
Perceived leadership effectiveness among selected predominantly black women administrators and institutional variables in higher education: an exploratory study. EdD U. of Tennessee, 1979.

NATERA,M. *784*
The employment of California women line administrators in K12 districts in the years 1968, 1972, and 1976. EdD U. of Southern California, 1977.

NEIDIG,M.B. *785*
Women applicants for administrative positions: attitudes held by administrators and school boards. PhD U. of Iowa, 1973,

NELSON,B.C. *786*
The relationship of selected variables to community college administrators' views of the feminine role. PhD U. of Connecticut, 1975.

NELSON,C.K. *787*
Factors influencing the promotion of women to the principalship in Arizona. EdD Northern Arizona U. 1982.

NIEBOER,N.S. *788*
The administrative woman in higher education. PhD United States International U. 1975.

NIETO,C. *789*
Factors for discontinuing pursuit of public elementary administration by once-aspiring female teachers. PhD Claremont Grad. Sch. 1980.

NOLL,N.L. *790*
Opinions of policy-making officials in two-year public educational institutions toward the employment of women administrators. PhD Arizona State U. 1973.

NORTON,J.S. *791*
A philosophic rationale of women's role in teacher education in the United States. EdD Boston U. Sch. of Educ. 1974.

ORT,V.K. *792*
The role of the school superintendent's wife. PhD Ohio State U. 1955.

OWENS,E.T. *793*
Perceived barriers to employment for women as educational administrators in South Carolina public schools. EdD U. South Carolina, 1975.

PACHECO,B.A. *794*
Barriers to advancement in educational administration as perceived by women administrators. EdD U. of the Pacific, 1982.

PADDOCK,S. *795*
Women's careers in administration. PhD U. of Oregon, 1977.

PAINE,L.T. *796*
A survey of current personnel practices in selected colleges and universities as related to the functions of the office of the dean of women. PhD Cornell U. 1950.

PASS,B.H. *797*
A study of administrative women in education. EdD U. of Virginia, 1976.

PAYNE,N.J. *798*
The status of black women in education administration. PhD Atlanta U. 1975.

PERRIN,E.H. *799*
Perceptions of women college faculty members toward careers in academic administration. PhD U. of Pittsburgh, 1974.

PETERSON,M.T. *800*
Status and trends in the promotion of women to secondary school principalships with special reference to black women. EdD Wayne State U. 1973.

PFIFFNER,V.T. *801*
Factors associated with women in major administrative positions in California community colleges. PhD U. of Southern California, 1972.

PHAGAN,P.A. *802*
Profile of the female president in higher education. EdD Loyola U., Chicago, 1982.

PICKER,A.M. *803*
Women educational administrators: career patterns and perceptions. EdD U. of California, Los Angeles, 1973.

PIGGOTT,L.C.J. *804*
The social characteristics and career patterns of women administrators in North Carolina colleges and universities. EdD U. of North Carolina at Greensboro, 1979.

PLATE,R.A.W. *805*
Perceived leadership behavior of women superintendents in Ohio in 1980. EdD U. of Toledo, 1980.

POLL,C. *806*
No room at the top: a study of the social processes

that contribute to the under-representation of women on the administration levels of the New York City school system. PhD U. of New York, 1978.

POPE,B.W. *807*
Factors influencing career aspirations and development of women holding administrative positions in public schools. EdD Temple U. 1979.

PORTER,D.J.H. *808*
An investigation into the perceived role conflict experienced by women administrators at the secondary school level in comparison to the perceived role conflict experienced by men administrators at the secondary level. PhD U. of Nebraska-Lincoln, 1978.

PRUITT,G.S. *809*
Women in leadership of alternative schools. EdD U. of Massachusetts, 1976.

RANSOM,G.B. *810*
Major factors influencing the status of black women in top level administrative positions in higher education 1969–1979. EdD Atlanta U. 1981.

RETTKE,J.H. *811*
A study of women's centers in selected institutions of higher education: the relationship of institutional and non-institutional funding sources to the center's organizational structure, operational budget, and programatic thrust. PhD Michigan State U. 1979.

RICHARDSON,J.A.M. *812*
Women superintendents of public schools in the United States: factors contributing to obtaining the position. EdD Drake U. 1979.

RIDEOUT,A.H. *813*
The upward mobility of women in higher education: a profile of women home economics administrators. EdD U. of Massachusetts, 1974.

ROBERTS,V.B. *814*
Administrative employment of black women in California public school districts, 1974, 1976 and 1978. EdD U. of Southern California, 1982.

ROBINSON,W.C. *815*
Secondary school women principals and assistant principals in Ohio: characteristics and aspirations. PhD U. of Toledo, 1978.

RODES,M.A. *816*
Women administrators of public secondary schools in three west coast states: their strengths and skills and other factors that have impact on promotion as perceived by four critical groups. EdD Seattle U. 1980.

ROLLINS,M.S. *817*
Critical aspects of the office of the director of women's intercollegiate athletics. EdD U. of Missouri-Columbia, 1982.

ROWE,M.F. *818*
The position of administrative assistant as held by women. EdD Indiana U. 1973.

ROWEN,I.B. *819*
Analysis of some elements of career patterns of 50 women administrators in higher education. EdD Rutgers U. 1981.

RUDD,F.G. *820*
Women educators in the State of Washington: status, qualifications and aspirations for educational leadership. EdD Brigham Young U. 1980.

SAMPLE,D.E. *821*
Some factors affecting the flow of women administrators in public school education. PhD U. of Michigan, 1976.

SANA'I,N. *822*
Self-perceived selected characteristics of female secondary school principals in Tennessee. PhD George Peabody Coll. for Teachers, 1981.

SANDORFF,P.I. *823*
Women administrators in public elementary education: factors for successful entry. PhD Claremont Grad. Sch. 1980.

SCALLY,Y.H. *824*
A comparison of the personality profiles and other background characteristics of selected female school district superintendents with those selected females aspiring to superintendencies. PhD Ohio U. 1982.

SCARLETTS,E.T. *825*
A historical study of women in public school administration from 1900–1977. EdD U. of North Carolina at Greensboro, 1979.

SCHLACK,M.J. *826*
A comparison of personal characteristics and leadership styles of university upper-management and middle-management women student personnel administrators. EdD Western Michigan U. 1974.

SCHUCH,B.M. *827*
Characteristics of women superintendents. EdD U. of Southern California, 1980.

SCHWARTZ,A.M.F. *828*
A study of the attitudes of school board members and superintendents toward the employment of women as public school administrators in New York State. PhD New York U. 1978.

SCRIVEN,A.L. *829*
A study of women occupying administrative positions in the central office of large school districts. EdD U. of Florida, 1973.

SEBREE,E.A. *830*
Women in student financial aid administration in institutions of higher education in nine southern states. PhD Florida State U. 1980.

SHAKESHAFT,C.S. 831
Dissertation research on women in educational administration: a synthesis of findings and paradigm for future research. PhD Texas A&M U. 1979.

SHUTTLESWORTH,V.M. 832
Women in administration in Texas public schools. EdD Baylor U. 1978.

SIMMONS,J.H. 833
Personality and background characteristics of female principals. EdD George Peabody Coll. for Teachers, 1981.

SIMMONS,P.A. 834
California women administrators in top-level public school positions: 1973–1979. PhD United States International U. 1979.

SLOAN,F.W. 835
A study of the aspirations of women teachers to become school administrators. EdD North Texas State U. 1979.

SMEY,B.A. 836
Social educators' perceptions of women in administrative roles and curriculum. EdD Rutgers U. 1980.

SMITH,A.P. 837
A study of administrators' perceptions of change in three private liberal arts women's junior colleges: Averett, Southern Seminary, Virginia Intermont in Virginia from 1966 to 1976. EdD Coll. of William and Mary in Virginia, 1978.

SMITH,J.A. 838
A study of women who are certified and employed as principals and assistant principals in Pennsylvania. EdD Temple U. 1977.

SPENCER,L.W. 839
Eleven years of change in the role of dean of women in colleges, universities and teachers' colleges. PhD Columbia U. 1952.

STEPHANZ,V.L. 840
Major obstacles to women's progress in educational administration: a comprehensive overview of major influences, developing trends, conclusions to be drawn and recommendations. EdD George Peabody Coll. for Teachers, 1979.

STEPHERSON,E.M. 841
A survey of the career patterns of women school superintendents. PhD Ohio State U. 1980.

STEVENSON,F.B. 842
Women administrators in ten big universities. PhD Michigan State U. 1973.

STILLER,E.S. 843
A profile analysis of women in central office positions in North Carolina public schools. EdD U. of North Carolina at Greensboro, 1979.

STOKES,M.J. 844
Professional development needs and organizational constraints reported by women administrators in the state universities of Florida. PhD Florida State U. 1981.

STRO,M.A. 845
An assessment of in-service needs as perceived by women and their immediate supervisors in educational administration. EdD United States International U. 1981.

SWAN,C. 846
A study of the effects of attitudes on the employment opportunities for women in administrative, managerial and other professional type positions in selected schools of higher education in California. PhD Claremont Grad. Sch. 1982.

TALBOT,J.T. 847
A woman in a key administrative position at a four-year institution of higher education: a microethnographic study. PhD U. of Connecticut, 1982.

TAYLOR,A.A. 848
The current status of black women in American higher education administration. PhD Arizona State U. 1977.

TAYLOR,M.M.M. 849
A psychosociological analysis of the graduate experiences of women graduate students in educational administration. PhD U. of Texas at Austin, 1980.

TAYLOR,S.S. 850
The attitudes of superintendents and board of education members in Connecticut toward the employment and effectiveness of women as public school administrators. PhD U. of Connecticut, 1971.

TESSLER,S.E. 851
Profiles of selected women college presidents reflecting the emerging role of women in higher education. PhD Boston Coll. 1976.

THOMAS,E.J. 852
Career patterns of black women administrators in historically negro senior colleges and universities. EdD Washington State U. 1976.

TIMMONS,J.E. 853
A study of attitudes toward women school administrators and the aspirations of women teachers for administrative positions in the State of Indiana. EdD Indiana U. 1973.

TIPPLE,M.E. 854
Sexual discrimination: attitudes toward the hireability of women for professional administrative positions in public education. PhD U. of Michigan, 1972.

TJOSVOLD,M.M. *855*
An analysis of selected factors in personnel management decisions which superintendents perceive as affecting the employment and promotion of women in public school administration in Minnesota. PhD U. of Minnesota, 1975.

TYLER,H.I. *856*
Personal characteristics and career paths of selected women administrators in higher education. PhD Kent State U. 1979.

TYSON,R.S. *857*
A descriptive study of factors influencing the professional mobility of black female administrators in public education in Louisiana between 1952 and 1978. EdD George Peabody Coll. for Teachers, 1980.

VIOLA,C.J. *858*
A study of Illinois community college board member attitudes toward women in administrative positions. EdD Northern Illinois U. 1982.

WALDO,K.R. *859*
An examination of attitudes toward women as manageresses in public schools. EdD Virginia Polytechnic Inst. and State U. 1982.

WALKER,D.M. *860*
Factors affecting the advancement of women within educational administration: managerial effectiveness, career aspirations, professional socialization, and the culture of the organization. PhD Michigan State U. 192.

WALKER,M.B. *861*
Perceptions and opinions about the employment of female administrators in the community college system of Pennsylvania. EdD U. of Pennsylvania, 1980.

WALSH,P.A. *862*
Career patterns of women administrators in higher education institutions in California. EdD U. of California, Los Angeles, 1975.

WARWICK,E.B. *863*
Attitudes toward women in administrative positions as related to curricular implementation and change. PhD U. of Wisconsin, 1967.

WATERS,K.G. *864*
A profile of black female office personnel in Southwestern Athletic Conference universities. PhD Kansas State U. 1976.

WEBB,D.E. *865*
Job-related factors as satisfiers and as dissatisfiers among women in leadership positions in elementary, secondary, and higher education in Mississippi. EdD Mississippi State U. 1981.

WEIR,V.J.T. *866*
Leadership among administrative women in public education in Nebraska. EdD U. of Nebraska-Lincoln, 1961.

WELLS,M.C. *867*
History and evaluation of the graduate course for women in student personnel administration at Syracuse University. PhD Syracuse U. 1950.

WEST,P.E. *868*
Women administrators in Wisconsin schools: a support-success theory. PhD U. of Wisconsin-Madison, 1978.

WHITE,D.B. *869*
A descriptive study of the status of women administrators in Texas public schools, 1968–1973. EdD U. of Houston, 1975.

WHITNEY,M.E. *870*
The women student personnel administrator: an anthropological approach to the study of one individual in a social system. EdD Columbia U. 1967.

WILLIAMS,R.E. *871*
Career patterns of women in educational fund-raising administration in American colleges and universities. PhD State U. of New York at Buffalo, 1981.

WIRTENBERG,T.J. *872*
Expanding girls' occupational potential: a case study of the implementation of Title IX's anti sex-segregation provisions in seventh grade practical arts. PhD U. of California, Los Angeles, 1979.

WONG,E.B. *873*
The career development of California school district female superintendents. EdD U. of San Francisco, 1979.

WOODS,B.B. *874*
Significant characteristics of professional women employed in public two-year and four-year higher education institutions in Michigan. PhD Michigan State U. 1979.

WOODS-FOUCHE,H. *875*
Selected parameters of potential geographic mobility of black women in higher education administration at traditionally black public colleges and universities. PhD Kansas State U. 1982.

WORDEN,P.E. *876*
Trends in placement of women administrators: Los Angeles unified school district. EdD Brigham Young U. 1979.

WRIGHT,A.B. *877*
Characteristics of institutions of higher education employing women in top-level administration and a profile of the women. PhD Iowa State U. 1980.

YAAP,S.S. *878*
A survey of the attitudes and opinions of a secondary school district certificated staff toward the utilization of female administrators. EdD United States International U. 1980.

YORKIS,K.L. *879*
Marital status, parenting, and pursuit of graduate

degrees: their relationship to and effect on the careers of women administrators in institutions of higher education. EdD American U. 1981.

ZIMDARS,S.R. *880*
Employment patterns of women and ethnic persons in school administrative positions in forty-nine districts in the seven-county Minneapolis-St Paul metropolitan area. PhD U. of Minnesota, 1976.

ZIMMERMAN,E.W. *881*
Characteristics of women public secondary school principals and assistant principals. EdD U. of Pennsylvania, 1979.

ZIMMERMAN,J.N. *882*
The status of women in educational administrative positions within the central offices of public schools. EdD Temple U. 1971.

ZUMBRUN,A.F. *883*
Comparison of attitudes of superintendents and board of education presidents in Indiana concerning the effectiveness of women as public school administrators. EdD Ball State U. 1976.

Teachers and teacher training

See also 28, 35, 99, 100, 106, 113, 118, 126, 128, 129, 162, 165, 215, 247, 270, 287, 325–402.

ALLAN,N.E. *884*
Attitudes of female kindergarten teachers and their perceptions of adjustment problems of kindergarten childen as related to preschool experience. PhD Michigan State U. 1977.

ALLAN,T.K. *885*
The relationship between supervisory ratings and the personality of female student-teachers. PhD U. of Maryland, 1966.

ALLEN,B.H. *886*
Development of children's stereotype of the female school teacher. PhD George Peabody Coll. for Teachers, 1962.

AMSTERDAM,A.R. *887*
A comparison of the effectiveness of three selected groups of married women elementary teachers. PhD New York U. 1967.

ANDRZEJEWSKI,J.R. *888*
The sexually disenfranchised: readings and the resources of educators and counselors. EdD U. of Northern Colorado, 1978.

ASBURY,J.W. *889*
Current profiles of women professors in Virginia, 1977–78. EdD U. of Virginia, 1979.

ATIENZA,M.F.E. *890*
A study of practices in home economics teacher education in selected colleges and universities in the United States with implications for the home economics teacher education program in the Philippine Women's University, Manila. PhD Michigan State U. 1959.

AUERBACH,A.W. *891*
Teachers' perceptions of the school psychologist as correlated with their attitudes toward women. PsyD Rutgers U. 1979.

BAIR,C.M.J. *892*
The cost of living of single self-supporting women teachers in the State of Connecticut and a plan to utilize this factor in state aid for schools. PhD Harvard U. 1950.

BASUALDO,E.A. *893*
The status and role of female vocational faculty in comprehensive high schools. DEd Pennsylvania State U. 1975.

BAYLEY,C.K. *894*
A study to assess the relationship between self-concept and career goals in education of female prospective teachers. EdD U. of Nebraska, 1981.

BEIGHLEY,K.E. *895*
A study of female college graduates certifying for elementary school teaching. PhD Michigan State U. 1963.

BENNETT,D.D. *896*
Selected attributes which influence commitment to teaching of female elementary teachers with different preparational backgrounds. EdD Indiana U. 1967.

BENOIT,S.S. *897*
Job satisfaction among faculty women in higher education in the state universities of Louisiana. PhD Louisiana State U. and A&M Coll. 1976.

BENTLEY,D.B. *898*
Edith Garland Dupré. PhD Louisiana State U. 1971.

BERWALD,H.D. *899*
Attitudes toward women college teachers in institutions of higher education accredited by the North Central Association (2 vols). PhD U. of Minnesota, 1962.

BLACKMORE,D.S. *900*
A comparison of selected personological attributes of women elementary teachers perceived during pre-service preparation and first-year teaching. EdD U. of California, Berkeley, 1963.

BLOCK,L.E. *901*
The history of the Public School Teachers' Association of Baltimore: a story of the internal practices of education. PhD Johns Hopkins U. 1972.

BOYD,M.V. *902*
Teacher training at St Hild's College, Durham, 1858–1910. MEd U. of Durham, 1977.

BROOKS,G.E.H. *903*
A phenomenological study of adult life development patterns of women educators. PhD U. of Connecticut, 1980.

BROWN,C.P. *904*
The effects of teacher education and continued university assistance on attitude of first-year teacher graduates from the Texas Woman's University. PhD Texas Woman's U. 1977.

BROWN,H.R. *905*
A study to determine the relationship between selected characteristics and the duration of continuous service of female public elementary school teachers. EdD American U. 1967.

CALLAHAN-SUMA,M. *906*
The relationship of specific variables in regard to a female educator's attainment of her position. EdD U. of Southern California, 1982.

CAMERON,S.W. *907*
Women faculty in academia: sponsorship, informal networks, and scholarly success. PhD U. of Michigan, 1978.

CAREY,J. *908*
An analysis of certain traits as exhibited by a group of women selected for elementary education at Syracuse University. EdD Syracuse U. 1954.

CARTER,S.B. *909*
Academic women revisited: an empirical study of changing patterns in women's employment as college and university faculty, 1890–1963. PhD Stanford U. 1981.

CASE,R.D. *910*
Married women and young women students at a day college of education, and in their first married year as teachers. MEd U. of Leicester, 1967.

CHAMP,J.M. *911*
A study of the attitudes of women (students, teachers and former teachers) towards teaching as a career. MA U. of London, Inst. of Educ. 1948.

CLARK,L.Y. *912*
A study of the relationship between the vocational home economics teacher-training curricula of a group of women's colleges and the expected responsibilities of beginning teachers. PhD Columbia U. 1934.

CLEVELAND,E.F. *913*
The relationship between feminist beliefs and classroom job assignments in elementary school teachers. PhD Case Western Reserve U. 1978.

COHEN,A. *914*
Attitude displacement from parent to female teacher and academic achievement. PhD Adelphi U. 1961.

COPPOLA,T.M. *915*
Dominant factors influencing acceptance of home economics teaching positions by young women trained for the profession: a study of a national sample of 1949 graduates. PhD Syracuse U. 1952.

DAILY,F.M. *917*
A study of female teachers' verbal behavior and peer group structure among classes of fifth grade children. PhD Kent State U. 1970.

DAVIS,E.K.C. *918*
A comparative study of demographic and personality characteristics of older and younger women students enrolled in a teacher preparation program. PhD U. of Texas at Austin, 1973.

DE CRESPO,P.C. *919*
Puerto Rican women teachers in New York: self-perception and work adjustment as perceived by themselves and by others. EdD Columbia U. 1965.

DIBLE,I.W. *920*
Factors related to success of women who seek elementary teaching credentials when they are between the ages of 30 and 45. PhD U. of California, Los Angeles, 1962.

DUNBAR,D.L. *921*
The effect of varying school placements on racial attitudes of white pre-service female elementary school teachers. EdD Fordham U. 1974.

DURAZZO,E.C. *922*
Welfare women trained as teacher-aides. PhD Pennsylvania State U. 1972.

DYE,C.A.S. *923*
A study of the influence of their spouses when beginning female elementary teachers seek counsel for school problems with recommendations for the elementary education undergraduate program. EdD U. of Mississippi, 1975.

ELLNER,C.L. *924*
Psychophysiological correlates of female teacher behavior and organizational outputs. PhD U. of California, Los Angeles, 1968.

ETHERIDGE,S.Y. *925*
Career profiles of women in university chemistry. PhD Florida State U. 1982.

FERGUSON,W.F. *926*
A comparison based on mean scores of certain pre-college tests and inventories of selected groups of female teachers and non-teacher graduates of the University of Mississippi. EdD U. of Mississippi, 1969.

FERNANDEZ,L.F. *927*
The effect of the federal affirmative action guidelines on the salary and promotion of women faculty at research universities. PhD U. of California, Berkeley, 1982.

FINGER,M.M. *928*
A study of freshman women in a teachers' college. PhD Northwestern U. 1940.

FREEMAN,B.L. *929*
A new political woman? A study of the politicization of faculty women. PhD U. of Wisconsin-Madison, 1975.

FRY,P.S. *930*
Curricular concomitants in the educational backgrounds of selected women leaders in education, fine arts, and literary fields. EdD U. of Southern California, 1968.

FURNELL,M.H. *931*
Relationship of career motivation and teacher effectiveness of female early childhood education teachers. PhD Florida State U. 1977.

GALLUP,R.S. *932*
A cross-sectional development study of the relationship between female elementary teachers' beliefs, academic preparation and experience in teaching. EdD U. of Florida, 1970.

GALVARRO,P.A. *933*
A study of certain emotional problems of women teachers. PhD Northwestern U. 1945.

GARVEY,R.M. *934*
The effects of self-perception upon occupational change: a comparative study of two groups of women teachers. EdD Ball State U. 1972.

GESSNER,J.K. *935*
Sex and attitudes toward women as factors affecting attitudes toward mathematics of elementary school teachers in two districts of New Jersey. EdD Rutgers U. 1977.

GIVENTER,L.L. *936*
A systems approach to the problem of sex discrimination in higher education faculty employment. PhD U. of Pittsburgh, 1977.

GRIFFIN,A. *937*
A portrait of the woman teacher in twentieth-century popular magazines. PhD Columbia U. 1961.

HARMSEN,H. *938*
A study of the comparison between the interpersonal values of sixth grade pupils and their female teachers. EdD U. of Missouri-Columbia, 1978.

HAYES,R.F. *939*
Standards of living of single women public school teachers in New York State. PhD New York U. 1936.

HENDERSON,J.C.G. *940*
Women as college teachers. PhD U. of Michigan, 1967.

HEWITT,S.A. *941*
The status of women faculty in departments of business education of NABTE institutions. EdD Utah State U. 1975.

HILTON,J.M. *942*
The relationships between sex-role stereotypes and career aspirations of elementary and secondary women teachers. EdD U. of Denver, 1977.

HRANITZKY,J.B. *943*
An examination of Soi trigraphs of teachers enrolled in gifted education at Texas Woman's University. PhD Texas Woman's U. 1981.

HULETT,S.A. *944*
Vertical mobility determiners of women educators in Missouri. EdD U. of Missouri-Columbia, 1976.

JENKINS,E.R. *945*
The role of the teacher: a three-year study of the role conceptions of students in a women's specialist college and four mixed colleges of education. MA U. of Wales,. Cardiff, 1972.

JOHNSTON,W.W. *946*
Dogmatism as a means of predicting insecurity, self-concept, meaning, attitude and effectiveness of female elementary teachers. EdD U. of South Dakota, 1967.

KARCH,J.Q. *947*
Characteristics of women teachers of education in institutions of higher learning in the USA. EdD U. of Washington, 1956.

KING,E.C. *948*
Perceptions of female vocational faculty members as seen by themselves and college administrators. PhD Pennsylvania State U. 1974.

KLEINPETER,E.B. *949*
An investigation of black female college faculty in the twenty largest private predominantly black colleges and universities. PhD Kansas State U. 1975.

LACEY,J. *950*
The influence of the department chairman in faculty employment as perceived by blacks and women in colleges of education at selected public universities in Illinois. PhD Southern Illinois U. at Carbondale, 1975.

LARKIN,R.F. *951*
The expectations of black female teachers and white female teachers toward black second- and third-grade pupils and effects of these expectations on black pupils' gains in reading scores in urban schools. EdD Rutgers U. 1978.

LAVICKA,R.M. *952*
A study of personality, environmental and perceptual factors influential in creative contributions of faculty women holding doctorates. PhD Kent State U. 1978.

LEAMING,M.P. *953*
Role perceptions of vocational female faculty in Colorado community colleges. PhD Colorado State U. 1979.

LEBOWITZ,R. *954*
The relationship of the views women elementary teachers have of their work and their attitudes

toward the feminist movement. PhD Columbia U. Teachers Coll. 1979.

LEONARD,Y.E. *955*
An analysis of the status of women as fulltime faculty members in coeducational colleges and universities of California. PhD U. of Southern California, 1963.

LETTS,O.I. *956*
A study of the roles of women teachers in the elementary schools with emphasis on teachers with children under eighteen years of age. PhD Michigan State U. 1975.

LINCOLN,S.A. *957*
A feminist process in teaching: a personal account. AD U. of Michigan, 1975.

LLOYD,L. *958*
Personality characteristics of selected women educators. EdD U. of Northern Colorado, 1976.

LONDON,A.P. *959*
Determinants of self-acceptance of black female school teachers selected from the Syracuse public school system and from Little Rock, Arkansas, public school system. PhD Syracuse U. 1975.

MCCULLOUGH,E.S. *960*
Changes in attitude of women student-teachers during differential elementary school assignments. EdD U. of Southern California, 1972.

MACDONALD,J.K. *961*
Upward job mobility for women in elementary education. PhD U. of Miami, 1975.

MCNAMARA,D.R. *962*
Socialization into an occupational role: some aspects of the case of female students training to be teachers in a college of education. PhD U. of Lancaster, 1973.

MALONEY,F.C. *963*
A study of the relationship between leadership behavior and particular personality characteristics of women elementary principals in public and Roman Catholic schools. EdD St John's U. 1978.

MARGOLIS,E. *964*
Relation of female teachers' self-definition of sex-role type to patterns of approval and disapproval behavior of seventh and eighth grade boys and girls. PhD U. of Georgia, 1980.

MASTERS,R.E. *965*
Perceptions of the academic community concerning selected effective teaching behaviors of women professors in masculinely-stereotyped and femininely-stereotyped teaching disciplines. EdD U. of Southern California, 1977.

MILLS,B.C. *966*
Relationship of career attitudes to stability in teaching among female elementary school teachers. EdD Indiana U. 1967.

MITRANO,B.S. *967*
Feminism and curriculum theory: implications for teacher education. EdD U. of Rochester, 1979.

MOREY,E.A. *968*
Vocational interests and personality characteristics of women teachers. PhD U. of California, Berkeley, 1948.

NASER,A.O. *969*
The educational philosophy of certain prospective American and Arab women teachers. EdD U. of Florida, 1966.

NAYLOR,F.M. *970*
A study of the supplemental incomes of women teachers in the public schools of Allegheny County, Pennsylvania. EdD U. of Pittsburgh, 1956.

NEVELS,J.N. *971*
An assessment of attitudes of faculty women and faculty men toward faculty women in selected departments at Michigan State University. PhD Michigan State U. 1980.

NORRIS,A. *973*
The wastage of married women teachers: a social survey. MSc U. of Salford, 1968.

PACHECO,A. *974*
A study of sex-role attitudes, job-involvement and job-satisfaction of women faculty at the University of Puerto Rico, Rio Piedras. PhD New York U. 1981.

PARTINGTON,G.G. *975*
The status of women in the teaching profession, 1918–1961. MEd* U. of Bristol, 1972.

PETERS,D.W. *976*
The status of the married woman teacher. PhD Columbia U. 1934.

PETERSON,W.A. *977*
Career phases and inter-age relationships: the female high school teacher in Kansas City. PhD U. of Chicago, 1956.

PETIT,R.M. *978*
Attitudinal study of faculty women in higher education in northwest United States. EdD U. of Montana, 1972.

PICKHARDT,C.E. *979*
Perceptions by self and other female black and white teachers from segregated and desegregated schools before and after a six-week training institute. PhD U. of Texas at Austin, 1970.

POLLARD,L.A. *980*
Women on college and university faculties: a historical survey and a study of their present academic status. EdD U. of Georgia, 1965.

QADRY,H.T. *981*
Problems of women teachers in Iraq. EdD Stanford U. 1957.

QUINT,C.I. *982*
The role of American negro women educators in the growth of the common school. EdD Boston U. 1970.

SARVAS,A.F. *983*
An analysis of the relationship between perceptions of vocational female faculty and administrators toward female faculty in four institutional types. EdD Pennsylvania State U. 1976.

SCHIRMER,E.E. *984*
The role of the elementary school teacher as perceived by freshmen women students. EdD Pennsylvania State U. 1965.

SCHNIEDEWIND,N. *985*
A model integrating personal and social change in teacher education: its implementation in a racism and sexism training program. EdD U. of Massachusetts, 1975.

SCOTT,M.H. *986*
An analytic study of certain motives and needs of prospective women teachers. EdD U. of Georgia, 1960.

SOMMERKORN,I. *987*
On the position of women in the university teaching profession in England: an interview study of 100 women university teachers. PhD U. of London, LSE 1967.

STEINER,L.L. *988*
A study of female kindergarten teachers' sex-role attitudes and their effect on kindergarten girls' sex-typed toy preferences. EdD U. of Houston, 1980.

STODT,M.M. *989*
Autonomy and complexity in women teachers in leadership positions. EdD Columbia U. 1972.

STRICKLER,J.W. *990*
An analysis of selected interview variables as predictors of teaching effectiveness among female elementary teacher candidates. EdD Ball State U. 1966.

SULLIVAN,J.C. *992*
A study of the social attitudes and information on public problems of women teachers in secondary schools. PhD Columbia U. 1940.

SULZER,W.E. *993*
An investigation of the relationship between conformity and mental health in women secondary school teachers. PhD New York U. 1964.

TOLBERT,S.R. *994*
Women faculty in American higher education: a study by institutional type. PhD Stanford U. 1975.

TOMEDY,F.J. *995*
The relationship of personality characteristics to measured interests of women teachers of English, social science, mathematics and physical science in certain senior high schools. PhD New York U. 1952.

TRAHAN,G.A. *996*
The relationship of dogmatism in preservice and inservice teachers to their willingness to describe Afro and Mexican-American women when given limited data. EdD U. of Houston, 1976.

URELL,C. *997*
The contentment of women teachers in elementary schools. PhD New York U. 1936.

WAITS,L.A. *998*
A study of the status of married women teachers in the public schools of Ohio: a comparative study of efficiency in teaching. PhD Ohio State U. 1932.

WAKEFIELD,S. *999*
A study of teacher attitudes toward female principals in Alexandria, Virginia. EdD George Washington U. 1972.

WARE,D.L. *1000*
The relationship of testosterone concentration, spatial ability and sex-role identification in women teaching secondary mathematics and primary grades. EdD U. of Houston, 1982.

WATSON,R.T. *1001*
A microstudy of female staff integration in a boys' secondary comprehensive school. MA U. of Sussex, 1973.

WEBB,S. *1002*
The training of women teachers in British India. MA U. of London, King's Coll., 1930.

WEINROTH,E.D. *1003*
Motivation, job satisfaction, and career aspirations of married women teachers at different career stages. PhD American U. 1977.

WEISS,G.D. *1004*
The education of women elementary teachers in relation to their role in society. EdD Pennsylvania State U. 1962.

WENBAN,J.E.A. *1005*
The employment of married women in teaching in primary and secondary schools in England and Wales, 1956–1966. MEd U. of Leeds, 1968.

WHEELER,D.W. *1006*
Some educational needs and aspirations of rural women educators in selected areas of south Mississippi. PhD U. of Southern Mississippi, 1978.

WHITE,K.P. *1007*
Professional career involvement among female elementary school teachers. PhD Indiana U. 1964.

WILLIAMS,C.C. *1008*
Feminine role as perceived by women teacher trainees. PhD Arizona State U. 1972.

WILSON,L.C. *1009*
A profile of female agricultural teachers in the future: farmers of America, eastern region, and

their job satisfaction level. EdD Virginia Polytechnic Inst. and State U. 1980.

WOOD,J.L. 1010
An historical and contemporary chronicle of women faculty and/or administrators at Miami University, 1902 through 1971. PhD U. of Miami, 1975.

YOUNG,E.T. 1011
A study of the opinions of deans and faculty members toward the effectiveness of women department chairmen in higher education. PhD U. of Southern Mississippi, 1974.

Educational psychology

General

ABRAMS,M.D. 1012
Leadership achievement among college women in coeducational organizations. PhD U. of Miami, 1975.

ALDRICH,A. 1013
A comparison of sectarian college women and university women in motor ability, personality adjustment, scholastic aptitude and background. EdD Pennsylvania State U. 1957.

ALKADRI,A.L.B. 1014
Schools as mediators in female role formation: an ethnography of a girls' school in Baghdad. PhD State U. of New York at Buffalo, 1979.

ALLEN,R.J. 1015
An analysis of the relationship between selected prognostic measures and achievement in the freshman program for secretarial majors at the woman's college of the University of North Carolina. EdD Pennsylvania State U. 1961.

AMIRI,S. 1016
Career motivation of Iranian high school females with an emphasis on social class, parents, and peers. PhD U. of Illinois at Urbana-Champaign, 1979.

ANDERSON,A.L. 1017
Female sex-role concepts and implications for American higher education. PhD U. of Southern California, 1975.

ANDERSON,E.R.P. 1018
The effects of motor practice and verbal information on recall of modeled behaviors by second and fifth grade girls. PhD U. of Minnesota, 1977.

ANDERSON,M.R. 1019
A descriptive study of values and interests of four groups of graduate women at the University of Minnesota. PhD U. of Minnesota, 1952.

ANDERSON,P.C. 1020
Sex-role factors and women's plans for graduate study. PhD Georgia State U. Coll. of Educ. 1976.

ARNOLD,V.D. 1021
Attitudes of high school business teachers, business students and parents of female business students toward the social, educational and economic roles of women. EdD U. of Florida, 1974.

ASCI,R. 1022
Personality characteristics of college women who choose investigative or enterprising majors. PhD Boston Coll. 1980.

ASH,B.L.F. 1023
An investigation of the relationship between field-dependent/field-independent cognitive style, sex-role identity, and personality type among young adult female community college office occupations and business administration majors. EdD Boston U. Sch. of Educ. 1982.

ASTANI,S.M. 1024
Women's education: a cross-cultural comparison of American and Iranian attitudes. PhD Iowa State U. 1981.

ATALLAH,S.S. 1025
Perceptions of problems encountered during doctoral study by selected women doctoral students. PhD U. of Illinois at Urbana-Champaign, 1976.

AYLWARD,B.M. 1026
The interests of a group of secondary modern schoolgirls in their leaving year. MA U. of Birmingham, 1956.

BADAN,L.A. 1027
An examination on some potential influences on the choice by girls of a full-time course of further education in office skills. MA* U. of Lancaster, 1971.

BAILEY,L.J. 1028
An investigation of vocational education students. EdD U. of Illinois at Urbana-Champaign, 1968.

BANCKE,L.L. 1029
Background antecedents of aggressiveness and assertiveness found in academically achieving women. PhD U. of Cincinnati, 1972.

BATESKO,M.L.B. 1030
A study of societal and familial variables which influence identity in older undergraduate women students at a women's college in New Jersey. EdD Rutgers U. 1982.

BATZ,E.T. 1031
Home environment and home-university relationships of a group of four-year home-resident women students in the University of Pittsburgh. PhD U. of Pittsburgh, 1941.

BEADLE,L.A. 1032
The college woman as her head resident sees her:

a study of the extent to which residents can see college women as they see themselves. PhD Syracuse U. 1952.

BEAMER,M.P. *1033*
A measurement of change in female freshmen: residence hall roommate compatibility, self-concept, and perception of university environment. PhD U. of Northern Colorado, 1974.

BEASLEY,M.W. *1034*
Autobiographical and attitudinal relationships among female secondary education students. PhD U. of Alabama, 1972.

BEKEV,S.W. *1035*
The performance of upper elementary school girls differentiated by two levels of giftedness and by placement in each of three grades on Piagetian tasks of concrete and formal operations. PhD U. of Southern California, 1980.

BELOW,H. *1036*
Life styles and roles of women as perceived by high school girls. PhD Indiana U. 1969.

BERGMANN,B.H. *1037*
The verbal concept formation and basic concept formation of groups of achieving female ninth grade readers. EdD Temple U. 1980.

BETHUNE,S.B. *1038*
Factors related to white females' choice of education as a field of study during college: an analysis of the national longitudinal study of the high school class of 1972. PhD U. of North Carolina at Chapel Hill, 1981.

BIKLEN,S.K. *1039*
Lessons of consequence: women's perceptions of their elementary school experiences – a retrospective study. EdD U. of Massachusetts, 1973.

BIOLETTI,P.A. *1040*
The influence of a girls' secondary school on the socialisation of its fourth year pupils. MEd U. of Newcastle upon Tyne, 1976.

BLAND,M.G.M. *1041*
A study of selected psychological and social factors for sorority and residence hall women at Oklahoma State University. EdD Oklahoma State U. 1972.

BLUMEN,J.L. *1042*
Selected dimensions of self-concept and educational aspirations of married women college graduates. PhD Harvard U. 1970.

BONE,M.M. *1043*
A personal guide for women students in elementary education. EdD New York U. 1949.

BRIDWELL,S.D. *1044*
Race and women's roles in higher education. EdD Indiana U. 1979.

BRODY,D.S. *1045*
Development factors affecting sociality traits and work habits among college women. PhD U. of Minnesota, 1952.

BROMBACH,C.T. *1046*
The effects of systematic group desensitization and marathon group desensitization on mathematics anxiety and confidence in learning mathematics in freshmen college females. EdD U. of New Orleans, 1980.

BROOKS,L.P. *1047*
The sex-role stereotyping of occupational perceptions by sixth-grade students. EdD Wayne State U. 1973.

BROUSSEAU,M.A. *1048*
Comparison of disciplined and non-disciplined women residents, Marquette University, 1967–1968. EdD Marquette U. 1969.

BROWN,B.J. *1049*
The relationship of selected biographical and psychometric characteristics for disadvantaged adolescent females to success in a compensatory education program for office occupations. EdD U. of Oklahoma, 1973.

BRUEMMER,R. *1050*
Academic differences and changes in major between female students enrolled in an orientation class and those not enrolled. EdD Brigham Young U. 1974.

BRUNSON,P.W. *1051*
The relationship between achievement of women in an all-female basic algebra class and the achievement of women in mixed-sex classes. PhD Indiana U. 1980.

BRUNSON,S.C. *1052*
Adolescent mothers' perceived needs to complete their high school education. PhD Ohio State U. 1981.

BRUYN,H. van O. *1053*
The need for vocational guidance: a study of three comparable groups of ex-secondary schoolgirls. MA U. of London, Inst. of Educ. 1948.

BUCHER,S. *1054*
A study of the thematic apperception test applied to a group of girls aged 11 to 13 years. MA U. of London, University Coll. 1953.

BUERK,D.D. *1055*
Changing the conception of mathematical knowledge in intellectually able, math avoidant women. EdD State U. of New York at Buffalo, 1981.

BURKE,J.L. *1056*
School and parental views of girls adopted or born to first versus later ordinal position. PhD Bryn Mawr Coll., 1976.

BURLING,J.W. *1057*
A comparison of the non-traditional academic discipline choices of female graduates of single-sex

and coeducational institutions of higher education. PhD Boston Coll. 1980.

CASE,C.M. 1058
Some sociological and psychological implications of the change to comprehensive schools in girls' secondary education. MEd U. of Leeds, 1967.

CATHIE,S.B. 1059
Black female participation and non-participation in vocational education in Trenton comprehensive high school. EdD Rutgers U. 1980.

CHAMPION,M.I.C. 1060
Needs of Oregon State College freshman women. PhD Oregon State U. 1955.

CHASE,G. 1061
Factors that interfered with the progress of women students at the State University of Iowa. PhD U. of Iowa, 1936.

CHESKA,A.T. 1062
The relationship of authoritarianism in women students to their perception of teachers' instructional behavior. PhD U. of California, Berkeley, 1961.

COLLINGS,J.A. 1063
A psychological study of female science specialists in the sixth form. PhD U. of Bradford, 1978.

COMEAU,L.H. 1064
The effect of teaching counseling skills and concepts to women college student advisors. EdD Boston U. Sch. of Educ. 1977.

CONNOLLY,L.M. 1065
Ego development of adolescent girls in ninth, tenth, and eleventh grades. PhD Fordham U. 1978.

COOK,B.I.W. 1066
Role aspiration as evidenced in senior women. PhD Purdue U. 1967.

COOK,E.A. 1067
Latent vs. aroused motive to avoid success and performance attributions, and expectancies among 5th-8th grade females. PhD Kent State U. 1980.

COOLEY,F.R.R. 1068
Women doctoral students: differential perceptions of their role behavior in the academic environment. PhD U. of Wisconsin, 1969.

COTTON,C.R. 1069
Sex-role concepts in young women: parental influences on sex-role concepts and the effects of sex-role concepts on achievement motivation, educational goals, desire to work, and career salience. PhD Ohio State U. 1980.

CRAMOND,B.L. 1070
Predicting mathematics achievement of gifted adolescent females. PhD U. of Georgia, 1982.

DASGUPTA,H.P. 1071
A survey of interests in groups of girls in secondary schools in relation to the curricula, social climate, and friendship patterns in their schools and classrooms. MA U. of London, Inst. of Educ. 1964.

DAUGHERTY,K.M. 1072
Development and utilization of a conceptual model to describe the relationship of selected research variables to female choice of occupational, vocational or technical programs. PhD U. of Pittsburgh, 1975.

DAVISON,M.B. 1073
Educational outcomes and implications of academically or vocationally focused small groups of undergraduate students in a women's residence hall. EdD Pennsylvania State U. 1964.

DEHAAS,P.A. 1074
Attention styles in teacher-identified hyperactive and normal girls. PhD Indiana U. 1981.

DEROSE,A.L. 1075
Perceptions of female seniors enrolled in cooperative office education in Michigan high schools. PhD Michigan State U. 1976.

DEVORE,A.B.C. 1076
Selected characteristics of successful and unsuccessful female paraprofessional students in a Baccalaureate degree program. EdD Fordham U. 1976.

DODGE,D.H. 1077
The relationship of personal adjustment, social adjustment, and self-concept of elementary school girls to sex-role preference measured by game choice. PhD U. of Alabama, 1979.

DORRIS,J.F. 1079
The effects upon freshman women of residency in an all-class hall. EdD Arizona State U. 1969.

DREYER,P.H. 1080
Sex-role perception, achievement motives and academic achievement among high school women. PhD U. of Chicago, 1973.

DUVAL,C.A. 1081
Differential teachers grading behavior toward female students of mathematics. EdD U. of Rochester, 1978.

DYE,F.H. 1082
Office work perceptions held by tenth grade female students enrolled in urban high schools serving disadvantaged youth. PhD Ohio State U. 1968.

EDGAR,R.M. 1083
Contingency contracting with high school females to reduce absenteeism: results and follow up. PhD U. of Tennessee, 1979.

EPPERT,A. 1084
A model program for college women and men at

Indiana State University, designed to increase awareness of stereotyped sex roles and to explore attitudes towards women. PhD Florida State U. 1975.

ESSMAN,C.S. *1085*
Pre-parental education: the impact of a short-term skills training course on female adolescents. PhD Pennsylvania State U. 1977.

FARMER,G.J. *1086*
The rationale design implementation and evaluation of a special program model for academically and/or economically disadvantaged students at a college for women. PhD U. of Pittsburgh, 1978.

FAUNCE,P.S. *1087*
Personality characteristics and vocational interests related to the college persistence of academically gifted women. PhD U. of Minnesota, 1966.

FEINSTEIN,T.R. *1088*
The measure of attendance at college by women as a variable relating to the stability of an existing marital relationship. EdD Boston U. Sch. of Educ. 1979.

FINKELSTEIN,E. *1089*
A study of female role definitions in a Yeshivah high school. [Jewish day school] PhD New York U. 1980.

FISH,V.K. *1090*
The relative contribution of perceived parental, science teacher, and best friend evaluation of science ability on the self-concept of science ability held by eighth grade females. PhD Western Michigan U. 1978.

FLORENCE,R.B. *1091*
Occupational sex stereotyping and curriculum choice by eighth grade girls. EdD Yeshiva U. 1979.

FOUDA,S.Z. *1092*
Effectiveness of two instructional designs based on Gagne's learning hierarchy and Ausubel's subsumption theory and two models of presentation in teaching the concept of 'mutualism in nature' to tenth grade girls in Egyptian high schools. EdD Temple U. 1980.

FORSYTHE,M.J. *1093*
An investigation of the effects of deferring sorority membership for freshman women. PhD Case Western Reserve U. 1963.

FOSTER,B.R. *1094*
An analysis of growth patterns among freshmen women students within various campus living arrangements. PhD U. of Alabama, 1973.

FOX,L.H. *1095*
Facilitating the development of mathematical talent in young women. PhD Johns Hopkins U. 1974.

FRANKLIN,J.F. *1096*
Social acceptance and individual factors in relation to adjustment after training at a residential school for girls. PhD U. of Michigan, 1949.

GALLAGHER,V.G. *1097*
A comparative study of the female image in selected elementary school science textbooks. EdD U. of the Pacific, 1981.

GALLUCCI,T.M. *1098*
A study of the effects of a deliberate curriculum intervention on the change in cognitive factors influencing women's achievement orientation. PhD U. of Minnesota, 1982.

GARNER,G.F. *1099*
Patterns of communication in a training school for adolescent girls. PhD U. of Oklahoma, 1969.

GASKELL,J.S. *1100*
The influence of the feminine role on the aspirations of high school girls. EdD Harvard U. 1973.

GENTRY,L. *1101*
Some intellectual attributes and educational interests of university women in various majors. PhD Ohio State U. 1959.

GILYARD,G.L. *1102*
Coping behavior, self-concept, and academic achievement of black high school females. EdD U. of Miami, 1975.

GLASS,G.T. *1103*
A study of mathematics anxiety among female college students. PhD Georgia State U. Coll. of Educ. 1982.

GLOGOWSKI,D.R. *1104*
An investigation of the relationships among age category, curriculum selected and measures of work values held and certainty of career choice for women students in a community college. EdD Indiana U. 1976.

GLUTZBACH,C.J. *1105*
Intellectual and nonintellectual characteristics associated with persistence of women in an elementary and nursery school teacher-education program. PhD U. of Minnesota, 1957.

GODKIN,R.L. *1106*
Anticipated job satisfaction: attitudinal bias among university female business majors. PhD North Texas State U. 1981.

GOODE,E.B. *1107*
Feminine affinity for program selection in the North Carolina community college system, 1979. EdD North Carolina State U. at Raleigh, 1980.

GORDON,G.L. *1108*
Divergent and spontaneous art strategy comparison profiles for art and non-art female college students. EdD Pennsylvania State U. 1966.

GORDON,J.M. *1109*
The organizational structures, funding patterns and future trends for women's programs at two-

year colleges in Florida. EdD Florida State U. 1979.

GORDON,L.D. *1110*
Women with missions: varieties of college life in the Progressive era. PhD U. of Chicago, 1980.

GRAHAM,M.F. *1112*
Factors bearing upon pursuit of higher education by junior and community college women graduates in Massachusetts: a needs assessment. EdD Boston U. Sch. of Educ. 1977.

GRANOWSKI,H.B. *1113*
The sociology of morality and education: a theoretical critique applied to an empirical study of moral judgement-making in a girls' comprehensive school. PhD U. of London, Inst. of Educ. 1981.

GRAY,P.E. *1114*
The relationship between fear of success and ego development in high school females. PhD Boston Coll. 1982.

GREENE,F.D. *1115*
A follow-up study of non-graduating women from the College of Education of the Ohio State University. PhD Ohio State U. 1943.

GUPTA,R.R. *1116*
The relationship between the psychological characteristics of a group of adolescent girls, their attitude towards science, and the measures of their scholastic attainment in science. MTech Brunel U. 1973.

HAGER,P.C. *1117*
The prediction of the educational choice of college women. PhD U. of Kentucky, 1974.

HAKKIO,J.S. *1118*
A comparison of 1958 and 1970 women student leaders at Northwestern University: their characteristics, self-concepts, and attitudes toward the university. PhD Northwestern U. 1972.

HALE,N.C. *1119*
Sex-typing: college women's perceptions of self and of doctoral women. PhD Syracuse U. 1981.

HAMPTON,B.C. *1120*
The motivation of female college business students to manage: a study of selected college business students in certain functional specialities. EdD U. of North Carolina at Greensboro, 1977.

HARDEMAN,C.H. *1121*
The effects on middle school students of 'mathco': a program to enhance young women's understanding of interdisciplinary uses of math in career choices. PhD U. of Oklahoma, 1979.

HART,S.J.. *1122*
The effects of student-centered orientation groups on situation-specific anxiety, self-actualization, and adjustment to school in high school freshman females. PhD Temple U. 1979.

HASTINGS,D.B. *1123*
The relationship of selected variables to the post-graduate educational plans to Memphis State University senior women. EdD Memphis State U. 1971.

HAUSMAN,A.L. *1124*
The influence of two cognitive styles on female pre-service teachers' perceptions of teacher-pupil interaction. PhD Fordham U. 1979.

HAWKINS,V.J. *1125*
A comparison of two methods of instruction: a saturated learning environment and traditional learning environment: its effects on achievement and retention among female adolescents in first-year algebra. PhD U. of Connecticut, 1984.

HEIDKE,J.D. *1126*
A study of cognitive-intellectual and psychosocial development of women at Kenyon College and the Ohio State University. PhD Ohio State U. 1982.

HIGGINS,D.K. *1127*
An assessment model for technology programs designed for women. EdD Columbia U. Teachers Coll. 1980.

HILDITCH,L. *1128*
A sociometric study of the integration of new entrants to a girls' secondary school. MEd U. of Manchester, 1966.

HILL,A.G. *1129*
Perceptions of women doctoral graduates in education at the University of Alabama relative to admission and selected academic and professional experience. EdD U. of Alabama, 1970.

HOLAHAN,C.A.K. *1130*
Relationship between stress in female doctoral students and needs for affiliation and support across academic departments varying in female representation. PhD U. of Texas at Austin, 1976.

HOLMAN,M.F. *1131*
Motivational causes of women dropouts in the extended degree program. PhD U. of Wisconsin-Madison, 1981.

HUMMELL,J.F. *1132*
A study of selected personality characteristics and science-related attitudes of ninth grade female students in urban parochial high schools. EdD Temple U. 1981.

HUMOTO,K.M. *1133*
Career counseling programs and procedures application and implication for women students at private liberal arts universities in Japan. EdD Boston Coll. 1980.

HUNT,B.E. *1134*
Characteristics, perceptions and experiences of married women students at Lansing Community College, 1965. EdD Michigan State U. 1966.

HUSTON,B.M. *1135*
A normative survey of the personal and academic characteristics of the freshman women students enrolled in Mary Hardin Baylor College, 1966–1967. EdD Baylor U. 1967.

IANNOTTI,M.M. *1136*
The relationship between certain noncognitive factors and the academic achievement of junior college women. PhD Fordham U. 1970.

ISTIPHAN,I. *1137*
Role expectations of American undergraduate college women in a western coeducational institution. PhD U. of Southern California, 1962.

JACKSON,C.L. *1138*
The effect of assertiveness training on the personality characteristics of high school girls. PhD Fordham U. 1979.

JAYASINGHE,H.S. *1139*
An exploratory study of methods of education guidance experimentally introduced into a government girls' secondary school in Ceylon. MA U. of London, Inst. of Educ. 1964.

JIMINEZ,C. *1140*
A proposed student personnel program for the Philippine Women's College. PhD Columbia U. 1982.

JONES,M.A. *1141*
The influence of the women's college fraternity on character development. PhD Yale U. 1935.

JORDAN,A. *1142*
Characteristics of University of Southern Mississippi adult undergraduate women and their perceived needs in selected student service areas. EdD U. of Mississippi, 1980.

JORDAN,A.W. *1143*
Relationship between selected collegiate experiences and beginning jobs for women. PhD Ohio State U. 1956.

JORDAN,M.L. *1144*
A study of perceived parental influence toward daughter choice of college academic major. EdD Oklahoma State U. 1978.

JOSSELSON,R.L. *1145*
Identity formation in college women. PhD U. of Michigan, 1972.

JULIAN,N.B. *1146*
An analysis of treatment of women in selected junior and senior high school United States history text-books. EdD New Mexico State U. 1979.

KALIA,N.N. *1147*
Sexism in Indian education: a comparative content analysis of sex-role models in the school textbooks of India. PhD Syracuse U. 1978.

KALISH,B.J. *1148*
Adult presence and reinforcement with girls in grades K, three and six. PhD Hofstra U. 1976.

KAYPAGHIAN,F.P. *1149*
A study of elementary school-girl dropouts and non-dropouts in Addis Ababa, Ethiopia. PhD Harvard U. 1960.

KELLEY.E.A. *1150*
Peer group friendships in one class of high school girls: change and stability. PhD Michigan State U. 1966.

KESLER,S.W. *1151*
Values of women college students in the Arab Middle East. PhD Cornell U. 1965.

KESSEL,E.J.M. *1152*
Values of women home economics students: a comparative study. EdD Washington State U. 1982.

KHALIDI,M.Z.I. *1153*
The use of technology-based adult basic education in developing the social roles of Arab-Muslim women: towards a policy prescription. PhD Indiana U. 1977.

KING,B.D. *1154*
Learning and orality: the relationship between oral receptivity and serial learning, verbal recall, and grade-point average in college women. EdD Boston U. 1970.

KING,C.R. *1155*
Attitudes of college women toward student organizations at the University of Oklahoma. EdD U. of Oklahoma, 1957.

KNAAK,N.K. *1156*
A study of the characteristics of academically successful and unsuccessful freshmen women who entered Northwestern University in the fall of 1954. PhD Northwestern U. 1956.

KNIGHT,E.L. *1157*
A study of the image of Mississippi State College for Women held by selected high school seniors in Mississippi and selected college seniors enrolled by Mississippi State College for Women. PhD U. of Alabama, 1973.

KNOTT,T.G. *1158*
Motivational factors in selected women candidates for the Master of Religious Education degree. PhD Boston U. 1964.

KUBISZYN,T.W. *1159*
The effects of knowledge of item difficulty, IQ and test anxiety on classroom text performance in undergraduate females. PhD U. of Texas at Austin, 1979.

LACAMPAGNE,C.B. *1160*
An evaluation of the Women and Mathematics (WAM) Program and associated sex-related differences in the teaching, learning and counselling of mathematics. EdD Columbia U. Teachers Coll. 1979.

LAURADUNN,G.D. *1161*
Development and evaluation of curriculum materials to teach secondary students about the changing roles of women through the use of poetry. EdD U. of Massachusetts, 1980.

LECKIE,J.T. *1162*
Self-image of competence, peer relations and anomie in a group of tenth grade girls. PhD New York U. 1957.

LEE,L.G. *1163*
Factors related to professional achievement of women: a study of California State university and college women. EdD U. of Southern California, 1975.

LEVINE,H.B. *1164*
Examination anxiety in women: a psychoanalytic approach. PhD New York U. 1981.

LEWIS,J.M. *1165*
The predictive validity of selected affective and cognitive variables on choice of major in a selected sample of college women. PhD U. of Connecticut, 1981.

LIDDICOAT,J.P. *1166*
Differences between under-achievers and over-achievers at a small liberal arts women's college. EdD Lehigh U. 1972.

LITTERBERG,R.A. *1167*
Role conflict in women pre-medical students. PhD Harvard U. 1976.

LONG,A.D. *1168*
The effect of co-education on the educational aspirations of girls. MEd U. of Leeds, 1981.

LONG,C.K. *1169*
Achievement motives, extrinsic personal motives, and the choice of credit/no credit courses by female college students. PhD U. of Pittsburgh, 1975.

LOVELACE,V.L.O. *1170*
The impact of sequential re-enactment on the observational learning of fifth grade girls viewing a prosocial television program. PhD U. of Michigan, 1980.

LOWNES,M.L.G. *1171*
A study of the existence of selected characteristics that may be necessary for entrepreneurial success among black female college students majoring in business. PhD George Peabody Coll. for Teachers, 1981.

LYNAM,M.L. *1172*
Informal groups among adolescent girls in the classroom situation. MA U. of Manchester, 1978.

LYNCH,L.R. *1173*
A comparison of the health and college adjustment problems of Jersey City State College freshman resident and non-resident women students. PhD New York U. 1972.

MCCLAREN,A.T. *1174*
Status change and consciousness: a case study of women in residential adult education in London. PhD U. of London, LSE 1979.

MCCLELLAN-GRUBBS,A.R. *1175*
The effects of sex bias and sex stereotyping in the urban school curriculum on the career aspirations of females and the implications for change. EdD U. of Southern California, 1980.

MCGEE,M. *1176*
Women college and university presidents: their personal and professional characteristics, career development patterns, and opinions about their roles. EdD U. of Florida, 1979.

MCKISSICK,E.C. *1177*
The relationship among the factors of academic ability, self-actualization and achievement of seniors in a four-year liberal arts college for women. EdD U. of Missouri-Columbia, 1975.

MACUS STRANGE,C.A. *1178*
The application of a paradigm for a rationale for curricular use of female adolescent novels. PhD U. of Pittsburgh, 1979.

MANICUR,A.R. *1179*
Problem areas and acceptability of student behavior as indicated by residence hall and sorority women at Indiana University. EdD Indiana U. 1960.

MARSALIS,L.W. *1180*
A study of the impact of attitudes on academic performance of students at the Mississippi State College for Women. EdD U. of Southern Mississippi, 1970.

MARSALIS,S.J. *1181*
Comprehensive nomenclature analysis: its effects on achievement in chemistry at the Mississippi State College for Women. EdD U. of Southern Mississippi, 1971.

MARTIN,B.H. *1182*
An investigation of the effect of the structured overview on achievement scores of a psychology unit test for eleventh and twelfth grade female students. EdD U. of New Orleans, 1977.

MARTIN,G.M. *1183*
Differences in evaluation of college climate between freshman and senior women at the University of Georgia. EdD U. of Georgia, 1966.

MARTIN,S. *1184*
The effect of perceived parental influence on need achievement of women in traditional and non-traditional academic majors. PhD U. of Oklahoma, 1975.

MASHA,G.S. *1185*
Occupational preferences, cognitive and affective factors in female students in Nigeria: a comparative study. PhD U. of Wales, Swansea, 1979.

MASON,P.C. *1186*
Sexist bias in the choice of role models for the professional psychology student. PhD California Sch. of Prof. Psych. 1978.

MATIS,E.E. *1187*
An analysis of differences in interests, personality needs, and personality structures between college women majoring in speech pathology and college women majoring in other professional areas. PhD U. of Alabama, 1968.

MAYER,E.A. *1188*
Study of the attitudes of a sample of the initial class of first-year women admitted to resident living at the University of Virginia. EdD U. of Virginia, 1971.

MEGGINSON,M.J.H. *1190*
The relationship of the Edwards personal preference schedule variables to the academic achievement of selected University of Mississippi female students within five ability levels. EdD U. of Mississippi, 1971.

METCALF,A.H.R. *1191*
The effects of boarding school on Navajo self-image and maternal behavior. PhD Stanford U. 1975.

MILLER,A.V. *1192*
The optimal allocation of time over the life cycle with an age-dependent utility function: implications for the female investment in education. PhD Northwestern U. 1974.

MILLER,E. *1193*
Factors contributing to the acquisition of information in certain fields: a study of certain factors in the background of 100 women students making extreme scores on a test of science, foreign literature, fine arts, and history and the social studies. PhD Columbia U. 1932.

MILLER,M.C. **1194**
An evaluation of concepts and their related competences for the study of the family in women's liberal arts colleges. PhD U. of Wisconsin, 1968.

MOODY,F.E. *1195*
The differential effects of teacher comments on college females' achievement as measured by test performance. EdD U. of Rochester, 1969.

MOORE,D.F. *1196*
A comparison of selected characteristics of LSU women graduates for the 1930s and 1950s: a study of changing roles and alienation. PhD Louisiana State U. 1976.

MOORE,J.H. *1197*
Fear of success and personal unconcern, sex-role attributes, and coeducation versus single-sex schooling in talented female adolescents. PhD Case Western Reserve U. 1979.

MORRIS,R.P. *1198*
A comparative analysis of selected characteristics of intellectual superior female students who persisted and those who did not persist in an advanced placement program. EdD North Texas State U. 1964.

MOSS,M.E. *1199*
The female undergraduate mathematics major: attitudes, experiences and aspirations. EdD Rutgers U. 1975.

MYERS,C.L. *1200*
Sexual harassment in higher education: a perceptual study of academic women in a state university system. PhD Florida State U. 1980.

NASH,J.M. *1201*
Prediction of academic achievement of women at a private junior college through use of certain intellective and family relationships measures. EdD Boston U. 1970.

NELSON,G.G. *1202*
Math avoidance in girls. PhD U. of Washington, 1979.

NOGVERA,R. *1203*
A proposal for a student personnel program for the Philippine Women's University. EdD Indiana U. 1954.

NUTTER,F.D. *1204*
Girls' perceptions of school subjects. MEd U. of Liverpool, 1979.

O'BRIEN,S.M. *1205*
Congruence of goals at a liberal arts college for women. EdD Indiana U. 1975.

OBST,F.M. *1206*
A study of selected psychometric characteristics of home economics and non-home economics women at the University of California, Los Angeles. PhD U. of California, Los Angeles, 1956.

O'NEILL,P.T.H. *1207*
Self-esteem and behavior of girls with convergent and divergent cognitive abilities in two types of schools. PhD Yale U. 1974.

OSHINSKY,J.C. *1208*
Sexual harassment of women students in higher education. PhD U. of Florida, 1980.

OSMOND,F.B. *1209*
Attitudes of specific groups in selected California communities regarding female participation in high school interscholastic programs. EdD U. of the Pacific, 1977.

PALMQUIST,M.J. *1210*
Some effects of the place of college residence on opportunities in social education for selected senior women at the Ohio State University. PhD Ohio State U. 1950.

PELOWSKI,J.F. *1211*
A study of the impact of the cross-cultural education program, the winter term abroad, on the

alumnae of Lake Erie College for Women from 1953 through 1978. PhD Michigan State U. 1979.

PETERS,C.E. 1212
A comparison of treatment for the reduction of math anxiety among eighth grade girls. PhD Ohio State U. 1982.

PHILLIPS,B.E. 1213
Fear of success and the female doctoral student: a study of the influence of age and marital status on women's experience. PhD California Sch. of Prof. Psych., Berkeley, 1977.

PHILLIPS,C.W. 1214
A national needs analysis of campus-based women's centers: implications for higher education. EdD U. of Massachusetts, 1978.

PONEAS,E.A. 1215
The university sorority: a study of the factors affecting intergenerational agreement on family culture. PhD Ohio State U. 1968.

PRICE,M.A. 1216
A study of motivational and perceptual factors associated with leadership behavior of young women in a private school. PhD Ohio State U. 1949.

RAPHAEL,D. 1217
An investigation into aspects of identity status of high school females. PhD U. of Toronto, 1975.

RAY,G.J. 1218
An investigation of students', faculty's and parents' attitudes towards a modified home economics curriculum from a feminist perspective. EdD U. of Massachusetts, 1980.

REINIGER-SHAPIRO,M.E.H. 1219
Traces of misogyny in women's schooling. EdD U. of Rochester, 1982.

ROBINSON,P.B. 1220
The motivations and expectations of mature women students entering a college of education. MPhil U. of Nottingham, 1975.

ROCKWOOD,C.A. 1221
The personal and family life needs of college women with implications for education. PhD U. of Chicago, 1952.

ROHALY,K.A. 1222
The relationship between movement participation, movement satisfaction, self-actualization, and trait anxiety in selected college freshmen women. PhD Ohio State U. 1971.

ROTHSCHILD,S.J.S. 1223
Factors influencing the mathematics-related attainment of a national sample of Hispanic, black, and white women. PhD Virginia Polytechnic Inst. and State U. 1981.

ROYSTER HORN,J.R. 1225
The academic and extracurricular undergraduate experiences of three black women at the University of Washington, 1935–1941. PhD U. of Washington, 1980.

SAGER,J.C. 1226
Making women visible in social studies textbooks: a curriculum design analysis of sex-role stereotypes. EdD State U. of New York at Buffalo, 1979.

SALIB,T.M.A. 1227
The effect of discovery and expository methods of teaching selected physical science concepts on science achievement and attitude of students in an Egyptian general preparatory school for girls. PhD Pennsylvania State U. 1978.

SANTIAGO-NAZARIO,N.I. 1228
Social psychological correlates of expected school drop-out among mainland Puerto Rican females. PhD U. of Massachusetts, 1981.

SCHMUCKLER,J.M. 1229
Psychosocial development of women college presidents. PhD Wright Inst. 1980.

SCHOLZ,N.T. 1230
Attitudes of women students toward residence hall experiences at the University of Georgia: a comparison of an honor hall and conventional halls. EdD U. of Georgia, 1970.

SCINTO,R.G. 1231
Measuring achievement motivation in high school girls. PhD Hofstra U. 1977.

SCOTT,E.D. 1232
Field of study choices of young female post-secondary students in four-year institutions. PhD Purdue U. 1982.

SCOTT,M.E. 1233
An exploration of the variable of open-mindedness in special and regular education female undergraduates. PhD Michigan State U. 1979.

SEAWARD,M.R. 1234
A comparison of the career maturity, self-concept and academic achievement of female cooperative vocational office training students, intensive business training students, and regular business education students in selected high schools in Mississippi. EdD Mississippi State U. 1976.

SELKOW,P. 1235
Effects of observational learning and symbolic verbalization on vocational aspirations of kindergarten and first-grade girls. PhD Fordham U. 1978.

SEVILLE,R.T. 1236
The application of systems analysis in identifying the patterns of professional abilities acquired by women students during initial courses for training for teaching in primary schools. PhD U. of Birmingham, 1974.

SHIEFF,J. *1237*
The objectives, activities, and outcome of school counselling: a classification using Tyler's possibility theory, based upon one counsellor's work in two girls' secondary schools. MA U. of Keele, 1974.

SHIELDS,L. *1238*
Factors influencing the maturity scores of students in a women's college of education. MEd U. of Manchester, 1970.

SHIN,K.Z. *1239*
A study of the determinants of higher educational aspirations of Korean women. PhD U. of Pittsburgh, 1981.

SITTHIPHONG,B.S. *1240*
A comparative study of work values between selected tenth grade Thai girls in Bangkok and Chiangmai, Thailand. EdD Oregon State U. 1981.

SMART,L.A. *1241*
Gender role identity, feminist ideology, and career and family commitment of twelfth grade girls in New England. PhD U. of Connecticut, 1979.

SMERD,S.J. *1242*
The relationship between inner-city high school girls' perception of academic competence and self-esteem. PhD U. of Pittsburgh, 1977.

SMITH,A.M.M. *1243*
An examination of relationships between femininity, anxiety, and achievement motivation in female university students. MEd U. of Aberdeen, 1975.

SPUNGIN,R.C. *1244*
The relationship of mathematics anxiety and problem solving attitude to the problem solving performance of female prospective early childhood teachers. EdD Boston U. Sch. of Educ. 1980.

SPURLIN,M.D. *1245*
A study of the relationship of sex, ability level, and biology preparation to achievement in freshman biology at Metropolitan State College. PhD U. of Colorado, 1968.

STALEY,K.H. *1246*
Family, educational, and personality influences on female pre-medical attrition: a longitudinal study. PhD U. of Iowa, 1976.

STAMP,M. *1247*
Girls and mathematics: parental influences. MSc U. of Lancaster, 1978.

STANG,G.E. *1248*
The effect of a micro-teaching experience on modifying the attitudes toward teaching science held by prospective women elementary school teachers. PhD U. of Minnesota, 1967.

STEIN,P.J. *1249*
The impact of selectivity: the college experience and the social-historical context on the attitudes of college women. PhD Princeton U. 1969.

STEPHENS,M.M. *1250*
Vocational preferences of secondary-modern school girls in a London suburb. MA U. of London, Inst. of Educ. 1957.

STEPHENSON,J.M. *1251*
The effect of a history of women text on high school students' sex discrimination and self-esteem attitudes. PhD Wright Inst. 1981.

STRONACH,B.W. *1252*
Achievement and affiliation motivation in Japanese college women. PhD Tufts U. 1980.

STROOPS,S.L. *1253*
Personality types and vocational interests of women students majoring in two different areas of teacher education. EdD U. of Alabama, 1971.

SWANN,C.C. *1254*
An educational and occupational study of 1971 Certificate of Merit women. EdD U. of Georgia, 1978.

SYMMS,D.E. *1255*
A survey of housing for women students and implications for educational development through housing experiences. EdD U. of Colorado, 1957.

TAYLOR,G.Y. *1256*
A study of certain characteristics of senior women students preparing to teach in three areas of education. PhD U. of Alabama, 1957.

THEMES,E.P. *1257*
Three methods of reducing math anxiety in women. PhD Kent State U. 1982.

THOMPSON,F.M. *1258*
Provisions for student activity programs in college residence halls for women. PhD U. of Chicago, 1947.

THOMPSON,S. *1259*
A comparative study of women students in home economics, arts and sciences and education with respect to certain social and personality characteristics. PhD Cornell U. 1941.

THRASH,P.A. *1260*
Women student leaders at Northwestern University: their characteristics, self-concepts, and attitudes toward the university. PhD Northwestern U. 1959.

THROWER,L. *1261*
A study of the effect of a doctoral program upon women as perceived by graduates and candidates in secondary education at the University of Alabama. EdD U. of Alabama, 1976.

TROTT,J.D. *1262*
Real and ideal perceptions of the environment of the University of Mississippi as reported by outstanding women leaders. EdD U. of Mississippi, 1972.

TURNER,M.A. 1263
An examination of the relationship between creative thinking and levels of self-acceptance among female college of education students. MA U. of Keele, 1975.

TYRRELL,L.A.A. 1264
Sex-role attitudes of young and returning female community college students. PhD U. of Michigan, 1976.

UNAN,V.S.S. 1265
A comparison of the effects of BSCS and traditional biological science on achievement, critical thinking ability, and attitude toward science, scientists, and scientific careers of female slow learners in an Egyptian preparatory school. PhD Pennsylvania State U. 1978.

URIOSTE,M.M. 1266
Multicultural experiential group counseling versus multicultural didactic instruction on the attitudes of high school females. PhD U. of Colorado at Boulder, 1978.

UTZ,V.R. 1267
The relation of certain personality value and interest factors to a choice of elementary or secondary teaching levels among women at the University of Oregon. EdD U. of Oregon, 1970.

VALDES,M.M. 1268
An exploratory story of reported personal problems of a group of women students in the College of Education, University of the Philippines. PhD State U. of New York at Buffalo, 1954.

VARSHNEY,S. 1269
Survey of attitudes of selected women towards education beyond high school. PhD U. of Utah, 1965.

WAGENSCHEIN,M. 1270
Institutional housing: selective clienteles, and social class of women students. EdD Stanford U. 1963.

WAHEED,Q. 1271
A study of the ideals, aspirations, and social development of girls in certain modern schools in an industrial area of London. MA U. of London, Inst. of Educ. 1962.

WALAWENDER,M.L. 1272
The behavior and role expectations of foreign and American graduate women. PhD Cornell U. 1964.

WALKER,B.W. 1273
An experiment to determine the effects of mathematical achievement and attitudes toward mathematics of prospective female elementary school teachers by the use of supplementary programmed instruction. EdD Memphis State U. 1981.

WALLACE,D.W. 1274
The effects of a systematic training program in responding skills on dental hygiene students at Texas Woman's University. PhD North Texas State U. 1977.

WALTHER,K.E.R. 1275
Effects of naturalistic settings on spontaneous verbal information-seeking behavior of sixth grade girls. PhD U. of Texas at Austin, 1978.

WARD,L.O. 1276
An investigation into the attitudes of pupils in a girls' grammar school to the moral aspects of historical events. MA U. of Wales, Cardiff, 1965.

WARE,N.C. 1277
Paradox, gender and professional life: a case study of women in dental school. PhD U. of Michigan, 1981.

WEISFELD,C.C. 1278
Boys and girls in competition: the context and communication of female inhibition. PhD U. of Chicago, 1980.

WERNER,L.I. 1279
Counselor education students' attitudes toward women. PhD U. of Florida, 1979.

WHITE,B.C. 1280
The perceptions of campus resource personnel held by undergraduate women at three private colleges. PhD Michigan State U. 1970.

WHITE,F.T. 1281
A description of the educational attainment, occupational status, and aspirations of young black women from the class of 1972. PhD U. of Maryland, 1981.

WHITFIELD,E.L. 1282
The effect of a planned curriculum on children's perceptions of the role of women in selected careers. EdD Texas Tech. U. 1978.

WILKINSON,F.J. 1283
Advisement in the program of development for the prototype demonstration school of the women's teacher training college in Ramallah, Jordan. PhD Harvard U. 1962.

WILKINSON,J.S. 1284
An investigation of the note-taking skills of selected female college students. EdD U. of Virginia, 1969.

WILLIAMS,D.B.E. 1285
An investigation into participation patterns of dependent African females in continuing education programs within selected university centers in Michigan. PhD Michigan State U. 1977.

WILLISON,N.A. 1286
A comparison of women in engineering technology and other major fields of study at Oklahoma State University on patterns of interest, scholastic aptitude, and demography. EdD Oklahoma State U. 1978.

WILSON,C.P. 1287
The characteristics of masculinity, femininity,

androgyny, age, and academic ability as factors in the retention of women students in college programs in business administration. PhD U. of Florida, 1981.

WINKLER,M.C. 1288
The life styles of women with earned Indiana University doctorates. EdD Indiana U. 1968.

WIRTZ,P.G. 1289
An analysis of attitude change among freshman women at the University of Nebraska as a result of an experimental sorority pledge education program. EdD U. of Nebraska-Lincoln, 1970.

WOLF,P.J. 1290
Problem solving of field dependent seventh and eighth grade girls under stress. PhD Loyola U., Chicago, 1969.

WOLFF,F.A. 1291
Self-parent similarity of high school girls in relation to teachers' judgements. PhD Columbia U. 1956.

WOOD,P.L. 1292
The relationship of the college characteristics index to achievement and certain other variables for freshmen women in the College of Education at the University of Georgia. EdD U. of Georgia, 1963.

WOODDELL,G.I. 1293
A study of the peer interactions of second grade girls at play using ethnographic methods. EdD U. of Cincinnati, 1982.

WOODS,S.L. 1294
Career patterns and attitudes of women who are college presidents. EdD Rutgers U. 1981.

WORK,G.G. 1295
Correlates of academic achievement for female sophomore elementary education majors. PhD U. of Ohio, 1977.

WORKMAN,K.R. 1296
Needs assessment of married student housing: a comparison of strategies. PhD Southern Illinois U. at Carbondale, 1982.

WORRALL,S.M. 1297
Mature women students: a study of social and educational factors determining their entry to university studies. PhD U. of Leeds, 1977.

WRAY,N.P. 1298
Effects of attention, incentive, and sequential repetition upon intentional and incidental learning in seventh grade girls. PhD U. of Wisconsin, 1966.

WRIGHT,F.III 1299
A multivariate analysis of the occupational interests and related temperament variables among 500 college women. EdD Temple U. 1974.

YATES,S.E.G. 1300
The relationship of self-concept and other variables to the work value orientation of black females enrolled in inner city vocational schools. EdD Virginia Polytechnic Inst. and State U. 1979.

YOUNG,R.A. 1301
Results of values clarification training on the self-concept of black female upper-class residence hall students at Mississippi State University. EdD Mississippi State U. 1977.

YOUSSEF,Z.A.H. 1302
An experimental study comparing effects of Biological Science Curriculum Study (BSCS) and traditional biology instruction in an Egyptian public secondary school for girls. PhD Pennsylvania State U. 1979.

ZIMMERMAN,R.L. 1303
Autobiographical studies of college freshman women for appraisal of personal and social adjustments. PhD U. of Wisconsin, 1949.

ZWEIFACH,M.S. 1304
Effects of a cross-age tutoring therapy program for disadvantaged adolescent girls. PhD Boston U. Grad. Sch. 1974.

Counselling in schools and colleges

ANDERSON,D. 1305
The effects of group counselling on the incidence of fear of success motives, role orientation, and personal orientation of college women. EdD Virginia Polytechnic Inst. and State U. 1977.

ANDERSON,R.L. 1306
An experimental investigation of group counseling with freshmen in a woman's college. PhD New York U. 1956.

ASHLEY,P.A. 1307
The effect of group counseling on the self-concept of high school females. EdD North Carolina State U. at Raleigh, 1974.

BALDWIN,G.W. 1308
The effects of consciousness-raising training for public school counselors on masculinity, femininity, and attitudes about women's role. PhD U. of Missouri-Kansas, 1981.

BAUM,P.B. 1309
Investigation of social conflicts of junior college women for counseling. PhD U. of Wisconsin, 1949.

BELDING,R.E. 1310
Guidance programs in smaller colleges for women. PhD Case Western Reserve U. 1953.

BLAKE,M.B. 1311
Guidance in colleges for women. EdD Harvard U. 1925.

BRAGDON,H.D. *1312*
The problems and process of counseling with special reference to the liberal arts college for woman. EdD Harvard U. 1928.

BUTLER,B.L. *1313*
The effects of three counseling procedures on the performance of low-achieving students in a small liberal arts college for women. PhD Atlanta U. 1972.

CUNINGHAM,M.L. *1314*
Dormitory counseling programs in selected colleges and universities which utilize undergraduate women counselors. EdD Northwestern U. 1958.

DURNALL,E.J.Jr. *1315*
A comparison of student personnel practices in junior colleges for women. PhD Oregon State U. 1953.

GEE,K.H. *1316*
An exploratory approach to an investigation of the role of the secondary guidance counselor in two private girls' schools in New York State. EdD Hofstra U. 1982.

GILLIAM,J.R. *1317*
The status of Texas high school counselors' attitudes toward the roles of women. EdD East Texas State U. 1975.

HANSON,J.C. *1318*
Feminine values and personality factors among women's liberation members, college women seeking personal counseling, and other college women. PhD Kent State U. 1974.

HARRIS,R.J. *1319*
Relationship of counseling factors to minority females' participation in mathematics and science. PhD U. of Wisconsin-Madison, 1980.

HEALEY,M.S. *1320*
College women's perceptions of counselors as a function of counselor sex, style and client problem type. PhD Fordham U. 1979.

HODGES,M.F.B. *1321*
Group counseling: its effect on ninth grade high school Hispanic females. EdD U. of Northern Colorado, 1981.

JACOBSON,R.F. *1322*
The organization and administration of special counseling programs for adult women in colleges and universities. EdD U. of Southern California, 1969.

KIDD,N.V.T. *1323*
The effect of group counseling and mini courses on women in a community college. DEd Pennsylvania State U. 1977.

LYNCH,A.Q. *1324*
The effects of basic encounter and task training group experiences on undergraduate advisors to freshman women. EdD U. of Florida, 1968.

MCBRAIR,M. *1325*
A study of the personnel program of Whittier Hall, a residence hall for graduate women. PhD Columbia U. 1952.

MCMILLAN,A.A. *1326*
Student personnel service for a small church-related woman's liberal arts college. EdD U. of Mississippi, 1967.

MAHONE,D.F. *1327*
An assessment of supportive needs of mature and traditional-aged women students at the Ohio State University. PhD Ohio State U. 1977.

MILLER,R.H. *1328*
The student personnel services for women in continuing education in Montgomery Community College. EdD George Washington U. 1973.

MYSINGER,L.J. *1329*
A study of the perceptions of counselors in the Birmingham (Alabama) public schools regarding the roles of women in the labor force with recommendations for educational administrators. PhD U. of Alabama, 1976.

NELSON,E.A. *1330*
A comparison of counseling and related needs as perceived by mature women students in selected community colleges: 1976 and 1980. PhD U. of Southern California, 1981.

OLSEN,J.E. *1331*
An analysis of short-term training effects upon female high school students' measured assertiveness. PhD Purdue U. 1975.

O'NEILL,M.B. *1332*
The effect of Glasser peer-group counseling upon academic performance, self- satisfaction, personal worth, social interaction, and self-esteem of low-achieving female college freshmen. PhD U. of Akron, 1973.

POPE,D. *1333*
Women and work: a comparison of graduate students in counseling and business on attitudes, factual knowledge, and androgyny. PhD Kent State U. 1982.

PUCKETT,D.E.W. *1334*
Educational counseling groups for black adolescent females from a low-income housing area. PhD U. of Michigan, 1976.

RASSIGA,E. *1335*
'Surviving in the pressure cooker: coping with academic stress and peer competition': developing a support/research group for women at a college counseling centre. EdD Boston U. Sch. of Educ. 1980.

REEVES,M.E. *1336*
Measurement of attitudes of deans of women toward principles of good counseling. EdD Boston U. 1960.

RILEY,B.G. *1337*
Secondary school counseling procedures, materials, and programs for female students as they relate to the guidelines established by Title IX. PhD Florida State U. 1979.

RIORDAN,R.J. *1338*
Feminine sex-role concepts among high school counselors and students. PhD Michigan State U. 1965.

SHANAHAN,J.E.Jr *1339*
Energy commitments of women counselors in schools, colleges, and agencies. EdD Ball State U. 1972.

SHUR,M.S. *1340*
A group counseling program for low self-esteem preadolescent females in the fifth grade. PhD U. of Pittsburgh, 1975.

SLANEY,F.J.M. *1341*
Some correlates of achievement motivation in women in student personnel work. PhD Ohio State U. 1972.

SOLLOWAY,J.G. *1342*
A clinical assessment of a community college affiliated guidance center for women. PhD Michigan State U. 1970.

STEFFEN,J.D. *1343*
The effects of two behavioral models of group counseling on the academic performance of selected college women. PhD U. of Minnesota, 1968.

TINSMAN,J.R. *1344*
Counselors' and students' perceptions of guidance services in a two-year private college for women. EdD U. of Virginia, 1971.

WALKER,S.H. *1345*
The relationship of birth-order to seeking counseling by undergraduate females at the University of Wyoming. PhD U. of Wyoming, 1972.

WALTHALL,N. *1346*
A study of the effectiveness of the resident counselor in the adjustment of a selected group of freshmen women. PhD Northwestern U. 1957.

WHITE,P.E.C. *1347*
A study of the status of women counselors in the Virginia community college system. EdD Coll. of William and Mary in Virginia, 1976.

WRIGHT,J.T. *1348*
A study of student personnel services in junior colleges for women in New England. EdD Boston U. 1967.

Mature and re-entry students

AMSTEY,F.H. *1349*
The relationship between continuing education and identity in adult women. EdD U. of Rochester, 1977.

AVERY,C.E. *1350*
An analysis of selected factors in relation to the program choices of adult undergraduate women in continuing education. PhD U. of Connecticut, 1977.

BAKER,L.D. *1351*
Characteristics, needs, motivations, and perceptions of mature women undergraduate students at three public four-year universities in Florida. PhD Florida State U. 1977.

BAVER,M.D. *1352*
An evaluation of the effects of a short-term educational program on the re-entry of adult women into education and employment. EdD Auburn U. 1982.

BERNE,P.A.E. *1353*
Characteristics of women enrolled in adult continuing education programs. PhD Saint Louis U. 1978.

BIGELOW,E.M. *1354*
Women returning to school: issues of adult development. PhD U. of California, Berkeley, 1981.

BLAUKOPF,P.A. *1355*
Life-change events: their impact on returning women college students. EdD Boston U. Sch. of Educ. 1981.

BOUDREAU,F.A. *1356*
Selves and significant others: a study of women who 'drop back in'. PhD U. of Connecticut, 1980.

BOWE,M.B. *1357*
The role of continuing education in the life of the married woman. PhD U. of Wisconsin, 1970.

BROWN,A.C.B. *1358*
A study of women influential in three Michigan communities: their attitudes towards and perceived ability to influence adult education practices. PhD U. of Michigan, 1963.

BURROUGH,T.R.B. *1359*
A proposed model for a re-entry program for mature women at a technical institute. PhD U. of Mississippi, 1979.

CALL,W.W. *1360*
The psychological needs and personality traits of Mormon women involved in formal continuing education and LDS Relief Society Education. PhD Arizona State U. 1975.

CAUSEY,P.M. *1361*
Differences in motivation between re-entry women students and traditional women students. EdD Mississippi State U. 1982.

CHICKERING,J.N. *1362*
Six years in the lives of six women who re-entered school and work after motherhood: the story of six

women's struggle to be. PhD Union for Experimenting Colleges and Universities, 1974.

CLARKSON,A.B. *1363*
A survey of the supports and problems perceived by returning women students at Portland Community College. PhD U. of Oregon, 1978.

CLAYTON,D.E. *1364*
A motivational typology of re-entry women. PhD Oregon State U. 1982.

COGGINS,J.H. *1365*
A comparison of selected cognitive and affective variables of adult women persisters and nonpersisters at Middlesex Community College. PhD U. of Connecticut, 1979.

COSTICK,R.M. *1366*
An exploratory study of the developmental processes of continuing education programs and services for women in selected Michigan community colleges. PhD Michigan State U. 1975.

DESMOND,N.E. *1367*
Life changes of women re-entering higher education. PhD Claremont Grad. Sch. 1982.

DIBNER,L.A. *1368*
Dumping the demons: a study of women over twenty-five years of age who are students at Dalen Community College: their goals, problems, and reference groups. EdD Columbia U. Teachers Coll. 1976.

DROZD,N.C. *1369*
Evaluative approaches to selected employment-training programs for unskilled, economically disadvantaged women at Davidson County Community College. PhD U. of North Carolina at Greensboro, 1981.

EMERSON,S.A. *1370*
Guilt feelings in returning women students. PhD U. of Michigan, 1977.

EVANS,C.G. *1371*
The returning woman student's degree of satisfaction with her university environment. EdD Oklahoma State U. 1980.

FARRELL,R.J. *1372*
An exploration of the reasons for initial enrolment in college courses by middle-aged women: twelve case studies. EdD State U. of New York at Albany, 1975.

FEDER-ALFORD,E. *1373*
'Doing' the role of the returning woman student: a study of the day-to-day management practices of a group of unique women. PhD U. of Texas at Austin, 1982.

FEENEY,H.M. *1374*
Interest values and social class as related to adult women who are continuing their education. PhD New York U. 1972.

FISHER,S.G. *1375*
The relationship between the roles of farm wives and patterns of educational participation. PhD U. of Minnesota, 1980.

FRALICK,M.A.F. *1376*
Characteristics of community college re-entry women preparing for traditional and non-traditional careers. EdD U. of Southern California, 1982.

GELWICK,B.P. *1377*
The adult woman student and her perceptions and expectations of the university environment. PhD U. of Missouri-Columbia, 1975.

GERSON,J.M. *1378*
Women returning to school: an analysis of role accumulation. PhD Cornell U. 1979.

GRIFFIN,D.R. *1379*
A comparative study of the educational/vocational profiles of mature women at the Pennsylvania State University. PhD Pennsylvania State U. 1977.

GRIFFIS,B.A. *1380*
Adult women students: the relationship of their life characteristics to enrolment in a bachelor's degree program. PhD Michigan State U. 1981.

GROSSBERG,M.F. *1381*
Re-entry women: an analysis of selected variables related to their re-entry decision. PhD U. of Connecticut, 1981.

HAIRSTON,S.H. *1382*
Sources of role conflict for black and white professional women in higher education. PhD U. of Pittsburgh, 1980.

HARGRAVE,L.J. *1383*
A follow-up study of mature women who completed bachelors degrees through the re-engagement program at Colorado Women's College, 1973–1976. PhD U. of Northern Colorado, 1977.

HEDSTROM,S.B. *1384*
An investigation of factors related to educational persistence of returning women students. EdD Northern Illinois U. 1977.

HETHERINGTON,C.G. *1385*
The effect of a skill-oriented group on returning women students. PhD Pennsylvania State U. 1978.

HETRICK,H.H. *1386*
A study of re-entry women at Auburn University and the relationship of selected characteristics to completion of undergraduate degrees. EdD Auburn U. 1980.

ILLFELDER,J.K. *1387*
Career decision, self-esteem and achievement styles of returning women students. PhD Ohio State U. 1980.

JACOBSON,M.D. *1388*
Follow-up study of women seen at the Center for Continuing Education of Women at the University of California, Berkeley. PhD U. of California, Berkeley, 1978.

JUPITER,B.S.A. *1389*
An evaluation of mothers' support groups for returning women students. EdD Boston U. Sch. of Educ. 1979.

KROM-BRAEN, J. *1390*
A comparative study of non-college age women who re-enter higher education in a traditional college, a contract learning college and a credit by examination institution. PhD State U. of New York at Buffalo, 1979.

LANTZ,J.B. *1391*
A comparison of adult women university students with other adult women on selected factors. PhD Michigan State U. 1969.

LAVACK,M.J. *1392*
A phenomenological exploration of older women's experience of higher education. PhD California Sch. of Prof. Psych. 1978.

LEFEVRE,C.J. *1393*
The mature woman as graduate student: a study of changing self-conceptions. PhD U. of Chicago, 1972.

LIND,E.M. *1394*
Re-entry mothers: 'life cycle' effects on returning undergraduate women. PhD U. of Pittsburgh, 1980.

LOESER,S.R. *1395*
The development of automomy in re-entry women. EdD U. of Maine, 1981.

MCCOLL,D.R.D. *1396*
A comparison of academic advancement in reading as a result of individual and group instruction with Job Corps women. EdD U. of Oregon, 1969.

MARPLE,D.J. *1397*
Motivational tendencies of women participants in continuing education. EdD Columbia U. 1969.

MASLIN,A. *1398*
Older undergraduate women at an urban university: a typology of motives, ego development, sex-typedness, and attitudes toward women's role. PhD Temple U. 1978.

MAY,D.A. *1399*
The mature woman student: pathway to growth. PhD Northwestern U. 1977.

MEARS,G.L. *1400*
Educational motivation of three groups of mature women in a metropolitan area. EdD U. of Mississippi, 1972.

MELIE,E.E. *1401*
Returning Nigerian and American college women: a cross-cultural analysis of their motivational orientations. PhD U. of Wisconsin-Madison, 1980.

MONAGHAN,L.K. *1402*
Continuing education programs for women: a spatial analysis of the personality characteristics and needs of mature women participants with implications for program models. EdD Memphis State U. 1974.

MOONEY,W.T. *1403*
Reducing anxiety and enhancing self-confidence in re-entry women. PhD State U. of New York at Albany, 1982.

NOLAN,B.I. *1404*
Characteristics, motivation, and barriers of re-entry women: a comparison of full-time and part-time students in transfer vocational and general education programs. EdD Brigham Young U. 1980.

OSBORN,K.H. *1405*
Characteristics, motivation, and problems of mature married women college students: a status study of selected students at the George Washington University. PhD U. of Chicago, 1963.

PAGE,M.J. *1406*
A descriptive analysis of selected attitudes, interests, and personality characteristics of mature college women. EdD North Texas State U. 1971.

PAUL,L.M.T. *1407*
The women's re-entry program as a recruitment device: a comparison of students in women's re-entry programs with mature women enrolled in traditional courses. EdD Columbia U. Teachers Coll. 1981.

REED,J.A. *1408*
The role of support systems in the educational attainment of mature women. PhD U. of Oklahoma, 1977.

REIMAL,M.W. *1409*
A study of factors affecting attrition among women re-entering formal education. EdD U. of Northern Colorado, 1976.

RENNER,H.L. *1410*
A comparison of the characteristics and institutional perceptions of mature married women persisters and non-persisters at a small urban college. PhD U. of Maryland, 1975.

RICHMOND,L.J. *1411*
A comparison of returning women and regular college age women at a community college. PhD U. of Maryland, 1972.

RUSLINK,D.H. *1412*
Married women's resumption of education in preparation for teaching: an investigation of selected factors that encourage and deter married women's entry or re-entry into two New Jersey colleges. PhD New York U. 1969.

SALKIN,B.A. *1413*
A follow-up study of 84 mature women graduates of Temple University. EdD Temple U. 1979.

SALTOUN,S.R. *1414*
Differences in perceived needs for educational training as a function of variations in self-esteem and role strain among demographically identifiable subpopulations of returning women students in community colleges. EdD U. of Southern California, 1982.

SCOTT,B.J. *1415*
An adult education model for surveying perceived roles and needs of rural women. PhD Kansas State U. 1977.

SILVER,E.S. *1416*
Involvement in college and selected student background characteristics as predictors of academic persistence for older women undergraduates. PhD U. of Maryland, 1977.

SITTS,M.R. *1417*
A study of the personality differences between a group of women who had participated in sewing classes in an adult education program and a group of their friends and neighbors who had not participated in any adult education activities. PhD Michigan State U. 1960.

SMALLWOOD,K.B. *1418*
The problems of mature women students enrolled in a selected community college. PhD North Texas State U. 1977.

SMITH,G.D. *1419*
Black women in continuing education: the effects of socioeconomic status and various psychological variables on specific functions within the innovation-decision process. EdD Temple U. 1977.

SPITZE,H.T. *1420*
The relation between selected women's knowledge and use of consumer credit: a basis for adult education program planning. EdD U. of Tennessee, 1961.

SPLAINE,P.A. *1421*
Analysis of selected characteristics that contribute to the success of returning women students. PhD U. of Maryland, 1979.

STONE,J.M. *1422*
Value characteristics of mature women students related to enrolment in a women's studies reentry program. PhD United States International U. 1975.

WATERS,E.B. *1423*
Exercising new options: adult women compared with men and younger women at a community college. EdD Wayne State U. 1973.

WEISS,K.L. *1424*
Effects of differential media treatments on newly admitted mature women students. PhD U. of Maryland, 1977.

WERLINICH,S. *1425*
Reported reasons for attending: withdrawal and return to college by a sample of females with a four-year college withdrawal – two-year college collegiate history. PhD U. of Pittsburgh, 1973.

WHITLEY,E.J. *1426*
The design, implementation and evaluation of an experiential leadership training program for continuing education women students. PhD U. of Pittsburgh, 1982.

WILKINS,J.G. *1427*
Characteristics of mid-career women enrolled in programs at the University of Pittsburgh through the office of continuing education for women from 1964–1968. PhD U. of Pittsburgh, 1968.

WILLIS,C.D. *1428*
Factors influencing female adult students to continue their education. PhD Iowa State U. 1977.

WILSON,L.C. *1429*
A study of the problems of mature women students enrolled in a selected rural junior college. EdD Auburn U. 1982.

WISCH,P.B. *1430*
A profile of mature returning women at Temple University in September 1974 and the effects of a special seminar on their levels of anxiety and potential for self-actualization during their first semester. EdD Temple U. 1976.

YANNESSA,C.J. *1431*
The perception of instructional and support services' adequacy for re-entry women at a two-year college. EdD U. of Cincinnati, 1981.

YATES,D.D. *1432*
An exploratory study of women who return to complete a high school education. PhD Michigan State U. 1962.

Vocational choice and commitment

See also **5** 323–626; **9** 488.

AHRONS,C.R. *1433*
A semantic differential study of career images of women held by high school counselors and academic women. PhD U. of Wisconsin-Madison, 1973.

ALMQUIST,E.M. *1434*
Occupational choice and career salience among college women. PhD U. of Kansas, 1969.

AMATEA,E.S. *1435*
A study of the effects of a career planning program for college women. PhD Florida State U. 1972.

APPELBAUM,L.R. *1436*
The female occupational selection process: atypicality of occupational choice. PhD U. of Illinois at Urbana-Champaign, 1980.

ARREDONDO,R. *1437*
The effect of vocational counseling on career maturity of female cooperative health education students. EdD Texas Tech. U. 1976.

ASHLEY-FOSTER,A. *1438*
A study of the relationship between career maturity and selected characteristics among urban black American high school females. PhD Kent State U. 1978.

BARBERY,M. *1439*
The development and initial construct-validation of the Women's Attitudes towards Careers Scale. PhD U. of South Florida, 1982.

BARNETT,R.C. *1440*
The vocational planning of college women: a psychosocial study. PhD Harvard U. 1964.

BARRETT,C.D. *1441*
Differences in career-related characteristics of women in selected career roles of higher education. PhD Purdue U. 1977.

BARUCH,R.W. *1442*
The achievement motive in women: a study of the implications for career development. EdD Harvard U. 1966.

BEN-DOR,T.R. *1443*
Career development of teenage girls as a process of integrating the vocational career concept with family plans. PhD U. of Toronto, 1979.

BENN,T.O. *1444*
Career choices of middle-class female adolescents: the influence of mothers, sex-role ideology, and occupational knowledge. EdD U. of Massachusetts, 1979.

BERNHARD,B.B. *1445*
Black adolescent females and the effects of maternal employment status and perceived intrafamilial variables on their career orientation. PhD Florida Inst. of Technology, 1982.

BERT,C.V. *1446*
Educational and occupational aspirations and expectations of adolescent girls in Florida. PhD Florida State U. 1967.

BIELBY,D.D. *1447*
Factors affecting career commitment of female college graduates. PhD U. of Wisconsin-Madison, 1975.

BLACKBURN,S.P.S. *1448*
Relationship of selected variables to occupational and educational aspirations and expectations of female high school seniors. EdD East Texas State U. 1974.

BLANK,S. *1449*
An investigation of personality variables of female junior college students choosing male and female dominated careers. PhD U. of Miami, 1974.

BOAZ,J.A. *1450*
A comparison of the interests of female professional personnel in community recreation to other occupations described by the Strong vocational interest blank for women. PhD U. of Minnesota, 1970.

BOEHMER,F.E. *1451*
Vocational continuity of college women: a study based on data secured from 6,466 women who matriculated in land-grant colleges between 1889 and 1922. PhD U. of Columbia, 1932.

BOLMAN,S.O. *1452*
Influences on the career development and life plans of undergraduates at a woman's college. EdD Columbia U. Teachers Coll. 1977.

BOTT,M.M. *1453*
Feminine identity and the educational vocational plans and preferences of adolescent girls attending parochial schools: a pilot study. PhD Michigan State U. 1962.

BRANDES,Z.J.M. *1454*
The effect of male attitudes on the career orientation, role choice, and aspirations of adolescent females. PhD Fordham U. 1982.

BRONK,C.G. *1455*
A comparison of the personal and professional characteristics of male and female leaders in vocational education. EdD Temple U. 1979.

BROWN,M.D. *1456*
The effects of background and college environment on women's careers. EdD Harvard U. 1980.

BRYAN,W.E. *1457*
A comparison of the career orientation of college women in contrasting majors. EdD Wayne State U. 1968.

BURLIN,F.D. *1458*
An investigation of the relationship of ideal and real occupational aspiration to locus of control and to other social and psychological variables in adolescent females. PhD Syracuse U. 1974.

BURROUGHS,L.V. *1459*
Occupational preferences and expectations as related to locus of control, sex-role contingency orientation, race, and family history among college women. EdD U. of Massachusetts, 1981.

BURSON,L.S. *1460*
Career maturity: a comparison of affective and cognitive programs with college freshmen women. EdD Mississippi State U. 1976.

CAPUANO,L.M. *1461*
The effect of vocational exploration group training on the vocational maturity of college women. PhD Fordham U. 1979.

CARITHERS,P.L. *1462*
The relationship of pupillometric response to career interests of female college students. PhD Indiana State U. 1975.

CARLSON,K.L. *1463*
Factors in vocational choices of liberal arts women. PhD Northwestern U. 1948.

CARLSON,N.L. *1464*
Occupational choice and achievement of women graduate students in psychology as a function of early parent-child interactions and achievement as related to birth order and family size. PhD U. of Kansas, 1970.

CARRINGTON,D.H. *1465*
An analysis of factors affecting the decision of college women seniors of the southeast to enter graduate school. EdD Florida State U. 1961.

CASSIDY,C.L. *1466*
The relationship of some attitudinal variables to career decision-making among college women. PhD U. of California, Berkeley, 1976.

CAWLEY,A.M. *1467*
A study of the vocational interest trends of secondary school and college women. PhD Catholic U. of America, 1951.

CHANDLER,T.M. *1468*
Factors which have influenced careers at Texas Woman's University. PhD Texas Woman's U. 1971.

COLLIER,H.V. *1469*
An investigation of the career choice patterns of female two-year college students from 1969 to 1973. EdD U. of Toledo, 1974.

COMBS,J.M. *1470*
Career development processes of undergraduate and graduate college women. PhD U. of Florida, 1978.

COVITZ,S.B. *1471*
A study to determine the effects of career counseling on subsequent job satisfaction in mature women returning to college. PhD Boston Coll. 1979.

DALY,E.M. *1472*
A theory for the vocational counseling of women. PhD Ohio U. 1970.

DANIEL,S.R.M. *1473*
A program for developing career consciousness among female adolescents. PhD U. of Pittsburgh, 1981.

DAVIS,M.S. *1474*
Sex-role factors in the career development of black female high school students. PhD U. of Cincinnati, 1977.

DAVIS,P.C. *1475*
Self-perceptions on sex-stereotypic attributes and the occupational aspirations and expectations of high school females. EdD U. of Houston, 1979.

DAVIS,R.S. *1476*
Influence of vocational guidance on freshman community college females. EdD U. of Missouri-Columbia, 1981.

DESMOND,A.H. *1477*
The effects of self-actualizing components on vocational aspiration, career orientation, and vocational maturity of adolescent girls. PhD Fordham U. 1979.

DICKERSON,K.G. *1478*
A study of female college students' academic and vocational aspirations and how they perceive that the faculty and administration of their institution see their roles as females. PhD Saint Louis U. 1972.

DICKEY,S. *1479*
Career orientation, future time perspective, and internality in college women. PhD Columbia U. 1975.

DI MATTIA,J.A. *1480*
Factors relating to educational aspirations of Princeton women. PhD U. of Pittsburgh, 1975.

DINUZZO,T.M. *1481*
Effects of a group career counseling model on vocational maturity and personal growth of female undergraduates over age 25. PhD U. of Florida, 1977.

DOHERTY,P.A. *1482*
Psychological sex-typing dimensions of achievement motivation and educational, career, and family plans of single traditional-age female college seniors. PhD U. of Iowa, 1979.

DONAHUE,T.J. *1483*
Discrimination against young women in career selection by high school counselors. PhD U. of Michigan, 1976.

DONOVAN,E.P. *1484*
The influence of the eighth grade science teacher's gender, classroom laboratory emphasis, level of understanding of science and career interest on eighth grade girls' science and engineering career interests. PhD Florida Inst. of Tech. 1982.

DORAN,L.E. *1485*
The effect of assertion training within a career awareness course on the sex-role, self-concepts and career choices of high school women. PhD U. of Illinois at Urbana-Champaign, 1976.

DRESSER,J.R. *1486*
Factors that influence the selection of a traditionally female occupation by women in Oregon community colleges. EdD Oregon State U. 1982.

DUTTON,R.P. *1487*
Commitment by women to educational careers. PhD Harvard U. 1955.

ECONOMOU,N. 1488
Relationships between identity confusion, identity crisis resolution, self-esteem, and career choice attitudes in freshmen college women. EdD Rutgers U. 1974.

EISLER,T.A. 1489
Parental influence on the career choices of women: some cohort differences. PhD Virginia Polytechnic Inst. and State U. 1981.

EKO,M.J. 1490
Factors influencing women's choices of industrial technical education in Arizona community colleges. EdD Arizona State U. 1980.

ELLIOTT,E.D. 1491
Effects of female role models on occupational aspiration levels of college freshman women.. PhD U. of Missouri-Columbia, 1972.

ELSTER,S.R. 1492
An evaluative study of a career information and advisory service for women. EdD George Washington U. 1975.

ESSLINGER,C.W. 1493
Educational and occupational aspirations and expectations and the educational, personal and family characteristics of selected twelfth-grade female students. EdD U. of Illinois at Urbana-Champaign, 1976.

ETHERINGTON,H.M. 1494
A comparative study of Onondaga community college women students making traditional and nontraditional business curricula choices. EdD Syracuse U. 1977.

FALK-DICKLER,F. 1495
Women and career choices: outcomes of a community college adult education program on decision-making. EdD Columbia U. Teachers Coll. 1981.

FEIFS,E.M. 1496
Selected factors related to the stability of occupational aspirations among women college graduates. EdD Duke U. 1981.

FORST,F.H. 1497
Design decisions of women after college. PhD U. of Pittsburgh, 1962.

FOX,B.L. 1498
Evaluation of the effectiveness of teaching: a process of career decision-making on college and post-college females. EdD U. of Tennessee, 1976.

FRIEDMAN,J.S. 1499
Determinants of career orientation among American females. PhD Illinois Inst. of Tech. 1975.

GALLOWAY,H.M. 1500
Female students and their aspirations. MSc U. of Edinburgh, 1975.

GARNER,G.O'D. 1501
The career development of college women through cooperative education. EdD Virginia Polytechnic Inst. and State U. 1980.

GASKELL,J.S. 1502
The influence of the feminine role on the aspirations of high school girls. EdD Harvard U. 1973.

GAZIANO-KANE,J.A. 1503
Sex-role identity, self-concept, and parental variables influencing college women juniors and seniors selecting traditional female and nontraditional female careers. PhD Boston Coll. 1982.

GERKEN,S.H. 1504
Identification and rating of components for a comprehensive career development program for mature female students in the community colleges of Virginia. EdD Virginia Polytechnic Inst. and State U. 1979.

GERRY,N.G. 1505
An analysis of female married college graduate NORC participants' career choices and their impact on curriculum construction. DEd Pennsylvania State U. 1978.

GOLDBERG,J.C. 1506
Just a housewife and mother: the perpectives of women in the process of educational and occupational counseling. EdD Rutgers U. 1982.

GOLDBERG,R.E. 1507
The influence of significant others, work values and background factors as related to the career orientations of freshmen and graduate women. PhD Ohio State U. 1982.

GOLDSTEIN,R.L. 1508
Effects of reinforcement and female career role models on the vocational attitudes of high school girls. EdD Boston Sch. of Educ. 1975.

GRACEY,J.S. 1509
Social, academic, and personal factors in the career aspirations of American female youth. PhD U. of Arizona, 1978.

GREEN,L.S. 1510
The effect of female potentiality training on the internal control perception by women resulting in an expansion of their vocational horizons. EdD U. of South Dakota, 1978.

GREEN,R.F. 1511
Factors influencing career orientation of female college graduates. PhD Columbia U. 1978.

GRENELL,B.H. 1512
Correlates of specialty choice of female medical students. PhD Columbia U. 1979.

GULLEDGE,E.N. 1513
A study of contributory factors to sex stereotyping of females in vocational education in Okaloosa and Walton counties, Florida. PhD Florida State U. 1978.

GUTTMACHER,M.J. *1514*
Individual and familial correlates of career salience among upwardly mobile college women. EdD Harvard U. 1979.

HABER,S.B. *1515*
Career/family orientations in female college seniors. PhD City U. of New York, 1976.

HALL,S.M. *1516*
An investigation of factors involved in girls' choices of science courses in the sixth form and of scientific careers. BLitt U. of Oxford, 1966.

HALL,W.J. *1517*
College women's identifications with their fathers in relation to vocational interest patterns. PhD U. of Texas at Austin, 1963.

HARRANGUE,M.D.S. *1518*
Developmental changes in vocational interests and work values as related to the vocational choices of college women. PhD Catholic U. of America, 1965.

HAWKINS,J.E. *1519*
The relationship of locus of control to academic achievement and occupational choice among college women. PhD North Carolina State U. at Raleigh, 1977.

HAWLEY,M.J. *1520*
The relationship of women's perceptions of men's views of the feminine ideal to career choice. PhD Claremont Grad. Sch. 1968.

HEINSOHN,A.L. *1521*
Work/career expectations of female college seniors having traditional and non-traditional sex-role equality attitudes. PhD Pennsylvania State U. 1974.

HELMS,N.E. *1522*
The effects of role modeling as a technique in counteracting sexual stereotyping in the occupational selection of high school girls. EdD Coll. of William and Mary in Virginia, 1982.

HIGGINBOTHAM,E.S. *1523*
Educated black women: an exploration into life chances and choices. PhD Brandeis U. 1980.

HOBSON,G.L. *1524*
Anxiety in women associated with a non-traditional or traditional career choice. PhD U. of Oklahoma, 1982.

HODGSON,M.L. *1525*
Intimacy and achievement needs in the career development of adult women. PhD State U. of New York, 1978.

HOLLEY,J.L. *1526*
An analysis of personality needs and certain background factors which may influence career choice of women business education majors. PhD U. of Mississippi, 1969.

HOPKINS,P.R. *1527*
A comparison of three variations of the non-sexist vocational card sort on the career choices and career exploration behaviors of high school girls. PhD U. of North Carolina at Chapel Hill, 1979.

IVERS,J.J. *1528*
The effect of counseling intervention and academic experience on the vocational maturity, job satisfaction, and self-actualization of adult female participants in a federal upward mobility system. EdD Temple U. 1978.

JABLONSKY,P.D. *1529*
The effect of variation of race and sex of mediated vocational role models upon black urban female junior high school students. PhD U. of Southern California, 1980.

JARMAN,B.J. *1530*
The effect of parental messages on the career patterns of professional women. PhD California Sch. of Prof. Psych. 1976.

JENNINGS,J.E. *1531*
The relationship between locus of control and career preference to academic achievement and perceptions of the feminine ideal held by men significant in the lives of senior high school girls. PhD St John's U. 1973.

JENSEN,M.A.C. *1532*
Career maturity and vocational self-esteem of traditional and returning college women. EdD Rutgers U. 1982.

JENSEN,N.L. *1533*
Relationship of risk taking and other variables to women's career choices. PhD Illinois Inst. of Technology 1981.

JOHNSON,J.R.C. *1534*
Family interaction patterns and career orientation in late adolescent females. EdD Boston U. Sch. of Educ. 1973.

JOHNSON,R.C. *1535*
An exploration of selected social factors related to high school women's consideration of engineering. EdD Columbia U. Teachers Coll. 1981.

KASL,E.S. *1536*
Relationship of undifferentiated interests and sex-role view of self to vocational development in re-entry women. PhD Columbia U. 1978.

KATSEKAS,B.S. *1537*
The effects of progressive relaxation and guided fantasy on the reduction of career anxiety in undergraduate women exploring nontraditional careers. EdD U. of Maine, 1979.

KENNEDY,J.J. *1538*
Familial and cultural factors influencing the occupational choice of women who are high academic achievers. PhD New York U. 1972.

KENNEY,P.J. *1539*
The influence of maternal identification on the traditional and non-traditional career choices of women. PhD Boston Coll. 1982.

KHOSH,M.S. *1540*
A study of the relationship to career objectives of interests, values, and selected personality factors of mature women enrolled in higher education. PhD Kent State U. 1976.

KIMBROUGH,F.H. *1541*
Effects of a group career/life planning counseling model on the sex role and career self-concept of female undergraduates. PhD Texas A&M U. 1981.

KITTREDGE,R.E. *1542*
Investigation of differences in occupational preferences, stereotyped thinking, and psychological needs among undergraduate women students in selected curricular areas. PhD Michigan State U. 1960.

KLARREICH,S.F. *1543*
Career counseling for college women: a new approach. PhD Case Western Reserve U. 1973.

KOTCHER,E.V. *1544*
Sex-role identity and career goals in adolescent women. PhD Hofstra U. 1975.

KREN,J.A. *1545*
Effects of non-traditional occupational role models on factors related to occupational choice of college women. PhD U. of Missouri-Columbia, 1979.

KRIPKE,C.F. *1546*
The motive to avoid success and its impact on vocational choices of senior college women. EdD Boston Sch. of Educ. 1980.

KUK,L.S. *1547*
Perceptions of work climate and their relationship to the career aspirations of women student affairs administrators. PhD Iowa State U. 1981.

KWAN YAN OI *1548*
A study of girls' attitudes and personality characteristics in relation to their vocational intentions. MPhil U. of London, Inst. of Educ. 1967.

LAWLER,A.C. *1549*
Career exploration with women using the non-sexist vocational card sort and the self-directed research. PhD U. of North Carolina at Chapel Hill, 1977.

LEINER,M. *1550*
Changes in selected personality characteristics and persistence in the career choices of women associated with a four-year college education at one of the colleges of the City University of New York. PhD New York U. 1964.

LEN,E.S.Y. *1551*
Factors influencing the career choice of selected college women in engineering. PhD Arizona State U. 1979.

LENTZ,L.P. *1552*
The career salience of women and college choice. EdD Temple U. 1977.

LEONARD,J.A.J. *1553*
Vocational aspirations of female undergraduate fashion merchandising majors at the Florida State University: an application of Holland's theory of vocational choice. EdD Auburn U. 1982.

LEVINE,A.G. *1554*
Marital and occupational plans of women in professional schools: law, medicine, nursing, teaching. PhD Yaif U. 1968.

LEWIS,L.C. *1555*
Significance levels of vocational inventory items as shown by selected women physical education teachers and professional students. PhD U. of Kentucky, 1958.

LEWIS,R.O. *1556*
Consistent career preferences, personality, and women's perceptions of male views of femininity. PhD Ohio State U. 1974.

LIGHTER,J.R. *1557*
The effects of maternal employment status and perceived intrafamilial variables on the career orientation of adolescent females. PhD Fordham U. 1980.

LINDBLOOM,C.G. *1558*
Factors influencing activity changes following career counseling with mature women. PhD U. of Oregon, 1974.

LONG,V.R. *1559*
Situation and person variables influencing professional career aspirations of black college women. PhD California Sch. of Prof. Psych., Los Angeles, 1982.

LUTZ,S.W. *1560*
The educational and vocational planning of talented college-bound women. EdD Texas Tech U. 1974.

LUXTON,E. *1561*
An evaluation of careers education and vocational guidance provided for able girls. MEd U. of Wales, Swansea, 1979.

LYON,E.R. *1562*
Career interests of married women with college degrees. PhD Northwestern U. 1967.

MCALLISTER,A.B. *1563*
A general model and proposed implementation plan for career education at Mississippi State College for Women. PhD U. of Alabama, 1973.

MCCANN,M.C. *1564*
A guidance based curriculum for a life planning/ career development program for adult women within an integration model. EdD U. of Massachusetts, 1977.

MCCORMICK,K.E. *1565*
The prediction of career commitment in female home economics undergraduates and the perceived stability of life style choice from graduation to age thirty. EdD U. of Illinois at Urbana-Champaign, 1981.

MCCOY,V.R. *1566*
Impact of a career exploration workshop for student wives on selected personality factors, career maturity, career decision-making, and career implementing behaviors. PhD Kansas State U. 1975.

MCDOWELL,J.M. *1567*
Academic productivity profiles, career choice: academic women. PhD U. of California, Los Angeles, 1979.

MCGRATH,E.M. *1568*
Female medical students and specialty interest. PhD George Washington U. 1975.

MCHUGH,W.T. *1569*
A study of the differences in self-concept and occupational role concepts of young women and middle-aged women in occupational training programs. PhD U. of Oregon, 1970.

MCKENNA,M.P. *1570*
Personality, occupational congruence, and vocational satisfaction: their relationship to mid-life career choices of women. PhD Fordham U. 1979.

MCLOUGHLIN,M.E. *1571*
Vocational maturity and the female career process. EdD U. of Tennessee, 1978.

MALIK,H.M. *1572*
A study of racism and sexism in career counseling, job selection and placement by vocational rehabilitation counselors in Alaska, Idaho and Oregon. PhD U. of Oregon, 1973.

MALIK,P.B.P. *1573*
Factors related to women's choices of careers in life sciences and letters: a comparison of a non-traditional with a traditional discipline. EdD Indiana U. 1981.

MARCANTEL,S.C. *1574*
A comparison of gifted and non-gifted adolescent girls for sex-role identity, attitudes toward the feminine role and stated career choices. EdD McNeese State U. 1981.

MARSHALL,S.J. *1575*
An investigation of the relationship of need for achievement and sex-role identity to career orientation among college women. PhD New York U. 1979.

MARTUCCI,M.E. *1576*
Difference in self-perceptions and role-perceptions in career oriented and non-career oriented college women. PhD U. of Notre Dame, 1972.

MASTERSON,A.C. *1577*
Advantaged and disadvantaged rural high school girls' perceptions of office work. PhD U. of Northern Colorado, 1968.

MATTHEWS,E.E. *1578*
The marriage-career conflict in the career development of girls and young women. PhD Harvard U. 1960.

MAYER,W.K. *1579*
Vocational interest patterns of teaching and non-teaching female college graduates. EdD U. of Florida, 1966.

MECKEL,D.A. *1580*
An investigation of career education for women in selected New England public high schools. EdD Harvard U. 1977.

MELDON,R.P. *1581*
A study of the influence of parental attitudes on the vocational aspirations of women, with special reference to girls in a selective secondary school and mature students in a teachers' training college. MA U. of London, Inst. of Educ. 1964.

MELILLO,D. *1582*
Role model and mentor influences on the career development of academic women. PhD United States International U. 1981.

MENSON,E.A. *1583*
Life career planning: a study of a method for increasing vocational maturity of high school girls. PhD Ohio U. 1978.

MEYER,G.W. *1584*
An analysis of selected factors and their relationship to vocational change of women. PhD U. of Connecticut, 1975.

MILANOVICH,N.J.A.D. *1585*
The extent to which female high school seniors' expressed vocational plans match their measured vocational interests. EdD U. of Houston, 1982.

MILLER,C.B. *1586*
The impact of group career counseling on career maturity and on stereotypical occupational choice of high school girls. PhD Purdue U. 1978.

MILLER,G.L. *1587*
A study of selected social processes on women's career motivation related to the declining number of women in the elementary school principalship. EdD Rutgers U. 1976.

MIYAHIRA,S.D. *1588*
College women's career orientations as related to work values and background factors. PhD Ohio State U. 1976.

MOLINA,J.C. *1589*
The influence of experiences as teacher aides on the level and direction of occupational aspirations of selected disadvantaged high school girls. PhD United States International U. 1968.

MOORE,F.B. 1590
The effects of a large group versus a small group vocational exploration group experience on the vocational knowledge, attitudes, and job search behaviors of high school females. PhD U. of Colorado at Boulder, 1976.

MORAN,M.M. 1591
An inquiry into the vocational interests of secondary school girls and a comparison of various methods of investigating these interests. MEd U. of Birmingham, 1963.

MOSBY,G.G. 1592
A study of the consistency of vocational choices of interests of black women graduates of a local liberal arts college, 1970–1974. PhD Atlanta U. 1977.

MOSS,J.D. 1593
Who influences women's career choices? PhD Iowa State U. 1978.

MULHOLLAND,J.D. 1594
A comparison of perceived career and educational influences of Masters of Business Administration (MBA) graduates for the purposes of counseling and recruiting women with implications for marketing and distributive education programs. EdD Temple U. 1982.

MUNDAY,D.A. 1595
The relationship of role models to the career orientation of female college students. PhD U. of Maryland, 1974.

NEWMAN,A.E. 1596
An investigation of the relationship of occupational aspiration to career maturity self-concept and locus of control in adolescent females. PhD Boston Coll. 1977.

NOLTING,E. 1597
A study of female vocational interests, pre-college to post-graduation. PhD U. of Minnesota, 1967.

O'DONNELL,J.A. 1598
A study of majors and career aspirations of a selected sample of undergraduate women in the university setting. EdD Washington State U. 1976.

OGILVIE,V.N. 1599
Evaluation of a group career counseling program for women. PhD U. of California, Los Angeles, 1975.

OKUN,B.F. 1600
A study of the variables affecting the occupational choice of women 12–20 years after college graduation. PhD Northwestern U. 1970.

PALMER,L.J. 1601
A comparative study of career planning and employment awareness of community college women. EdD Northern Illinois U. 1980.

PARKER,A.W. 1602
A comparative study of selected factors in the vocational development of college women. EdD Indiana U. 1961.

PARLATO,M.L. 1603
A comparative study of the educational and occupational aspirations of five selected groups of women in elementary education in the Detroit metropolitan area. EdD Wayne State U. 1966.

PAULSEN,D.L. 1604
The career commitment of twelfth grade girls. PhD Yale U. 1967.

PEARLMAN,V.A. 1605
Influences of mothers' employment on career orientation and career choice of adolescent daughters. PhD U. of Minnesota, 1980.

PEDRO,J.D. 1606
The relative efficacy of career maturity and gender specific role variables as predictors of planning involvement in high school females. PhD U. of Iowa, 1978.

PETERS,A.J. 1608
Correlates of persistence of occupational choice among a selected group of college women. PhD St John's U. 1956.

PETERSEN,L.E. 1609
Career aspirations of freshman women enrolled in community college office occupations curricula. EdD U. of North Dakota, 1976.

PETERSON,K.L. 1610
Factors in vocational choice by college women. PhD Iowa State U. 1980.

POOLE,R.R. 1611
Evaluation of a small group teaching-learning procedure designed to facilitate the occupational preparation of black undergraduate university women. PhD U. of Oregon, 1973.

POPE,S.K. 1612
Effects of female career role models on occupational aspirations, attitude and personalities of high school seniors. PhD U. of Missouri-Columbia, 1971.

PORTER,J.B. 1613
The vocational choice of freshmen college women as influenced by psychological needs and parent-child relationships. PhD U. of Oklahoma, 1967.

RAND,L.M. 1614
Characteristics of career-oriented and home-making-oriented college freshman women. PhD U. of Iowa, 1966.

RASKIN,B.L. 1615
The relative effect of occupational and socio-occupational information on high school girls' expressed opinions of women scientists and science as a career. PhD Johns Hopkins U. 1968.

RATHBURN,C.R. 1616
The effects of a career development workshop on

the career maturity of undecided female college students. PhD U. of Maryland, 1981.

RAUNER,T.M. *1617*
A study of occupational choices of college women. PhD Fordham U. 1959.

RAY,M.D. *1618*
Career counseling with the mature woman. PhD U. of Oregon, 1972.

REEHLING,J.E. *1619*
A longitudinal study of outcomes of the educational experience and resulting employment of a select group of adult women college students. PhD Kansas State U. 1979.

REMLEY,N.E. *1620*
Women medical students: their attitudes toward professional and sex roles. PhD Northwestern U. 1979.

RICHARDSON,M.S. *1621*
Self-concepts and role-concepts in the career orientation of college women. PhD Columbia U. 1972.

RITENOUR,W.M. *1622*
Personality trait rating as a predicator of job success of female graduates of selected high schools. EdD U. of Pittsburgh, 1958.

SAYER,L.A. *1623*
Career awareness of grade nine girls: evaluation of treatment programs. PhD U. of Toronto, 1980.

SCHAEFER,E.C. *1624*
The bearing of psycho-social familial factors on the choice between traditional and pioneer fields of female siblings in post secondary education. PhD Catholic U. of America, 1977.

SCHROCK,L.L. *1625*
The relationship of adolescent females' career choices to locus of control and perceptions of femininity. EdD Virginia Polytechnic Inst. and State U. 1981.

SCHWARTZ,J.L. *1626*
A study of guidance counselor sex biases in the occupational recommendations made for female students of superior intelligence. PhD New York U. 1974.

SEDLACEK,C.G. *1627*
Selected factors affecting certainty and persistence of vocational choice for college women. PhD U. of North Dakota, 1968.

SHAK,G.M. *1628*
An application of Holland's model of vocational development to a sample of employed women. PhD New York U. 1980.

SHELOV,M.L. *1629*
Traditionality of occupational choice among college women: a study of selected demographic and personality factors in relation to occupational choice. PhD New York U. 1978.

SHERRATT,N.M. *1630*
Occupational choice for girls: a sociological study of the constraints on the routes taken by a small group of girls in a college of further education. MPhil Open U. 1982.

SHERRILL,S.J. *1631*
The impact of a consciousness-raising program on career and life choices of graduates from a four-year private women's college. [Meredith College] EdD North Carolina State U. at Raleigh, 1982.

SIMPSON,G. *1632*
The daughters of Charlotte Ray: an investigation into the process of vocational development in black female attorneys. EdD Columbia Teachers Coll. 1979.

SIMPSON,W.A. *1633*
Self-concept and career choice among black women. EdD Oklahoma State U. 1975.

SLAUGHTER,P.S. *1634*
A comparison of self-concept, femininity, and career aspirations of college senior women preparing for typical and atypical occupations. EdD Mississippi State U. 1976.

SMITH,L.D. *1636*
Manifest personality needs as correlates of the vocational maturity of black and white freshmen women in a select university. PhD U. of Alabama, 1979.

SORG,S.E. *1637*
The development of a model to identify needs associated with sex-role stereotype in vocational education in Florida. PhD Florida State U. 1978.

SPEARE,K.H. *1638*
The patterns of role model influence on women's career development. PhD Northwestern U. 1978.

STEINBRUNN,J.B. *1639*
An investigation of psychological androgyny, achievement motivation, and vocational interests in college women. PhD U. of Nebraska, Lincoln, 1980.

SULLIVAN,J.M. *1640*
Women's career aspirations: a national survey of traditional and non-traditional aspirations of college freshmen. PhD Florida State U. 1981.

SULLIVAN,K.A. *1641*
Changes in girls' perceptions of the appropriateness of occupations for females through films which counter sex stereotyping. PhD Fordham U. 1975.

SULLIVAN,P.C. *1642*
The effects of short-term vocational group counseling on career change skills, feminine values, and career commitment of flight attendants. EdD Boston U. 1976.

SULLIVAN,V.J.M. *1643*
Self-reports of graduates of a traditionally female

program: career aspirations, level of position, and employment status of Michigan State University office administration majors. PhD Michigan State U. 1977.

SUMMERVILLE,B.E. *1644*
Career orientation of Washington community college women. PhD Washington State U. 1970.

SVINTH,M.K. *1645*
An exploratory study of the effects of an assertion training program on the assertion level, work motivation, and career information-seeking behavior of undergraduate college women. PhD U. of Oregon, 1976.

SWOPE,M.R. *1646*
High school guidance counselors' perceptions of selected careers for women college graduates. EdD Columbia U. 1963.

SYWAK,M.A. *1647*
Career development of college women, 1957–1971. PhD U. of California, Berkeley, 1981.

TANGRI,S.F.S. *1648*
Role-innovation in occupational choice among college women. PhD U. of Michigan, 1969.

THOMAS,A.H. *1649*
Counselor response to divergent vocational goals of a female client in terms of acceptance appropriateness and need for further counseling. PhD Michigan State U. 1967.

THOMPSON,J.N. *1650*
Stability and change in measured attitudes and vocational interests of women in a teacher education program. EdD U. of Missouri-Columbia, 1967.

THORN,I.M. *1651*
The effects of a career planning workshop on career subidentity growth of women employees. PhD U. of Maryland, 1980.

TOUCHTON,J.G. *1652*
Using Holland's theory to predict vocational behavior of college-educated women: an eight-year longitudinal study. PhD U. of Maryland, 1978.

TULLOS,C.E. *1653*
The interrelationships between sex-role identities, educational and career aspirations, and parental educational levels of women in a science careers workshop. EdD U. of Southern Mississippi, 1980.

TURNBOW,S.P. *1654*
The effectiveness of a guidance-based career exploratory program related to skilled trades occupations for internal-external locus of control in middle school females. PhD Oregon State U. 1982.

TUTTEROW,H.R. *1655*
The socio-demographic factors influencing career aspirations of the North Carolina agricultural extension service professional women in pursuing the county chairman position. EdD North Carolina State U. at Raleigh, 1982.

VERES,H.C. *1656*
Two-year college women: dimensions of career choice and career commitment. PhD Cornell U. 1974.

WALCH,E.S. *1657*
Utah high school sophomore attitudes toward women's roles and non-traditional vocational career choices. EdD Utah State U. 1980.

WALSH,M.A.E. *1658*
A study of participation in a career internship program for women. EdD Columbia U. Teachers Coll. 1980.

WARREN,P.A. *1659*
Vocational interests and the occupational adjustment of college women. PhD U. of California, Berkeley, 1958.

WARTHEN,C.O. *1660*
Factors related to women's participation in community college career selection. EdD Illinois State U. 1978.

WAUGH,J.A. *1661*
A descriptive study of the career choices of women majoring in education and engineering as related to self-concept, value system, and life structure. PhD U. of Pittsburgh, 1976.

WEATHERS,M.B. *1662*
Perceptions of prestige borrowing in relationship to occupational aspiration and career commitment in college senior women. PhD U. of Miami, 1978.

WEIHE,L.S. *1663*
Career decision-making among re-entry women: a study on the influence of modeling on information-seeking behavior and career decision-making. PhD U. of Iowa, 1980.

WEISHAAR,M.E. *1664*
Peer groups for women in nontraditional majors: facilitating career planning. PhD Pennsylvania State U. 1982.

WELLIVER,T.J. *1666*
Risk-taking judgments and other related variables of college women who are highly decided or highly undecided about their career goals. EdD Albany U. 1973.

WERNIG,S.R. *1667*
Personal and work values of women as related to choice of college and career orientation. PhD Boston Coll. 1980.

WHITE,B.J. *1668*
The relationship of self-concept and parental identification to women's vocational interests. PhD U. of California, Berkeley, 1958.

WHITESEL,L.S. *1669*
Career commitments of women art students. PhD U. of California, Berkeley, 1974.

WIGHTWICK,M.I. *1670*
Vocational interest patterns: a developmental study of a group of college women. PhD Columbia U. 1946.

WILKINSON,E.G. *1671*
Construction and validation of instruments for diagnosing counseling needs of women preparing for a career. PhD U. of California, Los Angeles, 1978.

WILLENSKY,M.K. *1672*
The effects of a career workshop on aspects of career exploratory behavior, locus of control, and self-concept of Jewish married women. EdD Boston U. 1979.

WILLIS,G.H. *1673*
The effect of occupational stereotypes and self-perceptions of college women, traditionalists and non-traditionalists, on occupational choice. PhD Georgia State U. Coll. of Educ. 1977.

WILLMARTH,J.G. *1674*
Factors affecting the vocational choice of women of different ages selecting clerical and secretarial occupations. EdD Washington State U. 1969.

WILSON,C.C. *1675*
Effects of a career exploration workshop on the vocational interests of androgynous and traditionally feminine high school girls. PhD U. of New Mexico, 1979.

WISSMANN,S.W. *1677*
Evaluation survey of placement media in the field of office work for women, with special reference to school placement and guidance programs. PhD Harvard U. 1950.

WITKIN,M.H. *1678*
The relationship between personality factors and attitudes toward women's roles and the career aspirations of female college students. PhD New York U. 1973.

WOLFE,L.K. *1679*
Traditionality of choice, sex-role orientation, performance, self-esteem, and career centeredness as moderators of the congruence of occupational choice in college women. PhD Ohio State U. 1982.

WOLFSON,K.T.P. *1680*
Career development of college women. PhD U. of Minnesota, 1972.

WOLKON,K.A. *1681*
Prediction of pioneer vocational choice in college women. PhD Boston Coll. 1970.

WOLPE,A.M. *1682*
Factors affecting the choice of engineering as a profession among women. MSc U. of Bradford, 1972.

WOODWARD,D.M. *1683*
The marriage and career orientations of women undergraduates. PhD U. of Cambridge, 1973.

YU,M. *1684*
An exploratory study of women in traditionally male professions and traditionally female professions and the role of creativity in their career choices. PhD U. of Michigan, 1972.

ZARRY,L.L. *1685*
The effect of videotaped cross-sex-typed career themes on career fantasy choices made by grade one pupils. PhD U. of Oregon, 1978.

ZISSIS,C. *1686*
The relationship of selected variables to the career-marriage plans of university freshman women. PhD U. of Michigan, 1962.

5 Employment

General

For psychological studies on all aspects of employment see below 323 ff.

See also **4** 136, 208; **9** 121, 149, 166,, 172, 181, 189, 210, 231, 279, 443, 486, 487, 519, 692; **12** 293; **19** 207, 214, 237; **21** 23.

AMRANAND,P. *1*
The determinants of individual turnover and unemployment among British women. PhD U. of London, LSE, 1979.

ANDERSON,P.Y. 2
Women and work: a study of female labor utilization in the United States. PhD U. of Chicago, 1977.

BARGHOUT,S.H. 3
Economic development and female participation in the labor force. PhD U. of Minnesota, 1970.

BENNETT,W.W. 4
Institutional barriers to the utilization of women in top management. PhD U. of Florida, 1964.

BIBB,R.C. 5
Sexual inequality of earnings in metropolitan blue-collar labor markets. PhD U. of Illinois at Urbana-Champaign, 1977.

BOOTHBY,D.W. 6
The determinants of earnings and occupation for young women. PhD U. of California, Berkeley, 1978.

BURKE,B.M. 7
Female labor force patterns in postwar Japan: 1955–1970. PhD U. of Pennsylvania, 1979.

CALWAY-FAGEN,N.J. *8*
Women's careers: a multivariate descriptive model. PhD George Peabody Coll. for Teachers, 1978.

CAPKA,D.D. 9
A comparative study of women employed in traditional, nontraditional, and non-sex-typed occupations. PhD California Sch. of Prof. Psych. 1977.

CARLSON,I.S. *10*
A comparison of employed and unemployed lower socioeconomic status women across several critical variables. PhD Purdue U. 1982.

CHESTERMAN,C.J. *11*
Women in part-time employment: an investigation of the growth of part-time employment in Britain since World War II, with particular reference to patterns of employment in Coventry. MA U. of Warwick, 1978.

CHIN,K.K.F. *12*
An examination of some aspects of women at work in clerical and manufacturing industries. MSc UMIST, Manchester, 1970.

COTE,N. *13*
Professional women and retirement. MPhil U. of Oxford, 1981.

DASKO,D.A. *14*
Incomes, income attainment, and income inequality among race-sex groups: a test of the dual industry theory. PhD U. of Toronto, 1982,

DATCHER,L.P. *15*
The effect of higher women's labor force participation rates on the relative earnings of black and white families. PhD Massachusetts Inst. of Technology, 1978.

DAWKINS,L.B. *16*
Women executives in business, industry, and the professions. PhD U. of Texas at Austin, 1962.

DEMAREST,J.L. *17*
Women minding their own businesses: a pilot study of independent business and professional women and their enterprises. PhD U. of Colorado at Boulder, 1977.

DEVANTER,I.V. *18*
The relative earnings of women in the United States. PhD New York U. 1968.

DIPIETRO,A.E. *19*
Competition or monosonistic discrimination: an analysis of the position of women in American labor markets. PhD U. of Pittsburgh, 1974.

DOUGLAS,P.H. *20*
Black working women. EdD Harvard U. 1981.

DRUMMOND,B.K. *21*
A study of problems relating to the employment of women 35 years of age or over in clerical occupations in Louisville, Kentucky. PhD Northwestern U. 1963.

ENGLANDER,F.J. *22*
Economic variables affecting the labor market status of blacks and women. PhD Rutgers U. 1975.

ERB,C.M. 23
Savings and investment decisions in the retirement plans of working women. PhD U. of Wisconsin, 1969.

FADAYOMI,T.O. 24
Black women in the labor force: an investigation of factors affecting the labor force participation of black women in the United States. PhD U. of Pennsylvania, 1977.

FAWDRY,M.K. 25
Formative instructional product evaluation of preretirement education modules for female service personnel. EdD Wayne State U. 1981.

FERNANDES,M.T. de S. 26
Women and the wage labor system: a theoretical approach to the sexual division of labor. PhD Brandeis U. 1982.

FEYISETAN,B.J. 27
The determinants of female labor force participation: the effects of the sectional composition of labor markets. PhD U. of Pennsylvania, 1982.

FITZGERALD,L.F. 28
Non-traditional occupations not for women only. PhD Ohio State U. 1979.

FURUGORI,T. 29
A micro labor supply model of women under the existence of discrimination. PhD State U. of New York at Buffalo, 1974.

GARVEY,N.A. 30
Job investment, actual and expected labor supply, and the earnings of young women. PhD Columbia U. 1980.

GIOVANNINI,M.J. 31
The effects of factory employment on the position of women in a Sicilian village. PhD Syracuse U. 1975.

GRAM,E.C. 32
How to raise women's wages: an evaluation of a women's liberation proposal within the context of a general equilibrium model. PhD U. of Wisconsin-Madison, 1975.

GREENWOOD,L.M. 33
Women, work, and powerlessness: a case study of the displaced homemaker. PhD U. of California, 1980.

HABER,S.E. 34
Trends in the share of females in the labor force. PhD Johns Hopkins U. 1958.

HABRYL,J.M. 35
An analysis of the labor force participation of women with college and graduate degrees in various occupational fields ranging from the traditionally male to the traditionally female professions. PhD Northwestern U. 1971.

HEATON,C.R. 36
Labor force behavior of women in nonmetropolitan labor markets. PhD U. of California, Davis, 1981.

HIBDON,N.L. 37
Employment factors and characteristics of women graduates of rural community colleges. PhD U. of Missouri-Columbia, 1979.

HIESTAND,D.L. 38
Economic growth and the opportunities of minorities: an analysis of changes in the employment of negroes and women. PhD Columbia U. 1963.

HOFFER,S.N. 39
The determinants of women's earnings. PhD U. of Illinois at Urbana-Champaign, 1972.

HOLCOMB,J.C. 40
Women in the labor force in the United States, 1940–1950. PhD U. of South Carolina, 1976.

HOLLEY,L.F. 41
Women in executive and managerial positions in Omaha, Nebraska. EdD U. of Colorado, 1960.

HOLMBERG,J.J. 42
Changing occupational status, 1960–70: the impact of increased female labor force participation. PhD Fordham U. 1977.

HUTCHINSON,E.J. 43
Women's wages: a study of the wages of industrial women, and measures suggested to increase them. PhD Columbia U. 1919.

IGBRUKE,J.U. 44
Labor market experience of young females: a regression analysis of individual differences in locus of control. PhD Southern Illinois U. at Carbondale, 1979.

JACKSON,A.R. 45
The high cost of being female: job segregation and earnings discrimination in contemporary America. PhD Vanderbilt U. 1978.

JEPHCOTT,A.P. 46
Studies of employment of adolescent girls in relation to their development and social background. MA U. of Wales, 1949.

JOHANSEN,E.J. 47
The sexual basis of the division of labor: interstate variation in labor force participation rates by sex in the United States. PhD U. of Texas at Austin, 1970.

JOHNSON,M.J. 48
A survey of women Master of Business Administration graduates in management positions. PhD U. of Pittsburgh, 1974.

JOHNSTON,R. 49
Mature women re-entering employment: the role of the Manpower Services Commission in meeting their needs. MPhil CNAA 1980.

KHAIRY,A.H.F. 51
The employment of women: evolution, pattern,

and composition with special reference to the United Kingdom. BPhil U. of St Andrews, 1973.

KOUTOUROUSHIS,P.C. 52
Participation of females in the Greek labour force: an economic analysis. MA* U. of Lancaster, 1968.

KUHLMANN,H.G. 53
A study of attitudes toward women in business. PhD Ohio State U. 1973.

LAMBIRI,J. 54
Women factory workers in a Greek rural area: a study of social change in Megara. PhD U. of London, LSE, 1962.

LARSON,D.A. 55
The components of non-market time and female labor supply patterns. PhD Washington U. 1979.

LAUTARD,E.H. 56
Occupational segregation by sex, and industrialization in Canada, 1891–1971. PhD U. of British Columbia, 1978.

LA VINA,L.Y. de 57
An assessment of World War II's impact on female employment: a study of the decade 1940–1950. PhD Rice U. 1982.

LEAPER,R.J. 58
Female labor force attachment: an analysis of unemployment rates in the United States and Canada. PhD Duke U. 1976.

LEDBETTER,R.B. 59
Current attitudes held by selected top corporate management regarding the role of women as executives. PhD California Sch. of Prof. Psych. Berkeley, 1970.

LORD,P.A. 60
The effects of variations in organization structure on the career patterns of female managers: a comparative study. MPhil U. of Surrey, 1976.

MCCARTHY,A.A. 61
Relative earnings mobility of women in the United States. PhD American U. 1982.

MARIOTTI,A.M. 62
The incorporation of African women into wage employment in South Africa, 1920–1970. PhD U. of Connecticut, 1980.

MARTINDALE,M.A. 63
Sex and residence in the socioeconomics of work: conceptualizations of labor and labor markets applied to women in non-metropolitan America. PhD U. of Texas at Austin, 1979.

MATSUURA,N.F. 64
Sexual discrimination in the post-World War II Japanese labor market, 1953–1973. DBA U. of Indiana, 1978.

MILLER,B.M. 65
Equal access to equal work: a study of interfirm variation in the occupational inequality of women. PhD U. of Illinois at Chicago Circle, 1980.

MILLER,D.L. 66
Structural determinants of women's work force participation in US cities, 1900 and 1970. PhD Temple U. 1978.

MISHRA,C.S. 67
Sex, race, and occupational inequalities in the United States. PhD U. of Florida, 1978.

MORRIS,M.F. 68
A study of women's occupations. PhD U. of Wisconsin, 1955.

MORRISON,A.H. 69
Women and their careers: a study of 306 women in business and the professions. PhD Bryn Mawr Coll. 1932.

NAGER,N.J.F. 70
Characteristics associated with annual earnings of women. PhD U. of Wisconsin-Madison, 1978.

ODITA,F.C.U. 71
Differences in pay, promotion, job title and other related factors between employed male and female college graduates as indicators of sex discrimination. PhD Ohio State U. 1972.

O'LEARY,J. 72
Women at work. MA National U. of Ireland, 1945.

O'LEARY,V.E. 73
The work acculturation of 72 black women into the labor force: trainee orientation. PhD Wayne State U. 1969.

ONDECK,C.M. 74
A study of female labor force attachment and discouragement. DBA George Washington U. 1978.

OPPENHEIMER,V.K. 75
The female labor force in the United States: factors governing its growth and changing composition. PhD U. of California, Berkeley, 1966.

ORMSBEE,H.G. 76
The young employed girl. PhD Bryn Mawr Coll. 1926.

PINCHES,C.R. 77
The industrial distribution of women's employment: an analysis of labor market segregation. PhD New Sch. for Social Research, 1979.

POULTON-CALLAHAN,C. 79
An analysis of the labor market experience of young women. PhD U. of Illinois at Urbana-Champaign, 1979.

RANKIN,C.H. 80
Essays on the labor market supply behavior of young women. PhD U. of Houston, 1980.

REAGAN,S.P. 81
Labor force participation of urban and rural small city females. PhD Louisiana Tech. U. 1980.

RECKNAGEL,H.J. 82
Women in white collar jobs: the study of an econ-

omic and social movement, 1910–1950. PhD New York U. 1953.

RENCE,C.C. *83*
Work, wages, and job changes: returns to labor market mobility for women. PhD U. of California, Berkeley, 1978.

ROBINSON,J.A. *84*
Women managers: aids and barriers in their career paths, performance, and advancement. PhD U. of California, Berkeley, 1974.

ROSS,R.T. *85*
Female labor supply in New Zealand. PhD Duke U. 1977.

ROTMAN,A. *86*
Professional women in retirement. PhD U. of Pittsburgh, 1981.

ROWLING,M. *87*
The study of women's employment with reference to the social and economic consequences. BCom* U. of Leeds, 1934.

RUBENSTEIN,P.D. *88*
Communications theory and pedagogy for working women in organizational structures. AD U. of Michigan, 1980.

RUSHER,E.M. *89*
A study of women in office management positions with implications for business education. PhD Ohio State U. 1957.

RYTINA,N.F. *90*
Female labor force participation and occupational status, 1965–1970. PhD Duke U. 1976.

SANSONI,M.B. *91*
Women entering traditionally male-dominated professions: an investigation of the process. PhD United States International U. 1982.

SANZGIRL,J.M. *92*
Professional women: an experimental and theoretical analysis. PhD U. of Pittsburgh, 1977.

SAWHILL,I. van D. *93*
The relative earnings of women in the United States. PhD New York U. 1968.

SCHLEY,S.G.G. *94*
An assessment of educational markets among female employees in firms of the Normandale community college service area. PhD U. of Minnesota, 1978.

SCHWARTZ,E.B. *95*
An evaluation of the application and implementation of Title VII as it applies to women in management. DBA Georgia State U. 1969.

SHACKETT,J.R. *96*
Experience and earnings of young women. PhD Harvard U. 1982.

SMITH,G.M. *97*
An empirical investigation of demand and supply in a local job market for women. PhD Rutgers U. 1964.

SOKOLOFF,N.J. *98*
Women in the labor market: a critique of theoretical perspectives in sociology, Marxism, and feminism. PhD City U. of New York, 1979.

SOLOMON,L.K. *99*
Labor force participation of women: a study of Arkansas. PhD U. of Arkansas, 1970.

SPECTOR,W.D. *100*
The adequacy of the private pension system for women: a look at survivor benefits and vesting provisions. PhD Brandeis U. 1981.

STADECKER,A.N. *101*
9 to 5: women office workers interpret a social movement. PhD Massachusetts Inst. of Technology, 1976.

STEVENSON,M.H. *102*
Determinants of low wages for women workers. PhD U. of Michigan, 1974.

SWAIN,J.D.Jr. *103*
Regional comparison of black and white women's economic activities in segmented labor markets: implications for social policy. PhD Syracuse U. 1977.

TANFER,K. *104*
Working women: a study of female labor force and determinants of participation in six large cities of Turkey, 1970. PhD U. of Pennsylvania, 1975.

TARG,D.B.E. *105*
Labor force participation of college-educated American women: the influence of early work commitment and later situational factors. PhD Purdue U. 1976.

TAYLOR,H. *106*
Labor substitution and the male-female earnings gap. PhD Yale U. 1982.

THOMAS,D.L. *107*
An investigation of the process by which women become employed. PhD U. of Iowa, 1963.

THOMPSON,A.R. *108*
Comparative occupational position of white and non-white females in the United States. PhD U. of Texas at Austin, 1973.

THOMPSON,L.A. *109*
Office service employment for women college graduates in metropolitan Oklahoma City. EdD U. of Oklahoma, 1961.

TOMJACK,L.J. *110*
The effects of post-secondary education on initial office employment for selected female employees in selected Midwest states for 1973, 1974 and 1975. EdD U. of Northern Colorado, 1976.

UNTIET,C.J. *111*
Hours of search and the reservation wage: a study

of the job search decisions of low income, non-working women. PhD Stanford U. 1978.

VERITY,T.E.A. *112*
Women in industry. MSc UMIST, Manchester, 1943.

VOGEL,L. *113*
Beyond domestic labor: women's oppression and the reproduction of labor power. PhD Brandeis U. 1981.

WAGNER,M.K. *114*
A study of female participation in the labor force in South Dakota, 1950–1970. PhD South Dakota State U. 1978.

WEAVER,V.L. *115*
Women preparing for skilled work in technology: correlates of success. EdD Boston U. Sch. of Educ. 1981.

WEINER,L.Y. *116*
From the working girl to the working mother: the debate over women, work, and morality in the United States, 1820–1980. PhD Boston U. Grad. Sch. 1981.

WOOD,A.M. *117*
Employment opportunities for women in California. PhD Stanford U. 1953.

WOODLEY,K.K. *118*
Women in management: current historical and future perspectives. PhD Union for Experimenting Coll. and U. 1981.

YASHIRO,N. *119*
Women in the Japanese labor market. PhD U. of Maryland, 1981.

YEHIA,M.A. *120*
Attitudes toward women's work commitment: changes from 1964 to 1975. PhD Wayne State U. 1976.

ZELLNER,H.S. *121*
The determinants of the occupational distribution of women. PhD Columbia U. 1975.

The employment of married women and mothers

See also **4** 973; **6** 816–955; **9** 653, 665; **19** 310, 343; **21** 9, 21, 41, 54

ALTMAN,S.H. *122*
Factors affecting the unemployment of married women: a study of the dynamics of the labor force behavior of secondary family workers. PhD U. of California, 1964.

ANDRESS,R.A. *123*
The role of attitudes in the labor force participation of married women. PhD U. of South Carolina, 1977.

ARAJI,S.K. *124*
Married women and the labor market. PhD Washington State U. 1978.

BEBENSEE,M.A. *125*
Income distribution effects of increased labor force participation by married women. PhD Duke U. 1977.

BECCUE,B.B. *126*
Determinants of the number of hours worked by the gainfully-employed married woman. PhD U. of Illinois at Urbana-Champaign, 1977.

BECK,E.L. *127*
An analysis of selected factors relevant to the employment status in business offices of married women college graduates. EdD Indiana U. 1963.

BECKETT-LAMON,J.O. *128*
Working wives: a racial analysis. PhD Bryn Mawr Coll. 1977.

BRAUNSTEIN,A.W. *129*
Labour supply behavior of female heads of households: extending the classical model to a dynamic framework. PhD Rutgers U. 1978.

BUNTING,F.A. *130*
The effect of employment among wives on the farmers' share of output in the food manufacturing sector. PhD U. of Maryland, 1981.

CAIN,G.G. *131*
Labor force participation of married women. PhD U. of Chicago, 1964.

CAIN,P.S. *132*
Determinants of the short-term labor supply response of young married women. PhD Johns Hopkins U. 1979.

CAUDLE,A.H. *133*
Financial management practices of employed and non-employed wives. PhD Florida State U. 1962.

CLARK,M.A.H. *134*
Female labor force attachment during the childbearing and childrearing years. PhD U. of Michigan, 1980

COGAN,J.F. *135*
Reservation wages, labor force participation rates, and hours of work of married women. PhD U. of California, Los Angeles, 1976.

CONLY,S.R. *136*
Subsidized day care and the employment of lower income mothers: a case study. PhD U. of South Carolina, 1974.

CORBETT,R.J. *137*
Predicting employability of AFDC mothers. DSW Catholic U. of America, 1973.

CORINDO,J. *138*
A labor market model: married women. PhD U. of Minnesota, 1970.

COX,D.C. *139*
The effects of career interruptions on the earnings of women: a longitudinal study. PhD Brown U. 1980.

DARIAN,J.C. *140*
Labor force participation of married women in the United States: an investigation of the role of occupation. PhD U. of Pennsylvania, 1972.

DAVIDOFF,L. *141*
The employment of married women in England, 1850–1950. MA U. of London, LSE, 1956.

DAVIES,R.G. *142*
Aspects of married female employment in Cray Valley industry, Bromley borough. MA U. of Sussex, 1969.

DELANO,P.J. *143*
Case studies of continuities and discontinuities in the employment-education-family patterns of women's lives. PhD Columbia U. 1961.

DEROW,E.O. *144*
Married women's employment and domestic labor. PhD U. of Toronto, 1977.

DEVANEY,B.L. *145*
The labor supply of married women: an analysis of the allocation of time to market and nonmarket activities. PhD U. of Michigan, 1977.

DIKMEN,H.L. *146*
Determinants of wife's satisfaction with her pay. PhD U. of Illinois at Urbana-Champaign, 1981.

DOUTHITT,R.A. *147*
Pension information and the retirement decisions of married women. PhD Cornell U. 1982.

FRAUNDORF,M.N. *148*
The labor force participation of married women at the turn of the century. PhD Cornell U. 1976.

GERNER,J.L. *149*
Economic implications of treating maternity leave as a temporary disability. PhD U. of Wisconsin-Madison, 1974.

GLENN,H.M. *150*
Attitudes of women regarding the gainful employment of married women. PhD Florida State U. 1958.

GORDON,H.A. *151*
Employment of women with preschool-age children. PhD U. of Maryland, 1976.

GREENHALGH,C.A. *152*
Labor supply and earnings in Great Britain with special reference to married women. PhD Princeton U. 1978.

GWARTNEY-GIBBS,P.A. *153*
Married women's work experience: intermittency and sex-typed occupations. PhD U. of Michigan, 1981.

HACKER,H.M. *154*
A functional approach to the gainful employment of married women. PhD Columbia U. 1962.

HANNA,S.D. *155*
Two structural models for family income: housing consumption, home ownership and the labor force participation of married women. PhD Cornell U. 1974.

HETRICK,B.J. *156*
The chaining roles of women: effects of women's employment on women and men in dual-earner couples. PhD U. of Maryland, 1979.

HILL,D.H. *157*
A dynamic analysis of the labor force participation of married women. PhD U. of Michigan, 1977.

HILL,M.A. *158*
Labor force participation of married women in urban Japan. PhD Duke U. 1980.

HIRSH,H.R. *159*
An exploration of the work participation decisions of college-educated married women. PhD U. of Maryland, 1980.

HOLMSTROM,L.L. *160*
Intertwining career patterns of husbands and wives in certain professions. PhD Brandeis U. 1970.

HONGVIVATANA,T. *162*
Employment decisions of married women. PhD Syracuse U. 1976.

HUGHES,G.S. *163*
Mothers in industry: wage earning by mothers in Philadelphia. PhD Bryn Mawr Coll. 1925.

HUNT,S.N. *164*
Women's labor force participation and family financial resources. PhD Texas Women's U. 1982.

HUNTER-HOLMES,J.C. *165*
Factors discriminating among occupational groups of 230 married women with children. PhD U. of Illinois at Urbana-Champaign, 1977.

HUTTON,C.R. *166*
Married women on fulltime shiftwork: some domestic and social consequences. MA U. of London, Bedford Coll. 1962.

INGLEHART,A.P. *167*
Married women and work, 1957–1976. PhD U. of Michigan, 1978.

JOHNSON,E.S. *168*
Middle-class, mid-aged, married mothers – their employment participation. PhD Boston Coll. 1976.

JONES,B.A.P. *169*
The contribution of black women to the incomes

of black families: an analysis of the labor force participation rates of black wives. PhD Georgia State U. Coll. of Business Administration, 1973.

JONES,C.D. *170*
The effect of free day care on women's labor force participation. PhD U. of Illinois at Urbana-Champaign, 1975.

KEIG,N.G. *171*
Labor force behavior: a case study of married women. PhD Ohio State U. 1961.

KIM,S. *172*
Determinants of the labor force participation among mature married women 30–44 years of age. PhD U. of Minnesota, 1971.

KRAFT,A. *173*
The labor supply of nonwhite married women. PhD State U. of New York at Buffalo, 1970.

LAFOLLETTE,C.T. *174*
A study of the problems of 652 gainfully employed married women homemakers. PhD Columbia U. 1935.

LEVINE,V. *175*
Work intensity and human capital accumulation: women with children. PhD Columbia U. 1980.

LICHTER,D.T. *176*
Household migration and the labor market experiences of married women. PhD U. of Wisconsin-Madison, 1981.

MCALISTER,P.R. *178*
Changes in employment status of women between the parental and postparental periods. DEd Pennsylvania State U. 1975.

MCCROSKEY,J. *179*
Working mothers and childcare: the context of childcare satisfaction for working women with pre-school children. DSW U. of California, Los Angeles, 1980.

MCINTYRE,E.L.G. *180*
The provision of day care in Ontario: responsiveness of provincial policy to children at risk because their mothers work. DSW U. of Toronto, 1979.

MEYER,J.A. *181*
Labor supply of women potentially eligible for family assistance. PhD Ohio State U. 1972.

MITCHELL,O.S. *182*
The postwar labor supply of nonmarried and married women. PhD U. of Wisconsin-Madison, 1978.

MOORE,S. *183*
The short-term effects of marital disruption on the labor supply behavior of young women. PhD Ohio State U. 1978.

MOUNTS,W.S.Jr. *184*
An analysis of the full-time/part-time work choice and wages of married women. PhD U. of Georgia, 1977.

NICHOLS,A.C. *185*
Factors in the labor force participation of mothers. PhD U. of California, Berkeley, 1977.

ORR,A.C.M.C. *186*
Three studies of the labor force behavior of married women: the effects of childcare costs, transitory income and past decisions. PhD U. of Pennsylvania, 1978.

POLLACK,S.D. *187*
Distributive justice and the working wife. PhD U. of Southern California, 1978.

POTTS,N.D. *188*
The relationship between married maternal women's employment and psychological stress. EdD U. of Houston, 1979.

QUESTER,A.O. *189*
The labor force behavior of wives: effect of the federal tax structure. PhD Tufts U. 1976.

REXROAT,C.A. *190*
Racial differences in wives' labor force participation. PhD U. of Illinois at Urbana-Champaign, 1980.

ROSEN,H.S. *191*
The impact of United States tax laws on the labor supply of married women. PhD Harvard U. 1974.

ROSENMAN,L.S. *192*
Marital status change and labor force readjustment: an analysis of female heads of families. PhD Washington U. 1976.

ROSETT,R.N. *193*
Working wives. PhD Yale U. 1957.

RUBIN,M.M. *194*
Labor force participation of suburban married women, 1970: selected metropolitan areas. PhD New York U. 1976.

SAMPSON,J.M. *195*
Determinants of the employment status of the wife-mother. PhD U. of Illinois at Urbana-Champaign, 1972.

SHANE,R.L. *196*
Labor supply of wives and young family members in the hired farm work force. PhD North Carolina State U. at Raleigh, 1976.

SKOULAS,N. *197*
Determinants of the participation rate of married women in the Canadian labour force: an econometric analysis. PhD Simon Fraser U. 1973.

SMITH,V.K. *198*
The employment and earnings of AFDC mothers: the first-year effect of the earnings exemption in two Michigan counties. PhD Michigan State U. 1973.

STIRLING,B.R. *199*
The interrelation of changing attitudes and changing conditions with reference to the labor force participation of wives. PhD U. of California, 1963.

TAYLOR,P.A. *200*
Women's labor force participation and marital stability in the United States: a panel study. PhD U. of Texas at Austin, 1976.

VAN VELSOR,E. *201*
Lifetime employment patterns of married women. PhD U. of Florida, 1980.

WILLIAMS,R.G. *202*
AFDC and work effort: the labor supply of low-income female heads of household. PhD Princeton U. 1974.

WILLIAMSON,V.K. *203*
Mothers at work: a study of the problems of opportunity restrictions encountered by working mothers with infant school children. MA(Econ) U. of Manchester, 1978.

WION,D.A. *204*
Increases in the proportion of working wives and the distribution of family earnings. PhD Pennsylvania State U. 1980.

WOLF,W.C. *205*
Occupational attainment of married women: do career contingencies matter? PhD Johns Hopkins U. 1976.

YAEGER,K.E. *206*
Model choice in the demand for childcare by working women: a multinominal logit analysis with quality adjustment. PhD Princeton U. 1978.

Labour law, labour reform, trade unions

See also **4** 99; **9** 179, 216, 218, 377, 561, 644; **11** 3.

ABICHT,M.M. *207*
Women's leadership roles in two selected labor unions in the United States and Belgium: a comparative, descriptive study. EdD U. of Cincinnati, 1976.

BAER,J.A. *208*
Protection, equality and justice: the judicial response to women's labor legislation. PhD U. of Chicago, 1974.

BAKER,E.F. *209*
Protective labor legislation with special reference to women in the State of New York. PhD Columbia U. 1925.

BARRETT,R.W. *210*
Administrative responsiveness to interest groups: a study in labor legislation protecting women and children in Massachusetts. PhD Radcliffe Coll. 1934.

BEINHAUER,M.T. *211*
State labor laws applicable to women and their effect on women's employment opportunities. PhD U. of Minnesota, 1955.

BLANKERTZ,L.E. *212*
Patriarchal capitalism: an application to the historical and contemporary participation of women in labor unions. PhD Bryn Mawr Coll. 1980.

BOOKMAN,A.E. *213*
The process of political socialization among women and immigrant workers: a case study of unionization in the electronics industry. PhD Harvard U. 1977.

BOONE,G. *214*
The Women's Trade Union Leagues in Great Britain and the United States of America. PhD Columbia U. 1942.

BRONFMAN,L.A.M. *215*
The impact of rules and regulations prohibiting sex discrimination in employment: a study of response patterns in Oregon. PhD U. of Oregon, 1973.

FEE,T.M. *216*
Enforcement of Title VII by the EEOC: a critical assessment of the federal government's efforts at eliminating sex discrimination in employment. PhD U. of California, Riverside, 1982.

FLORER,J.H. *217*
NOW: the formative years. The national effort to acquire federal action on equal employment rights for women in the 1960s. PhD Syracuse U. 1972.

FONOW,M.M. *218*
Women in steel: a case study of the participation of women in a trade union. PhD Ohio State U. 1977.

GOUGH,C.L. *219*
Pay, parity and policy: an appraisal of past and present sex discrimination legislation in Britain and its consequences for women workers. MSc U. of Wales, Cardiff, 1979.

HANCOCK,W.L.B. *220*
An analysis of the impact of federal laws and regulations on opportunities for women in management. DBA Mississippi State U. 1973.

HARDY,R.J. *221*
The impact of civil rights policies on achieving racial and sexual income equality, 1948–76. PhD U. of Iowa, 1978.

LEDGERWOOD,D.E. *222*
An analysis of the satisfaction/dissatisfaction of United States female unionists with their local trade union organizations: a view of the Coalition of Labor Union Women. PhD U. of Oklahoma, 1980.

LEMAN,P. *223*
Organizing women workers: the campaign for women's rights in three trade unions. [ACTT, NALGO and NAT FHE] MA U. of Warwick, 1980.

LEVENHAK,S.T. *224*
Trade union membership among women and girls in the United Kingdom, 1920–1965. PhD U. of London, LSE, 1971.

LONG,T.M. *225*
The impact of minimum wages on the employment and labor force participation of adult women. PhD Iowa State U. 1980.

MATTHEWS,L.R. *226*
Women in trade unions in San Francisco. PhD U. of California, Berkeley, 1912.

MEEHAN,E.M. *227*
Public policy: equal employment opportunities for women in Britain and America. DPhil U. of Oxford, 1982.

MOORE,E.A.P. *228*
'Life and Labor': Margaret Dreier Robins and the Women's Trade Union League. PhD U. of Illinois at Chicago Circle, 1981.

PAIGE,D.M. *229*
The Coalition for Women in State Service: a case study of a self-help group. DPA Southern California, 1979.

PEARLSON,J.S. *230*
Equal pay for women: its development in the United States. PhD Radcliffe Coll. 1953.

POMURA,G.M. *231*
The Allied occupation of Japan: reform of Japanese government labor policy on women. PhD U. of Hawaii, 1978.

PRYWES,R.W. *232*
A study of the development of the non-standard work week for women. PhD Bryn Mawr Coll. 1974.

PRZYBYLA,B.A. *233*
The experience of taking responsibility in leadership roles among selected labor union women. PhD U. of Michigan, 1980.

ROBBINS,A.R. *234*
Politics, unions, and the new middle class: a study of white-collar workers in Britain. [Inc. study of women at work and relations with trade unions] PhD U. of British Columbia, 1982.

RUGGIE,M. *235*
Women and work in Britain and Sweden: the role of the state in social change. PhD U. of California, Berkeley, 1980.

SEALANDER,J.A. *236*
The Women's Bureau, 1920–1950: federal reaction to female wage earning. PhD Duke U. 1977.

SMITH,V.F. *237*
The guidance implications for high school and college students, counselors, teachers, administrators, and employers, of Colorado laws relating to employment and employment practices and opportunities for women in five selected areas of Colorado. EdD U. of Colorado, 1955.

STEVENS,E.V. *238*
Some developments in national equal wage and employment policy for women with emphasis on the years 1962–1966. PhD U. of Illinois at Urbana-Champaign, 1967.

TANABE,P.A.W. *239*
Views of women's work in public policy in the United States: social security and equal pay legislation, 1935–1967. PhD Bryn Mawr Coll. 1973.

THORNTON,L.H.F. *240*
The legal right to equal pay, with special reference to European Community law. LLM U. of Manchester, 1975.

THORNTON,L.H.F. *241*
The legal status of working women (*la femme au travail*) in the European Economic Community. PhD U. of London, Queen Mary Coll. 1979.

WYLDE-BROWN,P.B. *242*
A consideration of the theory of women's wages and an attempt to test the truth of certain reasons which have been adduced by economic writers for the relatively lower wage-level of women in industry as compared with that of men. MA U. of Birmingham, 1930.

ZELMAN,P.G. *243*
Development of equal employment opportunity for women as a national policy, 1960–1967. PhD Ohio State U. 1980.

Specific occupations

Excluding those covered under: The educational professions, **4** 589–1011; The medical professions, **8** 477–558; Media **13** *passim*; Women religious, **18** 156–239; The ordination of women, **18** 242–61; Social work, **21** 265–308. *See also* **9** 1642.

AAGAARD,A.A. *244*
A study for the recruitment of women in industrial arts. EdD U. of Northern Colorado, 1975.

ALFKE,D.E. *245*
Professional opportunities for women in conservation and natural science. PhD Cornell U. 1953.

ALLEN,R.A. *246*
The labor of women in the production of cotton. PhD U. of Chicago, 1934.

ALLINSON,M. *247*
Dressmaking as a trade for women in Massachusetts. PhD Columbia U. 1916.

ANTLER,E.P. *248*
Fisherman, fisherwoman, rural proletariat: capitalist commodity production in the Newfoundland

fisheries. [Inc. study of sexual division of labour within fishery households and evaluation by value of women's work] PhD U. of Connecticut, 1982.

ATKINSON,A.C. *249*
Women in British librarianship: a survey with a historical introduction. DipLib* U. of Sheffield, 1965.

AYOUB,A.M.H. *250*
Absenteeism among manual women workers in engineering: a case study. MSc UMIST, Manchester, 1970.

BOCHER,R.B. *251*
A study into the representation of women at the middle management levels of the Pennsylvania State Government Civil Service. PhD Temple U. 1980.

BRIDGWOOD,A. *252*
Women workers in contemporary Britain: a study of workshop behaviour with special reference to a printing firm in Bradford. MSc U. of Bradford, 1978.

BRIGGS,F. *253*
The development of nursery nursing and the changing role of the nursery nurse, 1870–1975. MA U. of Sheffield, 1978.

BRUCE,M.J. *254*
Women in British Airways. MSc U. of Bath, 1975.

BRYON,F. *255*
Women's traditions in the Leeds tailoring industry. MA U. of Leeds, 1981.

CAPLETTE,M.K. *256*
Women in book publishing: a study of careers and organizations. PhD State U. of New York at Stony Brook, 1981.

COSTON,R.D. *257*
An investigation of the economic effects of the four-day work week on women apparel workers in Georgia. PhD U. of Arkansas, 1973.

DERBY,D.A. *258*
Black women basket makers: a study of domestic economy in Charleston County, South Carolina. PhD U. of Illinois at Urbana-Champaign, 1980.

DILL,B.T. *259*
Across the boundaries of race and class: an exploration of the relationship between work and family among black female domestic servants. PhD New York U. 1979.

EATON,M.S. *260*
Domestic workers in hospitals: a field of women's employment. PhD U. of London, LSE 1948.

ENARSON,E.P. *261*
Sexuality in the workplace: a study of outdoor women workers in the forest service. PhD U. of Oregon, 1981.

FENNEL,J.C. *262*
A career profile of women directors of the largest academic libraries in the United States: an analysis and description of the determinants. PhD Florida State U. 1978.

FOX,B. *263*
Women's domestic labour and their involvement in wage work: twentieth-century changes in the reproduction of daily life. PhD U. of Alberta, 1980.

FURIO,C.M. *264*
Immigrant women and industry: a case study of Italian immigrant women and the garment industry, 1880–1950. PhD New York U. 1979.

GILHAM,S.C. *265*
Equity and job satisfaction: the effects of education and training inputs among female civil service workers at the University of Kansas. PhD U. of Kansas, 1975.

GURNEY,G.S. *266*
Women veterinarians: a study of job satisfaction and professional practice patterns. PhD Iowa State U. 1980.

GURR,M.N. *267*
A study of women executives and professional administrators. PhD Northwestern U. 1956.

HEDGES,A.C. *268*
Wage worth of school training: an analytical study of 600 women workers in textile factories. PhD Columbia U. 1914.

HEYL,B.S. *269*
The house prostitute: a case study. PhD U. of Illinois at Urbana-Champaign.

HOWARD,J.K. *270*
Validation of the airman classification battery for women of the Air Force. PhD U. of Southern California, 1952.

HUTCHINSON,M.B. *271*
The semi-professions: case studies of approaches to professionalism: childcare, midwifery, and university librarianship. MSc U. of Lancaster, 1982.

INSKEEP,G.C. *272*
The selection process and its relationship to observed productivity, tenure, and absenteeism among women garment workers. PhD Columbia U. 1967.

JONES,N. *273*
Sex equality in engineering. MSc U. of Bath, 1978.

KENNEDY,J.C. *274*
Anne Sybil Cooke, 1895–1971: her life and work in county librarianship. MA U. of Loughborough, 1980.

KING,E.M. *275*
The range livestock industry through women's eyes. PhD Texas A&M U. 1978.

KIRK,K.W. 276
A national survey of women pharmacists: their attitudes, career practice patterns, and vocational interests. PhD U. of Wisconsin, 1972.

KOLODNER,H.J. 277
Industrial safety programming for female employees in fibers manufacturing plants. PhD New York U. 1973.

LE MARE,M.W. 278
Girl entrants to industry, with special reference to the training of girls aged 15 to 18 for semi-skilled work. BLitt U. of Oxford, 1959.

LEVITT,E.S. 279
A study of four career patterns and associated life history characteristics among female professional librarians. PhD New York U. 1970.

LEWIS,J. 280
Policewomen: a study of the workings of the women police. MA* U. of Sheffield, 1973.

LISS,M. 281
Prostitution in perspective: a comparison of prostitutes and other working women. EdD Northern Illinois U. 1981.

LITTRELL,J.J. 282
Employment requirements and opportunities for women as technicians in the St Louis labor market area. EdD U. of Missouri, 1958.

LIVINGSTON,O.F. 283
A study of women executives in life insurance companies owned and operated by negroes, with implications for business education. EdD New York U. 1964.

MCDONNELL,J.J. 284
The employment of women in selected positions in local New Jersey governmental and educational sub-divisions. EdD Rutgers U. 1975.

MASSON,G.A. 285
Elements of organizational discrimination: the Air Force response to women as military pilots. PhD U. of Southern California, 1976.

MEKKY,S.I. 286
A comparative study of the health of women employed in the English and Egyptian cotton industries. PhD U. of London, Sch. of Hygiene, 1968.

MILDWID,M.E. 287
Women in male-dominated professions: a study of bankers, architects, and lawyers. PhD Wright Inst. 1982.

MORTON,J.B. 288
A study of the employment of women as correctional officers in state level adult male correctional institutions. DPA U. of Georgia, 1980.

NELSON,H. 289
Women workers and the labour policy: a case study of the garment industry in the north-west. MA U. of Manchester, 1981.

NUOM,P.K. 290
Women in municipal management: Milwaukee municipal workforce. PhD U. of Wisconsin-Madison, 1982.

OELRICH,E.S. 291
The position of the female secretary in the United States from 1900 through 1967: an historical study. PhD U. of North Dakota, 1968.

PAUL,G.W. 292
Impact of female employees in adult all-male correctional institutions. MA U. of Houston, 1971.

PERLSTEN,G.R. 293
An exploratory analysis of certain characteristics of policewomen. PhD Florida State U. 1971.

PERRY,L. 294
The millinery trade in Boston and Philadelphia: a study of women in industry. PhD Bryn Mawr Coll. 1913.

PERUN,P.J. 295
A study of productivity in academic women social scientists. PhD U. of Chicago, 1977.

REEKUBGM,O.A. 296
Undergraduate female students as potential recruits to the library profession. PhD Columbia U. 1969.

REMMINGTON,P.L.W. 297
The Atlanta police: an ethnographic study of the introduction of female officers. PhD U. of Pittsburgh, 1978.

REYNOLDS,J.T. 298
The preretirement educational needs of retired black women who were domestic workers in Dallas, Texas. PhD East Texas State U. 1981.

ROBINSON,M.B.H. 299
The woman veterinarian: origins, education, and career. PhD Ohio State U. 1978.

ROSS,P.J. 300
Farmwomen's participation in United States agricultural production. PhD Ohio State U. 1982.

RUSTAD,M.L. 301
Women in khaki: a study of the American enlisted woman. PhD Boston Coll. 1981.

SALTZSTEIN,G.H. 302
Employment of females in municipal governments: the influence of female workforce characteristics, city characteristics, organizational structure, and hiring agents' attitudes on changes in representation levels. PhD U. of California, Riverside, 1979.

SAYIN,A.F. 303
A study of the operation of the home work system in the knitted outerwear and the women's apparel industries. PhD Bryn Mawr Coll. 1945.

SCHRAMM,D.G. 304
A study of the older woman worker who has

attempted to enter or re-enter the white collar labor force through the assistance of community training programs in clerical occupations. PhD U. of California, Los Angeles, 1969.

SMITH,C.J. *305*
Work and use of government benefits: a case study of Hispanic women workers in New York's garment industry. DSW Adelphi U. Sch. of Social Work, 1980.

SOFTLEY,E.M. *306*
Word processing and female employment. MSc U. of Manchester, 1979.

SOLOMON,L.D. *307*
Female doctoral chemists: sexual discrepancies in career patterns. PhD Cornell U. 1972.

STANES,D.F. *308*
The employment of women in supervisory and managerial positions in the cotton, clothing, biscuit, cocoa, chocolate and sugar confectionery industries in England with a historical introduction from 1900. MSc U. of London, LSE, 1955.

STROSNIDER,C.S. *309*
Leadership by women in criminal justice: there is room at the top. PhD Sam Houston State U. 1978.

SUMMER,P. *310*
The career pattern of women graduates of the University of Buffalo medical, dental and law schools, 1895–1915. PhD State U. of New York at Buffalo, 1980.

TAYLOR,W. *311*
Noise and hearing: a study of loom noise and hearing loss in a population of female jute weavers. MD U. of Edinburgh, 1968.

TIMPER,P.J.T. *312*
The relationship between the adoption of modern farm practices and the participation of farm women in farm tasks. PhD Utah State U. 1981.

UTECHT,K.M. *313*
An examination of the factors affecting recruitment, selection, and turnover of female operatives in a biscuit factory in the northwest of England. MA* U. of Lancaster, 1973.

VAIL,D.R. *314*
Effectiveness of US navy work groups which include women in non-traditional jobs, and all-male groups. DBA George Washington U. 1979.

VICE,J.A. *315*
Career development of women in engineering: factors influencing a nontraditional career. PhD Ohio State U. 1977.

VIETRI,L.T. *316*
Women in the higher civil service: a re-examination of representative bureaucracy. PhD U. of Maryland, 1981.

VINNICOMBE,S.M. *317*
The private secretary: an analysis of her gatekeeper role in the managing director's communication structure. PhD U. of Manchester, 1978.

WALING,A.M.B. *318*
An analysis of labor force experience and market work commitment of women interested in management training. PhD Purdue U. 1979.

WALLISCH,W.J.Jr. *319*
The admission and integration of women into the United States Air Force Academy. EdD U. of Southern California, 1977.

WARE,H.R.E. *320*
The recruitment, regulation and role of prostitution in Britain from the middle of the nineteenth century to the present day. PhD U. of London, 1970.

WINSPUR,P. *321*
Women and law enforcement: a study of policewomen in Britain. MPhil U. of Edinburgh, 1977.

ZAVELLA,P.J. *322*
Women, work and family in the Chicano community: cannery workers of the Santa Clara Valley. PhD U. of California, Berkeley, 1982.

ZIMMER,L.E. *322a*
Female guards in men's prisons: creating a role for themselves. PhD Cornell U. 1982.

Vocational and occupational psychology

See also 59; **4** 1433–1686; **6** 911, 940; **20** 138; **21** 90.

ABRAMS,D.L. *323*
Determinants of young women's career outcomes. PhD U. of Delaware, 1980.

ADAMS,J.M. *324*
Outstanding successful women: an in-depth study regarding the attitudes of successful executive women in achieving their status. PhD U. of Colorado at Boulder, 1975.

ALPERT,B.E. *325*
Psychological temperament adjustment and cross-situational coping in professional women. PhD Illinois Inst. of Technology, 1982.

AMAEWHULE,W.A. *326*
Managerial motivation among females: a status study of black American females. PhD Georgia State U. Coll. of Educ. 1982.

AMITIN,K.G. *327*
A correlational analysis of selected career development competencies and personality characteristics among low income black women. PhD Georgia State U. Coll. of Educ. 1978.

ANDERSEN,L.K. 328
The careers of adult women: psychological profiles from a development perspective. PhD U. of Minnesota, 1980.

ARBOGAST,K.A. 329
The procurement of women for the armed forces: an analysis of occupational choice. PhD George Washington U. 1974.

ARVIS,P.F. 330
Factors affecting the recruitment and advancement of women in managerial positions in federal agencies. PhD American U. 1973.

ASWELL,K.M.S. 331
Working women in transition: changing attitudes and behaviors regarding work, partnership and family. PhD Wright Inst. 1982.

AYLMER,D.G. 332
Prediction of success and satisfaction of women Masters in Business Administration using the Strong-Campbell interest inventory. PhD Boston Coll. 1978.

AYRES,G.A.L. 333
Self-efficacy theory: implications for the career development of women. PhD Ohio State U. 1980.

AZIMI ANARAKI,S. 334
Female managers: satisfaction, motivations and problems. PhD United States International U. 1980.

BANFIELD,E.E.C. 335
Women in middle management positions: characteristics, training, leadership style, limitations, rewards and problems. PhD United States International U. 1976.

BARBEE,M.S. 336
Skill assessment and training for women managers. PhD Colorado State U. 1976.

BARCLAY,L.A. 337
An examination of attitudes toward jobs and equal employment opportunity by traditionally and non-traditionally employed females. PhD Wayne State U. 1981.

BARNARD,W.K. 338
A study of female employees' responses on an attitude survey. PhD North Texas State U. 1978.

BAUMAN,R. 339
A study of Mexican American women's perceptions toward factors that impede academic and professional goal attainment. EdD U. of Houston, 1980.

BEATTY,M.A.M. 340
Employment outcomes among graduates of nontraditional skills training programs for disadvantaged women. PhD U. of Maryland, 1982.

BECKER,S.J. 341
A comparison of body attitudes in women with masculine vocational interests and those with feminine vocational interests. PhD U. of Maryland, 1971.

BEGALLA,M.A.E. 342
The comparison of the performance and achievement value of work, volunteer, and homemaking behaviors of supervisory male and female employees, non- supervisory female employees, and female volunteer workers. EdD U. of Tennessee, 1976.

BENEDICT,K.M. 343
When women succeed: organizational settings and the structure of careers. PhD Stanford U. 1980.

BERKOWITZ,A.D. 344
Role conflict in farm women. PhD Cornell U. 1981.

BERTRAND,U.S. 345
Personal and organizational correlates of role stress and job satisfaction in female managers. PhD U. of Wisconsin, 1981.

BICKEL,H.E. 346
An analysis of the work values of women: implications for counseling. EdD State U. of New York, 1969.

BIRD,N. 347
Relationships between experience factors, test scores and efficiency as shown by a study of four selected groups of women office workers. PhD Columbia U. 1931.

BLAKE,C.H. 348
Women's mobility and their motivations for working in the Madison, Wisconsin, labor market. PhD U. of Wisconsin, 1966.

BLUMENSTEIN,L.R. 349
The effects of Singer's job survival skills program on the self-concept and work attitudes of disadvantaged females. PhD Georgia State U. Coll. of Educ. 1976.

BOPP,M.L. 350
Professional women and their career networks. EdD Columbia U. Teachers Coll. 1981.

BOSE,C.E. 351
Women and jobs: sexual influences on occupational prestige. PhD Johns Hopkins U. 1973.

BOTTOMS,L.W. 352
The interrelationships among sex-role orientations, self-actualization and significant issues of high-achieving, executive women. PhD Georgia State U. Coll. of Educ. 1982.

BOYD,B.J. 353
A study of the relationship between the job satisfactions of women and selected demographic characteristics. PhD Kansas State U. 1974.

BRANDT,S.J. 354
Psychological correlates of occupational choice in women. PhD Adelphi U. 1977.

BRANNEN,K.C. *355*
A study of the intraorganizational diffusion of an external authority-decision innovation: the Women in Management (WIM) concept. PhD U. of Nebraska-Lincoln, 1979.

BRENNER,O.C. *356*
Traits and reported behaviors of female managers: must the female be similar to the male in order to become a manager? PhD Stevens Inst. of Technology, 1977.

BRITTAIN,K.H. *357*
Analysis and comparison of communication styles of executive women in traditional roles. EdD Memphis State U. 1981.

BROOKE,M.J. *358*
Status incongruence and support for change in sex-role ideology: a study of women in various professions. PhD Loyola U., Chicago, 1976.

BROOKS,M.B. *359*
The effect of employment on individual modernity among women in four societies. PhD Case Western Reserve U. 1976.

BRUNER,J.M. *360*
Role-conflict and self-concept congruency in working women. PhD California Sch. of Prof. Psych. 1980.

BRYCE,R.A. *361*
Characteristics of women holding executive, managerial, and other high level positions in four areas of business. EdD U. of Northern Colorado, 1969.

BURNS,P.J.H. *362*
Profiles in achievement-related behaviors in career and noncareer women. PhD Fordham U. 1976.

BUTLER,V.W. *363*
The effect of an experimental treatment on male attitudes toward female-intensive business occupations. PhD Florida State U. 1980.

CAINE,R.L. *364*
Women in the labor force and suicide rates. PhD U. of Georgia, 1979.

CARROLL,C.A. *365*
The relationship between sex role and professional advancement in women. PhD U. of South Carolina, 1980.

CASHEL,W.F. *366*
The perception of the USAF company grade officer role by women officer trainees. PhD Ohio State U. 1975.

CAVALLARO,M.L. *367*
Correlates of perceived job deprivation and life satisfaction among retired women of different occupational groups. PhD Ohio State U. 1980.

CHAPPELL,C.B. *368*
The status attainment process: women in the labor force of middletown. PhD Brigham Young U. 1979.

CHAPPELL,N.L. *369*
Work, commitment to work and self-identity among women. PhD McMaster U. 1978.

CHARLES,M.T. *370*
An evaluation of female recruit performance and male/female recruit perceptions of the female trooper's role in the 90th Michigan State Police Training Academy. PhD Michigan State U. 1978.

CHENOWETH,L.C. *371*
The career patterns and intragenerational mobility processes for mature American women. PhD Texas A&M U. 1980.

CHERNE,F.P. *372*
An exploratory study of selected personality characteristics of professional women in traditional and nontraditional occupations. EdD U. of California, San Francisco, 1982.

CHILD,J. *373*
Public schools and the changing cultural dynamics of women and work in the United States: a study of points of view. PhD U. of Oregon, 1981.

CLOSE,A.S. *374*
A comparative study of work attitudes of married and single women in manual and clerical occupations. MA U. of London, Birkbeck Coll. 1966.

COLEMAN,V.D. *375*
The self-esteem and vocational maturity of females. EdD Rutgers U. 1979.

COMBS,M.J. *376*
Personal characteristics influencing the hiring, promotion, and discharge of women in selected groups of occupations in Clarke County, Georgia. EdD U. of Georgia, 1974.

COOK,S.M.H. *377*
Personal value profile of selected women executives. DBA Texas Tech. U. 1973.

COOPER,J.F. *378*
Impact of the Strong-Campbell interest inventory and the vocational card sort on career salience and vocational exploration behavior of women. PhD U. of Maryland, 1975.

CORBETT,B.M. *379*
Social and personality factors influencing career choice of women in nontraditional, blue collar skilled trades. EdD Boston U. Sch. of Educ. 1981.

COYLE,J.M. *380*
Job involvement, work satisfaction, and attitudes toward retirement of business and professional women. PhD Texas Woman's U. 1976.

CRAWFORD,J.D. *381*
A comparative study of feminine role perception, selected personality characteristics, and career development. PhD Texas Tech U. 1975.

CURKENDALL,E.S. *382*
Relationships among ego development level, sex-role definition, and occupational status of women. PhD California Sch. of Prof. Psych., Los Angeles, 1978.

DAVIS,H.C. *383*
The impact of orientation to entry level coal mining occupations upon the self-concept of women seeking training for entry level coal mining occupations. PhD Ohio State U. 1980.

DEFABAUGH,G.L. *384*
Attitudes of potential professional women toward women's unconventional occupations. PhD U. of Rochester, 1975.

DENNIS,E.M. *385*
Women in selected male dominated trades: their perceptions of social workers and clerical workers. EdD U. of Cincinnati, 1981.

DIAMOND,H.A. *386*
Suicide by women professionals. PhD California Sch. of Prof. Psych. 1977.

DIFFLEY,J.H. *387*
A study of women business owners and the importance of selected entrepreneurial competencies related to educational programs. PhD U. of Oklahoma, 1982.

DIXON,B.L.B. *388*
Competence perceptions of female non-traditional occupation aspirants. PhD Florida State U. 1982.

DOLLASE,R.H. *389*
The new woman leader: a case study in leadership adaptation in a professional organization. EdD Boston U. Sch. of Educ. 1976.

DONOVAN,M.W. *390*
Beliefs of women in role innovative and traditional professions about themselves and their female colleagues. PhD George Washington U. 1976.

DOUCE,L.A. *391*
Career aspirations and career development of women in relation to adventure scale scores of the Strong-Campbell interest inventory. PhD U. of Minnesota, 1977.

DOWDALL,J.A. *392*
Employment and sex-role orientation of Rhode Island women. PhD Brown U. 1972.

DUBOY'S,T. *393*
Consistency, congruency, differentiational and job satisfaction among female clerical workers. PhD Fordham U. 1976.

DUPREE,C.M. *394*
Career orientation of women as related to selected personality characteristics. EdD U. of Georgia, 1976.

EDWARDS,K.L. *395*
The influence of management function and environmental support on stress and job satisfaction in black females in management. PhD U. of Cincinnati, 1979.

ELLIOTT,A.G.P. *396*
Sex and selection: a psychological study of the employment interview. PhD Trinity Coll. Dublin, 1980.

ELLIS,E.E. *397*
A study of the correlates of upward social mobility among unmarried career women. PhD Ohio State U. 1951.

ENRIQUEZ-WHITE,C. *398*
Attitudes of Hispanic and Anglo women managers toward women in management. EdD La Verne U. 1982.

EPSTEIN,S.H. *399*
Sex-role identification nurturance, birth order and women's employment in nontraditional careers. PhD Fordham U. 1981.

EYDE,L.D. *400*
Work values and background factors as predictors of women's desire to work. PhD Ohio State U. 1959.

FARAH,C.F. *401*
Work-related support and a balanced sex group: potential solutions to women managers' slow advancement. PhD California Sch. of Prof. Psych., Los Angeles, 1980.

FARNSWORTH,K.E. *402*
The vocational interests of women: a factor analysis of the woman's form of the Strong vocational interest blank. PhD Iowa State U. 1968.

FELMAN,I.R. *403*
Role models of women choosing role innovative, moderately innovative, and traditional professions. PhD California Sch. of Prof. Psych. Berkeley, 1981.

FELMLEE,D.H. *404*
Women's job transitions: a dynamic analysis of job mobility and job leaving. PhD U. of Wisconsin-Madison, 1980.

FELSTEHAUSEN,J.T. *405*
The mentoring of nonprofessional, nonmanagerial women who are pursuing upward career mobility. EdD U. of Illinois at Urbana-Champaign, 1982.

FERGUSON,E. *406*
The relationship of work motivation to selected demographic characteristics of black female workers. EdD U. of Houston, 1976.

FERGUSON,T.C. *407*
Successful women: a comparison of self-perceived factors influencing successful contemporary women and successful women born 1910–1915. PhD U. of California, Los Angeles, 1982.

FEULNER,P.N. *408*
Women in the professions: a social-psychological study. PhD Ohio State U. 1973.

FILLMAN,J.A. *409*
Childhood antecedents of career patterns in middle-aged women. PhD California Sch. of Prof. Psych. 1980.

FINCH,M.R. *410*
A study of the relationship between aspirations and aptitudes for managerial positions of women in the work force of Nashville, Tennessee. PhD George Peabody Coll. for Teachers, 1981.

FLAHERTY,J.D. *411*
Women historians in the 1970s: a study of socioeconomic backgrounds, motivations, and attitudes about the profession. PhD Northern Arizona U. 1982.

FLEXMAN,N.A. *412*
Women of enterprise: a study of success and failure incidents from self-employed women using the perspectives of Bakan's constructs of agency and communion and attribution theory. PhD U. of Illinois at Urbana-Champaign, 1980.

FOWLER,M.G. *413*
Personality dynamics and biographical factors associated with occupational role-innovation in females. PhD U. of Florida, 1976.

FRANKEL,P. *414*
Working women and minorities: a study of education and promotability as perceived by managers and females and minority employees. PhD Northwestern U. 1979.

FULLER,D.J.D. *415*
A study of differences between licensed professional women and licensed professional career women on selected characteristics: a status study. PhD U. of Colorado at Boulder, 1977.

GADDY,C.D. *416*
The woman in the dual-career family: personality differences and the impact of children on career development. PhD Catholic U. of America, 1982.

GARLAND,T.O. *417*
A study of anxiety and physical stress among factory girls. MD U. of Cambridge, 1938.

GARRETT,L.B. *418*
A comparison of personality characteristics and coping strategies between nurse managers and business women managers. PhD U. of Denver, 1982.

GARVIN,M. *419*
Factory women: sexual equality and the role of work. PhD Boston Coll. 1981.

GERHART,U.C. *420*
Job satisfaction and some stresses and strains of female lawyers, social workers and clerical workers. EdD Rutgers U. 1976.

GHAFFARI-SAMAI,P. *421*
An analysis of selected factors related to occupational aspirations and expectations of adult women. PhD U. of Connecticut, 1979.

GIDIO,J.M.de S. *422*
Gender specific problems of women in apprenticeship training. PhD U. of Oregon, 1980.

GILBERT,G. *423*
Career maturity of vocationally undecided middle-aged women. EdD U. of South Dakota, 1976.

GINN,F.W. *424*
Career motivation and role perception of women as related to parental role expectation and parental status discrepancy. PhD Catholic U. of America, 1968.

GLITZER,B.M. *425*
Job satisfaction and its relation to sources of self-esteem in working women. EdD Rutgers U. 1979.

GLOSSER,E.A. *426*
The consistency of like-indifferent-dislike response sets and related scales on the Strong vocational interest blank for women. PhD Indiana U. 1966.

GOLDBERG,R. *427*
Dissatisfaction and consciousness among office workers: a case study of a working women's organization. PhD American U. 1981.

GOLDMAN,B.S. *428*
The economics of job search and employment behavior of WIM women. PhD American U. 1982.

GOLTZ,D.L. *429*
The relationship of perceptions of sex roles and occupational choice among women. PhD U. of Oklahoma, 1977.

GOTS,L.S. *430*
Life stress, work tension and illness in managerial women. PhD Illinois Inst. of Technology, 1982.

GRAHAM,R.L. *431*
A follow-up study evaluating two speech programs for career officers in the United States Women's Army Corps. EdD U. of Maryland, 1964.

GREENBERG,G. *432*
Exploration of personalities, needs, and attitudes of female child care workers. PhD Illinois Inst. of Technology, 1970.

GREENFIELD,S.T. *433*
Attitudes toward work and success of women employed in male versus female dominated jobs. DBA U. of Southern California, 1978.

GREENWALD,H. *434*
A study of deviant sexual occupational choice by twenty New York women. PhD Columbia U. 1956.

GREY,M.C. *435*
The relationship of sex-role attitudes and personal circumstances/characteristics to level of occupational aspirations of working women PhD U. of Maryland, 1982.

GRINA,A.A.M. *436*
The effect of group experience on women in a management development course. PhD U. of Pittsburgh, 1978.

GRINNELL,G.C. *437*
Work-related stress among black female professionals. PhD United States International U. 1982.

GROSS,H.E. *438*
Self-perceptions of abilities relating to the employability of women between ages 40 to 65. PhD Kansas State U. 1981.

GUILLET.R.D. *439*
The status of women in administrative positions in the province of Ontario. EdD Wayne State U. 1982.

HADJIGHASEM,M.M. *440*
Predictors of woman's occupational attainment. EdD U. of Houston, 1979.

HAIRE,J.B. *441*
An investigation of selected sociopsychological variables in relation to the traditional or nontraditional occupational choice of middle-age women. PhD Southern Illinois U. at Carbondale, 1981.

HAIRSTON,S.H. *442*
Sources of role conflict for black and white professional women. PhD U. of Pittsburgh, 1980.

HALL,R.D. *443*
Sex differences in perceptions of competencies required to manage United States-based international corporations. [Position of women in management] PhD Arizona State U. 1982.

HARBINGER,B. *444*
Sexual harassment of women in the workplace: perception and reality. PhD United States International U. 1982.

HAREL,F. *445*
Perception et actualisation des facteurs de promotion chez les femmes cadres des grandes enterprises québecoises francophones du secteur privé. PhD U. of Montreal, 1982.

HASKINS,M.E.W. *446*
A comparative study of perceptions pertaining to the deterrents to women entering non-traditional occupations. PhD Florida State U. 1982.

HAVASSY,Y.J. *447*
Reactions to professional women as a function of attractiveness and level of competence. PhD California Sch. of Prof. Psych. 1981.

HAYSLIP,J.B. *448*
Developing career mobility for women with physical disabilities. EdD George Peabody Coll. for Teachers, 1981.

HEASTON,P.Y.W. *450*
An analysis of selected role perceptions among successful black women in the professions. PhD Northwestern U. 1975.

HENNIG,M.M. *451*
Career development for women executives. PhD Harvard U. 1971.

HENNY,C.Y. *452*
Women's evaluation of careers as a function of sex-stereotype, mathematical content, and opportunity for interpersonal contact. PhD American U. 1981.

HERNANDEZ,E.J. *453*
Perceptions of females by males in law enforcement: femininity, competence and attraction. PhD U. of California, Riverside, 1979.

HIRSCHFELD,M.A. *454*
The impostor phenomenon in successful career women. PhD Fordham U. 1982.

HODGSON,M.L. *455*
The career development of college-educated women as influenced by variations in intimacy and achievement needs over the adult life span. PhD State U. of New York at Buffalo, 1978.

HOPKINS,P.F. *456*
The relative validities of traditionally used job satisfaction and organizational commitment measures versus women-specific measures for the prediction of female tenure in a male-dominated job. PhD Wayne State U. 1976.

HORTON,J.A. *457*
The personality characteristics of professional career women: a study of the concurrent validity of John Holland's theory of vocational choice. PhD Ohio State U. 1975.

HOYTE,S.K. *458*
The Women's Job Corps: patterns of behavior relating to success or failure. DSW Catholic U. of America, 1969.

HUGHES,E.C. *459*
Sex discrimination in America's legal profession: an analytical study of male professionals' attitudes toward their female counterparts in the field of law. PhD United States International U. 1979.

HUGHES,M.A.E. *460*
An investigation of the aspirations, attitudes, apprehensions, and strategies for success of selected women executives in business, government, and education. PhD Kansas State U. 1981.

HUNT,P.J. *461*
Women supervisors: a study of their performance and the group interaction in a simulated organization. PhD U. of Akron, 1974.

HUNT,P.L. 462
Female child-care workers: their feminine identity congruence, attitudes toward women, self-actualization, and marital status. PhD Indiana State U. 1975.

HUNTER,C.S. 463
Attitudes of professional women as a function of self-esteem and defensiveness. PhD U. of Southern Mississippi, 1980.

HUTTON,S.S. 464
Occupational interest and the motivation for occupational achievement among women. PhD Arizona State U. 1978.

IRVINE,J.J. 465
The relationships among androgynous masculine, feminine, and undifferentiated sex-role orientations and attitudes toward women in a specified and in an unspecified occupational role. PhD Georgia State U. Coll. of Educ. 1979.

JOHNSTON,K.M. 466
The relationship of women's career choice to sex-role orientation, fear of success, and selected demographic variables. PhD Hofstra U. 1980.

JONES,J.A. 467
The attributes distinguishing women displaying a high degree of work stability. PhD Louisiana Tech U. 1977.

JONES,L.J. 468
Career planning for employed women: a counseling intervention and evaluation. PhD U. of Minnesota, 1979.

JURAN,S. 469
Stereotyped attributions of occupation, status and gender, or the anomaly of the high-status woman. PhD City U. of New York, 1979.

KANGAS,P.E. 470
The single professional woman: a phenomenological study. PhD California Sch. of Prof. Psych., San Diego, 1976.

KARMAN,F.J. 471
Women: personal and environmental factors in role identification and career choice. EdD U. of California, Los Angeles, 1972.

KATZ,D.R. 472
Changing values of women towards work: will tomorrow's young female managers differ from their older counterparts? PhD Temple U. 1982

KATZ,E.A. 473
Women in professional training: a study of the influence of mentors and sex ratio. PhD California Sch. of Prof. Psych., Los Angeles, 1980.

KEENAN,K.M. 474
Reasons for joining and early termination of service in the Women's Royal Army Corps: an attitude study. MPhil U. of London, Birkbeck Coll. 1978.

KIDD,T. 475
An investigation into the attitudes of a sample of young women joining HM Forces towards some moral issues and the relationship between these and their declared religious practice. MPhil U. of Nottingham, 1972.

KIM,M. 476.
Levels and determinants of female job satisfaction for a national sample of females. PhD U. of Georgia, 1982.

KIRK,K.W. 477
A national survey of women pharmacists: their attitudes, career practice patterns, and vocational interests. PhD U. of Wisconsin, 1972.

KISSEL,P.J. 478
A study in role balancing: female corrections officers on the job. PhD U. of Colorado at Boulder, 1980.

KNOTTS,R.E.L. 479
Manifest needs of professional female workers in business-oriented occupations. PhD Texas A&M U. 1972.

KNOX,N.B. 480
Sex-role orientation and self-esteem in career-committed and home-oriented women. PhD California Sch. of Prof. Psych., Berkeley, 1977.

KOESTER,J. 481
Rhetorical visions of female managers in popular self-help books. PhD U. of Minnesota, 1980.

KOLT,L.J. 482
The influence of female career role models on the self-concept and role conflict of women in male-dominated professions. PhD California Sch. of Prof. Psych., San Diego, 1982.

KRANE,J.C. 483
Experiences for women leading to successful entry into the post-secondary cooperative work experience management program. EdD U. of Northern Colorado, 1980.

KREBS,S.D. 484
Job satisfaction of department store women's wear buyers. PhD Texas Woman's U. 1979.

LACY,G.P.F. 485
An evaluation of attitudes toward women as managers in a government setting. PhD U. of Wisconsin-Madison, 1979.

LAFKY,B.L. 486
Women's intragenerational occupational mobility: a retrospective analysis of career patterns. PhD U. of California, Riverside, 1979.

LAHAT,M.B. 487
A woman's decision to work: demographic, cognitive and personality variables. PhD Temple U. 1976.

LEGGON,C.B. 488
The black female professional: role strains and status inconsistencies. PhD U. of Chicago, 1975.

LEIBOWITZ,A.S. 489
Women's allocation of time to market and non-market activities: differences by education. PhD Columbia U. 1972.

LELAND,C.A. 490
Women – men – work: women's career aspirations as affected by the male environment. PhD Stanford U. 1966.

LEMKAU,J.P. 491
Personality and background characteristics of women in asextypical occupations. PhD U. of Rhode Island, 1978.

LITTLE,D.M. 492
The effects of modeling of career counseling and sex of counselor on interest in non-traditional occupations for women. PhD Texas A&M U. 1973.

LOVE,B.B. 493
Self-esteem in women related to occupational status: a biracial study. PhD Northwestern U. 1974.

MCAFEE,J.W. 494
A study of the characteristics of women who select non-traditional occupational roles. PhD U. of California, Berkeley, 1973.

MCBRIDE,A.R. 495
The effects of an experiential workshop on professionally employed female and male college students' attitudes toward women in management. EdD Wayne State U. 1981.

MCCARTY,P.A. 496
One more time: why aren't women making it to the top? An investigation of the relationship between sex, self-confidence and feedback. PhD U. of Tennessee, 1981.

MCCLELLAN,H.E.H. 497
Women's roles and careers: conflict, compromise or fulfillment. PhD U. of Michigan, 1973.

MCILWEE,J.S. 498
Occupational segregation and the entry of women into non-traditional non-professional occupations. PhD U. of California, San Diego, 1980.

MCNEAL,I.M. 499
Occupational status and aspirations of women employees in selected occupations. EdD U. of Arkansas, 1976.

MACPHERSON,L.I. 500
The effects of social class on females' perceptions of traditional sex-role adherence in occupations. PhD Arizona State U. 1971.

MCPHERSON,M.B. 501
Bringing women in (finally): an analysis of women's effects and achievements in the American occupational structure. PhD U. of Nebraska-Lincoln, 1977.

MADANS,J.H. 502
Occupational segregation by sex: an analysis of the determinants of occupational sex composition among female workers. PhD U. of Michigan, 1978.

MALONE,B.L. 503
Relationship of black female administrators' mentoring experience and career satisfaction. PhD U. of Cincinnati, 1982.

MARCONI,K.M. 504
Predicting the occupational behavior of American women. PhD George Washington U. 1976.

MARSH,C.E. 505
The relationship of values, abilities, and selected demographic characteristics to career orientation in adult women. PhD U. Minnesota, 1981.

MARTIN,C.A. 506
Factors important to the vocational development of women police officers. EdD Andrews U. 1977.

MARTIN,R.P.T. 507
Self-disclosure of successful women administrators in Las Vegas, Nevada. PhD United States International U. 1981.

MATTHEWS,D.F. 508
Test of the concurrent validity of Holland's theory of careers with non-professional working women. PhD Ohio State U. 1977.

MAUPIN,R.J. 509
An analysis of job satisfaction and professional practice patterns of women certified public accountants. PhD U. of Arkansas, 1982.

MAZEN,A.M.M. 510
Personality, satisfaction, and models of occupational preferences and choices of women in female and male typical occupations. PhD Purdue U. 1982.

MELLON,S.J. 511
Instrumentality expectancy theory of work motivation: a modification and empirical test of its implications for disadvantaged black females in job training programs. PhD U. of Houston, 1975.

MISSIRIAN,A.K. 512
The process of mentoring in the career development of female managers. PhD U. of Massachusetts, 1980.

MOHSEN,A.S.A. 513
Job-seeking behavior and reemployability of female industrial workers. PhD Wayne State U. 1971.

MONKS,K.M. 514
Women in factory jobs: absenteeism, job satisfaction and work commitment of a sample of women workers. MLitt U. of Dublin, Trinity Coll. 1979.

MOORE,L.M. *515*
Distinguishing characteristics of women managers. PhD Wayne State U. 1977.

MOORE-WEST,M. *516*
Family, friends and partners: the search for intimacy and autonomy: a network analysis of working women's lives. PhD Bryn Mawr Coll. 1980.

MORGAN,D.H.J. *517*
Theoretical and conceptual problems in the study of social relations at work: an analysis of the differing definitions of women's roles in a Northern factory. PhD U. of Manchester, 1969.

MORGAN,K.C. *518*
A longitudinal study of the career patterns of women following the birth of a child. PhD Ohio State U. 1981.

MORGAN,M.R. *519*
A comparison of selected personality, biographical, and motivational traits among women athletes, physicians, and attorneys. PhD Ohio State U. 1973.

MORNEAU,R.H. *520*
Women in law enforcement: a social-psychological study. PhD U. of Southern California, 1975.

MOTTERN,J.A. *521*
A longitudinal study of factors affecting career plans of women. PhD U. of Illinois at Chicago Circle, 1980.

MOULLIET,D.K. *522*
Women employed in managerial and clerical occupations: differences in personality characteristics and role orientations. EdD U. of Cincinnati, 1979.

NELSON,M.C.W. *523*
The information channels used by certain professional women to gain employment: Arlington County, Virginia. PhD American U. 1973.

NIELSEN,L.H. *524*
An exploratory-descriptive study of mid-life women who have created first-time independent businesses. PhD U. of Oregon, 1981.

O'BRIEN,P.J. *525*
The American dual occupational structure as an influence on the sex differential in migration. PhD U. of Cincinnati, 1979.

O'REILLY,V.M. *526*
Personal adjustment and perceived locus of control in three groups of professional women. PhD California Sch. of Prof. Psych., Berkeley, 1977.

PARKER,S.R. *527*
The yin and the yang: do women managers have the best of both worlds? PhD Louisiana State U. and A&M Coll. 1976.

PARROW,A.A. *528*
Labor sectors and the status attainment process: race and sex comparisons. PhD Duke U. 1981.

PARSONS,H.D. *529*
Occupational role choices of graduate educated married women. PhD U. of Missouri-Columbia, 1972.

PATRICK,P.A. *530*
An investigation of the progress and problems of women in managerial positions in businesses and other institutions in the New Orleans area. PhD U. of Mississippi, 1979.

PATRICK,T.A. *531*
Personality and family background characteristics of women who enter male dominated professions. EdD Columbia U. 1973.

PATTERSON,R.A. *532*
Women in management: an experimental study of the effects of sex and marital status on job performance ratings, promotability ratings, and promotion decisions. PhD U. of Minnesota, 1975.

PATTISON,M.C. *533*
The relationship of competency as part of the self-concept to occupational role: a comparison study of females in three occupational roles. EdD Western Michigan U. 1982.

PEARSON,B.E. *534*
Women's entry into managerial positions at human service agencies: effect of applicant's locus of control and leadership style on employer preference for applicants. EdD U. of Maine, 1980.

PELLEGRINO,E.T. *535*
A case study of perceived formative and operational problems encountered by female entrepreneurs in retail and service firms located in the Roanoke, Virginia, standard metropolitan statistical area (SMSA). EdD Virginia Polytechnic Inst. and State U. 1979.

PEREZ,P.T. *536*
Problems of employed women in certain professional groups in the Philippines and their educational implications. PhD U. of Minnesota, 1954.

PERRY,M.P.H. *537*
Beyond suffrage and ideology: a study of achieving women in male intensive occupations in Orange County, New York. PhD Syracuse U. 1980.

PHILLIPS,L.E. *538*
Mentors and protégés: a study of the career development of women managers and executives in business and industry. PhD U. of California, Los Angeles, 1977.

PINCE,H.L. *539*
An assessment of attitudes of Wyoming counselors toward women and work. PhD U. of Wyoming, 1981.

POLLERT,A. 540
Women on the shopfloor: a study of women factory workers' experience and consciousness. PhD U. of Bristol, 1981.

PRATT,A.B. 541
Meanings of popular and unpopular occupations on the Strong vocational interest blank for women. PhD U. of Minnesota, 1970.

QUINN,B.J.C. 542
The influence of same-sex and cross-sex mentors on the professional development and personality characteristics of women in human services. EdD Western Michigan U. 1980.

RAMOS,M.C. 543
A study of black women in management. EdD U. of Massachusetts, 1981.

REED,C.B. 544
Professional women today: the relationship of their sex-role identities to anxiety, depression, hostility, and selected demographic variables. PhD U. of Florida, 1979.

REED,M.M. 545
A model of motivation for women in management. DBA Louisiana Tech U. 1981.

RETTIG,J.L. 546
Vocational choice patterns and personality characteristics of women in three occupational groups. PhD U. of California, 1962.

RIPLEY,T.M. 547
Discrimination against women professionals in a male-dominated profession by women consumers. PhD U. of Oregon, 1971.

ROBINSON,E. 548
Strain and dual role occupation among women. PhD City U. of New York, 1977.

ROBINSON,S.B. 549
The occupational aspirations of young black and white females: levels, atypicality and work commitment. PhD U. of Texas at Austin, 1978.

ROSENBERG,L.A. 550
Women and work in transition: their work participation, social class, sex role, and political attitudes and alienation. PhD U. of New Hampshire, 1981.

ROSENFELD,R.A. 551
Women's employment patterns and occupational achievements. PhD U. of Wisconsin, 1976.

ROSENTHAL,E.R. 552
Structural patterns of women's occupational choice. PhD Cornell U. 1974.

SAFAVI,Y.E. 553
The causes and degree of stress in female bank teller personnel in Southern California. PhD United States International U. 1980.

SAVAGE,H.L.H. 554
Field-dependence-independence and selected aspects of the academic and career evolution of women students in a broad-gauge discipline. PhD U. of Iowa, 1980.

SAWER,B.J. 555
Predictors of the wife's involvement in farm decision-making. EdD U. of British Columbia, 1972.

SAZAMA,R.M. 556
An investigation of the degree to which selected socio-psychological variables distinguish between young women who choose traditional occupations and young women who choose nontraditional occupations. PhD Southern Illinois U. at Carbondale, 1979.

SCHAFFER,K.T. 557
A study to examine the degree of self-fulfillment a woman experiences within her career goals and her awarenes of her own potential. PhD North Texas State U. 1978.

SCHAIN,W.S. 558
Psychodynamic factors affecting women's occupational choice: parent-child relations, expressed needs and level of ego development. EdD George Washington U. 1974.

SCHIFFER,D. 559
The interrelationship of sex-role stereotyping, locus of control, and organizational success among women in business. PhD New York U. 1977.

SCHINDLER,G.L. 560
Testosterone concentration, personality patterns, and occupational choice in women. EdD U. of Houston, 1979.

SCHISSEL,R.F. 561
Differential interest characteristics of career women. EdD U. of Nebraska, 1967.

SCHLESINGER,P.F. 562
A study of the lives of women managers at mid-career. EdD Boston U. Sch. of Educ. 1981.

SCHRADER,E.M. 563
Personality characteristics of the woman-to-woman mentor in the career arena. PhD U. of Colorado at Boulder, 1980.

SEASE,D.R. 564
An analysis of career development patterns among selected groups of women. PhD U. of Colorado at Boulder, 1979.

SEDER,M.A. 565
Vocational interest patterns of professional women. PhD U. of Minnesota, 1939.

SEGAL,J. 566
Profiles of successful women working in non-traditional occupations with special reference to their androgynous characteristics. PhD Fielding Inst. 1980.

SELVIDGE,N.J. *567*
Communication of influence: management style of women executives. PhD U. of Texas at Austin, 1977.

SHEA,K.V. *568*
Psychological health of high-achieving women executives. PhD Northwestern U. 1979.

SHELTON,P.B. *569*
Achievement motivation in professional women. PhD U. of California, Berkeley, 1967.

SHEPHERD,M.D. *570*
Analysis of practice patterns, stereotyping of women as managers, and perceptions of women in pharmacy by men and women pharmacy school graduates. PhD Purdue U. 1980.

SHERMAN,L.O. *571*
Women in the labor force: relationships among occupational attachments, family statuses, and poverty. PhD U. of Georgia, 1973.

SHERWOOD,E.B. *572*
The antecedents of career choice for women in two professions. PhD U. of Maryland, 1975.

SHURMER,P. *573*
Form and content: a study of social interaction in a business and professional women's club in Portsmouth. PhD U. of London (External), 1979.

SKVORC,L.R. *574*
Women in industry: alienation, satisfaction and change. PhD Case Western Reserve U. 1975.

SMITH,J.L. *575*
The effectiveness of values clarification training on selected personality dimensions and clarification of work values in women. PhD U. of Missouri-Kansas City, 1979.

SNYDER,D.F. *576*
A study of relationships between certain socio-economic factors and the Strong vocational interest blank for women. PhD U. of Minnesota, 1953.

SNYDER,P.P. *577*
Personality achievement variables and dogmatism level difference between androgynous and traditional feminine career professional women. PhD Catholic U. of America, 1977.

SNYDER,S.L. *578*
Perceived parental influence on women who choose male-dominated, sexually-equally chosen and traditional vocations. PhD U. of Iowa, 1975.

SOLOMON,G.N. *579*
Attitude towards retirement: a study of state employed females of Iowa. PhD Iowa State U. 1981.

STAFFORD,I.P. *580*
Sex-role attitudes as a moderator of women's occupational behaviour and self-esteem. EdD Rutgers U. 1982.

STAFFORD,R.L. *581*
An analysis of consciously recalled motivating factors and subsequent professional involvement for American women in New York State. EdD New York U. 1967.

STANFORD,S.M. *582*
Attitudes towards women: critical background predictors and the effect of a managerial development and feminist awareness seminar. PhD Northwestern U. 1975.

STEFANICS,E.T. *583*
Management-related success factors in the socialization processes of women in the field of leisure services. PhD U. of Minnesota, 1981.

STEINBERG,J.A. *584*
Climbing the ladder of success – in highheels: backgrounds of professional women. PhD Ohio State U. 1978.

STEVENSON,S.E. *585*
The effects of soloness on perceptions of the work environment by females in professional work groups. PhD U. of Cincinnati, 1980.

STOLESEN,S.N. *586*
Identity and intimacy development in working women. PhD California Sch. of Prof. Psych. Berkeley, 1981.

STRAND,K.J. *587*
Status attainment and sex segregation: a critique and reformulation of female occupational attainment research. PhD U. of Maryland, 1980.

SYLVESTER,M.A. *588*
The effects of parental occupational status, age at first fertility and educational attainment on the occupational prestige of young women. PhD U. of Colorado at Boulder, 1980.

TAYLOR,M.C. *589*
Sex and suicide: a study of female labor force participation and its effects upon rates of suicide. PhD Bowling Green State U. 1978.

TENZER,A. *590*
Parental influences on the occupational choice of career women in male dominated and traditional occupations. EdD Columbia U. Teachers Coll. 1977.

TEWARI,K.C. *591*
A study of women managers' need for achievement, affiliation, and power. PhD U. of Cincinnati, 1977.

THOMSON,S.G. *592*
Job attitudes of women in the labor force: structural and role-related correlates. PhD Bryn Mawr Coll. 1977.

TINSLEY,D.E.J. *593*
Characteristics of women with different patterns of career orientation. PhD U. of Minnesota, 1972.

TODD,J.P. 594
An analysis of predictor variables for completion of women soldiers' initial training in nontraditional service areas of the US army. EdD Catholic U. of America, 1981.

TOPOROFF,R. 595
Generating role types concerning the occupational participation of women in the twentieth century. PhD Washington State U. 1972.

TREAS,J.J. 596
Occupational attainment processes of mature American women. PhD U. of California, Los Angeles, 1976.

TUCKER,B.Z. 597
Feminine sex-role and occupational choice: a study of self and intergroup perceptions of three groups of women. EdD Temple U. 1970.

VANCE,C.L. 598
Comparison of the career development of women executives in institutions of higher education with corporate women executives. EdD Indiana U. 1978.

VANZANT,L.R. 599
Achievement motivation, sex-role, self-acceptance, and mentor relationship of professional females. EdD East Texas State U. 1980.

WADDELL,F.T. 600
Factors affecting choice, satisfaction and success in the female self-employed. PhD Ohio State U. 1982.

WALT,D.E. 601
The motivation for women to work in high level professional positions. PhD American U. 1962.

WARD,C.M. 602
The concurrent validity of Holland's theory for non-college-degreed black working women. PhD Ohio State U. 1980.

WARREN,C.E. 603
Perceptions of achievement: a study of women in two occupations in England and Canada. PhD U. of London, Goldsmith's Coll. 1979.

WEBER,E. 604
Characteristics of selected women managers: personal, educational, and career. EdD Columbia U. Teachers Coll. 1978.

WEIL,M.W. 605
A study of the factors affecting the role and role expectations of women participating or planning to participate in the labor force. PhD New York U. 1959.

WELSH,J.M. 606
Career development of women through adult life stages. PhD Arizona State U. 1978.

WERNER,J.E. 607
A study of Holland's theory of vocational choice as it applies to selected working women. EdD State U. of New York at Buffalo, 1969.

WEST,V.V.H. 608
Changes in motivation in girls in the first two years of employment. MA U. of London, Birkbeck Coll. 1959.

WESTRUM,H.J. 609
Self-concepts of gainfully employed women in two colleges in Washington State. EdD Oregon State U. 1975.

WHISLER,E.S. 610
Women's perceptions of factors affecting the nature and attachment of their ambitions: a three-generational study. PhD Indiana U. 1982.

WIERSMA,J.K. 611
Women's mid-life career change: on the methodology of personal transformation (2 vols). PhD U. of Michigan, 1979.

WILLIAMS,C.A. 612
An experimental study of the effects of assertiveness in the interpersonal communication style of a woman manager on perceptions of managerial effectiveness, credibility ratings, and attitudes towards women as managers. PhD Florida State U. 1979.

WILLIAMS,E. 613
Job satisfaction and self-concept as perceived by black female paraprofessional trainees. EdD U. of Miami, 1972.

WILLIAMS,S.E.W. 614
Relationship of personal characteristics and typicalness of occupation to occupational success of females. EdD Oklahoma State U. 1980.

WILSON,W.E.Jr. 615
A comparison of women clerical workers applying for a formal career change program with their non-applying peers on selected circumstantial and intrapersonal variables. PhD American U. 1979.

WISNIEWSKI,L.J. 616
Choosing a man's job: the effect of socialization on female occupational entry. PhD McMaster U. 1977.

WITYAK,N.L. 617
Occupational attainment resources and the life cycle patterns of young women. PhD George Washington U. 1982.

WOLF,R.V. 618
The value change theory of female educational participation and professional employment: a critique in the light of the evidence. PhD U. of California, Berkeley, 1977.

WOLFE,E.C. 619
Sex-role and moral judgment: a comparison of development in adult professional women. EdD Boston U. Sch. of Educ. 1982.

WOOD,E.M. *620*
Professional socialization experiences of women in non-traditional professions. PhD Georgia State U. Coll. of Arts and Sciences, 1980.

WOOD,M.E. *621*
Work values and job satisfaction of women office workers. PhD New York U. 1981.

WOOD,S.L. *622*
Let the army make a man of you: a cultural and situational analysis of women entering combat support occupations. PhD U. of Missouri-Columbia, 1978.

WRIGHT,M.S. *623*
Parent-child relations, achievement motivation and sex-role attitudes among black and white professional women in traditional and pioneer occupations. PhD State U. of New York at Buffalo, 1981.

YOGEV,S. *624*
Self-concept and role overload conflicts of professional women. PhD Northwestern U. 1979.

ZUCKERMAN,E.L. *625*
Attitudes toward power of management and non-management women. PhD City U. of New York, 1978.

6 Family Dynamics

General

See also **7** 20; **9** 373, 434, 596.

ANTHONY-WELCH,L.D. *1*
A comparative analysis of the black woman as transmitter of black values based on case studies of families in Ghana and among Jamaicans and Afro-Americans in Hartford, Connecticut. EdD U. of Massachusetts, 1976.

BALL,R.E. *2*
Expressive functioning and the black family life and domain satisfaction of black women. PhD U. of Florida, 1980.

BOLIN,W.D.W. *3*
Past ideals and present pleasures: women, work and the family, 1920–1940. PhD U. of Minnesota, 1976.

BROWN,A.H.III *4*
Modifying aggressive behaviors in families with pre-adolescent girls. PhD Brigham Young U. 1976.

DHALIWAL,M.S. *5*
Preferences in the size of family among senior girls in black segregated high schools in south, central and western parts of Mississippi. PhD Utah State U. 1970.

FOREMA N,M.A.L. *6*
The impact of Marxism and psychoanalysis on the concepts of woman and the family in the twentieth century. MA U. of Sheffield, 1977.

HIPPLER,A.E. *7*
Family structure and social structure: matrifocality in Hunter's Point. PhD U. of California, 1968.

HOLLANDER,M.R. *8*
Communication patterns in families with acting-out, depressed and normal adolescent daughters: a pilot study. PhD Michigan State U. 1979.

HUDSON,J.B. *9*
Feminine roles and family norms in a small city. PhD Cornell U. 1963.

LEPPEL,K. *10*
The relations among child quality, family structure, and the value of the mother's time. PhD Princeton U. 1980.

MILLER,J.R. *11*
Family communication and academic achievement of black adolescent females. PhD U. of Maryland, 1974.

MONSON,R.G. *12*
The relationship between nuclear family structure and female achievement. PhD U. of Florida, 1972.

MUDRICK,N.R. *14*
Income dynamics of families in the transition from male to female head. PhD Brandeis U. 1976.

MURPHY,M.D. *15*
Between the virgin and the whore: local community and the nuclear family in Seville, Spain. PhD U. of California, San Diego, 1978.

MUSA,K.E.E. *16*
Female role definitions, attitudes concerning appearance, and wife's family role. PhD U. of Wisconsin-Madison, 1973.

PETRONIO,S.S. *17*
The effect of interpersonal communication in the family on the family role satisfaction of the married woman. PhD U. of Michigan, 1979.

PRATT,L.V.V. *18*
The relationship of non-familial activity of wives to some aspects of family life. PhD U. of Michigan, 1955.

RODRIGUES,J. *19*
Continuity and change in urban Portuguese women's roles: emerging new household structures. PhD Columbia U. 1979.

RUTLEDGE,E.M. *20*
Marital and family relations of black women. PhD U. of Michigan, 1974.

SALAMON,S.B. *21*
In the intimate arena: Japanese women and their families. PhD U. of Illinois at Urbana-Champaign, 1974.

SHARP,S.A.A. *22*
The relationship between health patterns in the family and married women's dependency. PhD Virginia Polytechnic Inst. and State U. 1980.

STEINBERG,A.G. *23*
The concept of the feminine role in the American family: a study of the concept of the feminine role of 51 middle-class American families (2 vols). PhD New York U. 1957.

STUBER,M.C. 24
Feminine roles from the husbands' and daughters' points of view. EdD North Carolina State U. at Raleigh, 1979.

TATJE,T.A. 25
Mother-daughter dyadic dominance in black American kinship. PhD Northwestern U. 1974.

WEINSTOCK,D. 26
Early familial influences on women's competence. PhD California Sch. of Prof. Psych. 1981.

WEISMAN,C.S. 27
An analysis of female dominance in urban black families. PhD Johns Hopkins U. 1973.

Daughter-parent relationships

See also 4, 8, 24, 25; **8** 5, 273; **9** 255; **12** 1441, 1501; **17** 200–302, 372; **19** 233, 323; **20** 9.

ACHESON,K.R. 28
The relationship of father's sex-type and father-acceptance to personal adjustment and heterosexual behavior in adolescent girls. PhD Rosemead Grad. Sch. of Prof. Psych. 1977.

AMALFITANO,R.M.M. 29
A psychological investigation of similarities and differences between the friendship values and reported numbers of friends of adult women and their mothers and fathers. PhD U. of Wisconsin-Madison, 1980.

ANDERSON,R.M. 30
Mothers and daughters: their adult relationship. PhD U. of Minnesota, 1982.

ARCHBOLD,P.G. 31
Impact of parent-caring on women. DNS U. of California, San Francisco, 1980.

BARUCH,G.K. 32
Women and their work: a study of maternal influences upon women's attitudes toward career achievement. PhD Bryn Mawr Coll. 1970.

BERTI,B.E. 33
Women's relationships to their mothers at two stages of adulthood. PhD U. of Michigan, 1981.

BLOOM,J.B. 34
The effect of parental object loss upon the course of female psychosexual development. PhD Boston Coll. 1981.

BOND,A.M.H. 35
Grandmothers' attitudes and mothers' concerns. PhD Columbia U. 1961.

BROFMAN,J.J. 36
Effects of maternal employment, intrafamilial reinforcement for women achieving, and autonomy on daughters' achievement and achievement need. PhD Fordham U. 1980.

BROMBERG,E.M. 37
Mother-daughter relationships in later life: an investigation of effect on mutual aid patterns. DSW Columbia U. 1982.

BRUCE,J.A. 38
Maternal involvement in the courtship of daughters. PhD U. of Minnesota, 1972.

CARPENTER,J.C. 39
Patterns of self-disclosure and confirmation in mother-daughter communication. PhD Ohio State U. 1970.

CASCIO,R.C. 40
Perceived mother/daughter relationships: their effect on the sex-role choice of the daughter. EdD Northern Illinois U. 1979.

CASTELLANO,V.M. 41
The effects of early father absence and the level of antisocial behavior on the development of social egocentrism in adolescent Mexican American girls. PhD U. of Southern California, 1978.

CHESIRE,I.C. 42
Differences in mother and father interactions with four-, seven- and ten-year-old daughters in a free play situation. PhD U. of Rochester, 1982.

COOK,J.C.O. 43
Father-daughter dyadic relationships and girls' academic achievement. PhD Florida State U. 1982.

COUFAL,J.D. 44
Preventive-therapeutic programs for mothers and adolescent daughters: skills training versus discussion method. PhD Pennsylvania State U. 1975.

CRASTNOPOL,M.G. 45
Separation-individuation in a woman's identity vis-à-vis mother. PhD U. of Cincinnati, 1980.

DARLINGTON,S.J. 46
Young women's phenomenological sense of father and parental marital relationship and their relation to paternal loss. PhD Michigan State U. 1979.

DAVID,R.S. 47
Perceived parental child-rearing behaviors and achievement attribution patterns in adolescent females. PhD Fordham U. 1979.

DECKER,D.C. 48
The effects of father-absence during childhood on females' current marital satisfaction. PhD California Sch. of Prof. Psych., Los Angeles, 1982.

DICKINSON,J.A. 49
The impact of college females' relationships with their fathers and other selected variables on their relationships with males. EdD U. of Northern Colorado, 1979.

DORTON,J.R. *50*
The relationship between mothers' and daughters' sex-role attitudes and self-concepts in three types of family environments. PhD U. of Tennessee, 1979.

DUNHAM, T.F.Y. *51*
The effects of verbal and material flattery on the performance of girls differing in reported extent of maternal love-oriented discipline. PhD Duke U. 1963.

ECHOLS,C.V. *52*
Self-esteem, identification, and sex-role attitudes of mothers and daughters. PhD California Sch. of Prof. Psych., Fresno, 1979.

EVANS,A.E. *53*
Daughters' perceptions of the effects of having lived with an emotionally distant father. PhD California Sch. of Prof. Psych., San Diego, 1979.

FARMER,S.A. *54*
Maternal correlates of adolescents' self-concepts and self-esteem. PhD Georgia State U. Coll. of Arts and Sciences.

FAUGHEY,K.P. *55*
Parental model identification and sex-role typing in the daughter. PhD Yeshiva U. 1981.

FERGUSON,K.D. *56*
Major life decisions and life satisfactions: mothers and their daughters. PhD Kansas State U. 1979.

FINK,A. *57*
Effects of father absence and maternal employment on creative thinking ability in adolescent females. PhD Fordham U. 1980.

FISH,K.D. *58*
Paternal availability, family role structure, maternal employment, and personality development in late adolescent females. PhD U. of Massachusetts, 1969.

FLEMING,C.M. *59*
Perceptions of parents among white and Indian adolescent females. PhD U. of North Carolina at Chapel Hill, 1979.

GLASER,S.C.F. *60*
Parental influences on sex-role orientation in adolescent girls. PhD George Washington U. 1982.

GRANBERG,M.B.W. *61*
Parental attitudes toward women's roles and daughters' sex-role development. PhD Oregon State U. 1980.

GRAYSON,H.T.Jr. *62*
Psychosexual conflict in adolescent girls who experienced early parental loss by death. PhD Boston U. 1967.

GREEN,M.B. *63*
The relation of girls' sex-role preferences and perceptions of mothers' attitudes toward sex typing to social class and mothers' education level. PhD Columbia U. 1961.

GUINAN,J.G. *64*
Perception of parental identification and parental sanctioning attitudes as factors in female adolescent behavior. PhD Fordham U. 1974.

HARRISON,M.D. *65*
The relationship between perceived paternal attitude toward the daughter during childhood and subsequent tendency toward emotional disorders in the daughter. PhD U. of Maryland, 1973.

HENRICHS,M.H. *66*
Daughters' responses to paternal bereavement: a study of women who were latency age when their fathers died. PhD U. of Tennessee, 1978.

HOLMAN,A.M. *67*
The impact of father absence on achievement motivation in women. D.S.W. Adelphi U. Sch. of Social Work, 1977.

HOROWITZ,J.A. *68*
The relationship of father absence/presence and daughter's perception of mother's gender-related traits to the daughter's views of her own gender-related traits and women's roles. PhD New York U. 1982.

HOUSMAN,D.K. *69*
The relationship between suicidal behavior in female adolescents and the lack of empathic capacity and differentiation on the part of the mothers. EdD Boston U. Sch. of Educ. 1981.

IAZZETTA,V.B. *70*
Perceptions of mother and daughter as they pertain to certain aspects of the self-concept. EdD U. of Colorado, 1980.

JOHNSON,Z.C. *71*
Parental childrearing attitudes and the development of achievement motivation in daughters. PhD Boston U. Grad. Sch. 1974.

JONES,D.D. *72*
Shame as a referent of nonverbal behavior in mothers' and daughters' interactions. PhD U. of Minnesota, 1981.

JONES,J.H. *73*
Shameproneness in mothers and their daughters and the dynamics of shame in mothers' and daughters' verbal interactions. PhD U. of Minnesota, 1980.

JOSEPHS,L. *74*
Bereavement during adolescence: a study of adult women whose fathers or mothers died during their adolescence. PhD U. of Tennessee, 1981.

KARTELL,S.K. *75*
The father's influence on the woman's develop-

ment in the post-oedipal period. PhD Smith Coll. Sch. for Social Work, 1981.

KOEHLER,J.D. *76*
Sexual arousability and the adolescent father/daughter relationship. PhD U. of Louisville, 1982.

KOHN,S.C. *77*
Activity preference in mid-latency age girls: its relationship to perceptions of father's approved activity choices as a function of sibling position. PhD Boston Coll. 1981.

KOZIK,L.A.W. *78*
Factors affecting communication between the eleventh grade girl and her mother. PhD Ohio State U. 1958.

KRASNOW,E.J. *79*
A study of the maternal identification of adolescent girls: a comparison of girls who are adopted with girls who are living with their biological parents. DSW Catholic U. of America, 1969.

KRISTAL,J.L. *80*
The influence of the early father-daughter relationship on feminine sexual behavior. PhD U. of Texas at Austin, 1978.

LABRECQUE,S.V. *81*
Childrearing attitudes and observed behaviors of black fathers with kindergarten daughters. PhD Florida State U. 1976.

LAMY,P.C. *82*
An investigation of the activities and attitudes of fathers in relationship to their three to five year old daughters. PhD U. of Pittsburgh, 1975.

LEONARD,E.A. *83*
Concerning our girls and what they tell us: a study of some phrases of the confidential relationship of mothers and adolescent daughters. PhD Columbia U. 1930.

LETOURNEAU,A.E. *84*
Changes in inferred identification and mother-daughter interaction as a function of adolescent development. PhD Boston U. Grad. Sch. 1974.

LIDDELL,M.A. *85*
An investigation of the ways in which adolescent girls identify with their mothers, and perceive the social role of mothers. MPhil U. of London, Birkbeck Coll. 1967.

LIPPERT,J.G. *86*
Parental childrearing attitudes and behaviors as antecedents of self-actualization in females. PhD U. of Nebraska-Lincoln, 1975.

LISOWSKI,S.J. *87*
A study of the father- daughter relationship in childhood: its effect upon women's decisions involving motherhood and career. PhD U. of Wisconsin-Milwaukee, 1981.

LYNCH,M.E. *88*
Paternal androgyny, daughters' physical maturity, and achievement socialization in early adolescence. PhD Cornell U. 1982.

MACLAUGHLIN,J.A.D. *89*
Parental fighting and evoked verbal aggressive behavior in college-aged women. PhD U. of Connecticut, 1978.

MARTIN,D.H. *90*
The expressive domain of the father-adolescent daughter relationship defined by their perceptions and desires. EdD U. of Northern Colorado, 1978.

MEYER,R.M. *91*
Parent-daughter relationships and daughters' sexual self-concept, sexual behavior, and sexual values. PhD Yale U. 1977.

MICKLESON,K.K. *92*
The effects of father-daughter relationships on the development of achievement orientation and psychological androgyny in females. PhD California Sch. of Prof Psych., Berkeley, 1976.

MILLER,S.R. *93*
An investigation of the relationship between mothers' general fearfulnes, their daughters' locus of control, and general fearfulness in the daughter. PhD New York U. 1974.

MONROE-COOK,E. *94*
The relationships between college women's sex-role identities and self-esteem and their perceptions of their parents' sex-role identities, self-esteem and the quality of the parent-daughter relationship. PhD Michigan State U. 1979.

MOORE,G.H. *95*
Father-daughter relationships and the sexual views of adolescent girls. PhD Duke U. 1980.

MURPHY,A.W. *96*
Identification and authoritarianism in parent-child relationships with particular reference to mothers and their daughters. Phd New York U. 1971.

MUSSER,J.M. *97*
The relationship of father parenting style and father absence to feminine heterosexual relationships and personality adjustment. Psy.D. Rosemead Grad. Sch. of Prof. Psych. 1982.

NAWY,M. *98*
Toward a social role theory of mother-daughter relationships and resultant effects on daughters' sense of self-efficacy. PhD U. of California, Berkeley, 1981.

NORRIS,C.S. *99*
The effect of early childhood maternal deprivation on adolescent females' ability to delay gratification as measured by their response to varying reward schedules. PhD United States International U. 1980.

PARNELL,G.C. *100*
Relationships of mothers and daughters. PhD California Sch. of Prof. Psych., San Diego, 1976.

PETERS,A. *101*
An investigation of the relationshp between the inability of some women in psychotherapy to accept their female role and their perception of their mothers' attitudes toward the female role. PhD New York U. 1960.

PHILLIPS,D.J. *102*
A study of the concepts of family life held by a group of adolescent girls. MA U. of London, Inst. of Educ. 1952.

PICKARD,S.K. *103*
Separation issues between the late adolescent female and her mid-life mother. PhD Northwestern U. 1982.

PIPHER,M.B. *104*
The effects of father absence on the sexual development and adjustment of adolescent daughters and their mothers. PhD U. of Nebraska, 1977.

PRESTON,G.A. *105*
Parental role perceptions and identification in adolescent girls. PhD U. of Michigan, 1965.

RAGLAND,E.K. *106*
Social and sexual self-esteem in women and perceived father-daughter relationship during early adolescence. PhD U. of Oklahoma, 1977.

RUSSELL,H.L. *107*
Perceptions of mothers and fathers by normal, school problem and illegitimately pregnant adolescent white females. PhD U. of Houston, 1966.

SALOMON,M.M. *108*
Daughters remember mothers. PhD U. of Chicago, 1980.

SCHNEIDER,L.R. *109*
The relationship between identification with mother and home or career orientation in women. PhD Columbia U. 1962.

SENGBUSH,L.R. *110*
The father- daughter relationship and its influence on the reworking of separation individuation issues of adult college-educated women. PhD United States International U. 1981.

SHAPIRO,J.A. *111*
Paternal death during early adolescence and its effects on women's subsequent relationships with men. PhD United States International U. 1980.

SPIELER,S.M. *112*
The early father-daughter relationship: missing link in the psychoanalytic understanding of women's love of men. PsyD U. of New Jersey, 1981.

STEINDEL,C.D. *113*
The relationship of self-esteem and life satisfaction to attachment between elderly mothers and their middle-aged daughters. PhD Michigan State U. 1982.

STEVENS,J.G. *114*
Determinants of the difference between mother's educational expectation for her daughter and the mother's own education. PhD U. of Illinois at Urbana-Champaign, 1980.

STRAGHAN,N.B. *115*
The relationships between ordinal position, reaction to failure and anger toward mother among first and second born females. PhD U. of Detroit, 1980.

STRINGER- MOORE,D.M. *116*
Effects of parental child-rearing attitudes and attitudes toward feminism on female children's self-esteem and attitudes toward feminism. PhD U. of California, Davis, 1981.

SWORDS,L.F. *117*
Body image: a study of the relationship between the body image of adult daughters and the body image of their mothers. PhD California Sch. of Prof. Psych., Berkeley, 1980.

TATJE,T.A. *118*
Mother- daughter dyadic dominance in black American kinship. PhD Northwestern U. 1974.

ULTON,M.P. *119*
A study of parent-child relationships with emphasis on home discipline as it affects the conduct and personality of a group of pre-adolescent girls. PhD Catholic U. of America, 1936.

URBANK,A.J. *120*
The relationship between level of object relations and degree of autonomy in mothers and their adult daughters. PhD United States International U. 1980.

VAN BERGEN,A. *121*
Relationship of early father absence on sexual attitudes and self-concept of adult women. PhD United States International U. 1976.

VIGNOLA,S.L. *122*
The American Jewish woman's socialization process: the study of mother-daughter relationship as it affects the daughter's future choice of a husband. DSW Catholic U. of America, 1979.

VOGELSONG,E.L. *123*
Preventive-therapeutic programs for mothers and adolescent daughters: a follow-up of relationship enhancement versus discussion and booster versus no-booster methods. PhD Pennsylvania State U. 1975.

WALSTEDT,J.J. *124*
The role of the father in the socialization of altruism and 'otherness' in women. PhD Rutgers U. 1974.

WEAVER,F.J. *125*
Selected aspects of father-daughter interaction and daughter's instrumentalness in late adolescence. EdD Pennsylvania State U. 1968.

WEISHAUS,S.S. *126*
Determinants of affect of middle-aged women towards their aging mothers. PhD U. of Southern California, 1978.

WILBURNE,C.N . *127*
The relationship between a mother's sex-role orientation, her satisfaction with that role, and her daughter's personality characteristics. PhD California Sch. of Prof. Psych. 1978.

WINER ,F. *128*
The relationship of certain attitudes toward the mother to sex-role identity. PhD New York U. 1981.

WINKELSTEIN,F. *129*
An experimental study to evaluate a course in general semantics for mothers and their adolescent daughters in terms of changes in speech patterns and habits. PhD Columbia U. 1961.

ZIFFER,J.M.W. *130*
Sex-role orientation and vocational orientation of mothers and daughters. PhD Iowa State U., 1980.

Marriage

General

See also 820, 829; **9** 147, 186, 201, 218, 364, 541; **18** 277, 281; **19** 183.

ALSBROOK,R.L. *131*
Sexual discrimination in marriage: women as a minority group member in the marital dyad. EdD U. of Tulsa, 1975.

AROCHO,A. *132*
Perceived marital adjustment of women with advanced degrees as related to their interpersonal relationships. PhD Texas Woman's U. 1980.

AYLING,R.I. *133*
The role anticipations of student ministers' wives. PhD Boston U. 1965.

BAHR,R.F.S. *134*
The marital power structure and attitudes toward women's liberation and marital equality. PhD Washington State U. 1977.

BAKER,B.J. *135*
Family change and coping patterns of wives of prisoners. PhD U. of Nebraska-Lincoln, 1980.

BAUER,J.W. *136*
Determinants of wife's estimate of and satisfaction with amount of family net worth. PhD U. of Illinois at Urbana-Champaign, 1981.

BELOTE,G.A. *137*
The role of the college president's wife. PhD Michigan State U. 1974.

BOCCELLARI,A.A. *138*
Sex-role orientation among working-class and professional middle-class women in relation to their husbands' power needs. PhD California Sch. of Prof. Psych., Berkeley, 1979.

BONTRAGER-LEHMAN,C. *139*
The sex-roles and life-styles of married women in relation to mental health indices of the California Psychological Inventory (CPI). PhD U. of Ottowa, 1980.

BROWN,E.C. *140*
An investigation of risk-taking and fear of failure in married and divorced women. PhD Texas Woman's U. 1978.

BRUMFIELD,D.R. *141*
Identifying and corroborating differential role expectations of the wife of the pastor/minister among the students and faculty at Gulf-Coast Bible College. DMin United Theological Seminary, 1980.

CORNETT,S.J.F. *142*
The effects of structured learning environments on coping abilities and cognitive achievement of wives whose husbands have suffered heart attacks. PhD Ohio State U. 1981.

CROSS,J.R. *143*
Characteristics of select married women who have male friends: a study of sex-role transcendence. EdD East Texas State U. 1978.

CRUTE,B .J. *144*
Wives of professional athletes: an inquiry into the impact of professional sport on the home and family. PhD Boston Coll. 1981.

DENTON,G.W. *145*
Role attitudes of the minister's wife. PhD Columbia U. 1959.

DONAHUE,M.A. *146*
Characteristics of American corporate wives in Taipei as related to satisfaction. PhD Michigan State U. 1980.

ETHRIDGE,V.K. *147*
Determinants of the wife's achieved and expected intergenerational social mobility. PhD U. of Illinois at Urbana-Champaign, 1978.

FINERAN,L.J. *148*
A study of the relationship of achievement motivation to attribution and activity characteristics of military wives. EdD Coll. of William and Mary in Virginia, 1979.

FINLAYSON,E.M. *149*
A study of the wife of the army officer: her academic and career preparation, her current employ-

ment, and volunteer services. EdD George Washington U. 1969.

FOSTER,L.W. *150*
A study of perceived coping skills of career military wives. PhD Kent State U. 1982.

FOWLKES,M.R. *151*
The wives of professional men: a study of the interdependency of family and careers. PhD U. of Massachusetts, 1977.

GOCHROS,J.S. *152*
When husbands come out of the closet: a study of the consequences for their wives. [Homosexual tendencies in husbands.] PhD U. of Denver, 1982.

HAMMOND,E.A. *153*
The relationships between selected factors and the adjustment of air force career officers' wives during separation created by unaccompanied PCS tours. PhD Ohio State U. 1975.

HARDER,J.M. *154*
Self-actualization, mood, and personality adjustment in married women. EdD Columbia U. 1969.

HEALEY,D.E. *155*
Attitudes, status, and psychological functioning of women in egalitarian and traditional marriages. PhD Boston U. Grad. Sch. 1980.

HELFRICH,M.L. *156*
The social role of the executive's wife. PhD U. of Pittsburgh, 1959.

HUCKABAY,M.A. *157*
Women and their marriages: perceptions of influence and the boundaries of self. PhD Case Western Reserve U. 1980.

HUGHES,M.A . *158*
Attitudes of wives of United States army officers in the continental United States toward their educational and employment opportunities. EdD Arizona State U. 1973.

IU,C.R. *159*
Ethnic and economic correlates of marital satisfaction and attitude towards divorce of Chinese American women. DSW U. of California, Los Angeles, 1982.

JERIES,N. *160*
Determinants of wife's perception of selected aspects of husband-wife verbal communication. PhD U. of Illinois at Urbana-Champaign, 1973.

JONES,S.B. *161*
When families move: adaptations of married women to geographic mobility. PhD U. of Washington, 1976.

JOSLIN,D. *162*
Working-class daughters, middle-class wives: social identity and self-esteem among women upwardly mobile through marriage. PhD New York U. 1979.

JUDD,L.C. *163*
Communication in marriage from the wife's perspective. PhD Hofstra U. 1980.

KATZ,S.M. *164*
American purdah: an examination of the role of executives' wives. DBA Golden Gate U. 1979.

KONANC,J.A.T. *165*
Adult married women: evaluative attitude towards other women as related to various self-attitudes, personality characteristics and behavior. PhD U. of North Carolina at Chapel Hill, 1972.

LEE,Y.K. *166*
Determinants of wife's satisfaction with husband's job. PhD U. of Illinois at Urbana-Champaign, 1980.

LEWIS,E.M. *167*
The effects of intensity and probability on the preference for immediate versus delayed aversive stimuli in women with various levels of inter-spousal conflict. PhD U. of Illinois at Chicago Circle, 1980.

MCCAIN,H.B.Jr. *168*
The social network and wife as companion. PhD Emory U. 1973.

MCEVOY,P.T. *169*
Navy wives' knowledge of, interest in, and willingness to utilize naval and civilian support services during deployments. PhD United States International U. 1982.

MCFADD,A.C.M. *170*
Rehabilitation of married male alcohol abusers and wives' level of participation in treatment. PhD California Sch. of Prof. Psych., San Diego, 1976.

MARQUIT,J.B. *171*
A comparison of self-concept and locus of control between wives of practicing physicians and wives of physicians in training. PsyD Nova U. Sch. of Prof. Psych. 1982.

MARTIN MATTHEWS,A.E. *172*
Wives' experiences of relocation: status passage and the moving career. PhD McMaster U. 1980.

MOWDE,J.L. *173*
Factors affecting female power in the conjugal relationship. PhD Ohio State U. 1981.

NESBITT,D.G. *174*
The role of the physician's wife in the practice location decision. PhD U. of Iowa, 1979.

NICE,F.E. *175*
The pastor's wife as a participant in a co-counseling ministry in the Mennonite church. DMin Drew U. 1982.

O'FARREL,T.J. *176*
Marital stability among wives of alcoholics: reported antecedents of a wife's decision to separate from or endure her alcoholic husband. PhD Boston U. Grad. Sch. 1975.

OLSEN,V.F. *177*
Loneliness in marriage: women's experiences and perceptions. EdD Columbia U. Teachers Coll. 1980.

OURSLER,J.D. *178*
The role of extramarital involvement in personal adjustment, marital adjustment, and counseling of middle-class women. PhD St John's U. 1981.

OWENS,L.H. *179*
Self-concepts of adult married women and their relationship to feminine adolescent identity resolution with implications for counselors. PhD U. of Toledo, 1967.

POWELL,G.S. *180*
The effects of training wives in communication skills upon the marital satisfaction of both spouses. PhD U. of Georgia, 1977.

PUSKAR,K.R. *181*
Reactions of women to a geographic move resulting from husband's job transfer. DrPH U. of Pittsburgh, 1981.

RAETZKE,C.P. *182*
The wife's perception of conjugal influence in urban disadvantaged families. PhD U. of Illinois at Urbana-Champaign, 1975.

RITTER,M.I.H. *183*
The minister's wife: an exploration study on role conflict and self-actualization. PhD Fielding Inst. 1981.

ROBINSON,E.S. *184*
The effects of social drinking and sex-role orientation on selected nonverbal behaviors of married women. EdD Indiana U. 1982.

SELZER,T. *185*
Selected factors and combination of factors which predict marital satisfaction for married women within selected stages across the family life cycle. PhD U. of Illinois at Urbana-Champaign, 1977.

SIPERSTEIN,J.W.R. *186*
An assessment of communications and role perceptions of career and non-career wives with their husbands. EdD Rutgers U. 1978.

SMITH,T.R. *187*
The pastor-husband and wife: correlates of theological perspectives. Marital adjustment, job satisfaction, and wife's participation in church activities. PhD Florida State U. 1976.

SPEDDING,J.V. *188*
Wives of the clergy: a sociological analysis of wives of ministers of religion in four denominations. PhD U. of Bradford, 1975.

STRUCKHOFF,D.R. *189*
Adjustment of prisoners' wives to separation. PhD Southern Illinois U. at Carbondale, 1977.

STARR,D.L. *190*
Wife dependency as related to marital adjustment, masculinity-femininity, and perceptual congruence. PhD U. of Florida, 1973.

STEIN,K.G. *191*
Development and validation of a woman's marital psychological abuse scale. PhD Hofstra U. 1982.

TRAVE-DANIELEWICZ,A.J. *192*
Determinants of the wife's perception of income adequacy. PhD U. of Illinois at Urbana-Champaign, 1978.

UNDERWOOD,C.C. *193*
Wives of recovering alcoholics: their personal concerns during their husbands' first eighteen months of sobriety. PhD U. of Southern California, 1982.

URBAN,T.S. *194*
Wives' needs as related to perceptions of the husbands' post mental hospital behavior. EdD Pennsylvania State U. 1968.

USHER,S. *195*
Self-esteem in the mature married woman as a function of working status and feminist attitudes. PhD York U. 1977.

WEBERSHAPIRO,D.G. *196*
The marriage relationship of women writing doctoral dissertations. PhD California Sch. of Prof. Psych., Berkeley, 1977.

WEBSTER,T.N. *197*
An investigation of female assertiveness in marital situations. PhD U. of Georgia, 1977.

WEHRLE,J.M. *198*
The marriage squeeze: perceptions and adaptations of black female doctorates. PhD Southern Illinois U. at Carbondale, 1982.

WILEN-BERG,E. *199*
The role conflicts of married women students: effects upon psychological stress and marital adjustment and influence of husband's role help. PhD Cornell U. 1982.

WIMBERLY,C.E. *200*
Self-actualization and the minister's wife. PhD United States International U. 1979.

YUEN,J .C. *201*
Determinants of the wife's perception of economic well-being among 'disadvantaged' families. PhD U. of Illinois at Urbana-Champaign, 1976.

Divorce and separation

See also **18** 284; **20** 13.

BALLARD,B.A. *202*
Role satisfaction of divorced mothers in single-parent families as a function of social networks and sex-role orientation. PhD California Sch. of Prof. Psych., Berkeley, 1980.

BROWN,P. *203*
Psychological distress and personal growth among women coping with marital dissolution. PhD U. of Michigan, 1976.

BURLAGE,D.D. *204*
Divorced and separated mothers: combining the responsibilities of breadwinning and childrearing. PhD Harvard U. 1978.

BUTZ,T.E. *205*
Adjustment to marital separation in women. PhD Indiana U. 1980.

COHEN,J.B.B. *206*
The impact of marital dissolution on the adjustment and childrearing attitudes of mothers. PhD California Sch. of Prof. Psych., Los Angeles, 1981.

COLLETTA,N.D. *207*
Divorced mothers at two income levels: stress, support, and childrearing practices. PhD Cornell U. 1978.

CUSICK,K.M. *208*
A comparison of the constructs and resource choices of divorced and married mothers. PhD California Sch. of Prof. Psych., San Diego, 1978.

GILIUS,T.A. *209*
Divorced mothers: transitional problems, patterns of resource utilization, and coping effectiveness. PhD U. of Texas at Austin, 1980.

GONGLA,P.A. *210*
Social relationships after marital separation: a study of women with children. PhD Case Western Reserve U. 1977.

GUADAGNO,M.A.N. *211*
Selected factors affecting perceived need for life insurance by divorced mothers. PhD Ohio State U. 1978.

HERRICK,J.E. *212*
An in-depth study of four divorced working-class women. EdD U. of Massachusetts, 1977.

ISENHART,M.A. *213*
Divorced women: a comparison of two groups who have retained or relinquished custody of their children. PhD California Sch. of Prof. Psych., San Diego, 1979.

JOHNSON,P.J. *214*
Non-routine management of employment and family responsibilities by divorced mothers. PhD Ohio State U. 1978.

KELLY,J.M. *215*
A phenomenological study of a woman's experience separating from marriage and developing a single lifestyle. PhD U. of Pittsburgh, 1979.

KIZER,E.J. *216*
An exploratory analysis of women's communicative behavior, adjustment, and role definition following divorce. PhD Purdue U. 1978.

KOHAN,E.G. *217*
An investigation into factors affecting postdivorce adjustment of mothers and their preschool age sons. PhD California Sch. of Prof. Psych., Los Angeles, 1980.

L'HOMMEDIEY,T.R. *218*
The divorce experience of working- and middle-class women: a descriptive study. PhD U. of Pittsburgh, 1981.

MCCABE,M.E. *219*
Coping strategies of urban divorced women at the time of divorce and six months later. PhD U. of Wisconsin-Madison, 1981.

MARTIN,D.A. *220*
Patterns of responses to divorce of custodial mothers and their children. PhD U. of Texas at Austin, 1980.

MEYERS,J.C. *221*
The adjustment of women to marital separation: the effects of sex-role identification and of stage in family life, as determined by age and presence or absence of dependent children. PhD U. of Colorado at Boulder, 1976.

MITCHELL,K.W.H. *222*
Sense of competence and well-being in suburban divorced and remarried mothers. EdD Harvard U. 1979.

PAIS,J.S. *223*
Social-psychological predictors of adjustment for divorced mothers. PhD U. of Tennessee, 1978.

PETIET,C.A. *224*
Grief in divorcees and widows: similarities, differences, and treatment implications. PhD California Sch. of Prof. Psych., Berkeley, 1982.

REINHART,G.E. *225*
One-parent families: a study of divorced mothers and adolescents using social climate and relationship styles. PhD California Sch. of Prof. Psych., Berkeley, 1977.

SCHOICKET,S.G. *226*
Affinal relationships of the divorced mother. EdD Columbia U. 1968.

STORM,C.L. *227*
The communication ecology of the social networks of separated women. PhD Purdue U. 1982.

TAKAI,R.T. *228*
Marital separation in first marriages and remar-

riages of women: an examination of divergent patterns. PhD Johns Hopkins U. 1981.

WIGGINS,B.L. 229
The meaning of motherhood and career for the divorced career mother. EdD Columbia U. Teachers Coll. 1981.

Widowhood

See also **9** 105; **12** 1749 **18** 270, 271, 279, 280, 284, 309.

ARLING,G.W. 230
Social involvement and morale: a study of elderly widows. PhD U. of Illinois at Urbana-Champaign, 1974.

ARONSON,M.K. 231
A bio-psycho-social survey of community elderly widows: implications for comprehensive care. EdD Columbia U. Teachers Coll. 1980.

BARRELL,L.M. 232
From wife to widow: the transitional process. PhD U. of Illinois at Chicago Circle, 1980.

BARRETT,C.J.C. 233
The development and evaluation of three therapeutic group interventions for widows. PhD U. of Southern California, 1974.

BAUM,J. 234
An exploration of widowhood: coping patterns adopted by a population of widows. PhD U. of Wisconsin, 1979.

BETTIS,S.R. 235
Assertiveness training for widowed women. PhD U. of Oregon, 1978.

BIGGER,T.A. 236
The relationship between the grief reaction of older widows and their level of ego development. PhD U. of Florida, 1981.

BOTTAR,T.A. 237
The economic well-being and social adjustment of mid-life widows. PhD Syracuse U. 1981.

BURDETTE-FINN,P.M. 238
Evaluation of a model for prevention of maladjustment in young widows. PhD Loyola U. of Chicago, 1980.

CONSTANTINO,R.E.B. 239
Nursing care of widows in grief and mourning through bereavement crisis intervention. PhD U. of Pittsburgh, 1979.

FARRA,R.R. 240
The widow/bureaucratic linkage during the transition to widowhood: an exploratory study. PhD Florida State U. 1982.

FERGUSON,T. 241
Conflict and the young widow. PhD Columbia U. 1970.

FITZELLE,G.T. 242
The personal adjustment of a selected group of widows of 55 years and older. PhD Cornell U. 1953.

FUDIN,C.E. 243
The stresses and strains experienced by women who have lost husbands to cancer. PhD Rutgers U. 1982.

GIBBS,J.M. 244
The social world of the older widow in the non-metropolitan community. PhD Kansas State U. 1979.

GOSSETT,R.R. 245
So few men: a study of black widowhood. PhD Syracuse U. 1976.

GULLO,S.V. 246
A study of selected psychological, psychosomatic, and somatic reactions in women anticipating the death of a husband. PhD Columbia U. 1974.

HARVEY,C.D.H. 247
Widowhood: predicting social-psychological consequences. PhD Washington State U. 1973.

HAYS,D.R. 248
Perceived needs for support of women who participate in a Red Cross widows' program. EdD Columbia U. Teachers Coll. 1977.

HEINEMANN, G.D.P. 249
Determinants of primary support system strength among urban, widowed women: does life stage make a difference? PhD U. of Illinois at Chicago Circle, 1980.

HELSING,K.J. 250
Factors associated with mortality after widowhood. ScD Johns Hopkins U. 1981.

HIRSCH,S.M. 251
An exploratory study of the social functioning of widows: the relationship between the presence or absence of forewarning, family life cycle stage, and locus of control of the widow. EdD Columbia U. Teachers Coll. 1980.

HORNUNG,K.L. 252
Loneliness among older urban widows. PhD U. of Nebraska-Lincoln, 1980.

KEITH,J.G.B. 253
The relationship between the adjustment of the widowed and social support, self-esteem, grief experience, and selected demographic variables. EdD U. of Tennessee, 1982.

KLINE,K.L. 254
Determinants of income change among non-elderly widowed women living in a metropolitan area. PhD U. of Illinois at Urbana-Champaign, 1973.

LAREAU,L.S. 255
Widowhood in a rural environment: adaptation as

role modification. PhD U. of Illinois at Urbana-Champaign, 1977.

MACDONALD,J.R. *256*
Widows de facto and de jure: AFDC and OASDI. DSW Yeshiva U. 1982.

MATTHEWS,S.H. *257*
Social-psychological aspects of being an old, widowed mother in American society. PhD U. of California, Davis, 1976.

MORGAN,L.A. *258*
Widowhood and change: a longitudinal analysis of middle-aged women. PhD U. of Southern California, 1979.

MOSS,W.D. *259*
An assessment of self-esteem and perceived needs of widowed and divorced women. EdD U. of Kentucky, 1981.

NEALE,A.V. *260*
Social and psychological well-being in widowhood. PhD Wayne State U. 1981.

PAUL,P.B. *261*
Adaptation in widowhood among older women. DSN U. of Alabama, Birmingham, 1981.

ROCHE,E. *262*
The widow, her children, and their worlds: changes in the pattern of relationships. MA U. of Newcastle upon Tyne, 1981.

ROOK,K.S. *263*
Social networks and well-being of elderly widowed women. PhD U. of California, Los Angeles, 1980.

ROWE,J.O. *264*
An ethnography of women's experiences with a dying husband and their grief and redefinition of self. PhD Georgia State U. Coll. of Educ. 1982.

SAUNDERS,J.M. *265*
A clinical study of widow bereavement involving various modes of death. DNS U. of California, San Francisco, 1979.

SMITH,W.J. *266*
The desolation of Dido: patterns of depression and death anxiety in the adjustment and adaptation behaviors of a sample of variably-aged widows. ScD Boston U. 1975.

STEIN,M.K. *267*
The relationship of psychological and physical symptomatology and conditions relating to widowhood. PhD Kent State U. 1982.

STEINHART,F.A. *268*
The occupational reengagement of widows in the Chicago standard metropolitan statistical area. PhD Loyola U. of Chicago, 1976.

STERNBERG,M.B. *269*
The long-term adaptations of young and middle-aged widows to the loss of a spouse. EdD Columbia U. Teachers Coll. 1982.

STOLL,M.L. *270*
Predictors of middle-aged widows' psychological adjustment. PhD California Sch. of Prof. Psych., Los Angeles, 1981.

TAICH,A.P. *271*
Reference to other associations and perceived stress among older widows. PhD Saint Louis U. 1980.

TATE,N.P. *272*
Social interactional patterns and life satisfaction of a group of elderly black widows. PhD Brandeis U. 1981.

THOMAS,J.A. *273*
The effect of a life management skills program on depression and grief in widows. PhD Michigan State U. 1982.

VACHON,M.L.S. *274*
Identity change over the first two years of bereavement: social relationships and social support in widowhood. PhD York U. 1979.

VANCOEVERING,V.G.R. *275*
An exploratory study of middle-aged and older widows to investigate those variables which differentiate high and low life satisfaction. PhD Wayne State U. 1973.

ZIMMER,J.L. *276*
Adjustment of older women to widowhood. PhD California Sch. of Prof. Psych., San Diego, 1975.

Motherhood

See also **2** 22, 43, 65; **5** 122–206; **18** 251–587; **10** 18; **12** 375, 2966; **13** 10.

General

ABBE,A.E. *277*
The relationship of maternal attitudes to the diagnostic category of the child: a descriptive study, as seen in the Queens College educational clinic during one year. PhD New York U. 1956.

ACKERMAN,J.Z. *278*
A study of the mother-infant relationship in the first year of life. PhD New Sch. for Social Research, 1975.

ADAMS,D.J. *279*
A comparison of confidence and degree of contentment in parental role of custodial and noncustodial stepmothers. PhD Florida State U. 1982.

ADJEL,K. *280*
Maternal behavior and cognitive development. PhD U. of Strathclyde, 1975.

ADLER,L.M. 281
Mother-toddler interaction: content, style, and relations to symbolic development. PhD Rutgers U. 1982.

ALBRECHT,H.G. 282
Maternal patterns of behavior management: a comparison of two models. PhD Georgia State U. Coll. of Educ. 1979.

ALLEN,W.M. 283
Maternal antecedents to important aspects of child self-structure. PhD U. of Pittsburgh, 1978.

ALPER,R. 284
Mother-infant interaction and infant cognitive competence. PhD Yeshiva U. 1982.

ALTMAN,C. 285
The relationships between patterns of maternal attitudes and child personality structure at latency age. PhD U. of Chicago, 1955.

ANAGNOSTOPOULOU,I. 286
Mother-infant interaction and attachment behavior: one-year-old infants of mothers with mental disorders and normal mothers. PhD U. of Rochester, 1974.

ANDERSON,C.J. 287
Informing mothers about the behavioral characteristics of their infants: the effects on mother-infant interaction. PhD U. of Texas at Austin, 1978.

ANDERSON,M.B. 288
Childrearing practices of negro migrant mothers in three Pennsylvania counties. EdD Pennsylvania State U. 1965.

ANTONELL, A. 289
The influence of mother-infant interaction on infant development to three months: a study of cognitive and physical development within a social relationship. PhD U. of Bristol, 1980.

APPELBAUM ,R. 290
Race, class, and maternal childrearing: a study of differential behavior in a metropolitan setting. PhD U. of Chicago, 1972.

APPLE,S. 291
The relationship among a woman's psychological adjustment, her marital satisfaction, and the presence or absence of cerebral palsy in her child. PhD Ohio U. 1980.

ARCO,C.M. 292
A change of pace: an investigation of the saliency of maternal temporal style in mother-infant play. PhD West Virginia U. 1978.

ARONOWITZ,E. 293
Associations between the self-observation capacity of children and maternal attitudes. PhD U. of Chicago, 1970.

ASSAD,C. 294
The effects of children's difficulty with achievement tasks on maternal behavior: a comparison of clinic and non-clinic samples. PhD U. of Toledo, 1979.

ATKIN, R.R. 295
Maternal antecedents of children's role taking. PhD U. of Chicago, 1975.

AUGUST,C. 296
Sex-role definition, professional work status, altruistic motivation for parenthood, and ego development in college graduate mothers of school-age children. PhD New York U. 1979.

BADGELEY,E.W. 298
Aspects of interaction between infants and mother-surrogates. EdD Columbia U. 1967.

BADOCK,N.G. 299
Mothers' attribution of responsibility for emotional illness and placement of children in psychiatric treatment. PhD Tulane U. 1967.

BAILEY,M.M. 300
An observational study of mothers' commands and their young children's responses. PhD Michigan State U. 1977.

BAKER,L.S. 301
The relationship of maternal understanding of the child and attitudes towards the child to the adjustment of the child. PhD New York U. 1955.

BANNON,J.A. 302
The social reinforcement network of the single mother: its relationship to adjustment. PhD U. of Utah, 1980.

BANVELOS,D.J. 303
A comparative study of maternal childrearing expectations among Mexican American, Mexican American migrant, Anglo parents and Anglo teachers of preschool, kindergarten, first and second grades. EdD Wayne State U. 1982.

BARAN,J.A. 304
The mutual regulation of mother-child phonological behavior. PhD Purdue U. 1979.

BARBER,B . 305
A study of the attitudes of mothers of mentally retarded children as influenced by socioeconomic status. PhD U. of Southern California, 1963.

BARDIN,A. 306
Maternal depression and the development of young children. PhD U. of Cambridge, 1983.

BARKER ,G.F. 307
Self-esteem of the unwed mother. EdD Boston U. 1967.

BARRETT,R.K. 308
A study of the effects of maternal self-esteem on maternal caregiving behavior and relational

esteem in the family system. PhD U. of Pittsburgh, 1977.

BARTH,R.P. *309*
Coping skills training for school-age mothers. DSW U. of California, Berkeley, 1982.

BAUDIN,J.M. *310*
Mother-infant relations in different ethnic groups living in London. PhD U. of London, Bedford Coll. 1982.

BEAVERS,W.J. *311*
A study of the mothers of retarded children and the concept of pathogenesis utilizing the thematic apperception test. PhD U. of Georgia, 1975.

BELLINGER,D. *312*
The structure of maternal speech acts. PhD Cornell U. 1977.

BERG,R.M. *313*
A study of a group of unwed mothers receiving aid to dependent children. DSW U. of Pennsylvania, 1962.

BERNARDUCCI,F.P.Jr. *314*
Attitudes of mothers of cerebral palsied children toward the habilitative therapies. EdD U. of Massachusetts, 1979.

BERRY,R.E. *315*
The relationship between infant temperament and the organizational pattern of infant-mother attachment behavior. PhD York U. 1980.

BIEBER,T.B. *316*
A comparison study of negro wed and unwed mothers. PhD Columbia U. 1963.

BIELKE,P.A. *317*
The relationship of maternal ego development to parenting behavior and attitudes. PhD U. of Minnesota, 1979.

BILKER,L.M. *318*
Locus of internal-external control expectancy and expectancy changes of disadvantaged mothers. PhD U. of Florida, 1970.

BIRD,H.R. *319*
The relationship between maternal attitudes towards sons, sons' self-attitudes, and maternal awareness of sons. PhD Columbia U. 1958.

BIRDENBAUM,A. *320*
Non-institutionalized roles and role formation: a study of mothers of mentally retarded children. PhD Columbia U. 1968.

BISHOP,L. *321*
Some relationships between mothers' and infants' behaviors. PhD U. of Chicago, 1960.

BLANK,M.S. *322*
Some affects of maternal behavior on infant development. PhD U. of Cambridge, 1962.

BLEICHELD,B. *323*
Psychophysiological responses to an infant produced auditory signal: a comparison of groups of women in different phases of the maternal cycle. PhD Tulane U. 1980.

BOLES,G. *324*
Personality factors in mothers of cerebral palsied children. PhD Columbia U. 1957.

BOOMER,M. *325*
Object permanence development in the infant-mother relationship: an investigation of the cognitive aspect of attachment. PhD U. of California, Berkeley, 1978.

BOYNTON,G.M. *326*
The relationship between identity development and attitudes towards motherhood in young married professional women. PhD Columbia U. 1979.

BRECKENRIDGE,J. *327*
A confluence model of mother-infant interaction. PhD U. of Houston, 1982.

BREIT,M. *328*
Anxious attachment in mothers of fearful latency-age children. PhD New York U. 1979.

BRODY,G.F. *329*
A study of the relationship between maternal attitudes and mother-child interaction. PhD American U. 1963.

BROUGHER,T.K. *330*
Women's attitudes about motherhood. PhD U. of Missouri, 1973.

BROWN,M. *331*
Attitudes and personality characteristics of mothers and their relation to infantile colic. PhD Vanderbilt U. 1961.

BROWN,T.P. *332*
Verbal versus direct training methods in child management for mothers of varying educational backgrounds. PhD East Texas State U. 1978.

BRUNELL,M.L. *333*
Play interactions between mothers identified as having obsessional or hysteroid character-styles and their preschool children. PhD U. of Tennessee, 1979.

BUCKLEY,M. *334*
Motivations for motherhood: a comparison of body-image and certain personality variables between women who wish for a child and women who wish to remain childless. PhD California Sch. of Prof. Psych., Berkeley, 1977.

BUDD,K.S. *335*
An analysis of multiple misplaced social contingencies in the mother of a preschool child. PhD U. of Kansas, 1975.

BUNTON,P.L. *336*
Mothers' and children's perception of the maternal role: single, dual career and traditional families. PhD U. of Michigan, 1979.

BURKE,J.P. 337
A comparative study of the relationship between children's ages and certain aspects of mother talk. PhD Southern Illinois U. at Carbondale, 1972.

BUSCH,N.A. 338
Parental development in first-time mothers of handicapped, at risk, and normal children. PhD Pennsylvania State U. 1979.

BUXTON,M.W. 339
Patterns of vertical interaction between mothers and pre-school children. MPhil U. of Nottingham, 1978.

BYRD,L.E.M. 340
Maternal attachment: a causal modeling approach. PhD State U. of New York at Stony Brook, 1982.

CALLAGHAN,J.W. 341
Anglo, Hopi, and Navajo infants and mothers: newborn behaviors, interaction styles, and childrearing beliefs and practices. PhD U. of Chicago, 1981.

CALLARD,E.D. 342
Achievement motive in the four-year-old child and its relationship to achievement expectancies of the mother. PhD U. of Michigan, 1964.

CAMPBELL,B.K. 343
An assessment of early mother-infant interaction and the subsequent development of the infant in the first two years of life. PhD California Sch. of Prof. Psych., Berkeley, 1977.

CAMPBELL,E.H. 344
Effects of mothers' anxiety on infants' behavior. PhD Yale U. 1957.

CARLSON,P.V. 345
The development of emotional behavior as a function of diadic mother-young relationships. PhD Purdue U. 1961.

CARPENTER,D. 346
A study of maternal attitudes and perceptions associated with the failure to thrive syndrome in young children. PhD U. of Chicago, 1972.

CARR,S.J. 347
Sex, day care, and mother-child attachment. PhD Georgia State U. Coll. of Arts and Sciences, 1973.

CAVA,E.L. 348
Differences between interactions of mothers with their more troublesome children and their less troublesome children. PhD Ohio State U. 1967.

CHAPLAN,A.A. 349
Mothers' practices and persuasibility in preschool children. PhD Columbia U. 1967.

CHODORKOFF,J.M. 350
Infant development as a function of mother-child interaction. PhD Wayne State U. 1960.

CHODOROW,N.J. 351
Family structure and feminine personality: the reproduction of mothering. PhD Brandeis U. 1975.

CHOL,E.S. 352
Mother-infant interaction among Korean and American mothers. PhD U. of Texas at Austin, 1981.

CHRISTENSEN,A.H. 353
Observations of maternal behavior during mother-child separations. PhD George Peabody Coll. for Teachers, 1982.

CLAIBORNE,R.B. 354
A study of mother attitudes in juvenile delinquency: an evaluation of mother attitudes toward their sons as a factor in the delinquency behavior of the sons. PhD New York U. 1954.

CLANCY,S.L. 355
Peer acceptance and rejection as a function of the quality of maternal/child relationship. PhD U. of Washington, 1981.

CLARK,B.S. 356
Verbal communication of adolescent mothers to their infants. PhD George Peabody Coll. for Teachers, 1982.

CLARKE-STEWART,K.A. 357
Interactions between mothers and their young children: characteristics and consequences. PhD Yale U. 1972.

CLAY,V.S. 358
The effect of culture on mother-child tactile communication. EdD Columbia U. 1966.

CLEBONE,B.L. 359
Attitude similarities and differences among daughters, mothers, grandmothers, and great-grandmothers of maternal lineage families. PhD Ohio State U. 1977.

COHEN,J.L. 360
A comparison of norms and behaviors of childrearing in Jewish and Italian-American mothers. PhD Syracuse U. 1977.

COHLER,B.J. 361
Character, psychopathology and childrearing attitudes in hospitalized and non-hospitalized mothers of young children. PhD Harvard U. 1967.

COLLARD,C.V. 362
Role-perception of the middle-class wife-mother: a rural-urban comparison. PhD Louisiana State U. and A&M Coll. 1973.

COLWELL,J.M. 363
The relation of controlling and hostile attitudes of mothers to certain personality traits in children. PhD American U. 1961.

CONFUSIONE,M.J. 364
Single mothers' parental attitudes, behaviors, and

sex-role orientations. PhD California Sch. of Prof. Psych., Fresno, 1979.

CONNORS,K.A. 365
De-differentiation of sex roles in the attitudes of feminist mothers and of their three- and four-year-old children. PhD U. of Maryland, 1982.

CONTI MARTINEX DE PINILLOS,G.M. 366
Mothers in dialogue: some discourse features of mothers with normal and language-impaired children. PhD U. of Texas at Dallas, 1982.

COOK,D.B. 367
An exploratory study of the effects of maternal personality and language style upon mother-infant interaction. PhD U. of Toronto, 1980.

COOK,J. A. 368
An inquiry into patterns of communication and control between mothers and their children in different social classes. PhD U. of London, Inst. of Educ. 1973.

COOK,M.N. 369
Communicative confirmation and interpersonal satisfaction of mothers and their adolescent sons. PhD U. of Denver, 1980.

CORRIGAN,E.M. 370
Childrearing practices of unwed mothers. DSW Columbia U. 1970.

COSTIGAN,B.H. 371
The unmarried mother – her decision regarding adoption. DSW U. of Southern California, 1964.

COUSINS,M.J. 372
Maternal attitudes and marital adjustment of organization mothers and non-organization mothers of mentally retarded children. PhD Florida State U. 1965.

CRASE,D.R .B. 373
The pre-teen child's perception of mother's and maternal grandmother's responses to children's misbehavior and children's expressed needs. PhD Ohio State U. 1967.

CROSS,M.S. 374
The effects of normal and atypical infants on maternal attitudes and expectations. PhD U. of South Florida, 1978.

CROW,L.J. 375
Organizational setting and caseworkers' attitudes about services to unwed mothers. PhD St John's U. 1972.

CRUMMETTE,A.B.D. 376
The maternal care of asthmatic children. PhD U. of Pittsburgh, 1978.

CURWOOD,S.T. 377
Role expectation as a factor in the relationship between mother and teacher. PhD Radcliffe Coll. 1956.

CUTRONA,M.P. 378
The relationship between working-class mothers' attitudes toward education and the educational achievement of their children with regard to sex, race, and residence. EdD Fordham U. 1974.

CUTTER,F. 379
Maternal behavior and childhood allergy. PhD Catholic U. of America, 1955.

DAMERON,L. 380
Mother-child interaction in the development of self-restraint in the fourth year: a study of socialization. PhD U. of Chicago, 1953.

D'ANDREA,M.J. 381
Becoming parents during adolescence: a transactional developmental analysis of the effects of parenthood among unmarried black females. EdD George Peabody Coll. for Teachers, 1981.

D'ANGELO,E.J. 382
Communication deviance, thought disorder, and attention dysfunction in mothers of children at risk for schizophrenia. PhD U. of Michigan, 1980.

D'ANTONIO,I.J. 383
Mothers' responses to the functioning and behavior of cardiac children in childrearing situations. PhD U. of Pittsburgh, 1976.

DANZIGER,F. 384
Verbal communication between mother and child and some aspects of cognitive decentering. PhD U. of Toronto, 1975.

DASHIFF,C.J. 385
Mother-child relationships in retarded and normal children. PhD Florida State U. 1977.

DAVIS,N .A. 386
Models of motherhood: the early mother-infant relationship. PhD U. of Tennessee, 1980.

DAYTON,L.S. 387
The relationship between ego development of mothers and their emotional, social, and cognitive support of their children. PhD Northwestern U. 1981.

DE MELLO,D.N. 388
Patterns of communication between malfunctioning children and their mothers. PhD U. of Chicago, 1975.

DEMETRE,J.D. 389
Mother-infant interaction around objects. PhD U. of Strathclyde, 1982.

DESCHNER,J.G. 390
The influence of mother-child interactions on early manifestations of competence. PhD U. of Houston, 1972.

DICICCO,F .V. 391
Levinson's psychosocial development in early and late mothers. PhD U.S. International U. 1982.

DISKIN,S.D. 392
Maternal style of expressiveness and prediction of parenting behavior. PhD U. of California, Los Angeles, 1979.

DOMASH,L.G. 393
Selected maternal attitudes as related to sex, sex-role preference, and level of psychological differentiation of the five-year-old child. PhD New York U. 1973.

DONOVAN,A.L. 394
Mother-child interaction and the development of representational skills in young children. PhD State U. of New York at Buffalo, 1975.

DONTAS,C.A. 395
Application of convergent analyses of mother-infant interaction research: implications for the study of individual differences in separation-induced protest. PhD U. of Minnesota, 1977.

DOUMANIS,M.C. 396
The cultural function of mother-child interaction. PhD U. of Lancaster, 1978.

DUBERLEY,J.D. 397
The adjustment of the mother with a child with leukaemia. MSc U. of Manchester, 1976.

DUGAN,A.B. 398
Kin, social supports and depression among women of Mexican heritage who are single parents. PhD Bryn Mawr Coll. 1982.

DUNCAN,R.L. 399
Maternal parameters in the development of social intelligence. PhD Loyola U. of Chicago, 1973.

DUNST,G.J. 400
Cognitive-social aspects of communicative exchanges between mothers and their Down's Syndrome infants and mothers and their non-retarded infants. PhD George Peabody Coll. for Teachers, 1979.

DUROCHER,L. 401
Observation du comportement socioaffectif de l'enfant de maternelle en milieu défavorisé. DPS U. of Montreal, 1977.

DUTTON,J.R. 402
Maternal speech style to hearing-impaired children. PhD U. of Pennsylvania, 1980.

DZIK,M.A. 403
Maternal response to infant behavior. PhD U. of Pittsburgh, 1978.

EAKINS,P.S. 404
Mothers in transition. PhD U. of Colorado at Boulder, 1980.

EBLING,L.D. 405
Maternal perceptions of real and ideal family environments in sole and shared custody families. PhD United States International U. 1982.

ECHEVERRIA,M.A.K. 406
The role of mother as a para-professional help in the pre-school setting. PhD U. of London, Inst. of Psych. 1980.

EDEL,R.R. 407
A study of the relationship between certain overt behavior in children and covert areas of personality in their mothers. PhD New York U. 1961.

EDWARDS,J.A. 408
Maternal attitudes and social reinforcement as factors in mother-child interaction. PhD U. of Tennessee, 1966.

EHLERS,W.H. 409
The moderately and severely retarded child: maternal perceptions of retardation and subsequent seeking and using services rendered by a community agency. DSW Brandeis U. 1962.

ELBAUM,K.K. 410
A study of the impact of community services upon the attitudes of mothers of children with cardiac handicaps. PhD Brandeis U. 1967.

ELEY,M.G. 411
Socioeconomic status differences in mother-child verbal interaction practices as related to the symbolic mediatory processes of the child. PhD U. of Alberta, 1973.

EMERY,G.N. 412
Mothers' speech to two-year-olds differing in linguistic maturity. PhD U. of North Carolina at Chapel Hill, 1979.

ESPLIN,P.A. 413
Self-concept and parental interactions of unwed mothers: their relationships to each other and to the Minnesota Multiphasic Personality Inventory. PhD U. of Utah, 1976.

EYLER,F.D. 414
Demonstration of premature infants' capabilities to improve maternal attitude and facilitate mother-infant interaction. PhD U. of Florida, 1979.

FAERSTEIN,L.J.M. 415
Coping and defense mechanisms of mothers of learning-disabled children. EdD Columbia U. Teachers Coll. 1979.

FAFOUTI,M.M. 416
Communicative exchanges between mothers and infants in early infancy. PhD Clark U. 1980.

FALENDER,C.A. 417
Patterns of mother-child interaction in families at risk for mental retardation. PhD U. of Wisconsin-Madison, 1973.

FALSEY,S.M. 418
Developmental characteristics and behavioral organization of mother-infant interaction from

newborn to twelve months. PhD George Peabody Coll. for Teachers, 1978.

FARR,R. *419*
Reaction styles of mothers from one-parent families during their son's performance on a stressful, achievement-oriented task. PhD St John's U. 1981.

FEIRING,C. *420*
The influence of the child and secondary parent on maternal behavior: toward a social systems view of early infant-mother attachment. PhD U. of Pittsburgh, 1976.

FELZEN,E.S. *421*
Mothers' adjustment to their mongoloid children. PhD Cornell U. 1970.

FERREIRA,M.C.T.R. *422*
Development of a method for the study of mother-child interaction during meal-times. PhD U. of London, Inst. of Educ. 1968.

FIELD,T.M. *423*
Face-to-face interactions between normal and high-risk infants and their mothers. PhD U. of Massachusetts, 1976.

FILLER,J.W.Jr. *424*
Modification of the teaching styles of mothers: the effects of task arrangement on the match-to-sample performance of young retarded children. PhD George Peabody Coll. for Teachers, 1974.

FINEMAN,K.R. *425*
The influence of field-dependence/field-independence on mothers' ability to implement behavior therapy with problem children. PhD U. of California, Los Angeles, 1972.

FINGER,I.P. *426*
The relationship between the quality of maternal behavior and cognitive development in developmentally delayed children. PhD U. of California, Los Angeles, 1982.

FINNEY,J.C.J. *427*
Some maternal influences on children's personality and character. PhD Stanford U. 1959.

FISCHER,L.R. *428*
When daughters become mothers. PhD U. of Massachusetts, 1979.

FITZGIBBONS,M.C. *429*
The effects of masculine sex-role characteristics on perceived control and conflict in families of single-parent mothers of adolescents. PhD Saint Louis U. 1982.

FLICK,L.H. *430*
Psychosocial development as a determinant of adolescent maternal behavior. DrPH U. of North Carolina at Chapel Hill, 1980.

FLIEGEL,N.E. *431*
An investigation into the relationship between mothers' attitudes toward childrearing and children's experiences of those attitudes. EdD New York U. 1956.

FLOGE,L.P. *432*
The importance of childcare for mothers' employment and fertility. PhD Columbia U. 1981.

FORTUNE,H.O. *433*
A study of the power position of mothers in contemporary negro family life in New York City. EdD New York U. 1963.

FOWLER,D.E. *434*
An exploratory investigation of the relationship between locus of control and parenting tasks among lower socioeconomic status black mothers. PhD U. of Florida, 1978.

FOX,M. *435*
The relationship between maternal locus of control and maternal involvement in the day treatment of emotionally disturbed children. DSW Adelphi U. Sch. of Social Work, 1980.

FRANKEL,I.J. *436*
The effects of instruction and reinforcement on relaxation task behaviors in mother-child dyads. PhD New York U. 1978.

FRANZINI,B.S. *437*
A multilevel assessment of personality and interpersonal behavior of mothers of asthmatic children as compared with mothers of non-asthmatic children. PhD New York U. 1965.

FREEARK-ZUCKER,K. *438*
The separation-individuation process: a longitudinal study of mother-toddler pairs. PhD Michigan State U. 1981.

FREESE,M.P. *439*
Assessment of maternal attitudes and analysis of their role in early mother-infant interactions. PhD Purdue U. 1975.

FREIBERG,K.L.H. *440*
Mother-child free play interactions: relationships of free play styles to maternal sex, education, religion, number of children, liberation, use of natural childbirth, and breast feeding; and age, sex, trust and persistence of the child. PhD Syracuse U. 1974.

FULLILOVE,C.A. *441*
The relationship between maternal reinforcement behavior for high- and low-achieving children. PhD Loyola U. Chicago, 1977.

GABEL,H.D. *442*
The effects of parent group-education and group-play psychotherapy on maternal childrearing attitudes. PhD U. of Rochester, 1973.

GALLIGAN,A.C. *443*
The relationship between maternal locus of control, child behavior patterns, and maternal acceptance. EdD Columbia U. Teachers Coll. 1981.

GARRARD,K.R. *444*
Mothers' control of normal and developmentally delayed children in communicative interaction. PhD U. of California, Berkeley, 1982.

GEDDES,E.W. *445*
An exploratory study of mothers' attitudes toward control of their children and parental practices in handling problem situations between the parents and their children. PhD Cornell U. 1951.

GERSON,M.J. *446*
Motivations for motherhood. PhD New York U. 1978.

GILPIN,B.L. *447*
The intercorrelation of amount of interaction and coping response in mothers of children with leukemia. PhD Northwestern U. 1979.

GIUFFRA,M.J.M. *448*
The relationship between a mother's ego strength, sophistication of body concept, and the accuracy of her perception of her child's developmental behavior. PhD New York U. 1973.

GOLDSMITH, J. *449*
A child of one's own: unmarried women who choose motherhood. PhD California Sch. of Prof. Psych., San Francisco, 1975.

GOLDSTEIN,J.A.C. *450*
Effects of parent effectiveness training and assertiveness training on self-assessed parental attitudes and behaviors of women. EdD Temple U. 1980.

GOLDSTEIN,S.J. *451*
Relationship between maternal self-report and rated behavior in mother-child interactions with clinic and nonclinic subjects. PhD U. of Utah, 1980.

GOLOMBOK,S.E. *452*
Children in lesbian and single parent heterosexual families: sexual identity and psychiatric state. PhD U. of London, Inst. of Psych. 1982.

GONZALEZ,T.A. *453*
A study of the relationship of the BEM sex-role inventory and the Rokeach dogmatism scale for mothers of preschool children. PhD Ohio U. 1975.

GOODMAN,D. *454*
Anxiety and rejection in the mother-child relationship. MPhil U. of Nottingham, 1975.

GORDON, K.C. *455*
Selected verbal behaviors in conversational discourse between mothers and their children, delayed or normal in learning language. PhD Ohio State U. 1975.

GOROVITZ,J.A.B. *456*
Comparison of the teaching styles of mothers of nonretarded children and mothers of retarded children. PhD Case Western Reserve U. 1973.

GRAVES,N.B. *457*
City, country, and childrearing: a tricultural study of mother-child relationships in varying environments. PhD U. of Colorado, 1971.

GRAVES,Z.R. *458*
The effect of context on mother-child interaction. PhD City U. of New York, 1981.

GRAY,J.B. *459*
The relationship of mothers' attitudes towards the maternal role and mothers' reports of infant behavior to mothers' impressions of infant temperament. PhD New York U. 1982.

GREEN,J.A. *460*
A developmental analysis of mother-infant interactions. PhD U. of North Carolina at Chapel Hill, 1979.

GREEN,J.H. *461*
The relationship of stress to infant-mother attachment. PhD U. of Virginia, 1980.

GREENLAND,B. *462*
Mother-child relationship: linguistic and visual discriminatory responses of four year olds. MEd U. of Bristol, 1979.

GRIFFIN,G.A. *463*
The effects of multiple mothering on the infant-mother and infant-infant affectional systems. PhD U. of Wisconsin, 1966.

GROSSMAN,P.I. *464*
Prematurity, poverty-related stress, and the mother-infant relation. PhD U. of Florida, 1979.

HAGESTAD,G.O. *465*
Middle-age women and their children: exploring changes in a role relationship. PhD U. of Minnesota, 1975.

HALL,D.M. *466*
Capacity for understanding children through adaptive ego regression and authoritarian attitudes of foster mothers who differ in mothering skill. PhD Saint Louis U. 1968.

HARPER,D.C. *467*
Perceived maternal behavior among cerebral palsied children. PhD U. of Iowa, 1971.

HARRIS,J. C. *468*
Language development and mental handicap: a comparative observational study of the language of Down's Syndrome children and their mothers. PhD U. of Nottingham, 1980.

HARRIS,N. *469*
Controlling maternal attitudes: clinical and sociocultural implications. PhD Yeshiva U. 1965.

HART,I. *470*
Maternal childrearing practices and authoritarian ideology. PhD Duke U. 1956.

HART,M.M. *471*
Becoming a mother: motherhood from the

woman's perspective. PhD Pennsylvania State U. 1981.

HASSARD,P.K. *472*
The mother-infant dyad: an investigation of parity, maternal and infant behaviors, and infant sex and age as determinants of the interactive cycle. PhD Georgia State U. Coll. of Educ. 1975.

HENDERSON,W.E. *473*
An investigation of the unwed mother's relationships with important people in early life and cross-sectionally. PhD U. of Tennessee, 1962.

HENDRICKS,L.E.Jr. *474*
The effect of family size, child spacing, and family density on stress in low-income black mothers and their preadolescent children. PhD U. of North Carolina at Chapel Hill, 1977.

HERNDON,K.M. *475*
Mother-child interactions as a determinant of Type A – Type B behavior. PhD U. of Texas at Austin, 1976.

HERZ,F.M. *476*
The effects of maternal powerlessness and isolation on the adjustment of children in single-parent families. PhD Rutgers U. 1978.

HESTICK,H.E. *477*
Adolescent mother-toddler interaction: attitude, knowledge, and behaviors examined. PhD George Washington U. 1982.

HILL,H.M. *478*
An investigation of indices of competent parenting in mothers of Afro-American descent. PhD Columbia U. 1982.

HILL,M.J. *479*
Effects of conscious and unconscious factors on childrearing attitudes of lesbian mothers. PhD Adelphi U. 1981.

HIMES,M.C. *480*
Language development and patterns of mother-child interaction. PhD U. of Toronto, 1978.

HIRSCH,I.S. *481*
Training mothers in groups as reinforcement therapists for their own children. PhD U. of Maryland, 1967.

HIRSCH,S.L. *482*
Home climate in the black single-parent mother-led family: a social-ecological, interactional approach. PhD United States International U. 1979.

HIRSCHFELT,R.N. *483*
Anxiety and authoritarian control in allergic and non-allergic mothers, and anxiety and dependency in high and low allergic sons. PhD St John's U. 1970.

HISLOP,C.E.B. *484*
Anxiety, self-esteem, and role satisfaction in mothers of 20 to 28–month-old children. PhD U. of Michigan, 1981.

HO,C.C. *485*
Overprotective tendency in mothers of moderately retarded preschool males through analysis of mother-child interaction. PhD Ohio State U. 1976.

HOEFFER,B. *486*
Lesbian and heterosexual single mothers' influence on their children's acquisition of sex-role traits and behavior. DNS U. of California, San Francisco, 1979.

HOLADAY,B.J. *487*
Maternal response to their chronically ill infant's attachment behavior of crying. DNS U. of California, San Francisco, 1979.

HOLSTEIN,S.J. *488*
The modification of maladaptive mother-child interaction through modeling and behavior rehearsal. PhD U. of North Carolina at Chapel Hill, 1974.

HOSACK,A.M. *489*
A comparison of crisis: mothers' early experiences with normal and abnormal first-born infants. PhD Harvard U. 1968.

HOSKINS,R.A. *490*
A comparative study of selected linguistic behaviors of mothers and their language-impaired children. PhD Southern Illinois U. at Carbondale, 1973.

HOVDA,P. *491*
Role expectations of new foster mothers. PhD U. of Chicago, 1971.

HOWELL,M.C. *492*
Some effects of chronic illness on children and their mothers. PhD U. of Minnesota, 1962.

HUANG,L.N. *493*
The perceptions and experiences of mothers of retarded children in the network of human services. PhD Yale U. 1980.

HULL,D.M. *494*
Examination of three maternal characteristics in relationship to sex-role development of father-present and father-absent children. PhD U. of Washington, 1975.

HUMPHREYS,C. A. *495*
Single mothers: an investigation of their experience as single parents. PhD U. of Toronto, 1980.

HUNT,B.J. *496*
The single-parent woman in transition: critical factors for effective functioning. PhD U. of Maryland, 1979.

HUNTER,P.C. *497*
The relationship of maternal readiness to observed adolescent maternal role performance. PhD U. of Maryland, 1981.

HUNTER,V. *498*
The impact of adolescent parenthood on black teenage mothers and their families and the influence of two alternative types of child care. PhD U. of California, Los Angeles, 1982.

HYNES,W.J. *499*
Single-parent mothers and distress: relationships between selected social and psychological factors and distress in low-income single-parent mothers. DSW Catholic U. of America, 1979.

IRVING,L.H. *500*
A study of environmental factors of the unmarried mother in Oklahoma. PhD U. of Oklahoma, 1970.

JACKSON, A.L.M. *501*
Correlates of foster mother adequacy and satisfaction. DSW Catholic U. of America, 1974.

JACKSON,K.W. *502*
Maternal behavior and children's motivation. PhD Washington U., 1975.

JACOBS,F.H. *503*
The social context of maternal role set conflict (by socio-economic status). PhD Boston U. 1972.

JACOBS,M.A. *504*
Fantasies of mother-child interaction in hay fever sufferers. PhD Boston U. 1963.

JAMESON- BLOOM,C. *505*
Assessments, goals, and expectations of mothers of children with Down's Syndrome enrolled in early intervention programs. PhD Brandeis U. 1980.

JARRETT,G.E. *506*
The relationship of maternal age to acceptance and control in childrearing practices of young mothers. PhD U. of Maryland, 1979.

JEFFREY,B.I. *507*
Maternal adequacy feeling and problems of child discipline: an exploratory study of the maternal role. PhD Pennsylvania State U. 1965.

JENKINS,Z. *508*
A longitudinal study of informal instructional transactions in mother-child dyads. PhD U. of Rochester, 1982.

JOFFE,S.S. *509*
The quality of mother-infant attachment and its relationship to compliance with maternal commands and prohibitions. PhD U. of Minnesota, 1980.

JOHNSEN,K. P. *510*
An analysis of factors contributing to within-class differences in maternal role change over two generations. PhD Purdue U. 1966.

JOHNSON,C.E. *511*
Language of mothers and children. PhD Pittsburgh U. 1976.

JONES,C.J. *512*
Differences and similarities between two-parent and mother-child black families residing in a lower socio-economic-status census tract. PhD Michigan State U. 1974.

JONES,R.L. *513*
The effects of person-environment fit, locus of control, and the mother's perception of the teaching behaviors of the significant other on the teaching behaviors of low-income black mothers. PhD Case Western Reserve U. 1981.

JONES,W.C. *514*
Correlates of social deviance: a study of unmarried mothers. PhD New York U. 1965.

KAGAN,S.G. *515*
Emotional communication patterns in asthmatic children and their mothers. PhD Yeshiva U. 1977.

KAHN,A.J. *516*
Effects of a procedural variation on maternal behavior in a standardized mother-child interaction situation. PhD U. of Houston, 1975.

KALISKI,J.P. *517*
Patterns in childrearing: an exploratory investigation of the effects of parental feminism on sex-role development, need-achievement and autonomy in children. PhD U. of Rhode Island, 1976.

KAMMERER,P.G. *518*
The unmarried mother. PhD Harvard U. 1920.

KAUFFMAN,A.L . *519*
Mothers' perceptions of the developmentally delayed label. PhD U. of Illinois at the Medical Center, 1982.

KEANE,M.W. *520*
Black mothers and their sons: correlates and predictors of cognitive development from the second to the sixth year of life. PhD City U. of New York, 1976.

KEENAN,D.M. *521*
The utilization of maternal perceptions to develop indicators of subsequent parenting problems. EdD West Virginia U. 1982.

KELLOG,N.F. *522*
Fulfillment of psychological deprivation needs through foster parenting by black women. PhD Claremont Grad. Sch. 1976.

KELLY,P.L. *523*
Maternal psychiatric status and infant temperament as determinants of mother-infant interaction patterns. PhD U. of Rochester, 1974.

KELMAN,H.R. *524*
The effects of a group of non-institutionalized mongoloid children upon their families as perceived by their mothers. PhD New York U. 1959.

KENNEDY,J.F. *525*
Implications of grief and mourning for mothers of

defective infants. DSW Smith Coll. Sch. for Social Work, 1969.

KENNEY,E.T. 526
Level of ego development and authoritarianism of mothers with children who differ in IQ and school adjustment. PhD Washington U. 1965.

KEZUR,B.A. 527
Mother-child communication patterns based on therapeutic principles. PhD Humanistic Psych. Inst. 1980.

KILBRIDE,J.E. 528
Mother-infant interaction and infant sensorimotor development among the Baganda of Uganda. PhD Bryn Mawr Coll. 1976.

KING,D.E. 529
Perceptions of motherhood among black pregnant and parenting adolescents and young mothers. EdD Columbia U. Teachers Coll. 1982.

KIRKPATRICK,R.L. 530
A study of the relationship among perceived female roles of mothers and the problem-solving behavior of their children. PhD Southern Illinois U. at Carbondale, 1973.

KIRYAKAS,I.F.H. 531
Socio-economic factors influencing Iraqi mothers' beliefs and practices concerning infant feeding and weaning. PhD U. of Wales, 1981.

KLEEMEIR,C.A.P. 532
The relationship between observed mother-child interactions and attending behaviors in children. PhD Emory U. 1976.

KOCH,W.J. 533
Maternal command rate and child compliance. PhD U. of Alberta, 1982.

KONTOS,S.J. 534
Metacognitive content of mothers' verbal directives to preschool children. PhD Iowa State U. 1980.

KOVACH,M.E. 535
Maternal attitude and infant smile. PhD U. of Kansas, 1981.

KOZAK,N.V. 536
Maternal turn-yielding signals in mother-infant interaction. EdD Harvard U. 1980.

KRIBS,N.E.D. 537
A comparison of characteristics of women who have adopted a black child and women who state an unwillingness to adopt a black child. PhD U. of Oregon, 1972.

KRONEN,J. 538
Maternal facial mirroring at four months. PhD Yeshiva U. 1982.

KUBASKA,C.A. 539
A longitudinal study of mothers' speech characteristics. PhD Brown U. 1982.

KUCHNER,J.R.F. 540
Chinese-American and European-American: a cross-cultural study of infant and mother. PhD U. of Chicago, 1981.

KUCZYNSKI,K.A. 541
Maternal attitudes, child behavior and child development intervention in southern Appalachia. DSW Catholic U. of America, 1979.

LAKIN,M. 542
An investigation of personality characteristics of mothers of excessively crying (colicky) infants. PhD U. of Chicago, 1955.

LAMB,W.A. 543
A comparison of various techniques of training mothers as language concept models for their children. PhD U. of Arizona, 1970.

LAMP,R.E. 544
The effects of maternal anxiety on the subsequent emotional and learning behavior of the offspring. PhD U. of Washington, 1966.

LANDY,S.E. 545
An investigation of teenage mothers, their infants, and the resulting mother-infant dyads. PhD U. of Regina, 1982.

LANEY,M.D. 546
Relationships between maternal stress, infant status, and mother-infant interactions. PhD George Peabody Coll. for Teachers, 1979.

LANGE,M.H. 547
Mothers as teachers and storytellers: another look at socialization practices. PhD Washington U. 1979.

LANGER,G.B. 548
Pregnancy and motherhood motivation in unmarried women: some intrapsychic interpersonal and behavioral factors. PhD Michigan State U. 1975.

LANGMAID,W. 549
Breastfeeding and health: a survey of knowledge, attitudes, and beliefs in young people aged 16–18. MPhil CNAA Leeds Polytechnic, 1983.

LAPERRIERE,K. 550
Maternal attitudes in different subcultural groups. PhD Washington U. 1962.

LA POINT,V.de V. 551
A descriptive survey of some perceptions and concerns of black female single-parent families in Lansing, Michigan. PhD Michigan State U. 1977.

LASSAR,B.T. 552
A study of the effects of group discussion on the attitudes of mothers toward their cerebral palsied children. PhD New York U. 1956.

LAUBE,J.J. 553
Personal and social characteristics associated with mothers' attitudes towards seeking professional problem-solving help. DSW Catholic U. of America, 1980.

LAW,T. *554*
Differential childrearing attitudes and practices of Chinese-American mothers. PhD Claremont Grad. Sch. 1973.

LAWRENCE,W.E. *555*
The mother family. PhD Yale U. 1930.

LEDUC,L. *556*
A comparative study of training programs for the establishment and maintenance of appropriate parental behaviors in mothers using programmed instruction techniques with videotapes. PhD U. of Montreal, 1976.

LEE,S.M. *557*
Styles of communication interaction used by mothers of deaf and hearing children and their relationship to linguistic competence in deaf children. PhD California Sch. of Prof. Psych. 1978.

LEIBOWITZ,E. *558*
Mother-infant behavior in two social classes. PhD U. of Rochester, 1972.

LEIFER,A.S.D. *559*
Effects of early temporary mother-infancy separation on later maternal behavior in humans. PhD Stanford U. 1970.

LELER,H.O. *560*
Mother-child interaction and language performance in young disadvantaged negro children. PhD Stanford U. 1970.

LEON,M.A. *561*
Phenomenal mediation of maternal behavior. PhD U. of Chicago, 1972.

LESCHEN,S. *562*
The effect of peer vs. adult frustration of boys and girls of middle childhood and its relation to attitudes towards mothers. PhD Florida Inst. of Technology, 1982.

LEVINE,L .W. *563*
Mother-child communication and the acquisition of deixis. PhD New York U. 1981.

LEWIS,W.V. *564*
Relationship between a mother's experiencing level and her perceptions of her child's behavior. PhD California Sch. of Prof. Psych. 1976.

LII,S.S.Y. *565*
Mother-infant interaction as a function of birth order and sex of infant. PhD Indiana U. 1979.

LINGER,S. *566*
The speech of mothers to young infants: some early sex differences. MA U. of Sussex, 1977.

LIU,C.Y. *567*
Time use patterns and satisfaction with life of single-parent families with special emphasis on the female, low-income and/or minority family-head. PhD Michigan State U. 1982.

LIVINGOOD,A.B. *568*
The depressed mother as a source of stimulation for her infant. PhD U. of Maryland, 1976.

LOEWENSTEIN,S.F. *569*
An observational study of mothers and their children. PhD Brandeis U. 1970.

LOGAN,R.D. *570*
Maternal childrearing and academic achievement. PhD U. of Chicago, 1972.

LOOKER,T.B. *571*
Maternal mood and mother-child attachment behavior. PhD Columbia U. 1981.

LOW,N.E. *572*
Family day care in early infancy: effects on the infant-mother relationship. PhD California Sch. of Prof. Psych. 1982.

LUBER,P. *573*
Correlates of maternal grieving after the loss of a child. PhD U. of Texas at Austin, 1981.

LYNCH,C.C. *574*
An investigation of the sharing of common fears between mothers and their four-year-old and five-year-old children in middle-class families. PhD New York U. 1973.

MCALISTER,I.R. *575*
Interference, immoderation, inconsistency and dependency: differences in the behavior of mothers toward first and later born children. PhD Columbia U. 1965.

MCCARTHY,M.E . *576*
Relationships among the competence of Down's Syndrome infants, maternal perceptions of infant temperament, and maternal attitudes toward childrearing. PhD U. of Maryland, 1981.

MCCRAE,M.M. *577*
The effects of a short-term didactic group in helping single-parent mothers cope with stress. PhD Boston Coll. 1980

MCDONOUGH,J.S. *578*
An investigation of the effect of double-blind instructions on perceptual functioning as a function of maternal childrearing behaviors. PhD U. of Arkansas, 1975.

MCGUIRE,B.N. *579*
The developmental process of mothering as perceived by mothers of preschool children aged two to five. PhD Fielding Inst. 1980.

MACK,J.E. *580*
Cognitive functioning in mothers of autistic children. PhD York U. 1980.

MACKEY,S.K. *581*
A study of the differences in attitudes and behavior between mothers of disabled and nondisabled children. PhD U. of Illinois at Chicago Circle, 1978.

MCKIN,M.K. *582*
Mother and child as problem solving unit: an analysis of the characteristics and determinants of reflective and impulsive behavior. PhD Carleton U. 1977.

MCMAHEN,L. *583*
Mothers of preschool children: some attitudes to the maternal role. PhD U. of Birmingham, 1967.

MADURO,E.A. *584*
Maternal adaptation in relation to value of children and support system: a study of Hispanic mothers. PhD California Sch. of Prof. Psych., Berkeley, 1982.

MALOUF,R.E. *585*
Social bases of power in single-mother and two-parent families. PhD U. of Utah, 1979.

MANDELCORN,B.S. *586*
Maternal expectation and mother-child interaction. PhD McGill U. 1972.

MANN,V.D. *587*
A study of the attitudes of mothers of cerebral palsied children toward child adjustment. PhD American U. 1957.

MARCUSE,J.J. *588*
Maternal responsiveness to emotions and symptoms among asthmatics. PhD Yeshiva U. 1976.

MARGOLIS,M.O. *589*
A psychological study of mothers of asthmatic children. PhD Michigan State U. 1959.

MARKLEY,E.R. *590*
Social class differences in mothers' attitudes toward childrearing. PhD Columbia U. 1958.

MAYRINK-SABINSON,M.L.T. *591*
A study of mother-child interaction with language-learning children: context and maternal interpretation. PhD State U. of New York at Buffalo, 1981.

MEGENITY,J.S. *592*
The effects of an intervention program on maternal behaviors and on mothers' views of themselves as mothers. PhD Georgia State U. Coll. of Educ. 1976.

MERING,F.H. *593*
Mother-child relationships among educated and professionally active women. PhD Radcliffe Coll. 1953.

MERRICK,R.A. *594*
The behavior of aggressive and normal mother-son dyads. PhD Kent State U. 1971.

MESSER,D.J. *595*
Mother-child interaction and the use of referential speech. PhD U. of Strathclyde, 1978.

MIKUS,K.C. *596*
Paradoxes of early motherhood. PhD U. of Michigan, 1981.

MILLER,A.D.G. *597*
Pressures towards deviance: the case of unwed mothers. PhD U. of Colorado, 1971.

MONRAD,D.M. *598*
An investigation of the cognitive and affective components of maternal teaching style. PhD Johns Hopkins U. 1979.

MONTALTO,F.D. *599*
Maternal behavior and child personaltiy: a Rorschach study. PhD U. of Cincinnati, 1950.

MORGENSTERN,M. *600*
Maternal attitudes and reactions of normal siblings in families with a cerebral palsied member. PhD New York U. 1964.

MORISEY,P.G. *601*
Professional advocacy, community participation and social planning: the case of the unmarried mother from the 'inside the ghetto' perspective. DSW Columbia U. 1970.

MOSENDE,L.C. *602*
Sociocultural correlates of the maternal teaching styles of selected Filipino women. PhD U. of Michigan, 1981.

MOSS,N.E. *603*
Learning to mother: the effects of hospital unit organization on maternal behavior. PhD Stanford U.

MUNSON,S.E. *604*
The relationship between perceived childrearing practices and depression in college-age women. PhD Rutgers U. 1974.

NAINIE,M. *605*
Maternal expectations and satisfactions with nursery school programs. PhD Cornell U. 1961.

NEWMAN,L.W. *606*
Childhood disability and mothers' perceptions of family disorganization, family environment, and maternal coping. PhD U. of Texas Health Science Center at Dallas, 1978.

NEWPORT,E.L. *607*
Motherese: the speech of mothers to young children. PhD U. of Pennsylvania, 1975.

NEWSOM,S. *608*
Assessment of foster mother-child relationship by brief playroom observations. PhD U. of Chicago, 1961.

NICKLAUS,C.H. *609*
An examination of the relationship between the acceptance of the traditional feminine role by women and the presence of psychological problems in women and their children. EdD Fairleigh Dickinson U. 1977.

NOBLE,L.A. *610*
Structural analysis of mothers' attitudes toward childrearing in four communities in Appalachia. PhD U. of North Carolina at Greensboro, 1969.

NOBLE,L.S. *611*
The impact of infant sex and birth order on the magnitude and direction of maternal expectation. EdD U. of Virginia, 1980.

NORMAN,E. *612*
Some correlates of behavioral expectations: a role study of mothers with children in foster care placement. PhD City U. of New York, 1972.

NOTTINGHAM,R.D. *613*
A psychological study of forty unmarried mothers. PhD Ohio State U. 1936.

NUTTALL,J.R. *614*
Maternal perceptual style and mother-infant interaction in a play setting. PhD Michigan State U. 1981.

O'DONNELL,L.N. *615*
Women as mothers: family, employment and community commitments. EdD Harvard U. 1982.

OLLEY,J.G. *616*
Mother-infant interaction during feeding. PhD George Peabody Coll. for Teachers, 1973.

OLSEN,S.P. *617*
Response interference as a function of social evaluation and maternal childrearing experience. PhD U. of Iowa, 1965.

OLSON,S.L. *618*
Mother-infant interaction and the development of cognitive and language competence. PhD Indiana U. 1980.

O'ROURKE,A.M. *619*
The psychological characteristics of mothers whose children are in foster boarding home care as compared with other mothers whose children are at home with them. DSW Catholic U. of America, 1976.

ORTIZ,A.A. *620*
A comparative study of the observed affective behavior towards their adopted and biological children among Puerto Rican mothers (Spanish text). PhD Caribbean Center for Advanced Studies, 1979.

OWEN,F.W. *621*
Asthma and maternal stimuli. PhD Stanford U. 1961.

PADESKY,C.A. *622*
Cognitive and behavioral aspects of maternal coping with first juvenile arrest. PhD U. of California, Los Angeles, 1981.

PAINTER,S.L. *623*
Maternal adaptation to parenthood in the second year. PhD U. of British Columbia, 1980.

PALECECK,G.C. *624*
Correlation of child self-concept, mother employment, mother self-concept, mother role satisfaction, and father influence in childrearing. PhD United States International U. 1979.

PASCHKE,R.E. *625*
The maternal environment and behavior. PhD Purdue U. 1969.

PATTI,E.F. *626*
The interface of selected verbal and nonverbal behaviors in mother-child dyadic interactions with normal and language disordered children. PhD Purdue U. 1978.

PAWLBY,S.J. *627*
A study of imitative interaction between mothers and their infants. PhD U. of Nottingham, 1977.

PAXTON,P.W.S. *628*
Effects of drug-induced behavior changes in hyperactive children on maternal attitude and personality. PhD U. of Minnesota, 1972.

PEDULLA,B.M. *629*
Mothers' perceptions of their retarded children's development: the relationship of selected mother and child variables to realism. PhD Boston Coll. 1975.

PENTZ,T.R. *630*
Facilitation of language acquisition: the role of the mother. PhD Johns Hopkins U. 1975.

PERRY,J.B.Jr. *631*
An exploratory study of the mother substitutes of preschool children of employed mothers in Spokane, Washington. PhD Washington State U. 1961.

PESSEN,B. *632*
Learning to be a mother: the influence of the medical profession. PhD Brandeis U. 1978.

PETERSEN,P.C. *633*
Stressors, outcome dysfunction, and resources in mothers of children with handicaps. PhD U. of Nebraska, 1981.

PETERSON,C.M. *634*
The impact of a mother-infant group experience on maternal adjustment. PhD U. of Oregon, 1980.

PETERSON,G.A. *635*
Maternal speech patterns: their relationshp to language development and language delay. PhD George Peabody Coll. for Teachers, 1978.

PETERSON,M.A. *636*
The study of a methodology for observing mother-infant interaction patterns during the second year of life. PhD Cornell U. 1975.

PETRIE,P.E. *637*
Children under 2 years looked after by child minders: a study of their experiences, including observations of their interactions with mothers and minders and some comparisons with day nursery children of a similar age. PhD U. of London, Inst. of Educ. 1982.

PHELPS,R.E. *638*
Mother-son interaction in single-parent families. PhD U. of Utah, 1981.

PHILIPP,C. 639
Attitude changes in mothers of handicapped children in preschool programs. DSW U. of California, Berkeley, 1977.

PHILLIPS,D.C. 640
An exploratory study of the relationship between mothers' individualization of their children and the children's developmental progress. DSW Washington U. 1971.

PHILLIPS,J.R. 641
Formal characteristics of speech which mothers address to their young children. PhD Johns Hopkins U. 1970.

PISTRANG,N.E. 642
Woman's work involvement and experience of new motherhood. PhD U. of California, San Francisco, 1981.

POGGENSEE,A.L. 643
A comparative psychological study of married and unmarried mothers. PhD New York U. 1965.

POHLY,S.R. 644
The development of object and person permanence as a correlate of dimensions of maternal care. PhD State U. of New York at Stony Brook, 1979.

POLEY,B.A. 645
Altering dyadic synchrony, maternal self-confidence, and maternal perception of the infant through a teaching-modeling intervention for primiparous mothers. PhD U. of Texas at Austin, 1978.

POLLOCK,E. 646
An investigation into certain personality characteristics of unmarried mothers. PhD New York U. 1957.

POPPER,E.T. 647
Structural and situational effects on mothers' responses to children's purchase requests. DBA Harvard U. 1978.

PORTA,J.M.U. 648
Application of a structural balance model to the relation between mothers' attitudes toward their neighbourhood group and their attitudes and practices in childrearing. PhD Stanford U. 1966.

PRINCE,B.F. 649
Mothers' childrearing styles and daughters' dependency: an examination of restrictive and democratic methods. PhD Syracuse U. 1981.

PROCYK,M.R. 650
Determinants of aggression between mother and child. PhD Loyola U., Chicago, 1969.

PUECHLER ,B.U. 651
First-time mother: a comparison of maternal age and interpersonal relationships. EdD Northern Illinois U. 1981.

QUIGLEY,G.L.S. 652
A comparative study of mothers of children with the cleft lip-palate birth defect and mothers of non-handicapped children on selected personality characteristics. PhD St John's U. 1972.

QUIRK,M.E. 653
Maternal values, childrearing beliefs, and mother-child transactions of mothers of handicapped and mothers of non-handicapped preschool boys. EdD Clark U. 1982.

RADIUS,S.M. 654
An empirical test of a sociobehavioral model to predict mothers' compliance with a regimen for pediatric asthmatics. PhD Johns Hopkins U. 1978.

RAINS,P.M. 655
Becoming an unwed mother. PhD Northwestern U. 1969.

RAPP,D.W. 656
Childrearing attitudes of mothers in Germany and in the United States. PhD Florida State U. 1960.

RASHMAN,S.E. 657
An integrative model of mother-child interaction: structural, cognitive, emotional and behavioral facets. PhD U. of Illinois, 1981.

RATWICK,S.H. 658
A comparison of mothers' speech to normal and Down's Syndrome children. PhD U. of Notre Dame, 1978.

RAWLINS,M.L. 659
Maternal control style and the competence of the young child as a function of maternal and child status. PhD U. of Rochester, 1979.

READING,J. 660
The interaction of psychosocial factors on the parenthood choice of preprofessional women. PhD U. of Florida, 1982.

REES,B.M.L. 661
Development of summated rating scales for measuring identification with the mothering role. PhD U. of Arizona, 1979.

REES,R.L. 662
A comparison of children of lesbian and single heterosexual mothers on three measures of socialization. PhD California Sch. of Prof. Psych., Berkeley, 1979.

REILLY,T.W. 663
Modeling the development of women's self-evaluations in parental roles. PhD Johns Hopkins U. 1982.

REMICK,H.L.W. 664
The maternal environment of linguistic development. PhD U. of California, Davis, 1971.

REMY,J.H. 665
A study of the relationship between maternal

overpossessiveness and dependency in young boys. PhD Adelphi U. 1960.

REXFORD,M.T. *666*
Single mothers by choice: an exploratory study. PhD U. of California, Los Angeles, 1976.

RICE,D.L. *667*
Maternal control and cognitive development: a replication. PhD U. of Michigan, 1970.

RICH,P. *668*
A comparative study of maternal separation reactions to the placement of two- and three-year-old children in day care centers. DSW Columbia U. 1978.

RICHARDSON,B.B. *669*
Racism and childrearing: a study of black mothers. PhD Claremont Grad. Sch. 1981.

RILEY,E.M.D. *670*
Psychology, politics, and policies: theories of the child and the mother in the history of psychology in Britain. DPhil U. of Sussex, 1981.

RINGLER,N.M. *671*
Mothers' language to their young children and to adults over time. PhD Case Western Reserve U. 1973.

ROBERTS,G.B. *672*
Early experience and the development of cognitive competencies and language skills: teaching low-income Afro-Western Indian immigrant mothers strategies for enhancing development. PhD U. of Toronto, 1982.

ROBERTSON,N.II *673*
Maternal teaching style as a determiner of child learning. PhD U. of Chicago, 1970.

ROBINSON,N.D. *674*
Adoptive mothers' perceptions of stress in the agency home study. DSW Columbia U. 1973.

ROMANO,E. *675*
The impact of mental retardation upon the self-concept of the mother: a comparative study of the self-regarding attitudes of mothers of trainable retarded children and selected mothers of non-retarded children. PhD Syracuse U. 1968.

ROSALES,N.E. *676*
Good kids and bad kids: a study of two borderline mothers and their latency-age children. PhD Wright Inst. 1982.

ROSENZWEIG,C. *677*
Maternal attitude and latency-age school achievement: a study of mother-child interaction in the developmental phases. DSW Smith Coll. Sch. for Social Work, 1968.

ROTH,E.F. *678*
An exploratory study of the psychodynamics of mothers who have autistic children. DSW Smith Coll. Sch. for Social Work, 1969.

ROTTER,M.F. *679*
Descriptive study of a group of mothers who are at home with their young children. PhD U. of South Carolina, 1982.

ROWLAND (O'NEIL),C.M. *680*
Communicative strategies of visually impaired infants and their mothers. PhD U. of Oklahoma, 1980.

RUBENSTEIN,J.L. *681*
Maternal attentiveness and subsequent exploratory behavior in the infant. PhD Boston U. 1967.

RUBIN,S. *682*
Bereavement and vulnerability: a study of mothers of Sudden Infant Death Syndrome children. PhD Boston U. Grad. Sch. 1977.

RUBOUITS ,P.C. *683*
Achievement training given to six-year-old boys and girls by lower-class and middle-class mothers. PhD U. of Illinois at Urbana-Champaign, 1978.

RUOFF,L.O. *684*
Mother-infant interactions during the first year of life. PhD U. of Washington, 1976.

RUSSELL,M. *685*
Effect of group counseling with mothers on their attitudes toward children and on their sons' reading disability: an educational therapeutic approach to parent attitudes and reading disability in a clinic situation. PhD New York U. 1959.

RYAVEC,L.P.S. *686*
Conceptions of motherhood: the effect of the maternal ego idea upon the experience of motherhood. PhD U. of Michigan, 1978.

SAMUELS,A.F. *687*
The effect of intensive group discussion on certain attitudes of mothers toward children with reading disabilities and the relationship of changed attitudes on the reading growth of their sons. PhD New York U. 1958.

SAMUELS,M.R. *688*
A study of maternal role performance in one-parent negro families. EdD Columbia U. 1970.

SANFORD,M.S. *689*
Disruption of the mother-child relationship in conjunction with matrifocality: a study of child-keeping among the Carib and Creole of British Honduras. PhD Catholic U. of America, 1971.

SAUR,W.G. *690*
Social networks and family environments of mothers of multiply, severely handicapped children. PhD Florida State U. 1980.

SAXE,R.M. *691*
The relationship between maternal behaviors and a child's curiosity and play behaviors. PhD Michigan State U. 1968.

SAYRES,A.L. *692*
A comparison of attitudes toward childrearing of

mothers who differ significantly in self-concepts. PhD New York U. 1958.

SCHAEFER,R. A. 693
Maternal choice of childrearing strategy and birth order of child. PhD Duke U. 1980.

SCHERER,N.J. 694
The role of mother's expansions in her child's conversation and language learning. PhD U. of Washington, 1980.

SCHLACHET,B.C. 695
An experimental investigation of the maternal role in the etiology of schizophrenia. PhD New York U. 1966.

SCHNEIDERMAN,M.H. 696
'Do what I mean, not what I say': mothers' action-directives to their young children. PhD U. of Pennsylvania, 1980.

SCHNEYER,B.B. 697
Mothering is a ticklish situation, or the contribution of a sense of humor to mothering. PhD Union for Experimenting Colleges and Universities, 1981.

SCOTT,W.J. 698
Attachment and child abuse: a study of social history indicators among mothers of abused children. PhD U. of Minnesota, 1974.

SCHREIBER,J.F. 699
The quality of maternal empathy: its definition and relation to identification and psychological differentiation. PhD California Sch. of Prof. Psych., Berkeley, 1981.

SCHROEDER,F.M. 700
An exploratory study of beliefs and practices of Jemez Pueblo Indians of New Mexico – pertaining to childrearing in the preschool years in relation to the educational status of the mother. PhD New York U. 1960.

SCHUMAKER,J.S.B. 701
Mothers' expansions: their characteristics and effects on child language. PhD U. of Kansas, 1976.

SCHVANEVELDT, J.D. 702
The development of a film text for the measurements of perceptions towards maternal overprotection. PhD Florida State U. 1964.

SCHWARTZ,M.M. 703
Effects of maternal sex-role attitudes on certain aspects of preschoolers' behavior. PhD Fordham U. 1982.

SCOTT,B.A. 704
Comparison of parental expectations: goals and childrearing patterns of mothers receiving aid to dependent children. PhD Iowa State U. 1967.

SEGAL,A.S.B. 705
The prediction of expressed attitude toward the mother. PhD U. of Michigan, 1954.

SELAVAN,A. 706
A comprehensive integrational theory of the maternal mode of existence. PhD Duquesne U. 1968.

SHANLEY,P.J. 707
The effects of maternal attendance in the care of young hospitalized children with a diagnosis of cancer. EdD Columbia U. Teachers Coll. 1981.

SHARBOROUGH,S.J. 708
The cult of the mother in Europe: the transformation of the symbolism of woman. PhD U. of California, Los Angeles, 1977.

SHARP,J.D. 709
A longitudinal study of mother-infant interaction in the first four months of life. PhD U. of Strathclyde, 1973.

SHEA, M.L. 710
A study of consistency and change in maternal behavior toward two children in the same family. PhD Catholic U. of America, 1950.

SHEPHERD,I.L. 711
Attitudes of mothers of schizophrenic patients. PhD Pennsylvania State U. 1958.

SHODELL, N.J. 712
Personalities of mothers of nonverbal and verbal schizophrenic children. PhD Yeshiva U. 1967.

SHRAGER,E.F. 713
An experimental investigation of mother-child telepathy and related personality variables. PhD New York U. 1977.

SILVERSTEIN ,S.M. 714
The transmission of values associated with the independent social functioning of young children: a comparison between value orientations of middle-class mothers and maternal grandmothers. PhD New York U. 1980.

SIMPSON,L.J. 715
The influence of maternal characteristics, child characteristics, secondary reinforcement effects and social comparison effects upon the mother-to-child relation. PhD U. of Pittsburgh, 1968.

SIMSARIAN,F.P. 716
Attitudes of women residing in the Bethesda area of Montgomery Country, Maryland, regarding caring for children not their own. DSW Catholic U. of America, 1963.

SITGRAVES,M.E. 717
Recent life event stress and patterns of mother-son interaction in high-risk versus low-risk black mothers. PhD Boston U. Grad. Sch. 1980.

SMITH,H.T. 718
A comparison of interview and observation measures of mother behavior. PhD Radcliffe Coll. 1953.

SMITH,K.V.R. *719*
Children raised by lesbian mothers. PhD U. of California, Los Angeles, 1981.

SMITH,M.B. *720*
Developmental and cross-contextual stability of mother-child interactive behavior. PhD U. of Colorado, 1981.

SMOLAR,H.T.E. *721*
Stress and demographic variables as related to mother's referral of children in need of treatment. DSW Columbia U. 1976.

SNOW,J.E. *722*
A heuristic study of black female heads of households and black females who are not heads of households and their involvement with their children's educational development, Camden, New Jersey. EdD Rutgers U. 1976.

SOLOMON,J. *723*
Mother's self-concept and its influence upon her perception of her children and other women. PhD California Sch. of Prof. Psych., San Diego, 1975.

SOLOMON,Z.H. *724*
Stress, vulnerability and social support: a study of depression and anxiety in mothers of pre-school children. PhD U. of Pittsburgh, 1980.

SPENCER,A.M. *725*
Children of lesbian mothers. DPhil U. of London, Inst. of Psych. 1978.

SPIRA,N.N. *726*
Relationship of maternal kinesic hand games and infant engagement level. PhD Yeshiva U. 1982.

SPITZNAGEL,A.M.S. *727*
Mothers' views of their hyperactive sons' behavior and control problems. PhD Duke U. 1981.

STEINBERGER,C.B. *728*
Persistence and change in the lifestyles of thirteen single adoptive mothers. EdD Columbia U. Teachers Coll. 1979.

STIFFMAN,A.R.R. *729*
Mother-son interaction: affection, control, and compliance. PhD Washington U. 1980.

STOVER,L. *730*
Efficacy of training procedures for mothers in filial therapy. PhD Rutgers U. 1966.

STRAIN,B.A. *731*
Early dialogues: a naturalistic study of vocal behavior in mothers and three-month-old infants. PhD George Peabody Coll. for Teachers, 1975.

STRATTHAUS,J.D. *732*
The intercorrelation of controlling maternal behavior, dependency, and efficacy expectation in children. PhD California Sch. of Prof. Psych., San Diego, 1981.

STUTSMAN,L .M. *733*
Conformance to norms governing the position of mother. DSW U. of California, Berkeley, 1966.

SWANSON,A.R. *734*
An investigation of the relationship between an 8½ to 10½ year-old child's general fearfulness and the child's mother's anxiety, self-differentiation, and accuracy of perception of her child's general fearfulness. PhD New York U. 1975.

SZAPOCZNIK,J. *735*
Role-conflict resolution in Cuban mothers. PhD U. of Miami, 1977.

TAYLOR,L.S. *736*
Communication between mothers and normal siblings of retarded children: nature and modification. PhD U. of North Carolina at Chapel Hill, 1974.

TEITEL,S. *737*
The relationships between maternal childrearing attitudes, atypical behavior among mentally retarded children to levels of severity of amentia. PhD Adelphi U. 1958.

TENDLER,R. *738*
Maternal correlates of differentiation in hearing children of the deaf. PhD Yeshiva U. 1975.

TENNIS,G.H. *739*
Verbal interaction patterns of mothers with their preschool children: an exploration of the sex differences in achievement motivation. PhD Georgia State U. Coll. of Arts and Sciences, 1978.

THEW,C.H.M. *740*
The role of mothers and firstborn female siblings in teaching and encouraging language skills. EdD U. of British Columbia, 1979.

THOMPSON,M.S. *741*
Adolescent motherhood: social support and parenting. PhD U. of Wisconsin-Madison, 1982.

TIMM,S.A. *742*
The behavioral correlates of mothers of low and high self-esteem. PhD U. of Nebraska-Lincoln, 1974.

TROTTA,J.O. *743*
A comparison of the achievement motivation of mothers of retarded readers and mothers of achieving readers. PhD Temple U. 1967.

TRUFANT,C.A. *744*
The effect of familial support systems on black mothers' childrearing attitudes and behaviors, and on their children's competence. PhD Michigan State U. 1977.

TULKIN,S.R. *745*
Mother-infant interaction in the first year of life: an inquiry into the influence of social class. PhD Harvard U. 1971.

URZUA,C.G. 746
A sociolinguistic analysis of the requests of mothers to their two-year-old daughters. PhD U. of Texas at Austin, 1977.

VIRDEN,S.B. 747
The effect of information about infant behavior on primiparas' maternal role adequacy. DNS U. of California, San Francisco, 1981.

VOGEL,M.D. 748
Maternal attitude change toward self and child as a result of training in behavior modification. PhD U. of Maryland, 1975.

VOGEL,S.R. 749
The role of learning in defense: mothers' reinforcement patterns and children's recall and repetition of success and failure tasks. PhD Clark U. 1964.

WALK ER,C.W. 750
Persistence of mourning in the foster child as related to the foster mother's level of maturity. DSW Smith Coll. Sch. for Social Work, 1970.

WALKER,L. 751
Matricentricity and delinquency: a study of the relation of female-based households to delinquency and non-delinquency among negro and white boys. PhD Ohio State U. 1964.

WALLACE-BENJAMIN,J.R. 752
Black mothers' attitudes toward their retarded children. PhD Brandeis U. 1980.

WARD,W.S. 753
Unmarried mothers' decisions about their babies: a social-psychological study. PhD U. of Utah, 1973.

WASSERMAN,G.A. 754
Infant behavior, maternal behavior and maternal report: a cross-situational examination of mothers and their year-old infants. PhD City U. of New York, 1977.

WATERS,E.B.Jr. 755
The stability of individual differences in infant-mother attachment. PhD U. of Minnesota, 1977.

WATFORD,V.W. 756
Mothers' aggressive responses toward their preschool children following insults from an adult male: a test of catharsis and displacement. PhD U. of California, Irvine, 1976.

WATKINS,D.M. 757
A comparison of student housewife/mothers with non-student housewife/mothers on the characteristics of self-perceived identity, self-esteem, marital adjustment, and attitude toward child-rearing. PhD U. of North Colorado, 1982.

WEAVER,C.T. 758
Characteristics of mothers' vocal pitch to younger and older children during mother-child interaction. PhD U. of Virginia, 1976.

WEDDLE,K.D. 759
Relationship between maternal attitudes toward hospitalization and children's behavioral reactions to hospitalization. PhD U. of Tennessee, 1982.

WEEKS,Z.R. 760
The relationship of teenager and late childbearing motherhood to subsequent IQ, educational achievement, and adjustment of offspring. PhD Indiana U. 1982.

WEISEL,J.E. 761
Single-mother attitudes and characteristics related to the self-esteem of her son. PhD California Sch. of Prof. Psych., Los Angeles, 1976.

WEISSMAN,J. 762
An exploratory study of communication patterns of lower-class negro and Puerto Rican mothers and preschool children. EdD Columbia U. 1966.

WELCH,C.E.III 763
The economic legacy of mothers as single parents. PhD U. of Georgia, 1981.

WETHERFORD,R.K. 764
Risk components and security of mother-infant attachment at twelve months. PhD U. of Houston, 1977.

WHEELER,M.A. 765
Mothers' speech in context: age changes and language lessons. PhD Duke U. 1980.

WHEELER,M.J. 766
A study of knowledge of local health services amongst a sample of mothers of 6–12-months-old babies. MSc U. of Manchester, 1974.

WHITE,G.D. 767
The effects of observer presence on mother and child behavior. PhD U. of Oregon, 1973.

WHITE,J.L.Jr. 768
Attitudes toward childrearing as related to some psychodynamic factors in mothers. PhD Michigan State U. 1961.

WHITEHEAD,M.C.M. 769
Psychological factors affecting compliance to a medical treatment program: a study of mother participation in home infusion therapy for hemophiliacs. PhD California Sch. of Prof. Psych., Los Angeles, 1981.

WHITFIELD,C.E.B. 770
Low-income black and white mothers' verbal communication patterns with their preschool children. PhD Arizona State U. 1980.

WHITTED,C. 771
Supports in the black community: black unmarried mothers who kept their babies and achieved their educational and/or professional goals. EdD Columbia U. Teachers Coll. 1978.

WIDERSTROM,A.H. 772
Mother's use of language as a function of the

infant's stage of sensorimotor development. PhD Temple U. 1980.

WIEDER,S. 773
The texture of early maternal experience, maternal control and affect in relation to the second year of life. PhD City U. of New York, 1972.

WILSON,E.C. 774
Developmental changes in maternal influence techniques. PhD DePaul U. 1980.

WINTER,R.M. 775
The separation-individuation negotiations of asthmatic toddlers and their mothers. PhD Smith Coll. Sch. for Social Work, 1982.

WONG,K.M. 776
Maternal teaching style and home environment and the reading achievement of kindergarteners. EdD Rutgers U. 1982.

WOZNIAK,J.A.F. 777
Interaction of mother-child relations with conditions of isolation. PhD U. of Illinois at Urbana-Champaign, 1978.

WRIGHT,W.T.Jr. 778
An investigation of an adjunctive two-therapist group therapy procedure designed to improve the process of consensual validation in the mother-child relationship: the mother. PhD U. of Denver, 1959.

YOUNG,D. 779
Social class differences in the framing of interchanges by mothers for their infants. PhD U. of Loughborough, 1979.

YOUNG,J.W. 780
The personality structure of mothers of male paranoid schizophrenics. PhD Northwestern U. 1952.

ZEGIOB,L.E. 781
Observer effects in mother-child interactions as a function of social class. PhD U. of Georgia, 1976.

ZUNICH,M. 782
Relationship between maternal behavior and attitudes toward family life. PhD Florida State U. 1959.

ZWIEBEL,S. 783
The relation between maternal behaviors and aggression in sons: black and Puerto Rican families. DSW Adelphi U. Sch. of Social Work, 1979.

Child battering and neglect

See also **9** 256.

CLARK,K.N. 784
Knowledge of child development and behavior interaction patterns of mothers who abuse their children. PhD Wayne State U. 1975.

DAVIS,E.E. 785
An investigation of the communication of mothers with assessed abuse potential to their children. PhD U. of Pittsburgh, 1976.

DORAN,L.D. 786
Mothers' disciplinary responses under controllable stress: a child abuse analogue. PhD U. of Washington, 1981.

EBAUGH,M.C. 787
Locus of control, depression and anger in child-abusing mothers. PhD Texas Woman's U. 1979.

EVANS,A.L. 788
Personality characteristics of child-abusing mothers. PhD Michigan State U. 1976.

FLOYD,L.M. 789
Personality characteristics of abusing and neglecting mothers. PhD Louisiana State U. and A&M Coll. 1975.

FRIEDRICH,W.N. 790
Personality and psychophysiological variables in maltreating mothers. PhD U. of North Dakota, 1980.

GAUDIN,J.M. 791
Mothers' perceived strength of primary group networks and maternal child abuse. PhD Florida State U. 1979.

GYNN-ORENSTEIN,J.S. 792
The relationship between moral reasoning, locus of control, emotional empathy, and parenting profile in physically abusing mothers. PhD California Sch. of Prof. Psych., Los Angeles, 1981.

JENSEN,R.F. 793
Early parent-child relationships as perceived by abusive mothers and non-abusive mothers. PhD U. of Wyoming, 1981.

JOHNSON,D.E. 794
Abusive vs. competent mothers: predicting parenting behaviors from self-reported life history variables. PhD Michigan State U. 1979.

KATZ,M.L. 795
A comparison of ego functioning in filicidal and physically child-abusing mothers. PhD California Sch. of Prof. Psych., Los Angeles, 1975.

KENIS,D.R. 796
A study of the personality characteristics of mothers of abused children and failure to thrive children. PhD Northwestern U. 1980.

KIRSCH,S.L. 797
Characteristics of child-abusing mothers. PhD Yeshiva U. 1978.

LOVELAND,R.J. 798
Distinctive personality and discipline characteristics of child-neglecting mothers. PhD U. of North Dakota, 1976.

ROSEN,B. 799
Self-concept incongruence and interpersonal values among abusive mothers. PhD United States International U. 1977.

SCHINDLER,F.E. *800*
Abusive mother-child interactions: a controlled assessment of parenting skills. PhD U. of Arizona, 1982.

SELFRIDGE,E.B. *801*
A comparative study of self-identified abusive mothers and system-identified abusive mothers. PhD United States International U. 1978.

SINCLAIR-BROWN,W. *802*
A TA/Redecision psychotherapy program for mothers who physically abuse and/or seriously neglect their children. PhD Fielding Inst. 1980.

STULTZ,S.L. *803*
Childrearing attitudes of abusive mothers: a controlled study. PhD Cornell U. 1976.

WALKER,L.M. *804*
Patterns of affective communication in abusive and non-abusive mothers. PhD Michigan State U. 1977.

WISNER,J.J. *805*
Mothers who neglect: differentiating factors of their daily lives. DSW U. of California, Berkeley, 1976.

WOOD,A.G. *806*
Differences in child management among court-identified abusive mothers, self-identified abusive mothers, and other mothers. PhD U. of Oklahoma, 1978.

Other family relationships

See also **2** 8.

ANGRES,S.B. *807*
Intergenerational relations and value congruence between young adults and their mothers. PhD U. of Chicago, 1974.

ATKINS,D.V. *808*
A comparison of older sisters of hearing-impaired and normally-hearing children on measures of responsibility and parental attention. PhD U. of California, Los Angeles, 1982.

CEBULA,J.L. *809*
The psychological dysfunction of the adolescent female as related to family dynamics. PhD California Sch. of Prof. Psych., San Diego, 1978.

FREUDENBERG,B.E. *810*
The effect of sisters on feminine development. PhD U. of Pittsburgh, 1982.

HOYE,D.D. *811*
Mother-in-law adjustment of young marrieds. PhD U. of North Carolina at Greensboro, 1971.

MULLALY,M.J. *812*
The structure and process of humor within adult sister relationships. PhD U. of California, Berkeley, 1981.

POMERANCE,R.M. *813*
Sibling loss in young adult women: a restrospective study. PhD Boston U. Grad. Sch. 1973.

ROSEBUD-HARRIS,M.C. *814*
A description of the interaction and subjective characteristics of the relationship between black grandmothers and their grandchildren enrolled in the University of Louisville. PhD U. of Iowa, 1982.

WISOTSKY,M. *815*
Marriage adjustment and inter-generational acceptance: the relationship between marital adjustment and acceptance of mother and mother-in-law. PhD Columbia U. 1960.

Women's employment and the family

See also **3** *passim*; **4** 1605; **5** 122–206, 323–626; **9** 146, 580; **21** 44.

ADLER,K.R. *816*
Marital and maternal role ambivalence and their relationship to the employment status of married women. PhD U. of Miami, 1976.

ALLEN,S.M. *817*
Professional women and marriage. PhD California Sch. of Prof. Psych., Berkeley, 1980.

ALTMAN,S.L. *818*
Women's career plans and maternal employment. PhD Boston U. Grad. Sch. 1975.

AMSLER,J.F. *819*
Responses to stress in early motherhood among employed and non-employed women of two social classes. PhD Harvard U. 1975.

ANSON,R.E. *820*
Spartan wives: the development of an educational program for the wives and children of students at Michigan State College. PhD Columbia U. 1955.

ARMSTRONG,M.W. *821*
The home responsibilities of girls in relation to the employment status of their mothers. EdD Columbia U. 1964.

ARMSTRONG,R.F. *822*
Working mothers and teenage children in an Iowa community. PhD U. of Iowa, 1966.

AVIOLI,P.S. *823*
The employment decision of married mothers of infants. PhD Rutgers U. 1982.

AXELSON,L.J. *824*
A study of the marital adjustment and role defini-

tions of husbands and working and non-working wives. PhD Washington State U. 1963.

BARTLETT,R.L. *825*
The impact of married women and related factors on the distribution of family earnings. PhD Michigan State U. 1974.

BEAUVAIS,C.A. *826*
The family and the work group: dilemmas for women in authority. PhD City U. of New York, 1976.

BEHRMAN,D.L. *827*
Family and/or career: plans made by women expecting their first child. PhD Northwestern U. 1980.

BENN,R.K. *828*
Working mothers and their infants: the relationship between maternal identity integration, childcare and infant attachment. PhD U. of Michigan, 1981.

BERKOVE,G.R.F. *829*
Husband support for women returning to higher education: predictors and outcomes. PhD U. of Michigan, 1978.

BOLLES,A.L. *830*
The impact of working-class women's employment on household organization in Kingston, Jamaica. PhD Rutgers U. 1981.

BRANSON, N.W. *831*
An investigation of the effects of work on the families of black, female registrants in the Baltimore City WIN program: a pilot study. PhD U. of Maryland, 1979.

BRINKMAN,J.E. *832*
The relationship between marital integration and the working wife-mother. PhD U. of Oregon, 1976.

BRIZARD,R.H. *833*
Two days in one: portraits of professional women with families in France and America. PhD Wright Inst. 1977.

BRODIE,J.S. *834*
The effect of selected family variables on the achievement motivation of employed married women. PhD U. of Minnesota, 1981.

BROOKINS,G.K. *835*
Maternal employment: its impact on the sex-role and occupational choices of middle- and working-class black children. PhD Harvard U. 1977.

BROWN,S.E. *836*
Husband's attitude toward and consequences of wife-mother employment. PhD Florida State U. 1970.

BURHANS,R.S. *837*
The industrial employment of women and its influence upon the family. PhD Southern Baptist Theological Seminary, 1945.

CARLSON,B.E. *838*
Shared vs. primarily maternal childrearing: effects of dual careers on families with young children. PhD U. of Michigan, 1980.

CASS,R.H. *839*
Maternal employment as a positive reaction of the modern urban middle-class married women to the situation of anomie. PhD Fordham U. 1964.

CHASE-LANSDALE,P.L. *840*
Maternal employment in a family context: effects on infant-mother and infant-father attachments. PhD U. of Michigan, 1981.

CHIU,G.Y. *841*
Mothers' employment and children's utilization of physician services. PhD U. of Chicago, 1978.

COINER,M.C. *842*
Employment and mothers' emotional states: a psychological study of women re-entering the work force. PhD Yale U. 1978.

COLLINS,N.R. *843*
Facilitators and constraints in home management of the part-time professionally employed wife and mother. EdD Oklahoma State U. 1978.

COMBS,L.G. *844*
Working women's attitudes toward the dual role of wage earner and family member. PhD Florida State U. 1977.

COOK,S.D. *845*
The relationship of wives' employment status and number of children to husbands' life satisfaction and health adjustment. PhD Rosemead Grad. Sch. of Prof. Psych. 1980.

COX,M.J. *846*
The effects of father absence and working mothers on children. PhD U. of Virginia, 1975.

COX,P.P. *847*
Relationships between age of their child, their attitudes toward their job, and employed mothers' perceptions of their feelings toward being separated from their child and their perceptions of their child's feelings about the separation. PhD U. of Maryland, 1981.

DAVIES, J.M. *848*
Sexual identification in daughters of professional and non-working women. PhD Adelphi U. 1979.

DUCKLES,M.M. *849*
Wives and mothers working. PhD Wright Inst. 1977.

DUFFY,M.G. *850*
Professionally employed mothers of infants: a phenomenological study of their experiences. EdD Boston U. Sch. of Educ. 1982.

DUVALL,E.B. *851*
Conceptions of mother roles by five-year-old and six-year-old children of working and non-working mothers. PhD Florida State U. 1955.

EARP,J.L. *852*
Older married women and work: a comparative study of the social, psychological and demographic differences between paid employees and full-time housewives. DSc Johns Hopkins U. 1974.

EASTERBROOKS,M.A. *853*
Toddler development in a family context: variations in maternal employment, father involvement, and parenting characteristics. PhD U. of Michigan, 1982.

ELMAN,M.R. *854*
Coping with conflict between the parental and professional roles: factors related to choice of coping strategy and coping effectiveness for professional women with preschool children. PhD U. of Texas at Austin, 1981.

FAIRHURST,C.P. *855*
The assessment of counselors' attitudes toward the combining of a career and marriage by women. PhD Ohio U. 1969.

FAREL,A.C. *856*
Effects of preferred maternal roles and maternal employment on school adjustment and competence. DrPH U. of North Carolina at Chapel Hill, 1979.

FINKELMAN,J.J. *857*
Maternal employment, family relationships and parental role perception. PhD Yeshiva U. 1965.

FOSTER,A.C. *858*
Wife's earnings as a factor in family net worth accumulation. PhD U. of Missouri-Columbia, 1979.

FRANCIS,B.R. *859*
Effect of maternal employment on the socialization of sex-role and achievement in New Zealand. PhD Cornell U. 1975.

FRANCIS,R.S. *860*
Selected satisfactions and values of working mothers. PhD U. of Tennessee, 1979.

FRANKEL,J. T. *861*
The security status of young children whose mothers are employed. PhD Ohio State U. 1958.

FREITASVANDO,R. *862*
Motherhood and work: the relationship of socioeconomic status and career commitment to stress and psychological well-being. PhD U. of California, Davis, 1980.

FRERKING,R.A. *863*
Occupational status of the mother as a determinant of achievement motivation in women. PhD U. of Alabama, 1974.

GARDINER,W. *864*
A study of role conflict in middle-aged married working women. PhD United States International U. 1982.

GENDELL,M. *865*
Swedish working wives. PhD Columbia U. 1964.

GILLETTE,T .L. *866*
The working mother: a study of the relationship between maternal employment and family structure as influenced by social class and race. PhD U. of North Carolina at Chapel Hill, 1961.

GIMIAN,J. *867*
Self-esteem and autonomy in the daughters of employed mothers. PhD California Sch. of Prof. Psych. Berkeley, 1978.

GLEN,M.L. *868*
The educated, working wife and the division of labor in the household. EdD U. of Toledo, 1977.

GOLDSTEIN,E.S. *869*
The relationship of sex-role, self-concept, attitudes toward women, job involvement, and marital satisfaction in wives of dual career couples with children. PhD New York U. 1978.

GORDON,P.B. *870*
Wives' labor force involvement and husbands' family work: a dual spousal perspective. PhD Ohio State U. 1981.

GOVER,D.A. *871*
Employment as a factor in the marital adjustment of middle-class and working-class wives. PhD U. of North Carolina at Chapel Hill, 1962.

GRANROSE,C.S. *872*
Pathways to intention: a model of college women's intention to remain in the labor force following childbirth. PhD Rutgers U. 1981.

GRAY,J.D. *873*
Role conflicts and coping strategies in married professional women. PhD U. of Pennsylvania, 1979.

GREENWALD,S.E. *874*
Family responsibilities of selected working mothers. PhD New York U. 1960.

GRIGGS,M.B. *875*
Attitudes of high school seniors toward mothers and wives working outside the home. EdD U. of Illinois at Urbana-Champaign, 1971.

HANSON,S.L. *876*
A dynamic family life cycle approach to the socioeconomic attainment and mobility of married women. PhD Pennsylvania State U. 1981.

HEENAN,C. *877*
The impact of a first child on a career woman in her thirties: a phenomenological study. EdD Boston U. Sch. of Educ. 1980.

HOFFMAN,L.N.W. 878
Some effects of the employment of mothers on family structure. PhD U. of Michigan, 1958.

HOOPER,J.O. 879
Responses of family systems to mother's return to school. PhD U. of Wisconsin Madison, 1977.

HOPKINS,J.M. 880
A comparison of wives in dual-career and single-career families. PhD U. of Tennessee, 1977.

HOWE,R.R. 881
Relationships between female role-concepts and anxiety among employed and non-employed mothers of preschool-age children. PhD Wayne State U. 1972.

HURST,V.F. 882
Children's occupational and educational aspirations and expectations: an exploration of the effects of maternal employment. PhD U. of Kentucky, 1978.

HUTH,C.M. 883
Married women's work status: the influence of parents and husbands. PhD Bryn Mawr Coll. 1977.

JOHNSON,C.L. 884
Leadership patterns in working and non-working mother middle-class families. PhD U. of Kansas, 1968.

JOSEPH,L.M. 885
Professional women in the first two years of motherhood: a study of female-to-female support, nurturance and autonomy. EdD U. of Massachusetts, 1982.

JUBELIER,J.R. 886
Professional maternal employment: potential egalitarian effects on family structure and the child. PhD California Sch. of Prof. Psych., Los Angeles, 1978.

KLIGLER,D.S. 887
The effects of the employment of married women on husband and wife role: a study in culture change. PhD Yale U. 1954.

KRIEGER,M.E. 888
The effects upon the family when a women returns to school as reported by wives and husbands. PhD Pittsburgh U. 1977.

KUIPER,S. 889
Work values and problem perceptions of young married women in clerical occupations. EdD Indiana U. 1976.

LEVINE,B.K. 890
Familial parameters of the adjustment of preschool children to maternal employment. PhD Temple U. 1981.

LICHT,R.G. 891
Facilitators and inhibitors of occupational change in middle-aged, married career-oriented women. EdD Columbia U. Teachers Coll. 1978.

LIGHT,J.H. 892
Women balancing careers and children: the female experience in the decision-making process. EdD Boston U. Sch. of Educ. 1982.

LORD, C.B. 893
The relationship of maternal employment and ethnic origin to the sex-role perception of Cuban-American and Anglo-American female adolescents. PhD U. of Miami, 1980.

LYMAN,R.A.F. 894
Occupational status of the mother as a determinant of achievement motivation in women. PhD U. of Alabama, 1974.

MAGZIS,L.R. 895
Maternal employment and self-esteem of children. PhD U. of Michigan, 1977.

MALLAN,L.B. 896
Financial patterns in households with working wives. PhD Northwestern U. 1968.

MANNING,D.E. 897
Viewpoints of male graduate students with respect to their wives working at different stages of the family life cycle. PhD U. of Illinois at Urbana-Champaign, 1967.

MEREDITH,J.C. 898
Comparative life-styles of women: secretarial career vs. career and marriage. PhD U. of Southern California, 1967.

MILLER,B.J. 900
Expressed beliefs and feelings of ninth grade girls toward wives and mothers working outside the home as related to selected environmental characteristics. EdD U. of Georgia, 1975.

MILLER,M.E. 901
Expert information sources and outside employment and facilitators and mother-role change. PhD Michigan State U. 1964.

MISHLER,S.A. 902
Dual congruence and the role orientation and vocational and marital satisfaction of married women. PhD Ohio State U. 1975.

MITCHELL,J.P. 903
Mothers' occupational choices and their effects upon maternal role performance and daughters' occupational expectations. PhD Georgia State U. Coll. of Arts and Sciences, 1982.

MIZE,J.W.Jr. 904
Impact of female employment on marital power and marital adjustment. PhD Ohio State U. 1980.

MOYNIHAN,M.M. 905
Extracurricular activities, maternal employment and the educational and occupational aspirations of females and males. PhD U. of Akron, 1979.

MYERS,F.A. *906*
Economic pressure, perceptions of income needs and the employment of married women. PhD Florida State U. 1981.

NEEDLE,M.P. *907*
Women's satisfaction with work and childcare in relationship to family functioning. PhD U. of Maryland, 1981.

NEYSMITH,S.M. *908*
Working and non-working mothers' perception of the provider role. DSW Columbia U. 1976.

OTA,P.A. *909*
Negotiating motherhood: a class analysis of combining work and parenting roles. PhD U. of Southern California, 1980.

PEREIRA,D.H. *910*
Ego development, coping, and conception and performance of roles in employed, married mothers. PhD New York U. 1978.

PETERS,J.R. *911*
Constituents of experience in job happiness and unhappiness in employed women. PhD Duquesne U. 1969.

PETERS,M.F. *912*
Nine black families: a study of household management and childrearing in black families with working mothers. EdD Harvard U. 1976.

PETERSON,E.T. *913*
The impact of maternal employment on the mother-daughter relationship and on the daughter's role-orientation. PhD U. of Michigan, 1959.

PICHE,L. *914*
La motivation au travail et l'orientation mariage-carrière de la femme selon son niveau hiérarchique. DPS U. of Montreal, 1978.

PLUNKETT,M.S.W. *915*
Working mothers of young children: a study of conflict and integration. PhD U. of Michigan, 1980.

POLOMA,M. *916*
The married professional woman: an empirical examination of three myths. PhD Case Western Reserve U. 1970.

POWELL,K.S. *917*
Maternal employment in relation to family life. PhD Florida State U. 1960.

PRESBY,S. *918*
Home conditions, home management, and the job involvement of employed married mothers. PhD New York U. 1979.

RABINOR,J.R. *919*
Maternal employment during a child's first three years of life: effects on children's social-emotional adjustment. PhD Fordham U. 1980.

REGAN,C.A.B. *920*
Attitudes toward parents and achievement motivation of freshmen women in a selective urban university in relation to mothers' career patterns. PhD U. of Pennsylvania, 1972.

REIBSTEIN,J.A. *921*
Adjustment to the maternal role for mothers leaving careers: the impact of their interactions with role colleagues. PhD U. of Chicago, 1981.

REIS,J.M. *922*
Maternal employment and children's prosocial behavior. PhD State U. of New York at Buffalo, 1979.

RIESCH,S.K. *923*
Occupational commitment, role conflict, and the quality of maternal-infant interaction. DNSC Rush U. Coll. of Nursing, 1981.

RODRIGUEZ,C.F.Q. *924*
Families of working mothers in Puerto Rico. PhD Ohio State U. 1976.

ROSE,S.C. *925*
Role changes: the effects of working wives on marital communication and sex-role ideology. PhD California Sch. of Prof. Psych., Los Angeles, 1982.

ROSENTHAL,D.M. *926*
Working and non-working mothers in intact and non-intact families and effects on the child's perception of the parent-child relationship, educational achievement, self-concept, occupational aspirations, and vocational maturity. PhD State U. of New York at Buffalo, 1978.

ROSSMANN,J.E. *927*
An investigation of maternal employment among college women: a twenty-five year follow-up. PhD U. of Minnesota, 1963.

ROWAN,J.B. *928*
A study of role overload, nonmarket time use, and coping strategies of middle-class, employed women in intact families. PhD U. of Illinois at Urbana-Champaign, 1982.

SENF,J.H. *929*
Women's employment and kinship patterns. PhD U. of Illinois at Chicago Circle, 1977.

SHAW-GEORGE,P.A. *930*
Maternal satisfaction of professional women. EdD Boston U. Sch. of Educ. 1980.

SHEHAN,C.L. *931*
Informative beliefs and work orientations of employed and nonemployed mothers of preschool children. PhD Pennsylvania State U. 1981.

SMITH,J.W. *932*
Marital consequences of women's educational and career re-entry. PhD U. of California, Davis, 1981.

SOBEL,W.K. *933*
Sex-role stereotypes in relation to self-actualization and maternal employment among prospective clinicians. PhD Boston Coll. 1977.

SOBOL,M.B.G. *934*
Correlates of present and expected future work status of married women. PhD U. of Michigan, 1961.

SONENSTEIN,F.L. *935*
The impact of a wife's employment on working-class families. PhD Boston U. Grad. Sch. 1976.

STAFFORD,K. *936*
An economic analysis of employed wives' time allocation decisions. PhD Cornell U. 1978.

STECZAK,C.L.W. *937*
The impact of availability of childcare arrangements on the career paths and eventual job satisfaction of women in vocational education. PhD Purdue U. 1980.

STROUD,J.G. *938*
Careers of middle-aged women in work and family, personal and social concomitants and antecedents. PhD U. of California, Berkeley, 1977.

SWAIN,R.E. *939*
Maternal employment status, parental attitude toward and satisfaction with that status, and the behavior of children in preschool. PhD U. of Illinois at Urbana-Champaign, 1981.

TARR,L.L. *940*
The influence of personality and power dimensions on the sexual harassment encountered by working women. PhD California Sch. of Prof. Psych., Fresno, 1981.

THOMOPOULOS,E.H.C. *941*
Parents of preschool children: the work status of the mother as it relates to marriage adjustment, anxiety, and egalitarianism. PhD Illinois Inst. of Technology, 1974.

THOMPSON,E.J. *942*
Employment and childbearing decisions of mothers of young children. PhD U. of Washington, 1979.

VILLADSEN,A.W. *943*
A study of the interactions between family responsibilities and careers of women administrators in selected Southern institutions of higher education. PhD U. of Alabama, 1979.

WALKER,R.A. *944*
Wife's hours of market work related to family saving behavior. PhD Purdue U. 1978.

WALSH,C.A. *945*
The relationship between maternal employment and the development of self-concept in children. PhD Marquette U. 1979.

WARSHAW,R. *946*
The effects of working mothers on children. PhD Adelphi U. 1976.

WEBB,N.B. *947*
Attachment relationships of preschoolers to parents and other familiar caretakers: implications for day care and working mothers. DSW Columbia U. 1979.

WEISKOPF-BOCK,S.A. *948*
The effects of maternal employment on mother-child interaction and parental childrearing attitudes: a comparison of working mother and non-working mother middle-income families. PhD Harvard U. 1982.

WHITE,A. *949*
The effect of non-domestic employment of women upon their maternal functions. MD U. of Edinburgh, 1924.

WHITEHURST,R.N. *950*
Employed mother's influences on working-class family structure. PhD Purdue U. 1963.

WIGG,J.P. *951*
Women's work and family commitment. PhD U. of Wisconsin-Milwaukee, 1981.

WINSTON,N.A.S. *952*
The consequences for role performance and husband-wife interaction when the wife's socio-economic status equals or exceeds her husband's. PhD Washington State U. 1980.

WOODS,M.B. *953*
The unsupervised child of the working mother. PhD Bryn Mawr Coll. 1968.

WRIGHT,M.S. *954*
Parent-child relations, achievement motivation, and sex-role attitudes among black and white professional women in traditional and pioneer occupations. PhD State U. of New York at Buffalo, 1981.

YOUNG,S.F. *955*
Paternal involvement as related to maternal employment and attachment behavior directed to the father by the one-year-old infant. PhD State U. 1975.

7 Feminism

See studies of the women's movement before c. 1945 see **9** History. Related studies from other chapters are too numerous to list.

ALLEN,B.A. *1*
Democracy in America revisited: an application of Tocqueville's political theory to feminist theory and action. PhD Indiana U. 1981.

AULT,J.M. *2*
Class differences in family structure and the social bases of modern feminism. PhD Brandeis U. 1981.

BAHN,A.K. *3*
The women's movement. PhD City U. of New York, 1979.

BAKER,A.J. *4*
Ideology and the structure of social movement organizations: a case study of lesbian-feminism. PhD Case Western Reserve U. 1979.

BAKER,B.J. *5*
Acceptance versus rejection of the traditional feminine role: consideration of women's liberation. PhD Wayne State U. 1972.

BANKS,W.R. *6*
Sexual authority: an educational, historical, philosophical and sociological study in support of women's equality. PhD Claremont Grad. Sch. 1975.

BARKER-BENFIELD,G.T. *7*
The horrors of the half known life: aspects of the exploitation of women by men. PhD U. of California, Los Angeles, 1968.

BARTHOLOMEW,C.G. *8*
Attitudes and responses towards men and women who affiliate with the women's movement: a simulation study. PhD Syracuse U. 1980.

BAUER,A.J. *9*
A study of self-concept with women who identify with either a gay lib or women's lib organization. EdD U. of Northern Colorado, 1973.

BLACHER,J. *10*
An exploration of androgyny, self-actualization and field-independence in lesbian feminist and non-feminist and non-lesbian feminist and non-feminist women. PhD California Sch. of Prof. Psych., Los Angeles, 1977.

BLUMHAGEN,G.K.O. *11*
The relationship between female identity and feminism. PhD Washington U. 1974.

BRIGHT,C. *12*
Feminist ideology: a philosophical critique. PhD U. of Washington, 1979.

BUCHWALTER,S.D. *13*
Feminism and female role-conflict as related to adjustment and self-acceptance. PhD Kent State U. 1976.

BYNUM,L.T.M. *14*
Black feminist theology: a new word about God. DMin Sch. of Theology at Claremont, 1980.

CALIX,E.C. *15*
The feminist as perceived by the mental health worker. PhD California Sch. of Prof. Psych., San Diego, 1980.

CASSELL,J.M. *16*
A group called women: recruitment and organization in contemporary American feminism. PhD Columbia U. 1975.

CAVICCHI,M.A. *17*
Liberal theories of representation and the women's movement. PhD Case Western Reserve U. 1976.

CAVIN,S.E. *18*
An historical and cross-cultural analysis of sex ratios, female sexuality, and homosexual segregation versus heterosexual integration of patterns in relation to the liberation of women. PhD Rutgers U. 1978.

CHURGIN,J.R. *19*
The quiet revolution: the new woman and the old academe. EdD Columbia U. Teachers Coll. 1976.

CLAVAN,S. *20*
Impact of feminism on American family structure. PhD Temple U. 1972.

CLINE,S.I. *21*
Lesbian feminist versions: construction of a new reality. MLitt U. of Lancaster, 1982.

CLINTON,K.B. *22*
Feminism: an analysis and assessment. PhD Kansas State U. 1972.

COLE,D. 23
A typological study of the women's rights movements: implications for black women and education. EdD Rutgers U. 1976.

CRIGLER,P.W. 24
Significant variables indicative of commitment to the women's movement. PhD Northwestern U. 1973.

CROSBY,J.A. 25
From rationality to liberation: a critique of feminist ideology. PhD U. of Texas at Austin, 1977.

DARPLI,F. 26
The relationship of involvement in the women's liberation movement and measured self-actualization. PhD U. of Pittsburgh, 1974.

DEMPEWOLFF,J.A. 27
Feminism and its correlates. PhD U. of Cincinnati, 1972.

EISENSTEIN,Z.R. 28
Species life in Marx and Durkheim: its import as an ideology for women in contemporary society. PhD U. of Massachusetts, 1972.

ELKINS,H.L. 29
Redefining women. PhD New Mexico U. 1977.

EVANS,S.M. 30
Personal politics: the roots of women's liberation in the civil rights movement and the new left. PhD U. of North Carolina at Chapel Hill, 1976.

FARLEY,J.T.T. 31
Women on the march again: the rebirth of feminism in an academic community. PhD Cornell U. 1970.

FARRELL,W.F. 32
The political potential of the women's liberation movement as indicated by its effectiveness in changing men's attitudes. PhD New York U. 1974.

FERRANDINO,M.M. 33
Patriarchy and biological necessity – a feminist and anarchist critique. PhD State U. of New York at Buffalo, 1977.

FERREE,M.M. 34
The emerging constituency: feminism, employment and the working class. PhD Harvard U. 1976.

FITZGERALD,L.E. 35
A comparison of the rhetorical proofs employed by selected speakers of two feminist movements in the United States: the woman's suffrage movement, 1869–1920, and the women's liberation movement, 1963–1973. PhD New York U. 1975.

FLAMMANG,J.A. 36
The political consciousness of American women: a critical analysis of liberal feminism in America. PhD U. of California, Los Angeles, 1980.

FLEMING,J.J. 37
Women against feminism: the social bases of women's opposition to change in women's rights and roles. PhD Stanford U. 1982.

FOSS,K.A. 38
Ideological manifestations in the discourse of contemporary feminism. PhD U. of Iowa, 1976.

FRANKLIN,D.W. 39
Correlates of participation and non-participation in the women's liberation movement. PhD U. of Chicago, 1975.

FREEMAN,J. 40
The politics of women's liberation: a case study of an emerging social movement and its relation to the policy process. PhD U. of Chicago, 1973.

FULLER,P.E. 41
Laura Clany and the women's rights movement. PhD U. of Kentucky, 1971.

FURGERI,L.M. 42
The lesbian/feminist movement and social change: female homosociality, a new consciousness. EdD Columbia U. Teachers Coll. 1977.

GALLAGHER,M.M.F. 43
Women's liberation: social movement in a complex society. PhD U. of Colorado at Boulder, 1973.

GAMMAGE,J.K. 44
Quest for equality: an historical overview of women's rights activism in Texas, 1890–1975. PhD North Texas State U. 1982.

GILL,M.J. 45
Self-esteem and males' receptiveness to persuasion toward women's liberation ideology. PhD Washington State U. 1975.

GILL,S.K. 46
Supporting equality for women: an analysis of attitudes toward the Equal Rights Amendment. PhD U. of Oregon, 1982.

GILLESPIE-WOLTEMADE,N.M. 47
The emergence of a feminist metaculture: women's liberation as a global movement. PhD Ohio State U. 1982.

GIRARD,K.L. 48
How schools fail women: a study of feminists' perceptions of their schooling experiences and women's schooling needs. EdD U. of Massachusetts, 1974.

GLENNON,L.M. 49
A sociology of knowledge analysis of the women's liberation movement. PhD Rutgers U. 1974.

GOLDSMITH,S.P.N. 50
Personality, ego development, and moral reasoning differences between feminists and non-feminists. PhD U. of Minnesota, 1978.

GORRINGE,R.A. *51*
The hero myth and the women's movement. PhD California Sch. of Prof. Psych., Berkeley, 1974.

GREEN,P.A. *52*
The feminist consciousness. PhD Southern Illinois U. at Carbondale, 1978.

GREVATT,M.V. *53*
Lesbian/feminism: a response to oppression. PhD Case Western Reserve U. 1975.

GRUENEBAUM,M.J. *54*
The emergence and transformation of protest movements: a study of the women's movement in the United States. PhD Columbia U. 1980.

HADLEY,C. *55*
Collective and individual problems of feminist leaders: an inquiry into social process factors affecting women's concerns in the southeastern US. PhD Florida State U. 1979.

HANLEY,E.G. *56*
Male and female elementary school teachers' attitude and their perception of the other sex's attitude toward the women's liberation movement: a 'Q' analysis. PhD Wayne State U. 1978.

HAYMES,H.J. *56a*
The relationship of selected non-fictional popular and scholarly literature about women in the post World War II period (1945 to 1962) to the ideas of noted writers of the American women's liberation movement (1963 to 1970). EdD New York U. 1971.

HEIDE, W.S. *57*
Feminism for the health of it. PhD Union for Experimenting Coll. and U. 1978.

HEMMONS,W.M. *58*
Towards an understanding of attitudes held by the black woman on the women's liberation movement. PhD Case Western Reserve U. 1973.

HODGES,G.F. *59*
Betty Friedan's role as reformer in the women's liberation movement, 1960–1970. PhD Bowling Green State U. 1980.

HOFFMANN,F.L. *60*
Foundations of feminist social theory: implications of Freudian and existentialist ontologies. PhD U. of Oregon, 1977.

JARDINE,L.L. *61*
Educational implications in the writings of certain contemporary feminist theoreticians. PhD Arizona State U. 1978.

JOANS,B. *62*
Women's liberation small groups: a study in behavioral anthropology. PhD City U. of New York, 1974.

KLEIN,E. *63*
A social learning perspective on political mobilization: why the women's liberation movement happened when it did. PhD U. of Michigan, 1980.

KNOCHE,C.F. *64*
Feminism and political participation: the role of ideology, 1972–76. PhD U. of Wisconsin-Madison, 1978.

KOPLEWITZ,J.F. *65*
Toward a theory of feminist-oriented education. PhD Union for Experimenting Coll. and U. 1982.

KROLL,B.S. *66*
Rhetoric and organizing the Twin Cities women's movement, 1969–1976. PhD U. of Minnesota, 1981.

LANDES,J.B. *67*
The theory behind women's liberation problems and prospects. PhD New York U. 1975.

LEIDIG,M.W. *68*
A comparative study of feminists and antifeminists with regard to current life style and attitudes. PhD U. of Colorado at Boulder, 1976.

LEX,L.A.M. *69*
The feminist movement: its impact on women in the state legislatures. PhD Iowa State U. 1977.

MCDERMOTT,P. *70*
Autonomy or anatomy: women and rights in two traditions of American political thought. PhD U. of Arizona, 1982.

MANDLE,J.D. *71*
Attitudes towards the women's liberation movement and their correlates: a case study of undergraduate women. PhD Bryn Mawr Coll. 1974.

MANLEY,B. *72*
Feminist orientation as related to empathy, locus of control, and demographic variables: a study of women. PhD California Sch. of Prof. Psych., Los Angeles, 1976.

MANNOLINI,C.A. *73*
Towards a philosophy of feminism: a matter of androgyny. PhD Southern Illinois U. at Carbondale, 1975.

MARTIN-GERHARDS,R.A. *74*
A comparison of feminist and non-feminist women on certain life-style characteristics. EdD Idaho State U. 1977.

MATARESE,S.M. *75*
Two views of equality: liberal and Marxist perspectives on 'the woman question'. PhD U. of Minnesota, 1979.

MICHAELSON,R.L. *76*
The effects of varied focus on women's issues on the attitudes of college women. EdD Boston U. Sch. of Educ. 1979.

MILES,A.R. *77*
The politics of feminist radicalism: a study of integrative feminism. PhD U. of Toronto, 1979.

MILLER,L .S. *78*
Implications of the women's liberation movement on the personal behavior of the Puerto Rican women residing in the City of New York. PhD Caribbean Center for Advanced Studies, 1979.

MONTGOMERY,D.A. *79*
An intellectual profile of Belle Case La Follette: progressive editor, political strategist, and feminist. PhD Indiana U. 1975.

MORAIN,T.J. *80*
The emergence of the women's movement, 1960–1970. PhD U. of Iowa, 1974.

MORGAN,C.S. *81*
Support for the goals of the women's rights movement among college students. PhD U. of Oklahoma, 1973.

MORRIS,M.B. *82*
The public definition of a social movement: women's liberation. PhD U. of Southern California, 1972.

MUDD,S.E. *83*
Conciliation and confrontation in feminist rhetoric: an analysis of contemporary feminist manifestoes. PhD U. of Minnesota, 1978.

NELSON,J.F. *84*
Some causes and consequences of female liberation attitudes in two Latin American metropolises: a causal analysis of non-interval data. PhD U. of Chicago, 1975.

NELSON,J .M. *85*
Attitude-behavior consistency among black feminist and traditional black women. PhD Kent State U. 1981.

NOEL,M.A. *86*
Charting and projecting the progress of women in the United States. PhD U. of Kansas, 1979.

NOLAN,A.M. *87*
A study of academic women's inventoried attitudes toward women's liberation. EdD U. of Illinois at Urbana-Champaign, 1977.

NORTHROP,A. *88*
The critical generation of feminists: a longitudinal analysis of college-educated men and women. PhD U. of Chicago, 1975.

ODENDAHL,T.J. *89*
The women's network: conflict and opportunity in a corporate structure. PhD U. of Colorado at Boulder, 1982.

O'KEEFE,B.E. *90*
Attitudes towards women's liberation: relationships between cooperation, competition, personality, and demographic variables. PhD Saint Louis U. 1971.

OLSEN,S.M. *91*
Sixteen middle-class mothers view the women's movement: its ideological relevance and psychological effects. PhD Humanistic Psych. Inst. 1980.

ONDERCIN,D.G. *92*
The compleat woman: the equal rights amendment and perceptions of womanhood, 1920–1972. PhD U. of Minnesota, 1973.

PALMER,B.B. *93*
The impact of the new feminism on marital interaction with implications for counselors. PhD Ohio State U. 1972.

PIAZZA,T.L. *94*
The sources of support for feminism. PhD U. of California, Berkeley, 1980.

PORTER,C.S. *95*
Locus of control and attitudes toward the women's liberation movement as a function of sex and marital status. EdD Rutgers U. 1977.

REICHENTHAL,C.A. *97*
Feminism: consciousness-raising and psychology. PhD State U. of New York at Buffalo, 1975.

RICHARD,P.B. *98*
Explaining involvement in the women's movement: a study of ten groups in Syracuse. PhD Syracuse U. 1975.

RICHMAN,P.A. *99*
A study of pluralistic ignorance in the context of the women's liberation movement. PhD U. of Ottawa, 1974.

RIGER,S. *100*
Changes in ideology and activity with participation in the women's movement. PhD U. of Michigan, 1973.

RINEHART,J.G. *101*
The feminist reflex: its implications for sociological theorizing. PhD New York U. 1981.

RINEHART,S.H. *102*
The anti-feminist impulse. PhD Purdue U. 1982.

RISCH,S.L.F. *103*
The true believer and the moral agent: alternative images of feminist action. PhD U. of Massachusetts, 1975.

ROOS,J.A.H. *104*
Berkeley single feminists: ideological and structural factors influencing women's network formation and role construction. PhD U. of Colorado at Boulder, 1978.

ROSENTHAL,K.M. *105*
Women in transition: an ethnography of a women's liberation organization as a case study of personal and cultural change. PhD Harvard U. 1972.

ROSENTHAL,N.B. *106*
Consciousness raising: individual change and social change in the American women's liberation

movement. PhD State U. of New York at Stony Brook, 1976.

ROSENTHAL,P.Z. *107*
(Part III) The rhetoric of women's lib. PhD Rutgers U. 1971.

ROTTMAN,M.N. *108*
The effects of a self-administered feminist literature package on attitudes toward sex-role stereotypes among third class cadets at the United States Coast Guard Academy. PhD U. of Connecticut, 1980.

RYAN,P. A. *109*
The ideology of feminism, 1900–1920: an anthology of feminist ideas of motherhood, birth control and sexuality. MSc U. Coll. Cardiff, 1979.

SABET,S.S. *110*
Whatever happened to yin? A political analysis of the fate of the feminine principle in the history of western civilization. PhD Claremont Grad. Sch. 1977.

SABO,D.F .Jr. *111*
Sexuality and social changes: male reactions to feminism. PhD State U. of New York at Buffalo, 1979.

SAMARA,B.M. *112*
Teachers' conceptions of children's sex roles as related to attitudes about the women's liberation movement and personal background data. PhD Temple U. 1974.

SCANLON,G.M. *113*
The feminist debate in modern Spain. PhD U. of London, King's Coll. 1973.

SCHMID,M. *114*
Feminist attitudes: dimensions and distribution by gender, religion and class. PhD Northwestern U. 1974.

SCHUMACHER- FINELL,J. *115*
The relationship between attitudes toward feminism and the sex, age, and background factors of the residents in a small town setting. PhD Columbia U. 1977.

SHERWIN,S.B. *116*
Moral foundations of feminism. PhD Stanford U. 1974.

SHORTSLEEVES,J.M. *117*
Feminists and nonfeminists: differences in their sex-role concepts and their orientations toward achievement. PhD U. of Massachusetts, 1977.

SINGER,M.A. *118*
Attitudes about sex roles and the women's liberation movement as predictors of psychological adjustment and eight case histories of modern and traditional women. PhD U. of Washington, 1976.

SMITH,C.M. *119*
Occupational structure and rewards: an examination of feminist claims. PhD U. of Texas at Austin, 1974.

SPENCER,M. *120*
Social power and the capacity for innovation: an exploratory study of adult socialization in the context of the women's movement. PhD U. of California, Berkeley, 1976.

STEPHENSON,M.G. *121*
Being in women's liberation: a case study in social change. PhD U. of British Columbia, 1975.

SWINGER,H.K. *122*
The black militant woman and intellectual functioning. PhD U. of Southern California, 1978.

TAFT,J.J. *123*
The woman movement from the point of view of social consciousness. PhD U. of Chicago, 1913.

TALEPOROS,E. *124*
Women's liberationists and pseudo-women's liberationists – their beliefs about social issues, and perceptions of male-female relations. PhD New York U. 1974.

TALLEN,B.S. *125*
Liberal equality and feminism: the implications of the thought of John Stuart Mill. PhD U. of Michigan, 1980.

TAVRIS,C. A. *126*
The unliberated liberals' attitudes toward the issues of women's liberation. PhD U. of Michigan, 1971.

TONKINSON,M.E. *127*
Changing consciousness: the impact of the women's liberation movement on non-activist women in a university community. PhD U. of Oregon, 1976.

TRASK,H.K. *128*
Eros and power: the promise of feminist theory. PhD U. of Wisconsin-Madison, 1981.

TYRAN,C.J. *129*
The response of Queens College to the women's movement. PhD Duke U. 1981.

VENKATESH,A. *130*
The significance of the women's movement to marketing – a life-style analysis. PhD Syracuse U. 1977.

VOLLMER,B.M. *131*
Psychosocial characteristics of college women involved in campus women's liberation groups. PhD U. of Denver, 1974.

WALKER,J. *132*
Women's agency: socialist revolution and women's liberation. PhD Cornell U. 1978.

WAUGH,B.R. *133*
The evolution of a women's liberation movement group from 1970 to 1980: a study of the women's program of a theological consortium. PhD Wright Inst. 1981.

WEINER,J.R. *134*
The family of woman: a mythological analysis of the rhetoric of contemporary feminist song. PhD State U. of New York at Buffalo, 1979.

WEISS,T.B. *135*
The rhetoric of radical feminism: a pentadic analysis of the inception of a rhetorical movement. PhD Temple U. 1978.

WEITZ,R. *136*
Feminist consciousness raising, self-concept and depression. PhD Yale U. 1978.

WHEELER, B.A. *137*
Attitudes of women in business education toward selected concepts pertaining to women's rights. EdD Arizona State U. 1972.

WILLIAMSON,D.K. *138*
Rhetorical analysis of selected modern black American spokespersons on the women's liberation movement. PhD Ohio State U. 1980.

WILLS,D. *139*
The effects of feminist rhetoric on low-income women of limited education. PhD U. of Oregon, 1980.

WOLF,D.G. *140*
Contemporary Amazons: a study of a lesbian feminist community. PhD U. of California, Berkeley, 1977.

WOLFF,S.S. *141*
Feminism as a development phase: the relationship of feminist involvement to the adult development of women. EdD U. of Massachusetts, 1981.

WOODS,J.V. *142*
Family conflicts in America resulting from the women's liberation movement of the 1960s and 70s. PhD Union for Experimenting Coll. and U. 1980.

YAMPOLSKY,F.N. *143*
The power of a dissident group, the women's movement, to insert its doctrines into a subsystem of the media over time. PhD U. of Southern California, 1974.

YATES,G.G. *144*
Ideologies of contemporary American feminism. PhD U. of Minnesota, 1973.

YERACARIS,F. *145*
Consistency of sex-role characteristics and values in feminist and traditional women and their husbands. PhD California Sch. of Prof. Psych. Los Angeles.

8 Health

Alcohol, drugs, tobacco: use and misuse

Alcohol

For studies of the early temperance movement see **9** History. *See also* **19** 145, 446, 477; **20** 98, 166, 198.

ANDERSON,S.C. *1*
Patterns of identification in alcoholic women. PhD Rutgers U. 1976.

BATES,M.F. *2*
Sex-role strain in alcoholic women. PhD Columbia U. 1981.

BEALL,B.S.M. *3*
The expressed and physiologically measured attitudes to alcoholic beverages of female social drinkers and non-drinkers. PhD Texas Woman's U. 1976.

BENDER,N.J. *4*
An investigation of selected pretreatment characteristics of female alcoholics as related to treatment completion or noncompletion. PhD United States International U. 1978.

BENSON,C.S. *5*
Coping and support among daughters of alcoholics. PhD Indiana U. 1980.

CARTER,A.J. *6*
Social and demographic characteristics of a selected group of black females who abuse alcohol. EdD George Peabody Coll. for Teachers, 1982.

COLMAN,C.J. *7*
Problem drinking women: aspects of their marital interaction and sex-role style. PhD Harvard U. 1975.

DANIELS,L.A. *8*
Drinking patterns among women: a sociological study. PhD U. of Washington, 1980.

DUNLAP,N.G. *9*
Alcoholism in women: some antecedents and correlates of remission in middle-class members of Alcoholics Anonymous. PhD U. of Texas at Austin, 1961.

EDDY,C.C. *10*
The effects of alcohol on anxiety in problem and nonproblem drinking women. PhD Cornell U. 1978.

FITZGERALD,M.C. *11*
Correlates of alcoholism among Roman Catholic nuns: psychological and attitudinal variables. PhD United States International U. 1982.

FLEMING,M. *12*
Hostility in recovering alcoholic women compared to non-alcoholic women, and the effect of psychodrama on the former in reducing hostility. PhD United States International U. 1974.

FORTIN,M.L. *13*
Symptom progression of alcohol addiction in females and correlates of loss of control over drinking. EdD U. of San Francisco, 1981.

GARRETT,G.R. *14*
Drinking behavior of homeless women. EdD Washington State U. 1971.

GEISLE R,P.M. *15*
Patients at the University of Utah alcoholism clinic, 1957–1963; part III: Women. PhD U. of Utah, 1963.

GUINLE,M.P. *16*
Counselor sex and program modes in the treatment of female alcoholics. PhD U. of Mississippi, 1979.

HAZEN,L.R. *17*
Alcohol use, knowledge and attitudes among freshman women. EdD Oregon State U. 1980.

HERZ,S.M. *18*
Development considerations relating to women: alcohol and social isolation. PhD Yeshiva U. 1980.

HERZOG,M.A. *19*
A multidimensional approach to the diagnosis of alcoholism in women. PhD Marquette U. 1979.

HITCHCOX,C.F. *20*
EMG biofeedback relaxation training of women alcoholics: an alternative coping response to stress and helplessness. PhD California Sch. of Prof. Psych., Berkeley, 1978.

HOAR,C.H. *21*
Field dependence, level of ego development, and female sex-role perceptions of alcoholic and

nonalcoholic women. EdD George Washington U. 1976.

HORN,D.L. 22
The use of alcohol by women as a stress reducer in interpersonal relations: the 86% proof solution. PhD U. of Tennessee, 1978.

IDLEBURG,D.A. 23
An exploratory study of treatment outcomes in a 12–year follow-up of black and white female alcoholics. PhD U. of Washington, 1982.

KINSEY,B.A. 24
Alcohol and women: a sociocultural study of 46 female inebriates at the Willmar State Hospital, Willmar, Minnesota. PhD U. of Nebraska-Lincoln, 1962.

KLEEMAN,B.E. 25
Women alcoholics in management: identification and intervention in the workplace. EdD Boston U. Sch. of Educ. 1982.

KRAUTHAMER,C.M. 26
The personality of alcoholic mothers and their children: a study of their relationship to birth order, mother-child attitude and socioeconomic status. PhD Rutgers U. 1973.

KREISWORTH,V.S. 27
The identification of personality traits of drinking and nondrinking female college students. PhD Purdue U. 1980.

LANSBERRY,C.R. 28
The relationship between alcohol consumption, satisfaction and experienced control among women. PhD New York U. 1980.

LEMAY,D.Y. 29
An analysis of factors involved in the treatment of alcoholic and drug-addicted women in a hospital-based detoxification and rehabilitation program. EdD U. of Maine, 1980.

LITZ,J.E. 30
Life stresses and alcoholism in women. PhD City U. of New York, 1978.

LOGAN,D. 31
Marital adjustment and interaction between recovered alcoholic wives and their husbands. PhD U. of Georgia, 1980.

MCGOWAN,M.N. 32
Psychological correlates of alcoholic beverage consumption in women. PhD New York U. 1980.

MAXSON,C.E. 33
Alcoholism and suicide among females. PhD U. of California, Los Angeles, 1981.

MENUSTIK,C.E. 34
Verbal and nonverbal interaction patterns of alcoholic women and their husbands. PhD U. of South Carolina, 1980.

MIRAGLIA,P.J. 35
Selected correlates of self-reported alcohol use in Catholic college women. PhD U. of Pennsylvania, 1975.

MOYAR,M.M. 36
Psychosocial aspects of recovering alcoholic women. PhD Case Western Reserve U. 1981.

MUCHOWSKI-CONLEY,P.M. 37
The effects of a systematic skills training program for female alcoholics and their significant others on selected rehabilitation outcome variables. ScD Boston U., Sargent Coll. of Allied Health Professions.

NEWCOMB,C.H. 38
An exploration of the experience of parental deprivation in low-income female alcoholics. PhD George Washington U. 1982.

PINHAS,V.L. 39
An investigation to compare the degree to which alcoholic and non-alcoholic women report sex guilt and sexual control. PhD New York U. 1978.

RASMUSSEN,R.K. 40
Perceived family climate and interpersonal characteristics of alcoholic women and their husbands. PhD California Sch. of Prof. Psych. Berkeley, 1979.

RIDLON,F. 41
Status insularity and stigmatization among female alcoholics. PhD Syracuse U. 1982.

SAQUET-SHIRE,J.L. 42
Time in the house: a study of alcoholic women in halfway house recovery. PhD Northwestern U. 1981.

SCHOENEBECK,B.J. 43
An exploratory study of problem recognition and treatment entry as experienced by recovering female alcoholics. EdD Boston U. Sch. of Educ. 1980.

SCHWEIGLER,J.L. 44
The effects of structured group therapy and assertion training on a female alcoholic population. EdD U. of Southern California, 1981.

SILBERSTEIN,J.A. 45
Neuropsychological impairment in women alcoholics. PhD U. of Illinois at Urbana-Champaign, 1981.

SILVER-HOFFMAN,L.G. 46
Factors underlying the use of alcohol among professional women and their policy implications: a multivariate approach. PhD Brandeis U. 1977.

SOYSTER,C.P. 47
The meaning of stressful life events and social class fluctuations for women alcoholics. PhD California Sch. of Prof. Pscyh., Berkeley, 1981.

SPARADEO,F.R. 48
Cognitive deficits in alcohol-troubled females: a

comparative study. PhD U. of Rhode Island, 1981.

STOKES,E.J. *49*
Alcoholic women in treatment: factors associated with patterns of help-seeking. PhD Brandeis U. 1977.

TALAN,B.S. *50*
Power and control: predictors for the alcoholic woman's choice and effectiveness of treatment. PhD U. of Detroit, 1981.

TEED,R.D. *51*
The effect of interpersonal contact with female alcoholics on the attitudes of counseling students. PhD Arizona State U. 1968.

THOMAS,D.A. *52*
A study of selected factors on successfully and unsuccessfully treated alcoholic women. PhD Michigan State U. 1971.

TONOWSKI,R.F. *53*
Depressed alcoholic women: personality characteristics and life events. PhD Rutgers U. 1975.

TRACEY,D. *54*
An experimental analysis of the behavior of female alcoholics. PhD Rutgers U. 1975.

TRUDEL,R.M. *55*
Group therapy with women alcoholics: a perspective for rehabilitation. ScD Boston U. Sargent Coll. of Allied Health Professions, 1978.

VOGT,J.L.W. *56*
An intensive design study to determine the effects of two self-control modalities on the behavior of alcoholic women. PhD U. of Colorado at Boulder, 1977.

VOLPE,J.N. *57*
Links to sobriety: adaptions of female alcoholics. PhD Catholic U. of America, 1978.

WARREN,G.A. *58*
A survey of the drinking patterns of never married college women. EdD U. of Tennessee, 1979.

WILLIAMS,L.J. *59*
A comparative study of self-actualization of female alcoholics in Alcoholics Anonymous. PhD United States International U. 1980.

WILSNACK,S.C. *60*
Psychological factors in female drinking. PhD Harvard U. 1972.

WOODS,C.P. *61*
Alcohol abuse among lesbians: an investigation of possible contributory factors. PhD United States International U. 1981.

Drugs

ANDERSON,C.R. *62*
A self-concept study of white women addicted to heroin. PhD California Sch. of Prof. Psych. San Diego, 1980.

BAUMAN,P.S. *63*
A controlled study of drug-addicted mothers' parenting and their children's development. PhD California Sch. of Prof. Psych., Berkeley, 1980.

BROOKS-FINN,L.W. *64*
A study of illegal substance use and rejection of female role stereotyping among first year community college students. PhD Wayne State U. 1975.

COCKERILL,C.S. *65*
Personality characteristics of female adolescent former heroin addicts. PhD St John's U. 1976.

CUFFARO,S.T. *66*
A discriminant analysis of sociocultural motivation and personality differences among black, Anglo and Chicana female drug abusers in a medium security prison. PhD United States International U. 1978.

DATESMAN,S.K. *67*
The criminality of female heroin users. PhD U. of Delaware, 1980.

DICK,K.V.Jr. *68*
Typological analysis of personality patterns of drug-abusing females. PhD Ohio State U. 1979.

FAITH,K. *69*
Drug addiction, from a study of women and criminal justice. PhD U. of California, Santa Cruz, 1981.

GOLDIN,G.M. *70*
A study of maternal childrearing attitudes and selected personality variables among drug-addicted and non-addicted Caucasian pregnant women. PhD St John's U. 1980.

LAPP,J.E. *71*
Contributors to female use of psychopharmacological agents: a multifactorial cognitive and social analysis. PhD McGill U. 1980.

LINDSEY,B.T. *72*
Toward a typology of drug use among housewives. PhD Mississippi State U. 1979.

MEREDITH,D.J. *73*
The resocialization of women addicts in residential therapeutic groups. PhD Rutgers U. 1981.

MILLER,B.A. *74*
Illegal drug use among women in detention. PhD State U. of New York at Albany, 1980.

PAGE,R.C. *75*
Marathon group counseling with imprisoned female drug abusers. PhD U. of Florida, 1976.

RAMSEY,M.L. *76*
An investigation of the special features and needs of incarcerated female drug offenders with implications of this investigation in the development of

a female drug treatment program at the Correctional Institution for Women, Clinton, New Jersey, and an educational workshop outline based upon these findings. EdD Fairleigh Dickinson U. 1977.

RAY,D.F. *77*
Women who recovered from drug abuse: twelve case studies. PhD California Sch. of Prof. Psych., Berkeley, 1976.

RICE,S.M. *78*
Psychodynamic and developmental correlates of drug of choice in female adolescent drug users. PhD Boston U. Grad. Sch. 1977.

ROSENBAUM,M. *79*
Funneling options: the career of the woman addict. PhD U. of California, San Francisco, 1979.

THORNTON,S.A. *80*
An evaluation study of women, incorporating substance abuse treatment program for females. EdD Boston U. Sch. of Educ. 1981.

TOBIN,F.M. *81*
A suggested drug abuse education program for freshman women students attending an urban college. EdD Columbia U. 1972.

TREECE,C.J. *82*
Narcotic use in relation to selected ego functions among incarcerated women. PhD Boston U. Grad. Sch. 1977.

WEBER,C.R. *83*
A study of the effects of structured short-term therapy employing G.A.S. on self-concept and internal-external locus of control with an incarcerated female substance abuse population. PhD St John's U. 1981.

Tobacco

See also **19** 254, 313, 380, 418, 419.

GOTTLIEB,N.H. *84*
Smoking behavior in college women. PhD Boston U. Grad. Sch. 1981.

LUTFORD,A.J. *85*
Attitudes to smoking amongst student nurses. MPhil U. of London, Inst. of Psych. 1981.

NEETZ,R.A. *86*
The effect of smoking deprivation on psychomotor performance, mood, and task perception of female smokers. PhD U. of South Dakota, 1979.

ROBERTS,S.M. *87*
Beliefs associated with smoking intentions of college women. PhD U. of Illinois at Urbana-Champaign, 1979.

SMITH,K.A. *88*
Cigarette smoking: a phenomenological analysis of the experience of women in their successful versus unsuccessful attempts to quit smoking. PhD U. of Pittsburgh, 1981.

WILLETT,W.C. *89*
Cigarette smoking and non-fatal myocardial infarction in women. DPh Harvard U. 1980.

General health care and knowledge

See also **12** 1354; **13** 28; **19** 446; **23** 119.

ALTHAUS,R.A. *90*
Women's health care and health education: a survey of women in selected YWCAs. PhD Ohio State U. 1975.

BERKMAN,S.L. *91*
Health care patterns of teenage mothers and their young children. DSW U. of Calfornia, Los Angeles, 1980.

CLARK,M.J. *92*
The work of the health visitor. MPhil U. of Reading, 1972.

COFFEY,R.M. *93*
The effect of time on the demand for female medical care services. PhD Southern Methodist U. 1980.

COMISAROW,R.W. *94*
Work motivation of female health field workers. PhD Case Western Reserve U. 1970.

DELOREY,C. *95*
Health care for midlife women. DPh Harvard U. 1981.

DREXLER,M.S. *96*
Attitudes toward the women's health movement: their relation to attitudes towards women, community health orientation, dogmatism, and professional affiliation. PhD New York U. 1982.

FRETWELL,A.F. *97*
Efficacy of a patient activation health education program for elderly women. PhD U. of Utah, 1977.

GLASCOCK,E.L. *98*
Access to the traditional health care system by nontraditional women: perceptions of a cultural interaction. PhD New York U. 1981.

HAMMER,M.E. *99*
Perception of female veterans: their health care needs in Veterans Administration Hospitals. DSW U. of Southern California, 1979.

HANSON,P.A. *100*
Organizational and individual factors associated with innovation about women's health issues in college and university health education courses. PhD New York U. 1982.

HARPER,D.C. *101*
The effect of a medication self-care program on

knowledge of medication, health locus of control, and self-care behavior among black elderly hypertensive women. PhD U. of Maryland, 1980.

HUNTER,D.Y.H. *102*
The development of an instrument to determine the amount and kinds of unfounded health beliefs held by corpswomen in residence at McKinney Job Corps Center for Women. EdD U. of Houston, 1973.

ITO,K.L. *103*
Symbolic conscience: illness retribution among urban Hawaiian women. PhD U. of California, Los Angeles, 1978.

KAY,M.A. *104*
Health and illness in the barrio women's point of view. PhD U. of Arizona, 1972.

KENNER,C. *105*
The provision of married working women's health care in Britain, 1918–39. MPhil U. of Sussex, 1979.

LATHAM,J.E. *106*
The relationship between health knowledge and health practices of freshman women at the University of Oregon. PhD U. of Oregon, 1965.

LONGRES,J.F. *107*
Social conditions related to the acceptance of modern medicine among Puerto Rican women. PhD U. of Michigan, 1970.

LUKER,D.K.A. *108*
Health visiting and the elderly: an experimental study to evaluate the effects of focused health visitor intervention on elderly women living alone at home. PhD U. of Edinburgh, 1980.

LYONS,M.D. *109*
Analysis of health knowledge of college women. PhD U. of Iowa, 1961.

MCBRIDE,L.G. *110*
Selected characteristics of university undergraduate women as predictors of health service utilization. PhD Southern Illinois U. at Carbondale, 1979.

MASLEY,J.W. *111*
An analysis of certain factors related to the health knowledge and health habits of college freshmen women. PhD Pennsylvania State U. 1950.

MORGEN,S.L. *112*
Ideology and change in a feminist health center: the experience and dynamics of routinization. PhD U. of North Carolina at Chapel Hill, 1982.

PHIPPS,E.J. *113*
Women's folklore and health: traditions at work. PhD U. of Pennsylvania, 1980.

ROSS,H.M. *114*
Women and wellness: defining, attaining, and maintaining health in eastern Canada. PhD U. of Washington, 1982.

RUZEK,S.K. *115*
The women's health movement: finding alternatives to traditional medical professionalism. PhD U. of California, Davis, 1977.

SLESINGER,D.P. *116*
The utilization of preventive medical services by urban black mothers: a sociocultural approach. PhD U. of Wisconsin-Madison, 1973.

STAGE,S.J. *117*
Female complaints: a social history of the Lydia E. Pinkham Medicine Company. PhD Yale U. 1975.

TRIPLETT,J.L. *118*
Characteristics and perceptions of low-income women as they affect use of preventive health services. EdD U. of Michigan, 1968.

VAN GINNEKEN,J.K. *119*
Social factors related to utilization of maternal and child health services by black families in Buffalo, New York. PhD State U. of New York at Buffalo, 1972.

WAKELY,L.K. *120*
Factors affecting mothers' understanding of medical information. PhD U. of Texas Health Science Center at Dallas, 1980.

YULE,B.M.G. *121*
Red Cross nursing: impact on health care. MPhil CNAA, 1982.

Mental Health

General

See also **9** 672; **19** 29, 72, 170, 227, 468.

ARFFA,M.S. *122*
An investigation of some criteria of adjustive behavior among chronic female psychiatric patients in a state mental hospital. EdD State U. of New York at Buffalo, 1963.

EAGLESTON,J.R. *123*
Measuring and altering social support in chronically stressed women. PhD Stanford U. 1982.

FRIED,C. *124*
The psychogenesis of paranoid delusions in women. PhD Harvard U. 1957.

GIL,R.M. *125*
Cultural attitudes toward mental illness among Puerto Rican migrant women and their relationship to the utilization of outpatient mental health services. DSW Adelphi U. Sch. of Social Work, 1980.

GILBERT,S.D. *126*
The female sexual partner surrogate as an emerging member of the mental health team. PhD United States International U. 1975.

GILES,D.A. *127*
An evaluation of assertion training with highly feminine stereotyped females in an acute psychiatric setting. PhD U. of Southern Mississippi, 1980.

GRANT,G.G.G. *128*
Black female leadership success in mental health – an exploration of determinants and coping behaviors. EdD Fairleigh Dickinson U. 1978.

HESS,J.G. *129*
Sex-role development in psychiatrically disturbed adolescent females and their parents. PhD U. of Rhode Island, 1975.

HIGDON,J.F. *130*
Power and sexual dynamics in female paranoids and nonparanoids assessed by interpersonal check-list, sex attitudes questionnaire, and thematic stimuli. PhD U. of Southern Illinois, 1972.

KENNEDY,M.J. *131*
Operant conditioning of elderly female psychiatric patients. PhD U. of London, Inst. of Psych. 1970.

LA VIGNE,G. *132*
Dominance and territoriality on a female mental ward. EdD Columbia U. Teachers Coll. 1977.

LIFF,S.B. *133*
The effects of mental health professionals' theoretical orientation, sex and age on their attitudes toward an ideal feminine role and the relationship between these attitudes and their clinical judgements of female clients. PhD New York U. 1976.

MAYFIELD,S.J. *134*
A comparison of verbal and visuospatial task performance of hysterical and obsessive-compulsive women under varying levels of stress. PhD U. of Northern Illinois, 1980.

MOLHOLM,L.H. *135*
Female mental patients and normal female controls: a restudy ten years later. PhD Ohio State U. 1970.

MOORE,M.T. *136*
The mental health problems and treatment of black women in an urban community mental health center. PhD Brandeis U. 1979.

NICKLAUS,C.H. *137*
An examination of the relationship between the acceptance of the traditional feminine role by women and the presence of psychological problems in women and their children. EdD Fairleigh Dickinson U. 1977.

O'KEEFE,M. *138*
Mental health education for religious women. PhD Loyola U. of Chicago, 1962.

OLIVE,R.O. *139*
Filicide as related to female oedipal problems. PhD Michigan State U. 1966.

PHAUP,M.R. *140*
A study of the self-concepts of a group of women patients who, though clinically in remission, remain in a mental hospital. PhD George Washington U. 1960.

RADOSEVICH,M.L. *141*
Treatment of women for mental illness. PhD U. of Iowa, 1982.

REINHARDT,A.M. *142*
Correlates of psychiatric impairment among mothers in Utah: a sociological approach to social psychiatry. PhD U. of Utah, 1968.

ROSENZWEIG,M.G. *143*
Overcontrolled hostility in assaultive and self-injurious women. PhD U. of Alabama, 1978.

SANDLER,I.N. *144*
Characteristics of women working as child-aides in a school-based preventive mental health program. PhD U. of Rochester, 1971.

SCOTT,J.F. *145*
The selective influence of social and psychological characteristics of mothers on information and attitude changes in mental health education. PhD Brandeis U. 1962.

SLAVIN,J.H. *146*
The role of power conflicts in the psychodynamics of paranoid women. PhD U. of Michigan, 1970.

SMITH,H.B. *147*
A study of the status of mental health of rural women. EdD U. of South Dakota, 1980.

STRAKOCSCH, F.M. *148*
Factors in the sex life of 700 psychopathic women. PhD Columbia U. 1935.

SURBER,G.P. *149*
A study of early ward socializing behavior and inter-patient attitudes in relation to improvement of female mental patients. PhD New York U. 1959.

TOWNSEND,J.K. *150*
Reports of parent behavior (RPBI) related to current behavior and MMPI scores in female psychiatric inpatients. PhD U. of North Carolina at Chapel Hill, 1968.

WILLIAMS,K.P. *151*
Physical attractiveness of women and perceptions of severity of emotional disturbance. PhD Florida State U. 1979.

WOODS,N.F. *152*
Women's roles, mental ill health, and illness behavior. PhD U. of North Carolina at Chapel Hill, 1978.

Counselling and therapy

See also **17** 45–174.

ABBOTT,M.M. *153*
Consequences of short-term psychotherapy with wives of first myocardial infarction patients. PhD California Sch. of Prof. Psych., San Diego, 1979.

ACKER,N.L. *154*
Effect of gender of the therapist on the self-perceptions of the female client. PhD California Sch. of Prof. Psych., San Diego, 1978.

APPLEGARTH,L.D. *155*
The effects of short-term feminist training of counsellor trainees. EdD Boston U. Sch. of Educ. 1975.

ASLIN,A.L. *156*
Feminist and community mental health center psychotherapists' mental health expectations for women. PhD U. of Maryland, 1974.

ATKINSON,S.J. *157*
A phenomenological study of women who seek therapy from a woman therapist at a women's center. PhD Pittsburgh U. 1982.

BELOTE,B.J. *158*
Sexual intimacy between female clients and male psychotherapists: masochistic sabotage. PhD California Sch. of Prof. Psych., Berkeley, 1974.

BOULETTE,M.T.R. *159*
Determining needs and appropriate counselling approaches for Mexican-American women: a comparison of therapeutic listening and behavioral rehearsal. PhD U. of California, Santa Barbara, 1972.

BOYLL,S. *160*
Sex-role category and sex-role bias in counselling students' responses to a female coached client. PhD Indiana State U. 1980.

BREW,A.P. *161*
Effects of a counselling workshop on adult women. PhD U. of Maryland, 1975.

BROCKWAY,J.S.F. *162*
A design for counselling adult women using a paradigm of rational decision-making. PhD U. of Oregon, 1974.

BROOKS,L. *163*
Beginnings: a phenomenological exploration of the pre-phase of therapy with women. PhD California Sch. of Prof. Psych., San Diego, 1977.

CAPALDO,T.F. *164*
An investigation of women's preferences for the sex of a counsellor. EdD Boston U., Sch. of Educ. 1979.

CHEW,S.K. *165*
The relationship between sex-role stereotypes, female client self-disclosure and counsellor facilitativeness. EdD Oklahoma State U. 1979.

CLINE-NAFFZIGER,C. *166*
A survey of counsellors' and other selected professionals' attitudes toward women's roles. PhD U. of Oregon, 1971.

CULLINAN,A.R. *167*
An evaluation of the value of a woman co-counsellor in an integrity therapy group of men with marital communication difficulties. EdD Southwestern Baptist Theological Seminary, 1974.

DU BOIS,B.R. *168*
Feminist perspectives on psychotherapy and psychology of women: an exploratory study in the development of clinical theory. PhD Harvard U. 1976.

FINNERAN,M.R. *169*
The relationship between therapists' and clients' assessments of therapists' levels of empathy and views of women. PhD Pittsburgh U. 1980.

GORDON,D.S. *170*
Women's experiences in feminist therapy. PhD Georgia State U. Coll. of Educ. 1981.

HART,L.E. *171*
An investigation of the effect of male therapists' views of women on the process and outcome of therapy with women. PhD Auburn U. 1981.

HUG,W.F. *172*
A comparison of two psychiatric consultation processes involving the participation or nonparticipation of the female client. PhD U. of Maryland, 1975.

HUGHEY,S.E. *173*
A study of transition in the lives of women in counsellor training. PhD U. of Washington, 1982.

JOHNSON,J.L. *174*
Women leaders in national guidance and counselling associations: some implications of their backgrounds and leadership roles. EdD U. of Wyoming, 1972.

JOHNSON,L.S. *175*
Selected critical leadership tasks for camp counsellors as perceived by camp community members in girl scout summer resident camps. EdD Temple U. 1982.

KAHN,L.G. *176*
Effects of sex and feminist orientation of therapists on clinical judgements. DSW Columbia U. 1976.

KASOWSKI,E.M. *177*
A follow-up appraisal of process and change in a group home treatment program for disturbed adolescent girls. PhD City U. of New York, 1976.

KNIGHT,P.H. *178*
Degree of client manifest anxiety as a function of interaction distance: an investigation of the female-female counselling dyad. EdD Western Michigan U. 1979.

LONDON,M. *179*
A study of the attrition-retention of counsellors

trained in a peer counsellor training program for women. EdD Boston U. Sch. of Educ. 1978.

LOYD,D.F. *180*
Women counselling women: an art and a philosophy. EdD U. of Massachusetts, 1974.

LUNDEGREN,H.M. *181*
Personality traits of successful and unsuccessful women counsellors in girls' private and agency camps. PhD U. of Iowa, 1960.

MARCUS,M.F. *182*
A feminist counselling collective and the practice of feminist therapy. PhD Wright Inst. 1976.

MAREISON,F.R. *183*
Assessing the use of a psychiatric unit for mothers with their babies: risks to the babies. MSc U. of Manchester, 1981.

MERRILL,H.D. *184*
Counsellor training using extrinsic and instrinsic feedback with females differing in locus of control. EdD Auburn U. 1979.

MOSS,L.E. *185*
A woman's way: a feminist approach to body psychotherapy. PhD Union for Experimenting Coll. and U. 1981.

NAFFZIGER,K.G. *186*
A survey of counsellor-educators' and other selected professionals' attitudes towards women's roles. PhD U. of Oregon, 1971.

NELSON,K.A.K. *187*
An investigation of counsellor attitudes towards roles of women. PhD U. of Minnesota, 1982.

NOONAN,B.A. *188*
Toward an existential approach to therapy with women. PhD U. of Alberta, 1980.

NORKUS,A.G. *189*
Sex of therapist as a variable in short-term therapy with female college students. PhD U. of Southern Illinois, 1976.

ORSO,D.P. *190*
Effects of counsellor self-disclosure on client self-disclosure as a function of female client extroversion or introversion. PhD American U. 1979.

PALEY,M.G. *191*
The evolution of a feminist therapist. PhD Union Grad. Sch., Ohio, 1976.

PERRY,S.L. *192*
Counsellor educators' and supervisors' information and attitudes regarding the sex-role of women. EdD East Texas State U. 1981.

PETERS,A. *193*
An investigation of the relationship between the inability of some women in psychotherapy to accept their female role and their perception of their mothers' attitudes toward the female role. PhD New York U. 1960.

PHILIPS,S.B. *194*
The contrasting abilities of field-dependent and field-independent women counselling students to match sensory imagery. EdD Boston U. Sch. of Educ. 1982.

QUAYTMAN,W. *195*
Motivation for psychotherapy: a comparative investigation of motivational factors in female neurotic outpatients who prematurely terminate and those who remain in psychotherapy. PhD New York U. 1961.

SABLOVE,M.F. *196*
A training model for feminist counsellors. EdD U. of Massachusetts, 1978.

SABOGAL-TORI,D. *197*
An examination of the psychotherapeutic experience of Latin women. PhD California Sch. of Prof. Psych., Berkeley, 1975.

SHAPIRO,J.F. *198*
Socialization of sex roles in the counselling setting: differential counsellor behavioral and attitudinal responses to typical and atypical female sex roles. PhD Stanford U. 1975.

SHERMAN,J.C. *199*
Views of women in theories of counselling and psychotherapy. EdD Idaho State U. 1977.

SMOLEN,B. *200*
Psychoanalysis and feminist scholarship: toward a women's studies curriculum in counselling and psychology. EdD U. of Massachusetts, 1979.

STAPLES,E.J. *201*
The influence of the sex of the therapist and of the co-therapist technique in group psychotherapy with girls. PhD New York U. 1958.

STATEN,B.J. *202*
The effect of counsellor gender and sex-role attitudes on change of female clients' sex-role attitudes. PhD U. of Southern California, 1974.

STEIER,F.A. *203*
The effects of a training module portraying sex bias and sex-role stereotyping in psychotherapy on counsellor trainee attitudes toward women. EdD Ball State U. 1980.

STEVENSON,J.E. *204*
Therapists' anxiety in response to black and white female clients. PhD U. of Maryland, 1980.

STONE,L.G. *205*
A study of the relationships among anxious attachment, ego functioning, and female patients' vulnerability to sexual involvement with their male psychotherapists. PhD California Sch. of Prof. Psych., Los Angeles, 1980.

STURDIVANT,S. *206*
Feminist therapy: a new philosophy of treatment. PhD Fielding Inst. 1977.

SULLIVAN,C.R. *207*
The effects of interviewer presumptuousness and interviewee sex on interviewee self-disclosure in a female-conducted counselling interview. EdD Texas Tech U. 1982.

WALKER,R.B. *208*
The perceptual characteristics of women counsellor trainees. EdD U. of Virginia, 1978.

Depression

ADAMS-ESQUIVEL,H. *209*
Operant modification of endogenous symptoms in depressed women. PhD California Sch. of Prof. Psych., San Diego, 1979.

AGUADO,R.R. *210*
The component of aggression in female depression. PhD U. of Southern California, 1982.

BART,P.B. *211*
Depression in middle-aged women: some sociocultural factors. PhD U. of California, Los Angeles, 1967.

BRONSON,N.L. *212*
Defensive projection in depressed married women. PhD Emory U. 1981.

BULATAO,J.C. *213*
The direction of aggression in clinically depressed women. PhD Fordham U. 1961.

BURKHAM,R. *214*
The effect of the subliminal presentation of two gratifying fantasies on female depressives. PhD Saint Louis U. 1981.

CARRINGTON,C.H. *215*
A comparison of cognitive and analytically oriented brief treatment approaches to depression in black women. PhD U. of Maryland, 1979.

CLARK,W.D. *216*
Quantification of Rorschach content and verbalizations to predict degree of depression in young depressed women. EdD Rutgers U. 1966.

COMAS-DIAZ,L. *217*
Effects of cognitive and behavioral group treatment on the symptomatology of depression in Puerto Rican women. PhD U. of Massachusetts, 1979.

DAVIS,M.S. *218*
Poetry group therapy versus interpersonal group therapy: comparison of treatment effectiveness with depressed women. PhD Wright Inst. 1978.

DOYNE,E.J. *219*
Aerobic exercise as a treatment for depression in women. PhD U. of Georgia, 1981.

EUSANIO,A.M. *220*
Personality characteristics of depressed women. PhD Rutgers U. 1977.

FARIA,G. *221*
A study of role loss among depressed women. PhD U. of Denver, 1980.

HARRIS,R.B. *222*
Communication and the awareness of needs within the marriage of women hospitalized with a reactive depression diagnosis. PhD United States International U. 1975.

HAUSSMANN,M.J. *223*
Women's roles and vulnerability to depression. EdD Western Michigan U. 1981.

HEDRICK,M.A. *224*
Depression and sex-role values in the women. PhD California Sch. of Prof. Psych., Berkeley, 1977.

HUNTER,P.A.B. *225*
The processing of experience and the evaluation of the self in depressed and nondepressed females. PhD Louisiana State U. and A&M Coll. 1981.

KEARNEY,D.A. *226*
Intimacy as a factor in depression among women. PhD U. of Georgia, 1982.

KINGSLAND,R.C. *227*
Cognitive aspects of depression in women. PhD U. of California, Davis, 1981.

KRAUSE,N .M. *228*
Married women and depressive symptoms. PhD U. of Akron, 1979.

LACALLE,T.M.D. *229*
Depression as a function of the female role. PhD United States International U. 1975.

MAGERS,B.D. *230*
Cognitive-behavioral short-term group therapy with depressed women. PhD California Sch. of Prof. Psych., Berkeley, 1977.

MORRISON,B.K. *231*
Differential effects of ambiguous and clear, positive feedback on severely, moderately, and nondepressed women. PhD Texas Technical U. 1977.

NEWHAUSER,D.I. *232*
Physical measures of female speech and voice variables as indices of retarded clinical depression. PhD U. of Southern California, 1976.

NEWMANN,J.P. *233*
Sex differences in depression: a test of alternative explanations for the greater vulnerability of women to depression. PhD U. of Wisconsin-Madison, 1982.

NISSENFELD,S.M. *234*
The effects of four types of subliminal stimuli on female depressives. PhD Yeshiva U. 1979.

PADFIELD,M.N.C. *235*
The comparative effects of two counselling

approaches on the intensity of depression among low socioeconomic status, rural women. PhD U. of Arizona, 1975.

PALMER,A.J. *236*
An experimental evaluation of the therapist role, peer interactions, and self-motivation in the treatment of depressed female psychiatric patients. EdD West Virginia U. 1973.

PEARCE,S.S. *237*
The effect of structured group counselling on levels of depression among retired women in institutional and non-institutional settings. PhD St John's U. 1978.

RAHDERT,E.R. *238*
Manifestations of anger in clinically depressed women. PhD Purdue U. 1980.

SAND,J.M. *239*
Identifying predictors of depression in freshman college women. PhD Boston U. Grad. Sch. 1973.

SIGURDSON,M.K. *240*
A multivariate study of depression in elderly Caucasian women. PhD Indiana State U. 1979.

SPENDLOVE,D.C. *241*
Depression in Mormon women. PhD U. of Utah, 1982.

SPREIOTT,J.E. *242*
The use of assertiveness training and consciousness-raising groups in the treatment of depression in women. PhD U. of Maryland, 1979.

STEINER,R.E. *243*
A cognitive-developmental analysis of depression: interpersonal problem-solving and event interpretation among depressed and non-depressed women. PhD Clark U. 1974.

YOUNG,K.A. *244*
Sex-role acceptance and depression in middle-aged women. PhD Florida State U. 1975.

WASLI,E.L.M. *245*
Dysfunctional communication response patterns of depressed wives and their husbands in relation to activities of daily living. DNSc Catholic U. America, 1977.

Phobias

BELKIN,B.M. *246*
Homophobia in women. PhD Adelphi U. 1982.

BILLINGS,S.B.D. *247*
Interpersonal constructs of agoraphobic women and their husbands: a study of change. PhD California Sch. of Prof. Psych., San Diego, 1982.

COOPER,W.L. *248*
A test of group semantic desensitization with moderate to highly fearful mixed phobic females. PhD U. of Louisville, 1975.

ENGUM,E.S. *249*
Behavioral mode, reinforcement mode, and success demand in treating rat phobic university women. PhD U. of South Dakota, 1977.

LIPKE,H.J. *250*
The effects of model role, model gender, and subject expression of desire to change on 'feminine' females' imitation of approach to a feared snake. PhD St Louis U. 1978.

SHOBERG,J.D. *251*
Systematic desensitization vs. implosive therapy in the treatment of phobic college females. PhD Southern Illinois U. 1971.

STANDAHL,J.R. *252*
The therapeutic effects of five types of modeling on snake-phobic women. PhD U. of North Carolina at Greensboro, 1972.

WEBSTER,A.S. *253*
The development of phobias in women. PhD U. of Tennessee, 1953.

Schizophrenia

See also **19** 402.

BABB,H.E. *254*
The verbal behavior of schizophrenic women in four types of group situations. PhD U. of Kentucky, 1962.

BRYANT,J.E. *255*
Visual form recognition learning deficit in paranoid schizophrenic women. PhD U. of Cincinnati, 1955.

CARRINGTON,P. *256*
Dream reports of schizophrenic and non-schizophrenic women. PhD Columbia U. 1969.

COCHEN,R.O. *257*
The effects of four subliminally-introduced merging stimuli on the psychopathology of schizophrenic women. PhD Columbia U. 1977.

CRAIG,J.E. *258*
Perceived parental attitudes and the effects of maternal versus paternal censure and approval in good and poor premorbid hospitalized female schizophrenics. PhD U. of Wisconsin, 1966.

DAMBACHER,B.M. *259*
Hostility and counter-transference nursing therapy of a schizophrenic woman. DNSc U. of Boston, 1965.

DEWITT,C.R. *260*
Some behavioral characteristics of a sub-group of female ambulatory schizophrenics. PhD U. of Houston, 1961.

HEALEY,D.F. *261*
The concept of the schizophrenogenic mother: an

historical analysis. PhD United States International U. 1980.

KATZ,P. *262*
Rated ward behavior as related to perception judgment among female chronic schizophrenics. PhD St John's U. 1964.

KNAPPENBERGER,R.R. *263*
Relation of environmental expectations, locus of control and patient behavior in a follow-up study of operant conditioning with schizophrenic women. PhD Case Western Reserve U. 1973.

KRAMER-DOVER,S.L. *264*
The similarity in psychopathology between schizophrenic mothers and their children. PhD George Washington U. 1981.

LERNER,M.S. *265*
The relationship of certain aspects of the body image of female schizophrenic patients to therapeutic success or failure. PhD New York U. 1960.

LESYK,J.J. *266*
Effects of intensive operant conditioning on belief in personal control in schizophrenic women. PhD Case Western Reserve U. 1968.

LEWIS,F.W. *267*
The relationship of sensory awareness and psychological deficit in chronic non-paranoid female schizophrenics. PhD Brigham Young U. 1971.

MCGHIE,A. *268*
A comparative study of the mother-child relationship in schizophrenia. PhD U. of Glasgow, 1960.

MITCHELL,K.M. *269*
An elaboration of a study of the schizophrenogenic mother concept by means of the thematic apperception test. PhD Michigan State U. 1965.

POTELUNAS-CAMPBELL,M.F. *270*
The development and evaluation of a social skills training program for supervisor/supervisee dyad interactions in a work adjustment program with female schizophrenic outpatients. PhD New York U. 1982.

PUGH,L.A. *271*
The effects of praise, censure, and noise on electrodermal and reaction time measures in chronic schizophrenic and normal women. PhD U. of Oklahoma, 1965.

SCHAEFFER,D.L. *272*
Patterns of pre-morbid and symptom behavior in schizophrenic and depressed women. PhD Rutgers U. 1968.

THOMAS,R.C. *273*
Mother-daughter relationships and the social behavior of a selected group of schizophrenic patients treated in St Elizabeth's Hospital. PhD Catholic U. of America, 1955.

Mental retardation

See also **15** 94; **17** 537; **19** 337.

BROGAN,W.G. *274*
A comparative analysis of the reading errors of retarded and non-retarded females. PhD U. of North Carolina at Chapel Hill, 1973.

CRAWFORD,J.W. *275*
The effect of art experiences on the self-concept of institutionalized adolescent female mental retardates. EdD Pennsylvania State U. 1961.

DEMERY,M.M. *276*
A comparison of the cognitive development of retarded women in the domains of human reproduction, physical causality, and physical conservation. PhD Wayne State U. 1977.

DORAN,F.M.B. *277*
A contextualistic analysis of the drawing processes of three trainable mentally retarded institutionalized female adults. DEd Pennsylvania State U. 1973.

GELLER,M. *278*
Group psychotherapy with girls institutionalized for mental deficiency: a study of psychotherapeutic process and effects. PhD New York U. 1953.

HAN,S.S. *279*
Use of socialization games to increase prosocial behavior of institutionalized retarded women. PhD Ohio State U. 1980.

HUGHES,G.R. *280*
A comparison of the effects of two paradigms of time-out under two schedules of positive reinforcement on antonym learning by severely retarded girls. PhD U. of Manitoba, 1973.

JOHNSON,M.S. *281*
An analysis of leisure behavior in a half-way house for retarded women. PhD Florida State U. 1975.

KARTYE,J.P.Jr. *282*
A behavior-shaping program for institutionalized severely and profoundly retarded females. PhD Texas A&M U. 1971.

KNAUS,W.J. *283*
An experimental study of three methods of programmed vocational instruction presented to mentally retarded adolescent females. EdD U. of Tennessee, 1967.

LEE,P.L. *284*
An analysis of food-preference behavior of the mildly to moderately retarded woman in a half-way house. PhD Florida State U. 1976.

PETRUSKI,R.A. *285*
The separate and combined effects of behavior rehearsal and modeling variations in the groom-

ing skill acquisition of mentally retarded women. PhD Pennsylvania State U. 1982.

SHUMAN-CARPENTER,B.S. *286*
The effects of two methods of therapy on the body image of emotionally disturbed, retarded female adolescents. EdD Temple U. 1977.

SLIS ,V.G. *287*
Instructional set and objective self-awareness: effects on task performance and causal attribution of mentally retarded adult females. PhD Hofstra U. 1975.

SMITH,A.L.Jr. *288*
Differential reinforcement of other behaviors as a ward management technique for aggressive, retarded women. PhD U. of Nebraska, Lincoln, 1981.

VANUXEM,M. *289*
Education of feeble-minded women. PhD Columbia U. 1925.

WEISS,B.S. *290*
The effects of a vocational training program on educationally handicapped female adolescents in an institutional setting. EdD U. of Southern California, 1975.

WILLIAMS,W.L. *291*
The effect of cooperation procedures on the acquisition and subsequent generalization of a sign language communication repertoire in severely and profoundly retarded girls. PhD U. of Manitoba, 1977.

WRIGHTON,P.A. *292*
Comparative effects of demerit tokens, response cost, and time-out to decrease self-stimulatory behavior during posture training with severely and profoundly retarded women. PhD U. of Manitoba, 1978.

ZOOK,S.M. *293*
Need for approval and responsiveness to verbal and token reinforcements in institutionalized mentally retarded female adults. DEd Pennsylvania State U. 1975.

Nutrition

General

ABOUL,E.J.E. *294*
Food preferences, nutritional knowledge and nutrient intake of university women. PhD Texas Woman's U. 1976.

ARMSTRONG,J.M. *295*
Food beliefs and practices of Mexican-American women: a study of diet of two orientation groups: emergent and traditional. PhD U. of California, Berkeley, 1972.

BAGLEY,R.T. *296*
Relationship of diet to physical/emotional complaints and behavioral problems reported by women students at two Southern California universities. PhD United States International U. 1980.

BRICKER,A.J. *297*
Some environmental influences on food habits of women clerical workers. PhD New York U. 1961.

CALENDER,I.H. *298*
Reliability of methods of recording dietary intake of women at constant weight. ScDHyg U. of Pittsburgh, 1963.

CAPPS,E.L.B. *299*
Factors influencing food selection patterns of young college women. PhD Texas Woman's U. 1967.

DAVIS.R.J. *300*
The relation between nutrition knowledge and the dietary intake of selected women: a basis for adult education program development. EdD U. of Illinois at Urbana-Champaign, 1971.

DENISCO,S.G. *301*
A comparative study of the nutritional adequacy of the morning food intake of women clerical workers and women factory workers. PhD New York U. 1962.

HAKOJARVI,A.J. *302*
The relationship of social interaction and functional health to dietary intake of elderly women living alone in low income public housing. EdD Columbia U. 1969.

HARPER,L.J. *303*
Dietary practices of three samples of women: a longitudinal and cross-sectional study. PhD Michigan State U. 1956.

KOLASA,K.M. *304*
Foodways of selected mothers and their adult-daughters in upper east Tennessee. PhD U. of Tennessee, 1974.

MITCHELL,G.S. *305*
Cross-cultural assessment of food habits and life-styles of urban black female adolescents in Georgetown, Guyana, and Washington DC. PhD Howard U. 1978.

ROBINSON,N.B. *306*
A study of the effect of improved diet and improved diet with programmed exercise on medical nutrition status of women 50 years of age and over. PhD Texas Woman's U. 1967.

STIEDEMANN,M.K. *307*
Relation of immune status to selected nutrients in elderly women. PhD Colorado State U. 1979.

STORZ,N.S. *308*
Desired body weight, body image and perception of relative desirability of weight control methods of adolescent females. EdD Temple U. 1981.

TERRY,R.D. *309*
Diet, anthropometric characteristics, and

diabetes-related attitudes and knowledge among women residing in Eastern Cherokee township of Snowbird (North Carolina). PhD U. of Tennessee, 1982.

VAN LANINGHAM,E.L. 310
A comparative study of snacking habits of two groups of college women. PhD Texas Woman's U. 1972.

Anorexia and bulimia

BASSECHES,H.I. 311
Autonomy in adolescent young women with eating disorders. PhD George Washington U. 1979.

BOSKIND-LODAHL,M. 312
The definition and treatment of bulimarexia: the gorging/purging syndrome of young women. PhD Cornell U. 1977.

BUTTERFIELD,P.S. 313
Discrimination analysis of the cognitive belief patterns and coping strategies of bulimic and sedative/depressant abusing females. PhD Ohio State U. 1982.

CLEMENT,P.F. 314
Psychological correlates of binge eating in college women. PhD U. of Texas at Austin, 1980.

DARMSTADTER,L.J. 315
Eating disturbance, perceptual defense style and life adjustment distinctions among groups of obese, normal, bulimarexic, and anorexic women. PhD Ohio State U. 1982.

GOODWIN,P.C. 316
Body-image and self-image in adolescence and anorexia nervosa. MPhil U. of Surrey, 1982.

HAGGENMACHER,C.B. 317
A comparison of bulimarexic and nonbulimarexic college women on behavioral, attitudinal, and personality variables. PhD Washington State U. 1981.

HICKS,C.F. 318
Family and cultural factors in the development of eating disorders: a study of feminine identity in twenty-four bulimarexic women. EdD U. of Massachusetts, 1982.

LWIN,R.B.R. 319
Anorexia nervosa: an investigation into appetite, eating behavior and personal history. MPhil U. of Edinburgh, 1982.

MALLICK,M.J. 320
The adverse effects of weight control in teenage girls. PhD Case Western Reserve U. 1980.

MORAN,J.S. 321
Assessment of stressful life events in women with anorexia nervosa. PhD U. of Minnesota, 1981.

NEVO,S. 322
Eating patterns and personality characteristics of bulimic and overweight women. PhD U. of California, Berkeley, 1982.

PERCIVAL,P.J. 323
Subclinical eating disturbance: anorexic-like attitudes and behaviors in college women. PhD State U. of New York at Buffalo, 1982.

SITNICK,T.I. 324
Anorexia nervosa: a composite case history and theoretical study from a feminist perspective. PhD California Sch. of Prof. Psych., San Diego, 1979.

STUCKEY,M.K. 325
The depressive experience of normal weight bulimic women. PhD Northwestern U. 1981.

STURZENBERGER,S.C. 326
A follow-up study of anorexia nervosa in adolescent females: the prediction of outcome. PhD California Sch. of Prof. Psych., Los Angeles, 1976.

THOMPSON,M.G. 327
Life adjustment of women with anorexia nervosa and anorexic-like behavior. PhD U. of Chicago, 1980.

Obesity and overweight

ADAMS,C.H. 328
Psychosocial factors and educational implications in the prevention of adult onset obesity in women. PhD U. of Connecticut, 1981.

ALLEN,D.E. 329
Relationships among obesity, socioeconomic status, and certain personality factors of college women. PhD Texas Woman's U. 1973.

BAILEY,W.L. 330
A comparsion of the effects of visual sensory commitment action group therapy with commitment action group therapy only and no treatment control group of obese university females. PhD Brigham Young U. 1971.

BEARCE,J.S. 331
The relationship of eating disorder patterns and personality variables in overweight women. EdD U. of Massachusetts, 1981.

BRADLEY,E.P. 332
Body image, movement concept and body composition of obese college women in a weight reduction program. DA Middle Tennessee State U. 1975.

CHAMPION,L.J. 333
Perceived parent-child relationships of obese and non-obese female college students. PhD U. of Tennessee, 1977.

CHWAST,R. 334
The interrelationship among accuracy of body size perception, body satisfaction, and the body image

in obese and non-obese women. PhD Case Western Reserve U. 1978.

CONOLEY,C.W. 335
The effects of vicarious reinforcement in assertive training on assertive behavior anxiety and food intake of underassertive obese females. PhD U. of Texas at Austin, 1976.

DAVIDSON,C.S. 336
Learned internalization as a treatment strategy for obesity in women: a comparative analysis. PhD U. of Southern Mississippi, 1978.

DONAHOE,C.P.Jr. 337
Explorations of the energy balance of overweight women during weight loss in a behavioral treatment program. PhD U. of Wisconsin-Madison, 1981.

FEINER,A.H. 338
A study of certain aspects of the perception of parental figures and sexual identifications of an obese adolescent female group. PhD New York U. 1954.

FITZPATRICK,V.B. 339
Body image and weight loss in chronically obese and late-onset obese black lower socioeconomic status adolescent girls. PhD Catholic U. of America, 1976.

FORD,W.E. 340
The manipulation of time and eating behavior: the effect of set-point on the amount eaten by normal weight, moderately obese, and high obese women. PhD U. of Massachusetts, 1973.

FRAMER,E.M. 341
Physiological responses to affective stimuli of obese and non-obese females differing in dietary restraint. PhD North Texas State U. 1981.

FRIEDMAN,J. 342
Psychological correlates of overweight, underweight, and normal weight college women. PhD Temple U. 1958.

GALLIFORD,J.E. 343
Eliminating self-defeating behavior: the effects of ESDB bibliotherapy compared to ESDB group therapy on weight control in women. PhD Brigham Young U. 1982.

GARRETT,L.D. 344
Group behavioral therapy versus family behavioral therapy in treatment of obese adolescent females. PhD U. of Pennsylvania, 1979.

HALL,S.A.M. 345
Self-control and therapist control in the treatment of overweight women. PhD Washington State U. 1971.

HANSEN,C.M. 346
Sensitivity to negative social stimuli in overweight women. PhD U. of Toronto, 1979.

HELFMAN,S.B. 347
Effects of different treatment modalities on the self-concept of overweight women. PhD California Sch. of Prof. Psych., San Diego, 1981.

HOLT,C.R. 348
The effects of two different small group treatment methods on selected overweight middle school girls. PhD Brigham Young U. 1981.

HOROWITZ,R.H. 349
The influence of various group counselling procedures on certain personality traits and weight control among obese women. PhD U. of Miami, 1973.

JANUS,N.G. 350
A comparison of conflict avoidance in families containing obese girls with families containing non-obese girls. EdD U. of Massachusetts, 1981.

KESSLER,H. 351
Body perceptions of obese women. PhD Wright Inst. 1978.

LANTZ,C.E. 352
Spouse involvement and energy balance manipulations in behavioral weight management: effects on short- and long-term weight loss in overweight women. PhD Fuller Theological Seminary, 1976.

LAZARUS,C.N. 353
Factors associated with attempted weight maintenance among formerly overweight women. PhD Adelphi U. 1978.

LEARY,J.E. 354
A comparison between normal and overweight women on reasons for eating, restraint in eating, and attitude toward obesity. DEd U. of Oregon, 1977.

LEVY,B.K. 355
Dimensions of personality as related to obesity in women. PhD U. of California, Berkeley, 1955.

LITROWNIK,R.L. 356
A comparison between a willpower operant self-control and structured placebo approach to weight control in overweight women. PhD U. of Illinois at Urbana-Champaign, 1976.

MADDEN,M.J. 357
The symbolic world of obesity: a study of the rhetorical visions of obese women. PhD U. of Minnesota, 1982.

MARTIN,A. 358
The effect of subliminal stimulation of symbiotic fantasies on weight loss in obese women receiving behavioral treatment. PhD New York U. 1975.

MASSARA,E.B. 359
Que Gorditai: a study of weight among women in a Puerto Rican community. PhD Bryn Mawr Coll. 1979.

MIGDOLE,S.M. 360
An investigation of orality, depression, and de-

nials in obese and non-obese adolescent females. EdD Boston U. 1967.

MOHON,M.S. 361
Social support systems and networks of overweight and normal weight women. PhD U. of Arkansas, 1980.

MORCK,L.M. 362
Field dependence-independence, body image, and intropunitiveness in juvenile and adult-onset obese women.. PhD California Sch. of Prof. Psych. 1976.

MORELLI,G. 363
The effects of behavior therapy, non-directive therapy, and personality factors upon weight loss in obese women. PhD New Sch. for Social Research, 1976.

PARENT,E.A. 364
Anger and weight control: a comparison of the effects of rational anger management versus relaxation training with obese females in conjunction with a behavior modification-exercise treatment program. PhD Brigham Young U. 1982.

PARGMAN,D. 365
The relationship of weight loss to strength changes in obese adult females. PhD New York U. 1966.

PEARCE,J.W. 366
The role of spouse involvement in the behavioral treatment of overweight women. PhD University of Manitoba, 1980.

PETERSON,M.A. 367
Obesity, age of onset, and physical self-esteem, and the outcome in a behavioral treatment program for women. PhD New York U. 1981.

PHALEN,D.L. 368
Personality, psychopathology, and obesity in females: a descriptive study. PhD Ohio State U. 1977.

RANKIN,E.A.D. 369
A study of the relationship between self-concept and reduction of percent body fat among obese females. PhD U. of Maryland, 1979.

RASMUSSEN,D.M. 370
A comparison of the effects of commitment to action group therapy with two other weight reduction programs and a no-treatment control group on obese university females. EdD Brigham Young U. 1968.

REIDY,D.P. 371
The effect of peer group helpers on adolescent females in a weight reduction program. PhD St John's U. 1975.

REISS,A.R.P. 372
Obesity and aggression in women. PhD City U. of New York, 1973.

ROSENTHAL,B.S. 373
The role of a significant other in the behavioral treatment of overweight women. PhD U. of Connecticut, 1975.

SCHREIBER,F.M. 374
The contribution of role-playing techniques to self-concept enhancement and weight loss in overweight college women. PhD U. of Florida, 1980.

SCHWARTZ,A. 375
The reference groups of dieting obese women. PhD Columbia U. 1965.

SCHWARTZ,R.A. 376
The sexual behavior of obese women. PhD Illinois Inst. of Technology, 1971.

SCOTT,M.W. 377
Patterns of influence on some known correlates of obesity in middle-class black women. PhD U. of Maryland, 1980.

SIMS,H.J. 378
A study to identify and evaluate the attitudes toward obesity among three ethnic groups of women in Oklahoma: black, white, and Indian. PhD U. of Oklahoma Health Sciences Center, 1979.

STEINBERG,C.L. 379
Personality, perceptual and biographical characteristics of normal weight women and overweight women of varying age of onset of overweight. PhD U. of Maryland, 1979.

STEPHENSON,P.A. 380
The relationship between food preferences and perceived patterns of mothering among a group of obese and normal weight females. PhD Adelphi U. 1975.

TEVLIN,H.E. 381
A comparison of daily activity patterns of obese and normal-weight women. PhD U. of Oregon, 1979.

TURIAN,J.E. 382
The relationships among four themes of psychological functioning, the age of onset of obesity and the degree of obesity in middle and upper middle class urban women. PhD St John's U. 1980.

WAITE,D.G. 383
A comparison of various weight reduction approaches with overweight university female students. EdD Western Michigan U. 1974.

WARREN,C.L. 384
An investigation of the group approach to weight reduction and improvement of physical fitness in college women. EdD U. of Texas at Austin, 1966.

WEAVER,C.P. 385
A study of personality characteristics of obese women of two age groups as compared with

paired controls of normal weight. PhD U. of Iowa, 1960.

WEET,C.R. *386*
The effect of field dependency as a subject variable in two behavioral treatments for obesity in females. PhD U. of Kentucky, 1976.

WEISZ,G.M. *387*
Sources of control and behavior change in overweight women. PhD U. of Western Ontario, 1976.

WIDERYNSKA,D.J. *388*
Effect of direct decision therapy on post-psychotic outpatient overweight women. PhD United States International U. 1981.

WOLF,P.R. *389*
A comparison of holistic and behavioral group approaches in facililating weight loss, personality change, and self-concept change in adult women. EdD New Mexico State U. 1962.

WOLLERSHEIM,J.P. *390*
The effectiveness of learning theory-based group therapy in the treatment of overweight women. PhD U. of Illinois at Urbana-Champaign, 1968.

Physical illness

See also **5** 311; **19** 179, 452, 453

General

ALBUKERK,L.D. *391*
Psychological profile comparison of women undergoing hysterectomy, cholescystectomy, other surgery and no surgery. PhD Hofstra U. 1980.

ALEXANDER,A.S. *392*
Psychosocial dynamics among adolescent females faced with life-threatening illness: a descriptive study. PhD California Sch. of Prof. Psych., Los Angeles, 1975.

BECKLES,G.L.A. *393*
The prevalence of characteristics referrant of cardio-vascular disease among urban women of different ethnic origins: Trinidad. MSc Welsh National School of Medicine, 1982.

BREWER DE POZOS,K.A. *394*
Chronic pain as a means of communicating alienation in American society. Alienated women and their pain: thematic case studies. PhD U. California, Berkeley, 1980.

BUTLER,F.R. *395*
Factors related to compliance with a treatment regimen in black elderly diabetic women. PhD U. of Maryland, 1980.

CLAUS,L.M. *396*
Illness and illness behavior of women. PhD Saint Louis U. 1978.

FISHER,S.C. *397*
The negotiation of treatment decisions in doctor-patient communication and their impact on the identity of women patients. PhD U. of California, San Diego, 1979.

FLAX,C.S.C. *398*
Comparison between married women with ileostomies and married women without ileostomies on sexual anxiety, control, arousability, and fantasy. PhD New York U. 1980.

GREENBERGER,E. *399*
Fantasies of women confronting death: a study of critically ill patients. PhD Radcliffe Coll. 1961.

HEED,M.R. *400*
A study of the masculinity-femininity dimension of personality in normal and pathological groups: an investigation of differences in MF test productions of hospitalized and non-hospitalized women. PhD Washington U. 1955.

HOFFMAN,D.A. *401*
Mortality and morbidity in women treated for Hyperthyroidism. PhD Johns Hopkins U. 1981.

HOOK,N.C. *402*
Relative power distribution as related to need satisfaction in families with a wife-mother who has a rheumatic disease. PhD Michigan State U. 1972.

KEARNEY,H.M. *403*
A study of certain psychosocial factors found in female rheumatoid arthritis patients as compared with non-arthritic sisters. EdD Boston U. 1962.

KREIGER,N. *404*
An epidemiologic study of hip fracture in post-menopausal women. PhD Yale U. 1980.

LAMBERT,V.A. *405*
Factors affecting psychology well-being in rheumatoid arthritic women. DNS U. of California, San Francisco, 1981.

LAVELL,S.K. *406*
The female patient's experience of aesthetic regenerative facial surgery. PhD United States International U. 1980.

LAZAROFF,B.S. *407*
The effects of assertion training on two groups of females with chronic physical illness. PhD Georgia State U. Coll. of Educ. 1981.

LOHKAMP,N.L. *408*
The morality of hysterectomy operations. PhD Catholic U. of America, 1956.

MAZURE,C.M. *409*
Differential treatment recommendations for stereotypic and counterstereotypic women. PhD Pennsylvania State U. 1980.

MEIER,R.M. *410*
Overdependency in epileptic girls. PhD Boston U. Grad. Sch. 1975.

MUHL,A.M. *411*
Fundamental personality trends in tuberculous women. PhD George Washington U. 1923.

PELLMAN,R.G. *412*
Clinicians and women patients: clinicians' warmth, empathy and genuineness, attitudes toward women and demographic characteristics in relation to their clinical judgments of women. PhD Rutgers U. 1980.

PIEPER,B.A.D. *413*
The relationship between health status and perceived sexuality among females with diabetes mellitus. PhD Wayne State U. 1980.

REINHARDT,S. *414*
Characteristics of moods in hospitalized and normally functioning women. PhD Columbia U. 1968.

RIVKIN,M.O. *415*
Contextual effects of families on female responses to illness. PhD Johns Hopkins U. 1972.

ROSENBERG,L. *416*
Hormonal risk factors for myocardial infarction in women. DSc Harvard U. 1978.

RUSSELL,M.E. *417*
A controlled study of the relationship between gynaecological illness and marital problems in a Belfast general practice. MD Queen's U. of Belfast, 1968.

SEGALL,A. *418*
Socio-cultural variation in illness behavior: a comparative study of hospitalized Anglo-Saxon Protestant and Jewish female patients. PhD U. of Toronto, 1972.

SELIGSON,S. *419*
A psychosomatic investigation of the influence of sex-role identity on the development of physical and gynecological symptoms in women. PhD California Sch. of Prof. Psych., Berkeley, 1976.

SMITH-BEVINGTON,K.A. *420*
Self-concept in women with atopic dermatitis. PhD California Sch. of Prof. Psych., Berkeley, 1981.

SZKLO,M. *421*
The relationship of sociocultural factors to myocardial infarction in white women. DPH Johns Hopkins U. 1974.

TALBOTT,E.E. *422*
A study of sudden death from atherosclerotic heart disease in white women aged 25–64 in Allegheny County. DrPH U. of Pittsburgh, 1976.

TAYLOR,B.J. *423*
The psychological and behavioral effects of genital herpes in women: high recurrers vs. low recurrers. PhD U. of Washington, 1978.

WILLE,R.L. *424*
A comparative study of women who express chronic head pain and those who do not with respect to selected variables. PhD New York U. 1980.

WILLIAMS,M.A. *425*
A comparative study of postsurgical convalescence among women of two ethnic groups: Anglo and Mexican-American. PhD U. of California, 1971.

Cancer

See also **18** 274.

ADAMS,G.K. *426*
The relationship of self-image to managing activities of living in women following mastectomy for breast cancer. DNS U. of California, San Francisco, 1980.

AGHADIUNO,P.U. *427*
Breast cancer in Nigeria. MD U. of Glasgow, 1979.

BAILIS,K.L. *428*
An exploratory study on women's reactions to PAP smear examinations. PhD U. of Missouri-Columbia, 1981.

BARD,M. *429*
The relationship of the personality factor of dependence to psychological invalidism in women following radical mastectomy. PhD New York U. 1953.

BERNS,G.P. *430*
Psychological differences associated with primary location of cancer in women. PhD United States International U. 1981.

BLUM,L.S. *431*
Mastectomy: a study of the reactions of women to feelings of being inadequately informed, helpless, and abandoned. PhD Northwestern U. 1976.

BOYD,M.T. *432*
Women with breast cancer and their sisters: a psychological and physiological profile from adolescence to menopause. DrPH U. of California, Berkeley, 1982.

BROWN,L.N.M. *433*
The effects of an interpersonal skills training program for reach-to-recovery volunteers on the rehabilitation of mastectomy patients. EdD Boston U. Sch. of Educ. 1977.

CHRISTENSEN,D.N. *434*
Post-mastectomy couple counselling: an outcome study of a structured treatment protocol. PhD Brigham Young U. 1981.

CLARKE,D.L. *435*
Rogerian conditions in group therapy with mastectomy patients. PhD U. of Detroit, 1978.

COFER,J.B. *436*
Phantom breast concomitants among mastectomy patients. PhD North Texas State U. 1980.

COLLINS,E.J. *437*
A decision model for breast screening in medical care. MSc U. of Manchester, 1973.

CRADDOCK,R.B. *438*
Women's health beliefs about breast cancer: an assessment of a five-year teaching program in breast self-examination. DSN Birmingham, Southern Coll. 1982.

CURRIE,J.B. *439*
Dizygous twinning and breast cancer in women. PhD Yale U. 1967.

DIEM,G. *440*
Barriers to the performance of breast self-examination among a select group of college women. EdD Columbia U. Teachers Coll. 1982.

FARASH,J.L. *441*
Effect of counselling on resolution of loss and body image disturbance following a mastectomy. PhD California Sch. of Prof. Psych., Los Angeles, 1978.

FRANK,S.J. *442*
Personality correlates of breast cancer: an exploration of extraversion-introversion in women who have had breast cancer. PhD California Sch. of Prof. Psych., Los Angeles, 1977.

GERARD,D.M. *443*
Physiological and phenomenological reactions to erotic stimuli in post-mastectomy women and matched controls. PhD Michigan State U. 1981.

GJORGOV,A.N. *444*
Barrier contraceptive practice and male infertility as related factors to breast cancer in married women: a retrospective study. PhD U. of North Carolina at Chapel Hill, 1978.

GRAMSE,C.A. *445*
The relationship of internal-external health expectancies, value of health, health beliefs, and health behavior regarding breast self-examination in women. PhD New York U. 1982.

HALLAL,J.C. *446*
The relationship of health beliefs, health locus of control, and self-concept of the practice of breast self-examination in adult women. DNSc Catholic U. of America, 1980.

HEUSINKVELD,K. *447*
A study of variables related to regular breast self-examination behavior in a selected group of women. DrPH U. of Texas Health Science Center, Houston Sch. of Public Health, 1978.

HURLBURT,K.E. *448*
Life change events as they relate to the onset of breast tumors in women. PhD U. of Oregon, 1974.

HUSSEIN,M. *449*
A statistical study of factors influencing the incidence of breast cancer in females. PhD U. of North Carolina at Chapel Hill, 1961.

JOHNSTONE-WYATT,B.G.M. *450*
A sexual and rehabilitative needs assessment of mastectomy couples. PhD U. of Pennsylvania, 1981.

KHEEL,I.M. *451*
The trend and rates of female breast cancer in the Denver metropolitan area. PhD U. of North Colorado, 1982.

KRANTZLER,N.J. *452*
Treatment for cancer: nurses and the sociocultural context of medical care. PhD U. of California, Berkeley, 1982.

LEE,P.C.Y. *453*
The psychosocial impact of cancer: an evaluation of laryngectomy, mastectomy, and ostomy rehabilitation service programs for cancer patients. DSW U. of California, Berkeley, 1980.

LEPPER,K.E. *454*
Problems and coping patterns of the household member caring for the adult female cancer patient in the home. EdD Columbia U. 1968.

LONG,N.J. *455*
The intitial effect of loss of body part on self-esteem in women hospitalized for breast biopsy and possible mastectomy. DNSc Catholic U. of America, 1975.

LOWE,R.M. *456*
The effect of modeled cognitive restructuring on the frequency of breast self-examination in women. PhD Georgia State U. Coll. of Educ. 1977.

MCDONOUGH,C.A. *457*
An examination of causal attribution, emotional expressiveness, and body image as indices of adjustment to mastectomy. PhD Illinois Inst. of Tech. 1979.

MCINNIS-BOWERS,C.V. *458*
Reported breast self-examination procedures in a selected sample of women. PhD Southern Illinois U. at Carbondale, 1981.

MACKINTOSH,S.L. *459*
Incidence of breast and cervical cancer among women and selected social and psychological variables. PhD U. of South Carolina, 1979.

MANTELL,J.E. *460*
The effects of social-demographics, media and interpersonal influence, and health beliefs on breast

cancer detection behavior among urban women. PhD U. of California, Los Angeles, 1982.

MEYEROWITZ,B.E. *461*
Postmastectomy psychosocial condition of women in two breast cancer treatment modalities. PhD U. of Colorado at Boulder, 1978.

MOHAMED,M.H. *462*
A statistical study of factors influencing the incidence of breast cancer in females. PhD U. of North Carolina at Chapel Hill, 1961.

PENMAN,D.T. *463*
Coping strategies in adaptation to mastectomy. PhD Yeshiva U. 1979.

PERSAUD,V. *464*
Cancer of the uterine cervix in Jamaica. MD U. of London (External), 1972.

RICHARDS,M.C.B. *465*
The relationship between breast cancer in women and their locus of control and hostility. EdD U. of Georgia, 1976.

RYAN,E.A. *466*
The psychological aspects of breast cancer and mastectomy. PhD Northwestern U. 1978.

SANGER,C.K. *467*
A comparison of the psychological effects of breast-saving procedures and modified radical mastectomy. PhD Fordham U. 1978.

SCHON,M. *468*
Psychological effects of hypophysectomy in women with metastatic breast cancer. PhD New York U. 1957.

SOPCHAK,A.L. *469*
Changes in sexual behavior, desire and fantasy in breast cancer patients under androgen and estrogen therapy. PhD Adelphi U. 1957.

STECCHI,J.H. *470*
The effects of the reach-to-recovery program on the quality of life and rehabilitation of women who have had a mastectomy. EdD Boston U. Sch. of Educ. 1979.

STORMAN,M.D. *471*
Marital satisfaction variables and female breast cancer patients' predictions of their life expectancies. PhD Pacific Grad. Sch. of Psych. 1982.

THOMAS,C.J. *472*
Psychosocial aspects of mastectomy. MSc U. of Manchester, 1980.

THOMPSON,L. *473*
Who or what influences women to have a cytotest? A comparison of health educators' opinions with women's reports. MSc U. of Manchester, 1977.

WAKEFIELD,J. *474*
Beliefs about cancer and other factors affecting the readiness of women to accept and doctors to provide a test for premalignant conditions of the uterine cervix. PhD U. of Manchester, 1972.

WHEELER,J.I. *475*
Psychological alteration following the administration of male sex hormones to women with malignant tumors of the breast. PhD U. of Texas at Austin, 1955.

ZINKER,J.C. *476*
Terminal illness as a source of personality change in a woman suffering from cancer. PhD Case Western Reserve U. 1963.

The medical professions

General

See also **4** 222, 273, 1167, 1213, 1246, 1274, 1277, 1554, 1568, 1620; **5** 310, 519; **9** 102, 134, 135, 272, 447, 449, 506, 592, 666; **17** 398, 621, 623, 654, 668.

BARNETT,L.R. *477*
Sex-role strain in women in medicine. PhD U. of Kentucky, 1981.

BHARGAVA,G. *478*
Becoming a doctor: a study in the professional identification of women medical students in India. PhD York U. 1978.

CARTWRIGHT,L.K. *479*
Women in medical school. PhD U. of California, Berkeley, 1970.

DAVIDSON,L.R. *480*
Sex roles, affect, and the woman physician: a comparative study of the impact of latent social identity upon the role of women and men professionals. PhD New York U. 1975.

DUCKER,D.G. *481*
The effects of two sources of role-strain on women physicians. PhD City U. of New York, 1974.

FLINT,R.T. *482*
The relationship of women's tenure in occupational therapy to strong vocational interest blank and demographic variables. PhD U. of Minnesota, 1970.

GLICK,R. *483*
Practitioners and non-practitioners in a group of women physicians. PhD Case Western Reserve U. 1965.

GOSWAMI,M.J. *484*
Women dentists in Manhattan: a comparison with men dentists. PhD Columbia U. 1978.

HAIGNERE,L. *485*
Admission of women to medical schools: a study of organizational response to social movement and public pressure. PhD U. of Connecticut, 1981.

HAMMOND,J.M. *486*
Women in medical school: the negotiation and management of status and identity of women in a male-dominated institution. PhD Syracuse U. 1977.

KOLEHMAINEN,R.L. *487*
Women physicians: FMGS and primary care. DrPH Harvard U. 1977.

JONES,J.G. *488*
Career patterns of women physicians. PhD Brandeis U. 1971.

MANDELBAUM,D.R. *489*
Factors related to persistence in practice by women physicians. PhD Bryn Mawr Coll. 1975.

ORBACH,N.R.F. *490*
The evolution of a professional: the case of women in dentistry. PhD U. of Illinois at Chicago Circle, 1977.

SCOTT,W.P. *491*
Variables which contribute to leadership among female occupational therapists. PhD U. of Chicago, 1981.

WILLIAMS,J.J. *492*
The professional status of women physicians. PhD U. of Chicago, 1950.

Nursing

See also **9** 171, 190, 194, 406, 419, 422, 428, 579, 595, 629, 630, 660, 670; **19** 86, 118, 422.

ADAMACHE,K.W. *493*
The impact of unions on the wages and employment of nurses by hospitals. PhD Vanderbilt U. 1982.

ALLISON,R.F. *494*
The role of the nurses' aide. PhD U. of Michigan, 1972.

ANDERSON,C.L. *495*
The effect of a workshop on attitudes of female nursing students towards male homosexuality. PhD U. of Missouri-Columbia, 1978.

AUNG,T. *496*
Aspects of nurse manpower planning with particular reference to the non-participation of married nurses in the labour force. PhD UMIST, Manchester, 1977.

AUSTIN,R. *497*
Occupation and profession in the organization of nursing. PhD U. Coll. Cardiff, 1976.

BLOCH,D.W. *498*
A theory of role conflict resolution: the community mental health nurse. PhD U. of Colorado, 1972.

BOBVLA,J.A. *499*
The hospital nurse: her self-perception as professional and as communicator. PhD Ohio State U. 1972.

BONAPARTE,B.H.G. *500*
An investigation of the relation between ego defensiveness and open-closed mindedness of female registered professional nurses and their attitude toward culturally different patients. PhD New York U. 1977.

BROOKS,A.M.T. *501*
An analysis of female self-concept, self-actualization, and power-related personality factors as dimensions of power in female nurses with earned doctoral degrees. DNSc Catholic U. of America, 1978.

BROSNEN,J. *502*
Effects of sex, professional status, and attitudes toward women on female student nurses' reactions to clinical professionals' success and failure. PhD U. of Southern California, 1977.

CARTER,S.A.V. *503*
An exploration of non-traditional predictors of achievement performance among black female baccalaureate nursing students. EdD Temple U. 1981.

CLARKE,M. *504*
Social relationships between British and overseas student nurses. MPhil U. of Surrey, 1976.

COURT,S.D.M. *505*
The health of nurses in hospital. MD U. of Birmingham, 1947.

COWEN,E.D.H. *506*
Nurses' health. MD U. of Cambridge, 1947.

DICKENS,M.R. *507*
The influence of the position of women in the society on the development of nursing as a profession in America. PhD U. of New Mexico, 1977.

DOBBINS,M.P. *508*
Feminism, professionalism, and unionism among New Orleans nurses. PhD Tulane U. 1974.

DULEWICE,S.V. *509*
A study of nurses' job attitudes. MPhil U. of London, 1970.

EUNICE,P.L. *510*
Participation in continuing education by nurses in Nebraska. PhD U. of Nebraska-Lincoln, 1982.

FARNWORTH,M. *511*
A study of the psychological aspects of the recruitment of nurses. PhD U. of London, 1958.

FELGATE,R.V.R. *512*
The emergence of militancy in the nursing profession, 1960–1972. PhD U. of Surrey, 1978.

FITZPATRICK,L. *513*
A history of the National Organization for Public Health Nursing, 1912–1952. EdD U. of Columbia, 1972.

FOGARTY,B.E. 514
Labor-force participation among women: the case of nurses. PhD Purdue U. 1977.

FRANK,E.D. 515
Images of nursing among college freshmen women in New Orleans. EdD Columbia U. 1969.

GRAY,P.A. 516
Leadership in nursing teams: its perception by team leaders and team members. PhD U. of North Carolina at Chapel Hill, 1982.

GREEN,P.H. 517
Response to the choice of nursing scale of the MMPI by female nurse students and non-nurse students in vocational associate diploma and baccalaureate programs. PhD Boston Coll. 1972.

GREENLEAF,N.P. 518
Labor force participation by age of registered nurses and women in comparable occupations. DNS Boston U. Sch. of Nursing, 1982.

HALL,B.A. 519
Occupational values and family perspectives: a study of premedical and prenursing women. PhD U. of Colorado at Boulder, 1974.

HEREFORD,J. 520
Self-concepts and childhood recollections of undergraduate women preparing for nursing or teaching. PhD U. of Chicago, 1972.

HOCKEY,L. 521
A study of district nursing. PhD London, City U. 1979.

HOPE,R.M. 522
A study of the factors influencing the career decisions of the newly qualified staff nurse and their implications for staff development. MSc U. of Bath, 1976.

HOSINSKI,M. 523
Self, ideal self, and occupational role perceptual congruence in vocationally committed college women: a cross-sectional study of self-perception, self-aspiration, and occupational perception among university nursing students. PhD U. of Notre Dame, 1964.

HOXENE,D.D. 524
Attitude modification through professional training and development: the alteration of death-related fears in nurses. PhD Wayne State U. 1982.

IPOCK,B.D. 525
Anger in the returning RN student: a descriptive survey. EdD Oklahoma State U. 1982.

JEFFERY,A.J.W. 526
The effect of a recruitment film on the attitude of school leavers to nursing as a career. MEd U. of Manchester, 1950.

KRAMER,S.S. 527
An exploratory study of the situational problems of a select group of older women in a diploma school of nursing. PhD U. of Oregon, 1975.

LANCASTER,A. 528
A study of professional values and attitudes among registered nurses. MSc U. of Edinburgh, 1967.

LARYEA,M.G.G. 529
The midwife's role in the post-natal care of primiparae and their infants in the first 28 days following childbirth. MPhil CNAA, 1970.

LAWRENCE,C.J. 530
University education for nursing in Seattle, 1912–1970: the inside story of the University of Washington School (esp. work of Elizabeth Sterling Soule). PhD U. of Washington, 1972.

LEWIS,B.R. 531
The marketing of nursing. PhD UMIST, 1979.

LIA-HOAGBERG,B.L. 532
Professional activities and personality characteristics of nursing faculty compared with those of other academic women. PhD U. of Minnesota, 1982.

LIFF,S.T. 533
Images of women in medical education. MSc U. of Manchester, 1976.

MCLENNAN,W.M. 534
Midwifery in a north-east of Scotland practice, 1949 to 1958. MD U. of Glasgow, 1961.

MANN,D.P. 535
An investigation of the effects of a training program for female student nurses in the recognition of emotion in the facial region. PhD Kansas State U. 1975.

MELOSH,B. 536
Skilled hands, cool heads, and warm hearts: nurses and nursing, 1920–1960. PhD Brown U. 1979.

MERKLE,C.L. 537
An analysis of the interests of a 1977 sample of female registered nurses as measured by the Strong-Campbell interest inventory. PhD Boston Coll. 1978.

MERRY,P.E. 538
A descriptive study of mature and younger women in an associate degree nursing program. PhD U. of Southern California, 1974.

MILLER,C.L. 539
Nurses and the courts of law from 1957 to 1967. PhD Indiana U. 1969.

NYGARD,M.W.F. 540
Effect of consciousness-raising groups versus lectures about women on the personalities and career interests and homemaking interests of female students in nursing. PhD U. of Iowa, 1973.

OGIER,M.E. 541
A study of the leadership style and verbal interac-

tion of ward sisters with nurse learners. PhD U. of London, Birkbeck Coll. 1980.

PARIETTI,E.S. *542*
Development of doctoral education for nurses: an historical survey. EdD Columbia U. Teachers Coll. 1979.

PARSONS,V. *543*
A descriptive survey of registered nurses' attitudes, knowledge, and skills related to sexual health care of older children. DNS U. of California, Los Angeles, 1979.

REHN,R.A. *544*
Relationship between dogmatism, self-esteem, locus of control and predisposition toward two instructional method among female nursing students. EdD U. of Northern Illinois, 1982.

REILLY,D.E. *545*
A comparative analysis of selected non-intellective characteristics of college graduate and non-college graduate women who entered a collegiate nursing program. EdD New York U. 1967.

ROSENOW,A.M. *546*
The dilemma of achievement in nursing: a woman's profession. PhD U. of Chicago, 1981.

SCHARE,B.L. *547*
A status study of the use of and attitude toward health assessment skills among a selected group of master prepared registered nurses. EdD U. of Cincinnati, 1982.

SILLIMAN,J.C. *548*
Academic achievement of Mexican-American females in a college of nursing. PhD U. of Arizona, 1974.

SMITH,C.E.K. *549*
Comparison of motives and challenge responses of nurses experiencing different levels of structure in the work setting. PhD U. of Minnesota, 1982.

SMYTH,M.P. *550*
A proposal for sister education in nursing. EdD Columbia U. 1965.

STEWART,F.I. *551*
The increasing college-age population of women in Ohio and its implications for nursing education in Ohio. PhD Columbia U. 1959.

STROMBORG,M.F. *552*
The relationship between image of nursing and sex-role identity for seniors in diploma, associate degree, and baccalaureate nursing programs. EdD Northern Illinois U. 1974.

TAYLOR,E.C. *553*
Job satisfaction among female nurses: an analysis of a theory. PhD U. of Florida, 1980.

WALKER,J.F. *554*
'Practitioners in their own right': an analysis of some aspects of the role of the midwife. MSc U. of Wales, Cardiff, 1979.

WHITE,R.F. *555*
Female identity and work roles: the case of nursing. PhD U. of Chicago, 1964.

WILEY,M.L. *556*
A study of the administrative organization of baccalaureate nursing education in sister formation of the religious Sisters of Mercy. EdD Columbia U. 1967.

WRENNALL,M.J. *557*
A study of some factors influencing the career decisions of military nurses. MPhil U. of London, Birkbeck Coll. 1975.

WYKLE,M.L.H. *558*
Development of autonomy in nursing students in a Catholic, Protestant and public black college. PhD Case Western Reserve U. 1981.

9 History

Africa

ARNETT,M.F. *1*
Qasim Amin and the beginnings of the feminist movement in Egypt. PhD Dropsie U. 1966.

BADRAN,M.A.F. *2*
Huda Sha' rawi and the liberation of the Egyptian woman. DPhil U. of Oxford, 1977.

FEGAN,E.S. *3*
Report of a tour to the west coast of Africa to study the education of women, 1928–29: some notes on the Buchama tribe, Nigeria, 1928. DipAnthropology U. of Cambridge, 1929.

RASHEED,N.S. *4*
Slave girls under the early 'Abbāsids. PhD U. of St Andrews, 1973.

STILLMAN,Y.K. *5*
Female attire of medieval Egypt: according to the trousseau lists and cognate material from the Cairo Geniza. PhD U. of Pennsylvania, 1972.

TUCKER,J.E. *6*
Women and the family in Egypt, 1800–1860: a study in changing roles and status. PhD Harvard U. 1981.

VAUGHAN,M.A. *7*
Social and economic change in southern Malawi: rural communities in the Shira Highlands and Upper Shira valley from the mid-nineteenth century to 1915. [Includes intensification of female labour] PhD U. of London, Sch. of Oriental and African Studies, 1981.

WHITE,E.F. *8*
Creole women traders in Sierra Leone: an economic and social history, 1792– 1945. PhD Boston U. Grad Sch. 1978.

The Ancient World

See also **1** 65.

ALPERN,G.K. *9*
Women in ancient Greek political thought. PhD Case Western Reserve U. 1975.

ARVITES,J.A. *10*
Irene, woman emperor of Constantinople: her life and times. PhD U. of Mississippi, 1979.

AVERY,W.T. *11*
Julia, daughter of Augustus: a biography. PhD Case Western Reserve U. 1937.

BOHN,M.T. *12*
Property rights of women in ancient Greece. PhD Yale U. 1906.

BUCKLER,G.G. *13*
The intellectual and moral standards of Anna Comnena. [Daughter of Emperor Alexius of Constantinople] DPhil U. of Oxford, 1927.

COLLIE,F.A. *14*
The history and nature of the dowry among the ancient Greeks. MA U. of Wales, 1905.

CORNWELL,A.J. *15*
Women and marriage in the writings of Tertullian. BLitt U. of Oxford, 1965.

DAVIES,L.T. *16*
Vicissitudes of the Greek – chiefly of the Athenian – woman. MA U. of London, 1906.

DUPRIEZ,F. *17*
La condition de la femme romaine dans le Haut-Empire et l'influence du Christianisme. PhD U. of Montreal, 1977.

GARLAND,B.J. *18*
Gynaikonomoi: an investigation of Greek censors of women. PhD Johns Hopkins U. 1981.

HALLGREN,E.L. *19*
The legal status of women in the *leges barbarorum*. PhD U. of Colorado at Boulder, 1977.

HARDY,L.C. *20*
The imperial women in Tacitus' *Annales*. PhD Indiana U. 1976.

HARWOOD,H.J. *21*
The political influence of women under the Julio-Claudian emperors. PhD State U. of New York at Buffalo, 1978.

HOFFSTEN,R.B. *22*
Roman women of the early Empire. PhD U. of Pennsylvania, 1939.

HOLMES,A.M. *23*
The position of women among the Romans. MA U. of London, University Coll. 1932.

JONES,G.M.L. *24*
Women in Roman history from 200 BC to AD 138. MA U. Coll. of N. Wales, Wales, Bangor, 1964.

JUST,F.P.R. *25*
Ideas about women in classical Athens. BLitt U. of Oxford, 1976.

KALDIS-HENDERSON,N.G. *26*
A study of women in ancient Elis. PhD U. of Minnesota, 1979.

KAMPEN,N.B. *27*
Images and status of Roman working women: second and third century reliefs from Ostia. PhD Brown U. 1978.

LIGHTMAN,M. *28*
Women: a mirror of social change in the years of the Roman Revolution. PhD Rutgers U. 1980.

MCCLEES,H. *29*
A study of women in Attic inscriptions. PhD U. of Columbia, 1920.

MILLARD,A. *30*
The position of women in the family and society in ancient Egypt with special reference to the Middle Kingdom. PhD U. of London, University Coll. 1976.

MOIR,K.M. *31*
Cornelia, mother of the Gracchi. MLitt, U. of Edinburgh, 1981.

PALMER,M.S. *32*
The position of women in ancient Egypt. MA U. of Manchester, 1929.

RAE,N.F.C. *33*
Julia Domna. PhD U. of St Andrews, 1932.

ROBERTS,M.L. *34*
The status of women in Roman law. PhD Boston U. 1896.

ROBINS,R.G. *35*
Egyptian queens in the 18th dynasty up to the end of the reign of Amenhofpe III. DPhil U. of Oxford, 1981.

SCHAPS,D.M. *36*
Women and property control in classical and Hellenistic Greece. PhD Harvard U. 1927.

SINGER,M.R.W. *37*
Octavia minor, sister of Augustus: an historical and biographical study. PhD Duke U. 1945.

SYMES,E. *39*
The education of women under the Roman Empire. MA U. of London, 1909.

TITCHENER,M. *40*
The guardianship of women in Egypt during the Ptolemaic and Roman eras. PhD U. of Wisconsin, 1920.

WILLIAMS,M.G. *41*
De Jvlia Domna. PhD U. of Michigan, 1897.

Asia

See also **1** 65; **12** 1260.

AGNEW,V. *42*
Elite women in the Indian Nationalist Movement, 1919–1947. PhD U. of Toronto, 1976.

AHMAD,Z.A. *43*
Women and child industrial labour in the Bombay Presidency. PhD U. of London, LSE 1935.

BANERJEA,R. *44*
The education of women in Bengal, with special reference to that of the nineteenth and twentieth centuries. MEd U. of Leeds, 1938.

BEAHAN,C.L. *45*
The women's movement and nationalism in late Ch'ing China. PhD Columbia U. 1976.

CHING-CHUNG,P.K.T. *46*
Political power and social prestige of palace women in the northern Sung (960–1126). PhD U. of Pennsylvania, 1977.

COLLINS,L.E. *47*
The new women: a psychohistorical study of the Chinese feminist movement from 1900 to the present. PhD Yale U. 1976.

ELLIOTT,V.C. *48*
The education of Hindu women from ancient days with its bearing on the preparation of the Hindu woman for her place in society. PhD Hartford Seminary Foundation, 1947.

FRENIER,M.D. *49*
Women and the Chinese Communist Party, 1921–1952: changes in party policy and mobilization techniques. PhD U. of Iowa, 1978.

HO,K.C. *50*
The status and the role of women in the Chinese Communist movement, 1946– 1949. PhD Indiana U. 1973.

HOSAIN,S. *51*
The social life of women in early medieval Bengal. PhD U. of London (External), 1965.

LAHIRI,K. *52*
Education of women in Bengal, 1849–1882, with special reference to missionary contributions. PhD U. of Pennsylvania, 1979.

MATHUR,R.B. *53*
The early history of female education in India. PhD U. of London, Sch. of Oriental and African Studies, 1947.

MICKELSON,J.M. *54*
British women in India, 1757–1857. PhD U. of Michigan, 1978.

MOLONY,K.S. *55*
One woman who dared: Chikawa Fusae and the Japanese women's suffrage movement. PhD U. of Michigan, 1980.

NAGY,M.M. *56*
'How shall we live?' Social change, the family institution and feminism in prewar Japan. PhD Washington U. 1981.

NATH PANIGRAHI,L. *57*
The practice of female infanticide in India and its suppression in the North Western Provinces. PhD U. of London, Sch. of Oriental and African Studies, 1965.

O'HARA,A.R. *58*
The position of women in early China. PhD Catholic U. of America, 1946.

PAL,A. *59*
A critical analysis of factors influencing the growth of female education in Bengal during the early twentieth century (1900–1939). MPhil U. of London, Inst. of Educ. 1967.

PAUL,G.B. *60*
Emancipation and education of Indian women since 1829. PhD U. of Pittsburgh, 1970.

RATTE,M.L. *61*
The lotus and the violet: attitudes toward womanhood in Bengal, 1792–1854. PhD U. of Massachusetts, 1977.

SARKAR,P. *62*
A historical study of the social influences on the education of women in India. MA U. of London, Inst. of Educ., 1958.

SHARDAMMA,M. *63*
Sati and its abolition. BLitt U. of Oxford, 1953.

SIU,B.C.Y. *64*
The women's movements in China, 1900–1949. PhD Carleton U. 1981.

WANKEN,H.M. *65*
'Woman's sphere' and Indian reform: the Women's National Indian Association, 1879–1901. PhD Marquette U. 1981.

The British Isles

*Up to c.*1700

See also **1** 88, 118, 238; **12** 64, 1235, 1354.

BARNETT,T.R. *66*
Queen Margaret and the influence she exerted on the Celtic Church in Scotland. PhD U. of Edinburgh, 1925.

BONE,Q.B. *67*
Henrietta Maria and the English Rebellion, 1609–1669. PhD U. of Illinois at Urbana-Champaign, 1954.

CAHN,G. *68*
Changing conceptions of women in sixteenth- and seventeenth-century England. PhD U. of Michigan, 1981.

CASPARY,M.H. *69*
Personal letters of English women from 1625–1760. PhD Stanford U. 1945.

CATLIN,J.G. *70*
The public non-parliamentary speeches of Queen Elizabeth I: an annotated bibliography and commentary. PhD U. of North Carolina at Chapel Hill, 1969.

CIONI,M.L. *71*
Women and law in Elizabethan England, with particular reference to the Court of Chancery. PhD U. of Cambridge, 1975.

COOK,A.M. *72*
The evidence for the reconstruction of female costume in the early Anglo-Saxon period in the south of England. MA U. of Birmingham, 1974.

DALE,M.K. *73*
Women in the textile industries and trade of fifteenth-century England. MA U. of London, 1928.

DE GRUNNE,J.D.de H. *74*
Feminine devotion in the English seventeenth century as illustrated by unpublished MSS in the Bodleian Library, and published and unpublished diaries, letters and treatises. BLitt U. of Oxford, 1960.

DOCHERTY,P.C. *75*
Isabella, Queen of England, 1296–1330. DPhil U. of Oxford, 1978.

DUEAN,M.B. *76*
The case of Mary Stuart. PhD Georgetown U. 1923.

DUNLAP,S.J. *77*
The social position of women in late thirteenth- and early fourteenth-century Scotland, 1283–1329. MLitt U. of St Andrews, 1977.

FARBER,E. *78*
The letters of Lady Elizabeth Russell (1540–1609). PhD Columbia U. 1977.

GALLAGHER,M.K. *79*
Some chapters on the education and position of women in the Middle Ages. PhD Fordham U. 1975.

GATHERER,W.A. *80*
An annotated edition of George Buchanan's account of the personal reign of Mary Stuart, with a critical introduction. PhD U. of Edinburgh, 1955.

GLANZ,L.M. 81
The legal position of English women under the early Stuart kings and the interregnum, 1603–1660. PhD Loyola U., Chicago, 1973.

HARVEY,S. 82
The Cooke sisters: a study of Tudor gentlewomen. PhD Indiana U. 1981.

HIGGINS,P.M. 83
Women in the English Civil War. MA U. of Manchester, 1966.

HOOD,S.J.R. 84
The impact of Protestantism on the Renaissance ideal of women in Tudor England. PhD U. of Nebraska-Lincoln, 1977.

HUGHEY,R.W. 85
Cultural interests of women in England from 1524 to 1640, indicated in the writings of the women: a survey. PhD Cornell U. 1932.

KITTEL,M.R. 87
Married women in thirteenth-century England: a study in common law. PhD U. of California, Berkeley, 1973.

KUSCHMIERZ,R.L.M. 88
The Instruction of a Christian woman: a critical edition of the Tudor translation. PhD U. of Pittsburgh, 1961.

MCELROY,M.M.D. 89
Literary patronage of Margaret Beaufort and Henry VII: a study of Renaissance propaganda (1483–1509). PhD U. of Texas at Austin, 1964.

MACFARLANE,A.D.J. 90
Witchcraft prosecutions in Essex, 1560–1680: a sociological analysis. DPhil U. of Oxford, 1967.

MENDELSON,S.H. 91
Women in seventeenth-century England: three studies. DPhil U. of Oxford, 1981.

MEYER,G.D. 92
Science for Englishwomen, 1650–1760: the telescope, the microscope, and the feminine mind. PhD Columbia U. 1941.

MONTGOMERY,M.D. 93
Eleanor of Provence, Queen of England, 1223–1291. PhD Mississippi State U. 1965.

MOORE,C.E. 94
Queen Emma and the role of women in Anglo-Saxon society. PhD U. of California, Santa Barbara, 1973.

MORGAN,L.I. 95
The Renaissance lady in England. PhD U. of California, Berkeley, 1932.

MULVIHILL,M.E. 96
Feminine portraiture, 1660–1714: ideologies of woman in English life and letters as a model of the emergence of liberal thought during the Restoration and reign of Queen Anne. PhD U. of Wisconsin-Madison, 1982.

MURRAY,L.H. 97
The ideal of the court lady in England, 1558–1625. PhD U. of Chicago, 1936.

MUSGRAVE,C.A. 98
Household administration in the fourteenth century with special reference to the household of Elizabeth de Burgh, Lady of Clare. MA U. of London, 1923.

NOTESTEIN,W. 99
A history of English witchcraft from 1558 to 1718. PhD Yale U. 1908.

REYNOLDS,T.J. 100
Queen Elizabeth in the writings of the Recusants. PhD Harvard U. 1956.

SCOTT,R.J. 101
Women in the Stuart economy. MPhil U. of London, LSE, 1973.

SMITH,D.S. 102
Tudor and Stuart midwifery. PhD U. of Kentucky, 1980.

SMITH,H.L. 103
Feminism in seventeenth-century England. PhD U. of Chicago, 1975.

SYPHER,S.S. 104
Mary of Lorraine at the end of the old alliance. PhD Cornell U. 1968.

TODD,B.H. 105
Widowhood in a market town: Abingdon, 1540–1720. DPhil U. of Oxford, 1983.

WATERSON,N.M. 106
Mary II of England and her life during the years 1689–1694: her influence on politics, on the Anglican Church, and on society. BLitt U. of Oxford, 1925.

WEIKEL,A. 107
Crown and council: a study of Mary Tudor and her Privy Council. PhD Yale U. 1966.

WILSON,A.F. 108
Childbirth in seventeenth- and eighteenth-century England. DPhil U. of Sussex, 1983.

WOOD,M. 109
Foreign correspondence with Marie de Lorraine, Queen of Scotland, from the originals in the Balcarres papers, 1537–48 and 1548–57. PhD U. of Edinburgh, 1923.

YOSHIOKA,B.G.S. 110
Imaginal worlds: woman as witch and preacher in seventeenth-century England. PhD Syracuse U. 1977.

After c.1700

See also below 416, 420, 539; **1** 52, 140, 141, 145, 191 237.

ADICKES,S.E. *111*
The social quest: the expanded vision of four women travelers in the era of the French Revolution. [Mary Wollstonecraft, Helen Maria Williams, Ann Radcliffe and Mary Berry.] PhD New York U. 1977.

AHRENDS,E. *112*
Radicalism and feminism in England in the early nineteenth century. MPhil CNAA, 1979.

AINSWORTH,E.M. *113*
Changing attitudes to the employment of women and children on the land between the 1830s and the 1870s with particular reference to the county of Sussex. MA U. of Sussex, 1970.

ALLEN,M. *114*
Women's place and World War II. MA U. of Essex, 1979.

ANDERSON,N.B.F. *115*
Eliza Lynn Linton and the woman question in Victorian England. PhD Tulane U. 1973.

AUBUCHON,A.Jr. *116*
Feminism and women's education in England, 1860–1890. PhD Harvard U. 1976.

AYERS,P.L. *117*
The public career of Lady Astor. PhD U. of Pittsburgh, 1958.

BALD,M.A. *118*
Representative Victorian women. PhD U. of Edinburgh, 1921.

BECKWITH,M.C. *119*
Catherine MacAulay, eighteenth-century English rebel: a sketch of her life and some reflections on her place among the historians and political reformers of her time. PhD Ohio U. 1953.

BERCH,B.E. *120*
Industrialization and working women in the nineteenth century: England, France and the United States. PhD U. of Wisconsin-Madison, 1976.

BILLINGHAM,J. *121*
Women's work and wages in the West Riding of Yorkshire, 1760–1830. MA U. of Sheffield, 1977.

BILLINGTON,H.C. *122*
The women's education and suffrage movement, 1850–1914: innovation and institutionalisation. PhD U. of Hull, 1976.

BOLSTER,E. *123*
Mother Mary Francis Bridgeman and the Irish Sisters of Mercy in the Crimean War. PhD National U. of Ireland, 1963.

BRAYBON,C.G. *124*
Attitudes to working women in British industry, 1914–1920. MPhil U. of Sussex, 1977.

BROOKES,B.L. *125*
Abortion in England, 1919–1939: legal theory and social practice. PhD Bryn Mawr Coll. 1982.

BRULEY,S. *126*
Socialism and feminism in the Communist Party of Great Britain, 1920–39. PhD U. of London, LSE, 1980.

BRYAN,S.M. *127*
Women's suffrage in the Manchester area, circa 1890–1906. MA U. of Manchester, 1974.

BUTLER,M.A. *128*
Images of women in political thought: from John Locke to John Stuart Mill. PhD Johns Hopkins U. 1979.

CARSON,R.K. *128a*
From teacups to terror: the rhetorical strategies of the Women's Social and Political Union, 1903–1918. PhD U. of Iowa, 1975.

COHN,S.R. *129*
Feminization of clerical labor in Great Britain: a contrast of two large clerical employers (1857–1937.) [General Post Office and Great Western Railway] PhD U. of Michigan, 1981.

CRAWFORD,F.W. *130*
Some aspects of the political and economic problems of women in English society, 1884–1901. PhD New York U. 1956.

DAMIANI,A.E.F. *131*
British travel attitudes to the Near East in the eighteenth and nineteenth centuries. [Includes Mary Wortley Montagu] PhD U. of Edinburgh, 1977.

DARKNELL,F.A. *132*
Democracy and parapolitics: the case of militant suffragists in Britain, 1905–1914. PhD U. of California, Berkeley, 1973.

DAVY,T. *133*
Female shorthand-typists and typists, 1900–1939. MA U. of Essex, 1980.

DONNISON,J.E. *134*
The development of the profession of midwife in England, 1754–1902. PhD(Econ) U. of London, LSE, 1974.

DOWLING,W.C. *135*
The Ladies Sanitary Association and the origins of the health visiting service. MA U. of London, LSE, 1963.

ENGELMAN,H. *136*
The ideal English gentlewomen in the nineteenth century, her education, conduct and sphere. PhD Northwestern U. 1956.

EWBANK,D.R. 137
The role of women in Victorian society: a controversy explored in six utopias, 1871–1895. PhD U. of Illinois, 1969.

FEE,E. 138
Science and the 'woman question', 1860–1920: a study of English scientific periodicals. PhD Princeton U. 1978.

FLORECKA,I. 139
A comparative study of the economic position of women in Great Britain and Poland in the inter-war period. PhD U. of Edinburgh, 1945.

FRIEDMAN,L.J. 139a
Mary Lamb, sister, seamstress, murderer, writer. PhD Stanford U., 1976.

GARDNER,J.C. 140
The origin and nature of the legal rights of spouses and children in the Scottish law of succession. PhD U. of Edinburgh, 1927.

GARNER,L. 141
The feminism of mainstream women's suffrage in early twentieth-century England: an evaluation. PhD U. of Liverpool, 1981.

GILLGANNON,M.M. 141a
The Sisters of Mercy as Crimean War Nurses. PhD U. of Notre Dame, 1962.

HALL,G.M. 142
Prostitution and sex promiscuity in several countries at the present time. MA U. of Liverpool, 1932.

HALL,V.J. 143
Women in journalism: a sociological account of the entry of women into the profession of journalism in Great Britain until 1930. PhD U. of Essex, 1979.

HAMMERTON,A.J. 144
A study of middle-class female emigration from Great Britain, 1830–1914. PhD U. of British Columbia, 1969.

HENDRICK,J.B. 145
The tailoress in the ready-made clothing industry in Leeds, 1889–99. MA U. of Warwick, 1971.

HERSTEIN,S. 145a
Barbara Leigh Smith Bodichon (1827–1891): a mid-Victorian feminist. PhD City U. of New York, 1980.

HEWITT,M. 146
The effect of married women's employment in the cotton textile districts on the organization and structure of the home in Lancashire, 1840–80. PhD U. of London, LSE, 1983.

HILLYER,R. 147
The parson's wife in history. MPhil U. of London, King's Coll. 1971.

HIRST,T.F. 148
An investigation of the incorporation of women into the engineering trades in South London between 1914 and 1918. MEd U. of Reading, 1976.

HOGG,S.H. 149
The employment of women in Great Britain, 1891–1921. DPhil U. of Oxford, 1968.

HOLCOMBE,L. 150
Middle-class working women in England, 1850–1914. PhD Columbia U. 1962.

HOLTON,S.M.J. 151
Feminism and democracy: the women's suffrage movement in Britain, with particular reference to the National Union of Women's Suffrage Societies, 1897–1918. PhD U. of Stirling, 1980.

HOLTZMAN,E.M. 152
Marriage, sexuality, and contraception in the British middle class, 1918–1939: the correspondence of Marie Stopes. PhD Rutgers U. 1982.

HUANG,F.S. 153
The role of women workers in the British textile industry, 1780–1850. MLitt U. of Cambridge, 1972.

HUFFMAN,J.E.B. 154
The British Labour Party and women's suffrage, 1884–1906. PhD Georgia State U. 1980.

HUME,L.P.B. 155
The National Union of Women's Suffrage Societies, 1893–1914. PhD Stanford U., 1979.

HUNT,F. 156
Women in the nineteenth-century bookbinding and printing trade, 1790–1914. MA U. of Essex, 1979.

INESON,A. 157
Science and technology, medicine, welfare and the labour process: women munition workers in the First World War. MPhil U. of Sussex, 1983.

JACOBY,R.M. 158
The British and American Women's Trade Union Leagues, 1890–1925: a case study of feminism and class. PhD Harvard U. 1977.

JOHN,A.V. 159
Women workers in British coal mines 1840–90 with special reference to West Lancashire. PhD U. of Manchester, 1976.

KAMINSKI,D.C. 160
The radicalization of a ministering angel: a biography of Emily Hobhouse, 1860–1926. PhD U. of Connecticut, 1977.

KANNER,S.B. 161
Victorian institutional patronage: Angela Burdett-Coutts, Charles Dickens and Urania Cottage reformatory for women, 1846–1858. PhD U. of California, Los Angeles, 1972.

KAPLAN-TUCKEL,B. *162*
A rhetorical analysis of four Parliamentary debates on women's suffrage in Great Britain, 1870–1897. PhD Pennsylvania State U. 1982.

KOSAK,M. *163*
Women munition workers during the First World War. PhD U. of Hull, 1976.

LEWER,S. *164*
Impact of the First World War on women's employment, with special reference to the city of Coventry. MA* U. of Warwick, 1974.

LANGLOIS,P.F.S. *165*
The feminine press in England and France, 1875–1900. PhD U. of Massachusetts, 1979.

LAWLEY,E.F.G. *166*
The post-war industrial position of women in Manchester. MComm U. of Manchester, 1933.

LINDLEY,M. *167*
Queen Caroline and literature. MA U. of Liverpool, 1927.

LOHMAN,J.S. *167a*
Sex or class? English Socialists and the woman question, 1884–1914. PhD Syracuse U., 1979.

MCCRONE,K.E. *168*
The advancement of women during the age of reform, 1832–1870. PhD New York U. 1971.

MCFADDEN,K.D. *169*
George Bernard Shaw and the woman question . PhD U. of Toronto, 1976.

MCNALLY,J.R. *170*
Socialism and sexual politics, 1884–1906. MA U. of Warwick, 1979.

MAGGS,C.J. *171*
Nursing: an aspect of women's work in the late nineteenth and early twentieth centuries in England. PhD U. of Bath, 1980.

MAINS,J.A. *171a*
British travellers in Switzerland with special reference to some women travellers between 1750 and 1850. PhD U. of Edinburgh, 1967.

MAPPEN,E.F. *172*
Women workers and unemployment policy in late Victorian and Edwardian London. PhD Rutgers U. 1977.

MARSHALL,C.T. *173*
Gertrude Bell: her work and influence in the Near East, 1914–1926. PhD Vanderbilt U. 1968.

MARTIN,C.E. *174*
Female Chartism: a study in politics. MA Univ. Coll. Swansea, 1974.

MELANI,L. *175*
Hidden motives: a study of power and women in British periodical fiction, 1864. PhD Indiana U. 1973.

MEYER,P.J.B. *175a*
No land too remote: women travellers in the Georgian age, 1750–1830. PhD U. of Massachusetts, 1978.

MODY,C.M.S. *176*
The political thought of Mrs Besant: the English years 1847–1893. PhD U. of Kansas, 1973.

MORGAN,C.E. *177*
Working-class women and labour and social movements in mid-nineteenth century England. PhD U. of Iowa, 1979.

MORGAN,D.R. *178*
The politics of women's suffrage in Britain and the United States of America, 1906–20. PhD U. of Cambridge, 1967.

MORRIS,J. *179*
The 'sweated traders' women workers and the Trade Boards Act of 1909: an exercise in social control. PhD U. of London, LSE, 1982.

NASH,S.D. *180*
Social attitudes towards prostitution in London from 1752 to 1829. PhD New York U. 1980.

NEFF,W.F. *181*
Victorian working women: an historical and literary study of women in British industries and professions, 1832–1850. PhD Columbia U. 1929.

NELSON,L.E. *182*
Types of women diarists in the reign of George III. PhD Trinity College, Dublin, 1952.

NOLAN,B.E. *183*
The political theory of Beatrice Webb. PhD Bryn Mawr Coll., 1978.

NORD,D.E. *184*
The apprenticeship of Beatrice Webb. PhD U. of Columbia, 1980.

NORRIS,M. *185*
Women and public protest, 1780–1844. MA* U. of Sheffield, 1981.

OTTO,P.C. *186*
Daughters of the British aristocracy: their marriage in the eighteenth and nineteenth centuries, with particular reference to the Scottish peerage. PhD Stanford U. 1974.

PALMER,D. *187*
The protracted foundations of a national maternity service: the failure to reduce maternal mortality in England and Wales, 1919–1939. MA* U. of Warwick, 1978.

PINCHBECK,I. *188*
The work of women in agriculture in the late eighteenth and early nineteenth centuries and the influence of the agrarian revolution thereon. MA U. of London, 1927.

PINCHBECK,I. *189*
Women workers and the industrial revolution, 1750–1950. PhD U. of London, LSE, 1930.

PRINCE,J.E. *190*
Florence Nightingale's reform of nursing, 1860–1887. PhD U. of London, LSE, 1982.

REISS,E. *191*
The rights and duties of Englishwomen: an investigation of present-day law and opinion. PhD U. of Manchester, 1924.

RILEY,L.W. *192*
The opposition to women's suffrage, 1867. BLitt U. of Oxford, 1977.

ROBBIE,M.L. *193*
Discovering the bluestockings: a neglected constellation of clever women. PhD U. of Edinburgh, 1947.

ROON,L.M. *194*
The history of nursing legislation in the British Commonwealth, 1891–1939. PhD Radcliffe Coll., 1952.

ROSEN,A.W. *194a*
The militant campaign of the Women's Social and Political Union, 1903–1914. PhD U. of California, Berkeley, 1972.

ROSS,E.M. *195*
Women and the Poor Law administration, 1857–1909. MA U. of London, LSE, 1956.

ROVER,C.M. *196*
The women's suffrage movement in Britain, 1866–1914. PhD U. of London (External), 1966.

SAMA,A. *197*
The Times and the women's suffrage movement, 1900–1918. MLitt U. of St Andrews, 1975.

SAVIDGE,A.W.J. *198*
The foundation and early years of Queen Anne's Bounty. MA U. of London, Birkbeck Coll. 1953.

SAYWELL,R.J.T. *199*
The development of the feminist idea in England, 1789–1933. MA U. of London, King's Coll. 1936.

SCOTT,J.C. *200*
Bradford women in organization, 1867–1914: an introductory study of their contribution to social, political and economic development. MA U. of Bradford, 1971.

SHKOLNIK,E.S. *201*
Leading ladies: a study of eight late Victorian and Edwardian political wives. PhD U. of Illinois at Urbana-Champaign, 1978.

SMITH,K.C. *202*
The militant suffragettes as a police problem, London, 1906–1914. PhD Ohio State U. 1974.

SOFTLEY,P. *203*
Changes in the social status of women in England: an analysis of the married women's property and divorce controversies, 1854–57. MA U. of Leicester, 1962.

SUMMERFIELD,P. *204*
Women workers in the Second World War: a study of the interplay in official policy between the need to mobilize women for war and conventional expectations about their roles at work and at home. DPhil U. of Sussex, 1982.

SUMNER,M. *205*
Prositution and images of women: a critique of the Victorian censure of prostitution. MSc(Econ), Wales (Aberystwyth), 1980.

TANK,S.P. *206*
Social change and social movements: working-class women and political activity in Britain, 1880–1921. PhD U. of London, LSE, 1981.

TAYLOR,B.G. *207*
The feminist theory and practice of the Owenite socialist movement in Britain, 1820–1845. DPhil U. of Sussex, 1981.

TAYLOR,P. *208*
Women domestic servants, 1919–1939: the final phase. MA U. of Birmingham 1976.

THOM,D. *209*
Women munition workers at Woolwich Arsenal in the 1914–18 War. MA* U. of Warwick, 1975.

THOM,D. *210*
The ideology of women's work, 1914–24, with special reference to the National Federation of Women Workers and other trade unions. PhD CNAA (Thames Polytechnic), 1982.

TOLPIN,M. *211*
The Darwinian influence on psychological definitions of femininity in England, 1871–1914. PhD Harvard U. 1972.

TRUSTRAM,M. *212*
Marriage and the Victorian army at home: the regulation of soldiers' relationships with women and the treatment of soldiers' wives. PhD U. of Bristol, 1981.

TURBIN,C. *213*
Woman's work and woman's rights: a comparative study of the woman's trade union movement and the woman suffrage movement in the mid-nineteenth century. PhD New Sch. for Social Research, 1978.

UTTRACHI,P.B. *214*
Health and household: material culture of middle-class women in nineteenth-century Britain. PhD Rutgers U. 1973.

WALKOWITZ,J.R. *214a*
'We are not beasts of the field': prostitution and the campaign against the Contagious Diseases Act, 1869–1886. PhD U. of Rochester, 1974.

WALTON,R.G. *215*
The place of women in the development of social work, 1860–1971. PhD U. of Manchester, 1972.

WATSON,S. 216
A comparative study of relations between the Women's Trade Union League and the Trades Union Congress in Britain and between the Women's Trade Union League and the American Federation of Labor in the USA, 1909–19. MA* U. of Warwick, 1980.

WEATHERHEAD,E.L. 217
A study of the physique of women in industry. MSc U. of London 1927.

WHIPP,R.T.H. 218
The women pottery workers of Staffordshire and trade unionism, 1890–1905. MA* U. of Warwick, 1979.

WORZALA,D.M.C. 219
The Langham Place Circle: the beginnings of the organized women's movement in England, 1854–1870. PhD U. of Wisconsin-Madison, 1982.

Continental Europe

General

HOWELL,M.C. 220
Women's work in urban economies of late medieval northwestern Europe: female labor status in male economic institutions. PhD Columbia U. 1979.

MACFARLANE,F.M. 221
The status of royal women in Dark Age Europe. MLitt U. of Glasgow, 1983.

MULLANEY,M.M. 222
The female revolutionary. The woman question and European socialism, 1871–1921. PhD Rutgers U. 1980.

France

See also **1** 41, 162.

ALTER,A.I. 223
Women are made not born: making bourgeois girls into women, France 1830–1870. PhD Rutgers U. 1981.

BACHRACH,S.D. 224
The feminization of the French postal service, 1750–1914. PhD U. of Wisconsin-Madison, 1981.

BARKER,N.N. 225
The influence of the Empress Eugénie on foreign affairs of the Second Empire. PhD U. of Pennsylvania, 1958.

BIDELMAN,P.K. 226
The feminist movement in France: the formative years, 1858–1889. PhD Michigan State U. 1975.

BOWERS,M.E. 227
The *Liber Manualis* of Dhuoda: advice of a ninth-century mother for her sons; edited with an introduction and translation. [Earliest literary work by a woman in the Frankish kingdom] PhD Catholic U. of America, 1977.

BOXER,M.J. 228
Socialism faces feminism in France, 1879–1913. PhD U. of California, Riverside, 1975.

BROOKING,J.T. 229
The influence of the trial notes on five major Joan of Arc plays. PhD Case Western Reserve U. 1956.

CAMERON,V.P. 230
Woman as image and image-maker in Paris during the French Revolution. PhD Yale U. 1983.

CARENS,G.G. 231
Cottage industry and women's work: a study of Auffay, France, 1750–1850. PhD U. of North Carolina at Chapel Hill, 1978.

COHEN,E.S. 232
The socialization of girls and young women in early modern France 1560–1700. PhD U. of Toronto, 1978.

DURHAM,M.J. 233
The *sans-jupons'* crusade for liberation during the French Revolution. PhD U. of Washington, 1972.

GODDARD,E.R. 234
Women's costume in French texts of the eleventh and twelfth centuries. PhD Johns Hopkins U. 1925.

GOLD,P.S. 235
Image and reality: women in twelfth-century France. PhD Stanford U. 1977.

GOLIBER,S.H. 236
The life and times of Marguerite Durand: a study in French feminism. PhD Kent State U. 1975.

GRAVES,W.L. 237
The politics of reform: Marguerite of Navarre. PhD Texas Christian U. 1979.

GRUNWALD,E. 238
Louis Philippe's France as seen by English women. PhD U. of London, University Coll. 1948.

HEDMAN,E.R. 239
Early French feminism from the eighteenth century to 1848. PhD New York U. 1954.

HELLERSTEIN,E.O. 240
Women, social order, and the city: rules for French ladies, 1830–1870. PhD U. of California, Berkeley, 1980.

HILDEN,P.J. 241
French socialism and women textile workers, 1880–1914: a regional study. [Lille, Roubaix, Tourcoing] PhD U. of Cambridge, 1981.

HULLEY,C. 242
Marie de Guise. PhD U. of Washington, 1944.

HUNT,P.C. *243*
Revolutionary syndicalism and feminism among teachers in France, 1900–1921. PhD Tufts U. 1975.

JONES,R.E.A. *244*
Marie Antoinette and the French Revolution. MA U. of Wales, 1947.

LEMBRIGHT,R.L. *245*
Louise of Savoy and Marguerite d'Angoule[c005]me: Renaissance patronage and religious reform. PhD Ohio State U. 1974.

LIGHTBODY,C.W. *246*
The judgments of Joan, 1431–1815. PhD Cornell U. 1951.

LIGHTMAN,H.L. *247*
Sons and mothers: queens and minor kings in French constitutional law. PhD Bryn Mawr Coll. 1981.

LOUGEE,C.E.C. *248*
Feminism and social stratification in seventeenth-century France. PhD U. of Michigan, 1972.

MCBRIDE,T.M. *249*
Rural tradition and the process of modernization: domestic servants in nineteenth-century France. PhD Rutgers U. 1973.

MCMILLAN,J.P. *250*
The effects of the First World War on the social conditions of women in France. DPhil U. of Oxford, 1976.

MEIJER,M.S. *251*
François Le Billon (1522–1564): feministe-nationaliste- secrétaire. PhD Catholic U. of America, 1972.

MOSES,C.G. *252*
The evolution of feminist thought in France, 1829–1889. PhD George Washington U. 1978.

OTIS,L.L. *253*
Nisi in postribulu: prostitution in Languedoc from the twelfth to the sixteenth century. PhD U. of Columbia, 1980.

PABST,L.B. *254*
The regency of Mary of Guise. PhD U. of Illinois, 1951.

POPE,B.C. *255*
Mothers and daughters in early nineteenth-century Paris. PhD Columbia U. 1981.

POTASH,J.R. *256*
The foundling problem in France, 1800–1869: child abandonment in Lille and Lyon. PhD Yale U. 1979.

PRICE,J.A. *257*
Marguerite de France: literary patroness of the Renaissance. PhD U. of Kentucky, 1974.

RAFFERTY,F.M. *258*
'Madame Séverine' 1855–1929. [Pen-name of Caroline Remy, a Parisian journalist] PhD U. of Notre Dame, 1974.

ROFFMAN,M.N. *259*
Working-class women in medieval France, 800–1300. PhD U. of Hawaii, 1977.

RUBIN,E.R. *260*
The heroic image: women and power in early seventeenth-century France, 1610– 1661. PhD George Washington U. 1977.

SCOUTEN,M.A.S. *261*
Villedieu: a feminist-advocate. PhD State U. of New York at Albany, 1982.

SMITH,B.G.S. *262*
The women of the Lille bourgeoisie, 1850–1914. PhD U. of Rochester 1976.

SOWERWINE,C. *263*
Women and socialism in France 1871–1921: socialist women's groups from Léonie Rouzade to Louise Saumoneau. PhD U. of Wisconsin-Madison, 1973.

STOCK,M.L. *264*
Poullain de la Barre: a seventeenth-century feminist. PhD Columbia U. 1961.

STRUMINGHER,L.S. *265*
Les Canutes: women workers in the Lyonese silk industry, 1836–48. PhD U. of Rochester, 1974.

TAYLOR,J.C. *266*
From proselytizing to social reform: three generations of French female teaching congregations, 1600–1720. PhD Arizona State U. 1980.

TURNER,G.D. *267*
The aristocratic widow in law and society according to the Canon Law of France during the twelfth and thirteenth centuries. PhD Michigan U. 1969.

WALKER,A.S. *268*
The life and status of a generation of French women, 1150–1200. PhD U. of North Carolina at Chapel Hill, 1958.

WAUGH,L.J. *269*
The images of woman in France on the even of the Loi Camille See, 1877–1880. PhD U. of Massachusetts, 1977.

WEBB,C.J. *270*
Royalty and reform: the predicament of Renée de France, 1510–1575. PhD Tufts U. 1969.

WESTON,E.A. *271*
Prostitution in Paris in the later nineteenth century: a study of political and social ideology. PhD State U. of New York at Buffalo, 1979.

WILSON,L.B. *272*
Les maladies des femmes: women, charlotary, and professional medicine in eighteenth-century France. PhD Stanford U. 1982.

Germany and Central Europe

BOAK,H.L. *274*
The status of women in the Weimar Republic. PhD U. of Manchester, 1983.

BOMNER,S.H. *275*
Margaret of Austria: her life and learning in Europe's high renaissance. PhD U. of Pittsburgh, 1981.

BOYD,C.E. *276*
'Nationaler Frauendienst': German middle-class women in service to the Fatherland, 1914–1918. PhD U. of Georgia, 1979.

EVANS,R.J. *277*
The women's movement in Germany, 1890–1919. DPhil U. of Oxford, 1973.

FESSENDEN,P.L. *278*
The role of woman deputies in the German National Constituent Assembly and the Reichstag: 1919–1933. PhD Ohio State U. 1976.

FRANZOI,B.A. *279*
Women and industrial work in the German Reich, 1871–1914. PhD Rutgers U. 1979.

HACKETT,A.K. *280*
The politics of feminism in Wilhelmine Germany, 1840–1918. PhD Columbia U. 1976.

HAMER,T.L. *281*
Beyond feminism: the women's movement in Austrian social democracy, 1890–1920. PhD Ohio State U. 1973.

HAUSNER,J. *282*
Irene Harand and the movement against racism, human misery and war, 1933– 1938. PhD Columbia U. 1974.

HONEYCUTT,K. *283*
Clara Zetkin: a left-wing socialist and feminist in Wilhelmian Germany. PhD Columbia U. 1975.

KAPLAN,M.A. *284*
German-Jewish feminism: the Judischer Frauenbund, 1904–1938. PhD Columbia U. 1977.

KARAFIOLE,E. *285*
The reforms of the Empress Maria Theresa in the provincial government of Lower Austria, 1740–1765. PhD Cornell U. 1965.

MIDELFORT,H.C.E. *287*
The social and intellectual foundations of witch hunting in southwestern Germany, 1562–1684. PhD Yale U. 1970.

NEUMAN,R.P. *288*
Socialism, the family and sexuality: the Marxist tradition and German Social Democracy before 1914. PhD Northwestern U. 1972.

PORE,R.E. *289*
The German Social Democratic Women's movement, 1919–1933. PhD West Virginia U. 1977.

QUATAERT,J.H. *290*
The German Socialist Women's Movement, 1890–1918: issues, internal conflicts and the main personages. PhD U. of California, Los Angeles, 1974.

RETZ,R.T. *291*
Austrian Trade Unions and the 'woman question': Socialist and Catholic approaches, 1890–1914. PhD U. of Oregon, 1976.

RICHARDS,M.D. *292*
Reform or revolution: Rosa Luxemburg and the Marxist movement, 1893–1919. PhD Duke U. 1969.

ROTHWELL,C.E. *293*
Rosa Luxemburg and the German Social Democratic Party. PhD Stanford U., 1938.

RULLKOETTER,W. *294*
Legal protection of women in ancient German society. PhD U. of Chicago, 1899.

RUPP,L.J. *295*
Woman's place is in the war: mobilization propaganda and public images of women in Germany and in the United States, 1939–1945. PhD Bryn Mawr Coll. 1976.

SANFORD,J.S. *296*
The origins of German feminism: German women, 1789–1870. PhD Ohio State U. 1976.

STEPHENSON,A.J.R. *297*
Women in German society, 1930–1940. PhD U. of Edinburgh, 1974.

STRAIN,J. *298*
Feminism and political radicalism in the German Social Democratic movement, 1890–1914. PhD U. of California, Berkeley, 1964.

WALINSKI-KIEHL,R.S. *299*
Prosecuting witches in early modern Germany, with special reference to the Bishop of Bamberg, 1595–1680. MPhil CNAA, 1981.

WEDDERSHUTS,N. *299a*
Motherhood for the Fatherland: the portrayal of women in Nazi propaganda. PhD U. of Wisconsin-Madison, 1982.

WHITE,G.L. *300*
Some phases of the social work of women in the North German states. PhD Cornell U. 1901.

WILMOT,L.H. *301*
National Socialist youth organisations for girls: a contribution to the social and political history of the Third Reich. DPhil U. of Oxford, 1980.

WOOD,M.W. *302*
Birth, death, and the pleasures of life: working women in Nuremberg, 1480–1620. PhD U. of Wisconsin-Madison, 1979.

Italy

GIBSON,M.S. 303
Urban prostitution in Italy, 1860–1915: an experiment in social control. PhD Indiana U. 1979.

HOWARD,J.J. 304
The woman question in Italy, 1861–1880. PhD U. of Connecticut, 1977.

RIEMER,E.S. 305
Women in the medieval city: sources and uses of wealth by Sienese women in the thirteenth century. PhD New York U. 1975.

Russia and Eastern Europe

ALLEN, R.V. 306
The Legislative Commission of Catherine II. PhD Yale U. 1950.

BOBROFF, A.L. 307
Working women, bonding patterns, and the politics of daily life: Russia at the end of the old regime (2 vols). PhD U. of Michigan, 1982.

CLEMENTS, B.E. 308
The revolution and the revolutionary: Aleksandra Mikhailovna Kollontai, 1912–23. PhD Duke U. 1971.

DAVIS, F.E. 309
Two centuries of the Ottoman lady. PhD Columbia U. 1968.

DENNY, S.L. 310
Sofia Lvovna Perovskaya, 1853–1881. [Leader of the Russian revolutionary organization 'People's Will'] MA U. of Sussex, 1975.

DRUMM, R.E. 311
The Bolshevik Party and the organization and emancipation of working women, 1914 to 1921: or a history of the Petrograd experiment. PhD Columbia U. 1977.

EDMONSON, L.H. 312
Feminism in Russia, 1900–17. PhD U. of London, 1981.

ENGEL, B.A. 313
From feminism to populism: a study of changing attitudes of women of the Russian intelligentsia, 1855–1881. PhD Columbia U. 1974.

GOLDBERG, R.L. 314
The Russian women's movement, 1859–1917. PhD U. of Rochester, 1976.

HAUGE, K. 315
Alexandra Mikhailovna Kollontai: the Scandinavian period, 1922–1945. PhD U. of Minnesota, 1971.

HAYDEN, C.E. 316
Feminism and Bolshevism: the Zhenotdel and the politics of women's emancipation in Russia, 1917–1930. PhD U. of California, Berkeley, 1979.

KNIGHT, A.W. 317
The participation of women in revolutionary movements in Russia, from 1890 to 1914. PhD U. of London, LSE, 1977.

LAVIGNA, C. 318
Anna Kuliscioff: from Russian populism to Italian reformism, 1873–1913. PhD U. of Rochester, 1971.

LIPSKI, A. 319
Russaia under Anna Ivanovna: a study of internal governmental policies during her reign. PhD U. of California, 1953.

MCNALLY, S.J. 320
From public person to private prisoner: the changing place of women in medieval Russia. PhD State U. of New York at Binghamton, 1976.

MORTON, B.T. 321
E.D. Kuskova: a political biography of a Russian democrat, part 1 (1869–1905). PhD Pennsylvania State U. 1981.

PERMENTOR, H.R. 322
The personality and cultural interests of the Empress Catherine II as revealed in her correspondence with Friedrich Melchior Grimm. PhD U. of Texas, 1969.

PERTZOFF, M.H. 323
'Lady in Red': a study of the early career of Alexandra Mikhailovna Kollontai. PhD U. of Virginia, 1968.

PETSCHAVER, P. 324
The education and development of an enlightened absolutist: the youth of Catherine the Great, 1729–1762. PhD New York U. 1969.

REED, M.E. 325
Croatian women in the Yugoslav Partisan Resistance, 1941–1945. PhD U. of California, Berkeley, 1980.

ROBINSON, L.C. 326
Czech feminism, 1848–1914. PhD U. of London, Sch. of Slavonic and East European Studies, 1980.

ROSS, D. 327
The role of the women of Petrograd in war, revolution and counter-revolution, 1914–1921. PhD Rutgers U. 1973.

SCEPANSKY, A.J. 328
Vera Ivanovna Zasulich: from revolutionary terror to scientific Marxism. PhD George Washington U. 1974.

SCOTT, M. 329
Her brother's keeper: the evolution of women Bolsheviks. PhD U. of Kansas, 1980.

STITES, R.T. 330
The question of the emancipation of women in nineteenth-century Russia. PhD Harvard U. 1968.

Scandinavia

DE ANGELIS,R.W. *332*
Ellen Key (1849–1926): a biography of the Swedish social reformer. PhD U. of Connecticut, 1978.

EAMES,E.S. *333*
The position of women in Norway in Viking times. MLitt U. of Cambridge, 1950.

FROLANDER-ULF,M.C. *333a*
The cattle keepers of Eastern Finland. An analysis of the economic and political roles of women in Kuusisaari village in the twentieth century. PhD U. of Pittsburgh, 1978.

STOREK,M.H. *334*
Women in the time of the Icelandic family saga. PhD Bryn Mawr Coll. 1946.

THOMAS,R.G. *335*
The position of women in the Icelandic life and social economy as shown in the Icelandic sagas. MA U. of Wales, 1939.

WELSCH,E.K. *336*
Feminism in Denmark, 1850–1875. PhD Indiana U. 1974.

Spain and Portugal

AL ABDEL,D.M. *337*
The status of women in Spain during the Arab domination. MLitt U. of Cambridge, 1956.

CANCIO,R.M. *338*
The function of Maria Christina of Austria's regency (1885–1902) in preserving the Spanish monarchy. PhD Saint Louis U. 1955.

DILLARD,N.P. *339*
Daughters of the reconquest: medieval women in Castilian town society, 1100– 1300. PhD U. of Virginia, 1979.

KESSLER,M.S. *340*
A Burkeian analysis of speeches and articles of Dolores Ibarruri. [Spanish Communist] 1936–1939. PhD New York U. 1974.

WYATT,L.S. *341*
D. Carlotta and the Regency affair. PhD U. of Florida, 1969.

Latin America and the Caribbean

ARROM,S.M. *342*
Women and the family in Mexico City, 1800–1857. PhD Stanford U. 1978.

BAUM,E. *343*
Empress Leopoldina: her role in the development of Brazil, 1817–1826. PhD New York U. 1965.

BUSH,B.J. *344*
Slave women in British West Indian slave society, 1650–1832. MPhil U. of Sheffield, 1980.

CHERPAK,E.M. *345*
Women and the independence of Gran Colombia, 1780–1830. PhD U. of North Carolina at Chapel Hill, 1973.

GRAHAM,S.L. *346*
Protection and obedience: the paternalist world of female domestic servants, Rio de Janeiro, 1860–1910. PhD U. of Texas Austin, 1982.

KENTNER,J.R. *347*
The socio-political role of women in the Mexican wars of independence, 1810–1821. PhD Loyola U. Chicago, 1975.

MILLER,B.A. *348*
The role of women in the Mexican Cristero rebellion: a new chapter. PhD U. of Notre Dame, 1981.

SOTO,S.A. *349*
The Mexican woman: a study of her participation in the revolution, 1910–1940. PhD U. of New Mexico, 1977.

North America

*Up to c.*1800

BARTLETT,H.R. *350*
Eighteenth-century Georgian women. PhD U. of Maryland, 1939.

BENSON,M.S. *351*
Women in eighteenth-century America. PhD Columbia U. 1935.

COBBLEDICK,M.R. *352*
The status of women in Puritan New England, 1630–1660: a demographic study. PhD Yale U. 1936.

COTT,N.F. *353*
In the bonds of womanhood: perspectives on female experience and consciousness in New England, 1780–1830. PhD Brandeis U. 1974.

DEXTER,E.W.A. *354*
Colonial women of affairs: a study of women in business and the professions in America before 1776. PhD Clark U. 1923.

FILIACI,A.M. *355*
Raising the republic: American women in the public sphere, 1750–1800. PhD State U. of New York at Buffalo, 1982.

HENRY,S.J. *355a*
Notes toward the liberation of journalism history: a study of five women printers in colonial America. PhD Syracuse U., 1976.

HOLLIDAY,C. *356*
Women's life in colonial days. PhD American U. 1922.

HULL,N.E.H. *357*
Female felons: women and serious crime in the superior courts of Massachusetts, 1673–1774. PhD Columbia U. 1981.

KARLSEN,C.F. *358*
The devil in the shape of a woman: the witch in seventeenth-century New England. PhD Yale U. 1980.

MALMSHEIMER,L.M. *359*
New England funeral sermons and changing attitudes towards woman, 1672–1792. PhD U. of Minnesota, 1973.

MANGES,F.M. *360*
Women shopkeepers, tavernkeepers, and artisans in colonial Philadelphia. PhD U. of Pennsylvania, 1958.

MARLOW,H.C. *361*
The ideology of the woman's movement, 1750–1860. PhD U. of Oklahoma, 1966.

SALMON,M. *362*
The property rights of women in early America: a comparative study. PhD Bryn Mawr Coll. 1980.

TRECKEL,P.A. *363*
English women on seventeenth-century American frontiers. PhD Syracuse U. 1978.

ULRICH,L.T. *364*
Good wives: a study in role definition in northern New England, 1650–1750. PhD U. of New Hampshire, 1980.

VAN KIRK,S.M. *365*
The role of women in the fur trade society of the Canadian West, 1700–1850. PhD U. of London, Queen Mary Coll. 1975.

WEISMAN,R.M. *366*
Witchcraft in seventeenth-century Massachusetts: the construction of a category of deviance. PhD U. of California, Berkeley, 1977.

After c.1800

See also above 120, 157, 178, 216, 295; **1** 5, 11, 19, 43, 86, 93, 109, 131, 142, 226; **5** 148; **7** 35, 96, 123; **12** 199, 274, 296, 464, 1079, 1235.

ABRAMOWITZ,M.W. *367*
Eleanor Roosevelt and Federal responsibility and responsiveness to youth, the negro and others in time of depression. PhD New York U. 1970.

ALLEN,M.M. *368*
Women and the West: a study of book-length travel accounts by women who travelled in the Plains and the Rockies, with special attention to general concepts that the women applied to the Plains, the mountains, westerners and the West in general. PhD U. of Texas at Austin, 1972.

ANCILLA,J. *370*
The political theory of Mercy Otis Warren: a study of American constitutionalism. PhD St John's U. 1968.

ANDERSON,J.R. *371*
The New Deal career of Frances Perkins, Secretary of Labor, 1933–1939. PhD Case Western Reserve U. 1968.

ANDERSON,K.L. *372*
Practical political equality for women: Anne Martin's campaigns for the US Senate in Nevada, 1918 and 1920. PhD U. of Washington, 1978.

ANDERSON,K.S.T. *373*
The impact of World War II in the Puget Sound area on the status of women and the family. PhD U. of Washington, 1975.

ANDOLSEN,B.H. *374*
Racism in the nineteenth and twentieth century women's movements: an ethical appraisal. PhD Vanderbilt U. 1981.

ANTLER,J. *375*
The educated woman and professionalization: the struggle for a new feminine identity, 1890–1920. PhD State U. of New York at Stonybrook, 1977.

ARON,C.S. *376*
To barter their souls for gold: female federal clerical workers in late nineteenth-century America. PhD U. of Maryland, 1981.

ASHER,N.L. *377*
Dorothy Jacobs Bellanca: feminist trade unionist, 1894–1946. PhD State U. of New York at Binghamton, 1982.

ASHLEY,B.L.R. *378*
Women and individualism: gender symbolism and feminism since the eighteenth century. PhD U. of Pittsburgh, 1981.

BACCHI,C.L. *379*
Liberation deferred: the ideas of the English-Canadian suffragists, 1877–1918. PhD McGill U. 1977.

BARNHART,J.B. *380*
Working women: prostitution in San Francisco from the Gold Rush to 1900. PhD U. of California, Santa Cruz, 1976.

BARON,A. *381*
Woman's 'place' in capitalist production: a study of class relations in the nineteenth-century newspaper printing industry. PhD New York U. 1981.

BARTLETT,E.A. *382*
Liberty, equality, sorority: origins and interpretations of American feminist thought: Frances Wright, Margaret Fuller, and Sarah Grimke. PhD U. of Minnesota, 1981.

BASCH,N. *383*
In the eyes of the law: married women's property

rights in nineteenth-century New York. PhD New York U. 1979.

BASS,D.C. *384*
'The best hopes of the sexes': the woman question in Garrisonian Abolitionism. PhD Brown U. 1980.

BEASLEY,M.H. *385*
Pens and petticoats: the story of the first Washington women correspondents. PhD George Washington U. 1974.

BECKER,S.D. *386*
An intellectual history of the National Woman's Party, 1920–1941. PhD Case Western Reserve U. 1975.

BEETON,B. *387*
Woman suffrage in the American West, 1869–1896. PhD U. of Utah, 1976.

BEHNKE,D.A. *388*
Created in God's image: religious issues in the woman's rights movement of the nineteenth century. PhD Northwestern U. 1975.

BENSMAN,M. *389*
Feminism and family ideologies: dilemmas and conflict in the women's movement to 1870. PhD New Sch. for Social Research, 1981.

BERG,B.J. *390*
The remembered gate: origins of American feminism. The woman and the city, 1800–1860. PhD City U. of New York, 1976.

BERMAN,H. *391*
Era of the Protocol: a chapter in the history of the International Ladies' Garment Workers' Union, 1910–1916. PhD Columbia U. 1956.

BIRTH,E.L. *392*
Edith Elmer Wood and the genesis of liberal housing thought, 1910–1942. PhD Columbia U. 1976.

BLAIR,K.J. *393*
The clubwoman as feminist: the woman's culture club movement in the United States, 1868–1914. PhD State U. of New York at Buffalo, 1976.

BLAND,S.R. *394*
Techniques of persuasion: the National Woman's Party and woman suffrage, 1913–1919. PhD George Washington U. 1972.

BONNER,H.L.W. *395*
The Jeannette Rankin story. PhD Ohio U. 1982.

BOWMAN,M.J. *396*
Economic aspects of the histories of reformatory women: a study of women committed to the Massachusetts State Reformatory from July 1, 1931 to July 1, 1933. PhD Radcliffe Coll. 1938.

BRAGAR,M.C. *397*
The feebleminded female: an historical analysis of mental retardation as a social definition, 1890–1920. PhD Syracuse U. 1977.

BREAULT,J.C. *398*
The odyssey of a humanitarian, Emily Howland, 1827–1929: a biographical analysis. PhD U. of Pennsylvania, 1974.

BRENZEL,B.M. *399*
The girls at Lancaster: a social portrait of the first reform school for girls in North America, 1856 to 1905. EdD Harvard U. 1978.

BREWER,P.B. *400*
Lillian Smith, thorn in the flesh of crackerdom. [Publisher of *South Today*] PhD U. of Georgia 1982.

BRUDIE,J.F. *401*
Family limitation in American culture, 1830–1900. PhD U. of Chicago, 1982.

BUECHLER,S.M. *402*
Social change and movement transformation: the de-radicalization of the Illinois women's rights/woman suffrage movement, 1850–1920. PhD State U. of New York at Stony Brook, 1982.

BUHLE,M.J. *403*
Feminism and socialism in the United States, 1820–1920. PhD U. of Wisconsin-Madison, 1974.

BURNS,A.V. *404*
An educational survey of the State Industrial Home for Girls in Missouri at Chillicothe. PhD U. of Missouri-Columbia, 1935.

BURNS,J.R. *405*
Community and change: a comparative study of the Afro-Americans and the woman suffragists as minority groups in American society, 1900–1929. MPhil U. of Sheffield, 1979.

BYTHEWAY,R.E. *406*
History of the development of the nursing service of the Veteran's Administration under the direction of Mrs Mary A. Hickey, 1919–1942. EdD Columbia U. 1972.

CAMHI,J.J. *407*
Women against women: American anti-suffragism, 1880–1920. PhD Tufts U. 1973.

CAMP,H.C. *408*
'Gurley:' a biography of Elizabeth Gurley Flynn, 1890–1964. PhD Columbia U. 1980.

CAMPBELL,B.K. *409*
Prominent women in the Progressive era: a study of life histories. PhD U. of Illinois at Chicago Circle, 1976.

CAMPBELL,D'A.M. *410*
Wives, workers, and womanhood: America during World War II. PhD U. of North Carolina at Chapel Hill, 1979.

CARLISLE,M.R. *411*
Prostitutes and their reformers in nineteenth-century Philadelphia. PhD Rutgers U. 1982.

CARPENTER,D.B. *412*
'The life of Lilian Jackson Emerson' by Ellen Tucker Emerson. PhD U. of Massachusetts, 1978.

CARRELL,E.P.H. *413*
Reflections in a mirror: the Progressive woman and the settlement experience. PhD U. of Texas at Austin, 1981.

CARRIGAN,D.O. *414*
Martha Moore Avery: the career of a crusader. PhD U. of Maine, 1966.

CARTWRIGHT,S.M. *416*
'Blessed drudgery': womanly virtue and nineteenth-century organizations. PhD U. of California, Davis, 1977.

CHAFÉ,W.H. *417*
From suffrage to liberation: the changing roles of American women, 1920– 1970. PhD Columbia U. 1971.

CHALLINOR,J.R. *418*
Louisa Catherine Johnson Adams (wife of John Quincy Adams): the price of ambition. PhD The American U. 1982.

CHAPMAN,M.E. *419*
Nursing education and the movement for higher education for women: a study in interrelationships, 1870–1900. EdD Columbia U. 1969.

CLAUS,R.F. *420*
Militancy in the English and American woman suffrage movements. PhD Yale U. 1975.

CLEYERDON,C.L. *421*
The woman suffrage movement in Canada. PhD U. of Columbia, 1950.

COCHRANE,C.E. *422*
The nineteenth-century women's rights movement and its relationship to the development of nursing education in the United States, 1857–1863. PhD U. of Texas at Austin, 1981.

COHEN,A.I. *423*
Mary Parker Follett: spokesman for democracy, philosopher for social group work, 1918–1933. DSW U. of Wisconsin, 1971.

COLE,M.S. *424*
Catherine Bauer and the public housing movement, 1926–1937. PhD George Washington U. 1975.

COLEMAN,R.E. *425*
A historical survey of the rhetorical proofs used by the women speakers of the suffrage organizations, 1869–1919. PhD Case Western Reserve U. 1968.

COLEMAN,W.M. *426*
Keeping the faith and disturbing the peace. Black women: from anti-slavery to women's suffrage. PhD U. of California, Irvine, 1982.

CONRAD,S.A.P. *427*
Perish the thought: intellectual women in romantic America. PhD U. of Texas at Austin, 1973.

COOKE,F. *428*
History of the Hospital Sisters of the Third Order of St Francis. PhD Marquette U. 1943.

COOMBS,C.L. *429*
The legal status of women in Nebraska, with comparative studies. PhD U. of Nebraska, 1933.

COOPER,F.A. *430*
Mary Parker Follett: the power of power-with. PhD U. of Southern California, 1981.

COULTER,T.C. *431*
A history of woman suffrage in Nebraska, 1856–1920. EdD Ohio State U. 1967.

CRAF,J.R. *432*
Women in war work: the study of an economic and social movement. PhD New York U. 1947.

CRANDELL,S.J. *433*
Social control techniques in the speeches of the Woman's Christian Temperance Union. PhD Northwestern U. 1946.

DALSIMER,M.H. *434*
Women and family in the Oneida community, 1837–1881. PhD New York U. 1975.

DALY,J.M. *435*
Mary Anderson, pioneer labor leader. PhD Georgetown U. 1968.

DANIELS,D.G. *436*
Lillian D. Wald (1867–1940): the progressive woman and feminism. PhD City U. of New York, 1977.

DARNEY,V.G. *437*
Women and world's fairs: American international expositions, 1876–1904. PhD Emory U. 1982.

DAVIES,M.W. *438*
Woman's place is at the typewriter: the feminization of clerical workers and changes in clerical work in the United States, 1870–1930. PhD Brandeis U. 1979.

DAWSON,V.M. *439*
Opinions of contemporary French travellers on the American woman. PhD U. of Pittsburgh, 1935.

DEAN,P.A. *440*
The meek get their licks: temperance literature of the early nineteenth century as an expression of private feminism. PhD U. of Minnesota, 1981.

DEBLASIO,D.M. *441*
Her own society: the life and times of Betsey Mix Cowles, 1810–1876. PhD Kent State U. 1980.

DELATTE,C.E. *442*
An American odyssey: a biography of Lucy Bakewell Audubon. [Wife of John Audubon, wri-

ter of *The birds of America*] PhD Louisiana State U. 1979.

DICKINSON,J.Y. *443*
The role of the immigrant women in the US labor force, 1890–1910. PhD U. of Pennsylvania, 1975.

DICKSON,L.F. *444*
The early club movement among black women in Denver: 1890–1925. PhD U. of Colorado at Boulder, 1982.

DILLON,M.E. *445*
The influence of Frances Willard on the woman's movement of the nineteenth-century. PhD Northwestern U. 1940.

DIXLER,E.J. *446*
The woman question: women and the American Communist Party, 1929–1941. PhD Yale U. 1974.

DONEGAN,J.B. *447*
Midwifery in America, 1760–1860: a study in medicine and morality. PhD Syracuse U. 1972.

DOYLE,W.T. *448*
Charlotte Perkins Gilman and the cycle of feminist reform. PhD U. of California, Berkeley, 1960.

DRACHMAN,V.G. *449*
Women doctors and the women's medical movement: feminism and medicine, 1850–1895. PhD State U. of New York at Buffalo, 1976.

DUBLIN,T.L. *450*
Women at work: the transformation of work and community in Lowell, Massachusetts, 1826–1860. PhD Columbia U. 1975.

DUBOIS,E.C. *451*
A new life: the development of an American woman suffrage movement, 1860–1869. PhD Northwestern U. 1975.

DUDLEY,J.W. *452*
A history of the Association of Southern Women for the Prevention of Lynching. PhD U. of Cincinnati, 1979.

DUFFY,A.D. *453*
Upper-class women: power, class and sex caste in New York City, 1880–1920. PhD McMaster U. 1979.

DYE,J.L. *454*
For the instruction and amusement of women: the growth, development and definition of American magazines for women, 1780–1840. PhD U. of Pennsylvania, 1977.

DYE,N.S. *455*
The Women's Trade Union League of New York, 1903–1920. PhD U. of Wisconsin-Madison, 1974.

ELDER,R.E. *456*
History of demobilization of the United States Navy Women's Reserve, 1945–1946. PhD U. of Chicago, 1948.

ENDELMAN,G.E. *457*
Solidarity for ever: Rose Schneiderman and the Women's Trade Union League. PhD U. of Delaware, 1978.

ENTRIKIN,I.W. *458*
Sara Josepha Hale and *Godey's Lady's Book*. PhD U. of Pennsylvania, 1943.

EVANS,V.L. *459*
The status of the American woman in sport, 1912–1932. PhD U. of Massachusetts, 1982.

EWEN,E.W. *460*
Immigrant women in the land of dollars, 1890–1920. PhD State U. of New York at Stony Brook, 1979.

FARRELL,J.C. *461*
'Beloved lady': a history of Jane Addams' ideas on reform and peace. PhD Johns Hopkins U. 1965.

FASTENAU,M.K. *462*
Maternal government: the social settlement houses and politicization of women's sphere, 1889–1920. PhD Duke U. 1982.

FELD,T.R. *463*
A comparative study of the suffrage phase and the women's liberation phase of the woman's movement: a case study of rhetorical adaptation. PhD Purdue U. 1972.

FILO,B.A. *464*
Reclaiming those poor unfortunates: the movement to establish the first federal prison for women. PhD Boston U. Grad. Sch. 1982.

FITZPATRICK,E.F. *465*
Academics and activitists: women social scientists and the impulse for reform, 1892–1920. PhD Brandeis U. 1981.

FRAUENGLASS,W. *466*
A study of attitudes toward woman suffrage found in popular humor magazines, 1911–1920. PhD New York U. 1967.

FREEDMAN,E.B. *467*
Their sisters' keepers: the origins of female corrections in America. PhD Columbia U. 1976.

FUS,D.A. *469*
Persuasion on the Plains: the woman suffrage movement in Nebraska. PhD Indiana U. 1972.

GALLAHER,R.A. *470*
Legal and political status of women in Iowa: an historical account of the rights of women in Iowa from 1838 to 1918. PhD U. of Iowa, 1918.

GARRISON,L.D. *471*
Cultural missionaries: a study of American public library leaders, 1876–1910. [Inc. study of feminization of librarianship] PhD U. of California, Irvine, 1973.

GAULARD,J.M. *472*
The rhetorical strategies of Margaret Sanger and

the American birth control movement, 1912 to 1938. PhD Indiana U. 1978.

GAY,D.A. *473*
The tangled skein of romanticism and violence in the old South: the Southern response to abolitionism and feminism, 1830–1861. PhD U. of North Carolina at Chapel Hill, 1975.

GEER,E.A. *474*
Lucy Webb Hayes: an unexceptionable woman. [Wife of President Hayes and temperance reformer] PhD Case Western Reserve U. 1962.

GELLES,E.B. *475*
Abigail Adams: domesticity and the American Revolution. [Wife of President John Adams] PhD U. of California, Irvine, 1978.

GIELE,J.Z. *476*
Social change in the feminine role: a comparison of women's suffrage and women's temperance, 1870–1920. PhD Radcliffe Coll. 1961.

GILLES,C.L. *477*
Materials on education in selected women's magazines, 1890–1899, 1930–1939, and 1947–1956. PhD U. of Pennsylvania, 1962.

GLEASON,C.J. *479*
Legislation for women in Oregon. PhD Catholic U. of America, 1924.

GOLDSTEIN,J.H. *480*
The effects of the adoption of woman suffrage: sex differences in voting behavior – Illinois 1914–1921. PhD U. of Chicago, 1973.

GORDON,F.D. *481*
After winning: the New Jersey suffragists, 1910–1947. PhD Rutgers U. 1982.

GRABINER,V.E. *482*
Woman's suffrage and social control. DCrim U. of California, Berkeley, 1976.

GRANT,M.H.
Private women, public person: an account of the life of Julia Ward Howe from 1819 to 1868. PhD George Washington, 1982.

GRAVES,L.L. *483*
The Wisconsin woman suffrage movement, 1846–1920. PhD U. of Wisconsin, 1954.

GRAY,V. *484*
Activities of Southern women, 1840–1860. PhD U. of Wisconsin, 1927.

GREEN,J.H. *485*
The rhetoric antecedent to the women's liberation movement from 1776–1850. PhD Florida State U. 1981.

GREENWALD,M.W. *486*
Women, war, and work: the impact of World War I on women workers in the United States. PhD Brown U. 1977.

GREGORY,C.W. *487*
The problem of labor during World War II: the employment of women in defense production. PhD Ohio State U. 1969.

GRIEDER,F.A. *488*
American women in the professions: a study of trends, 1870–1940, and their implications for counselling college women. PhD Stanford U. 1950.

GRIFFITH,E. *489*
Elizabeth Cady Stanton, self sovereign: a biography based on social learning theory. PhD American U. 1981.

GRIM,H.E. *490*
Susan B. Anthony: experiment of freedom. PhD U. of Wisconsin, 1938.

HALL,B.L. *491*
Mothers' assistance in Philadelphia: actual and potential costs. PhD Bryn Mawr Coll. 1929.

HALL,J.D. *492*
Revolt against chivalry: Jessie Daniel James and the women's campaign against lynching. PhD Columbia U. 1974.

HAMILTON,T.K.B. *493*
The National Association of Colored Women, 1896–1920. PhD Emory U. 1978.

HARLEY,S. *494*
Black women in the District of Columbia, 1890–1920. PhD Howard U. 1981.

HARRIS,T.C. *495*
Jeannette Rankin: suffragist, first woman elected to Congress, and pacifist. PhD U. of Georgia, 1972.

HARRISON,C.E. *496*
Prelude to feminism: women's organizations, the federal government and the rise of the women's movement, 1942 to 1968. PhD Columbia U. 1982.

HARRISON,D.I. *497*
The Consumers' League of Ohio: women and reform, 1909–1937. PhD Case Western Reserve U. 1975.

HARTMANN,H.I. *498*
Capitalism and women's work in the home, 1900–1930. PhD Yale U. 1974.

HAY,M.P. *499*
Madeline McDowell Breckinridge: Kentucky suffragist and progressive reformer. PhD U. of Kentucky, 1980.

HENDERSON,J.K. *501*
Four nineteenth-century professional women. [Harriot Hunt, Elizabeth Blackwell, Maria Mitchell, and Ellen Swallow Richards] EdD Rutgers U. 1982.

HENSLEY,F.S. *503*
'Change and continuity' in the American

women's movement, 1848–1930: a national and state perspective. PhD Ohio State U. 1981.

HEWITT,N.A. *505*
Women's activism and social change: the case of Rochester, New York, 1822–1872. PhD U. of Pennsylvania, 1981.

HIESTAND,W.C. *506*
Midwife to nurse-midwife: a history. The development of nurse-midwifery education in the continental United States to 1965. EdD Columbia U. Teachers Coll. 1977.

HODGES,J.R. *507*
A study of *The Female Spectator*, (1744–1746). PhD U. of North Carolina at Chapel Hill, 1950.

HOGELAND,R.W. *508*
Femininity and the nineteenth-century post-Puritan mind. PhD U. of California, Los Angeles, 1968.

HONEY,M.E. *509*
Popular magazines, women and World War II: the use of popular culture as propaganda. PhD Michigan State U. 1979.

HUFF,R.P. *510*
Social Christian clergymen and feminism during the Progressive era, 1890–1920. PhD Union Theological Seminary, 1978.

HUMMEL,M.D. *511*
The attitude of Edward Bok and the *Ladies' Home Journal* toward woman's role in society, 1889–1919. PhD North Texas State U. 1982.

HUMMER,P.M. *512*
The decade of elusive promise: professional women in the United States, 1920–1930. PhD Duke U. 1976.

HUTTON,M.G.B. *513*
The rhetoric of Ida B. Wells: the genesis of the anti-lynch movement. PhD Indiana U. 1975.

HYNES,T.M. *514*
The portrayal of woman in selected magazines from 1911–1930. PhD U. of Wisconsin-Madison, 1975.

JABLONSKY,T.J. *515*
Duty, nature and stability: the female anti-suffragists in the United States, 1894–1920. PhD U. of Southern California, 1978.

JACKSON,E.L.M. *516*
Petticoat politics: political activism among Texas women in the 1920s. PhD U. of Texas at Austin, 1980.

JACOBS,E.E. *517*
A study of the physical vigor of American women. PhD Clark U. 1917.

JAMES,J.W. *518*
Changing ideas about women in the United States, 1776–1825. PhD Radcliffe Coll. 1954.

JANIEWSKI,D.E. *519*
From field to factory: race, class, sex, and the woman worker in Durham, 1880–1940. PhD Duke U. 1979.

JENNINGS,R.B. *520*
A history of the educational activities of the Women's Educational and Industrial Union from 1877–1927. EdD Boston Coll. 1978.

JOHNSON,E.G.Z. *521*
Protective legislation and women's work: Oregon's ten-hour law and the Muller v. Oregon case, 1900–1913. PhD U. of Oregon, 1982.

JOHNSON,K.R. *522*
The woman suffrage movement in Florida. PhD Florida State U. 1966.

JOHNSON,P.C. *523*
Sensibility and Civil War: the selected diaries and papers, 1858–1866, of Frances Adeline (Fanny) Seward. PhD U. of Rochester, 1964.

JOSEPH,M.L. *524*
Changes in women's daytime dress as related to other selected cultural factors during the first and the third decades of the twentieth century. PhD Pennsylvania State U. 1962.

JOYCE,R.O. *525*
A woman's place: the life history of a rural Ohio grandmother. [Life history of Sarah Flynn Penfield] PhD Ohio State U. 1980.

KALEDEN,E.O. *526*
The educational Clover Adams. [Marian Hoop (Clover) Adams, wife of Henry Adams] PhD Boston U. Grad. Sch. 1977.

KANOWITZ,L. *527*
Sex-based discrimination in American law. PhD Columbia U. 1969.

KATZ,D.H. *528*
Carrie Chapman Catt and the struggle for peace. PhD Syracuse U. 1973.

KATZ,E. *529*
Grace Hoadley Dodge: women and the emerging metropolis, 1856–1914. PhD New York U. 1980.

KAVANAGH,M.A. *530*
A comparative study of leaders and non-leaders among Catholic girl scouts. PhD Fordham U. 1944.

KEARNEY,J.R. *531*
Anna Eleanor Roosevelt: years of experiment. PhD U. of Wisconsin, 1967.

KENEALLY,J.C. *532*
The opposition to women's suffrage in Massachusetts, 1868–1920. PhD Boston Coll. 1963.

KENNEDY,D.M. *533*
Birth control: its heroine and its history in America – the career of Margaret Sanger. EdD Yale U. 1968.

KESSLER,L.J. 534
A siege of the citadels: access of woman suffrage ideas to the Oregon press, 1884–1912. PhD U. of Washington, 1980.

KIRK,B.M. 535
The critical evaluation of present practices in the Women's Athletic Association in the United States. PhD New York U. 1936.

KIRKBY,D.E. 536
Alice Henry: the National Women's Trade Union League of America and progressive labor reforms, 1906–1925. PhD U. of California, Santa Barbara, 1982.

KLACZYNSKA,B.M. 537
Working women in Philadelphia, 1900–1930. PhD Temple U. 1975.

KLEINBERG,S.J. 538
Technology's stepdaughters: the impact of industrialization upon working-class women, Pittsburgh, 1865–1890. PhD U. of Pittsburgh, 1973.

KLINE,R.F. 539
Domestic servants on the New York and London stages: 1880–1920, with an emphasis on costume. PhD U. of Illinois at Urbana-Champaign, 1980.

KOERIN,B.B. 540
Images of women: mirrors of change. (Nineteenth century). PhD U. of Virginia, 1982.

KOLLER,M.R. 541
A statistical study of changes occurring in selected aspects of courtship among three married female generations, central Ohio. PhD Ohio State U. 1950.

KOLMERTEN,C.A. 542
Unconscious sexual stereotyping in utopian thought: a study of the American Owenite communities, 1825–1829. PhD Purdue U. 1978.

KRADITOR,A.S. 543
The ideas of the woman suffrage movement, 1890–1920. PhD Columbia U. 1962.

KRATZ,A.H. 544
Prosecutions and treatment of women offenders and the economic crisis: Philadelphia 1925–1934. PhD U. of Pennsylvania, 1940.

KRONE,H.L. 545
Dauntless women: the story of the woman suffrage movement in Pennsylvania, 1910–1920. PhD U. of Pennsylvania, 1946.

KUGLER,I. 546
The woman's rights movement and the National Labor Union (1866–1872): what was the nature of the relationships between the National Labor Union and what may serve to explain periods of cooperation and subsequent divergence. PhD New York U. 1954.

LABBE,D.E. 547
Women in early nineteenth-century Louisiana. PhD U. of Delaware, 1975.

LAGANKE,L. 548
The National Society of the Daughters of the American Revolution: its history, policies and influences, 1890–1949. PhD Case Western Reserve U. 1951.

LASSER,C.S. 549
Mistress, maid and market: the transformation of domestic service in New England, 1790–1870. PhD Harvard U. 1982.

LAZAROU,K.E. 550
Concealed under petticoats: married women's property and the law of Texas 1840–1913. PhD Rice U. 1980.

LEACH,W.R. 551
For better or worse: the social ideas of the American feminist movement, 1850–1875. PhD U. of Rochester, 1976.

LEBSOCK,S.D. 552
Women and economics in Virginia: Petersburg, 1784–1820. PhD U. of Virginia, 1977.

LEHRER,S. 553
Origins of protective labor legislation for women, 1900–1925. PhD State U. of New York at Binghamton, 1980.

LEIBY,G.M. 554
The prevalence of syphilis among parturient women in the Eastern Health District during 1937. Johns Hopkins U. 1938.

LEIGH,M.H. 555
The evolution of women's participation in the Summer Olympic Games, 1900–1948. PhD Ohio State U. 1974.

LEMONS,J.S. 556
The new woman in the new era: the woman's movement from the Great War to the Great Depression. PhD U. of Missouri, 1967.

LERNER,E. 557
Immigrant and working-class involvement in the New York City woman suffrage movement, 1905–1917: a study in Progressive era politics. PhD U. of California, Berkeley, 1981.

LERNER,G. 558
Abolitionist from South Carolina: a life of Sarah and Angelina Grimke. PhD Columbia U. 1966.

LEVINE,S.B. 559
Their own sphere: women's work, the Knights of Labor, and the transformation of the carpet trade,1870–1890. PhD City U. of New York, 1979.

LICHTMAN,S.T. 560
Women at work, 1941–1945: wartime employment in the San Francisco Bay area. PhD U. of California, Davis, 1981.

LIEBERMAN,J.A. *561*
Their sisters' keepers: the women's hours and wages movement in the United States, 1890–1925. PhD Columbia U. 1971.

LINDIG,C.M. *562*
The women's movement in Louisiana, 1879–1920. PhD North Texas State U. 1982.

LINTNER,M.D.L. *563*
The height of fashion: the construction of ladies fashion headwear, 1830–1914. PhD U. of Michigan, 1979.

LOCKE,M.L. *564*
'Like a machine or an animal': working women of the late nineteenth-century urban far west, in San Francisco, Portland, and Los Angeles. PhD U. of California, San Diego, 1982.

LOUIS,J.P. *566*
Woman suffrage and progressive reform: the fight for the Nineteenth Amendment, 1913–1920. PhD Harvard U. 1968.

LUNARDINI,C.A. *567*
From equal suffrage to equal rights: the National Women's Party, 1913–1923. PhD Princeton U. 1981.

LYNN,M.C. *568*
Some aspects of the changing position of women in America, 1920–1929. PhD U. of Rochester, 1974.

MCBRIDE,S.E. *569*
Woman in the popular magazines for women in America, 1830–1956. PhD U. of Minnesota, 1966.

MCCAULEY,E.B. *570*
The New England mill girls' feminine influence in the development of public libraries in New England, 1820–1860. PhD Columbia U. 1972.

MCCREESH,C.D. *571*
On the picket line: militant women campaign to organize garment workers, 1880–1917. PhD U. of Maryland, 1975.

MCCRONE,K.E. *572*
The advancement of women during the age of reform, 1832–1870. PhD New York U. 1971.

MCDONALD,P.A. *574*
Baltimore women, 1870–1900. PhD U. of Maryland, 1976.

MCMAHON,T.S. *575*
Women and economic evolution or the effects of industrial changes upon the status of women. PhD U. of Wisconsin, 1909.

MADSEN,A.B. *576*
The 1867 campaign for woman suffrage in Kansas: a study in rhetorical situation. PhD U. of Kansas, 1975.

MADSON,L.P. *577*
The rhetoric, strategy and style of a liberationist: Victoria C. Wordhull, 1838–1927. PhD Ohio U. 1974.

MALINO,S.S. *578*
Faces across the counter: a social history of female department store employees, 1870–1920. PhD Columbia U. 1982.

MARSHALL,H.E. *579*
Dorothea Lynde Dix: a forgotten Samaritan. [Humanitarian crusader for the mentally ill and superintendent of army nurses in the American Civil War] PhD Duke U. 1934.

MASEL-WALTERS,L.J. *580*
Their rights and nothing less: the history and thematic content of the American woman suffrage press, 1868–1920. PhD U. of Wisconsin-Madison, 1977.

MASTELLER,J.C. *581*
Marriage or career, 1880–1914: a dilemma for American women writers and their culture. PhD U. of Minnesota, 1978.

MAXINE,M. *582*
Margaret Fuller: from liberal to radical; a foreshadowing of the feminist movement. PhD U. of New Mexico, 1973.

MAXWELL,W.J. *583*
Frances Kellor in the Progressive era: a case study in the professionalization of reform. EdD Columbia U. 1968.

MEAD,J.L. *584*
A rhetorical analysis of representative speeches of selected women speakers in America, 1850–1860. PhD U. of Denver, 1979.

MECKEL,R.A. *585*
The awful responsibility of motherhood: American health reform and the prevention of infant and child mortality before 1913. PhD U. of Michigan, 1980.

MELDER,K.E. *586*
The beginnings of the women's rights movement in the United States, 1800–1840. PhD Yale U. 1964.

MERK,L.B. *587*
Massachusetts and the woman suffrage movement. PhD Radcliffe Coll. 1956.

MEZVINSKY,N. *588*
The White-Ribbon reform, 1870–1920. [Women's Christian Temperance Union] PhD U. of Wisconsin, 1959.

MICKISH,J.E. *589*
Legal control of socio-sexual relationships: creation of the Mann White Slave Traffic Act of 1910. PhD Southern Illinois U. at Carbondale, 1980.

MINER,M.E. *590*
Slavery of prostitution: a plea for emancipation. PhD Columbia U. 1917.

MITCHINSON,W.L. *591*
Aspects of reform: four women's organizations in nineteenth-century Canada. PhD York U. 1977.

MOLDOW,G.M. *592*
The gilded age, promise and disillusionment: women doctors and the emergence of the professional middle class, Washington DC, 1870–1900. PhD U. of Maryland, 1980.

MOREHOUSE,W.M. *593*
The speaking of Margaret Sanger in the birth control movement from 1916 to 1937. PhD Purdue U. 1968.

MORRISON,G.E. *594*
Women's participation in the 1928 presidential campaign. PhD U. of Kansas, 1978.

MOTTUS,J.E. *595*
New York nightingales: the emergence of the nursing profession at Bellevue and New York Hospital, 1850–1920. PhD New York U. 1980.

MOTZ,M.F. *596*
True sisterhood: the female family in nineteenth-century Michigan. PhD U. of Michigan, 1981.

MOYNIHAN,R.B. *597*
Abigail Scott Duniway of Oregon: woman and suffragist of the American frontier. PhD Yale U. 1979.

MUSMANN,V.K. *598*
Women and the founding of social libraries in California. PhD U. of Southern California, 1982.

NELSON,M. *599*
Ladies in the streets: a sociological analysis of the National Woman's Party, 1910–1930. PhD State U. of New York at Buffalo, 1976.

NEWSOME,C.G. *600*
Mary McLeod Bethune in religious perspective: a seminal essay. PhD Duke U. 1982.

NICKLESS,P.J. *601*
Changing labor productivity and the utilization of native women workers in the American cotton textile industry, 1825–1860. PhD Purdue U. 1976.

NISSENBAUM,S.W. *602*
Careful love: Sylvester Graham and the emergence of Victorian sexual theory in America, 1830–1840. PhD U. of Wisconsin, 1968.

NUGENT,E.R. *603*
The relationship of fashion in women's dress to selected aspects of social change from 1850 to 1950. PhD Louisiana State U. and A&M Coll. 1962.

O'CONNOR,L.M.F. *604*
Rhetorical proof in speeches of women of the reform platform, 1828–1861. PhD Columbia U. 1952.

OGLE,S.F. *605*
Anna Louise Strong: progressive and propagandist. PhD U. of Washington, 1981.

OGNIDENE,E.R. *606*
Women to women: the rhetoric of success for women, 1860–1920. PhD Rensselaer Polytechnic Inst. 1979.

OLMSTED,A.P. *607*
Agitator on the left: the speechmaking of Elizabeth Gurley Flynn, 1904–1964. PhD Indiana U. 1971.

OSBORNE,J.S. *608*
Class and sex: a simulation model in women's history. EdD U. of Massachusetts, 1977.

PALMER,P.M. *609*
Frances Wright D'Arusmont: case study of a reformer. PhD Ohio State U. 1973.

PARKER,P.L. *610*
A critical biography of Susanna Haswell Rowson. PhD New York U. 1981.

PAUL,A. *611*
The legal position of women in Pennsylvania. PhD U. of Pennsylvania, 1912.

PAUL,A. *612*
Towards equality: a study of the legal position of women in the States. DCL American U. 1928.

PEAL,E. *613*
The atrophied rib: urban middle-class women in Jacksonian America. PhD U. of Pittsburgh, 1970.

PEASE,J.H. *614*
The freshness of fanaticism: Abby Kelley Foster: an essay in reform. PhD U. of Rochester, 1969.

PETRIK,P.E. *615*
The bonanza town: women and family on the Rocky Mountain mining frontier, Helena, Montana, 1865–1900. PhD State U. of New York at Binghamton, 1982.

POLCI,M.W. *617*
The role and development of the League of Women Voters in Connecticut: an organizational response to the changing status of women. PhD U. of Connecticut, 1981.

POPKIN,A.H. *618*
'Bread and Roses': an early movement in the development of socialist feminism. PhD Brandeis U. 1978.

PORTER,M.A.H. *619*
Charlotte Perkins Gilman: a feminist paradox. PhD McGill U. 1975.

POTTS,M.J. *620*
Charlotte Perkins Gilman: a humanist approach to feminism. PhD North Texas State U. 1976.

PRINDLE,P.G. *620a*
An analysis of the rhetoric in selected representa-

tive speeches of Anna Elizabeth Dickinson. Stanford U. 1972.

PRINGLE,R.W. 621
Anna Louise Strong: propagandist of Communism. PhD U. of Virginia, 1970.

PUETT,A.E. 622
Melville's wife: a story of Elizabeth Shaw Melville. PhD Northwestern U. 1969.

PUMPHREY,M.W. 623
Mary Richmond and the rise of professional social work in Baltimore: the foundations of a creative career. DSW Columbia U. 1956.

PUZ,S.K. 624
Women's role in the quest for justice in American history: a civic education curriculum. DA Carnegie-Mellon U. 1981.

QUINN,R.J. 625
The modest seduction: the experience of pioneer women on the trans- Mississippi frontier. PhD U. of California, Riverside, 1977.

RANLETT,J.B. 626
Sorority and community: women's answer to a changing Massachusetts, 1865–1895. PhD Brandeis U. 1974.

RAPONE,A.J. 627
Clerical labor force formation: the office woman in Albany, 1870–1930. PhD New York U. 1981.

REVERBY,S.M. 629
The nursing disorder: a critical history of the hospital – nursing relationship, 1860–1945. PhD Boston U. Grad. Sch., 1982.

REZNICK,A.E. 630
Lillian D. Wald: the years at Henry Street. [Nurse and social reformer] PhD U. of Wisconsin, 1973.

RHODES,M. 631
Dried flowers: the history of women's culture at Cotter College, 1884–1965. PhD Ohio State U. 1981.

RICHARDS,W.L. 632
A review of the life and writings of Elizabeth Oakes Smith: feminist, author, and lecturer, 1806–1893. PhD Ball State U. 1928.

RILEY,G.L.G. 633
From chattel to challenger: the changing image of the American women, 1828–1848. PhD Ohio State U. 1976.

RITTER,D.M. 634
The letters of Louise Ritter from 1893–1925: a Swiss-German immigrant woman to Antelope County, Nebraska. PhD U. of Nebraska-Lincoln, 1979.

ROBERTS,J.E. 635
A New England family: Elizabeth P. Peabody, 1804–1894; May T. Peabody, 1806–1887; Sophia A. Peabody, 1809–1871. PhD Case Western Reserve U. 1937.

ROBINS,T.H.R. 636
Women in the American prohibition movement, 1870–1920. MPhil CNAA, 1978.

ROSEN,R.E. 638
The lost sisterhood: prostitution during the Progressive era. PhD U. of California, Berkeley, 1976.

ROSENBERG,R.L.N. 639
The dissent from Darwin, 1890–1930: the new view of women among American social scientists. PhD Stanford U. 1974.

ROSS,B.S. 640
Adaptation in exile: loyalist women in Nova Scotia after the American Revolution. PhD Cornell U. 1981.

ROTELLA,E.J. 641
Women's labor force participation and the growth of clerical employment in the United States, 1870–1930. PhD U. of Pennsylvania, 1977.

ROTH,D.R. 642
Matronage: patterns in women's organizations, Atlanta, Georgia, 1890–1940. PhD George Washington U. 1978.

ROYDHOUSE,M.W. 644
The 'universal sisterhood of women': women and labor reform in North Carolina, 1900–1932. PhD Duke U. 1980.

RUDNICK,L.P. 645
The unexpurgated self: a critical biography of Mabel Dodge Luhan. PhD Brown U. 1977.

RUEGAMER,L. 646
'The paradise of exceptional women': Chicago women reformers, 1863–1893. PhD Indiana U. 1982.

RUOFF,J.C. 647
Southern womanhood, 1865–1920: an intellectual and cultural study. PhD U. of Illinois at Urbana-Champaign, 1976.

RURY,J.L. 648
Women, cities, and schools: education and the development of an urban female labor force, 1890–1930. PhD U. of Wisconsin-Madison, 1982.

SAFIER,G.S. 649
Jessie Bernard, sociologist. PhD U. of Kansas, 1972.

SAUCEDA,J.B. 652
From the inner circle: the relationship of the space occupied, past and present, by Southwest American Indian women to the Southwest Indo-Hispano women of yesteryear and today. PhD U. of Colorado at Boulder, 1979.

SCHARF,L. 653
The employment of married women during the

Depression, 1929–1941. PhD Case Western Reserve U. 1977.

SCHOFIELD,A. *654*
The rise of the pig-headed girl: an analysis of the American labor press for their attitudes toward women, 1877–1920. PhD State U. of New York at Binghamton, 1980.

SCHOLTEN,P.L.C. *655*
Militant women for economic justice: the persuasion of Mary Harris Jones, Ella Reeve Bloor, Rose Pastor Stokes, Rosa Schneiderman, and Elizabeth Gurley Flynn. PhD Indiana U. 1979.

SEALE,W.Jr. *656*
Margaret Lea Houston, 1819–1867: the first lady of Texas. PhD Duke U. 1965.

SHADWELL,D.G. *657*
A rhetorical analysis of selected speeches by Jane Addams. PhD U. of Illinois at Urbana-Champaign, 1967.

SHARP,K.A. *658*
Rose Pastor Stokes: radical champion of the American working class, 1879–1933. PhD Duke U. 1979.

SHERRICK,R.L. *659*
Private visions, public lives: the Hull House women in the Progressive era. PhD Northwestern U. 1980.

SHIELDS,E.A. *660*
A history of the United States Army Nurse Corps (female), 1901–1937. EdD Columbia U. Teachers Coll. 1980.

SHOUB,R.D. *661*
Social and occupational expectations: women, blacks and immigrants, 1890–1929. PhD Arizona State U. 1981.

SHROCK,A.A. *662*
Feminists, flappers and the maternal mystique: changing conceptions of women and their roles in the 1920s. PhD U. of North Carolina at Chapel Hill, 1974.

SILVERMAN,E.L. *663*
Theodore Roosevelt and women: the inner conflict of a President and its impact of his ideology. PhD U. of California, Los Angeles, 1973.

SKLAR,K.K. *664*
Household divinity: a life of Catherine Beecher. PhD U. of Michigan, 1969.

SKOLD,K.L.B. *665*
Women workers and child care during World War II: a case study of the Portland, Oregon, shipyards. PhD U. of Oregon, 1981.

SLAIGHT,W.R. *666*
Alice Hamilton: first lady of industrial medicine. PhD Case Western Reserve U. 1974.

SLOAN,L.A. *667*
Some aspects of the suffrage movement in Indiana. PhD Ball State U. 1982.

SMITH,A.W. *668*
Anne Martin and a history of woman suffrage in Nevada, 1869–1914. PhD U. of Nevada, Reno, 1976.

SMITH,M.R. *669*
Almshouse women: a study of 228 women in the city and county almshouse of San Francisco. PhD Stanford U. 1896.

SMITH,N.B. *670*
The women who went to the war: the Union army nurse in the Civil War. PhD Northwestern U. 1981.

SOCHEN,J. *671*
Now let us begin: feminism in Greenwich Village, 1910–1920. PhD Northwestern U. 1967.

SPALDING,M.J. *672*
Dorothea Dix and the care of the insane from 1841 to the Pierce Veto of 1854. PhD Bryn Mawr Coll. Grad. Sch. of Social Work and Social Research, 1976.

SPENCER,R.W. *673*
Dr Anna Howard Shaw: the evangelical feminist. PhD Boston U. Grad. Sch. 1972.

SPIGGLE,S. *674*
The emergence of a social movement: nineteenth-century women's rights. PhD U. of Connecticut, 1980.

SQUIRES,M.L. *675*
Womanhood, competitive sport and the 'cult of true womanhood': a paradox at the turn of the century. PhD Texas Woman's U. 1977.

SREBNICK,A.G. *676*
True womanhood and hard times: women and early New York, industrialization 1840–1860. PhD State U. of New York at Stony Brook, 1979.

STANSELL,M.C. *677*
Women of the laboring poor in New York City, 1820–1860. PhD Yale U. 1979.

STAPEN,C.H. *678*
The novel form and *Woodhull & Claflin's Weekly*, 1870–1876: a little magazine edited by women and published for suffragists, socialists, free lovers and other radicals. PhD U. of Maryland, 1979.

STEINBERG,S.E.H. *679*
Reformer in the market place. Edward W. Bon and the *Ladies' Home Journal*, 1889–1919. PhD Johns Hopkins U. 1971.

STEINER,L.C. *680*
The women's suffrage press, 1850–1900: a cultural analysis. PhD U. of Illinois at Urbana-Champaign, 1979.

STEINSON,B.J. *681*
Female activism in World War I: the American women's peace, suffrage, preparedness, and relief movements. PhD U. of Michigan, 1977.

STEPHENS,B.J. *682*
May Wright Sewall (1844–1920). PhD Ball State U. 1977.

STRAUB,E.F. *683*
Government policy toward civilian women during World War II. PhD Emory U. 1973.

STRICKER,F.A. *684*
Socialism, feminism and the new morality: the separate freedoms of Max Eastman, William English Walling and Floyd Dell, 1910–1930. PhD Princeton U. 1974.

STRONG-BOAG,V.J. *686*
The Parliament of women: the National Council of Women of Canada, 1893–1929. PhD U. of Toronto, 1975.

STUCKER,J.J. *687*
The impact of woman suffrage on patterns of voter participation in the United States: quasi-experimental and real-time analyses, 1890–1920. PhD U. of Michigan, 1973.

SVARLIEN,O. *688*
International control of the traffic in women: a study of international organization. PhD U. of North Carolina at Chapel Hill, 1942.

TAYLOR,A.E. *689*
The woman suffrage movement in Tennessee. PhD Vanderbilt U. 1943.

TAYLOR,P.C. *690*
The entrance of women into party politics: the 1920s. PhD Harvard U. 1967.

TEDESCO,M. *691*
Science and feminism: conceptions of female intelligence and their effect on American feminism, 1869–1920. PhD Georgia State U. 1978.

TENTLER,L.W. *692*
Women and work: industrial employment and sex roles, 1900–1929. PhD U. of Michigan, 1975.

TERBORE-PENN,R.M. *693*
Afro-Americans in the struggle for woman suffrage. PhD Howard U. 1977.

THOMPSON,M. *694*
Ida B. Wells-Barnett: an exploratory study of an American black woman, 1893–1930. [Leader in the anti-lynch movement] PhD George Washington U. 1979.

TODD,H.C. *695*
Women's organizations in the United States – their development and present status. PhD American U. 1925.

TRUBEY,L.P. *696*
The public speaking career of Ida M. Tarbell. PhD U. of Florida, 1972.

TWIN,S.L. *697*
Jock and Jill: aspects of women's sports history in America, 1870–1940. PhD Rutgers U. 1978.

UNGER,S. *698*
A history of the National Women's Christian Temperance Union. PhD Ohio U. 1933.

VANCE,L.D.M. *699*
May Maria Jennings, Florida's genteel activist. PhD U. of Florida, 1980.

WAGGENSPACK,B.M. *700*
Elizabeth Cady Stanton's reform rhetoric, 1848–1854: a Perelman analysis of practical reasoning. PhD Ohio State U. 1982.

WAGNER,R.R. *701*
Virtue against vice: a study of moral reformers and prostitution in the Progressive era. PhD U. of Wisconsin, 1971.

WAGNER,S.M.R. *702*
That word is liberty: a biography of Matilda Joslyn Gage. PhD U. of California, Santa Cruz, 1978.

WARBASSE,E.B. *704*
The changing legal rights of married women, 1800–1861. PhD Radcliffe Coll. 1960.

WARE,S.W. *705*
Political sisterhood in the New Deal: women in politics and government, 1933–1940. PhD Harvard U. 1978.

WARES,L.J. *706*
Dress of the African American woman in slavery and freedom: 1500 to 1935. PhD Purdue U. 1981.

WATERMAN,W.C. *707*
Prostitution and its repression in New York City, 1900–1931. PhD Columbia U. 1932.

WEDEL,J.M. *708*
The origins of state patriarchy during the progressive era: a sociological study of the Mothers' Aid Movement. PhD Washington, 1975.

WEIN,R. *709*
Educated women and the limits of domesticity, 1830–1918. PhD New York U. 1974.

WHITAKER,F.M. *710*
A history of the Ohio Women's Christian Temperance Union, 1870–1920. PhD Ohio State U. 1971.

WHITE,D.G. *711*
Ain't I a woman? Female slaves in the antebellum South. PhD U. of Illinois at Chicago Circle, 1979.

WHITES,L. *712*
Southern ladies and millhands: the domestic economy and class politics: Augusta, Georgia, 1870–1890. PhD U. of California, Irvine, 1982.

WILLIAMS,P.A.O. *713*
Self-made and unself-made: the myth of the self-made man and the ideologies of the true woman, new woman and Amazon, 1820–1920. PhD U. of New Mexico, 1982.

WILSON,M.G. *714*
Women and the city, 1870–1920. PhD U. of Southern California, 1977.

WLADAVER-MORGAN,S. *715*
Young women and the New Deal: camps and residence centers, 1933–1943. PhD U. of Indiana, 1982.

WUCHENICH,J.G. *716*
The social and educational progress of the American woman as reflected in the cookbook, 1776–1899. PhD U. of Pittsburgh, 1978.

YOAKAM,D.G. *717*
An historical study of the public speaking activity of women in America from 1828 to 1860. PhD U. of Southern California, 1935.

YOUNG,A.N. *718*
Interpreting the dangerous trades: workers' health in America and the career of Alice Hamilton, 1910–1935. PhD Brown U. 1982.

YOUNG,I.S. *719*
Jane Addams and child welfare reforms, 1889–1899. DSW Catholic U. of America, 1967.

YOUNG,J.H. *720*
Anne Elizabeth Dickinson and the Civil War. PhD U. of Illinois, 1941.

ZIMMERMAN,L. *721*
Women in the economy: a case study of Lynn, Massachusetts, 1760–1974. PhD Brandeis U. 1977.

ZINGMAN,B.G. *722*
An index to *The Dial*, 1920–1929. PhD U. of Louisville, 1971.

ZOPHY,A.M.H. *723*
For the improvement of my sex: Sarah Josepha Hale's editorship of *Godey's Lady's Book*, 1837–1877. PhD Ohio State U. 1978.

10 Language

Several related studies are to be found under Motherhood **6** 277–806. *See also* **17** 181, 183, 639, 753; **18** 98; **19** 222; **20** 184.

ADAMS,G.C.S. *1*
Words and descriptive terms for woman and girl in French and Provençal border dialects. PhD North Carolina at Chapel Hill, 1950.

BRIONES,R.G. *2*
Semantic conditioning of Filipino women's evaluations of heterosexual behaviors. PhD Fordham U. 1981.

BROWN,R.E. *3*
A use of the semantic differential to study the feminine image of girls who participate in competitive sports and certain other school-relating activities. PhD Florida State U. 1965.

COOPER,E.J. *4*
A sociosemantic study of language about females. PhD U. of North Carolina at Chapel Hill, 1976.

DUFFY,R.J. *5*
The vocal pitch characteristics of eleven year old, thirteen year old and fifteen year old female speakers. PhD U. of Iowa, 1958.

GRUNDEN,R.S. *6*
Towards a description of a female movement vocabulary. PhD Ohio State U. 1978.

HART,A.K.M. *7*
Relationships among social and cognitive variables and the use of language by adolescent girls. PhD U. of Cambridge, 1973.

HORTON,J.R. *8*
A comparison of oral assertiveness of inexperienced versus experienced female students in speech pathology. EdD U. of Georgia, 1980.

KATZ,H.A. *9*
The effects of previous exposure to pornographic film, sexual instrumentality, and guilt on male verbal aggression against women. PhD U. of Connecticut, 1971.

KODISH,D.G. *10*
'Never had a word between us': pattern in the verbal art of a Newfoundland woman. PhD U. of Texas at Austin, 1981.

KOMNENICH,P. *11*
Hormonal influences on verbal behavior in women. PhD U. of Arizona, 1974.

KREFTING,C.E. *12*
Objective studies in the oral style of American woman speakers. PhD Louisiana State U., 1937.

KUHN,S.E.A. *13*
The relationship of formal operations and syntactical complexity in oral language of adult women. EdD U. of Georgia, 1978.

LEIGHT,T. *14*
Comparisons of articulation between young college women and their mothers. PhD Columbia U. 1960.

LINDO,B.Z. *15*
The Women's Rights Movement and the sociolinguistic application to sexism in standard American English. PhD United States International U. 1977.

LINKE,C.E. *16*
A study of pitch characteristics of female voices and their relationship to vocal effectiveness. PhD U. of Iowa, 1953.

LINVILLE,S.E. *17*
Acoustic characteristics of adult women's voices with advancing age: a production and perception study. PhD Northwestern U. 1981.

MCDONALD,L.O. *18*
A functional analysis of individual differences in conversational style among mothers. PhD U. of Oregon, 1979.

MCFARLIN,A.S. *19*
Hallie Quinn Brown: black woman elocutionist 1845(?)-1949. PhD Washington State U., 1975.

NALIBOW,K.L. *20*
The declensional patterns of feminine professional working titles and surnames in contemporary standard Polish. PhD U. of Pennsylvania, 1970.

NEWMAN,M.A.T. *21*
An analysis of the rhetorical characteristics of the public speech of selected women. PhD Pennsylvania State U. 1982.

SCHOLL,H.H. *22*
Comparisons of voice between young college women and their mothers. PhD Columbia U. 1959.

STROMBERG,C.E. *23*
Semantic differentiation of social behavior of valued persons by female college groups. PhD U. of Texas at Austin, 1962.

TATMAN,C. *24*
A survey of the speaking activities of a liberal arts college for Women. PhD U. of Iowa, 1958.

11 Law

Several related studies will be found under **2** Criminology. *Historical studies will be found under* **9** History. *For abortion law see* **19** 1–132 *passim; for labour law see* **5** 207–243 *passim. See also* **4** 273, 1554, 1632; **5** 287, 420, 459, 519; **19** 13, 22, 48, 99, 120, 127; **23** 196, 231, 241.

BESSMER,S. *1*
The laws of rape. PhD Stanford U. 1976.

CHICO,B.B. *2*
The Colorado Case in historical perspective using the 1975 United States National Women's Conference Act Public Law 94–167 as a vehicle for social change. DA U. of Northern Colorado, 1979.

CREIGHTON,W.B. *3*
The development of the legal status of women in employment in Great Britain. PhD U. of Cambridge, 1975.

DAW,R.C. *4*
The equal rights of men and women in international law. DPhil U. of Oxford, 1971.

DICKS,V.I. *5*
A rhetorical analysis of the forensic and deliberative issues and strategies in the Angela Davis trial. PhD Ohio State U. 1976.

HELEINE,F. *6*
Les pouvoirs ménagers de la femme mariée en droit québecois. PhD U. of Montreal, 1972.

JOHNSTON,A.F. *7*
Litigation bearing upon women in secondary education. EdD U. of Oklahoma, 1977.

LIPETZ,M.J. *8*
Routine justice: the impact of the courtroom workgroup on the processing of cases in women's court. PhD Northwestern U. 1980.

LUNN,J. *9*
Private and public maintenance for the wife. MPhil CNAA, 1978.

MCCANN,K.E. *10*
The legal response to wife abuse: a study of sex bias. MPhil U. of Sheffield, 1983.

MCCOMISKEY,T.E. *11*
The status of the secondary wife: its development in ancient Near Eastern law. A study and comprehensive index. PhD Brandeis U. 1965.

MULLIGAN,J.E. *12*
Three federal interventions on behalf of childbearing women: the Sheppard-Towner Act, Emergency Maternity and Infant Care, and the Maternal and Child Health and Mental Retardation Planning Amendments of 1963. PhD U. of Michigan, 1976.

NEWBY,L. *13*
The sociology of the law of rape. MA* U. of Sheffield, 1976.

O'CONNOR,K.P. *14*
Litigation strategies and policy formulation: an examination of organized women's groups use of the courts, 1869–1977. PhD State U. of New York at Buffalo, 1979.

O'GRADY,R.A. *15*
Caring work and women's OAS/Benefits: an analysis of proposed changes in the Social Security Law. PhD Brandeis U. 1982.

PETRIE,J. *16*
Women: equal citizens or dependent wives? A discussion of two contrasting notions of women, their roles, rights and duties within the law, with particular reference to current attempts to resolve them in relation to the supplementary benefits scheme. MA* U. of Sheffield, 1979.

RABKIN,P.A. *17*
The silent feminist revolution: women and the law in New York State from Blackstone to the beginnings of the American womens' rights movement. PhD State U. of New York at Buffalo, 1975.

RISKIN,S. *18*
The *Moredet:* a study of the rebellious wife and her status in initiating divorce in Jewish law. PhD New York U. 1982.

ROBY,P.A. *19*
Politics and prostitution: a case study of the formulation, enforcement, and judicial administration of the New York State penal law on prostitution, 1870–1970. PhD New York U. 1971.

ROJAS,M.H. *20*
The ideological distinction between sex and race discrimination as found in selected Supreme Court cases and briefs of counsel. EdD Virginia Polytechnic Inst. and State U. 1982.

SION,A. *21*
Prostitution and the law. PhD U. of Cambridge, 1971.

SIVARAMAYYA,B. *22*
Women's rights of inheritance: a comparative study of the Hindu, Muslim, New York and Quebec laws. DCL McGill U. 1971.

THOMAS,K.J. *23*
Feminist theory and legal analysis. MA* U. of Sheffield, 1981.

12 Literature

(*Note:* Lack of space forces us to omit critical editions and other edited texts, studies of works with a female figure as title character (*Madame Bovary, Anna Karenina, Pamela*) unless the content is specifically related to women's studies, and comparative dissertations considering one woman author among several men. Comparative studies and studies of women in works by men are grouped at the front of each section. Studies of individual female writers follow.)

Comparative and general studies

Up to c.1600

ABOUL-ENEIN,A.M. *1*
Cleopatra in French and English drama from Yodelle to Shakespeare. PhD Trinity Coll. Dublin, 1954.

ASHBY,W.D. *2*
The lady of the fountain: a study of a medieval myth. PhD U. of Miami, 1976.

DREYFUSS,C.A.S. *3*
Femina sapiens in drama: Aeschylus to Grillparzer. PhD U. of Michigan, 1975.

EGGERZ-BROWNFELD,S. *4*
Anti-feminist satire in German and English literature of the late Middle Ages. PhD Catholic U. of America, 1981.

HARRISON,R.H. *5*
The spirited lady through Nicolete to Rosalind. PhD U. of Oregon, 1974.

KINTER,W.L. *6*
Prophetess and fay: a study of the ancient and medieval tradition of the Sibyl. PhD Columbia U. 1958.

KNIGHT,E.E. *7*
The role of women in Don Juan and Faust literature. PhD Florida State U. 1973.

MACCURDY,M.M. *8*
The polarization of the feminine in Arthurian and troubadour literature. PhD Syracuse U. 1980.

MCMILLIAN,.A.H. *9*
'Evere an hundred goode ageyn oon badde': catalogues of good women in medieval literature. (Boccaccio, Christine de Pisan and Chaucer). PhD Indiana U. 1979.

PAOLUCCI,A. *10*
The women in the *Divine comedy* and *The faerie queene*. PhD Columbia U. 1963.

PAROTTI,P.E. *11*
The female warrior in the renaissance epic. PhD U. of New Mexico, 1972.

ROBINSON,L.S. *12*
Monstrous regiment: the lady knight in sixteenth-century epic. [Ariosto's Bradamente, Tasso's Clorinda and Spenser's Britomart] PhD Columbia U. 1974.

SCANIO,V.A. *13*
The doctrine of the lady in Italian medieval and renaissance treatises. PhD U. of Michigan, 1977.

SCHWARTZ,J.I. *14*
Studies in Marian verse, 1534–1900. PhD Yale U. 1944.

SUZUKI,M. *15*
Helen's daughters: woman as emblem in the matter of Troy. [Helen in Virgil's *Aeneid*, Spenser's *Faerie queene* and Shakespeare's *Troilus and Cressida*.] PhD Yale U. 1982.

THADEN,M. *16*
Medea: a study in the adaptability of a literary theme. PhD Pennsylvania State U. 1972.

UNRUE,J.C. *17*
Hali Meidenhad and other virginity treatises. PhD Ohio State U. 1970.

UTLEY,F.L. *18*
Satire on women in Greek, Latin and Middle English. PhD Harvard U. 1936.

WINSOR,E.J. *19*
A study in the sources and rhetoric of Chaucer's *Legend of good women* and Ovid's *Heroides*. PhD Yale U. 1963.

ZAK,N.C. *20*
The portrayal of the heroine in Chretien de Troye's *Erec et Enide*, Gottfried von Strassburg's *Tristan* and *Flamenca*. PhD U. of California, Berkeley, 1981.

ZIEGLER,G. *21*
The characterization of Guinevere in English and

French medieval romance. PhD U. of Pennsylvania, 1974.

After c.1600

BAER,E.R. *22*
'The pilgrimage inward': the quest motif in the fiction of Margaret Atwood, Doris Lessing and Jean Rhys. PhD Indiana U. 1981.

BELTRAN,L. *23*
The old woman and authority: evolution and meaning of a literary character. PhD Michigan U. 1966.

BORISOFF,D.J. *24*
Changing aspects in twentieth-century Faustian works: the woman as illuminator and liberator of the isolated hero. PhD New York U. 1981.

BURDNER,M.S. *25*
The woman as artist in twentieth-century fiction. PhD Ohio State U. 1979.

CHASE,L.B. *26*
The *'willing victim'*: female masochism in modern novels. PhD U. of Connecticut, 1978.

CLARK,N.B. *27*
The black aesthetic reviewed: a critical examination of the writings of Imamu Amiri Baraka, Gwendolyn Brooks and Toni Morrison. PhD Cornell U. 1980.

CLEMON-KARP,S. *28*
The female androgyne in tragic drama. PhD Brandeis U. 1980.

COHEN,S.H. *29*
The Electra figure in twentieth-century American and European drama. PhD U. of Indiana, 1968.

COURTIVRON,I.de. *30*
Androgyny, misogyny, and madness: three essays on women in literature. PhD Brown U. 1973.

CROUCH,I.M. *31*
Joan of Arc and four playwrights: a rhetorical analysis for oral interpretations. [Shakespeare's *Henry VI* Part I, Shaw's *St Joan*, Maxwell Anderson's *Joan of Lorraine* and Anouilh's *L'Alouette*.] PhD U. of Southern Illinois, 1972.

DAWSON,W.M. *32*
The female characters of August Strindberg, Eugene O'Neill, and Tennessee Williams. PhD U. of Wisconsin, 1964.

DIORIO,M.A.L.G. *33*
'Vessels of experience': a comparative study of women in selected novels of Gustave Flaubert and Henry James. PhD U. of Kansas, 1977.

DIRKS,M.D. *34*
The tragic heroine in the mythological drama, 1800–1960.

EIRICH,S.H. *35*
Lire au feminin: une etude du discours feminin dans les Romans de Duras, Woolf, et Sarraute. PhD State U. of New York at Buffalo, 1978.

FOX,S.D. *36*
The novels of Virginia Woolf and Nathalie Sarraute. PhD Emory U. 1970.

FUCCI,M.L. *37*
Women's novels of the seventies in the United States and France. PhD U. of Michigan, 1976.

GARCIA,E.R. *38*
The picaresque tradition of the female rogue: differences from and similarities to the *picaro*. PhD Columbia U. 1973.

GARDINER,E.P. *39*
Translations of selected poems by ten contemporary French and Spanish women poets, with a critical introduction. PhD Ohio U. 1975.

GOODE,A. *40*
Mothers and daughters and the novel. [*Dombey and son, Portrait of a lady, House of mirth, The voyage out, Night and day* and *To the lighthouse*.] PhD State U. of New York at Stony Brook, 1979.

GOROWARA,K.K. *41*
The treatment of the unmarried woman in comedy, 1584–1921. PhD Glasgow U. 1962.

GREENE,M.S.E. *42*
Love and duty: the character of the Princess de Cleves as reflected in certain later English and American novels. [Studies in Richardson's *Clarissa Harlowe*; Jane Austen's *Sense and sensibility* and *Persuasion*, Charlotte Brontë's *Jane Eyre*; George Eliot's *Middlemarch*, and Henry James's *The wings of the dove* and *The portrait of a lady*.] PhD U. of New Mexico, 1965.

GUGAW,D.M. *43*
The female warrior heroine in Anglo-American popular balladry. PhD U. of California, Los Angeles, 1982.

HAMBLIN,E.N. *45*
Adulterous heroines in nineteenth-century literature: a comparative literature study. [Leopoldo Alas's *La regenta*, Flaubert's *Madame Bovary*, Tolstoy's Anna Karenina and Hawthorne's *The scarlet letter*.] PhD Florida State U. 1977.

HANDY,P.M. *46*
The woman as hero in twentieth-century women's fiction. [Edith Wharton, Virginia Woolf, Sylvia Plath and Eudora Welty, Lois Gould, May Sarton and Margaret Atwood.] PhD Bowling Green State U. 1979

HARRISON,R. *47*
Women and romantic fiction: subordination and resistance. MLitt U. of Birmingham, 1981.

HERRMANN,A.C. *48*
Towards a female dialogue. Virginia Woolf and Christa Wolf. PhD Yale U. 1983.

HERZOG,C.J. *49*
Nora's sisters: female characters in the plays of Ibsen, Strindberg, Shaw and O'Neill. PhD U. of Illinois at Urbana-Champaign, 1982.

HICKEY,M.V. *50*
The early adolescent's reactions to the literary and cultural portrayal of women. EdD Rutgers U. 1974.

HOMANS,M.B. *51*
Studies in the feminine poetic imagination: Dorothy Wordsworth, Emily Brontë, and Emily Dickinson. PhD Yale U. 1978.

HOWARD,U.E. *52*
The mystical trends in the poetry of Emily Dickinson and Annette von Droste-Hülshoff. PhD U. of Illinois at Urbana-Champaign, 1974.

JEDERMAN,J.E. *53*
The sexual stereotype of women in children's literature. EdD Northern Illinois U. 1974.

JELINEK,E.C. *54*
The tradition of women's autobiographies. (Comparative study with specific concentration on Elizabeth Cady Stanton, Gertrude Stein, Lillian Hellman and Kate Millet.) PhD State U. of New York at Buffalo, 1977.

JENSEN,M.A. *55*
Women and romantic fiction: a case study of Harlequin Enterprise, romances and readers. PhD McMaster U. 1980.

JOHNSTON,S.A. *56*
Mothers and daughters in twentieth-century women's fiction. PhD U. of British Columbia, 1981.

JURGRAU,T.L. *57*
'Pastoral' and 'rustic' in the country novels of George Sand and George Eliot. PhD City U. of New York, 1976.

KELLEY,M.B. *59*
The unconscious rebel: studies in feminine fiction, 1820–1880. PhD Iowa State U. 1974.

KRAFT,S.B. *60*
Women and society in the novels of George Eliot and Edith Wharton. PhD U. of Rochester, 1973.

LABUVITZ,E.K. *61*
The female *Bildungsroman* in the twentieth century, a comparative study: Dorothy Richardson, Simone de Beauvoir, Doris Lessing, Christa Wolf. PhD New York U. 1982.

L'ENFANT,J.C. *62*
Edith Wharton and Virginia Woolf: tradition and experiment in the modern novel. PhD Louisiana State U. 1974.

LENOWITZ,K. *63*
The controversy over character: an examination of the novels of Iris Murdoch and Nathalie Sarraute. PhD U. of Colorado at Boulder, 1980.

LEONARD,D. *64*
Mary Stuart, the historical figure in English and American drama. PhD Columbia U. 1964.

LEVINE-KEATING,H. *65*
Myth and archetype from a female perspective: an exploration of twentieth- century North and South American women poets. PhD New York U. 1980.

LINDAU,B. *66*
Feminism in the English novel: George Eliot, Virginia Woolf, Doris Lessing. PhD U. of South Carolina, 1979.

LUBIN,A.M. *67*
(Part II) Becky Sharp's role playing in *Vanity Fair* and (Part III) Grotesques in the fiction of Flannery O'Connor. PhD Rutgers U. 1973.

MACKAY,B. *69*
The new women in the drama of Buchner, Ibsen, Strindberg and Brecht. PhD Yale U. 1974.

MADISON,E.C. *70*
Reality and imagery in the novels of Virginia Woolf and Nathalie Sarraute. PhD Indiana U. 1974.

MAGLIN,N.B. *71*
Rebel women writers, 1894–1925. PhD Union Grad. Sch., Ohio, 1975.

MAROTTA,K.R. *72*
The literary relationship of George Eliot and Harriet Beecher Stowe. PhD Johns Hopkins U. 1974.

MARTIN,E.A. *73*
Uncommon women and the common experience: fiction of four contemporary French and German women writers. [Marie Cardinal, Ingeborg Drewitz; Christina Brückner and Françoise Mallet-Joris.] PhD Indiana U. 1982.

MODLESKI,T. *75*
Popular feminine narratives: a study of romances, gothics, and soap operas. PhD Stanford U. 1980.

MUNITZ,B. *76*
Joan of Arc and modern drama. [Shaw, Kaiser, Brecht, Anouilh and Anderson.] PhD Princeton U. 1968.

NEWSOME,E. *77*
Women as dramatists. MSc U. of Bradford, 1974.

NOONAN,P.E. *78*
Women and love: feminine perspectives on love and sexuality in the fiction of 19th and 20th century women writers. PhD U. of Denver, 1979.

PANARO,L.A. *79*
Desperate women: murderers and suicides in nine modern works. [Kate Chopin's *The awakening*, Wharton's *The house of mirth*, Mauriac's *Thérèse Desqueynoux*, Julien Green's *Adrienne Mesurat* Glasgow's *The sheltered wife*, Beavoir's *L'invité*, Moravia's *Leambizioni sbagliate*, Elizabeth Bowen's

To the north and Natalia Ginzburg's *E stato cosi.*] PhD New York U. 1981.

PARISH,M.H. *80*
Women at work: housewives and paid workers as mothers in contemporary realistic fiction for children. PhD Michigan State U. 1976.

PARK,H.J. *81*
The search beneath appearances: the novels of Virginia Woolf and Nathalie Sarraute. PhD Indiana U. 1979.

PECK,E.M.M. *82*
Exploring the feminine: a study of Janet Lewis, Ellen Glasgow, Anaîs Nin and Virginia Woolf. PhD Stanford U. 1974.

RIGNEY,B.H. *83*
Madness and sexual politics in the feminist novel: studies of Charlotte Brontë, Virginia Woolf and Doris Lessing. PhD Ohio State U. 1977.

ROMIG,E.M. *84*
Women as victims in the novels of Charles Dickens and William Faulkner. PhD Rice U. 1978.

RONNING,K.A. *85*
Above all a nice girl: the heroines of best-sellers, 1895–1920. PhD U. of Nebraska-Lincoln, 1980.

ST ANDREWS,B.A. *86*
Forbidden fruit: the relationship between mother and knowledge. PhD Syracuse U. 1980.

SABISTON,E.J. *87*
The provincial heroine in prose fiction: a study in isolation and creativity. [Jane Austen's Emma, Flaubert's Emma Bovary, George Eliot's Dorothea Brooke and Henry James's Isabel Archer.] PhD Cornell U. 1969.

SCANLON,L. *87a*
Essays on the effect of feminism and socialism upon the literature of 1880–1914. PhD Brandeis U. 1973.

SHABKA,M.G. *88*
The writer's search for identity: a redefinition of the feminine personality from Virgina Woolf to Margaret Drabble and Doris Lessing. PhD Kent State U. 1981.

SHAW,E.B. *89*
The comic novels of Ivy Compton-Burnett and Nathalie Sarraute. PhD U. of Colorado at Boulder, 1974.

SOUBLY,D.M. *90*
The sun and stars nearer roll: Jungian individuation and the archetypal feminine in the epics of William Blake and James Joyce. PhD Wayne State U. 1981.

STANBACK,T.W. *91*
A study of twelve 'unsympathetic' women characters in modern drama. PhD Cornell U. 1953.

STEWART,G. *92*
A new mythos[x]: the novel of the artist as heroine, 1877–1977. PhD Wayne State U. 1977.

SUKENICK,L. *93*
Sense and sensibility in women's fiction: studies in the novels of George Eliot, Virginia Woolf, Anais Nin and Doris Lessing. PhD City U. of New York, 1974.

SULLIVAN,K.L. *94*
The muse of fiction: fatal women in the novels of W.M. Thackeray, Thomas Hardy and John Fowles. PhD Johns Hopkins U. 1973.

TAUB,M. *96*
The martyr as tragic heroine: the Joan of Arc theme in the theater of Schiller, Shaw, Anouilh and Brecht. PhD U. of North Carolina at Chapel Hill, 1982.

TAYLOR,N.M. *97*
Conscious construction: the concept of plot in five novels by women. PhD Loyola U. of Chicago, 1977.

TODD,J.M. *98*
Dark Lady, Fair Lady: variations in the use of the conventions of the double heroine among selected nineteenth-century British and American novelists. PhD Harvard U. 1976.

TOEGEL,E.M. *99*
Emily Dickinson and Annette von Droste-Hülshoff: poets as women. PhD U. of Washington, 1980.

VAIL,M.I. *100*
Transformation of narrative structure in relation to the role of the female protagonist in the eighteenth-century novel. [*Manon Lescaut, Mémoires du comte de Comminge, Moll Flanders, La réligieuse, La vie de Marianne.*] PhD Cornell U. 1978.

WELLS,J.L. *101*
Madness and women: a study of the themes of insanity and anger in modern literature by women. [Doris Lessing, Anna Karan, Shirley Jackson, Christina Stead.] PhD U. of California, Berkeley, 1976.

WICHMANN,B. *102*
From sex-role identification toward androgyny: a study of major works of Simone de Beauvoir, Doris Lessing and Christa Wolf. PhD Purdue U. 1978.

WILD,R.S. *103*
Studies in the shorter fiction of Elizabeth Bowen and Eudora Welty. PhD U. of Michigan, 1965.

WILLIAMS, S. *104*
Women and creativity: a study of selected plays of Ibsen, Strindberg, Wedekind and Shaw. PhD U. of East Anglia, 1974.

WINSTON,E. *105*
Women and autobiography: the need for a more

inclusive theory. [British and American especially Gertrude Stein and Edith Sitwell.] PhD U. of Wisconsin-Madison, 1977.

Feminist criticism

Many other studies in this chapter are also relevant. See, for example, 35, 391, 418, 462, 478, 744, 898, 902.

ARBUTHNOT,L.B. *106*
Main trends in feminist criticism in film, literature, and art history: the decade of the 1970s. [Berger, Haskell, Millett, Rosen.] PhD New York U. 1982.

BAHM,R.M. *197*
The influence of non-sexual cues, sexual explicitness and sex guilt on females' erotic response to literature. PhD U. of Massachusetts, 1972.

BAMMER,A. *108*
Visions and re-visions: the utopian impulse in feminist fiction. PhD U. of Wisconsin-Madison, 1982.

BARTKNOSKI,F. *109*
Towards a feminist ethos: readings in feminist utopian fiction. PhD U. of Iowa, 1982.

BROWN,J.P. *110*
Feminist drama: definition and critical analysis. PhD U. of Missouri-Columbia, 1978.

CARUSO,B.A . *111*
Circle without boundaries: feminist criticism and the contemporary woman poet. PhD Bowling Green State U. 1977.

CICARD O,B.J. *112*
The mystery of the American Eve: alienation of the feminine as a tragic theme in American letters. PhD Saint Louis U. 1971.

CORNILLON,S.K. *113*
Development and implementation of a feminist literary perspective. PhD Bowling Green State U. 1975.

CUNNINGHAM,J.A. *114*
Charles Brockden Brown's pursuit of a realistic feminism: a study of his writings as a contribution to the growth of women's rights in America. EdD Ball State U. 1971.

DICK,D.M. *115*
Writers' creativity in relation to sex-role identity and ego permissiveness. PhD California Sch. of Prof. Psych. Los Angeles, 1978.

ESPLUGAS,C.C. *116*
Female sexual encounters in works by Sherwood Anderson and Manuel Pluig and existential themes and literary techniques in Sherwood Anderson's and Manuel Pluig's works. PhD U. of Toledo, 1981.

FERNANDO,L. *117*
Feminism and the novelist's imagination. PhD U. of Leeds, 1964.

FISH,S.L. *118*
A phenomenology of women. PhD U. of Southern Illinois at Carbondale, 1975.

FLYNN,E.A. *119*
Feminist critical theory: three models. PhD Ohio State U. 1977.

GHINGER,C.F. *120*
Alienation and the quest for self: the powerful heroine of fiction. PhD U. of Colorado at Boulder, 1978.

HALISCHAK,K. *121*
Recent voices in American feminist literature. PhD U. of Notre Dame, 1982.

IANNONE,C.A. *122*
Feminist literary criticism, 1968–1980: a reappraisal. PhD State U. of New York, 1981.

JACOBS,M.S. *123*
Beyond the castle: the development of the paradigmatic female study. PhD American U. 1980.

KAPLAN,B.M. *124*
Women and sexuality in utopian fiction. PhD New York U. 1977.

KNEPPER,M.S. *125*
Radical and revisionary: an examination of feminist literary criticism; its theory, style and politics. PhD U. of Nebraska-Lincoln, 1982.

KRIER,W.J. *126*
A pattern of limitations: the heroine's novel of the mind. PhD Indiana U. 1973.

LANSER,S.S. *127*
Point of view as ideology and technique: women writers and narrative voice. PhD U. of Wisconsin-Madison, 1979.

MARTIN,O.E. *128*
Curriculum and response: a study of the images of the black woman in black fiction. PhD U. of Chicago, 1980.

MATZA,D. *129*
A critique of the new feminist criticism. PhD Case Western Reserve U. 1979.

MESSICK,J.H. *130*
Reading as if for life: the female Quixote. PhD U. of California, Santa Barbara, 1982.

MIDDLETON,U.S. *131*
The exiled self: women writers and political fiction. [Mary Shelley, George Eliot, Virginia Woolf, Doris Lessing.] PhD U. of California, Berkeley, 1979.

MILLER,M.P. *132*
A phenomenological investigation of the creative process of women poets: the structure, nature and

antological significance of the creative process. PhD California Sch. of Prof. Psych., Berkeley, 1981.

MILLER,N.K. *133*
Gender and genre: an analysis of literary femininity in the eighteenth-century novel. PhD Columbia U. 1974.

MORGAN,E.E. *134*
Neo-feminism and modern literature. PhD U. of Pennsylvania, 1972.

PAELIA,C.A. *135*
Sexual personae: the androgyne in literature and art. PhD Yale U. 1974.

REGISTER,C. *136*
Feminist ideology and literary criticism in the United States and Sweden. PhD U. of Chicago, 1973.

ROLLER,J.M. *137*
The feminist novel: the politics and ideology of style. PhD U. of Michigan, 1981.

ROSINSKY,N.M. *138*
Feminist theory in women's speculative fiction, 1966–81. PhD U. of Wisconsin-Madison, 1982.

ROTH,M.B. *139*
Tiresias their muse: studies in sexual stereotypes in the English novel. PhD Syracuse U. 1973.

SAYRES,S. *140*
Susan Sontag and the practice of modernism. PhD State U. of New York at Buffalo, 1982.

SCHWEICKART,P.P. *141*
A theory for feminist criticism. PhD Ohio State U. 1980.

SHEDD,P.T. *142*
The relationship between attitude of the reader towards women's changing role and response to literature which illuminates women's role. PhD Syracuse U. 1976.

SNOW,K. *143*
Feminism and finalism: the history of an idea. PhD U. of Kentucky, 1979.

TALBERT,L.L. *144*
Witchcraft in contemporary feminist literature. PhD U. of Southern California, 1979.

TERRY,P.C. *145*
Female individuation in the twentieth-century as seen through contemporary fiction. PhD California Sch. of Prof. Psych., San Diego, 1977.

ZAK,M.W. *146*
Feminism and the new novel. PhD Ohio State U. 1973.

African literature

General studies

See also **4** 185; **23** 125.

BELATECHE,M. *147*
Voix et visages de femmes dans le roman algérien de langue française. PhD George Washington U. 1982.

EL-RABIA,M.B. *148*
Women writers and critics in modern Egypt, 1888–1963. PhD U. of London, Sch. of Oriental and African Stud. 1965.

GITHAE-MUGO,M.M. *149*
Visions of Africa in the fiction of Chinua Achebe, Margaret Laurence, Elspeth Huxley and Ngugi Wa Thiong'o. PhD U. of New Brunswick, 1973.

GITHII,E.W. *150*
Literary imperialism in Kenya: elements of imperial sensibility in the African works of Isak Dinesen and Elspeth Huxley. PhD Tufts U. 1980.

HAMMOND,T.N. *151*
The image of women in Senegalese fiction. PhD State U. of New York at Buffalo, 1976.

JONES,P.P. *152*
Nommo Spirit: Africanisms in the poetry of Afro-Diaspo women. PhD U. of Pittsburgh, 1980.

LEE,S.M. *153*
L'image de la femme dans le roman francophone de l'Afrique occidentale. PhD U. of Massachusetts, 1974.

LIPPERT,A. *154*
The changing role of women as viewed in the literature of English-speaking and French-speaking West Africa. PhD Indiana U. 1972.

MACK,B.B. *155*
Wakokin mata: Hausa women's oral poetry. PhD U. of Wisconsin-Madison, 1981.

SARVAN,C.P. *156*
Aspects of freedom in Southern African fiction: a study of the works of Olive Schreiner, Sarah Millin, Doris Lessing and Nadine Gordimer. PhD U. of London (External), 1979.

SMYLEY,K.M. *157*
The African woman: interpretations of Senegalese novelists Aboulaye Sadji and Ousmane Sembene. PhD City U. of New York, 1977.

UMEH,M.A. *158*
Women and social realism in the novels of Buchi Emecheta. PhD U. of Wisconsin-Madison, 1981.

Individual writers

Nadine Gordimer

BOYLE,J.W. *159*
The international novel: aspects of its develop-

ment in the twentieth century with emphasis on the work of Nadine Gordimer and V.S. Naipaul. PhD U. of Pittsburgh, 1983.

COOK,J.W. *160*
The novels of Nadine Gordimer. PhD Northwestern U. 1976.

ESSA,A. *161*
Postwar South African fiction in English: Abrahams, Paton, and Gordimer. PhD U. of Southern California, 1969.

HOLLAND,R.W.H. *162*
The edge of possibility: a study of the interrelationships of political, religious and existential beliefs in the writings of Alan Paton and Nadine Gordimer. MPhil U. of Sussex, 1978.

Out-El-Kouloub

GHATTAS,S.R. *163*
Visages de femmes égyptiennes: étude sociolinguistique de l'oeuvre de Out-El-Kouloub. PhD U. of California, Irvine, 1979.

Doris Lessing

ALCORN,N.E. *164*
Vision and nightmare: a study of Doris Lessing's novels. PhD U. of California, Irvine, 1971.

BEARD,L.S. *165*
Lessing's Africa: geographical and metaphorical Africa in the novels and stories of Doris Lessing. PhD Cornell U. 1979.

BONOMO,J. *166*
The free woman and the traditional woman in novels by Doris Lessing: analysis and poetry. EdD Rutgers U. 1980.

BROOKS,E.W. *167*
Fragmentation and integration: a study of Doris Lessing's fiction. PhD New York U. 1971.

BUDHOS,S. *168*
An examination of the theme of enclosure with emphasis on marriage in selected works by Doris Lessing. PhD St John's U. 1980.

BURKOM,S.R. *169*
A reconciliation of opposites: a study of the works of Doris Lessing. PhD U. of Minnesota, 1970.

BURNISTON,S. *170*
A reading of *The golden notebook* by Doris Lessing. PhD U. of Birmingham, 1979.

CAREY,A.A. *171*
Doris Lessing: the search for reality. A study of the major themes in her novels. PhD U. of Wisconsin-Madison, 1965.

CEDERSTROM,L. *172*
From Marxism to myth: a developmental study of the novels of Doris Lessing. PhD U. of Manitoba, 1978.

CLEARY,R.D. *173*
A study of marriage in Doris Lessing's fiction. PhD State U. of New York at Stony Brook, 1981.

DRAINE,M.E. *174*
Stages of consciousness in Doris Lessing's fiction. PhD Temple U. 1977.

GAGE,D.B. *175*
Fictive figurings: meta commentary on Doris Lessing's *Children of violence*. PhD Arizona State U. 1978.

GRANT,V.F. *176*
The quest for wholeness in novels by Doris Lessing. EdD Rutgers U. 1974.

HALLIDAY,P.A.Y. *177*
The pursuit of wholeness in the work of Doris Lessing: dualities, multiplicities, and the resolution of patterns in illumination. PhD U. of Minnesota, 1973.

KILDAHL,K.A. *178*
The political and apocalyptical novels of Doris Lessing: a critical study of *Children of violence, The golden notebook, Briefing for a descent into hell*. PhD U. of Washington, 1974.

KROUSE,A.N. *179*
The feminism of Doris Lessing. PhD U. of Wisconsin-Madison, 1972.

KURILOFF,P.C. *180*
Doris Lessing: the practice of realism in the novel. PhD Bryn Mawr Coll. 1979.

MANION,E.C. *181*
Transcendence through disorder: a study of the fiction of Doris Lessing. PhD McGill U. 1980.

MARCHINO,L.A. *182*
The search for self in the novels of Doris Lessing. PhD U. of New Mexico, 1972.

MITCHELL,T.K. *183*
The irrational element in Doris Lessing's fiction. PhD Boston U. Grad. Sch. 1978.

MORGAN,D.D. *184*
The unity of human life: the meaning of the novels of Doris Lessing. PhD Occidental Coll. 1972.

NAUMER,M.A.S. *185*
The city and the veld: a study of the fiction of Doris Lessing. PhD U. of Oregon, 1973.

REID,M. *186*
Form and space in the fiction of Doris Lessing. PhD Tufts U. 1979.

ROSE,E.C. *187*
Doris Lessing's *Children of violence* as a *Bildungsroman*. PhD U. of Massachusetts, 1974.

SCHLUETER,P.G. *188*
A study of the major novels of Doris Lessing. PhD Southern Illinois U. 1968.

SELIGMAN,C.D. *189*
The autobiographical novels of Doris Lessing. PhD Tufts U. 1975.

SIMS,S.K.S. *190*
Repetition and evolution: an examination of themes and structures in the novels of Doris Lessing. PhD U. of Oregon, 1978.

SMITH,D.E.S. *192*
A thematic study of Doris Lessing's *Children of violence*. PhD Loyola U. Chicago, 1971.

WALTER,D.J. *193*
Twentieth-century woman in the early novels of Doris Lessing. PhD U. of Tennessee, 1978.

WELLS,D.B. *194*
The unity of Doris Lessing's *Children of violence*. PhD Tulane U. 1976.

Flora Nwapa

ASANBE,J. *195*
The place of the individual in the novels of Chinna Achebe, T.M. Aluno, Flora Nwapa and Wole Soyinka. PhD Indiana U. 1979.

Olive Schreiner

RIVE,R.M. *196*
Olive Shreiner (1855–1920): a biographical and critical study. DPhil U. of Oxford, 1974.

American Literature

General studies

ALBERT,M.L.H. *197*
Children of the Confederacy: a study of New South themes in Porter, Welty, McCullers and O'Connor. PhD U. of Hawaii, 1982.

ALLEN,M.I. *198*
The necessary blankness: women in major American fiction of the sixties. PhD U. of Maryland, 1973.

ALLEN,M.M. *199*
Women in the west: a study of book-length travel accounts by women who travelled in the Plains and Rockies. PhD U. of Texas at Austin, 1972.

ANDERSON,D.R. *200*
Failure and regeneration in the New England of Sarah Orne Jewett and Mary E. Wilkins Freeman. PhD U. of Arizona, 1974.

ARMES,N.R. *201*
The feeder: a study of the fiction of Eudora Welty and Carson McCullers. PhD U. of Illinois at Urbana-Champain, 1975.

AUGUST,B.T. *202*
The poetic use of womanhood in five modern American poets: Moore, Millay, Rukeyser, Levertov, and Plath. PhD New York U. 1978.

BARRETT,P.W. *203*
More American Adams: women heroes in American fiction. PhD U. of Rhode Island, 1978.

BAXTER,M.R. *204*
Modern woman as heroine in representative plays by S.N. Behmura. PhD U. of Wisconsin, 1973.

BEHRMAN,A.L.R. *205*
The heroine of our common scene: portrayals of American women in four novels by Edith Wharton and Henry James. PhD U. of Michigan, 1976.

BEIS,P.S. *206*
Cold fire: some contemporary American women poets. PhD Saint Louis U. 1972.

BENT,N.P. *207*
Romance and irony in Henry James's view of women. PhD Syracuse U. 1980.

BERKSON,D.W. *208*
The ordeal of the American girl: female initiation in Henry James's fiction. PhD U. of Illinois at Urbana-Champaign, 1978.

BLACKBURN,R.L. *209*
Conscious agents of time and self: the lives and styles of African-American women as seen through their autobiographical writings. PhD U. of New Mexico, 1978.

BLOOMER,D.E. *210*
An individual response to person, place and time: the local colour fiction of Sarah Orne Jewett, Hamlin Garland and Willa Cather. MA U. of Manchester, 1977.

BORDNER,M.S. *211*
The woman as artist in twentieth-century fiction. PhD Ohio State U. 1979.

BORENSTEIN,L. *212*
The place of femininity in the creative imagination: a study of Henry James, Robert Musil and Marcel Proust. DPhil U. of Sussex, 1976.

BOWERS,J.P. *212a*
The writer in the theatre: the plays of Gertrude Stein. PhD U. of California, Berkeley, 1981.

BRADLEY,J. *213*
Valedictory performances of three American women novelists. [Gertrude Atherton, Ellen Glasgow and Edith Wharton.] PhD State U. of New York at Stony Brook, 1981.

BRADSHER,F.K. *214*
Women in the works of James Fenimore Cooper. PhD Arizona State U. 1978.

BREMER,S.L.N. *215*
Woman in the works of William Dean Howells. PhD Stanford U. 1971.

BREWTON,B.E. *216*
Richard Wright's thematic treatment of women in

Uncle Tom's children, Black boy and *Native son*. EdD Rutgers U. 1978.

BROADWELL,E.P. *217*
Male authority and female identity in the poetry of Sylvia Plath, Anne Sexton and Adrienne Rich. PhD U. of North Carolina at Chapel Hill, 1981.

BROMBERGER,E.A. *218*
An odour of old maid: Boston as literary symbol. PhD U. of California, Los Angeles, 1976.

BROWN,E. *219*
Six female black playwrights: images of blacks in plays by Lorraine Hansberry, Alice Childress, Sonia Sanchez, Barbara Molette, Martie Charles, and Ntozake Shange. PhD Florida State U. 1980.

BROWN,M.H. *221*
Images of black women: family roles in Harlem renaissance literature. DA Carnegie-Mellon U. 1976.

BROWN,S.R. *222*
'Mothers' and 'sons': the development of autobiographical themes in the plays of Eugene O'Neill. PhD U. of Connecticut, 1975.

BURNS,M.A. *223*
The development of women characters in the works by William Faulkner. PhD Auburn U. 1974.

CALDWELL,R.M. *224*
Liberation for women in the fiction of Henry James. PhD Kansas State U. 1976.

CARLSON,C.H. *225*
Heroines in certain American novels. PhD Brown U. 1971.

CELLA,C.R. *226*
Two reactions against the stereotype of the old-fashioned girl in American novels, 1890–1920. PhD U. of Kentucky 1968.

CLARK,J.W. *227*
The tradition of Salem witchcraft in American literature, 1820–1870. PhD Duke U. 1970.

CLEARY,B.A.R. *228*
The Scarlet Amulet: the woman's limitations as redeemer in Hawthorne's major fiction. PhD U. of Nebraska-Lincoln, 1975.

COWELL,P.L. *229*
Women poets in pre-revolutionary America, 1650–1775. PhD U. of Massachusetts, 1977.

CRAMER,C.K. *230*
The new democratic protagonist: American novels and women main characters, 1960–1966. PhD Texas Christian U. 1980.

CROTTY,M.M. *231*
The mother in the fiction of Henry James. PhD Fordham U. 1962.

CROUTHER,L.A. *232*
Returning home: heroines as rebuilders and victims in American fiction written by women. [Willa Cather, Ellen Glasgow, Zora Hurston, Nella Larsen.] PhD Indiana U. 1982.

CULBERT,G.A. *233*
Hamlin Garland's image of woman: an allegiance to ideality. PhD U. of Wisconsin-Madison, 1974.

CURRY,J.A. *234*
Women as subjects and writers of nineteenth-century American humor. PhD U. of Michigan, 1975.

DALEY,N.K. *235*
The image of the woman in the contemporary American novel: 1950–1954 and 1968–1972. PhD Wayne State U. 1975.

DALKE,A.F. *236*
'Had I known her to be my sister, my love would have been more regular': incest in nineteenth-century American fiction. PhD U. of Pennsylvania, 1982.

DAVENPORT,M.L. *237*
Woman in nineteenth-century American fiction: ideals and stereotypes in the novels of John William De Forest. PhD U. of Texas at Austin, 1972.

DAVIS,N.H. *238*
The women in Theodore Dreiser's novels. PhD Northwestern U. 1969.

DAVIS,S.D. *239*
The female protagonist in Henry James's fiction, 1870–1890. PhD Tulane U. 1974.

DEAN,S.W. *240*
Lost ladies: the isolated heroine in the fiction of Hawthorne, James, Fitzgerald, Hemingway, and Faulkner. PhD U. of New Hampshire, 1973.

DEEGAN,D.Y. *241*
The stereotype of the single woman in American novels: a social study with implications for the education of women. PhD Columbia U. 1952.

DEEN,C.A.S. *242*
Women in the novels of John Updike: a critical study. PhD Texas A&M U. 1980.

DEROUNIAN,K.Z. *243*
Genre, voice, and character in the literature of six early American women writers, 1650–1812. PhD Pennsylvania State U. 1980.

DESHAZER,M.K. *244*
The woman poet and her muse: sources and images of female creativity in the poetry of H.D., Louise Bogan, May Sarton, and Adrienne Rich. PhD U. of Oregon, 1982.

DEWITT,J.F. *245*
The beautiful thing: William Carlos Williams and women. PhD U. of Connecticut, 1973.

DOBBS,J. *246*
Not another poetess: a study of female experience in modern American poetry. PhD U. of New Hampshire, 1973.

DOVE,J.R. *247*
Howells' rationalism as exhibited in his treatment of his female characters. PhD U. of Texas at Austin, 1957.

DRESNER,Z.Z. *248*
Twentieth-century American women humorists. PhD U. of Maryland, 1982.

DRUCKER,S.A. *249*
What melts in the pot: Jewish women writers in America. PhD State U. of New York at Buffalo, 1980.

DUGAW,D.M. *250*
The female warrior heroine in Anglo-American popular balladry. PhD U. of California, Los Angeles, 1982.

DUHLING,S.R. *251*
Women in the tales of Henry James: a study of his changing attitudes toward Europe and America. PhD U. of Georgia, 1976.

EDGERTON,J.M. *252*
Woman Manquée and Woman Triumphant in the poetry of Randall Jarrell. PhD U. of North Carolina at Chapel Hill, 1970.

EDWARDS,M.E.P. *253*
(Part I) Henry James and the woman novelist: the double standard in the tales and essays. PhD U. of Virginia, 1978.

EGOLF,R.H. *254*
Faulkner's men and women: a critical study of male-female relationships in his early Yoknapatawpha County novels. PhD Lehigh U. 1978.

EHRLICH,C. *255*
Evolutionism and the female in selected American novels, 1885–1900. PhD U. of Iowa, 1973.

ELLIOTT,K.S. *256*
The portrayal of the American Indian woman in a select group of American novels. PhD U. of Minnesota, 1979.

ELLSWORTH,M.E.T. *257*
Two New England writers: Harriet Beecher Stowe and Mary Wilkins Freeman. PhD Columbia U. 1981.

FAIRBANKS,C.L. *258*
Garmented with space: American and Canadian Prairie women's fiction. PhD U. of Minnesota, 1982.

FARLEY,P. *259*
Form and function: the image of woman in selected works of Hemingway and Fitzgerald. PhD Pennsylvania State U. 1973.

FERGUSON,P.M. *260*
Women dramatists in the American theatre, 1901–1940. PhD U. of Pittsburgh, 1958.

FESMIRE,B.L. *261*
The blaze within: forms of pilgrimage in the poetry of Denise Levertov, Anne Sexton, Sylvia Plath and Adrienne Rich. PhD Florida State U. 1981.

FINGER,L.L. *262*
Elements of the grotesque in selected works of Welty, Capote, McCullers and O'Connor. PhD George Peabody Coll. for Teachers, 1972.

FISHER,J.B. *263*
The minority woman's voice: a cultural study of black and Chicana fiction. PhD American U. 1978.

FLETCHER,M. *264*
The Southern heroine in the fiction of representative Southern women writers, 1850–1960. PhD Louisiana State U. 1963.

FOWLER,E.T. *265*
Annotated edition of the letters of Vachel Lindsay to Nellie Vieira. PhD U. of Tennessee, 1968.

FRICK,M.J.B. *266*
Women writers along the rivers, 1850–1950: the roles and images of women in Northwestern Missouri and Northeastern Kansas as evidenced by their writings. PhD U. of Missouri at Kansas City, 1982.

FRIEDMAN,S.P. *267*
Feminist concerns in the works of four twentieth-century American women dramatists: Susan Glaspell, Rachel Crothers, Lillian Hellman and Lorraine Hansberry. PhD New York U. 1977.

FRISBY,J.R. *268*
New Orleans writers and the negro, 1870–1900. [Includes Grace King, Ruth McEnery Stuart and Kate Chopin.] PhD Emory U. 1972.

FRYER,J.J. *269*
The faces of Eve: a study of women in American life and literature in the nineteenth century. PhD U. of Minnesota, 1973.

GABELNICK,F. *270*
Making connections: American women poets on love. PhD American U. 1974.

GARSON,H.S. *271*
The fallen woman in American naturalistic fiction from Crane to Faulkner. PhD U. of Michigan, 1967.

GASTON,K.C. *272*
The theme of female self-discovery in the novels of Judith Rossner, Gail Godwin, Alice Walker and Toni Morrison. PhD Auburn U. 1980.

GEARY,S.E. *273*
Scribbling women: essays on literary history and popular literature in the 1850s. PhD Brown U. 1976.

GHERMAN,D.L. *274*
From parlor to tepee: the white squaw on the American frontier. PhD U. of Massachusetts, 1975.

GILLETTE,J.B. *275*
Medusa/Muse: women as images of chaos and order in the writings of Henry Adams and Henry James. PhD Yale U. 1972.

GLADSTEIN,M.R. *276*
The indestructible woman in the works of Faulkner, Hemingway, and Steinbeck. PhD U. of New Mexico, 1973.

GLENN,E.W. *277*
The androgynous woman character in the American novel. PhD U. of Colorado at Boulder, 1980.

GOLDMAN,M. *278*
American women and the Puritan heritage: Anne Hutchinson to Harriet Beecher Stowe. PhD Boston U. Grad. Sch. 1975.

GONSHER,D.A. *279*
Stereotypes of women in contemporary American drama: 1958–1978. PhD City U. of New York, 1980.

GOODENBERGER,M.E.M. *280*
William Faulkner's compleat woman. PhD U. of Nebraska-Lincoln, 1976.

GOULD,D.S. *281*
'Hens that won't sit' women in the novels of Harold Frederic. PhD Pennsylvania State U. 1977.

GRAHAM,R.J. *282*
Concepts of women in American literature, 1813–1871. PhD U. of Pennsylvania, 1973.

GRAHAM,T.R. *283*
Woman as character and symbol in the work of William Carlos Williams. PhD U. of Pennsylvania, 1974.

GRANT,N.M. *284*
The role of women in the fiction of Ernest Hemingway. PhD U. of Denver, 1968.

GRAY,P.K. *285*
The lure of romance and the temptation of feminine sensibility: literary heroines in selected popular and 'serious' American novels, 1895–1915. PhD Emory U. 1981.

GREENWALD,F.T. *286*
The young girls in the novels of W.D. Howells and Henry James. PhD New York U. 1974.

GUEST,C.B. *287*
The position of women as considered by representative American authors since 1800. PhD U. of Wisconsin, 1943.

HAMMER,A.G. *288*
Recitations of the past: identity in novels by Edith Wharton, Ellen Glasgow, and Carson McCullers. PhD U. of California, Davis, 1981.

HASANAIN,A.G.A. *289*
Women in Ernest Hemingway. PhD U. of Toledo, 1981.

HATCH,D.H. *290*
A reader response study of the grotesque in the fiction of Eudora Welty, Flannery O'Connor, and Carson McCullers. PhD U. of Massachusetts, 1982.

HEALY,M. *291*
A study of non-rational elements in the works of Henry Adams as centralized in his attitude toward woman. PhD U. of Wisconsin, 1956.

HENSLEY,D.E. *292*
Jack London's real and fictional women: a study of attributes. PhD Ball State U. 1982.

HERSH,B.B. *293*
The image of employed women in current fiction. EdD New York U. 1978.

HERZOG,K.K.H. *294*
The American Eve and romantic primitivism: images of women and of ethnic or exotic characters in mid-nineteenth-century American novels. PhD U. of North Carolina at Chapel Hill, 1980.

HILL,T.S. *295*
Frank Norris's heroines. PhD U. of Wisconsin, 1960.

HILL,V.L. *296*
Strategy and breadth: the socialist-feminist in American fiction. PhD State U. of New York at Buffalo, 1979.

HOEKSTRA,E.L.J. *297*
The characterization of women in the novels of Charles Brockden Brown. PhD Michigan State U. 1975.

HOERCHNER,S.J. *298*
'I have to keep the two things separate': polarity in women in the contemporary American novel. PhD Emory U. 1973.

HOPKINS,K. *299*
Virgins and whores: the feminine in the works of William Carlos Williams. PhD U. of New Hampshire, 1972.

HORNSTEIN,J. *300*
Literary history of New England women writers: 1630–1800. PhD New York U. 1978.

HOUSE,E.B. *301*
Robert Frost on women and marriage. PhD U. of South Carolina, 1975.

HOUSTON,N.B. *302*
Nathaniel Hawthorne and the eternal feminine. PhD Texas Tech. U. 1965.

HUNT,G.A. **303**
Feminism and the modern family: Howells as domestic realist. PhD Brandeis U. 1976.

IFKOVIC,E.J. *304*
God's country and the woman: the development of an American identity in the popular novel, 1893–1913. PhD U. of Massachusetts, 1972.

INGRAM,E.D. *305*
Black women: literary self-portraits. PhD U. of Oregon, 1980.

JAN-ORNI,C. *306*
The characterization of women in Tennessee Williams' works. PhD U. of Nebraska-Lincoln, 1979.

JESSUP,J.L. *307*
Fate of our feminists: Edith Wharton, Ellen Glasgow and Willa Cather. PhD Vanderbilt U. 1948.

JOHNS,B.A. *308*
The spinster in five New England women regionalists. PhD U. of Detroit, 1979.

JOHNSON,B.V. *309*
The treatment of the negro woman as a major character in American novels, 1900–1950. PhD New York U. 1955.

JONES,A.G. *310*
'Tomorrow is another day': women, men and society in selected fiction of seven Southern women writers. PhD U. of North Carolina at Chapel Hill, 1977.

JONES,R.B. *311*
Symbolist aesthetics in modern American fiction: studies in Gertrude Stein and Jean Toomer. PhD U. of Wisconsin-Madison, 1981.

JOUAY,A. *312*
The treatment of women in the fiction of Ernest Hemingway. MLitt U. of Strathclyde, 1981.

KAMMER,J.H. *313*
Repression, compression and power: six women poets in America, 1860–1960. [Emily Dickinson, H.D., Marianne Moore, Elizabeth Bishop, Sylvia Plath and Denise Leuertov.] DA Carnegie-Mellon U. 1976.

KAYE,F.W. *314*
The roles of women in the literature of the post civil war American frontier. PhD Cornell U. 1973.

KAZMARK,M.E. *315*
The portrayal of women in American theatre, 1925–1930. PhD U. of California, Los Angeles, 1979.

KEDESDY,D.A.L. *316*
Images of women in the American best seller: 1870–1900. PhD Tufts U. 1976.

KELLY,R.G. *317*
Mother was a lady: strategy and order in selected American children's periodicals, 1865–1890. PhD U. of Iowa, 1970.

KENNEDY,P. *318*
The pioneer woman in Middle Western fiction. PhD U. of Illinois at Urbana-Champaign, 1968.

KIMBEL,E. *319*
Chopin, Wharton, Cather and the new American fictional heroine. PhD Temple U. 1980.

KINNEBREW,M.J. *320*
Dialect in the fiction of Carson McCullers, Flannery O'Connor, and Eudora Welty. PhD U. of Houston, 1983.

KOGEN,M. *321*
Howells and the woman question. PhD Southern Illinois U. at Carbondale, 1978.

KOOLISH,L.L. *322*
A whole new poetry beginning here: contemporary American women poets. PhD Stanford U. 1981.

KRAUS,W.K. *323*
A critical survey of the contemporary adolescent-girl problem novel. PhD Southern Illinois U. at Carbondale, 1974.

LADD,M.J. *324*
The feminine perspective: six early American women writers. PhD U. of Delaware, 1982.

LANT,K.M. *325*
Behind a mask: a study of nineteenth-century American fiction by women. PhD U. of Oregon, 1982.

LEDER,P.G. *326*
'Snug contrivances': the classic American novel as reformulated by Kate Chopin, Sarah Orne Jewett, and Edith Wharton. PhD U. of California, Irvine, 1981.

LETTENEY,A.V. *327*
Hawthorne's heroines and popular magazine fiction. PhD U. of Connecticut, 1980.

LEVY,H.F. *328*
No hiding place on earth: the female self in eight modern American women authors. PhD U. of Michigan, 1982.

LEWIS,T.S.W. *329*
Hart Crane's correspondence with his mother and grandmother. PhD Columbia U. 1970.

LEWIS,V.C. *330*
The Mulatto woman as major female character in novels by black women, 1892– 1937. PhD U. of Iowa, 1981.

LINDEROTH,L.W. *331*
The female characters of Ernest Hemingway. PhD Florida State U. 1966.

LYCETTE,R.L. *332*
Diminishing circumferences: feminine responses in fiction to New England decline. PhD Purdue U. 1970.

LYONS,A.W. *333*
Myth and agony: the Southern woman as belle. PhD Bowling Green State U. 1974.

MCALPIN,S. *334*
Enlightening the commonplace: the work of Sarah Orne Jewett, Willa Cather and Ruth Suckow. PhD U. of Pennsylvania, 1971.

MCCADDEN,J.F. 335
The hero's flight from women in the novels of Saul Bellow. PhD Fordham U. 1979.

MCCLURE,C.S. 336
The American Eve: a tragedy of innocence. [Margaret Fuller, Gertrude Atherton, Willa Cather and Kate Chopin.] PhD U. of New Mexico, 1973.

MCDONALD,S.S.W. 337
Writing and identity: autobiographies of American women novelists, 1930–1955. PhD Saint Louis U. 1981.

MCDOWELL,D.E. 338
Women on women: the black women writer of the Harlem renaissance. PhD Purdue U. 1979.

MCELHINEY,A.B. 339
The image of the pioneer woman in the American novel. PhD U. of Denver, 1978.

MCGINITY,S.S. 340
The image of the Spanish-American woman in recent Southwestern fiction. PhD East Texas State U. 1968.

MCGINTY,S.L. 341
The development of the American heroine in the short fiction of Henry James. PhD U. of Denver, 1977.

MACHANN,V.S.B. 342
American perspectives on women's initiations: the mythic and realistic coming to consciousness. PhD U. of Texas at Austin, 1979.

MCKENZIE,B. 343
Region and world: the achievement of American women writers of fiction since 1930. PhD Florida State U. 1963.

MACKINTOSH,E.M. 344
The women characters in the novels of Saul Bellow. PhD Kansas State U. 1979.

MALONE,G.S. 345
The nature and causes of suffering in the fiction of Paula Marshall, Kristin Hunter, Toni Morrison, and Alice Walker. PhD Kent State U. 1979.

MANSFIELD-KELLEY,D. 346
Oliver la Farge and the Indian woman in American literature. PhD U. of Texas at Austin, 1979.

MARSHALL,K.L.K. 347
A study, for oral interpretation, of selected poetry by contemporary American women. PhD Syracuse U. 1978.

MARTIN,G.M. 348
Women in the criticism and fiction of William Dean Howells. PhD U. of Wisconsin-Madison, 1982.

MASSEY,T.M. 349
Faulkner's females: the thematic function of women in the Yoknapatawpha cycle. PhD U. of Nevada, Reno, 1969.

MATTHEWS,B.A. 350
Frontier women as portrayed in the humor of the old southwest. PhD U. of Arkansas, 1979.

MATTON,C.G. 351
The role of women in three of Faulkner's families. PhD Marquette U. 1974.

MELTON,S.L.G. 352
Women and the idea of the feminine in some major works by Henry Adams. PhD Kansas State U. 1980.

MENGERT,G.K. 353
The quest for wholeness in three modern writers. [Eudora Welty, Carson McCullers and Flanney O'Connor.] PhD Emory U. 1978.

MINER,M.M. 354
On the rack: twentieth-century American women's bestsellers. PhD State U. of New York at Buffalo, 1982.

MITCHELL,B.E. 355
Women and the male quester in Herman Melville's *Typee, Mardi* and *Pierre*. PhD Northwestern U. 1979.

MONTGOMERY,J.H. 356
Pygmalion's image: the metamorphosis of the American heroine. PhD Syracuse U. 1971.

MORGAN,E.E. 357
Neo-feminism and modern literature. PhD U. of Pennsylvania, 1972.

MORGAN,P.B. 358
The use of female characters in the fiction of Vladimir Nabokov. MA U. of Wales, Lampeter, 1980.

MORRIS,L.A.F. 359
Women vernacular humorists in nineteenth-century America: Ann Stephens, Frances Whitcher, and Marietta Holley. PhD U. of California, Berkeley, 1978.

MRAZ,D.J. 360
The changing image of female characters in the works of Tennessee Williams. PhD U. of Southern California, 1967.

MUSSELL,K.J. 361
The world of modern gothic fiction: American women and their social myths. PhD U. of Iowa, 1973.

NAULT,M. 362
Women characters in the fiction of Saul Bellow. PhD U. of Birmingham, 1979.

NELSON-CAVE,W. 363
Representative women playwrights of America, 1757–1964. PhD U. of Birmingham, 1977.

NEWTON,S.E. 364
An ornament to her sex: rhetorics of persuasion in early American conduct literature for women and the eighteenth-century American seduction novel. PhD U. of California, Davis, 1976.

NIEMTZOW,A. *365*
The marital whip: literary reactions to the new woman in Hawthorne, James, and Adams. PhD Harvard U. 1973.

NORMAN,R.L. *366*
Autobiographies of American women writers to 1914. PhD U. of Tennessee, 1979.

O'BANNER,B.M. *367*
A study of black heroines in four selected novels (1929–1959) by four black American women novelists: Zora Neale Hurston, Nella Larsen, Paule Marshall, Ann Lane Petry. PhD U. of Southern Illinois at Carbondale, 1981.

OLAUSON,J.L.B. *368*
Representative American women playwrights, 1930–1970: and a study of their characters. PhD U. of Utah, 1976.

OSBORNE,R. *369*
The browning of the flower: a study of the women characters in the novels of Robert Penn Warren. PhD U. of Alabama, 1980.

OWENS,E.S. *370*
The phoenix and the unicorn: a study of the published private writing of May Sarton and Anne Morrow Lindbergh. PhD Ohio State U. 1982.

OYLER,M.M. *371*
An examination of the heroine of the junior novel in America as revealed in selected junior novels, 1850–1960. EdD Columbia U. 1970.

PACKMAN,D.B. *372*
Structures of desire: Vladimir Nabokov's *Lolita, Pale fire* and *Ada*. PhD New York U. 1979.

PAGE,S.R. *373*
Woman in the works of William Faulkner. PhD Duke U. 1969.

PAPPWORTH,J. *374*
The American woman in the mid-nineteenth-century as evinced in the work of Nathaniel Hawthorne and women writers of his acquaintance. DPhil U. of Oxford, 1980.

PARKER,J. *376*
Uneasy survivors: five women writers, 1896–1923. [Sarah Orne Jewett, Mary E. Wilkins Freeman, Willa Cather, Ellen Glasgow, and Edith Wharton.] PhD U. of Utah, 1973.

PARKER,P.L. *377*
The search for autonomy in the works of Kate Chopin, Ellen Glasgow, Carson McCullers, and Shirley Ann Grau. PhD Rice U. 1982.

PARKS,K.I. *378*
Faulkner's women: archetype and metaphor. PhD U. of Pennsylvania, 1980.

PATTERSON,A. *379*
The women of John Steinbeck's novels in the light of humanistic psychology. PhD US International U. 1974.

PEARCE,B.M. *380*
Texas through women's eyes, 1823–1860. PhD U. of Texas at Austin, 1965.

PEONTEK,L.L. *381*
Images of women in Saul Bellow's novels. PhD Saint Louis U. 1980.

PERRY,C.M. *382*
Adolescence, autonomy, and vocation: heroines of *Kunstlerromane* by modern American women. PhD Indiana U. 1982.

PERSON,L.S. *383*
Aesthetic headaches: images of women in American fiction. PhD Indiana U. 1977.

PEVITTS,B.B. *384*
Feminist thematic trends in plays written by women for the American theatre: 1970–1979. Phd Southern Illinois U. at Carbondale, 1980.

POGGI,G.E. *385*
The awakening: the female in business in the twentieth-century American novel. PhD U. of Southern California, 1982.

POPE,D. *386*
The pattern of isolation in contemporary American women's poetry: Louise Bogan, Maxine Kumin, Denise Levertov, Adrienne Rich. PhD U. of Wisconsin-Madison, 1979.

QUART,B. *387*
The treatment of women in the work of three contemporary Jewish-American writers: Mailer, Bellow, and Roth. PhD New York U. 1979.

RECHNITZ,R.M. *388*
Perception, identity and the grotesque: a study of three Southern writers. [Flannery O'Connor, Carson McCullers, Eudora Welty.] PhD Colorado State U. 1967.

REDLE,K.G. *389*
Amy Lowell and Harriet Monroe: their correspondence. PhD Northwestern U. 1967.

REINER,S.L. *390*
'It's love that makes reality reality': women through the eyes of Saul Bellow's protagonists. PhD U. of Cincinnati, 1980.

REIRDON,S.R. *391*
An application of script analysis to four of William Faulkner's women characters. EdD East Texas State U. 1974.

ROBERTS,P.L.B. *392*
The female image in the Caldecott Medal award books. EdD U. of the Pacific, 1975.

ROCCO,C.J. *393*
Flannery O'Connor and Joyce Carol Oates: violence as art. PhD U. of Illinois at Urbana-Champaign, 1975.

ROMINES,M.A. *394*
House, procession, river: domestic ritual in the

fiction of Seven American women, 1877–1972. PhD George Washington U. 1977.

ROSS,M.C. *396*
Moral alues of the American woman as presented in three major American authors. [Hawthorne, James and Faulkner], PhD U. of Texas at Austin, 1964.

ROTUNDO,B.R. *397*
Mrs James T. Fields, hostess and biographer. [Best known for her biographies of Celia Thaxter, Sarah Orne Jewett and Harriet Beecher Stowe.] PhD Syracuse U. 1968.

ROYSTER,B.H. *398*
The ironic vision of four black women novelists: a study of the novels of Jessie Fauset, Nella Larsen, Zora Neale Hurston and Ann Petry. PhD Emory U. 1975.

RUNDLE,M.A. *399*
The concept of the lady in the American novel, 1850–1900. PhD U. of Cincinnati, 1956.

RUSSELL,H.J. *400*
Social comment as depicted in the plays of American woman dramatists. PhD U. of Denver, 1959.

SAMUELSON,J.W. *401*
Patterns of survival: four American women writers and the proletarian novel. [Edith Summers Kelley, Agnes Smedley, Tillie Olsen, Harriette Arnow.] PhD Ohio State U. 1982.

SANDERS,S.L.C. *402*
Admiration and condemnation: Washington Irving's ambivalence toward women and marriage in his work. PhD U. of Georgia, 1981.

SATTERWHITE,J.N. *403*
Godey's lady's book and fiction 1830–1850. PhD Vanderbilt U. 1961.

SCARBOROUGH,M.N. *404*
Songs of Eleusis: the quest for self in the poetry of Sylvia Plath, Anne Sexton and Adrienne Rich. PhD Washington U. 1978.

SCHAFFER,P.W. *405*
The position of women in society as reflected in serious American drama from 1890 to 1928. PhD Stanford U. 1965.

SCHREIBER,S.O. *406*
Art and life: the novels of black women. PhD U. of New Mexico, 1981.

SCOTT,S.M. *407*
Thematic study of the writings of Puritan women from the time of the original settlers to 1770. PhD Southern Illinois U. at Carbondale, 1984.

SEE,F.G. *408*
metaphoric and metonymic imagery in nineteenth-century American fiction. Harriet Beecher Stowe, Rebecca Harding Davis, and Harold Frederic. PhD U. of California, Berkeley, 1967.

SEIDEL,K.L. *409*
The Southern Belle: her fall from the pedestal in fiction of the Southern renaissance. PhD U. of Maryland, 1976.

SHANNON,A.W. *410*
Women on the color line: subversion of female stereotypes in the fiction of Cable, King and Chopin. PhD U. of Nebraska-Lincoln, 1979.

SHINN,T.J. *411*
A study of women characters in contemporary American fiction 1940–1970. PhD Purdue U. 1972.

SIDES,S.D. *412*
Women and slaves: an interpretation based on the writings of Southern women. PhD U. of North Carolina at Chapel Hill, 1969.

SILVERSTEIN,L.R. *413*
The American heroine. PhD Harvard U. 1971.

SINCLAIR,S.D. *414*
Hawthorne's 'New Revelation': the female Christ. PhD Duke U. 1981.

SKILLMAN,B.L. *415*
The characterization of American women in twentieth-century American literature for children. PhD Ohio U. 1975.

SMITH,J.R. *416*
Hawthorne's women and weeds: what really happens in the garden. PhD Indiana U. 1979.

SMITH,J.T. *417*
Feminism in the novels of Floyd Dell. PhD U. of Texas at Dallas, 1970.

SNOW,K. *418*
Feminism and dualism: the history of an idea. PhD U. of Kentucky, 1979.

SODOWSKY,A.L. *419*
The images of women in the novels of Sinclair Lewis. PhD Oklahoma State U. 1977.

SPIGEL,H.T. *420*
The sacred image and the new truth: a study in Hawthorne's women. PhD U. of Washington, 1969.

SPITZER,M. *421*
Hawthorne's women: female influences on the life and fiction of Nathaniel Hawthorne. PhD New York U. 1974.

STAID,M.P. *422*
The academic woman in the American college novel. PhD Arizona State U. 1975.

STANTON,R.B. *423*
The significance of the women in Hawthorne's American romances. PhD Indiana U. 1953.

STEPHENS,J.L. *424*
The central female characters in the Pulitzer Prize plays, 1918 to 1949. PhD Kent State U. 1977.

STOCKARD,J.L. 425
The role of the American black woman in folktales: an interdisciplinary study of identification and interpretation. PhD Tulane U. 1980.

STRATTON,K.A.A. 426
Woman as B: woman as A. PhD Indiana U. of Pennsylvania, 1982.

STUECHER,D.D. 427
Double jeopardy: nineteenth-century German American women writers. PhD U. of Minnesota, 1981.

SUMNER,M.R. 428
Women in business and office occupations as depicted in the American novel, 1890–1950. EdD Rutgers U. 1977.

TALBOTT,B.M. 429
The material ideal: women as symbols of success in selected American fiction. PhD U. of Wisconsin-Milwaukee, 1978.

TALIAFERRO,J.H. 430
the emergence of the political female character as revealed in selected American plays from 1762 to 1850. PhD New York U. 1976.

TAYLOR,J.K. 431
Patterns of destruction in several women characters in American fiction since 1950. PhD Indiana U. of Pennsylvania, 1978.

TAYLOR,J.N. 432
The struggle for work and love: working women in American novels, 1890–1925. PhD U. of California, Berkeley, 1977.

THETFORD,M.L. 433
Vocational roles for women in junior fiction. EdD Rutgers U. 1974.

THOMAS,M.A. 434
An overview of Miss Anne: white women as seen by black playwrights. PhD Florida State U. 1973.

THOMAS,R. 435
Dominated, isolated, and submerged women in the fiction of Anais Nin and Carson McCullers. PhD U. of Utah, 1976.

THORESON,T.R. 436
Women in the writings of Mark Twain. PhD Northwestern U. 1976.

THORNTON,P.E. 437
The prison of gender: sexual roles in major American novels of the 1920s. PhD U. of New Brunswick, 1976.

TITUS,C.F. 438
Depiction of women in the novels of William Dean Howells. PhD U. of Missouri-Columbia, 1955.

TOMLINSON,D.O. 439
Women in the writing of Charles Brockden Brown: a study in the development of an author's thought. PhD U. of North Carolina at Chapel Hill, 1974.

TOTH,S.E.A. 440
More than local color: a re-appraisal of Rose Terry Cooke, Mary Wilkins Freeman and Alice Brown. PhD U. of Minnesota, 1969.

TURNBULL,M.T. 441
Women in the theater in the novel: 1880–1915. PhD U. of Chicago, 1978.

TURNER,S.H.R. 442
Images of black women in the plays of black female playwrights, 1950–1975. PhD Bowling Green State U. 1982.

TWIGG,C.A. 443
The social role of Faulkner's women: a materialist interpretation. PhD State U. of New York at Buffalo, 1978.

UDOSEN,W.B. 444
Image of the black woman in black American drama: 1900 to 1970. EdD East Texas State U. 1979.

UBA,G.R. 445
Native grains: marriage and family in the fiction of W.D. Howells. PhD U. of California, Los Angeles, 1982.

VARGA-COLEY,B.J. 446
The novels of black American women. PhD State U. of New York at Stony Brook, 1981.

VOGELBAUM,A.D.van O. 447
The new heroines: the emergence of sexuality in the treatment of the American fictional heroine, 1890–1900. PhD Tulane U. 1978.

VON TORNOW,G.J. 448
The heroine in American drama and theatre down to the Civil War and her relation to life and the novels of the times. PhD Cornell U. 1945.

VOTH,R.A. 449
The lyric strain: a study of the heroine of the Old South. PhD George Washington U. 1970.

VUNOVICH,N.W. 450
The women in the plays of Eugene O'Neill. PhD U. of Kansas, 1966.

WADE-GAYLES,G.J. 451
The narrow space and the dark enclosure: race and sex in the lives of black women in selected novels written by black women, 1946–1976. PhD Emory U. 1981.

WALKER,C.L. 452
The women's tradition in American poetry. PhD Brandeis U. 1973.

WALOWIT,K.M. 453
Wonder woman: enigmatic heroine of American popular culture. PhD U. of California, Berkeley, 1974.

WARD,H.M. 454
The black woman as character: images in the American novel, 1852–1953. PhD U. of Texas at Austin, 1977.

WARREN,J.W. 455
The American Narcissus and the woman as a non-person: a study in nineteenth- century American literature. PhD Columbia U. 1981.

WASHINGTON,M.H. 456
Black-eyed Susans: classic stories by and about black women. PhD U. of Detroit, 1976.

WASHINGTON,S.M. 457
An annotated bibliography of black women biographies and autobiographies for secondary school students. PhD U. of Illinois at Urbana-Champaign, 1980.

WASSERSTROM,W. 458
Heiress of all the ages. PhD Columbia U. 1951.

WATERS,M.A. 459
The role of women in Faulkner's *Yoknapatawpha*. EdD Columbia U. Teachers' Coll. 1975.

WATSON,C.M. 460
The novels of Afro-American women: concerns and themes: 1891–1965. PhD George Washington U. 1978.

WEISS,J. 461
The feminine assertion: women in the world of William Carlos Williams. PhD U. of California, Los Angeles, 1973.

WELLING,E.B. 462
Edith Wharton and Ellen Glasgow: a critique of the small society. PhD Harvard U. 1977.

WERLOCK,A.H.P. 463
From Margaret Powers Mahon to Linda Snopes Kohl: an examination of 'incorrigibly individual' women in the novels of William Faulkner. DPhil U. of Sussex 1981.

WEST,B.J. 464
Attitudes toward American women as reflected in American literature between the two world wars. PhD Cornell U. 1954.

WHITE,B.A. 465
Growing up female: adolescent girlhood in American literature. PhD U. of Wisconsin-Madison, 1974.

WHITE,I.B. 466
The American heroine, 1789–1899: nonconformity and death. PhD U. of Kentucky, 1978.

WHITE,R.L. 467
Fitzgerald's women. MA U. of Kent, 1974.

WILEY,C.G. 468
A study of the American women as she is presented in the American drama of the nineteen-twenties. PhD U. of New Mexico, 1957.

WILKINS,J.W. 469
Robert Anderson's women: their ritual role. PhD Ohio State U. 1976.

WILLETT,M. 470
Salem witchcraft in American literature. PhD Brandeis U. 1959.

WILLIAMS,D.L. 471
William Faulkner and the mythology of woman. PhD U. of Massachusetts, 1973.

WILLIAMS,M. 472
The pastoral in New England local color: Celia Thaxter, Sarah Orne Jewett, Alice Brown. PhD Stanford U. 1972.

WILSON,B.H. 473
Quiet realism: women writers in the William Dean Howells' tradition. PhD U. of North Carolina at Chapel Hill, 1965.

WOLF,C.S.B. 474
A study of prose by nineteenth-century Texas women. PhD Texas Tech. U. 1982.

WRIGHT,D.C. 475
Visions and revisions of the 'New Woman' in American realistic fiction from 1880 to 1920: a study in authorial attitudes. PhD U. of North Carolina at Chapel Hill, 1971.

WUNSCH,M.A. 476
Walls of Jade: images of men, women and family in second generation Asian- American fiction and autobiography. PhD U. of Hawaii, 1977.

WYMAN,M. 477
Women in the American realistic novel, 1860–1893: literary reflection of social fact. PhD Radcliffe Coll. 1950.

YACO,R.M. 478
Suffering women: feminine masochism in novels by American women. PhD U. of Michigan, 1975.

ZAHLER,W.P. 479
The husband and wife relationship in American drama from 1919 to 1939. PhD Kent State U. 1973.

ZASTROW,S.V.H. 480
The structure of selected plays by American women playwrights: 1920–1970. PhD Northwestern U. 1975.

Individual writers

Louisa May Alcott

ALBERGHENE,J.M. 481
From Alcott to *Abel's island*: the image of the artist in American children's literature. PhD Brown U. 1980.

DIAMANT,S.E. 482
Louisa May Alcott and the woman problem. PhD Cornell U. 1974.

GRUBEL,M.W. *483*
A comparative analysis and evaluation of sex roles exemplified in certain juvenile novels about family life. [Includes *Little women*] PhD New York U. 1968.

MCCURRY,N.A. *484*
Concepts of childrearing and schooling in the March novels of Louisa May Alcott. PhD Northwestern U. 1976.

MARSELLA,J.A. *485*
Fulfilling destiny: the world of children and women in the short stories of Louisa May Alcott. PhD U. of Hawaii, 1981.

SHULL,M.I.S. *486*
The novels of Louisa May Alcott as commentary on the American family. PhD Bowling Green State U. 1975.

Bess Streeter Aldrich

FOREMAN,R.J. *487*
The fiction of Bess Streeter Aldrich. DA Drake U. 1982.

Harriette Arnow

GRIFFIN,J.R. *489*
Fiddle tunes, foxes and a piece of land: region and character in Harriette Arnow's Kentucky trilogy. PhD U. of Nebraska-Lincoln, 1982.

Gertrude Atherton

FORREY,C.D. *490*
Gertrude Atherton and the new woman. PhD Yale U. 1971.

Mary Hunter Austin

ALTMAN,D.J. *491*
Mary Hunter Austin and the roles of women. PhD State U. of New York at Albany, 1979.

BALLARD,R.G. *492*
Mary Austin's *Earth horizon*: the imperfect circle. PhD Claremont Grad. Sch. 1977.

MCCLANAHAN,M.H. *493*
Aspects of southwestern regionalism in the prose work of Mary Austin. PhD U. of Pittsburgh, 1941.

THOROUGHGOOD,I.T. *494*
Mary Hunter Austin, interpreter of the western scene, 1888–1906. PhD U. of California, Los Angeles, 1950.

WATERS,L.W. *495*
Mary Austin as nature essayist. PhD Texas Tech. U. 1974.

WYNN,D.T. *496*
A critical study of the writings of Mary Hunter Austin (1868–1934). PhD New York U. 1940.

Elizabeth Bishop

BRYAN,N.L. *497*
A place for the genuine: Elizabeth Bishop and the factual tradition in modern American poetry. PhD Claremont Grad. Sch. 1973.

ESTESS,S.P. *498*
Discoveries of travel: Elizabeth Bishop and the Poetry of Process. PhD Syracuse U. 1976.

GREENHALGH,A.M. *499*
Elizabeth Bishop's primary vocabulary: a lexical study and concordance. PhD U. of Pennsylvania, 1982.

LUDINIGSON,C.R. *500*
Fire buried in the mirror: the poetry of Elizabeth Bishop. PhD Northern Illinois U. 1978.

MULLEN,K.R. *501*
Manipulation of perspective in the poetry of Elizabeth Bishop. PhD U. of Texas at Austin, 1977.

MULLEN,R.F. *502*
The Map-Maker's colors: a study of the form and language of Elizabeth Bishop's poetry. PhD Columbia U. 1979.

NEWMAN,A.R. *503*
Elizabeth Bishop: a study of form and theme. PhD U. of South Carolina, 1974.

ROBINSON,P.L. *504*
The textures of reality: a study of the poetry of Elizabeth Bishop. PhD Rutgers U. 1978.

SCHWARTZ,L. *505*
'That sense of constant readjustment': Elizabeth Bishop's 'North and South'. PhD Harvard U. 1976.

TRAVISANO,T.J. *506*
Elizabeth Bishop: introspective traveler. PhD U. of Virginia, 1981.

WYLLIE,D.E. *507*
A critical study of Elizabeth Bishop's poetry. PhD Bowling Green State U. 1977.

Louise Bogan

COOKSON,S. *508*
'All has been translated into treasure': the art of Louise Bogan. PhD U. of Connecticut, 1980.

RIDGEWAY,J.C. *509*
The poetry of Louise Bogan. PhD U. of California, Riverside, 1977.

Kay Boyle

GADO,F. *510*
Kay Boyle: from the aesthetics of exile to the polemics of return. PhD Duke U. 1968.

JACKSON,B.K. *511*
The achievement of Kay Boyle. PhD U. of Florida, 1964.

Anne Bradstreet

DURR,J.C.S. *512*
Anne Bradstreet in the tradition of English women writers. PhD U. of Mississippi, 1978.

GARCIA-ROUPHAIL,M. *513*
Anne Bradstreet, her poetry, and the policies of exclusion: a study of the developing sense of poetic purpose. PhD Ohio State U. 1982.

ROWLETTE,E.J.H. *514*
The works of Anne Bradstreet. PhD Boston U. 1964.

WHITE,A.S. *515*
The poetry of Anne Bradstreet. PhD U. of California, Los Angeles, 1962.

WHITE,E.W. *516*
A study of the life and works of Anne Bradstreet, 1612–1672. BLitt U. of Oxford, 1953.

Gwendolyn Brooks

HANSELL,W.H. *517*
Positive themes in the poetry of four negroes. PhD U. of Wisconsin, 1972.

HEMMINGWAY,B.S. *518*
'The universal wears contemporary clothing': the works of Gwendolyn Brooks. PhD Florida State U. 1981.

SCHUCHAT,M.J.S. *519*
Gwendolyn Elizabeth Brooks: a Janus poet. PhD Texas Woman's U. 1982.

SHAW,H.B. *520*
Social themes in the poetry of Gwendolyn Brooks. PhD U. of Illinois at Urbana-Champaign, 1972.

Alice Brown

LANGILL,E.D. *521*
Alice Brown: a critical study. PhD U. of Wisconsin-Madison, 1975.

Frances Hodgson Burnett

THREADGOLD,A.R. *522*
The adult novels of Frances Hodgson Burnett. MA U. of Birmingham, 1977.

Roane Fleming Byrnes

PREVOST,V.L. *523*
Roane Fleming Byrnes: a critical biography. PhD U. of Mississippi, 1974.

Hortense Calisher

ISLAS,A. *524*
The work of Hortense Calisher: on middle ground. PhD Stanford U. 1971.

Rachel Carson

JOHNSON,K. *525*
The lost Eden: the new world in America nature writing. [Includes a study of *Silent spring*]. PhD U. of New Mexico, 1973.

Willa Cather

ADAMS,T.S. *526*
Six novels of Willa Cather: a thematic study. PhD Ohio State U. 1961.

ALLEN,D.A. *527*
Willa Cather: a critical study. PhD U. of Denver, 1972.

ARNOLD,M. *528*
Self-division and self-unity in the novels of Willa Cather. PhD U. of Wisconsin, 1968.

BAKER,B.P. *529*
Image and symbol in selected works of Willa Cather. PhD Texas Christian U. 1968.

BARBA,S.R. *530*
Willa Cather: a feminist study. PhD U. of New Mexico, 1973.

BASH,J.R. *531*
Willa Cather: a study in primitivism. PhD U. of Illinois at Urbana- Champaign, 1954.

BOHKLE,L.B. *532*
'Seeking is finding': Willa Cather and religion. PhD U. of Nebraska- Lincoln, 1982.

CHARLES,Sister P.D. *533*
Love and death in the novels of Willa Cather. PhD U. of Notre Dame, 1965.

COOPER,C.B. *534*
Willa Cather: the nature of evil and its purgation. PhD Florida State U. 1969.

CREUTZ,K.E. *535*
The genesis of Willa Cather's *The Song of the lark*. PhD U. of California, Los Angeles, 1968.

CURTIN,W.M. *536*
The relation of ideas and structure in the novels of Willa Cather. PhD U. of Wisconsin, 1959.

DANIELSON,J.C. *537*
A 'sense of a sense' of place in the works of Willa Cather. PhD Bowling Green State U. 1968.

DAUGHADAY,C.H. *538*
Willa Cather's happy experimenting: artistic fusion of themes and structure in the novels of Willa Cather. PhD U. of Kentucky, 1967.

DINN,J.N. *539*
'Only two or three human stories': recurrent patterns of action in the major fiction of Willa Cather. PhD U. of Notre Dame, 1973.

EICHORN,H.B. *540*
Willa Cather: stranger in three worlds. PhD Stanford U. 1968.

FINESTONE,H. 542
Willa Cather's apprenticeship. PhD U. of Chicago, 1954.

FLEMING,P.J. 543
The integrated self: sexuality and the double in Willa Cather's fiction. PhD Boston U. Grad. Sch. 1974.

FOX,C.M. 544
Revelation of character in five Cather novels. PhD U. of Colorado, 1963.

GEHRKI,B.A. 545
Willa Cather's families: fictions and facts in her Plains' writings. PhD U. of Nebraska-Lincoln, 1981.

GERBER,P.L. 546
Willa Cather: novelist of ideas. PhD U. of Iowa, 1952.

GIANNONE,R.J. 547
Music in Willa Cather's fiction. PhD U. of Notre Dame, 1964.

GREEN,G.W. 548
Elements of form in the novels of Willa Cather. PhD Harvard U. 1956.

HARRIS,R.C. 549
Energy and order in Willa Cather's novels. PhD U. of North Carolina at Chapel Hill, 1974.

HUMES,D.B. 550
The importance of the solitary individual:a study of solipsism in Willa Cather's protagonists. PhD Columbia U. 1980.

KRAUSE,J.B. 551
Self-actualizing women in Willa Cather's Prairie novels. PhD U. of Nebraska-Lincoln, 1978.

LAMBERT,M.E. 552
Theme and craftsmanship in Willa Cather's novels. PhD U. of North Carolina at Chapel Hill, 1965.

LAUERMAN,D.A. 553
The garden and the city in the fiction of Willa Cather. PhD Indiana U. 1972.

LEWISON,N.V. 554
The achievement of Willa Cather. PhD U. of Iowa, 1944.

MACHEN,M.R. 555
Home as motivation and metaphor in the works of Willa Cather. PhD U. of New Mexico, 1979.

MCLAY,C.N. 556
Willa Cather: the search for order in her major fiction. PhD U. of Alberta, 1970.

MASSEY,D.G. 557
Simplicity with suggestiveness in Willa Cather's revised and republished fiction. PhD Drew U. 1979.

MOSELEY,A. 558
The voyage perilous: Willa Cather's mythic quest. PhD U. of Oklahoma, 1974.

MURPHY,M.W. 559
The complex past in Willa Cather's novels of the twenties. PhD U. of Texas at Austin, 1974.

O'BRIEN,S. 560
Stronger vessels: Willa Cather and her pioneer heroines. PhD Harvard U. 1975.

O'CONNOR,M.A. 561
Willa Cather and the short story. PhD U. of California, Davis, 1971.

PETTY,A.M. 562
Biblical allusions in the fiction of Willa Cather. PhD U. of Nebraska, 1973.

PLUNKETT,K.M. 563
The symbol of the frontier in selected novels of Willa Cather. PhD U. of Rhode Island, 1982.

PRENDERGAST,A.F. 564
One of ours: Willa Cather's successful failure. PhD U. of Pittsburgh, 1971.

RANDALL,J.H. 565
Willa Cather's search for value: a critical and historical study of her fiction. PhD U. of Minnesota, 1957.

ROSS,J. 566
Willa Cather and the realistic movement in American fiction. PhD U. of Iowa, 1960.

SCHMITTLEIN,A.E. 567
Willa Cather's novels: an evolving art. PhD U. of Pittsburgh, 1962.

SCHNEIDER,L. 568
Willa Cather's 'land-philosophy' in her novels and short stories. PhD U. of Notre Dame, 1967.

SCHROETER,J. 569
Willa Cather's literary reputation. PhD U. of Chicago, 1959.

SCOTT,J.C. 570
Between fiction and history: an exploration into Willa Cather's *Death comes for the Archbishop*. PhD U. of New Mexico, 1980.

SELTZER,S. 571
The family in the novels of Willa Cather. PhD St. John's U. 1982.

SMITH,A.H. 572
The persistent hardness of life in Willa Cather's major fiction: a study of her dominant stays against the hard realities. PhD State U. of New York at Albany, 1971.

THOMPSON,B.L.A. 573
Continuity in the work of Willa Cather. PhD U. of Nebraska-Lincoln, 1974.

THORBERG,R. 574
Willa Cather: a critical interpretaion. PhD Cornell U. 1954.

THROCKMORTON,J.L. *575*
Willa Cather: artistic theory and practice. PhD U. of Kansas, 1954.

THRONE,M.E. *576*
The two selves: duality in Willa Cather's protagonists and themes. PhD Ohio State U. 1969.

TOLER,C. *577*
Man as creator of art and civilization in the works of Willa Cather. PhD U. of Notre Dame, 1965.

VIERNEISEL,K.H. *578*
Fugitive matriarchy: Willa Cather's life and art. PhD U. of Chicago, 1977.

WHITE,H.N. *579*
Willa Cather's apprenticeship: a collection of her writings in the *Nebraska state journal* 1891–1895. PhD U. of Texas at Austin, 1955.

WHITTINGTON,C.C. *580*
The use of inset narratives in the novels of Willa Cather. PhD Vanderbilt U. 1972.

YONGUE,P.L. *581*
The immense design: a study of Willa Cather's creative process. PhD U. of California, Los Angeles, 1972.

ZEIGEL,J.S. *582*
The romanticism of Willa Cather. PhD Claremont Grad. Sch. 1967.

ZWICK,R.C. *583*
The agrarian ethos in Willa Cather's Nebraska stories and novels: from memory to vision. PhD U. of Nebraska-Lincoln, 1982.

Mary Hartwell Catherwood

PRICE,R. *584*
A critical biography of Mrs Mary Hartwell Catherwood: a study of middle western regional authorship, 1847–1902. PhD Ohio State U. 1943.

Elizabeth Margaret Chandler

JONES,M.P. *585*
Elizabeth Margaret Chandler: poet, essayist, abolitionist. PhD U. of Toledo, 1981.

Mary Ellen Chase

DODGE,E.C. *586*
A critical study of the writings of Mary Ellen Chase. PhD Boston U. 1963.

Mary Boykin Chestnut

MUHLENFELD,E.S. *587*
Mary Boykin Chestnut: the writer and her work. PhD U. of South Carolina, 1979.

Lydia Maria Child

LAMBERTON,B.G. *588*
A biography of Lydia Maria Child. PhD U. of Maryland, 1953.

TAYLOR,L.C. *589*
To make men free: an interpretative study of Lydia Maria Child. PhD Lehigh U. 1956.

Kate Chopin

ARNER,R.D. *590*
Music from a farther room: a study of the fiction of Kate Chopin. PhD Pennsylvania State U. 1970.

BONNER,T. *591*
A critical study of the fiction of Kate Chopin: the formal elements. PhD Tulane U. 1975.

BUTLER,H.S. *592*
Sexuality in the fiction of Kate Chopin. PhD Duke U. 1979.

CLATWORTHY,J.M. *593*
Kate Chopin: the inward life which questions. PhD State U. of New York at Buffalo, 1979.

DYER,J.A. *594*
Kate Chopin's use of natural correlatives as psychological symbols in her fiction. PhD Kent State U. 1977.

GARITTA,A.P. *595*
The critical reputation of Kate Chopin. PhD U. of North Carolina at Greensboro, 1978.

KOLOSKI,B.J. *596*
Kate Chopin and the search for a code of behavior. PhD U. of Arizona, 1972.

LALLY,J.M. *597*
Kate Chopin: four studies. PhD U. of Utah, 1973.

LATTIN,S.P.H. *598*
Method and vision in Kate Chopin's fiction. PhD U. of Kentucky, 1977.

MARTIN,R.A. *599*
The fictive world of Kate Chopin. PhD Northwestern U. 1971.

PETERSEN,P.J. *600*
The fiction of Kate Chopin. PhD U. of New Mexico, 1972.

RANKIN,D. *601*
Kate Chopin and her Creole stories. PhD U. of Pennsylvania, 1932.

ROUMM,P.G. *602*
Portraits of suffering womanhood in representative nineteenth-century American novels: the contribution of Kate Chopin. PhD Kent State U. 1977.

VAN SITTERT,B.C. *603*
Social institutions and biological determinism in the fictional world of Kate Chopin. PhD Arizona State U. 1975.

SKAGGS,P.D. 604
A woman's place: the search for identity in Kate Chopin's female characters. PhD Texas A&M U. 1972.

TOTH,E. 605
That outward existence which conforms: Kate Chopin and literary convention. PhD Johns Hopkins U. 1975.

Mary Colum

RIMO,P.A. 606
Mary Colum: woman of letters. PhD U. of Delaware, 1982.

Rose Terry Cooke

SMITH,R.L. 607
'These poor weak souls': Rose Terry Cooke's presentation of men and women who were converts to the social gospel in the gilded age. PhD U. of Wisconsin-Milwaukee, 1978.

Susan Fenimore Cooper

KURTH,R.T. 608
Susan Fenimore Cooper: a study of her life and works. PhD Fordham U. 1974.

Adelaide Crapsey

SMITH,S.S. 609
The poems of Adelaide Crapsey: a critical edition with an introduction and notes. PhD U. of Rochester, 1972.

Rachel Crothers

BALI,O.P. 610
The treatment of marriage in the plays of Rachel Crothers. PhD Miami U. 1979.

WILLIAMS,M. 611
The changing role of the woman as represented in selected plays by Rachel Crothers: 1899–1937. PhD U. of Denver, 1971.

Mollie E. Moore Davis

WILKINSON,C.W. 612
The broadening stream: the life and literary career of Mollie E. Moore Davis. PhD U. of Illinois, 1947.

Rebecca Harding Davis

SHEAFFER,H.W. 613
Rebecca Harding Davis: pioneer realist. PhD U. of Pennsylvania, 1948.

Sidonie de la Houssaye

PERRET,J.J. 614
A critical study of the life and writings of Sidonie de la Houssaye, with special emphasis on the unpublished works. PhD Louisiana State U. 1966.

Emily Dickinson

See also **1** 42, 81.

AHRENS,K.L. 615
The function of religious imagery in the poetry of Emily Dickinson. PhD Fordham U. 1973.

ANSELMO,P.N. 616
Renunciation in the poems and letters of Emily Dickinson. PhD U. of Notre Dame, 1965.

ARP,T.R. 617
Dramatic poses in the poetry of Emily Dickinson. PhD Stanford U. 1962.

BARKER,W.B. 618
Lunacy of light: Emily Dickinson and the female tradition. PhD U. of California, Davis, 1981.

BRETZ,A.C. 619
Blossom of the brain: religious experience in the poetry of Emily Dickinson. PhD U. of Chicago, 1973.

BUCKINGHAM,W.J. 620
Emily Dickinson: an annotated bibliography. PhD Indiana U. 1971.

CAMERON,S. 621
Emily Dickinson's poetry: a study of tone. PhD Brandeis U. 1973.

CAPPS,J.L. 622
Emily Dickinson's reading, 1836–1886: a study of the sources of her poetry. PhD U. of Pennsylvania, 1963.

CARTER,C.W. 623
'In sumptuous solitude': a study of method and design in the love poems of Emily Dickinson. PhD U. of North Carolina at Chapel Hill, 1972.

CHALIFF,C. 624
Emily Dickinson against the world: an interpretation of the poet's life and work. PhD New York U. 1967.

CHAPPELL,D.L. 625
The selection of Emily Dickinson's poems in college textbooks, anthologies, 1890–1976. PhD U. of Tennessee, 1979.

COGGESHALL,R.H. 626
Emily Dickinson: the problem poems. PhD U. of North Carolina at Chapel Hill, 1978.

COPPLE,L.B. 627
Three related themes of hunger and thirst, homelessness, and obscurity as symbols of privation, renunciation and compensation in the poems of Emily Dickinson. PhD U. of Michigan, 1954.

CRENSHAW,B.T. *628*
A fairer house than prose: the poems of Emily Dickinson. PhD U. of California, Irvine, 1980.

CROSTHWAITE,J.F. *629*
'Confident despair': some aspects of theology implicit in the poetry of Emily Dickinson. PhD Duke U. 1972.

DAVIS,W.F. *630*
The art of peace: the moral vision of Emily Dickinson. PhD Yale U. 1964.

DI SALVO,L.P. *631*
The arrested syllable: a study of the death poetry of Emily Dickinson. PhD U. of Denver, 1965.

DOYLE,C.M. *632*
The 'Experiment of Green': Emily Dickinson's evolving concept of nature. PhD Kent State U. 1973.

EDMUNDS,L.E. *633*
Emily Dickinson's wonderland: the uses of fantasy in her poetry. PhD Pennsylvania State U. 1979.

FAST,R.R. *634*
Emily Dickinson's art of evanescence. PhD U. of Minnesota, 1979.

FEIT,J. *635*
'Another way to see': Dickinson and her English romantic precursors. PhD Yale U. 1974.

FINKELSTEIN,M.R.B. *636*
Emily Dickinson and the practice of poetry. PhD State U. of New York at Stony Brook, 1970.

FLES,R.A. *637*
Round the steep air: visual and kinesthetic imagery in the poetry of Emily Dickinson. PhD Michigan State U. 1972.

FLICK,R.G. *638*
Emily Dickinson: mystic and skeptic. PhD U. of Florida, 1967.

FORD,T.W. *639*
The theme of death in the poetry of Emily Dickinson. PhD U. of Texas at Austin, 1959.

FRANK,B. *640*
The wiles of words: ambiguity in Emily Dickinson's poetry. PhD U. of Pittsburgh, 1965.

FRANK,E. *641*
Perception of an object: varieties of lyrical form in the poetry of Emily Dickinson. PhD U. of California, Berkeley, 1973.

FRANKLIN,R.W. *642*
Editing Emily Dickinson. PhD Northwestern U. 1965.

FREDERICKSON,C.A. *643*
Emily Dickinson: a word made flesh. PhD State U. of New York at Binghamton, 1980.

FREEMAN,M.H. *644*
Emily Dickinson's prosody: a study in metrics. PhD U. of Massachusetts, 1972.

GALLOWAY,E.W. *645*
Herself herself diversify: Dickinson's compositional choices. PhD Boston U. Grad. Sch. 1982.

GARBOWSKY,M.M. *646*
Emily Dickinson's literary community. PhD Drew U. 1979.

GELPI,A.J. *647*
The business of circumference: the mind and art of Emily Dickinson. PhD Harvard U. 1962.

GIMMESTAD,N.C. *648*
Lamps and lenses: Emily Dickinson and her adolescent audience. PhD U. of Michigan, 1972.

GOUDIE,A.K. *649*
'The earth has many keys': a study of Emily Dickinson's responses to nature. PhD Indiana U. 1969.

GREENE,E.P. *650*
The splintered crown: a study of Eve and Emily Dickinson. PhD U. of Minnesota, 1969.

GREGOR,N. *651*
The luxury of doubt: a study of the relationship between imagery and theme in Emily Dickinson's poetry. PhD U. of New Mexico, 1965.

GVERRA,J.G. *652*
Emily Dickinson's metaphoric art. PhD Purdue U. 1981.

GUTHRIE,J.R. *653*
'Compound vision' in the poetry of Emily Dickinson. PhD State U. of New York at Buffalo, 1979.

HAENNI,C.H. *654*
The associative mind of Emily Dickinson: color imagery, fascicle unity, and psychological continuity. PhD Florida State U. 1978.

HAGER,J.S. *655*
A holistic reading of Emily Dickinson's poetry. PhD U. of North Carolina at Chapel Hill, 1982.

HALL,M.L. *656*
The relation of love and death in the poetry of Emily Dickinson. PhD Loyola U. of Chicago, 1971.

HARDY,M.C. *657*
A word made flesh: Emily Dickinson's poetic strategies. PhD U. of Washington, 1980.

HIGGINS,D.J.M. *658*
Portrait of Emily Dickinson: the poet and her prose. PhD Columbia U. 1961.

JASTER,F. *659*
The illusions of time in the poetry of Emily Dickinson. PhD Tulane U. 1977.

JOHNSON,G.R. *660*
Emily Dickinson: perception and the poet's quest. PhD Emory U. 1979.

JONES,B.H. *661*
'Experience is the Angled Road': patterns of spiritual experience in the poetry of Emily Dickinson. PhD Bryn Mawr Coll. 1972.

JONES,R.R. *662*
Emily Dickinson's flood subject: immortality. PhD Northwestern U. 1960.

KAPPEL,L. *663*
Emily Dickinson and the private vision. PhD Indiana U. 1972.

KARLSON,K.J. *664*
Jamaicas of remembrance: Emily Dickinson and the female experience in America. PhD U. of Minnesota, 1980.

KELLY,L.K. *665*
A concordance of Emily Dickinson's poems. PhD Pennsylvania State U. 1951.

KHER,I.N. *666*
The landscape of absence: Emily Dickinson's poetry. PhD U. of Alberta, 1970.

KNOX,H.M. *667*
The alien dimension: a study of metaphor and metonymy in the poetry of Emily Dickinson. PhD U. of California, Berkeley, 1979.

KRIESBERG,R.M. *668*
The poetry of Emily Dickinson. PhD New York U. 1965.

LAIR,R.L. *669*
Emily Dickinson's fracture of grammar. PhD Ohio State U. 1966.

LAMBERT,R.G. *670*
The prose of a poet: a critical study of Emily Dickinson's letters. PhD U. of Pittsburgh, 1968.

LEONARD,D.J.N. *671*
Emily Dickinson: the weight of consciousness. PhD U. of Wisconsin- Madison, 1981.

LILLIEDAHL,A.M. *672*
Emily Dickinson in Europe: her literary reputation in selected countries. PhD U. of Houston, 1979.

MCINTOSH,M.M. *673*
Emily Dickinson's poems about pain: a study of interrelated moral, theological, and linguistic freedoms. PhD Harvard U. 1967.

MANN,J.S. *674*
The leashed serpent: a study of Emily Dickinson's poetry. PhD U. of Pennsylvania, 1972.

MARCUS,M. *675*
Nature symbolism in the poetry of Emily Dickinson. PhD U. of Kansas, 1958.

MOLSON,F.J. *676*
The forms of god: a study of Emily Dickinson's search for and test of God. PhD U. of Notre Dame, 1965.

MONTGOMERY,B. *677*
Emily Dickinson and the meditative tradition. PhD State U. of New York at Stony Brook, 1981.

MOREY,P.L. *678*
Emily Dickinson's literary history. PhD Howard U. 1970.

MOSSBERG,B.A.C. *679*
When a writer is a daughter: aesthetics of identity in the life and art of Emily Dickinson. PhD Indiana U. 1977.

MUDGE,J.M. *680*
Emily Dickinson and the image of home. PhD Yale U. 1973.

NIMS,I.D. *681*
Tone in the poetry of Emily Dickinson: a linguistic analysis with pedagogical reflections. PhD Indiana U. 1971.

OBERHAUS,D.H. *682*
The religious voice of Emily Dickinson. PhD City U. of New York, 1980.

OLIVER,V.H. *683*
Apocalypse of green: a study of Emily Dickinson's eschatology. PhD U. of Houston, 1982.

OLPIN,L.R. *684*
The comic spirit of Emily Dickinson. PhD U. of Massachusetts, 1971.

O'SHEA,D.J. *685*
Dickinson's search for metaphors: a study of selected images. PhD U. of Oregon, 1972.

PHELAN,J.D'A. *686*
Puritan tradition and Emily Dickinson's poetic practice. PhD Bryn Mawr Coll. 1972.

PHILLIPS,E.J. *687*
Mysticism in the poetry of Emily Dickinson. PhD Indiana U. 1967.

POLLAK,V.R. *688*
Emily Dickinson's early poems and letters. PhD Brandeis U. 1969.

PORTER,D.T. *689*
The art of Emily Dickinson's early poetry. PhD U. of Rochester, 1964.

RASHID,F.D. *690*
'Minor nations': Emily Dickinson and the entomological. PhD U. of Detroit, 1980.

RICHMOND,L.J. *691*
Success in circuit: the poetic craft of Emily Dickinson. PhD Syracuse U. 1970.

RUDDICK,N. *692*
Emily Dickinson's spectrum: an analysis of the significance of color imagery in the poems and letters. PhD McMaster U. 1980.

SHERWOOD,W.R. *693*
Circumference and circumstance: stages in the mind and art of Emily Dickinson. PhD Columbia U. 1964.

SIEGFRIED,R. 694
Conspicuous by her absence: Amherst's religious tradition and Emily Dickinson's own growth in faith. PhD Saint Louis U. 1982.

SLETTO,A.D. 695
Emily Dickinson's poetry: the fascicles. PhD U. of New Mexico, 1975.

STEGER,C.H. 696
Phonological patterning and syntactic structure in the literary criticism for fifteen poems by Emily Dickinson. PhD New York U. 1977.

SUDOL,R.A. 697
Elegy in the poetry of Emily Dickinson. PhD State U. of New York at Stony Brook, 1976.

TAYLOR,M.B. 698
Polarity and resolution: the fiction-making process of Emily Dickinson. PhD U. of Iowa, 1976.

TERRIS,V.R. 699
Emily Dickinson and the genteel critics. PhD New York U. 1973.

THOMAS,O.P. 700
The very press of imagery: a reading of Emily Dickinson. PhD U. of California, Los Angeles, 1960.

TODD,J.E. 701
Emily Dickinson's use of the persona. PhD U. of Wisconsin, 1965.

WEISBUCH,R.A. 702
Compound vision: Emily Dickinson's poetic strategies and patterns. PhD Yale U. 1972.

WHEATCROFT,J.S. 703
Emily Dickinson and the orthodox tradition. PhD Rutgers U. 1960.

WILSON,S.M. 704
Structure and imagery patterns in the poetry of Emily Dickinson. PhD U. of Southern California, 1959.

WYLDER,E.P. 705
The voice of the poet: selected poems of Emily Dickinson with an introduction to the rhetorical punctuation of the manuscripts. PhD U. of New Mexico, 1967.

Hilda Doolittle

DESY,P.M. 706
H.D. and the search for the absolute. PhD Kent State U. 1978.

DIPACE FRITZ,A. 707
Thematic development in the poetry of H.D. PhD Washingston State U. 1982.

FRIEDMAN,S.S. 708
Mythology, psychoanalysis, and the occult in the later poetry of H.D. PhD U. of Wisconsin, 1973.

GREGSON,I.E. 709
H.D.: her struggle against imagism. PhD U. of Hull, 1981.

HOLLAND,J.M. 710
H.D.: the shape of a career. PhD Brown U. 1967.

KAUFMAN,J.L. 711
Theme and meaning in the poetry of H.D. PhD Indiana U. 1959.

MILKIA,J. 712
The fiction of H.D. PhD Columbia U. 1972.

ROBINSON,J.S. 713
H.D.'s *Helen in Egypt*: a recollection. PhD U. of California, Santa Cruz.

SCOGGAN,J.W. 714
De(con)structive poetics: readings of Hilda Doolittle's *The war trilogy*. PhD U. of British Columbia, 1982.

SWANN,T.B. 715
The classical world of H.D. PhD U. of Florida, 1960.

ZAJDEL,M.M. 716
The development of a poetic vision: H.D.'s growth from imagist to mythologist. PhD Michigan State U. 1979.

Alice Dunbar

METCALF,E.W. 717
The letters of Paul and Alice Dunbar: a private history. PhD U. of California, Irvine, 1973.

WILLIAMS,R.O. 718
An in-depth portrait of Alice Dunbar-Nelson. PhD U. of California, Irvine, 1974.

Sarah Barnwell Elliott

MACKENZIE,C.C. 719
Sarah Barnwell Elliott: a biography. PhD Case Western Reserve U. 1971.

MANESS,D.G. 720
The novels of Sarah Barnwell Elliott: a critical study. PhD U. of South Carolina, 1974.

Edna Ferber

SHAUGHNESSY,M.R. 721
Women and success in American society in the works of Edna Ferber. PhD U. of Chicago, 1973.

Dorothy Canfield Fisher

MCCALLISTER,L. 722
Dorothy Canfield Fisher: a critical study. PhD Case Western Reserve U. 1969.

Zelda Sayre Fitzgerald.

COOPER,D.M. *723*
Form and function: the writing style of Zelda Sayre Fitzgerald. PhD U. of Delaware, 1979.

MILFORD,N.W. *724*
Zelda: a biography. PhD Columbia U. 1972.

Mary E. Wilkins Freeman

AVILA,C.M. *725*
A study of socio-economic issues in the novels of Mary E. Wilkins Freeman. PhD Florida State U. 1980.

BAILEY,R.B. *726*
The celebration of self-reliance in the fiction of Mary Wilkins Freeman. PhD U. of Alberta, 1975.

DIOMEDI,C.A. *727*
Mary Wilkins Freeman and the romance-novel tradition. PhD U. of Maryland, 1970.

GLASSER,L.B. *728*
'In a closet hidden': the life and work of Mary Wilkins Freeman. PhD Brown U. 1982.

KENDRICK,B.L. *729*
The infant Sphinx: collected letters of Mary E Wilkins Freeman (September 1875–December 1901). (Volumes I and II). PhD U. of South Carolina, 1981.

KNIPP,T.R. *730*
The quest for form: the fiction of Mary E. Wilkins Freeman. PhD Michigan State U. 1966.

Alice French

RUSHTON,L.E. *731*
The Arkansas fiction of Alice French. PhD U. of Arkansas, 1982.

L. Virginia French

PECK,V.L. *732*
Life and works of L. Virginia French. PhD Vanderbilt U. 1940.

Jean Fritz

HOSTETLER,E.A.R. *733*
Jean Fritz: a critical biography. PhD Toledo U. 1981.

Margaret Fuller

BERGER,P.F. *734*
Margaret Fuller: critical realist as seen in her works. PhD Saint Louis U. 1972.

BRAUN,F.A. *735*
The influence of Goethe on Margaret Fuller. PhD U. of Illinois at Urbana-Champaign, 1909.

BURTON,R.C. *736*
Margaret Fuller's criticism: theory and practice. PhD U. of Iowa, 1942.

DURNING,R.E. *737*
Margaret Fuller, citizen of the world: an intermediary between European and American literatures. PhD U. of North Carolina at Chapel Hill, 1965.

EBBITT,W.R. *738*
The critical essays of Margaret Fuller from the *New York Tribune*: with introduction and notes. PhD Brown U. 1944.

FAY,F.M. *739*
Margaret Fuller. PhD St John's U. 1951.

GOLEMBA,H.L. *740*
The balanced view in Margaret Fuller's literary criticism. PhD U. of Washington, 1971.

KEARNS,F.E. *741*
Margaret Fuller's social criticism. PhD U. of North Carolina at Chapel Hill, 1961.

URBANSKI,M.M.O. *742*
Margaret Fuller's *Woman in the nineteenth century*. PhD U. of Kentucky, 1973.

Martha Gellhorn

ORSAGH,J.E. *743*
A critical biography of Martha Gellhorn. PhD Michigan State U. 1978.

Ellen Glasgow

ALLSUP,J.L. *744*
Feminism in the novels of Ellen Glasgow. PhD U. of Southern Illinois U. at Carbondale, 1974.

ATTEBERRY,P.D. *745*
Ellen Glasgow: the shape of her early career. PhD U. of Washington, 1983.

BATES,R.D. *746*
Changing views: a study of Ellen Glasgow's fluctuating social philosophy. PhD U. of South Carolina, 1966.

BECKER,A.W. *747*
Ellen Glasgow: her novels and their place in the development of Southern fiction. PhD Johns Hopkins U. 1956.

BECKHAM,B.S. *748*
The satire of Ellen Glasgow. PhD U. of Georgia, 1972.

BRESSLER,M.J. *749*
A critical study of the published novels of Ellen Glasgow. PhD U. of Nebraska-Lincoln, 1965.

BRINEY,M.M. *750*
Ellen Glasgow: social critic. PhD Michigan State U. 1956.

DERRIG,P.A. *751*
Ellen Glasgow's role in American fiction: a reinterpretation. PhD St John's U. 1963.

DILLARD,R.H.W. *752*
Pragmatic realism: a biography of Ellen Glasgow's novels. PhD U. of Virginia, 1965.

DUNN,N.E. *753*
Ellen Glasgow's search for truth. PhD U. of Pennsylvania, 1968.

EDWARDS,H.W. *754*
A study of values in selected published prose of Ellen Glasgow. PhD New York U. 1960.

FREY,C.E. *755*
The evolution of the lone heroine in the novels of Ellen Glasgow. PhD U. of Illinois at Urbana-Champaign, 1976.

GATLIN,J.T. *756*
Ellen Glasgow's artistry. PhD U. of Iowa, 1969.

GODBOLD,E.S. *757*
Ellen Glasgow and the woman within. PhD Duke U. 1970.

GOLTS,R.R. *758*
The face of everywoman in the writings of Ellen Glasgow. PhD Temple U. 1977.

GORE,L.Y. *759*
Ellen Glasgow's *Beyond defeat*: a critical edition. Vol. I: Editor's Introduction. PhD U. of Virginia, 1964.

HERTH,H.E. *760*
Ellen Glasgow's ideal of the lady with some contrasts in Sidney Lanier, George W. Cable and Mark Twain. PhD U. of Wisconsin, 1956.

HUGHES,N.E. *761*
Ellen Glasgow and the literature of place. EdD Columbia U. 1970.

KELLY,W.W. *762*
Struggle for recognition: a study of the literary reputation of Ellen Glasgow. PhD Duke U. 1957.

KISH,D. *763*
An immortal part in this place-setting in Ellen Glasgow's novels. PhD U. of Pittsburgh, 1970.

KREIDER,T.M. *764*
Ellen Glasgow: southern opponent to the Philistine. PhD U. of Cincinnati, 1952.

LEBEDUN,F.J. *765*
Mature artistry: textual variants in the collected novels of Ellen Glasgow. PhD U. of Missouri-Columbia, 1978.

LITWHILER,S.J.D. *766*
A comparative study of the chivalric satire of Ellen Glasgow and James Branch Cabell. PhD Auburn U. 1976.

MENDOZA,H.N. *767*
The past in Ellen Glasgow. PhD U. of Minnesota, 1966.

MEYER,E.V. *768*
The art of Ellen Glasgow. PhD U. of Denver, 1955.

MOAKE,F.B. *769*
Problems of characterization in the novels of Ellen Glasgow. PhD U. of Illinois at Urbana-Champaign, 1957.

MURPHY,D.M. *770*
Vein of ambivalence: structural, stylistic and personal dualisms in Ellen Glasgow's major novels. PhD Princeton U. 1969.

PATTERSON,D.W. *771*
Ellen Glasgow's use of Virginia history. PhD U. of North Carolina at Chapel Hill, 1959.

RAPER,J.R. *772*
Ellen Glasgow and Darwinism, 1873–1906. PhD Northwestern U. 1966.

RICHARDS,M.K. *773*
The development of Ellen Glasgow as a novelist. PhD Columbia U. 1961.

ROUSE,H.B. *774*
Studies in the works of Ellen Glasgow. PhD U. of Illinois at Urbana-Champaign, 1942.

SANTAS,J.F. *775*
Ellen Glasgow's American dream. PhD Cornell U. 1963.

SCURA,D. *776*
Ellen Glasgow and James Branch Cabell: the record of a literary friendship. PhD U. of North Carolina, 1973.

SHELTON,J.K. *777*
A literary biography of Ellen Glasgow. PhD U. of Birmingham, 1968.

WHITE,J.E. *778*
Symbols in the novels of Ellen Glasgow. PhD U. of Boston, 1964.

Susan Glaspell

NOE,M.A. *779*
A critical biography of Susan Glaspell. PhD U. of Iowa, 1976.

WATERMAN,A.E. *780*
A critical study of Susan Glaspell's works and her contributions to modern American drama. PhD U. of Wisconsin, 1956.

Carolina Gordon

BROWN,S.A. *781*
Carolina Gordon and the impressionist novel. PhD Vanderbilt U. 1958.

CHAPPELL,C.M. *782*
The hero figure and the problem of unity in the novels of Carolina Gordon. PhD Emory U. 1973.

FRAISTAT,R.A.C. *783*
Carolina Gordon as novelist and woman of letters. PhD U. of Pennsylvania, 1980.

ROCKS,J.E. *784*
The mind and art of Carolina Gordon. PhD Duke U. 1966.

Shirley Ann Grau

CHIOGIOJI,E.N. *785*
A matter of houses: structural unity in the works of Shirley Ann Gray. PhD U. of Maryland, 1981.

Angelica Wilde Grimke

STUBBS,C.A. *786*
Angelica Wilde Grimke: Washington poet and playwright. PhD George Washington U. 1978.

Louise Imogen Guiney

MURPHY,M.A. *787*
Louise Imogen Guiney. PhD Fordham U. 1939.

PARRISH,S.M. *788*
Currents of the nineties in Boston and London: Fred Holland Day, Louise Imogen Guiney and their circle. PhD Harvard U. 1954.

Lorraine Hansberry

GRANT,R.H. *789*
Lorraine Hansberry: the playwright as warrior-intellectual. PhD Harvard U. 1982.

Bernice Kelly Harris

GLOVER,E.W. *790*
Salt of the Earth: plain people in the novels of Bernice Kelly Harris. PhD U. of North Carolina at Chapel Hill, 1977.

Constance Cary Harrison

MAXWELL,S. *791*
Constance Cary Harrison: American woman of letters, 1843–1920. PhD U. of North Carolina at Chapel Hill, 1977.

Lillian Hellman

ACKLEY,M.E. *792*
The plays of Lillian Hellman. PhD U. of Pennsylvania, 1969.

ANGERMEIR,C.B. *793*
Moral and social protest in the plays of Lillian Hellman. PhD U. of Texas at Austin, 1971.

BLITGEN,C. *794*
The overlooked Hellman. PhD U. of California, Santa Barbara, 1972.

BROCKINGTON,J. *795*
A critical analysis of the plays of Lillian Hellman. PhD Yale U. 1962.

CARLSON,E.T. *796*
Lillian Hellman's plays as a reflection of the Southern mind. PhD U. of Southern California, 1975.

HALLER,C.D. *797*
The concept of moral failure in the eight original plays of Lillian Hellman. PhD Tulane U. 1967.

HUNGERFORD,R.W. *798*
Minutes in Lillian Hellman's *The children's hour*: composition of the play from inception to publication. PhD U. of South Carolina, 1980.

JOHNSON,A.B. *799*
A study of recurrent character types in the plays of Lillian Hellman. PhD U. of Massachusetts, 1971.

KELLER,A.J. *800*
Form and content in the plays of Lilliam Hellman: a structural analysis. PhD Stanford U. 1965.

LARIMER,C.D.M. *801*
A study of female characters in the eight plays of Lillian Hellman. PhD Purdue U. 1970.

LONG,N.R. *802*
Creative autonomy of the literary woman: the case of Lillian Hellman. PhD U. of Maryland, 1977.

MCPHERSON,M.L. *803*
Lillian Hellman and her critics. PhD U. of Denver, 1976.

MOONEY,T.R. *804*
'Southern' influences in four plays by Lillian Hellman. PhD Tulane U. 1981.

PATRAKA,V.M. *805*
Lillian Hellman: dramatist of the second sex. PhD U. of Michigan, 1977.

WHITESIDES,G.E. *806*
Lillian Hellman: a biographical and critical study. PhD Florida State U. 1968.

Josephine Herbst

GURLIE,J.M. *807*
The evolution of form in the works of Josephine Herbst. PhD New York U. 1975.

KEMPTHORNE,D.Q. *808*
Josephine Herbst: a critical introduction. PhD U. of Wisconsin-Madison, 1973.

Marietta Holley

BLYLEY,K.G. *809*
Marietta Holley. PhD U. of Pittsburgh, 1937.

WINTER,K.H. *810*
Snow and roses: the life of Marietta Holley. PhD State U. of New York at Albany, 1982.

Fannie Hurst

BRANDIMARTE,C.A. *811*
Fannie Hurst and her fiction: prescriptions for America's working women. PhD U. of Texas at Austin, 1980.

Zora Neale Hurston

HOLLOWAY,K.F.C. *811a*
A critical investigation of the literary and linguistic structures in the fiction of Zora Neale Hurston. PhD Michigan State U. 1978.

JENKINS,J.O. *812*
To make a woman black: a critical analysis of the women characters in the fiction and folklore of Zora Neale Hurston. PhD Bowling Green State U. 1978.

JOHNSON,G.J. *813*
Hurston's folk: the critical significance of Afro-American folk tradition in three novels and the autobiography. PhD U. of California, Irvine, 1977.

SCHMIDT,R.T. *814*
'With my sword in my hand?': the politics of race and sex in the fiction of Zora Neale Hurston. PhD U. of Pittsburgh, 1983.

Helen Hunt Jackson

MARTIN,M.L. *815*
Helen Hunt Jackson in relation to her time. PhD Lousianna State U. 1940.

ODELL,R. *816*
Helen Hunt Jackson and her times. PhD U. of Nebraska-Lincoln, 1937.

Laura Riding Jackson

BURNS,A.W. *817*
Robert Graves and Laura Riding: a literary partnership. PhD Boston U. Grad. Sch. 1969.

JACOBS,M. *818*
The work of Laura (Riding) Jackson: the primary vision. PhD U. of Leicester, 1977.

MASOPUST,M.A. *819*
The poetry of Laura Riding: a survey. DPhil U. of Oxford, 1981.

WEXLER,J.P. *82–*
Construing the word: an introduction to the writings of Laura (Riding) Jackson. PhD Northwestern U. 1974.

Shirley Jackson

MILLER,R.R. *821*
Shirley Jackson's fiction: an introduction. PhD U. of Delaware, 1974.

PARKS,J.G. *822*
The possibility of evil: the fiction of Shirley Jackson. PhD U. of New Mexico, 1973.

Sarah Orne Jewett

BISHOP,F. *823*
The mind and art of Sarah Orne Jewett. PhD U. of Wisconsin, 1955.

FAGAN,S.J.M. *824*
Sarah Orne Jewett's fiction: a reevaluation from three perspectives. PhD U. of Oregon, 1982.

FROST,J.E. *825*
Sarah Orne Jewett. PhD U. of New York, 1953.

FULTZ,M.C. *826*
The narrative art of Sarah Orne Jewett. PhD U. of Virginia, 1968.

MCGUIRE,M.A. *827*
Sarah Orne Jewett. PhD Columbia U. 1964.

NAGEL,G.L. *828*
Women and preservation in the works of Sarah Orne Jewett. PhD Tufts U. 1979.

NAIL,R.W. *829*
Place and setting in the work of Sarah Orne Jewett. PhD U. of North Carolina at Greensboro, 1980.

Josephine W. Johnson

WILK,M.B.L. *830*
The inland woman: a study of the life and major works of Josephine W. Johnson. PhD U. of Massachusetts, 1978.

Mary Johnston

HARTLEY,G.M. *831*
The novels of Mary Johnston: a critical study. PhD U. of South Carolina, 1972.

Grace Elizabeth King

SLAYTON,G.C. *832*
Grace Elizabeth King: her life and works. PhD U. of Pennsylvania, 1974.

Carolina M. Kirkland

KEYES,L.C. *833*
Carolina M. Kirkland: a pioneer in American realism. PhD Harvard U. 1936.

Clare Kummer

FINIZIO,V.L. *834*
Clare Kummer: an analysis of her plays and musicals. PhD U. of Iowa, 1965.

Emma Lazarus

ZEIGER,A. *835*
Emma Lazarus: a critical study. PhD New York U. 1951.

Ursula le Guin

BITTNER,J.W. *836*
Approaches to the fiction of Ursula K. le Guin. PhD U. of Wisconsin-Madison, 1979.

HARE,D.E. *837*
In this land there be dragons: Carl G. Jury, Ursula K. le Guin and narrative prose fantasy. PhD Emory U. 1982.

Denise Levertov

BLOCK,S.J. *838*
The archetypal feminine in the poetry of Denise Levertov. PhD Kansas State U. 1978.

SAUTTER,D. *839*
Perception in process: a study of Denise Levertov's poetic practice. PhD Syracuse U. 1980.

Deborah Norris Logan

BARR,M.S. *840*
The 'worthy' and the 'irrelevant': Deborah Norris Logan's Diary. PhD State U. of New York at Buffalo, 1980.

Amy Lowell

BELL,B.R. *841*
The correspondence of Amy Lowell and John Gould Fletcher. PhD Texas Christian U. 1974.

RUIHLEY,G.R. *842*
Amy Lowell: symbolic impressionist. PhD U. Wisconsin, 1969.

Mina Loy

KOUDIS,V.M. *843*
The cerebral foreigner: an introduction to the poetry of Mina Loy. PhD U. of Iowa, 1972.

Carson McCullers

BAUERLY,D.M. *844*
Patterns of imagery in Carson McCullers' major fiction. PhD Marquette U. 1973.

BLUEFARB,S. *845*
The escape motif in the modern American novel: Mark Twain to Carson McCullers. PhD U. of New Mexico, 1967.

CARLSON,J.G. *846*
The dual vision: paradoxes, opposites, and doubles in the novels of Carson McCullers. PhD Case Western Reserve U. 1976.

CARLTON,A.R. *847*
Patterns in Carson McCullers' portrayal of adolescence. EdD Ball State U. 1972.

CARNEY,C.F. *848*
A study of themes and techniques in Carson McCullers' prose fiction. PhD Columbia U. 1970.

CARR,V.S. *849*
Carson McCullers and the search for meaning. PhD Florida State U. 1969.

CLARK,C.K. *850*
Carson McCullers and the tradition of romance. PhD Louisiana State U. 1974.

ECKARD,R.D. *851*
The sense of place in the fiction of Carson McCullers. EdD Ball State U. 1975.

EVERETT,H.D. *852*
Love and alienation: the sad, dark vision of Carson McCullers. PhD U. of New Mexico, 1975.

GILLESPIE,S. *853*
Dialectical elements in the fiction of Carson McCullers: a comparative critical study. PhD New York U. 1976.

HARRISON,A. *854*
An assessment of Carson McCullers' fiction. MA U. of Kent, 1980.

HUNT,T.H. *855*
Humour in the novels of Carson McCullers. PhD Florida State U. 1972.

JOHNSON,T.S. *856*
The horror in the mansion: Gothic fiction in the works of Truman Capote and Carson McCullers. PhD U. of Texas at Austin, 1973.

JOHNSTONEAUX,R.B. *857*
Abandonment in the major works of Carson McCullers. PhD George Peabody Coll. for Teachers, 1980.

JOYCE,E.T. *858*
Race and sex: opposition and identity in the fiction of Carson McCullers. PhD State U. of New York at Stony Brook, 1973.

MILLICHAP,J.R. *859*
A critical reevaluation of Carson McCullers' fiction. PhD U. of Notre Dame, 1970.

ROGERS,A.T. *860*
The search for relationships in Carson McCullers. PhD Saint Louis U. 1971.

SHAPIRO,A.M. *861*
Carson McCullers: a descriptive bibliography. PhD Indiana U. 1977.

SMITH,C.M. *863*
Self and society: the dialectic of themes and forms in the novels of Carson McCullers. PhD U. of North Carolina at Greensboro, 1976.

SMITH,S.M. *864*
Carson McCullers: a critical introduction. PhD U. of Pennsylvania, 1964.

SULLIVAN,M.S. *865*
Carson McCullers, 1917–1947: the conversion of experience. PhD Duke U. 1966.

WALKER,S.B. *866*
A science of love: love, music, and time in the work of Carson McCullers. PhD Tulane U. 1979.

WALLACE,H.J. *867*
'Lifelessness is the only abnormality': a study of love, sex, marriage, and family in the novels of Carson McCullers. PhD U. of Maryland, 1976.

WHITT,M.A. *868*
A study of the adolescent in Carson McCullers' fiction. PhD U. of Alabama, 1974.

Catherine McDowell

FRANK,W.L. *869*
Catherine Sherwood Bonner McDowell: a critical biography. PhD Northwestern U. 1964.

Emma Bell Miles

EDWARDS,G.T. *870*
Emma Bell Miles: Appalachian author, artist, and interpreter of folk culture. PhD U. of Virginia, 1981.

Elizabeth Shaw Melville

PUETT,A.F. *871*
Melville's wife: a study of Elizabeth Shaw Melville. PhD Northwestern U. 1969.

Josephine Miles

LIANG,V.H. *872*
Coming to terms: the poetry and criticism of Josephine Miles. PhD U. of Ohio, 1980.

Edna St Vincent Millay

KING,G.H. *873*
The development of the social consciousness of Edna St Vincent Millay as manifested in her poetry. PhD New York U. 1943.

MINOT,W.S. *874*
Edna St Vincent Millay: a critical revaluation. PhD U. of Nebraska, 1970.

PATTON,J.J. *875*
Edna St Vincent Millay as a verse dramatist. PhD Colorado U. 1962.

PETTIT,J.M. *876*
Edna St Vincent Millay: a critical study of her poetry in its social and literary milieu. PhD Vanderbilt U. 1956.

Harriet Monroe

WILLIAMS,E. *877*
Harriet Monroe and the poetry renaissance: the first ten years of *Poetry: a magazine of verse*, 1912–1922. PhD U. of Chicago, 1970.

Marianne Moore

ABBOTT,C.S. *878*
Marianne Moore: a descriptive bibliography. PhD U. of Texas at Austin, 1973.

CANNON,P.R. *879*
Marianne Moore: poetics and the quest for poetry. PhD U. of Chicago, 1972.

CAREY,M.C. *880*
The poetry of Marianne Moore: a study of her verse, its sources and its influence. PhD U. of Wisconsin, 1959.

COSTELLO,B. *881*
Sincerity and gusto: the descriptive poetry of Marianne Moore. PhD Cornell U. 1977.

GARELICK,J.S. *882*
Marianne Moore, modern poet: a study of Miss Moore's relationships with William Carlos Williams, e.e. Cummings, T.S. Eliot, Wallace Stevens, and Ezra Pound. PhD Harvard U. 1972.

GUILLORY,D.L. *883*
A place for the genuine: the poetics of Marianne Moore. PhD Tulane U. 1972.

HADAS,P.G. *884*
Efforts of affection: the poetry of Marianne Moore. PhD Washington U. 1973.

JASKOSKI,H.M. *885*
'A method of conclusions': a critical study of the poetry of Marianne Moore. PhD Stanford U. 1969.

KINDLEY,J.B. *886*
Efforts of affection: the poetry of Marianne Moore. PhD Columbia U. 1971.

KOELLING,R.W. *887*
Marianne Moore and the verse essay: structural patterns in the early poetry of Marianne Moore. PhD U. of Nebraska-Lincoln, 1982.

LOURDEAUX,S.J. *888*
The poetry of Marianne Moore: from visual arts to personal politics, 1909– 1935. PhD U. of Chicago, 1979.

REES,R. *889*
The imagery of Marianne Moore. PhD Pennsylvania State U. 1956.

ROSS,B. *890*
Fables from the peaceable kingdom: the poetry of Marianne Moore. PhD State U. of New York at Buffalo, 1982.

SCHULMAN,G.J. *891*
Marianne Moore: the poetry of engagement. PhD New York U. 1971.

SLATIN,J.M. *892*
'The savage's romance': the poetry of Marianne Moore, 1915–1925. PhD Johns Hopkins U. 1979.

SPROUT,R.A.J. *893*
Marianne Moore: the poet as translator. PhD Tufts U. 1980.

STRUTHERS,E.A. *894*
The fragrance of iodine: Marianne Moore's techniques. PhD U. of Iowa, 1980.

WARLOW,F.W. *895*
Marianne Moore: unfalsifying sun and solid gilded star. PhD U. of Pennsylvania, 1959.

Mary Elizabeth Moragne

CRAVEN,D.M. *896*
Mary E. Moragne, her journal and its environment. A study in Upper South Carolina culture. PhD U. of Tennessee, 1952.

Anna Cora Mowatt

BLESI,M. *897*
The life and letters of Anna Cora Mowatt. PhD U. of Virginia, 1935.

Anais Nin

BROWN,H.G. *898*
Animus and the fiction of Anais Nin: a feminine interpretation of logos. PhD Emory U. 1980.

EDKINS,C.A. *899*
The necessary link: mediation in the works of Anais Nin. PhD U. of Texas at Austin, 1980.

HOLDER,O.E. *900*
Anais Nin's fiction: proceeding the dream outward. PhD U. of New Mexico, 1981.

LUNDBERG,C. *901*
Narrative voice in Anais Nin's *Cities of the interior*. PhD Northwestern U. 1982.

MCMATH,W.V. *902*
Feminine identity in Anasis Nin's *Cities of the interior*. PhD U. of Tennessee, 1978.

MERCHANT,H.D. *903*
Anais Nin's texts of pleasure: a woman's *Ta erotika*. PhD Purdue U. 1981.

NOVINGER,E.A. *904*
Neurosis and transformation: a study of women's roles in the fiction of Anais Nin. PhD Florida State U. 1982.

PAINE,S.J. *905*
Sense and transcendence: the art of Anais Nin, Vladimir Nabokov, and Samuel Beckett. PhD Syracuse U. 1979.

POTTS,M.L. *906*
The genesis and evolution of the creative personality: a Rankian analysis of *The diary of Anais Nin*. Volumes I-V. PhD U. of Southern California, 1973.

THOMAS,R. *907*
Transcendental reality in the fiction of Anais Nin. PhD U. of Utah, 1980.

ZEE,N.S. *908*
Anais Nin: beyond the mask. PhD Brown U. 1973.

Joyce Carol Oates

ARROWOOD,G.F. *909*
Execution, obsession, and extinction: the short fiction of Joyce Carol Oates. PhD U. of Maryland, 1981.

BENDER,E.T. *910*
The artistic vision, theory and practice of Joyce Carol Oates. PhD U. of Notre Dame, 1977.

BLOOM,K.B. *911*
The grotesque in the fiction of Joyce Carol Oates. PhD Loyola U. of Chicago, 1979.

DUCAS,P.C. *912*
Determinism in Joyce Carol Oates's novels, 1964–1975. PhD U. of Wisconsin-Madison, 1979.

FRIEDMAN,E. *913*
'Dreaming America': the fiction of Joyce Carol Oates. PhD New York U. 1978.

GRANT,M.K. *914*
The tragic vision of Joyce Carol Oates. PhD Indiana U. 1974.

HODGE,M.C. *915*
What moment is not terrible?: an introduction to the work of Joyce Carol Oates. PhD U. of Tennessee, 1974.

MARTIN,A.C. *916*
Toward a higher consciousness: a study of the novels of Joyce Carol Oates. PhD U. of Northern Illinois, 1974.

MESINGER,B.M. *917*
Dissonance and indeterminacy in the critical writings and fiction of Joyce Carol Oates: implications for the interpreter. PhD Wayne State U. 1977.

MISTRI,Z. *918*
Joyce Carol Oates: transformation of 'Being' toward a center. PhD Purdue U. 1977.

ORENSTEIN,S.B. *919*
Angle of fire: violence, self and grace in the novels of Joyce Carol Oates. PhD New York U. 1978.

PETITE,J.M. *920*
The interrelatedness of marriage, passion and female identity in the fiction of Joyce Carol Oates. PhD Kansas State U. 1976.

ROZGA,M.G. *921*
Development in the short stories of Joyce Carol Oates. PhD U. of Wisconsin-Madison, 1977.

SCOTT,P.E. *922*
An interpreter's approach to the language behavior of literary speakers: a sociolinguistic analysis of Joyce Carol Oates' poetry. PhD U. of Southern Illinois U. at Carbondale, 1977.

STEVENS,C.C. *923*
The imprisoned imagination: the family in the fiction of Joyce Carol Oates, 1960–1970. PhD U. of Illinois at Urbana-Champaign, 1974.

WILSON,M.A. *924*
The image of self in selected works of Joyce Carol Oates. PhD Louisiana State U. 1977.

Flannery O'Connor

See also **1** 172, 256.

ALLEN,S.T. *925*
'The mind and heart of love': Eros and Agape in the fiction of Flannery O'Connor. PhD U. of Detroit, 1976.

ASALS,F.J. *926*
Flannery O'Connor: an interpretive study. PhD Brown U. 1967.

AU,B.G. *927*
The dragon by the side of the road: a study of the fiction of Flannery O'Connor. PhD Claremont Grad. Sch. 1977.

BAUMBACH,G.A. *928*
The psychology of Flannery O'Connor's fictive world. PhD Ohio State U. 1972.

BLACKWELL,A.L. *929*
The artistry of Flannery O'Connor. PhD Florida State U. 1966.

BLACKWELL,H.A. *930*
Technique and the pressure of belief in the fiction of Flannery O'Connor. PhD U. of Chicago, 1976.

BORGMAN,P.C. *931*
The symbolic city and Christian existentialism in fiction by Flannery O'Connor, Walker Percy, and John Updike. PhD U. of Chicago, 1973.

BOYD,Z.M. *932*
The literary apprenticeship of Flannery O'Connor. PhD U. of Massachusetts, 1977.

BREWSTER,R.A. *933*
The literary devices in the writings of Flannery O'Connor. PhD East Texas State U. 1968.

BUNTING,C.T. *934*
The Christian elements in the writings of Flannery O'Connor. PhD U. of Southern Mississippi, 1971.

CALSER,P.A. *935*
The fiction of Flannery O'Connor. PhD U. of Pennsylvania, 1970.

CARLSON,T.M. *936*
Flannery O'Connor: the Manichaean Dilemma. PhD U. of North Carolina at Chapel Hill, 1973.

CHARD,G.E.H. *937*
Flannery O'Connor's fiction: materials and selected structures. PhD Northwestern U. 1975.

CHARNIGO,R.T. *938*
A structural analysis of the short fiction of Flannery O'Connor. PhD Bowling Green State U. 1975.

CHEW,M.E. *939*
Aesthetic integration in the works of Flannery O'Connor. PhD Boston U. Grad. Sch. 1976.

CLEVE LAND,C.L. *940*
Psychological violence: the world of Flannery O'Connor. PhD Saint Louis U. 1972.

CONNOLLY,J.M. *941*
The fiction of Flannery O'Connor. PhD Columbia U. 1956.

CRUSER,P.A. *942*
The fiction of Flannery O'Connor. PhD U. of Pennsylvania, 1970.

DARRETTA,J.L. *943*
The idea and image of retribution in the fiction of Flannery O'Connor. PhD Fordham U. 1972.

DENNIS,J.D. *944*
Tableaux, processions, and journeys in Flannery O'Connor's fiction. PhD Southern Illinois U. at Carbondale, 1975.

DIBBLE,T.J. *945*
The epiphanal vision in the short fiction of Flannery O'Connor. PhD U. of Nebraska- Lincoln, 1971.

DINNEEN,P.M. *946*
Flannery O'Connor: realist of distances. PhD Pennsylvania State U. 1967.

DULLEA,C.M . *947*
The vision of faith and reality in the fiction of Flannery O'Connor. EdD Ball State U. 1977.

DUNN,F.M. *948*
Functions and implications of setting in the fiction of Flannery O'Connor. PhD Catholic U. of America, 1966.

DUNN,R.J. *949*
A mode of good form and philosophy in the fiction of Flannery O'Connor. PhD U. of Michigan, 1971.

EBRECHT,A.D. *950*
Flannery O'Connor's moral vision and *The things of this world*. PhD Tulane U. 1982.

FOX,W.H. *951*
Opposition to reader humanism in the fiction of Flannery O'Connor and Walker Percy. PhD Emory U. 1979.

GARRETT,P.L. *952*
Flannery O'Connor's artistry: techniques of characterization. PhD Indiana U. of Pennsylvania, 1975.

GATTUSO,J.F. *953*
The fictive world of Flannery O'Connor. PhD Columbia U. 1968.

GREGORY,D.L. *954*
An internal analysis of the fiction of Flannery O'Connor. PhD Ohio State U. 1967.

GULLEY,E.F. *955*
Peacocks, pigs, and prophets: ironic iconography in the short fiction of Flannery O'Connor. PhD Lehigh U. 1975.

HAM,M.E. *956*
Children as victims, demons, seers: Flannery O'Connor's *Wise blood*. DA U. of Mississippi, 1977.

HAND,J.T. *957*
Letters to the Laodiceans: the romantic quest in Flannery O'Connor. PhD Kent State U. 1971.

HAU SER,J.D. *958*
The broken cosmos of Flannery O'Connor: the design of her fiction. PhD U. of Pennsylvania, 1973.

HEGARTY,C.S.J. *959*
Vision and revision: the art of Flannery O'Connor. PhD U. of Chicago, 1973.

HOPKINS,K.J. *960*
An exercise in adjudication: interpretations of Flannery O'Connor's *The violent bear it away*. PhD Bowling Green State U. 1982.

JOHNSON,R.E. *961*
A translation of silence: the fiction of Flannery O'Connor. PhD State U. of New York at Buffalo, 1973.

KATZ,C.R. *962*
Flannery O'Connor: a rage of vision. PhD U. of California, Berkeley, 1975.

KEANE,M. *963*
Structural irony in Flannery O'Connor instrument of the writer's vision. phD Loyola U. of Chicago, 1970.

KELLER,J.C. *964*
The comic spirit in the works of Flannery O'Connor. PhD Tulane U. 1970.

LANGFORD,R.B. *965*
The comic sense of Flannery O'Connor. PhD Duke U. 1974.

LEAVER,J.M. *966*
The finite image: attitudes toward reality in the works of Flannery O'Connor. PhD U. of Wisconsin-Madison, 1976.

LEE,M.J. *967*
Clowns and captives: Flannery O'Connor's images of the self. PhD U. of New Hampshire, 1978.

LEESON,R.M. *968*
The iconoclastic art of Flannery O'Connor. PhD U. of Oregon, 1982.

MALLON,A.M.G. *969*
Mystic quest in Flannery O'Connor's fiction. PhD U. of Nôtre Dame, 1981.

MARTIN,C.W. *970*
The convergence of actualistics: themes in the fiction of Flannery O'Connor. PhD Vanderbilt U. 1967.

MATCHIE,T.F. *971*
The mythical Flannery O'Connor: a psychomythic study of *A good man is hard to find*. PhD U. of Wisconsin-Madison, 1974.

MAYER,D.R. *972*
The hermaphrodite and the host: incarnation as vision and method in the fiction of Flannery O'Connor. PhD U. of Maryland, 1973.

MEHL,D.P. *973*
Spiritual reality in the works of Flannery O'Connor. PhD Saint Louis U. 1974.

MOORE,D.L. *974*
(Part II) Limitations in the fiction of Flannery O'Connor PhD Rutgers U. 1977.

MORTON,M.L. *975*
With ground teeth: a study of Flannery O'Connor's women. PhD Louisiana State U. 1980.

MULLER,G.H. *976*
Flannery O'Connor and the Catholic grotesque. PhD Stanford U. 1967.

NISLY ,P.W. *977*
Flannery O'Connor and the gothic impulse. PhD U. of Kansas, 1974.

OLSON,C.J. *978*
The dragon by the road: an archetypal approach to the fiction of Flannery O'Connor. PhD U. of New Mexico, 1975.

ORVELL,M.D. *979*
An incarnational art: the fiction of Flannery O'Connor. PhD Harvard U. 1970.

PADGETT,T. E. *980*
The irony in Flannery O'Connor's fiction. PhD U. of Missouri, 1972.

QUINN,J.J. *981*
The tragic vision in the writings of Flannery O'Connor: a study of her analogical imagination. PhD U. of London, King's College, 1970.

RACKY,D.J. *982*
The achievement of Flannery O'Connor: her

system of thought, her fictional techniques, and an explication of her thought and techniques in *The violent bear it away*. PhD Louisiana State U. 1968.

RAST,J.W. *983*
Flannery O'Connor: biblical education in the home. PhD Duke U. 1980.

RAY,D.L. *984*
(Part III) Flannery O'Connor's satires on American liberalism. PhD Rutgers U. 1976.

REEVES,J.M. *985*
An experiment using fictional literature as a resource for preaching with particular reference to Flannery O'Connor. DMin Drew U. 1982.

ROUT,K.J.K. *986*
The development of Flannery O'Connor's social consciousness. PhD Stanford U. 1975.

RUSS,D.D. *987*
Family in the fiction of Flannery O'Connor. PhD Georgia State U. Coll. of Arts and Sciences, 1981.

SHLOSS,C. *988*
The limits of inference: Flannery O'Connor and the representation of 'Mystery'. PhD Brandeis U. 1974.

SHORT,D.A. *989*
The concrete is her medium: the fiction of Flannery O'Connor. PhD U. of Pittsburgh, 1969.

SMITH,J.C. [*990*
Written with zest: the comic art of Flannery O'Connor. PhD Harvard U. 1974.

STEPHENS,M.T. *991*
An introduction to the work of Flannery O'Connor. PhD Indiana U. 1968.

TATE,J.O. *992*
Flannery O'Connor and *Wise blood*: the significance of the early drafts. PhD Columbia U. 1975.

THOMAS,M.D. *993*
The quest: motif in Flannery O'Connor's short stories. PhD Purdue U. 1982.

WELLING,L.C. *994*
The centre cannot hold: a close textual analysis of Flannery O'Connor's *Wise blood* to reveal its mythopoeic dimensions and the informing archetypes that create richness and density and carry the ambiguity. DA Carnegie-Mellon U. 1975.

WRAY,V.F. *996*
Flannery O'Connor in the American romance tradition. PhD U. of South Carolina, 1979.

YORDON,J.E. *997*
The double motif in the fiction of Flannery O'Connor. PhD U. of Southern Illinois at Carbondale, 1977.

Medora Field Perkerson

DEMARCO,K.A. *998*
Medora Field Perkerson: a study of her literary career and especially of her friendship with Margaret Mitchell. PhD U. of Georgia, 1978.

Julia Peterkin

LANDESS,T.H. *999*
Julia Peterkin: a critical study. PhD U. of Southern California, 1972.

Ann Petry

ISAACS,D.S. *1000*
Ann Petry's life and art: piercing stereotypes. EdD Columbia U. Teachers Coll. 1982.

Elizabeth Stuart Phelps

BENNETT,M.A. *1001*
Elizabeth Stuart Phelps, 1844–1911. A critical biography. PhD U. of Pennsylvania, 1938.

KELLY,L.D. *1002*
'Oh the poor women': a study of the works of Elizabeth Stuart Phelps. PhD U. of North Carolina at Chapel Hill, 1979.

KESSLER,C.F. *1003*
'The woman's hour': life and novels of Elizabeth Stuart Phelps (1844–1911). PhD U. of Pennsylvania, 1977.

Sarah Morgan Piatt

HANAWALT,J.A. *1004*
A biographical and critical study of John James and Sarah Morgan (Bryan) Piatt. PhD U. of Washington, 1981.

Sylvia Plath

AIRD,E.M. *1005*
Sylvia Plath: an introduction to her life and art. MLitt U. of Newcastle-upon Tyne, 1969.

BALITAS,V.D. *1006*
Sylvia Plath, poet. PhD U. of Pennsylvania, 1973.

BARNARD,C.K. *1007*
God's lioness: the poetry of Sylvia Plath. PhD Brown U. 1973.

BENJAMIN,O. *1008*
The self as icon in the work of Sylvia Plath. MPhil U. of Liverpool, 1982.

CAPEK,M.E.S. *1009*
Perfection is terrible: a study of Sylvia Plath's poetry. PhD U. of Wisconsin, 1973.

DALEY,P.C.W. *1010*
Art and identity in the poetry of Sylvia Plath. MA U. of Birmingham, 1978.

JONES,E.H. *1011*
The woman as hero: a study of the poetry and fiction of Sylvia Plath. PhD U. of Essex, 1972.

MEGNA,J.F. *1012*
The two-world dimension in the poetry of Sylvia Plath. EdD Ball State U. 1972.

ROSENSTEIN,H.C. *1013*
Sylvia Plath, 1932–1952. PhD Brandeis U. 1972.

STAINTON,R.T. *1014*
The magician's girl: power and vulnerability in the poetry of Sylvia Plath. PhD Rutgers U. 1975.

Katherine Anne Porter

ADAMS,R.H. *1015*
The significance of point of view in Katherine Anne Porter's *Ship of fools*. PhD U. of Southern California, 1965.

BUNKERS,S.L. *1016*
Katherine Anne Porter: a re-assessment. PhD U. of Wisconsin- Madison, 1980.

CROWDER,E.G.B. *1017*
Image, metaphor, and symbol in Katherine Anne Porter's short fiction. PhD New York U. 1974.

DEMOUY,J.K. *1018*
The seeds of the pomegranate: a study of Katherine Anne Porter's women. PhD U. of Maryland, 1978.

FARRINGTON,T.A. *1019*
The control of imagery in Katherine Anne Porter's fiction. PhD U. of Illinois at Urbana-Champaign, 1972.

GIVNER,J.M. *1020*
A critical study of the works of Katherine Anne Porter. PhD U. of London, External 1973.

HERTZ ,R.N. *1021*
Rising waters: a study of Katherine Anne Porter. PhD Cornell U. 1964.

KIERNAN,R.F. *1022*
The story collections of Katherine Anne Porter: sequence as context. PhD New York U. 1971.

KRISHNAMURTHI,M.G. *1023*
Katherine Anne Porter: a study in themes. PhD U. of Wisconsin, 1966.

LEDBETTER,N.W.T. *1024*
The thumbprint: a study of people in Katherine Anne Porter's fiction. PhD U. of Texas at Austin, 1966.

LUGG,B. *1025*
Mexican influences on the work of Katherine Anne Porter. PhD Pennsylvania State U. 1976.

LYONS,M.P. *1026*
Art and politics in the writings of Katherine Anne Porter. PhD U. of Rhode Island, 1981.

MILES,L.R. *1027*
Unused possibilities: a study of Katherine Anne Porter. PhD U. of California, Los Angeles, 1973.

NANCE,W.L. *1028*
The principle of rejection: a study of the thematic unity in the fiction of Katherine Anne Porter. PhD U. of Notre Dame, 1963.

REDDEN,D.S. *1029*
The legend of Katherine Anne Porter. PhD Stanford U. 1965.

SCHWARTZ,E. *1030*
The fiction of Katherine Anne Porter. PhD Syracuse U. 1954.

SUGISAKI,K. *1031*
Harmonious motion of life: a comparative study of the works of Katherine Anne Porter and Kinoto Okamoto. PhD Occidental Coll. 1973.

VIDA,A.R.V. *1032*
The shape of meaning: a study of the development of Katherine Anne Porter's fictional form. PhD Pennsylvania State U. 1968.

VLIET,V.A.R. *1033*
The shape of meaning: a study of the development of Katherine Anne Porter's fictional form. PhD Pennsylvania State U. 1968.

WALDRIP,L.D.B. *1034*
A bibliography of works of Katherine Anne Porter. PhD U. of Texas at Austin, 1967.

YOSHA,L.W. *1035*
The world of Katherine Anne Porter. PhD U. of Michigan, 1961.

Lizette Woodward Reese

KLEIN,L.R.M. *1036*
Lizette Woodworth Reese: a critical biography. PhD U. of Pennsylvania, 1943.

GILES,R.K. *1036a*
Lizette Woodworth Reese: the quality and influence of her poetic voice. PhD Auburn U. 1981.

Agnes Repplier

STOKES,G.S. *1037*
Agnes Repplier: a critical biography. PhD U. of Pennsylvania, 1941.

VAUGHN,A.C. *1038*
Agnes Repplier: social critic. PhD Michigan State U. 1957.

Adrienne Rich

BRACEWELL,M. *1039*
From androgyny to community in the poetry of Adrienne Rich. PhD U. of Texas at Austin, 1980.

DIAZ-DIOCARETZ,M. *1040*
Reading and writing in the act of translation: the poetry of Adrienne Rich. PhD State U. of New York at Stony Brook, 1982.

HUDSON-MARTIN,C.A. *1041*
Moments of change: the poems of Adrienne Rich. PhD U. of Notre Dame, 1979.

KEYES,C.J. *1042*
The aesthetics of power: a stylistic approach to the poetry of Adrienne Rich. PhD U. of Massachusetts, 1980.

MCMILLEN,B.F. *1043*
A study of the formal and thematic uses of film in the poetry of Parker Tyler, Frank O'Hara and Adrienne Rich. PhD Ohio U. 1976.

MORRISON,M. *1044*
Adrienne Rich: poetry of 're-vision'. PhD George Washington U. 1977.

SEGAL,C.F. *1045*
Natural resources: Adrienne Rich's early works. PhD Lehigh U. 1981.

STEIN,K.F. *1046*
'Home and wanderer': transformation of the self in Adrienne Rich's poetry. PhD U. of Connecticut, 1982.

WHELCHEL,M. *1047*
'Re-forming the crystal': the evolution of Adrienne Rich as feminist poet. PhD U. of Connecticut, 1977.

Laura E. Richards

ALEXANDER,A.S. *1048*
Laura E. Richards, 1850–1943: a critical biography. PhD Columbia U. 1979.

Elizabeth Madox Roberts

HAWLEY,I.L. *1049*
Elizabeth Madox Roberts: her development as self-conscious narrative artist. PhD U. of North Carolina at Chapel Hill, 1970.

NILLES,M.E. *1050*
The rise and decline of a literary reputation: vagaries in the career of Elizabeth Madox Roberts. PhD New York U. 1972.

ROVIT,E.H. *1051*
Elizabeth Madox Roberts: her symbolism and philosophic perspective. PhD Boston U. 1957.

SPEARS,W. *1052*
Elizabeth Madox Roberts: a biographical and critical study. PhD U. of Kentucky, 1953.

Elizabeth Robins

MARCUS,J.C. *1053*
Elizabeth Robins: a biographical and critical study. PhD Northwestern U. 1973.

Mary Rowlandson

DEBOLD,R.K. *1054*
A critical account of Mrs Mary Rowlandson's captivity account. PhD Yale U. 1972.

KESTLER,F.R. *1055*
Mary White Rowlandson: the significance of her narrative in American literature. PhD St John's U. 1982.

Susanna Haswell Rowson

BRANDT,E.B. *1056*
Susanna Haswell Rowson: a critical biography. PhD U. of Pennsylvania, 1974.

PARKER,P.L. *1057*
A critical biography of Susanna Haswell Rowson. PhD New York U. 1981.

WEIL,D.Z. *1058*
Susanna Rowson, the young lady's friend. PhD U. of Cincinnati, 1974.

Muriel Rukeyser

CURTIS,J.E. *1059*
Muriel Rukeyser: the woman writer confronts traditional mythology and psychology. PhD U. of Wisconsin-Madison, 1981.

HUDSON,N. *1060*
A woman of words: a study of Muriel Rukeyser's poetry. PhD U. of California, Berkeley, 1978.

Zoe Akins Rumbold

MIELECH,R.A. *1061*
The plays of Zoe Akins Rumbold. PhD Ohio State U. 1974.

Mari Sandoz

MATTERN,C. *1062*
Mari Sandoz: her use of allegory in *Slogum House*. PhD U. of Nebraska-Lincoln, 1981.

STAUFFER,H.A.W. *1063*
Mari Sandoz: a study of the artist as a biographer. PhD U. of Nebraska-Lincoln, 1974.

WALTON,K.O.D. *1064*
Mari Sandoz: an initial critical appraisal. PhD U. of Delaware, 1970.

May Sarton

CLEWETT,B.J. *1065*
Creativity and the Daimonic in Mann's *Doctor Faustus* and two Sarton novels. PhD Northwestern U. 1982.

FUNCK,S.B. *1066*
The finely woven web of interaction: human relationships in the nucli of May Sarton. PhD U. of Texas at Arlington, 1982.

Dorothy Scarborough

NEATHERLIN,J.W. *1068*
Dorothy Scarborough: form and milieu in the work of a Texas writer. PhD U. of Iowa, 1973.

Zelda Sears

BETTISWORTH,D.L. *1069*
The life and career of Zelda Sears. [Playwright, screenwriter and actress.] PhD U. of Georgia, 1974.

Anne Douglas Sedgwick

SWANSON,G.E. *1070*
The novels of Anne Douglas Sedgwick. PhD New York U. 1956.

Catharine Maria Sedgwick

GIDEZ,R.B. *1071*
A study of the works of Catharine Maria Sedgwick. PhD Ohio State U. 1958.

WELSH,N.M. *1072*
Catharine Maria Sedgwick, her position in American literature and thought up to 1860. PhD Catholic U. of America, 1937.

Anne Sexton

BIXLER,F.B. *1073*
The achievement of Anne Sexton. PhD U. of Arkansas, 1980.

CAPO,K.E.M. *1074*
Redeeming words: a study of confessional rhetoric in the poetry of Anne Sexton. PhD Northwestern U. 1978.

FELDMAN,R. *1075*
Anne Sexton: a study of her poetry. PhD New York U. 1979.

NUCIFORA,J.E. *1076*
'The awful babble of that calling': the personal myth of the madwoman in the poetry of Anne Sexton. PhD U. of Wisconsin-Madison, 1978.

QUEBE,R.E. *1077*
The questing self: a study of Anne Sexton's poetry. PhD U. of Texas at Austin, 1979.

Elizabeth Oakes Smith

RICHARDS,W.L. *1079*
A review of the life and writings of Elizabeth Oakes Smith, feminist, author, and lecturer 1806–1893. PhD Ball State U. 1981.

WYMAN,M.A. *1080*
Two American pioneers: Seba Smith and Elizabeth Oakes Smith. PhD Columbia U. 1927.

Mrs Southworth

BOYLE,R.L. *1081*
Mrs E.D.E.N. Southworth, novelist. PhD Catholic U. of America, 1938.

SILVERBLATT,A.M. *1082*
Mrs E.D.E.N. Southworth and Southern mythic society. PhD Michigan State U. 1980.

Anne Spencer

GREENE,J.L. *1083*
Anne Spencer: a study of her life and poetry. PhD U. of North Carolina at Chapel Hill, 1974.

Harriet Prescott Spofford

HALBEISEN,E.K. *1084*
Harriet Prescott Spofford, a romantic survival. PhD Pennsylvania U. 1934.

Jean Stafford

AVILA,W.E. *1085*
The ironic fiction of Jean Stafford. PhD U. of Maryland, 1980.

Gertrude Stein

See also **1** 134.

ARMATAGE,E.K. *1086*
The mother of us all: the woman in the writings of Gertrude Stein. PhD U. of Toronto, 1974.

BAINUM,M.I. *1087*
Gertrude Stein's theatre. PhD U. of Wisconsin-Madison, 1981.

BERGMANN,H.F. *1088*
Gertrude Stein: identity, event and time. PhD State U. of New York at Albany, 1976.

BLOMME,G.C.B. *1089*
Gertrude Stein's concepts of the self and her literary characters. PhD U. of Michigan, 1973.

BOWERS,J.P. *1090*
The writer in the theatre: the plays of Gertrude Stein. PhD U. of California, Berkeley, 1981.

COPELAND,C.F. *1091*
Narrative techniques in the works of Gertrude Stein. PhD U. of Iowa, 1973.

DAVIS,E.H. *1092*
Gertrude Stein's return to narrative. PhD Harvard U. 1970.

DEKOVEN,M. *1093*
Explaining Gertrude Stein: a criticism for experimental style. PhD Stanford U. 1976.

DOANE,J.L. *1094*
Silence is so windowful: the early novels of Gertrude Stein. PhD State U. of New York at Buffalo, 1981.

DUBNICK,R.K. *1095*
Gertrude Stein and Cubism: a structural analysis of obscurity. PhD U. of Colorado at Boulder, 1976.

EDGINGTON,K.A. *1096*
Abstraction as a concept in the criticism of Gertrude Stein and Wassily Kandinsky. PhD American U. 1976.

GARVIN,H.R. *1097*
Gertrude Stein: a study of her theory and practice. PhD U. of Michigan, 1950.

HOFFMAN,M.J. *1098*
The development of abstractionism in the writing of Gertrude Stein to 1913. PhD U. of Pennsylvania, 1963.

HUNKER,M.B.S. *1099*
Gertrude Stein: a rationale and content for an introduction to the aesthetics of modernism. PhD Ohio State U. 1980.

KATZ,L. *1100*
The first making of *The making of Americans*: a study based on Gertrude Stein's notebooks and early versions of her novel (1902–1908). PhD Columbia U. 1963.

LANDON,R.B. *1101*
Extremes of parataxis: nonrationalism in the writing of Gertrude Stein and Thomas Berger. PhD U. of Texas at Austin, 1978.

LOWE,F.W. *1102*
Gertrude's web: a study of Gertrude Stein's literary relationships. PhD Columbia U. 1957.

MACKINLAY,P.W. *1103*
Gertrude Stein and the art of portraiture. PhD U. of Chicago, 1977.

MCMENIMAN,L.J. *1104*
Design and experiment in *The making of Americans* by Gertrude Stein. PhD U. of Pennsylvania, 1976.

ROBERTS,M.J. *1105*
The meditative mode in Gertrude Stein's experimental work. PhD U. of Texas at Austin, 1981.

ROE,N.E. *1106*
Gertrude Stein: rhetoric and the modern composition. PhD U. of Michigan, 1971.

STEINER,W.L. *1107*
Gertrude Stein's portrait form. PhD Yale U. 1974.

THIGPEN,J. *1108*
A manual for teaching counselor trainees existential concepts through an exploration of the life and writings of Gertrude Stein. PhD East Texas State U. 1971.

TOWNSEND,J.B.L. *1109*
The singing self: philosophy, autobiography and style in Gertrude Stein's lyrical Mallorcan works (1915–1916). PhD Wayne State U. 1977.

WALKER,J.L. *1110*
Gertrude Stein and her objects: from *Melanctha* to *Tender buttons*. PhD U. of California, Berkeley, 1975.

Kate Stephens

HABEIN,M. *1111*
Kate Stephens: a study of her life and writings. PhD U.of Kansas, 1952.

Elizabeth Barstow Stoddard

MATLACK,J.M. *1112*
The literary career of Elizabeth Barstow Stoddard. PhD Yale U. 1968.

Harriet Beecher Stowe

ADAMS,J.R. *1113*
The literary achievements of Harriet Beecher Stowe. PhD U. of Southern California, 1940.

HOVET,T.R. *1114*
Harriet Beecher Stowe's holiness crusade against slavery. PhD U. of Kansas, 1970.

KIMBAL,G.H. *1115*
The religious ideas of Harriet Beecher Stowe: her gospel of womanhood. PhD U. of California, Santa Barbara, 1976.

KIRKHAM,E.B. *1116*
Harriet Beecher Stowe and the genesis, composition, and revision of *Uncle Tom's cabin*. PhD U. of North Carolina at Chapel Hill, 1968.

MILLER,E.A. *1118*
The Christian philosophy in the New England novels of Harriet Beecher Stowe. PhD U. of Nevada Reno, 1970.

VEACH,C.W. *1119*
Harriet Beecher Stowe: a critical study of her early novels. PhD Indiana U. 1967.

Caroline Strickland

RIORDAN,D.G. *1120*
The concept of simplicity in the works of Mrs Caroline Strickland. PhD U. of North Carolina at Chapel Hill, 1973.

Ruth McEnery Stuart

FLETCHER,M.P. *1121*
A biographical and critical study of Ruth McEnery Stuart. PhD Louisiana State U. 1955.

Ruth Suckow

STEWART,M.O. *1122*
A critical study of Ruth Suckow's fiction. PhD U. of Illinois, 1960.

Mary Virginia Terhune

WRIGHT,M.H. *1123*
Mary Virginia Hawes Terhune (Marian Harland). PhD U. George Peabody Coll. for Teachers, 1935.

Megan Terry

WAGNER,P.J. *1124*
Megan Terry: political playwright. PhD U. of Denver, 1972.

Octave Thanet

MCMICHAEL,G.L. *1125*
Minor figure: a biography of Octave Thanet. [Pseudonym of Alice French.] PhD Northwestern U. 1959.

Celia Thaxter

DE PIZA,M.D. *1126*
Celia Thaxter: poet of the Isles of Shoals. PhD U. of Pennsylvania, 1955.

Eunice Tietjens

LOVE,W.N.S. *1127*
Eunice Tietjens: a biographical and critical study. PhD U. of Maryland, 1960.

Mabel Loomis Todd

WHITE,S.N. *1129*
Mabel Loomis Tood: gender, language and power in Victorian America. PhD Yale U. 1982.

Sophie Treadwell

WYNN,N.E. *1130*
Sophie Treadwell: the career of a twentieth-century American feminist playwright. PhD City U. of New York, 1982.

Amelie Rives Troubetsky

LONGEST,G.C. *1131*
Amelie Rives Troubetsky: a biography. PhD U. of Georgia, 1969.

Anne Tyler

NESANOVICH,S.A. *1132*
The individual in the family: a critical introduction to the novels of Anne Tyler. PhD Louisiana State U. 1979.

Hulda Saenger Walter

SCROGIN,B.J.C. *1133*
An edition of selected poems by Hulda Saenger Walter. EdD East Texas State U. 1982.

Mary Ward

SNIPES,H.J. *1134*
May Ward: poet of the prairie and its people. PhD Kansas State U. 1973.

Mercy Otis Warren

HUTCHESON,M.M. *1135*
Mercy Warren: a study of her life and works. PhD American U. 1951.

Eudora Welty

APPEL,A. *1136*
The short stories of Eudora Welty. PhD Columbia U. 1963.

ARNOLD,St.G.T. *1137*
Consciousness and the unconscious in the fiction of Eudora Welty. PhD Stanford U. 1975.

BENADE,W. *1138*
Dream and the interior world in the early short stories of Eudora Welty. PhD U. of Chicago, 1972.

BROOKHART,M.H. *1139*
The search for lost time in the early fiction of Eudora Welty. PhD U. of North Carolina at Chapel Hill, 1981.

CALLAWAY,K. *1140*
In her time, in her place: caste and class in the fiction of Eudora Welty. PhD U. of Virginia, 1977.

CARSON,F. *1141*
Eudora Welty's *The golden apples* and the problem of the collection novel. PhD U. of Chicago, 1972.

CARSON,G.R. *1142*
Primitivism and the visionary imagination: Eudora Welty's comic romantic art. PhD Harvard U. 1974.

CHRONAKI,B. *1143*
Breaking the *Quondam obstruction*: place as an aspect of meaning in the work of Eudora Welty. PhD Duke U. 1976.

DAVIS,C.E. *1144*
Eudora Welty's art of naming. PhD Emory U. 1969.

FELD,B.D. *1145*
The short fiction of Eudora Welty. PhD Columbia U. 1978.

FOLSOM,G.R. *1146*
Form and substance in Eudora Welty. PhD U. of Wisconsin, 1960.

FOREMAN,F.B. *1147*
Women's choices: a study of the feminine characters in the novels of Eudora Welty. PhD U. of South Florida, 1981.

FULLINWIDER,C.M. *1148*
Eudora Welty's fiction: its unconventional rela-

tionship to the Southern literary tradition. PhD State U.of New York at Albany, 1975.

GARBARINE,A. *1149*
The feast itself: a study of narrative technique in the fiction of Eudora Welty. PhD St John's U. 1977.

GOELLER,A.D. *1150*
The pastorals of Eudora Welty. PhD Temple U. 1978.

GRIFFITH,A.J. *1151*
Eudora Welty's fiction. PhD U. of Texas at Austin 1959.

HARRIS,J.L. *1152*
Eudora Welty: the achieved worlds of her early stories. PhD Ohio U. 1976.

HEMBREE,C.W. *1153*
Narrative technique in the fiction of Eudora Welty. PhD U. of Oklahoma, 1974.

HERLONG,R.P. *1154*
A study of human relationships in the novels of Eudora Welty. PhD U. of South Carolina, 1975.

HINTON,J.L. *1155*
Out of all times of trouble: the family in the fiction of Eudora Welty. PhD Vanderbilt U. 1974.

HOWARD,Z.T. *1156*
Meaning through rhetoric in Eudora Welty's *A curtain of green, The wide net* and *The golden apples*. EdD U. of Northern Colorado, 1970.

KAREM,S.S. *1157*
Mythology in the works of Eudora Welty. PhD U. of Kentucky, 1977.

KING,W.P. *1158*
A thematic study of the fiction of Eudora Welty. PhD George Peabody Coll. for Teachers, 1972.

KREYLING,M.P. *1159*
The novels of Eudora Welty. PhD Cornell U. 1975.

LAING,J.B. *1160*
The Southern tradition in the fiction of Eudora Welty. PhD U. of Kansas, 1980.

LEMIEUX,E.R. *1161*
Sexual symbolism in the short stories of Eudora Welty. PhD State U. of New York at Binghamton, 1979.

MCGOWAN,M.P. *1162*
Patterns of female experience in Eudora Welty's fiction. PhD Rutgers U. 1977.

MILLSAPS,E.M. *1163*
The family in four novels of Eudora Welty. PhD U. of Tennessee, 1976.

NASH,C.C. *1164*
The theme of human isolation in the works of Eudora Welty. PhD U. of Minnesota, 1975.

NOSTRANDT,J.R. *1165*
Survival by endurance: a motif in the short fiction of Eudora Welty. PhD U. of North Carolina at Chapel Hill, 1975.

PRENSHAW,P.J.W. *1166*
A study of setting in the fiction of Eudora Welty. PhD U. of Texas at Austin, 1970.

RANDISI,J.L. *1167*
Eudora Welty's Southern romances: the novels of Eudora Welty viewed within the Southern romance tradition. PhD State U. of New York at Stony Brook, 1979.

ROUSE,S.A. *1168*
Place and people in Eudora Welty's fiction: a portrait of the deep South. PhD Florida State U. 1962.

SMITH,C.P. *1169*
The journey motif in the collected works of Eudora Welty. PhD U. of Maryland, 1971.

TAPLEY,P.A. *1170*
The portrayal of women in selected short stories by Eudora Welty. PhD Louisiana State U. 1974.

THOMPSON,V.H. *1171*
Life's impact is oblique: a study of obscurantism in the writings of Eudora Welty. PhD Rutgers U. 1972.

TURNER,C.L. *1172*
Eudora Welty's short fiction: a survey of structural and narrative techniques. PhD Georgia State U. 1978.

VINSON,C.M. *1173*
Imagery in the short stories of Eudora Welty. PhD Northwestern U. 1970.

WEINER,R.V. *1174*
Reflections of the artist in Eudora Welty's fiction. PhD U. of North Carolina at Chapel Hill, 1978.

Edith Wharton

AMMONS,E.M. *1175*
Edith Wharton's heroines: studies in aspiration and compliance. PhD U. of Illinois at Urbana-Champaign, 1974.

ANDERSON,L.C. *1176*
Edith Wharton's heroes. PhD U. of Kansas, 1982.

ANDREWS,M.E. *1177*
Initiation and growth in Edith Wharton's fiction. PhD U. of Texas at Austin, 1979.

ASKEW,M.W. *1178*
Edith Wharton's literary theory. PhD U. of Oklahoma, 1957.

BARIL,J.R. *1179*
Vision as metaphorical perception in the fiction of Edith Wharton. PhD U. of Colorado, 1969.

BELL,M. *1180*
Edith Wharton: studies in a writer's development. PhD Brown U. 1955.

BRETSCHNEIDER,M.A. *1181*
Edith Wharton: patterns of rejection and denial. PhD Case Western Reserve U. 1969.

CARTWRIGHT,F.C.W. *1182*
The age of innocence by Edith Wharton: a critical and annotated edition. PhD U. of Nebraska, 1970.

COLLINS,A. *1183*
The death of the soul: a study of Edith Wharton's fiction. PhD U. of Calgary, 1979.

FRITZ,A.J. *1184*
The use of the arts of decoration in Edith Wharton's fiction: a study of her interests in architecture, interior decoration and gardening and of the language in which she exploited them. PhD U. of Wisconsin, 1956.

GARRISON,S.M. *1185*
A descriptive bibliography of Edith Wharton. PhD U. of South Carolina, 1982.

GIMBEL,W. *1186*
Edith Wharton: orphancy and survival. PhD Fordham U. 1982.

GLEASON,J.J. *1187*
After innocence: the late novels of Edith Wharton. PhD Ohio State U. 1969.

GODFREY,D.A. *1188*
A real relation to life: self and society in Edith Wharton's major novels. PhD U. of Kentucky, 1982.

GREENWOOD,F.J.V. *1189*
A critical study of Edith Wharton's short stories and nouvelles. PhD Stanford U. 1962.

GREENWOOD,W.B. *1190*
Edith Wharton: her materials and methods. PhD U. of Cincinnati, 1942.

HEMMER,J.M. *1191*
A study of setting in the major novels of Edith Wharton. PhD Fordham U. 1964.

HENRY,M.J. *1192*
The theme of success in the writings of Edith Wharton. PhD Harvard U. 1976.

HORTON,R.W. *1193*
Social and individual values in the New York stories of Edith Wharton. PhD New York U. 1945.

JACOBY,V.A.D. *1194*
A study of class values and the family in the fiction of Edith Wharton. PhD Stanford U. 1972.

JONES,E.K. *1195*
Prototypes of liberation: the novels of Edith Wharton. MA U. of Manchester, 1974.

KOPRINCE,S.J.F. *1196*
The fictional houses of Edith Wharton. PhD U. of Illinois at Urbana- Champaign, 1981.

LEACH,N.R. *1197*
Edith Wharton: critic of American life and literature. PhD U. of Pennsylvania, 1952.

LEWIS,K.A. *1198*
Satire and irony in the later novels of Edith Wharton. PhD Stanford U. 1968.

LINDBERG,G.M. *1199*
Edith Wharton and the rhetoric of manners. PhD Stanford U. 1967.

LYDE,M.J. *1200*
The relation of convention and morality in the work of Edith Wharton. PhD U. of Chicago, 1957.

MCMANIS,J.A. *1201*
Edith Wharton's treatment of love: a study of conventionality and unconventionality in her fiction. PhD Louisiana State U. 1967.

MAYNARD,N. *1202*
The Medusa's face: a study of character and behavior in the fiction of Edith Wharton. PhD New York U. 1971.

MILLER,C.A. *1203*
Natural magic: irony as a unifying strategy in the fiction of Edith Wharton. PhD U. of Oklahoma, 1980.

MOLLEY,C.N. *1204*
The Artemis Athene and Venus polarity in the works of Edith Wharton: a mythological dimension with psychological implications. PhD Pennsylvania State U. 1971.

MOORE,P. *1205*
The fiction of Edith Wharton. PhD U. of Leicester, 1974.

MORANTE,L.M. *1206*
Edith Wharton: the house of the past. PhD New York U. 1979.

PETERMAN,M.A. *1207*
The post-war novels of Edith Wharton, 1917–1938. PhD U. of Toronto, 1977.

PITLICK,M.L. *1208*
Edith Wharton's narrative technique: the major phase. PhD U. of Wisconsin, 1965.

PLANTE,P.R. *1209*
The critical reception of Edith Wharton's fiction in America and England with an annotated enumerative bibliography of Wharton criticism from 1900 to 1961. PhD Boston U. 1962.

RICE,M.L. *1210*
The moral conservatism of Edith Wharton. PhD U. of Minnesota, 1953.

SASAKI,M. *1211*
The sense of horror in Edith Wharton. PhD Yale U. 1973.

SAUNDERS,T. *1212*
Moral values in the novels of Edith Wharton. PhD U. of Pittsburgh, 1954.

SEIFERT,C.S. *1213*
Houses of mirth: Edith Wharton's hieroglyphic world. PhD U. of Chicago, 1980.

SEMEL,A. 1214
A study of the thematic design in the four major novels of Edith Wharton. PhD U. of Notre Dame, 1971.

TURNER,J. 1215
The ideology of women in the fiction of Edith Wharton 1899–1920. PhD U. of Wisconsin-Madison, 1975.

TUTTLETON,J.W. 1216
Edith Wharton and the novel of manners. PhD U. of North Carolina at Chapel Hill, 1963.

TYLER,J.L. 1217
The novelist's building site: the use of point of view in the novels and novellas of Edith Wharton. MPhil U. of Oxford, 1980.

TYREE,W. 1218
Puritan in the drawing-room: the Puritan aspects of Edith Wharton and her novels. PhD Princeton U. 1979.

WERSHOVEN,C.J. 1219
The female intruder in the novels of Edith Wharton. PhD U. of Florida, 1979.

WHALEY,R.M. 1220
Landscape in the writing of Edith Wharton. PhD Harvard U. 1982.

WOLFE,R.F. 1221
The restless women of Edith Wharton. EdD Columbia U. 1974.

ZILVERSMIT,A.C.S. 1222
Mothers and daughters: the heroines in the novels of Edith Wharton. PhD New York U. 1980.

Phillis Wheatley

HOLDER,K.R. 1223
Some linguistic aspects of the heroic couplet in the poetry of Phillis Wheatley. PhD North Texas State U. 1973.

Sarah Helen Whitman

VARNER,J.G. 1224
Sarah Helen Whitman, seeress of Providence. PhD U. of Virginia, 1941.

Laura Ingalls Wilder

DYKSTRA,R.R. 1225
The autobiographical aspects of Laura Ingalls Wilder's *Little house* books. EdD State U. of New York at Buffalo, 1980.

SPAETH,J.L. 1226
'Over the horizon of the years': Laura Ingalls Wilder and the *Little house* books. PhD U. of North Dakoka, 1982.

Augusta Evans Wilson

FIDLER,W.P. 1227
The life and works of Augusta Evans Wilson. PhD U. of Chicago, 1947.

Thyra Saunter Winslow

WINEGARD,R.C. 1228
Thyra Saunter Winslow: a critical assessment. PhD U. of Arkansas, 1971.

Constance Fenimore Woolson

GINGRAS,R. 1229
Constance Fenimore Woolson's literary achievement as a short story writer. PhD Florida State U. 1980.

GRAY,S.C. 1230
The literary achievement of Constance Fenimore Woolson. PhD U. of Wisconsin, 1955.

KERN,J.D. 1231
Constance Fenimore Woolson, literary pioneer. PhD U. of Pennsylvania, 1933.

MILLEDGE,L.U. 1232
Theme and characterization in the fiction of Constance Fenimore Woolson. PhD U. of Georgia, 1971.

STEPHAN,P.M. 1233
Comparative value systems in the fiction of Constance Fenimore Woolson. PhD U. of New Mexico, 1976.

WEDDELL,A.L. 1234
Internationalism in the European short stories of Constance Fenimore Woolson. PhD Texas A&M U. 1974.

Frances Wright

FOLLIS,J.T. 1235
Frances Wright: feminism and literature in antibellum America. PhD U. of Wisconsin-Madison, 1982.

Elinor Wylie

BROWN,M.G. 1236
Elinor Wylie and the religion of art: poetry and social attitudes in the 1920s. PhD Emory U. 1979.

COLLURA,J.M. 1237
Elinor Wylie's prose: a study in conflict. PhD U. of Pittsburgh, 1962.

FARR,J.B. 1238
Language from spirit: the art of Elinor Wylie. PhD Yale U. 1966.

GRAY,T.A. 1239
The poetry of Elinor Wylie: a critical study. PhD Syracuse U. 1967.

HELMICK,E.T. 1240
Elinor Wylie: the woman in her work. PhD U. of Miami, 1969.

HILT,K.F. 1241
Elinor Wylie's fiction: a study of the novels and shorter pieces. PhD U. of Maryland, 1978.

HOMSLEY,B.S. 1242
The life of Elinor Wylie. PhD U. of Wisconsin-Madison, 1970.

POTTER,N. 1243
Elinor Wylie: a biographical and critical study. PhD Boston U. 1954.

WRIGHT,E.V. 1244
A bibliographic study of Elinor Wylie. PhD Loyola U. of Chicago, 1954.

Anzia Yezierska

SULLIVAN,R.M. 1245
Anzia Yezierska, an American writer. PhD U. of California, Berkeley, 1975.

Asian literature

Chinese literature

ANDERSON,C.M. 1246
Two modern Chinese women: Ping Hsin and Ting Ling. PhD Claremont Grad. Sch. 1954.

BJORGE,G.J. 1247
Ting Ling's early years: her life and literature through 1942. PhD U. of Wisconsin-Madison, 1977.

CAHILL,S.E. 1248
The image of the goddess Hsi Wang Mu in medieval Chinese literature. PhD U. of California, Berkeley, 1982.

CH'EN,T.Y. 1249
Women in Confucian society: a study of three T'an-Tz'u narratives. PhD Columbia U. 1974.

GOLDBLATT,H.C. 1250
A literary biography of Hsiao Hung (1911–1942). [Pen-name of Chang Nai-Ying.] PhD Indiana U. 1974.

LINDFORS,S.A. 1251
Private lives: an analysis of the short stories of Ouyang Tzu, a modern Chinese writer. PhD U. of Texas at Austin, 1982.

WU,P.Y. 1252
The white snake: the evolution of a myth in China. [Tragic heroine in Chinese literature.] PhD Columbia U. 1969.

Indian and Persian literature

BLACKWELL,F.W. 1253
The characterization of women in three contemporary Hindi playwrights: Jai Shankar Prasad, Lakshmi Narain Lal and Mohan Rakesh. PhD U. of Wisconsin-Madison, 1973.

HANDLER,E. 1254
The feminine paradigms of the gadya kavyas: a study in literary conventions. [Women of *Vasavadatta, Harsacarita, Kadambari* and *Dasakumacarita.*] PhD U. of Pennsylvania, 1966.

MILANI,F.M.Z. 1255
Forugh Farrokhzad: a feminist perspective. PhD U. of California, Los Angeles, 1979.

PARAMESWARAN,U.G. 1256
A study of representative Indo-English novelists. [Includes Kamala Markandaya.] PhD Michigan State U. 1972.

POULOS,S.M. 1257
Feminine sense and sensibility: a comparative study of six modern women short fiction writers in Hindi and Urdu: Rashid Jahan, Ismat Chughtai, Qurratul-Ain Hyder, Mannu Bhandari, Usha Priyamvada, Vijay Chauhan. PhD U. of Chicago, 1975.

RAO,K.S.N. 1258
The new harvest: the Indian novel in English in the post-independence era: women at work; Kamala Markandaya. PhD Pennsylvania State U. 1968.

ROHLICH,T.H. 1259
Hamamatsu Chunagon Monogatari: an introduction and translation. PhD U. of Wisconsin-Madison, 1979.

SEN,J. 1260
Changes in the status of women during the nineteenth century as reflected in Bengali literature. PhD U. of London, 1924.

THOMAS,M.G. 1261
The luminous web: a critical survey of Mrs Sarojini Naidu. PhD U. of Pennsylvania, 1953.

Japanese literature

BRAZELL,K.W. 1262
A study and partial translation of *Towazugatari.* [Autobiography of Lady Nijo, a Japanese court lady in the Kamakura period, concubine to the retired Emperor Gofukakusa and later a wandering nun.] PhD Columbia U. 1969.

CRANSTON,E.A. 1263
The *Izumi Skikibu Nikki*: a study and translation. [Diary of Izumi Shikibu, a Japanese poetess.] PhD Stanford U. 1966.

NAKAGAWA,V.V. *1264*
Three Japanese women writers: Higuchi Ichiyo, Sata Ineko, and Kurahashi Yumiko. PhD U. of California, Berkeley, 1981.

SILVERMAN,E.A. *1265*
A waste of effort: psychological projection as a primary mode of alientation in selected novels by Kawabata Yasunari. [A fictional male narrator on the question of the ideal woman.] PhD U. of Southern California, 1977.

Vietnamese literature

CONG HUYEN TON NU THI,N. *1266*
The tradition roles of women as reflected in oral and written Vietnamese literature. PhD U. of California, Berkeley, 1973.

YEAGER,J.A. *1267*
The Vietnamese francophone novel: a literary response to colonialism. [Includes a study of the literary function of the women characters.] PhD U. of Wisconsin-Madison, 1982.

Australasian literature

LIDOFF,J.E. *1268*
Obscure griefs: the autobiographical fiction of Christina Stead. PhD Harvard U., 1976.

TAYLOR,R. *1269*
The indigenous voice: the expression of indigenous culture in the literary works of José María Arguedas, Vincent Eri, Wito Ihimimuera, and Patricia Grace. PhD U. of British Columbia, 1981.

Canadian literature

General studies

See also above 258.

CHAWLA,S. *1270*
Canadian fiction: literature as role explanation: an analysis of novels written by women 1926–1974. PhD York U. 1981.

HOY,H.E. *1271*
The portrayal of women in recent English-Canadian fiction. PhD U. of Toronto, 1977.

HUGHES,T.R. *1272*
Gabrielle Roy et Margaret Laurence: deux chemins, une recherche. PhD McGill U. 1980.

IRVINE,L.M. *1273*
Hostility and reconciliation: the mother in English-Canadian fiction. PhD American U. 1977.

MALLINSON,A.J. *1274*
Versions and subversions: formal strategies in the poetry of contemporary Canadian women. PhD Simon Fraser U. 1981.

RACKOWSKI,C.S. *1275*
Women by women: five contemporary English and French-Canadian novelists. PhD U. of Connecticut, 1978.

TANASZI,M.J. *1276*
Feminine consciousness in contemporary Canadian fiction with special reference to Margaret Atwood, Margaret Laurence and Alice Munro. PhD U. of Leeds, 1977.

TURNER,G.P. *1277*
The protagonists' initiating experiences in the Canadian *Bildungsroman* 1908–1971. PhD U. of British Columbia, 1979.

URBAS,J. *1278*
Le personnage feminin dans le roman canadien français de 1940 a 1967. PhD U. of Toronto, 1971.

VERDUYN,C. *1279*
L'idée de la découverte de soi dans le roman feminin canadien depuis 1960: étude d'oeuvres quebecoises et canadiennes-anglaises. PhD U. of Ottowa, 1979.

Individual writers

Margaret Avison

MANSBRIDGE,F. *1280*
The poetry of Raymond Souster and Margaret Avison. PhD U. of Ottowa, 1975.

Marie-Claire Blais

MORIN,Y. *1281*
Une saison dans la vie d'Emmanuel: les structures de l'oeuvre et le style de Marie-Claire Blais. PhD U. of Montreal, 1972.

SAHEB,A. *1282*
Ironie, dire et vouloir-dire chez Roch Carrier, Marie-Claire Blais, Réjean Ducharme. PhD U. of Montreal, 1979.

Louise Morey Bowman

PRECOSKY,D.A. *1283*
Canadian poetry 1910 to 1925: the beginnings of modernism. [Includes Louise Morey Bowman.] PhD U. of New Brunswick, 1979.

Laure Conan

RODEN,L.S. *1284*
Laure Conan: the first French-Canadian woman novelist (1845–1924). PhD U. of Toronto, 1956.

Isabella Crawford

BURNS,R.A. *1285*
The intellectual and artistic development of Isabella Valancy Crawford. PhD U. of New Brunswick, 1982.

Sara Jeannette Duncan

FORTIER,D.N. *1286*
The European connection: a study of Thomas Haliburton, Gilbert Parker, and Sara Jeannette Duncan. PhD U. of Toronto, 1981.

MCKENNA,I.K. *1287*
Sara Jeannette Duncan: the New Woman: a critical biography. PhD Queen's U. at Kingston, 1981.

Anne Hébert

CHIASSON,A.P. *1288*
The tragic mood in the works of Anne Hébert. PhD Tufts U. 1974.

EMOND,M. *1289*
Le monde imaginaire d'Anne Hébert dans *Les chambres de bois, Kamouraska* et *Les enfants du Sabbat*. PhD Laval U. 1981.

JVERY,R. *1290*
Oeuvres en prose d'Anne Hébert: essai de semiotique narrative et discursive de *La robe corail* et de *Kamouraska*. PhD U. of Ottowa, 1977.

PATERSON,J.M. *1291*
L'Architexture des *Chambres de bois*: modalités de la représentation chez Anne Hébert. PhD U. of Toronto, 1981.

THERIAULT,S. *1292*
La quéte d'équilibre dans l'oeuvre romanesque d'Anne Hébert: étude psychostructurale. PhD U. of Ottowa, 1978.

Margaret Laurence

CURRY,G.C. *1293*
Journeys toward freedom: a study of Margaret Laurence's fictional women. PhD Indiana U. 1980.

Marie LeFranc

CHARTRES,S.M. *1294*
Circle of solitude: the life and works of Marie LeFranc. PhD U. of Virginia, 1972.

Gabrielle Roy

BABBY,E.R. *1295*
The language of spectacle and the spectacle of language in selected texts of Gabrielle Roy. PhD Yale U. 1980.

Classical literature

See also above 15, 16, 18, 19.

AKINLUYI,E.O. *1296*
The role of female characters in Vergil's *Aeneid*. MA U. of Durham, 1966.

BARRY,T.C. *1297*
'To Megkon': the function of the choral stasion in Euripides' *Helen*. PhD Yale U. 1972.

BOEDEKER,D.D. *1298*
Aphrodite's entry into Greek epic. PhD Saint Louis U.,, 1973.

BRAUN,R.E. *1299*
Docta puella fuit: resentment and reprisal in Propertius. PhD U. of Texas at Austin, 1969.

CLADER,L.L. *1300*
Helen: the evolution from divine to heroic in Greek epic tradition. PhD Harvard U. 1974.

COLLINS,L.L. *1301*
Neikeos Arkhé: Helen and heroic ethics. PhD Cornell U. 1982.

CRYSTAL,P. *1302*
An investigation into whether differences in attitude to women are reflected in the work of Lucretius, Catullus, Propertius, the corpus Tibullianum, Horace and Ovid. MPhil CNAA, 1983.

FREIERT,W.K. *1303*
The motifs of confrontation with women in Homer's *Odyssey*. PhD U. of Minnesota, 1972.

GARRIGUES,J.T. *1304*
Cicero's references to women, and their role in Roman society. PhD U. of Chicago, 1968.

GENOVESE,E.N. *1305*
Attis and Lesbia: Catullus' Attis poem as a symbolic reflection of the Lesbia cycle. PhD Ohio State U. 1970.

GROTEN,F.J. *1306*
The tradition of the Helen legend in Greek literature. PhD Princeton U. 1955.

HAMILTON,J.D.B. *1307*
The characterization and function of Helen in Euripidean drama. PhD U. of Minnesota, 1973.

HILL,A. *1308*
The women of Sophocles and Aeschylus. MA U. of London, 1910.

JACOBSON,H. *1309*
Studies in Ovid's *Heroides*. (Esp. Penelope and Briseis.) PhD U. of Columbia, 1967.

KURMALLY,M.Y. *1310*
Martial's attitude towards women. PhD Ohio State U. 1971.

MACK,A.M. *1311*
Mulieres comicae: female characters in Plautus and his predecessors. PhD Harvard U. 1967.

MACKINNON,J.K. 1312
The presentation of women in early Greek heroic poetry and the three tragedies. BLitt U. of Oxford, 1969.

MARQUARDT,P.A. 1313
Ambivalence in Hesiod and its relationship to feminine deities. PhD U. of Wisconsin-Madison, 1976.

MORROW,L.S. 1314
Euripides' treatment of women: an androgynous answer. PhD Ohio State U. 1974.

NUGENT,M.R. 1315
The literary treatment of virginity in the first four centuries of Greek Christian literature. PhD Catholic U. of America, 1942.

ODOM,W.L. 1316
A study of Plutarch: the position of Greek women in the first century after Christ. PhD U. of Virginia, 1964.

PAGE,A. 1317
Women in ancient comedy. MA U. of Manchester, 1947.

PATTICHIS,P.L. 1318
Euripides' Helen and the romance tradition. PhD U. of Columbia, 1963.

POOLE,H.M. 1319
The unity of Euripides' *Hecuba* by way of the image of Hecuba as an earth mother. PhD Florida State U. 1979.

POWELL,B. 1320
Erichthonius and the three daughters of Cecrops. PhD Cornell U. 1905.

PROST,W.A. 1321
The 'Eidolon' of Helen: diachronic edition of a myth. PhD Catholic U. of America, 1977.

SMITHSON,M.A. 1322
The position of women in New comedy. MA U. of Nottingham, 1965.

TOY,K.N. 1323
The women of Sophocles. MA U. of Birmingham, 1911.

TROUSDELL,R. 1324
The ethical women in six Euripidean tragedies. PhD Yale U. 1974.

VELISSARIOU,A. 1325
Representations of women in Aeschylus. PhD U. of Essex, 1982.

VISSER,M.A.B. 1326
The Erinyes: their character and function in classical Greek literature and thought. [Mythological female revenge figures.] PhD U. of Toronto, 1980.

WATTS,M. 1327
The characterization of women in Plautus and Terence and the fragments of Menander. MA U. of London, 1919.

WEST,G.S. 1328
Women in Vergil's *Aeneid*. PhD U. of California, Los Angeles, 1975.

WILLIAMS,J.M. 1329
The theme of the deserted heroine in classical literature. MA U. of Wales, 1935.

YIALOUCAS,C.S. 1330
The conflict of Doxa and Aletheia in Euripides and his predecessors. PhD U. of California, Berkeley, 1981.

English, Irish and Welsh literature

Up to 1500

ANDERSON,J.E. 1331
Strange, sad voices: the portraits of Germanic women in the old English 'Exeter Book'. PhD U. of Kansas, 1978.

APROBERTS,R.P. 1332
Criseyde and the moral of Chaucer's Troilus. PhD U. of California, Berkeley, 1950.

ATKINSON,C.W. 1333
'This creature': a study of *The book of Margery Kempe*. PhD Boston Coll. 1979.

BEACH,J.W. 1334
The loathly lady: a study in the popular elements of the Wife of Bath's tale: with a view to determining its story type. PhD Harvard U. 1907.

BELANOFF,P.A. 1335
The changing image of women in Old English poetry. PhD New York U. 1982.

BERKELEY,G.A. 1336
Julian of Norwich: the rhetoric of revelation. PhD Princeton U. 1982.

BURKE,L.B. 1337
Women in the medieval manuals of religious instruction and John Gower's *Confessio amantis*. PhD Columbia U. 1982.

CARTER,P.N. 1338
An edition of William of Malmesbury's *Treatise on the miracles of the virgin*, with an account of its place in his writing and in the development of Mary legends in the twelfth century. DPhil U. of Oxford, 1960.

CA VALCANTI,L.N.T. 1339
Sovereignty in love or obedience in marriage: an analysis of the sovereignty obedience theme and its relationship to the characterization of women in the major works of Geoffrey Chaucer. PhD Pennsylvania State U. 1962.

CHAUVIN,J. 1340
The role of Mary Magdalene in medieval drama. PhD Catholic U. of America, 1951.

CLAYTON,M. 1341
The cult of the Blessed Virgin Mary in Anglo-Saxon England, with particular reference to the vernacular texts. DPhil U. of Oxford, 1983.

CODER,R.V. 1342
Chaucer's Wife of Bath. PhD U. of Iowa, 1942.

CONROY,A.R. 1343
The isle of ladies: a fifteenth-century English Chaucerian poem. PhD Yale U. 1976.

CORTINA,L.R. 1344
Composition and meaning of the *Vita de Santa Maria Egipciaca*. PhD Case Western Reserve U. 1972.

DOYLE,T.A. 1345
Classical and baroque elements of spirituality in mediaeval didactic works for women. PhD Fordham U. 1948.

EGGEBROTEN,A.M. 1346
Women in the 'Katherine' group and *Ancrene Riwle*. PhD U. of California, Berkeley, 1979.

ESTRICH,R.M. 1347
A study of the sources and interpretation of Chaucer's Legend of Good Women. PhD Ohio State U. 1935.

FRANK,M.H.L. 1348
The Prioress and the Puys: a study of the cult of the virgin and the medieval Puys in relation to Chaucer's prioress and her tale. PhD U. of Colorado, 1970.

GANGULY,S. 1349
A study of Chaucer's diction and terms for womanly beauty. PhD U. of London, University College, 1940.

GARTH,H.M. 1350
St Mary Magdalene in medieval literature. PhD Johns Hopkins U. 1949.

GOULD,M.A. 1351
Women's roles in Anglo-Saxon and Eddic poetry. PhD U. of Oregon, 1974.

HALLER,R.S. 1352
The old whore and mediaeval thought: variations on a convention. PhD Princeton U. 1960.

HUGHES,H.H. 1353
Chaucer's Criseyde and her ancestry. PhD U. of Texas, 1948.

HUGHES,M.J. 1354
Women healers in medieval life and literature. PhD Columbia U. 1942.

JANNARELLI,C.T. 1355
Marian lyrics in Middle English. PhD U. of Pennsylvania, 1957.

JESMOK,J.M. 1356
Malory's women. PhD U. of Wisconsin-Milwaukee, 1979.

KENNEDY,T.C. 1357
Anglo-Norman poems about love, women and sex from British Museum Ms Harley 2253. PhD Columbia U. 1973.

KISER,L.J. 1358
In service of the flower: Chaucer and the Legend of Good Women. PhD U. of Virginia, 1977.

KLINCK,A.L. 1359
Female characterisation in Old English poetry. PhD U. of British Columbia, 1976.

KNITTEL,F.A. 1360
The women in Chaucer's Fabliaux. PhD U. of Colorado, 1961.

LANDRUM,M.H. 1361
A fourfold interpretation of the Wife's lament. PhD Rutgers U. 1963.

LEWIS,L.E. 1362
The play of Mary Magdalene. PhD U. of Wisconsin, 1963.

LUCKETT,R. 1363
The legend of St Cecilia and English literature: a study. PhD U. of Cambridge, 1972.

MCDERMOTT,J.J. 1364
Mary Magdalene in English literature from 1500 to 1650. PhD U. of California, Los Angeles, 1964.

MCELWEE,K.M.M. 1365
The change in the poet's conception of ideal womanhood subsequent to contact with French literature at the Norman Conquest. MA National U. of Ireland, 1952.

MCMASTER,H.N. 1366
The legend of St Cecilia in Middle English literature. PhD Yale U. 1936.

MALVERN,M.M. 1367
The Magdalen: an exploration of the shaping of myths around the Mary Magdalene of the New Testament canonical gospels and an examination of the effects of the myths on the literary figure, particularly on the heroine of the fifteenth-century Digby play. PhD Michigan State U. 1969.

MANNING,S.J. 1368
Ten Middle English Mary-lyrics. PhD Johns Hopkins U. 1956.

MAYNADIER,G.H. 1369
The Wife of Bath's tale: a study of its sources and the tales related to them. PhD Harvard U. 1898.

MONTGOMERY,A.E. 1370
Devotion to the Blessed Virgin Mary in English life and literature before 1300. PhD Northwestern U. 1937.

MORLEY,K.E. 1371
The role of women in Middle English versions of the downfall of the fellowship of the Round Table. MA U. of Manchester, 1977.

MULRODNEY,C.R. 1372
The cultus of the Blessed Virgin Mary in the Middle English lyrics. PhD St John's U. 1942.

MURPHY,M.A. 1373
The heritage of Cordelia: the early influences which have moulded the later poets' conception of woman. MA National U. of Ireland, 1932.

OLSTEAD,M.M. 1374
The role and evolution of the Arthurian enchantress. PhD U. of Florida, 1959.

PENNAR,A.M. 1375
Women in medieval Welsh literature: an examination of some literary attitudes before 1500. DPhil U. of Oxford, 1975.

POLLARD,L.M.S. 1376
Swa Icweme to Good: a study of the use of the Virgin Martyr legend in Medieval English literature with particular reference to Cynewulf's *Juliana* and *The Liflade ant te Passiun of Seinte Iuliene*, PhD Brown U. 1980.

PRYOR,C.L. 1377
The role of the Virgin Mary in the Coventry, York, Chester and Towneley cycles. PhD Catholic U. of America, 1933.

PULLIAM,W. 1378
The relationship of Geoffrey Chaucer's work to the antifeminist tradition. PhD Tulane U. 1967.

RAMSEY,R.V. 1379
Tradition and Chaucer's unfaithful woman. PhD U. of Oklahoma, 1964.

REED,G.H.V. 1380
Chaucer's women: commitment and submission. PhD U. of Nebraska-Lincoln, 1973.

ROBERTO,N.M. 1381
Making the mold: the roles of women in the Middle English metrical romance. PhD New York U. 1976.

ROBERTSUN,E.A. 1382
The triumph of female spirituality: a study of the Katherine group and its contexts. PhD Columbia U. 1982.

ROMER,K.T. 1383
Alceste as a figure of wisdom: a new interpretation of Chaucer's Legend of Good Women. PhD Harvard U. 1968.

ROWE,D.W. 1384
Chaucer's Legend of Good Women. PhD Harvard U. 1968.

SARGENT,A.M. 1385
The penitent prostitute: the tradition and evolution of the *Life of St Mary the Egyptian*. PhD U. of Michigan, 1977.

SCHRIEBER,E.G. 1386
The figure of Venus in late Middle English poetry. PhD U. of Illinois, 1969.

SHANER,M.C.E. 1387
An interpretive study of Chaucer's Legend of Good Women. PhD U. of Ilinois at Urbana-Champaign, 1973.

SHEA,V.A. 1388
Nat every vessel al of Gold: studies in Chaucer's legend of Good Women. PhD U. of Connecticut, 1971.

SHORT,A.J. 1389
Woman and womanhood in Chaucer's works. MLitt U. of Aberdeen, 1968.

SMAGOLA,M.P. 1390
Spek wel of love: the role of woman in Chaucer's Legend of Good Women. PhD Case Western Reserve U. 1972.

STARGARDT,U. 1391
The influence of Dorothea von Montau on the mysticism of Margery Kempe. PhD U. of Tennessee, 1981.

STONE,R.K. 1392
Middle English prose style: Margery Kempe and Julian of Norwich. PhD U. of Illinois at Urbana-Champaign, 1963.

SUTTON,J.W. 1393
A reading of Chaucer's Legend of Good Women based on its Ovidian sources. PhD Indiana U. 1979.

TALBOT,A.C. 1394
The search for the Otherworld Maiden, a mythic theme in early Norse and Celtic literature, with special reference to *Svipdagsmál*. PhD U. of Lancaster, 1976.

WADE,C.L. 1395
The Middle English Marian lyrics. PhD U. of Washington, 1982.

WALKER,B.M. 1396
The portrayal of women in Anglo-Saxon literature. MA U. of Leeds, 1955.

WEIR,E.G. 1397
The vernacular sources of the Middle English plays of the Blessed Virgin Mary. PhD Stanford U. 1942.

WRAY,D. 1398
The Virgin Mary and the courtly lady: a study in correspondence in the Middle English lyrics. MA U. of Keele, 1977.

1500–1700

General studies

ANGELL,C.F. 1399
'The Center Attractive': the function of women in Ben Jonson's comedy. PhD U. of Massachusetts, 1974.

ARBERY,G.C. 1400
Women, Christianity, and the stage in four Shakespearean comedies. PhD U. of Dallas, 1982.

AULD,I.B. 1401
Woman in the Renaissance: a study of the attitude of Shakespeare and his contemporaries. PhD U. of Iowa, 1939.

BABB,M.C.F. 1402
Declarations of independence: the rebel heroine, 1684–1800. PhD U. of Washington, 1973.

BANDEL ,B. 1403
Shakespeare's treatment of the social position of women. PhD Columbia U. 1951.

BARRANGER,M.S. 1404
Woman as tragic focus in Elizabethan and Jacobean drama. PhD Tulane U. 1964.

BARRATT,H.S. 1405
'The Rose Distilled': virginity, fertility and marriage in Shakespeare. PhD U. of Western Ontario, 1975.

BEITH-HALAHMI,E.Y. 1406
Angell fayre or strumpet lewd: the theme of Jane Shore's disgrace in ten sixteenth-century works. PhD Boston U. 1971.

BJORK,G.F. 1407
The renaissance mirror for fair ladies: Samuel Daniel's 'Complaint of Rosamond' and the tradition of the feminine complaint. PhD U. of California, Irvine, 1973.

BLOY,B.J.M. 1408
'Women's exercise': studies in the female personae of Elizabethan miscellanies. PhD U. of Tennessee.

BROOK,C.K. 1409
Mary Manley and Catherine Trotter: two late Restoration dramatists. PhD Harvard U. 1976.

BROOKS,C.B. 1410
The dramatization of attitudes toward women 1585–1595. PhD U. of California, Berkeley, 1955.

BROWNE,M.C. 1411
Shakespeare's Lady Macbeth and Cleopatra: women in a political context. PhD Brown U. 1976.

BUELER,L.W.E. 1412
The dramatic uses of women in Jacobean tragedy. PhD U. of Colorado at Boulder.

BUFTON,A.E. 1413
Female characterization in Jacobean tragedy, with special consideration of the tragedies of Heywood, Webster, Middleton, Beaumont and Fletcher. MA U. of Wales, 1939.

BURROWS,M.M. 1414
The position of woman in the seventeenth century and her influence on the literature. MA U. of Birmingham, 1912.

CASHDOLLAR,P.M. 1415
'My female friends': an examination of women and women's roles in the writings of Jonathan Swift. PhD U. of Rhode Island, 1978.

CHERRY,C.L. 1416
Women in the plays of Thomas Middleton. PhD U. of North Carolina at Chapel Hill, 1968.

CHILDRES,C.F. 1417
Feminine character and sexual roles in the plays of Thomas Middleton 1580–1627. PhD Northwestern U. 1973.

COOK,D.A. 1418
The role of the heroine in six Shakespearean comedies. PhD U. of Connecticut, 1977.

CUNNINGHAM,R. 1419
A study of *The myroure of oure ladyre*. PhD Fordham U. 1957.

DAVIES, R. 1420
Shakespeare's treatment of woman as wife in the tragedies and the final plays. MA U. of Wales (Cardiff), 1978.

DELUCA,D.M. 1421
Forgetful of her yoke: the woman warrior in three Renaissance epics. [*Orlando Furioso, Gerusalemme liberata, The faerie queene.*[PhD U. of Washington, 1981.

DOHERTY,G.T. 1422
The Renaissance liberation of women: studies in the theme of 'female dominance' in the poetry of the sixteenth and seventeenth centuries. PhD U. of London, University College, 1973.

DUSINBERRE,J. 1423
Attitudes to women in Jacobean drama. PhD U. of Warwick, 1970.

FALK,S.I. 1424
The vogue of the courtesan play, 1602–1610. PhD U. of Chicago, 1948.

FEIL,D. 1425
The female page in Renaissance drama. PhD Arizona State U. 1971.

FISHER,S.A. 1426
Circe as the fatal woman in Milton's poetry: Milton's concept of the Renaissance woman. PhD U. of Minnesota, 1971.

FLANNAGAN,R.C. 1427
Milton's Eve. PhD U. of Virginia, 1966.

FRIEDMAN,S. 1428
Some Shakespearian characterizations of women and their tradition. PhD Yale U. 1973.

GAGEN,J.E. 1429
Foreshadowings of the New Woman in English drama of the seventeenth and early eighteenth century. PhD Columbia U. 1950.

GEORGE,D.H. 1430
Is she also the divine image? Values for the femi-

nine in Blake, Milton and Freud. PhD State U. of New York at Buffalo, 1979.

GIBALDI,J. *1431*
The Baroque muse: Mary Magdalene in European literature, 1500 to 1700. PhD New York U. 1973.

GILBERT,M.A. *1432*
The shrew and the disguised girl in Shakespeare's comedies. PhD Indiana U. 1969.

GIRS,C.R. *1433*
Shakespeare's Venus figures and Renaissance tradition. PhD American U. 1975.

GLASSMAN,S.F. *1434*
The emancipated woman in John Dryden's comedies. PhD U. of Rhode Island, 1978.

GOLDBERG,L.A. *1435*
The role of the female in the drama of Lyly, Greene, Kyd, and Marlowe. PhD Northwestern U. 1969.

GOLDMAN,L.N. *1436*
Attitudes toward the mistress in five Elizabethan sonnet sequences. PhD U. of Illinois at Urbana-Champaign, 1964.

GRISE,M.S. *1437*
Shakespeare's comic heroines as women and as wives: a study of the limits of Shakespeare's feminism. PhD U. of Kentucky, 1979.

HANSEN,C.L. *1438*
Woman as individual in English Renaissance drama: a defiance of the masculine code. PhD Arizona State U. 1975.

HARNER,J.L. *1439*
Jane Shore: a biography of a theme in Renaissance literature. PhD U. of Illinos at Urbana-Champaign, 1972.

HASILKORN,A.M. *1440*
Prostitution in Elizabethan and Jacobean comedy. PhD St John's U. 1979.

HEIMS,N.S. *1441*
Fathers and daughters in the plays of Shakespeare. PhD City U. of New York, 1978.

HELTON,T. *1442*
The concept of woman's honour in Jacobean drama. PhD U. of Minnesota, 1952.

HENGERER,J.H. *1443*
The theme of the slandered woman in Shakespeare. PhD U. of Wisconsin, 1966.

HOEY, M.J.F. *1444*
Shakespeare and two women: a study of Eleanor of Aquitaine and Margaret of Anjou. PhD St John's U. 1950.

HORN,C.P .C *1446*
The tragic heroine and the theme of seduction in Jacobean drama. MA U. of Birmingham, 1977–78.

INGRAM,A.J.C. *1448*
Changing attitudes to 'bad' women in Elizabethan and Jacobean drama. PhD U. of Cambridge, 1978.

JAMES,K.H. *1449*
The widow in Jacobean drama. PhD U. of Tennessee, 1973.

JOHNSON,H.L. *1450*
A study of Congreve's theory of humour in comedy as it pertains to women characters. PhD Northern Illinois U. 1980.

JOH NSON,J.E. *1451*
The persecuted heroine in English Renaissance tragicomedy. PhD Columbia U. 1969.

JOHNSON,M.L. *1452*
Images of women in the works of Thomas Heywood. PhD Temple U. 1974.

JONES,M.B. *1453*
Self-images: a study of female autobiography written in England from 1680 to 1800. PhD U. of North Carolina at Chapel Hill, 1977.

KAHIN,,H.A. *1454*
Controversial literature about women: a survey of the literature of this type with special reference to the writings of the English Renaissance. PhD U. of Washington, 1934.

KATANKA,M.C. *1455*
Women of the underworld: a study of prostitutes and women criminals in popular literature, 1600–1700. MA U. of Birmingham, 1974.

KAYE,M. *1456*
'The Sword Philippan: woman as hero in Stuart tragedy. PhD U. of California, Berkeley, 1975.

KELLY,K.A. *1457*
'Amongst the Red, the White, the Green': woman, nature, and metaphor in Stuart love poetry. PhD Ohio State U. 1978.

KLINGER,G.C. *1458*
English she-tragedy, 1680–1715: its characteristics and its relationship to the sentimental tradition PhD Columbia U. 1970.

KOHLER,C. *1459*
The Elizabethan woman of letters: the extent of her literary activities. PhD U. of Virginia, 1936.

KRAUSE,J.J. *1460*
Elizabeth and Isis: Spenser's vision of *The faerie queene*. PhD Ohio U. 1975.

LICHTENBERG,S. *1461*
Images for the presentation of women in English Renaissance drama. PhD Rutgers U. 1977.

LIGHTFOOT,J.E. *1462*
The treatment of women in Restoration comedy of manners. PhD Texas Tech. U. 1973.

LITTLE,J .E. *1463*
Erring 'Humanium genus' and the providential

heroine in *The two gentlemen of Verona, The Merchant of Venice* and *The winter's tale*. PhD U. of Illinois at Urbana-Champaign, 1979.

LYNCH,D.E. *1464*
Woman as metaphor in George Herbert. PhD Fordham U. 1979.

LYTLE,T.A. *1465*
'More dissemblers besides women' by Thomas Middleton. PhD U. of Toronto, 1976.

MACCARTHY,B.G. *1465a*
Women's share in the development of the English novel, 1621–1818. PhD National U. of Ireland, 1939.

MCCOLLEY,D.K. *1466*
'Daughter of God and Man': the callings of Eve in *Paradise Lost*. PhD U. of Illinois at Urbana--Champaign, 1974.

MCDONALD,M.L. *1467*
The independent woman in the Restoration comedy of manners. PhD U. of Colorado at Boulder, 1975.

MACDONALD,R.A. *1468*
The widow: a recurring figure in Jacobean and Caroline comedy. PhD U. of New Brunswick, 1978.

MCFEELY,M.C. *1469*
Elizabethan views of women and Shakespeare's comic heroines. PhD City U. of New York, 1981.

MACKENZIE,A.M. *1470*
The women in Shakespeare's plays: a critical study from the dramatic and psychological points of view, and in relation to the development of Shakespeare's art. DLitt U. of Aberdeen, 1924.

MCKEWIN,C. *1471*
The subtile mirror: the function of feminine characterization in Ben Jonson's comedy. PhD U. of Maryland, 1977.

MAGAW,B.L. *1472*
The female characters in prose chivalric romance in England, 1475–1603: their patterns and their influences. PhD U. of Maryland, 1973.

MAYBERRY,S.N. *1473*
The adulterous wife in Renaissance drama. PhD U. of Tennessee, 1982.

MOODY,J. *1474*
Britomart, Imogen, Perdita, the Duchess of Malfi: a study of women in English Renaissance literature. PhD U. of Minnesota, 1971.

MORGAN,F.H. *1475*
A biography of Lucy, Countess of Bedford, the last great literary patroness. PhD U. of Southern California, 1958.

MORRELL,J.M. *1476*
Women in Elizabethan and Jacobean tragedy: a study of the principal conventions and influences governing the treatment of women characters in English tragedy. MA U. of London, Royal Holloway Coll. 1931.

MUSTAFA,K.A.M. *1477*
The comedy of contract; or, the second sex in early and late Restoration comedy. MLitt U. of Bristol, 1972.

MUTH,M.F. *1478*
Elizabethan praise of the queen: dramatic interaction in Royal panegyric. PhD Ohio State U. 1977.

NAFF,M.L. *1479*
The woman as object, partner, and 'persona' Renaissance conventions of love in English poetry of the sixteenth and seventeenth centuries. PhD U. of Oregon, 1978.

NICKLES,M.A. *1480*
The women in Congreve's comedies: characters and caricatures. PhD New York U. 1972.

NORVELL,B.J.G. *1482*
'O mother, mother, what have you done?' Shakespeare's mothers in relation to catastrophe. PhD U. of West Virginia, 1982.

O'SULLIVAN,J.P. *1483*
The disguised heroine in six Shakespearean comedies. PhD U. of Connecticut, 1970.

PATELLA,D.R. *1484*
Jacobean women and the comic stage. PhD U. of Oregon, 1978.

PATTON,J.F. *1485*
Elizabethan she-tragedies or female-complaints. PhD U. of Ohio, 1969.

PEAKE,R.H. *1486*
The stage prostitute in the English dramatic tradition from 1558 to 1625. PhD U. of Georgia, 1966.

PECZENIK,F. *1487*
Adam's other self: a reading of Milton's Eve. PhD City U. of New York, 1981.

PERRY,R. *1488*
Women, letters and the origins of English fiction: a study of the early epistolary novel (1660–1740). PhD U. of California, Santa Cruz, 1974.

PETER,L.A. *1489*
Women as educative guardians in Shakespeare's comedies. PhD Indiana U. 1975.

PETKO,C.M. *1490*
Positive and negative mutability in Books III and IV of Edmund Spenser's *The Faerie Queene*: a study of the four main female characters. PhD Florida State U. 1978.

POMERLAU,C.S. *1491*
'Resigning the needle for the pen': a study of autobiographical writings of British women before 1800. PhD U. of Pennsylvania, 1974.

RICHTER,T.L. *1492*
Anti-feminism in English literature, 1500–1660. PhD Northwestern U. 1934.

RILEY,M.G. *1493*
Infinite variety in Milton: a study of John Milton's concept of woman as shown in his works. PhD Rutgers U. 1962.

RUEDY,S.W. *1494*
Spenser's Britomart. PhD Duke U. 1975.

SALMAN,P.C. *1495*
Spenser's representatin of Queen Elizabeth I. PhD U. of Columbia, 1968.

SAXON,P.J. *1496*
The limits of assertiveness: modes of female identity in Shakespeare and the Stuart dramatists. PhD U. of Texas at Austin, 1977.

SALTER,N.K.C. *1497*
Masks and roles: a study of women in Shakespeare's drama. PhD U. of Connecticut, 1975.

SHEPHERD,S.L.G. *1498*
Some types of independent women in Jacobean drama. MLitt U. of Oxford, 1981.

SHIRK,H.N. *1500*
Iconography of the Goddess Natura in Spenser's *Faerie queene*. PhD Bryn Mawr Coll. 1973.

SINNOTT,B.S. *1501*
The father-daughter theme in Shakespeare's plays. PhD U. of North Carolina at Chapel Hill, 1972.

SMITH,K.D. *1502*
Women of the nobility in Shakespeare's English history plays. PhD Northwestern U. 1975.

SMITH,S.F. *1503*
Diana and the Renaissance allegory of love. PhD Princeton U. 1979.

SPROAT,K.B.V. *1504*
A reappraisal of Shakespeare's view of women. PhD Ohio State U. 1975.

STAUFFER,R.M. *1505*
The relation of women to English literature from 1558 to 1660. PhD Radcliffe Coll. 1942.

STONE,C.W. *1506*
John Ford's women: the moral center of his drama. PhD Kent State U. 1975.

SULLIVAN,J.M. *1507*
Women, wine and song: three minor genres of seventeenth-century British poetry. PhD U. of Minnesota, 1981.

TABB,M.M. *1508*
The female protagonist in Jacobean tragedy. PhD U. of Connecticut, 1976.

TAYLOR,J.R. *1509*
Lucy, Countess of Bedford, Jonson and Donne. PhD McMaster U. 1979.

TAYLOR,P.M. *1510*
Modest maids, matrons, and miscreants: the women in the chastity plays of John Fletcher. PhD Southern Illinois U. at Carbondale, 1981.

TAYLOR,W.E. *1511*
The villainess in Elizabethan drama. PhD Vanderbilt U. 1957.

WEINKAUF,M.S. *1512*
The two faces of Eve: the ideal and the bad Renaissance wife in *Paradise lost*. PhD U. of Tennessee, 1966.

WESSELS,E.J. *1513*
A mythic light on Eve: the function of mythological allusion in deepening her character and role in the epic action of *Paradise lost*. PhD Fordham U. 1972.

WILSON,E.C. *1515*
The idealization of Queen Elizabeth in the poetry of her age. PhD Harvard U. 1934.

WINDT,J.H. *1516*
Not cast in other women's mold: strong women characters in Shakespeare's *Henry VI* trilogy, Drayton's *England's Heroicall Epistles* and Jonson's poems to ladies. PhD Stanford U. 1974.

YOUNG,D.M. *1517*
The virtuous women in the Restoration playworld: the concept of marriage and the social status of women in the comedies of Etherege, Wycherley, and Congreve. PhD Florida State U. 1977.

ZIMMER,R.K. *1518*
A study of the heroines in the dramatic pieces of James Shirley. PhD U. of Kentucky, 1972.

ZINN,Z. *1519*
Love and marriage in the novels of English women: 1740–1840. PhD U. of Wisconsin, 1935.

Individual writers

Aphra Behn

BARRETT,A.G. *1520*
Plot, characterization and theme in the plays of Aphra Behn. PhD U. of Pennsylvania, 1965.

HARGREAVES,H.A. *1521*
The life and plays of Mrs Aphra Behn. PhD Duke U. 1960.

HOGAN,F.T. *1522*
The Spanish comedia and the English comedy of

intrigue with special reference to Aphra Behn. PhD Boston U. 1955.

LASSWELL,T. *1523*
Two plays of Aphra Behn: *The rovers* Part One and *The feign's curtezans*: a theatrical defence of the author and the comedy of intrigue. PhD U. of Oregon, 1982.

LEJA,A.E. *1524*
Aphra Behn Tory. PhD U. of Texas at Austin, 1962.

LINDQUIST,C.A. *1525*
The prose fiction of Aphra Behn. PhD U. of Maryland, 1970.

MEYER,A.G. *1526*
Romance and realism in the novels of Aphra Behn and previous prose fiction. PhD Ohio U. 1967.

O'DONNELL,M.A. *1527*
Experiments in the prose fiction of Aphra Behn: Behn's use of narrational voice, character, and tone. PhD Florida U. 1979.

QUANTRILL,E.M. *1528*
Alphra Behn: a Restoration writer of popular fiction. MA U. of Liverpool, 1974.

SAUL,S.M. *1529*
The comic art of Aphra Behn. PhD Harvard U. 1977.

SCOTT,C.S. *1530*
Aphra Behn: a study in dramatic continuity. PhD Texas Christian U. 1972.

SHEFFEY,R.T. *1531*
The literary reputation of Aphra Behn. PhD U. of Pennsylvania, 1959.

WAKEFIELD-RICHMOND,M.K. *1532*
The life and works of Mrs Alphra Behn, with a special study of *Oroonoko*. BLitt U. of Oxford, 1949.

ZUTHER,S.K. *1533*
The world of love and its ethic in Aphra Behn's comedies. PhD U. of Kansas, 1980.

Margaret Cavendish

COCKING,H.M. *1534*
Originality and influence in the work of Margaret Cavendish, first duchess of Newcastle. MPhil U. of Reading, 1973.

Mary Herbert, Countess of Pembroke

JACKSON,P.J. *1535*
An Elizabethan translator: the Countess of Pembroke with particular attention to her *Discourse of life and death*. PhD U. of Washington, Seattle, 1940.

NEWCOMB,E.A. *1536*
The Countess of Pembroke's circle. PhD U. of Wisconsin, 1938.

SHEPPERD,S.J. *1537*
The forbidden muse: Mary Sidney Herbert and Renaissance poetic theory and practice. PhD Texas Woman's U. 1980.

WYNNE,B.Y. *1538*
(Part II): The education of Mary Sidney. PhD Rutgers U. 1979.

YOUNG,F.C. *1539*
Mary Sidney, Countess of Pembroke. PhD U. of Wisconsin, 1911.

Katherine Philips

SOUERS,P.W. *1540*
Mrs. Katherine Philips, the matchless Orinda. PhD Harvard U. 1928.

WOODWARD,A. *1541*
The life and works of Katherine Philips. CertLit* U. of Oxford, 1920.

The eighteenth century

General and comparative studies

ALLEN,M.J. *1542*
'A contradiction still': some eighteenth-century characterizations of women. PhD U. of Oregon, 1976.

BARRON,S.S. *1543*
Female difficulties: woman's role and woman's fate in eighteenth- century English women's fiction. PhD Ohio State U. 1982.

BRICK,G. A. *1544*
Samuel Johnson and four literary women. [Elizabeth Carter, Charlotte Lennox, Fanny Burney and Hannah More.] PhD Arizona State U. 1979.

BROWN,R.G. *1545*
The role of the Duchess of Marlborough in Augustan literature. PhD Rochester U. 1972.

BUTLE R,M.E. *1546*
The rhetoric of self-consciousness and of self-knowledge in *Moll Flanders, Evelina, Anna St Ives* and *Emma*. PhD Stanford U. 1979.

CLANCEY,R.W. *1547*
The Augustan fair-sex debate and the novels of Samuel Richardson. PhD U. of Maryland, 1966.

COLEMAN,V.J. *1548*
English dramatic adaptations of Richardson's *Pamela* in the 1740s. PhD U. of Arkansas, 1969.

DAMMERS,R.H. *1549*
Female characters and feminine morality in the tragedies of Nicholas Rowe. PhD U. of Notre Dame, 1971.

DERDERIAN,N.C. *1550*
Against the patriarchal pomp! A study of the feminine principle in the poetry of William Blake. PhD State U. of New York at Buffalo, 1974.

DICK,M. *1551*
Fathers and daughters in eighteenth-century British drama. PhD Columbia U. 1982.

DUKE,K.M. *1552*
Women's education and the eighteenth-century British novel. PhD U. of Arkansas, 1980.

EPES,A.R. *1553*
Her fertile fancy and her feeling heart: the anatomy of the eighteenth-century English woman novelist. PhD Fordham U. 1964.

FINDLEY,S. *1554*
Feminist politics and the fiction of Eliza Fenwick, Mary Hays and Mary Wollstonecraft. PhD U. of Essex, 1982.

FISHER,W.R. *1555*
The unfortunate female: a study of the penitent prostitute type in English literature of the third quarter of the eighteenth-century. PhD Princeton U. 1922.

FOSTER,J.C. *1556*
Daniel Defoe and the position of women in eighteenth-century England: a study of *Moll Flanders* and *Roxana*. PhD U. of New Mexico, 1972.

FOSTER,M.J. *1557*
Margaret Montgomerie: her influence on the life and writings of James Boswell. PhD Florida State U. 1971.

FULBRIGHT,J.S. *1558*
William Blake and the emancipation of woman. PhD U. of Missouri-Columbia, 1973.

HALL,K.G. *1559*
The exalted heroine and the triumph of order: class, women and religion in the English novel, 1740–1800. PhD U. of Edinburgh, 1981.

HOAGLAND,F.M. *1560*
The women of Steele and Addison: a critical and literary interpretation of their status in the early eighteenth-century. PhD Cornell U. 1933.

HOFFELD,L. *1560a*
The servant heroine in eighteenth and nineteenth century British fiction: the social reality and its image in the novel. PhD New York U. 1975.

HOWELLS,C.A. *1561*
The presentation of emotion in the English Gothic novels of the late eighteenth and early nineteenth centuries, with particular reference to Ann Radcliffe's *The mysteries of Udolpho*, M.G. Lewis's *Monk*, Mary Shelley's *Frankenstein*, C.R. Maturin's *Melmoth the wanderer*, Charlotte Brontë's *Jane Eyre* and works by the minor Minerva Press novelists Regina Roche and Mary Ann Radcliffe. PhD U. of London, 1969.

HUEBNER,W.V. *1562*
Convention and innovation in the satirical treatment of women by the major satirists of the early eighteenth century. PhD U. of Minnesota, 1964.

HUGHES,B.E. *1563*
Women novelists before Jane Austen. MA U. of Wales, 1915.

HUKE,I.R. *1564*
The Gothic novels of the Radcliffe school: a study of the novels written between 1788 and 1800 by Mrs Ann Radcliffe and her imitators with special attention to the relationship between these novels and the themes of the sublime evolved by Edmund Burke and others. MPhil U. of East Anglia, 1977.

JACOBSON,M.C.K. *1565*
Women in the novels of Defoe, Richardson, and Fielding. PhD U. of Connecticut, 1975.

KIMBALL,J.G. *1566*
A structural analysis of the women in *Gulliver's travels*. PhD Case Western Reserve U. 1962.

KRIER,W.J. *1567*
A pattern of limitations: the heroine's novel of the mind. PhD Indiana U. 1973.

KUTRIEN,M.G. *1568*
Popular British romantic women poets (1790–1832). PhD Bowling Green State U. 1974.

LACY,K .W. *1569*
An essay on feminine fiction, 1757–1803. PhD U. of Wisconsin, 1972.

LAL,R.R. *1570*
Women in the novels of Miss Fanny Burney, Mrs Charlotte Smith, Mrs Ann Radcliffe and Miss Maria Edgeworth. MA U. of London, 1965.

LARSON,E.S. *1571*
Early eighteenth-century English women writers: their lives, fiction and letters. PhD Brandeis U. 1987.

LOTT,J.R. *1572*
The vogue of the betrayed woman theme in English fiction, 1740–1775. PhD Duke U. 1962.

MCCORD,N.O.N. *1574*
Smollett's quest for character: a study of his use of types of the feminine. PhD Auburn U. 1979.

MASON,S.R. *1575*
Daniel Defoe's paradoxical stand on the status of women. PhD U. of Utah, 1974.

MATTERN,E.R. *1576*
Samuel Richardson and feminism: a study of the secondary relationships in *Clarissa*. PhD Michigan State U. 1979.

METCALFE,J.E. *1577*
Jonathan Swift and the stage of the world: a study of Swift's poetry, with particular reference to the poems about women. PhD U. of Florida, 1974.

MISE,R.W. *1578*
The Gothic heroine and the nature of the Gothic novel. PhD U. of Washington, 1970.

MURPHY,K.M. *1579*
The emanations of the four Zoas: Ahania, Enion, Vala, Enitharmon. [Feminine representations in Blake.] PhD U. of Toledo, 1979.

NEEDHAM,G.B. *1580*
The old maid in the life and fiction of eighteenth-century England. PhD U. of California, Berkeley, 1938.

NORTON,H.R. *1580a*
The archetypal feminine in the poetry of Percy Bysshe Shelley. PhD Syracuse U. 1976.

O'DONNELLY,S.R. *1581*
'Born to know, to reason, and to act': Samuel Johnson's attitude toward women as reflected in his writings. PhD U. of Arizona, 1979.

PLATT,C.M. *1582*
Patrimony as power in four eighteenth-century women's novels: Charlotte Lennox's *Henrietta* 1758, Fanny Burney's *Evelina* 1778, Charlotte Smith's *Emmeline* 1788, Ann Radcliffe's *The mysteries of Udolpho* 1794. PhD U. of Denver, 1980.

POLLACK, E.M. *1583*
Perspectives on a myth: women in the verse of Swift and Pope. PhD Columbia U. 1979.

PYKARE,N.C. *1584*
The female part of the species: a study of women in Fielding. PhD Kent State U. 1976.

ROBERTS,B.B. *1585*
The Gothic romance: its appeal to women writers and readers in late eighteenth-century England. PhD U. of Massachusetts, 1975.

ROGERS,K.M. *1586*
Jonathan Swift's attitude toward women. PhD Columbia U. 1957.

RUDOLF,J.E. S. *1587*
The novels that taught the ladies: a study of popular fiction written by women, 1702–1834. PhD U. of California, San Diego, 1972.

RUSSELL,A.Z. *1588*
The image of women in eighteenth-century English novels. PhD Brandeis U. 1974.

SCOWCRO FT,R.P. *1589*
Anti-Pamela: the problem of retribution as it affected women in the eighteenth-century novel. PhD Harvard U. 1947.

SEEMAN,I.L. *1590*
Clarissa: the history of a baroque Magdalen. PhD U. of Iowa, 1978.

SHEVELOW,K. A. *1590a*
'Fair-sexing it': Richard Steele's *Tatler* and the evolution of a feminized prose in English periodical literature. PhD U. of California, San Diego, 1981.

SIMONS,J.A. *1591*
The treatment of women in selected novels from Richardson to Jane Austen. MA U. of Manchester, 1972.

SMEDMAN,M.S. *1592*
A portrait of the ladies: women in popular English fiction, 1730–1750. PhD Indiana U. 1975.

SMITH,E. *1593*
Some pioneer women novelists and their contribution to the eighteenth-century novel, 1688–1740. PhD U. of London, 1926.

SPENCER,J. *1594*
Minor women novelists and their presentation of a feminine ideal, 1744–1800; with special reference to Sarah Fielding, Charlotte Lennox, Frances Brooke, Elizabeth Griffith, Harriet Lee, Clara Reeve, Charlotte Smith, Mary Wollstonecraft and Jane West. DPhil U. of Oxford, 1982.

STASKIEL,M.P. *1595*
The divine Clarissa: secular sanctity in the eighteenth century. PhD Duquesne U. 1972.

STEPTO,M.L. *1596*
Blake, Urizen, and the feminine: the development of a poetic logic. PhD U. of Massachusetts, 1978.

SWANSON,G.R. *1597*
Henry Fielding and the psychology of womanhood. PhD U. of South Carolina, 1976.

TAYLOR, A.R. *1598*
'Fellows without Breeches': male authors and their female narrators in the eighteenth- and nineteenth-century novel. PhD U. of California, Berkeley, 1975.

TODD-NAYLOR,U.. *1599*
Richardson's influence on the women novelists of the eighteenth century. PhD U. of London, University Coll. 1935.

WALLACE,J.W. *1600*
The Augustan poets and the fair sex. PhD Columbia U. 1954.

WATSON,A.F. *1601*
British women writers and the origins of the feminist movement in England in the latter part of the eighteenth century. MA U. of Manchester, 1964.

WEBER,D.L. *1602*
Fair game: rape and sexual aggression on women in some early eighteenth-century prose fiction. PhD U. of Toronto, 1980.

WHITE, R.B. *1602a*
A study of the *Female Tatler* 1709–1710. PhD U. of North Carolina at Chapel Hill, 1966.

Individual writers

Mary Astell

SMITH,F.M. *1603*
Mary Astell. PhD Columbia U. 1915–16.

Anna Letitia Barbauld

MOORE,C.E. *1604*
The literary career of Anna Letitia Barbauld. PhD U. of North Carolina at Chapel Hill, 1969.

Fanny Burney

BENKOVITE,M.J. *1605*
Fanny Burney, novelist. PhD Yale U.,1951.

BROWN,M.G. *1606*
Fanny Burney's three eighteenth-century romances: *Evelina, Cecilia* and *Camilla*. PhD U. of North Carolina at Greensboro, 1980.

FISCHER,F.W. *1607*
The novels of Fanny Burney: a formal analysis. PhD U. of California, Berkeley, 1972.

GERMAN,H.L. *1608*
Fanny Burney and the late eighteenth-century novel. PhD Ohio State U. 1957.

HARRIS,H.R. *1609*
Realism in the fiction of Frances Burney. PhD U. of Southern California, 1957.

HEMLOW,J. *1610*
The courtesy book element in Fanny Burney's works. PhD Radcliffe Coll. 1948.

KVERN ES,D.M. *1611*
A critical study of Fanny Burney. PhD U. of Minnesota, 1967.

MORRISON,M.L. *1612*
Fanny Burney and the theatre. PhD U. of Texas at Austin, 1957.

MULLIKEN,E.Y. *1613*
The influence of the drama on Fanny Burney's novels. PhD U. of Wisconsin, 1969.

ROSS,D.L. *1614*
Female difficulties: the struggle between author and woman in the novels of Fanny Burney. PhD U. of Rochester, 1980.

WADDELL,J.N. *1615*
The language of Fanny Burney. PhD U. of Leicester, 1977.

WHITE,E. *1616*
Fanny Burney, novelist, a study in technique. PhD U. of Illinois at Urbana-Champaign, 1951.

Elizabeth Carter

HAMPSHIRE,G.I. *1617*
An edition of some unpublished letters of Elizabeth Carter (1717–1806), and a calendar of her correspondence. BLitt U. of Oxford, 1972.

Susanna Centlivre

BOWYER,J.W. *1618*
The life and works of Mrs Susanna Centlivre. PhD Harvard U. 1928.

BURKE,T.W. *1619*
Susanna Centlivre's *A bold stroke for a wife*: a re-evaluation. PhD Case Western Reserve U. 1971.

HOOR,H.Ten *1620*
A reexamination of Susanna Centlivre as a comic dramatist. EdD U. of Michigan, 1963.

MARKEL ,S.A. *1621*
The cook's wife reconsidered: an evaluation of the comedies of Susanna Centlivre. PhD U. of Kansas, 1982.

STATHAS,T. *1622*
A critical edition of three plays by Susanna Centlivre. PhD Stanford U. 1965.

Hester Chapone

ROBINSON,I.H. *1623*
The life and works of Hester Chapone. BLitt U. of Oxford, 1936.

Mary Mitchell Colyer

HUGHES,H.S. *1624*
The life and works of Mary Mitchell Colyer. PhD U. of Chicago, 1917.

Elizabeth Elstob

COLLINS,S.H. *1625*
Elizabeth Elstob: a biography. PhD Indiana U. 1970.

Sarah Fielding

NEEDHAM,A.E. *1626*
The life and works of Sarah Fielding. PhD U. of California, Berkeley, 1943.

PARRISH,A.M. *1627*
Eight experiments in fiction: a critical analysis of the works of Sarah Fielding. PhD Boston U. Grad. Sch. 1973.

RAYNAL,M.I. *1628*
A study of Sarah Fielding's novels. PhD U. of North Carolina at Chapel Hill, 1970.

WITTHAUS,R.L. *1629*
Sarah Fielding. BLitt U. of Oxford, 1951.

Elizabeth Griffith

ESHLEMAN,D.H. *1630*
Elizabeth Griffith: a biographical and critical study. PhD U. of Pennsylvania, 1947.

Eliza Haywood

ERICKSON,J.P. *1631*
The novels of Eliza Haywood. PhD U. of Minnesota, 1961.

MAYRENT,S.L. *1632*
'A champion of the sex': Eliza Haywood's contribution to the development of the English novel. PhD U. of Kent, 1978.

SCHOFIELD,M.A. *1633*
Quiet rebellion: the fictional heroines of Eliza Fowler Haywood. PhD U. of Delaware, 1979.

WHICHER,G.F. *1634*
The life and romances of Mrs Eliza Haywood. PhD Columbia U. 1915.

Elizabeth Inchbald

DUGAN,J.S. *1635*
A critical study of the plays of Elizabeth Inchbald. PhD U. of Toronto, 1979.

JOUGHIN,G.L. *1636*
The life and work of Elizabeth Inchbald. PhD Harvard U. 1932.

MCKEE,W. *1637*
Elizabeth Inchbald, novelist. PhD Catholic U. of America, 1935.

SIGL,P.M. *1638*
The literary achievement of Elizabeth Inchbald (1753–1821). PhD U. of Wales (Swansea), 1981.

Charlotte Ramsay Lennox

KYNASTON,A .M. *1639*
The life and writings of Charlotte Lennox, 1720–1804. MA U. of London, 1936.

SMALL,M.R. *1640*
The life and literary relations of Charlotte Lennox. PhD Yale U. 1925.

TODD-NAYLOR,U. *1641*
Charlotte Lennox. BLitt U. of Oxford, 1931.

Mary de La Rivière Manley

ANDERSON,P.B. *1642*
Mary de La Rivière Manley: a cavalier's daughter in Grub Street. PhD Harvard U. 1931.

DUFF,D.A.C. *1643*
Materials toward a biography of Mary de La Rivière Maney. PhD Indiana U. 1965.

Elizabeth Montagu

EWERT,L.H. *1644*
Elizabeth Montagu to Elizabeth Carter: literary gossip and critical opinions from the pen of the 'Queen of the Blues'. PhD Claremont Grad. Sch. 1968.

HANSON,M. *1645*
Elizabeth Montagu: a biographical sketch and a critical edition of her writings. PhD U. of Southern California, 1982.

Lady Mary Wortley Montagu

GRUNDY,I.M. *1646*
A critical edition of the verse of Lady Mary Wortley Montagu. DPhil U. of Oxford, 1971.

HALSBAND,R. *1647*
The literary career of Lady Mary Wortley Montagu. PhD Northwestern U. 1949.

MAHAFFEY,L.K. *1648*
Alexander Pope and his Sappho: Pope's relationship with Lady Mary Wortley Montagu and its influence on his work. PhD U. of Texas at Austin, 1963.

SCHWARTZ, K.C. *1649*
The rhetorical resources of Lady Mary Wortley Montagu. PhD Ohio State U. 1976.

Ann Radcliffe

DURANT,D.S. *1650*
Ann Radcliffe's novels: experiments in setting. PhD U. of North Carolina at Chapel Hill, 1971.

EPSTEIN,L. *1651*
Ann Radcliffe's Gothic landscape of fiction and the various influences upon it. PhD New York U. 1971.

GARRETT,J. *1652*
Gothic stains and bourgeois sentiments in the novels of Mrs Ann Radcliffe and her imitators. PhD Dalhousie U. 1973.

KEEBLER,L.E. *1653*
Ann Radcliffe: a study in achievement. PhD U. of Wisconsin, 1967.

MCINTYRE,C.F. *1654*
Ann Radcliffe in relation to her time. PhD Yale U. 1918.

POUND,E.F. *1655*
The influence of Burke and the psychological critics on the novels of Ann Radcliffe. PhD U. of Washington, 1963.

SHERMAN,L.F. *1656*
Ann Radcliffe and the Gothic romance: a psychoanalytic approach. PhD State U. of New York at Buffalo, 1975.

SMITH,N.C. *1657*
The art of Gothic: Ann Radcliffe's major novels. PhD U. of Washington, 1967.

STOLER,J.A. *1658*
Ann Radcliffe: the novel of suspense and terror. PhD U. of Arizona, 1972.

SWIGART,F.H. *1659*
A study of the imagery in the Gothic romances of Ann Radcliffe. PhD U. of Pittsburgh, 1966.

TOMPKINS,J.G. *1660*
The work of Mrs Radcliffe and its influence on later writers. MA U. of London, 1921.

VALLEY,J.B. *1661*
Characterization of the Gothic heroine in Ann Radcliffe's works. PhD Howard U. 1981.

VIDYARTHY,D.P. *1662*
Sentiment and sensibility in English prose fiction from Samuel Richardson to Ann Radcliffe with special reference to character delineation. PhD U. of London, King's Coll. 1949.

WEISSMAN,A. *1663*
Thoughts in things: Ann Radcliffe as a psychological novelist. PhD City U. of New York, 1981.

Clara Reeve

GADSBY,E.J. *1664*
Clara Reeve. MA U. of London, 1926.

REEVES,J.K. *1665*
The novels of Clara Reeve. BLitt U. of Oxford, 1932.

SANTMYER,H.H. *1666*
Clara Reeve: her life and works. BLitt U. of Oxford, 1927.

Mary Robinson

FORRY,J.H. *1667*
A study of the novels of Mrs Mary Robinson, 1758–1800. PhD U. of Pittsburgh, 1952.

Sarah Scott

CRITTENDEN,W.M. *1668*
The life and writings of Mrs Sarah Scott – novelist, 1723–1795. PhD U. of Pennsylvania, 1931.

ONDER LYZER,G.E. *1669*
Sarah Scott: her life and work. PhD U. of California, Berkeley, 1957.

Mrs Sheridan

BARNES,M.E.W. *1670*
Mrs Frances Sheridan, her life and works, including a study of her influence on Richard Brinsley Sheridan's plays and an edition of her comedy *The discovery*. PhD Yale U. 1914.

CHEW,S.P. *1671*
The life and works of Frances Sheridan. PhD Harvard U. 1937.

Charlotte Smith

FRY,C.L. *1672*
Charlotte Smith: popular novelist. PhD U. of Nebraska, 1970.

MARTIN,S.R. *1673*
Charlotte Smith, 1749–1806: a critical survey of her works and place in English literary history. PhD U. of Sheffield, 1980.

TURNER,R.P. *1674*
Charlotte Smith: new light on her life and literary career. PhD U. of Southern California, 1966.

Mary Wollstonecraft

FORRER,S.S. *1675*
The literary criticism of Mary Wollstonecraft. PhD U. of Colorado at Boulder, 1979.

HAYDEN,L.K. *1676*
A rhetorical analysis of Mary Wollstonecraft's *A vindication of the rights of woman*. PhD U. of Michigan, 1971.

The nineteenth century

General and comparative studies

ADAMS,R.M. *1677*
The Victorian woman in fact and fiction: 1871–1901. PhD Radcliffe Coll. 1951.

AGRESS,L.J. *1678*
The feminine irony: treatments of women by women in early nineteenth-century literature. PhD U. of Massachusetts, 1975.

ALAYA,F.M. *1679*
William Sharp's *Fiona MacLeod* 1855–1905: a study in later Victorian cosmopolitanism. PhD Columbia U. 1965.

ALDERMAN,J.J. *1680*
The treatment of women characters in some novels of Meredith and Hardy. MPhil U. of London, King's Coll. 1970.

ARAKAWA,S.R. *1681*
The relationship of father and daughter in the novels of Charles Dickens. PhD Yale U. 1977.

AUERBACH,N.J. *1682*
Reality as vision in the novels of Jane Austen and George Eliot. PhD Columbia U. 1970.

BADINJKI,T. *1683*
Some differing conceptions of the heroine in selected mid-Victorian novels. MLitt U. of Edinburgh, 1981.

BALLARD,G.P. *1684*
Thomas Hardy's tragic heroes and heroines. PhD U. of Illinois at Urbana-Champaign, 1979.

BALL STADT,C.P.A. *1685*
The literary history of the Strickland family: Elizabeth, 1794–1875; Agnes, 1796–1874; Jane Margaret, 1800–1888; Catherine Parr, 1802–1899; Susanna, 1803–1885; Samuel, 1809–1867. PhD U. of London, University Coll. 1965.

BHATT,P.B. *1686*
Thomas Hardy's women: a study in relationships. PhD Catholic U. of America, 1972.

BIDDISTON,L.T. *1687*
The *femme fatale* as symbol of the creative imagination in late Victorian fiction. PhD Louisiana State U. 1969.

BILLINGSLEY,B.A. *1688*
Take her up tenderly: a study of the fallen woman in the nineteenth-century English novel. PhD U. of Texas at Austin, 1962.

BISHOP,N.H. *1689*
The mother archetype in Arnold's *Merope* and Swinburne's *Atalanta in Calydon*. PhD U. of Wisconsin-Madison, 1972.

BOKEN,J.B. *1690*
Byron's ladies: a study of *Don Juan*. PhD Columbia U. 1970.

BOUMELHA,P.A. *1691*
Female sexuality, marriage and divorce in the fiction of Thomas Hardy, with special reference to the period 1887–1896. DPhil U. of Oxford, 1981.

BROWN,D.D. *1692*
From the queen's garden into the world: the concept of women in the novels of Charles Kingsley. PhD Georgia State Coll. of Arts and Sciences, 1981.

BRUNSON,M.L.C. *1693*
Toward 'fin de siècle' emancipation: the development of independence in Thomas Hardy's Wessex women. PhD Texas Tech. U. 1967.

BUTERY,K.A. *1694*
The Victorian heroine: a psychological study. PhD Michigan State U. 1980.

CAHILL,P.A.E. *1695*
Beginning the world: women and society in the novels of Dickens. PhD U. of Massachusetts, 1978.

CHARD,M.J. *1696*
Spiritual pilgrimage: a study of its sources and thematic significance in the novels of Charlotte Brontë, Elizabeth Gaskell, and George Eliot. PhD U. of Edinburgh, 1982.

CHEEK,E.R. *1697*
Dickens' views of women. PhD U. of North Carolina at Chapel Hill, 1967.

CLIFT,J.D. *1698*
Little Nell and the lost feminine: an archetypal analysis of some projections in Victorian culture. PhD U. of Denver, 1978.

COHEN,P.M. *1699*
Heroinism: the woman as the vehicle for values in the nineteenth-century English novel from Jane Austen to Henry James. PhD Columbia U. 1981.

CONDRAY,M.J. *1700*
Woman's one career: Trollope's view of the character and proper role of woman. PhD U. of Texas at Austin, 1969.

CONROY,E. *1701*
The women of George Meredith. MA U. of Wales, 1912.

COOK,M. *1702*
The odd woman in late-Victorian literature. MA U. of Sussex, 1976.

COPE,D.G. *1703*
The women characters of W.S. Landor. MA U. of Birmingham, 1917.

COSTIC,L.A.S. *1704*
Education in the novels of Charlotte Brontë Elizabeth Gaskell and George Eliot. PhD U. of Delaware, 1980.

COUGH,R.L. *1705*
Women and Thomas Hardy: a study of sex-linked qualities in the characters. PhD Oklahoma State U. 1975.

CRABBE,J.K. *1706*
The noblest gift: women in the fiction of Thomas Love Peacock. PhD U. of Oregon, 1973.

CROXT ON,C.I.R. *1707*
Thackeray's use of irony in characterizing women in his major novels. EdD Ball State U. 1978.

CULROSS,J.L. *1708*
The prostitute and the image of prostitution in Victorian fiction. PhD Louisiana State U. 1970.

CUNNINGHAM,A.R. *1709*
The emergence of the new woman in English fiction, 1870–1914. DPhil U. of Oxford, 1975.

DANIELS,E.A. *1710*
George Meredith's women: a study of changing attitudes in Victorian England. PhD New York U. 1954.

DAVIES,B.F. *1711*
The social status of the middle class Victorian woman as it is interpreted in representative mid-nineteenth century novels and periodicals. PhD Stanford U. 1943.

DAVIES,S. *1712*
Women in the works of women novelists in the second half of the nineteenth century. MA U. of Manchester, 1971.

DAVIS,R.R. *1713*
Anglican evangelicalism and the feminine literary tradition: from Hannah More to Charlotte Brontë. PhD Duke U. 1962.

DAVIS,S.de S. *1714*
The female protagonist in Henry James's fiction, 1870–1890. PhD Tulane U. 1974.

DENTON,R.L. *1715*
Female selfhood in Anthony Trollope's Palliser novels. PhD U. of Kentucky, 1977.

DETTER,H.M. *1716*
The female sexual outlaw in the Victorian novel: a stray in the conventions of fiction. PhD Indiana U. 1971.

DOLAN,E.M. *1717*
The greater women novelists of the Victorian age. MA National U. of Ireland, 1945.

DOLOGITE,D.G. *1718*
The evolution of Swinburne's *femme fatale* mythology. PhD St John's U. 1978

DUFFY,B.M. *1719*
The female archetypes in Swinburne's early work, 1857–1871. PhD Louisiana State U. 1981.

DYLLA,S.M. *1720*
Jane Austen and George Eliot: the influence of their social worlds on their women characters. PhD U. of Wisconsin-Milwaukee, 1974.

ELIASBERG,A.P. *1721*
The Victorian anti-heroine: her role in selected novels of the 1860s and 1870s. PhD City U. of New York, 1975.

ENZER,S.S. *1722*
Maidens and matrons: Gissing's stories of women. PhD State U. of New York at Stonybrook, 1978.

ESSEX,R. *1723*
A study of the role of the woman in Thomas Hardy's novels. PhD New York U. 1976.

EVANS,E. *1724*
The characterization of women in the English novels from Richardson to the Brontës. MA U of Wales, 1931.

EWBANK,D.R. *1725*
The role of woman in Victorian society: a controversy explored in six Utopias, 1871–1895. PhD U. of Illinois at Urbana-Champaign, 1968.

FOX,M.R. *1726*
The woman question in selected Victorian fiction, 1883–1900. PhD City U. of New York, 1975.

FRANCONE,C.B. *1727*
Women in rebellion: a study of the conflict between self-fulfillment and self-sacrifice in *Emma*, *Jane Eyre* and *The Mill on the floss*. PhD Case Western Reserve U. 1975.

GAINES,K.H. *1728*
'Equivocal heroines': women in Victorian sensation fiction. PhD Northwestern U. 1982.

GANDESBERY,J.J. *1729*
Versions of the mother in the novels of Jane Austen and George Eliot. PhD U. of California, Davis, 1976.

GEARY,S.E. *1730*
Scribbling women: essays on literary history and popular literature in the 1850s. PhD Brown U. 1976.

GOFF,B.M. *1731*
Artists and models: Rossetti's images of women. PhD Rutgers U. 1976.

GOLLA,M. *1732*
The emerging woman: tension between Anthony Trollope's theory and art, 1864–1880. PhD U. of Illinois at Urbana-Champaign, 1973.

HARRIS,K.S. *1733*
The new woman in the literature of the 1890s. PhD Columbia U. 1963.

HARRISON,S.T.C. *1734*
Irish women writers, 1800–1835. PhD Trinity Coll. Dublin, 1947.

HARTLEY,J. *1735*
A study of some mid-nineteenth century women novelists and their heroines. PhD U. of Essex, 1976.

HARTLEY,S.R. *1736*
The later novels of George Meredith: women's struggle for emancipation. PhD Florida State U. 1973.

HAYDOCK,J.J. *1736a*
The woman question in the novels of George Gissing. PhD U. of North Carolina at Chapel Hill, 1965.

HAZEN,L.S. *1737*
Vessels of salvation: fathers and daughters in six Dickens novels. PhD U. of Wisconsin-Madison, 1978.

HICKOK,K.K. *1738*
Representations of women in the work of nineteenth-century British women poets. PhD U. of Maryland, 1977.

HOFF,C.M. *1739*
Images of mid-Victorian women: the popular fiction of Yonge, Craik and Oliphant. PhD Indiana U. 1981.

HOFFMANN,L.N. *1740*
A delicate balance: the resolutions to conflict of women in the fiction of four women writers of the Victorian period. [Charlotte Brontë, George Eliot, 'George Egerton', Olive Schreiner.] PhD Indiana U. 1974.

HULL,G.T. *1741*
Women in Byron's poetry: a biographical and critical study. PhD Purdue U. 1972.

HUNT,L.S. *1742*
Ideology, culture and the female novel tradition: studies in Jane Austen, Charlotte Brontë and

George Eliot as nineteenth-century women writers. PhD U. of California, Berkeley, 1977.

HUNTER,S.K. *1743*
Transformation of pastoral: studies in the idyllic fiction of Mary Russell Mitford, Elizabeth Gaskell, George Eliot and Thomas Hardy. PhD U. of Warwick, 1981.

JARMUTH,S.L. *1744*
Dickens' use of women in his novels. PhD New York U. 1966.

JEKEL,P.L. *1745*
Thomas Hardy's heroines: a chorus of priorities. PhD U. of Virginia, 1981.

JONES,I.M. *1746*
Merched llen Cymru o 1850 i 1914. (The women of the literature of Wales from 1850 to 1914.) MA U. of Wales, 1935.

JOSEPHS,L.S. *1747*
A historical and critical study of Diana, heroine of *Diana of the crossways* by George Meredith. PhD U. of Pittsburgh, 1966.

KANDELA,A.A. *1748*
Tennyson's idea of women in relation to contemporary and Eastern influences. PhD U. of Dundee, 1975.

KATZ,J.N. *1748a*
Rooms of their own: forms and images of liberation in five novels. (*Evelina; Pride and prejudice; Jane Eyre; Middlemarch* and *The waves*. PhD Pennslyvania State U. 1972.

KENNEDY,J.D. *1749*
Trollope's widows: beyond the stereotypes of maiden and wife. PhD U. of Florida, 1975.

KEYSER,L.J. *1750*
Joan of Arc in nineteenth-century English literature. PhD Tulane U. 1970.

KILLHAM,E.J. *1751*
Tennyson's *The princess*: a study, with special reference to the 'woman question'. MA U. of London, University Coll. 1953.

KOWALESKI,E.A. *1752*
The dark night of her soul: the effects of Anglican Evangelicalism on the careers of Charlotte Elizabeth Tonna and George Eliot. PhD Columbia U. 1981.

KROESE,I .B. *1753*
The beauty and the terror: Shelley's visionary women. PhD U. of Ohio, 1966.

LAWSON,M.S. *1754*
Class structure and the female character in Anthony Trollope's *The way we live now*. PhD Bowling Green State U. 1975.

LOCKER,K.C.O. *1755*
The definition of woman: a major motif in Browning's *The ring and the book*. PhD U. of Illinois at Urbana- Champaign.

LUCAS,N.B. *1756*
Women and love relationships in the changing fictional world of Anthony Trollope. PhD U. of Illinois at Urbana-Champaign, 1973.

MCDANIEL,J.A. *1757*
Fettered wings half loose: female development in the Victorian novel. PhD Tufts U. 1975.

MCGAHAN,E.C. *1758*
An examination of the methods of Dickens and Thackeray in the characterization of women. MA U. of Wales, 1946.

MATTUS,M.E. *1759*
The 'fallen woman' in the *fin de siècle* English drama, 1884–1904. PhD Cornell U. 1974.

MEERS,G.M. *1760*
Victorian schoolteachers in fiction. PhD Northwestern U. 1953.

MELLICK,M.J.V. *1762*
Divergent melodramatic heroines of the mid-Victorian play: or, the woman who doesn't faint. PhD Ohio State U. 1976.

MEKEWETHER,J.A. *1763*
The burning chain: the paradoxical nature of love and women in Byron's poetry. PhD Wayne State U. 1969.

MITCHELL,S.H. *1764*
The unchaste woman in early fiction, 1835–1880. DPhil U. of Oxford, 1977.

MURPHY,M.J. *1765*
Dickens' 'other women': the mature women in his novels. PhD U. of Louisville, 1975.

MYERS,K.M. *1766*
Female archetypes in selected longer poems of Shelley. PhD Northern Illinois U. 1977.

NASH,S.A . *1767*
'Wanting a situation': governesses and Victorian novels. PhD Rutgers U. 1980.

NATOV,R.L. *1768*
The strong-minded heroine in mid-Victorian fiction. PhD New York U. 1975.

NESTOR,P.A. *1769*
Female friendships and communities: a study of women writers, 1840–1880. DPhil U. of Oxford, 1983.

NICHOLSON THOMPSON,M.P. *1770*
The changing ideal of womanhood in the novel and its relation to the feminist movement from 1837 to 1873. PhD U. of Cambridge, 1947.

NUNNALLY,J.C. *1771*
The Victorian femme *fatale*: mirror of the decadent temperament. PhD Texas Tech. Coll. 1968.

O'HEAR,M.F. *1772*
The constant dream: Coleridge's vision of woman and love. PhD U. of Maryland, 1970.

ONSLOW,B. *1773*
Environment and the social scene in the works of Mrs Gaskell with some comparison with the novels of Jane Austen and George Eliot. MA U. of Manchester, 1973.

OWEN S,G. *1774*
Town and country in the life and work of Mrs Gaskell and Mary Russell Mitford. MA U. of Wales, 1953.

PAGE,J.I. *1775*
Enduring Alice. [The Lewis Carroll heroine.] PhD U. of Washington, 1970.

PARRA,N. *1776*
Dickens and his heroines. PhD U. of Chicago, 1973.

PHILBIN,A.I. *1777*
The literary *femme fatale* – a social fiction: the wilful female in the deterministic vision of Thomas Hardy and in the psychological vision of Henry James. PhD Southern Illinois U. at Carbondale, 1977.

PIKE,H.A. *1778*
A study of the role of women in *David Copperfield*. MPhil CNAA 1983.

POINTON,M.C. *1779*
The growth of women's sport in late Victorian society as reflected in contemporary literature. MEd U. of Manchester, 1978.

PRESS,H.B. *1780*
Behind the looking glass: the heroine as a vehicle for literary and social satire in Thackeray's major novels. PhD New York U. 1979.

PUTZELL,S.M. *1781*
Victorian views of man in the novels of Charlotte Brontë and George Eliot. PhD Emory U. 1977.

RENSHAW,B.A. *1782*
Reason and imagination in the work of Jane Austen and Charlotte Brontë. MA U. of Liverpool, 1973.

RIBMAN,R.B. *1783*
John Keats: the woman and the vision. PhD U. of Pittsburgh, 1962.

RICHERT,E.S. *1784*
Perception of women's roles in Thomas Hardy's novels. PhD Brown U. 1976.

RICKERT,M. *1785*
The fallen woman in the Victorian novel. PhD U. of Colorado at Boulder, 1979.

RINEHART,N.M. *1786*
Anthony Trollope's treatment of women, marriage, and sexual morality seen in the context of contemporary debate. PhD U. of Maryland, 1975.

ROBINSON,E.W. *1786a*
Gissing's odd women: a study of marriage and feminism in the middle-class novels of George Gissing. PhD Ball State U. 1981.

RORABACHER,L.E. *1787*
Victorian women in life and fiction. PhD U. of Illinois at Urbana-Champaign, 1942.

ROSE,C .P. *1788*
Shelley's view of woman. PhD Claremont Grad. Sch. 1959.

ROSE,P.A. *1789*
The social position of women as reflected in the fiction of the period, 1880–1895. MA U. of London, External 1962.

ROWELL,G.R. *1790*
The dramatic treatment of women's social status, 1865–1914. BLitt U. of Oxford, 1951.

RUDM AN,C.F. *1791*
Wasted woman: the irony of sex in George Meredith. PhD State U. of New York at Stony Brook, 1979.

SANTANIELLO,A.E. *1792*
Charles Dickens' *Little Dorrit*: a study of the heroine as victim and savior. PhD Harvard U. 1961.

SATTERWHITE,J.N. *1793*
Godey's *Lady's book* and fiction, 1830–1850. PhD Vanderbilt U. 1954.

SAUNDERS,V.D. *1794*
Gentle spirits: female writers of the supernatural. PhD Princeton U. 1982.

SCANNELL,J.M.A. *1796*
The treatment of emotion in Jane Austen and Charlotte Brontë. DPhil U. of Oxford, 1975.

SCHAPIRO,B.A. *1797*
The romantic mother: ambivalent images of women in Romantic poetry. PhD Tufts U. 1979.

SCHLOSSTEIN,S.E. *1798*
Byron: the inverted role of the female in his poetry. PhD U. of Cincinnati, 1974.

SEIPLE, J.A.M. *1799*
Charles Dickens and the self-denying woman. EdD East Texas State U. 1979.

SENF,C.A. *1800*
Daughters of Lilith: an analysis of the vampire motif in nineteenth-century English literature. PhD State U. of New York at Buffalo, 1979.

SEPEDA,T. *1801*
Yeats and women: the nineteenth century. PhD U. of Reading, 1981.

SHOWALTER,E.C. *1802*
The double standard: criticism of women writers in England, 1845–1880. PhD U. of California, Davis, 1970.

SIEFERT,S.E. *1803*
The dilemma of the talented woman: a study in nineteenth century fiction. PhD Marquette U. 1974.

SONSTROEM,D.A. *1805*
Four fair ladies of heaven and hell: the fantasy and morality of Dante Gabriel Rossetti. PhD Harvard U. 1965.

SPORN,P. *1806*
The transgressed woman: a critical description of the heroine in the works of George Gissing, Thomas Hardy and George Moore. PhD State U. of New York at Buffalo, 1967.

SWANSON,J.M.B. *1806a*
Speaking in a mother tongue: female friendship in the British novel. (Jane Austen's *Persuasion*, Charlotte Brontë's *Shirley*, Meredith's *Diana of the crossways* and Virginia Woolf's *Mrs Dalloway*. PhD U. of California, Santa Barbara, 1981.

STEIN,S.G. *1807*
'Woman and her master': the feminine ideal as social myth in the novels of Charles Dickens, William Thackeray and Charlotte Brontë. PhD Washington U. 1976.

STEVENSON,R.C. *1808*
The heroine and the comic spirit: a study of the early novels of George Meredith. PhD Harvard U. 1969.

STINE,P.W. *1809*
The changing image of Mary Queen of Scots in nineteenth-century British literature. PhD Michigan State U. 1972.

STRICKLAND,E.P.M. *1810*
Metamorphoses of the muse: a study of woman as symbol of the romantic imagination. PhD York U. 1976.

STUBBS,P.J.E. *1811*
The portrayal of women in English fiction, 1880–1918. MA U. of Sheffield, 1974.

SYMES,D.S. *1812*
The heroine's search for salvation in late nineteenth-century British popular fiction. PhD U. of New Mexico, 1973.

THOM SON,M.P.N. *1813*
The changing ideals of womanhood in the novel and its relation to the feminist movement, 1837–73. PhD U. of Cambridge, 1947.

TRUDGILL,E. *1814*
Madonnas and magdalens: the origins and development of Victorian sexual attitudes in literature and society. PhD U. of Leicester, 1973.

TRUSSLER,G. *1815*
A comparative examination of the treatment of the theme of renunciation in the novels of Charlotte Brontë and George Eliot. MPhil U. of London, University Coll. 1968.

VAUGHAN,L.M. *1816*
Aspects of Hertha: Swinburne's symbol of the woman. PhD U. of Alberta, 1978.

WAIDNER,M.L. *1817*
From reason to romance: a progression from an emphasis on neoclassic rationality to romantic intuition in three English woman novelists. [Jane Austen, Charlotte and Emily Brontë.] PhD Tulsa U. 1973.

WALTERS,K.K. *1818*
Ladies of leisure: idle womanhood in the Victorian novel. PhD U. of Oregon, 1980.

WIDMER,E.J.R. *1819*
Love and duty: the heroines of Jane Austen and Charlotte Brontë. PhD U. of Washington, 1958.

WIJESINHA,R. *1820*
Marriage and the position of women as presented by some of the early Victorian novelists. DPhil U. of Oxford, 1979.

WINSOR,D.A. *1820a*
The continuity of the gothic: the gothic novels of Charlotte Brontë, Emily Brontë and Iris Murdoch. PhD Wayne State U. 1979.

WOOD,H. *1821*
Minor Victorian didactic fiction, 1850–1900, examined and described with especial reference to the publications of the tract societies and to the work of Hesba Stretton and Emma Jane Worboise. MA U. of Manchester, 1978.

YELIN,L. *1822*
Women, money and language: *Dombey and son* and the 1840s. PhD Columbia U. 1977.

YOUNGREN,V.R. *1823*
Moral life in solitude: a study of selected novels of Jane Austen, Charlotte Brontë, Elizabeth Gaskell and George Eliot. PhD Rutgers U. 1977.

Individual writers

Eugenia de Acton (Alethea Lewis, née Brereton)

SHIPPEN,E.P. *1824*
Eugenia de Acton, 1749–1827. PhD U. of Pennsylvania, 1944.

Jane Austen

ACABAL,P.G. *1825*
Jane Austen's moral vision: form and function. PhD Indiana U. 1973.

ALLAN,H. *1826*
The pastoral idea in the novels of Jane Austen. PhD U. of London, University Coll. 1972.

ANDERSON,W.E. *1827*
Jane Austen's novels as represented actions. PhD U. of California, Berkeley, 1968.

ARTHURS,A. *1828*
Arrangements with the earth: Jane Austen's landscapes. PhD Bryn Mawr Coll. 1972.

AUGUST,R.K. *1829*
(Part III) Family politics in Jane Austen's novels. PhD Rutgers U. 1978.

BABB,H.S. *1830*
Techniques of conversation in Jane Austen's novels. PhD Harvard U. 1955.

BANDE R,E. *1831*
Jane Austen's readers. PhD McGill U. 1981.

BEACH,L. *1832*
A rhetorical analysis of Jane Austen's novels. PhD Stanford U. 1971.

BEATTIE,T.C. *1833*
From *Pride and prejudice* to *Emma*: a story of Jane Austen as moralist. PhD U. of Michigan, 1968.

BENNETT,P. *1834*
Family relationships in the novels of Jane Austen: PhD U. of Washington, 1980.

BERNTSEN,C. *1835*
The discomforts of reading Jane Austen: punitive and subversive rhetoric in the six novels. PhD U. of California, Berkeley, 1971.

BINKLEY,W.D. *1836*
Comic self-discovery in Jane Austen's novels. PhD U. of Wisconsin, 1961.

BLUM,B.M. *1837*
A study of Jane Austen's juvenilia as a response to late eighteenth-century fiction and in light of her later work. MPhil U. of Oxford, 1979.

BRADBROOK,F.W. *1838*
Jane Austen: novelist of tradition. PhD U. of Wales (Bangor), 1965.

BRAMER,G.R. *1839*
The quality of love in Jane Austen's novels. PhD U. of Notre Dame, 1966.

BROWN,J.P. *1840*
The bonds of irony: a study of Jane Austen's novels. PhD Columbia U. 1975.

BROWN,L.W. *1841*
The novels of Jane Austen: a study of the language of comedy. PhD U. of Toronto, 1967.

BROWN, W.L. *1842*
The function of the family in Jane Austen's novels. PhD U. of California, Berkeley, 1953.

BRYANT,R.C.W. *1843*
Jane Austen's *Emma*: art and image. PhD U. of Texas at Austin, 1970.

BURROWS,J.F. *1844*
Jane Austen's *Emma*: a study of narrative art. PhD U. of London, Birkbeck Coll. 1967.

CANTRELL,D.D. *1845*
The twentieth-century criticisms of Jane Austen's *Mansfield Park* and *Emma*. PhD U. of Tennessee, 1970.

CHABOT,C.B. *1846*
The vicissitudes of desire: Jane Austen and the concept of style. PhD State U. of New York at Buffalo, 1972.

CHILLMAN,D. *1847*
Jane Austen's juvenilia as a key to the structure of her first three mature novels. PhD U. of Texas at Austin, 1963.

CONSTANTINE,A.V. *1848*
Wit in Jane Austen's novels: an expression of the conflict between duty and desire. PhD U. of Illinois at Urbana-Champaign, 1972.

CORWIN,L.J. *1849*
The concept of the self in the novels of Jane Austen. PhD U. of Pennsylvania, 1970.

CRAIK,W .A. *1850*
Pattern in the novels of Jane Austen. PhD U. of Leicester, 1963.

CUNNINGHAM,J.C. *1851*
Delicacy and decorum: Jane Austen and the eighteenth-century mentors of manners and morals. PhD U. of Chicago, 1970.

DARMA,B. *1852*
Character and moral judgment in Jane Austen's novels. PhD Indiana U. 1980.

DAVIE,J.N. *1853*
Jane Austen and her relationship to some aspects of eighteenth-century literature. BLitt U. of Oxford, 1965.

DELANEY ,J.F. *1854*
Chapter design in Jane Austen's novels. PhD Temple U. 1970.

DEVOR,A.N. *1855*
Jane Austen-student and teacher: a study of Jane Austen's use of educational ideas in her novels. PhD U. of Kansas, 1978.

DRAFFAN,R.A. *1856*
Jane Austen: an approach to her novels. MA U. of Liverpool, 1964.

DRIVER,R.E. K. *1857*
A study of Jane Austen's techniques of structure and exposition in her six major novels. MA U. of Manchester, 1958.

DRY,H. *1858*
Syntactic reflexes of point of view in Jane Austen's *Emma*. PhD U. of Texas at Austin, 1975.

DUCKWORTH,A.M. *1859*
The improvement of the estate: self and inheritance in Jane Austen's major fiction. PhD Johns Hopkins U. 1967.

DUFFY,J.M. *1860*
Jane Austen and the nineteenth-century critics of fiction, 1812–1913. PhD U. of Chicago, 1955.

DURGUN,L.K.H. *1861*
Jane Austen's art of adjustment: symbolic presentation in four novels. PhD Syracuse U. 1980.

EDGE,C.E. *1862*
Jane Austen's novels: a study of the theme of isolation. PhD Duke U. 1958.

EISNER,S.A. *1863*
Jane Austen's characters: manners of being. PhD U. of Pennsylvania, 1973.

ERICKSON,E.J.Q. *1864*
The significance of *Persuasion*. PhD U. of Washington, Seattle, 1970.

FAHNESTOCK,M.L. *1865*
The reception of Jane Austen in Germany: a miniaturist in the land of poets and philosophers. PhD Indiana U. 1982.

FERGUS,J.S. *1866*
Jane Austen's early novels: the educating of judgment and sympathy. PhD City U. of New York, 1975.

FIELDEN,R.D.S. *1867*
Jane Austen and the novel of manners, 1778–1830. MA U. of Manchester, 1953.

FLYNN,T.P. *1868*
The growth of community in Jane Austen's *Mansfield Park*. PhD Ohio U. 1977.

FOWLER,M.E. *1869*
Patterns of prudence: courtship conventions in Jane Austen's novels. PhD U. of Toronto, 1970.

FRAWLEY,J. *1870*
Jane Austen: satirist. MA National U. of Ireland, 1953.

FREEDMAN,F.S. *1871*
'Ceremonies of life': manners in the novels of Jane Austen. PhD Tufts U. 1979.

FRYWELL,D.R. *1872*
The patterns of Jane Austen's novels. PhD U. of Kentucky, 1953.

GLEASON,G.D. *1873*
Dramatic affinities in the life and work of Jane Austen. PhD U. of Iowa, 1956.

GLUCKSMAN,S. *1874*
The happy ending in Jane Austen. PhD State U. of New York at Stony Brook, 1973.

GRAEBER,G. *1875*
Comic, thematic, and mimetic impulses in Jane Austen's *Persuasion*. PhD Michigan State U. 1977.

GROSSMAN,M. *1876*
Jane Austen: the testing of wit. PhD Columbia U. 1978.

HARTZLER,S.K.K. *1877*
Marriage as theme and structure in Jane Austen's novels. PhD Indiana U. 1971.

HAWKES,D. *1878*
Jane Austen: heroines and horizons. PhD Rutgers U. 1978.

HELMS,A.E. *1879*
(Part II) Sensibility and sense in Jane Austen's *Persuasion*. PhD Rutgers U. 1971.

HILL,P.A.N. *1880*
The function of setting in Jane Austen's novels. PhD Auburn U. 1971.

HIRST,C.S. *1881*
Jane Austen's *Mansfield Park*. PhD Notre Dame U. 1973.

HOLLY,M.V. *1882*
Jane Austen and the uniqueness of *Emma*. PhD Washington State U. 1969.

HORWITZ,B.J. *1883*
Jane Austen and the writers on women's education. PhD State U. of New York at Stony Brook, 1979.

IRVINE,I.M. *1884*
Figurative representation in the novels of Jane Austen: a study of style. PhD U. of Pennsylvania, 1972.

JACKEL,D.A. *1885*
Jane Austen and the concept of the novelist's art, 1775–1820. PhD U. of Toronto, 1970.

JOHNSON,C.L. *1886*
Using the mind well: the moral life in Jane Austen's novels and the heritage of Johnson and Locke. PhD Princeton U. 1981.

JONES,F.L. *1887*
The structure of the novel in Jane Austen and its relationship to the work of her predecessors. MA U. of London, Queen Mary Coll. 1935.

JONES,H.H. *1888*
Jane Austen and eight minor contemporaries: a study in the novel, 1800–1820. [The minor contemporaries include Mary Brunton, Elizabeth Hamilton, Amelia Opie, Lady Morgan, Anna Maria Porter, Jane Porter and Charlotte Dacre.] PhD U. of Newcastle-upon Tyne, 1979.

KANTROV,I.M. *1889*
'A deep and enlightened piety': the religious background of Jane Austen's fiction. PhD Tufts U. 1980.

KESTNER,J.A. *1890*
Jane Austen seven themes in variation. PhD Columbia U. 1969.

KILEY,A.W. *1891*
The art of living: Jane Austen's social aesthetic. PhD U. of Wisconsin 1968.

KIRKHAM,C.M. *1892*
A critical study of the novels of Jane Austen in relation to the popular literature of her time, especially drama. MLitt U. of Bristol, 1973.

KOPPEL,G.S. *1893*
The moral basis of Jane Austen's novels. PhD Washington U. 1965.

LAVIN,M.J. *1894*
The contruction of the novel and Jane Austen. MA National U. of Ireland, 1936.

LAW,D.R. *1895*
Education to perfection in the novels of Jane Austen. PhD U. of Wisconsin-Madison, 1977.

LEVIN,J.A. *1896*
Marriage in the novels of Jane Austen. PhD Yale U. 1975.

LINK,F.M. *1897*
The reputation of Jane Austen in the twentieth century with an annotated enumerative bibliography of Austen criticism from 1811 to June 1957. PhD Boston U. 1958.

LYNCH,C.M. *1898*
The reader as guest: Jane Austen's audience. PhD U. of Pittsburgh, 1974.

MCILROY,E.L. *1899*
Realism and anti-realism in the novels of Jane Austen. PhD Syracuse U. 1963.

MCKINSTRY,S.J. *1900*
Rational creatures: the process of fictionalizing in Jane Austen's novels. PhD U. of Michigan, 1982.

MARKHAM,A. *1901*
Jane Austen's view of marriage as expressed in her novels. MA U. of Nottingham, 1971.

MARTIEN,N.G. *1902*
(Part II) *Mansfield Park* and Jane Austen's heroine. PhD Rutgers U. 1969.

METCALFE,A.C. *1903*
Sense and sensibility: a study of its similarity to *The history of Sir Charles Grandison*. PhD U. of Kent, 1970.

MILECH,B.H. *1904*
Narrative transactions: Jane Austen's novels and the reader's role in the construction of narrative meaning. PhD Indiana U. 1979.

MILL ER,K.F. *1905*
The archetype in the drawing room: fairy tale structures in the novels of Jane Austen. PhD Brown U. 1980.

MOLE R,K.L. *1906*
Jane Austen's novels and their literary milieu. PhD Harvard U. 1964.

MONAGHAN,D.M. *1907*
The theme of initiation and the form of social occasion in Jane Austen's novels. PhD U. of Alberta, 1970.

MORAHAN,R.E. *1908*
(Part III) Jane Austen's endings. PhD Rutgers U. 1971.

MUDRICK,M. *1909*
The achievement of Jane Austen: a study in ironic process. PhD U. of California, Berkeley, 1949.

MUELLERLEKE,StA., Sister *1910*
The unconventional Miss Austen or a study of Jane Austen's use of the conventions of popular English fiction, 1770–1800. PhD U. of Chicago, 1968.

MURRAH,C. *1911*
Jane Austen's treatment of background and setting. PhD Harvard U. 1955.

NARDIN,J.B. *1912*
The concept of propriety in Jane Austen's novels. PhD State U. of New York at Buffalo, 1971.

NEWMAN,R.B. *1913*
Life style in the novels of Jane Austen. PhD U. of Michigan, 1972.

PATY,P.K. *1914*
Jane Austen: her relationship to the romantic and the realistic traditions of English fiction. PhD U. of Minnesota, 1963.

PENRITH,M.C. *1915*
Sub-style in *Emma*: the nature and values of idiolects and narrative. MLitt U. of Lancaster, 1980.

PICKERING,J.E. *1916*
Comic structure in the novels of Jane Austen. PhD Stanford U. 1973.

PODIS,J.M. *1917*
'The way they should go': family relationships in the novels of Jane Austen. PhD Case Western Reserve U. 1974.

POST,A.P. *1918*
Jane Austen and the 'loiterer': a study of Jane Austen's literary heritage. PhD U. of North Carolina at Chapel Hill, 1972.

RAZ,R.W. *1919*
Syntactic variations in Jane Austen's dialogue. PhD U. of Michigan, 1970.

RILEY,M. *1920*
Reduction and redemption: the meaning of *Mansfield Park*. PhD Ohio U. 1973.

ROSENBAUM,J.E. *1921*
On trial and found wanting: the heroine and her society in Jane Austen's novels. PhD U. of Pittsburgh, 1977.

RUBINSTEIN,E.L. *1922*
Jane Austen's novels: the microcosm and the world beyond. PhD Columbia U. 1964.

SANDERS,H.M. *1923*
Jane Austen's novels: a study in narrative method. PhD Syracuse U. 1954.

SANDSTROM,E.A. *1924*
Deception and undeception in the novels of Jane

Austen. PhD U. of Illinois at Urbana-Champaign, 1956.

SATZ,M.G. *1925*
Deities and translucent volleyballs: an epistemological approach to *Pride and prejudice* and *Die Marquise von O.* PhD U. of Texas at Dallas, 1982.

SLATTERY,M.P. *1926*
The technique of balance in the construction of character in the novels of Jane Austen. PhD Catholic U. of America, 1966.

SOUTHAM,B.C. *1927*
A critical study of the writings of Jane Austen which survive in manuscript. BLitt U. of Oxford, 1961.

SPENCE,J.H. *1928*
From prudence to romance: some aspects of Jane Austen's evolving views of nature and society. PhD U. of London, King's Coll. 1976.

STEIN,M.J. *1929*
Reality-perception and self-knowledge in Jane Austen: a study of the six novels. PhD U. of Chicago, 1978.

STOLLER,A.L. *1930*
Jane Austen's rhetorical art: a revaluation. PhD Brown U. 1974.

STOVEL,J.B. *1931*
Jane Austen's moral beliefs and their background with special reference to *Mansfield Park.* PhD Harvard U. 1971.

TAGOE ,V.R.W. *1932*
The technique of comedy in the novels of Jane Austen. MPhil U. of London, Royal Holloway Coll. 1971.

TALLMADGE,A.L. *1933*
Sense and sensibility: Austenian gleanings. PhD Northwestern U. 1935.

TAYLOR,R. *1934*
The narrative technique of Jane Austen: a study in the use of point of view. PhD U. of Texas at Austin, 1975.

TEN HARMSEL,H. *1935*
Jane Austen's use of literary conventions. PhD U. of Michigan, 1962.

TURNER,B. C. *1936*
The polite novel after Jane Austen. BLitt U. of Oxford, 1944.

WEINSHEIMER,J.C. *1937*
Three assays of Jane Austen's novels. PhD Ohio U. 1973.

WEISSMAN,C.A. *1938*
Character and pattern in Jane Austen's fiction. PhD Cornell U. 1981.

WHEALLER,S.C. *1939*
The use of distance in Jane Austen's novels. PhD Purdue U. 1982.

WHITE,E.M. *1940*
Jane Austen and the art of parody. PhD Harvard U. 1960.

WHITTEN,B.G. *1941*
Jane Austen's 'comedy of feeling': a critical analysis of *Persuasion.* PhD U. of California, Davis, 1971.

WILHELM,A.E. *1943*
Word clusters in Jane Austen's major novels. PhD U. of North Carolina at Chapel Hill, 1971.

WILLIAMS,M.J. *1944*
Jane Austen: the novels as six fictional methods. DPhil U. of Oxford, 1982.

WILLIS,L.H. *1945*
Vision and judgment as means of character definition in Jane Austen's novels. PhD U. of Alberta, 1971.

WOODS,M.StF. *1946*
Jane Austen and the omniscient narrative voice. PhD Catholic U. of America, 1965.

WRIGHT,A. *1947*
Jane Austen's novels: language and structure. MLitt U. of Bristol, 1970.

WRIGHT,A.H. *1948*
Irony in Jane Austen's novels. PhD Ohio State U. 1951.

ZIMMERMAN,E. *1949*
Jane Austen and sensibility: a study of tradition and technique. PhD Temple U. 1966.

Joanna Baillie

LAMB,V.B. *1950*
Joanna Baillie: her relevant place in the history of England's drama. PhD U. of Kent, 1972.

Mary Elizabeth Braddon

NYBERG,B.M. *1951*
The novels of Mary Elizabeth Braddon 1837–1915: a reappraisal of the author of *Lady Audley's secret.* PhD U. of Colorado, 1965.

The Brontës

ALEXANDER,C.A. *1952*
A study of the early prose writings of Charlotte Brontë, accompanied by a diplomatic edition of those which are unpublished. PhD U. of Cambridge, 1979.

ARNDT,F.C. *1953*
Villette: with the turn of the wheel. PhD Duke U. 1972.

ARTHUR,B.B. *1954*
Psychological dualism in the novels of Charlotte Brontë. PhD U. of Houston, 1982.

BLOOMER,N.H. *1955*
Despair and love in the works of Emily Jane Brontë. PhD State U. of New York at Buffalo, 1976.

BOWEN,B.M. *1956*
Emily Brontë. MA U. of Birmingham, 1947.

BOWERING,G. *1957*
A reappraisal of Anne Brontë's novels in the light of nineteenth and twentieth-century critical opinions. MPhil U. of London, Birkbeck Coll. 1978.

BRAMMER,M.M. *1958*
A critical study of Charlotte Brontë's *The professor,* with special consideration of its relation to previous novels. MA U. of London, Bedford Coll. 1958.

BRAYFIELD,P.L. *1959*
A new feminist approach to the novels of Charlotte Brontë. PhD Southern Illinois at Carbondale, 1973.

BROMLEY,L.A. *1960*
(Part III) The Victorian 'good woman' and the fiction of Charlotte Brontë. PhD Rutgers U. 1973.

BURNS,L.O. *1961*
Alienation and unification: relationships in the novels of Charlotte Brontë. PhD U. of Ohio, 1978.

BYERS,D.M. *1962*
An annotated bibliography of the criticism on Emily Brontë's *Wuthering Heights* 1847–1947. PhD U. of Minnesota, 1973.

CHITHAM,E. *1963*
The poems of Anne Brontë: an edition with notes on the poems. MA U. of Warwick, 1977.

COOPER,D.J. *1964*
Emily Brontë, with special reference to her poems. MA U. of Leeds, 1946.

COSTELLO,P .H. *1965*
The parson's daughters: the family worlds of Charlotte, Emily and Anne Brontë. PhD Union for Experimenting Coll. and U. 1982.

CROSBY,C. *1966*
The haunting of the text: the case of Charlotte Brontë's *Villette*. PhD Brown U. 1982.

CURRY,C.M. *1967*
Fantasy and prophesy: a comparative study of the similarities and differences in the development, personal and artistic, of the sisters Charlotte and Emily Brontë and the way in which these considerations affect the reading of the sisters' mature creative works. MA U. of Wales (Aberystwyth), 1974.

DESSNER,L.J. *1968*
The homely web of truth: a study of Charlotte Brontë's novels. PhD New York U. 1969.

DOOLEY,L. *1969*
Psychoanalysis of Charlotte Brontë as a type of the woman of genius. PhD Clark U. 1916.

DOWNEY,M.J. *1970*
Studies in Charlotte Brontë. PhD U. of Illinois at Urbana-Champaign, 1938.

DUGAS,J.H. *1971*
The literary reputation of the Brontës 1845–1951. PhD U. of Illinois at Urbana-Champaign, 1951.

EASON,S.L.B. *1972*
Ambivalent views toward woman's role in the novels of Charlotte Brontë. PhD Bowling Green State U. 1977.

FISHER,C. *1973*
The narration and structure of Charlotte Brontë's novels. PhD U. of Wisconsin-Madison, 1980.

FISHER,C.L. *1974*
Charlotte Brontë, formalist: a study of the novels as thematic unities. PhD State U. of New York at Albany, 1975.

FLAHIFF,F.T.C. *1975*
Formative ideas in the novels of Charlotte and Emily Jane Brontë. PhD U. of Toronto, 1965.

FRANK,K.V. *1976*
The empty mirror: a biography of Emily Brontë. PhD U. of Iowa, 1979.

GEORGE,R.F. *1977*
The evangelical revival and Charlotte Brontë's *Jane Eyre*. PhD U. of Florida, 1981.

GILL,A.M. *1978*
The religious attitudes of Patrick Brontë and his daughter, Anne, as reflected in their works. MA U. of Manchester, 1975.

GORDON,J. A. *1979*
The dramatic scene in the novels of Charlotte Brontë, with special reference to her use of theatrical and pictorial elements. BLitt U. of Oxford, 1969.

GOULD,G.L. *1980*
Emily Brontë's relation to Gondalas subject of *Wuthering Heights*. PhD City U. of New York, 1974.

HOWARD,M.A. *1981*
Charlotte Brontë's novels: an analysis of their thematic and structural patterns. PhD U. of Washington, 1962.

HUDSON,A.R. *1982*
The religious temper of Charlotte Brontë's novels. PhD U. of Toronto, 1981.

ISAAC,M.R. *1983*
A comparative study of the writing of Emily and Anne Brontë. MA U. of Wales (Cardiff), 1976.

ISENBERG,D.R. *1984*
The work of Emily Brontë. MA U. of Liverpool, 1960.

JOHNSTON,R.D. *1985*
Charlotte Brontë's adaptation and enlargement of autobiographical narrative. PhD New York U. 1980.

JUERS,E.M. *1986*
Biography and literary criticism the case of Emily Brontë and *Wuthering Heights*. PhD U. of Essex, 1980.

KEENAN,G. *1987*
Realism in the novels of Anne Brontë. MA Queen's U. of Belfast, 1971.

KNIES,E.A. *1988*
The art of Charlotte Brontë: a study of point of view in her fiction. PhD U. of Illinois at Urbana-Champaign, 1964.

LAMBERT,D.E.D. *1989*
The shaping spirit: a study of the novels of Emily and Charlotte Brontë. PhD Stanford U. 1967.

LINDER,C.A. *1990*
Narrative techniques in the novels of Charlotte Brontë. MA U. of Exeter, 1976.

LOXTERMAN,A.S. *1991*
The giant's foot: a reading of *Wuthering Heights*. PhD Ohio State U. 1971.

MACCOBY,D.H. *1992*
The poetry of Emily Brontë in the context of the Romantic movement. MLitt U. of Oxford, 1979.

MCKNEELY,L.M. *1993*
Anne Brontë, novelist of reform. PhD Emory U. 1956.

MADEWELL,V.D.A. *1994*
Emily Brontë's word artistry: symbolism in *Wuthering Heights*. PhD North Texas State U. 1981.

MARSDEN,H. *1995*
The north of England in the novels of the Brontës. PhD U. of London, Birkbeck Coll. 1968.

MARSDEN,H. *1996*
Wuthering Heights: character, plot, and background in studies in the factual sources. BLitt Trinity Coll. Dublin, 1954.

MORRIS,P.O. *1997*
Charlotte Brontë. MA National U. of Ireland, 1945.

MOSS,F.K. *1998*
Characterization in Charlotte Brontë's fiction. PhD U. of Wisconsin, 1969.

NEUFELDT,V.A. *1999*
The shared vision of Anne and Emily Brontë: the context for *Wuthering Heights*. PhD U. of Illinois at Urbana-Champaign, 1969.

O'DO M,K.C. *2000*
The Brontës and romantic views of personality. PhD U. of Wisconsin, 1961.

OGDON,J.A.H. *2001*
Libido-symbolism and Emily Brontë's writings. MA U. of Liverpool, 1956.

OLDFIELD,J. *2002*
The lonely web of truth: the achievement of a sense of reality in the Brontë novels. MA U. of Birmingham, 1973.

PASSEL,A.W. *2003*
Charlotte Brontë's novels: the artistry of their construction. PhD U. of the Pacific, 1967.

PETERS,M.M. *2004*
Four essays on the style of Charlotte Brontë. PhD U. of Wisconsin, 1969.

PUIREK,J.E. *2005*
The female self in the novels of Charlotte Brontë: the dynamics of change. PhD U. of California, Irvine, 1982.

PLATT,C. V. *2006*
The female quest in the works of Anne, Charlotte and Emily Brontë. PhD U. of Illinois at Urbana-Champaign, 1974.

QUERTE RMOUS,H.M. *2007*
The Byronic hero in the writings of the Brontës. PhD U. of Texas at Austin, 1960.

RANDALL,J.A.M. *2008*
Sexual symbolism as a function of repression in *Jane Eyre*. PhD Case Western Reserve U. 1971.

REYNOLDS,M.R. *2009*
Wuthering Heights: levels of reality. MA U. of Exeter, 1974.

ROSS,A.M. *2010*
The dreamer in the landscape: a critical study of Emily Brontë's poetry. PhD U. of California, Los Angeles, 1980.

SADIQ,E.A. *2011*
Brontë's journey to the East: the romantic quest in her fiction. PhD Wayne State U. 1982.

SCHWARTZ,R.C. *2012*
The search after happiness: a study of Charlotte Brontë's fiction. PhD Wayne State U. 1968.

SEN,S. *2013*
The evidence of Eden: art and vision in the novels of Charlotte Brontë. PhD U. of Rochester, 1980.

SHAPIRO,A. *2014*
A study in the development of art and ideas in Charlotte Brontë's fiction. PhD Indiana U. 1965.

STENBERG,R.A. *2015*
The novels of Anne Brontë. PhD U. of Minnesota, 1980.

STEPHENS,M.A.W. *2016*
Mysticism in the works of Emily Jane Brontë. PhD Case Western Reserve U.

SHRUBB,V.C. *2017*
Religion and moral consciousness in the novels of Charlotte Brontë. MPhil U. of Oxford, 1981.

SIGEL,J.E. *2018*
Passionate craftsmanship: the artistry of Charlotte Brontë's *Jane Eyre* and *Villette*. PhD State U. of New York at Binghamton, 1976.

STOWELL,R. *2019*
The origins and use of some major patterns and types of imagery in Charlotte Brontë's novels. BLitt U. of Oxford, 1972.

SULLIVAN,P.C. *2020*
Studies in Charlotte Brontë. PhD Harvard U. 1974.

THORBURN,D.B. *2021*
The effects of the Wesleyan movement on the Brontë sisters, as evidenced by an examination of certain of their novels. PhD New York U. 1947.

WARD,M.L. *2022*
Anguish and resolution: a study of myth in the work of Emily Brontë. PhD U. of Iowa, 1981.

WEST,C.L. *2023*
Aspects of time in *Wuthering Heights*. PhD Yale U. 1980.

WILLIAMS,J.M. *2024*
Observation, insight, and perception in the novels of Charlotte Brontë. PhD U. of Toronto, 1979.

WILLS,J.C. *2025*
Charlotte Brontë's literary theories. PhD U. of Delaware, 1966.

WINNIFRITH,T.J. *2026*
The Brontës: fiction and fact. PhD U. of Liverpool, 1971.

ZAGARELL,S.A. *2027*
Charlotte Brontë from fantasy to social and psychological reality. PhD Columbia U. 1976.

Rhoda Broughton

COLE,T.F.W. *2028*
Rhoda Broughton. DPhil U. of Oxford, 1963.

Elizabeth Barrett Browning

BORG,J.M.W. *2029*
The fashioning of Elizabeth Barrett Browning's *Aurora Leigh*. PhD Northwestern U. 1979.

COOPER,H.M. *2030*
Elizabeth Barrett Browning: a theory of women's poetry. PhD Rutgers U. 1982.

DONALDSON,S.M. *2031*
Elizabeth Barrett Browning's poetic and feminist philosophies in *Aurora Leigh* and other poems. PhD U. of Connecticut, 1977.

GOLDSTEIN,M. *2032*
Elizabeth Barrett Browning's *Sonnets from the Portuguese* in the light of the Petrarchan tradition. PhD U. of Wisconsin, 1958.

GRAY,L.L.B. *2033*
The texts of Elizabeth Barrett Browning's *Sonnets from the Portuguese*: a structural reading. PhD U. of Detroit, 1978.

HARRINGTON,E.R. *2034*
A study of the poetry of Elizabeth Barrett Browning. PhD New York U. 1977.

HILL,C.B.T. *2035*
A study of spiritualism in the life and work of Elizabeth Barrett Browning. PhD U. of Birmingham, 1978.

KINTNER,E.E. *2036*
A preliminary study for a definitive edition of the letters of Robert Browning and Elizabeth Barrett Browning. PhD Yale U. 1953.

STEINMETZ,V.R.V. *2037*
The development of Elizabeth Barrett Browning's juvenile self-images and their transformation in *Aurora Leigh*. PhD Duke U. 1979.

WILSEY,M. *2038*
The composition of *Aurora Leigh*. PhD Yale U. 1938.

WING-SHEUNG LEUNG,J. *2039*
The poet in Elizabeth Barrett Browning's *Aurora Leigh*. MPhil U. of Oxford, 1981.

Claire Clairmont

KINGSTON,M.J. *2040*
Claire Clairmont: a biographical and critical study. PhD Duke U. 1952.

Mary Coleridge

RUSSELL,R.W. *2041*
The poetry of Mary Elizabeth Coleridge. BLitt U. of Oxford, 1952.

Sara Coleridge

GRANTZ,C.L. *2042*
Letters of Sara Coleridge: a calendar and index to her manuscript correspondence in the University of Texas library. PhD U. of Texas at Austin, 1968.

Marie Corelli

GUTZEIT,J.C. *2043*
The novels of Marie Corelli. PhD U. of Chicago, 1965.

HUFF,C.C. *2044*
The novels of Marie Corelli: their themes and their popularity as an index of popular taste. PhD U. of Colorado, 1970.

Dinah Mollock Craik

MAID,B.M. *2045*
Dinah Mollock, the author of *John Halifax, gentleman*: an introduction. PhD U. of Massachusetts, 1980.

Maria Edgeworth

BRENNAN,P.J. *2046*
The Edgeworth novels: today and yesterday. MA National U. of Ireland, 1960.

BREWSTER,D.G. *2047*
Maria Edgeworth and the moral tale: a critical and comparative study. MA U. of Sheffield, 1956.

BUTLER,M.S. *2048*
Education and public life: major themes in the novels of Maria Edgeworth. DPhil U. of Oxford, 1967.

CRAIG,C.R. *2049*
Maria Edgeworth and the common sense school. PhD U. of Nebraska-Lincoln, 1971.

EISENSTADT,E.R. *2050*
A study of Maria Edgeworth's fiction. PhD Washington U. 1975.

EWENS,E.G. *2051*
Maria Edgeworth and the novel. PhD Trinity Coll. Dublin, 1946.

GOODMAN,T. *2052*
Maria Edgeworth: novelist of reason. PhD New York U. 1936.

HOUSTON,J.M.M. *2053*
A critical survey of the principal works of Maria Edgeworth. BLitt U. of Oxford, 1965.

LYNCH,P.A. *2054*
The world of the Edgeworth novels: the society aspect. MA National U. of Ireland, 1972.

MACCARTHY,E.M. *2055*
Maria Edgeworth: a study in Anglo-Irish literature. MA National U. of Ireland, 1934.

MCWHORTER,O.E. *2056*
Maria Edgeworth's art of prose fiction. PhD U. of Arkansas, 1965.

MOOD,R.G. *2057*
Maria Edgeworth's apprenticeship. PhD U. of Illinois at Urbana-Champaign, 1939.

SAMSON,E.M.F. *2058*
Maria Edgeworth: her place in the history of the English novel. BLitt U. of Oxford, 1925.

UNTHANK,L.T.B. *2059*
Essence of common sense: a comparative study of some of Maria Edgeworth's fiction for children. PhD U. of Liverpool, 1974.

YATES,T.V. *2060*
Maria Edgeworth and the art of education. PhD Purdue U. 1976.

George Egerton

STETZ,M.D. *2061*
'George Egerton': woman and writer of the eighteen-nineties. (Pseudonym of Mary Chavelita Dunne.) PhD Harvard U. 1982.

George Eliot

ADAM,I.W. *2062*
Themes of isolation and restoration in George Eliot's fiction. MA U. of London, Birkbeck Coll. 1960.

ALLEY,H.M. *2063*
Middlemarch and *Daniel Deronda*: heroes of erudition and experience. PhD Cornell U. 1971.

ALTHAUS,D.C. *2064*
The love triangle as a structural principle in the novels of George Eliot. PhD Ohio U. 1971.

ANDERSON,R.F. *2065*
Formative influences on George Eliot, with special reference to George Henry Lewes. PhD U. of Toronto, 1963.

ANDRONE,M.J.P. *2066*
Legacies of clerical life: a study of clerical, artistic and domestic figures in the novels of George Eliot. PhD U. of Pennsylvania, 1977.

ATKINS,D.J. *2067*
George Eliot and Spinoza. PhD U. of Nebraska-Lincoln, 1977.

AUSTEN,H. *2068*
Local habitations: regionalism in the early novels of George Eliot. PhD Harvard U. 1966.

AZMY,I. *2069*
George Eliot as an analyst of the social life of England in the nineteenth century. MA U. of Sheffield, 1949.

BAKER,W. *2070*
The Jewish elements of George Eliot's *Daniel Deronda*: a study of George Eliot's interest in, and knowledge of, Judaism. MPhil U. of London, Royal Holloway Coll. 1970.

BARRY,J.D. *2071*
The literary reputation of George Eliot. PhD Northwestern U. 1955.

BEATY,J. *2072*
Middlemarch, from notebook to novel: a study of George Eliot's creative method. PhD U. of Illinois at Urbana-Champaign, 1956.

BEAVEN,G.P. *2073*
Marriage in the novels of George Eliot. MPhil U. of York, 1979.

BELL,B.J.H. *2074*
The figure of the child in the novels of George Eliot. PhD U. of South Carolina, 1974.

BELL,S. 2075
George Eliot: a study in the intellectual development of her novels. PhD U. of Wisconsin, 1972.

BENSON,J.D. 2076
The moral aesthetic problem in George Eliot's fiction. PhD U. of Toronto, 1969.

BLYTHE,D.E. 2077
Household gods: domesticity in the novels of George Eliot. PhD U. of North Carolina at Chapel Hill, 1977.

BOLSTAD,R.M. 2078
The passionate self in George Eliot: *Adam Bede, The mill on the Floss* and *Daniel Deronda*. PhD U. of Washington, 1975.

BONAPARTE,F. 2079
George Eliot: tragedy in a minor key. PhD New York U. 1970.

BRADLEY,A.G. 2080
Pastoral in the novels of George Eliot. PhD State U. of New York at Buffalo, 1972.

BRAIDWO OD,T.E. 2081
Levels of narration in the major novels of George Eliot: a consideration of the narrative functions of techniques used to present character in George Eliot's exploration of ideas about community and fellowship. MLitt U. of Cambridge, 1978.

BRITZ,J.P. 2082
French criticism of George Eliot's novels. PhD U. of Minnesota, 1956.

BUDGEN,V.J. 2083
The influence of Evangelicalism on George Eliot's life and work. MA U. of Manchester, 1965.

BURDICK,N.R. 2084
The incarnate idea: character and purpose in George Eliot's fiction. PhD U. of Wisconsin-Madison, 1979.

BURNS,J.S. 2085
The wider life: a study of the writings of George Eliot. PhD Rice U. 1964.

BEDIENT,C.B. 2086
The fate of the self: self and society in the novels of George Eliot, D.H. Lawrence and E.M. Forster. PhD U. of Washington, 1964.

BUSH ,G.E.B. 2087
Middlemarch and the tradition of the English provincial novel. PhD U. of Wisconsin, 1974.

BUTLER,P.A. 2088
Despondency corrected: George Eliot, romantic. PhD U. of Texas at Austin, 1976.

BUZAN,M.M. 2089
Tragedy and parable in George Eliot's novels. PhD U. of Texas at Austin, 1981.

CARROLL,D.R. 2090
Themes and structural symbols in the novels of George Eliot. PhD U. of Durham, 1962.

CARTER,D.A. 2091
The drama of self: role- playing as theme in the novels of George Eliot. PhD U. of Illinois at Urbana-Champaign, 1974.

CARTWRIGHT,J.D. 2093
Authorial commentary in the novels of George Eliot as primarily exemplified in *Adam Bede, The mill on the Floss* and *Middlemarch*. PhD U. of Wisconsin, 1969.

CASEY,F.W. 2094
George Eliot's practice as a novelist in relation to her critical theory. PhD U. of Wisconsin, 1951.

CATE,H.L. 2095
The literary reception of George Eliot's novels in America (1858–1882). PhD U. of Georgia, 1962.

CAWLEY,F.S. 2096
George Eliot and Germany . PhD Harvard U. 1916.

CHANDER,J. 2097
Religious and moral ideas in the novels of George Eliot. PhD U. of Wisconsin, 1963.

CHASE,L.D. 2098
Preaching without book: the rhetoric of religion in the novels of George Eliot. PhD Marquette U. 1980.

CHEN,A.W.S.W. 2099
The mind of George Eliot. PhD U. of Pennsylvania, 1966.

CLARK,R.N. 2100
The idealist, the missionary and the overreacher in the novels of George Eliot. PhD Florida State U. 1969.

COHEN,S.R. 2101
'The family procession': generational structures in the novels of George Eliot. PhD Yale U. 1978.

COLLINS,R.L. 2102
The present past: the origin and exposition of theme in the prose fiction of George Eliot. PhD Stanford U. 1961.

COMBS,J.R. 2103
George Eliot's mind and the clerical characters in her fiction. PhD U. of Texas at Austin, 1968.

CONNORS,P.E. 2104
A mythic analysis of George Eliot's *Adam Bede*. PhD U. of Detroit, 1978.

CONWAY,R.H . 2105
The difficulty of being a woman: a study of George Eliot's heroines. PhD U. of Denver, 1973.

COOKSEY,G.W. 2106
The novelist and moral responsibility: a study of George Eliot. MA U. of Wales, 1953.

COOLEY,E.M. 2107
The uses of melodrama in George Eliot's fiction. PhD U. of California, Berkeley, 1962.

CORTESE,R. *2108*
George Eliot and Dante. PhD U. of Wisconsin-Madison, 1981.

COUGH,J.P. *2109*
George Eliot in France. PhD Yale U. 1954.

CREEL,G.W. *2110*
The poetry of George Eliot. PhD U. of California, Berkeley, 1948.

DALY,M.G. *2111*
Foundresses of nothing: narrators, heroines and renunciation in George Eliot's novels. PhD Yale U. 1977.

DAVIES,R.G. *2112*
George Eliot: a study in mid-Victorian pessimism. PhD Ohio State U. 1936.

DAVIS,N.J. *2113*
Pictorialism in George Eliot's art. PhD Northwestern U. 1972.

DEAKIN,B.Y. *2114*
The effect of George Eliot the thinker on George Eliot the novelist. MA U. of Manchester, 1947.

DEEGAN,T.P. *2115*
George Eliot's historical thought and her novels of the historical imagination. PhD Northwestern U. 1970.

DEL GUERICO,T. *2116*
Ethics in George Eliot's letters, essays and fiction. PhD U. of Pennsylvania, 1951.

DEMERI TT,W. *2117*
George Eliot as a tragic novelist: her theory and practice. PhD Rutgers U. 1970.

DENEAU,D.P. *2118*
From Amos Barton to Daniel Deronda: studies in the imagery of George Eliot's fiction. PhD U. of Notre Dame, 1959.

DIAMOND,N.J. *2119*
Vision and the role of the past in the novels of George Eliot. PhD U. of Washington, 1959.

DODD,V.A. *2120*
Some religious and philosophical influences upon the nature of George Eliot's imagination, with particular reference to Thomas Carlyle and John Stuart Mill. BLitt U. of Oxford, 1975.

DODGE,K.A. *2121*
Transformation: deliverance or death, structure and theme of George Eliot's *Daniel Deronda*. PhD U. of Texas at Austin, 1976.

DOGRAMACI,E. *2122*
George Eliot and Emancipation: a Turkish view. PhD U. of Edinburgh, 1957.

DOYLE,M.E. *2123*
Distance and narrative technique in the novels of George Eliot. PhD U. of Notre Dame, 1968.

DSEAGU,S.A. *2124*
Tragedy in the novels of George Eliot. MPhil U. of Leeds, 1971.

DUNCAN,C.F. *2125*
Time-levels and value-structures in George Eliot's novels. PhD Emory U. 1965.

DUNHAM,R .H. *2126*
Wordsworthian themes and attitudes in George Eliot's novels. PhD Stanford U. 1971.

DURING,S.C. *2127*
Daniel Deronda and psychology: a contextual study. PhD U. of Cambridge, 1982.

EASTMAN,R. *2128*
George Eliot's *Daniel Deronda*: it's place in the development of her fiction. PhD U. of Chicago, 1953.

EISNER,G. *2129*
George Eliot: the problem novels. PhD U. of California, Irvine, 1974.

EKMAN,J.K. *2130*
Humour in George Eliot. MLitt U. of Edinburgh, 1975.

ELKINS,M.J. *2131*
Definition and control: the exercise of power in the novels of George Eliot. PhD Southern Illinois U. at Carbondale, 1979.

EMERY,L.C. *2132*
Creative conflict in George Eliot's middle novels. PhD U. of California, Berkeley, 1973.

ENGEL,M.T.J. *2133*
The literary reputation of George Eliot in Germany, 1857–1970. PhD U. of Detroit, 1973.

ERM ARTH,E. *2134*
Conversion in George Eliot. PhD U. of Chicago, 1971.

EUWEMA,B. *2135*
The development of George Eliot's ethical and social theories. PhD U. of Chicago, 1935.

FAIREY,W.W. *2136*
The relationship of heroine, confessor, and community in the novels of George Eliot. PhD Columbia U. 1975.

FEENEY,M.E. *2137*
Women in the major fiction of George Eliot. PhD U. of Massachusetts, 1973.

FISHER,P. *2138*
The disappearance of society: a study of the novels of George Eliot. PhD Harvard U. 1971.

FITZPATRICK,T.D. *2139*
Alienation and mediation in the novels of George Eliot. PhD Rutgers U. 1979.

FREY,B.G. *2140*
Love, sex and artists in George Eliot's works. PhD City U. of New York, 1978.

FUERMANN,W. B. 2141
The novels of George Eliot: a critical commentary. PhD U. of Illinois at Urbana-Champaign, 1974.

FULMER,C.M. 2142
She being dead yet speaketh: a study of George Eliot's moral aesthetic. PhD Vanderbilt U. 1970.

FURNISS,J.N. 2143
George Eliot and the Protestant work ethic. PhD Duke U. 1973.

GANIM,V.L. 2144
Limitation and responsibility in the fiction of Goethe and George Eliot. PhD Emory U. 1978.

GEI BEL,J.W. 2145
An annotated bibliography of British criticism of George Eliot, 1858–1900. PhD Ohio State U. 1969.

GELLEY,A. 2146
Symbolic setting in the novel: studies in Goethe, Stendhal and George Eliot. PhD Yale U. 1965.

GOLDSBERRY,D.M. 2147
George Eliot's use of the tragic mode. PhD U. of North Carolina at Chapel Hill, 1972.

GOTTLIEB,A.H. 2148
George Eliot: a biographical and intellectual study. PhD U. of Cambridge, 1971.

GRANT,J.A.S. 2149
The nature of duty and the problem of passion in the works of George Eliot. PhD U. of Toronto, 1974.

GRAVER,S.L. 2150
George Eliot and the idea of community. PhD U. of Massachusetts, 1976.

GREEN,J.M. 2151
Creative ambivalence: George Eliot's narrative stance. PhD State U. of New York at Buffalo, 1978.

GRIFFITH,G.V. 2152
The idea of progress and the fiction of George Eliot. PhD U. of Southern Illinois at Carbondale, 1975.

GROSSMAN,R.H. 2153
Drama and background in George Eliot's *Scenes of clerical life*. PhD U. of California, San Diego, 1972.

HAKAMY,A.A. 2154
The struggle between traditionalism and modernism: a study in the novels of George Eliot and Najib Mahfuz. PhD U. of Michigan, 1979.

HAMMAD,W.A. 2155
George Eliot's works in relation to the intellectual movements of her time. PhD U. of Manchester, 1964.

HANDLEY,G.R. 2156
A critical study of *Daniel Deronda*: its relation to George Eliot's fiction and to its time. PhD U. of London, Bedford Coll. 1962.

HARRIS,M.D. 2157
George Eliot and the problems of agnosticism: a study of philosophical psychology. PhD State U. of New York at Buffalo, 1971.

HATTON,J.C. 2158
Sympathy and form in George Eliot's early novels. PhD U. of California, Berkeley, 1973.

HEINDEL,L.H. 2159
Daniel Deronda: Eliot's debt to Feuerbach. PhD Lehigh U. 1976.

HELLENBERG,N.M. 2160
The role of nature in George Eliot's fiction. PhD U. of Oregon, 1975.

HENNELLY,M.M. 2161
Sibyl in the gloom: a study of guilt in the life and novels of George Eliot. PhD Saint Louis U. 1970.

HERRON,J.S. 2162
Reading George Eliot. PhD Indiana U. 1980.

HESTER,W.E. 2163
George Eliot's technique as a novelist. PhD U. of North Carolina at Chapel Hill, 1961.

HIGDON,D.L. 2164
The sovereign fragments: a study of George Eliot's epigraphs. PhD U. of Kansas, 1968.

HOFFM AN,B.H. 2165
The credibility of George Eliot's major characters: a study of character, moral patterns and the nature of society in her novels. PhD State U. of New York at Buffalo, 1970.

HOLLAND,J.G. 2166
George Eliot's *Daniel Deronda* with particular consideration of the Jewish elements. PhD U. of North Carolina at Chapel Hill, 1972.

HOOTON,J.W.M. 2167
George Eliot's idea of community: a comparative study of *Silas Marner* and *Daniel Deronda*. MPhil U. of London, External, 1975.

HOROWITZ,L.W. 2168
Present, past and future: the vision of society in George Eliot's novels. PhD Cornell U. 1971.

HORR,C.H. 2169
George Eliot's theory of the novel, 1857–1880. PhD Ohio U. 1981.

HUDSON,S.M. 2170
George Henry Lewes' evolutionism in the fiction of George Eliot. PhD U. of Southern California, 1970.

HURLBURT,R.F. 2171
The ethical teachings of George Eliot. PhD Boston U. 1896.

HURLEY,E.T. 2172
The family as an instrument for theme and structure in the fiction of George Eliot. PhD U. of Michigan, 1966.

HUTCHINGS,P.A. *2173*
From truism to truth: George Eliot's changing use of the narrator. PhD U. of Iowa, 1978.

HUTCHINSON,A.G. *2174*
George Eliot and the *Westminster review*. MA U. of Durham, 1968.

HUZZARD,J.A. *2175*
George Eliot and Italy: a comprehensive study of *Romola*. PhD Pennsylvania State U. 1956.

IRWIN,T.J. *2176*
'A process and an unfolding': character-formation in the fiction of George Eliot. PhD U. of Cambridge, 1983.

JABBI,B.B. *2177*
The coherence of *Daniel Deronda*. MA U. of Sussex, 1971.

JAYNE,V.D. *2178*
The technique of George Eliot's novels. PhD U. of Minnesota, 1903.

JOHN,J. *2179*
Pan-humanism in the novels of George Eliot. PhD Marquette U. 1974.

JONES,J.C. *2180*
The use of the bible in George Eliot's fiction. PhD North Texas State U. 1975.

JONES,P.H.C. *2181*
The spontaneous wisdom of mankind: the influence of August Comte on the novels of George Eliot. MA Wales (UWIST), 1976.

KABIR,Z. *2182*
Society and the individual in the writings of George Eliot. MA U. of Bristol, 1963.

KAYE,R.W. *2183*
Character and value in Georce Eliot's novels. PhD Stanford U. 1978.

KEARNEY,J.P. *2184*
George Eliot's treatment of time. PhD U. of Wisconsin, 1968.

KENNEY,E.J. *2185*
George Eliot's presence in *Middlemarch*. PhD Cornell U. 1968.

KER,I.T. *2186*
The interaction of certain evangelical and romance influences on the works of George Eliot. MLitt U. of Cambridge, 1972.

KILCULLEN,E. A. *2187*
George Eliot's treatment of marriage. PhD U. of Toronto, 1968.

KISCHNER,M.S. *2188*
Spinozism in three novels of George Eliot: *Adam Bede, The mill on the Floss* and *Silas Marner*. PhD Washington U. 1976.

KITCHEL,A.T. *2189*
Scientific influences in the work of Emile Zola and George Eliot. PhD U. of Wisconsin, 1921.

KLEPFISZ,I. *2190*
The uses of history in George Eliot's fiction: a study of *Romola* and its place in George Eliot's development. PhD U. of Chicago, 1971.

KNOEPFLMACH ER,U.C. *2191*
The Victorian novel of religious humanism: a study of George Eliot, Walter Pater, and Samuel Butler. PhD Princeton U. 1961.

KRIEFALL,L.H. *2192*
A Victorian apocalypse: a study of George Eliot's *Daniel Deronda* and its relation to David F. Strauss's *Das Leben Jesu*. PhD U. of Michigan, 1966.

KULERMAN,R.M. *2193*
Theme and structure in George Eliot's early fiction. PhD City U. of New York, 1979.

LAIN G,R.C. *2194*
Humor in George Eliot's novels. PhD U. of Pittsburgh, 1961.

LEDLIE,O. *2195*
George Eliot's narrative techniques in the dramatic delineation of her mentors. PhD Rice U. 1974.

LEE,F.M. *2196*
George Eliot. MA U. of Birmingham, 1941.

LEMKE,F.D. *2197*
George Eliot and her predecessors in village literature. PhD U. of Illinois, 1933.

LEVENSON,S.F. *2198*
The artist and the woman in George Eliot's novels. PhD Brandeis U. 1975.

LEVINE,G.L. *2199*
Determinism in the novels of George Eliot. PhD U. of Minnesota, 1959.

LINEHAN,K.B. *2200*
George Eliot's use of comedy and satire. PhD Stanford U. 1973.

LINKOVICH,S.A. *2201*
The romantic image in the novels of George Eliot. PhD U. of Toronto, 1977.

LITVAK,J.D. *2202*
Poetry in the novel: the poetics of disunity in George Eliot and Flaubert. PhD Yale U. 1981.

LOWE,S.W.J. *2203*
The later novels of George Eliot. MA U. of Manchester, 1977.

LYONS,R.S. *2204*
A study of *Middlemarch*. PhD Princeton U. 1960.

MCCOBB,E. A. *2205*
George Eliot's knowledge of German culture and its influence on her novels. PhD U. of Hull, 1979.

MCCORMACK,K. *2206*
Characters' reading and changing reality in the novels of George Eliot. PhD U. of Miami, 1981.

MCGRATH,D.J. *2207*
George Eliot and the wisdom of the child: a study of innocence and its importance in the novels of George Eliot. MPhil U. of London, Westfield Coll. 1980.

MCGUINN,N. *2208*
A study of the women in the novels of George Eliot, considered in relation to nineteenth-century feminism and to contemporary scientific and sociological thought upon the nature and role of women. DPhil U. of Oxford, 1980.

MCKINLEY,L.E. *2209*
Family affection and female principles in the novels of George Eliot. MPhil U. of Liverpool, 1980.

MCMAHON,C.R. *2210*
George Eliot and the feminist movement in nineteenth century England. PhD Stanford U. 1961.

MCMANUS,J.A. *2211*
The moral philosophy of George Eliot. MA U. of Warwick, 1972.

MANN,K.L.B. *2212*
Definition through form: the embodiment of George Eliot's beliefs in the early novels. PhD U. of Pennsylvania, 1971.

MANSE LL,D.L. *2213*
George Eliot's theory of fiction. PhD Yale U. 1963.

MARKIN,A. *2214*
George Eliot and education. PhD U. of Calgary, 1981.

MARTIN,B.K. *2215*
Standards of behavior in George Eliot's fiction. PhD U. of Cincinnati, 1967.

MASON,K.M. *2216*
George Eliot and the question of tragic redemption: a study of imaginative sympathy in *The mill on the Floss* and *Daniel Deronda*. PhD Cornell U. 1972.

MATTHEWS,C.E. *2217*
George Eliot on art and artists. PhD Harvard U. 1968.

MATUS,J.L. *2218*
Accommodating the actual: determinism and modes of writing in the novels of George Eliot. PhD U. of Toronto, 1981.

MEIKLE,S. *2219*
Issues of masculinity and feminity in three novels of George Eliot. PhD. of Leicester, 1982.

MIDLER,M.S. *2220*
The 'he and she of it': self-division as shaping force in George Eliot's fiction. PhD Rutgers U. 1980.

MILDER,G.E. *2221*
'Sublime resignation': George Eliot and the role of women. PhD Harvard U. 1974.

MINTZ,A.L. *2222*
George Eliot and the novel of vocation in England. PhD Columbia U. 1975.

MINTZ,M.J.R. *2223*
George Eliot and metaphor: creating a narrator in the mid-nineteenth-century novel. PhD U. of Chicago, 1982.

MOLDSTAD,D.F. *2224*
Evangelical influences on George Eliot. PhD U. of Wisconsin, 1954.

MORGAN,L. *2225*
Projecting and remembering: a study of narratives in three novels by George Eliot. PhD U. of London, University Coll. 1972.

MYERS,W.F.T. *2226*
Ideas of mental and social evolution in the treatment of character in George Eliot's novels. BLitt U. of Oxford, 1965.

NACHLAS,J.R. *2227*
Moral problems and social integration in the later novels of George Eliot. PhD U. of Toronto, 1980.

NAWALANIC,L.A. *2228*
George Eliot's ecological consciousnes in *Middlemarch*. PhD U. of Houston, 1979.

NEWTON,K.M. *2229*
George Eliot and romanticism. PhD U. of Edinburgh, 1972.

NIXEN,L.de B. *2230*
George Eliot: Clio as a novelist: an investigation into the uses of history in three of George Eliot's novels: *Romola, Middlemarch* and *Daniel Deronda*. PhD U. of Redlands, 1971.

NJOKU,M.C. *2231*
George Eliot: the technique of unfolding character from within. PhD U. of Alberta, 1977.

NOBLE,T.A. *2232*
A study of George Eliot's *Scenes of clerical life*. PhD Yale U. 1959.

NORMAN,L. *2233*
The novel as moral experiment: George Eliot's novels. PhD Brandeis U. 1967.

O'CLAIR,R.M. *2234*
A critical study of George Eliot's *Middlemarch*. PhD Harvard U. 1956.

OESTEREICHER,M.H. *2235*
On George Eliot and the meaning of *Middlemarch*. MPhil U. of Sussex, 1977.

OLDFIELD,D.E. *2236*
The prose style of *Middlemarch*. MA U. of London, Birkbeck Coll. 1964.

OLP HERT,L. *2237*
The role and status of women in the novels of George Eliot. MA U. of Ulster, 1974.

O'NEAL,E.M. *2238*
George Eliot's novels: confronting the fathers. PhD U. of California, Berkeley, 1979.

OWENS,R.J. *2239*
George Eliot's readers and critics, 1857–1902. PhD U. of Liverpool, 1958.

PALKO,A.J. *2240*
Latter-day saint: George Eliot's new St Theresa in image and symbol. PhD U. of Notre Dame, 1973.

PAPE,O.W. *2241*
Fictional rhetoric in George Eliot, Trollope and Fontane. MPhil U. of Sussex, 1973.

PARIS,B.J . *2242*
Experiments in life: George Eliot's reconciliation of realism and moralism. PhD Johns Hopkins U. 1959.

PAXTON,N.L. *2243*
Evolution and the mother in the novels of George Eliot. PhD Rutgers U. 1982.

PECK,S.C. *2244*
George Eliot's development as a psychological novelist. PhD U. of Wisconsin, 1972.

PELL,N.A. *2245*
'A flight from home': displacement as feminist critique in George Eliot's expatriate fiction. PhD State U. of New York at Buffalo, 1980.

PERRY,J.M. *2246*
George Eliot's voice in *Scenes of clerical life* and *Daniel Deronda*. MPhil U. of London, Birkbeck Coll. 1971.

PETERSON,V.A. *2247*
Moral growth in the heroines of George Eliot. PhD U. of California, Los Angeles, 1960.

PINNEY,T.C. *2248*
Wordsworth's influence on George Eliot. PhD Yale U. 1960.

POSTLETHWAITE,D.L. *2249*
The novelist as a woman of science: George Eliot and contemporary psychology. PhD Yale U. 1975.

POUND,A.H. *2250*
A critical study of four mid-Victorian political novels: *Sybil* by Benjamin Disraeli, *Alton Locke* by Charles Kingsley, *Felix Holt the Radical* by George Eliot and *Phineas Finn* by Anthony Trollope. MA U. of Manchester, 1971.

PRATT,J.C. *2251*
A *Middlemarch* miscellany: an edition with introduction and notes of George Eliot's 1868–1871 notebook. PhD Princeton U. 1965.

PRICE,T. *2252*
The ugly duckling: recurrent themes in George Eliot. PhD Rutgers U. 1975.

QUICK,J.R. *2253*
A critical edition of George Eliot's *Silas Marner*. PhD Yale U. 1968.

RAHMAN,A.M.A. *2254*
English criticism of George Eliot's novels between 1857 and 1881. MA U. of Manchester, 1959.

REDFERN,M.A. *2255*
Historical process and historical purpose in the novels of George Eliot. MPhil U. of Liverpool, 1979.

REISEN,D.M.C. *2256*
Pilgrims of mortality: the quest for identity in the novels of George Eliot. PhD Columbia U. 1972.

REISHMAN,J.V. *2257*
Six moral fables: a study of the redemptive vision in George Eliot's short fiction. PhD U. of Virginia, 1971.

RENWICK,R. *2258*
The intellectual background of George Eliot's early writings. PhD Harvard U. 1950.

RICHARDSON,M . *2259*
A study of *Felix Holt*. MA U. of Birmingham, 1973.

ROBERTS,N.J. *2260*
Studies in the social criticism of Dickens and George Eliot. PhD U. of Cambridge, 1973.

ROBERTSON,L.K. *2261*
George Eliot's ideas on education. PhD U. of Arkansas, 1982.

ROBINSON,C.L. *2262*
The ideology of sympathy: a study of George Eliot's later phase. PhD Brandeis U. 1965.

ROQUEMORE,J.H. *2263*
Historicism in George Eliot's fiction. PhD State U. of New York at Buffalo, 1974.

ROUNDS,S.R. *2264*
George Eliot's progressive alienation from English life. PhD Indiana U. 1970.

RUST,J.D. *2265*
George Eliot's periodical contributions. PhD Yale U. 1945.

RYAN,M.A. *2266*
George Eliot as a literary critic. PhD Boston U. 1941.

SANTAN GELO,G.A. *2267*
The background of George Eliot's *Romola*. PhD U. of North Carolina at Chapel Hill, 1962.

SCHNEIDER,R.L. *2268*
George Eliot: her search for order. PhD Cornell U. 1954.

SCHUTZ,F.C. *2269*
Sense and sensibility: a study of reason and emotion as elements of character and conduct in the novels of George Eliot. PhD U. of California, Berkeley, 1960.

SEIDENFEL D,B.B. *2270*
Vision and envisioning: subjectivity in the novels

of George Eliot. PhD Union Grad. Sch. Midwest, 1978.

SHUMAKER,R.C. *2271*
The rhetoric of George Eliot's fiction. PhD U. of Pittsburgh, 1974.

SHUTTLEWORTH,S. *2272*
Organicism and narrative structure: a study of George Eliot's novels. PhD U. of Cambridge, 1980.

SIFF,D.H. *2273*
The choir invisible: the relation of George Eliot's poetry and fiction. PhD New York U. 1968.

SIMPKIN,E. *2274*
George Eliot's literary criticism – especially as seen in her contributions to periodicals. MA U. of London, Bedford Coll. 1957.

SMITH,C.A. *2275*
George Eliot and the romantic enterprise. PhD U. of Missouri-Columbia, 1974.

SORENSON,K.M. *2276*
Drama in George Eliot: a model for imaginative expression. PhD Yale U. 1978.

SOUTHGATE,D. S. *2277*
George Eliot: a study of her novels. MPhil U. of Nottingham, 1977–8.

STEELE,K.B. *2278*
Social change in George Eliot's fiction. PhD Brown U. 1974.

STEINHOFF,W.R. *2279*
Recurrent patterns in George Eliot's novels. PhD U. of California, Berkeley, 1948.

STEINLIGHT,S.M. *2280*
The social vision of George Eliot's fiction. DPhil U. of Sussex, 1978.

STEVENS,J. *2281*
Towards Zion: George Eliot's artistic assessment of contemporary liberalism. PhD U. of Wales (Swansea), 1980.

STONEMAN,P.M. *2282*
A study of the development of George Eliot's methods of presenting character from *Scenes of clerical life* to *Romola* with special reference to linguistic aspects of her technique. MA U. of London, University Coll. 1964.

STUMP,R.J . *2283*
Vision as imagery, theme, and structure in George Eliot's novels. PhD U. of Washington, 1957.

SULLIVAN,W.J. *2284*
George Eliot and the fine arts. PhD U. of Wisconsin, 1970.

SWANN,B.S.F. *2285*
George Eliot and realism: the development of a concept of symbolic form. PhD Princeton U. 1970.

SZANTO,A.A. *2286*
Between liberalism and democracy: George Eliot's novels and the structure of mid-Victorian social reality. PhD U. of California, San Diego, 1973.

SZIROTNY,J.M.S. *2287*
The religious background of George Eliot's novels. PhD Stanford U. 1966.

TEMPLIN,C.H. *2288*
The treatment of community in the novels of George Eliot. PhD Indiana U. 1972.

TEMPLIN,L.H. *2289*
George Eliot: a study of the omniscient point of view in her fiction. PhD Indiana U. 1964.

TES LER,R.W. *2290*
George Eliot and the inner self. PhD New York U. 1975.

THOMSON,F.C. *2291*
The entail of nemesis: a study of *Felix Holt, the Radical*. PhD Yale U. 1957.

THUENTE,D.R. *2292*
Channels of feeling: George Eliot's search for the natural bases of religion. PhD U. of Kentucky, 1973.

TODD,J. *2293*
On the role of the reader: the theory and practice of the reader, and the fiction of George Eliot. DPhil U. of York, 1982.

TUCKER,H.C. *2294*
George Eliot's ideal self: a study of subjective influences on her prose fiction. PhD Vanderbilt U. 1960.

TURNER,W.H. *2295*
George Eliot's narrative technique. PhD U. of Toronto, 1969.

VONVILLAS,B.A. *2296*
George Eliot and feminism. PhD U. of Rhode Island, 1980.

WADDELL,M.J. *2297*
The idea of nature: George Eliot and her intellectual milieu. PhD U. of Cambridge, 1977.

WADE,D.E. *2298*
A study of the authorial commentary in *Scenes of clerical life, Felix Holt, Middlemarch* and *Daniel Deronda* by George Eliot, examining the frequency and recurrent topics of the 'author's voice' in the narrative. MPhil U. of London, Birkbeck Coll. 1976.

WARD,S.S. *2299*
Pattern and personality: a study of split structure in the novels of George Eliot. PhD Harvard U. 1973.

WARNER,F.C. *2300*
Toward *Middlemarch*: the heroine's search for guidance as motif in the earlier novels of George

Eliot. PhD U. of Illinois at Urbana-Champaign, 1974.

WATSON,K.M. *2301*
The use of religious diction in the nineteenth-century novel, with special reference to George Eliot. DPhil U. of Oxford, 1971.

WHEATLEY,J.H. *2302*
George Eliot and the art of thought: studies in the early novels. PhD Harvard U. 1960.

WHITE ,K.A.M. *2303*
Irredeemable egoism in the novels of George Eliot. EdD Ball State U. 1978.

WILLEY,F.W. *2304*
George Eliot and the conventions of the novel: studies of a writer in the traditions of fiction. PhD Harvard U. 1962.

WILLIAMS,D.H.H. *2305*
The figure of the counsellor in the novels of George Eliot. MA U. of London, External 1972.

WILSON,J.H. *2306*
George Eliot in America, her vogue and influence, 1858–1900. PhD U. of North Carolina at Chapel Hill, 1965.

WILSON,L. *2307*
George Eliot and the Victorian ideal. PhD Ohio U. 1968.

WOLF,E.V. *2308*
George Eliot's liberal menagerie: natural history, biology and value in the early novels. PhD Harvard U. 1969.

WOLFE,T.P. *2309*
The inward vocation: an essay on George Eliot's *Daniel Deronda*. PhD Rutgers U. 1973.

WOLFF,M.J. *2310*
Marian Evans to George Eliot: the moral and intellectual foundations of her career. PhD Princeton U. 1958.

WOODCOCK,J.A. *2311*
The moral dimension of beauty in George Eliot's heroines. PhD State U. of New York at Stony Brook, 1971.

WRIGHT,T.R. *2312*
George Eliot and the religion of humanity. DPhil U. of Oxford, 1977.

YEE,C.Z. *2313*
Feminism and the later heroines of George Eliot. PhD U. of New Mexico, 1977.

ZICHY,F.A. *2314*
The novelist's purpose: sympathy and judgment in the novels of George Eliot. PhD Harvard U. 1976.

ZIMMERMAN,B.S. *2315*
Appetite for submission: the female role in the novels of George Eliot. PhD State U. of New York at Buffalo, 1974.

Horatia Ewing

BAILEY,D.V. *2316*
A critical study of the work of Juliana Horatia Ewing (1841–1885). PhD U. of London, Bedford Coll. 1980.

BINDING,P.M. *2317*
Mrs Ewing: a critical appreciation of her work. BLitt U. of Oxford, 1969.

Susan Ferrier

EDWARDS,J.G. *2318*
The novels of Susan Ferrier considered in relation to the work of some other women novelists of her period. MA U. of Wales, 1954.

VALDES,H.J.M. *2319*
Style in the novels of Susan Ferrier. PhD U. of Texas at Austin, 1961.

WARREN,M.L. *2320*
The life and works of Susan Edmonstone Ferrier. PhD Cornell U. 1942.

Marianne Francis

MENAGH,D. *2321*
An edition of the letters of Marianne Francis (1790–1832) to Hester Lynch Piozzi (1741–1821), 1808–10. PhD City U. of New York, 1975.

Lady Georgina Fullerton

LEONARD,R.S. *2322*
Lady Georgina Fullerton. PhD St John's U. 1955.

Elizabeth Gaskell

AL-KOUREITI,M.I. *2323*
The contemporary reception of Mrs Gaskell as novelist and biographer, with special reference to reviews of her work. PhD U. of Hull, 1979.

AXE,K.J. *2324*
Elizabeth Cleghorn Gaskell: a critical evaluation of her novels. PhD U. of Kansas, 1973.

BICK,S. *2325*
Towards a female *Bildungsroman*: the protagonist in the works of Elizabeth Gaskell. PhD U. of California, Berkeley, 1976.

BOGGS,W.A. *2326*
Reflections of Unitarianism in Mrs Gaskell's novels. PhD U. of California, Berkeley, 1951.

BOYLE,P.M. *2327*
Elizabeth Gaskell: her development and achievement. PhD U. of Pennsylvania, 1970.

BRYANT,A.N. *2328*
Ideas and social themes in the works of Mrs Gaskell: a study of their relationship to social and literary background. MLitt U. of Strathclyde, 1971.

CARWELL,V.A. *2329*
Serialization and the fiction of Mrs Gaskell. PhD Northwestern U. 1965.

CLARKE,C.M. *2330*
Mrs Gaskell's short stories and sketches in relation to the periodicals where they first appeared. MPhil U. of London, Bedford Coll. 1973.

CRICK.J.B. *2331*
Daughters and wives: Mrs Gaskell's heroines. PhD U. of Leeds, 1975.

DAVIS,M.T. *2332*
An annotated bibliography of criticism on Elizabeth Cleghorn Gaskell. PhD U. of Mississippi, 1974.

DIGLIO,A.R. *2333*
Mrs Gaskell, social critic: with especial reference to *Mary Barton* and *North and south*. BPhil U. of Oxford, 1968.

DONALD,A.J. T. *2334*
The treatment of 'fallen women' in the novels of Dickens and Mrs Gaskell. BLitt U. of Oxford, 1969.

EIFRIG,G.M. *2335*
Growing out of motherhood: the changing role of the narrator in the works of Elizabeth Gaskell. PhD Bryn Mawr Coll. 1982.

ELBANNA,E. A. *2336*
The family in the novels of Mrs Gaskell. MLitt U. of Edinburgh, 1981.

FRANKS,P. *2337*
The emergence of harmony: development in the novels of Mrs Gaskell. PhD Temple U. 1973.

GALLAGHER,C.M. *2338*
Elizabeth Gaskell: the social novels. MA U. of Liverpool, 1963.

GARRETT,M.D. *2339*
The country village and the industrial city in Elizabeth Gaskell's fiction. PhD George Washington U. 1979.

GREEN,R.C. *2340*
One and many in the writings of Elizabeth Gaskell: increments of a comprehensive vision. PhD U. of Rochester, 1980.

GREENUP,G.D. *2341*
An assessment of the reviews of Mrs Gaskell's novels. PhD U. of Arizona, 1977.

HODGSON,J. *2342*
Mrs Gaskell's short stories. MA U. of Kent, 1978.

LANCASTER,J.T. *2343*
Mrs Gaskell, with special reference to the social reform novel, 1830–1850. MLitt U. of Cambridge, 1927.

LAUN,E.M. *2344*
'Couchant' lion under glass: a study of Elizabeth Gaskell's shorter fiction. PhD U. of Pittsburgh, 1979.

MCVEAGH,J. *2345*
The novels of Mrs Gaskell. PhD U. of Birmingham, 1967.

MANTOVANI,J.M. *2346*
The feminine world view of Elizabeth Cleghorn Gaskell. PhD U. of Southern California, 1974.

MEYER,E. *2347*
Growing amid change: Elizabeth Gaskell's vision of personal development. PhD Boston Coll. 1982.

MIRZA,Z. *2348*
The theme of Mrs Gaskell's *Ruth* and the reception of the novel. MPhil U. of London, Birkbeck Coll. 1967.

NESTOR,P.A. *2349*
Women in the novels and short stories of Elizabeth Gaskell. MPhil U. of Oxford, 1980.

NICKEL,M.A. *2350*
The reconciliation of opposites in the work of Elizabeth Gaskell. PhD Notre Dame U. 1974.

OWENS,G. *2351*
Town and country life in the life and works of Mrs Gaskell and Mary Russell Mitford. MA U. of Wales, 1953.

PANUSKA,J. *2352*
Character artistry in the novels of E.C. Gaskell. PhD U. of Alberta, 1973.

PIKE,A.J. *2353*
The Victorian scene in the writings of Mrs Gaskell. MA U. of Sheffield, 1958.

RAFF,A.D. *2354*
Elizabeth Gaskell: a critical study. PhD Cornell U. 1966.

RAILTON,W.K. *2355*
Mrs Gaskell: life and works. MA U. of Wales, 1940.

RAY NER,D.F. *2356*
Mrs Gaskell's *North and south* considered as a social novel and in relation to her development as a novelist. PhD U. of London, Bedford Coll. 1968.

RECCHIO,T.E. *2357*
The shape of Mrs Gaskell's fiction: realism into myth. PhD Rutgers U. 1982.

RICHARDS,R.P. *2358*
Some aspects of Mrs Gaskell's art: *Wives and daughters*. MPhil U. of London, Birkbeck Coll. 1975.

ROBINSON,D.L. *2359*
A study of Elizabeth Gaskell's artistic theory and practice in her major works. PhD U. of London, Royal Holloway Coll. 1976.

ROTHER,A.H. *2360*
Mrs Gaskell's art. PhD U. of Colorado, 1967.

SAWDEY,B.C.M. 2361
Between two worlds: a study of the heroine in the novels of Elizabeth Gaskell. PhD U. of Illinois at Urbana-Champaign, 1975.

SCHNURER, C. 2362
Mrs Gaskell's fiction. PhD U. of Pittsburgh, 1932.

SCHWARTZ,S.L. 2363
Elizabeth Gaskell: the novelist as artist. PhD U. of Rochester, 1971.

SETON,J. 2364
The importance of the heroine's personal relationships in the novels of Mrs Gaskell. MA U. of Manchester, 1968.

SHARPS,J.G. 2365
Observation and invention in the work of Mrs Gaskell. BLitt U. of Oxford, 1964.

SHELSTON,A.J. 2366
Elizabeth Gaskell: a study of four major works. MA U. of London, King's Coll. 1968.

STEELE,A. 2367
The fictional treatment of industrial relations from 1827 to 1879, with special reference to the novels of Mrs Gaskell. *BLitt U. of Oxford, 1965.*

TARRATT,M.M. 2368
Elizabeth Gaskell's attitude to the art of fiction as revealed in her later works (1855–65). BLitt U. of Oxford, 1967.

WELCH,J. E. 2369
The reputation of Elizabeth Gaskell: an annotated bibliography, 1929–1975. PhD U. of Michigan, 1978.

WHEELER,M.D. 2370
Elizabeth Gaskell's use of literary sources in *Mary Barton* and *Ruth*. PhD U. of London, Royal Holloway Coll. 1975.

WHITFIELD,A.S. 2371
Elizabeth Cleghorn Gaskell: a study of her writings. BLitt U. of Oxford, 1926.

WILL ENS,S.P. 2372
The novels of Elizabeth Gaskell: the comic vision. PhD Catholic U. of America, 1973.

WILLIAMS,W.T. 2373
Women's roles as delineated by Victorian society: a study of heroines in the major novels of Mrs Elizabeth Gaskell. PhD Florida State U. 1975.

WRIGHT,E. 2374
Mrs Gaskell: a study of her attitudes and beliefs in relation to her development as a novelist. PhD U. of London (Royal Coll. Nairobi), 1965.

Mary Hays

LURIA,G.M. 2375
Mary Hays: a critical biography. PhD New York U. 1972.

Felicia Hemans

JANNE,P.E. 2376
The life and works of Felicia Dorothea Hemans, 1793–1835. MA U. of London, King's Coll. 1963.

LESLIE,M.I. 2377
Felicia Hemans: the basis of a biography by Temple Lane (pseud.). PhD Trinity Coll. Dublin, 1943.

WILSON,E.G. 2378
Felicia Hemans. PhD Harvard U. 1952.

Barbara Hofland

BUTTS,D. 2379
Mrs Barbara Hofland, 1770–1844: a biographical and literary study. MPhil U. of Sheffield, 1981.

Mary Howitt

WOODRING,C. R. 2380
William and Mary Howitt and their circles. PhD Harvard U. 1949.

Emily Lawless

BREWER,B.W. 2381
Emily Lawless: an Irish writer above all else. PhD U. of North Carolina at Chapel Hill, 1982.

LINN,W.J. 2382
The life and works of the Hon. Emily Lawless: first novelist of the Irish literary revival. PhD New York U. 1971.

Elizabeth Lynn Linton

BELFLOWER,J.R. 2383
The life and career of Elizabeth Lynn Linton (1822–1898), Victorian woman of letters. PhD Duke U. 1967.

Harriet Martineau

ANDERSON,M.R. 2384
Harriet Martineau, a representative didactic writer of the nineteenth century. PhD U. of Pittsburgh, 1932.

ARBUCKLE,E.M. 2385
Harriet Martineau's letters to Fanny Wedgwood, 1837–1871. PhD U. of Edinburgh, 1978.

BENNETT,S.M. 2386
Harriet Martineau; historian of ideas. MA U. of Birmingham, 1977.

COSTAI N,K.M. 2387
The fictional works of Harriet Martineau. MA U. of Nottingham, 1961.

REA,E. 2388
A study of Harriet Martineau. MA U. of Birmingham, 1970.

RIVENBURG,N.E. *2389*
Harriet Martineau, an example of Victorian conflict. PhD Columbia U. 1932.

SANDERS,V.R. *2390*
Harriet Martineau: the significance of her literary contribution with special reference to her influence and relationship to nineteenth-century society and literature. DPhil U. of Oxford, 1983.

SEAT,W.R. *2391*
Harriet Martineau in America. PhD Indiana U. 1957.

Mary Russell Mitford

COLES,W.A. *2392*
The correspondence of Mary Russell Mitford and Thomas Noon Talfourd (1821–1825). PhD Harvard U. 1957.

RAUSCH,M.S. *2393*
Mary Russell Mitford and regional reliasm. PhD U. of Minnesota, 1968.

Margaret Oliphant

BUCKINGHAM,M.S. *2394*
The use of religious elements in the fiction of Margaret Wilson Oliphant. PhD Cornell U. 1938.

GRAY,M.K. *2395*
The fiction of Margaret Oliphant. PhD U. of Glasgow, 1979.

MOSIER,W.E. *2396*
Mrs Oliphant's literary criticism. PhD Northwestern U. 1967.

Amelia Opie

HARMON,L. *2397*
Amelia Opie and contemporary thought. PhD New York U. 1934.

MACGREGOR,M.E. *2398*
The life and works of Mrs Amelia Opie. PhD U. of London, King's Coll. 1932.

Anne Benson Proctor

THOMAS,L.A. *2399*
Letters of Anne Benson Proctor, with introduction and notes. MA U. of Birmingham, 1968.

Henry Handel Richardson

NICHOLS,J.R. *2400*
Theme and technique in Henry Handel Richardson: a discussion of the relationship between theme and technique in the major novels of Henry Handel Richardson. [Pen-name of Ethel Florence Richardson.] PhD U. of North Caroline, 1969.

Regina Maria Roche (née Dalton)

SCHROEDER,N.E. *2401*
Regina Maria Roche: popular novelist, 1789–1834. PhD Northwestern U. 1978.

Christina Rossetti

BAUMBACH,F.E. *2402*
Relativity and polarity in Christina Rossetti. PhD U. of Wisconsin, 1968.

BRUCK,M.D. *2403*
The poetry and prose of Christina Rossetti. PhD U. of Wisconsin, 1955.

CANTALUPO,C.M. *2404*
Continuities of faith and style in Christina Rossetti's poetry. PhD Rutgers U. 1983.

CHARLES,E.K. *2405*
A comparative study of nineteenth and twentieth century criticism of selected poems of Christina Rossetti. PhD New York U. 1978.

COOK,W.J. *2406*
The sonnets of Christina Rossetti: a comparative prosodic analysis. PhD Auburn U. 1971

CROWLEY,A.P.O. *2407*
D.G. and C. Rossetti. MA National U. of Ireland, 1940.

D'AMICO,D.R. *2408*
'O Hope deferred, hope still': the poetry of Christina Rossetti. PhD U. of Wisconsin-Madison, 1980.

ERDLE,M.G. *2409*
A revaluation of the poetry of Christina Rossetti. PhD St John's U. 1965.

FESTA,C.D. *2410*
Studies in Christina Rossetti's *Goblin Market* and other poems. PhD U. of South Carolina, 1969.

JIMENEZ,N. *2411*
Concordance of the bible and the poetry of Christina Rossetti. PhD State U. of New York at Albany, 1977.

JUHNKE,A.K. *2412*
Dante Gabriel and Christina Rossetti: the poetry of love, death and faith. PhD Indiana U. 1966.

KAMEN,A. *2413*
Christina Rossetti as a lyrical poet. MA U. of Wales, 1927.

KMETZ,G. *2414*
With stillness that is almost paradise: romanticism and mysticism in the poetry of Christina Rossetti. PhD Columbia U. 1973.

KOHL,J.A. *2415*
Sparks of fire: Christina Rossetti's artistic life. PhD U. of Delaware, 1969.

KOMPERDA,C.L. *2416*
The religious poetry of Christina Rossetti: a study of quality. PhD Lehigh U. 1980.

LAMOUREUX,P.E. *2417*
The development of theme and image in Christina Rossetti's poetry and fictional prose. PhD Harvard U. 1978.

LEDER,S. *2418*
The image of woman in Christina Rossetti's poetry. PhD New York U. 1979.

MCCANN,H. *2419*
The influence of the 'dolce stil nuovo' on the poetry of Christina Rossetti. PhD U. of Wisconsin-Madison, 1978.

MCLOUGHLIN,J.E. *2420*
Christina Rossetti. MA National U. of Ireland, 1947.

PACKER,L.M. *2421*
Beauty for ashes: a biographical study of Christina Rossetti's poetry. PhD U. of California, Los Angeles, 1957.

PARSONS,D.M. *2422*
Christina Rossetti: the imagery in her English poetry. MA U. of London, King's Coll. 1948.

QUILL,K.M. *2423*
The poetry of Christina Rossetti: a study in the creative imagination. PhD U. of Rochester, 1977.

SHALKHAUSER,M.D. *2424*
The poetry and prose of Christina Rossetti. PhD U. of Wisconsin, 1955.

THOMAS,E.W. *2425*
Christina Georgina Rossetti. PhD Columbia U. 1931.

UFFELMAN,L.K. *2426*
Christina Rossetti's *A pageant and other poems*: an annotated critical edition. PhD Kansas State U. 1969.

WEIDEMAN,R.S. *2427*
A critical bibliography of Christina Rossetti. PhD U. of Texas at Austin, 1970.

WION,A.H. *2428*
'Give me the lowest place': the poetry of Christina Rossetti. PhD Cornell U. 1976.

Elizabeth Sewell

LADNER,B.M. *2429*
Elizabeth Sewell: poetic method as an instrument of thinking and knowing. PhD Duke U. 1971.

FRERICHS,S.C. *2430*
Elizabeth Missing Sewell: a minor novelist's search for the 'via media' in the education of women in the Victorian era. PhD Brown U. 1974.

Mary Shelley

CALLAGHAN,C.M. *2431*
Mary Shelley's *Frankenstein*: a composition of romanticism. PhD Stanford U. 1936.

EL-SHATER,S.M. *2432*
The novels of Mary Shelley. MA U. of Liverpool, 1963.

FELDMAN,P.R. *2433*
The journals of Mary Wollstonecraft Shelley. PhD Northwestern U. 1974.

GRAY,D.K. *2434*
Frankenstein and the development of the English novel. PhD U. of Dallas, 1979.

NEUMANN,B.R. *2435*
Mary Shelley. PhD U. of New Mexico, 1972.

OZOLIN,S. *2436*
The novels of Mary Shelley: from *Frankenstein* to *Falkner*. PhD U. of Maryland, 1972.

POWERS,K.R. *2437*
The influence of William Godwin on the novels of Mary Shelley. PhD U. of Tennessee, 1972.

TROOP,M. *2438*
Mary Shelley's monster: a study of *Frankenstein*. PhD Boston U. Grad. Sch. 1973.

WADE,P.T. *2439*
Influence and intent in the prose fiction of Percy and Mary Shelley. PhD U. of North Carolina at Chapel Hill, 1966.

Dora Sigerson Shorter

SMITH,M.E. *2440*
A biographical and critical study of Dora Sigerson Shorter, 1866–1918. PhD U. of Pennsylvania, 1954.

May Sinclair

GILLESPIE,D.M.F. *2441*
Female artists as characters and creators: the dual concern with feminine role and feminine fiction in the work of May Sinclair. PhD U. of Alberta, 1974.

KINNAMON,R.A. *2442*
May Sinclair's fiction of the supernatural. PhD Duke U. 1974.

TAYLOR,C.Y. *2443*
A study of May Sinclair, woman and writer, 1863–1946; with an annotated bibliography. PhD Washington State U. 1969.

ZEGGER,H.D. *2444*
May Sinclair's psychological novels. PhD New York U. 1970.

Caroline Anne Southey

SCHONERT,V.L. 2445
The correspondence of Caroline Anne Bowles Southey to Mary Anne Watts Hughes. PhD Harvard U. 1957.

Emily Sellwood, Lady Tennyson

HOGE,J.O. 2446
The letters of Emily Lady Tennyson. PhD U. of Virginia, 1970.

Anne Thackeray, Lady Ricthie

FREEMAN,J.E. 2447
A critical appreciation of the life and works of Anne Thackeray, Lady Ritchie. MA U. of Liverpool, 1968.

HUIE,J. 2448
Anne Thackeray, afterwards Lady Ritchie. PhD U. of London, University Coll. 1961.

PREUS,O.J.H. 2449
Anne Thackeray Ritchie and the Victorian literary aristocracy. PhD U. of Minnesota, 1958.

Frances Trollope

GARDINER,N.B. 2450
A critical study of the work of Frances Milton Trollope. PhD U. of London, 1969.

GRIFFIN,R.A. 2451
Frances Milton Trollope: a study of a literary reputation. PhD Case Western Reserve U. 1940.

Mrs Humphrey Ward

BUTTERWORTH,J.R. 2452
The novels of Mrs Humphrey Ward: a study in form. PhD U. of California, Los Angeles, 1959.

COGHLA N,K.A. 2453
Mrs Humphrey Ward: novelist and thinker. PhD Boston U. 1957.

COLACO,J.H. 2454
Mrs Humphrey Ward: studies in three novels. BLitt U. of Oxford, 1976.

COLLISTER,P. 2455
The major novels of Mrs Humphrey Ward, 1888–1900. PhD U. of Reading, 1981.

DUNBAR,G.D.S. 2456
The faithful recorder: Mrs Humphrey Ward and the foundation of her novels. PhD Columbia U. 1953.

GARNETT,P. 2457
Mrs Humphrey Ward: claims to intellectual power and formal literary excellence. MA U. of Birmingham, 1966.

MUSIL,C.M. 2458
Art and ideology: the life and times of Mrs Humphrey Ward. PhD Northwestern U. 1974.

MYERS,J.S. 2459
Mary Ward's *Helbeck of Bannisdale* and English Catholicism. PhD U. of Pennsylvania, 1981.

REYNOLDS,L.A. 2460
Mrs Humphrey Ward and the Arnold heritage. PhD U. of California, Los Angeles, 1952.

UNIKEL,G. 2461
The religious Arnoldism of Mrs Humphrey Ward. PhD U. of California, Berkeley, 1951.

WILLIAMS,K.E. 2462
Faith, intention and fulfillment: the religious novels of Mrs Humphrey Ward. PhD Temple U. 1969.

Florence Wilson

BAKER-SMITH,M.P.D. 2463
The writings of Florence Wilson in relation to Evangelical Humanism. PhD U. of Cambridge, 1970.

Mrs Henry Wood

LAWSON,J.R. 2464
The domestic-sensational novels of Mrs Henry Wood. PhD U. of California, Berkeley, 1956.

Dorothy Wordsworth

KINCAID-EHLERS,E. 2465
Blue woman on a green field: a consideration of Dorothy Wordsworth. PhD U. of Rochester, 1978.

ROGERS,J.E. 2466
'Dearest friend': a study of Dorthy Wordsworth's journals. PhD Pennsylvania State U. 1973.

THOMPSON,F. 2467
Dorothy Wordsworth: her mind and art. MA U. of Birmingham, 1926.

Charlotte Yonge

DEMIS,V.T. 2468
The novels of Charlotte Yonge: a critical introduction. PhD Michigan State U. 1980.

GREEN, C.E. 2469
The novels of Charlotte Yonge, 1850–65: a case for religious fiction. BLitt U. of Oxford, 1974.

INNERD,J.A. 2470
An investigation into the effects of the Victorian notions of duty and obedience on the domestic novels of Charlotte Mary Yonge. PhD U. of Durham, 1974.

The twentieth century

General and comparative studies

ALLENE,E. 2471
Women as signifier in the novels of Henry James. DPhil U. of Sussex, 1981.

ANDERSON,P.G. 2472
The female principle in the fiction of Wyndham Lewis. PhD U. of Alberta, 1979.

BAILIE,E. 2473
Women for liberation in the plays of Sean O'Casey. PhD Indiana U. 1974.

BANNISTER,I.L. 2474
Sirens, wise women and sorcerers: a study of women in the plays of Bernard Shaw. PhD Trinity Coll., Dublin, 1979.

BERKSON, D.W. 2475
The ordeal of the American girl: female initiation in Henry James's fiction. PhD U. of Illinois at Urbana-Champaign, 1978.

BESANT,L. 2476
Shaw's women characters. PhD U. of Wisconsin, 1964.

BRAENDLIN,B.H. 2477
Bildung and the role of woman in the Edwardian *Bildungsroman*: Maugham, Bennett and Wells. PhD Florida State U. 1978.

BROSS,A.W. 2478
Joseph Conrad's female characters in selected fiction. PhD Louisiana State U. 1967.

BURC HARD,G.M. 2479
D.H. Lawrence and the 'femme fatale'. PhD U. of Illinois at Urbana-Champaign, 1982.

CASH,J.L. 2480
The treatment of women characters in the complete works of Joseph Conrad. PhD Texas Tech. U. 1972.

CHESSMAN,H.S. 2481
Talk and silence in the novels of Virginia Woolf, Elizabeth Bowen, and Ivy Compton-Burnett. PhD Yale U. 1979.

CORE,D.L. 2482
The atmosphere of the unasked question: women's relationships in modern British fiction. PhD Kent State U. 1981.

CRANE,G.M. 2483
The characterization of the comic women characters of George Bernard Shaw. PhD Indiana U. 1968.

CROTTY,M.M. 2484
The mother in the fiction of Henry James. PhD Fordham U. 1962.

CURTLER,E.S. 2485
A woman young and old: love in Yeat's vision. PhD Duke U. 1977.

CWIAKALA,J. 2486
Some English and Polish women novelists of the inter-war period, 1918–39. BLitt U. of Oxford, 1970.

DICKINSON,J.E. 2487
Women novelists and war: a study of the responses of seven women novelists, 1914–1940. MLitt U. of Edinburgh, 1980.

ECKLEY,G.E.W. 2488
Anna Livia Plurabelle: the continuum of *Finnegan's wake*. PhD Kent State U. 1970.

EDWARDS,M.E.P. 2489
(Part I) Henry James and the woman novelist: the double standard in the tales and essays. PhD U. of Virginia, 1978.

FEDOR,J.R. 2490
The importance of the female in the plays of Samuel Beckett, Harold Pinter, and Edward Albee. PhD U. of Washington, 1976.

FIN KELSTEIN,B.B. 2491
The role of women in the novels of E.M. Forster with parallels to the role of homosexuals in *Maurice*. PhD Columbia U. 1972.

GALENBECK,S.L.C. 2492
Women, manners, and morals: Henry James's plays and the comedy of manners on the turn of the century British stage. PhD U. of Oregon, 1980.

GIBSON,S.M. 2493
Love and the vote: fiction of the suffrage movement in Edwardian England. PhD U. of Massachusetts, 1975.

GRIMES,M.L. 2494
The archetype of the great mother in the novels of William Golding. PhD U. of Florida, 1976.

GRUMMAN,J.M. 2495
Henry James's great 'bad' heroines. PhD Purdue U. 1972.

HORAN,T.J. 2497
The figure of Mary in *Finnegan's wake*. PhD Temple U. 1976.

HORNEY,L.J. 2498
The emerging woman of the twentieth century: a study of the women in D.H. Lawrence's novels *The rainbow* and *Women in love*. EdD Ball State U. 1972.

HOVET,G.O. 2499
The *Bildungsroman* of the middle-aged woman: her emergence as heroine in British fiction since 1920. PhD U. of Kansas, 1976.

KAPLAN,S.J. 2500
The feminine consciousness in the novels of five

twentieth-century British women. [Dorothy Richardson, May Sinclair, Virginia Woolf, Rosamond Lehmann, Doris Lessing.] PhD U. of California, Los Angeles, 1971.

KESTER,D.A. 2501
Shaw and the Victorian 'problem' genre: the woman side. PhD U. of Wisconsin- Madison, 1973.

KETCHAM,M.D. 2502
E.M. Forster's women characters: a psychoanalytic study. PhD U. of California, Berkeley, 1973.

KHAWAJA,M.M. 2503
Graham Greene: design of irony and the role of the female. PhD West Virginia U. 1979.

KOO TKA,M. 2504
The old woman: one phase of the character poem in contemporary British verse. PhD U. of Pennsylvania, 1931.

LIDSTO NE-SINHA,M.J. 2505
'Female', 'femme' and 'feminist' in the work of twentieth-century women novelists. [Predominantly British; includes Doris Lessing, Michele Roberts and Ursula Le Guin.] PhD U. of Keele, 1981.

LITTLE,S.B. 2506
The relationship of the woman figure and views of reality in three works by James Joyce. PhD Arizona State U. 1971.

LUNDVALL,S.D. 2507
Joseph Conrad: the feminine perspective. PhD U. of Nebraska-Lincoln, 1978.

MERRICK,.A.H. 2509
Conrad and the true lie: the role of women in the political novels and *Chance*. PhD Harvard U. 1967.

MONAHAN,M.J. 2510
The position of Molly Bloom in *Ulysses*. PhD U. of Kent, 1971.

NASSIF PAYVANDI,C.A. 2511
A study of contemporary women playwrights in Britain. [Enid Bagnold, Shelagh Delaney, Doris Lessing, Ann Jellicoe, Jane Arden and Maureen Duffy.] PhD U. of Iowa, 1978.

O'DONNELL,B. 2512
Synge and O'Casey women: a study in strongmindedness. PhD Michigan State U. 1976.

PALLISER ,C. 2513
The early fiction of Virginia Woolf and her literary relations with Katherine Mansfield. BLitt U. of Oxford, 1975.

PAN ETTA,E.H. 2514
The anti-heroine in the fiction of Henry James. PhD U. of Notre Dame, 1980.

PHELPS,T.G. 2515
Empress of the Labyrinth: the feminine in David Jones's poetry. PhD U. of Notre Dame, 1980.

RICHARD,J.M. 2516
The modern British *Bildungsroman* and the woman novelist: Dorothy Richardson, May Sinclair, Rosamond Lehmann, Elizabeth Bowen and Doris Lessing. PhD U. of North Carolina at Chapel Hill, 1981.

ROBERTS,H. 2517
Women and fiction: a sociological study of British fiction by and for women since the turn of the century. DPhil U. of Sussex, 1976.

RUNNELS,J.A. 2519
Mother, wife and lover: symbolic women in the work of W.B. Yeats. PhD Rutgers U. 1973.

SCHWALDE,D.J. 2520
H.G. Wells and the superfluous woman. PhD U. of Colorado, 1962.

SCHWER TMAN,M.P. 2521
Henry James's portraits of ladies. PhD U. of North Carolina at Chapel Hill, 1968.

SCOTT,M.D. 2522
Many ghosts to fight: the image of women in British society between the wars as reflected in the novels of English women authors. PhD Boston U. Grad. Sch. 1974.

SHIELDS,J.L. 2523
Shaw's women characters: an analysis and a survey of influences from life. PhD Indiana U. 1958.

SIEMENS,R.G. 2524
The role of the woman in the artist's development in certain British artist-hero novels of the nineteenth and early twentieth centuries. PhD U. of Wisconsin, 1966.

SIMPSO N,H. 2525
D.H. Lawrence and feminism, 1900–1930. PhD U. of Reading, 1979.

STARNES,J.A.H. 2526
A study of the female characters in William Golding's novels. PhD Georgia State U. 1980.

STEPHENS,E.D. 2527
The novel of personal relationships: a study of three contemporary British women novelists. [Edna O'Brien, Penelope Mortimer and Margaret Drabble.] PhD Emory U. 1976.

STRAGUE,K. 2528
From a troubled heart: T.H. White and women in *The once and future king*. PhD U. of Texas at Austin, 1978.

STUBBS,P.J.A. 2529
A comparative study of the fiction of Iris Murdoch and Muriel Spark. MPhil U. of London, University Coll. 1969.

STUBBS,P.J.A. 2530
The treatment of moral values in the work of four contemporary novelists: Graham Greene, Muriel

Spark, Iris Murdoch, Doris Lessing. PhD U. of London, University Coll. 1978.

SURYANARAYAN,Z. 2531
A parallel study of two British women poets: Ruth Pitter and Elizabeth Jennings. PhD U. of Rhode Island, 1980.

TOMBS,E. 2532
John Cowper Powys: escapism and women. MA U. of Wales (Aberystwyth), 1980.

TUDOR,K. R. 2533
The androgynous mind in W.B. Yeats, D.H. Lawrence, Virginia Woolf and Dorothy Richardson. PhD U. of Toronto, 1972.

VANDERHAAR,M.M. 2534
Yeats's relationships with women and their influence on his poetry. PhD Tulane U. 1966.

WATSON,B.B. 2535
A Shavian guide to the intelligent woman. PhD Columbia U. 1963.

WEDWICK,C.C. 2536
The treatment of women in the plays of William Butler Yeats. PhD Bowling Green State U. 1975.

WELLS,G.L. 2537
The role of the female in relation to the arist in the works of Joyce Cary. PhD U. of Mississippi, 1975.

WILSON,A.M. 2539
Dolls and angels: a study of Joseph Conrad's female characters. PhD U. of Pittsburgh, 1978.

Individual writers

Elizabeth von Arnim

WILENS,P. 2540
'Elizabeth' and the tragic-comic vision of femininity. [Pseudonym of Mary Annette Beauchamp, Countess von Arnim and later Countess Russell.] PhD New York U. 1981.

Enid Blyton

RAY,S.G. 2541
A study of the growth of critical attitudes amongst adults towards Enid Blyton since 1936 related to an examination of the reasons for her popularity amongst children. MPhil CNAA 1980.

Maud Bodkin

MONTELLA,I.H.Z. 2542
Images of encounter: Maud Bodkin's journal and her psychology of literary response. PhD Syracuse U. 1978.

Elizabeth Bowen

BLODGETT,H.H. 2543
Circles of reality: a reading of the novels of Elizabeth Bowen. PhD U. of California, Davis, 1968.

BROWN,P.H. 2544
After the fall: innocence and experience in eight novels by Elizabeth Bowen. PhD U. of Pittsburgh, 1982.

DOSTAL,R.M. 2545
Innocence and knowledge in the novels of Elizabeth Bowen. PhD U. of Notre Dame, 1964.

GARNE R,M.P. 2546
The fiction of Elizabeth Bowen and its relation to other fiction by women, 1919–1965. DPhil U. of Oxford, 1980.

HANN A,J.G. 2547
Elizabeth Bowen and the art of fiction: a study of her theory and practice. PhD Boston U. 1961.

HEATH,W.W. 2548
Elizabeth Bowen and the tradition of the novel. PhD U. of Wisconsin, 1956.

KENDRIS,T. 2549
The novels of Elizabeth Bowen. PhD Columbia U. 1964.

KIRKPATRICK,L.J. 2550
Elizabeth Bowen and company: a comparative essay in literary judgment. PhD Duke U. 1965.

LAWSON,J.A. 2551
Professionalized susceptibilities: imagination in the early novels of Elizabeth Bowen. PhD U. of Iowa, 1979.

MCDOWELL,A.B. 2552
Identity and the past: major themes in the fiction of Elizabeth Bowen. PhD Bowling Green State U. 1971.

MCGOWAN,M.J. 2553
Lyric design in the novels of Elizabeth Bowen. PhD Boston U. 1971.

MILLER,D.W. 2554
Scene and image in three novels by Elizabeth Bowen. PhD Columbia U. 1967.

NARDELLA,A.E.R. 2555
Feminism, art and aesthetics: a study of Elizabeth Bowen. PhD State U. of New York at Stony Brook, 1975.

ROSSEN,J.A. 2556
The early novels of Elizabeth Bowen: an existential reading. PhD U. of Minnesota, 1982.

RUPP,R.H. 2557
The achievement of Elizabeth Bowen: a study of her fiction and criticism. PhD Indiana U. 1963.

SOLDANI,L.N. 2558
To live how one can: a thematic study of Elizabeth Bowen's short fiction. PhD U. of Notre Dame, 1967.

Brigid Brophy

DOCK,L.A. 2559
Brigid Brophy, artist in the baroque. PhD U. of Wisconsin-Madison, 1976.

Ivy Compton-Burnett

O'REILLY,W.M. 2560
Nature and convention in the novels of Ivy Compton-Burnett. PhD U. of Connecticut, 1972.

Margaret Drabble

MORAN,M.H. 2561
Existing within structures: Margaret Drabble's view of the individual. PhD U. of New Mexico, 1980.

SAYLORS,R.D. 2562
Moral development and fictional technique in the novels of Margaret Drabble. PhD U. of Houston, 1981.

Florence Farr

JOHNSON,J.A. 2563
Florence Farr: biography of a new woman. PhD U. of Leeds, 1972.

Lady Gregory

DONOVAN,D.C. 2564
Lady Gregory and the Abbey theatre. MA U. of Ireland, 1951.

MULLET,O.G. 2565
The war with women and words: Lady Gregory's destructive, Celtic folklore woman. PhD U. of Wisconsin-Madison, 1973.

MURPHY,D.J. 2566
The letters of Lady Gregory to John Quinn. PhD Columbia U. 1961.

PICK,M. 2567
The work of Lady Gregory: her contribution to the Irish dramatic and literary revival. MA U. of London, Bedford Coll. 1940.

REGAN,M.J . 2568
Lady Gregory: the dramatic artist. MA National U. of Ireland, 1953.

SEXTON,H.I. 2569
A critical assessment of Lady Gregory's achievement as a dramatist. MA U. of Manchester, 1963.

STEVENSON,M.L.K. 2570
Lady Gregory: a character study. PhD U. of North Carolina at Chapel Hill, 1977.

TANNER,W.E. 2571
A study of Lady Gregory's translations of Molière. PhD U. of Tulsa, 1972.

YOUNG,L.D. 2572
The plays of Lady Gregory. PhD Trinity Coll., Dublin, 1958.

Radclyffe Hall

FRYE,J.C. 2573
Radclyffe Hall: a study in censorship. PhD U. of Missouri-Columbia, 1972.

Norah Hoult

GIST,J.D. 2574
Characterization in the works of Norah Hoult. PhD U. of Arkansas, 1970.

Katherine Tynan Hinkson

MOLONEY,F.I. 2575
Katherine Tynan Hinkson: a study of her poetry. PhD Pennsylvania State U. 1952.

Elizabeth Jennings

HARRISON,J.E. 2576
The quiet pursuit: poetry of Elizabeth Jennings. PhD Ohio U. 1968.

Mary Lavin

ROARK,B.J. 2577
Mary Lavin: the local and the universal. PhD U. of Colorado, 1968.

STANLEY,A.A. 2578
Mary Lavin's widow stories. PhD U. of Georgia, 1982.

Frieda Lawrence

HOLLAND,J. E. 2579
The memoirs of Frieda Lawrence. PhD U. of Texas at Austin, 1976.

Rosamond Lehmann

LESTOURGEON,D.E. 2580
The novels of Rosamond Lehmann. PhD U. of Pennsylvania, 1960.

Rose Macaulay

DAVIES,M.G. 2581
Rose Macaulay: a study of six of her novels. MPhil U. of Southampton, 1973.

KUEHN,R.E. 2582
The pleasures of Rose Macaulay: an introduction to her novels. PhD U. of Wisconsin, 1962.

MARROCCO,M.J. 2583
The novels of Rose Macaulay: a literary pilgrimage. PhD U. of Toronto, 1978.

PASSTY ,J.N. 2584
Eros and androgny: the writings of Rose Macaulay. PhD U. of Southern California, 1982.

RIZZO,P.L. 2585
Rose Macaulay: a critical survey. PhD U. of Pennsylvania, 1959.

Katherine Mansfield

BERKMAN,S.L. 2586
Katherine Mansfield: a study of her life and work. PhD Radcliffe Coll. 1942.

BRAEKKAN,E.M. 2587
From feminist to 'feminine': a comparative study of Katherine Mansfield's short stories. PhD U. of Warwick, 1981.

CHATTERJEE,M.F. 2588
The relationship between Katherine Mansfield's criticism and her fiction. PhD New York U. 1979.

DOWLING,D.H. 2589
Katherine Mansfield: her theory and practice of fiction. PhD U. of Toronto, 1976.

GARL INGTON,J.D. 2590
Literary theory and practice in the short stories of Katherine Mansfield. PhD U. of Wisconsin, 1954.

HANKIN,C.A. 2591
Katherine Mansfield: a psychological inquiry. PhD U. of California, Berkeley, 1971.

KLEINE,D.W. 2592
Method and meaning in the stories of Katherine Mansfield. PhD U. of Michigan, 1961.

KOMINARS,S.B. 2593
Katherine Mansfield: the way to Fontainebleau. PhD Boston U. 1966.

KURYLO,C.C. 2594
Chekhov and Katherine Mansfield: a study in literary influence. PhD U. of North Carolina at Chapel Hill, 1974.

MASON,N.B. 2595
Intimacy and isolation: a tension which informs the work of Katherine Mansfield. PhD Purdue U. 1980.

MORSE,L.M. 2596
Juxtaposition in the short stories of Katherine Mansfield. EdD Oklahoma State U. 1971.

PATTINSON,P.M. 2597
Vision and design in the short stories of Katherine Mansfield. MA U. of Liverpool, 1968.

SERVAIS,Y. 2598
The art of Katherine Mansfield. MA National U. of Ireland, 1937.

WALKER,N. 2599
Stages of womanhood in Katherine Mansfield's *Prelude*. PhD U. of Massachusetts, 1976.

YEN,Y.S. 2600
Katherine Mansfield's use of point of view. PhD U. of Wisconsin, 1967.

ZINM AN,T.S. 2601
The snail under the leaf: Katherine Mansfield's ironic vision. PhD Temple U. 1973.

Alice Meynell

CALLAN,C .E. 2602
Alice Meynell. MA U. of Birmingham, 1926.

ELMES,T.I. 2603
Alice Meynell. MA National U. of Ireland, 1949.

GRAHAM,M. 2604
The works of Alice Meynell. MA U. of Birmingham, 1942.

MCLERNAN,M.C. 2605
The works of Alice Meynell. MA U. of Liverpool, 1937.

MEDFURD,E.R. 2606
Alice Meynell. PhD U. of Texas at Austin, 1968.

MURPHY,M.C. 2607
Alice Meynell. MA National U. of Ireland, 1969.

TUELL,A.K. 2608
Mrs Meynell and her literary generation. PhD Columbia U. 1925.

Naomi Mitchison

SMITH,D.A. 2609
Possible worlds: the fiction of Naomi Mitchison. PhD U. of Edinburgh, 1982.

Iris Murdoch

AIKEN,G.E. 2610
This accidental world: the philosophy and fiction of Iris Murdoch. PhD U. of Tennessee, 1979.

ANDERSON,T.K. 2611
Concepts of love in the novels of Iris Murdoch. PhD Purdue U. 1970.

ASHDOWN,E.A. 2612
Form and myth in three novels by Iris Murdoch: *The flight from the enchanter, The bell* and *The severed head*. PhD U. of Florida, 1974.

BEAMS,D.W. 2613
Form in the novels of Iris Murdoch. PhD Columbia U. 1978.

BELLAMY,M.O. 2614
The artist and the saint: an approach to the aesthetics and the ethics of Iris Murdoch. PhD U. of Wisconsin-Madison, 1975.

BIRDSALL,N.E. 2615
Art, beauty and morality in the novels of Iris Murdoch. PhD U. of Minnesota, 1980.

CLARK,J.A. *2616*
A complexity of mirrors: the novels of Iris Murdoch. PhD U. of Wisconsin-Milwaukee, 1978.

FAS T,L.E. *2617*
Self-discovery in the novels of Iris Murdoch. PhD U. of Oregon, 1970.

FOLEY,B.M. *2618*
Iris Murdoch's use of works of art as analogies of moral themes. PhD Wayne State U. 1979.

GILLIGAN,J.T. *2619*
The fiction and philosophy of Iris Murdoch. PhD U. of Wisconsin-Milwaukee, 1973.

GOSHGARIAN ,G. *2620*
From fable to flesh: a study of the female characters in the novels of Iris Murdoch. PhD U. of Wisconsin-Madison, 1972.

HAGUE,A. *2621*
Iris Murdoch's comic vision. PhD Florida State U. 1979.

HAYWOOD,H. *2622*
Chance and control in the novels of Iris Murdoch. PhD U. of East Anglia, 1981.

HENDERSON,G.A.M. *2623*
Dionysus and Apollo: Irish Murdoch and love. PhD Georgia State U. 1974.

HUMES,W.M. *2624*
The problem of identity in the novels of Iris Murdoch. PhD U. of Aberdeen, 1972.

KAPLAN,M.N. *2625*
Iris Murdoch and the Gothic tradition. PhD Columbia U. 1969.

KEATES,L.S. *2626*
Varieties of the quest-myth in the early novels of Irish Murdoch. PhD U. of Pennsylvania, 1972.

KEMP,B.P. *2627*
Fantasy and symbol in the works of Iris Murdoch. MPhil U. of London, King's Coll. 1968.

KUHNER,A.E. *2628*
The alien god in the novels of Iris Murdoch. PhD U. of Washington, 1978.

MARTINDA LE,K.M. *2629*
For love of the good: moral philosophy in the later novels of Iris Murdoch. PhD U. of Toronto, 1981.

MOHAN,R.E. *2630*
Through myth to reality: a study of the novels of Iris Murdoch. PhD Purdue U. 1977.

ROCKEFELLER,L.J. *2631*
Comedy and the early novels of Iris Murdoch. PhD Bowling Green State U. 1968.

STIMPSON,C.R. *2632*
The early novels of Iris Murdoch. PhD Columbia U. 1967.

STINSON,J.J. *2633*
The uses of the grotesque and other modes of distortion: philosophy and implication in the novels of Irish Murdoch, William Golding, Anthony Burgess and J.P. Donleavy. PhD New York U. 1971.

STRANG,S.M. *2634*
Iris Murdoch: novelist of moral intent. PhD Brown U. 1981.

SULLIVAN,Z.T. *2635*
Enchantment and the demonic in the novels of Iris Murdoch. PhD U. of Illinois at Urbana-Champaign, 1970.

WOLF,N.C. *2636*
Philosophical ambivalence in the novels of Iris Murdoch.m PhD U. of Connecticut, 1972.

Edith Nesbit

ARMSTRONG,D.L. *2637*
E. Nesbit: an entrance to *The magic city*. PhD Johns Hopkins U. 1974.

CROXON,M. *2638*
A study of Edith Nesbit. MA U. of Birmingham, 1972.

Violet Paget

GARDNER,B.H. *2639*
Violet Paget: an essay in biographical criticism. PhD Harvard U. 1954.

Kathleen Raine

NETTERVILLE,H.E. *2640*
Kathleen Raine: the heart in flower. PhD Florida State U. 1980.

ROSEMERGY,J.M.C. *2641*
Kathleen Raine, poet of Eden: her poetry and criticism. PhD U. of Michigan, 1981.

Jean Rhys

ASHCOM,J.N. *2642*
The novels of Jean Rhys: two kinds of modernism. PhD Temple U. 1982.

EMERY,M.L. *2643*
Modernism and the marginal woman: a socio-critical approach to the novels of Jean Rhys. PhD Stanford U. 1982.

HACKER,L.L. *2644*
A study of Jean Rhys's fiction. MA U. of Birmingham, 1974–75.

JONES,A.B. *2645*
Europe and the West Indies: a confrontation in the work of Jean Rhys. PhD U. of Wales (Aberystwyth), 1980.

LANE,M.L. *2646*
Jean Rhys: the work and the cultural background. PhD Tufts U. 1978.

Dorothy Richardson

BANGS,C.J. *2647*
The open circle: a critical study of Dorothy Richardson's *Pilgrimage*. PhD U. of Oregon, 1977.

BLAKE,C.R. *2648*
A critical study of Dorothy M. Richardson's *Pilgrimage*. PhD U. of Michigan, 1958.

GLI KIN,G.H. *2649*
Dorothy Richardson's *Pilgrimage*: a critical study. PhD New York U. 1961.

HANSCOMBE,G.E. *2650*
Feminist consciousness: a study of the work of Dorothy Miller Richardson. DPhil U. of Oxford, 1979.

LINDSAY,S. *2651*
The technique of Dorothy Richardson. MPhil U. of London, Birkbeck Coll. 1967.

ROSE,S. *2652*
The social and aesthetic views of Dorothy M. Richardson: a study of *Pilgrimage* and her miscellaneous writings in the light of her theoretical and practical views of socialism and literary art. PhD U. of London, Royal Holloway Coll. 1967.

WALTERS,D.A. *2653*
Man, woman and God in Dorothy Richardson's *Pilgrimage*. PhD U. of Arkansas, 1982.

Victoria Sackville-West

EDWARDS,M.I. *2654*
Inheritance in the fiction of Victoria Sackville-West. PhD U. of Michigan, 1976.

MACKNIGHT,N.M. *2655*
Vita: a portrait of V. Sackville-West. PhD Columbia U. 1972.

TOOKER,S.M. *2656*
A world of one's own: the novels of V. Sackville-West. PhD Boston Grad. Sch. 1973.

Dorothy L. Sayers

BURLESON,J.B. *2657*
A study of the novels of Dorothy L. Sayers. PhD U. of Texas at Austin, 1965.

DONOVAN,G.M. *2658*
Dorothy L. Sayers' detective fiction: fable to myth. PhD St John's U. 1981.

FAIRMAN,M.B. *2659*
The neo-medieval plays of Dorothy L. Sayers. PhD U. of Pittsburgh, 1961.

SOLOWAY,S.L. *2660*
Dorothy Sayers: novelist. PhD U. of Kentucky, 1971.

Edith Sitwell

BENNETT,G.W. *2661*
The form and sensibility of Edith Sitwell's devotional poems: a study of baroque tradition. PhD U. of Kansas, 1969.

BROPHY,J. *2662*
Empire of shade: a reading of Edith Sitwell's poetry. PhD Columbia U. 1965.

FALK,C.J.T. *2663*
The poetic vision of Edith Sitwell. PhD U. of North Dakota, 1970.

HUSAIN,F.N.Y.J. *2664*
Edith Sitwell in the symbolist tradition. PhD U. of Minnesota, 1965.

MCKENNA,J.P. *2665*
The early poetry of Edith Sitwell. PhD Columbia U. 1963.

ODEGARD,M.B. *2666*
The development of the poetry of Edith Sitwell. PhD U. of Wisconsin, 1956.

OWER,J.B. *2667*
Alienation and atonement in the poetry of Edith Sitwell. PhD U. of Alberta, 1972.

Edith Somerville

LAURIE,H. *2668*
The correspondence of Edith Somerville and Violet Martin with their literary agent James B Pinker, 1896–1922. MA Queen's U. of Belfast, 1969.

WATSON,C.S. *2669*
The novels of Edith Somerville and Martin Ross. PhD Trinity Coll., Dublin, 1953.

Muriel Spark

JONES,J.A. *2670*
The absurd in the fiction of Muriel Spark. PhD U. of Pennsylvania, 1974.

KEYSER,B.E.Y. *2671*
The dual vision of Muriel Spark. PhD Tulane U. 1971.

LAFFIN,G.S. *2672*
Unresolved dualities in the novels of Muriel Spark. PhD U. of Wisconsin, 1973.

MCLEOD,P.G. *2673*
Vision and the moral encounter: a reading of Muriel Spark's novels. PhD Rice U. 1973.

MANSFIELD,J.G. *2674*
Another world than this: the Gothic and Catholic in the novels of Muriel Spark. PhD U. of Iowa, 1973.

QUINN,J.A. *2675*
A study of the satiric element in the novels of Muriel Spark. PhD Purdue U. 1969.

SMITH,R.A. *2676*
The novels of Muriel Spark. PhD Queen's U. of Belfast, 1973.

WHITTAKER,R. *2677*
Faith and fictionability in the novels of Muriel Spark. PhD U. of East Anglia, 1979.

WRIGHT, S.J.P. *2678*
Forms and themes in the novels of Muriel Spark. MA U. of Birmingham, 1978.

Mary Stewart

REAVES,M.R. *2680*
The popular fiction tradition and the novels of Mary Stewart. DA Middle Tennessee State U. 1978.

Helen Waddell

FRIMAN,A.E. *2681*
A critical survey of Helen Waddell's medieval studies. PhD U. of Tennessee, 1964.

Mary Webb

DEHN,F.J. *2682*
The novels of Mary Webb as an expression of a mythology. PhD Kent State U. 1982.

MAY,H.E. *2683*
Life as lyric drama in the fiction of Mary Webb. PhD Florida State U. 1982.

MORLEY,L. *2684*
Folklore in Mary Webb's novel *Precious bane*. PhD U. of Pennsylvania, 1977.

STUDLEY,J. *2685*
The novels of Mary Webb: a reading and interpretation. PhD U. of Toronto, 1977.

Rebecca West

REDD,T.N. *2686*
Rebecca West: master of reality. PhD U. of South Carolina, 1972.

Virginia Woolf

ALEXANDER,S.J. *2687*
Outsiders and educated men's daughters: the feminist as heroine in six novels of Virginia Woolf. PhD Florida State U. 1975.

BAILLARGEON,G.V. *2688*
The logical imagination: the novels of Virginia Woolf. PhD U. of British Columbia, 1980.

BAIN,P.H. *2689*
Poetry into prose: the meaning of writing for Virginia Woolf. PhD U. of Chicago, 1972.

BALDANZA,F. *2690*
The novels of Virginia Woolf. PhD Cornell U. 1954.

BANCROFT,K.R. *2691*
Virginia Woolf: experiment and tradition. MA U. of Exeter, 1978.

BARNETT,A.W. *2692*
Who is Jacob? The quest for identity in the writing of Virginia Woolf. PhD Columbia U. 1962.

BAZIN,N.G.T. *2693*
The aesthetics of Virginia Woolf. PhD Stanford U. 1969.

BELL,C.W. *2694*
A study of Virginia Woolf's *Moment of vision*. PhD U. of Texas at Austin, 1972.

BENFORD,J.L. *2695*
The evolution of the theme and structure of *The waves* by Virginia Woolf. PhD Bryn Mawr Coll. 1969.

BISHOP,E.L. *2696*
Toward the far side of language: a study of Virginia Woolf's fiction. PhD Queen's U. at Kingston, 1978.

BLUMENTHAL,H.E. *2697*
Collaboration and contact: city life in *Ulysses* and *Mrs Dalloway*. PhD U. of Pennsylvania, 1982.

BUSHOFF,P.P. *2698*
Virginia Woolf's verbal alchemy: feeling in form. PhD Purdue U. 1980.

BRADY,E.I. *2699*
Rhythm in the fiction of Virginia Woolf. PhD U. of London, University Coll. 1972.

BREWER,W.M.E. *2700*
Virginia Woolf and the painter's vision. PhD Colorado State Coll. 1968.

BROWN,D.A.D. *2701*
The aesthetics of feminism in Virginia Woolf's fiction. PhD U. of California, Berkeley, 1976.

BROWN,R.C. *2702*
The world of Virginia Woolf: a study of her view of reality. PhD Rutgers U. 1959.

BUCKEZ,D. *2703*
Stasis and progression in the novels of Virginia Woolf. PhD U. of Chicago, 1976.

BULLOCK,R.R. *2704*
Language into myth: the major fiction of Virginia Woolf. PhD U. of North Carolina at Chapel Hill, 1981.

BUNYAN,D.C. *2705*
Virginia Woolf's views of consciousness in relation to art and life. MLitt U. of Durham, 1971.

CHALFANT,T.H. *2706*
The marriage of granite and rainbow: Virginia Woolf as biographer. PhD U. of Wisconsin, 1971.

CHAPMAN,M.D. *2707*
Virginia Woolf's recurrent imagery: an approach to the world of her imagination. PhD U. of New Brunswick, 1970.

CONDON,T.J. *2708*
Image as vision: a study of the experimental nature of Virginia Woolf's early fiction. PhD U. of Rhode Island, 1978.

CONKLIN,A.M. *2709*
Historical and sociocultural elements in the novels of Virginia Woolf. PhD U. of North Carolina at Chapel Hill, 1974.

CONSTEIN,C.F. *2710*
Relativity in the novels of Virginia Woolf. EdD Temple U. 1957.

CORDISH,P.S. *2711*
The view from on high: a study of metaphor of perception in the work of Virginia Woolf. PhD Johns Hopkins U. 1973.

COUCH,F.A. *2712*
Methods and principles in the literary criticism of Virginia Woolf. PhD U. of London, Birkbeck Coll. 1970.

CULVER,S.E. *2713*
Nature and human nature in the major novels of Virginia Woolf. PhD Michigan State U. 1980.

CUMINGS,M.F. *2714*
Visionary ritual in the novels of Virginia Woolf. PhD U. of Wisconsin-Madison, 1972.

CUR RIER,S. *2715*
Virginia Woolf: a whole vision and a whole aesthetic. PhD U. of Massachusetts, 1979.

CURTIN,J.F. *2716*
'Colour burning on a framework of steel': form and identity in the novels of Virginia Woolf. PhD U. of Virginia, 1975.

DAUGHERTY,B. R. *2717*
Virginia Woolf's use of distance against patriarchal control of women, death, and character. PhD Rice U. 1982.

DAZIEL ,B.D. *2718*
'The sentence in itself beautiful': a study of Virginia Woolf's mannerist fiction. PhD Boston U. Grad. Sch. 1975.

DEIMAN, W.J. *2719*
Virginia Woolf's *Between the acts*: the culmination of a career and the resolution of a vision. PhD Yale U. 1967.

DESALVO,L.A. *2720*
From *Melymbrosia* to *The voyage out*: a description and interpretation of Virginia Woolf's revisions. PhD New York U. 1977.

DIBATTISTA,M.N. *2721*
The romance of the self: the early novels of Virginia Woolf. PhD Yale U. 1973.

DIBONA,H.R. *2722*
The fiction of Virginia Woolf: a quest for reality. PhD U. of California, Berkeley, 1970.

DISBROW,S.K. *2723*
To lyricise the argument: Virginia Woolf, novelist and feminist. PhD U. of Nebraska-Lincoln, 1982.

DRUFF,J.H. *2724*
Artistic self-consciousness in the fiction of Sterne, Joyce and Woolf. PhD U. of California, Berkeley, 1979.

DRYUD,M.A. *2725*
Rending the veil: dreams in five novels by Virginia Woolf. PhD Purdue U. 1980.

EISENBERG,N.G. *2726*
'The far side of language': the search for expression in the novels of Virginia Woolf. PhD Columbia U. 1976.

ESPINOLA,J.C. *2727*
Point of view in selected novels by Virginia Woolf. PhD Northwestern U. 1970.

FEREBEE,R.S. *2728*
Virginia Woolf as an essayist. PhD U. of New Mexico, 1981.

FLAHERTY,L. *2729*
Woman as peacemaker in Virginia Woolf's novels. PhD U. of Iowa, 1977.

FRYE,J.M.S. *2730*
Toward a form for paradox: image and idea in the novels of Virginia Woolf. PhD Indiana U. 1974.

FULLER,C.D. *2731*
The relation between theory and practice in the novels of Virginia Woolf. MLitt U. of Aberdeen, 1979.

GAIRDNER,W.D. *2732*
Consciousness in the novels of Virginia Woolf. PhD Stanford U. 1970.

GALLAGHER,S.van S. *2733*
The fiction of the self: Virginia Woolf and the problem of biography. PhD State U. of New York at Buffalo, 1979.

GALTON,J. *2734*
The desertion of character in Virginia Woolf's novels. PhD U. of Rochester, 1967.

GLEITER,K.J. *2735*
Similes in Virginia Woolf's fiction: *The voyage out, To the lighthouse, The waves, Between the acts*. PhD U. of North Carolina at Chapel Hill, 1977.

GODWIN,J.L. *2736*
Virginia Woolf: moments of vision in *Mrs Dalloway, To the lighthouse* and *Between the acts*. PhD U. of Texas at Austin, 1980.

GOLDMAN,M.I. *2737*
Virginia Woolf and the art of criticism. PhD U. of Minnesota, 1959.

GOLDSMITH,B.Z.A *2738*
The enormous burden of the unexpressed language as theme in the novels of Virginia Woolf. PhD Ohio State U. 1978.

GOLUB,J.E. *2739*
The production of a reading: self and world in selected texts by Virginia Woolf. MPhil U. of London, Royal Holloway Coll. 1979.

GOODENOUGH,E.N. *2740*
Marvellous are the innocent: a study of youth in Virginia Woolf. PhD Harvard U. 1982.

GORSKY,S.R. *2741*
'The central shadow': dualism in form and meaning in *The waves*. PhD Case Western Reserve U. 1969.

GOTTLIEB,S.P. *2742*
(Part III) 'Life and death, sanity and sanity': a reading of *Mrs Dalloway*. PhD Rutgers U. 1974.

GRAHAM,J.W. *2743*
The mind and art of Virginia Woolf. PhD U. of Toronto, 1953.

HAFLEY,J.R. *2744*
Virginia Woolf as novelist. PhD U. of California, Berkeley, 1952.

HALLER,E.H. *2745*
The search for 'life itself': characterization and its relation to form in the novels of Virginia Woolf. PhD Emory U. 1968.

HAMWEE,L.A. *2746*
The impact of English post-impressionism and the aesthetics of pure form on Virginia Woolf's fiction. PhD U. of London, King's Coll. 1973.

HARAKAS,T. *2747*
Dualism in the novels of Virginia Woolf. PhD Michigan State U. 1982.

HARTWELL,D.J. *2748*
Human relationships in the novels of Virginia Woolf. BPhil U. of St Andrews 1966.

HAZEL,B.R. *2749*
The development of narrative techniques in the fiction of Virginia Woolf, 1915–1925. MPhil U. of Southampton, 1972.

HENIG, S. *2750*
The literary criticism of Virginia Woolf. PhD New York U. 1968.

HILSINGER,S.S. *2751*
Insubstantial pageant: a reading of Virgina Woolf's novels. PhD U. of Connecticut, 1964.

HUNGERFORD,E.A. *2752*
The narrow bridge of art: Virginia Woolf's early criticism, 1905–1925. PhD New York U. 1960.

JAMES,S. *2753*
The art of Virginia Woolf. MA U. of Manchester, 1977.

JEWISON,D.B. *2754*
Virginia Woolf: 'reforming' the novel through imagery. PhD U. of Manitoba, 1974.

JULIEN,H. *2755*
Virginia Woolf: post-impressionist novelist. PhD U. of New Mexico, 1968.

KATZ,L.S. *2756*
A rhetorical analysis of Virginia Woolf's feminist tracts and her novels. PhD Rensselaer Polytechnic Inst. 1976.

KELLEY,A.van B. *2757*
Fact and vision: a study of the novels of Virginia Woolf. PhD City U. of New York, 1971.

KENNEY,S.M. *2758*
Fin in the water: a study of Virginia Woolf. PhD Cornell U. 1968.

KING,M.P. *2759*
The price of awareness: Virginia Woolf as a practitioner critic. PhD U. of Texas at Austin, 1962.

KNEUBUHL,B.J. *2760*
Channel crossings: Virginia Woolf in France 1920–1977. PhD U. of Massachusetts, 1979.

LANE,D.E. *2761*
A study of the development of the fiction of Virginia Woolf with particular reference to 'vision' and 'design'. MA U. of London, University Coll. 1958.

LASKIN,M.M. *2762*
The evolution of Virginia Woolf's visionary histories: *The years* and *Between the acts*. PhD State U. of New York at Stony Brook, 1979.

LAURANS,P. *2763*
Fictions about fictions: the study of a modern literary development in the novels of Virginia Woolf. PhD Harvard U. 1975.

LEVENBACK,K.L. *2764*
A chasm in a smooth road: a study of the effect of the Great War on Virginia Woolf. PhD U. of Maryland, 1981.

LEWIS,F.C. *2765*
Significant deformity: art and life in Virginia Woolf's novels and art criticism. PhD U. of Edinburgh, 1975.

LILIENFELD,C.J. *2766*
The necessary journey: Virginia Woolf's voyage to the lighthouse. PhD Brandeis U. 1975.

LUKENS,C.D. *2767*
The woman artist's journey: self-consciousness in the novels of Virginia Woolf. PhD U. of Washington, 1981.

LYON,M.C. *2768*
Virginia Woolf as a critic. PhD Radcliffe Coll. 1957.

MCKILLOP,L.T. *2769*
The process of critical articulation: narrator, char-

acter and symbol in Virginia Woolf. PhD U. of Virginia, 1980.

MCLAUGHLIN,A.L. 2770
A fin in a waste of waters: a study of symbolic transformation in *The waves* by Virginia Woolf. PhD American U. 1978.

MCLAURIN,A. 2771
A sense of repetition: an essay on the novels of Virginia Woolf. MA U. of Wales (Cardiff) 1969.

MCLAURIN,A. 2772
Aesthetics and Bloomsbury with special reference to the works of Virginia Woolf. PhD U. of Wales (Cardiff), 1971.

MCNETT,J.M. 2773
Virginia Woolf on biography: theory and praxis. PhD U. of Massachusetts, 1980.

MCNICHOLS,S. 2774
Between the acts: a critical study of Virginia Woolf's last novel. MLitt U. of Newcastle, 1970.

MAJUMD AR,R. 2775
The critical reception of Virginia Woolf's novels, 1915–1960. PhD U. of London, Queen Mary Coll. 1968.

MARDER,H. 2776
The androgynous mind: feminism in the works of Virginia Woolf. PhD Columbia U. 1964.

MARSHALL,P.A. 2777
Private vision made public: style and structure in four novels by Virginia Woolf. PhD Indiana U. 1978.

MENDEZ,C.W. 2778
Language, mystery and selfhood in the novels of Virginia Woolf. PhD Syracuse U. 1972.

MOR,S. 2779
An inquiry into madness: the meaning of madness in the works of Virginia Woolf. PhD U. of Southern California, 1979.

MORGENSTERN,B.S. 2780
Like a work of art: the narrative voices in the novels of Virginia Woolf. PhD Pennsylvania State U. 1971.

NAREMORE,J.O. 2781
The world without a self: style in the novels of Virginia Woolf. PhD U. of Wisconsin, 1970.

NEILEN,D. 2782
The search for intimacy: feminist reconciliations in the fiction of Virginia Woolf. PhD Syracuse U. 1980.

NOVAK,J. 2783
The search for the razor edge of balance: the shaping principle of Virginia Woolf's fiction and criticism. PhD U. of Chicago, 1971.

OVERSTREET,L.K. 2784
'This globe, full of figures': an archetypal study of Virginia Woolf's *The waves*. PhD U. of Arkansas, 1982.

PARASVRAM,L.S. 2785
Virginia Woolf: the treatment of natural phenomena in six novels. PhD U. of Kentucky, 1972.

PETERS,C. 2786
Virginia Woolf as biographer. MPhil U. of London, Birkbeck Coll. 1970.

PHILLIPS,A.H. 2787
The anonymous self: a study of Virginia Woolf's novels. PhD Stanford U. 1971.

POIRIER,S. 2788
Characterization and theory of personality in the novels of Virginia Woolf. PhD U. of Nebraska-Lincoln, 1978.

PROUDFIT,S.L.W . 2789
The fact and the vision: Virginia Woolf and Roger Fry's post-impressionist aesthetic. PhD U. of Michigan, 1967.

RADBIL,A . 2790
Impressionism and Virginia Woolf. PhD Florida State U. 1979.

RADIN,G.P. 2791
The Years by Virginia Woolf: the evolution of a novel. PhD City U. of New York, 1977.

RAHMAN,S. 2792
Virginia Woolf and reality: the artist, the intellectual and the mystic in the novels. PhD City U. of New York, 1973.

RAKOWSKY,C.H. 2793
To inhabit eternity: Virginia Woolf's coming to terms with death. PhD Case Western Reserve U. 1978.

REA,P.S.L. 2794
A study of the figure of the artist in the novels of Virginia Woolf. PhD U. of London, Royal Holloway Coll. 1979.

RETTIG,C.B. 2795
The continuing battle against the Philistines: Virginia Woolf's cultural criticism. PhD U. of Michigan, 1980.

RICHARDSON,R.O. 2796
Virginia Woolf's *The waves*: a reading. PhD Cornell U. 1969.

RICHTER,H.C. 2797
Modes of subjectivity in the novels of Virginia Woolf. PhD New York U. 1967.

ROBERTS,R.M. 2798
Significant form in Virginia Woolf. MA U. of Birmingham, 1973.

ROBINSON,D.S. 2799
'Frigidity' and the aesthetic vision: a study of Karen Horney and Virginia Woolf. PhD U. of Rochester, 1974.

ROCK,M.L. *2800*
Electronic storytelling: a study of narrative techniques in the novel and video adaptation of *To the lighthouse*. PhD New York U. 1981.

ROGAT,E.G.H. *2801*
The lifted veil: Virginia Woolf and women's consciousness. PhD Stanford U. 1974.

ROSEN,A. *2802*
The pulse of colour: a study of Virginia Woolf. PhD State U. of New York at Buffalo, 1981.

RUBENSTEIN,R. *2803*
Virginia Woolf's response to Russian literature. PhD U. of London, Birkbeck Coll. 1969.

SACKS,M.C.H. *2804*
The starling- pelted tree: image and idea in the novels of Virginia Woolf. PhD Northwestern U. 1955.

SAINT PAER,E.M.DE *2805*
Virginia Woolf's moments of vision: their implications for the artist figures in her novels. MA U. of Birmingham, 1973.

SAMUELSON,R.E. *2806*
Virginia Woolf as critic. PhD U. of Washington, 1956.

SATZ,M.E. *2807*
Virginia Woolf as a literary critic. PhD Boston U. 1951.

SCHAEFER,J.A.O. *2808*
The three-fold nature of reality in the novels of Virginia Woolf. PhD Stanford U. 1962.

SCHEIBER,H.J. *2809*
Functions of imagery in Virginia Woolf's *The waves*: a study of the language and rhetoric of the text. PhD New York U. 1978.

SCHLACK,B.A. *2810*
Literary allusions in selected novels of Virginia Woolf: a study in criticism. PhD New York U. 1974.

SCHULKIND,J.C. *2811*
Virginia Woolf, novelist. DPhil U. of Sussex, 1971.

SHANAHAN,M.S. *2812*
Order and chaos in the novels of Virginia Woolf. PhD U. of Wisconsin, 1970.

SIEK,B.L. *2813*
Virginia Woolf's theory of fiction. PhD U. of Chicago, 1980.

SILVER,B.R. *2814*
Virginia Woolf and the Elizabethans: a study of her Elizabethan criticism in the context of her growth as critic and novelist. PhD Harvard U. 1973.

SIMMONS,S.B. *2815*
The linguistic analysis of a literary text. Virginia Woolf: 'The Russian point of view'. PhD State U. of New York at Buffalo, 1979.

SMITH,M.A. *2816*
The personality of the essayist: Virginia Woolf and Thomas Mann. PhD U. of Oregon, 1974.

SPELTZ,A.L. *2817*
The voyage out and Virginia Woolf's struggle for autonomy: imagery of separation and dependency. PhD State U. of New York at Stony Brook, 1982.

SQUIER,S.M. *2818*
The politics of street haunting: Virginia Woolf and the city. PhD Stanford U. 1977.

STRONG,P. *2819*
The light in the garden: imagery in *Mrs Dalloway, To the lighthouse* and *The waves*. PhD U. of Wisconsin, 1973.

THAKUR,N.C. *2820*
The symbol in the novels of Virginia Woolf. BLitt U. of Oxford, 1963.

TILBERRY,J.H. *2821*
The literary method of Virginia Woolf: a phenomenological approach. PhD Case Western Reserve U. 1982.

TOBIN,G.J. *2822*
Virginia Woolf's *The waves* and *The years* as novel of vision and novel of fact. PhD U. of Wisconsin-Madison, 1973.

TRANSUE,P.J. *2823*
Feminism and fiction: the aesthetic dilemma: a study of Virginia Woolf. PhD Ohio State U. 1981.

TRIVEDI,H. *2824*
Virginia Woolf and the tradition of the English novel: a study of her criticism of fiction. PhD U. of Wales (Bangor), 1975.

TROMBLEY,S. *2825*
Virginia Woolf and her doctors. PhD U. of Nottingham, 1980.

VANDERWERFF,W.G. *2826*
Virginia Woolf as equilibrist: the moment of vision and the androgynous mind. PhD U. of North Carolina at Greensboro, 1978.

WARNER,E.D. *2827*
Some aspects of romanticism in the works of Virginia Woolf. DPhil U. of Oxford, 1980.

WEEMS,B.F. *2828*
Virginia Woolf's use of imagery in her search for values. PhD Columbia U. 1962.

WHITE,R. F. *2829*
The literary reputation of Virginia Woolf: history of British attitudes toward her work, 1915–1955. PhD U. of Pennsylvania, 1959.

WHITEHEAD,J. *2830*
A study of the relationship between Virginia

Woolf's novels and the intellectual interests of her time. DPhil U. of Oxford, 1979.

WILKOTZ,J.N. 2831
A psychoanalytic study of the novels of Virginia Woolf. PhD U. of California, Berkeley, 1973.

WILSON,J.L. 2832
'A house that fits us all': search for form in *Jacob's room, Orlando* and *The waves*. PhD U. of California, Berkeley, 1969.

WORRELL,E. 2833
The short works of Virginia Woolf: a study for the oral interpreter. PhD Northwestern U. 1955.

WYATT,J.M. 2834
The technique of literary allusion in the novels of Virginia Woolf. PhD Harvard U. 1969.

YEAMANS,B.L. 2835
Woolfian reality: her vision of unity examined in *The voyage out* and *To the lighthouse*. MA U. of Exeter, 1976.

YUNIS,S.S. 2836
Obligatory pilgrimages: garden strolls, train rides and other rituals in the later novels of Virginia Woolf. PhD Case Western Reserve U. 1982.

French literature

General and comparative studies

See also **9** 227, 234.

ADAMS,D.J. 2837
La femme dans les contes et les romans de Voltaire. MA U. of Manchester, 1972.

ALTHOFER,B.A. 2838
Aspects of the archetypal feminine in the plays of Michel de Ghelderode. PhD U. of California, Berkeley, 1976.

ALVES,D.L. 2839
Love and the resources of style in Julie's letters in Rousseau's *Nouvelle Héloise*. PhD Catholic U. of America, 1974.

ANDERSON,D.L. 2840
The development of the Héloise motif and *La nouvelle Héloise*. PhD U. of North Carolina at Chapel Hill, 1969.

BEAMISH-THIRIET,F.M.O. 2841
The myth of woman in Baudelaire and Blok. PhD U. of Washington, 1973.

BERG,E.L. 2842
Classical depictions: figures of woman in French classicism. [Women in literature and painting in France, *c.*1660–80.] PhD Cornell U. 1982.

BERNECK,B. 2843
Feminism in the works of Beaumarchais. PhD Yale U. 1973.

BLEUZE,R.A. 2844
Romancières et critiques: étude du Prix Femina, 1904–1968. PhD U. of Colorado at Boulder, 1977.

BUGLIANI,A.C. 2845
Women and the feminine principle in Claudel's works. PhD Northwestern U. 1973.

BUTLER,M.L. 2846
Rousseau's vision of woman. PhD U. of Connecticut, 1980.

CALO,J.E. 2847
La création de la femme chez Michelet. PhD U. of Pennsylvania, 1971.

CAMPBELL,C.E. 2848
The *entremetteuse* in French Renaissance comedies. PhD U. of Missouri-Columbia, 1982.

CAROS,J. 2849
Diderot and the *Salonnières*. PhD Columbia U. 1968.

CARRELL,S.L. 2850
Le soliloque de la passion féminine: étude d'une formule monophonique de la littérature épistolaire. PhD U. of Virginia, 1977.

CHARNEY,D.J. 2851
Woman as mediatrix in the prose works of André Pieyre de Mandiargues. PhD Duke U. 1976.

CHESSHER,J.L. 2852
The portrayal of woman in the French naturalist novel. PhD U. of London, Birkbeck Coll. 1962.

COOK,M. 2853
The odd woman in the French naturalist novel. MA U. of Sussex, 1976.

COOPER,C.B. 2854
Women poets of the twentieth century in France: a critical bibliography. PhD Columbia U. 1944.

COURTNEY,S. 2855
Les jeunes filles dans le théâtre d'Alfred de Musset. MA National U. of Ireland, 1950.

CROSSLEY,R.P.A. 2856
Women in Camus. PhD Stanford U. 1976.

DE COURTIVRON,I. 2857
Androgny, misogny and madness: three essays on women in literature. [Nineteenth- and twentieth-century literature, French.] PhD Brown U. 1973.

DARROCH,A.G.B. 2858
Paul Éluard's *La rose publique*: a critical study. PhD U. of Toronto, 1973.

DESMOND,M.J. 2860
The concept of narrative among twelfth-century vernacular hagiographers: a comparison of the *Vie de Sainte Marguerite*, the *Vie de Saint Gilles* and the *Vie de Sainte Osith* with their Latin sources. PhD U. of Wisconsin-Madison, 1978.

DEZIO,J. *2861*
Woman as outsider in Giraudoux's theatre from *Siegfried* to *Electre*. PhD New York U. 1979.

DOCK,T.S. *2862*
Woman in the *Encyclopédie*. PhD Vanderbilt U. 1979.

D'ORSSAUD,S. *2863*
Le caractère de l'honnête femme d'après la littérature du dix-septième siècle. PhD Radcliffe Coll. 1941.

DEROSIERS,N.S. *2864*
Visages de l'héroine corneliènne dans les tragédies et tragi-comédies (1659–1674). PhD U. of Massachusetts, 1980.

DOHERTY,L.G. *2865*
The women of Musset's theater. PhD U. of Wisconsin-Madison, 1977.

DOW,B.H. *2866*
The varying attitude toward women in French literature of the fifteenth century: the opening years. PhD Columbia U. 1937.

DUPÊCHER,D.R. *2867*
L'image du convent dans le roman français du XVIIe siècle. PhD Princeton U. 1973.

EASTERLY,J.E.T. *2868*
Women in the novels of Paul Bourget. PhD Vanderbilt U. 1973.

EMPLAINCOURT,M. *2869*
La femme damnée: a study of the lesbian in French literature from Diderot to Proust. PhD U. of Alabama, 1977.

EPSTEIN,E.S. *2870*
The crisis of the poetic ideal: woman and muse in Parnassian poetry. PhD Harvard U. 1967.

FAILLIE,M.H. *2871*
La femme et le Code civile dans *La comédie humaine* d'Honoré de Balzac. PhD New York U. 1964.

FALLANDY,Y.M. *2872*
The role of the Blessed Virgin in the *Miracles de Nostre Dame par personnages*. PhD U. of California, Los Angeles, 1958.

FARNSWORTH,W.O. *2873*
Uncle and nephew in the Old French *chansons de geste*: a study in the survival of matriarchy. PhD Columbia U. 1913.

FEAL,G. *2874*
Le théâtre de Crommelynck: érotisme et spiritualité. PhD U. of Michigan, 1972.

FERRIOT,J.C. *2875*
The epistolary art of Diderot: the letters to Sophie Volland. PhD Tulane U. 1969.

FLEDER,L.W. *2876*
Female physiology and psychology in the works of Diderot and the medical writers of his day. PhD Columbia U. 1978.

FLOYD,J.H. *2877*
Women in the life of Honoré de Balzac. PhD Columbia U. 1921.

FORBES,E. *2878*
L'importance dramatiques des femmes dans le théâtre de Jean Giraudoux. MA U. of Liverpool, 1962.

FOSS,N.E.M. *2879*
Female characters in the comedies of Charles Rivière Dufresny. PhD U. of Minnesota, 1980.

FRASURE,D.E.M. *2880*
The function of women and the theme of love in the novels of Georges Bernanos. PhD Duke U. 1976.

FRIEDMAN,L.M. *2881*
The nature and role of women as conceived by representative authors of eighteenth-century France. PhD New York U. 1970.

FULLMAN,S.C. *2882*
The imperilled idea: the evolution of woman and the court in the romances of Chrétien de Troyes. PhD Rutgers U. 1976.

GADDY,B.E. *2883*
Women in the fictional works of André Gide. PhD U. of North Carolina at Chapel Hill, 1967.

GIBSON,M.T. *2884*
Les femmes selon Dumas: une étude. MA U. of Birmingham, 1915.

GIBSON,W. *2884a*
The role of women in French drama 1628–1643. PhD U. of Birmingham, 1973.

GONTIER,F. *2885*
Les images de la femme dans le roman français de l'entre-deux-guerres. PhD U. of Virginia, 1973.

GRAINGER,I.E. *2886*
Women in the imaginative works of Albert Camus. PhD U. of North Carolina at Chapel Hill, 1973.

GRUBER,L.S. *2887*
L'ange femme et la fin du mal dans L'épogée romantique. PhD Harvard U. 1974.

GRUZINSKA,A. *2888*
La femme et ses 'paysages d'âme': dans l'oeuvre romanesque d'Octave Mirbeau. PhD Pennsylvania State U. 1973.

GUTERMUTH,M.E. *2889*
Feminism in Louis Aragon's novels. PhD U. of Missouri-Columbia, 1965.

HART,K.D. *2890*
A critical history of the psychological portraiture of women in French literature through the eighteenth century. PhD U. of Texas at Austin, 1955.

HARTNET T,B.C. *2891*
Le rôle de la femme dans le théâtre de Paul Claudel. MA National U. of Ireland, 1959.

HEMPHILL,V.C. *2892*
Corneille's heroines. MA U. of Southampton, 1958.

HENDERSON,M.W. *2893*
Woman in the medieval French epic. PhD New York U. 1965.

HENDERYCKSEN,H.R. *2894*
La condition féminine dans les théâtres de Corneille et Racine. PhD Rutgers U. 1979.

HERMEY,C.W. *2895*
Contemporary French women poets: a bilingual and critical anthology. [Andrée Chedid, Thérèse Plantier, Annie Salager, Denise Grappe, Yvonne Caroutch and Marie-Françoise Prager.] PhD State U. of New York at Binghamton, 1975.

HIGSON,J. *2896*
La femme dans la vie et l'oeuvre de Stendhal. PhD Laval U. 1960.

HOLMES,D. *2897*
The image of women in selected French fiction of the interwar period: a study of literary responses to the changing role of women, 1918–1939. DPhil U. of Sussex, 1977.

HUNTING,C. *2898*
Innocence ou culpabilité? Trois figures féminines dans le roman français au dix-huitième siècle. PhD Harvard U. 1972.

INGLER,J.B. *2899*
Woman as myth in the works of Gérard de Nerval. PhD Oklahoma State U. 1966.

INSDORF,C. *2900*
Montaigne and feminism. PhD City U. of New York, 1972.

JACKS,S.R. *2901*
Women and passion in the novels of Julien Green. PhD U. of Georgia, 1979.

JARDINE,A.A. *2902*
Gynesis: configurations of woman in the contemporary imagination. American feminist readings/ French text of modernity. PhD Columbia U. 1982.

JENNINGS,L.C.B. *2903*
Les romanciers naturalistes et la question de l'émancipation féminine. PhD Wayne State U. 1969.

JOHN,M.L.F. *2904*
Images of woman in selected Molière plays. PhD Pennsylvania State U. 1978.

JOHNSON,L. *2905*
La femme dans l'oeuvre dramatique de Paul Claudel, 1882–1898. MA U. of Manchester, 1968.

JONES,S.E. *2906*
Ethics and the novel as studied in the works of woman novelists from the publication of the *Princesse de Clèves*, 1678 until the end of the reign of Louis XIV, 1715. PhD U. of London, Bedford Coll. 1962.

JOURLAIT,A.O.M. *2907*
Woman and feminine presence in selected poems of Paul Éluard and Vicente Aleixandre: a thematic study. PhD U. of Michigan, 1973.

KEIDEL,G.C. *2908*
The *Evangile aux femmes*: an Old French satire on women; edited with an introduction and notes. PhD Johns Hopkins U. 1895.

KHETTRY,F.M.C. *2909*
Evolution de la conception de l'amour conjugal dans la comédie française de Molière à Beaumarchais. PhD Toronto, 1977.

KINGHAM,P.M. *2910*
Péguy's concept of woman. MPhil U. of London, External 1980.

KLENKE,M.A. *2911*
Nicholas Bozon's lives of Martha and Mary Magdalene. PhD Yale U. 1940.

KLIN,G. *2912*
Woman in eighteenth-century French fiction. PhD Wayne State U. 1963.

LACHMANN,A.D.P. *2913*
Leon Frapie romancier, précurseur du mouvement populiste et de l'émancipation de la femme. PhD Bryn Mawr Coll. 1973.

LACY,K.W. *2914*
An essay on feminine fiction, 1757–1893. (Mme de Riccoboni, Mme de Charrière, Mme de Souza, Mme Cottin and Mme de Krüdener.) PhD U. of Wisconsin, 1972.

LARSEN,E. *2915*
The role of women in the plays of Giraudoux. PhD U. of Wisconsin, 1958.

LEE,B.G. *2916*
Victorian adventuress: changing perspectives on the courtesan of the nineteenth-century French stage. PhD Florida State U. 1972.

LERNER,J.K. *2917*
Rabelais and woman. PhD City U. of New York, 1976.

LIPTON,V.A. *2918*
Women in today's world: a study of five French women novelists. [Célia Bertin, Marguerite Duras, Violette Leduc, Françoise Mallet-Joris, Christiane Rocheforte.] PhD U. of Wisconsin-Madison, 1972.

MACLEAN,I.W.F. *2919*
Feminism and literature in France. DPhil U. of Oxford, 1972.

MAGNIN,P.K.DE *2920*
The cast of Helen: metaphorical woman in the text of Rousseau. PhD Cornell U. 1975.

MARKIEWICZ,S. *2921*
The question of feminine liberty in the writings of Denis Diderot. PhD Stanford U. 1973.

MARSHALL,R.G. *2922*
The role of love in the comedy of Marivaux. PhD Yale U. 1950.

MARTIN,S.M. *2923*
The development of the female dramatic character in Jodelle and Garnier. PhD Boston Coll. 1981.

MASON,F. *2924*
La femme dans le théâtre de Sartre. MA U. of Exeter, 1970.

METCALF,C.P. *2925*
Women in the novels of Guy de Maupassant. MA U. of Birmingham, 1981.

MICHAEL,C.V. *2926*
La femme et le mal dans *Les liaisons dangereuses* de Choderlos de Laclos. PhD U. of Wisconsin-Madison, 1973.

MITCHELL-CARON,M.A. *2927*
Eros et l'aveu féminin dans la littérature française (entre 1550 et 1630). PhD U. of California, Irvine, 1973.

MORLEY,K.M. *2928*
Female roles in the romances of Chrétien de Troyes. MA U. of Birmingham, 1973.

MORRISON,A.J. *2929*
Character study in Old French Romans d'aventures: the heroine. PhD Johns Hopkins U. 1903.

MOULD,W.A. *2930*
The figure of the mother in Racinian tragedy. PhD U. of Kansas, 1968.

MOVASSAGHI,M.B. *2931*
The role of women in the French baroque theater. PhD Louisiana State U. 1978.

MULLER,D.E.M.N. *2932*
Zola's attitude towards women as revealed in his novels. PhD U. of London, University Coll. 1968.

MURATORE,M.J. *2933*
The evolution of the Cornelian heroine. PhD U. of California, Davis, 1979.

MYKYTA,L.A . *2934*
Vanishing point: the question of the woman in the works of Maurice Blanchot. PhD State U. of New York at Buffalo, 1980.

NEFF,T.L. *2935*
La satire des femmes dans la poésie lyrique française du moyen âge. PhD U. of Chicago, 1896.

NOT ,P.V. *2936*
La femme dans l'oeuvre romanesque et théâtrale de Camus. MA U. of Exeter, 1981.

OHAYON,R. *2937*
The function of femininity in selected novels of the Abbé Prévost. PhD Columbia U. 1980.

OHAYON,V.A. *2938*
Les jeunes filles dans *La comédie humaine*; mythe ou réalité? PhD New York U. 1970.

PICARD,G.L. *2939*
Les soeurs des anges: le développement de l'idéal féminin chez les premiers romantiques. PhD Harvard U. 1942.

PISANO,A.P. *2940*
La Nouvelle Béatrice: the role of woman in the life and writings of Jules Michelet, 1848–1860. PhD U. of Notre Dame, 1974.

PONCHIE,J.P. *2941*
De la sensibilité de quelques personnages féminins de Molière. PhD Michigan State U. 1972.

POPE,D. *2942*
The development of feminist consciousness in women's writings in France in the first half of the nineteenth century. [Esp. Germaine de Staël, George Sand and Flora Tristan.] PhD U. of Bristol, 1980.

PRICE,J.A. *2943*
Marguerite de France: literary patroness of the Renaissance. PhD U. of Kentucky, 1974.

RABINE,L .R. *2944*
The other side of the ideal: women writers of mid-nineteenth-century France. [George Sand, Daniel Stern, Hortense Allart and Flora Tristan.] PhD Stanford U. 1973.

RADFORD,C.B. *2945*
The role of woman in twentieth-century French theatre. PhD Queen's U. of Belfast, 1970.

RAVA,S.R. *2946*
Talking to women: narrative structures in Proust and Flaubert. PhD Washington U. 1977.

RENICK,K. *2947*
The role of women in the works of Villiers de L'Isle-Adam. PhD U. of Southern California, 1979.

RICHARDSON,L.M. *2949*
The forerunners of feminism in French literature of the Renaissance from Christine of Pisan to Marie de Gournay. PhD Johns Hopkins U. 1927.

ROSENBERG,R.A.R. *2950*
Zola's imagery and the archetype of the Great Mother. PhD U. of Michigan, 1969.

RUDLOFF,S.L.M. *2951*
The woman as a figure in the works of Pierre Louÿs. PhD Tulane U. 1975.

SANDHU-CENDRES,M.M. *2952*
Le féminisme et les romanciers de l'époque romantique. PhD Yale U. 1969.

SAYEG H,A. *2953*
The concept and role of woman in the works of André Breton. PhD U. of Pennsylvania, 1974.

SCHMIDT,J.A. *2954*
Corneille's tragic heroines, 1637–1643: a feminist interpretation. PhD U. of Virginia, 1980.

SCHMITZ,B.A. *2955*
French women writers and their critics: an analysis of the treatment of women writers in selected histories of French literature. PhD U. of Wisconsin-Madison, 1977.

SCHONFELDER,L.M. *2956*
Woman in the plays of Jean Giraudoux. PhD U. of London, University Coll. 1968.

SHERMAN ,S.E. *2957*
A portrait of woman through the eyes of Denis Diderot. PhD Columbia U. 1968.

SIEGEL,I.E. *2958*
Feminism in the French popular playwrights, 1830–1848. PhD U. of Missouri-Columbia, 1975.

SIENKEWICZ,A.W. *2959*
Two women of letters. Mme de Sévigné and Mme Du Deffand. PhD Johns Hopkins U. 1978.

SIMON-MILLER,F.L. *2960*
Instances du féminin au XVIIe siècle. PhD Yale U. 1980.

SMITH,E.M .P.R. *2961*
Nana, Santa, and *Nacha Regules*: trois courtisanes modernes. PhD U. of Georgia, 1974.

SMITH,P.H. *2962*
The more complicated sex: Diderot's view of the feminine universe. PhD U. of Exeter, 1973.

SPILLMAN,M.S.F. *2963*
Beles, Avenanz et de Franc Corage: 'notatio' of female characters in the Arthurian works of Chrétien de Troyes. PhD Tulane U. 1981.

STEINBERGER,E.M. *2964*
Balzac's portrayal of woman: a study in the role of women in his fictional works before 1842. PhD City U. of New York, 1977.

STEINER,L.F. *2965*
The role of the 'grand dame' in the *milieu* of the French salon, as represented in selected works of Marcel Proust and Jean Anouilh. PhD U. of Minnesota, 1977.

STEINLIGHT,C.E. *2966*
The function and image of motherhood in the works of Balzac. PhD U. of London, University Coll. 1976.

SULLIVAN,P.A. *2967*
The heroine in twelfth-century French literature: the portrayal of women characters in epic and romance. PhD U. of Wales, Cardiff, 1981.

SZABO,G.J. *2968*
The feminine image in Victor Hugo's *Les misérables*. PhD U. of Toronto, 1976.

TANENBAUM,J.de L. *2969*
The role of women in the *Song of Roland*. PhD Florida State U. 1982.

TARR,K.R. *2970*
Love and marriage in the *Miracles de Nostre Dame par personnages*. PhD U. of Kansas, 1976.

TAYLOR,S.E. *2971*
The Saracen princess in the medieval *chanson de geste*. MA U. of Sheffield, 1952.

THIERMAN,L.M. *2972*
Sainte-Beuve and women of the eighteenth century. PhD U. of Michigan, 1959.

THOMPSETT,E. *2972a*
Social and literary aspects of the theme of seduction in the French *roman mondain* of the eighteenth century with particular reference to *Les liaisons dangereuses* and its predecessors. PhD U. of London, Bedford Coll. 1972.

TURRIN,H.J. *2973*
Figures of the feminine ideal in medieval writings with special reference to the Virgin Mary in the Latin tradition and the troubadour's *Domna* in the twelfth-century Provençal love lyric. PhD U. of Cambridge, 1979.

TWIGHT,A.G. *2974*
Women of the seventeenth-century French classics as seen by the nineteenth century. PhD Northwestern U. 1898.

VALETTE,F.C. *2975*
La tradition antiféministe dans la littérature française du moyen âge et sa continuation dans les contes du seizième siècle. PhD U. of Illinois, 1966.

VICKERS,N.J. *2976*
Preface to the *Blasons anatomiques*: the poetic and philosophical contexts of descriptions of the female body in the Renaissance. PhD Yale U. 1976.

WALLACE,A.H. *2977*
The fatal woman in French literature of the nineteenth century. PhU. of North Carolina at Chapel Hill, 1960.

WATTS,M.E. *2979*
The representation of woman in selected poetry and plastic arts of the Renaissance in France,. PhD U. of Toronto, 1977.

WEBB,S.J. *2979*
Aspects of fidelity and infidelity in the eighteenth century French novel from Chasles to Laclos. PhD Indiana U. 1977.

WILLIAMS, R.de W. *2980*
Women in the theater of Alexandre Hardy. PhD U. of North Carolina at Chapel Hill, 1979.

WILLIS,J. 2981
Proust and the female fantasy. MPhil Brunel U. 1981.

YOUNG,E. *2982*
A study of the 'femme fatale' of French decadent-symbolist literature and painting. MPhil U. of Nottingham, 1979.

ZYLAWY,R.I. *2983*
Aspects of women's ideology and the rise of feminine ethics from the seventeenth century to the

eighteenth century as reflected in the works of Marivaux and Prévost. PhD U. of Colorado at Boulder, 1973.

Individual writers

Louise Ackermann

JENKINS,E.M. *2984*
Mme Louise Ackermann. MA U. of Leeds, 1928.

Marie d'Agoult

BROOK,E.S. *2985*
The social and political ideas of Countess d'Agoult (Daniel Stern). PhD Columbia U. 1969.

GARNETT,M.A. *2986*
Pseudonym and identity: the literary and psychological itinerary of Marie d'Agoult. PhD U. of Wisconsin-Madison, 1980.

Mme d'Aulnoy

BEELER, J.R. *2987*
Mme d'Aulnoy, historical novelist of the late seventeenth century. PhD U. of North Carolina at Chapel Hill, 1964.

DEGRAFF,A.V. *2988*
The tower and the well: a study of form and meaning in Mme d'Aulnoy's fairy tales. PhD U. of Virginia, 1979.

MITCHELL,J.T. *2989*
A thematic analysis of Mme d'Aulnoy's *Contes de fées*. PhD U. of North Carolina at Chapel Hill, 1973.

PALMER,M.D. *2990*
Mme d'Aulnoy in England. PhD U. of Maryland, 1969.

WILLIAMS,E.D. *2991*
The fairy tales of Mme d'Aulnoy. PhD Rice U. 1982.

Mme de Beauharnais

LEWIS,B.A.M.G. *2992*
The prose fiction of Mme de Beauharnais: a critical study. MLitt U. of Oxford, 1882.

TURGEON,F.K. *2993*
Fanny de Beauharnais. PhD Harvard U. 1930.

Simone de Beauvoir

ACOSTA,D.G. *2994*
Le couple dans l'oeuvre de Simone de Beauvoir. PhD City U. of New York, 1978.

D'AVANZO,N.M. *2995*
A study of the will in the works of Simone de Beauvoir. PhD Rutgers U. 1967.

BEAUDET-ZEPAIR,L. *2996*
Le féminisme de Simone de Beauvoir: hier et aujourd'hui. PhD City U. of New York, 1981.

DAVIDSON,B. *2997*
Patterns and problems in our relations with others: a study of the novels of Simone de Beauvoir. MPhil U. of Leicester, 1979.

EISENBERG,H.L. *2998*
The theme of female demission in the works of Simone de Beauvoir. PhD U. of California, Berkeley, 1978.

FONG,A.C. *2999*
Exis and praxis: woman's dilemma in the works of Simone de Beauvoir. PhD Duke U. 1974.

GOOD,R.J. *3000*
Le thème de l'échec dans l'oeuvre de Simone de Beauvoir. PhD U. of Colorado at Boulder, 1973.

HOLLINGSWORTH,W.J. *3001*
The fiction of Simone de Beauvoir: the pursuit of the absolute. PhD Case Western Reserve U. 1979.

LABAT,J. *3002*
La liberté et la mort dans les romans de Simone de Beauvoir. PhD U. of Missouri-Columbia, 1971.

LASOCKI,A.M.B. *3003*
Simone de Beauvoir: écrire: une enterprise essai de commentaire par les textes. PhD U. of California, Los Angeles, 1968.

LEIGHTON,J.U. *3004*
The conception of woman in the works of Simone de Beauvoir. PhD Case Western Reserve U. 1969.

MICHALEK,B.B. *3005*
Les hommes vus par Simone de Beauvoir: analyse critique de la présentation des hommes dans l'oeuvre de Simone de Beauvoir. MA U. of Essex, 1981.

MOSTOVYCH,A.M. *3006*
The intellectual in the works of Simone de Beauvoir. PhD Indiana U. 1982.

NAHAS,H. *3007*
Étude de la femme dans la littérature existentielle française: Jean-Paul Sartre et Simone de Beauvoir. PhD U. of Minnesota, 1954.

NAUGHTON,M.C. *3008*
The divided self: Simone de Beauvoir's autobiography. MLitt U. of Cambridge, 1975.

O'SULLIVAN,D.A. *3009*
Janus and Narcissus: woman's situation as depicted in *The second sex*, the works of fiction and the autobiography of Simone de Beauvoir. PhD U. of Arizona, 1972.

PAǦES,I.M. *3010*
Le roman de l'existence et le thème de la séparation dans l'oeuvre de Simone de Beauvoir. PhD U. of Wisconsin, 1971.

RUBINO,E.A. *3011*
Restrictions of freedom themes in the fictional works of Simone de Beauvoir. PhD Case Western Reserve U. 1973.

SHERINGHAM,S.C. *13011a*
Les thèmes de l'enfarce et la puérilité dans l'oeuvre de Simone de Beauvoir. MA U. of Exeter, 1978.

WARREN,D.L. *3012*
Simone de Beauvoir: towards a female subject. PhD U. of California, Los Angeles, 1979.

Catherine Bernard

KINSEY,S.R. *3013*
Catherine Bernard: a study of fiction and fantasy. PhD Columbia U. 1979.

Mme de Charrière

BRAUNROT,C .P. *3015*
Mme de le Charrière and the eighteenth-century novel: experiments in epistolary techniques. PhD Yale U. 1973.

MINIER-BIRK,S.C. *3016*
L'oeuvre romanesque de Mme de Charrière: réflexion systématique et création dans les *Lettres neuchâteloises, Mistriss Henley* et les *Lettres écrites de Lausanne*. PhD U. of Connecticut, 1977.

MYINTO O,T.L. *3017*
Mme de Charrière. Témoignage et engagement féminins dans le roman du XVIIe siècle. PhD U. of California, Berkeley, 1980.

WOOD,D.M. *3018*
The novels of Mme de Charrière (1740–1805). PhD U. of Cambridge, 1975.

Christine de Pisan

BUMGARDNER,G.H. *3019*
Tradition and modernity from 1380 to 1405: Christine de Pisan. PhD Yale U. 1970.

EDMONDS,B.P. *3020*
Aspects of Christine de Pisan's social and political ideas. PhD U. of Maryland, 1972.

FINKEL,H.R. *3021*
The portrait of the woman in the works of Christine de Pisan. PhD Rice U. 1972.

MARGOLIS,N. *3022*
The poetics of history: an analysis of Christine de Pisan's *Livre de la mutacion de fortune*. PhD Stanford U. 1977.

RENO,C.M. *3023*
Self and society in *L'avision-Christine* of Christine of Pisan. PhD Yale U. 1972.

ROSIER,M.F. *3024*
Christine de Pisan as a moralist. PhD U. of Toronto, 1945.

WILSON,N.S. *3025*
A revaluation of Christine de Pisan as a literary figure. PhD Stanford U. 1952.

WISMAN,J.A. *3026*
L'humanisme dans l'oeuvre de Christine de Pisan. PhD Catholic U. of America, 1976.

Colette

HARPER,P. *3027*
The importance of the past in the work of Colette. MLitt U. of Edinburgh, 1975.

KIRKHAM,E. *3028*
The epithet and Colette. MA U. of Leeds, 1942.

MARKS,E. *3029*
Colette: a critical study. PhD New York U. 1968.

OLKEN,I.T. *3030*
Colette: aspects of imagery. PhD U. of Michigan, 1960.

PHILBRICK,A.L. *3031*
Space as metaphor and theater: the individual's search for space in selected works of Colette. PhD Brown U. 1979.

SLAHY-SUTTON,C. *3032*
Communication avec le non-humain chez Colette. PhD Indiana U. 1980.

SOKOLOWSKI ,R. *3033*
L'échec du couple dans les romans de Colette. PhD State U. of New York at Albany, 1979.

TIDWELL,J.B. *3034*
Imagery in the works of Colette. PhD U. of Alabama, 1969.

VIRK,R.S. *3035*
The poetic imagination of Colette. PhD U. of Southern California, 1974.

WRIGHT,E.O. *3036*
Matériaux et perceptions dans l'oeuvre de Colette. MA U. of Manchester, 1959.

Mme Cottin

HORNICEK,J. *3037*
Mme Cottin: a study of the pre-romantic novel in France. PhD Harvard U. 1922.

SYKES,L.C. *3038*
Mme Cottin et le roman sentimental. DPhil U. of Oxford, 1940.

Hélisenne de Crenne

BERGAL,I.M. *3039*
Hélisenne de Crenne, a sixteenth-century French novelist. PhD U. of Minnesota, 1966.

JORDAN,M.F. *3040*
The *Angoysses douloureuses* of Hélisenne de Crenne. PhD Harvard U. 1969.

LORIENTE,S.M.M. 3041
Angoysses douloureuses qui procedent d'amours d'Hélisenne de Crenne. PhD U. of Southern California, 1982.

SECOR,H.R. 3042
Hélisenne de Crenne: *Les Angoysses douloureuses qui procedent d'amours* (1538): a critical edition based on the original text with introduction notes and glossary. PhD Yale U. 1957.

WALDSTEIN,H. 3043
Hélisenne de Crenne: a woman of the Renaissance. PhD Wayne State U. 1965.

Marie Louise Denis

WILLEN,C.K. 3044
Métromanie et mechanceté: une étude de *La coquette punie* de Marie Louise Denis. PhD Harvard U. 1979.

Mme Deshoulières

BORGLUM,G.P. 3045
Mme Deshoulières (1638–1694). PhD Yale U. 1939.

Mme Du Deffand

DUISIT,L.R. 3046
Mme Du Deffand epistolière. Valeur littéraire de la correspondance. PhD Yale U. 1960.

Pernette Du Guillet

SODERSTROM,R.A. 3047
The poetry of Pernette Du Guillet and its Italian sources and inspirations. PhD Vanderbilt U. 1982.

YAMAMOTO,K.K. 3048
The evolution of love in Pernette Du Guillet's *Rymes*. PhD Northwestern U. 1979.

Mme de Duras

CRICHFIELD,G. 3049
Three novels of Mme de Duras: *Ouirika, Edouard* and *Olivier*. PhD U. of Wisconsin, 1972.

Marguerite Duras

ALLEYNE,B.E. 3050
A study of the works of Marguerite Duras. MSc U. of Salford, 1974.

BRATTON,J.S. 3051
The novels of Marguerite Duras. PhD Columbia U. 1968.

COHEN,A. 3052
La dialectique du solipsisme et de l'altérité dans l'oeuvre de Marguerite Duras (essai de phénoménologie critique). PhD U. of California, Los Angeles, 1969.

COHEN,S.D. 3053
Marguerite Duras and the art of the novel. PhD New York U. 1982.

DRUON,M.V. 3054
La scène triangulaire dans l'oeuvre romanesque de Marguerite Duras. PhD U. of California, Los Angeles, 1981.

GLASSMAN,D.N. 3055
Marguerite Duras's 'Indian Cycle': a fantasy text. PhD Yale U. 1982.

HULES,V.T. 3056
La dynamique du devenir dans le théâtre de Marguerite Duras. PhD Harvard U. 1976.

HUSSERL-KAPIT,S.L. 3057
Le monde psychologique des romans de Marguerite Duras. PhD Harvard U. 1973.

KARAGEORGE, Y.V. 3058
Fictional and cinematic treatment of time in five French authors, 1955–1976. [Incl. Marguerite Duras.] PhD Indiana U. 1978.

KEMPO,O. 3059
Politique et poétique chez Marguerite Duras. PhD U. of British Columbia, 1974.

MORGAN,J.M. 3060
Marguerite Duras: the novelist as film maker. PhD Indiana U. 1982.

MURPHY,C.J. 3061
Trois 'états' de l'écriture romanesque de Marguerite Duras: une étude de l'aliénation et de l'absence. PhD U. of Pennsylvania, 1974.

OLSON,R.L. 3062
The expanding significance of the shrinking hero in the novels of Marguerite Duras. PhD U. of Oklahoma, 1981.

REDHEAD,G.B. 3063
Marguerite Duras: a thematic and critical study. PhD U. of Kent, 1972.

TERRY,L.P. 3064
Le thème de l'ennui dans les romans de Marguerite Duras. PhD Middlebury Coll. 1975.

Isabelle Eberhardt

ENSLEN,D. 3065
Isabelle Eberhardt et l'Algérie. PhD U. of Southern California, 1979.

Mme d'Épinay

SIMHA,E.S. 3066
An eagle in a cage of gauze: Mme d'Épinay's *Histoire de Madame de Montbrillant*. PhD Yale U. 1968.

TRAPENLL,M. 3067
The *Histoire de Madame de Montbrillant*: a critical analysis of Madame d'Épinay's confession and self-justification. PhD U. of Pittsburgh, 1972.

Jeanne Flore

BINFORD,R.K. 3068
The *Comptes amoureux* of Jeanne Flore: a critical study. PhD U. of Iowa, 1972.

Mme de Genlis

LABORDE,A.M. 3069
L'oeuvre de Mme de Genlis. PhD U. of California, Los Angeles, 1965.

SANDERS,J.B. 3070
Madame de Genlis and juvenile fiction in England. PhD Indiana U. 1965.

Mlle de Gournay

FLYNN,J.W. 3071
A critical edition of some literary responses by Mlle de Gournay. PhD U. of Manchester, 1979.

HOLMES,P.P. 3072
The life and literary times of Marie le Jars de Gournay. PhD U. of London, King's Coll. 1952.

Mme de Graffigny

BARROWS,P.S. 3073
Mme de Graffigny's *Lettres d'une Péruvienne* and the mid-eighteenth-century French novel. MPhil U. of London, 1977.

Eugénie de Guérin

CINIPHÉIC ,A.M.de 3074
La sensibilité d'Eugenie de Guérin. MA National U. of Ireland, 1947.

Anne Catherine d'Helvétius

ALLAN,P. 3075
Une édition critique de la correspondence de Madame Helvétius avec introduction biographique. PhD U. of Toronto, 1975.

Simone Jacquemard

TEST,M.L. 3076
Une analyse des romans de Simone Jacquemard. PhD U. of California, Los Angeles, 1973.

Mme de Krüdener

NEY,E.W. 3077
Additional light on Mme de Krüdener's life and writings. PhD New York U. 1953.

Louise Labé

HANISCH,G.S. 3078
Love elegies of the Renaissance: Marot, Ronsard and Louise Labé. PhD City U. of New York, 1976.

LARACY,E.D. 3079
Louise Labé. MA National U. of Ireland, 1940.

SIGAL,S.C. 3080
Le platonisme et le sensualisme dans l'oeuvre de Louise Labé. PhD Tulane U. 1975.

SPODARK,E. 3081
The *Défense et illustration* of Louise Labé. PhD Northwestern U. 1982.

WOODS,C.L. 3082
The three faces of Louise Labé. PhD Syracuse U. 1976.

Mme de Lafayette

BÁRCZAY-MILLAR,C. 3083
La Princesse de Clèves and the tragic dimension of classicism. PhD State U. of New York, 1974.

CAMPBELL,J. 3084
The language of Madame de Lafayette: a study of the literary function of key-words. PhD U. of Glasgow, 1979.

HALL,D.R. 3085
A structural analysis of the fictional works of Mme de Lafayette. PhD U. of Maryland, 1968.

KUIZENGA,D. 3086
Aspects of style and language in *La Princesse de Clèves*. PhD City U. of New York, 1974.

MCNEILL,I.F.E. 3087
L'univers dramatique de Mme de Lafayette. PhD Stanford U. 1970.

MOORE,A.M. 3088
Le temps fatal: temporal structure in *La Princesse de Clèves*. PhD U. of Oregon, 1980.

REDHEAD,R.W. 3089
Love and death in the fictional works of Mme de Lafayette. PhD U. of Minnesota, 1971.

RODINO,S. 3090
Mme de Lafayette and the Italian tradition of the courtier. PhD City U. of New York, 1977.

TIEFENBRUN,S.W. 3091
A structural stylistics analysis of *La princesse de Clèves*. PhD Columbia U. 1971.

WOSHINSKY,B.R. 3092
The creative use of literary convention in the novels of Mme de Lafayette. PhD Yale U. 1968.

Violette Leduc

STOCKINGER,J.G. 3093
Violette Leduc: the legitimization of *la batarde*. PhD U. of Wisconsin-Madison, 1979.

Ninon de Lenclos

MARTIN-THERAULT,A. *3094*
Les *Lettres de Ninon de Lenclos au Marquis de Sévigné*: étude stylistique et historique. PhD McGill U. 1973.

Marie Leneru

PEACOCK,V.L. *3095*
The works of Marie Leneru. PhD Cornell U. 1930.

Marie-Jeanne Leprince de Beaumont

REBSTOCK,B.M. *3096*
La multiple image: les romans de Marie-Jeanne Leprince de Beaumont. PhD Georgetown U. 1982.

Marguerite de Lussan

CUFF,D.A. *3097*
Marguerite de Lussan and the historical novel in the first half of the eighteenth century. PhD U. of Cambridge, 1932.

Françoise Mallet-Joris

DAVIS,M.T.L. *3098*
Thèmes clefs et procedes littéraires dans l'oeuvre romanesque de Françoise Mallet-Joris: le motif de l'aspiration vers l'absolu. PhD Catholic U. of America, 1975.

ROBERTS,L.J. *3099*
Major image and vocabulary patterns in the first five novels of Françoise Mallet-Joris. PhD Columbia U. 1977.

Marguerite de Navarre

ALLAIRE,J.L. *3100*
L'évangélisme de Marguerite de Navarre. PhD Wayne State U. 1966.

ANSERMIN,S.L. *3101*
La poésie réligieuse de Marguerite de Navarre et de Vittoria Colonna. PhD U. of Colorado, 1966.

ATANCE,F.R. *3102*
Marguerite de Navarre et la réforme. PhD U. of Western Ontario, 1970.

BERNARD,R.W. *3103*
Renaissance attitudes on marriage, love, and sexual mores as found in the *Heptaméron*. PhD U. of Kansas, 1968.

BERNARDO,R.M. *3104*
The problem of perspective in the *Miroir de l'âme pêcheresse,* the *Prisons* and the *Heptaméron* of Marguerite de Navarre. PhD U. of New York at Binghamton, 1979.

COLLINS,H.G. *3105*
The fiction of truth: a study of the *Heptaméron* of Marguerite de Navarre. PhD Rutgers U. 1975.

DAVIS,B.J. *3106*
The *Devisants* and their personal relationships in Marguerite de Navarre's *Heptaṁeron*. PhD Columbia U. 1974.

FOURNEIR,H.S. *3107*
Style in the non-dramatic verse of the *Marguerites de la Marguerite des Princesse*. PhD U. of Western Ontario, 1976.

FRIEDTURNES,U. *3108*
L'Heptaméron de Marguerite de Navarre: analyse structurale des nouvelles de la première journée. PhD Pennsylvania State U. 1979.

GELERNT,J. *3109*
World of many loves: the *Heptaméron* of Marguerite de Navarre. PhD Columbia U. 1963.

HENDERSON,C.E. *3110*
Analysis and comparison of an anonymous seventeenth-century reproduction with the original *Heptaméron* of Marguerite de Navarre. PhD Case Western Reserve U. 1972.

JONES,E.M. *3111*
The inspiration and sources of Marguerite de Navarre. MA U. of Wales, 1929.

KLAUSENBURGER,L.E.H. *3112*
Ambiguity in the *Heptaméron*: structures and technique. PhD U. of Michigan, 1974.

LECKMAN,H.H. *3113*
Mysticism in the poetry of Marguerite de Navarre. PhD Catholic U. of America, 1982.

MIRABEL,C.M. *3114*
The religious attitude of Marguerite de Navarre in her last works. MPhil U. of London, Warburg Inst. 1977.

MORRIS,P.A. *3115*
The role of women in politics and social life as viewed by Marguerite de Navarre in the *Heptaméron* and her secular drama. PhD City U. of New York, 1978.

ORIS,J. *3117*
Mysticism in the work of Marguerite de Navarre. PhD U. of London, Birkbeck Coll. 1981.

REYNOLDS,R.P. *3118*
Les devisants de *L'Heptaméron:* contribution à l'étude de la pensée politique et sociale de Marguerite de Navarre. [French text.] PhD U. of Texas at Austin, 1970.

ROMER,B.J.W. *3119*
The *Heptaméron* of Marguerite de Navarre: scriptural context and structure. PhD U. of North Carolina at Chapel Hill, 1977.

SHERRARD,L.A.O. *3120*
The love poems of Marguerite of Navarre. MPhil U. of London, Warburg Inst. 1982.

TOENES,S.J. 3121
The *Heptaméron* of Marguerite de Navarre: a classification of the nouvelles. PhD U. of Wisconsin, 1970.

WALKER,J.C. 3122
Characteristics of French syntax of the sixteenth century as exemplified in the language of Marguerite de Navarre. PhD Cornell U. 1898.

WALSH,M.R. 3123
Marguerite of Navarre and her circle. PhD Niagara U. 1938.

Marie de France

ALLEN,M.V. 3124
The literary craftsmanship of Marie de France. PhD U. of Virginia, 1954.

BLACK,B.P. 3125
Irony in the *lais* of Marie de France. PhD Tulane U. 1978.

BRIGHTENBACK,E.K. 3126
Aspects of organicity in old French romance narrative: the prologue and narrative modalities in the *lais* of Marie de France. PhD Princeton U. 1974.

BROOKES,B.S. 3127
A stylistic analysis of the *lais* of Marie de France. PhD Columbia U. 1967.

BULLOCK-DAVIES,C. 3128
Marie de France and South Wales. PhD U. of Wales, Bangor, 1963.

DAVIES,J.B. 3129
The syntax of Marie de France as studied in her *lais*. MA U. of Wales, 1938.

FITZ,B.E. 3130
Desire and language: textual metaphor in the *lais* of Marie de France. PhD Yale U. 1973.

GOURAIGE,A. 3131
Le merveilleux dans les lais de Marie de France. PhD State U. of New York at Albany, 1973.

GREEN,R.B. 3132
The growth of love: a study of reality and symbolism in the lays of Marie de France. PhD Rutgers U. 1971.

HARRIS,J.E. 3133
The lays *Gugemar*, *Lanval* and a fragment of *Yone* with a study of the life and work of the author. PhD Columbia U. 1930.

ILLINGWORTH,R.N. 3134
A study of the *lais* of Marie de France and Celtic analogues. BLitt U. of Oxford, 1960.

MICHEL,R.A. 3135
From symbol to self: the *lais* of Marie de France. PhD City U. of New York, 1979.

TWIFORD,L.K.C. 3136
Reality and convention in the *lais* of Marie de France. PhD Rice U. 1978.

WEINGARTNER,R. 3137
The authorship of the Old- French *lai*: *Guingamor*. PhD Princeton U. 1968.

WENNBERG,B. 3138
Marie de France and the anonymous *lais*: a study of the narrative *lai* in the twelfth and thirteenth centuries. PhD U. of Pennsylvania, 1956.

WOLF,L. 3139
The implied author in the *lais* of Marie de France. PhD U. of Pittsburgh, 1974.

Marie Noël

CHARTERS,E.M. 3140
Marie Noël: her life and works. PhD Columbia U. 1966.

O'DONOGHUE,M.A.N. 3141
Le thème de l'amour malheureux dans la poésie de Marie Noël. MA National U. of Ireland, 1967.

Anne de Marquets

SEILER,M.H. 3142
Anne de Marquets: poétesse réligieuse du seizième siècle. PhD Catholic U. of America, 1932.

Mme de Noailles

ALLARD,H.G. 3143
Anne de Noailles, nun of passion: a study of the novels of Anne de Noailles. PhD Yale U. 1973.

HAI GIS,R.E. 3144
Sensations and images in the poetry of Mme de Noailles. PhD Radcliffe Coll. 1939.

NANCIN,J.H. 3145
Mme de Noailles: a study of her life and works. PhD Case Western Reserve U. 1938.

Mme Riccoboni

CRAGG,O.B. 3146
The novels of Mme Riccoboni. PhD Bryn Mawr Coll. 1970.

CROSBY,E.A. 3147
Mme Riccoboni: her life and works; her place in the literary history of the eighteenth century. MA U. of London, 1919.

MORGAN,M.C. 3148
Mme Riccobini par rapport au roman de son époque et son attitude envers les femmes. PhD State U. of New York at Binghamton, 1979.

ROSE,P. 3149
Introduction to the life and works of Mme Riccoboni. PhD Columbia U. 1973.

Christiane Rochefort

STECKEL,A. *3150*
Narration and metaphor as ideology in the novels of Christiane Rochefort. PhD U. of Wisconsin-Madison, 1975.

Mme Roland

CISAR,M.A. *3151*
The image of the self: autobiographical space in the works of Mme Roland. PhD Brown U. 1979.

YOUNG,C.E. *3152*
A comparison of the letters and the memoirs of Mme Roland: an introductory study for a biography. PhD Cornell U. 1927.

Marie de Romieu

WINANDY,A.E. *3153*
Marie de Romieu *Les premières oeuvres poétiques*: étude et édition critique. PhD Pittsburgh U. 1968.

Mme de Sablé

GUIDARELLI,V.C. *3154*
The salon of Mme de Sablé: foyer of literary Jansenism. PhD Fordham U. 1979.

George Sand

BIRTWELL,M.H. *3155*
Les idées politiques de George Sand. MA U. of Manchester, 1926.

BLOUNT,P.G. *3156*
The reputation of George Sand in Victorian England. PhD Cornell U. 1961.

BOWES,M.E. *3157*
George Sand and the feminist movement. PhD U. of Pennsylvania, 1952.

BROWN,R.J. *3158*
A study of the double motif in George Sand's writing. PhD Yale U. 1977.

COULLOUX,M.M. *3159*
Aspects du merveilleux chez George Sand: les *Contes d'une grandmère*. PhD U. of Colorado at Boulder, 1978.

DALY ,P. *3160*
George Sand: l'écriture au féminin. PhD Washington U. 1981.

FAIRCHILD,S.L. *3161*
George Sand, historian of her time in her *Correspondance* (1812–June 1835). PhD Wayne State U. 1980.

GIBSON,M.B. *3162*
Les romans champêtres de George Sand. MA Queen's U. of Belfast, 1940.

GLASGOW,J.M. *3163*
Psychological realism in George Sand's early novels and short stories (1831–1835). PhD U. of California, Los Angeles, 1966.

GRAY,Y.G. *3164*
Le féminisme de George Sand. MA U. of Birmingham, 1954.

HERRMANN,L.S. *3165*
George Sand and the nineteenth-century Russian novel: the quest for a heroine. PhD Columbia U. 1979.

HILDEBRAN, K.B. *3166*
Elements of realism in the novels of George Sand, 1832–1848. PhD U. of Chicago, 1939.

HYSLOP,F. *3167*
Les compagnons du tour de France par George Sand et les milieux ouvriers sociaux contemporains. MA U. of Manchester, 1920.

IRR,M. *3168*
Les structures psychologiques dans les romans de George Sand. PhD Laval U. 1971.

KARP,C.S. *3169*
George Sand's reception in Russia, 1832–1881. PhD U. of Michigan, 1976.

KREITMAN,L.R. *3170*
George Sand's symbolic vision: a fading yet future fantastic. PhD U. of Pennsylvania, 1976.

MERKER,R. *3171*
Exociticism in the works of George Sand. PhD New York U. 1967.

PÉCILE,M.J. *3172*
George Sand: la vocation et la formation d'une femme écrivain au dix-neuvième siècle. PhD U. of Massachusetts, 1976.

PERRY,A.C. *3173*
George Sand, feuilletoniste: 1844–1848. PhD Washington U. 1973.

PETOUKHOFF,V.G. *3174*
George Sand et le drame philosophique: *Aldo le Rimeur, Les sept cordes de la lyre, Gabriel, Les Mississipiens, Le diable aux champs*. PhD U. of Pennsylvania, 1975.

POWLES,L.V. *3175*
The mysticism of George Sand. PhD U. of London, External 1939.

ROSEN BERG,R.P. *3176*
George Sand in Germany, 1832–1848: the attitude towards her as a woman and a novelist. PhD U. of Wisconsin, 1933.

SCHUTZ,A.H. *3178*
Peasant vocabulary in the works of George Sand. PhD U. of Chicago, 1922.

STALEY,E.M. *3179*
George Sand and Jean-Jacques Rousseau. PhD John Hopkins U. 1926.

STOW,H.K. *3180*
Narrative and thematic structure in George Sand's *Horace*. PhD U. of Wisconsin-Madison, 1979.

TEMCHIN,S.I. *3181*
Straining the structures of romanticism: George Sand's *Lélia* reconsidered. PhD Tufts U. 1981.

TUCKER,A.K. *3182*
George Sand as a political theorist. MA U. of London, 1922.

WALL,N.R. *3183*
The persuasive style of the young George Sand. PhD George Washington U. 1974.

WENTZ,D.L. *3184*
Fait et fiction: les formules pedagogiques des *Contes d'une grandmère* de George Sand. PhD U. of Connecticut, 1980.

Nathalie Sarraute

BELL,S.M. *3185*
The fiction of Nathalie Sarraute: a study of her work from *Tropismes* to *Vous les entendez?* PhD U. of Glasgow, 1976.

BLOCK,D.Z. *3186*
Imagery in the works of Nathalie Sarraute. PhD Rutgers U. 1973.

CALIN,F.D.G. *3187*
La vie retrouvée: étude de l'oeuvre romanesque de Nathalie Sarraute. PhD Stanford U. 1972.

CASEY,A.H. *3188*
L'imagination de Nathalie Sarraute. PhD Georgetown U. 1973.

COTHRAN,J.A. *3190*
Narrative structures in the novels of Nathalie Sarraute. PhD U. of Pennsylvania, 1974.

COUGH LIN-MIEVILLE,J.M. *3191*
Étude structurale et thématique des metaphores dans *Les fruits d'or* de Nathalie Sarraute. PhD Emory U. 1978.

CRAWFORD,M.A. *3192*
An existential vision of man in the fiction of Witold Gombrowicz and selected novels by Sartre, Sarraute, Robbe-Grillet and M. Butor. PhD New York U. 1972.

FLEMING,J.A. *3193*
The imagery of tropism in the novels of Nathalie Sarraute: an index with commentary. PhD Harvard U. 1966.

HANSON,S.A. *3194*
The strategies of suspicion in the novels of Nathalie Sarraute. PhD Johns Hopkins U. 1981.

HO,D.K. *3195*
Les principes structuraux dans les romans de Nathalie Sarraute. PhD Northwestern U. 1978.

JAMES,G.L. *3196*
Dialogue and reality in the fiction of Nathalie Sarraute. PhD U. of Arizona, 1979.

JEFFERSON, A.M. *3197*
Aspects of the poetics of fiction: the novels of Nathalie Sarraute. DPhil U. of Oxford, 1975.

MCMEANS,R.M. *3198*
Language and structure in the novels of Nathalie Sarraute. PhD Case Western Reserve U. 1977.

MEGNA,R. *3199*
Nathalie Sarraute: the novelist as social psychologist. PhD Rice U. 1978.

NELSON,J.A. *3200*
Order and chaos in the novels of Nathalie Sarraute. PhD Michigan State U. 1977.

OBERST,B.S. *3201*
Nathalie Sarraute: the images of tropism. PhD Case Western Reserve U. 1973.

ST. AMOUR,D. *3202*
Point of view in the novels of Nathalie Sarraute: 1948–1968. PhD U. of Michigan, 1973.

VERNIÈRE-PLANK,L. *3203*
Nathalie Sarraute tradition et 'modernité' d'une oeuvre contemporaine. PhD Fordham U. 1967.

VINEBERG,E. *3204*
Au-delà des tropismes: étude des romans de Nathalie Sarraute. PhD U. of California, Irvine, 1973.

WRIGHT,M.G. *3205*
Nathalie Sarraute: *Entre la vie et la mort*; une interprétation linguistique. PhD U. of Wisconsin-Madison, 1973.

Mlle de Scudéry

AUBÉ,L.A. *3206*
Aspects of reality in the *Grand Cyrus* of Madeleine de Scudéry. PhD Case Western Reserve U. 1970.

CIS ON,M.B. *3207*
The *Samedis* of Mlle de Scudéry. PhD Fordham U. 1967.

KEATING,R.T. *3208*
The literary portraits in the novels of Mlle de Scudéry. PhD Yale U. 1970.

NUNN,R.R. *3209*
Mlle de Scudéry's *Clélie*. PhD Columbia U. 1966.

Comtesse de Ségur

KILLIP,E.H. *3210*
The stories of the Comtesse de Ségur and her contribution to children's literature. PhD U. of Bristol, 1957.

Mme de Sévigné

ALLENTUCH,H.M.R. 3211
A descriptive analysis of the personality of Mme de Sévigné. PhD Columbia U. 1962.

ARSENAULT,P.E. 3212
The literary opinions of Mme de Sévigné. PhD Princeton U. 1959.

CUMING,L.M.B. 3213
Mme de Sévigné and the intellectual life of her times. MA U. of London, Bedford Coll. 1956.

GOLDSMITH,E.C. 3214
Bridging distances: writing as displacement and location in the letters of Mme de Sévigné. PhD Cornell U. 1978.

GUENOUN,S. 3215
La *Correspondance* de Mme de Sévigné et de Mme de Guenoun: une separation littéraire. PhD Princeton U. 1981.

HOWARD,C.R. 3216
Mme de Sévigné en France au dix-huitième siècle. PhD Stanford U. 1977.

LAWRENCE,T.H. 3217
Les lectures de Mme de Sévigné. MA U. of Leeds, 1934.

MENSHER, G.B. 3218
Problems of time and existence in the letters of Mme de Sévigné. PhD U. of Iowa, 1977.

NICOLICH,R.N. 3219
Mme de Sévigné and the problem of reality and appearances. PhD Michigan State U. 1965.

RECKER,J.A.M. 3220
'Appelle-moi Pierrot': wit and irony in the 'letters' of Mme de Sévigné. PhD Ohio State U. 1982.

Marquise de Souza-Botelho

VINCENS,S. J. 3221
Vestiqes du classicisme au temps de Chateaubriand les romans de Mme de Souza (1761–1836). PhD U. of Colorado, 1969.

Mme de Staël

COLSON,L.C. 3222
Étude de la société dans *Corinne ou l'Italie* de Mme de Staël. PhD Case Western Reserve U. 1970.

DISTANCE,D. 3223
L'Angelterre dans l'oeuvre de Mme de Staël. MA Queen's U. of Belfast, 1935.

FORSBERG,R.J. 3224
Mme de Staël: the English period. PhD U. of Southern California, 1970.

GILON,L. 3225
Mme de Staël-De Launay: femme de théâtre. PhD U. of Massachusetts, 1978.

GOLIN,S.J. 3226
Mme de Staël and the rejection of happiness: a study in the end of the Enlightenment. PhD Brandeis U. 1968.

GRANT,I.L.D. 3227
Mme de Staël: the significance of her Weimar period. PhD U. of Southern California, 1940.

GUTWIRTH,M. 3228
Mme de Staël as a novelist. PhD Bryn Mawr Coll., 1952.

GWYNNE,G.E. 3229
Mme de Staël et les idéologies. MA U. of Wales, 1949.

HARMON,D.S. 3230
The antithetical world view of Mme de Staël: ideology, structure and style in *Delphine* and *Corinne*. PhD George Washington U. 1975.

HEKMATPANAH,L. 3231
Mme de Staël and literature: theory and practice. PhD U. of Chicago, 1978.

JAECK, E.G. 3232
Mme de Staël and the spread of German literature. PhD U. of Illinois at Urbana-Champaign, 1910.

JOHNSON,D.P.C. 3233
Origines et développement du cosmopolitisme de Mme de Staël à travers son théâtre (avec des inédits provenant des archives de Coppet et des archives Jean le Marois). PhD U. of Illinois at Urbana-Champaign, 1977.

JONES,R.A. 3234
Mme de Staël and England: a study of Mme de Staël's English acquaintances, and of her reputation and influence in England. MA U. of London, 1928.

LEIN,M.E. 3235
Les sources des théories littéraires de Mme de Staël. PhD U. of Chicago, 1949.

MCKENZIE,E.D. 3236
An evaluation of Mme de Staël's judgment of German literature in her book *De l'Allemagne*. PhD U. of Pittsburgh, 1949.

MICHAELS,M.S. 3237
Feminist tendencies in the works of Mme de Staël. PhD U. of Connecticut, 1977.

MORROS,L .M.S. 3238
Woman in the expository works of Mme de Staël. PhD U. of Washington, 1975.

PALMUNEN,K.F. 3239
Mothers and daughters in the fiction of Mme de Staël. PhD Brown U. 1979.

POCQUET,E.J. *3240*
L'Allemagne de Mme de Staël et celle de Henri Heine. PhD U. of Colorado, 1971.

PRATT,T. *3241*
Italy in the life and work of Mme de Staël. MA U. of Wales (Aberystwyth), 1968.

SHINALL,S.L. *3242*
Mme de Staël's concept of the novel. PhD U. of Illinois at Urbana-Champaign, 1966.

STANDRING,E.M. *3243*
Le féminisme de Mme de Staël. MA U. of Manchester, 1941.

STONGE,S.H.S. *3244*
Evolution of the religious thought in the works of Mme de Staël. PhD Vanderbilt U. 1971.

THOMAS DE PANGE,V.M.J. *3245*
Mme de Staël and her English correspondents. DPhil U. of Oxford, 1956.

TOURTEBATTE,B.W. *3246*
Répertoire chronologique de la correspondance de Mme de Staël. PhD U. of Chicago, 1949.

TRAIL,M.C. *3247*
Mme de Staël: her Russian- Swedish journey. PhD U. of Southern California, 1946.

UNDERWOOD, G.A. *3248*
Rousseauism in the works of Mme de Staël. PhD Harvard U. 1914.

Mme de Tencin

SADLER MOORE,P.A. *3249*
The birth of the corrupt heroine: gestation in the novels of Madame de Tencin. PhD U. of Florida, 1980.

Elsa Triolet

BREED,N.J. *3250*
Feminine self-consciousness and masculine referent: the image of woman in the novels of Elsa Triolet. PhD Princeton U. 1979.

CASEY,B.B. *3251*
Elsa Triolet: a study in solitude. PhD Northwestern U. 1974.

SHARRATT,F.M.S. *3252*
L'oeuvre romanesque d'Elsa Triolet. PhD U. of Edinburgh, 1980.

ZINN,J.A. *3253*
Elsa Triolet: romancière et témoin de sonépoque. PhD U. of Nebraska-Lincoln, 1972.

Mme de Villedieu

MORRISETTE,B.A. *3254*
The life and works of Marie-Catherine Des Jardins (Mme de Villedieu), 1632–1683. PhD Johns Hopkins U. 1938.

SCOUTEN,M.A.S. *3255*
Mme de Villedieu: a feminist advocate. PhD State U. of New York at Albany, 1982.

Renée Vivien

MANNING,J.L. *3256*
Rhetoric and images of feminism in the poetry of Renée Vivien. [Pseudonym of Pauline Tarn.] PhD Yale U. 1981.

Simone Weil

BUGLER,M.B. *3257*
Literary ideas and aesthetics in the writings of Simone Weil. MA Queen's U. of Belfast, 1975.

BUR FORD,W.S. *3258*
Simone Weil's *Venise sauvée.* PhD Johns Hopkins U. 1966.

CABAUD,J.M. *3259*
L'expérience vécue de Simone Weil. PhD Columbia U. 1956.

DAHIR,K.L. *3260*
Simone Weil: violence and the intellectual: a personal odyssey. PhD U. of Wisconsin, 1971.

MAL AN,I.R. *3261*
L'enracinement de Simone Weil: essai d'interprétation. PhD U. of Kansas, 1957.

MONSEAU,C. *3262*
L'humanisme de Simone Weil dans *La condition ouvrière.* PhD Laval U. 1956.

MONSEAU,M. *3263*
L'humanisme de Simone Weil après *La condition ouvrière.* PhD Laval U. 1958.

Monique Wittig

SHAKTINI,N. *3264*
The problem of gender and subjectivity posed by the new subject pronoun 'J/E' in the writing of Monique Wittig. PhD U. of Calfornia, Santa Cruz, 1982.

WOODHULL,W. *3265*
Politics, the feminine, and writing: a study of Monique Wittig's *Les guérillères* and *Brouillon pour une dictionnaire des amantes.* PhD U. of Wisconsin-Madison, 1979.

Marguerite Yourcenar

HAFNER BURTON,K.A. *3266*
Deep structure and narrative text coherence: a reading of *Comment Wang-Fo fut sauvé* by Marguerite Yourcenar. [Pseudonym of Marguerite de Crayencour.] PhD U. of Wisconsin-Madison, 1980.

German literature

General and comparative studies

ALLAN,L. *3267*
Naturalists and the woman question: images of middle-class *Emanzipierte* in German and Scandinavian drama. PhD Brown U. 1982.

AMBROSE,M.J. *3268*
An examination of the independent role of women in Friedrich Hebbel's major dramas. PhD U. of Pennsylvania, 1977.

ARENDT,W.E.W. *3269*
Die Gestalt der Mutter in den *Nachtwachen von Bonaventura*. PhD Queen's U. at Kingston, 1982.

BACH,M.G. *3269a*
Wieland's attitude toward woman and her cultural and social relations. PhD Columbia U. 1922.

BAILLIET,T.S. *3270*
Die dichterische Gestaltungen der heidnischen und Christlichen Frau im Werk Eichendorffs. PhD Washington U. 1969.

BALINKIN,A. *3271*
The central women figures in Carl Zuckmayer's dramas. PhD U. of Cincinnati, 1976.

BARBER,E.D. *3272*
The position of women as reflected in the medieval German didactic literature. MA U. of Manchester, 1940.

BELKA,R.W. *3273*
A functional definition of satire applied to women in the *Fastnachtspiele* of Hans Sachs. PhD Brigham Young U. 1975.

BENNETT,V.J. *3274*
The role of the female in the works of Hermann Hesse. PhD U. of Utah, 1972.

BIGGE,A.E. *3275*
Heinrich Laube's woman characters: a study in development. PhD U. of Michigan, 1930.

BLACKWELL,L.J. *3276*
Bildungsroman mit Dame: the heroine in the German *Bildungsroman* from 1770 to 1900. PhD Indiana U. 1982.

BÖHM,G.S. *3277*
Die Bedeutung der Frau in dem erzählerischen Werk René Schickeles. PhD Tulane U. 1965.

BURGESS,A.V. *3278*
The female characters in Grillparzer's drama, as contrasted with those in Goethe's and Schiller's. MA U. of Wales, 1907.

CARDOZA,M.P. *3279*
The presentation of women in sixteenth-century Lutheran biblical drama. PhD U. of California, Los Angeles, 1968.

CARNE,E.M.E. *3280*
Die Bedeutung der Frauengestalten in Epos Hartmanns von Aue. PhD U. of Colorado, 1968.

CARR,E.W. *3281*
Arthur Schnitzler's *Therese: Chronik eines Frauenlebens.*. PhD State U. of New York at Binghamton, 1979.

CARR,F.H.T. *3282*
Courasche and her contemporaries: a contribution to the study of the novel in Germany in the seventeenth century. MA U. of Hull, 1969.

CRONIN,M.J. *3283*
The politics of Brecht's women characters. PhD Brown U. 1974.

CUMINGS,E.C. *3284*
Woman in the life and work of Theodor Mundt. PhD U. of Chicago, 1936.

DAHME,L.F. *3285*
Women in the life and art of Conrad Ferdinand Meyer. PhD Columbia U. 1937.

DOUTHIT,D.A.B. *3286*
The concept of women in Ernst Barlach's dramas. PhD U. of Texas at Austin, 1967.

DROST,C.L. *3287*
The major female characters in Georg Buechner's dramas. PhD Louisiana State U. 1974.

ELARDO,R.J. *3288*
The Chthonic woman in the novellas and fairytales of E.T.A. Hoffmann. PhD U. of Michigan, 1979.

EVELAND,S.A.N. *3289*
The divine lover of Mira Bai and Mechthild von Magdeburg: a study of two women's literary descriptions of a mystical relationship with God. PhD U. of Texas at Austin, 1978.

EZERGAILIS,I.M. *3290*
An ambiguous dialectic: the female principle in Thomas Mann's work. PhD Cornell U. 1969.

FOOT,R. *3291*
The phenomenon of speechlessness in the poetry of Marie Luise Kaschnitz, Günther Eich, Nelly Sachs and Paul Celan. PhD U. of Alberta, 1980.

FRANKE,E.K. *3292*
Die Bedeutung der Frau in Dürrenmatts Dramen. PhD Rochester U. 1979.

GIBBS,M.E. *3293*
A study of the women characters in the novels of Wolfram von Eschenbach. MA U. of London, Bedford Coll. 1965.

GOCKLEY,G.E. *3294*
Goethe's stylistic presentation of the main women characters in *Wilhelm Meisters Lehrjahre*. PhD Indiana U. 1963.

GOODMAN,K.R. *3295*
German women and autobiography in the

nineteenth century: Louise Aston, Fanny Lewald, Malwida von Meysenbug and Marie von Ebner-Eschenbach. PhD U. of Wisconsin-Madison, 1977.

GRAVES,R.A. *3296*
The integral personality: the relationship between the female characters and the world in selected works of Theodor Fontane and Wilhelm Raabe. MLitt U. of Bristol, 1979.

HARE,M.F. *3297*
The role of women in Fontane's novels of Berlin society. MA U. of Keele, 1975.

HEINEMANN,M.E. *3298*
Women prose writers of the Nazi holocaust. PhD Indiana U. 1981.

HEPTNER,E.M. *3299*
Two nineteenth-century conceptions of womanhood: a comparison of the attitudes of Kleist and Hebbel. PhD Washington U. 1975.

HESSLER,M.G. *3300*
The nun in German literature. PhD U. of Illinois at Urbana-Champaign, 1944.

HIRSCH,S.K. *3301*
Heinrich Boll's female trinity and the 'restauration': evolution of a response. PhD U. of Texas at Austin, 1976.

HODGES,J.L. *3302*
The treatment of women, love and marriage in the works of Hans Sachs. PhD U. of North Carolina at Chapel Hill, 1951.

HOFFMAN,H.J. *3303*
The image of women in the drama of the German Democratic Republic, 1949–1971. PhD U. of Massachusetts, 1980.

HOVE,D.A. *3304*
Lessing's heroines and their literary models. PhD U. of Iowa, 1973.

HUNT,I.E. *3305*
Mutter und Muttermythos in Günter Grass' Roman *Der Butt*. PhD Washington U. 1982.

INGLIS,F.J.G. *3306*
Female characters in the works of H.J.C. von Grimmelshausen. MLitt U. of Oxford, 1978.

JOHNSTON,K. *3307*
An analysis of the female protagonists in the novels and Erzählungen of Theodor Fontane. MLitt U. of Newcastle-upon-Tyne, 1974.

KIENBAUM,B.E. *3308*
Die Frauengestalten in Theodor Fontanes Berliner Romanen: Rolle und Funktion in der Darstellung du Konflickt zwischen Individuum und Gesellschaft. PhD Michigan State U. 1978.

KING,E.D. *3309*
Women in the works of Gottfried Keller. PhD U. of Wisconsin, 1938.

KIRCHBERGER,E.L. *3310*
The role of the woman as mother in the German epic of the twelfth and early thirteenth centuries. PhD U. of Wisconsin, 1949.

KOLB,J. *3311*
Wine, women and song: sensory referents in the works of Heinrich Heine. PhD Yale U. 1979.

KRIS CIOKAITIS,I. *3312*
The woman in the works of Friedrich Hebbel: a reevaluation. PhD Michigan State U. 1968.

KUPLIS,A. *3313*
The image of woman in Bertolt Brecht's poetry. PhD U. of Wisconsin-Madison, 1976.

LANGEROVA,V.Z. *3314*
Women characters in the works of Uwe Johnson. PhD Vanderbilt U. 1976.

LEVIN,T.J. *3315*
Political ideology and aesthetics in neo-feminist German fiction: Verena Stefan, Elfriede Jelinck, Margot Schroeder. PhD Cornell U. 1979.

MCCOMBS,N.K. *3316*
Earth spirit, victim, or whore? The figure of the prostitute in German literature, 1880–1925. PhD U. of California, San Diego, 1982.

MCCULLAR,S.Y. *3317*
'Ideal' versus 'real' womanhood as portrayed in the literature and correspondence of early German romanticism. PhD Rice U. 1979.

MACINNES,I.S. *3318*
The influence of feminism on the German women novelists of the nineteenth century. PhD U. of California, Berkeley, 1921.

MOELLER,A.J.K. *3319*
The woman as survivor: the development of the female figure in Heinrich Böll's fiction. PhD U. of Nebraska-Lincoln, 1979.

NEIKIRK,J.C. *3320*
The role of the woman in the works of Ödön von Horváth. PhD U. of Wisconsin, 1971.

NEWPORT,C.M.P. *3321*
Woman in the thought and work of Friedrich Hebbel. PhD U. of Wisconsin, 1908.

NOVAK,S.G.S. *3322*
Images of womanhood in the works of German female dramatists: 1892–1918. PhD Johns Hopkins U. 1971.

NUSSBAUM,L.K. *3323*
The image of woman in the work of Bertolt Brecht. PhD U. of Washington, 1977.

OLSON,S.K. *3324*
Aspects of personality in marriage: connubiality in the epic works of Hartmann von Aue. PhD U. of Texas at Austin, 1982.

PAUL SELL,P.M.R. *3325*
The relationship of 'Young Germany' to questions of women's rights. PhD U. of Michigan, 1976.

PEKARY,C.H. *3326*
The feminist movement in Germany as reflected in the contemporary novels of German women. PhD Cornell U. 1925.

PLACE,M.E. *3327*
The characterization of women in the plays of Frank Wedekind. PhD Vanderbilt U. 1977.

POTASH,G.S. *3328*
Die Wandlungen des Frauenbildes in der Lyrik Heinrich Heines. PhD U. of Illinois at Urbana-Champaign, 1980.

PRANDI,J.D. *3329*
Spirited women heroes of the *Goethezeit*: women protagonists in the dramas of Goethe, Schiller and Kleist. PhD U. of California, Berkeley, 1981.

REMYS ,E. *3330*
Hermann Hesse's *Das Glasperlenspiel*: a concealed defence of the mother world. PhD U. of Cincinnati, 1975.

RESNIK,B. *3331*
The role of women in Jakob Julius David's *Novellen*. PhD U. of Southern California, 1972.

RITCHIE,G.M.F. *3331a*
Caroline Schlegel-Schelling im biographischen Roman. PhD U. of Michigan, 1965.

RODNER,F.A. *3332*
Women in Gotthelf's short stories. PhD Harvard U. 1976.

ROSE,I.B. *3333*
Social stereotypes and female actualities: a dimension of the social criticism in selected works by Fontane, Hauptmann, Wedekind, and Schnitzler. PhD Princeton U. 1976.

ROSS ,C.J. *3334*
Schiller and Hebbel: characters and ideas and the portrayal of women. PhD U. of Toronto, 1974.

ROWE,M.L. *3335*
A typology of women characters in the German naturalist novel. PhD Rice U. 1981.

SANDERS,R.H. *3336*
The virtuous woman in the comedies of the early Germany enlightenment. PhD State U. of New York at Stony Brook, 1975.

SCHECK,I.E. *3337*
Die Isolation der Frau in der zeitgenossischen deutschen Prosa. PhD U. of Oregon, 1982.

SCHMIDT,W.E. *3338*
The changing role of women in the works of Arthur Schnitzler. PhD U. of Wisconsin, 1973.

SCHNECK,E.H. *3339*
Goethe's attitude toward women in his utterances after 1800. PhD U. of Wisconsin, 1934.

SCHREIBER,S.E. *3340*
The German woman in the age of enlightenment: a study in the drama from Gottsched to Lessing. PhD Columbia U. 1949.

SCHWEIZER,E.J. *3341*
Woman in North Germanic heroic legend. PhD Yale U. 1965.

SCOTT,A.G. *3342*
Goethe's Zuleika, Marianne von Willemer and her world. PhD Columbia U. 1954.

SEITZ,J. *3343*
Die Frau und ihre Stellung im Werk Johann Beers. PhD U. of Minnesota, 1971.

SHEERAN,J.G. *3344*
Women and the freedom-to-be in selected works of Schiller and the romantics. PhD U. of Minnesota, 1976.

STEEL,J.C. *3345*
Female characters and their functions in the works of Wolfram von Eschenbach. MSc U. of Wales (Cardiff), 1977.

STERLING,S.B. *3346*
Witty heroines and lovely victims: changing ideals of femininity in eighteenth century German drama. PhD U. of California, Berkeley, 1975.

TEUSCHER,G. *3347*
Frauengestalten in Grimmelhausens *Vogelnest* I and II. PhD State U. of New York at Buffalo, 1975.

THEURER,W. *3348*
Heinrich Mann and the 'femme fatale'. PhD Columbia U. 1976.

THORNTON,H.L.H. *3349*
The situation of women in Gerhart Hauptmann's early naturalistic works. PhD Vanderbilt U. 1981.

TUBACH,S.P. *3350*
Female homoeroticism in German literature and culture. PhD U. of California, Berkeley, 1980.

VANOVITCH,K.A.L. *3351*
Female roles in East German drama, 1949–1977. PhD U. of Cambridge, 1981.

WARD,D.C. *3353*
The two Marys: a study of the women in Hermann Hesse's fiction. PhD Columbia U. 1976.

WEIERHEUS ER,W.J. *3354*
The mother in the life and works of Hebbel. PhD U. of Iowa, 1955.

WERNER,O.H. *3355*
The unmarried mother in German literature with special reference to the period 1770–1800. PhD Columbia U. 1917.

YATES,D. *3356*
Grillparzer and his early tragic heroines: Sappho, Medea, Hero. MA U. of Birmingham, 1925.

ZIVERS,I.M. *3357*
Undine: tradition and interpretation of an archetypal figure in German literature. PhD Rutgers U. 1974.

Individual writers

Ilse Aichinger

FLEMING ,M.E. *3358*
Ilse Aichinger: 'Die Sicht der Entfremdung' – ein Versuch, die symbolik Ihres Werkes von dessen Gesamtstruktur her zu erschliessen. PhD U. of Maryland, 1974.

Bettina von Arnim

MALONE,M.I. *3359*
Bettina von Arnim. MA National U. of Ireland, 1924.

WALDSTEIN,E.J. *3360*
Bettina von Arnim and the literary salon: women's participation in the cultural life of early nineteenth century Germany. PhD U. of Washington, 1982.

Louise Aston-Meier

CARICO,M.E. *3361*
The life and works of Louise Aston-Meier. PhD U. of Tennessee, 1977.

Charlotte Birch-Pfeiffer

EVANS,C.A. *3362*
Charlotte Birch-Pfeiffer: dramatist. PhD Cornell U. 1982.

Lily Braun

SAUERLANDER,A.M. *3363*
Lily Braun: a study of her personality, her socialistic and literary acitivity and an estimate of her place in German literature. PhD Cornell U. 1936.

Hilde Domin

STERN,D.C. *3364*
Hilde Domin: from exile to ideal. PhD Indiana U. 1977.

Annette von Droste-Hülshoff

GENSCH,H.M. *3365*
Versuch einer statistischen Stilanalyse von Gedichten der Annette von Droste-Hülshoff. PhD U. of Cincinatti, 1967.

LOBDEU,W.Y. *3366*
The animal world of Annette von Droste-Hülshoff. PhD Vanderbilt U. 1968.

MATTHEWS,E. *3367*
Women writers in Germany in the beginning of the nineteenth century, with special reference to Annette von Droste-Hülshoff. MA U. of Wales, 1925.

MILLER,J.W. *3368*
Poetic strategy and metaphorical structure: a study of Annette von Droste-Hülshoff's *Geistliches Jahr*. PhD Vanderbilt U. 1965.

MORGAN,M.E. *3369*
Annette von Droste-Hülshoff: a woman of letters in a period of transition. PhD U. of London, Birkbeck Coll. 1978.

SMITH,L.von Z. *3369a*
Nature in the works of Annette von Droste-Hülshoff. U. of London, University Coll. 1932.

TUSKEN,L.W. *3370*
Annette von Droste-Hülshoff's *Die Judenbuche*: a new study of its background. PhD Columbia U. 1966.

Marie von Ebner-Eschenbach

DOYLE,M.R. *3371*
Catholic atmosphere in Marie von Ebner-Eschenbach. PhD Catholic U. of America, 1936.

KHAWAJA,R. *3372*
The treatment of love and marriage in the prose fiction of Marie von Ebner-Eschenbach. MA U. of Exeter, 1974.

LLOYD,D.E.S. *3373*
A woman looks at man: the male psyche as depicted in the works of Marie von Ebner-Eschenbach. PhD U. of Pennsylvania, 1969.

Luise Gottsched

RICHEL,V.C. *3374*
Luise Gottsched: a reconsideration. PhD Yale U. 1968.

Catharina Regina von Greiffenberg

SLOCUM,M.K. *3375*
Untersuchungen zu Lob und Spiel in den *Sonnetten* der Catharina Regina von Greiffenberg. PhD Cornell U. 1970.

Hildegard of Bingen

NEWMAN,B.J. *3376*
O Feminea Forma: god and woman in the works of St Hildegard 1098–1179. PhD Yale U. 1981.

Anna Owena Hoyers

ROE,A.B. *3377*
Anna Owena Hoyers, a poetess of the seventeenth century. PhD Bryn Mawr Coll., 1915.

Hrotsvitha

BUTLER,M.M. 3378
Hrotsvitha: the theatricality of her plays. [10th-century nun of Gandersheim.] PhD U. of Michigan, 1959.

Ricarda Huch

BERNSTEIN,J. 3379
Bewusstwedung in Romanwerk der Ricarda Huch. PhD Case Western Reserve U. 1973.

FRANK,M.H. 3380
Ricarda Huch and the German women's movement. PhD New York U. 1977.

RUSSELL,R.J. 3381
Ricarda Huch and E.G. Kolbenheyer as historical novelists: a contribution to the problem of the development of the historical novel in Germany. MA U. of London, University Coll. 1937.

SEADLE,I.P.C. 3382
The role of nature in Ricarda Huch's creative prose works. PhD U. of Michigan, 1965.

Marie Luise Kaschnitz

ELLIOTT,J.L.C. 3383
Character transformation through point of view in selected short stories of Marie Luise Kaschnitz. PhD Vanderbilt U. 1973.

Elizabeth Langgässer

BEHRENDT,J.E. 3384
Die Einheit von Elizabeth Langgässers Weltbild in der markischen Argonauten fahrt. PhD Ohio State U. 1963.

BREARLEY,M.B. 3385
The image of childhood in the novels of Elizabeth Langgässer. PhD U. of Connecticut, 1982.

RENER,F.M. 3386
Man in the thought of Elizabeth Langgässer. PhD U. of Toronto, 1958.

TERHAAR,J.A.A. 3387
The concept of nature in Elizabeth Langgässer's *Das unausloeschliche Siegel*. PhD U. of Iowa, 1957.

Else Lasker-Schüler

BERG,H.R. 3388
The child faces crisis: a study of thematic relationships in the early poety of Else Lasker-Schüler and in the *Menschheitdämmerang* anthology. PhD U. of Chicago, 1974.

COHN,H.W. 3389
The 'broken world' of Else Lasker-Schüler. PhD U. of London, External 1966.

CURTIS,J.E. 3390
Else Lasker-Schüler's drama *Dark river*; a translation into English and a critical commentary. PhD Catholic U. of America, 1982.

KLUSENER, E.A. 3391
Else Lasker-Schüler: eine Biographie oder ein Werk? PhD Washington U. 1979.

MACHT,R.M. 3392
Motifs of Judaic mysticism in the poetry of Else Lasker-Schüler. PhD Indiana U. 1968.

SULL,Y.S. 3393
Die lyrik Else Lasker-Schülers stilelemente und themenkreise. PhD George Washington U. 1980.

ZIMMERMANN,I.M.E. 3394
Der Mensch im Spiegel des tierbildes Untersuchungen zum Werk Else Lasker-Schülers. PhD U. of Kansas, 1980.

Christine Lavant

BLAIR,B.M. 3395
Die Sprachfigur in der Lyrik Christine Lavants: der Pfauenschrei-die Bettlerschale-Spindel in Mond. PhD Rutgers U. 1981.

Gertrud von le Fort

BAECKER,A.F. 3396
The treatment of history in the works of Gertrud von le Fort. PhD U. of Cincinnati, 1956.

FIHN,J.A. 3397
An analysis of character types in the narratives of Gertrud von le Fort. PhD U. of Michigan, 1954.

HILTON,I. 3398
Gertrud von le Fort: a Christian writer. PhD U. of Southampton, 1962.

HUFMAN,D.M. 3399
Aspects of 'caritas' in the prose narratives of Gertrud von le Fort. PhD New York U. 1956.

NETT,M.L.E. 3400
Dimensions of love in the narrative works of Gertrud von le Fort. PhD U. of Colorado, 1966.

O'BOYLES,M.I. 3401
Gertrude von le Fort: a critical study. BLitt U. of Oxford, 1962.

Mechthild von Magdeburg

FRANKLIN,J.C. 3402
Love and transition: water and the imagery of liquids in the work of Mechthild von Magdeburg. PhD Case Western Reserve U. 1972.

Emil Marriot

BYRNES,J.F. 3403
The short fiction of Emil Marriot. [Pseudonym of Emile Mataja.] PhD Johns Hopkins U. 1977.

Agnes Miegel

FUHRIG,A.M. *3404*
Die Sprachgestaltung in der erzühlerden Prosa Agnes Miegels: eine Strunturanalipe. PhD Michigan State U. 1972.

Gabriel e Reuter

SCHNEIDER,G.A. *3405*
Portraits of women in selected novels by Gabriele Reuter. PhD Syracuse U. 1982.

Luise Rinser

LEE,E. *3406*
The idea of humanity in the short stories of Luise Rinser. PhD Vanderbilt U. 1974.

Sibylle Schwarz

ZIEFLE,H.W. *3408*
Sibylle Schwarz: Leben und Werk. PhD U. of Illinois at Urbana-Champaign, 1973.

Anna Seghers

ALWARD,K.V. *3409*
Anna Seghers and socialist realism. PhD McGill U. 1972.

KALEYIAS,G.P. *3410*
Reflections of history: the stories of Anna Seghers in Weimar Germany and in exile, 1924–1947. PhD U. of Maryland, 1981.

KOPPY,I.M. *3411*
Anna Seghers and her works in the context of socialist realism. PhD Florida State U. 1973.

LABAHN,K.J. *3412*
Anna Seghers' exile literature: the Mexican years (1941–1947). PhD U. of Washington, 1983.

Ina Seidel

FOULGER,L.E. *3413*
The prose works of Ina Seidel. PhD U. of Leeds, 1970.

MCKITTRICK,M. *3414*
Woman in the work and thought of Ina Seidel. PhD U. of Wisconsin, 1938.

Regina Ullman

STEPHENS,D.S. *3415*
Regina Ullman: biography, literary reception, interpretation. PhD U. of Texas at Austin, 1980.

Clara Viebig

CARPENTER,V.W. *3416*
A study of Clara Viebig's *Novellea*. PhD U. of Pennsylvania, 1978.

DEDNER,D.S. *3417*
From infanticide to single motherhood: the evolution of a literary theme as reflected in the works of Clara Viebig. PhD Indiana U. 1979.

Martin a Wied

BERRY,J.L. *3418*
Martina Wied: Austrian novelist, 1882–1957. PhD Vanderbilt U. 1966.

Gabrielle Wohmann

MORRIS-FARBER,N. *3420*
Critical reception of the works of Gabrielle Wohmann in West Germany, Switzerland and Austria. PhD New York U. 1979.

Christa Wolf

DRIVER,M.K.M. *3421*
De Omnibus dubitandum: zur burgerlichen und Marxistischen Rezeption von Christa Wolfs Roman *Der geteilte Himmel* 1963–1978. PhD Rutgers U. 1980.

KINGSBURY,A.V.M. *3422*
The writings of Christa Wolf: from objective to subjective authenticity. PhD Michigan State U. 1981.

Sidonia Hedwig Zäunemann

DE BERDT,A.J.J. *3423*
Sidonia Hedwig Zäunemann: poet laureate and emancipated woman 1714–1740. PhD U. of Tennesse, 1977.

Hebrew literature

AL-DAUSARI,A.M.A. *3424*
The woman as portrayed in modern Hebrew literature in Mapu and Mendele. MPhil U. of London, Sch. of Oriental and African Studies, 1980.

Islamic and Arabic literature

STERN,G.H. *3425*
The life and social conditions of women in the primitive Islamic community as depicted in the eighth volume of Ibn Sa'd's *Tabaqat al Kubra* and the sixth volume of Ibn Hanbal's *Musnad*. PhD U. of London, Sch. of Oriental and African Studies, 1937.

TIBI,A. *3426*
A study of Al-Ma'âfici's biography of famous women in early Islam. DPhil U. of Oxford, 1975.

ZEIDAN,J.T. *3427*
Women novelists in modern Arabic literature. PhD U. of California, Berkeley, 1982.

ZERBE,E .A. *3428*
Veil of shame: role of women in the modern fiction of North Africa and the Arab world. PhD Indiana U. 1974.

Italian literature

See also above 1421.

BIELLOCH,P. *3429*
A thematic study of Italian contemporary women writers. PhD Rutgers U. 1982.

BOYERS,W.H. *3430*
The ladies of Dante's *Rime*. PhD U. of Chicago, 1929.

FAHI,C.F. *3432*
The intellectual status of women in Italy in the late sixteenth century, with special reference to treatises on women and the position of women in literary academies. PhD U. of Manchester, 1964.

GAMBACORTA,F. M. *3433*
The Dantean *figura* of Matelda: a new interpretation. PhD Rutgers U. 1970.

MAXFIELD,C.M. *3434*
Valorose donne: the emerging woman in the nineteenth century Italian novel. PhD Cornell U. 1977.

MOTT,L.F. *3435*
The system of courtly love; studied as an introduction to the *Vita nuova* of Dante. PhD Columbia U. 1896.

O'HEALY,A.M . *3436*
A woman writer in contemporary Italy: Natalia Ginzburg. PhD U. of Wisconsin-Madison, 1976.

PICCHIONE,L. *3437*
The complexities of the naîf element in Natalia Ginzburg's works. PhD U. of Toronto, 1976.

SATIN,J.H. *3438*
Gaspara Stampa. PhD Columbia U. 1952.

SHAPIRO,M.G. *3439*
Woman, earthly and divine, in the *Comedy* of Dante. PhD Columbia U. 1968.

SICILIANO,E.A. *3440*
The modern woman in the novels of Neera. PhD Harvard U. 1946.

WILBANKS,E.R. *3441*
The changing images of women in the works of Petrarch, Boccaccio, Alberti and Catiglione. PhD U. of Chicago, 1977.

Latin American and Caribbean literature

General and comparative studies

BIRKEMOE,D.S. *3442*
Contemporary women novelists of Argentina 1945–1967. PhD U. of Illinois at Urbana-Champaign, 1968.

CLASS,B.M. *3443*
Fictional treatment of politics by Argentine female novelists. PhD U. of New Mexico, 1974.

DIAZ,G.J. *3444*
Images of the heroine: development of the female character in the novels of Beatriz Guido, Marta Lynch and Syria Poletti. PhD U. of Texas at Austin, 1981.

GANTT,B.N. *3444a*
The women of Macondo: feminine archetypes in García Márquez *Cien años de soledad*. PhD Florida State U. 1977.

GARFINKEL,L.G. *3444b*
La imagen de la madre ausente en la poseía de Césur Vallejo. PhD Stanford U. 1972.

HANDELSMAN,M.H. *3445*
Amazons and artists: a study of Ecuadorian women's prose. PhD U. of Florida, 1976.

JACK SON,M.G. *3446*
The roles and portrayal of women in selected prose works by six female writers of Peru. PhD U. of Kentucky, 1982.

LATORTUE,R.A. *3447*
The woman in the Haitian novel. PhD Yale U. 1982.

LOUSTAUNAU,M.O. *3448*
Mexico's contemporary women novelists. PhD U. of New Mexico, 1973.

OHARA,M.C. *3449*
La heroina en Jesus Lara. PhD U. of Washington, 1981.

PACIFICO,P. *3450*
El nino y el adolescente en la narrativa femenina de la Argentina. PhD U. of Puerto Rico, Rio Piedras, 1976.

PERCAS,M. *3451*
Women poets of Argentina (1810–1950). PhD Columbia U. 1951.

RODRIGUEZ,M.C. *3452*
The role of women in Caribbean prose fiction. PhD City U. of New York, 1979.

ROSENBAUM,S.C. *3453*
Modern woman poets of Spanish America: the precursors – Delmira Agustini, Gabrielea Mistral, Alfonsina Storni, Juana de Ibarbourou. PhD Columbia U. 1946.

SALDIVAR,S.G. 3454
El desarrollo del personaje femenino en la novela mexicana contemporanen: Azuela, Yanez y Fuentes. PhD New York U. 1978.

SHAW,L.R. 3455
The feminine principle in a masculine world: a study of contemporary Argentine fiction by women writers, 1950–1970. PhD U. of Tennessee, 1978.

THORPE,M.R. 3456
The image of the women in West Indian fiction. PhD Queen's U. at Kingston, 1976.

WALLIS,M.P. 3457
Modern women poets of Brazil. PhD U. of New Mexico, 1947.

YOUNG,R.B.S. 3458
Six representative women novelists of Mexico 1960–1969. PhD U. of Illinois at Urbana-Champaign, 1975.

Individual writers

Delmira Agustini

EAST,L.K.D. 3459
The imaginary voyage: evolution of the poetry of Delmira Agustini. PhD Stanford U. 1981.

STEPHENS,D.T. 3460
Delmira Agustini and the quest for transcendence. PhD U. of Tennessee, 1974.

TARQUINIO,L. T. 3461
A poesía de Delmira Agustini. PhD Stanford U. 1968.

Gertrudis Goméz de Avellaneda

PINERA,E.A. 3462
El teatro romántico de Gertrudis Goméz de Avellaneda. PhD New York U. 1974.

ROSELLÓ,A.J. 3463
La poesía lírica de Gertrudis Goméz de Avellaneda. PhD U. of Southern California, 1973.

María Luisa Bombal

AGOSIN,M.S. 3464
Las protagonistas en la narrativa de María Luisa Bombal. PhD Indiana U. 1982.

LIRA,G.G. 3465
María Luisa Bombal: realidad y fantasia. PhD U. of California, Los Angeles, 1981.

SERROS,R. 3466
La felicidad vista atraves del amor: la soledad y la muerte en la obra literaria de María Luisa Bombal. PhD U. of Southern California, 1971.

Silvina Bullrich

FROUMAN-SMITH,E.M. 3467
Female roles in the fiction of Silvina Bullrich. PhD U. of New Mexico, 1979.

TUSA,B.M. 3468
The works of Silvina Bullrich. PhD Tulane U. 1972.

Rosario Castellanos

PARHAM,M.H. 3469
Alienation in the fiction of Rosario Castellanos. PhD U. of California, Los Angeles, 1979.

REBOLLEDO,T.D. 3470
The wind and the tree: a structural analysis of the poetry of Rosario Castellanos. PhD U. of Arizona, 1979.

ROBINSON,G.A.StJ. 3471
Indigenism and feminism in the prose fiction of Rosario Castellanos. PhD Louisiana State U. 1981.

ROMAN-LOPEZ,A.N. 3472
Conflicto cultural y existencial en *Oficio de Tinieblas* de Rosario Castellanos. PhD Tulane U. 1982.

SCHERR,R.L. 3473
A voice against silence: feminist poetics in the early work of Rosario Castellanos. PhD U. of California, Berkeley, 1979.

WASHINGTON,T. 3474
The narrative works of Rosario Castellanos: in search of history in confrontations with myth. PhD U. of Minnesota, 1982.

Madre Castillo

ANTONI,C.G. 3475
A comparative examination of style in the works of Madre Castillo. [Nun of the Order of St Clare 1671–1742.] PhD City U. of New York, 1979.

Sor Juana Ines de la Cruz

CATALA,R.E. 3476
Syncretism in the Latin American baroque and its expression in the works of Juana Ines de la Cruz. PhD New York U. 1982.

DANIEL,L.A . 3477
A 'Terra incognita': Sor Juana's theatre. PhD Texas Tech U. 1979.

PÉREZ,M.E. 3478
Lo Americano en el teatro de Sor Juana Ines de la Cruz. PhD New York U. 1972.

SABAT DE GUERNICA,G. 3479
El *Primero Sueño* de Sor Juana Ines de la Cruz: tradicuones literarias y originalidad. PhD Johns Hopkins U. 1968.

Griselda Gambario

KISS,M.F. *3480*
The labyrinth of cruelty: a study of selected works of Griselda Gambario. PhD Rutgers U. 1982.

MCALEER,J.K. *3481*
Contradictory semantics of verbal and non-verbal language in the theatre of Griselda Gambario. PhD U. of Wisconsin-Madison, 1982.

Carmen Gándara

DE RODRÍGVEZ,C.R.S. *3482*
Carmen Gándara: pensamiento temática, y estilo. PhD U. of Oklahoma, 1975.

Elena Garro

PARR,C.S. *3483*
Narrative technique in the prose fiction of Elena Garro. PhD U. of Southern California, 1978.

Beatriz Guido

GIBSON,C.M . *3484*
Cinematic technique in the prose fiction of Beatriz Guido. PhD Michigan State U. 1974.

Luisa Josefina Hernandez

BRANN,S.J. *3485*
El teatro y las novelas de Luisa Josefina Hermandez. PhD U. of Illinois at Urbana-Champaign, 1969.

KNOWLES,J.K. *3486*
Luisa Josefina Hernandez: a study of her dramatic theory and practice. PhD Rutgers U. 1970.

Carmen Lira

CANTILLANO,O.A. *3487*
Carmen Lira y los *Cuentos: de mi tía Panchita*: aspectus folklóricos, literarias, y lingüísticas. PhD U. of Arizona, 1972.

Marta Lynch

BENNETT,B.L. *3488*
Narrative structure in the novels of Marta Lynch. PhD U. of California, Davis, 1981.

KAMINSKY,A.S.K. *3489*
Marta Lynch: the expanding political consciousness of an Argentine woman writer. PhD Pennsylvania State U. 1975.

MOSIER,M.P. *3490*
An ideological study of the novels of Marta Lynch, 1962–1974. PhD U. of Wisconsin-Madison, 1979.

Cecilia Meireles

IGEL,R. *3491*
O terra da morte na poesía de Cecilia Meireles. PhD U. of New Mexico, 1973.

Gabriela Mistral

CAIMANO,E.M. *3492*
'Mysticism' in Gabriela Mistral – a clarification. PhD St John's U. 1967.

GAZARIAN,M.L. *3493*
The prose of Gabriela Mistral: an expression of her life and personality. PhD Columbia U. 1967.

HERNANDEZ,M.F.B. *3494*
Gabriela Mistral and the standards of American criticism. PhD U. of New Mexico, 1964.

Alfonsina Storni

TITIEV,J.T.G. *3495*
A critical approach to the poetry of Alfonsina Storni. PhD U. of Michigan, 1972.

Elizabeth Borton de Trevino

VICKERS,P.S. *3496*
Mexico in the works of Elizabeth Borton de Trevino. PhD Texas Tech. U. 1972.

Clorinda Matto de Turner

DE MELLO,G. *3497*
The writings of Clorinda Matto de Turner. PhD U. of Colorado, 1968.

Concha Urquiza

WILMOT,E.B. *3498*
Pensamiento y poesía de Concha Urquiza. PhD U. of Southern California, 1968.

Russian, Turkish and East European literature

ADLER,R. *3499*
The image of woman in the works of Y.L. Peretz: a sociopsychological study. PhD New York U. 1974.

AWDZIEWICZ,M.C. *3500*
The compositional techniques of Anna Nikolaevna Korol'kova: a study of repetition. PhD Brown U. 1975.

BAUER,N.C. *3501*
V.F. Panova: a study of conflicting ethics in post-war Soviet society. MA U. of Liverpool, 1974.

BENSON,R.C. *3502*
The ideal and the erotic: Tolstoy's heroines in love and marriage. PhD Yale U. 1969.

BROWNING,B.J. *3503*
The portrayal of women in modern Turkish literature. MA U. of Durham, 1981.

CHRISTENSEN,J. A. *3504*
The shaping of the Russian philosophical heroine: feminine images of beauty in Russian philosophical aesthetics and the heroines of Nikolai Gogol. PhD U. of California, Berkeley, 1978.

CLYMAN,T.W. *3505*
Women in Chekhov's prose works. PhD New York U. 1971.

COOPER,H.R. *3506*
Tasso's women: the Slavic literary epic. PhD Columbia U. 1974.

DOINSETT,C.F. *3507*
A study in conceptual and expressive spontaneity: the prose of Mariana Ivanovna Tsvetaeva. MPhil U. of Essex, 1981.

DRIVER,S.N. *3508*
The poetry of Anna Axmatova, 1912–1922. PhD Columbia U. 1967.

GREEDAN,R.C. *3509*
Mirra Lokhvitskaia's 'duality' as a 'romantic confict' and its reflection in her poetry. PhD U. of Pittsburgh, 1982.

HARTMAN,C.F. *3510*
Weather, water, light and Sophia in the poetry of V.S. Solov'ev. PhD U. of Pennsylvania, 1972.

HAIGHT,A.V. *3511*
Anna Akhmatova: life and work. PhD U. of London, Sch. of Slavonic and East European Studies, 1972.

HASTY,O.P. *3512*
Marina Cvetaeva's encounter with Rainer Maria Rilke. PhD Yale U. 1980.

KARLINSKY,S. *3513*
Marina Cvetaeva; her life and art. PhD U. of California, Berkeley, 1964.

KESARCODI-WATSON,I. *3514*
F.M. Dostoevsky's soteriology related to some female types in his fiction. PhD Northwestern U. 1978.

KING,J.M. *3515*
Marina Cvetaeva's mythobiographical childhood: an analysis of four late prose works. PhD Harvard U. 1978.

KLIMOV,A. *3516*
Three faces of Russian Acmeism: Gamilev, Axmatova, and Mandel'stam. PhD New York U. 1973.

KOLODZIEJ,J.S. *3517*
Eliza Orzeszkowa's feminist and Jewish works in Polish and Russian criticism. PhD Indiana U. 1975.

KOSACHOV,N. *3518*
Literary and related art: biography by Marietta Shaginian. PhD U. of Ottowa, 1973.

LLEWELL YN SMITH,V. *3519*
Women in Chekhov's work and life. DPhil U. of Oxford, 1970.

LONGMIRE,R.A. *3520*
Princess Dashkova and the intellectual life of eighteenth century Russia. MA U. of London, Sch. of Slavonic and East European Studies, 1955.

MCCORMACK,K.L. *3521*
Images of women in the poetry of Zinaida Gippius. PhD Vanderbilt U. 1982.

MAY,S.R. *3522*
The image of rural woman in contemporary Soviet prose. MLitt U. of Oxford, 1983.

MOODY,C. *3523*
Vera Panova and her Soviet critics. MA U. of Leeds, 1962.

SENDICH,M. *3524*
The life and works of Karolina Pavlova. PhD New York U. 1968.

TAUBMA N,J.A. *3525*
'Between letter and lyric': the epistolary poetic friendships of Marina Cvetaeva. PhD Yale U. 1972.

TROUPIN,M.A. *3526*
Marina Cvetaeva's *Remeslo*: a commentary. PhD Harvard U. 1974.

TUMAS-RICHTER,E.A. *3527*
A comparative analysis of women characters in *The Quiet Don* by M. Sholokhov and *The peasants* by W. Reymont. PhD U. of Colorado at Boulder, 1977.

VITINS,I. *3528*
Escape from earth: a study of the four elements and their associations in Marina Cvetaeva's work. PhD U. of California, Berkeley, 1974.

WILSON,N.L. *3529*
Women in Goncharov's fiction. PhD U. of Alberta, 1981.

Scandinavian and Icelandic literature

General and comparative studies

ASMUNDSSON,D.R. *3530*
Fredrika Bremer in England. PhD Columbia U. 1964.

BALI CE,V.J. *3531*
A study of the female as wife and mother in Ibsen's dramas. PhD Purdue U. 1971.

SVERRE,T.B. *3532*
Mothers and daughters as portrayed by Nor-

wegian women writers from 1854 to the present. PhD U. of Texas at Austin, 1981.

YEH,S.L.S. 3533
The portrayal of women in the Icelandic family sagas. PhD U. of Iowa, 1974.

Individual writers

Isak Dinesen

DESIMONE,S.C. 3534
Alpenglow: Isak Dinesen and the sense of history. PhD U. of Kentucky, 1977.

JAMES,S.V. 3535
Caged birds . . . and free: women in the works of Isak Dinesen. PhD State U. of New York at Buffalo, 1978.

NORRIS,C.L. 3536
Literary allusion in the tales of Isak Dinesen. PhD U. of California, San Diego, 1982.

WHISSEN,T.R. 3537
Isak Dinesen as critic: a study of the critical principles contained in her major works. PhD U. of Cincinnati, 1969.

Amalie Skram

CRENSON-JONES,M.J.V. *3537a*
Amalie Skram: life and works: a study in disillusionment. PhD U. of Cambridge, 1977.

Sigrid Undset

DUNN,M.M. 3538
Sigrid Undset's novels: cycles of religious conversion. PhD Fordham U. 1966.

KELLY,R.P. 3539
Sigrid Undset: her spiritual development as revealed in her novels. PhD St John's U. 1956.

Spanish and Portuguese literature

General and comparative studies

AGUIRRE,A.M. 3540
El personaje femenino en el teatro de Manuel y Antonio Machado. PhD Stanford U. 1968.

ALVAREZ,E.D. 3541
La obra de Ramón Sender: (estudio de los personajes femeninos). PhD Michigan State U. 1971.

BUSCH,C.L. 3542
Women in the novels of Unamuno. PhD U. of Maryland, 1965.

CARTER,M.R. 3543
The image of woman in selected plays of Jacinto Benavente y Martínez. PhD Saint Louis U. 1965.

CATRON,D.L. 3544
Saint Mary Magdalene in Spanish and Portuguese literature of the sixteenth and seventeenth centuries. PhD U. of Michigan, 1972.

CHEW,J.M. 3545
The portrayal of feminine life in the novels of Fernán Caballero, Alarcón, Pereda, and Valera viewed against the background of woman's position in nineteenth-century Spain. PhD Pennsylvania State U. 1958.

COLECCHIA,F.M. 3546
The treatment of woman in the theater of Federico García Lorca. PhD U. of Pittsburgh, 1954.

CONTRERAS,M. 3547
'Two interpreters of Galicia': Rosalia de Castro and Emilia Pardo Bazàn. PhD U. of Pittsburgh, 1960.

DASH,A.E. 3548
Un estudio de algunos personajes femeninos en el teatro de Jacinto Benavente y Martínez. PhD Middlebury Coll. 1964.

DAVIS,M.S. 3549
Proyecoines estilisticas en los personajes femeninos de Jose Cid. PhD Purdue U. 1979.

DAVIS,W.R. 3550
The role of the Virgin in the *Cantigas de Santa Maria*. PhD U. of Kentucky, 1969.

DAVISON,D.D. 3551
The role of the woman in Miguel Mihura's plays. PhD Florida State U. 1974.

DELBUSTO,M. 3552
La mujer liberada en la obra de Galdó's. PhD U. of Miami, 1974.

DI MAIO,C. 3553
Antifeminism in selected works of Ernique Jardiel Poncela. PhD Michigan State U. 1974.

DODSON,R .G. 3554
The Marian legend in the religious theater of Tirso de Molina. PhD U. of Southern California, 1969.

DOYAGA,E. 3555
La mujer en los ensayos de Unamuno. PhD New York U. 1967.

FRIESNER,E.M. 3556
The mirror of Queens: the queen in the theatre of Lope de Vega. PhD Yale U. 1977.

GREENBER G,I.F. 3559
The woman of the *romance viejo novelesco*: her presentation and purpose. PhD U. of California, Los Angeles, 1982.

GUERRINI,M.C. 3560
Galdós and nineteenth-century Spanish feminism: women and marriage in the *Novelas contemporáneas* (1881–1915). PhD U. of Pennsylvania, 1978.

HADJOPOULOS,T.M. *3561*
Four women novelists of postwar Spain: Matute, Laforet, Quiroga and Medio. PhD Columbia U. 1974.

HEALEY,A.V. *3562*
Spanish women novelists of the post-war era. MA National U. of Ireland, 1968.

HEATHCOTE,A.A . *3563*
The portrayal of women characters in the religious plays of Tirso de Molina. MA U. of Manchester, 1956.

HELLER,S.R. *3564*
The characterization of the Virgin Mary in four thirteenth-century narrative collections of miracles: Jacobus de Voragine's *Legenda Aurea,* Gonzalo de Berceo's *Milagros de Nuestra Señora,* Gautier de Coinci's *Miracles de Nostre Dame,* and Alfonso el Sabio's *Cantigas de Santa Maria.* PhD New York U. 1975.

HETAK,W .D. *3565*
The eulogy of the lady in the early poetry of the *Cancionero de Baena.* PhD Case Western Reserve U. 1971.

KELLEY,L.M. *3566*
An analysis of the development of the feminine image in selected novels by Machado de Assis. PhD Saint Louis U. 1978.

KOROS,C.M.S. *3567*
The image of the woman in nonfiction and the 'Comedia' during the Golden Age in Spain. PhD U. of Pennsylvania, 1973.

KUZMA,M.K. *3568*
The feminine literary figures in the works of the Marqués de Santillana. PhD Case Western Reserve U. 1977.

LAHR-WELL,A.M. *3569*
The Don Juan and feminist myths in Unamuno: a struggle towards consciousness. PhD Saint Louis U. 1975.

LAMONTE,R.S. *3570*
The characterization of woman in the novels of Pío Baroja. PhD Columbia U. 1974.

LANGSTON,C.A.L. *3571*
Female primary characters in several of Blasco's Valencian novels. PhD Louisiana State U. 1979.

LEBREDO,G.G. *3572*
Fermin de Pas y Ana Ozores en *La Regenta.* PhD Florida State U. 1970.

LEE,A .A. *3573*
Portrait of Lozana: the lusty Andalusian woman by Francisco Delicado; translated, introduction and notes. PhD U. of South Carolina, 1979.

LINDSAY,M.B. *3574*
Socio- psychological characterization of women in selected novels by Benito Pérez Galdós. PhD U. of Illinois at Urbana-Champaign, 1979.

LOPEZ ,D. *3575*
The portrayal of women in the theatre of Alejandro Casona. PhD U. of Toronto, 1981.

LUNDELIUS,M.R. *3576*
The *Mujer varonil* in the theater of the siglo de oro. PhD U. of Pennsylvania, 1969.

MCKEGNEY,J.C. *3577*
Female characters in the novels of José Rubén Romero and Gregorio López y Fuentes a comparative study. PhD U. of Washington, 1959.

MANDEL,A.S. *3578*
A thematic survey of La Celestina studies 1824–1968. PhD U. of California, Los Angeles, 1970.

MARQUEZ,H.P. *3579*
La representation de les personajes femeninos en el Quijote. PhD U. of California, Riverside, 1979.

MARTÍNEZ,J.R. *3580*
Estudio de la mujer en las comedias novelescas auténticas y de fecha conocida de Lope de Vega entre 1600 y 1620. PhD Florida State U. 1971.

MARTINEZ,R.C. *3581*
La mujer en la obra de Leopoldo Alas. PhD U. of Virginia, 1971.

MERCER,L.E. *3582*
Martínez Sierra's conception of woman's role in modern society. PhD Ohio State U. 1941.

MOLHO,L.S. *3583*
The mother in the theatre of Jacinto Benavente. PhD Case Western Reserve U. 1963.

MONTERO-PAULSON,D. *3584*
La jerarquia femenina en la obra de Perez Galdós. PhD U. of Pennsylvania, 1981.

MORALES GALÁN,C. *3585*
El tema maternal ena l concepcion Unamunesca de la mujer. PhD Louisiana State U. 1971.

MOSLEY,M.K. *3586*
Women in fifteenth-century *cancioneros.* PhD U. of Missouri- Columbia, 1976.

NATAL,M.J.M. *3587*
Los años formativos del ciclo de la vida femenina: una aproximación antropológica en algunas obras de la narrativa española contemporánea. PhD U. of Florida, 1980.

NORRIS,N.A. *3588*
Personajes femeninos característicos de los escritores del noventayocho. PhD Indiana U. 1978.

O'CONNOR,P.W. *3589*
Women in the theatre of Gregorio Martínez Sierra. PhD U. of Florida, 1962.

ODD,F.L. *3590*
The women of the *romancero.* PhD U. of Colorado, 1974.

OKTABA,N.I. *3591*
Development of the female character in

nineteenth century Spanish drama. PhD U. of Toronto, 1982.

ORDONEZ,E.J. *3592*
Woman as protagonist and creator in the contemporary Spanish novel. PhD U. of California, Irvine, 1976.

ORSAG,S.A. *3593*
Galdós' presentation of women in the light of naturalism. PhD U. of Pittsburgh, 1971.

PATTERSON,M.S. *3594*
Woman-victim in the theater of Spanish women playwrights of the twentieth century. PhD U. of Kentucky, 1980.

PLATT,J. *3595*
The maternal theme in Garcia Lorca's four tragedies. PhD U. of Southern California, 1973.

POOLE,R.H. *3596*
Women in early Spanish literature with special emphasis on the women in the medieval Spanish ballad. PhD Stanford U. 1950.

RATCLIFFE,M.E. *3597*
The role of women in medieval Spanish history and epic literature: Jimena, wife of Rodrigo. PhD U. of Toronto, 1981.

ROCKWOOD,R.E. *3598*
Don Juan Manuel: his conception and consideration of women. PhD Harvard U. 1924.

RODRIGUEZ,F. *3599*
La mujer en la sociedad española en la novelística de Concha Aloś. PhD U. of Arizona, 1973.

RODRIGUEZ,L.M. *3600*
Women in twenty-five plays of Rojas Zorrilla. PhD U. of New Mexico, 1981.

RONQUILLO,P.J.de. *3601*
Hacia una definicia de la pícara del siglo XVII en España. PhD Louisiana State U. 1969.

SÁNCHEZ-DÍEZ,F.J. *3602*
La novela picaresca de protagonista femenino en España durante el siglo diez siete. PhD U. of North Carolina at Chapel Hill, 1972.

SCHNEIDER,J.F. *3603*
The image of women in selected Spanish Golden Age Byzantine romances. PhD U. of Georgia, 1978.

SCHOMBER,J.H. *3604*
Juan Luís Vives and women's liberalism. PhD Florida State U. 1975.

SIMS,E.N. *3605*
El anti feminismo en la literatura española hasta 1560. PhD Catholic U. of America, 1970.

SLOVER,L.E. *3606*
The three Marias: literary portrayals of the situation of women in Portugal. PhD Harvard U. 1977.

SPONSLER,L.A. *3607*
The presence of women in medieval Spanish poetry: the epic and lyric traditions. PhD Yale U. 1969.

STEFFEN,C.C. *3608*
Women in *Las siete partidas* of Alfonso X de Castilla y León. PhD U. of Texas at Austin, 1979.

STEVENS,L.E. *3609*
Feminine protagonists in Manuel Gálvez's novels. PhD Indiana U. 1964.

STOUT,E.T. *3610*
Women in the novels of Benito Pérez Galdós. PhD U. of New Mexico, 1951.

SZAUTNER,K.A.M. *3611*
The mystery of woman in the works of Blaise Cendrars. PhD Bryn Mawr Coll. 1970.

TORREYSON,D. *3612*
Woman in the Spanish comedia of the Golden Age. PhD U. of Pittsburgh, 1934.

TRACHMAN,S.E. *3613*
Cervantes' women of literary tradition. PhD Columbia U. 1932.

TURMAND,M.E. *3614*
Women and society in the nineteenth-century Spanish novel. PhD Yale U. 1974.

VALLUE,G. *3615*
Los personajes femeninos en los dramas de Cristobal de Virués. PhD Emory U. 1978.

WARD,M.I. *3616*
Themes of submission, dominance, independence and romantic love: the female figure in the post *avante-garde* plays of Miguel Mihura. PhD U. of Colorado, 1974.

WATTS,S. *3617*
Women in the novels of Galdós. MPhil U. of Leeds, 1976.

WOOD,C.N. *3618*
The mother image in selected works of Miguel de Unamuno. PhD U. of Virginia, 1975.

Individual writers

Julia de Burgos

QUIROGA,C .L. *3619*
Julia de Burgos: el desarrollo de la conciencia femenina en la expresión póetica. PhD New York U. 1980.

Rosalía de Castro

BARTA,J.B. *3620*
The traditional Peninsular lyric as reflected by Rosalía de Castro (affinities of subject and form in *Cantares gallegos, Follas novas*'. PhD U. of Minnesota, 1965.

FOSTER,G.R. 3621
Nature and emotion in Rosalía de Castro's *En las orillas del Sar*. PhD U. of Wisconsin-Madison, 1979.

GIBLIN,D.J. 3622
Rosalía de Castro and her vision of the world. MPhil U. of Leeds, 1976.

MAESTAS,M. L. 3623
Critical reaction to the poetry of Rosalía de Castro. PhD U. of Missouri-Columbia, 1973.

PIERCE,V.P. 3624
Rosalía de Castro. PhD U. of Kansas, 1961.

RICHARDS ,J.M. 3625
Sentiments and imagination in the poetry of Rosalía de Castro. MA U. of Birmingham, 1970.

STEVENS,J.R. 3626
The poetry of Rosalía de Castro: a psychological and philosophical interpretation of its imagery. PhD U. of Wisconsin, 1971.

STEVEN S,S. 3627
Rosalía de Castro: literary and social origins of the Galician poetry. PhD U. of Michigan, 1982.

Carmen LaForet

MATEU,W.F. 3628
The new Spanish feminism in the writings of Carmen LaForet. PhD U. of Alabama, 1982.

Ana María Matute

ACEVEDO,M.A. 3629
La creacion literara infantil de Ana María Matute. PhD Texas Tech. U. 1979.

ALVIS,J.E. 3630
La traición en la obra de Ana María Matute. PhD U. of Oklahoma, 1976.

CANNON,E.T. 3631
Childhood as theme and symbol in the major fiction of Ana María Matute. PhD Ohio State U. 1972.

CHACON,M.A. 3632
The Spanish Civil War in the works of Ana María Matute. PhD U. of California, Los Angeles, 1974.

DOYLE,M.S. 3633
Los mercaderes: a literary world by Ana María Matute. PhD U. of Virginia, 1981.

FERNANDEZ,M.A. 3634
Temas bíblicos en la obra de Ana María Matute: su expresión y significado. PhD U. of Colorado at Boulder, 1979.

FLORES-JENKINS,R.G. 3635
La mujer como individuo y como tipo en la novelistica de Ana María Matute. PhD U. of Connecticut, 1980.

LING,J.P. 3636
Time in the prose of Ana María Matute. PhD U. of Wisconsin-Madison, 1972.

PLASE NCIA,G. 3637
Deporte y juegos en el ensayo hispánico contemporáneo. [Includes Ana María Matute.] PhD City U. of New York, 1979.

SHELBY,J.T. 3638
Alienation in the novels of Ana María Matute. PhD U. of Washington, 1976.

ULYATT,P. 3639
Allegory, myth and fable in the work of Ana María Matute. MLitt U. of Newcastle-upon Tyne, 1977.

WEITZNER,M.E. 3640
The novelistic world of Ana María Matute: a pessimistic vision of life. PhD U. of Wisconsin, 1963.

Dolores Medio

CASEY,H.L. 3641
Language and communication as thematic elements in the works of Dolores Medio. PhD U. of Oklahoma, 1975.

Emilia Pardo Bazán

BARROSO,F.J. 3642
La intención naturalista y reformadora en la novelistica de Emilia Pardo Bazán. PhD U. of Virginia, 1970.

BRADFORD,C.A.A. 3643
Emilia Pardo Bazán and Russian literature: its impact on her last three novels. PhD Vanderbilt U. 1972.

BROWN,D.F. 3644
The influence of Emile Zola on the novelistic and critical work of Emilia Pardo Bazán. PhD U. of Illinois at Urbana-Champaign, 1935.

CANNON,H.L. 3645
Stylistic technique and thematic preferences as reflected in the short stories of Emilia Pardo Bazán. PhD U. of Minnesota, 1973.

CHANDLER,A.A. 3646
The role of literary tradition in the novelistic trajectory of Emilia Pardo Bazán. PhD Ohio State U. 1956.

COOK,T.A. 3647
El feminismo en la novelística de Emilia Pardo Bazán. PhD U. of Virginia, 1974.

DANDLIKER,J.D. 3648
Artistic and moral intent in the short stories of Emilia Pardo Bazán. PhD U. of Colorado at Boulder, 1973.

FARLOW,C.E. 3649
Emilia Pardo Bazán and the theater. PhD U. of Wisconsin-Madison, 1977.

GILES,M.E.G. *3650*
Descriptive artistry in the novels of Emilia Pardo Bazán. PhD U. of California, Berkeley, 1961.

GOWIN,K.A. *3651*
Shifts in narrative voices in four novels of Emilia Pardo Bazán. PhD Louisiana State U. 1981.

GUTTMAN,J.M. *3652*
Representative women in the narrative works of Emilia Pardo Bazán. PhD U. of New Mexico, 1978.

HEMINGWAY,M.J. *3653*
Pardo Bazán, the novelist, and spiritual naturalism: theory and practice. DPhil U. of Oxford, 1976.

HORRIGAN,J. *3654*
The literary personality of Emilia Pardo Bazán, as revealed in her principal short stories. MA U. of Manchester, 1974.

KEGLER,L.S. *3655*
Lo trágico en el cuento de Emilia Pardo Bazán. PhD Middlebury Coll. 1970.

KIRBY,H.L. *3656*
Evolution of thought in the critical writings and novels of Emilia Pardo Bazán. PhD U. of Illinois at Urbana-Champaign, 1963.

MCLEAN,E.F. *3657*
Objectivity and change in Pardo Bazán's treatment of priests, agnostics, Protestants and Jews. PhD Duke U. 1961.

O'CONNELL,E.P. *3658*
La condesa Emilia Pardo Bazán: novelista. MA National U. of Ireland, 1948.

OSBORNE,R.E. *3659*
The critical ideas of Emilia Pardo Bazán. PhD Brown U. 1948.

PASCOE,D.J. *3660*
Individualism in the late *Novelas breves* of Emilia Pardo Bazán. MA U. of Exeter, 1977.

RICHARDS,H.J. *3661*
True and perverted idealism in the works of Emilia Pardo Bazán. PhD U. of Minnesota, 1964.

RIDGWAY,E.L.G. *3662*
The *Novelas breves* of Emilia Pardo Bazán. PhD Louisiana State U. 1970.

RODRIGUEZ,A.R. *3663*
La cuestión feminista en los ensayos de Emilia Pardo Bazán. PhD Tulane U. 1982.

RUI Z,C. *3664*
Modernismo y psicología en *La Quimera, La sirena negra* y *Dulce dueno*. PhD Case Western Reserve U. 1974.

SANCHEZ,P. *3665*
Emilia Pardo Bazán: a contrast study between the novelist and the short story writer. PhD U. of California, Los Angeles, 1964.

SCONE,E.L. *3666*
Cosmopolitan attitudes in the works of Emilia Pardo Bazán. PhD U. of New Mexico, 1959.

TAYLOR,M.E. *3667*
Religious problems in the novels of Emilia Pardo Bazán. PhD U. of Kentucky, 1973.

Elena Quiroga

MCGLOIN,G.G. *3668*
Elena Quiroga's *La careta*: time and the mask. PhD Saint Louis U. 1971.

Teresa of Avila, St

MAHOMEY,M. *3669*
Symbolism in the *Interior castle* of Saint Teresa of Avila. PhD Fordham U. 1972.

PELLIGRO,M.A. *3670*
Luz y sombra en la vida y obra de Santa Teresa de Avila. PhD U. of Connecticut, 1975.

RECIO,I. *3671*
La lengua poética de Santa Teresa. PhD U. of California, Riverside, 1971.

María de Zayas y Sotomayor

CHARRON,G. *3672*
María Zayas de Sotomayor: novelista española del siglo diez y siete. PhD U. of California, Los Angeles, 1975.

FOA,S.M. *3673*
Feminismo y forma narrativa: estudio del tema y las técnicas de María de Zayas y Sotonayor. PhD Princeton U. 1975.

PLACE,E.B. *3674*
A study of the works of Salas Barbadillo and María de Zayas. PhD Harvard U. 1919.

ROBERTS,S.B. *3675*
María de Zayas – novelista cortesana. MA U. of Wales (Cardiff), 1970.

RODRIGUEZ,J.A. *3676*
Técnicas literarias y costumbrismo en la obra de María de Zayas y Sotumayor. PhD U. of Southern California, 1972.

STACKHOUSE,K.A. *3677*
Narrative roles and style in the *novelas* of María de Zayas y Sotomayor. PhD U. of Florida, 1972.

SYLVANIA,L.E.V. *3678*
Dona María de Zayas of Sotomayor: a contribution to the study of her works. PhD Columbia U. 1922.

VASILESKI,I.V. *3679*
La creación novelística de Dona María de Zayas y Sotomayor. PhD Florida State U. 1971.

13 Media

Studies of the periods before c.1945 are to be found under **9** history. *See also* **2** 33; **4** 153, 937; **7** 143; **12** 317; **19** 13, 83; **22** 63.

AKPAN, E.D. *1*
News photos and stories: men's and women's roles in two Nigerian newspapers. [How Nigerian women are presented in *The Daily Times* and *New Nigerian*] PhD Ohio State U. 1975.

ALPERN, S. *2*
A woman of *The Nation*. Freda Kirchwey. PhD U. of Maryland 1978.

BAHN, A.K. *3*
Changes and continuities in the transitional status of bride into wife: a content analysis of bridal magazines, 1967–1977, the decade of the women's movement. PhD City U. of New York, 1979.

BASS, M.H. *4*
Sex-role stereotyping on television programmes popular with children. PhD York U. 1980.

BENDLER, D.D. *5*
The female in cartoonland: a content analysis of sex-role models in Saturday morning cartoon programs. PhD Ohio State U. 1974.

BOOZER, J.L. *6*
Early childhood as portrayed in women's magazines, 1945–1970. PhD U. of Pittsburgh, 1971.

BOWMAN, W.W. *7*
Distaff journalists: women as a minority group in the news media. PhD U. of Illinois at Chicago Circle, 1974.

BRYER, J.R. *8*
'A trial-track for racers': Margaret Anderson and the *Little Review*. PhD U. of Wisconsin, 1965.

DREIBELBIS, G.C. *9*
A case study of Joan Ganz Cooney and her involvement in the development of the Children's Television Workshop. EdD Northern Illinois U. 1982.

ESSA, E.L. *10*
The impact of television on mother-child interaction and play. PhD Utah State U. 1977.

FILLOSO, K.L. *11*
Female adolescents' perceptions of self, of their television fictional role models and of their real world role models: an exploratory study. PhD Ohio State U. 1974.

FREDERICKS, C. *12*
A study of the responses of a group of adult female listeners to a series of educational radio programs. PhD New York U. 1954.

GELFMAN, J.S. *13*
Women in television news: the on-air woman newscaster in New York. EdD Columbia U. 1974.

GIRARD, C.F. *14*
American women's magazines and the concept of marriage, 1901–1951. PhD Saint Louis U. 1955.

GRENIER, J.A. *15*
The origins and nature of progressive muckraking. [Inc. study of Ida Tarbell] PhD U. of California, Los Angeles, 1965.

GRIEVE, C.A. *16*
Working-class female role modelling as influenced by parent-child interaction and television viewing. PhD U. of Denver, 1979.

GUEST, P.H. *17*
Television as a variable in citizenship activities of women. PhD Pennsylvania State U. 1954.

HAYES, E.J. *18*
Women in management: an analysis of attitudes toward women in television management. PhD Southern Illinois U. at Cardondale, 1980.

HEARN, P.H. *19*
Images of women in the leisure reading c
young people. PhD Southern Illinois U. 19.

JEWELL, K.S.W. *20*
An analysis of the visual development of stereotype: the media's portrayal of Mammy and Aunt Jemima as symbols of black womanhood. PhD Ohio State U. 1976.

JOHNSTON, A. *21*
Abortion in women's magazines: a case study of their approach to socio-political issues. MA (I.S.)* U. of Sheffield, 1980.

KROCK, L.A. *22*
The relationship between measures of ego development for female television viewers and

their preferred female television characters. EdD Boston U. Sch. of Educ. 1981.

LEONHARD-SPARK, A.J. *23*
A content analysis of food ads appearing in women's consumer magazines in 1965 and 1977. EdD Columbia U. Teachers College, 1980.

LOGIE, I.R. *24*
Careers for women in journalism: a personnel study of 881 women experienced as salaried writers in journalism, advertising, publicity, and promotion. PhD Columbia U. 1939.

MAKOSKY, D.R. *25*
The portrayal of women in wide-circulation magazine short stories, 1905–1955. PhD U. of Pennsylvania, 1966.

MATHER, L.L. *26*
The education of women: images from popular magazines. EdD U. of Pennsylvania, 1977.

MEEHAN, D.M. *27*
An interpretive communication study of images and roles of women in selected situation comedies from 1950 to 1975. PhD U. of Southern California, 1979.

MILLER, A.E. *28*
A descriptive analysis of health-related articles in the six leading women's magazines: content, coverage and readership profile. PhD Southern Illinois U. 1980.

MILLUM, T.G. *29*
Advertising in women's magazines: an analysis of visual communication. PhD U. of Birmingham, 1971.

NERNEY, B.J. *30*
Katharine S. White, *New Yorker* editor: her influence on the *New Yorker* and on American literature. PhD U. of Minnesota, 1982.

OERTON, S.J. *31*
The feminist press in Britain since 1970. MA U. Coll. Swansea, 1981.

REYNOLDS, P.K.C. *32*
Opinion journals and the women's movement, 1968–1977. PhD U. of Texas at Austin, 1982.

RICHARDSON, G.C. *33*
Portrayal of birth in an American medium: nonfiction content in popular women's magazines. PhD Indiana U. 1978.

ROYES, H.H. *34*
Television and traditional culture: a survey of the Afroamerican women on St Helena Island, South Carolina. PhD U. of Wisconsin–Madison, 1980.

SCHOLTES, M.C. *35*
A study of the careers of 100 women who prepare and present television programs for homemakers. PhD Columbia U. 1957.

SEITER, E.E. *36*
The promise of melodrama: recent women's films and soap operas. PhD Northwestern U. 1981.

SHAW, S.J. *37*
Retail press publicity with major emphasis on merchandise publicity found on women's pages of newspapers. PhD New York U. 1955.

SHEIFER, I.C. *38*
Ida M. Tarbell and morality in big business: an analysis of a Progressive mind. PhD New York U. 1967.

SMITH, E.V. *39*
Content analysis of middle-class women's fiction from 1901 to 1960 as indicative of changing cultural values related to middle-class birth rates. PhD Purdue U. 1961.

SMITH, R.B. *40*
Functions of mass media for Wisconsin farm women. PhD U. of Wisconsin, 1967.

SPRAFKIN, J.N. *41*
Sex and sex-role as determinants of children's television selections and attention. PhD State U. of New York at Stony Brook, 1975.

VOLPER, R.J. *42*
Feminist goals as depicted in the behavior of the husband versus the wife in selected American family comic strips from 1960–1974: a content analysis. PhD New York U. 1975.

WATT, M.S. *43*
A critical analysis of the roles of women in a local media industry. PhD State U. of New York at Buffalo, 1979.

ZIMMERMAN, D.E. *44*
The portrayal of women in mass media, 1949 to 1956: the Du Mont television network versus popular films, books, magazines and songs. PhD Union for Experimenting Colleges and Universities, 1979.

14 Philosophy

See also **4** 83, 98, 107, 137; **7** 60, 116; **16** 19, 36, 47; **18** 218; **19** 18, 35, 59.

BERUBE, R.N. *1*
Symbol, art and sacrament: the art symbol according to Susanne K. Langer and its analogy with sacrament. PhD Catholic U. of America, 1982.

BUFFORD, S.L. *2*
Susanne K. Langer's two themes of art. PhD U. of Texas at Austin, 1969.

BURNS, C.F. *3*
Thinking and the construction of emotion: a case study of the creative thought of Mary Wollstonecraft. PhD Rutgers U. 1978.

CRAIG, C.E. *4*
Simone de Beauvoir's *The Second Sex* in the light of the Hegelian master-slave dialectic and Sartrian existentialism. PhD U. of Edinburgh, 1979.

DICKASON, M.A. *5*
Sophia denied: philosophy, women, and theories of human nature. PhD U. of Colorado at Boulder, 1977.

DIETZ, M.G. *6*
Between the human and the divine: the political thought of Simone Weil. PhD U. of California, Berkeley, 1982.

DIONNE-LEGAULT, D. *7*
Simone Weil, miroir d'une pensée existentialiste; ou, L'agir dans une philosophie de l'irréductibilité. PhD U. of Montreal, 1975.

FISCHER, C.B. *8*
The fiery bridge: Simone Weil's theology of work. PhD Graduate Theol. Union, 1979.

FOX, S.F. *9*
Political, abstract, and domestic spheres: why have women been underrepresented in political philosophy? PhD Claremont Grad. Sch. 1978.

GAGNON, L.M. *10*
An analysis and evaluation of the role of symbol and semblance in the philosophy of art of Susanne K. Langer. PhD U. of Notre Dame, 1971.

GOLDSCHLAGER, A.J. *11*
L'influence de Spinoza sur la pensée religieuse de Simone Weil. PhD U. of Toronto, 1975.

GOOCH, A.S. *12*
Metaphysical ordination: reflections on Edith Stein's *Endliches und ewiges sein*. PhD U. of Dallas, 1982.

GRAVES, J.B. *13*
A theory of musical comedy based on the concepts of Susanne K. Langer. PhD U. of Kansas, 1981.

HAMBLIN, M.W. *14*
Simone Weil: concept of a self-emptying god with special reference to the problem of human suffering. PhD U. of Southern California, 1976.

HORAN, S.J. *15*
Female status: a hologeistic study. PhD State U. of New York at Buffalo, 1980.

MANNOLINI, C.A. *16*
Toward a philosophy of feminism: a matter of androgyny. PhD Southern Illinois U. at Carbondale, 1975.

MAYEAUX, A.R. *17*
A phenomenology of woman. PhD Emory U. 1975.

O'CONNOR, C.L. *18*
Women and cosmos: the feminine in the thought of Pierre Teilhard de Chardin. PhD Fordham U. 1970.

OKIN, S.M. *19*
Women and citizens: the status of women in the history of political philosophy. PhD Harvard U. 1975.

OLSEN, G.R. *20*
The effort to escape from temporal consciousness as expressed in the thought and work of Hermann Hesse, Hannah Arendt and Karl Loewith. PhD U. of Arizona, 1973.

OSBORNE, M.L. *21*
Plato's feminism. PhD U. of Tennessee, 1978.

PELLERIN, G. *22*
Le problème religieux et la mort chez Simone de Beauvoir. PhD U. of Ottawa, 1980.

ROACH, T.S. *23*
Appearance in history: Hannah Arendt's metaphorical logic of the person. PhD Duke U. 1981.

ROBERT, E.R. *24*
Women's roles: a Marxist-existentialist analysis. PhD Western Michigan U. 1973.

SPRINGSTED, E.O. *25*
Christus mediator: the Platonic doctrine of mediation in the religion and philosophy of Simone Weil. PhD Princeton Theological Seminary, 1980.

TURCOTTE, L. *26*
L'importance des données biologiques dans *Le deuxième sexe* de Simone de Beauvoir et *La femme* de F.J.J. Buytendijk: étude comparative et analyse de texte. PhD U. of Montreal, 1982.

VISCARDI, L.G. *27*
A feminist theory of authenticity. PhD U. of Florida, 1981.

WARREN, D.L. *28*
Simone de Beauvoir: towards a female subject. PhD U. of California, Los Angeles, 1979.

WAWRYTKO, S.A. *29*
The philosophical systematization of a 'feminine' perspective in terms of Taoism's 'tao te ching' and the works of Spinoza. PhD U. of Washington, 1976.

WENDELL, S.D. *30*
The subjection of women today. [A contemporary perspective on John Stuart Mill's arguments] PhD U. of British Columbia, 1976.

WHITE, S.P. *31*
Moral history of women. PhD Syracuse U. 1935.

YOUNG, J.M. *32*
The concept of 'worldlessness' in the thought of Hannah Arendt. PhD Florida State U. 1982.

15 Physiology

See also **9** 217, 517; **10** 11; **12** 2876, 2976; **22** 3, 14, 27, 113, 136, 173.

ABDO, S.H.A. *1*
Leg strength and height-weight factors in relation to cardiovascular efficiency of college women. PhD Louisiana State U. 1965.

AIERSTOCK, B.A. *2*
Effects of exercise upon selected physiological responses to a psychic stressor in college women. EdD Temple U. 1972.

AL DABBAGH, Z.M.A. *3*
The establishment of average body measurements for Saudi Arabian women and the development of basic garment patterns. PhD Texas Woman's U. 1980.

ALTERI, R.E. *4*
The effects of interval and endurance running upon anthropometric and physiological parameters in college-aged females. DA Middle Tennessee State U. 1975.

ANDERSON, E.T. *5*
The effect of a selected jogging and a selected walking program on maximum oxygen uptake body composition and total body strength of female college students. EdD Brigham Young U. 1974.

BALSHAN, I.D. *6*
A factorial study of muscle tension and personality in a woman. PhD U. of California, Los Angeles, 1962.

BARDWICK, J.M. *7*
Uterine contractions as a function of anxiety, sexual arousal and menstrual cycle phase. PhD U. of Michigan, 1964.

BARTON, J.R. *8*
The effects of physical exertion on immediate and delayed mental performance of adult females. PhD Texas A&M U. 1979.

BAUCHMOYER, S.L. *9*
The effects of social reinforcement and experimenter sex on the performance of college women on a novel motor task. PhD U. of Iowa, 1974.

BEAM, A.L. *10*
Comparison of motor ability of females with older siblings over six years of physical growth. EdD U. of Alabama, 1979.

BECKER, B.J. *11*
Construction of a muscular strength test for college women. PhD U. of Oregon, 1968.

BELL, A.C. *12*
Prediction of maximal oxygen intake in women 20 to 40 years of age. PhD Texas Woman's U. 1972.

BENNETT, C. *13*
The relative contributions of modern dance, folk dance, basketball and swimming to selected and general motor abilities of college women. PhD Indiana U. 1956.

BIRD, A.M. *14*
The effects of social facilitation upon the performance of two psychomotor tasks by female subjects. PhD U. of Colorado, 1972.

BLACKINTON, M. *15*
The value of a height-weight classification plan as a predictor of the motor ability of college women. EdD U. of Utah, 1965.

BLAIR, D.A. *16*
The energy expenditure and activity levels of lean adult-onset and child-onset obese women. PhD Cornell U. 1980.

BLUCKER, J.A. *17*
A comparison of selected physiological parameters between exercising and non-exercising young and older women. PhD Florida State U. 1972.

BOSWORTH, J. *18*
Relationships between the vertical jump performance of college women and selected anthropometric measurements and strength variables. PhD Springfield Coll. 1964.

BOTTGER, J.E. *19*
A study of the relationship between the percentage of buccal cell nuclei containing Barr bodies and the psychological masculinity-femininity indices of 100 freshman and sophomore college women. PhD Texas Woman's U. 1970.

BOWMAN, T.E. *20*
Electrocortical and behavioral aspects of visuospatial processing and cognitive orientation in

young, middle-aged and elderly females. PhD U. of Southern California, 1981.

BRANDON, M.E. *21*
Morphological variation and its association with some retrospective and present parameters in female college graduates. PhD U. of Wisconsin–Madison, 1980.

BROWN, E.W. *22*
Biomechanical analysis of the running patterns of girls, three to ten years of age. PhD U. of Oregon, 1978.

BRUSH, F.C. *23*
Patterns of movement and associated electrical muscle activity in college women of high and low motor ability. PhD U. of Maryland, 1966.

BUCKBEE, B.E. *24*
The effects of selected resistance training equipment and regimens on strength in college-age women. DPE Springfield Coll. 1981.

BURIAN, R.J. *25*
A study of the relationship between female body physique and a number of psycho-sexual-social correlates. EdD Arizona State U. 1969.

BURRIS, B.J. *26*
Measurement of aerobic capacity in college women. PhD U. of Wisconsin, 1970.

BURRIS, M.S. *27*
The effects of a six-week aerobic dance and folk dance program vs the effects of a six-week aerobic jogging program on the cardiovascular efficiency and percent of body fat in postpubescent girls. EdD U. of Southern Mississippi, 1979.

BUTTON, S.G. *28*
Investigation of leg density changes of college-age females comparing a low resistance-low repetition exercise program to a high resistance-high repetition exercise program. PhD U. of Utah, 1974.

CARPENTER, J.R. *29*
The effect of exercise on several physiological and psychological variables among three elderly female subjects. EdD West Virginia U. 1982.

CATON, I.J. *30*
Influence of systematic weight training upon women's strength and performance of basic motor skills. EdD U. of Tennessee, 1962.

CAVANAUGH, D.J. *31*
Acute and chronic effects of exercise on plasma concentrations of prolactin and hematological parameters in women runners, aged 18–37. PhD Ohio State U. 1982.

CHIRA, Y. *32*
Hematological responses and work capacity after iron supplementation in sedentary and trained women. PhD U. of Southern California, 1980.

CLOSS, E.L. *33*
Isokinetic measurement of strength in black and in white university women. PhD Texas Woman's U. 1977.

CLOWER, M.A. *34*
The relationships of self-concept, movement concept, and physical fitness for college women. EdD U. of Georgia, 1978.

COHEN,J.S. *35*
Effects of physical training in a cool environment and heat acclimatization on thermoregulation of women during mild exercise in the heat. PhD U. of Iowa, 1978.

COOLEY, S.J. *36*
Construction of a muscular strength test on the universal gym machine for college women. PhD U. of Oregon, 1974.

CORDAIN, L. *37*
Effects of an aerobic training program on ventilatory muscle strength in untrained women. PhD U. of Utah, 1981.

CRAGIN, W.E. *38*
Generality and specificity of motor performance as affected by practice and analysis of acquisition curves of college women on three gross motor tasks. PhD Louisiana State U. 1968.

CRESS, C.L. *39*
Morthological bisexuality as a factor in the motor performance of college women. PhD Springfield Coll. 1984.

CRIST, D.M. *40*
Effects of physical training on the electrical excitability of ventral-horn motorneurons in women. PhD U. of New Mexico, 1981.

DARBY, L.A. 41
The effects of anaerobic and aerobic training on the appetite, food intake, and body composition of untrained women. PhD Ohio State U. 1982.

DAVIS, D. *42*
Attitudes of females toward multi-dimensional physical activity as a function of achievement motivation, movement satisfaction, race and socioeconomic level. PhD U. of Maryland, 1978.

DAVIS, J.B. *43*
Reflex premotor and reaction times of black and white females to a kinesthetic stimulus. PhD Texas Woman's U. 1975.

DEGUZMAN, J.A. *44*
The effects of a semester of modern dance on the cardiovascular fitness and body composition of college women. EdD, Columbia U. 1979.

DICKERSCHEID, J.D. *45*
Development of a method of measuring the effects of a preschool child on the mother's heart rate. PhD Ohio State U. 1967.

DOLGENER, F.A. *46*
The evaluation and prediction of maximum aero-

bic power in females. PhD U. of Texas at Austin, 1973.

DOROCIAK, J.J. *47*
Validity of running tests of 4, 8 and 12 minutes duration in estimating aerobic power for college women of different fitness levels. PhD Louisiana State U. and A&M Coll. 1981.

DOSWELL, W.M. *48*
Physiology and behavior: an investigation of the relation between race, repression-sensitization and systolic blood pressure response in female registered nurses. PhD New York U. 1982.

DOUGLAS, R.L. *49*
Differences in anxiety levels, neuroticism, and extraversion associated with three levels of physical fitness in females. PhD U. of Southern Mississippi, 1975.

DOWDY, D.B. *50*
The effects of aerobic dance, on physical work capacity, cardiovascular function and body composition of middle-aged women. EdD U. of Georgia, 1982.

DURRANT, E. *51*
The effects of jogging, rope jumping, and aerobic dance on body composition and maximum oxygen uptake of college females. EdD Brigham Young U. 1975.

EDGLEY, B.M. *52*
The validation of workloads at 180 and 190 heart rate as predictors of maximal oxygen consumption for college women. EdD Oklahoma State U. 1977.

EDWARDS, M.A. *53*
A study to determine the effects of training at predetermined heart-rate levels in college women. PhD U. of Pittsburgh, 1970.

EGAN, N.J. *54*
The MMPI MF scale in college women – an empirical investigation of some clinical assumptions. PhD Michigan State U. 1981.

EISENMAN, P.A. *55*
A comparison of effects of training on aerobic capacity in girls and young women. PhD Kent State U. 1973.

EWING, J.L. *56*
Effects of varying levels of fatigue on the rate of force development in females. PhD U. of Minnesota, 1982.

FEIN, J.T. *57*
Effects of continuous and intermittent work on heat acclimatization of women. PhD U. of Iowa, 1972.

FLAGG, T. *58*
Self-modification of aerobic exercise behavior in women. PhD U. of Michigan, 1982.

FLEDER, L.W. *59*
Female physiology and psychology in the works of Diderot and the medical writers of his day. PhD Columbia U. 1978.

FRINGER, M.N. *60*
Changes in selected cardiorespiratory parameters during periods of conditioning and deconditioning in young adult females. PhD U. of Maryland, 1972.

FUCHS, C.Z. *61*
The effect of the temporomandibular joint position on isometric muscle strength and power in adult females. EdD Boston U. Sch. of Educ. 1981.

GARRITY, H.M. *62*
The relationship of somatotypes of college women to physical fitness performance. EdD Boston U. 1959.

GENCH, B.E. *63*
Cardiovascular adaptations of college women to training at predetermined individualized heart-rate levels for varied durations. EdD U. of Northern Colorado, 1974.

GIBBONS, E.S. *64*
The effects of various training intensity levels on anaerobic threshold, aerobic power and aerobic capacity in young females. PhD Texas A&M U. 1981.

GLOSS, M.G.W. *65*
The capacity of women to perform strenuous work. PhD North Carolina State U. 1977.

GODLASKY, C.A. *66*
The development of fitness in college women. EdD Pennsylvania State U. 1962.

GOLDMAN, M.F. *67*
The learning retention and bilateral transfer of a motor skill by college women as a function of mental practice, physical practice and mixed practice. PhD New York U. 1972.

GUILLIAMS, G.R. *68*
Cardio-respiratory responses during exercise as related to females of different training levels. PhD Ohio State U. 1971.

HARRIS, D.V. *69*
An investigation of psychological characteristics of university women with high and low fitness indices. PhD U. of Iowa, 1965.

HARRY, D.S. *70*
The differences in exogenous and endogenous fat utilization between trained and untrained women during rest and moderate exercise and recovery from exercise. PhD U. of Illinois at Urbana-Champaign, 1972.

HART, E.K. *71*
A comparative study of personality traits related

to attitudes toward physical activity as expressed by university women. PhD U. of Utah, 1974.

HART, M.S. *72*
The relationship between reported satisfaction with body image, anxiety, and the occurrence of physiological deviations among healthy college females. PhD New York U. 1967.

HAYS, J.C.P. *73*
The contribution of beginning modern dance to cardiovascular fitness in college women. PhD U. of Texas at Austin, 1971.

HIGGS,S.L. *74*
Endurance performance of good and average women competitors under self-motivated and competitive conditions. PhD U. of Minnesota, 1971.

HINSON, M.M. *75*
An electromyographic study of the push-up for women. PhD U. of Minnesota, 1966.

HO, M.A. *76*
Sex hormones and the sleep of women. PhD Yeshiva U. 1972.

HOFF, B.A. *77*
Relationships between the work efficiency of college women and their strength: predicted maximal oxygen consumption, ventilation equivalent and heart rate. PhD U. of Oregon, 1970.

HOLLEN, E. *78*
Estimations of the daily energy expenditure of women from records of activity and of pulse rate. PhD Iowa State U. 1963.

HOYMAN, A.S. *79*
Prediction of physical endurance of college women from metabolic variables. PhD U. of Illinois at Urbana-Champaign, 1963.

HUTCHINS, G.L. *80*
The relationship of selected strength and flexibility variables to the antero-posterior posture of college women. PhD U. of Oregon, 1963.

HYATT, I.M. *81*
The effects of two endurance programs on the body composition of college females. EdD U. of Houston, 1982.

JAEGER, M. *82*
Some aspects of relationship between motor coordination and personality in a group of college women. PhD Columbia U. 1957.

JENNINGS, S.E. *83*
The effects of a 9-week conditioning program on slow wave sleep and mood states of physically inactive women. PhD Pennsylvania State U. 1981.

JERVERY,A.A. *84*
A study of the flexibility of selected joints in specified groups of adult females. PhD U. of Michigan, 1961.

JOHNSON,K.M. *85*
The effect on passive audiences on the motor performance and autonomic arousal level of college women. PhD U. of Southern California, 1974.

JONES,B.C. *86*
The effect of isokinetic training on the force-velocity relationship and maximal power in female forearm flexor muscles. PhD U. of Alberta, 1977.

JONES,B.J. *87*
The effects of 53 hours of continuous wakefulness on the performance of balance strength and psychomotor tasks by college females. PhD Florida State U. 1972.

KEISER, M.B. *88*
Relationship of posture to energy expenditure and other physiological responses of women ascending and descending stairways. PhD Ohio State U. 1959.

KELLY, G.N. *89*
Analysis of college females' perception of liquid horizontality. PhD Washington State U. 1979.

KINDIG, L.E. *90*
Estimation of body fat of college women from densitometric and anthropometric measurements. EdD Temple U. 1967.

LANGFORD, F. *91*
Influence of age and body weight on energy expenditure of women during controlled physical activity. PhD Iowa State U. 1960.

LEBE-NERON, R.M.C. *92*
Effects of an isometric resistance training program on passive abduction of the hip joint in college women. PhD Florida State U. 1980.

LEE, E.J. *93*
The validity of a submaximal cardiovascular step test for women. EdD Louisiana State U. and A&M Coll. 1974.

LEWIS, D.M. *94*
The effects of participation in an individualized instructional program on the physical fitness of severely retarded female adolescents. EdD U. of Virginia, 1982.

LIFE, M.L. *95*
The effects of supplementary isometric exercises with swimming and golf on selected physiological factors of college women. PhD Lousiana State U. and A&M Coll. 1964.

LITTLE, D.E. *96*
A self-instructional course in body and figure control for college women. EdD East Texas State U. 1973.

LITTLE, M.J. 97
Performance of young adult women of three body builds on selected cardiovascular endurance texts. EdD U. of Texas at Austin, 1969.

LIU,N.Y.S. 98
Effects of training on some selected physical fitness variables of middle-aged women. PhD U. of Illinois at Urbana-Champaign, 1970.

LLEWELLYN, J.G. 99
Physiologic response to stressful challenge in type A women. DNSc. Rush U. Coll. of Nursing, 1982.

LOVE, P.A. 100
Remediation of collateral knee ligament looseness by isometric exercises in females with defined ligament variability. PhD Texas Woman's U. 1977.

MCKINNEY, E.D. 101
The relationship between certain factors of personality and selected components of physical fitness of college freshmen women. EdD Boston U. 1958.

MCPEAK, C.T. 102
Effects of an interval training program on aerobic, anaerobic, and anthropometric parameters of women. PhD Ohio State U. 1977.

MANNING, J.M. 103
Fatigue and recovery patterns of women following an intermittent isometric and isokinetic exercise. PhD U. of Maryland, 1981.

MARBLESTONE, R.A. 104
Psychological effects of fitness running in normal women. PhD Adelphi U. 1980.

MASON, W.F. 105
An investigation of the relationship between the self-concept and physical fitness of white, American-Indian and black women college students. EdD U. of Arkansas, 1979.

MAYFIELD, D.M. 106
An investigation of the effects of a ten-week aerobic dance. program on cardio-respiratory functioning, body composition and self-actualization of selected females. PhD George Peabody Coll. for Teachers, 1981.

MERSEREAU, M.R. 107
The relationship between measures of dynamic process, output and dynamic stability in the development of running and jumping patterns of preschool age females. PhD Purdue U. 1977.

METIVIER, J.G. 108
The effects of five different physical exercise programs on the blood serum cholesterol of adult women. PhD U. of Illinois at Urbana-Champaign, 1960.

METTERNICH, K.A. 109
The effects of aerobic training on the plasma lipids and lipoproteins, functional capacity and body composition of sedentary adult women. PhD U. of Southern Mississippi, 1982.

MILLER, E.A. 110
The effects of hemoglobin supplements upon maximal oxygen uptake in females. EdD U. of Arkansas, 1978.

MOLSTAD, S.M. 111
Reentry women: the relationship of Q-Ach extraversion-introversion and locus of control to physical persistence on two psychomotor tasks. EdD U. of North Carolina at Greensboro, 1981.

MUNTZING, E.P. 112
The effects of two training loads on specified fitness parameters in sedentary adult women ages 20–30, 31–40 and over 41. EdD Brigham Young U. 1980.

MYNATT, C.V. 113
A study of the differences in selected physical performance test scores of women in Tennessee colleges. PhD U. of Michigan, 1959.

OTTO, R.M. 114
Metabolic response of young females to training and maintenance/detraining. PhD Ohio State U. 1977.

OYSTER, N.A. 115
An investigation of the influence of selected anthropometric measurements on the ability of college women to perform on the 35-yard dash. PhD U. of Oregon, 1971.

PATTERSON, C.A. 116
Selected body measurements of women aged 65 and older. PhD Florida State U. 1981.

PAUL, M.J. 117
Differences in motor ability of college women. EdD U. of Alabama, 1966.

PEREZ, C.D.O. 118
The relationship between oxygen consumption and cardiovascular and pulmonary measurement in adult women. PhD Texas Woman's U. 1973.

PETERSON, A.J. 119
The effect of aerobic and aerokinetic training on serum lipids and lipoproteins in college-aged women. EdD U. of Arkansas, 1981.

PETTERSEN, P.C. 120
Interrelationship of kinesthetic flexibility joint angulation and motor ability in college women. EdD U. of Georgia, 1970.

PICCIONE, C. 121
The effects of structured hypnotic imagery on the perception and reduction of ischemic pain by hypnotizable female students grouped as high and low imagers. PhD U. of Montana, 1980.

PICKEL, D.R. 122
The effects of two interval running programs and

duration of training on selected running tests by college women. PhD U. of Oregon, 1978.

PLOWMAN, S.A. *123*
A comparison of Cureton's low and middle gear training program and Cooper's aerobics in young adult women. PhD U. of Illinois at Urbana-Champaign, 1970.

PRATHER, M.E.S. *124*
Body composition of women. PhD Iowa State U. 1963.

PRATT, M. *125*
Physiological differentiation of erotic and anxiety arousal patterns in women. PhD U. of Iowa, 1981.

PRICE, R.L. *126*
The effect of the Inch Master exerciser on body girth, subcutaneous fat, and selected physiological variables of adult women. EdD Oklahoma State U. 1973.

PURVIS, G.J. *127*
The effect of three levels of duration and intensity of exercise upon the peripheral vision and depth perception of women. PhD Louisiana State U. and A&M Coll. 1973.

RANDOLPH, G.L. *128*
The differences in physiological response of female college students exposed to stressful stimulus, when simultaneously treated by either therapeutic touch or casual touch. PhD New York U. 1980.

REITER, M.A. *129*
Effects of a physical exercise program on selected mood states in a group of women over age 65. EdD Columbia U. Teachers Coll. 1981.

RHODES, J.W. *130*
Development of a cardiovascular fitness test for college women based on an index of work equivalency. EdD North Texas State U. 1970.

RICHARDSON, R.H. *131*
Stimuli in homemaking activities associated with heart-rate changes in women from two socio-economic levels. PhD Ohio State U. 1969.

RICHARDSON, R.J. *132*
Changes in creatinine output and the physical condition of college women enrolled in a program of conditioning exercises. PhD Texas Woman's U. 1967.

RINGO, M.B. *133*
An investigation of some aspects of abdominal strength, trunk extensor strength, and antero-posterior erectness in college women. PhD U. of Oregon, 1957.

RITCHEY, E.A. *134*
The effects of an exercise training program on serum cholesterol and triglyceride levels in women using oral contraceptives. EdD Virginia Polytechnic Inst. and State U. 1976.

RYAN, B.J. *0135*
The status of stability of the medial and lateral collateral knee ligaments of pre-pubescent and post-pubescent women. EdD U of Oklahoma, 1964.

SANDERS, R.T. *136*
The effects of a program of progressive resistance exercise on strength, muscle girth and body composition of college women. EdD Oklahoma State U. 1975.

SANKOWSKY, M.H. *137*
The effect of a treatment based on the use of guided visuo-kinesthetic imagery on the alteration of negative body-cathexis in women. EdD Boston U. Sch. of Educ. 1981.

SCHUELE, M.K. *138*
The relationship of physical fitness in women to self-esteem and locus of control. PhD U. of Missouri, Kansas City, 1979.

SELL, D.L. *139*
The effects of practice emphasis and feedback on a speed and accuracy task by aged females. PhD U. of Southern California, 1976.

SHELDAHL, L.M. *140*
Effects of exercise in cool water on body weight loss and thermoregulation of women. PhD Pennsylvania State U. 1978.

SHIRREFFS, J.H. *141*
The relationship between exposure to complex environmental sounds and temporary threshold shifts in women. PhD Texas Woman's U. 1974.

SMITH, S.A. *142*
A study of the influence of a motivational device on the gross motor performance of adolescent females. EdD U. of New Mexico, 1969.

SPANDE, M.S. *143*
A factorial analysis of body flexibility in university women with a view to determining the relationship of isolated factors with motor performance. PhD New York U. 1954.

SPEARS, C.D. *144*
Analysis of physiological effects on college women of two programs of regular exposures to extreme heat. EdD Louisiana State U. and A&M Coll. 1969.

STANDEVEN, M.V. *145*
The effect of a long-term physical fitness program on selected biochemicals and their personality correlates in women. PhD Purdue U. 1979.

STEVENS, C.J. *146*
Circulatory adjustments of females to interval training and detraining. PhD Ohio State U. 1977.

STEVENSON, J.I. *147*
Physiological responses of college females to maximal treadmill and bicycle exercises with special reference to oxygen pulse. PhD U. of Southern California, 1978.

STONER, L.J. *148*
Cardiovascular efficiency of Minnesota women aged 46–60 engaged in a moderate exercise program. PhD U. of Minnesota, 1966.

TAYLOR, L.R. *149*
The validity of predicting the maximal oxygen uptake of young females using selected submaximal estimators. EdD West Virginia U. 1980.

TERBIZAN, D.J. *150*
The effect of set-repetition combinations on strength gain using isotonic strength training in females age 18–35. PhD Ohio State U. 1982.

THOMPSON, G.S. *151*
The effects of dietary supplements on bone density and nutritional status of elderly women. PhD U. of Tennessee, 1973.

TRAHAN, B.J. *152*
The effects of two specific exercise programs on the body composition of women. EdD U. of Houston, 1973.

TREADAWAY, B.M. *153*
A study of the changes in traits of temperament, motor ability, and fundamental skills of body movement of 150 women enrolled in classes in fundamental skills of body movement; Southeastern State College, Durant, Oklahoma, during the academic year 1958–1959. PhD Texas Woman's U. 1960.

TUFTS, S.A. *154*
The effects of diet and physical activity on selected measures of college women. PhD U. of Iowa, 1969.

UNDERWOOD, C.S. *155*
The relationship between body type and body fat and personality factors of college women. EdD Temple U. 1970.

UPTON, S.J. *156*
A comparison of cardiorespiratory fitness of trained and untrained middle-aged women. PhD Texas Woman's U. 1981.

VAN ANNE, N.M. *157*
An electromyographic study of the relationship between neuromuscular hypertension and flexibility in college women. PhD U. of Oregon, 1962.

VAN DER MERWE, M.S. *158*
The relationship between physical fitness and the health status of selected Canadian college women. PhD Ohio State U. 1981.

VOGAN, D.R. *159*
Selected physiological responses of untrained women training in water at different depths. EdD Brigham Young U. 1981.

WATSON, L. *160*
A study of the relationship between the ability to relax and athletic ability among college women. PhD U. of Oregon, 1952.

WEESNER, M.L. *161*
A comparison of two approaches in the teaching of conditioning and its effects upon the fitness knowledge and attitude of college women. PhD U. of Oregon, 1972.

WHITE, J.A. *162*
An investigation of the relationships between the aerobic capacity of undergraduate college women and their performances on walk-run field tests of 8, 10 and 12 minutes' duration. PhD U. of Oregon, 1973.

WHITE, M.K. *163*
The effects of walking and aerobic dancing on the skeletal and cardiovascular systems of postmenopausal females. EdD West Virginia U. 1981.

WILKS, B.L.B. *164*
Effects of calisthenics on heart rate of college women. EdD U. of Georgia, 1974.

WILLIAMS, J.C. *165*
The relationship between a four-week exercise program and urinary catecholamines in women. PhD Texas Woman's U. 1974.

WIRTH, J.C. *166*
The relationship of static muscle strength and endurance with the use of oral contraceptives, phase of the menstrual cycle, and vitamin B-6 status. PhD U. of Illinois at Urbana-Champaign, 1978.

WOOTEN, E.P. *167*
The comparison of oxygen uptake of women while walking in various types of footwear. PhD Ohio State U. 1961.

WYNN, M.J. *168*
Relationship of heart rate and oxygen uptake of college women at selected work loads. PhD U. of Oregon, 1971.

YARBROUGH, E.I. *169*
The effect of breakfast on the motor performance and blood glucose level of university women. EdD U. of Arkansas, 1973.

YOCOM, R.D. *170*
An analysis of the physical and physiological characteristics and endurance performance of young women. PhD New York U. 1951.

ZINGHEIM, P.K. *171*
Discriminative control of the vaginal vasomotor response in women: its relationship to behaviour. PhD Ohio State U. 1976.

ZUTI, W.B. *172*
Effects of diet and exercise on body composition of adult women during weight reduction. PhD Kent State U. 1972.

16 Politics

For studies of periods before c.1945 see **9** History. *See also* **7** *passim;* **14** *passim;* **19** 48, 56, 74, 100, 102; **23** 67, 237.

ABA-MECHA, B.W. *1*
Black woman activist in twentieth-century South Carolina: Modjeska Monteith Simkins. PhD Emory U. 1978.

ARMSTRONG, K.V. *2*
The participation of Scottish women in village politics. PhD U. of Pittsburgh, 1976.

BANTHIN, J.M. *3*
The New York State women's political caucus: a case study in organizational behavior. PhD U. of Michigan, 1973.

BASHEVKIN, S.B. *4*
Women and change: a comparative study of political attitudes in France, Canada, and the United States. PhD York U. Ontario 1981.

BATTO, B.F. *5*
Studies on women at Mari: politics and religion. PhD Johns Hopkins U. 1972.

BAXTER, S.K. *6*
Women and politics: the parties, the League of Women Voters and the electorate. PhD U. of Michigan, 1977.

BECKWITH, K.L. *7*
Patterns of mass political participation among American women, 1952–1976. PhD Syracuse U. 1982.

BERGER, J. *8*
A New Deal for the world: Eleanor Roosevelt and American foreign policy, 1920–1962. PhD City U. of New York, 1979.

BRODIE, M.J. *9*
Pathways to public office: Canadian women in the post-war years. PhD Carleton U. 1981.

BRUMBAUGH, S.B. *10*
Democratic experience and education in the National League of Women Voters. PhD Columbia U. 1977.

BUCKLEY, M.E.A. *11*
Ideology and Soviet women. PhD Vanderbilt U. 1981.

BUNETTA, T.H. *12*
Margaret Thatcher, Britain's spokesman for a new Conservatism: a rhetorical analysis of the Party Conference speeches (1975–1978). PhD Louisiana State U. 1979.

BURT-PINTAR, S.D. *13*
The political participation of women in Ontario. PhD York U. 1981.

CARROLL, S.J. *14*
Women as candidates: campaigns and elections in American politics. PhD Indiana U. 1980.

COOKE, R.J.C. *15*
The political career of Anna Eleanor Roosevelt: a study of the public conscience. DSS Syracuse U. 1965.

DIAMOND, I.G. *16*
Women and the state legislatures: a macro and micro analysis. PhD Princeton U. 1975.

DUNKLE, D.E. *17*
Women and politics: the political role expectations of adolescent females. PhD State U. of New York at Buffalo, 1974.

EATON, E.T. *18*
The Belgian Leagues of Working-Class Women. PhD Catholic U. of America, 1955.

EDWARDS, S.E. *19*
The political thought of Hannah Arendt: a study of thought and action. PhD Claremont Grad. Sch. 1984.

ELSHTAIN, J.B. *20*
Women and politics: a theoretical analysis. PhD Brandeis U. 1973.

FALLON, J.F. *21*
A Burkeian analysis of the rhetoric of Margaret Thatcher. PhD Ohio State U. 1981.

FEAGANS, I. *22*
Female political elites: case studies of female legislators. PhD Howard U. 1972.

FIEDLER, M.E. *23*
Sex and political participation in the United States: a comparative analysis of masses and elites. PhD Georgetown U. 1977.

FOOTE, F.L. *24*
Role stress and cultural resources: a study of the

role of the woman member of Congress. PhD Michigan State U. 1967.

FOREMAN, N.R.H. 25
The First Lady as a leader of public opinion: a study of the role and press relations of Lady Bird Johnson. PhD U. of Texas at Austin, 1971.

GARVEY, B.O. 26
A rhetorical-humanistic analysis of the relationship between First Ladies and the way women find a place in society. PhD Ohio State U. 1978.

GEORGE, E.L. 27
The women appointees of the Roosevelt and Truman administrations: a study of their impact and effectiveness. PhD American U. 1972.

GRAHAM, S.R. 28
Political recruitment of women into urban governmental roles: a study of social sex roles. PhD U. of Cincinnati, 1975.

HAREVEN, T.K. 29
The social thought of Eleanor Roosevelt. PhD U. of Ohio, 1965.

HARRIS, L.A.H. 30
Margaret Chase Smith: an examination of her public speaking with emphasis on the 'Declaration of conscience, 1950' and the 'Declaration of conscience, 1970'. PhD Southern Illinois U. at Carbondale, 1974.

HUNTLEY, R.T. 31
Events and issues of the Angela Davis dismissal. EdD U. of Southern California, 1976.

JENKINS, W.G. 32
The extent to which trends that emerged during the United Nations first development decade, 1960–1970, relative to educational opportunities for women are still prevalent during the United Nations second development decade. PhD Florida State U. 1976.

JOHNSON, D.E. 33
Organized women and national legislation. PhD Case Western Reserve U. 1960.

JURKOVIC, L.D. 34
The life and public career of Eleanor Lansing Dulles. PhD Kent State U. 1982.

KEEFE, S.E. 35
Women in power: Anglo and Mexican-American female leaders in two Southern California communities. PhD U. of California, Santa Barbara, 1974.

KHAN, V.S. 36
Hannah Arendt: a study in anti-utopia. PhD U. of Michigan, 1971.

KIM, H. 37
A comparative study of the US House of Representatives and the National Assembly of Korea: a cross-cultural study focusing on role analysis of female politicians. PhD U. of Hawaii, 1975.

KYLE, P.A. 38
Political sex role distinctions: motivations, recruitment, and demography of women party elite in North Carolina. PhD Georgetown U. 1973.

LALL, B.G. 39
The foreign policy program of the League of Women Voters of the United States' methods of influencing government action, effects on public opinion and evaluation of results. PhD U. of Minnesota, 1964.

LANGE, L.M.A. 40
Women and democratic theory. PhD U. of Toronto, 1980.

LEE, M.M. 41
The participation of women in suburban politics: a study of the influence of women as compared to men in suburban governmental decision-making. PhD Tufts. U. 1973.

LEVITT, M.T. 42
Political attitudes of American women: a study of the effects of work and education on their political role. PhD U. of Maryland, 1965.

LIPSON, S.L. 43
Consensus building in the League of Women Voters of East State. PhD Columbia U. 1980.

MACHEN, M.G. 44
Images of Joan of Arc: their political uses in modern France. PhD Johns Hopkins U. 1959.

MCINTYRE, D.I. 45
Sexual harassment in government: the situation in Florida and the nation. PhD Florida State U. 1982.

MCKEE, M.J. 46
Congress woman Clare Boothe Luce: her rhetoric against Communism. PhD U. of Illinois at Urbana-Champaign, 1962.

MCKENNA, G.N. 47
A critic of modernity: the political thought of Hannah Arendt. PhD Fordham U. 1917.

MAGGENTI-MILANO, M.E. 48
The National Women's Political Caucus: its role as a reference group for the woman state legislator. PhD Pennsylvania State U. 1977.

MEANS, I.N. 49
Norwegian political recruitment patterns and recruitment of women. PhD U. of Washington, 1971.

MICHELMAN, C. 50
The Black Sash of South Africa, 1955 to 1969: a case study in liberation. PhD U. of Massachusetts, 1971.

MILLER, J.W. 51
The organization and significance of women and young people within the major British political parties. PhD U. of Minnesota, 1948.

MILLETT, K. *52*
Sexual politics. PhD Columbia U. 1970.

NICHOLSON, J.B. *53*
Perceptions of organizational goals and effectiveness: a study of four metropolitan Washington women's commissions. PhD Johns Hopkins U. 1976.

NUCKOLS, M.L. *54*
A comparative analysis of selected United Nations documents related to educational opportunity for women during the first development decade (1960–1970). PhD Florida State U. 1975.

O'SULLIVAN, E. *55*
The relationship of reference groups and self-esteem to women's political participation. PhD U. of Maryland, 1974.

PAGET, K.M.E. *56*
A woman in politics: change in role perception. PhD U. of Colorado at Boulder, 1975.

PHARR, S.T. *57*
Sex and politics: women in social and political movements in Japan. PhD Columbia U. 1975.

PRIMAVERA, J.M. *58*
Factors that led Congress to include provisions for elimination of sex bias, sex discrimination and stereotyping in vocational education in the Educational Amendments of 1976. PhD U. of Missouri–Columbia, 1978.

ROSE, J.J. *59*
Women's political attitudes. PhD U. of Missouri–Columbia, 1977.

ROSENBERG, M.C.B. *60*
Women in politics: a comparative study of Congresswomen Edith Green and Julia Butler Hansen. PhD U. of Washington, 1973.

RUSSELL, A. *61*
Patsy Takemoto Mink: political woman. [Hawaiian Congresswoman] PhD U. of Hawaii, 1977.

SAPIRO, V. *62*
Socialization to and from politics: political gender role norms among women. PhD U. of Michigan, 1976.

SHANLEY, R.A. *63*
The League of Women Voters: a study of pressure politics in the public interest. PhD Georgetown U. 1955.

SHORT, C.K. *64*
Women in American politics: what's a nice girl like you . . . ? PhD Claremont Grad. Sch. 1981.

SMITH, K.S. *65*
The characteristics and motivation of American women who seek positions of political leadership. PhD New Sch. for Social Research, 1976.

SPEICHER, K.L. *66*
Women, politics and the life cycle: a study of New Jersey political activists. PhD New Sch. for Social Research, 1977.

STEINMO, K.A. *67*
The silenced majority: women and American democracy. PhD U. of California, Davis, 1971.

STEWART, D.W. *68*
Public policy and decision processes: the impact of women's policy issues on decision-making in the North Carolina legislature. PhD U. of North Carolina at Chapel Hill, 1975.

STOBAUGH, B.P. *69*
Women candidates for the British parliament, 1918–1970: statistical analyses and three case studies. [Ellen Wilkinson, Duchess of Atholl and Eleanor Rathbone] PhD Boston U. Grad. Sch. 1975.

STRAVRAKIS, B.D. *70*
Women and the Communist Party in the Soviet Union. PhD Case Western Reserve U. 1961.

VOGEL, L. *71*
Beyond domestic labor: women's oppression and reproduction of labor power. PhD Brandeis U. 1981.

WASHINGTON, P.L. *72*
The black woman's agenda: an investigation into strategies for change. PhD Arizona State U. 1978.

WEBSTER, A.A. *73*
French women and politics: the involvement of women in the fight for contraception reform. 1953–1968. PhD Princeton U. 1974.

WELLS, A.S. *74*
Female attitudes toward women in politics: the propensity to support women. PhD U. of Florida, 1972.

WOLCHIK, S.L. *75*
Politics, ideology, and equality: the status of women in Eastern Europe. PhD U. of Michigan, 1978.

17 Psychology

Studies on educational psychology and occupational psychology are to be found at **4** 1012–1304 *and* **5** 323–626 *respectively.*

General psychology

See also **1** 17, 245; **4** 46; **9** 211; **12** 1656, 1663, 1694, 2251, 2591, 2876, 3163, 3168.

History, philosophy and theories

ABRAHAM, R. *1*
Freud and 'mater': the influence of Sigmund Freud's mother on his life and work. PhD U. of California, Davis, 1979.

BUCKLEY, N.L. *2*
Women psychoanalysts and the theory of feminine development: a study of Karen Horney, Helen Deutsch and Marie Bonaparte. PhD U. of California, Los Angeles, 1982.

COREY-SEIBOLD, M.L. *3*
Psychology's foremothers: case studies of six women who shaped the development of American psychology. PhD Fuller Theological Seminary, Sch. of Psych. 1982.

DANAAN, J.M. *4*
The image and the soul: an inquiry into Jungian thought, feminine mind and personality. PhD U. of California, Santa Cruz, 1979.

FIELD, R.A. *5*
The return of the goddess: the feminine principle in theosophic thought and transpersonal psychology. PhD California Inst. of Integral Studies, 1981.

FISHER, E.E. *6*
A critical evaluation of the Freudian theories of feminine psychology. PhD New York U. 1957.

LAIDLAW, T.A. *7*
Concepts of femininity, 1890–1930: reflections of cultural attitudes in psychological theories. PhD U. of Alberta, 1978.

MCLAUGHLIN, K.J. *8*
The concept of the mother goddess and its significance: the feminine principle from the perspectives of Jungian psychology, the Hindu Tantra, and Christianity. PhD U. of California, Inst. of Asian Studies, 1977.

SUPER, S.I. *9*
Florence Hollis and the development of psychosocial casework theory: an intellectual biography, 1927–1940. DSW U. of Illinois at Chicago Circle, 1980.

WHARTON, J.A. *10*
Freud on feminine hysteria – a re-examination. PhD U. of California, Santa Cruz, 1975.

YOUNG, E.B. *11*
Transforming psychology: the integration of the feminine. A presentation and analysis of a therapeutic model. PhD U. of California, Berkeley, 1979.

Psychometrics: test construction and validation

BANK, R.K. *12*
Formulation, application, and analysis of a method to study female underachievement. EdD Harvard U. 1970.

BILLS, L.E. *13*
The development and validation of an instrument to measure the attitudes of women toward joining a consciousness-raising group. PhD U. of Maryland, 1975.

CASEY, T.J. *14*
The development of a leadership orientation scale on the Strong vocational interest blank for women. PhD U. of Notre Dame, 1974.

COLLINS, A.M. *15*
The attitudes toward women scale: validity, reliability and subscore differentiation. PhD U. of Maryland, 1973.

CRISP-YEAGER, C.R.S. *16*
Development of a method to explore achievement identity in women. PhD California Sch. of Prof. Psych. San Diego, 1982.

GERNES, E.A. *17*
A factual analysis of selected items of the Strong

vocational interest blank for women. PhD U. of Nebraska–Lincoln, 1941.

GLOVER, E.G. *18*
A motor creativity test for college women. EdD U. of North Carolina at Greensboro, 1974.

HARMON, L.A.W. *19*
The measurement of women's interests: the effect of using married women as occupational criterion groups on the women's Strong vocational interest blank. PhD U. of Minnesota, 1965.

HARVEY, D.W.H. *20*
The validity of Holland's vocational preference inventory for adult women. PhD U. of Connecticut, 1971.

HOLBROOK, J.E. *21*
Situational effects on the measurement of women's fear of success. PhD U. of Houston, 1974.

HOPKINS, L.B. *22*
Construction and initial validation of a test of ego identity status for females. PhD Temple U. 1977.

JACOBS, M.K. *23*
Women's moral reasoning and behavior in prisoner's dilemma. PhD U. of Toledo, 1975.

LEVIN, R.B. *24*
The psychology of women: an empirical test of a psychoanalytic construct. PhD Syracuse U. 1962.

LONG, A.M. *25*
The dimensionality of the locus-of-control construct for women. PhD U. of Utah, 1974.

O'BRIEN, M.J.H. *26*
A study to determine the accuracy of the Holland types for women employed in realistic and social occupations. PhD Catholic U. of America, 1977.

ROBINSON, E.A. *27*
The development and validation of an inventory of traditional and non-traditional feminine behavior. PhD U. of South Carolina, 1977.

SANNITO, T. *28*
A factor analysis of the Thorne femininity scale. PhD Loyola U. Chicago, 1970.

SHERMAN, N.R. *29*
The competitive direct achieving style among young women – an experimental validation study of an inventory. PhD Stanford U. 1982.

SISSON, V.S. *30*
The development of a leadership orientation scale for college women based on the Strong–Campbell interest inventory. EdD Auburn U. 1981.

WILKINS, P.E. *31*
A validity study of selected scales of the Strong vocational interest blank for women. PhD U. of Iowa, 1966.

Experimental psychology: cognitive processes, perception and motor processes, consciousness states

BEHRENS, M.G. *32*
Effects of global-analytic style, female role orientation, and fear of success on problem-solving behavior. PhD Claremont Grad. Sch. 1973.

BRABECK, M.M.K. *33*
The relationship between critical thinking skills and development of reflective judgement among adolescent and adult women. PhD U. of Minnesota, 1980.

COVINGTON, M.I. *34*
The effects of a cognitive task on the perception phenomenon employing females. PhD Baylor U. 1976.

FEIN, S.R. *35*
Conceptual tempo and abstract reasoning in college students: a study of the effects of individual differences in speed and confidence of judgement on abstract reasoning performance of college females. PhD New York U. 1970.

GANUNG, C.A. *36*
Motivational determinants of verbal learning in older women. PhD Duke U. 1971.

JACK, R.M. *37*
The effect of reinforcement value in mixed and unmixed lists on the learning style of overachieving and underachieving female college students. PhD Purdue U. 1974.

JACOBSEN, C.H. *38*
Field dependent–independent learning style: perceptions of personal and ideal learning style by college women using a structured Q-sort procedure. PhD Bryn Mawr Coll. 1982.

MCCABE, S.A. *39*
Prediction of female problem-solving skill from cognitive style measures under motivating task-orienting conditions. PhD Purdue U. 1976.

MOODY, D.L. *40*
Imagery differences among women of varying levels of experience, interests and abilities in motor skills. PhD Pennsylvania State U. 1965.

NAU, K.L. *41*
Intrasensory and intersensory processing in young and old adult females. PhD Texas Tech U. 1980.

SCARBOROUGH, K.L. *42*
Central processing of adult females of divergent age and activity levels. PhD U. of Texas at Austin, 1973.

STURGIS, B.J. *43*
Correlates of problem-solving in women. PhD U. of Missouri–Columbia, 1977.

WIGHTMAN, B.K. *44*
The effects of providing a cognitive structure on the performance of field-independent and field-dependent women on an affective sensitivity task. PhD Ball State U. 1982.

Behaviour Therapy and Behaviour Modification

See also 829–883; **8** 153–208.

ABRAMS, M.A.M. *45*
The efficacy of behavior modification with emotionally handicapped adolescent girls. EdD Fordham U. 1979.

ADAMS, K.A. *46*
Assertiveness training, androgyny, and professional women. PhD U. of Texas at Austin, 1976.

ALVES-MASTERS, J. *47*
Changing self-esteem of women through Middle Eastern dance. PhD U. of Georgia, 1979.

BAER, R.A. *48*
Phenomenological and behavioral consequences of assertiveness training for women. PhD Northwestern U. 1976.

BAILEY, J.P. *49*
Consciousness-raising groups for women: implications of Paulo Freire's theory of critical consciousness for psychotherapy and education. EdD U. of Massachusetts, 1977.

BALL, P.G. *50*
The effect of group assertiveness training on selected measures of self-concept for college women. EdD U. of Tennessee, 1976.

BALLOU, M.B. *51*
A study of the effectiveness of leaderless, consciousness-raising groups for women – process dimension. PhD Kent State U. 1976.

BARNETT, E.H. *52*
The development of personal power for women: an exploration of the process of empowerment. EdD Boston U. Sch. of Educ. 1981.

BARRETT, S.E. *53*
Women's empowerment: a conceptual framework for feminist therapy. PhD Union for Experimenting Coll. and U. 1980.

BEAMISH, P.M. *54*
The effects of assertive training and power-base training on manifest and latent power for women. EdD West Virginia U. 1979.

BERAH, E.F. *55*
The influence of differential scheduling of sessions on the effectiveness of an assertion training program for women. PhD U. of Cincinnati, 1977.

BERLIN, S.B. *56*
An investigation of the effects of cognitive-behavior modification treatments on problems of inappropriate self-criticism among women. PhD U. of Washington, 1978.

BILLINGHAM-PARKER, K.A. *57*
The behavioral manifestations of fear of success with women and the modification of such behaviors via a modeling procedure. PhD De Paul U. 1978.

BOWMAN, P.R. *58*
The relationship between attitudes toward women and the treatment of activity and passivity. EdD Boston U. Sch. of Educ. 1976.

BZDEK, V.M. *59*
Effects of a self-esteem skill building program on a group of women. PhD U. of Oregon, 1980.

CAREW, I.B. *60*
The effect of a leadership training program on women's values, attitudes and leader behavior. EdD U. of Massachusetts, 1979.

CARLOCK, C.J. *61*
Development and analysis of a weekend workshop for the personal development of women. PhD Florida State U. 1975.

CARPER-KUNSTEL, I. *62*
Investigating the effectiveness of a taped, leaderless consciousness-raising group for women: outcome dimension. PhD Kent State U. 1977.

COLLINS, E.R. *63*
A role-playing workshop as a facilitator of change in attitudes toward women. EdD Boston U. Sch. of Educ. 1975.

CONNER, C.N. *64*
The effectiveness of bibliotherapy on teaching initiator dating skills to females. PhD Oklahoma State U. 1981.

CORDAHL, M.A. *65*
The efficacy of effectiveness training for women: a program evaluation. PhD California Sch. of Prof. Psych. San Diego, 1980.

CUCINOTTA, P. *66*
Changing sex-role behavior in women by assertive training. PhD Purdue U. 1978.

DEITCH, I.M. *67*
Cognitive-behavioral treatment of mathematics anxiety in college women. PhD Yeshiva U. 1981.

DELANGE, J.M. *68*
Relative effectiveness of assertive skill training and desensitization for high and low anxiety women. PhD U. of Wisconsin–Madison, 1976.

DELPORTILLO, C.T. *69*
The effectiveness of minimal success on positive attitude change among Latino women. EdD U. of San Francisco, 1981.

DILEO, J.C. 70
Influences on women's sex-role attitudes, assertiveness, modes of interaction, self-concept and self-esteem: evaluation of a training program. PhD Tulane U. 1975.

DOLECKI, L.S. 71
The effects of alpha feedback training on anxiety in internally and externally controlled female students. PhD U. of Georgia.

DONALDSON, C.S. 72
The effects of self-defense training on women's self-esteem and locus-of-control orientation. PhD California Sch. of Prof. Psych., Berkeley, 1978.

DORN, R.S. 73
The effects of sex-role awareness groups on fear of success, verbal task performance and sex-role attitudes of undergraduate women. EdD Boston U. Sch. of Educ. 1975.

EBENSTEIN, N. 74
The effect of a group counseling program on the self-concept and the sense of independence in women. PhD Wayne State U. 1976.

ENGLISH, D. 75
Effectiveness of a stress reduction training program for women. PhD North Texas State U. 1982.

ERB, M.E. 76
Toward women's fuller humanness: self-actualization of women as related to sex-role values, psychological qualities and relationships. PhD California Sch. of Prof. Psych. 1976.

ERICKSON, V.L. 77
Psychological growth for women: a cognitive developmental curriculum intervention. PhD U. of Minnesota, 1973.

EVANS, K.A. 78
A study of the effects of assertion training on psychological androgyny in female undergraduate students. EdD U. of South Dakota, 1979.

EVANS, L.E. 79
The influence of relaxation techniques on the varying level of tension in college women. PhD U. of Iowa, 1954.

FOLLINGSTAD, D.R. 80
Decreasing conforming behavior in women: an intervention utilizing male support for females' abilities and an exploration of personality variables influencing levels of conformity. PhD U. of Colorado at Boulder, 1974.

FREIBERG, P.A. 81
Modeling and assertive training: the effect of sex and status of model on female college students. PhD U. of Maryland, 1974.

GEMBOL, D.J.C. 82
Effects of assertive training on self-concept and locus of control of women. PhD Kansas State U. 1981.

GOLDMAN, E. 83
Prostitution diversion program: a program evaluation. PhD California Sch. of Prof. Psych. 1978.

GREEN, L.S. 84
The effect of female potentiality training on the internal control perception by women, resulting in an expansion of their vocational horizons. EdD U. of South Dakota, 1978.

GULANICK, N.A. 85
A group program for highly feminine women aimed at increasing androgyny. PhD Southern Illinois U. at Carbondale, 1976.

GUN, B.R. 86
A study of the effect of a sex-role stereotype workshop on education students' attitudes towards women. EdD Boston U. Sch. of Educ. 1975.

HALL, B.A.W. 87
The effect of sex of the leader on the development of assertiveness in women undergoing group assertive training. PhD U. of Missouri at Kansas City, 1975.

HAMMER, R.L. 88
The effectiveness of three levels of 'tension intervals' in fostering relaxation training of highly anxious college women. PhD U. of Washington, 1975.

HANDS, S.L. 89
An evaluation of a course for women directed toward the development of self-actualizing life styles. PhD U. of Texas Health Science Center at Dallas, 1974.

HANSEN, S.L. 90
Effects of assertive training on assertive behaviors and sense of personal efficacy in women. PhD California Sch. of Prof. Psych., San Diego, 1976.

HARNESS, L.J. 91
The effects of assertiveness training for women as expressed by changes in assertiveness and self-acceptance. PhD U. of North Dakota, 1976.

HARRINGTON, J.A. 92
The effects of assertiveness training on aggressive female college students. PhD Ball State U. 1979.

HART, L.B. 93
Training women to become effective leaders: a case study. EdD U. of Massachusetts, 1974.

HARTWELL, L.J. 94
The effects of an assertiveness training group on the levels of assertiveness and anxiety in females. PhD U. of Tennessee, 1980.

HAYNES, J.S. 95
A study to determine the impact of a sex-roles

course on changing attitudes towards self and women. PhD West Virginia U. 1976.

HEGARTY, M.N. *96*
Self-study group discussions and their effect on attitudes of adolescent females toward self and others. PhD Boston Coll. 1967.

HEGEMAN, E.B. *97*
Choice shift and attitude change in a field setting: women's consciousness-raising groups. PhD New York U. 1974.

HEGI, D. *98*
Strengthening the interpersonal support systems of single females through relationship enhancement training. PhD Texas Tech. U. 1979.

HENDERSON, J.M. *99*
The effects of assertiveness training on self-actualization in women. EdD U. of Northern Colorado, 1975.

HOMES, A.M. *100*
Change in women's consciousness-raising groups: a study of four types of change and of some factors associated with them. DSW U. of Toronto, 1978.

JACKSON, J.D.S. *101*
Assertion training: rational-emotive therapy vs. self-instructional coping therapy in the facilitation of refusal behavior among women. PhD Stanford U. 1980.

JETTE, N.M. *102*
The effect of modern dance and music on body image and self-concept in college women. EdD Brigham Young U. 1975.

JOHNSON, J.W. *103*
The effect of group assertiveness training on assertiveness, self-concept, and sex-role stereotypy in married women. PhD U. of Arkansas, 1976.

JONES, M.E. *104*
A study of the effect of the 1981 NEA/TEA women's leadership training program on the perceptions of competencies and aspirations of participants. PhD George Peabody Coll. for Teachers, 1982.

KELLEN, B.G. *105*
The training and development of success relevant traits in women: an evaluation of a commercial career/personal development. PhD Columbia U. 1981.

KEMPNER, S. *106*
The effects of a cognitive-behavioral treatment on the social assertiveness of single women. PhD Florida State U. 1979.

KINCAID, M.L.B. *107*
Effects of a group consciousness-raising program on the attitudes of adult women. PhD Arizona State U. 1973.

KING, V.G. *108*
The effects of a short-term training workshop on the self-concept of low-assertive college females. PhD American U. 1977.

KNOEPELI, H.E. *109*
The origin of women's autonomous learning groups. PhD U. of Toronto, 1971.

KULLMAN, S.B. *110*
The effect of a body integration group on woman's attitudes toward self and other women. PhD U. of Pittsburgh, 1978.

L'HERISSON, L.A. *112*
Effects of the sex of group leaders on women participants in assertion training. PhD Louisiana State U. and A & M Coll. 1978.

LANG, P.H. *113*
The use of feedback and behavioral assignments in assertive training groups for women. PhD U. of Georgia, 1976.

LANGBERG, M.D. *114*
The effects of structured group sessions on married college women's real and ideal perceptions of their sex roles. PhD Temple U. 1977.

LEBEWOHL, M.G. *115*
The effect of participation in an internship program on the self-esteem of adult women. PhD Boston Coll. 1980.

LEHRER, S.K.S. *116*
The effects of a woman's conference on participant attitudes toward women's roles in society. PhD U. of Southern Mississippi, 1981.

LEVINE-WELSH, P.C. *117*
The effects of three treatments which incorporate rational-emotive techniques and assertion skills training upon locus of control and assertive behavior in adult women. EdD Virginia Polytechnic Inst. and State U. 1982.

LEWITTES, H.J. *118*
Assertiveness training for women in mixed-sex small group discussions. PhD Stanford U. 1976.

LINGIS, M. *119*
The effects of a group values clarification procedure on low-income adolescent girls. EdD Clark U. 1981.

LISS-LEVINSON, N. *120*
Sexual assertiveness for women: an investigation of the effects of sexual assertion training and consciousness-raising groups. PhD Southern Illinois U. at Carbondale, 1976.

LITTLE, G.G. *121*
The impact of assertive training on the anxiety and symptomization of women referred by physicians. PhD U. of Florida, 1978.

LUNCEFORD, R.D. *122*
Self-concept change of black college females as a

result of a weekend black experience encounter workshop. PhD United States International U. 1973.

MAAS, J.P. *123*
Ego diffusion in women with behavioral disorders and the integrating effects of psychodrama in identity consolidation. PhD U. of Southern California, 1964.

MCCUISTION, S.L. *124*
The effect of the self-help clinic experience on body ownership in women. PhD California Sch. of Prof. Psych., Los Angeles, 1973.

MANDERINO, M.A. *125*
Effects of a group assertive training procedure on undergraduate women. PhD Arizona State U. 1974.

MATTHEWS, B.C. *126*
Effects of a choice awareness experiential workshop on locus of control, performance self-esteem, and self-oriented attributions in a woman/woman dyadic model. EdD U. of Tennessee, 1980.

MEHNERT, I.B. *127*
The effects of an abbreviated training paradigm on females learning assertive behavior. EdD U. of South Dakota, 1974.

MERTENS, J.S. *128*
The effects of mental hygiene motion pictures on the self-regarding attitudes and self-perceptions of college girls. PhD Pennsylvania State U. 1951.

MOINAT, S.M. *129*
Client characteristics: service, delivery and outcome for female diversion clients. PhD Claremont Grad. Sch. 1979.

NOVINCE, L.C. *130*
The contribution of cognitive restructuring to the effectiveness of behavior rehearsal in modifying social inhibition in females. PhD U. of Cincinnati, 1977.

O'LEARY, M.J.K. *131*
The effects of assertion training on fear of success, locus of control and self-acceptance in women. PhD U. of Missouri–Kansas City, 1977.

PALEY, S.G. *132*
Cognitive-behavioral assertiveness training for socially withdrawn female adolescents. PhD Syracuse U. 1981.

PARMELY, C.A. *133*
Behavioral and self-concept change in adult women resulting from an assertive training program. EdD Boston U. Sch. of Educ. 1978.

PEARMAN, F.C. *134*
A short-term training program to decrease sex-role stereotyping toward women. PhD U. of Oklahoma, 1980.

PEARSON, D.F. *135*
Effects of teaching assertiveness skills to women by correspondence. PhD Brigham Young U. 1981.

PERTZBORN, A.M. *136*
The effect of Gestalt therapy on self-actualization, anxiety and muscle tension in female college students. PhD Fielding Inst. 1979.

PETERSON, N. *137*
Effects of two distinct life-planning group models upon several personal and vocational outcome measures in adult women. EdD U. of Cincinnati, 1978.

PHINNEY, A.L. *138*
The effects of assertion training and bibliotherapy with married women. PhD State U. of New York at Stony Brook, 1977.

PITKIN, E.R. *139*
An investigation of the differential effects of three types of behavior training in job seeking for women. ScD Boston U. 1978.

POSLUNS, E. *140*
The change process of women becoming liberated from sex-role stereotypes. EdD U. of Toronto, 1981.

REILLY, C.J. *141*
The effects of assertiveness and career/life planning training on personal assertiveness, locus of control, and self-concept of disadvantaged women. EdD Boston U. Sch. of Educ. 1981.

REISMAN, B.L. *142*
Short-term effects of 'seminar counseling women' on attitudes and behaviors towards women held by its participants. PhD Kent State U. 1977.

REITER, M.J. *143*
Effects of postural training on self-concept of selected college women. PhD U. of Utah, 1972.

RICHEY, C.A. *144*
Increased female assertiveness through self-reinforcement. PhD U. of California, Berkeley, 1974.

RIEGLER, E. *145*
The effect of pre-treatment instructions and sex of roleplayer on the assertive training of college females. PhD U. of Alabama, 1977.

RUDNER, R.A. *146*
The effects of jogging and assertiveness training on self variables and assertiveness in women. PhD U. of Florida, 1979.

RUDOLPH, S.G. *147*
The effect on the self-concept of female college students of participation in hatha yoga and effective interpersonal relationship development classes. PhD Ball State U. 1981.

RYAN, F.P. *148*
Modifying highly external locus of control, reduc-

ing anxiety, and increasing assertive behavior among women students. PhD Pennsylvania State U. 1975.

SCHUBERT, M. *149*
The impact of consciousness-raising groups on women and their committed relationships. PhD Southern Illinois U. at Carbondale, 1977.

SCHWARTZ, P.L. *150*
An investigation of assertiveness, locus of control, and response to stress in streetwalkers as compared to other working women. PhD, U. of Miami, 1981.

SINGER, J.E. *151*
Sexual mythology: a social learning approach to the elimination of sex-role stereotyped behavior in women. PhD U. of Colorado at Boulder, 1975.

SMITH, N.A. *152*
The dramatic synthesis group process as a facilitator of personal growth: a group experience for women revolving around the cooperative creation of a play. EdD U. of Arkansas, 1982.

STALLWORTH, A.J. *153*
The relative effect of rational behavior training on the anxiety level of women college students. EdD Mississippi State U. 1982.

STEEL, C.M. *154*
The effects of group assertive skill training on the development, maintenance, and generalization of assertive skills in unassertive female undergraduates. PhD U. of Missouri–Columbia, 1976.

STEVENSON, N.A.T. *155*
Effects of assertiveness training on the achievement motivation levels of women in transition. EdD East Texas State U. 1979.

STIGLITZ, E.A. *156*
An evaluation of a women's consciousness-raising group: the process of change. PhD Purdue U. 1976.

STRAUSS, E.R. *157*
Analysis of change in female self-esteem as the result of participation in the Crystal and Bolles method of career/life planning. EdD Northeastern U. 1977.

STRIEGEL, Q.B. *158*
Self-reported behavioral and attitudinal changes influenced by participation in women's consciousness-raising groups. PhD U. of Kansas, 1975.

TAIT, H.S. *159*
The effect of assertion training on selected personality dimensions of women. PhD U. of Missouri–Kansas City, 1976.

TALAN, B.S. *160*
Power and control: predictors for the woman's choice and effectiveness of treatment. PhD U. of Detroit, 1981.

TALBURTT, M.A. *161*
Promoting creative risk-taking in women. PhD U. of Michigan, 1976.

TERRILL, M.J. *162*
The effects of assertion training and cognitive restructuring on the assertive behavior and situational discomfort of college women. PhD U. of Illinois at Urbana–Champaign, 1978.

THOMAS, A.G. *163*
Assertion training for professional women: a case study. EdD U. of Massachusetts, 1976.

THOMPSON, P.E. *164*
Locus of control, body articulation and sexual differentiation in women as modified by self-help and sex education programs. PhD Michigan State U. 1980.

TILLMANN, G.Y. *165*
The effects of peer feedback on assertive training outcomes with female adolescents. PhD Fordham U. 1981.

TINSLEY, J.R. *166*
The differential effects of an audio program learning tape and open group discussion on women's attitudes toward women and work. PhD U. of Missouri, 1973.

WALKER, P.M. *167*
Women's consciousness-raising groups: an exploratory study of demographic and other related variables. PhD U. of Texas at Austin, 1977.

WALL, K.E. *168*
Effects of all-female and mixed-sex assertion training groups on the assertive behavior of females. PhD U. of Miami, 1977.

WEINBERG, C.C. *169*
The creative process as a vehicle for personal growth: a small-group experience for women revolving around the cooperative creation of a slide/tape show. PhD Michigan State U. 1977.

WILCOXON, L.A. *170*
Therapeutic effects of self-instructional training for nonassertive women. PhD Pennsylvania State U. 1976.

WILMOTH, P.B. *171*
Effects of sex composition of the group on assertion training outcomes for women. PhD U. of Missouri–Columbia, 1979.

WONG, J.M.B. *172*
A staff development model for adult women: three sequential interventions and followup data. PhD U. of Minnesota, 1980.

WORKMAN, J.F. *173*
Changes in self-esteem, locus of control, and anxiety among female college students related to assertion training. PhD U. of Southern California, 1982.

WYSOCKI, S.R. *174*
Differential effects of three group treatments on self-actualization and attitudes toward the sex roles of women. PhD U. of Southern California, 1975.

Developmental psychology

Childhood

ANDERSON, D.E. *175*
Psycho-social correlates of locus of control expectancies in female children. PhD U. of Alberta, 1976.

BOOTH, S.D. *176*
Perceived similarity of sex-role characteristics among preadolescent and adolescent girls. PhD Columbia U. 1963.

BRODIE, J.R. *177*
Predictors of the imaginary companion phenomenon in preschool girls. PhD Wayne State U. 1981.

CALHOUN, G.C. *178*
The effects of short-term group counseling using assertiveness training techniques on nonassertive preadolescent girls. EdD, George Peabody Coll. for Teachers, 1980.

CLAMAR, A.J. *179*
A comparative study of selected personality characteristics of 8- to 12-year-old adopted and non-adopted girls. PhD New York U. 1979.

DEUTSCH, F. *180*
Cognitive and social determinants of female preschoolers' empathic ability, helping, and sharing behavior. PhD Pennsylvania State U. 1972.

DIAMOND, K.E. *181*
Discrimination of English and nonsense words by 16-week and 32-week old female infants. PhD Ohio State U. 1974.

DOZIER, A.L. *182*
Interaction of race and age of model, and race of subjects, on imitative behavior in girls. PhD Hofstra U. 1975.

GILLAM, K.C.B. *183*
A comparative study of the language of two sisters over the same period of four months between the ages of two years one month and two years five months. MEd U. of Liverpool, 1963.

GLENISTER, D.A. *184*
An investigation of the scientific interests of girls aged 12–13 years. MA U. of London, Day Training Coll. 1932.

GOFFMAN, M.L.M. *185*
Management of aggression in preadolescent girls: its effect on certain aspects of ego functioning. PhD U. of Michigan, 1961.

LUDEKE, R.J. *186*
Teaching behaviors of 11-year-old and 9-year-old girls in same-age and mixed-age dyads. PhD U. of Minnesota, 1978.

LYNN, R. *187*
Sex-role preference and mother-daughter fantasies in young girls. PhD U. of Denver, 1961.

MOELLER, T.P. *188*
Cooperative behaviors of four-year-old girls in nursery school settings. PhD U. of Michigan, 1974.

MORRISSETTE, M.P. *189*
The use of categories by bright, normal and subnormal pre-adolescent girls on the Pikunas graphoscopic scale and the Stephens categorization tasks. PhD U. of Oklahoma, 1967.

MULAWKA, E.J. *190*
Sex-role typing in the elementary school classroom as reinforcement of sex-role sterotypes learned at home. PhD Wayne State U. 1972.

OETZEL, R.L.M. *191*
The relationship of aggression anxiety to sex-typing in ten-year-old girls. PhD Stanford U. 1964.

RALEY, A.L. *192*
Responses of girls to the humor of cartoons. PhD Fordham U. 1942.

RASHBA, S.J.M. *193*
Antecedent conditions in the development of empathy and style of approach in eight-year-old girls. PhD U. of Florida, 1975.

ROEHL, K.L. *194*
Preadolescent and adolescent female sex-role identity as a function of ego development level and parental sex-role identity. PhD U. of Minnesota, 1980.

SAMS, F.A.S. *195*
Locus of control, peer group size, and feedback and conformity in nine-year-old females. PhD Emory U. 1976.

SPARER, E.A. *196*
Gender identity of three-year-old girls in two diverse groups: children of single mothers and children of couples. PhD California Sch. of Prof. Psych., Berkeley, 1978.

SQUIRES, M.F. *197*
Empathic, nurturant and abusive behavior of normally and abnormally reared girls. PhD Indiana U. 1979.

SUBER, C.J. *198*
The effect of certain social variables on sex role preference and gender identification in preschool age girls. PhD U. of Maryland, 1975.

WOOD, H.D. *199*
Predicting behavioral types in preadolescent girls from psychosocial development and friendship values. PhD U. of Windsor, 1976.

Adolescence

See also **2** 76–172; **4** 168–203; **6** 28–130; **8** 294–390; **19** 14–234 and 495–570.

ADLER, I.S. *200*
A profile of the runaway-prone adolescent girl and a psychodiagnostic instrument for her detection. PhD U. of California, Los Angeles, 1979.

ALLEN, J. *201*
Identity formation in late-adolescent women. PhD City U. of New York, 1973.

ALLSOP, J.F. *202*
The effect of extraversion, neuroticism and psychoticism on measures of anti-social behaviour in secondary schoolgirls. MSc U. of Birmingham, 1973.

ALTMAN, L.D. *203*
Changes in girls' school performance and attitudes toward achievement during the years spanning adolescence. PhD City U. of New York, 1974.

ANDREOLI, M. of St. V. *204*
Experimental aggression and self-punishment in three contrasted groups of adolescent girls. PhD Fordham U. 1964.

AURITT, J.Y. *205*
The relationship between a behavioral manifestation of fear of success and sex-appropriate achievement behavior in early adolescent females. PhD Temple U. 1976.

BLANCHARD, P.M. *206*
The adolescent girl: a study from the psychoanalytic viewpoint. PhD Clark U. 1919.

BLODGETT, H.E. *207*
An experimental approach to the measurement of self-evaluation among adolescent girls. PhD U. of Minnesota, 1953.

BLOOM, A.R. *208*
Achievement motivation and occupational choice: a study of adolescent girls. PhD Bryn Mawr Coll. 1971.

BRINKERHOFF, R.S. *209*
Ego development in adolescent girls. PhD U. of Chicago, 1972.

BURNS, R. *210*
Perceptual cognitive development and its relation to activity in adolescent girls. PhD Catholic U. of America, 1974.

BUTLER, I.C. *211*
Self-concept, race and social class in adolescent females. PhD U. of Washington, 1977.

CAMPBELL, P.B. *212*
Feminine intellectual decline during adolescence. PhD Syracuse U. 1973.

CAPWELL, D.F. *213*
Personality patterns of adolescent girls who show improvement in IQ. PhD U. of Pennsylvania, 1944.

CHASEN, B.Z. *214*
The sex-role socialization of working-class adolescent girls: thematic analysis of role-change behavior in writing children's stories. EdD Harvard U. 1981.

CHASSIN, L. *215*
Sex-role identification, sex-role preference and psychopathology in lower-class black adolescent girls. PhD Columbia U. 1977.

CHISHOLM, J.F. *216*
Alienation and interpersonal perception among female adolescent runaways and truants. PhD U. of Massachusetts, 1978.

COLEMAN, C.E. *217*
An investigation of girls' job perceptions. MEd U. of Liverpool, 1977.

COWEY, D.W. *218*
A study of low achievement motivation among girls in a selected area. MEd U. of Newcastle upon Tyne, 1972.

CZESCIK, B. *218a*
A comparative study of the object relations of early maturing girls and their latency-aged female peers. PhD California Sch. of Prof. Psych., San Diego, 1980.

DAKOSKE, J.C. *219*
Temporal estimates and perspectives in female adolescents with inhibitive impulsive personality characteristics. PhD Fordham U. 1968.

DALSIMER, K.K. *220*
The development, in adolescent girls, of fear of academic success. PhD New York U. 1973.

DENO, E.D. *221*
Changes in the home activities of junior high school girls over a 27-year period. PhD U. of Minnesota, 1958.

DOCKRAY, D.B. *222*
An inquiry into some of the personal problems of adolescent girls in the fourth year of secondary schools. MEd U. of Newcastle upon Tyne, 1972.

DOCTORS, S.R. *223*
The symptom of delicate self-cutting in adolescent females: a developmental view. PhD Yeshiva U. 1979.

DODSON, E.A. *224*
The effects of female role models on occupational exploration and attitudes of adolescents. PhD Michigan State U. 1973.

DOHERTY, P.M. *225*
Self-acceptance as a function of same-sex peer relationships in adolescent and young adult women. EdD Boston U. Sch. of Educ. 1976.

DOROFF, D.R. *226*
Attempted and gestured suicide in adolescent girls. EdD Rutgers U. 1968.

DOTY, S.A. *227*
Runaway behavior and perceived resource availability in adolescent females. PhD U. of Texas at Austin, 1979.

DUBOIS, C.A. *228*
Girls' adolescence observances in North America. PhD U. of California, Berkeley, 1933.

EGAN, G.V. *229*
Antecedents and consequents of cross-identification in adolescent females. PhD Saint Louis U. 1964.

FAUST, M.S. *230*
Developmental maturity as a determinant in prestige of adolescent girls. PhD Stanford U. 1957.

FEINSTEIN, P.E. *231*
Cognitive stage and psychosocial concern in early latency-aged girls. PhD Yeshiva U. 1980.

FITCH, R.S. *232*
Examination of selected MMPI profiles of four groups of Spanish-American and Anglo-American adolescent females. EdD Baylor U. 1972.

FORD, V.B. *233*
An investigation of the selection process and drug treatment of explosively aggressive adolescent females.

FORTENBERRY, M.M. *234*
The experience of latency-aged girls from intact and divorced families. PhD Fielding Inst. 1982.

GATHRON, M.K. *235*
An analysis of variables affecting the self-concept in unmarried teenage girls. EdD Oklahoma State U. 1981.

GEORGE, V.D. *236*
An investigation of the occupational aspirations of talented black adolescent females. PhD Case Western Reserve U. 1979.

GHOSH, D. *237*
An investigation into the development of value judgements and factors influencing it among groups of girls in secondary modern schools. MA U. of London, Inst. of Educ. 1964.

GUPTA, S.P. *238*
A study of various aspects of the psychological development of groups of adolescent girls in certain secondary modern schools in the London area. MA U. of London, Inst. of Educ. 1964.

HEMMING, C.J. *239*
Some problems of adolescent girls (an analysis of the contents of letters to a journal). PhD U. of London, Birkbeck Coll. 1957.

HILLERY, M.P. *240*
The religious life of adolescent girls. PhD Catholic U. of America, 1939.

HOFFMAN, B.R. *241*
Sex-role perceptions, sex-role self-concepts and future plans of teenage girls. PhD Boston U. Graduate Sch. 1973.

HUNTER, M.G. *242*
The reactions of young adolescent girls and their parents to puberty. PhD Boston U. Grad. Sch. 1974.

IRESON, C.J. *243*
Effects of sex-role socialization on the academic achievement, educational expectations, and interpersonal competence of adolescent girls. PhD Cornell U. 1975.

JAQUISH, G.A. *244*
Divergent thinking and perceived complexity of the life-structure among female adolescents. PhD Cornell U. 1981.

KENNEDY, E.A. *245*
Personality needs in the experience behavior and life plans of gifted girls. EdD Columbia U. 1964.

KILOSO, K.L. *246*
Female adolescents' perceptions of self, of their television fictional role models and of their real world role models: an exploratory study. PhD Ohio State U., 1974.

KIRSHNER, K.S. *247*
Factors contributing to the psychological importance of work to adolescent females. EdD Boston U. Sch. of Educ. 1982.

KNOEBBER, M.M. *248*
The adolescent girl: an analysis of her attitudes, ideals, and problems. PhD Saint Louis U. 1934.

KRUSE, M.A. *249*
Ordinal position and the occurrence of Holland's personality types among talented adolescent females. PhD Case Western Reserve U. 1979.

LAHIRY, M. *250*
A study of the attitudes of adolescent girls to their own physical, intellectual, emotional and social development. MA U. of London, Inst. of Educ. 1960.

LATTIMORE, C.L. *251*
The relationship of selected antecedent conditions and locus of control among black adolescent females. PhD Duke U. 1978.

LINDEN, B.W. *252*
Personality characteristics, family variables, and ego-development in runaway girls. PhD U. of Wyoming, 1979.

MCCONNON, A.M. *253*
Self-acceptance, self-concepts and perception of family relations in adolescent girls attending con-

vent grammar schools. MEd U. of Manchester, 1968.

MCEWAN, C.C. *254*
Some medical and social aspects of the female adolescent years as observed in the City of Glasgow in the early 1960s. MD U. of Glasgow, 1965.

MCGAUGHEY, M.V. *255*
The formation of learning set as a function of creativity and intelligence in adolescent females. PhD U. of Georgia, 1968.

MALTAS, C.P. *256*
Feminine self-concepts and self-esteem in the transition to adolescence. PhD Boston U. Grad. Sch. 1975.

MANDAL, U. *257*
A study of the influence of identification and the self-concept on the attitudes and values of girls aged 10–15. MA U. of London, Inst. of Educ. 1963.

MANTHEI, D.W. *258*
Disengagement from childhood in late adolescent females. PhD Boston U. 1972.

MARTHAS, M. *259*
A study of the process of sexual identity formation in adolescent females. EdD Boston U. Sch. of Educ. 1980.

MINAHAN, N.M. *260*
Relationships among self-perceived physical attractiveness, body shape and personality of teenage girls. PhD U. of Illinois at Urbana–Champaign, 1971.

MISTRY, Z.D. *261*
A study of the self-picture held by selected groups of adolescent girls prior to and after school-leaving age. MA U. of London, Inst. of Educ. 1960.

MOSES, H.M. *262*
The relationship of degree of autonomy to degree of cognitive expansiveness in adolescent girls. PhD City U. of New York, 1968.

MULHOLLAND, A.J. *263*
Adolescent girls' perception of parents and teachers. MSc Queen's U. of Belfast, 1971.

NEWMAN, S.J. *264*
The female adolescent psychopath and her parents: an examination of their interpersonal relationship. PhD Brigham Young U. 1981.

NILES, F.S. *265*
The influence of parents and peers on adolescent girls. MEd U. of Manchester, 1969.

O'BYRNE, J.G. *266*
Effects of Kohlbergian and Rogerian treatments on the moral development and logical reasoning of adolescent girls. PhD Catholic U. of America, 1976.

O'CONNOR, M. *267*
An investigation into psychological stress in school-going adolescent girls. MEd U. of Dublin, Trinity College, 1978.

PEACOCK, R.A. *268*
Situational determinants of assertiveness in depressed and nondepressed girls. PhD U. of Alabama, 1981.

PIERIS, H.E. *269*
A comparative study of the interests of adolescent girls in certain urban and rural areas. MA U. of London, Inst. of Educ. 1949.

PIPITONE, P.L. *270*
The function of self-esteem, attitudes toward school and teachers' perceptions among above average fifth-grade girls. PhD Kent State U. 1974.

PIXELL, M. *271*
An inquiry into the apparent narrowing of interests of girls on entering adolescence. MA U. of London, Inst. of Educ. 1966.

PRICE, H.H. *272*
Securing valid and reliable evidence of the ability of the adolescent girl to make intelligent decisions concerning the use of personal resources. PhD Ohio State U. 1939.

RANKIN, P.P. *273*
Looking at change in the area of body image and self-concept in adolescent females after exposure to two types of small group counseling experiences. EdD U. of Southern California, 1974.

REAVELY, G. *274*
Adult attitudes toward sex-role discontinuity in adolescent and preadolescent girls. PhD California Sch. of Prof. Psych., Los Angeles, 1977.

RICHMOND, W.V. *275*
The adolescent girl: a clinical study. PhD Clark U. 1919.

ROFF, C. *276*
The self-concept in adolescent girls. PhD Boston U. 1959.

ROSKAM, A. *277*
Patterns of autonomy in high-achieving adolescent girls who differ in need for approval. PhD City U. of New York, 1972.

ROWE, R.L. *278*
A study of differential developmental factors in the behavioral history of female adolescents as criteria in special education grouping practices. EdD U. of Oregon, 1965.

ROY, K. *279*
Relation between the role of the girl in the club and her role in the family. PhD Cornell U. 1940.

RYAN, H.M. *280*
The problems and personality adjustments of adolescent girls. PhD Fordham U. 1953.

SACHS, B.A. 281
The relationship of cognitive development to interpersonal problem solving abilities in female adolescents. PhD Wayne State U. 1981.

SAFRIN, R. 282
Primary process thought in the Rorschachs of girls at the oedipal, latency, and adolescent stages of development. PhD New York U. 1974.

SCHUTZ, R.E. 283
Patterns of personal problems of adolescent girls. PhD Columbia U. 1957.

SCOTT, L.E.U. 284
The effects of mixed-sex and single-sex cooperative grouping and individualization on science achievement and attitudes of early adolescent females. PhD U. of Minnesota, 1982.

SELINGER, S. 285
Stages of ego and psychodynamic development in female adolescents. PhD Ohio State U. 1976.

SHORTER, D.L. 286
The relationship between political activism and psychosocial development in late adolescent black women. PhD U. of Maryland, 1978.

SHUKERT, A.B.H. 287
Ego identity achievement and academic achievement motivation in adolescent females. PhD U. of Texas at Austin, 1979.

SMART, L.S. 288
Gender-role identity, feminist ideology, and career and family commitment of twelfth-grade girls in New England. PhD U. of Connecticut, 1979.

SMOKLER, C.B.S. 289
The development of self-esteem and femininity in early adolescence. PhD U. of Michigan, 1974.

STACEY, M.W. 290
An enquiry into the stability of attitudes and interests of a group of adolescent girls. MA U. of London, Inst. of Educ. 1948.

STEELE, C.I. 291
Institutional placement during adolescence and its relationship to the girl's task of sexual identification. DSW Smith Coll. Sch. for Social Work, 1969.

STEIN, N.D. 292
Interplay: a psycho-social study of sex-role beliefs and attitudes and the physical activities of working-class adolescent girls. EdD Harvard U. 1981.

STERLING, D.H. 293
The experience of being me for black adolescent females: a phenomenological investigation of black identity. PhD U. of Pittsburgh, 1974.

STRUTT, B.E. 294
The influence of Outward Bound courses on the personality of girls. MEd U. of Manchester, 1965.

TERRAZAS, O.E. 295
The self-concept of Mexican-American adolescent females. PhD Wright Inst. 1980.

THOMAS, N.L.V. 296
The effects of a sensitivity-encounter group experience upon self-concept and school achievement in adolescent underachieving girls. PhD Loyola U. of Chicago, 1974.

TORDA, F.R. 297
Heterosexual, marital and maternal orientations of late adolescent negro and white girls. PhD U. of Chicago, 1969.

TYLER, L.E. 298
Factors conditioning the development of interests in adolescent girls. PhD U. of Minnesota, 1941.

WESTCOTT, R.H. 299
Guidance in life problems for the adolescent girl student. EdD U. of California, Berkeley, 1923.

WINTERSTEINER, G.S. 300
The effects of a sex-role stereotyping awareness workshop on the level of ego development, occupational aspiration and sex-role attitudes of adolescent females. EdD Boston U. Sch. of Educ. 1979.

WOOTON, P.A. 301
Factors influencing the moral judgements made by secondary school girls. MEd U. of Manchester, 1973.

WRCHOTA, R.J. 302
Oral passive aims in acting out adolescent girls in relationship to the developmental task of sexual identification. DSW Smith Coll. Sch. for Social Work, 1973.

Adult development

General

ACKERMAN, W.B.H. 303
Women's search for roles. PhD State U. of New York at Buffalo, 1975.

ADELMAN, S.C. 304
Field independence and feminine identity. PhD Harvard U. 1974.

ADELSON, B.M. 305
Moral judgment in women as a function of field independence, feminist attitudes, and subjective adult experience. PhD New York U. 1975.

ALEXANDER, K.L. 306
Psychosocial development of women in early adulthood. EdD Boston U. Sch. of Educ. 1980.

AMENT, R.B.G. 307
Female sex-role attitudes and the occupational rating of sex-announced profiles. PhD St John's U. 1982.

ARMSTRONG, A.M. 308
The relationship among need for power, sex of subject, career choice, and the social and psychological barriers that limit leadership opportunities for women. PhD Fielding Inst. 1978.

AUSUBEL, J.E. 309
Fear of success in women and its relation to unresolved dependency needs and the inhibition of aggression. PhD Adelphi U. 1981.

BAEFSKY, P.M. 310
Self-sacrifice, cooperation, and aggression in women of varying sex-role orientations. PhD U. of Southern California, 1974.

BAKER, L.G. 311
A comparison of the personal and social adjustment of 38 never-married women and 38 married women. PhD Oregon State U. 1967.

BARNETT, B.A. 312
Anger in women: the difference between actual and ideal response styles. PhD California Sch. of Prof. Psych., Berkeley, 1976.

BARRON, C.R. 313
Female expectations and attributions for success outcomes as a function of sex-role orientation, private self-consciousness, and sex-linkage of task. PhD Ohio State U. 1980.

BERMAN, F.D. 314
Rorschach assessment of abusive and non-abusive women: a study of border-line personality organization. EdD U. of Tulsa, 1982.

BERNER, A.J. Jr. 315
Women in transition: the self-concept of women at four phases of the adult life cycle. PhD Claremont Grad. Sch. 1981.

BERNSTEIN, A.M.W. 316
Fear of failure and role congruence: an investigation into the nature of achievement motivation in women. PhD Michigan State U. 1975.

BEUTELL, N.J. 317
An investigation of inter-role conflicts and coping with role conflict among married women. PhD Stevens Inst. of Technology, 1979.

BINION, V.J. 318
An analysis of factors influencing the development of sex-role identity and sex-role attitudes of contemporary black women. PhD U. of Michigan, 1981.

BIRNBAUM, J.L.A. 319
Life patterns, personality style and self-esteem in gifted family-oriented and career-committed women. PhD U. of Michigan, 1971.

BOILEN, M.G. 320
The third phase of separation individuation in women. PhD Wright Inst. 1981.

BOSSI, E.B. 321
Women's self-images: an experimental study. EdD U. of Massachusetts, 1977.

BROTHERS, C.A. 322
An attributional analysis of the sex-role incongruent female. PhD U. of Maryland, 1978.

BROZOVICH, C.J. 323
A systematic idiographic investigation of a woman in the process of change. PhD California Sch. of Prof. Psych., Berkeley, 1975.

BRUNS-HILLMAN, M.E. 324
Traditional and nontraditional female achievers: factors which may account for divergent modes of expression of achievement motivation. PhD Loyola U., Chicago, 1980.

BURK, J. 325
A psychological approach to cosmetic surgery in women: self-consistency. PhD California Sch. of Prof. Psych., Los Angeles, 1975.

BURNLEY, C.S. 326
Selves, careers, and relationships of never married women. PhD U. of Tennessee, 1979.

CARR, K.A.S. 327
Sex-role orientation as it relates to persuasibility of females: an experimental study. PhD Bowling Green State U. 1974.

CHERRY, E.F. 328
On success avoidance in women: a comparative study of psychoanalytic theories. PhD Adelphi U. 1977.

CHERRY, R.W. 329
A comparative study of the psychosocial development of adult women in four occupations. PhD Wayne State U. 1981.

CHIESA, M.J. 330
Ego development and conceptual development systems and their relationship to coping and defense processes in women. PhD Fordham U. 1980.

CHRISTY, L.C.T. 331
Culture and control orientation: a study of internal-external locus-of-control in Chinese and American-Chinese women. PhD U. of California, Berkeley, 1977.

CLEMENTSON-MOHR, J.A. 332
Academic women: well-being, personality variables and attitudes toward women. PhD U. of Minnesota, 1978.

COKIN, L.A. 333
Educated women in their thirties: an exploratory psychosocial study. PhD George Washington U. 1982.

CONDRIN, B.D. 334
Successful women: a study in the development of

female competence. PhD California Sch. of Prof. Psych., Berkeley, 1975.

COOPER, L.D.P. *335*
Aspirations, attitudes and changing roles of black women in American society. EdD Wayne State U. 1975.

COWAN, M.L. *336*
Personality factors in women affecting their degree of political involvement. PhD Oklahoma State U. 1974.

CRABLE, P.G. *337*
Women and self: an initial investigation of the feminine essence using sandplay. PhD United States International U. 1976.

CRIMMINGS, A.M. *338*
Female causal attribution for success and failure outcomes as a function of sex-role identity and degree of competitiveness in the achievement situation. PhD Ohio State U. 1978.

CROSSON, C.W. *339*
Age and creativity among manifestly creative women. PhD U. of Maryland, 1982.

DAVIES, E.T. *340*
The effect of sex, need for achievement, women's role orientation and normative information upon causal attribution of success. PhD Loyola U., Chicago, 1980.

DAVIS, M.J. *341*
A comparison of traditional and non-traditional identities in women. PhD Brigham Young U. 1981.

DEALMEIDA, E.E. *342*
A descriptive and analytical study of the early adult roles of black and white women. PhD Duke U. 1977.

DE RIDDER, J.A. *343*
Sex-related roles, attitudes and orientation of Negro, Anglo and Mexican-American women over the life cycle. PhD North Texas State U. 1976.

DE ROOY, J.L. *344*
'Ego' as a master trait: an investigation of women's sex-role identification, attitudes toward women, and achievement motivation, as they relate to conforming ego development. EdD U. of Houston, 1980.

DESJARDINS, C.D. *345*
Self-perceptions of women over the adult life cycle. PhD Arizona State U. 1978.

DESMOND, S.E. *346*
Personality orientation, work values and other characteristics of pioneer and traditional academic women. PhD U. of Pittsburgh, 1975.

DICKEY, E.D. *347*
Life events, social support, and adjustment in women: a field study. EdD U. of Massachusetts, 1977.

DOHERTY, A. *348*
The relationship of dependency and perception of parents to the development of feminine sex role and conscience. PhD Catholic U. of America, 1969.

DOYLE, J.A. *349*
A study of the relationships between mental health, field dependency and attitudes toward the female's role. PhD U. of Regina, 1973.

EICHLER, L.S. *350*
'Feminine narcissism': an empirical investigation. PhD Boston U. Grad. Sch. 1973.

EISENBUD, R.J. *351*
Factors influencing the repudiation of femininity. PhD Radcliffe Coll. 1952.

ELLMAN, C.S. *352*
An experimental study of the female castration complex. PhD New York U. 1970.

ERICKSON, J.A. *353*
Work attachment and home role among a cohort of American women. PhD U. of Pennsylvania, 1976.

ESTES, B.J. *354*
A descriptive study of the developmental phase of women in their 30s. PhD U. of Pittsburgh, 1977.

FARONE, P.A. *355*
The adult developmental patterns of career-committed women who make a transition to an integrated lifestyle. PhD U. of Pittsburgh, 1981.

FAVER, C.A. *356*
Women and achievement orientation across the life-cycle. PhD U. of Michigan, 1979.

FEIGENBAUM, R. *357*
The impact of physical attractiveness on actor attributions achievement-related behavior in women. PhD Fordham U. 1981.

FELDMAN, S.M. *358*
The competent woman: a multivariate investigation of sex roles, achievement motivation, self-esteem and locus of control. PhD California Sch. of Prof. Psych., Fresno, 1980.

FISHER, C.B. *359*
Developmental patterns of mid-life career interested women: a life history study. PhD U. of Maryland, 1980.

FLECKLES, S. *360*
Life-cycle development in women: a social-clinical psychology perspective. PhD Wright Inst. 1980.

FONTANA, G.L.J. *361*
An investigation into the dynamics of achievement motivation in women. PhD U. of Michigan, 1970.

FOSTER, N.J. *362*
Women: locus of control and attitudes toward femininity and masculinity. PhD Northwestern U. 1974.

FRANK, E.A. *363*
Employment, homemaking, and married women: the relationship between personality styles, life patterns, and moods. PhD City U. of New York, 1980.

FRANKEL, P.S. *364*
The relationship of self-concept, sex-role attitudes and the development of achievement need in women. PhD Northwestern U. 1969.

GAMA, E.M.E. *365*
Differential effects of achievement and affiliation arousal on achievement of females of differing motivational configurations. PhD U. of Minnesota, 1979.

GANNAWAY, L.L. *366*
Community involvement and values as related to ego development in women. EdD U. of Arkansas, 1982.

GARCIA, D. *367*
Stress, coping and strain in women. PhD Rutgers U. 1981.

GILMORE, B. *368*
Women's need achievement and need to avoid success: relationships with other variables. PhD Illinois Inst. of Technology, 1974.

GITTMAN, B. *369*
The relationships of women's perceptions of self-esteem and locus-of-control orientation to (A) self-role orientation, (B) employment status, (C) dissonance and (D) selected demographic variables. PhD Hofstra U. 1978.

GLASS, C.A. *370*
The differences of individuals with type A and type B behavior patterns and the women's awareness seminar of self-actualization and flexibility. EdD Coll. of William and Mary in Virginia, 1981.

GOLD, D.W. *371*
Disadvantaged women's ego identity status as related to achievement, self-esteem, and demographic information. PhD U. of Pittsburgh, 1980.

GOLDSTEIN, A.B. *372*
Women's fear of success as it relates to the mother-daughter relationship, fear of loss of affiliation, and a fear of competition. PhD California Sch. of Prof. Psych., Berkeley, 1980.

GORDON, A.T. *373*
Self-esteem, sex-role orientation, and career orientation of women in two stages of development: childbearing stage and beyond. PhD U. of California, Berkeley, 1978.

GOTTFRIED, R.B. *374*
Carving new paths: young women's journey to selfhood. PhD Brandeis U. 1982.

GRALEWSKI, C.M. *375*
Sex-role attitudes, perceived competence related to role, and role satisfaction in women differing in traditionality of role. PhD U. of Illinois at Chicago Circle, 1978.

GRAVILL, C.M. *376*
Female stereotypes. MA U. of Essex, 1972.

GREEN, L.H. *377*
An investigation of factors which influence the vocational classification of career-oriented and home-oriented women. PhD Ohio State U. 1971.

GRODNER, S. *378*
The relationship of body image, attitude toward female role and fear of success in adult women. PhD United States International U. 1981.

GRODSKY, P.B. *379*
Models of womanhood: a multivariate approach. PhD City U. of New York, 1975.

HALAS, C.M. *380*
Sex-role stereotypes: perceived childhood socialization experiences and the attitudes and behaviors of mature women. PhD Arizona State U. 1974.

HANCOCK, E. *381*
Women's development in adult life. EdD Harvard U. 1981.

HANCOCK, K.A. *382*
A study of locus of control and psychological androgyny in women as a function of age and feminism. PhD California Sch. of Prof. Psych., Berkeley, 1978.

HANLOM, J.E. *383*
Contributions toward a theory of competence in women. PhD Columbia U. 1978.

HARRIS, M.M. *384*
Personal constructions of sex-typed roles and need achievement among black and white women. PhD U. of Pittsburgh, 1974.

HARTZ-KARP, J.F. *385*
Never married women: the experience, expectations and effects of never marrying and role adaptations to a negatively evaluated status. PhD U. of California, Los Angeles, 1981.

HAVLICK, M.J. *386*
Life styles of single women. PhD Temple U. 1975.

HAWKINS, I.L. *387*
Achievement motivation, race and social class influences upon female attributions. PhD California Sch. of Prof. Psych., 1979.

HECHT, S.L. *388*
An investigation into the dynamics of female

masochistic character structure. PhD U. of California, Berkeley, 1981.

HERBERT, J.C. *389*
Manifest and latent constructions of power in black and white working-class women. PhD New Sch. for Social Research, 1976.

HICKEY, R.M. *390*
A description of adult development in single women following a career-committed life pattern. PhD U. of Pittsburgh, 1981.

HIGGINS-TRENK, M.A. *391*
A descriptive study of women's lifestyles and attributions. PhD Pennsylvania State U. 1979.

HOLLANDER, L.S. *392*
The other woman: personality characteristics and parent-child relationships of single women repeatedly involved with married men. PhD California Sch. of Prof. Psych. 1976.

HOLMES, I.H. *393*
The allocation of time by women without family responsibilities. EdD Columbia U. Teachers Coll. 1981.

HORN, M.L. *394*
The integration of negative experience by high and low functioning women. PhD U. of Florida, 1975.

HOWARD, M.R. *395*
Ego identity status in women, fear of success and performance in a competitive situation. PhD State U. of New York at Buffalo, 1975.

HUDSON, J.O. *396*
Aggression and directionality in manifest dream content across level of ego development in female adults. EdD U. of Houston, 1979.

HUGHES, C.B. *397*
Stressors, role strain and coping mechanisms in the continuously employed nurse-mother. EdD Columbia U. Teachers Coll. 1980.

HYMAN, R.B. *398*
The relationship of inner-direction and time-competence to four stages of adulthood in a sample of women in the mental health professions. PhD Hofstra U. 1978.

INGRAM, R.P. *399*
The effects of locus of control and sex-role preferences on the achievement orientation of females. EdD U. of Georgia, 1980.

IVERSON, K.R. *400*
The acculturation process among academic women. PhD U. of Wisconsin–Madison, 1977.

JABURY, D.E. *401*
Identity diffusion as a function of sex roles in adult women. PhD Michigan State U. 1967.

JACOBSON, S.F. *402*
Sex-role identity and sex-role attitudes as related to achievement motivation in women. PhD New York U. 1977.

JAKOUBEK, J.T. *403*
Sex-role conceptualization, self-descriptions and role strain in women as related to ego development. PhD U. of Arkansas, 1979.

JENKINS, S.R. *404*
Person-situation interaction and women's achievement-related motives. PhD Boston U. Grad. Sch. 1982.

JOHNSON, L.J. *405*
A comparative study of the womanhood experiences of black young adult females and white young adult females. PhD U. of South Carolina, 1976.

JOHNSON, M.M. *406*
Instrumental and expressive components in the personalities of women. PhD Radcliffe Coll. 1955.

JOHNSON, P.A. *407*
The relationships of trait anxiety, personality characteristics and values to assertiveness in the adult woman. PhD Ohio State U. 1976.

JOHNSTON, A.D. *408*
Sex role and self-actualization in women over 30 years of age. PhD United States International U. 1981.

KANTER, M.K. *409*
Psychological implications of never-married women who live alone. PhD California Sch. of Prof. Psych., Berkeley, 1977.

KAPLAN, S.R. *410*
An exploratory study of adult development of educated women: social and psychological factors related to continuing education in graduate and professional programs. PhD U. of California, Berkeley, 1980.

KAYE, A.L. *411*
An investigation of early adult and midlife structure for women living a traditional life pattern. PhD U. of Pittsburgh, 1981.

KEYS, E.J. *412*
Women's roles: an attitudinal and behavioral survey. PhD U. of Cincinnati, 1976.

KERR, M. *413*
Emotional fluctuations in women. PhD U. of London, Bedford Coll. 1938.

KIEFFER, C.M. *414*
The never-married mature academic woman: a life history analysis. PhD U. of Missouri–Columbia, 1979.

KIMELMAN, J. *415*
Woman's search for identity. PhD U. of Cincinnati, 1973.

KIMLICKA, T.M. *416*
A comparison of androgynous, feminine, mascu-

line, and undifferentiated women on sex guilt, self-esteem and body satisfaction. PhD Washington State U. 1978.

KLEIN, H.M. *417*
Psychological masculinity and femininity, self-consciousness, and typical and maximal dominance expression in women. PhD U. of Texas at Austin, 1978.

KNOX, N.B. *418*
Sex-role orientation and self-esteem in career-committed and home-oriented women. PhD California Sch. of Prof. Psych., Berkeley, 1977.

KRIGER, S.F. *419*
Need achievement and perceived parental child-rearing attitudes of career women and homemakers. PhD Ohio State U. 1971.

KROHN, K.H. *420*
The need to achieve and the need to nurture in women in different life stages. PhD City U. of New York, 1979.

KULICK, F.B. *421*
Affect and expectancy of females high and low in achievement motivation as a function of causal beliefs. PhD U. of Miami, 1978.

LACKEY, B.C. *422*
Perceptions of the quality of family life of career women and their families and non-career women and their families. PhD United States International U. 1981.

LANDESMAN, C.F. *423*
Some personality traits of high-achieving women: an exploratory study. PhD California Sch. of Prof. Psych., Los Angeles, 1976.

LARSON, M.S.F. *424*
Female achievement conflict related to parental sex-typing and identification. PhD Michigan State U. 1969.

LINK, M.C. *425*
A description of the relationship between day-dreaming patterns of women and cognitive style, sex-role orientation and anxiety. PhD U. of Pittsburgh, 1982.

LOBBAN, G.M. *426*
Some patterns of adult feminine identity and their preoedipal and oedipal antecedents. PhD City U. of New York, 1982.

LORING, J.B. *427*
Modern traditional role ideology related to selected aspects of women's lifestyles. EdD American U. 1974.

MCCLOSKY, M.G. *428*
Women at educational and professional cross-roads: an exploratory investigation of their attitudes, self-perceptions and personal goals. PhD U. of California, Berkeley, 1975.

MCFARLANE, B.F. *429*
New directions: a study of adult women. PhD Wright Inst. 1976.

MCKINLEY, M.C. *430*
The effect of a psychology of personal growth course on levels of self-actualization and psychological androgyny in mature women students. PhD Loyola U., Chicago, 1978.

MCMURRY, M.J. *431*
Religion and women's sex-role traditionalism. PhD Indiana U. 1975.

MANNING, T.T. *432*
Career motivation, ego development and self-actualization in adult women. PhD Catholic U. of America, 1973.

MARSHALL, P.S. *433*
Personal power and mental health in women of an energy-impacted town. PhD Colorado State U. 1980.

MARTIN, M.A. *434*
Strategies of adaptation: coping patterns of the urban transient female. DSW Columbia U. 1982.

MATTEI, N.M. *435*
Education for ego and sex-role development in young women. EdD Boston U. Sch. of Educ. 1979.

MEGINNIS, S.K. *436*
Correlation of selected sociodemographic and psychological variables with indicators of sex-role orientation of young adult women. PhD U. of North Carolina at Chapel Hill, 1979.

MICHAEL, C.N. *437*
A phenomenological study of female adult development through age thirty-four. PhD U. of Connecticut, 1981.

MILLER, E.S. *438*
Achievement motivation in women: a developmental perspective. PhD Loyola U., Chicago, 1977.

MOONEY-GETOFF, M.J. *439*
Women and personal power: decisions which open and close future lines of action. PhD Pennsylvania State U. 1979.

MORGAN, D.D. *440*
Perception of role conflicts and self-concepts among career and noncareer college-educated women. PhD Columbia U. 1962.

MORGAN, S. *441*
Contradictions and conflicts in sex-role expectations as a function of ego development: a study of women volunteering in decision-making positions. PhD U. of California, Berkeley, 1979.

MORRIS, E.F. *442*
The personality traits and the psychological needs of educated homemakers and career women. EdD Arizona State U. 1974.

MUNRO, M.E. 443
The effects of sex of partner, role model and androgyny on female competitiveness. PhD U. of Florida, 1978.

MURPHY, M. 444
The third decade: developmental concerns of women between the ages of thirty and forty. PhD California Sch. of Prof. Psych., Berkeley, 1976.

MYERS, L.W. 445
A study of the self-esteem maintenance process among black women. PhD Michigan State U. 1973.

NASH, L.J. 446
Relation between sexual object choice of women and ego development, neuroticism, and conscious and unconscious sexual identity. PhD Hofstra U. 1976.

NASON, M.W. 447
Field dependence and nurturance in women: a study of mode of field approach and adult developmental issues. PhD Harvard U. 1974.

NELLE, S.V. 448
Cognitive social learning of sex-roles and self-concepts in women. PhD U. of Washington, 1975.

NORRIS, W.L. 449
A path model for feelings of personal efficacy for black employed male and female familyheads, employed female non-familyheads and housewives. PhD U. of Michigan, 1980.

O'CONNELL, A.A.N. 450
Determinants of women's life styles and sense of identity: personality, attitudes, significant-others, and demographic characteristics. PhD Rutgers U. 1974.

O'NEILL, M.S. 451
An investigation of women's sex-role conflict and the predictability of modes of conflict resolution. PhD Boston Coll. 1974.

ORLASKY, C.L. 452
A study of fear of success among adult women. PhD Kent State U. 1979.

PACE, M.A. 453
A descriptive study of the characteristics of the never-married female including self-concept and family interaction. PhD Florida State U. 1975.

PAPILLON, J.S. 454
Skin color and self-concept among black women. PhD California Sch. of Prof. Psych., Berkeley, 1976.

PARSONS, P.F. 455
Research on black female self-concept: origins, issues, and directions. PhD Claremont Grad. Sch. 1974.

PECHTEL, J.D. 456
Type of education and other factors in the adjustment of blind women. PhD Northwestern U. 1951.

PHILLIPS, W.E. 457
The motive to achieve in women as related to perception of sex role in society. PhD U. of Maryland, 1974.

PIZZI, R.E. 458
The impact of role stereotypes on the socialization of women. PhD U. of Washington, 1982.

PORJESZ, Y.R. 459
The femininity-achievement conflict: an expanded formulation of the motive to avoid success in females. PhD City U. of New York, 1974.

PORTER, M.L. 460
Psychodynamic correlates of sex-role attributes in women. PhD U. of California, Santa Barbara, 1978.

POWELL, B. 461
Role-conflict and symptoms of psychological distress in college-educated women. PhD Fordham U. 1975.

PREFONTAINE, M. 462
Women's role orientation in three types of French Canadian educational institutions. PhD Cornell U. 1969.

PUDER, M.A. 463
An empirical investigation of an expanded formulation of the motive to avoid success in females. PhD City U. of New York, 1976.

RAFFE, D. 464
Competitive behavior in women: the influence of unconscious factors. PhD Northwestern U. 1980.

RAND, J.E. 465
Feminine ego style: a psychosocial adaption. PhD California Sch. of Prof. Psych., San Diego, 1980.

REESE, R.E.S. 466
A process-oriented study of psychosocial development in women age thirty-two to forty-five. PhD U. of Wisconsin–Milwaukee, 1982.

REILLY, S.J. 467
The relation of sex-role orientation in women to coping style and cognitive response to stress. PhD U. of Southern California, 1981.

REYNOLDS, J.L. 468
A comparison of the effects of self-as-a-model/others-as-a-model on assertion and androgyny in females. EdD Mississippi State U. 1982.

RICHMAN, J.A. 469
Psychological and psychophysiological distress in employed women and housewives: class, age and ethnic differences. PhD Columbia U. 1978.

RIEGER, M.P. 470
Life patterns, coping strategies and support

systems in high and low creative women. PhD U. of Georgia, 1981.

ROEBUCK, R.E. *471*
The relationship between level of ego development and dogmatism in women. PhD Boston Coll. 1981.

ROEHL, J.E. *472*
Stressful life events of re-entry women students. PhD Arizona State U. 1981.

RUSHING, L.H. *473*
Independence – conformity: a comparative study of white and black women. PhD New Sch. for Social Research, 1982.

SALLEY, K.L. *474*
The development of competitiveness in women. PhD U. of Arkansas, 1977.

SCHAEFFER, J.A. *475*
The relationship between women's self-esteem and their affiliation need. PhD Loyola U. of Chicago, 1982.

SCHENKEL, S. *476*
The relationship between ego identity status, field-independence, and traditional femininity. PhD State U. of New York at Buffalo, 1973.

SCHIFF, E. *477*
The relationship of women's sex-role identity to self-esteem and ego development. PhD U. of Maryland, 1977.

SEIDER, J.A. *478*
A psychohistorical exploration of the psychoanalytic psychology of women. PhD U. of Tennessee, 1976.

SEINFELD, S. *479*
Achievement motivation in women as related to the altruistic other orientation, sex-role attitudes, and traditionality and nontraditionality of vocational choice. PhD New York U. 1981.

SELF, P.A.P. *480*
Self-concepts, attitudes, and values of women honor students. PhD Texas A&M U. 1973.

SELZER, S. *481*
Relationships between developmental experience and choice of defensive behavior; study II: females. PhD U. of Houston, 1956.

SERKIN, E.J. *482*
Personality development in highly educated women in the years eighteen to forty-five. PhD Wright Inst. 1980.

SHANSKY, C.R. *483*
The personality correlates of hypertension and field dependence in black women. PhD Illinois Inst. of Technology, 1976.

SHERLOCK, P.K. *484*
The relationship of Wolff's archetypal feminine images to time orientation and related psychological variables. PhD Pacific Grad. Sch. of Psych. 1980.

SHOFF, S.P. *485*
The significance of age, sex and type of education on the development of reasoning in adults. PhD U. of Utah, 1979.

SIDEL, C.M.M. *486*
The evolution of life decisions in three generations of suburban upper middle class women. PhD Northwestern U. 1977.

SIMS, J.M. *487*
Rural women's mental health and sex-role conflict. PhD California Sch. of Prof. Psych., Fresno, 1979.

SMITH, M.A. *488*
Compliance and defiance as it relates to role conflict in women. PhD U. of Michigan, 1961.

SMITH, S.J. *489*
Dimensions of women's locus-of-control beliefs in relation to academic achievement and expectation, vocational aspiration and attitudes toward the women's movement. PhD U. of California, Berkeley, 1977.

SOYSA, N. *490*
Self-concept and role conflict: a study of some aspects of women's self-perception and self-evaluation in relation to their attitudes towards their sex-role. PhD Cornell U. 1961.

SPRICER, R. *491*
Developmental tasks of adult women. PhD U. of Alberta, 1981.

STEINDORF, D.R. *492*
Compliance and age in women. PhD Illinois Inst. of Technology, 1971.

STEWART, W.A. *493*
A psychosocial study of the formation of the early adult life structure in women. PhD Columbia U. 1977.

STOCKARD, A.J. *494*
The development of sex-role related attitudes and behaviors of young women. PhD U. of Oregon, 1974.

STRAUB, C.A. *495*
An exploration of Chickering's theory and women's development. PhD Ohio State U. 1982.

STRAUSS, M.D. *496*
Women about women: a descriptive study of the psychological impact of the feminine sex-role stereotype. PhD U. of Texas at Austin, 1971.

STUART, J.E. *497*
Vulnerability to learned helplessness and sex-role stereotyping in women. PhD Southern Illinois U. at Carbondale, 1977.

SUGARMAN, L. *498*
Women in early adulthood: developmental tasks and stages. PhD U. of London, Birkbeck Coll. 1982.

TAYLOR, J.P. *499*
Differences and similarities in the self-concepts and sex-role perceptions of black women from non-college, college-student and college-graduated educational categories. PhD U. of Cincinnati, 1979.

TAYLOR, S. *500*
Seven lives: women's life structure evolution in early adulthood. PhD City U. of New York, 1981.

TROCKI, K.F. *501*
The process of social change: the case of women's roles. PhD U. of Pittsburgh, 1977.

TUCCILLO, E. *502*
Women's self-perceived sex-role identification and reactions to perceived frustration. PhD City U. of New York, 1977.

TURNER, M.E.L. *503*
Sex-role attitudes and fear of success in relation to achievement behavior in women. PhD Fordham U. 1974.

TUSKA, S.A. *504*
Self-conception and identification among women planning and not planning to teach. PhD U. of Chicago, 1964.

VAHANIAN, T. *505*
How women feel about being women. PhD Columbia U. 1954.

VIGILANTI, M.A. *506*
The effects of sex-role attitudes on women's self-actualization and life satisfaction. EdD Western Michigan U. 1980.

VOLGY, S.S. *507*
Sex-role orientation and measures of psychological well-being among feminists, housewives and working women. PhD U. of Arizona, 1976.

WARD, L. *508*
The interaction of moral reasoning and motivation on women's behavior in a conflict situation: the moral lens paradox. PhD Case Western Reserve U. 1977.

WEIS, S.J.F. *509*
Self-esteem and self-implementation in role saliency of women. PhD Pennsylvania State U. 1969.

WEISS, J.B. *510*
Fear of success and the female castration complex: an empirical study. PhD California Sch. of Prof. Psych., Los Angeles, 1981.

WEISSKOPF, S.C. *511*
The psychoanalytic theory of female development: a review and a critique. PhD Harvard U. 1972.

WHITE, R.E. *512*
The twenty-nine year old never-married woman: response to a deviant social status. PhD California Sch. of Prof. Psych., Berkeley, 1974.

WHITESIDE, H. *513*
A study of the concerns of a selected group of unmarried women. PhD Columbia U. 1955.

WILKINSON, T.E. *514*
The role of aggression in the psychic development of women. PhD California Sch. of Prof. Psych., Berkeley, 1979.

WILLIAMS, B.F. *515*
Relationship of female acceptance or rejection of double sex standards to selected variables. PhD North Texas State U. 1977.

WILLIAMS, L.A. *516*
Black women and self-image: a phenomenological existential case history approach. PhD California Sch. of Prof. Psych., San Diego, 1976.

WILLIAMS, M.C. *517*
An exploratory study of needs for continuing self-development as perceived by wives of school superintendents in the greater Boston suburban area. EdD Boston U. 1964.

WILSON, L.S. *518*
Women's role innovation, role conflict, and well-being. PhD California Sch. of Prof. Psych., Los Angeles, 1979.

ZARO, J.S. *519*
An experimental study of role conflict in women. PhD U. of Connecticut, 1971.

ZIEBARTH, C.A.M. *520*
Feminine role conflict – the influence of models and expectations of others. PhD U. of Colorado, 1970.

College years

See also 45–174

ADAMS, N.A. *521*
A study by class rank of high ability female education majors over a period of fifteen years. PhD U. of Wyoming, 1981.

ADRIAN, M.J. *522*
Selected motor and psychological changes in college women. PhD Springfield Coll. 1965.

AGUREN, C.T. *523*
An exploration of self-actualization, self-concept, locus of control, and other characteristics as exhibited in selected mature community college women. EdD North Texas State U. 1974.

ALLEN, M.E. *524*
Selected dimensions of coping behavior in black

female college freshmen. PhD Northwestern U. 1981.

ALEXANDER, W.R.H. *525*
A study of body types, self-image and environmental adjustment in freshman college females. EdD Indiana U. 1967.

ALTHOF, S.E. *526*
A study of the personality variables related to fear of success in college women. PhD Oklahoma State U. 1975.

ASTLEY, M.R. *527*
Sex-role self-concept and anxiety style in college women. EdD Harvard U. 1978.

BAKKE, L.H. *528*
A study of the relationship of aesthetic judgment to self-esteem and security in university women. PhD Syracuse U. 1971.

BALLASH, C.L. *529*
Achievement aspirations and socialization patterns in college women. PhD Claremont Grad. Sch. 1981.

BELDNER, J. *530*
Fear of success in college women and its relation to performance in achievement situations. PhD New York U. 1976.

BERLIN, A.M.M. *531*
Depression, locus of control, and rationality-irrationality in college women. PhD Kent State U. 1980.

BICKMAN, L.D. *532*
Personality constructs of senior women planning to marry or to live independently soon after college. PhD U. of Pennsylvania, 1975.

BIRD, D.J. *533*
An analysis of psychological needs of groups of college freshmen woman by SVIB-W patterns. PhD U. of Kansas, 1959.

BLACK, J.D. *534*
The interpretation of MMPI profiles of college women. PhD U. of Minnesota, 1953.

BOGGS, K.R. *535*
The effects of scholastic ability, role orientation, fear of success, need for approval, and cultural values on the college major choices of women. PhD U. of Utah, 1978.

BOLTON, I.A. *536*
The problems of negro college women. PhD U. of Southern California, 1949.

BOROVAY, R.F. *537*
An investigation of the relationships among depression, locus of control, and assertive behavior in freshman college women. PhD U. of Miami, 1977.

BRAILEY, J.A. *538*
The identity experience of college women: some contributing factors. PhD U. of Michigan, 1973.

BROWN, F.G. *539*
The effect of autonomy on the daydreams and sex-role identification of black college women. PhD Adelphi U. 1982.

BUEHLMANN, B.B. *540*
The relationship between avoidance of success and other selected characteristics of college females. PhD Illinois State U. 1974.

BURGEMEISTER, B.B. *541*
The permanence of interests of women college students: a study in personality development. PhD Columbia U. 1941.

BURKE, C.M.H. *542*
Achievement motivation of women with traditional and non-traditional majors in a community college. PhD U. of Wyoming, 1979.

BURROUGHS, L.V. *543*
Occupational preferences and expectations as related to locus of control, sex-role contingency orientation, race, and family history among college women. EdD U. of Massachusetts, 1981.

BURTON, E.C. *544*
State and trait anxiety, achievement motivation and skill attainment in college women. PhD Ohio State U. 1970.

CALHOUN, H.D. *545*
Community college women students: characteristics, motivations, and aspirations. PhD U. of Alabama, 1975.

CANTER, R.J. *546*
An analysis of achievement-related expectations and aspirations in college women. PhD U. of Colorado at Boulder, 1975.

CARDER, C.E. *547*
Needs for achievement and affiliation as a function of age and career salience in women college students. PhD Ohio State U. 1977.

CAREY, P.M. *548*
Causal attribution for success and failure in black and white female graduate students. PhD New York U. 1982.

CLARK, P.E. *549*
The social unadjustment problems of a selected group of junior college girls. PhD U. of Southern California, 1943.

CLOUGH, L.B. *550*
A factor analysis of variables related to female college achievement. PhD U. of Connecticut, 1965.

CORRINGTON, S.A. *551*
Psychological characteristics of college women

exhibiting high and low fear of success. PhD United States International U. 1976.

CRUMMER, M.L. 552
Sex-role identification, 'motive to avoid success', and competitive performance in college women. PhD U. of Florida, 1972.

DANIELS, R.R. 553
Perceived and behavioral levels of creativity for university women. PhD U. of Nebraska–Lincoln, 1980.

DELISLE, F.H. 554
A study of the relationship of the self-concept to adjustment in a selected group of college women. PhD Michigan State U. 1953.

DIGNAN, M.H. 555
Ego identity, identification, and adjustment in college women. PhD Fordham U. 1963.

DOMINGUES, P.M. 556
Self-concept and socio-economic background of the mature female undergraduate student. PhD Northwestern U. 1971.

DUA, P.S. 557
Identification of personality characteristics differentiating elected women leaders from non-leaders in a university setting. PhD Pennsylvania State U. 1963.

DUGGER, J.A. 558
A study of measurable personal factors of leaders and non-leaders among university freshmen women. PhD Florida State U. 1969.

DUNBAR, D.S. 559
Sex-role identification and achievement motivation in college women. PhD Ohio State U. 1959.

DUNBAR, S.M.B. 560
College women's self-esteem and attitudes toward women's roles. PhD Michigan State U. 1975.

DUNKERLEY, M.D. 561
A statistical study of leadership among college women. PhD Catholic U. of America, 1940.

ESPIN, O.M. 562
Critical incidents in the lives of female college students: a comparison between women of Latin America and the United States. PhD U. of Florida, 1974.

FAGERBURG, J.E. 563
A comparative study of undergraduate women in relation to selected personal characteristics and certain effects of educational interruption. PhD Purdue U. 1967.

FANNIN, P.M. 564
Ego identity status and sex-role attitude, work-role salience, atypicality of college major and self-esteem in college women. PhD New York U. 1977.

FERRIER, M.-J. 565
Self-actualization and achievement motivation in college women. PhD Boston Coll. 1973.

FIGURELLI, J.C. 566
Effect of sex-role identification and fear of success on achievement behavior in college women. PhD Fordham U. 1977.

FISCHETTI, C.M. 567
Influencing achievement in college-aged women. PhD Purdue U. 1977.

FISHER, R.L. 568
An empirical typology of college women's personal role-conceptions. PhD U. of California, Berkeley, 1973.

FLYNN, S.K. 569
An analysis of the recreational behavior and personality characteristics of a select group of college women who exhibited atypical social behavior. EdD, U. of North Carolina at Greensboro, 1972.

FOX, L.L.W. 570
A comparative analysis of internal-external locus of control and sex-role concepts in black and white freshman women. EdD East Texas State U. 1975.

GARDNER, C.J.L. 571
A comparative study on the assertiveness of black and white women at the university level. PhD Southern Illinois U. at Carbondale, 1977.

GIBBONS-CARR, M.V. 572
Individuation status and projected sense of future self in college women. PhD Boston U. Grad. Sch. 1982.

GILL, M.K. 573
Psychological feminity of college women as it relates to self-actualization, feminine role attitudes, and selected background variables. EdD St John's U. 1974.

GINSBURG, S.D. 574
Ego identity status in college women: its relationship to ego development, ego strength and locus-of-control orientation. PhD U. of Missouri–Saint Louis, 1978.

GLATFELTER, M. 575
Identity development, intellectual development and their relationship in re-entry women students. PhD U. of Minnesota, 1982.

GREENSPAN, L.J. 576
Sex-role orientation, achievement motivation, and the motive to avoid success in college women. PhD Case Western Reserve U. 1974.

GREENWALD, D.P. 577
A multitrait-multimethod assessment of social inadequacy in female college students. PhD U. of Cincinnati, 1976.

GUBER, S. 578
A cross-cultural study of the perceived feminine role and self-concept of college women in the United States and Israel. PhD New York U. 1965.

HAGEY, S.J.J. 579
Risk-taking, self-complexity, and role choice at two stages in the lives of college women. PhD U. of Oregon, 1970.

HAMILTON, E.D. 580
An attributional approach to achievement-related behavior in female college students. PhD Claremont Grad. Sch. 1979.

HAGLUND, S.V. 581
Relationships among adjustment variables and sex-role orientation in college women: a constructed validation study of psychological androgyny. PhD Ohio U. 1977.

HANSON, J.C. 582
Feminine role values and personality factors among women's liberation members, college women seeking personal counseling, and other college women. PhD Kent State U. 1974.

HERNANDEZ, A.R. 583
A comparative study of fear of success in Mexican-American and Anglo-American college women. PhD California Sch. of Prof. Psych., Los Angeles, 1976.

HILL, R.C. 584
Suicidal superachievers: a study of some surrogate-family-oriented college women. PhD Wright Inst. 1982.

HUGHES, B.C. 585
Sex-role perception and depression in college women. PhD Brigham Young U. 1981.

JACKSON, M.L. 586
The relationship between self-concept and academic achievement among college women. EdD George Washington U, 1979.

KAHN, D.G. 587
Fantasy as sex-role exploration: building blocks of identity formation and career orientation in college women. PhD Case Western Reserve U. 1978.

KALKA, B.S. 588
A comparative study of feminine role concepts of a selected group of college women. EdD Oklahoma State U. 1967.

KOWATSCH, C.A. 589
An investigation of the inter-relationships between self-esteem, social intelligence, and word association styles in female college students. PhD Loyola U. of Chicago, 1974.

KRESOJEVICH, I.Z. 590
Motivation to avoid success in women as related to year in school, academic achievement and success context. PhD Michigan State U. 1971.

LANGSTON, K.F. 591
The relationship between body image and body composition of college females. EdD U. of Houston, 1979.

LAWRENCE, G.L. 592
Behaviors and attitudes of college females differing in parent identification. EdD George Peabody Coll. for Teachers, 1968.

LEE, J.B. 593
Variables differentiating between the selection of a predominantly white university and a predominantly black college by black women. PhD U. of Alabama, 1979.

LENTZ, M.E. 594
The relationship between fear of success and situational conditions in college females. PhD Kansas State U. 1976.

LIPINSKI, B.G. 595
Sex-role conflict and achievement motivation in college women. PhD U. of Cincinnati, 1965.

LOKITZ, B.D. 596
Crisis, competition and sacrifice: a look at the experiences of undergraduate women during their first two years of college. PhD Washington U. 1980.

LOUDERMILK, J.L. 597
A comparison of leadership styles and other selected characteristics associated with women in higher education. EdD U. of Georgia, 1979.

LOWRIE, K.H. 598
Factors which relate to the extra-curricular performance of college women. PhD U. of Iowa, 1943.

LYONS, L. 599
The relationship of need achievement, need affiliation, parental reinforcement, and parental modeling to the program enrollment of female graduate students. PhD Fordham U. 1976.

MCGAVERN, M.L. 600
The effects of cognitive self-instruction on the creative performance and self-concept of college women. PhD U. of Texas at Austin, 1977.

MCKAY, C.F. 601
A test of Holland's theory of vocational choice using a sample of rural, urban and suburban female community college students. EdD Virginia Polytechnic Inst. and State U. 1977.

MANTELL, M.R. 602
Catastrophic fantasies, fear of negative evaluation, and assertiveness/nonassertiveness among undergraduate women. PhD U. of Pennsylvania, 1976.

MARKSBERRY, M.L. 603
Educational implications of attitudes of college women toward their possible roles in life. PhD U. of Chicago, 1951.

MARPLE, B.L.N. *604*
Adult women students compared with younger students on selected personality variables. PhD Boston Coll. 1974.

MARSHALL, S.J. *605*
An investigation of the relationship of need for achievement and sex-role identity to career orientation among college women. PhD New York U. 1979.

MASH, D.J. *606*
The relationship of women's life-style preference and personality during college. PhD Ohio State U. 1974.

MATTHEWS, L.J. *607*
Comparisons of self-actualization among three groups of college women. EdD Oregon State U. 1979.

MAYS, V.M. *608*
Academic achievement and resultant achievement motivation as related to the racial and sex-role attitudes of college-level black women. PhD U. of Massachusetts, 1979.

MIRKESELL, S.G.S. *609*
College women's sex-role identity, reported participation in cross-sex behavior and perceived willingness to encourage cross-sex behavior in school-age children. PhD U. of Maryland, 1981.

MILLER, F.S. *610*
Biographical variables, racism, sexism and the personality development of black female undergraduates: an exploratory investigation. PhD Texas Christian U. 1981.

MIRABILE, J.J. *611*
Sex-role classification, flexibility and appropriateness of behavioral response in college-age women. PhD U. of Georgia, 1981.

MONTAGUE, A.C. *612*
A factoral analysis of the basic interest patterns of 200 women college students in various curriculum groups. PhD Temple U. 1960.

MOORE, H.B. *613*
Race and social class: sociocultural factors in the development of the achievement motive in college women. PhD Boston Coll. 1977.

MULVIHILL, F.X. *614*
Sex matriarchy and academic achievement of black students. PhD Michigan State U. 1974.

OHRT, B.A. *615*
An analysis of self-concept change in adult women students in community college. PhD Washington State U. 1982.

OLIVER, L.W. *616*
The relationship of familial variables to career and homemaking orientation in college women. PhD U. of Maryland, 1974.

PAGEL, L.H. *617*
Correlates of achievement conflict in college women. EdD U. of California, Los Angeles, 1975.

PATTY, R.S.A. *618*
The arousal of the motive to avoid success in college women. PhD U. of Nebraska–Lincoln, 1973.

PENN, L.S. *619*
Current sex-role identification, sex-role stereotypes, and role conflict in university women. PhD Adelphi U. 1975.

PHILIPS, N.B. *620*
Sex-role reasoning in college women and its relationship to masculinity, femininity, moral judgement, need for social approval and authoritarianism. PhD New York U. 1982.

PHILLIPS, B.E. *621*
Fear of success and the female doctoral student: a study of the influence of age and marital status on women's experience of graduate school. PhD California Sch. of Prof. Psych., Berkeley, 1977.

PHILLIPS, F.A. *622*
An evaluation of a basic skills course for college women. PhD Springfield Coll. 1966.

PODHORETZ, H. *623*
Motivation of female doctoral students: manifest needs, perceived parenting and locus of control. PhD Fordham U. 1974.

PORTER, J. *624*
Sex-role concepts: their relationships to psychological well-being and to future plans in female college seniors. PhD U. of Rochester, 1967.

PROULX, M.C. *625*
Personal, family and institutional factors associated with attitudes toward women's roles among French-Canadian college students. PhD Michigan State U. 1976.

PUGH, C.A. *626*
Psychological dimensions of masculinity and femininity and attitudes toward women among black, Hispanic and white female college students. EdD U. of Massachusetts, 1982.

REINHARD, P.Z. *627*
Perceived maternal child-rearing patterns and employment as predictors of fear of success in college women. PhD Fordham U. 1978.

RICE, V.G. *628*
On the course and correlates of personality development in college women. PhD Harvard U. 1982.

RITIGSTEIN, J.M. *629*
The relationship of defense mechanisms to trait anxiety and state anxiety in female college students. PhD New York U. 1974.

ROBBINS, R.B. *630*
Achievement performance and fantasy arousal in college women as a function of the motive to avoid success, problem format, and relationship to experimenter. PhD Temple U. 1973.

ROGERS, N.-S. *631*
A study of certain personality characteristics of sorority and non-sorority women at the University of California, Los Angeles. PhD U. of California, Los Angeles, 1953.

ROMANO, N.C. *632*
Relationships among identity confusion and resolution, self-esteem, and sex-role perceptions in freshman women at Rutgers University. EdD Rutgers U. 1975.

RONEY, L.K. *633*
The relationship of identity achievement and person-environment congruence to psychological adjustment in college women. PhD U. of Texas at Austin, 1979.

SAXON, S.V. *634*
Test profile characteristics of selected behavioral pattern groups of freshmen women residents on the Minnesota counseling inventory. PhD Florida State U. 1963.

SCARATO, A.M. *635*
Self-confidence, self-acceptance and sexual behavior in college women: an exploratory study. PhD U. of Maryland, 1975.

SCHRADER, M.M. *636*
A comparison of the self-concept, achievement motivation, and feminine role perception between traditional college-age women and nontraditional college-age women in a small college environment. PhD Ohio State U. 1977.

SCOTT, M.E. *637*
An exploration of the variable of open-mindedness in special and regular education female undergraduates. PhD Michigan State U. 1979.

SILVERMAN, M.C. *638*
Sex-role identity, fear of success and academic achievement in female college students. PhD Columbia U. 1980.

SIMCOX, C.Q. *639*
The effect of facial attractiveness upon the evaluation of fictitious black and white potential female dropouts by the faculty of selected Pennsylvania community colleges: a psycholinguistic investigation. PhD Pennsylvania State U. 1975.

SIMMONS, W.D. *640*
Superior women college students: a study of their self-concepts and academic motivation. EdD U. of Illinois at Urbana–Champaign, 1968.

SITZMAN, C.-J. *641*
The effects of role models on ego strength and self-concept of graduate school women. PhD Catholic U. of America, 1979.

SKILLINGS, R.E. *642*
Situational determinants of assertive behaviors in college females. PhD U. of Pittsburgh, 1977.

SKINNER, A.B. *643*
Evolving life patterns of college-educated women: motive dispositions in context. PhD Harvard U. 1977.

SLAUGHTER, M.H. *644*
An analysis of the relationship between somatotype and personality profiles of college women. PhD U. of Illinois at Urbana–Champaign, 1968.

SLOTKIN, J.H. *645*
Role conflict among selected Anglo and Mexican-American female college graduates. PhD U. of Arizona, 1976.

SMITH, L.D. *646*
Manifest personality needs as correlates of the vocational maturity of black and white freshmen women in a select university. PhD U. of Alabama, 1979.

SNYDER, J.J. *647*
Factors relating to self-actualization and motivation to achieve in learning among college women. PhD Fordham U. 1978.

SOLOMON, A. *648*
Identification, differentiation, and extension of self: a study of perceptions of self, mother, and daughter in a sample of college women. PhD Cornell U. 1955.

STACK, S.L. *649*
The relationship between locus of control and perceived obstacles in graduate school for female students. PhD United States International U. 1981.

STEINBERG, C.L. *650*
Sex-role orientation and fear of failure motivation in college women. PhD State U. of New York at Albany, 1976.

STEWART, A.J. *651*
Longitudinal prediction from personality to life outcomes among college-educated women. PhD Harvard U. 1975.

STEWART, D.G. *652*
The social adjustment of black females at a predominantly white university. PhD U. of Connecticut, 1971.

STOCK, M.J.S. *653*
Separation anxiety in college women. PhD Saint Louis U. 1969.

STODDARD, H.A. *654*
Characteristics, attitudes, aspirations and problems of women doctoral students at Indiana University, Bloomington, EdD Indiana U. 1977.

STUTLER, D.L. *655*
The interrelationship between academic achievement of college freshmen women and measures of anxiety and ability. PhD Oregon State U. 1973.

THOMAS, R.J.T. *656*
Background and personality characteristics of creative college women. EdD Mississippi State U. 1977.

TOBACYK, J.J. *657*
Personality structure and mood in female college students. PhD U. of Florida, 1977.

TRADER, D.D. *658*
A study of college women's attitudes toward the feminine role. PhD U. of North Carolina at Greensboro, 1972.

ULRICH, A.C. *659*
Measurement of stress evidenced by college women in situations involving competition. PhD U. of Southern California, 1957.

VASQUEZ, M.J.T. *660*
Chicana and Anglo university women: factors related to their performance, persistence and attrition. PhD U. of Texas at Austin, 1978.

VEREARA, A. *661*
A critical study of a group of college women's response to poetry. PhD U. of Columbia, 1947.

VICKLAND, A.F. *662*
College satisfaction of mature college women. PhD Texas A&M U. 1976.

VILLIS, C.A. *663*
A developmental assessment of undergraduate women's needs. PhD U. of Southern Illinois at Carbondale, 1980.

WAGNER, M.L. *664*
The adult minority women in the community college. EdD Rutgers U. 1980.

WATERS, C.C. *665*
Sex-role attitudes and the manifest needs of college women. PhD Fordham U. 1976.

WATSON, J. *666*
The relationship between family environment and ego development in the creative thinking of college-age females. PhD Boston Coll. 1982.

WEBSTER, S.R. *667*
Anxiety as a function of differing sex-role expectations of female college students. PhD U. of Southern Mississippi, 1977.

WEISSMAN, E.I. *668*
The relationship between the marital status, feminine identity conflict, and self-actualization of women doctoral students. EdD Boston U. Sch. of Educ. 1974.

WHITE, S.E. *669*
Perceptions of higher education of a selected group of academically successful college women. EdD U. of Denver, 1961.

WIGGINS, C.A. *670*
The relationship of anxiety and tolerance of ambiguity to the curricular choices of female university students. PhD U. of Connecticut, 1971.

WILLIAMS, E.C. *671*
Black college women's dignity and leadership quest: an evaluation of a program to motivate degree completion. EdD Wayne State U. 1973.

WILLIAMS, J.A.M. *672*
Sex-role conflict and academic achievement: a study of superior women students. EdD U. of Illinois at Urbana–Champaign, 1970.

WILSON, M.S. *673*
Conformity and noncomformity of college girls to the standard of their parents. PhD U. of Pennsylvania, 1952.

WILSON, P.P. *674*
College women who express futility: a study based on fifty selected life histories of women college graduates. PhD Columbia U. 1951.

WRIGHT, M.E.P. *675*
Self-concept and the coping progress of black graduate and undergraduate women at a predominantly white university. PhD U. of Michigan, 1975.

YOUNG, S.P.A. *676*
The introduction of moral and ethical judgements into the teaching of issues in child development and education to a group of selected college women. PhD Georgia State U. Coll. of Educ. 1974.

ZAKI, L.N. *677*
The relationship between self-concept, social and economic values and attitudes toward the elderly among lower division female college students. PhD New York U. 1980.

ZUCKER, R.A. *678*
Normal dependency in self report and overt behavior: a study of college women. PhD Harvard U. 1966.

Midlife

See also **4** 404–31; **6** *passim*; **8** 211, 244; **19** 235–50.

ANDERSON, E. *679*
Fifteen hundred women look at life after forty. PhD Columbia U. 1952.

ARMSTRONG, B.N. *680*
A comparison of the attitudes and adjustment of middlescent mothers and their ninth and tenth grade adolescents. PhD Ohio State U. 1970.

ARTSON, B.F.S. *681*
Mid-life women: homemakers, volunteers, profes-

sionals. PhD California Sch. of Prof. Psych., Berkeley, 1978.

BEGGS, J.J. *682*
Personality shift in women at a choice point in middle life. PhD U. of Oregon, 1967.

BENNETT, S.K. *683*
Social change and women's social roles: life patterns and situational determinants in extra-familial roles at mid-life. PhD U. of North Carolina at Chapel Hill, 1978.

BENZIES, B.J. *684*
Maternal status and mental health in later life. PhD Illinois Inst. of Technology, 1980.

BOEDECKER, A.L. *685*
Women's life patterns, role involvements, and satisfaction at mid-life. PhD Pennsylvania State U. 1978.

BOYACK, V.L. *686*
Middle-aged women: their use of leisure time and perceptions of their middle years. PhD U. of Southern California, 1977.

BROWN, B.E. *687*
Married academic women in mid-life transition. EdD Temple U. 1982.

CORL, N.S. *688*
Mid-life distress in women: psychosocial factors. PhD California Sch. of Prof. Psych., Berkeley, 1980.

COX, C.B. *689*
Illness behavior in mid-life women. DSW U. of Maryland Baltimore Professional Schools, 1980.

DANNENBAUM, D.K. *690*
Mid-life women and achievement patterns associated with role change. EdD Temple U. 1981.

DEGUIRE, K.S. *691*
Activity choice, psychological functioning, degree of satisfaction and personality factors in educated middle-aged women. PhD Fordham U. 1974.

DOWNS, D. *692*
A comparison of 16 personality factors of women, retired or retiring from the motherhood role. PhD United States International U. 1981.

DROEGE, R. *693*
A psychosocial study of the formation of the middle adult life structure in women. PhD California Sch. of Prof. Psych., Berkeley, 1982.

ELLETT, S.E. *694*
An investigation of identity and self-esteem in traditional married women during their middle years, and the impact of the life planning seminar. PhD Virginia Commonwealth U. 1981.

FARMER, P.H.U. *695*
An exploratory investigation into the nature of the mid-life transition of a group of selected women. EdD Temple U. 1979.

FREVERT, R.L. *696*
Effects of life career pattern on self-esteem and life satisfaction of college educated women in the middle years. PhD Iowa State U. 1982.

GASS, G.D.Z. *697*
The attitudes of 85 women in their middle years toward their narrowing role and the relationship of these attitudes to their contentment. PhD U. of Michigan, 1957.

GERVER, J.M. *698*
Multiple role behavior and perception of ambiguous pictures in middle-aged women: satisfaction, flexibility, and control. PhD City U. of New York, 1981.

GOODMAN, S.F. *699*
Women in their later years: a study of the psychosocial development of women between 45–60. EdD Boston U. Sch. of Educ. 1980.

HIGGINS, D.H. *700*
Self-concept and its relation to everyday stress in middle-aged women: a longitudinal study. PhD Illinois Inst. of Technology, 1977.

HOLT, M.E. *701*
A comparison of self-esteem for mid-life women who are homemakers or employed persons participating in continuing education programs. EdD Georgia U. 1979.

HUMPHREY, L.H. *702*
A survey of women's goal-emphases and satisfaction during the postparental period. PhD Michigan State U. 1969.

JACKSON, P.F. *703*
Disruption and change in mid-life: an exploratory study of women in their fifth decade. PhD U. of Pittsburgh, 1974.

JOHNSON, R.B. *704*
Psychodynamic and developmental considerations of childless older women. PhD Northwestern U. 1981.

KAHNWEILER, J.B. *705*
Developmental concerns of women returning to school at mid-life based on a concept of the mid-life transition. PhD Florida State U. 1979.

KAUFFMAN, J.K. *706*
The caring role of middle-aged employed women with elderly mothers: an exploratory study with implications for home economics educational programming. PhD Michigan State U. 1982.

KITCHING, J.C. *707*
The self-concept of middle-aged women. PhD Florida State U. 1972.

LEWIS-ORE, P.B. *708*
Self-concept and sex-role identification in midlife

traditional and feminist women. EdD Idaho State U. 1977.

LISS, B.E. *709*
Life satisfaction: a comparison of retired and employed women. U. of Texas Health Science Center at Houston Sch. of Public Health, 1982.

LIVSON, F.B. *710*
Evolution of self: patterns of personality development in middle-aged women. PhD Wright Inst. 1974.

MCRAE, C.R. *711*
Psychological processes in the normal aging of middle-class, middle-aged women. PhD Fielding Inst. 1977.

MELTZER, L.M. *712*
The aging female: a study of attitude toward aging and self-concept held by pre-menopausal, menopausal and post-menopausal women. PhD Adelphi U. 1974.

MILLER, C.A. *713*
The life course patterns of Chicago area women: a cohort analysis of the sequencing and timing of related roles through the middle years. PhD Loyola U. of Chicago, 1982.

MILLER, K.R. *714*
Midlife women and self-esteem. PhD California Sch. of Prof. Psych., Berkeley, 1980.

NOBERINI, M.R. *715*
Adaptive behavior in middle-aged women: a follow-up study. PhD U. of Chicago, 1976.

RICE, S. *716*
Single older childless women: a study of social support and life satisfaction. DSW U. of California, Los Angeles, 1982.

ROGERS, J.L. *717*
Women in middle age: an examination of the interaction of life stage, social roles, and locus of control. PhD Ohio State U. 1980.

ROSENAUER, L.L. *718*
Stress in middlescent women: a comparison of the perceptions of therapists and middlescent women. PhD United States International U. 1982.

ROSENSTEIN, B. *719*
Activity patterns of middle-class women in their mid-years – with implications for adult education. EdD U. of California, Los Angeles, 1967.

SCHOENHOLZ, D.R. *720*
Life-style selection and personal satisfaction among empty nest women. PhD U. of Southern California, 1981.

SEGALLA, R.A. *721*
Departure from traditional roles: current life-styles of six groups of educated mid-life women. PhD George Washington U. 1979.

SHAPIRO, M.T. *722*
The effects of a confluent pre-retirement education program on women in midlife. PhD U. of California, Santa Barbara, 1979.

SINGER, N.G. *723*
An exploratory study of the early and midlife adult development of women following a re-entry life pattern. PhD U. of Pittsburgh, 1981.

THEOBALD, C. *724*
Prose memory of middle-aged women: an exploratory study. PhD Arizona State U. 1982.

THOMAS, D.A. *725*
Intragroup comparisons of middle-age women. PhD Ohio State U. 1981.

THOMPSON, I.J.A. *726*
A tentative model of the life structures of a selected sample of women ages forty to fifty. EdD U. of Tennessee, 1982.

THOMPSON, M.J. *727*
Identity attainment in mid-life females: an assessment scale. PhD U. of Georgia, 1980.

VOELZ, D.B. *728*
Development tasks of women in their middle years. PhD United States International U. 1974.

WASKEL, S.A. *729*
The ability of women in the mid-years to generate alternatives in the applied and abstract sense. PhD U. of Nebraska–Lincoln, 1979.

WEISHAUS, S.S. *730*
Determinants of affect of middle-aged women towards their aging mothers. PhD U. of Southern California, 1978.

WIERSMA, J.K. *731*
Women's mid-life career change: on the methodology of personal transformation. PhD U. of Michigan, 1979.

WOOD, V.I. *732*
Patterns of role change and life styles of middle-aged women. PhD U. of Chicago, 1963.

ZACKS, H. *733*
The self-concept of college graduate women in midlife. PhD Case Western Reserve U. 1982.

ZUBROD, L.A.C. *734*
A study of the psychosocial development of women: transition into middle adulthood. EdD Boston U. Sch. of Educ. 1980.

Old age

See also **6** 230–76.

CALDWELL, B.M. *735*
Psychological effects of sex hormone replacement in aged women. PhD Washington U. 1951.

CHAPMAN, S.C. *736*
A social-psychological analysis of morale in a select population of low-income elderly black females. PhD Pennsylvania State U. 1979.

EDMONDS, M.M. *737*
Social class and the functional health status of the aged black females. PhD Case Western Reserve U. 1982.

ELDERJUCKER, P.L. *738*
Effects of group therapy on self-esteem, social interaction and depression of female residents in a home for the aged. PhD Temple U. 1979.

ENGLE, V.F. *739*
A study of the relationship between self assessment of health function, personal tempo and time perception in elderly women. PhD Wayne State U. 1981.

FLETCHER, S. *740*
An investigation of the relationship of locus of control and social opportunity to life satisfaction and purpose in life among elderly women. PhD New York U. 1981.

GIESEN, C.B. *741*
Perceptions of aging: women's views of their change over time. PhD West Virginia U. 1980.

HALE, N. *742*
Present and retrospective learning needs elicited from the autobiographies of ten women over age sixty. EdD Indiana U. 1981.

IRVIN, Y.F. *743*
The role of age and adjustment on the subjective well-being in older black women. PhD U. of Pittsburgh, 1981.

JOHNSTON, R.A. *744*
The relationship between locus of control and psychological well-being in elderly female nursing home residents. PhD U. of Maryland Baltimore Professional Schools, 1981.

KELLEY, N.L. *745*
Socialization for body transcendence: a study of elderly religious women. PhD Medical Coll. of Pennsylvania, 1978.

KETTELL, M.E. *746*
Integrity of ego processes in aged females. PhD Boston U. 1964.

LITWIN-GRINBERG, R.R. *747*
Lives in retrospect: a qualitative analysis of oral reminiscence as applied to elderly Jewish women. DSW U. of California, Berkeley, 1982.

MACKERACHER, D.M. *748*
A study of the experience of aging from the perspective of older women. PhD U. of Toronto, 1982.

MASO, E.F. *749*
Fear of death in elderly black women. PhD Boston U. Grad. Sch. 1979.

MROTEK, D.D. *750*
Women 62–82: a contextual analysis in an adult developmental framework. PhD Northwestern U. 1982.

NAGY, M.C. *751*
Attributional differences in health status and life satisfactions of older women: a comparison between widows and non-widows. PhD U. of Oregon, 1982.

NEWSOM-CLARK, S.K. *752*
A study of the communicative efficiency in institutionalized and non-institutionalized aged females. PhD U. of Tennessee, 1980.

PETTAS, M. *753*
An exploratory study of oral communication characteristics in a population of aged women. PhD U. of Florida, 1963.

RUBIN, K.B. *754*
Stressful life changes and adaptation among aging women. PhD Ohio State U. 1977.

SCOTT, M.R. *755*
A comparison of the life satisfaction of aged career women and aged housewives. PhD U. of Florida, 1979.

SKINNER, R.J. *756*
The relationship between sex-role identity and perceived health in elderly females. PhD U. of Texas at Austin, 1979.

STEIGER, T.-R.B. *757*
Antecedents to successful senescence: a study of institutionalized aged women. PhD Bryn Mawr Coll. 1981.

STOJANOVIC, E.J. *758*
Morale and its correlates among aged black and white rural women in Mississippi. PhD Mississippi State U. 1970.

TAYLOR, S.P. *759*
Aging in black women: coping strategies and lifeways within an urban population. PhD U. of Massachusetts, 1978.

THOMPSON, D.O. *760*
A comparison of morale in a single female population, aged 65 to 75, as related to age-integrated versus age-segregated housing. PhD Southern Illinois U. 1978.

Social psychology

Group and interpersonal processes

ANZAFAME, L.J. *761*
The effect of fear of success and significance of the male partner on female performance on an intellectual decision-making task. PhD U. of Connecticut, 1973.

ARD, M.A. *762*
Mate selection preferences of black single college females with reference to selected variables. PhD Indiana State U. 1979.

AXELROD, J. *763*
The effect of sex-role attitude, status and sex of the addressee on the nonverbal communication of women. PhD New York U. 1980.

BARRON, A.S. *764*
The effects of three styles of interviewing on the response of women from two contrasting socio-economic groups. PhD Columbia U. 1957.

BECKER, C.S. *765*
A phenomenological explication of friendship as exemplified by most important college women friends. PhD Duquesne U. 1973.

BELL-KING, B.A. *766*
A symbolic interactionist approach to the social world of women achievers. PhD United States International U. 1978.

BENDER, L.R. *767*
Women as leaders: the impact of leader attributes of masculinity and femininity, and of follower attitudes toward women on leadership effectiveness. PhD State U. of New York at Buffalo, 1980.

BERGMAN, L.S. *768*
Interpersonal attraction as a situational determinant for the arousal of motive to avoid success in the college female. PhD Hofstra U. 1975.

BLOCK, J. *769*
Women's experience of injustice in the context of interpersonal inequality. PhD City U. of New York, 1982.

BURR, R.L. *770*
The effects of same-sex and mixed-sex growth groups on measures of self-actualization and verbal behavior of females. EdD, U. of Tennessee, 1974.

BURROUGHS, W.A. *771*
A study of white females' voting behavior toward two black female corroborators in a modified leaderless group discussion. PhD U. of Tennessee, 1969.

CARDI, M.W. *772*
The relationship between sex-role stereotype and trust among women as measured by co-operation and competition. PhD Ohio State U. 1972.

CHANDLER, E. *773*
A psychosocial study of group membership in the lives of four women: revealing and revising the family metaphor. PhD City U. of New York, 1975.

CORNFELD, J.L. *774*
Role model influences on the life style aspirations of female graduate students. PhD U. of Maryland, 1978.

COWAN-ARONSON, S.R. *775*
An exploration of the nature of support: a 'human connection' for women going against the grain. EdD Boston U. Sch. of Educ. 1982.

DAVIDSON, S.L. *776*
The therapeutic dimensions of friendship between women. PhD U. of Utah, 1978.

DONAGHY, W.C. *777*
An experimental study of the effects of anxiety on nonlexical verbal behavior in female dyad groups. PhD Northwestern U. 1969.

EDWARD, D.A. *778*
Girls' camp cross-age helping: a study of self and situation effects and influences. PhD U. of Texas at Austin, 1981.

EHRHARDT, M. *779*
A sociometric study of the friendship status of college women. EdD Indiana U. 1955.

FEHR, B.J. *780*
The communication of evaluation through the use of interpersonal gaze in same and inter-racial female dyads. PhD U. of Delaware, 1981.

FERGUSON, K.E. *781*
Self, society and womankind: the politics of self-other relations. PhD U. of Minnesota, 1976.

FIELDS, P.J. *782*
Parent-child relationships, childhood sexual abuse, and adult interpersonal behavior in female prostitutes. PhD California Sch. of Prof. Psych., Los Angeles, 1980.

FREESE, F. *783*
Differential perceptions of interpersonal relationships among dormitory women. PhD U. of Texas at Austin, 1955.

GILBERT, B.R.G. *784*
Women's leisure-time associates at a small woman's college and a large coed university. PhD U. of Kansas, 1973.

GOULDNER, H.B. *785*
The organization woman: patterns of friendship and organizational commitment. PhD U. of California, Los Angeles, 1960.

GRACE, J.G. *786*
The influence of male peers on the achievement and performance of females in pressured and non-pressured task situations. PhD U. of Southern Mississippi, 1977.

HAEBERLE, A.W. *787*
Friendship as an aspect of interpersonal relations: a study of friendship among the women residents of a small community. PhD New York U. 1956.

HAYES, M.M. *788*
A comparative study of spontaneity as observed in group relationships and group activities in two

parallel classes of a girls' county technical school. MA U. of London, Inst. of Educ. 1952.

HEJINIAN, C.L. 789
An exploration of the role of same sex close friendship in women's adult development. PhD Wright Inst. 1981.

HERETICK, D.M.L. 790
Effects of modeling experiences and generalized expectancies on female achievement behaviors in mixed-sex competition. PhD Virginia Commonwealth U. 1978.

HOWARD, H.L. 791
Prejudice against women and homosexuals. PhD U. of Washington, 1980.

JACKSON, A.D. 792
Militancy and black women's competitive behavior in competitive vs. non-competitive conditions. PhD Rutgers U. 1978.

JANNEY, J.E. 793
An effort to measure feminine sociality at the college level. PhD Ohio State U. 1935.

JEAN, P.J. 794
The effect of male presence on female self-consciousness, body image, and mood. PhD U. of Nebraska–Lincoln, 1981.

KEZSBOM, D.S. 795
Inconsistent status characteristics in determining female leadership in mixed-sex problem-solving groups. PhD Fordham U. 1981.

KIRSH, S.L. 796
Emotional support systems of working-class women. PhD U. of Toronto, 1981.

LEGGETT, L.S. 797
The social integration of a woman in transition. PhD Kent State U. 1981.

LINDLE, G.A. Jr 798
The effects of interpersonal performance on females in a simulated selection interview. EdD U. of Tennessee, 1979.

LOOMIS, M.D. 799
The effect of female competence on self-disclosure reciprocity in males. PhD Catholic U. of America, 1979.

MARR, J.A. 800
Effects of dominance and submissiveness on communication patterns of women in mixed-sex dyads. PhD Florida State U. 1981.

MILES, I.G. 801
Competitive achievement performance in women as a function of achievement motivation, sex-role attitudes and sex appropriateness of the achievement task in intra and inter sex competitive situations. PhD Catholic U. of America, 1976.

MOORE, L.L. 802
The relationship of academic group membership to the motive to avoid success in women. EdD U. of Virginia, 1971.

MOORE, M.M. 803
Nonverbal behavior in women as a function of situation and sex of partner(s). PhD U. of Missouri–Columbia, 1981.

NAFFZIGER, N.K. 804
Women in small groups: an examination of the effects of integrative, expressive, and instrumental group experiences. PhD Southern Illinois U. at Carbondale, 1975.

NAIMARK, E.S. 805
The relationship of women's liberation, wife's work status and masculinity-femininity to husband-wife verbal interaction during problem-solving. PhD Purdue U. 1972.

NELSON, A.A. 806
A qualitative assessment of perceived communication correlates of female homosociality and success. PhD U. of Colorado at Boulder, 1980.

NETT, S.R. 807
Crossroads: a study of caring relationships in a residential program for women. PhD Humanistic Psych. Inst. 1979.

NYLAND, J.L. 808
The effect of exposure to female role models on women's self-perception and career. PhD U. of Hawaii, 1981.

OSBORNE, N. 809
An analysis of female mentor relationships. PhD Arizona State U. 1981.

PADDOCK-ELLARD, K. 810
Characteristics of self-perceived inter-personal competency in adult females. PhD, Florida State U. 1981.

PELLETIER, C.S. 811
The relationship between reported affiliative needs of women and their self-disclosure tendencies and affiliative behaviors. PhD Ohio U. 1974.

PENDLETON, L.R. 812
Interpersonal attraction and anxiety responses to female assertiveness. PhD Colorado State U. 1977.

PEPLAU, L.A. 813
The impact of fear of success, sex-role attitudes and opposite-sex relationships on women's intellectual performance: an experimental study competition in dating couples. PhD Harvard U. 1974.

RUBINSTEIN, R.B. 814
Female prostitution: relationship of early separation and sexual experiences. PhD California Sch. of Prof. Psych. 1980.

SARGENT, J.L. 815
Female leaders in small groups: the effect of three leadership styles on perceived leader behavior,

group member satisfaction, and group interaction. PhD Florida State U. 1977.

SCOTT, S. *816*
Self-esteem in women as a function of participation in groups. PhD United States International U. 1975.

SELF, R.L. *817*
Black male/white female relationship implications for black females. PhD United States International U. 1978.

SIEGEL, H.D. *818*
The effect of attitude similarity and need gratification on romantic attraction toward males in females. PhD Hofstra U. 1977.

SLOTE, G. *819*
Feminine character and patterns of interpersonal perception. PhD New York U. 1962.

SMITH, L.L. *820*
Women's friendships with other women: a reflection of object relations. PhD Boston U. Grad. Sch. 1982.

SMITH, S.J.G. *821*
Communication barriers between black and white women. PhD U. of Michigan, 1980.

TEAGUE, M.C. *822*
Competency and non-competency as determinants of interpersonal attraction in biased and unbiased women. PhD Colorado State U. 1973.

VERMILYEA, C.J. *823*
The nature of emotional support for ten young women living alone. PhD U. of Illinois at Urbana–Champaign, 1979.

WERNIKOFF, I.N. *824*
The effect of fear of success and male attitudes towards female competency on female performance in a mixed-sex decision-making situation. PhD Northwestern U. 1979.

WHITE, J.E. *825*
Dimensions of conformity and evasion in residence halls for university women: a sociological analysis of normative behavior in a large-scale social organization. PhD U. of Illinois at Urbana–Champaign, 1962.

WILLIAMS, J.H. *826*
Primary friendship relations of housewives in two social status areas, Columbia, South Carolina. PhD Vanderbilt U. 1956.

YERBY, J. *827*
Female leadership in small problem-solving groups: an experimental study. PhD Bowling Green State U. 1972.

YUAN, Y.-Y. T. *828*
Assimilation and isolation in the neighborhood world of women. PhD Harvard U. 1973.

Social perception and attitudes

See also 45–174.

ADAMS, C.H. *829*
Male acceptance: antidote to fear of success in women? PhD U. of Alabama, 1978.

ADAMS, K.A. *830*
Family and fantasy: dread of the female and the narcissistic ethos in American culture. PhD Brandeis U. 1980.

ARRINGTON, G.E. *831*
Attitudes of superintendents towards the rights and roles of women in contemporary society. EdD U. of Virginia, 1980.

ASMUNDSSON, R. *832*
Social workers' attitudes about women at work: traditional or egalitarian. DSW Columbia U. 1977.

ASTLE, D.J. *833*
United States men and women's attitudes towards female sex roles: an analysis of 1972–1977 National Opinion Research Center general social surveys. PhD Oklahoma State U. 1978.

BAKSHY, J.B. *834*
Men's perceptions of the achieving female: a thematic analysis of affiliative and instrumental role functioning. PhD Illinois Inst. of Technology, 1977.

BECKER, S.J. *835*
A comparison of body attitudes in women with masculine vocational interests. PhD U. of Maryland, 1971.

BURNS, A. *836*
The perceived inter-relation of physical attractiveness, likeability and perceived age in women. PhD City U. of New York, 1978.

BUSS, A.C. *837*
Liberal women's estimates of the average woman in relation to own self-esteem. PhD Michigan State U. 1974.

BUTLER, L.C. *838*
Some correlates of attitudes toward women among undergraduate males. PhD U. of Florida, 1976.

CHAPLAN, R. *839*
Differences between opinions and emotions about women's changing role. PhD Yeshiva U. 1976.

CONWAY, R. *840*
Pseudo and genuine liberal attitudes toward women: relationship to diagnostic sex-role bias and several demographic variables. PhD New York U. 1979.

ENGEL, J.W. *841*
Changing attitudes toward the dual work/home roles of women: University of Minnesota freshmen. PhD U. of Minnesota, 1978.

FORD, D.S. 842
The relationship between multidimensional locus of control, sex role, self-actualization and feminist/ traditional attitudes toward women. PhD California Sch. of Prof. Psych. 1981.

GIBNER, J.W. 843
An analysis of factors associated with work-leisure attitudes and perceptions of three groups of women. PhD U. of Michigan, 1973.

GOLDBERG, L.H. 844
Attitudes of clinical psychologists toward women. PhD Illinois Inst. of Technology, 1973.

HAAS,S.F. 846
Perceptions of male and female competence as a function of sex of subject and traditionality of attitudes toward women. PhD U. of Cincinnati, 1976.

HAYES, M.L. 847
The effect of sex and race upon the perception of physical attractiveness, social desirability and employability of women. EdD Rutgers U. 1980.

HEFFNER, P.A. 848
The impact of policewomen on patrol: contributions of sex-role stereotypes to behavior in an astereotypic setting. PhD Wayne State U. 1976.

HEMPEL, U.E. 849
Cognitive bias in stereotyping (the effects of attractive versus unattractive female faces on the recognition of socially desirable versus undesirable behaviors). PhD U. of Oregon, 1975.

HOWELL, C.D. 850
Black concepts of the ideal black woman. PhD U. of California, Berkeley, 1978.

HUCK, J. 851
Determinants of assessment center ratings for white and black females and the relationship of these dimensions to subsequent performance effectiveness. PhD Wayne State U. 1974.

ISAACS, M.B. 852
Sex-role stereotyping and the evaluation of the performance of women. PhD U. of California, 1974.

IZENBERG, S.D. 853
Attitudes toward women's roles and grade and sex of adolescents. EdD Columbia U. Teachers Coll. 1978.

JORDAN, B.K. 854
Discerning real and ideal perceptions of women in Michoacan and Montana. PhD U. of Oregon, 1978.

KATIMS, P.A. 855
Male reaction to females labeled assertive. PhD U. of Washington, 1977.

KELLY, M.K. 856
Scottish and American teenagers' attitudes toward the female role. PhD U. of Pennsylvania, 1977.

LANGFORD, E.P. 857
The sex-role of the female as perceived by Anglo and negro children. PhD East Texas State U. 1969.

LAVENTURE, R.O. 858
The relationship between attitudes towards women and perceptions of aggression and resultant aggressive behavior. PhD Southern Illinois U. at Carbondale, 1977.

LIRETTE, N.M. 859
Psychological health, assertive behavior, and attitudes toward women's role. PhD California Sch. of Prof. Psych., Fresno, 1979.

MCFALL, M.E. 860
The effects of response style and situational variations on perceptions of assertive behavior in females. PhD U. of Montana, 1981.

MCKAY, B.J. 861
An empirical study of feminine attitudes toward feminine achievement. PhD Northwestern U. 1974.

MELLMAN, S. 862
The attribution of female assertive behavior as it relates to judged physical attractiveness. PhD Saint Louis U. 1979.

NEATH, J.F. 863
Women's social and sexual devaluation of women. PhD U. of Kansas, 1981.

PAPALEO, S. 864
A psychological study of the image of woman as a sexual object: stepping into the moon. PhD California Sch. of Prof. Psych., San Diego, 1978.

PAVEK, B.J. 865
Perceived models, selected characteristics and values by two samples of North Dakota women. EdD U. of North Dakota, 1975.

PHIBBS, S.B. 866
The relationship of self-esteem and locus of control to acceptance of women in nontraditional role situations. PhD Georgia State U. Coll. of Educ. 1979.

PINCHES, S.K. 867
Sexism in women's judgements of arguments between women and men. PhD Michigan State U. 1978.

PORTERFIELD, E.A. 868
Maidens, missionaries and mothers: American women as subjects and objects of religiousness. PhD Stanford U. 1975.

RAWLES, J.L. 869
Perceptions of nontraditional women: factors influencing ratings of femininity and likability. PhD California Sch. of Prof. Psych., Los Angeles, 1981.

ROSS, A.A. *870*
Sentiments toward rather than away from women: an empirical analysis. PhD U. of Texas at Austin, 1975.

SLAVIN, M.O. *871*
The theme of feminine evil: the image of women in male fantasy and its effect on attitudes and behavior. PhD Harvard U. 1972.

SNOW, B.M. *872*
An analysis of the relationship of certain factors to the social acceptance status of college freshman women. EdD Pennsylvania State U. 1957.

SOHLER, P.R.G. *873*
The relationship of sex, self-esteem, masculinity-femininity orientation, and attitudes toward women to the self-induced helplessness phenomenon. PhD Oklahoma State U. 1980.

STEIN, A.A. *874*
Images of contemporary American women as reflected by programs and activities of auxiliaries of professional associations. EdD U. of Northern Colorado, 1974.

TODER, N.L. *875*
The effect of the sexual composition of a group on sex-role attitudes and discrimination against women. PhD U. of California, Los Angeles, 1974.

TOWNSEND, A.L. *876*
The effects of gender centrality on women's gender-related attitudes. PhD U. of Michigan, 1982.

TRAIL, B.M. *877*
Comparison of attitudes towards women and measures of interests between feminist, traditional female and male university students. PhD Texas A&M U. 1975.

TRILLING, B.A. *878*
Factors related to women's prejudice against women. PhD Fordham U. 1975.

UGUCCIONI, S.M. *879*
The concept of femininity and its relationship to attitudes concerning the roles of women in present-day society. PhD Duke U. 1978.

WARD, J.L. *880*
An investigation of middle school students' attitudes toward women's sex-roles. EdD Northern Illinois U. 1979.

WELSCH, M.C.B. *881*
Expectancy of success and attribution of performance as a function of women's perception of man's ideal woman. PhD U. of Alabama, 1976.

WILLIAMS, J.M. *882*
An analysis of subtle discrimination as perceived by a group of college women. EdD Virginia Polytechnic Inst. and State U. 1981.

WILSON, K.K. *883*
Perceptions of women in traditional and non-traditional occupational and social roles. PhD Arizona State U. 1980.

18 Religion

See also **4** *passim;* **17** 240; **19** 96, 127.

Ancient and primitive religions

ARTHUR, R.H. 1
Feminine motifs in eight *Nag Hammadi* documents. ThD Graduate Theological Union, 1979.

DEMAN, E.B. van 2
The cult of Vesta Publica and the vestal virgins. PhD U. of Chicago, 1898.

DUTRA, J.A. 3
Hera: literary evidence of her origin and development as a fertility goddess. PhD Tufts U. 1966.

EATON, A.W. 4
The goddess Anat: the history of her cult, her mythology, and her iconography. PhD Yale U. 1964.

EBIN, V.A. 5
The Aowin priestesses, vessels of the gods: a study of spirit mediums in south-west Ghana. PhD U. of Cambridge, 1978.

EISNER, R.E. 6
Ariadne in religion and myth, prehistory to 400 BC PhD Stanford U. 1971.

GRETHER, G.E. 7
The divinity of women in the Roman imperial families, 27 BC – 235 AD. PhD Cornell U. 1939.

GROSS, R.M. 8
Exclusion and participation: the role of women in aboriginal Australian religions. PhD U. of Chicago, 1975.

HEYOB, S.K. 9
The cult of Isis among women in the Greco-Roman world. PhD Catholic U. of America, 1973.

KAFFER, R.E. 10
Contemporary witchcraft: a sociological examination of witches and of their practice and concept of witchcraft. PhD U. of California, Berkeley, 1973.

KRAEMER, R.S. 11
Ecstatics and ascetics: studies in the functions of religious activities for women in the Greco-Roman world. PhD Princeton U. 1976.

LIEBERMAN, S.R. 12
The Eve motif in ancient Near Eastern and classical Greek sources. PhD Boston U. Grad. Sch. 1975.

LLOYD, S.M. 13
The occult revival: witchcraft in the contemporary United States. PhD U. of Missouri, Columbia, 1978.

MELLOR, R.J. 14
Dea Roma: the development of the idea of the Goddess Roma. PhD Princeton U. 1967.

PRITCHARD, J.B. 15
Palestinian figurines of the female figure: the problem of its relation to certain goddesses known through literature. PhD U. of Pennsylvania, 1942.

SHARBROUGH, S.J. 16
The cult of the mother in Europe: the transformation of the symbolism of woman. PhD U. of California, Los Angeles, 1977.

SLADEK, W.R. 17
Inanna's descent to the netherworld. [Mesopotamian goddess] PhD Johns Hopkins U. 1974.

SMITHSON, I. 18
The great mother: past and present. PhD U. of California, Davis, 1977.

WALTERS, E.J. 19
Attic grave reliefs that represent women in the dress of Isis (Greece). PhD New York U. 1982.

Buddhism

CISSELL,K.A.A. 20
The Pi-Ch'Iu-Ni Chuan biographies of famous Chinese nuns from 317–516 C.E. PhD U. of Wisconsin–Madison, 1972.

PAUL,D.M. 21
A prolegomena to the *Srimaladevi Sutra* and the Tathagatagarbha theory: the role of women in Buddhism. PhD U. of Wisconsin–Madison, 1974.

Christianity

The New Testament period and the early Church

ADAMS, M.G. 22
The hidden disciples: Luke's stories about women in his gospel and in Acts. DMin San Francisco Theological Seminary, 1981.

AUSTIN, M.D. *23*
The place of women in early Christian thought and activity. PhD Southern Baptist Theological Seminary, 1913.

BALCH, D.L. *24*
'Let wives be submissive . . .': the origin, form and apologetic function of the household duty code (Haustafel) in I Peter. PhD Yale U. 1974.

COKER, H.E. *25*
Women and the gospel in Luke and Acts. PhD Southern Baptist Theological Seminary, 1955.

DUTILE, G. *27*
A concept of submission in the husband-wife relationship in selected New Testament passages. PhD Southwestern Baptist Theological Seminary, 1980.

EMREY, E.V. *28*
Paul's ethics and feminism in light of I Corinthians. DMin School of Theology at Claremont, 1980.

EVANS, M.J. *29*
The place of women in the New Testament Church. MPhil CNAA, 1978.

FOSTER, H.E. *30*
Jewish and Graeco-Roman influences upon Paul's attitude toward women. PhD U. of Chicago, 1934.

FREERKSEN, J.A. *31*
The biblical role of woman with an exegesis of I Corinthians 2: 2–16. ThD Grace Theological Seminary and Coll. 1980.

HALL, S.E. *32*
A survey of the status of women in Christianity during the first four centuries with special reference to the non-Orthodox movements. PhD U. of St Andrews, 1982.

JAYNE, D.T. *33*
The status of women in first-century Christianity. MPhil U. of Nottingham, 1980.

KIRWIN, G.F. *34*
The nature of the Queenship of Mary. STD Catholic U. of America, 1973.

KISHPAUGH, M.J. *35*
The Feast of the Presentation of the Virgin Mary in the temple: an historical and literary study. PhD Catholic U. of America, 1941.

LESLIE, W.N. *36*
The concept of woman in the Pauline Corpus in light of social and religious environment of the first century. PhD Northwestern U. 1976.

LOUGEE, D.A. *37*
The status of women as seen in the earlier Latin patristic writers. PhD U. of Illinois at Urbana–Champaign, 1923.

MALONE, M.T.P. *38*
Christian attitudes towards women in the fourth century: background and new directions. PhD U. of Toronto, 1971.

MORE O'FERRALL, M.M. *39*
Monica, the mother of Augustine in Augustine's *Confessions*. MA University Coll., Dublin, 1973.

RYRIE, C.C. *40*
The status of women in the life of the Church during the first three centuries. PhD U. of Edinburgh, 1954.

SCHIERLING, M.J. *41*
Woman, cult, and miracle recital: Mark 5: 24–34. PhD Saint Louis U. 1980.

SIDDONS, P.A. *42*
Biblical feminism: a New Testament perspective in the quality of women. DMin Colgate Rochester Divinity Sch. 1980.

SMITH, H.L. *43*
Women in the Pauline churches. PhD Southern Baptist Theological Seminary, 1950.

SWOGGER, M.P. *44*
The holy women at the tomb. MLitt U. of Aberdeen, 1972.

VAKMANIC, M.C. *45*
The Marian question in the light of Vatican II: a critique and a proposal. ThD Southern Baptist Theological Seminary, 1972.

WILLIAMS, F.W. *46*
The teaching of the New Testament concerning the nature, role and rights of women. PhD Bob Jones U. 1981.

WITHERINGTON, B. *47*
Women and their roles in the Gospels and Acts. PhD U. of Durham, 1968.

WOODHALL, J.A. *48*
The socio-religious role of women according to Hippolytus in the light of the early Christian fathers. PhD Fordham U. 1980.

WOODRUFF, M. *49*
Underlying factors contributing to Paul's teaching concerning women. PhD Southwestern Baptist Theological Seminary, 1950.

The Middle Ages

See also **1** 225, 230; **9** 66; **12** 1341, 1370.

BARRETT, B.C. *50*
Santa Teresa y sus obras. MA National U. of Ireland, 1948.

BEHREN, R.L. von *51*
Women in late medieval society: Catherine of Siena – a psychological study. PhD U. of California, Davis, 1972.

BELL, C.J. *52*
The role of monastic women in the life and letters of early medieval England and Ireland. PhD U. of Virginia, 1975.

BONSNES, M.P. *53*
The pilgrimage to Jerusalem: a typological metaphor for women in early medieval religious orders. PhD New York U. 1982.

BOURDILLON, A.F.C. *54*
The order of Minoresses in England. MA U. of Manchester, 1925.

BOYD, C. *55*
A Cistercian nunnery in Italy in the thirteenth century. PhD Radcliffe Coll. 1934.

BUGGE, J.M. *56*
The theological ideal of virginity in Middle English devotional literature for women. PhD Harvard U. 1970.

BYRNE, SISTER MARY *57*
The nun tradition in medieval England. PhD Catholic U. of America, 1932.

COOKE, K. *58*
Shaftesbury Abbey in the eleventh and twelfth centuries: the nuns and their estates. MLitt U. of Oxford, 1982.

EDWARDS, A.J.M. *59*
Odo of Ostia's history of the translation of St Milburga and its connection with the early history of Wenlock Abbey. MA U. of London, Royal Holloway Coll. 1960.

ELKINS, S.K. *60*
Female religious in twelfth-century England. PhD Harvard U. 1977.

GRIPKEY, M.V. *62*
The Blessed Virgin Mary as mediatrix in the Latin and Old French legends prior to the fourteenth century. PhD Catholic U. of America, 1938.

HASSALL, W.O. *63*
A study of the nunnery of St Mary Clerkenwell and its property with an edition of its cartulary. DPhil U. of Oxford, 1941.

HEIMMEL, J.P. *64*
'God is our mother': Julian of Norwich and the medieval image of Christian feminine divinity. PhD St John's U. 1980.

HOCHSTETLER, D.D. *65*
A conflict of traditions: consecration for women in the early Middle Ages. PhD Michigan State U. 1981.

HYLKEMA, M.R. *66*
Medieval popularity of St Anne. PhD Niagara U. 1937.

JACKA, H.T. *67*
The dissolution of the English nunneries. MA U. of London, 1917.

KEHOE, T.R. *68*
The work of the nuns in education during the Middle Ages. PhD Boston U. 1938.

L'HEUREUX, Mother A.G. *69*
The mystical vocabulary of Venerable Mère Marie de l'Incarnation and its problems. PhD Catholic U. of America, 1958.

NICHOLS, J. A. *70*
The history and cartulary of the Cistercian nuns of Marham Abbey, 1249–1536. PhD Kent State U. 1974.

POWER, E.E. *71*
Some chapters in the history of English nunneries in the late Middle Ages. MA U. of London, 1906.

RUDDER, P.S. *72*
Will and humility in Santa Teresa de Jesús. PhD U. of Minnesota, 1968.

STEIN, F.M. *73*
The religious women of Cologne, 1120–1320. PhD Yale U. 1977.

VINJE, P.M. *74*
An understanding of love according to the anchoress Julian of Norwich. PhD Marquette U. 1982.

Protestantism

See also **9** 74, 84, 88.

BAILEY, F.A. *75*
The status of women in the Disciples of Christ movement, 1865–1900. PhD U. of Tennessee, 1979.

BARNES, J.N. *76*
The mind-body concept in the thinking of Ellen G. White. PhD New York U. 1965.

CUTLER, D.R. *77*
Birth ceremonies and practices: a cross-cultural study developed from a comparison of contemporary Episcopal infant baptism and churching of women, and equivalent ceremonies in the 1549 English prayer book. PhD Harvard U. 1965.

DAVIS, S.T. *78*
Woman's work in the Methodist church. PhD U. of Pittsburgh, 1963.

DICK, E.N. *79*
The Adventist crisis, 1843–1844. [Ellen G. White] PhD U. of Wisconsin, 1930.

EASTON, B.L. *80*
Women, religion and the family: revivalism as an indicator of social change in early New England. PhD U. of California, Berkeley, 1975.

EDMONSON, L.D. *81*
Fundamentalist sects of Los Angeles, 1900–1930. PhD School of Theology at Claremont, 1969.

FOX, M.Q. *82*
Power and piety: women in Christian Science. PhD New York U. 1973.

FRANCIS, M. *83*
Selina Countess of Huntingdon. BLitt U. of Oxford, 1958.

GADT, J.C. *84*
Women and Protestant culture: the Quaker dissent from Puritanism. PhD U. of California, Los Angeles, 1974.

GOTTSCHALK, S. *85*
The emergence of Christian Science in American religious life, 1885–1910. [Mary Baker Eddy] PhD U. of California, Berkeley, 1969.

GRAHAM, E.D. *86*
The contribution of Lady Glenorchy and her circle to the Evangelical revival. BD U. of Leeds, 1965.

GRIPE, E. *87*
The professionally trained woman in the Presbyterian church in the USA, 1900–1972: the role of power in the achievement of status and equality. EdD Columbia U. 1975.

HANSEN, P. *88*
Woman's hour: feminist implications of Mary Baker Eddy's Christian Science Movement, 1885–1910. PhD U. of California, Irvine, 1981.

HARDESTY, N.A. *89*
'Your daughters shall prophesy': revivalism and feminism in the age of Finney. PhD U. of Chicago, 1976.

HENRY, I.S. *90*
A study of the educational policy and effort of the woman's division of Christian service of the Methodist church. EdD New York U. 1960.

HILL, P.R. *91*
One unbroken household: the definition and embodiment of a rhetoric of mission among Protestant women in America. PhD Harvard U. 1981.

HOPKINS, J.K. *92*
Joanna Southcott: a study of popular religion and medical politics, 1789–1914. PhD U. of Texas at Austin, 1972.

HULL, J.E. *93*
The controversy between John Wesley and the Countess of Huntingdon: its origin, development and consequences. PhD U. of Edinburgh, 1959.

INSKO, W.R. *94*
A study of women directors of Christian education in the parishes of the Episcopal church in the continental United States. EdD Duke U. 1960.

JONES, I.A. *95*
A recommended program of training for Baptist women lay leaders. PhD U. of Pennsylvania, 1947.

KLEINKE, J.A. *96*
The self-reported problems and support systems of adult women of the Church of Jesus Christ of Latter-Day Saints. EdD Brigham Young U. 1982.

LACEY, B.E. *97*
Women and the Great Awakening in Connecticut. [Eighteenth-century revivalist movement] PhD Clark U., 1982.

LAWLESS, E.J. *98*
Women's speech in the Pentecostal religious service: an ethnography. PhD Indiana U. 1982.

LEISERING, K.J. *99*
An historical and critical study of the Pittsburgh preaching career of Kathryn Kuhlman. PhD Ohio U. 1981.

LESHER, W.R. *100*
Ellen G. White's concept of sanctification. PhD New York U. 1970.

LETSINGER, N.H. *101*
The women's liberation movement: implications for Southern Baptists. ThD Southern Baptist Theological Seminary, 1973.

LINDLEY, S.H. *102*
Woman's profession in the life and thought of Catherine Beecher: a study of religion and reform. PhD Duke U. 1974.

LUDLOW, D.P. *103*
'Arise and be Doing': English 'preaching' women, 1640–1660. PhD Indiana U. 1978.

MILLER, I.T. *104*
Frances Elizabeth Willard: religious leader and social reformer. PhD Boston U. Grad. Sch. 1978.

MCDOWELL, J.P. *105*
A social gospel in the south: the woman's Home Mission movement in the Methodist Episcopal church, South, 1886–1939. PhD Duke U. 1979.

MARTIN, P.S. *106*
Hidden work: Baptist women in Texas, 1880–1920. PhD Rice U. 1982.

MILLER, P.P. *107*
The evolving role of women in the Presbyterian church in the early nineteenth century. PhD U. of Maryland, 1979.

MONTOVANI, M.R. *108*
The impact of the women's movement on the communication within the United Presbyterian Women's Organization: a participant observation study. PhD Ohio U. 1982.

MOORE, A.L. *109*
Ellen G. White's concept of righteousness by faith as it relates to contemporary SDA issue. PhD New York U. 1980.

OLIPHANT, C.A. *110*
Seventh-Day Adventist publishing and Ellen G.

White's journalist principles. PhD U. of Iowa, 1968.

PRICE, M.G. *111*
A study of some of the effects of nineteenth-century revivalism on the status and accomplishments of women in the Evangelical Convent church of America. EdD Boston U. Sch. of Educ. 1977.

RAKOW, M.M. *112*
Melinda Rankin and Magdalen Hayden: Evangelical and Catholic forms of nineteenth-century Christian spirituality. PhD Boston Coll. 1982.

ROOKER, N.B. *113*
Mary Ann Burnham Freeze; Utah evangelist. PhD U. of Utah, 1982.

RUACH, S.W.N. *114*
Communication effectiveness and extent of adoption of an organizational innovation in local units of United Methodist women. EdD Indiana U. 1975.

SETTA, S.M. *115*
Woman of the Apocalypse: the reincorporation of the feminine through the Second Coming of Christ in Ann Lee. PhD Pennsylvania State U. 1979.

SHAW, H.J. *116*
A rhetorical analysis of the speaking of Mrs Ellen G. White, a pioneer leader and spokeswomen of the Seventh Day Adventist Church. PhD Michigan State U. 1959.

SPANN, A.L. *117*
The ministry of women in the Society of Friends. PhD U. of Iowa, 1945.

TEESDALE, W.H. *118*
Ellen G. White, pioneer, prophet. PhD U. of California, Berkeley, 1933.

TIBBETS, J.W. *119*
Women who were called: a study of the contributions to American Christianity of Ann Lee, Jemima Wilkinson, Mary Baker Eddy, and Aimee Semple McPherson. PhD Vanderbilt U. 1976.

TOBIN, P.J. *120*
The Southcottians in England, 1782–1895. [Followers of Joanna Southcott, English religious fanatic] MA U. of Manchester, 1978.

TURNER, R.E. *121*
A critical analysis of the concept of preaching in the thought of Ellen G. White. PhD School of Theology at Claremont, 1979.

VERDESI, E.H. *122*
The professional trained woman in the Presbyterian church: the role of power in the achievement of status and equality. EdD Columbia U. Teachers Coll. 1975.

WALLACE, C.M. *123*
Daughters of God: meanings of womanhood in the Church of Jesus Christ of Latter-Day Saints. PhD U. of Washington, 1982.

WATTS, J.D. *124*
A proposed psychological support system for ministers' wives of the Seventh Day Adventist Church in North America. DMin Andrews U. 1982.

WELCH, P.M. *125*
An educational program designed to change attitudes concerning women speaking in mixed public assemblies at Cherry Corner Baptist Church, Murray, Kentucky. DMin Southern Baptist Theological Seminary, 1976.

WILKINSON, J.T. *126*
The Revd Richard Baxter and Margaret Charlton: being an examination of *The breviate of a life of Margaret Charlton* by Richard Baxter (1681) together with kindred material. MA U. of Birmingham, 1930.

WILSON, N.C. *127*
A study of Ellen G. White's theory of urban religious work as it relates to Seventh Day Adventist work in New York City. PhD New York U. 1981.

WILSON, R.F. *128*
Human liberation and theology: an examination of the theology of Gustavo Gutierrez, James H. Cone and Mary Daly. PhD Southern Baptist Theological Seminary, 1982.

WINSLOW, G.H. *129*
Ellen Gould White and Seventh Day Adventism. PhD Clark U. 1933.

WOODS, R.G. *130*
Evelyn Underhill's concept of worship. ThD Southern Baptist Theological Seminary, 1971.

WRIGHT, E.P. *131*
A descriptive catalogue of the Joanna Southcott Collection at the University of Texas. PhD U. of Texas at Austin, 1966.

WUTERICH, J.G. *132*
Juan Luís Vives, *The instruction of the Christian woman*: a critical evaluation and translation. PhD Boston Coll. 1969.

Roman Catholicism

See also **4** 324–403; **9** 100.

ANDERSON, R.D. *133*
The character and communication of a modern day prophet: a rhetorical analysis of Dorothy Day and the Catholic Worker movement. PhD U. of Oregon, 1979.

BERRIDGE, D.M. *134*
The function of religion at adolescence in Roman Catholic girls. PhD U. of London, Bedford Coll., 1967.

BRENNAN, L.M. *135*
The correlation of self-actualization, selected background variables, and involvement in social organizations and activities of women in three national Catholic organizations. PhD Boston Coll. 1973.

BROWN, A.V. *136*
The Grail movement in the United States, 1940–1972: the evolution of an American Catholic laywomen's community. PhD Union Theological Seminary, 1982.

CREWS, C.F. *137*
The role of Miss Maude Petre in the modernist movement. [English Catholic modernism] PhD Fordham U. 1972.

FARWELL, L.J. *138*
Betwixt and between: the anthropological contributions of Mary Douglas and Victor Turner toward a renewal of Roman Catholic ritual. PhD Claremont Grad. Sch. 1976.

FRARY, T.D. *139*
The ecclesiology of Dorothy Day [co-founder of *The Catholic Worker* and the Catholic Worker movement]. PhD Marquette U. 1972.

GIBBS,J. *139a*
The visions and locations of St Theresa [of Avila]. BLitt U. of Oxford, 1940.

HUFFHINES, K.L.D. *140*
Family of origin and differentiation of self of selected Catholic women: a case study. EdD East Texas State U. 1981.

KANGER, K.E. *141*
Change in religious attitudes of freshmen Catholic women after one year on a small religiously-oriented campus, a large religiously-oriented campus, and a large secular campus. PhD U. of Northern Colorado, 1972.

KELLY, A.E. *142*
Catholic women in campus ministry: an emerging ministry for women in the Catholic church. PhD Boston U. Grad. Sch. 1975.

LAVRIN, A.I. *143*
Religious life of Mexican women in the eighteenth century. PhD Harvard U. 1963.

MCCARTHY, J.B. *144*
Death anxiety, intrinsicness of religion and purpose in life among nuns and Roman Catholic female undergraduates. PhD St John's U. 1973.

MCDERMOTT,R.M. *145*
The legal position of women in the Roman Catholic church: shifting policies and norms. JCD Catholic U. of America, 1979.

MCINNIS, M.A. *146*
The contribution of Catholic women to Catholic thought in the Catholic literary periodicals of the United States in the nineteenth century. PhD Boston Coll. 1939.

MCKENNA, M.H.V. *147*
Religious attitudes and personality traits in four groups of Catholic women. PhD Fordham U. 1958.

MEAGHER, K.M. *148*
The status of women in the post-conciliar Church. PhD U. of Ottawa, 1977.

NEELY, A.E. *149*
Girlhood in the Catholic Church: Spanish, French and American autobiographies 1902–1978. PhD U. of Wisconsin–Madison, 1981.

ORSI, R.A. *150*
The Madonna of 115th street: faith and community in Italian Harlem, 1880–1950. PhD Yale U. 1982.

RICHTER, J.B. *151*
Currents of spirituality in eighteenth-century France: nuns, sisters, and *philosophes*. PhD U. of Wisconsin, 1972.

ROBERTS, W.L. *152*
Dorothy Day and *The Catholic Worker*, 1933–1982. PhD U. of Minnesota, 1982.

SHIODA, M.J.B. *153*
Cultural bases for teaching religion in Catholic women's colleges in Japan. PhD Saint Louis U. 1967.

SMITH, M.L. *154*
Catholic viewpoints about the psychology, social role, and higher education of women. PhD Ohio State U. 1961.

WORLAND, C.E. *155*
American Catholic women and the church to 1920. PhD Saint Louis U. 1982.

Women religious

See also **8** 138, 556; **9** 123, 600.

AGUDO, P.R. *156*
Contributions of Wilfried Daim and Viktor Frankl to counselling in the context of a religious community of women. PhD Boston U. Grad. Sch. 1975.

ALVAREZ, J. *157*
Psychological androgyny among Catholic sisters. EdD U. of Northern Colorado, 1978.

BARNHISER, J.A. *158*
A study of the authority structures of three nineteenth-century apostolic communities of religious women in the United States. JCD Catholic U. of America, 1975.

BATISTE, S.A.P. *159*
Creativity among women religious changing careers. EdD U. of Massachusetts, 1981.

BENNETT, F.A. *160*
Avowed happiness in communities of religious women. PhD U. of Utah, 1971.

BERES, M.E. *161*
Change in a women's religious organization: the impact of individual differences, power and the environment. PhD Northwestern U. 1976.

BONNER, D.W. *162*
Extern sisters in monasteries of nuns. PhD Catholic U. of America, 1964.

BRUCKEN, C.S. *163*
Body image and habit change in religious women. PhD Loyola U., Chicago, 1971.

BURNS, M.S. *164*
A comparative study of social factors in religious vocations to three types of women's communities. PhD Catholic U. of America, 1958.

BURSTON, W.J. *165*
A study of religious women-novices with the Bernreuter personality inventory. MPsychSc National U. of Ireland, 1970.

CALABRO, W.V. *166*
Some organizational determinants of orientation to change: a case study of the attitudes of women religious to the call for *Aggiornamento* in the Catholic Church. PhD New York U. 1976.

CALMUS, M.E. *167*
A study of the perceptions and attitudes of the members of a congregation of religious women regarding goals, priorities, and future directions for that organization. PhD U. of Colorado at Boulder, 1978.

CAMPBELL, M.A.F. *168*
Bishop England's sisterhood, 1829–1929. PhD Saint Louis U. 1968.

CHRISTIAN, H.M. *169*
Attitudes of women religious who elect to work in the inner city. PhD State U. of New York at Buffalo, 1978.

CLARK, P.M. *170*
Real-ideal residence environment: perceptions of older women religious. EdD Columbia U. Teachers Coll. 1981.

COLL, R.A. *171*
Paulo Freire and the transformation of consciousness of women in religious congregations. EdD Columbia U. Teachers Coll. 1982.

CONNOLLY, P.F. *172*
The development of a ministry to Dominican religious women experiencing vocational change. DMin Drew U. 1980.

CREAMER, M.J. *173*
Development of pre-service collegiate nursing education for the Sisters of Saint Joseph of Wichita, Kansas. PhD Columbia U. 1961.

DONAHUE, E.A. *174*
Perceptions of community life in a congregation of religious women. PhD Fordham U. 1970.

ELSIKDUITS, R.V. *175*
The Sisters of Our Lady of Charity of the Good Shepherd, 1835–1977: a study in cultural adaptation. PhD U. of Minnesota, 1978.

FAHEY, M.R. *176*
The inservice training of religious secondary school teachers in congregations of women in the United States. PhD Fordham U. 1960.

FARREL, B.F.F. *177*
The rights and duties of the local ordinary regarding congregations of women religious of pontifical approval. PhD Catholic U. of America, 1941.

FECHER, C.J. *178*
The longevity of members of Catholic religious sisterhoods. PhD Catholic U. of America, 1927.

FITZPATRICK, M.B. *179*
The sister social worker: an integration of two professional roles. PhD U. of Notre Dame, 1962.

FOREST, C.A. *180*
The religious academic woman: a study of adjustment to multiple roles. PhD Fordham U. 1966.

FORTKORT, M. *181*
Changes in educational and occupational patterns within a province of religious sisters. PhD State U. of New York at Buffalo, 1978.

FUCHS, H.R. *182*
From Utopia to voluntary organization: effects of organizational change upon membership commitment in religious orders of women in the United States. PhD Columbia U. 1975.

HAIRE, P.A. *183*
An investigation of psychological differences among Roman Catholic sisters with respect to life styles, years in religious service, and degree of commitment to religious life. PhD United States International U. 1981.

HAMMERSMITH, S.K. *184*
Being a nun: social order and change in a radical community. PhD Indiana U. 1976.

HARMER, C.M. *185*
Change in religious communities of women: an analysis of some variables involved. PhD Temple U. 1974.

HEBARD, R.D. *186*
A nunnery movement in Oklahoma. PhD Southern Baptist Theological Seminary, 1949.

HILL, B. *187*
Women and religion: a study of socialization in a community of Catholic sisters. PhD U. of Kentucky, 1967.

HOWARD, M.P. *188*
Intimacy and power: their relationship as per-

ceived by Catholic nuns. PhD Catholic U. of America, 1982.

HUESMANN, M.A. *189*
A study of the relationship of death anxiety, age, and rigidity-flexibility in Roman Catholic women religious. PhD Saint Louis U. 1980.

JANCOSKI, L.K. *190*
Religion and commitment: a psycho-historical study of creative women in Catholic religious communities. PhD U. of Chicago, 1976.

JEAN, M. *191*
Évolution des communautés religieuses de femmes au Canada, 1639–1973. PhD U. of Ottawa, 1974.

JOHNSON, M.M. *192*
An exploration of approaches to retirement in communities of religious sisters. EdD Columbia U. 1972.

JOSEPH, M.V. *193*
A study of self-role congruence and role-role congruence on the integration of the religious role and the social work role of the sister social worker. DSW Catholic U. of America, 1974.

JOYCE, M.U. *194*
An empirical investigation of Erikson's developmental crises of ego identity, intimacy, and generativity in religious women. PhD Fordham U. 1970.

KEALY, T.M. *195*
Dowry of women religious. PhD Catholic U. of America, 1941.

KEENAN, E. *196*
Survival and attrition in religious women. PhD Marquette U. 1976.

KENNEDY, C. *197*
A study of the charism operative in Mary Josephine Rogers (1882–1955) as foundress of the Maryknoll Sisters. PhD Saint Louis U. 1980.

KENWEY, F.J. *198*
Mary's spiritual maternity according to modern writers. PhD Catholic U. of America, 1957.

KERBRAT, D.J. *199*
Identification of designated talents among a group of sisters from the Province of Manitoba using the TSCs and the POI. PhD U. of Kansas, 1975.

LEWIS, M.A. *200*
Actual and perceived age differences in self-concept and psychological well-being for Catholic sisters. PhD Syracuse U. 1972.

LINDER, I.C. *201*
Some factors influencing women to choose church-related vocations: a study in occupational sociology. PhD U. of Iowa, 1956.

LUCASSEN, M.R. *202*
Appraisal of potential leadership qualities among young women religious. PhD Loyola U. of Chicago, 1963.

MCAULEY, E.A.N. *203*
Vows, commitment, and Roman Catholic sisters: a descriptive study of a congregation. PhD United States International U. 1975.

MCCARTHY, E.T.S. *204*
A study of the expectations of members of a religious community and lay professional women on retirement as a basis for planning a pre-retirement education program. PhD Saint Louis U. 1969.

MCGANN, J.R.S. *206*
Interests of a group of women religious on the Strong vocational interest blank. PhD St John's U. 1963.

MASTEJ, M.M. *207*
A study of the influence of religious life on the personality adjustment of religious women as measured by a modified form of the Minnesota Multiphasic Personality Inventory. PhD Fordham U. 1954.

MERCILLE, M.M.R. *208*
An investigation of the response of religious women to counselling practices used by religious superiors. PhD Fordham U. 1964.

MISNER, B. *209*
A comparative social study of the members and apostolates of the first eight permanent communities of women religious within the original boundaries of the United States, 1790–1850. PhD Catholic U. of America, 1981.

MODDE, M.M. *210*
A canonical study of the Leadership Conference of Women Religious (LCWR) of the United States of America. JCD Catholic U. of America, 1977.

MONAHAN, D.R. *211*
Educating women religious: the history of Marillace College, 1955–69. PhD Saint Louis U. 1972.

MOORE, M.E. *212*
The relationship between ego and moral development in adult lay and religious women. PhD Illinois Inst. of Technology, 1975.

MORAN, R.E. *213*
Death and rebirth: a case study of reform efforts of a Roman Catholic sisterhood. PhD U. of California, Santa Barbara, 1972.

MOTTE, M.M. *214*
An exploratory study of the types of commitment among members of a religious community of women. PhD Boston Coll. 1972.

MULLANEY, J.W. *215*
Fifteen treatment programs provided by the Sisters of the Good Shepherd in the New York province with particular reference to the teachings

of Mother Euphrasia. DSW Catholic U. of America, 1963.

MUNICH, J. *216*
Unforeseen retirement: a community of nuns in transition. PhD U. of Southern California, 1977.

MURPHY, W.V. *217*
A study of the relations between internal-external control, and selected personality variables among Catholic women religious: those living traditional life-styles and those living non-traditional life-styles. PhD St John's U. 1975.

OBEN, F.M. *218*
An annotated edition of Edith Stein's papers on woman. [Religious and philosophical thoughts of a German Carmelite sister killed in Auschwitz in 1942] PhD Catholic U. of America, 1979.

O'BRIAN, A.G. *219*
The dynamics of organizational behavior in communities of religious women. PhD Syracuse U. 1975.

O'TOOLE, M.G. *220*
Sisters of Mercy of Maine: a religious community as a social system. PhD Catholic U. of America, 1964.

PENDERGAST, M.C. *221*
Assessment of a psychological screening program for candidates to a religious congregation of women. PhD Fordham U. 1968.

PETERSON, S.C. *222*
The Presentation Sisters in South Dakota, 1880–1976. PhD Oklahoma State U. 1979.

PITZER, S.E. *223*
A study of the rhetoric employed by a community of nuns during the charges of renewal. PhD Pennsylvania State U. 1972.

RIDICK, J. *224*
Intrapsychic factors in the early dropping out of female religious vocationers. PhD U. of Chicago, 1972.

RIGGS, F.M. *225*
Attitudes of missionary sisters toward American Indian acculturation. PhD Catholic U. of America, 1967.

RUFFT, E. *226*
Stages of adult development for women religious and married women. PhD Virginia Commonwealth U. 1981.

SANCHEZ, J.A. *227*
The community of love: a study of the process of change in a congregation of nuns in Puerto Rico. PhD Tulane U. 1975.

SANGIOVANNI, L.F. *228*
The ex-nuns: an exploration of emergent status transition. PhD Rutgers U. 1974.

SELLMEYER, F.M. *229*
The Southern Province of the School Sisters of Notre Dame, 1925–1965. PhD Saint Louis U. 1967.

SFERRELLA, J.M. *230*
The response of women religious to Vatican II: an exploratory investigation utilizing Etzioni's theory of societal guidance. PhD Wayne State U. 1981.

SMILEY, M.A. *231*
Attitudes of women religious before and after participation in a pre-retirement education program. PhD Texas A&M U. 1977.

SMITH, D.A. *232*
A comparative case study of the relationship of change strategies and perceptions of leader roles to the attainment of a renewal mandated for religious communities of women by the documents of Vatican II. EdD State U. of New York at Buffalo, 1979.

SPRINGSTEAD, M.T. *233*
Problems of postulants and novices in selected communities of religious women. PhD Fordham U. 1970.

TARLETON, M.R.B. *234*
The relation of perceived attitudes of reference group members to personal attitudes toward and decisions to enter Roman Catholic sisterhoods. PhD Catholic U. of America, 1968.

VAUGHAN, R.P. *235*
A comparative study of personality differences between contemplative and active religious women. PhD Fordham U. 1956.

WATSON, F. *236*
Monastic ritual: social dramas of revitalization in a community of American Benedictine women. PhD U. of Kansas, 1982.

WEDGE, R.B. *237*
The occupational milieu of the Catholic sister. PhD St John's U. 1966.

WHITE, M.R. *238*
A follow-up study of candidates in a religious community of women. PhD Fordham U. 1970.

YOYCE, M.U. *239*
An empirical investigation of Erickson's development crises of ego-identity intimacy and generativity in religious women. PhD Fordham U. 1970.

Feminist Christianity

See 42, 89, 128, 305; **2** 280; **4** 32; **7** 14, 133; **9** 388, 510, 673; **12** 985.

BOHLER, C.J. *240*
The politics of prayer: feminist perspectives for expanding Christian prayer. PhD School of Theology at Claremont, 1982.

HOGAN, D.C. *241*
Woman and the Christian experience: feminist ideology, Christian theology and spirituality. PhD Boston U. Grad. Sch. 1975.

The ordination of women

BOHN, C.R. *242*
Women in theological education: realities and implications. EdD Boston U. Sch. of Educ. 1981.

ENGELMAN, K.L. *243*
An inquiry into the attitudes of local church members towards ordained women ministers serving local congregations. PhD U. of Wisconsin–Madison, 1974.

FLOOD, M.W. *244*
The place of women in the ministerial offices of the church as witnessed by ecclesial tradition and rites of ordination. PhD U. of St Michael's, Inst. of Christian Thought, 1977.

GAYLOR, C.C. *245*
The ordination of women in the Episcopal Church in the United States: a case study. PhD St John's U. 1982.

GOMAN, J.G. *246*
The ordination of women: the Bible and the Fathers. DMin School of Theology at Claremont, 1976.

HEATH, L.F. *247*
A study of the New Testament attitude towards the ministry of women and its implications for Church leadership. DMin Fuller Theological Seminary, 1975.

HUYCK, H.A. *248*
To celebrate a whole priesthood: the history of women's ordination in the Episcopal church. PhD U. of Minnesota, 1981.

JOWERS, M.R. *249*
Equal rights for women: a study of the problems associated with the ordination and acceptance of women in ministerial positions in the Southern Baptist Convention, with implications for the local church and district association. DMin San Francisco Theological Seminary, 1981.

KLICK, R.C. *250*
The female diaconate in recent American Lutheranism. STD Temple U. 1949.

KNUTSON, K.E. *251*
Ordained women in the Danish Church: a case history of the twentieth century. DMin U. of Chicago, 1972.

MARRETT, M.M. *252*
The historical background and spiritual authority of the Lambeth conferences and their impact on the Protestant Episcopal church in the United States of America with particular emphasis on the ordination of women to the priesthood. PhD New York U. 1980.

MORRISON, S.M. *253*
Ministry shaped by hope: towards wholeness: the woman as ordained minister. PhD Wesley Theological Seminary, 1979.

NORPEL, M.L. *254*
The relevance of the Lutheran deaconess tradition in America for post-conciliar religious life among Roman Catholic women. PhD Catholic U. of America, 1971.

PAGE, F.S. *255*
Toward a biblical ethic of women in ministry. PhD Southwest Baptist Theological Seminary, 1980.

PROKES, M.T. *256*
The flesh was made word: an initial exploration of this proposition as it applies to women's ministries in the light of four post-Vatican II orientations with the Roman Catholic church. PhD U. of St Michael's Inst. of Christian Thought, 1976.

RHODES-WICKETT, S.K. *257*
Your daughters did prophesy (women clergy). DMin School of Theology at Claremont, 1981.

SARTORI, S.L. *258*
Conflict and institutional change: the ordination of women in the Episcopal church. PhD State U. of New York at Albany, 1978.

SCHMIDT, M.M. *259*
Effects of group interaction on the self-perception of women in religious life. PhD U. of Illinois at Urbana–Champaign, 1970.

STEININGER, R.F. *260*
History of the female diaconate in the Lutheran church in America. PhD U. of Pittsburgh, 1934.

WAHL, J.A. *261*
The exclusion of woman from holy orders. PhD Catholic U. of America, 1959.

Overseas missions

EKAM, A.G. *262*
The contributions of the Holy Child Sisters to women's education in the cross-river state of Nigeria from 1930 to 1967. PhD Catholic U. of America, 1980.

HAWKINS, D.C. *263*
The development and influence of the Women's

Missionary Training School in Brazil. PhD Southwestern Baptist Theological Seminary, 1958.

HURLEY, J.R. *264*
The Franciscan Sisters as a Westernizing influence in Uganda. PhD St John's U. 1981.

MURRAY, J.M. *265*
The Kikuyu female circumcision controversy, with special reference to the Church Missionary Society's 'sphere of influence'. PhD U. California, Los Angeles, 1974.

SCHINTZ, M.A. *266*
An investigation of the modernizing role of the Maryknoll Sisters in China. PhD U. of Wisconsin–Madison, 1978.

SCHROER, C.R. *267*
Christian women's influence can enable the church in the Tohoku to be more effective in its ministry and its mission to the world. DMin Eden Theological Seminary, 1980.

WILLIAMSON, H.R. *268*
All for China: an account of the life and labour of Mrs E.H. Edwards of Taiynanfu, Shensi. MA U. of London, 1922.

Pastoral care

See also **6** 145.

BENNETT, K.I. *269*
Clinical pastoral education: an opportunity in theological education for women. DMin Columbia Theological Seminary, 1979.

BRANDON, R.W. *270*
The church as a healing community for the bereaved widow. PhD Eden Theolological Seminary, 1976.

CHARNIN, R.A. *271*
A tape ministry to supplement pastoral care with widows in the Homewood Reformed Church. DMin Trinity Evangelical Sch. 1979.

COLLINS, D.C. *272*
Pastoral counselors and the crying woman: a study of differences in responses between male and female pastoral counselors. PhD Graduate Theological Union, 1980.

DURKIN, M.G. *273*
The responsible Christian woman: toward a pastoral theology for suburban upper middle-class women. PhD U. of Chicago, 1974.

FRIBERG, N.C. *274*
An assessment of the religious coping of women cancer patients for purposes of pastoral counseling. PhD U. of Iowa, 1977.

GOSS, J.U. *275*
A pastoral awareness of dreams in the age thirty transition in women. DMin Colgate Rochester Divinity Sch./Bexley Hall/Crozer Theological Seminary, 1981.

HOLCOMB, L.R.P. *276*
Role concepts and self-esteem in church women with implications for pastoral counseling. PhD Syracuse U. 1974.

INMAN, C.S. *277*
Developing a deacon wife approach to pastoral ministry. DMin Southwestern Baptist Theological Seminary, 1980.

MCCONNELL, M.T. *278*
Women's experience: implications for theology and pastoral care. DMin Southern Methodist U. 1981.

NYGREN, R.E. *279*
Empowering widows to become care-givers. DMin Princeton Theological Seminary, 1981.

REED, C.A. *280*
Developing a ministry to the widow in the local church. DMin Southwestern Baptist Theological Seminary, 1980.

SADLER, E.K. *281*
A team ministry deacon wife approach to ministering. DMin New Orleans Baptist Theological Seminary, 1977.

SARGENT, F.A. *282*
Sex-role stereotyping and current pastoral counseling practice. PhD Boston U. Grad. Sch. 1979.

SIMMONS, T.E. *283*
The role of the woman pastoral associate in parish ministry. DMin Catholic U. of America, 1981.

YEAGER, G.L. *284*
Developing a manual for ministering with a congregation having widowed, separated or divorced persons. DMin Drew U. 1982.

Hinduism and Indian religion

AJGAONKAR, S.N. *285*
The position of women in ancient India according to the *Dharmásaestras*. BLitt U. of Oxford, 1925.

AJGAONKAR, S.N. *286*
The social and legal position of women in ancient India as represented by a critical study of the epics: the *Mahabharata* and the *Ramayana*. DPhil U. of Oxford, 1927.

BOAZ, G.D. *287*
The psychological role of the mother in the origin of religious sentiment: a psychological study of

the mother-goddess cults, with special reference to India. DPhil U. of Oxford, 1942.

BROWN, C.M. *288*
The development of a feminine theology: an historical and theological study of the *Brahmavaivarta Purana*. PhD Harvard U. 1973.

CHAUDHURI, J. *289*
The position of women in the Vedic ritual. PhD U. of London, Sch. of Oriental and African Studies, 1934.

HENDRICKS, N.C. *290*
Simone Weil and the Indian religious tradition. PhD McMaster U. 1972.

HERMAN, P.K. *291*
Ideal kingship and the feminine power: a study of the depiction of *Ramarajya* in the Valmiki *Ramayana*. PhD U. of California, Los Angeles, 1979.

LESLIE, J. *292*
The religious role of women in ancient India. MPhil U. of Oxford, 1982.

PINKHAM, C.M.W. *293*
The status of woman in Hinduism as reflected in the *Puranas*, the *Mahabharata*, and the *Ramayana*. PhD Columbia U. 1941.

RAO, S. *294*
The position of women in early India as it appears in the Vedic literature and the sacred law. BLitt U. of Oxford, 1936.

REYNOLDS, H.B. *295*
'To keep the Tâli strong': women's rituals in Tamilnad, India. PhD U. of Wisconsin–Madison, 1978.

ROBBINS, M.E. *296*
Indo-European female figures. [Goddesses and mythological heroines] PhD U. of California, Los Angeles, 1978.

SOLIMENE, A.A. *297*
The divine feminine in the theologies of the Hindu tradition: a study in the theology of religion. PhD Fordham U. 1982.

Islam

CHUN, C. *298*
An exploration of the community model for Muslim missionary outreach by Asian women. DMiss, Fuller Theological Seminary, 1977.

HUSSEIN, H.S. *299*
The Koran and courtly love: a study of the Koran and its influence on the development of divine and courtly love. PhD U. of Southern California, 1971.

JONES, L.B. *300*
The status of women in Islam. MA U. of Wales, 1941.

SMITH, M. *301*
The life and teachings of Rābia' al-'Adawiyya al-Qayriyya of Basra, together with some account of the place of women saints in Islam. PhD U. of London, 1928.

Judaism

See also **11** 18; **12** 249, 2070, 2166; **20** 109; **21** 121, 122.

ARCHER, L.J. *302*
The social and legal positions of the Jewish woman in Palestine during the inter-testamental and Mishnaic period: a survey of life from birth to marriage. PhD U. of London, 1983.

BRITT, R.N. *303*
The role of Turkish and Rhodes Sephardic women in the Seattle Sephardic community. PhD Union for Experimenting Colleges and Universities, 1981.

BROOTEN, B.J. *304*
Inscriptional evidence for women as leaders in the ancient synagogue. PhD Harvard U. 1982.

CAMP, C.V. *305*
Wisdom and the feminine in the Book of Proverbs. PhD Duke U. 1982.

COLLINS, O.E. *306*
The stem 'ZNH' and prostitution in the Hebrew Bible. PhD Brandeis U. 1977.

DIXON, S.A. *307*
The position of women among the early Hebrews. PhD Boston U. 1908.

ELWELL, E.S.L. *308*
The founding and early programs of the National Council of Jewish Women: study and practice as Jewish women's religious expression. PhD Indiana U. 1982.

HAVICE, H.K. *309*
The concern for the widow and the fatherless in the ancient Near East: a case study in Old Testament ethics. PhD Yale U. 1978.

FINE, I.A. *310*
Developing a Jewish studies program for women: a springboard to history. PhD Union for Experimenting Colleges and Universities, 1980.

LEWIS, T.N. *311*
Woman under Rabbinic Judaism. PhD Hebrew Union Coll. 1949.

PERITZ, I.J. *312*
Woman's relation to the ancient Hebrew cult. PhD Harvard U. 1898.

SMITH, C.A. *313*
The barren women of the Old Testament. MA U. of Exeter, 1982.

UMANSKY, E.M. *314*
Lily H. Montagu and the development of Liberal Judaism in England. PhD Columbia U. 1981.

WEINBERGER, P.M. *315*
The social and religious thought of Grace Aguilar (1816–1847). [Relationship between Judaism and Christianity] PhD New York U. 1970.

19 Reproduction

Abortion, contraception and family planning

See also 257, 483, 513–16, 559; **9** 125, 472, 533, 573; **15** 134; **20** 15, 37; *related studies are also to be found in* **3** Demography and **23** Women in the Third World.

ABELL, P.K. *1*
Voluntary sterilization and moral development of women. EdD Boston U. Sch. of Educ. 1980.

ADLER, N.E. *2*
Reactions of women to therapeutic abortion – a social-psychological analysis. PhD Harvard U. 1974.

ALBANO, S.J. *3*
Locus of control of increasing specificity, reinforcement value and contraceptive use among sexually experienced college females who are knowledgeable about contraception. PhD New York U. 1981.

ALTER, R.C. *4*
Abortion outcome as a function of sex-role identification. PhD U. of Florida, 1979.

AUGER, J.A.R. *5*
A psychophysiological study of the normal menstrual cycle and of some possible effects of oral contraceptives. PhD U. of California, Los Angeles, 1967.

BELENKY, M.F. *6*
Conflict and development: a longitudinal study of the impact of abortion decisions on moral judgements of adolescent and adult women. EdD Harvard U. 1978.

BISCONTI, E. *7*
Psychological aftermath of female voluntary sterilization: a comparison of client and agency perceptions. PhD United States International U. 1980.

BRASHEAR, D.L.B. *8*
A study of contraceptive practices among white female college students. PhD Purdue U. 1971.

BROWNER, C. *9*
Poor women's fertility decisions: illegal abortion in Cali, Colombia. PhD U. of California, Berkeley, 1976.

BURGESS, R.B. *10*
Effects of attitudes about premarital sex on contraceptive risk-taking among low-income, unmarried teenagers. PhD Emory U. 1979.

BURNHILL, M.S. *11*
Hospitalized abortion patients: a demographic study. PhD State U. of New York at Albany, 1971.

BUTTS, J.D. *12*
Perceptions of the experience of tubal ligation: an exploratory study in fertility control among twenty low-income black women. EdD Columbia U. 1969.

BUUTAP, N. *13*
Legislation, public opinion, and the press: an interrelationship reflected in the *New York Times* reporting of the abortion issue. PhD U. of Chicago, 1979.

CHANDLER, L.J. *14*
Women's social networks: their effects on the anxiety of abortion. PhD U. of Michigan, 1975.

CLARK, C. *15*
Race, motherhood, and abortion. PhD Columbia U. 1979.

COLEMAN, S.J. *16*
Induced abortion and contraceptive method choice among urban Japanese marrieds. PhD Columbia U. 1978.

CONNOR, L.M. *17*
Comparison of moral and ego development in women: a quantitative and qualitative study of the reconstruction of the abortion decision. EdD Boston U. Sch. of Educ. 1982.

COTTAM, W.S. *18*
Abortion, moral philosophy and education. PhD U. of Utah, 1973.

CRABTREE, P.H. *19*
Personality correlates of the delayed abortion decision. PhD Adelphi U. 1980.

CRESSY, M.K. *20*
Factors related to the use of family planning services by low-income teenage mothers. EdD Columbia U. Teachers Coll. 1976.

CUNNINGHAM, M. *21*
Attitudes of Catholic college students toward abortion. EdD Columbia U. 1973.

DAVIS, N.J. *22*
The abortion market: transactions in a risk commodity. PhD Michigan State U. 1973.

DEUTSCH, M.B. *23*
Personality factors, self-concept, and family variables related to first-time and repeat abortion-seeking behavior in adolescent women. PhD American U. 1982.

DIRKS, M.J. *24*
Psychological outcomes of abortion: an exploration of knowledge, conflict, and expectancies. PhD U. of Cincinnati, 1979.

DIXON, S.S. *25*
An analysis of the uses of key 'life words' in the present abortion debate in the USA. PhD Temple U. 1974.

DRUCKER, C.A. *26*
The psychological aspects of contraceptive choice among single women. PhD Adelphi U. 1975.

ELIOT, S.V. *27*
The determinants of psychological response to abortion. PhD Yeshiva U. 1975.

FIGA-TALAMANCA, I.P. *28*
Induced abortion in Italy. PhD U. of California, Berkeley, 1972.

FINGERER, M.E. *29*
Psychological sequelae of abortion – anxiety and depression. PhD Adelphi U. 1972.

FISCH, M.A. *30*
Internal versus external ego orientation and family planning effectiveness among poor black women. PhD Columbia U. 1973.

FISHER, N.B. *31*
Abortion: a study of the perceptions of 60 abortion applicants and 20 service givers in Denver, Colorado. DSW U. of Denver, 1976.

FRANCOME, C.S. *32*
Social forces and the abortion law. PhD CNAA, 1980.

FREEMAN, E.W. *33*
Women as agents: abortion and motivation to contracept. PhD Bryn Mawr Coll. 1976.

GARNER, A.L.H. *34*
Factors affecting the adoption of modern family planning techniques, as perceived by adult women in Barranquilla, Colombia. PhD Florida State U. 1974.

GELLMAN, M.A. *35*
The ethics of abortion. PhD Northwestern U. 1981.

GERRARD, C.O.C. *36*
Sex guilt and contraceptive use in abortion patients. PhD U. of Texas at Austin, 1974.

GILCHRIST, L.D. *37*
Coping with contraception: a cognitive behavioral approach to prevention of unwanted teenage pregnancy. PhD U. of Washington, 1981.

GILL, V.D. *38*
Family planning program effects and attitudes of adolescent females toward authority. PhD U. of Kansas, 1979.

GREGORY, M.S. *39*
Abortion and adoption: fetal value beyond the parenthood debate. PhD Vanderbilt U. 1982.

GRIFFIN, C.R. *40*
Antecedents affecting contraceptive behavior of teenage females. PhD U. of Utah, 1980.

GUTTMACHER, S.J. *41*
Patients delay in seeking health care: social factors associated with delayed abortion. PhD Columbia U. 1976.

HALL, E.E. *42*
Contraceptive risk-taking among women entering a family planning clinic. PhD Southern Illinois U. at Carbondale, 1977.

HARMAN, J.D. *43*
Rights, obligations, and social freedom: the case of abortion. PhD U. of Wisconsin–Madison, 1978.

HARRISON, A.P.G. *44*
Social pressure and health education: an exploratory intervention study of health education dealing with the problem of abortion. MSc U. of Manchester, 1978.

HEMBREE, J.D. *45*
Pre-abortion psychological experience and its relationship to post-abortion psychological outcome. PhD U. of Florida, 1978.

HIRSCH, M.B. *46*
Contraceptive method switching among American female adolescents, 1979. PhD Johns Hopkins U. 1982.

HUGHES, B.R. *47*
Abortion: perception and contemporary genocide myth: a comparative study among low-income pregnant black and Puerto Rican women. PhD New York U. 1973.

HUMPHRIES, D. *48*
The politics of abortion: a case study of New York's abortion law. PhD U. of California, Berkeley, 1973.

HUNTER, E.K. *49*
The role of fantasies about the fetus in abortion patients: an adaptive process. PhD California Sch. of Prof. Psych., Fresno, 1979.

HUTCHERSON, J.R. *50*
The self-concept of women at the time of elective abortion. PhD U. of Maryland, 1972.

IMBER, J.B. *51*
Strategies of despair: abortion in America and in

American medicine. PhD U. of Pennsylvania, 1979.

JAIN, A.K. *52*
Single service organizations: a comparative study of twelve abortion clinics in Ohio. PhD Case Western Reserve U. 1977.

JONES, A.M. *53*
Attitudes of abortion counselors and their work role. PhD U. of Michigan, 1982.

JONES, P.G. *54*
Ethical issues related to induced abortion. ThD, Southwestern Baptist Theological Seminary, 1976.

KEARING, Y.E. *55*
Reflective decision-making: an empirical phenomenological study of the decision to have an abortion. PhD Duquesne U. 1980.

KEISER, G.L. *56*
Dynamics of policy politics: the cases of abortion funding and family planning in the State of Oregon. PhD U. of Oregon, 1981.

KNOTT, S.G. *57*
Demographic factors and contraceptive practices of repeatedly aborting women. PhD United States International U. 1979.

KOO, H.P.C. *58*
Use of induced abortion and contraception in Taiwan: a multivariate analysis. DrPH U. of Michigan Sch. of Public Health, 1973.

LAKE, R.A. *59*
The ethics of rhetoric and the rhetoric of ethics in the abortion controversy. PhD U. of Kansas, 1982.

LEAHY, P.J. 60
The anti-abortion movement: testing a theory of the rise and fall of social movements. PhD Syracuse U. 1975.

LEE, N.H. *61*
Acquaintance networks in the social structure of abortion. PhD Harvard U. 1968.

LEIBOWITZ, L. *62*
Repression-sensitization in abortion patients: the effects of encouraging emotional expression. PhD Long Island U. 1979.

LEVINSON, R.A. *63*
Teenage women and contraceptive behavior: focus on self-efficacy in sexual and contraceptive situations. PhD Stanford U. 1982.

LINCOLN, E. *64*
A care study of the reproductive experience of women who have had three or more induced abortions. PhD U. of Pittsburgh, 1982.

LINDERMANN, C. *65*
Birth control behavior of young, unmarried women. PhD U. of California, Los Angeles, 1972.

LIVELY, B.T. *66*
The relationship of knowledge to perceived benefits and risks of oral contraceptives among college women. EdD West Virginia U. 1979.

LUKER, K.C. *67*
Patterns of pregnancy: towards a theory of contraceptive risk-taking. PhD Yale U. 1974.

LYNCH, M.C. *68*
A psychological study of premaritally pregnant college women seeking abortion. PhD Wayne State U. 1972.

LYNCH, P.T.C. *69*
Abortion politics and family life: an interpretation. PhD U. of Massachusetts, 1981.

MCCAMMON, S.L. *70*
The theory of reasoned action and the health belief model applied to contraception of college women. PhD U. of South Carolina, 1981.

MCCORMICK, E.P. *71*
Attitudes toward abortion among women undergoing legally induced abortions. PhD Catholic U. of America, 1973.

MCQUOWN, D.I. *72*
Psychological factors contributing to abortion distress. PhD City U. of New York, 1974.

MARDFIN, D.W. *73*
Economics of abortion demand by pregnant married women: the ultimate fertility choice. PhD U. of Hawaii, 1979.

MARKSON, S.L. *74*
Citizens united for life: status politics, symbolic reform and the anti-abortion movement. PhD U. of Massachusetts, 1979.

MARTIN, C.D. *75*
Psychological problems of abortion for the unwed teenage girl. PhD United States International U. 1972.

MELCHING, D.E. *76*
Factors affecting the adoption of oral contraceptives. PhD Bryn Mawr Coll. 1977.

MICHELMAN, D.K. *77*
Abortion: a psychological study. PhD Michigan State U. 1971.

MILLER, G.G. *78*
Attitudes of educated women toward the use of oral contraception. EdD U. of Tulsa, 1970.

MILLIGAN, S.E. *79*
An analysis of access to contraceptive care in western Pennsylvania. PhD U. of Pittsburgh, 1982.

MININGER, L.S. *80*
Personality aspects of teenage abortion. PhD United States International U. 1974.

MOLDANADO, S.A. *81*
Trends and patterns in the attitudes of the public toward legal abortion in the United States, 1972–1978. PhD U. of Illinois at the Medical Center, 1982.

MOORE, E.C. *82*
Abortion: ambivalence and ambiguity. PhD Columbia U. 1973.

MOORE, M.R. *83*
Affects of a film model on the psychological and physical stress of abortion. PhD U. of Utah, 1979.

MUHR, J.R. *84*
Psychological adjustment to first-trimester abortion. PhD Northwestern U. 1978.

MURAMATSU, M. *85*
Studies on induced abortion in Japan. PhD Johns Hopkins U. 1959.

NAUFUL, B.B. *86*
Nursing students' attitudes toward and knowledge of abortion before and after a supervised clinical experience with patients having abortions. EdD U. of South Carolina, 1978.

NEAL, C.E. *87*
Compliance and the state legislature: an empirical analysis of abortion and aid to non-public schools in Illinois and Minnesota. PhD U. of Minnesota, 1980.

NEEF, M.H. *88*
Policy formation and implementation in the abortion field. PhD U. of Illinois at Urbana–Champaign, 1979.

NELSON, J.A. *89*
Abortion and the causal theory of names. PhD State U. of New York at Buffalo, 1980.

NIES, C.M. *90*
Social psychological variables related to family planning among Mexican-American females. PhD U. of Texas at Austin, 1974.

NOBLE, L.D. *91*
Personality characteristics associated with contraceptive behavior in women seeking abortion under liberalized California law. PhD California Sch. of Prof. Psych., Berkeley, 1972.

OBENG, B.B. *92*
Five hundred consecutive cases of abortion. MD U. of London, 1967.

OSTERBUSCH, S.E. *93*
An exploration of factors affecting referral of adolescent girls to a planned parenthood clinic. DSW U. of Illinois at Chicago Circle, 1977.

PAIGE, K.E. *94*
The effects of oral contraceptives on affective fluctuations associated with the menstrual cycle. PhD U. of Michigan, 1969.

PEACOCK, N.B. *95*
An empirical assessment of a decision-making model of contraceptive use and nonuse among adolescent girls. PhD Purdue U. 1981.

PETT, M.E. *96*
Religion and the abortion patient: a study of anxiety as a function of religious belief and participation and the decision-making process. PhD U. of Iowa, 1975.

PLATTNER, S. *97*
Conceptual systems and sex-role attitudes and beliefs and their effect on short-term abortion outcome. PhD U. of Colorado at Boulder, 1979.

PROUD, E. Jr *98*
A comparison of the effects of anxiety on self-concept between pregnant women seeking an abortion and pregnant women not seeking an abortion. PhD United States International U. 1979.

PUTKA, J.S. *99*
The Supreme Court and abortion: the socio-political impact of judicial activism. PhD U. of Cincinnati, 1979.

RAILSBACK, C.M.C. *100*
The contemporary American abortion controversy: a study of public argumentation. PhD U. of Iowa, 1982.

RAM, E.R. *101*
Mothers' perception of communication barriers in family planning between parents and their children. PhD U. of North Carolina at Chapel Hill, 1971.

REEDY, C.D. *102*
The Supreme Court and Congress on abortion: an analysis of comparative institutional capacity. PhD U. of Minnesota, 1982.

REKANT, M.J. *103*
Unwanted pregnancy: an exploratory investigation of women who have therapeutic abortions. PhD Boston U. Grad. Sch. 1973.

RICKETTS, S.A. *104*
Contraceptive use among teenage mothers: evaluation of a family planning program. PhD U. of Pennsylvania, 1973.

RUTLEDGE, M.S. *105*
The effects of counseling on university women requesting abortion. EdD Northern Illinois U. 1978.

SACHDEV, S.P. *106*
Factors relating to the abortion decision among premaritally pregnant females. PhD U. of Wisconsin–Madison, 1975.

SALTZMAN, K.A.I. *107*
Abortion referral and counseling service of Colorado. DA U. of Northern Colorado, 1974.

SANTE, B.A. 108
A comparison of two methods of obtaining abortion data from fertility surveys. PhD Columbia U. 1982.

SCHARF, K.R. 109
Abortion and the body politic: an anthropological analysis of legislative activity in Massachusetts. PhD Boston U. Grad. Sch. 1981.

SCHWYHART, W.R. 110
Psychological adjustment of women using sterilization for contraception. PhD California Sch. of Prof. Psych., Berkeley, 1974.

SEE, E.M. 111
Professional management of the client with spoiled identity: the abortion patient. PhD U. of Kansas, 1973.

SHALABY, L.M. 112
How women feel about abortion: psychological, attitudinal, and physical effects of legal abortion. PhD U. of Iowa, 1975.

SHEA, J.A. 113
Social support for contraceptive utilization in adolescence. PhD Pennsylvania State U. 1981.

SHUSTERMAN, L.E.R. 114
Psychosocial factors of the abortion experience. PhD Northwestern U. 1974.

SILVERMAN, H.A. 115
The prediction of utilization of subsidized family planning services by AFDC mothers in Pennsylvania. PhD Bryn Mawr Coll. 1970.

SMETANA, J.G. 116
Personal and moral concepts: a study of women's reasoning and decision-making about abortion. PhD U. of California, Santa Cruz, 1978.

SMITH, A.P. 117
The 'Roe v. Wade' and 'Doe v. Bolton' decisions on abortion: an analysis, critique and examination of related issues. PhD Drew U. 1981.

SMITH, E.D.I. 118
Attitudes among baccalaureate nursing students in New York City regarding women seeking elective abortions. EdD Columbia U. Teachers Coll. 1975.

SMITH, E.M. 119
Psychosocial correlates of regular contraceptive use in young unmarried women. PhD Washington U. 1978.

SMITH, L.J.F. 120
The abortion controversy, 1936–77: a case study in 'emergence of law'. PhD U. of Edinburgh, 1980.

SOMERS, R.L. 121
Risk of admission to psychiatric institutions among Danish women who experience induced abortion: an analysis based on national record linkage. PhD U. of California, Los Angeles, 1979.

SPAIN, J.S. 122
Psychological dimensions of effective and ineffective contraceptive use in adolescent girls. PhD City U. of New York, 1977.

SPRAGUE, J.B. 123
The impact of legalized abortion upon hospitals in New York State. PhD U. of North Carolina at Chapel Hill, 1974.

STEINLAUF, B. 124
Attitudes and cognitive factors associated with the contraceptive behavior of young women. PhD Wayne State U. 1977.

STROVER, S.L. 125
Making decisions under stress: the case of adolescents seeking birth control. PhD Stanford U. 1982.

SUPANNATAS, S. 126
Some factors affecting the non-acceptance of a birth control method in the postpartum period among Thai married women who already have two children. DrPH U. of California, Berkeley, 1975.

TRAINA, F.J. 127
Diocesan mobilization against abortion law reform. PhD Cornell U. 1975.

ULRICH, C.O. 128
Counseling needs of university female students concerning conception control and related sexual information. HSD Indiana U. 1975.

VIGLIONE, M. 129
Contraceptive choice and maternal image. PhD California Sch. of Prof. Psych., Berkeley, 1982.

WARD, L. 130
The right to choose: a study of women's fight for birth control provisions. PhD U. of Bristol, 1981.

ZIMMERMAN, M.K. 131
Passage through abortion: a sociological analysis. PhD U. of Minnesota, 1976.

ZWEBEN, J.E. 132
Psychological and psychosomatic responses to the oral contraceptive. PhD U. of Michigan, 1971.

Infertility

Related studies are also to be found in **3** Demography.

ALLISON, J.R. 133
Infertility and role conflict: a phenomenological study of women. PhD California Sch. of Prof. Psych., Los Angeles, 1976.

BRODY, H. 134
Psychologic factors associated with infertility in women: a comparative study of psychologic factors in women afflicted with infertility includ-

ing groups with and without a medical basis for their condition. PhD New York U. 1955.

COOPER, S.L. *135*
Female infertility: its effect on self-esteem, body image, locus of control and behavior. EdD Boston U. Sch. of Educ. 1979.

EISNER, B.G. *136*
Some psychological differences on the Rorschach scale between infertility patients and women with children. PhD U. of California, 1957.

HUNT, S.J.P. *137*
A comparative analysis of childless women with low birth expectations. PhD Oregon State U. 1979.

MAGNER, J.R. *138*
The relationship of ambivalence and motivation for pregnancy in psychophysiologic infertility. PhD United States International U. 1980.

MOSENA, P.W. *139*
Application of a waiting-time model to the measurement of sterility among a noncontracepting sample of women in Latin America. PhD U. of Tennessee, 1975.

RICHARDSON, I.M. *140*
A comparative study of personality characteristics of functionally infertile and fertile women. EdD Texas Tech U. 1972.

TAYLOR, W.J.C. *141*
Infertility investigations: a study of the effects of group counselling on mood change and social functioning. MPhil U. of Edinburgh, 1982.

Menstruation

See also 5, 94, 255; **15** 7; **20** 106; **22** 114; **23** 184.

General

ALTENHAUS, A.L. *142*
The effect of expectancy for change on performance during the menstrual cycle. PhD Rutgers U. 1978.

ANASTASIO, M.M. *143*
The relationship of selected personality characteristics to the chronology of the menstrual cycle in women. PhD New York U. 1959.

ANDERSON, E.I. *144*
Cognitive performance and mood change as they relate to menstrual cycle and estrogen level. PhD Boston U. 1972.

ASCHER-SVANUM, H. *145*
Alcohol use and psychological distress during the menstrual cycle. PhD U. of Minnesota, 1982.

ATCHESON, L.P. *146*
Menstruation, myth, taboo, belief and fact: a psycho-anthropological study of evaluations of female role character and behavior. PhD City U. of New York, 1977.

BECK, A.C. *148*
Chronological fluctuations of six premenstrual tension variables and their relation to traditional modern sex-role stereotypes. PhD Purdue U. 1970.

BERDY, M.D. *149*
Toward an attributional perspective of menstrual symptomatology. PhD Temple U. 1979.

BRENNAN, B.M. *150*
The effect of menstrual cycle phase and instructional set on self-report of current and retrospective states. PhD U. of Texas at Austin, 1980.

BROCKWAY, J.A. *151*
Prediction of premenstrual symptomatology using the MOOS menstrual distress questionnaire. PhD U. of Iowa, 1975.

BURKE, A.J. *152*
Menstrual cycle and caffein effects on physiological and psychological processes. PhD North Texas State U. 1980.

CORCORAN, T.M. *153*
The influence of four phases of the menstrual cycle on selected motor abilities of high school girl athletes and nonathletes. EdD Boston U. 1969.

CRABBE, J.L. *154*
Menstruation as stigma. PhD U. of Colorado at Boulder, 1975.

DEWITT, P.H. *155*
Comparison of group training procedures for coping with menstrual distress. PhD Purdue U. 1981.

DI NARDO, P.G. *156*
Psychological correlates of the menstrual cycle. PhD Saint Louis U. 1974.

DUGAN, S.M. *157*
The relationship of personality to emotional fluctuations associated with the menstrual cycle. PhD U. of Missouri, 1981.

DUSON, B.M. *158*
Effectiveness of relaxation desensitization and cognitive restructuring in teaching the self-management of menstrual symptoms to college women. PhD U. of Texas at Austin, 1976.

ENGLANDER-GOLDEN, P. *159*
A longitudinal study of cyclical variations in moods and behaviors as a function of repression and the menstrual cycle. PhD U. of Nebraska, 1977.

ERICKSON, B.E.D. *160*
An examination of sexual behavior and of differences among women in patterns of emotional, cognitive and physical change during the menstrual cycle. PhD U. of North Carolina at Chapel Hill, 1977.

ERNSTER, V.L. *161*
Attitudes and expectations about menstruation

among girls of menarcheal age. PhD Columbia U. 1977.

FEKETE-MACKINTOSH, A. *162*
Dream content and the menstrual cycle in ovulatory and anovulatory cycles. PhD Yeshiva U. 1979.

FERGUSON, J.H. *163*
The effects of relaxation training on menstrual pain and locus of control in a selected group of women. EdD East Texas State U. 1980.

FLINT, M.P. *164*
Menarche and menopause of Rajput women. PhD City U. of New York, 1974.

FULLER, B.A. *165*
The behaviors of selected middle school aged females in relation to the menarcheal process. EdD Lehigh U. 1980.

FUTTERMAN, L.A. *166*
Psychological differentiation and the premenstrual tension syndrome. PhD U. of California, San Diego, 1982.

GEISEN, L. *167*
The relationship of menstrual distress to sex-role orientation, sex-role acceptance, and self-assertion. PhD Adelphi U. 1980.

GOLUB, S.B. *168*
The effect of premenstrual hormonal changes on mood, personality and cognitive function. PhD Fordham U. 1974.

GREENSTEIN, B.H. *169*
Observations of premenstrual women's behavior: a comparison of informed and uninformed raters' perceptions. PhD U. of California, Berkeley, 1981.

GREGORY, B.A.J.C. *170*
Menstruation in psychiatric patients. MD U. of Cambridge, 1956.

HAFT, M.S. *171*
An exploratory study of early adolescent girls' body image self-acceptance, acceptance of the traditional female role, and response to menstruation. PhD Columbia U. 1973.

HART, R.M. *172*
Attitudinal aspects of premenstrual tension. PhD Auburn U. 1981.

HECZY, M.D. *173*
Effects of biofeedback and autogenic training on menstrual experiences: relationships among anxiety, locus of control, and dysmenorrhea. PhD City U. of New York, 1978.

HERLIHY, C.S. *174*
Menstrually related fluctuations in estrogen and progesterone and their relationship to observed nurturant and control behaviors and subjective ratings of mood states. PhD Ohio State U. 1977.

HOFFMAN, C. *175*
Menstruation and the unconscious: a content analysis of dreams. PhD U. of California, Los Angeles, 1976.

HOUSMAN, H.S. *176*
A psychological study of menstruation. PhD U. of Michigan, 1955.

JARETT, L.R. *177*
Psychosocial and biological influences on menstruation, menstrual synchrony, menstrual cycle length, and menstrual regularity. PhD New York U. 1978.

KAHN, R.J. *178*
Sensory threshold fluctuations as a function of menstrual cycle phase. PhD Yeshiva U. 1965.

KAMER, J.M. *179*
Epilepsy and the menstrual cycle: the contribution of stressful life experiences and the menstrual cycle to epileptic seizures. PhD Loyola U., Chicago, 1980.

KAMPER, A.A. *180*
The effect of functional periodicity upon the mental efficiency of college women. PhD U. of Pennsylvania, 1932.

KATZENSTEIN, V.N. *181*
The effects of the menstrual cycle on dream reports. PhD Case Western Reserve U. 1975.

KEHOE, P. *182*
Psychological factors in the experience of premenstrual and menstrual symptomatology. PhD U. of Texas at Austin, 1977.

KESSLER, J.A. *183*
Marital interaction, social networks, and the menstrual cycle. PhD U. of Notre Dame, 1976.

KOCEL, K.M. *184*
Socio-cultural influences on the psychological concomitants of the menstrual cycle. PhD U. of Hawaii, 1978.

KOESKE, R.K.D. *185*
The interaction of social-cognitive and physiological factors in premenstrual emotionality. PhD Carnegie–Mellon U. 1977.

LANDERS, A.D. *186*
A longitudinal investigation of clinical concomitants of the menstrual cycle. PhD Michigan State U. 1973.

LAZAROV, S. *187*
The menstrual cycle and cognitive function. PhD Yeshiva U. 1982.

LEDERMAN, M.J. *188*
Menstrual cycle and fluctuation in cognitive perceptual performance. PhD Boston U. Grad. Sch. 1974.

MCKENNA, W.B. 189
The menstrual cycle, motivation and performance. PhD City U. of New York, 1974.

MCLEAN, E.J.R. 190
Autonomic functions and mood during the menstrual cycle. PhD U. of Oklahoma Health Sciences Center, 1982.

MCMAHON, E.J. 191
Cognitive style and its relationship to menses duration and sex-role identity. PhD Case Western Reserve U. 1979.

MARINI, D.C. 192
The relationship of stress arousal and stress-prone personality traits to menstrual distress. PhD U. of Maryland, 1978.

MAYER, C.R. 193
The menstrual cycle, attitude and spatial test performance. PhD Yeshiva U. 1982.

MECCARELLO, J.C. 194
Premenstrual tension and menarcheal experience. PhD State U. of New York at Buffalo, 1979.

MEYER, B.M. 195
A psychological study of some of the factors in the menstrual histories of 100 women. PhD Ohio State U. 1937.

MONTGOMERY, J.D. 196
A phenomenological investigation of the premenstrual phase of the menstrual cycle. PhD U. of California, Berkeley, 1980.

MOORHEAD, M.A. 197
The experience of dysmenorrhea: a qualitative study in female psychology. EdD Boston U. Sch. of Educ. 1980.

MUNCHEL, M.E. 198
The effects of symptom expectations and response styles on cognitive and perceptual motor performance during the premenstrual phase. PhD Indiana U. 1978.

O'ROURKE, M.W. 199
The subjective appraisal of psychological well-being and self-reports of menstrual and non-menstrual symptomatology in employed women. DNS U. of California, San Francisco, 1980.

PAULSON, M.J. 200
Psychological concomitants of premenstrual tension. PhD U. of Kansas, 1956.

PICCOLO, D. 201
Menstrual cycle distress: a study of its relation to feminine identity and sexual inhibition. PhD U. of Windsor, 1981.

PISTILLI, J.A. 202
Stereotype perceptions of women as a function of menstrual cycle phase and physical attractiveness. PhD Kent State U. 1975.

POLSON, D.L. 203
Effects of biofeedback and autogenic training on symptoms of menstrual distress. PhD United States International U. 1981.

PORACH, L.B. 204
The relationship of masculine and feminine identification to dream scores and to menstrual cycle reactions. EdD U. of Virginia, 1970.

PRATOLA, S. 205
The effect of menstrual cycle saliency on causal attribution for success and failure. PhD U. of South Carolina, 1980.

RASHAD, N.M. 206
The menstrual cycle and accident causation during participation in sports activities. HSD Indiana U. 1979.

REDGROVE, J.A. 207
Work and the menstrual cycle. PhD U. of Birmingham, 1968.

REIME, V.A. 208
The relationship between degree of premenstrual distress and changes in agility and endurance that occur during the menstrual cycle. PhD New York U. 1978.

RUSS, C.A. 209
Thermal biofeedback and menstrual distress. PhD U. of California, 1976.

SCHROEDER, W.B. 210
A meta-analysis of menstrual cycle phenomena from an attributional perspective. PhD Rosemead Grad. Sch. 1982.

SEAGULL, E.A.W. 212
An investigation of personality differences between women with high and low premenstrual tension. PhD Michigan State U. 1973.

SHEKELLE,R.B. 213
Changes in mood during the menstrual cycle in normal women. PhD U. of Chicago, 1963.

SMITH,A.J. 214
Menstruation and industrial efficiency. PhD U. of California, Los Angeles, 1946.

SMITH,M.A. 215
Menstrual disorders: incidence and relationship to attitudes, manifest needs and scholastic achievement in college freshman women. EdD U. of Denver, 1970.

SMITH-MARDER,P.J. 216
A study of selected dream contents in the dreams of adolescent and mature women during menstruation. PhD California Sch. of Prof. Psych., Los Angeles, 1978.

SNYDER, D.A.B. 217
The relationship of the menstrual cycle to certain aspects of the perceptual cognitive functioning. PhD Purdue U. 1977.

SOMMER, B.A.B.W. *218*
Behavioral and affective correlates of the menstrual cycle. PhD U. of California, Davis, 1972.

STEINGARTEN, K.A. *219*
The relationship between psychological variables and menstrual distress. PhD U. of Georgia, 1977.

STRUTHERS,A.B. *220*
Functional periodicity and efficiency: an experimental study of the efficiency of junior high school girls during the menstrual period. PhD U. of Southern California, 1936.

TARPIN, J. *221*
The effect of the modification of sexual attitudes on premenstrual distress. PhD U. of Miami, 1975.

TEITLER, K.H. *222*
The menstrual cycle and verbal aggression. PhD Long Island U., Brooklyn Center, 1979.

THOMPSON, C.T. *223*
Influence of developmental age on menstrual cycle disruption among women entering college. PhD U. of Pittsburgh, 1973.

THORBECK, J.E. *224*
Menarche and body image in young adolescent girls. EdD Boston U. Sch. of Educ. 1978.

TIKTIN, M. *225*
Menstrual tensions and marital satisfaction. PhD U. of Oregon, 1966.

VILA-CASTELLAR, J. *226*
Vulnerability to acquisition of neurotic symptoms: an experimental study of conditioning effects on the human menstrual cycle. PhD U. of Manchester, 1977.

WACHS, K.M. *227*
Personality changes as a function of menstrual cycle and medication in normal and psychiatric inpatient women. PhD U. of South Dakota, 1980.

WAGGEMER. E.L. *228*
Social and psychological influences on premenstrual tension. PhD U. of Cincinnati, 1980.

WALKER, M.L. *229*
The menstrual cycle: its socially and psychologically mediated behavioral correlates. PhD Tulane U. 1980.

WARNER, B.L. *230*
A study of the impact of menarche on self-esteem, level of anxiety, body image and psychological masculinity and femininity in young adolescent girls. EdD Boston U. Sch. of Educ. 1982.

WEBSTER, S.K. *231*
Attributional approaches to the relationship of symptoms to cognitive performance across the menstrual cycle. PhD U. of Southern Illinois at Carbondale, 1979.

WEYLAND, C.J. *232*
Primary dysmenorrhea and its relation to sexual attitudes. PhD Catholic U. of America, 1976.

WIGDERSON, D.M. *233*
Menstrual information: a study concerning the transmission of information and attitudes about the menstrual function in fifty mother-daughter pairs. EdD Columbia U. 1971.

WINEMAN, E.W. *234*
Some psychophysiological correlates of the human menstrual cycle. PhD U. of California, Los Angeles, 1967.

The menopause

See also 164.

DAVIS, D.L. *235*
Women's experience of menopause in a Newfoundland fishing village. PhD U. of North Carolina at Chapel Hill, 1980.

DOWTY, N.G. *236*
Women's attitudes towards the climacterium in five Israeli sub-cultures. PhD U. of Chicago, 1971.

FITZGERALD, T.J. *237*
Characteristics of menopausal women in the labor force. PhD Saint Louis U. 1969.

JACKSON, B.B.H. *238*
Life satisfaction in black climacteric women in relation to specific life events. PhD U. of Pittsburgh, 1982.

KRAINES, R.J. *239*
The menopause and evaluations of the self: a study of middle-aged women. PhD U. of Chicago, 1963.

LEVIT, L. *240*
Anxiety and the menopause: a study of normal women. PhD U. of Chicago, 1963.

LINCOLN, N.L. *241*
Women's attitudes toward menopause as related to self-esteem. PhD U. of Michigan, 1980.

MITTENES, L.S. *242*
The social definition of bodily state changes: the menopause. PhD Pennsylvania State U. 1979.

NOVAK, P.J. *243*
Symptomatology of menopause as a function of estrogen replacement therapy and sex role. PhD Oklahoma State U. 1980.

PATRICK, M.L. *244*
A study of middle-aged women and menopause. DPH U. of California, Los Angeles, 1970.

PAYNE, S.L. *245*
Predicting adjustment to the female menopause. PhD U. of Miami, 1981.

PERLMUTTER, E.S. *246*
Women's views of menopause: an experimental attributional approach. PhD Northwestern U. 1981.

STAFFORD, L.J. *247*
A descriptive exploration study of some variables influencing psychological symptoms in climacteric women. PhD United States International U. 1976.

WILBUSH, J. *248*
The female climacteric. DPhil U. of Oxford, 1980.

WRIGHT, A.L. *249*
Cultural variability in the experience of menopause: a comparison of Navajo and Western data. PhD U. of Arizona, 1980.

YOUNG, E.L. *250*
Extraversion-introversion and the relationship to menopausal symptomatology. PhD U. of Maryland, 1978.

Pregnancy and childbirth

General

See also 98; **2** 9; **6** 446, 449, 531, 548, 549; **9** 102, 108; 187, 585; **11** 12; **12** 447; **23** 50, 64, 175, 210, 253.

AFFONSO, D.D. *251*
Assessment of women's postpartal adaptation as indicator of vulnerability to depression. PhD U. of Arizona, 1982.

AL-NAHI, Q.N. *252*
Aspects of antenatal care in the East Sussex Health Area. PhD U. of London, Guy's Hospital Medical Sch. 1980.

ANDREWS, C.M. *253*
Maternal postures and fetal position. PhD Wayne State U. 1977.

ANDREWS, J. *254*
A community study of obstetrics with special reference to smoking, illegitimacy and the use of a computer. MD London Hospital and Medical Coll. 1973.

ANZALONE, M.K. *255*
Postpartum depression and premenstrual tension, life stress, and marital adjustment. PhD Boston U. Grad. Sch. 1977.

ARBEIT, S.A. *256*
A study of women during their first pregnancy. PhD Yale U. 1975.

ARIES, N.R. *257*
The fragmentation of reproductive health policy: the case of maternity care and birth control. PhD Brandeis U. 1982.

ASKERN, M.F. *258*
Psychological aspects of pregnancy: the sequential progression of interpersonal focus. PhD U. of Nevada, Reno, 1979.

ATKIN, L.C. *259*
Mother-infant interaction with low and full birth-weight infants. PhD Cornell U. 1978.

AUERBACH, K.G. *260*
Behavior during pregnancy: a sociological analysis. PhD U. of Minnesota, 1976.

AUSTIN, S.H. *261*
Coping and psychological stress in pregnancy, labor and delivery with 'natural childbirth' and 'medicated' patients. PhD U. of California, Berkeley, 1974.

AYRES, B.C. *262*
A cross-cultural study of factors relating to pregnancy taboos. PhD Radcliffe Coll. 1956.

BAILEY, R.L. *263*
Fashions in pregnancy: an analysis of selected cultural influences, 1850–1980. PhD Michigan State U. 1981.

BALDWIN, M.S. *264*
Basic values and decisions about pregnancy. PhD Texas Woman's U. 1977.

BALLOU, J.W. *265*
The influence of object-relational paradigms on the experiences of pregnancy and early motherhood. PhD U. of Michigan, 1975.

BANKS, J. *266*
Maternal reactions to caesarean section. PhD California Sch. of Prof. Psych., Berkeley, 1978.

BARBIERI, P. *267*
Women's attitudes toward infant care before and after the birth of the child. PhD Stanford U. 1978.

BARCLAY, R.L. *268*
Modification of pregnancy anxieties: some comparisons between pregnant and non-pregnant women. PhD Wayne State U. 1972.

BAUMAN, B.C. *269*
Personality characteristics of women who elect a program of educated childbirth as compared to those who do not elect such a program. PhD Columbia U. 1960.

BEAUDOIN, M.A. *270*
Prediction of postpartum maternal self-esteem by demographic data, personality, attitude, pregnancy, and childbirth variables. PhD U. of Northern Colorado, 1981.

BELSON, R. *271*
Shame in pregnancy. DSW Adelphi U. School of Social Work, 1977.

BENNETTS, A.B. *272*
Out-of-hospital childbearing centers in the United States: a descriptive study of the demographic and medical obstetric characteristics of women beginning labor therein, 1972–1979. DrPH U. of Texas Health Science Center, Houston Sch. of Public Health, 1981.

BEST, E.K. 273
Grief in response to prenatal loss: an argument for the earliest maternal attachment. PhD U. of Florida, 1981.

BLUMBERG, N.L. 274
Early maternal postpartum adjustment: a study of the effects of neonatal risk, maternal attitude toward pregnancy, and childbirth and maternal cognitive style. PhD New York U. 1978.

BOSIC, D.J. 275
Effect of relaxation training on anxiety manifestations displayed by pregnant women. PhD United States International U. 1981.

BRACK, D.C. 276
Why women breastfeed: the influence of cultural values and perinatal care on choice of infant feeding methods and success at breastfeeding. PhD City U. of New York, 1979.

BRADLEY, C.F. 277
The effects of hospital experiences on postpartum feelings and attitudes of women. PhD U. of British Columbia, 1976.

BREEN, D. 278
Changes in women's self-concept with the birth of a first child. DPhil U. of Sussex, 1973.

CARDILLO, M.J. 279
Attitudes and expectations toward pregnancy and childbirth in primiparae. PhD Hofstra U. 1981.

CHANDRABHA, V. 280
The effect of sleep on the mood manifestations of postpartum women. PhD U. of Pittsburgh, 1975.

CHAO, Y.Y. 281
Maternal concept formation about the baby and the self of newly delivered mothers in the presence of their newborn babies. PhD U. of Pittsburgh, 1979.

CHOWDHURY, A.K.M.A. 282
Pregnancy: a direct method of estimating fertility. ScD Johns Hopkins U. 1980.

CLARK, E.M.F. 283
Selected personality characteristics of primapara and multipara unmarried and married lower-class negro women. PhD St John's U. 1972.

COLEMAN, M. 284
The effects of parity, prenatal attachment, and early postnatal contact on maternal attachment behaviors at one to three months postpartum. PhD U. of California, Davis, 1981.

COLMAN, L.L. 285
Delayed childbearing: a descriptive study of pregnancy and the postpartum in 12 primiparous women over 30 years old. PhD Wright Inst. 1978

CONE, K.L. 286
An investigation of stress experienced by first-time mothers during the first month post partum and the implications for the training of mental health professionals. PhD U. of Pittsburgh, 1982.

CORBIN, J. 287
The process of adaptation in women with a pregnancy superimposed upon a medical complication. DNS U. of California, San Francisco, 1979.

CORNELL, M.M. 288
Psychological variables in the mother related to infant feeding patterns. PhD U. of Southern California, 1968.

COUNTER, B.C. 289
Daughters becoming mothers: the relationship between maternal identification and the development of pregnant women's sense of themselves as mothers. PhD California Sch. of Prof. Psych., Los Angeles, 1981.

CRAIG, S.M.S. 290
The effects of early, extra contact on maternal perception and infant behavior. PhD U. of Texas Health Science Center at Dallas, 1980.

CURRY, M.A.H. 291
The effect of skin-to-skin contact between mother and infant during the first hour following delivery on the mother's maternal attachment behavior and self-concept. DNS U. of California, San Francisco, 1979.

DALING, J.R. 292
Subsequent pregnancy outcome following induced abortion. PhD Washington U. 1977.

DAMRATOWSKI, F.J. 293
Blood pressure patterns of pregnant women. PhD U. of Maryland, 1982.

DART, M.T. 294
The effects of three prenatal psychological interventions on the course and outcome of pregnancy. PhD Harvard U. 1977.

DECOTEAU, M.J. 295
Psychological implications of pregnancy and early parenthood on a selected group of urban women. EdD U. of California, San Francisco, 1982.

DESPRES, M.A. 296
Factors associated with favorable and unfavorable attitudes towards pregnancy in primiparae. PhD U. of Chicago, 1963.

DIGGES, J.L. 297
Psychosocial stress as a factor in the assessment of risk in pregnancy. PhD U. of Oklahoma Health Sciences Center, 1978.

DIXON, R.D. 298
Out-of-wedlock conceptions: illegitimate births and alternative resolutions among young, poor, urban, black females. PhD Emory U. 1976.

DOBROFSKY, L.R. 299
Social control as implemented in the decision-

making process of pregnant women. PhD Saint Louis U. 1972.

DOERING, S.G. *300*
Femininity scales and first pregnancy. PhD Johns Hopkins U. 1975.

DRAKE, D.I. *301*
Parity and human maternal behavior in the first postpartum hour. PhD George Peabody Coll. for Teachers, 1981.

DUFFUS, G.M. *302*
Maternal adaptations to pregnancy and their relationships to the birth weight of the baby. MD U. of Aberdeen, 1969.

EDWARDS, K.R. *303*
Psychological changes associated with pregnancy and obstetric complications. PhD U. of Miami, 1969.

EPSTEIN, L.S. *304*
Dreams of pregnant women. PhD U. of Kansas, 1969.

FISH, D.G. *305*
An obstetric unit in a London hospital: a study of relations between patients, doctors and nurses. PhD U. of London, LSE, 1967.

FITZGERALD, C.M. *306*
Nausea and vomiting in pregnancy: some psychosocial correlates. MPhil U. of Edinburgh, 1981.

FOX, M.L. *307*
Unmarried adult mothers: a study of the parenthood transition from late pregnancy to two months postpartum. EdD Boston U. Sch. of Educ. 1979.

FRANK, S.T. *308*
The effect of husbands' presence at delivery and childbirth preparation classes on the experience of childbirth. PhD Michigan State U. 1973.

FRIEDMAN, L.C. *309*
Marital determinants of anxiety and psychosomatic symptoms in pregnancy. PhD U. of Houston, 1979.

FRUMAN, E.B. *310*
The effect of resumption of employment, dependence on job satisfaction, role conception, and environmental stress on postpartum adjustment in the primiparous woman. PhD U. of Southern California, 1982.

FURNEY, S.F. *311*
A comparison of childbirth preparation and non-preparation on selected physiological variables and attitudes to pregnancy and delivery in private patients. EdD U. of Tennessee, 1980.

GADALLA, F.R.A. *312*
A study of motivational factors and barriers related to the utilization of prenatal care by mothers delivered at Alameda County Hospital. PhD U. of California, Berkeley, 1962.

GANTZ, R. *313*
Smoking patterns during pregnancy. DrPH Harvard U. 1979.

GARCIA MANZANEDO, H.B. *314*
Mother, child, and culture: selected problems in maternal and child health in a Mexican-American population. DrPH U. of California, Berkeley, 1967.

GAULIN-KREMER, M.E. *315*
Infant and mother in the first postnatal hours: descriptive and experimental observations. PhD U. of Connecticut, 1976.

GLADIEUX, J.D. *316*
The transition to parenthood: satisfaction with the pregnancy experience as a function of the marital relationship and the social network. PhD U. of California, Berkeley, 1975.

GODFREY, E.P. *317*
Antecedents of poor neonatal pregnancy outcome, Rhode Island, 1965–1966. PhD Brown U. 1978.

GOFSEYEFF, M.H. *318*
Pregnancy and maternal adaptation in women with different childbearing motivations. PhD Boston U. Grad. Sch. 1977.

GORDON, S.J. *319*
Relationships among anxiety, expressed satisfaction with body image, and maladaptive physiological responses in pregnancy. PhD New York U. 1976.

GRAHAM, H.M. *320*
Having a baby: women's experiences of pregnancy, childbirth and early motherhood. DPhil U. of York, 1981.

GRAY, L.C. *321*
A study of pregnancy: body image and anxiety. PhD California Sch. of Prof. Psych., Los Angeles, 1977.

GREEN, J.M. *322*
The relationship between self-perceived sex-role identification, relevant concept meanings, feelings about being pregnant and the childbirth process. PhD City U. of New York, 1979.

GREEN, R.T. *323*
Perceived styles of mother-daughter relationship and the prenatal adjustment of the primagravida. PhD George Washington U. 1973.

GREENBERG, S.H. *324*
The relationship of cognitive development to unplanned pregnancy. PhD U. of Washington, 1982.

GROTEFEND, M.E. *325*
Determinants of patient participation in maternity clinics. PhD American U. 1966.

GRUBB, C.A. *326*
Perceptions of time by multiparous women in relation to themselves and others during the first postpartal month. PhD U. of Pittsburgh, 1979.

GULICK, E.E. *327*
The relationship between expectant mothers' sex-role orientation, nurturance, maternal attitudes, information on breastfeeding, and success in breastfeeding. PhD New York U. 1981.

GUNTER, L. *328*
Self-concept and physiological adaptation: a study of mothers of premature infants. PhD U. of Chicago, 1960.

HACKMAN, E.M. *329*
Intergenerational factors in pregnancy outcome. PhD U. of Washington, 1980.

HAMILTON, E.B. *330*
The relationship of maternal patterns of stress, coping, and support to quality of early infant-mother attachment. PhD U. of Virginia, 1980.

HAMFORD, J.M. *331*
Patterns of variables involved in differing outcomes of pregnancy. PhD Pennsylvania State U. 1971.

HAUGHEY, D.W. *332*
Need conflicts of pregnancy and the learning of need-related stimuli. PhD Boston U. 1960.

HAWTHORNE AMICK, J.T. *333*
The effect of different routines in a special care baby unit on the mother-infant relationship: an intervention study. PhD U. of Cambridge, 1982.

HERRERO, I.J.A. *334*
Effectiveness and decision-making in a health planning context of measures for the prevention of perinatal mortality and morbidity: the case of out-patient ante-natal care. MLitt U. of Oxford, 1981.

HILLIARD, M.E. *335*
A descriptive study of selected mother and infant behaviors on the day of delivery. PhD U. of Florida, 1973.

HITTLEMAN, J.H.F. *336*
Adult-neonate mutual gaze as a function of the infant's sex and adult stimulation: implications for the mother-infant interaction. PhD Columbia U. 1975.

HOLTGREWE, M.M. *337*
Child outcome of Missouri high-risk maternity and child-care program: implications for mental retardation policy. PhD Saint Louis U. 1981.

HOPKINS, J.B. *338*
The effect of early and extended neonatal contact on mother-infant interaction. PhD George Peabody Coll. for Teachers, 1978.

HOPPER, S.S. *339*
Birth among strangers: pregnancy, delivery and perinatal care of poor women in an American city. PhD U. of Washington, 1979.

HORN, B.M. *340*
An ethnoscientific study to determine social and cultural factors affecting native American Indian women during pregnancy. PhD U. of Washington, 1975.

HOSETH, P.E. *341*
The effect of a childbirth education course on specific stressors, related to the childbirth experience in primipara women. EdD U. of Oregon, 1977.

HOTT, J.R. *342*
An investigation of the relationship between psychoprophylaxis in childbirth and changes in self-concept of the participant husband and his concept of his wife. PhD New York U. 1972.

IRONS, E.S. *343*
The causes of unwanted pregnancy: a psychological study from a feminist perspective. EdD U. of Massachusetts, 1977.

ISENALUMHE, A.E. *344*
A study of the relationship between breastfeeding and four specific sources of information on infant feeding practices among low socioeconomic status mothers. PhD New York U. 1979.

JACQUES, N.C.S. *345*
The role of early mother-infant contact in the development of mother-child relationship. MSc U. of Cambridge, 1979.

JESSUP, H.J. *346*
The effect of pregnancy on self-concept, marital satisfaction, and body density. PhD Texas A&M U. 1980.

JIMENEZ, M.H. *347*
Relationships between job orientation in women and adjustment to the first pregnancy and postpartum period. PhD Northwestern U. 1977.

JOHNS, B.L. *348*
Maternal childbearing attitudes: identification, measurement, and relation to parity and other variables. PhD Hofstra U. 1975.

JOHNSTONE, F.D. *349*
The assessment of maternal nutrition and its effect on pregnancy. MD U. of Aberdeen, 1977.

JONES, A.C. *350*
Psychological assessment as an adjunct to obstetrical screening of high-risk pregnancies: an exploratory study. PhD U. of Iowa, 1974.

JONES, C. *351*
An exploratory study of women's manifest

dreams during first pregnancy. PhD Columbia U. 1978.

JONES, C.C. 352
Social and psychological factors in pregnancy. MA U. of Liverpool, 1967.

JONES, F.A. 353
Maternal attachment to infants during postnatal period: effects of additional infant-mother contact and information about infant competency. PhD Oklahoma State U. 1977.

JONES, M.E. 354
An anthropological assessment of bonding: mother/infant attachment behavior in a study of forty adolescent black and white mothers from delivery through six months. PhD Southern Methodist U. 1981.

JURA, M.B. 355
Mother-infant interaction related to holding during the first three months. PhD Boston U. Grad. Sch. 1978.

KALTENBACH, K.A. 356
Neonatal characteristics and their effect on mother-infant interaction during the second and third day of life. PhD Temple U. 1982.

KAPLAN, D.M. 357
Predicting outcome from situational stress on the basis of individual problem-solving patterns: a study of maternal coping patterns in the psychological stress situation posed by premature birth, relating these coping patterns to the early mother-child relationship. PhD U. of Minnesota, 1961.

KARMEL, M.O. 358
Maternal attitudes in women trained for childbirth by Lamaze techniques and women receiving no formal prenatal training. PhD U. of North Carolina at Greensboro, 1974.

KARMEL, R. 359
Body image characteristics of late pregnancy and changes observed at the postnatal period. PhD U. of Ottowa, 1976.

KAUFMAN, L.R. 360
The interaction of acculturation and pregnancy. PhD U. of California, Los Angeles, 1963.

KAUFMAN, S.P. 361
Unplanned pregnancy: a dilemma for college students. PhD U. of Pennsylvania, 1981.

KEAN, W.L. 362
Patterns of medical care utilization: childbirth in three Texas towns. PhD U. of Texas at Austin, 1980.

KENNEDY, E.T. 363
Evaluation of the impact of women, infants and children's supplemental feeding program on prenatal patients in Massachusetts. DSc Harvard U. 1979.

KIKUCHI, J.F. 364
Assimilative and accomodative responses of mothers to their newborn infants with congenital defects. PhD U. of Pittsburgh, 1979.

KIRGIS, C.A. 365
A study of health care and health education for Navajo pregnant women. PhD U. of Utah, 1978.

KITE, J.V. 366
First pregnancies in women over 30. PhD California Sch. of Prof. Psych., Berkeley, 1976.

KLEIN, H.T. 367
Maternal anxiety and abnormalities of birth: relationship between anxiety level during pregnancy and maternal-fetal complications. PhD Yeshiva U. 1963.

KONTOS, D.J.K. 368
The effects of mother-infant separation in the early postpartum hours and days on later maternal attachment behavior. PhD U. of Toronto, 1977.

KRASA, N.R. 369
A psychosocial study of the relation between recent object loss, separation anxiety, and 'accidental' conception of pregnancy. PhD New York U. 1980.

KRUEDELBACH, N.G. 370
Dimensions of pregnancy: a factor analytic study. PhD Ohio State U. 1975.

LANGHORST, B.H. 371
Maternal accommodation: a quantitative look at a qualitative phenomenon. PhD Purdue U. 1981.

LAUKARAN, V.H. 372
The relationship of maternal attitude to pregnancy outcome and child health: a cohort study of unwanted pregnancy. DrPH U. of California, Los Angeles, 1978.

LEBO, M.A. 373
Mood structure and change: the P-technique analysis of five pregnant women. PhD West Virginia U. 1972.

LEIFER, M. 374
Psychological changes accompanying pregnancy and motherhood. PhD U. of Chicago, 1972.

LEWIS, C.S. 375
Socio-cultural influences on the pregnancy experience: an analysis of the differences between hypertensive and normotensive women. PhD Northwestern U. 1980.

LEWIT, E.M. 376
Experience with pregnancy: the demand for prenatal care and the production of surviving infants. PhD City U. of New York, 1977.

LINN, P.L. 377
Newborn environments and mother-infant interactions. PhD U. of Kansas, 1979.

LISMAY, J.V. 378
Dreams and dream work during pregnancy: their relationship to birth outcome. PhD California Sch. of Prof. Psych., Berkeley, 1980.

LUBIC, R.W. 379
Barriers and conflict in maternity care innovation. PhD Columbia U. Teachers Coll. 1979.

MACARTHUR, C. 380
Smoking in pregnancy: the health educational aspects. PhD U. of Manchester, 1978.

MCCABE, S.N. 381
The effect of infant behavior, infant sex, and prenatal education on maternal satisfaction with breastfeeding. PhD U. of Maryland, 1979.

MCCLELLAN, M.S. 382
Effects of early infant contact on maternal perceptions, attitudes, and behaviors. PhD Arizona State U. 1979.

MCCRAW, R.K. 383
Attitudinal, personality and demographic factors in the selection of childbirth preparation classes and the effects of preparation on the mother and infant. PhD U. of South Florida, 1981.

MCGUIRE, T.L. 384
Changing mothers' perceptions of their preterm or small-for-gestational-age infants: the neonatal behavioral assessment scale. PhD Fuller Theological Seminary Sch. of Psych. 1981.

MCKEVITT, T.K. 385
Medical intervention in pregnancy and childbirth in Britain and the Soviet Union. MPhil U. of Birmingham, 1982.

MCLAUGHLIN, F.J. 386
The effect of the mother's observation of a neonatal assessment on subsequent mother-infant interaction. PhD George Peabody Coll. for Teachers, 1979.

MCSWAIN, D.B. 387
Social networks and natural childbirth. PhD U. of California, Davis, 1980.

MARIESKIND, H.I. 388
Gynaecological services: their historical relationship to the women's movement with recent experience of self-help clinics and other delivery modes. DrPH U. of California, Los Angeles, 1976.

MARTINDALE, L.J. 389
The pregnant role: an examination of the Parsonian model of the patient-physician role as it applies to pregnancy. PhD Wayne State U. 1977.

MATHES, S. 390
A comparative study of the relationship between Leboyer, natural and routine deliveries: maternal attitudes towards infants. PhD Temple U. 1982.

MAZEN, F.R.A. 391
Communicator similarity and acceptance of recommendations: a study of attitudes and behavior of pregnant women. PhD Yale U. 1967.

MILLER, R.S. 392
Pregnancy: the social meaning of a physiological event. PhD New York U. 1973.

MOBURG, B.J. 393
The relationship between the quality of a woman's childbirth experience and the patterns of mother-infant attachment. PhD Southern Illinois U. Carbondale, 1981.

MOK, M.M.C. 394
Experience in childbirth: a statistical analysis. MSc U. of Glasgow, 1979.

MONDLICK, R.S. 395
Postpartum depression and early parental relationship, marital adjustment and self-concept. PhD U. of New Mexico, 1981.

MONTGOMERY, G. 396
An enquiry into the value of ante natal care. MD U. of Glasgow, 1930.

MOORE, D.E. 397
Identification of women at obstetrical risk from measures of prenatal psychological stress. PhD George Peabody Coll. for Teachers, 1977.

MORGINSKY, C. 398
Psychological and attitudinal reactions to childbirth of recently parturient women. PhD Fordham U. 1982.

MOWDAY, E.W. 399
The experience of first pregnancy in married mental health professionals in supervision. PhD Pacific Grad. Sch. of Psych. 1981.

MOYES, B.A. 400
Perceptions of pregnancy. PhD U. of Edinburgh, 1976.

MUNTO, W.F. 401
The value of ante-natal clinics and infant welfare centres. MD U. of Aberdeen, 1929.

MURA, E.L. 402
Pregnancy and delivery complications in schizophrenic women. PhD New Sch. for Social Research, 1971.

NARAGON, C.A. 403
Childbirth at home: a descriptive study of 675 couples who chose home births. PhD California Sch. of Prof. Psych., Berkeley, 1980.

NATH, C.L. 404
The effect of prenatal classes on attitudes toward pregnancy. EdD West Virginia U. 1982.

NEWTON, N.R. 405
Attitudes of mothers of newborn babies towards their biological feminine functions. PhD Columbia U. 1952.

NICHOLS, B.L.A. *406*
Nutritional practices and health competency levels of pregnant and lactating women in a tri-county area of Alabama. EdD Auburn U. 1976.

NICHOLSON, M.E. *407*
Maternity care as perceived by newly delivered mothers under the care of nurse-midwives and those under the care of obstetricians. EdD Columbia U. Teachers Coll. 1976.

NUCKOLLS, K.B. *408*
Psychosocial assets, life crisis, and the prognosis of pregnancy. PhD U. of North Carolina at Chapel Hill, 1970.

NUSSBAUM, H.R. *409*
Psychological androgyny and maternal role conflict and maternal role satisfaction in primiparous women during the neomaternal period. EdD Columbia U. Teachers Coll. 1980.

ORR, R.M. *410*
Patterns of nutritional care in pregnancy. DSc Harvard U. 1979.

OSTRUM, A.E. *411*
Psychological factors influencing women's choice of childbirth procedure. PhD Columbia U. 1971.

PEOPLES, M.D. *412*
Impact evaluation of programs for mothers and infants: implications from an evaluation of the maternity and infant care project in North Carolina. DrPH U. of North Carolina at Chapel Hill, 1981.

PEPPER, A.G. *413*
Maternal care: its receipt and value for a population of primiparous women. PhD Yale U. 1972.

PERES, K.E. *414*
Emotional aspects of the pregnancy experience: anxiety, life changes, and feminine identification. PhD U. of Florida, 1978.

PEREZ, R.G. *415*
Stress and coping as determinants of adaptation to pregnancy in Hispanic women. PhD U. of California, Los Angeles, 1982.

PETROWSKI, D.D. *416*
Effectiveness of instruction in postpartum care during the prenatal and postnatal phases of pregnancy. PhD U. of Maryland, 1974.

PHILPOTT, L.L. *417*
A descriptive study of birth practices and midwifery in the lower Rio Grande valley of Texas. DrPH U. of Texas Health Science Center, Houston Sch. of Public Health, 1979.

PICONE, T.A. *418*
The effects of maternal weight gain and cigarette smoking during pregnancy on pregnancy outcome and neonatal behavior. PhD U. of Connecticut, 1980.

PIRAN, B.B.K. *419*
The effects of cigarette smoking during pregnancy on the mother and on the baby. MD U. of Aberdeen, 1976.

PORTER, A.M.D. *420*
Planning maternity care. MPhil U. of Durham, 1972.

PRICE, G.M. *421*
Influencing maternal care through discussion of videotapes of maternal-infant feeding interaction. PhD Boston U. Grad. Sch. 1975.

PRIDE, M.W. *422*
Patterns of interaction between nurses and patients in labor on two maternity services. DNSc Catholic U. of America, 1976.

PYE, C.J. *423*
Postpartum depression: a prospective multivariate study of normal primiparous women. PhD Queen's U. of Kingston, 1981.

RAND, C.S. *424*
Psychological perspectives of childbearing: the relationships of personality and attitude variables and type of obstetrical caretaker to maternal response to pregnancy and childbirth. PhD Johns Hopkins U. 1982.

RAUSCH, L.L. *425*
Chlorination of drinking water and pregnancy outcomes in New York villages, 1968–1977. PhD Columbia U. 1980.

RENEE, N. *426*
Relationships between maternal attitudes and the Leboyer method of childbirth. PhD Adephi U. 1978.

RICH, O.J. *427*
Temporal and spatial experience as reflected in the verbalization of multiparous women during labor. PhD U. of Pittsburgh, 1972.

RICHARDSON, P.S. *428*
Approach and avoidance behaviors enacted toward persons by women in labor. PhD U. of Pittsburgh, 1977.

RIFFATERRE, B.B. *429*
Determination of pregnancy depression and its relation to marital status and group affiliation in a single ethnic group. PhD Yeshiva U. 1961.

ROBBINS, J.M. *430*
Dissonance factors in illegitimate pregnancy resolution. PhD Emory U. 1978.

ROBSON, K.M. *431*
A study of mothers' emotional reactions to their newborn babies. PhD U. of London, Inst. of Psych. 1981.

RONCOLI, M.T. *432*
An investigation of the relationship between the magnitude of life stress, appraisal of adjustment

to life stress and the occurrence of conception among women of childbearing age. PhD New York U. 1980.

ROSE, A.H. 433
An estimation of in utero drug exposure by determinates of frequency and distribution of maternal drug consumption. DrPH U. of Texas Health Science Center at Houston, 1980.

ROSS-HARRISON, D. 434
A study of early, extended contact on the development of the maternal-infant bond in elective, repeat cesarean section women. PhD U. of Southern California, 1982.

RUBENSTEIN, A.H. 435
A longitudinal study of psychological changes occurring during pregnancy. PhD U. of Toronto, 1976.

RYLANDS, J.M. 436
Maternal perception and neonatal behaviour. MPhil U. of Edinburgh, 1982.

SALTER, M. 437
Maternal expectations and perceptions of newborns. PhD Loyola U., Chicago, 1982.

SANDELOWSKI, M.J. 438
Under the influence: a study of the problem of pain relief in childbirth in the United States with emphasis upon the natural childbirth movement, 1914–1960. PhD Case Western Reserve U. 1982.

SARGENT, S.P. 439
Prepartum maternal attitudes, neonatal characteristics, and postpartum adaptation of mother and infant. PhD Boston U. Grad. Sch. 1977.

SCHROER, T.A. 440
Archetypal dreams and a critical life phase: a study of dreams during first pregnancy. PhD California Sch. of Prof. Psych., San Diego, 1981.

SCHUSTER, C.S. 441
The relationship of prenatal and perinatal factors to the mother's perception of her one-month-old infant. PhD Ohio State U. 1981.

SCHWARTZ, J.F. 442
Pregnancy history and body image. PhD California Sch. of Prof. Psych., Berkeley, 1976.

SEARS, B.A. 443
An historical study of selected popular beliefs and practices pertaining to pregnancy and childbirth in the state of Texas from 1845 through 1968. PhD Texas Woman's U. 1968.

SELEVAN, S.G. 444
Evaluation of data sources for occupational pregnancy outcome studies. PhD U. of Cincinnati, 1980.

SHAW, N.S. 445
So you're going to have a baby: institutional processing of maternity patients. PhD Brandeis U. 1972.

SHEPHERD, W.P. 446
An evaluation of women's beliefs and behavior concerning alcohol consumption during pregnancy. PhD U. of Nebraska, 1980.

SHERWEN, L.N. 447
An investigation into the effects of psychoprophylactic method training and locus of control on fantasy production and body cathexis in the primiparous woman. PhD New York U. 1980.

SHULMAN, D.A.R. 448
Relationship between neonatal soothability and expectant mother's anxiety levels and heart rates. PhD Syracuse U. 1977.

SIMON, C.L. 449
Marital pair pregnancy-related problem-solving skill and the wife's adjustment to her first pregnancy. PhD George Washington U. 1974.

SIMPSON, C.E. 450
Comparison of pregnancy outcome related to prenatal care between private and service negro patients in Oklahoma County. PhD U. of Oklahoma, 1968.

SMITH, B.J. 451
The reasons women receive or do not receive prenatal care and the reasons they receive early or late prenatal care. EdD Columbia U. 1971.

SMITH, H.E. 452
Syphilis and pregnancy. MD U. of Manchester, 1950.

SOLER, N.G. 453
Diabetes in pregnancy. MD U. of Birmingham, 1978.

SOPHIAN, G.J. 454
Toxaemia of pregnancy. MD U. of London, St Bartholomew's Hospital Medical Sch. 1950.

SPINX, M.J.P. 455
Experiences of first pregnancy and use of antenatal services in São Paulo, Brazil. PhD U. of London, LSE, 1982.

STARK, A.J. 456
Styles of health care offered to pregnant women and mother-child health outcomes. PhD U. of North Carolina at Chapel Hill, 1976.

STEIN, G.S. 457
An inquiry into the nature of the maternity blues. MPhil U. of London, Inst. of Psych. 1980.

STEINER, J.R. 458
The effect of family-centered versus wife-centered obstetrical care upon family life. PhD Ohio State U. 1972.

STERN, R.S. 459
A study of pregnancy of 500 women delivering at the Yale-New Haven Hospital. PhD Yale U. 1970.

STEVENS, P.L.B. 460
A social psychological study of pregnant women. PhD U. of Texas at Austin, 1954.

SUH, K. 461
Rural health in a developing nation: a study of the utilization of maternal health care services in Korea. PhD Brandeis U. 1978.

SULLIVAN, D.L. 462
Effects of early contact and postpartum training on level of maternal attachment behaviors, mothers' self-confidence and competence, and mutuality of mother-infant interaction. PhD California Sch. of Prof. Psych., Los Angeles, 1979.

SULLIVAN, P.L. 463
Primary health education during pregnancy: a programmed approach. PhD U. of Alberta, 1976.

TALLY, F.M.C. 464
From the mystery of conception to the miracle of birth: an historical survey of beliefs and rituals surrounding the pregnant woman in Germanic folk tradition, including modern American folklore. PhD U. of California, Los Angeles, 1978.

TANZER, D.R.W. 465
The psychology of pregnancy and childbirth: an investigation of natural childbirth. PhD Brandeis U. 1967.

TAYLOR, S.H. 466
The association between pregnancy anxiety and self-concept in married primigravidae. EdD U. of Northern Colorado, 1980.

TELLES, C.A. 467
Psychological and physiological adaptation to pregnancy and childbirth in low-income Hispanic women. PhD Boston U. Grad. Sch. 1982.

TETLOW, C. 468
Mental illness in relation to child-bearing (with special reference to aetiology). MD U. of Manchester, 1962.

THOME-BERTELSSON, M. 469
A descriptive of characteristics of nursing mothers who breast-fed for different lengths of time. MSc U. of Manchester, 1977.

THOMSON, E.D. 470
The relationship between locus of control and other psychological variables in childbirth. MSc U. of Manchester, 1978.

TIERSON, F.D. 471
Influences of dietary cravings and aversions during pregnancy on maternal diet and pregnancy outcome. PhD State U. of New York at Albany, 1982.

TILDEN, V.P. 472
The relationship of single status during pregnancy to life stress, social support, and emotional disequilibrium. DNS U. of California, San Francisco, 1981.

TODD, A.D. 473
The medicalization of reproduction: scientific medicine and diseasing of the healthy woman. PhD U. of California, San Diego, 1982.

TONES, K. 474
An analysis of some motivational determinants of the decision to breastfeed, with special reference to the 'health belief model'. PhD U. of Leeds, 1980.

VANDALE, S.E. 475
Socio-cultural factors associated with infant feeding in a group of Mexican mothers. PhD U. of Northern Carolina at Chapel Hill, 1979.

VAN GEMERT, J.A. 476
Changes in interpersonal perceptions, locus of control, attitudes, and knowledge during pregnancy and the first year following birth in married couples who voluntary participated in childbirth preparation classes. PhD California Sch. of Prof. Psych., Los Angeles, 1976.

VAUGHN, J.S. 477
The effect of information and influences on health beliefs regarding the fetal alcohol syndrome of pregnant women receiving prenatal care in a medical care center. PhD U. of Pittsburgh, 1979.

VEEDER, N.W. 478
Prenatal care utilization and persistence patterns in a developing nation: a study of 185 pregnant women attending two prenatal clinics in Kingston, Jamaica, West Indies. PhD Brandeis U. 1974.

VENEZIE, D.J. 479
Correlates of body attitude change in pregnancy. PhD Washington U. 1972.

VINAL, D.J.F. 480
Childbirth education programs: a study of women participants and non-participants. PhD U. of Nebraska, 1981.

WATTS, P.L. 481
First pregnancy: its impact on sex-role orientation, career orientation, and body image. PhD Michigan State U. 1980.

WEINSTOCK, R.C. 482
The relationship of sex roles, anxiety, and prenatal complications during pregnancy. PhD Florida Inst. of Technology, 1981.

WESTHEIMER, R.K. 483
An investigation of the effectiveness of paraprofessionals in increasing the use of postpartum and family planning services by women from lower socioeconomic backgrounds in an urban setting. EdD Columbia U. 1970.

WHITE, S.E. 484
Psychosexual and nurturant aspects of pregnancy: a prospective study. PhD New Mexico State U. 1980.

WIDMAYER, S.M. 485
An intervention for mothers and their preterm infants. PhD U. of Miami, 1979.

WILL, J.A. 486
Neonatal cuddliness and maternal handling patterns in the first month of life. PhD West Virginia U. 1977.

WILLIAMS, R.L. 487
Outcome-based measurements of medical care output: the case of maternal and infant health. PhD U. of California, Santa Barbara, 1974.

WILNER, S.I. 488
Maternity care in two health care systems: a comparison of a health maintenance organization with fee-for-service practices. DSC Harvard U. 1981.

WILSON, M.L.B. 489
Energy expenditure of pregnant and lactating women. PhD U. of California, Berkeley, 1974.

WOODHILL, J.M. 490
The influence of maternal diet upon the course and outcome of pregnancy in a group of Australian women. PhD Harvard U. 1951.

WOROBEY, J. 491
The experimental enhancement of maternal involvement in the mother-newborn dyad. PhD Pennsylvania State U. 1980.

YOUNG, C.L. 492
Maternal perceptions of the psychosocial consequences of a high-risk birth. PhD U. of Pittsburgh, 1979.

ZEMLICK, M.J. 493
Maternal attitudes of acceptance and rejection during and after pregnancy. PhD U. of Washington, 1952.

ZUCKERBERG, J. 494
An exploration into feminine role conflict and body symptomatology in pregnancy. PhD Long Island U., Brooklyn Center, 1972.

Teenage pregnancy

See also **20** 1, 15, 34.

BAIZERMAN, M.L. 495
A study of agency interaction among comprehensive programs for pregnant teenagers and other human service agencies. PhD U. of Pittsburgh, 1972.

BANIGAN, M.J. 496
Adolescent pregnancy in Utah, 1905–1977. PhD U. of Utah, 1980.

BIRDWHISTELL, M.C. 497
The incidence of educational attrition of pregnant students in two Virginia public school systems as related to counseling and health factors. EdD U. of Virginia, 1969.

BLAU, R.R. 498
The pregnant teenager and her mother. PhD California Sch. of Prof. Psych., Los Angeles, 1978.

BOYKIN, N.M. 499
Sex discrimination in public education: comparative analysis of comprehensive education programs for pregnant high school students in selected urban school districts of California and Michigan. PhD U. of Michigan, 1976.

BRENNAN, M.M. 500
Self-concept change among pregnant adolescent girls as a result of small group counseling. PhD United States International U. 1977.

BRISSETT, D.D. 501
Development and validation of a model for retaining pregnant adolescent and school-age parents in the Jamaican school system. EdD Western Michigan U. 1981.

BURNETT, H.R. 502
A comparative study of the adolescent pregnancy programs in Texas and their relationships to the public school administrator. PhD Texas A&M U. 1974.

CHILDS, R.D. 503
The pregnant public school student: legal implications for school administrators. EdD U. of Denver, 1972.

CLARK, E.S. 504
The administration of a comprehensive school program for school-age, pregnant girls. PhD U. of Southern California, 1972.

COHEN, I. 505
The need for attachment and its relationship to teenage pregnancy. PhD California Sch. of Prof. Psych., Los Angeles, 1980.

CONLEY, M.M. 506
Motivation for parenthood, need satisfaction, and romantic love: a comparison between pregnant and non-pregnant teenagers. PhD Virginia Polytechnic Inst. and State U. 1979.

COOPER, R.S. 507
Application of CPI and interview data in understanding adolescent pregnancy. PhD U. of North Carolina at Chapel Hill, 1977.

COWART, L.W. 508
An exploratory study: the self-perceived needs and intentions of one population of pregnant adolescents who are involved with the criminal justice system. EdD Syracuse U. 1980.

CRAWFORD, G. 509
Teen social support patterns and the stress of pregnancy. PhD Case Western Reserve U. 1980.

DAHMANN, J.D. *510*
Psychological effects of three alternatives of adolescent unmarried women faced with unwanted pregnancies. PhD Florida Inst. of Technology, 1980.

DAILEY, A.L. *511*
Group counseling parameters for pregnant nonresidential high school students. PhD U. of Pittsburgh, 1971.

DEWITT, J. *512*
Follow-up study of school-age unwed pregnant girls in Escambia County, Florida. EdD Florida State U. 1979.

DIXON, B.D. *513*
Teenage pregnancy and adolescent risk-taking: the influence of alienation, feminist ideology, contraceptive orientation, socioeconomic status, and traditional/fundamentalist religion upon the adolescent woman's decision whether to contracept. PhD American U. 1981.

DIXON, V.L. *514*
Teenage pregnancy: a personality comparison of prenatal and abortion groups. EdD Columbia U. Teachers Coll. 1977.

EATON, L.F. *515*
The relationship of unwanted teenage pregnancy to sex knowledge, attitudes toward birth control, acceptance of one's sexuality, parental acceptance, risk taking, and age. PhD U. of Michigan, 1979.

EMODI, S.O.R. *516*
Knowledge of reproduction, attitudes toward contraception, and self-esteem of teenage pregnant girls in southeastern Michigan. PhD U. of Michigan, 1981.

EPSTEIN, M.B. *517*
Public school services for pregnant students in North Carolina: preferences of administrators and school system practices. PhD Ohio State U. 1981.

FISCHER, K.P.J. *518*
Precocious pregnancies: patterns of sexuality among white adolescent women in the rural South. PhD U. of Florida, 1979.

FISCHMAN, S.H. *519*
Factors associated with the decision of unwed black pregnant adolescents to deliver or abort. DPH Johns Hopkins U. 1974.

GOLANT, M.C. *520*
The effects of group counseling on locus of control with pregnant teenagers. PhD U. of Southern California, 1979.

GRICE, R.C. *521*
The impact of family concept on selective determinants of early pregnancy among adolescent females in an urban community. DSW Howard U. 1980.

GUYATT, D.E. *522*
Adolescent pregnancy: a study of pregnant teenagers in a suburban community in Ontario. DSW U. of Toronto, 1976.

HAGELIS, J.P. *523*
Unwed adolescent pregnancy and contraceptive practice. PhD California Sch. of Prof. Psych., Los Angeles, 1973.

HANAFI, H.B.O. *524*
A study of prenatal care initiation of adolescent mothers. DrPH U. of California, Berkeley, 1981.

HARICH, M.V.F. *525*
Life histories of school-age pregnant students as a basis for the health educator's role in the prevention of pregnancy and its attendant problems. PhD U. of Maryland, 1972.

HART, B.R. *526*
Rorschach indicators of pregnancy risk in sexually active adolescents. PhD Yeshiva U. 1982.

HATCHER, S.L.M. *527*
The adolescent experience of pregnancy and abortion: a developmental analysis. PhD U. of Michigan, 1972.

HELD, L.P. *528*
Self-esteem and social network of the pregnant teenager. DrPH U. of Texas Health Science Center, Houston Sch. of Public Health, 1979.

HENDERSON, G.H. *529*
Perceptions of selected school-age mothers, their parents and school personnel regarding school activities and educational practices. PhD Ohio State U. 1978.

HONEYMAN, B.W. *530*
A multivariate investigation of the family system in families of unwed pregnant and non-pregnant adolescents. PhD U. of California, Fresno, 1981.

INMAN, L.D. *531*
The role of personality and family relationship factors in adolescent unwed pregnancy. PhD U. of North Carolina at Chapel Hill, 1977.

JOHNSON, R.A. *532*
An analysis of the attitudes of Minnesota secondary school principals toward the issue of school-age pregnant girls receiving continuing education in their own high school throughout their pregnancy. EdD U. of Minnesota, 1971.

KIPP, M.J. *533*
A study of the adjustment and attitudinal changes undergone in an urban area by unwed, pregnant girls in a special educational center as compared with those remaining in a regular school setting. PhD St John's U. 1973.

KNIPE, I.S. *534*
A discriminant analysis of success factors among pregnant teenage mothers. PhD U. of Virginia, 1978.

KOONTZ, A.M. 535
Relationship of biologic maturation and birthweight in adolescent pregnancy. DrPH Johns Hopkins U. 1978.

KRUBINER, P. 536
Cultural factors in risk for adolescent pregnancy. PhD Yeshiva U. 1982.

KUNKES, C.H. 537
Adolescent pregnancy: factors determining its cause and resolution. PhD Yeshiva U. 1978.

LENZ, E.S. 538
An assessment of current policies and practices regarding the continuing education of pregnant students in the Hamilton County (Ohio) public schools. EdD U. of Cincinnati, 1974.

LIGHT, L. 539
Characteristics of low-income adolescent primiparas associated with nutritional status and the outcomes of pregnancy. EdD Columbia U. Teachers Coll. 1974.

MEAD, A.J. 540
A study to identify the adolescent with a high risk probability of pregnancy. PhD Fielding Inst. 1978.

MOSKO, R.D. 541
The effect of self-control awareness training on the self-control of teenage expectant mothers. PhD Marquette U. 1981.

ORTIZ, C.G. 542
Teenage pregnancy: factors affecting the decision to carry or terminate pregnancy among Puerto Rican teenagers. EdD U. of Massachusetts, 1982.

PATTERSON-STEELE, C.G. 543
Biological and social needs of black teenage girls as revealed by black pregnant teenagers. PhD Union for Experimenting Colleges and Universities, 1982.

PERRY, A.V. 544
Attitudes of public school officials toward twelve cases of high school age marriage and pregnancy. PhD U. of Iowa, 1970.

POLLACK, R.I. 545
An examination of selected vocational behaviors of twelfth-grade school-age pregnant girls. PhD Wayne State U. 1976.

PRATHER, F. 546
Family environment, self-esteem and the pregnancy status of adolescent females. PhD State U. of New York at Buffalo, 1981.

RILEY, B.L. 547
A study of value choices among unmarried pregnant teenage girls in five Texas cities. PhD Texas Woman's U. 1973.

ROLAND, J.E. 548
Knowledge and attitudes of administrators, board members, and teachers regarding the education of pregnant students in Illinois. EdD U. of Illinois, Urbana–Champaign, 1973.

ROOSA, M.W. 549
A comparison of the childbearing and initial childrearing experiences of teenage and older mothers. PhD Michigan State U. 1980.

RUEBEL, M.V. 550
The effects of valuing process training on the self-concept of pregnant teenage girls attending a special school for pregnant minors. PhD United States International U. 1975.

RYAN, K.J. 551
The effects of different therapeutic techniques on the self-concept of the pregnant minor and unwed mother. PhD United States International U. 1975.

SILK, S.D. 552
Psychosocial aspects of adolescent pregnancy: developmental, cognitive and social dimensions. PhD Wayne State U. 1979.

SINGER, J.M. 553
A program for pregnant school-age girls in the East Baton Rouge, Louisiana, school district: a follow-up study with implications for functional education. EdD Louisiana State U. and A&M Coll. 1974.

SINGLETON, N.C. 554
Adequacy of diets of pregnant teenagers: educational, nutritional and socioeconomic factors. PhD Louisiana State U. and A&M Coll. 1974.

SITKIN, E.M. 555
Measurement of prospective fantasy and other factors in pregnant black teenage girls. PhD Columbia U. 1972.

SNYDER, J.A. 556
An investigation of certain personality needs and relational patterns in a group of 70 premaritally pregnant girls. EdD U. of Pennsylvania, 1967.

STAGGERS, P.S. 557
A comparative study of the attitudes of pregnant girls enrolled in special schools and pregnant and nonpregnant girls enrolled in regular schools toward self, parents, peers, school and community. PhD Purdue U. 1974.

SUKANICH, A.C. 558
Measures of physical maturity and outcome of pregnancy in girls less than 16 years of age. DrPH U. of Pittsburgh, 1981.

SWEENEY, K.M. 559
A study of adolescent aborters and adolescent expectant mothers regarding their perceptions of their mothers' and fathers' parenting behavior. PhD United States International U. 1981.

THORMANN, M.S. 560
An exploratory investigation of the childbearing attitudes in a population of pregnant teenagers. EdD George Washington U. 1981.

TUCKER, J.S. *561*
Measuring knowledge and attitudes of 15–21 year-olds concerning recognition of pregnancy and care during pregnancy. MPH U. of Dundee, 1981.

TUCKER, O.D. *562*
The perceptions of students, teachers, and administrators regarding unwed, pregnant students in the public secondary schools of the State of Alabama. PhD U. of Alabama, 1980.

WALTERS, L.W.H. *563*
Locus of control and anomia in male and female adolescents when considered with selected background variables: the special case of pregnant adolescent girls. PhD U. of Georgia, 1978.

WAXLER, T.T. *564*
A comparative study of the self-concepts and aspirations of three groups of pregnant adolescents. PhD Michigan State U. 1978.

WELTI, V.S. *565*
Adolescent pregnancy and motherhood: a case study investigation. PhD California Sch. of Prof. Psych., Berkeley, 1975.

WESTNEY, O.E. *566*
The comparative effects of a group discussion program and a lecture program on the self-concept, attitudes toward pregnancy, and manifest anxiety of unwed primigravida negro adolescent girls. PhD U. of Maryland, 1972.

WILKENS, D. *567*
Identification through regression analysis of some variables that characterize pregnant high school girls. PhD Southern Illinois U. at Carbondale, 1974.

WISE, S.J. *568*
Pregnancy adaptation and the development of attachment in adolescent mothers. PhD Boston U. Grad. Sch. 1979.

WOESSNER, G.M.D. *569*
Attitudes and perceptions of selected groups of school administrators toward programs for pregnant minors in California. EdD Northern Arizona U. 1979.

ZABIN, L.S. *570*
Pregnancy risk to adolescent girls in early years of intercourse. PhD John Hopkins U. 1979.

Motivation for parenthood

See also 506.

DIETZ, T.M. *571*
Factors influencing childlessness among American women. PhD U. of California, Davis 1979.

EVANSON, S.E. *572*
Motivations for pregnancy and parenthood: an expectancy value analysis. PhD U. of California, Santa Cruz, 1975.

FORTNEY, J.A. *573*
Role preference and fertility: an exploration of motivations for childbearing. PhD Duke U. 1971.

GERSON, K. *574*
Hard choices: how women decide about work, career, and motherhood. PhD U. of California, Berkeley, 1981.

HALE, S.M. *575*
Women who choose not to have children: an exploratory profile. PhD California Sch. of Prof. Psych., San Diego, 1979.

HILL, L.E. *576*
The baby dilemma: how homosexual and heterosexual women are handling this decision. PhD Wright Inst. 1980.

HOUSEKNECHT, S.K. *577*
Wives but not mothers: factors influencing the decision to remain voluntarily childless. PhD Pennsylvania State U. 1977.

JONES, S.L.H. *578*
Towards a psychological profile of voluntary childfree women. PhD California Sch. of Prof. Psych., Los Angeles, 1978.

KELLER, F.O. *579*
The childless mother: an evaluation of deviancy as a concept in contemporary culture. PhD California Sch. of Prof. Psych., Berkeley, 1975.

LEVINE, J.O. *580*
Voluntarily childfree women and mothers: a comparative study. PhD Michigan State U. 1978.

LIND, M.C. *581*
Motherhood as option or destiny: pregnancy decision-making among childless women. PhD U. of Hawaii, 1977.

SCOTT, L.H. *582*
Intentionally childless women: an exploration of psychosocial and psychosexual factors. PhD Fielding Inst. 1979.

TEICHOLZ, J.G. *583*
A preliminary search for psychological correlates of voluntary childlessness in married women. EdD Boston U. Sch. of Educ. 1977.

TOOMEY, B.G. *584*
College women and voluntary childlessness: a comparative study of women indicating they want to have children and those indicating they do not want to have children. PhD Ohio State U. 1977.

VEEVERS, J.E. *585*
Voluntarily-childless wives: an exploratory study. PhD U. of Toronto, 1973.

WELDS, K.M. *586*
Voluntary childlessness in professional women. PhD Harvard U. 1976.

WILLIAMS, S.L. *587*
Reproductive motivation and feminine identifications. PhD California Sch. of Prof. Psych., Los Angeles, 1981.

20 Sexuality

General

See also **12** 1814; **19** 160.

ALLISON-TOMLINSIN, M. *1*
A study of some educational and sociological conditions: a survey of sexual knowledge and attitudes of pregnant and nonpregnant inner-city teenage girls. EdD Wayne State U. 1981.

ANDERSEN, B.L. *2*
A comparison of systematic desensitization and directed masturbation in the treatment of primary orgasmic dysfunction in females. PhD U. of Illinois at Urbana–Champaign, 1980.

ATWATER, L. *3*
Women in extramarital relationships: a case study in sociosexuality. PhD Rutgers U. 1978.

BAHM, R.M. *4*
The influence of non-sexual cues, sexual explicitness and sex guilt on females' erotic responses to literature. PhD U. of Massachusetts, 1972.

BARBACH, L.G. *5*
Groups for treatment of preorgasmic women. PhD Wright Inst. 1974.

BARBOUR, C.G. *6*
Women in love: the development of feminine gender identity in the context of the heterosexual couple. PhD U. of Michigan, 1981.

BARTON, E.N. *7*
An examination of the conflict between sexual exclusivity and sexual non-exclusivity in married women. PhD Fielding Inst. 1981.

BEGGS, V.E. *8*
Effects of anxiety on female sexual arousal. PhD U. of Georgia, 1979.

BLOCH, D. *9*
Attitudes and practices of mothers in the sex education of their daughters. DrPH U. of California, Berkeley, 1970.

BRENNER, L.L. *10*
The effect of a sexuality enhancement workshop on the self-concept, body image, and satisfaction with sexual relationships of female graduate students. PhD Georgia State U. Coll. of Educ. 1978.

BREWER, B.G. *11*
Individual differences in female orgasmic functioning: an exploration of the physiological and psychological correlates of sexual response in women. PhD U. of Cincinnati, 1979.

BUSKIRK, S.S. VAN *12*
Female sexual orientation, behavior and developmental history. PhD North Texas State U. 1979.

CAMPOLI-STONE, M. *13*
A comparative study of the sexual attitudes of college students from intact and divorced families. EdD Temple U. 1982.

CERNY, J.A. *14*
Biofeedback and the voluntary control of sexual arousal in females. PhD Northern Illinois U. 1976.

CHARNOWSKI, K.M. *15*
Adolescent sexuality, contraceptive and fertility decisions. PhD U. of Chicago, 1982.

CHAVOOR, S.M. *16*
Sexual identity, object choice, and life styles among women. PhD U. of Tennessee, 1981.

CLARK, A.L. *17*
A study of factors associated with wives' sexual responsiveness. PhD Stanford U. 1960.

CLIFFORD, R.E. *18*
Female masturbation in sexual development and clinical application. PhD State U. of New York at Stony Brook, 1975.

COFFMAN, R.J. *19*
Sexual attitudes and behaviors of female partners of spinal cord-injured males. PhD United States International U. 1981.

COUREY, L.S. *20*
The role of genital vasocongestive changes in the labelling of sexual arousal in women. PhD Concordia U. 1981.

DANIELSON, D.W. *21*
The relationship between perceived self-actualization, perceived orgastic frequency, and sexual knowledge in women. PhD Texas Woman's U. 1980.

DAVENPORT, F.I. *22*
A study of the trends of sexual interest and status

of knowledge of young women in their late adolescence. PhD Columbia U. 1923.

DAVIDSON, A.D. *23*
The relationship of reported sexual daydreaming to sexual attitude, sexual knowledge, and reported sexual experience in college women. PhD U. of Cincinnati, 1974.

DAVIS, E.G. Jr *24*
Sexual responsivity of androgynous vs. sex-typed females to affectional vs. libidinous themes of visual erotica. PhD Southern Illinois U. at Carbondale, 1979.

DOLLER, D.L. *25*
The effects of treatment on high and moderate sex guilt college females. PhD Arizona State U. 1981.

DUNCAN, D.J. *26*
An assessment of the effects on self-concept and sexual attitudes of a time-limited female sexuality group. PhD American U. 1974.

DUNKELBLAU, E. *27*
The effect of permission instructions on women with elevated sex guilt while they view a sex therapy film. PhD U. of Kansas, 1981.

DER EB, C.W. VAN *28*
Self-esteem, sexual standards, and sexual behavior in a group of college freshman women. PhD Northwestern U. 1974.

ECHEANDIA, D.M. *29*
The drive-facilitation role of sexual fantasy: effects of female-active sexual fantasy rehearsal upon female-active sexual arousal and response. PhD U. of California, Los Angeles, 1982.

ERSNER-HERSFIELD, R.R. *30*
Evaluation of two components of group treatment for pre-orgasmic women: couples versus women format and massed versus distributed spacing. PhD Rutgers U. 1978.

EVANS, L.L. *31*
Factors related to female orgasmic capacity in sexual intercourse. PhD U. of California, Irvine, 1977.

FAULK, M. *32*
A survey of married women presenting at an outpatient clinic complaining of dissatisfaction with their sexual experience in marriage. MPhil U. of London Inst. of Psych. 1969.

FOWLER, J.L. *33*
A comparison of physiological and self-reported arousal in orgasmic and inorgasmic females. PhD U. of Georgia, 1980.

FRIED, E.R. *34*
Psychosexual development in pregnant and never-pregnant adolescents. PhD Fielding Inst. 1981.

FRIEDEMAN, J.S. *35*
Relationships of selected variables to sexual knowledge in a group of older women. PhD U. of Cincinnati, 1978.

GALLAND, V.R. *36*
Bisexual women. PhD California Sch. of Prof. Psych., Berkeley, 1975.

GARBLIK, P.B. *37*
Acceptance or rejection of sex-role stereotypes as a factor in adolescent female sexual behavior and use of contraception. EdD U. of Cincinnati, 1978.

GILAIE, H. *38*
The relationship between physical activity, sexual anxiety and outcome of group treatment for pre-orgasmic women. PhD Wright Inst. 1981.

GLASER, C.G. *39*
Post-orgasmic experiences in married and unmarried women. PhD California Sch. of Prof. Psych. 1979.

GOLDSTINE, H.B. *40*
The relationship of hysteria and psychopathology to female sexual dysfunction. PhD California Sch. of Prof. Psych., Berkeley, 1977.

GOOD, G.E. *41*
Masculinity-femininity and related psychosexual dynamics in women who compete for the title of Miss America. PhD Rosemead Grad. Sch. of Prof. Psych. 1981.

GOREN, E.R. *42*
A psychophysiological analysis of female sexual arousal: the perception and voluntary control of vaginal blood volume. PhD Rutgers U. 1977.

GOSPODINOFF, E.R. *43*
Bodily contact and sexual response in adult females. PhD U. of Pennsylvania, 1979.

GREENE, D.M. *44*
Loving women: an exploration into feelings and life experiences. PhD City U. of New York, 1976.

GREENHOUSE, E.M. *45*
The relationship between identity status and several aspects of heterosexual relationships in college women. PhD Columbia U. 1975.

GROSS, M.W. *46*
Female sex-role identity and female sexual satisfaction. PhD U. of Maryland, 1981.

GROVE, H.V. *47*
Social-psychological predictors of attitudes towards premarital sexual permissiveness among college women. PhD U. of Tennessee, 1980.

HARBET, S.C. *48*
Attitudes and behaviors of college women concerning female masturbation. HSD Indiana U. 1978.

HARITON, E.B. *49*
Women's fantasies during sexual intercourse with

their husbands: a normative study with tests of personality and theoretical models. PhD City U. of New York, 1972.

HARRIS, C.W. *50*
Discrimination and facilitation of sexual responding in women: the application of biofeedback training. PhD State U. of New York at Stony Brook, 1978.

HASSELL, F.J. *51*
Women's sexual orientation as related to Jungian psychological type, biographical factors, and current life style. PhD Georgia State U. Coll. of Arts and Sciences, 1978.

HEINRICH, A.G. *52*
The effect of group and self-directed behavioral-educational treatment of primary orgasmic dysfunction in females treated without their partners. PhD U. of Colorado at Boulder, 1976.

HENDERSON, J.A. *53*
The content of women's reported sexual fantasies as a function of personality type and sex guilt. PhD U. of Manitoba, 1982.

HENSON, D.E. *54*
Objective measurement of human female eroticism: a new approach. PhD Southern Illinois U. at Carbondale, 1976.

HORTON, D.J. *55*
Sex-role orientation, sexual behavior and sexual satisfaction in women. PhD George Washington U. 1982.

HOYT, L.L. *56*
Socio-psychological aspects of sexuality among older women. PhD Arizona State U. 1979.

HUNTLEY, D. *57*
The role of love-object dependability in the sexual arousal of married females. PhD Northern Illinois U. 1976.

HUSTED, J.R. *58*
The effect of methods of systematic desensitization and presence of sexual communication in the treatment of female sexual anxiety by counter-conditioning. PhD U. of California, Los Angeles, 1972.

JACKSON, T.H. *59*
The effectiveness of state guilt reduction via cognitive coping instructions in high sex guilt females following sexual stimulation. PhD U. of Kansas, 1975.

JACOBSON, B.A. *60*
Sex roles and sexual attitudes and behavior in women: 21 case studies. PhD United States International U. 1977.

JANKOVICH, R.A. *61*
Treatment of orgasmic dysfunction using women's groups. PhD U. of Nevada, Reno, 1974.

JOACHIM, M.J. *62*
Social support, masturbatory guilt and success of education treatment groups for primary orgasmic dysfunction. U. of California, Los Angeles, 1979.

KALLEN, S.L. *63*
Sexual behavior and self-esteem in college women. PhD Michigan State U. 1982.

KAY-RECZEK, C.E. *64*
The relationship between dominance and sexuality in college women. PhD U. of Vermont and State Agricultural Coll. 1977.

KIDOGUCHI, L.E. *65*
An investigation of women's reactions to events involving sexual intimacy and force. PhD U. of Hawaii, 1978.

KIRKPATRICK, C.S. *66*
Femininity, feminism, and sexual satisfaction in women. PhD U. of Oregon, 1974.

KRAC, A. *67*
Social scripts and female masturbatory behavior: a causal model. HSD Indiana U. 1978.

KURIANSKY, J.B. *68*
Women with orgasmic dysfunction and their response to a short-term behavioral group therapy: a long-term follow-up study. PhD New York U. 1980.

LASTORIA, M.D. *69*
The relationship of religiosity to the sexual attitudes, perceived sexual attitudes, and sexual behavior of single undergraduate students. EdD Loyola U, Chicago, 1982.

LEFF, J.J. *70*
Relationship between mode of masturbatory activity and subsequent mode of achieving orgasm during coitus in women. PhD U. of Southern California, 1979.

LINEBARGER, L.T. *71*
An evaluation of selected factors that have influenced the single female student's education for human sexuality prior to entering college. PhD Texas Woman's U. 1973.

LUDEMAN, K. *72*
The sexuality of the older postmarital woman. PhD Humanistic Psych. Inst. 1979.

MCCANDLISH, B.M. *73*
Object relations and dream content of bisexual, homosexual and heterosexual women. PhD Harvard U. 1976.

MCCULLOUGH, R.C. *74*
Rhythms of sexual desire and sexual activity in the human female. PhD U. of Oregon, 1973.

MCDERMOTT, G.W. *75*
An examination of the relationship between androgyny and the use of fantasy by females

during masturbation. PhD United States International U. 1982.

MCMAHON, J.W. 76
Sex guilt, reported heterosexual behavior, and attitudes toward premarital permissiveness among women. PhD Washington U. 1972.

MARKUS, E.B. 77
An examination of psychological adjustment and sexual preferences in the female. PhD U. of Missouri at Kansas City, 1980.

MARSHALL, G.J. 78
The efficacy of vicarious extinction as a treatment for sex anxiety in women. PhD U. of Texas at Austin, 1976.

MEADOW, R.M. 79
Factors contributing to the sexual satisfaction of married women: a multiple regression analysis. PhD Arizona State U. 1982.

MILES, J.J. 80
The effect of behavioral self-management treatments on nonorgasmic women without partners. PhD U. of Calgary, 1981.

MITCHELL, P.A. 81
An investigation of treatment effects on the untreated male partners of women who participate in pre-orgasmic therapy. PhD Fielding Inst. 1980.

MOEN, E.W. 82
Household structure, family socialization and the premarital sexual behavior of US adolescent females. PhD Johns Hopkins U. 1975.

MOORE, J.I. 83
The effects of participation in a human sexuality seminar upon self-concept in women. PhD U. of Missouri at Kansas City, 1979.

MOREAULT, D.M. 84
Women's sexual fantasies as a function of sex guilt and experimental sexual stimulation. PhD U. of South Carolina, 1977.

MOROKOFF, P.J. 85
Female sexual arousal as a function of individual differences and exposure to erotic stimuli. PhD State U. of New York at Stony Brook, 1980.

MOULD, D.E. 86
A study of women and orgasm. PhD U. of Texas at Austin, 1980.

NACHBAHR, G.M. 87
Gender role and sexuality in transsexual women as compared to homosexual and heterosexual women. PhD Catholic U. of America, 1977.

NEDERLANDER, C.E.B. 88
A sex education program for females incorporating graphic expression in the modification of sexual behavior. PhD U. of Michigan, 1976.

NEELEY, R.E. Jr 89
Sexual knowledge and permissiveness among unmarried mothers. PhD Florida State U. 1971.

NELSON, A.J. 90
A typology of female sexuality. PhD U. of California, Berkeley, 1980.

NEMEYER, L. 91
Coming out: identity congruence and the attainment of adult female sexuality. EdD Boston U. Sch. of Educ. 1980.

OLASOV, J.T. 92
Bodily experience and sexual responsivity in women. PhD U. of Tennessee, 1975.

PAYN, N.M. 93
Beyond orgasm: a study of the effect of couple systems of group treatment for preorgasmic women. PhD Wright Inst. 1976.

PEELER, W.H. Jr 94
Women's subjective responses to sexual orgasm. PhD U. of California, Los Angeles, 1978.

PEUKERT, M.J. 95
A psychological comparison of sexual styles of women. PhD United States International U. 1981.

PICKERING, S. 96
Women with sexual problems: their attitudes and expectations. MSc U. of Aberdeen, 1982.

PIERCE, D.K. 97
The adjustment of female transsexuals following surgical and hormonal sex reassignment. PhD Rutgers U. 1977.

PINHAS, V.L. 98
An investigation to compare the degree to which alcoholic and non-alcoholic women report sex guilt and sexual control. PhD New York U. 1978.

RABEN, R.S. 99
Sexual knowledge, attitudes and behavior, and attitudes toward feminism: a cross-cultural study. PhD U. of North Carolina at Greensboro, 1979.

RANKER, J.E. Jr. 100
An investigation of the relationship between women's attitude toward sex in marriage and their conformity to selected patterns of erotic behavior in dating and courtship before marriage. PhD U. of Southern California, 1966.

ROBINSON, C.H. 101
The effects of observational learning on sexual behaviors and attitudes in orgasmic dysfunctional women. PhD U. of Hawaii, 1974.

ROTHSTEIN, R. 102
Men's perception of sexuality and kindness in a woman. PhD U. of Massachusetts, 1959.

ROTKIN, K.F. 103
The social construction of female sexual experience. PhD U. of California, Santa Cruz, 1978.

RUBIN, A.M. *104*
Sex attitudes of female sex educators. EdD Columbia U. 1970.

SCHAEFER, L.C. *105*
Sexual experience and reactions of a group of 30 women as told to a female psychotherapist. EdD Columbia U. 1964.

SCHREINER-ENGEL, P. *106*
Female sexual arousability: its relation to gonadal hormones and the menstrual cycle. PhD New York U. 1980.

SCHUETZ, C.W. *107*
Characteristics of masturbators and non-masturbators in a female population. PhD Southern Illinois U. at Carbondale, 1977.

SCHWARZWALD, L.E. *108*
GSR arousal, blocking and subjective arousal in high and low assertive females as a function of assertive and nonassertive roles in sexual and non-sexual fantasies. PhD California Sch. of Prof. Psych., Los Angeles, 1976.

SEGAL, J. *109*
Premarital sexual activity and religious practice of Jewish female college students attending south central United States universities. EdD U. of Houston, 1973.

SELTZER, J.R. *110*
Premarital sexual attitudes of young women in the United States, 1971–1976. PhD Johns Hopkins U. 1981.

SHAFER, D.A. *111*
Dimensions of female sexual functioning. PhD U. of Delaware, 1980.

SHANOR, K.I.N. *112*
Social variables of women's sexual fantasies. PhD United States International U. 1974.

SHOPE, D.F. *113*
A comparison of selected college females on sexual responsiveness and nonresponsiveness. EdD Pennsylvania State U. 1966.

SILVERBERG, J.A. *114*
Study of the relationship of sex-role attitude, sexual control, and variety of sexual behaviors with the frequency of orgasmic response in women. PhD New York U. 1981.

SIZEMORE, L.F. *115*
Female orgasm and erotic fantasy. PhD Northwestern U. 1975.

SKAGGS, E.W. *116*
Psychosocial concomitants of human female sexual dysfunction (2 vols). PhD U. of Texas at Austin, 1980.

SMITH, A.D. *117*
Effects of focus of attention on female sexual arousal. PhD U. of Georgia, 1979.

SNOW, L.J. *118*
Sex-role orientation and female sexual functioning. PhD Arizona State U. 1978.

SORELL, G.T. *119*
Masculinity and femininity in traditional and nontraditional adult women: a test of the parental imperative. PhD Pennsylvania State U. 1982.

STEELE, D.G. *120*
Female responsiveness to erotic films and its relation to attitudes, sexual knowledge and selected demographic variables. PhD Baylor U. 1973.

STERN, A.B. *121*
Enchancement of female sexual arousal through hypnosis. PhD Michigan State U. 1976.

STOCKTON, M.T. *122*
Three-scale comparative analysis of sexual dysfunction: single women reared by a mother and father or by a divorced mother. PhD United States International U. 1980.

SUTER, B.A. *123*
Masculinity-feminity in creative women. PhD Fordham U. 1971.

SWANSON, C.H. *124*
Female sexual careers: the paths and processes in becoming sexually active. PhD U. of Connecticut, 1975.

TALBUT, R.M.R. *125*
A romantic appraisal of sexual activities and erotic fantasies in women. MSc U. of Manchester, 1978.

TAPPER, S.E. *126*
An exploration of the effects of small group discussion upon attitudes toward premarital sexual risk-taking behavior. EdD Temple U. 1975.

THOENNES, D.A. *127*
EMG measures of frontalis muscle tension for sexually satisfied and sexually dissatisfied females. PhD U. of Arizona, 1976.

THOMAS, D.B. *128*
A study of female orgasmic dysfunction with special reference to pastoral counseling. EdD New Orleans Baptist Theological Seminary, 1977.

WARNER, J.E. *129*
A factor analytic study of the physical and affective dimensions of peak of female sexual response in partner-related sexual activity. EdD Columbia U. Teachers Coll. 1981.

WEBSTER, E.C. *130*
Personality correlates of sexual responsiveness and patterns of orgasmic functioning in black women. PhD New York U. 1978.

WEISS, P. *131*
Some aspects of femininity. PhD U. of Colorado, 1962.

WELCHES, L.J. 132
Study of factors influencing the sexual behavior of girls during adolescence. DNS U. of California, San Francisco, 1976.

WELLS, B.L. 133
Female nocturnal orgasms: an exploratory study. PhD Southern Illinois U. at Carbondale, 1979.

WELSHER, J.M. 134
Differential characteristics of primary and situational anorgastic Caucasian women. PhD Wright Inst. 1981.

WEST, J.E. 135
Internal and external factors related to sexual arousal in females. PhD Southern Illinois U. at Carbondale, 1981.

YOUNG-HYMAN, D.L. 136
Family dynamics of sexual activity in adolescent females. PhD Adelphi U. 1977.

ZUCKERMAN, M.D. 137
The repudiation of femininity: an empirical study of the female castration complex. PhD Adelphi U. 1975.

Androgyny

See also **7** 10, 73; **18** 157; **17** 581; **22** 25; **23** 265.

BORNMANN, M.A. 138
Self-esteem, androgyny, and occupational preference in women. EdD Rutgers U. 1981.

CUST, M.A. 139
Self-actualization and psychological androgyny in a sample of university women. PhD U. of Alberta, 1978.

CREW, S.K.B. 140
Androgyny in adult women: a developmental-integrative view. PhD U. of Cincinnati, 1982.

FRENZEL, E.G. 141
Effects of sex composition of groups on androgyny in women. PhD Colorado State U. 1979.

GARZA, L.M. 142
The relationship between innovative career choice and androgyny in a selected group of women. EdD East Texas State U. 1978.

JACOBS, M.R. 143
The antecedents of androgyny in women: perceived parental nurturance and sex-role model attributes of parents. PhD U. of Maryland, 1978.

MURRAY, B.A. 144
Androgyny and sex-role stereotypes: women's real and ideal self-perceptions and perceptions of psychological health in others. PhD California Sch. of Prof. Psych., Fresno, 1976.

OTT, T.J. 145
Androgyny, sex-role stereotypes, sex-role attitudes and self-actualization among college women. PhD U. of Notre Dame, 1976.

POLAK, D.S. 146
Perceived parental behaviors and attributes and their relationship to female androgyny: an exploratory study. PhD California Sch. of Prof. Psych., Los Angeles, 1980.

POTASH, M.S. 147
Androgyny and its relation to behavioral rigidity and self-actualization in women college students. EdD Boston U. Sch. of Educ. 1978.

PUIG-CASAURANC, M.D.C. 148
Personality and interest characteristics of females in traditional and non-traditional relationship to psychological androgyny. PhD Washington State U. 1976.

RADLOVE, S.K. 149
Androgyny and sexual functioning in women. PhD U. of Miami, 1976.

SCHAEFER, M.B. 150
A study of androgyny in creative female adolescents and their parents. PhD St John's U. 1979.

SCHOECH, H.M. 151
Androgyny in middle-aged women. PhD California Sch. of Prof. Psych., Berkeley, 1977.

SMITH, G.P. 152
Psychological androgyny and attitudes toward feminism in relation to the perception of dominance and sexuality. PhD U. of Windsor, 1981.

STECKLER, P.J. 153
The relationship of androgyny in psychotherapists to authoritarianism and clinical judgement of female patients. PhD Case Western Reserve U. 1980.

Lesbian sexuality

See also 73, 87; **2** 122; **7** 21, 42, 53, 140; **12** 2869.

ADELMAN, M.R. 154
Adjustment to aging and styles of being gay: a study of elderly gay men and lesbians. PhD Wright Inst. 1980.

ARMON, V. 155
Some personality variables in overt female homosexuality. PhD U. of Southern California, 1958.

BEACH, B.J. 156
Lesbian and non-lesbian women: profiles of development and self-actualization. PhD U. of Iowa, 1980.

BLUM, A.C. 157
Lesbians' sexual preference: the meaning of the

origins question in the lives of gay women. PhD Wright Inst. 1982.

BROOKS, V.R. *158*
Minority stress and adaptation among lesbian women. PhD U. of California, Berkeley, 1977.

CLEAVE, C. VAN *159*
Self-identification, self-identification discrepancy and environmental perspectives of women with a same-sex sexual preference. EdD Ball State U. 1977.

CROUCH, A.M. *160*
A comparison of parental home and family relationships and family constellations of adult female homosexuals and adult female heterosexuals. EdD U. of New Mexico, 1977.

EDMOND, N.J. *161*
The consequences of the lesbian label on social workers' judgements of the lesbian. PhD U. of Denver, 1978.

ELLIOT, P.E. *162*
Lesbian identity and self-disclosure. PhD U. of Windsor, 1981.

FITZPATRICK, G. *163*
Self-disclosure of lesbianism as related to self-actualization and self-stigmatization. PhD United States International U. 1982.

FOGARTY, E.L. *164*
'Passing as Straight': a phenomenological analysis of the experience of the lesbian who is professionally employed. PhD U. of Pittsburgh, 1980.

FREEDMAN, M.J. *165*
Homosexuality among women and psychological adjustment. PhD Case Western Reserve U. 1967.

HAVEN, M.J. *166*
Alcoholism and self-esteem among women with a female sex object preference. PhD California Sch. of Prof. Psych., Los Angeles, 1981.

HEDBLOM, J.H. *167*
The social career of the female invert. PhD State U. of New York at Buffalo, 1971.

HOFFMAN, A.J. *168*
The Freudian theory of the relationship between paranoia and repressed homosexual wishes in women. PhD Case Western Reserve U. 1975.

HOWARD, S.J. *169*
Determinants of sex-role identifications of homosexual female delinquents. PhD U. of Southern California, 1962.

KASL, C.E. *170*
Psychotherapy outcome of lesbian women as related to therapist attitude toward and knowledge of lesbianism. PhD Ohio U. 1982.

KNAPP, G.I. *171*
A reconstituted lesbian family: an ethnographic study to formulate a grounded theory of closeting behavior. PhD Michigan State U. 1982.

KUBA, S.A. *172*
Being in a lesbian family: the preadolescent child's experience. PhD California Sch. of Prof. Psych., Fresno, 1981.

KUNZ, A.M. *173*
Women as seen through their personal documents: a study of lesbians and non-lesbians. PhD U. of New Mexico, 1975.

LEVY, T. *174*
The lesbian: as perceived by mental health workers. PhD California Sch. of Prof. Psych., San Diego, 1978.

LISAGOR, N.L. *175*
Lesbian identity in the subculture of women's bars. PhD U. of Pennsylvania, 1980.

LOFTIN, E.C. *176*
The study of disclosure and support in a lesbian population. PhD U. of Texas at Austin, 1981.

MARCER, B.L. *177*
Attitudes towards female homosexuality: a phenomenological study of Caucasian heterosexual women with different educational backgrounds. PhD California Sch. of Prof. Psych., Berkeley, 1980.

MONTEFLORES, C. DE *178*
Lesbian sexuality: a phenomenologically based approach. PhD California Sch. of Prof. Psych., Berkeley, 1978.

MOSES, A.E. *179*
Playing it straight: a study of identity management in a sample of lesbian women. DSW U. of California, Berkeley, 1977.

MURPHY, B.C. *180*
Intergenerational contact and the impact of parental attitudes on lesbian and married couples: a comparative study. EdD Boston U. Sch. of Educ. 1982.

NELSON, C.I. *181*
A study of homosexuality among women inmates at two state prisons. PhD Temple U. 1974.

OBERSTONE, A.K. *182*
Dimensions of psychological adjustment and style of life in single lesbians and single heterosexual women. PhD California Sch. of Prof. Psych., Los Angeles, 1974.

O'CAROLAN, R.J. *183*
An investigation of the relationship of self-disclosure of sexual preference to self-esteem, feminism, and locus of control in lesbians. PhD U. of Missouri at Kansas City, 1982.

PAINTER, D.S. *184*
A communicative study of humor in a lesbian

speech community: becoming a member. PhD Ohio State U. 1978.

PERKINS, M.W. *185*
Biobehavioral aspects of female homosexuality. PhD Southern Methodist U. 1976.

PONSE, B.R. *186*
Identities in the lesbian world. PhD U. of Southern California, 1976.

POOLE, K.A. *187*
A sociological approach to the etiology of female homosexuality and the lesbian social scene. PhD U. of Southern California, 1970.

RAPHAEL, S.M. *188*
'Coming out': the emergence of the movement lesbian. PhD Case Western Reserve U. 1974.

SHACHAR, S.A. *189*
Lesbianism and role conflict: an investigation of coping strategies and psychological variables. PhD U. of Texas at Austin, 1979.

SIMONDS, D.S. *190*
Romanticism as construed by homosexual and heterosexual women. PhD U. of Texas at Austin, 1978.

SPAULDING, E.C. *191*
The formation of lesbian identity during the 'coming out' process. PhD Smith Coll. for Social Work, 1982.

STEPHENS, C.A. *192*
The management of a female homosexual identity. MScEcon U. of Wales (Cardiff), 1982.

SWARTZ, S.S. *193*
Counseling lesbian couples: significant factors involved in maintaining a lesbian dyad. EdD Boston U. Sch. of Educ. 1980.

TANNER, D.M. *194*
The formation and maintenance of lesbian dyadic households in an urban setting. PhD U. of Illinois at Chicago Circle, 1976.

VANCE, B.K. *195*
Female homosexuality: a social psychological examination of attitudinal and etiological characteristics of different groups. PhD Oklahoma State U. 1977.

WESTON, A.E. *196*
Sexual and social interaction patterns in lesbian and heterosexual women. PhD U. of California, Berkeley, 1978.

WILSON, M.L. *197*
A new female homosexuality scale. EdD U. of Northern Colorado, 1973.

21 Sociology

Domestic and household organization

General

See also **3** 122–206 *passim*; **6** 816–955 *passim*; **9** 498.

BANE, M.A. *1*
Household division of labor, market work and the non-market economic contributions of married women. PhD Florida State U. 1982.

BERGER, P.S. *2*
Variables associated with teenage girls' attitudes toward selected homemaking activities. EdD Pennsylvania State U. 1968.

BIRD, G.W. *3*
Sex-role orientation, role salience, income, and family type as determinants of wife-husband sharing of family tasks. PhD Oklahoma State U. 1981.

BOUQUET, M.R. *4*
The sexual division of labour: the farm household in a Devon parish. PhD U. of Cambridge, 1980.

BRUMMER, M.A. *5*
Relationship between the concept married female college graduates have of homemaking and the satisfaction they manifest with homemaking. PhD United States International U. 1969.

CHARLES, N. *6*
Analysis of the ideology of women's domestic role and its social effects in modern Britain. PhD U. of Keele, 1979.

DAVIS, E.P. *7*
Aspects of the economics of housewives' travel. MPhil U. of Oxford, 1981.

EZEU, M.P. *8*
Family members' perceptions of household production in relation to quality of life. PhD Michigan State U. 1982.

GOLDSMITH, E.B. *9*
Time use of beginning families with employed and unemployed wives. PhD Michigan State U. 1977.

GRAMM, W.L. *10*
A model of the household supply of labor over the life cycle: the labor supply decision of married school teachers. PhD Northwestern U. 1971.

GREEN, C.A. *11*
The estimate of household production functions: an inspired way to examine production in the non-market sectors. PhD U. of Illinois at Urbana–Champaign, 1982.

HOBSON, D. *12*
A study of working-class women at home: femininity, domesticity and maternity. MA U. of Birmingham, 1979.

IMAMURA, A.E. *13*
Kanai or Kagai? The Japanese urban housewife – her image of and involvement in her community. PhD Columbia U. 1980.

JACKSON, D.P. *14*
The determinants of household time allocations for husbands and wives. PhD Cornell U. 1981.

JOHNSTON, D.K. *15*
Women's attitude towards the kitchen. PhD U. of Surrey, 1981.

KALISH, M.S. *16*
Family work: the utilization of time in the maintenance of single parent and working mother families. PhD Michigan State U. 1981.

KAO, R.S. *17*
Sharing of homemaking tasks between New York City Puerto Rican working-class husbands and wives as related to the wife's family life attitudes and her employment or non-employment. PhD New York U. 1974.

KLIEJUNAS, J.M. *18*
Being of use: the value of housework in the household and in the economy. PhD Stanford U. 1982.

LO, S.N. *19*
Effects of self-reinforcement and goal setting on the affect and personal orientation of housewives. PhD Fuller Theological Seminary Grad. Sch. of Psych., 1971.

LUXTON, M.J. *20*
Why women's work is never done: a case study from Flin Flon, Manitoba, of domestic labour in

industrial capitalist society. PhD U. of Toronto, 1978.

MCCALLISTER, L.S. *21*
Planning for mothers' work: jobs, childcare and homemaking in four middle American neighborhoods. PhD U. of California, Berkeley, 1982.

MCKEE, J.D. *22*
The housewife: class and class-related attitudes. PhD York U. 1982.

MARK, A.E. *23*
Some aspects of the relationship between the labor force participation of women and changes in household technology, 1920–1960. PhD U. of Illinois at Urbana–Champaign, 1963.

MILLER, M.K. *24*
A statistical study of 29 activities of 952 housewives for the purpose of finding their groupings. PhD Syracuse U. 1954.

MUKHOPADHYAY, C.C. *25*
The sexual division of labor in the family: a decision making approach. PhD U. of California, Riverside, 1980.

NELSON, E.N. *26*
Women's work – jobs and housework. PhD U. of California, Los Angeles, 1975.

OAKLEY, A.R. *27*
Work attitudes and work satisfaction of housewives. PhD U. of London, Bedford Coll. 1975.

OLSON, J.L.T. *28*
The impact of housework on child-care and the role conflict between the two. PhD Northwestern U. 1978.

PENNINGTON, S.L. *29*
Women as homeworkers: an analysis of the housework labour force in England from 1850 until the present day. PhD U. of Essex, 1981.

PINDER, R.H. *30*
Transmission of sex roles relating to household division of labor. PhD Florida State U. 1971.

PORTER, M. *31*
Experience and consciousness: women at home, men at work. PhD U. of Bristol, 1979.

RICHARDSON, A. *32*
Work and housework: temporal aspects of two of women's roles. PhD U. of Wisconsin, 1973.

ROSE, E.B. *33*
A study of factors influencing selection and satisfaction in use of major household appliances as indicated by three selected groups of married women graduates of the Ohio State University. PhD Ohio State U. 1959.

RUSHWORTH, M.J. *34*
Social networks and social origins: a study of the relational patterns and activities of fifty middle-class housewives. MSc U. of Edinburgh, 1979.

SCHWAB, L.O. *35*
Self-perceptions of physically disabled homemakers. EdD Nebraska Teachers Coll. 1966.

SEIDEL, H.A. *36*
Housework organisation, marital relationship and the availability of confidants to young housewives. MPhil U. of London, Inst. of Psych. 1978.

SELL, K.D. *37*
Household sex roles over two generations perceived and expected. PhD Florida State U. 1968.

SHAMSEDDINE, A.H. *38*
Expansion of imputations in national income and product accounts: with a case study on the value of housewives' services in the United States. PhD George Washington U. 1968.

SMITH, C.S. *39*
A study of social relationships of housewives in two communities. MSc U. of London, LSE, 1947.

VANEK, J. *40*
Keeping busy: time spent in housework, United States, 1920–1970. PhD U. of Michigan, 1973.

Women as consumers

See also **13** 23, 38

BENNETT, S.C. III *41*
Differences in supermarket shopping patterns of working and nonworking wives. PhD Georgia State U. Coll. of Business Administration, 1973.

BRAUN, B.S. *42*
Consumer economic knowledge of older women. PhD U. of Missouri–Columbia, 1979.

CUNNINGHAM, S.M. *43*
The role of perceived risk in brand commitment and product discussion among housewives. PhD Harvard U. 1965.

DUKER, J.M. *44*
Some aspects of working wife family consumer behavior. PhD U. of Chicago, 1968.

EDGERTON, A.E. *45*
Health claims in advertising, with special reference to beliefs of certain women consumers. PhD New York U. 1938.

GOULET, J.C. *46*
Credit availability to women. PhD U. of Notre Dame, 1975.

HAMM, B.C. *47*
A study of the differences between self-actualization scores and product perceptions among female consumers. PhD U. of Texas at Austin, 1967.

HOVERMALE, R.L. *48*
Spending patterns of single women with emphasis on clothing. PhD Ohio State U. 1962.

HULL, K.B. *49*
Differences in consumer credit attitudes, knowledge and experiences among married and non-married women in Des Moines, Iowa. PhD Iowa State U. 1978.

MCCALL, S.H. *50*
An investigation of the differential in consumer behavior of the working woman as opposed to the non-working woman and the resulting impact on the performance of marketing functions and institutions. PhD North Texas State U. 1974.

METZEN, E.J. *51*
The importance of consumer competencies for young women and implications for consumer education. EdD U. of Missouri–Columbia, 1963.

MURPHY, J.H. II *52*
An empirical investigation of informal primary group conformity influence on female consumer behavior. PhD U. of Texas at Austin, 1974.

NELSON, J.E. *53*
An empirical investigation of the nature and incidence of ecologically responsible consumption of housewives. PhD U. of Minnesota, 1974.

NOYES, M.B. *54*
Employed vs. non-employed wives: a comparison of credit behavior. PhD Colorado State U. 1982.

SKINNER, L.E. *55*
Disaggregated analysis of women's shopping trip generation. MPhil U. of Edinburgh, 1975.

TRIER, H.E. *56*
Sociological variables, personality traits, and buying attitudes related to role perception and conflicts among 242 Michigan wives. PhD Michigan State U. 1960.

Dress

See also above 48; **9** 5, 72, 145, 563, 706

BOYLE, M.M. *57*
A study of the termination of use of selected items of women's clothing as related to attitudes on saving and use of clothing. PhD Pennsylvania State U. 1965.

CHEN, J.H. *58*
Clothing attitudes of Chinese and American college women. PhD Pennsylvania State U. 1970.

CONRAD, G. *59*
Clothing values and their relation to personality factors and to selected demographic variables for two groups of Canadian university women. PhD Pennsylvania State U. 1973.

DARDEN, L.A. *60*
Personality correlates of clothing interest for a group of non-incarcerated and incarcerated women ages 18 to 30. PhD U. of North Carolina at Greensboro, 1975.

DEEMER, E.M. *61*
Clothing and appearance: self and ideal self-images related to an index of adjustment and values for a group of college women. PhD Pennsylvania State U. 1967.

DILLON, L.S.S. *62*
A preference analysis of appropriate business dress for corporate women professionals. PhD Ohio State U. 1979.

DITTY, D.D. *63*
Social psychological aspects of clothing preferences of college women. PhD Ohio State U. 1962.

EDMONDS, L.L. *64*
Clothing buying practices and life-style differentials between employed black and white women. PhD Virginia Polytechnic Inst. and State U. 1979.

EVANS, L.R. *65*
Fashion colors in women's apparel as related to business cycles and individual attitudes. PhD Texas Woman's U. 1976.

FARQUHAR, D.M. *66*
The availability of ready-to-wear clothing incorporating design features preferred by elderly arthritic women. PhD Florida State U. 1981.

FLOTTMAN, E.L. *67*
In-home purchasing of personal clothing by women. PhD Purdue U. 1974.

FLYNN, J.Z. *68*
Dress of older Italian-American women: documentation of dress and the influence of sociocultural factors. PhD Ohio State U. 1979.

FORSYTHE, S.M. *69*
Influence of female applicants' mode of dress on interviewers' perception of personal characteristics and subsequent hiring recommendations for middle management positions. PhD U. of Tennessee, 1981.

FRANCIS, E.M.C. *70*
Selected clothing usage and buying practices of a specified group of college women and their mothers. PhD Pennsylvania State U. 1971.

FRANCIS, S.K. *71*
Extent of clothing purchase planning as a determinant of women's satisfaction with their purchases of selected outerwear. PhD Ohio State U. 1981.

GATES, R.E. *72*
Clothing behavior associated with types of mobility and with extrinsic-reward orientation among a specified group of non-employed wives. PhD Pennsylvania State U. 1960.

HARRISON, E.V. *73*
Clothing selection practices, interest, knowledge

and perception for a group of educated women consumers in India. PhD Pennsylvania State U. 1969.

HEATH, H.A. *74*
A factor analysis of women's measurements taken for garment and pattern construction. PhD U. of Chicago, 1951.

HOFFMAN, A.M. *75*
Clothing behavioral factors for a specific group of women related to aesthetic sensitivity and certain socio-economic and psychological background factors. PhD Pennsylvania State U. 1956.

HOLMAN, R.M.H. *76*
Communicational properties of women's clothing: isolation of discriminable clothing ensembles and identification of attributions made to one person wearing each ensemble. PhD U. of Texas at Austin, 1976.

HOVERMALE, R.L. *77*
Spending patterns of single women with emphasis on clothing. PhD Ohio State U. 1962.

KAHNG, H. *78*
Clothing interests and clothing aspirations associated with selected social psychological factors for a group of college women in Korea. PhD Pennsylvania State U. 1971.

KARHOFF, N.I. *79*
Clothing-related attitudes and the body image as perceived and expressed by business and professional women. PhD Ohio State U. 1979.

KIBARIAN, B. *80*
A definitive study of the women's costume-jewelry industry from a managerial viewpoint. PhD New York U. 1958.

KING, S.E. *81*
Perception and creativity in clothing and social experiences for selected groups of university women. PhD Pennsylvania State U. 1969.

LARRIMER, J.A. *82*
A comparative study of body-cathexis and statements about clothing of feminist and nonfeminist women. PhD U. of Missouri–Columbia, 1977.

LUSK, J.R. *83*
Shoe preferences of women relative to comfort, fashion, market satisfaction, and foot health. PhD Texas Woman's U. 1979.

MCCULLOUGH, J.H. *84*
A multivariate profile of fashion-conscious college women. PhD Purdue U. 1977.

MOORE, E.L. *85*
Apparel purchasing problems of the middle-aged woman. PhD Texas Woman's U. 1982.

MOORE, M.H. *86*
The clothing market of older women. PhD Purdue U. 1968.

OLLINGER, N.M. *87*
Clothing use by women at middle age as related to self-process. PhD Ohio State U. 1974.

PENALIS, F.M. *88*
Self-esteem and conformity in clothing of adolescent girls as reflected by brand name awareness and preference. EdD Pennsylvania State U. 1968.

ROACH, M.E. *89*
The influence of social class on clothing practices and orientation at early adolescence: a study of clothing-related behavior of 7th grade girls. PhD Michigan State U. 1960.

ROGERS, E.L. *90*
Women's apparel relative to self-concept and appropriateness to profession. PhD Texas Woman's U. 1982.

SHEIKH, N.A. *91*
Textile buying practices of a selected group of female Pakistani consumers related to selected background factors and clothing behaviors. PhD Pennsylvania State U. 1970.

SILVERMAN, S.S. *92*
Clothing and appearance: their psychological implications for teen-age girls. PhD Columbia U. 1946.

SNYDER, J.K. *93*
Differences in selected aspects of clothing behavior for college educated young, mature, and elderly women in the southeast. PhD Florida State U. 1966.

STANFORD, D.H. *94*
The sex appeal of women's clothing as evaluated by young adult women and men. PhD Texas Woman's U. 1974.

STEINHAUS, N.H. *95*
Apparel promotion for women and model age in relation to source credibility, interpersonal attraction and purchase intent. PhD Ohio State U. 1980.

STEMM, F.A.E. *96*
Clothing attitudes and evaluative criteria used by employed women differing in feminine-role orientation and work orientation: emphasis on the single-again adult. PhD Ohio State U. 1980.

TERRY, L.M. *97*
Analysis of the relationship between specified clothing profiles and selected demographic variables for elderly women and women of other age groups. PhD U. of North Carolina at Greensboro, 1978.

TWETEN, B.J. *99*
An analysis of the clothing interest levels and purchasing styles of employed and nonemployed women. PhD U. of Nebraska–Lincoln, 1980.

WARDEN, J.A. *100*
Some factors affecting the satisfactions and dissatisfactions with clothing of women students in

the College of the Liberal Arts. PhD Pennsylvania State U. 1955.

WARNING, M.C. *101*
The implications of social class for clothing behavior: the acquisition and use of apparel for girls seven, eight and nine years of age in three social classes in Des Moines, Iowa. PhD Michigan State U. 1956.

WRIGHT, P. *102*
A design for a woman's clothing inventory. PhD Columbia U. 1963.

Ethnic, migrant and minority communities

See also 68; **4** 280, 409; **5** 264, 305; **9** 5, 72, 145, 443, 563, 661, 706; **18** 225; **23** 44, 157, 167, 172, 184

ARIAS, M.C. *103*
A case study of the program of the Overseas Education Fund Institute in leadership development for Latin American women in the United States from 1963 to 1970. EdD Boston U. 1972.

BAKER, N.R.-T. *104*
American Indian women in an urban setting. PhD Ohio State U. 1982.

BALDWIN, N.T. *105*
Cultural adaptations of international student wives at the University of Florida. PhD U. of Florida, 1970.

BIGGERS, J.T. *106*
The negro woman in American life and education: a mural presentation. EdD Pennsylvania State U. 1954.

BINDERMAN, M. *107*
Factors in desegregation decisions of black mothers. PhD U. of North Carolina at Chapel Hill, 1970.

BRETTELL, C.B. *108*
Hope and nostalgia: the migration of Portuguese women to Paris. PhD Brown U. 1978.

BROWN, M.I. *109*
Changing maternity care patterns in migrant Puerto Ricans: a study of acculturation in a group of Puerto Rican born women in New York City. PhD New York U. 1961.

CARREIRO, M.C. *110*
The participation of the Portuguese immigrant female in higher education. PhD Boston Coll. 1980.

CHANG, L.L.H. *111*
Acculturation and emotional adjustment of Chinese women immigrants. DSW Columbia U. 1980.

COE, S.N. *112*
A study of identity patterns among three generations of black women. PhD Northwestern U. 1982.

COLEMAN, A.C. *113*
Organizational norms, power opportunities and power styles exercised by black women. PhD Boston U. Grad. Sch. 1980.

COLON RIVERS, M.M. de *114*
Familial-cultural influences on participation of United States Spanish-speaking women in adult education. EdD Michigan State U. 1978.

CORTESE, M. *115*
Self-disclosure by Mexican-American women: the effects of acculturation and language of therapy. PhD North Texas State U. 1979.

DANE, N.A. *116*
Social environment and pyschological stress in Latin American immigrant women. PhD California Sch. of Prof. Psych., Berkeley, 1980.

DAVIS, D.J. *117*
The effect of homework activities on English proficiency of foreign student wives participating in a conversational English program. PhD Kansas State U. 1982.

DEGARMO, E.R. *118*
An exploratory study of Mexican-American women in an urban community. PhD U. of California, Berkeley, 1975.

DOUGHERTY, M.C. *119*
Maturation and motherhood: becoming a woman in rural black culture. PhD U. of Florida, 1973.

FOWLER, A.C. *120*
The contemporary negro subculture: an exploratory study of lower-class negro women of New Orleans. PhD Tulane U. 1970.

FRANK, B.B. *121*
The American orthodox Jewish housewife: a generational study in ethnic survival. PhD City U. of New York, 1975.

FRYMER-BLUMFIELD, H. *122*
The maintenance of ethnic identity among Jewish women in an urban setting. PhD American U. 1977.

GARCIA, M.A. *123*
The effects of spiritualism and *santería* as a cultural determinant in New York Puerto Rican women, as reflected by their use of projection. PhD Adelphi U. 1979.

GHAHREMAN, M. *124*
A comparative study of life satisfaction and self-confidence between American and Iranian women in the United States. PhD United States International U. 1982.

GONZALEZ, A.M. *125*
Psychological characteristics associated with bi-

culturalism among Mexican-American college women. PhD U. of Texas at Austin, 1978.

GOULD-STUART, J. *126*
The use of state services by Latin American immigrant woman in New York City. PhD City U. of New York, 1981.

HARRISON, E.S. *127*
Women in Navajo myth: a study in the symbolism of matriliny. PhD U. of Massachusetts, 1973.

HIRAYAMA K.K. *128*
Effects of the employment of Vietnamese refugee wives on their family roles and mental health. DSW U. of Pennsylvania, 1980.

HOFFMAN, D.V. *129*
Asian women learning English in Leicester: the challenges of a changing world. MEd U. of Manchester, 1981.

INCLAN, J.E. *130*
Family organization, acculturation and psychological symptomatology in second generation Puerto Rican women of three socioeconomic class groups. PhD New York U. 1979.

INFANTE, I.M. *131*
Politicalization of immigrant women from Puerto Rico and the Dominican Republic. PhD U. of California, Riverside, 1977.

JOHNSTON, A.A. *132*
The ethnic identity experience of Chamorro women. PhD California Sch. of Prof. Psych., San Diego, 1980.

JORDAN, R.A. *133*
The folklore and ethnic identity of a Mexican-American women. PhD Indiana U. 1975.

KABERRY, P.M. *134*
The position of women in Australian aboriginal society. PhD U. of London, LSE, 1938.

KATAOKA, S.M. *135*
Issei women: a study in subordinate status. PhD U. of California, Los Angeles, 1977.

KHATTAB, H.A.S. *136*
Current roles of Ramah Navajo women and their natality behavior. PhD U. of North Carolina at Chapel Hill, 1974.

KIKUMURA, A. *137*
The life history of an Issei woman: conflicts and strain in the process of acculturation. PhD U. of California, Los Angeles, 1979.

KIM, J. *138*
Processes of Asian American identity development: a study of Japanese American women's perceptions of their struggle to achieve positive identities as Americans of Asian ancestry. EdD U. of Massachusetts, 1981.

KIN, S.D. *139*
Interracially married Korean women immigrants: a study in marginality. PhD U. of Washington, 1979.

LADNER, J.A. *140*
On becoming a woman in the ghetto: modes of adaptation. PhD U. of Washington, 1968.

LAFRIEDA, D.F. *141*
The relationship between special programs and the community adaptation and marital adjustment of wives of foreign students. PhD U. of Miami, 1973.

LEWIN, E. *142*
Mothers and children: Latin American immigrants in San Francisco. PhD Stanford U. 1975.

LOPEZ-GARRIGA, M.M. *143*
Strategies of self-assertion: the Puerto Rican woman. PhD City U. of New York, 1976.

MANCUSO, A. *144*
Women of old town. [Italian-American ethnic enclave in large Eastern city.] EdD Columbia U. Teachers Coll. 1977.

MONTENEGRO, R. *145*
Educational implications of cultural values and attitudes of Mexican-American women. PhD Claremont Grad. Sch. 1973.

MOORE, C.T. *146*
The effect of assertive training on the assertive behavior of foreign women in a US environment. EdD Temple U. 1979.

MUGRAUER, B.M.M. *147*
A cultural study of ten negro girls in an alley. PhD Catholic U. of America 1951.

MUNOZ-VAZQUEZ, M. *148*
The effect of role expectation on the marital status of young urban Puerto Rican women: a study of the impact of cultural core shift in a transitional society. PhD U. of Missouri–Columbia, 1978.

MURAI, E. *149*
The enhancement of the alien's adjustment through interpersonal relationships within the ethnic group toward the socialization into the host society: Japanese women's case. PhD U. of Michigan, 1972.

PITMAN, D.E. *150*
Reactions to desegregation: a study of negro mothers. PhD U. of North Carolina at Chapel Hill, 1960.

POEHLMAN, J. *151*
Culture change and identity among Chamorro women of Guam. PhD U. of Minnesota, 1979.

RAGUCCI, A.T. *152*
Generational continuity and change in concepts of health curing practices and ritual expressions of the women of an Italian American enclave. PhD Boston U. 1971.

RAMOS, M. 153
A micro-ethnographic study of Chicana mother and daughter socialization practices. PhD U. of Colorado, Boulder, 1982.

RASHID, S. 154
The socialisation and education of Pakistani teenage girls in London. MPhil U. of London, Sch. of Oriental and African Studies, 1981.

REED, D. 155
Leisure time of girls in a 'Little Italy': a comparative study of the leisure interests of adolescent girls of foreign parentage, living in a metropolitan community, to determine the presence or absence of interest differences in relation to behavior. PhD Columbia U. 1932.

REGULSKA-PONIZ, J.M. 156
Women's role in metropolitan and non-metropolitan migration trends. PhD U. of Colorado at Boulder, 1982.

REYES, E.A. 157
The interrelationships of role-taking, social competence, sex-role concept, acculturation and trait anxiety among Puerto Rican women in New York City: a developmental approach. PhD U. of Texas at Austin, 1981.

RICHARDS, C.E. 158
The role of Iroquois women: a study of the Onondaga Reservation. PhD Cornell U. 1957.

RIVERA, E. 159
The adjustment of male children of Puerto Rican immigrants as a function of mother's acculturation and adjustment. PhD Kent State U. 1979.

RIVERA, J.-A.M. 160
Bilingualism and personality differences in Puerto Rican females. PhD Adelphi U. 1978.

ROGOZEN, F. 161
The influences of stress on the health of American women in Israel during the process of acculturation. PhD Fielding Inst. 1981.

SAMANIEGO, S. 162
The motive to avoid academic and vocational success in Hispanic American women. PhD City U. of New York, 1980.

SATTERFIELD, D.M.O. 163
Acculturation and marriage role patterns: a comparative study of Mexican-American women. PhD U. of Arizona, 1966.

SHIRLEY, B.Z. 164
A study of ego strength: the case of the Hispanic immigrant woman in the United States. EdD Boston U. Sch. of Educ. 1981.

SHUKRY, L.S. 165
The role of women in a changing Navaho society. PhD Cornell U. 1954.

SMITH, B.J. 166
Home economics program development related to problems of foreign student wives and families in cultural adaptation. PhD Kansas State U. 1979.

SOTO, E. 167
Sex-role traditionalism, assertiveness, and symptoms in first and second generation Puerto Rican women living in the United States. PhD New York U. 1979.

SPINDLER, M.L. 168
Women and culture change: a case study of the Menomini Indians. PhD Stanford U. 1956.

STEWART, A. 169
'Las mujeres de Aztlan': a consultation with elderly Mexican-American women in a socio-historical perspective. PhD California Sch. of Prof. Psych., Berkeley, 1973.

SUMAZA-LABORDE, I.S. 170
The effects of an assertiveness training program for Puerto Rican college women planning to emigrate to the United States. EdD Temple U. 1979.

TERRAZAS, L.M. 171
The psychological effects of adult basic education programs on locus of control and socialization with Mexican-born Mexican-American women. PhD United States International U. 1977.

THEOPHANO, J.S. 172
'It's really tomato sauce but we call it gravy': a study of food and women's work among Italian-American families. PhD U. of Pennsylvania, 1982.

TORRES-MATRULLO, C. 173
Acculturation and psychopathology among Puerto Rican women in mainland United States. PhD Rutgers U. 1974.

TURNER, D.M. 174
A study of the home tuition of Asian women immigrants in West Yorkshire. PhD U. of Liverpool, 1977.

UNNI, V.K. 175
A study of selected characteristics of consumption, life style and social class concepts among wives of negro blue-collar industrial workers in selected Louisiana parishes. DBA Louisiana Tech U. 1973.

WAGNER, J.K. 176
An examination and description of acculturation of selected individual American Indian women in an urban area. PhD New York U. 1972.

WATKINS, F.E. 177
Crafts and industries of the American Indian women of California and the southwest. PhD U. of Southern California, 1942.

WHITE, J.V. 178
The impact of women on desegregation in Boston. EdD Boston U. Sch. of Educ. 1977.

WIDER, J.S. *179*
Indonesian women in The Hague: colonial immigrants in the metropolis. PhD New York U. 1967.

WONG, A. *180*
A study of the initial adjustment to American society of six Chinese immigrant females in high school. PhD Wright Inst. 1980.

YOUNG, A.G.T. *181*
Suicide among black women: a longitudinal analysis. PhD Harvard U. 1979.

Leisure

See also 155; **12** 1819; **13** 19

FRYER, L.P. *182*
Women and leisure: a study of social waste. PhD Columbia U. 1924.

GALLAGHER, J.E. *183*
A study of the use of leisure by college women. PhD Loyola U. of Chicago, 1975.

HACKER, S.L.S. *184*
Patterns of work and leisure: an investigation of the relationships between childhood and current styles of leisure and current career behavior among young women graduates in the field of public school education. PhD U. of Chicago, 1969.

HARLEY, J.L. *185*
Report of an enquiry into the occupations, further education and leisure interests of girl wage-earners from elementary and central schools in the Manchester district, with special reference to the influence of school training on their use of leisure. MEd U. of Manchester, 1937.

KALINSKI, C.W. *186*
Food, women, and leisure. MSc U. of Salford, 1982.

MERRITT, M.A. *187*
The relationship of selected physical, mental, emotional and social factors to the recreational preferences of college women. PhD U. of Iowa, 1961.

MORGAN, O.I. *188*
A study of the training for leisure occupations offered in a senior girls' school in an industrial area, together with an industrial enquiry into the use made of this training by the girls after their entry into employment. MEd U. of Manchester, 1942.

REYNOLDS, L.W. *189*
Leisure-time activities of a selected group of farm women. PhD U. of Chicago, 1935.

ROEDER, H.H. *190*
A comparison between the leisure reading patterns of female teachers and female non-teachers in an industrial city. EdD State U. of New York at Buffalo, 1968.

WATSON, T.O. *191*
A comparison of the leisure reading habits of female teachers and non-teachers. EdD North Texas State U. 1971.

Social class, role and status

See also **4** 199; **9** 608, 662

BLUMBERG, A.S. *192*
Academic women and issues of unequal treatment. PhD City U. of New York, 1981.

BOULDING, E.M.B.-H. *193*
The effects of industrialization on the participation of women in society. PhD U. of Michigan, 1969.

CANADAY, M.H. *194*
The social roles of married middle-aged women with implications for adult education. EdD Pennsylvania State U. 1966.

CLOWERS, L. E. *195*
A sociological study of birth order and attitudes concerning female sex role equality. PhD Tulane U. 1976.

COOVER, E.R. *196*
Status and role change among women in the United States, 1940–1970: a quantitative approach. PhD U. of Minnesota, 1973.

DANFORTH, S.C. *197*
Reform for women in the Turkish Republic: processes of social change. PhD U. of Chicago, 1977.

DISCH, E. *198*
Women's roles and economic structures in southern Italy. PhD Tufts U. 1976.

DWORKIN, R.J. *199*
The female-American: social structure, awareness, and ideology. PhD Northwestern U. 1974.

EHRMANN, W.W. *200*
Cultural determinants of the status of woman. PhD Yale U. 1983.

FAHERTY, W.B. *201*
Recent popes on woman's position in society. PhD St Louis U. 1949.

FINK, D.R. *202*
Women's work and change in a Danish community. PhD U. of Minnesota, 1979.

GOLDMAN, M.S. *203*
Gold diggers and silver miners: prostitution and the fabric of social life on the Comstock Lode. PhD U. of Chicago, 1977.

GRAY, G.R. *204*
Women's proper place: a content analysis of sixty-

five commencement addresses delivered to women. PhD U. of Oregon, 1981.

HIGHTOWER, N. van *205*
The politics of female socialization. PhD New York U. 1974.

HORAN, S.J. *206*
Female status: a hologeistic study. PhD State U. of New York at Buffalo, 1980.

JODY, N. *207*
Production, reproduction and the status of women. PhD State U. of New York at Stony Brook, 1978.

KAPLAN, I.M. *208*
Family life cycle and women's satisfaction with their community. PhD Princeton U. 1980.

KLINE, R.O. *209*
Women in the bar: norm and situation in a northern Italian hamlet. PhD U. of California, Davis, 1976.

KUHNS, E.P. *210*
Institutional participation of women in a California town in the structures of economic allocation, of integration, and of expression. PhD Syracuse U. 1954.

KUSANO, K. *211*
Industrialization and the status of women in Japan. PhD U. of Washington, 1973.

LEAHY, M.E. *212*
Quality and inequality in capitalist and socialist societies: comparative studies of women and national development in the U.S., Mexico, the U.S.S.R. and Cuba. PhD U. of Southern California, 1981.

LEE, L.J. *213*
The social world of the female prostitute in Los Angeles. PhD United States International U. 1982.

LEONARD, C.A. *214*
Prostitution and changing norms in America. PhD Syracuse U. 1979.

LUCIANO, D.R. *215*
The proto-Indo-European concept of woman: a study in comparative philology, anthropology and comparative religion. PhD U. of Connecticut, 1974.

MATTHAEI, J.A. *216*
Womanhood and economic life: a study in American economic history. PhD Yale U. 1978.

MILNER, C.A. *217*
Black pimps and their prostitutes: social organization and value system of a ghetto occupational subculture. PhD U. of California, 1971.

MURPHY, K.M. *218*
Women in three societies: a comparison of the political and economic status of women in a communist, national socialist and liberal society. PhD Fordham U. 1953.

NUSS, S.A. *219*
International indicators of the position of women: a capitalist-socialist comparison. PhD U. of Colorado at Boulder, 1975.

NYUN-HAN, E. *220*
The socio-political roles of women in Japan and Burma. PhD U. of Colorado at Boulder, 1972.

OSTRANDER, S.A. *221*
The upper class woman: a study in social power. PhD Case Western Reserve U., 1976.

OWENS, E.J. *222*
A comparative study of environment and social factors in the respective backgrounds of black and white women of achievement. EdD U. of San Francisco, 1982.

PERRY, L.L. *223*
Mothers, wives, and daughters in Osaka: autonomy, alliance and professionalism. PhD Pittsburgh U., 1976.

PUSHKIN, R. *224*
The relationship between family size and the role and structure of the family: a study of women's work status and family life in a Lancashire town. MSc U. of Manchester, 1981.

REINARTZ, K.F. *225*
American women and Swedish women: changes since World War II. PhD U. of New Mexico, 1973.

ROSENHAN, M.S. *226*
Women's place and cultural values in Soviet children's readers: an historical analysis of the maintenance of role division by gender, 1920s and 1970s. PhD U. of Pennsylvania, 1981.

RUSSELL, A. *227*
Female working-class youth culture in a work situation. MPhil U. of Aston, 1982.

SCHIRMIER, J.G. *228*
Work, family and class: Danish urban women and the welfare state. PhD U. of Washington, 1980.

SELBY, L.G. *229*
The nature of American woman: a cultural account. PhD U. of Texas at Austin, 1972.

SHURMAN, G.M. *230*
Japanese women: history, role transformation, and cases of the achievement of eminence. PhD United States International U. 1978.

SLEPACK, D.G. *231*
Women in the German Democratic Republic: a field study and comparative analysis of sex bias in USA and GDR children's reading. EdD U. of Cincinnati, 1976.

STERNER, J.A. *232*
Women's post-college socioeconomic activities. PhD Ohio State U. 1963.

THOMAS, C.P. 233
Social participation of women: labor force, formal, informal. PhD Michigan State U. 1974.

TOMLINSON, S. 234
A theoretical examination of knowledge about women in industrial societies. MSocSc. U. of Birmingham, 1975.

TSUCHIGANE, T.R. 235
Discrimination against women in the United States. PhD U. of Maryland, 1972.

UNTEREGGER-MATTENBERGER, J. 236
The roots of a social movement – an exploratory study of women's self-conceptions and changing sex roles in Switzerland. PhD U. of Minnesota, 1975.

WOOTEN, M.L. 238
The status of women in Texas: PhD U. of Texas at Austin, 1941.

YAMIN ESFANDIARI, F.-M. 239
Cross-cultural comparison of attitude towards women in England and Iran. PhD U. of Manchester, 1980.

ZILBERGELD, G.W. 240
Personal troubles and public solutions among Jews and women in America. PhD U. of Miami, 1975.

Voluntary work, voluntary organizations and clubs

Studies of periods before 1945 are to be found **9** History. *See also* **5** 137; **18** 193; **23** 271.

BADEAUX, L.M. 241
An evaluation of a general semantics approach in teaching situational leadership theory in women's volunteer service organizations. PhD Louisiana State U. and A&M Coll. 1981.

BARTLETT, L.R. 242
Problems and satisfaction of women active in volunteer community service. PhD Columbia U. 1959.

BAUER, C.E.C. 243
Voluntary associations among women of two classes in urban Colorado. PhD U. of Colorado at Boulder, 1975.

BERRY, F.A. 244
Survey of a selected number of women's organizations in Tampa, Florida, and their contributions to education. EdD U. of Florida, 1975.

BUCKMAN, R.O. 245
Interaction between women's clubs and institutions in Greater Lafayette, Indiana. PhD U. of Chicago, 1953.

CONKLIN, E.N. 246
Women's voluntary associations in French Montreal: a study of changing institutions and attitudes. PhD, U. of Illinois at Urbana–Champaign, 1972.

DEMOS, V.P. 247
Women volunteers: the relationship between the female role and participation in women's organizations. PhD U. of Notre Dame, 1978.

FERRARI, M.M. 248
Project special grandparents: effects of interaction of first-grade boys and older women in a school setting. PhD Case Western Reserve, U. 1973.

FLETTY, V. 249
Public services of women's organizations. PhD Syracuse U. 1953.

GARDNER, M.E.E. 250
The negro woman: her role as participant in volunteer community activities in Westchester communities. EdD New York U. 1961.

JACKS, O. 251
The development of girls' 4–H club work in Texas. PhD U. of Texas at Austin, 1947.

JOHNSON, L.B. 252
The role orientation of women in voluntary associations in Raleigh, North Carolina. PhD North Carolina State U. at Raleigh, 1972.

MCCOURT, K. 253
Women and grass-roots politics: a case study of working-class women's participation in assertive community organizations. PhD U. of Chicago, 1975.

MINNICK, A.K. 254
The effect of girl scout conventional organizational practices on the retention of girl members. PhD U. of Michigan, 1972.

MINNIS, M.S. 255
The relationship of women's organizations to the social structure of a city. PhD Yale U., 1951.

PATTERSON, V.C. 256
Characteristics and motivational factors of volunteer club leaders in evangelical churches: an analysis of pioneer girls' club leaders. EdD Northern Illinois U., 1978.

PUERTA, R.A. 257
A quasi-experimental design to test an explanatory model for program impact: the housewives clubs in Honduras. PhD Cornell U., 1982.

SCHRAM, V.R. 259
Determinants of volunteer work participation by married women. PhD U. of Illinois at Urbana–Champaign, 1980.

STENZEL, A.K. 260
A study of girl scout leadership training: non-professional leaders of adults as continuous learners. PhD U. of California, Berkeley, 1963.

STRONG, W.A. 261
The origin, development and current status of the Oklahoma Federation of Colored Women's Clubs. EdD U. of Oklahoma, 1957.

TOMPKINS, J.B. 262
Reference groups and status values as determinants of behavior: a study of women's voluntary association behavior. PhD U. of Iowa, 1955.

WILLIAMS, B.L. 263
Voluntary association and the political behavior of women. PhD Rice U. 1976.

WILSON, K.K. 264
Expectations about learning experiences in nonformal education: girl scout leaders in Hawaii. PhD Michigan State U. 1978.

WOLVERTON, M.E. 265
Influence of all states encampments on local girl scout council senior program. EdD U. of Cincinnati, 1963.

Welfare and social work

See also **9** 491, 623, 669; **19** 115, 339, 362

ALMANZOR, A.C. 266
Volunteer and staff participation in a voluntary social welfare association in the United States: a study of the National Young Women's Christian Association. DSW Columbia U., 1961.

ALTROGGE, P.D. 267
Empirical study of the female insured unemployed. PhD U. of Missouri–Columbia, 1975.

AMERMAN, D. 268
Vocational and social adjustments of clients rehabilitated by state divisions of vocational rehabilitation, 1957–1959. Part I: employed and unemployed females. PhD U. of Utah, 1963.

ANDERSON, M.C. 269
A case study of a new organizational subunit's development: the UCSB Women's Center. PhD U. of California, Santa Barbara, 1981.

ARMBRUSTER, R.A. 270
Personality characteristics of contemporary American female social workers as compared to those of Bertha Pappenheim. PhD Florida Inst. of Technology, 1982.

AUSTIN, J.P. 271
Poor women's sorority: social life among women in low income public housing. PhD Boston U. Grad. School, 1981.

BATAINAH, S.M. 272
Vocational and social adjustment of clients rehabilitated by state divisions of vocational rehabilitation, 1957–1959. Part II: fully employed females. PhD U. of Utah, 1963.

BERNARD, S.E. 273
The economic and social adjustment of low-income female-headed families. PhD Brandeis U. 1965.

BISHOP, E.S. 274
The self-concept of the welfare mother: some sociological correlates. PhD Florida State U. 1972.

CALKIN, C.L. 275
Women administrators: an exploration of critical factors in women's advancement in social work. PhD U. of Denver, 1982.

DABROWSKI, I.J. 276
Working-class women as paid workers and community volunteers: an ethnographic study. PhD Washington U. 1979.

FISHER, V. 277
Women, dependency, and social security: aspects of the role of the state in patriarchal and capitalist relations. MA* U. of Sheffield, 1979.

FORMAN, R.Z. 278
Let us now praise obscure women: a comparative study of publicly supported unmarried mothers in government housing in the United States and Britain. PhD Boston U. Grad. Sch. 1979.

GILKES, C.L.T. 279
Living and working in a world of trouble: the emergent career of the black woman community worker. PhD Northeastern U. 1979.

GRUBER, A.R. 280
A comparative study of the utilization of mature college-graduated women employed half-time as caseworkers in an urban public welfare department. DSW Columbia U. 1971.

HAND, J.E. 281
Shopping bag women of Manhattan. [A study of homeless vagrant women.] PhD New Sch. for Social Research, 1982.

HAYDEN, M.J. 282
Waiting for child care: a survey of mothers on waiting lists for publicly subsidized day care. PhD Claremont Grad. Sch. 1980.

HEARD, C.R. 283
Vocational and social adjustments of clients rehabilitated by state divisions of vocational rehabilitation, 1957–1959. Part III: part-time employed females. PhD U. of Utah, 1963.

HERTZ, S.V.H. 284
A study of the organization and politics of the Welfare Mothers Movement in Minnesota. PhD U. of Minnesota, 1974.

HONIG, M.H. 285
The impact of the welfare system on labor supply and family stability: a study of female heads of families. PhD Columbia U. 1971.

JOYCE, T.D. 286
An exploratory study of the relationships between

welfare dependency and the attitudinal characteristics of welfare mothers. PhD Cornell U. 1973.

KELLY, R.F. *287*
Urban labor markets and the determination of welfare dependency among female-headed low-income families: a comparative analysis of path models. PhD Rutgers U. 1979.

KRAFT, G.S. *288*
Age differences in stability, extraversion, and openness to experience among women social workers. PhD U. of Maryland, 1982.

LONGFELLOW, C.J. *289*
Social support and mother-child interactions. EdD Harvard U. 1979.

NALL, E.W. *290*
Social movement to social organization: a case study of a women's center. PhD Michigan State U. 1976.

OLDANI, J.L. *291*
The woman as reformer: a facet of the American character. PhD Saint Louis U. 1967.

OZAKI, R.H. *292*
A study of certain maternal attitudes influencing mothers' availability to pupil welfare workers. DSW Washington U. 1960.

PAGE, M.H. *293*
Women in social work: perceptions of status and role change. PhD U. of Pittsburgh, 1978.

PHILLIPS, M.H. *294*
The impact of the declaration procedure upon the perceptions and attitudes of mothers receiving aid to families with dependent children. DSW Columbia U. 1972.

PURVIS, M.L. *295*
St Louis women of achievement and community. PhD Saint Louis U. 1973.

RICE, B.C. *296*
A study of professional career satisfaction of women social workers in relation to career patterns, career saliency, professional role conception, congruence, and race. DSW Catholic U. of America, 1980.

RICHMAN, D.R. *297*
A comparison of cognitive and behavioral group counseling techniques for job finding with welfare women. PhD Hofstra U. 1979.

ROSE, S.A. *298*
Independent family day care mothers in the black community. EdD, Columbia U. Teachers Coll. 1976.

ROSEN, P.C. *299*
A profile of Renaissance House: a group home for dependent/deprived adolescent girls. EdD U. of Pennsylvania, 1982.

ROSS, J.A. *300*
The effect of recommendations made by an expert to negro mothers of low socioeconomic status when recommendations are supported or negated by a peer. PhD Hofstra U. 1971.

SHEPPARD, J.W. *301*
A comparison of selected factors in describing the mature paraprofessional woman as an indigenous community resource in an urban educational community. EdD Temple U. 1973.

SHOMO, E.W. Jr *302*
Social insurance for women. PhD Rutgers U. 1968.

SHORES, J.W. *303*
A study of independence and hostility in female welfare clients as indicated by interpersonal word list and video tape. PhD Kansas State U. 1975.

SIGVARDT, B.A. *304*
Vocational and social adjustment of females with mental disabilities rehabilitated by state divisions of vocational rehabilitation, 1957–1959. Part VI: social adjustment. PhD U. of Utah, 1963.

SNYDER, R.S. *305*
The effect of ADC work-incentives on labor force participation of ADC mothers in Indiana. PhD Indiana U. 1976.

TRIEFF, M.S. *306*
Psychological needs and coping ability of women in a training program at a center for displaced homemakers. EdD U. of Houston, 1979.

VARTY, J.W. *307*
Prior characteristics, community college interactions and after college status of 180 female ADC recipients. PhD U. of Michigan, 1979.

WAXLER, I. *308*
Women's perceptions of women's roles: a study of female welfare clients. DSW Columbia U. 1980.

WEST, M.P. *309*
The national welfare rights movement: social protest of welfare women (1966–1976). PhD Rutgers U. 1978.

22 Sport

General

See also **4** 432–562; **6** 144; **9** 459, 535, 555, 697; **12** 1779; **19** 206.

ADKINS, V.B.L. *1*
The development of negro female Olympic talent. PED Indiana U. 1967.

BALAZS, E.K. *2*
A psycho-social study of outstanding female athletes. EdD Boston U. Sch. of Education. 1974.

BARNES, M.J. *3*
An investigation of relationships between certain physiological-psychological capacities and motor abilities of high school girl athletes and non-athletes in selected schools. EdD Boston U. 1961.

BATTAGLIA, R.M. *4*
A comparison of motivational traits of selected community college female athletes with other selected groups of athletes. PhD U. of Utah, 1976.

BOHREN, J.M. *5*
The role of the family in the socialization of female intercollegiate athletes. PhD U. of Maryland, 1977.

BUTCHER, J.E. *6*
Physical activity participation of adolescent girls. PhD U. of Alberta, 1980.

CAMPBELL, L.E. *7*
The female athlete: a study to distinguish androgynous sex role, locus of control, and perceived parenting. EdD U. of Oregon, 1977.

CHADWICK, I.F. *8*
A comparison of the personality traits and kinesthetic augmentation and reduction of college female athletes and non-athletes. PhD Florida State U. 1972.

CLARK, E.K. *9*
Self-perceived sex role and female involvement in sport. PhD U. of New Mexico, 1980.

COLLINS, E.L. *10*
Sex-role perceptions and self-actualization among high school female athletes and non-athletes. PhD U. of Florida, 1979.

CONE, S.L. *11*
The relationship between self-concept and selected physical characteristics among female varsity athletes and non-participants. PhD Texas A&M U. 1979.

COOK, N.L. *12*
Criteria for professional preparation of women coaches. PhD U. of California, Berkeley, 1972.

CORBETT, D.R. *13*
The relationship between androgyny, self-concept and social status among minority female athletes and non-athletes. PhD U. of Maryland, 1981.

CRANFORD, M.L. *14*
Blood lactate concentrations in female athletes performing various types and intensities of work. PhD Ohio State U. 1972.

DANIELS, M.A. *15*
The historical transition of women's sports at the Ohio State University, 1885–1975, and its impact on the national women's intercollegiate setting during that period. PhD Ohio State U. 1977.

DUDA J.E. *16*
A comparison of personality characteristics of adult women athletes, young adult women athletes and college women athletes: a study of assertive behavior in sport. EdD Boston U. 1980.

DUQUIN, M.E. *17*
Institutional sanction for girls' sport programs: effects on female high school students. PhD Stanford U. 1975.

FAHEY, B.W. *18*
Woman and sport: an existential analysis. PhD Ohio State U. 1973.

FARISS, A.V. *19*
The effect of autocratic and democratic leadership styles on the success of high school female sport participants. PhD U. of Connecticut, 1978.

FARR, J. *20*
Women, sport and American society. PhD U. of Utah, 1979.

FAULKNER, M.E. *21*
The sex-role orientations of women intercollegiate coaches in eight sports. EdD U. of Northern Colorado, 1978.

FINN, J.A. 22
Perception of violence among high-hostile and low-hostile women athletes and non-athletes before and after exposure to sport films. DPE Springfield Coll. 1976.

FOSS, P.M. 23
Factors related to urban adult female participation in physical activity programs. PhD Michigan State U. 1979.

GORDON, R.D. 24
Effects of hypnosis relaxation training or music on state anxiety and stress in female athletes. EdD U. of Utah, 1981.

GREENDORFER, S.L. 25
The nature of female socialization into sport: a study of selected college women's sport participation. PhD U. of Wisconsin, Madison, 1974.

GRIFFIN, M.R. 26
An analysis of state and trait anxiety experienced in sports competition by women at different age levels. EdD Louisiana State U. and A&M Coll. 1971.

GRIMMETT, D.A. 27
Psychological and physiological comparisons between female athletes and non-athletes. EdD Brigham Young U. 1979.

GROSS, R.M. 28
The effect of stimulus and movement complexity upon reaction time and movement time of college women and athletes. PhD Springfield Coll. 1974.

HABIGER, T.M. 29
Femininity and the female varsity athlete. EdD U. of Tennessee, 1982.

HARRIS, B.L. 30
Sex-role orientation, fear of success, and competitive sport performance of high school athletes. EdD U. of North Carolina at Greensboro, 1978.

HEBERT-MARTIN, F. 31
The effect of a 'health and fitness package' on the increase in attitudes toward, knowledge about and involvement in physical activity among an adolescent girls target population. DNS U. of California, San Francisco, 1979.

HIGGINSON, D.C. 32
A sociological investigation of the female athletes who took part in the Empire State Games. EdD Syracuse U. 1980.

HILL, S.L. 33
The temperament traits of women who coach team sports and individual sports on the intercollegiate level. EdD U. of North Carolina at Greensboro, 1978.

HUNT, D.M. 34
A study of administrative duties and their importance by those who administer inter-collegiate athletic programs for women in Tennessee. DA Middle Tennessee State U. 1976.

JONES, A.K. 35
The female athlete, her image in fact and fiction: a study in sociology through literature. PhD U. of Alberta, 1981.

JONES, D.C. 36
The relationship of sex-role orientations to stereotypes held for female athletes in selected sports. EdD West Virginia U. 1979.

JONES, H.B. 37
Athletic motivation inventory of female athletes and non-athletes. PhD California Sch. of Prof. Psych., Berkeley, 1974.

KELLOGG, P.G. 38
Title IX of the Education Amendments of 1972: a factor in increased participation by females in interscholastic sports. EdD U. of Northern Colorado, 1979.

KILDEA, A.E. 39
Meaningfulness in life: locus of control and sex-role orientation of selected female athletes and non-athletes. PhD Southern Illinois U. at Carbondale, 1979.

KRATZ, L.E. 40
A study of sports and the implications of women's participation in them in modern society. PhD Ohio State U. 1958.

LAIRD, E.M. 41
The comparison of the aggressive responses of women athletes and non-athletes at three educational levels. PhD Springfield Coll. 1971.

LEMEN, M.G. 42
The relationship between selected variables and attitudes of college women toward physical education and certain sports. PhD U. of Iowa, 1962.

LEWIS, V.F. 43
A study of the informational needs of college women sports spectators. PhD Ohio State U. 1953.

LEYHE, N.L. 44
The attitudes of the women members of the American Association of Health, Physical Education, and Recreation towards competition in sports for girls and women. PhD Indiana U. 1956.

LORENTZEN, D. 45
Psychological characteristics of successful and less successful junior female athletes participating in an open and closed skill sport. PhD U. of Nebraska, 1981.

MACKEY, A. 46
A national study of women's intramural sports in teachers' colleges and schools of education. EdD Boston U. 1957.

MAGOON, E.J. *47*
The influence of music on the performance of female beginner and advanced players in selected sports skills. EdD Boston U. Sch. of Educ. 1975.

MALUMPHY, T.M. *48*
The personality and central characteristics of women athletes in intercollegiate competition. PhD Ohio State U. 1966.

MARKERT, J.E. *49*
The body composition of female athletes. EdD U. of Kansas, 1978.

MENOFF, B.R. *50*
An investigation of competitive and cooperative behavior in female athletes and non-athletes. PhD California Sch. of Prof. Psych., Los Angeles, 1975.

MOORE, S.L. *51*
A study of perceived locus of control in college women athletes in team and individual sports. PhD U. of Oregon, 1980.

MORRIS, P.C. *52*
A comparative study of physical measures of women athletes and unselected college women. EdD Temple U. 1960.

MORRISON, L.L. *53*
A test of basic sports skills for college women. PED Indiana U. 1964.

MYERS, F.R.J. *54*
A descriptive study of college women's performing groups: groups of sixteen or more girls who perform precision drilling and/or twirling and/or dancing at college. EdD Columbia U. 1966.

PASSMORE, B.A. *55*
Assertiveness of women intercollegiate athletes. PhD Ohio State U. 1977.

PRICE, M.A. *56*
The role of United States women's participation in the modern Olympic Games. PhD Columbia U. 1953.

PROCTOR, A.J. *57*
Predicting group membership of ninth grade female athletes in selected sports. PhD U. of Utah, 1978.

RAMIREZ, M.D. *58*
Self-perception of personality among selected female athletes. EdD Brigham Young U. 1980.

REMLEY, M.L. *59*
Twentieth-century concepts of sports competition for women. PhD U. of Southern California, 1970.

RICHARDSON, D.A. *60*
Women and physical activity: a sociocultural investigation of primary involvement. EdD U. of Georgia, 1974.

SCHMITT, P.A. *61*
Personality profiles of intercollegiate women in team and individual sports as measured by the personal orientation inventory. PhD Texas Woman's U. 1974.

SHENTON, P.A. *62*
Women in sport: a comparative study of Britain and the USSR. MEd U. of Liverpool, 1979.

SLATTON, Y.L. *63*
The role of women in sport as depicted through advertising in selected magazines, 1900–1968. PhD U. of Iowa, 1970.

STEWART, F.O. *64*
Interactionist strategies for assessing personality and behavior differences among female intercollegiate athletes and non-athletes. PhD Virginia Commonwealth U. 1981.

STOVALL, J.C. *65*
Effects of perceived competence and audience gender on motor task persistence in athletic and non-athletic women. PhD U. of Michigan, 1981.

THRONEBERRY, C.A. *66*
A comparison of sex-role concepts and self-actualization of college female athletes and non-athletes. PhD Texas Woman's U. 1979.

WATKINS, M.B.S. *67*
Historical and biographical studies of women Olympic participants at Tennessee State U., 1948–1980. EdD George Peabody Coll. for Teachers, 1980.

WATTS, D.P. *68*
Changing conceptions of competitive sports for girls and women in the United States from 1880 to 1960. PhD U. of California, Los Angeles, 1961.

WELCH, P.D. *69*
The emergence of American women in the Summer Olympic Games, 1900–1972. EdD U. of North Carolina at Greensboro, 1975.

Athletics

BATES, B.T. *70*
The development of a computer program with application to a film analysis: the mechanics of female runners. PhD Indiana U. 1972.

BROOKE, W.O. Jr. *71*
Assessing the impact of Title IX and other factors on women's intercollegiate athletic programs, 1972–1977: a national study of four-year AIAW institutions. EdD Arizona State U. 1979.

BUSH, J.J *72*
A study of the relationship of pre-test anxiety and performance of college women gymnasts. PhD Springfield Coll. 1970.

CLAY, J.T. *73*
Personality traits of female intercollegiate athletes and female intercollegiate athletic coaches. PhD U. of Utah, 1974.

COHEN, K. *74*
Metabolic alterations with sprint versus endurance interval training in females. PhD Ohio State U. 1975.

COLE, D.S. *75*
Psychosocial factors related to marathon running in women. EdD Boston U. Sch. of Educ. 1980.

CONLEY, E.O. *76*
An analysis of women's intercollegiate athletics as a factor in the college selection process with specific attention given to small private colleges. PhD State U. of New York at Buffalo, 1981.

COPELAND, D.A. *77*
The effects of an isokinetic power training program for women on vertical jumping ability. PhD U. of Iowa, 1977.

DECARIA, M.D. *78*
The effect of cognitive rehearsal training on performance and on self-report of anxiety in novice and intermediate female gymnasts. PhD U. of Utah, 1977.

DEUTSCH, H.M. *79*
A comparison of women's throwing patterns. PhD U. of Illinois at Urbana–Champaign, 1969.

DREIDAME, R.E. *80*
A survey of the organization and administration of women's intercollegiate athletic programs in the 1973–1974 AIAW active member schools. PhD Ohio State U. 1974.

EGGERT, S.R. *81*
Coaching success in women's athletics: the relationship of selected factors in preparation of coaches. EdD Brigham Young U. 1978.

FRECK, K.A. *82*
The status, authority and responsibilities of women's athletic directors in merged and unmerged athletic departments. PhD U. of Iowa, 1981.

FREDERICKS-DAYS, K.A. *83*
A futuristic investigation of women's athletics: using a modified Delphi application. PhD U. of Southern California, 1982.

GARFIELD, D.S. *84*
Strength gains in women intercollegiate athletes using the Nautilus training system. EdD Syracuse U. 1972.

GERARD, C.L. *85*
Women distance runners: androgyny and self-esteem. EdD U. of Northern Colorado, 1982.

GEROU, N.E. *86*
A survey of the educational background and professional experience of women's athletic directors in the United States. EdD U. of Colorado at Boulder, 1977.

GOODLOE, N.R. *87*
A study of the perceived qualifications of women athletic directors. EdD U. of Oregon, 1978.

HALL, J.B. *88*
Preparing beginning judges of women's gymnastics. PhD U. of Utah, 1975.

HAVEN, B.H. *89*
Changes in the mechanics of the running patterns of highly skilled women runners during competitive races. PED Indiana U. 1977.

HILL, G.H. *90*
Participation of twelfth grade females in interscholastic athletics. EdD Rutgers U. 1981.

HODGDON, P.D. *91*
An investigation of the development of interscholastic and intercollegiate athletics for girls and women from 1917–1970. PhD Springfield Coll. 1973.

HOVIOUS, B.W. *92*
Women's intercollegiate athletic programs in selected universities and colleges in the southeastern region of the United States. EdD Louisiana State U. and A&M Coll. 1977.

HUNT, V. *93*
Governance of women's intercollegiate athletics: an historical perspective. EdD U. of North Carolina at Greensboro, 1976.

JONES, B.A.S. *94*
Impact of Title IX on women's athletic programs of selected state universities in Texas: a critical assessment. EdD Texas Southern U. 1979.

KEARNEY, J.F. *95*
The history of women's intercollegiate athletics in Ohio, 1945–1972. PhD Ohio State U. 1973.

KEYES, M.E. *96*
The history of the Women's Athletics Committee of the Canadian Association for Health, Physical Education and Recreation, 1940–1973.
PhD Ohio State U. 1980.

KIMURA, I.F. *97*
The high jump as performed by the 1979 United States outdoor female record holder: a biochemical analysis. PhD Texas Woman's U. 1981.

KNOPPERS, A. *98*
A behaviorally based appraisal of coaching performance in women's athletics at Michigan State University. EdD U. of North Carolina at Greensboro, 1978.

LAIRD, N.L. *99*
The evolution of competitive distance running programs for women in the United States. EdD U. of Houston, 1978.

LESLIE, M.E. *100*
Principles of women's intercollegiate athletics. PhD U. of Southern California, 1979.

LESMES, G.R. *101*
Metabolic response of young females to different frequencies of sprint versus endurance interval training. PhD Ohio State U. 1976.

MARTIN, C.E. *102*
An analysis of the attitudes of elementary school teachers and administrators towards athletics for females. PhD Ohio State U. 1979.

MASSIE, L.O. *103*
Selected practices for the conduct of women's intercollegiate athletics in Kentucky colleges. PED, Indiana U. 1970.

NEEDELS, E.L. *104*
Women's athletics and innovative career choice. PhD Duke U. 1981.

O'BRIEN, C.M. *105*
An investigation of the processes which produce elite women gymnasts in the USSR. PhD Ohio State U. 1979.

OKRANT, M.J. *106*
An examination of the significance of educational and regional factors in explaining women's intercollegiate athletic program quality. EdD Oklahoma State U. 1975.

OLCOTT, S.C. *107*
The development of an instrument to measure attitudes toward women's participation in track and field. EdD Boston U. Sch. of Educ. 1980.

RUSSELL, W.L. *108*
The legal aspects of girls' interscholastic athletics: a summary of litigation involving the participation, rules, and regulations of the Interscholastic High School Athletic Associations in each state from 1971–1977. EdD U. of North Carolina at Greensboro, 1978.

RUTHERORD, J.K. *109*
Women's intercollegiate athletics in the United States: a geographical examination, 1971–1977. EdD Oklahoma State U. 1977.

SCHMIDT, D.H.K. *110*
Basic mechanics of women's gymnastics. PhD U. of Iowa, 1975.

SCOTT, G.D. *111*
A comparative study of standards and policies in athletics for girl and women. PhD Case Western Reserve U. 1963.

SEIBERT, M.E. *112*
Attitudes of members of the Association for Intercollegiate Athletics for Women toward critical issues in athletics. EdD Indiana U. 1978.

SELLERS, W.J.S. *113*
A study of selected physical characteristics of the legs and feet of female athletes with shin splints. EdD U. of Mississippi, 1977.

SELYA, M. *114*
The psychological characteristics of women distance runners and secondary amenorrhea associated with running. PhD Boston Coll. 1980.

SIMPSON, C. *115*
Personality traits and performance in women's gymnastics. PED Indiana U. 1974.

SISLEY, B.L. *116*
Measurement of attitudes of women coaches toward the conduct of intercollegiate athletics for women. EdD U. of North Carolina at Greensboro. 1973.

SMITH, K.I. *117*
Program planners' perceptions of cost and effectiveness variables affecting girls' interscholastic athletic programs. EdD U. of Southern California, 1980.

THAXTON, N.A. *118*
A documentary analysis of competitive track and field for women at Tennessee State A & I University and Tuskegee Institute. PhD Springfield Coll. 1970.

USHER, M.M. *119*
A history of women's intercollegiate athletics at Florida State University from 1905–1972. PhD Florida State U. 1980.

WAHL, J.K. *120*
The programmatic status of women's intercollegiate athletics and relationships associated with institutional characteristics and affiliations with athletic governing bodies. EdD U. of Colorado at Boulder, 1981.

WANDZILAK, T.M. *121*
A study of the women's intercollegiate athletic program and its participants at the Ohio State University, during the 1976–1977 academic year. PhD Ohio State U. 1977.

WHIDDON, N.S. *122*
A model for undergraduate professional preparation programs for women athletic coaches in southeastern senior colleges and universities. EdD Florida Atlantic U. 1977.

WILSON, J. *123*
A cinematographical analysis of selected sprint starts in track for women. PhD U. of Minnesota, 1972.

WOOD, N.E. *124*
An analysis of the leadership of the Association for Intercollegiate Athletics for Women, 1971–1980. PhD U. of Utah, 1980.

Specific sports and games

ADDISON, C.F. *125*
Effects of variations of target size, distance and

shooting technique on archery performance by college women beginners. EdD Temple U. 1972.

ALEXANDER, A.V. *126*
The enhancement of the self-concept of young black females through field hockey and the omega module. EdD Temple U. 1981.

ARRASMITH, J.L. *127*
Swimming classification test for college women. PhD U. of Oregon, 1968.

BOBB, M. *128*
Characteristics of women field hockey players according to positions played and levels of competition. EdD U. of Georgia, 1977.

BROWN, D.P. *129*
The effect of augmenting instruction with an improvised teaching aid for college women in learning selected badminton skills. PED Indiana U. 1969.

CHAPMAN, N.L. *130*
An investigation of the prediction of success in women's field hockey. EdD U. of North Carolina at Greensboro, 1979.

CHASE, M. *131*
Relationships between selected biological rhythm and performances of professional women golfers. PhD U. of Utah, 1976.

COHEN, D.A. *132*
An epidemiological study of women's high school basketball injuries. PhD U. of Illinois at Urbana–Champaign, 1977.

COTTER, L.L. *133*
Group cohesiveness and team success among women's intercollegiate basketball teams. PED Indiana U. 1978.

CROGAN, C.A. *134*
The reported preferences and practices of teachers of golf for women at the college level. EdD U. of Michigan, 1953.

CURTIS, J.M. *135*
The effects of four methods of spare conversion involving variations in points of aim on bowling achievement of college women. PED Indiana U. 1970.

DIEHL, P.S. *136*
Effects of a season of training and competition on selected physiological parameters in female college basketball players. PhD Ohio State U. 1974.

DOWNING, M.R. *137*
Women's basketball: an historical review of selected organizations which influenced its ascension toward advanced competition in the United States. PhD Texas Woman's U. 1973.

DRYSDALE, K.J. *138*
A socio-historical analysis of the stigmatization of the high-level female softball competitor. PhD U. of Iowa, 1978.

ECKLUND, J.A. *139*
A comparison of the effect of variation in task difficulty in the transfer of basketball shooting accuracy among college, senior high, and junior high females. PhD U. of Minnesota, 1975.

FOSTER, E.G. *140*
Personality traits of highly skilled basketball and softball women athletes. PED Indiana U. 1972.

GORDON, P.A. *141*
Prediction of basketball-playing ability of college women by selected tests. EdD U. of Arkansas, 1978.

GRASTORF, J.E. *142*
Nonverbal behaviors of collegiate female volleyball and basketball coaches as recalled by athletes and coaches. EdD U. of North Carolina at Greensboro, 1980.

GRAVES, M.L. *143*
Stress in college women basketball players and coping techniques of coaches. EdD U. of Arkansas, 1981.

GIFFIN, N.S. *144*
A comparison of the heart rates of female college participants in field hockey and basketball. PhD U. of Oregon, 1967.

GROPPEL, J.L. *145*
A kinematic analysis of the tennis one-handed and two-handed backhand drives of highly skilled female competitors. PhD Florida State U. 1978.

GUNDEN, R.E. *146*
A comparison of selected measurements of high and low skill achievers among college women in tennis and golf classes. PhD U. of Iowa, 1967.

IRWIN, J. *147*
The effect of selected audiovisual aids in teaching beginning tennis skill and knowledge to college women. PhD Indiana U. 1959.

JENSEN, J.L. *148*
The development of standards for women's athletics and their influence on basketball competition in the State of New York. PhD Ohio State U. 1972.

JONES, P.L. *149*
A survey of Southeastern Conference women's basketball coaches and Ohio Valley Conference women's basketball coaches on the overall effects of pre-season weight training. DA Middle Tennessee State U. 1979.

JONES, R.J. *150*
The effects of contingency management on competitive game, practice and selected managerial behaviors at girls' basketball camp. PhD Ohio State U, 1979.

KLATT, L.A. *151*
Kinematic and temporal characteristics of a successful penalty corner in women's field hockey. PED Indiana U. 1977.

LEILICH, A.F. *152*
The primary components of selected basketball tests for college women. PhD Indiana U. 1953.

LEWIS, A.E. *153*
A comparison of three methods of teaching bowling to college women. EdD George Peabody Coll. for Teachers, 1965.

LEWIS, K. *154*
Leadership: a success factor for women volleyball coaches. EdD Brigham Young U. 1978.

LISKEVYCH, T.N. *155*
A comparative study of women's volleyball at the international level. PhD Ohio State U. 1976.

LOWRY, C.D.E. *156*
Leadership, power, and sources of group attraction in women's intercollegiate team sports groups. PhD Texas Woman's U. 1972.

LUMPKIN, A. *157*
The contributions of women to the history of competitive tennis in the United States (1874–1974). PhD Ohio State U. 1974.

MASON, G.I. *158*
Superordinate and subordinate role preferences of peer-selected leaders and their teammates on women's intercollegiate volleyball teams. PhD Ohio State U. 1977.

MESSIER, S.P. *159*
Relationships among selected kinetic parameters, bat velocities, and three methods of striding by female softball batters. PhD Temple U. 1982.

MIDTLYNG, J. *160*
Stress responses of women in advanced hunt horsemanship at Indiana University. PED North Texas State U. 1971.

MILLER, W. *161*
Achievement level in tennis knowledge and skill for women physical education major students. PhD Indiana U. 1952.

MOYER, L.J. *162*
The construction of films designed for practice in officiating women's basketball. PhD U. of Iowa, 1968.

MUSHIER, C.L. *163*
A cross-sectional study of the personality factors of girls and women in competitive lacrosse. PhD U. of Southern California, 1970.

O'CONNOR, P.T. *164*
A study of speed and skill in relation to success achieved by college women engaged in badminton singles competition. PhD Texas Woman's U. 1966.

PARCHMAN, L.L. *165*
Cinematographical and mechanical analysis of the golf swing of female golfers. EdD Louisiana State U. 1970.

PETERSON, P.M. *166*
History of Olympic skiing for women in the United States: a cultural interpretation. PhD U. of Southern California, 1967.

PHILLIPS, M.P. *167*
Standardization of a badminton knowledge test for college women. PhD U. of Wisconsin, 1945.

PIPER, M.F. *168*
The relationship between selected softball statistics and the win-loss record of major women's softball teams. EdD Brigham Young U. 1975.

POSTON, B.L. *169*
Social class of women collegiate swimmers. PhD U. of Utah, 1977.

RABKE, M.L. *170*
The relationship of vision, quickness of arm and leg movement, point control of foil, length of lunge, and general fencing ability of women enrolled in beginning fencing classes in Texas Woman's University, Denton, Texas. PhD Texas Woman's U. 1960.

RENICK, J. *171*
An analysis of women's basketball rules. PhD U. of Southern California, 1972.

RHODES, W.M. *172*
Effects of variations in number of strokes taught and equipment used on tennis achievement by college women. PED Indiana U. 1962.

RIDINGER, R.R. *173*
Chronic intensive physical training and cardiac function in female swimmers. PhD Ohio State U. 1975.

RUSSELL, J.A. *174*
Tennis and the woman player: why the changes? EdD U. of Georgia, 1981.

SAPPINGTON, C.E. *175*
The role of the women's basketball official as perceived by selected groups of subjects. PhD U. of Iowa, 1976.

SCHUMAKER, E.J. *176*
An analysis of the general attributional schemata of female volleyball players. DPE Springfield Coll. 1981.

SEXTON, M. *177*
Implications of the All-American Girl Baseball League for physical educators in the guidance of highly skilled girls. PhD Columbia U. 1954.

SHAMBAUGH, M.E. *178*
The objective measurement of success in teaching folk dancing to university women. PhD U. of California, Berkeley.

SHELTON, J.C. *179*
Assertion in women's intercollegiate tennis singles. EdD U. of North Carolina at Greensboro, 1979.

SHICK, J.M. *180*
The effects of mental practice on selected volleyball skills for college women at the University of Minnesota. PhD U. of Minnesota, 1968.

SHIEBON, R. *181*
The effects of aerobic dancing on women's vocational self-concepts. PhD Purdue U. 1982.

SMITH, C.F. *182*
Effect of anxiety levels of women intercollegiate basketball players on their performance in a laboratory setting and a game situation. PhD Texas Woman's U. 1973.

STALLARD, M.L. *183*
Female intercollegiate basketball players' perceptions of their coaches. PhD U. of Utah, 1974.

STEWART, H.E. *184*
A test for measuring field hockey skill of college women. PED Indiana U. 1965.

THEBERGE, N. *185*
An occupational analysis of women's professional golf. PhD U. of Massachusetts, 1977.

THORPE, J.A.L. *186*
A study of intelligence and skill in relation to the success achieved by college women engaged in badminton and tennis singles competition. PhD Texas Woman's U. 1965.

TONER, M.K. *187*
The relationship of selected physical fitness, skill, and mood variables to success in female high school basketball candidates. EdD Boston U. Sch. of Educ. 1981.

ULIBARRI, V.D. *188*
The interrelationship of selected kinetic energy and vision measures in distinguishing skill level of female softball batters. PhD U. of Connecticut, 1981.

WEISS, E.S. *189*
The value and use of instructional television in teaching women beginning golfers. EdD Arizona State U. 1971.

WILSON, V.E. *190*
The effects of competitive emphasis, grading policies, and anxiety levels on the skill, knowledge, and course satisfaction of beginning women tennis players. PhD U. of Oregon, 1971.

ZARDUS, J.L. *191*
The effect of a relaxation training program on the development of badminton skills in college women. EdD Boston U. 1972.

ZIMMERMAN, P.A. *192*
The effect of selected visual aids on the learning of badminton skills by college women. PhD U. of Iowa, 1970.

23 Women in the Third World

See also **1** 228 *passim*; **4** 276, 305, 312, 1002, 1149, 1151, 1153, 1185; **19** 164, 461.

ABBOTT, S. *1*
Full-time farmers and week-end wives: change and stress among rural Kikuyu women. PhD U. of North Carolina, 1974.

ACASIO, L.C. *2*
A study of factors related to rural women's participation in development programs in Nueva Ecija, Central Luzon, Philippines. PhD Kansas State U. 1982.

ACKERMAN, S.E. *3*
Cultural process in Malaysian industrialization: a study of Malay women factory workers. PhD U. of California, San Diego, 1980.

AKHTAR, S. *4*
Theoretical and empirical evidence of female labor force participation rates in low-developed countries: a cross-cultural comparison. PhD CNAA, 1980.

ALAUDDIN, F.B. *5*
Need for development education as expressed by the rural women of Bangladesh. PhD U. of Michigan, 1979.

AL-BAADI, H.M. *6*
Social change, education, and the roles of women in Arabia. PhD Stanford U. 1982.

AL-BANNA, R.R. *7*
Planning for utilization of womenpower from secondary level education in Iraq. EdD Harvard U. 1974.

ALKADHL, A.L.B. *8*
Schools as mediators in female role formation: an ethnography of a girls' school in Baghdad. PhD State U. of New York at Buffalo, 1979.

ALLAGHI, F.A. *9*
Rural women and decision making: a case study in the Kufra Settlement project, Libya. PhD Colorado State U. 1981.

ALMANA, A.M. *10*
Economic development and its impact on the status of women in Saudi Arabia. PhD U. of Colorado at Boulder, 1981.

AL-MARZOOQ, S.M. *11*
A study of social change in Kuwait with special reference to the status of women. MA U. of Durham, 1975.

ALONSO, J.A. *12*
The domestic seamstresses of Neza Hual Coy Otl: a case study of feminine overexploitation in a marginal urban area. PhD New York U. 1979.

ALPHONSO, V.I. *13*
Female education in Bengal. MA U. of London, King's Coll. 1981.

AMECHI, E.E.A. *14*
The legal status of Nigerian women with special reference to marriage. PhD U. of London, LSE, 1980.

ANDERSON, J.M. *15*
The middle-class woman in the family and the community, Lima, Peru. PhD Cornell U. 1978.

ANDORS, E.B. *16*
The Rodi: female associations among the Gurung of Nepal. PhD Columbia U. 1976.

ARENAS DE COSTA, D.M. *17*
The female labor force in Venezuela: factors determining labor force participation rates. PhD Ohio State U. 1980.

ARNEY-EBEID, F.J. *18*
The social effects of the employment of women in the Egyptian textile industry. DPhil, U. of Oxford, 1981.

ARNOLD, M. *19*
Mexican women: the anatomy of a stereotype in a mestizo village. PhD U. of Florida, 1973.

ARNTSEN, A. *20*
Women and social change in Tunisia (2 vols). PhD Georgetown U. 1977.

ASHRAF, S.H. *21*
Non-formal education and the integration of women into rural development: a statistical analysis of project design; case study: Iran. PhD Michigan State U. 1978.

ASOMANI, C.A.G. *22*
A descriptive survey of the university women of Ghana and their attitudes towards the women's liberation movement. EdD George Washington U. 1977.

AUERBACH, L.S. 23
Women's domestic power: a study of women's roles in a Tunisian town. PhD U. of Illinois at Urbana–Champaign, 1980.

AUMAITRE, L.A. 24
The ideas of Teresa de la Parra on the social development of women in Venezuela. PhD New York U. 1980.

AZINGE, D.F. 25
The education of women and girls in Nigeria: a survey. MEd U. of Hull, 1972.

BABB, F.E. 26
Women and marketing in Huaraz, Peru: the political economy of petty commerce. PhD State U. of New York at Buffalo, 1981.

BALAKRISHNAN, R. 27
Productive activities and economic contributions to family income of El Salvador women. PhD Ohio State U. 1981.

BARNETT, W.K. 28
An ethnographic description of Sanleitsun, Taiwan, with emphasis on women's roles overcoming research problems caused by the presence of a great tradition. PhD Michigan State U. 1970.

BARTHEL, D.L. 29
The impact of development on women's status in Senegal. PhD Harvard U. 1977.

BAUER, J.L. 30
Changes in the behavior and consciousness of Iranian women (1963–1978): a social structural application of social learning theory (2 vols). PhD Stanford U. 1981.

BAY, E.G. 31
The royal women of Abomey. PhD Boston U. Grad. Sch. 1977.

BENNETT, L. 32
Mother's milk and mother's blood: the social and symbolic roles of women among the Brahmans and Chetris of Nepal. PhD Columbia U. 1977.

BERGER-SOFER, R.E. 33
Pious women: a study of the women's roles in a Hasidic and pious community: Meah She'Arim. PhD Rutgers U. 1979.

BICK, M.J.A. 34
Power and the allocation of rights in women in African societies. PhD Columbia U. 1974.

BIERY, A.S. 35
Domestic authority and female autonomy in matrilineal societies. PhD Northwestern U. 1971.

BIRAIMAH, K.C. 36
The impact of gender-differentiated education on Third World women's expectations: a Togolese case study. PhD State U. of New York at Buffalo, 1982.

BIRI, E.A. 37
Men's attitudes toward women's roles in Libya: an indicator of social change. PhD U. of Akron, 1981.

BLACHMAN, M.J. 38
Eve in an adamocracy: the politics of women in Brazil. PhD New York U. 1976.

BLEDSOE, C.H. 39
Women and marriage in Kpelle society. PhD Stanford U. 1976.

BOONE, S.A. 40
Sowo art in Sierra Leone: the mind and power of women on the plane of the aesthetic disciplines. PhD Yale U. 1979.

BOSSEN, L.H. 41
Women and dependent development: a comparison of women's economic and social roles in Guatemala. PhD State U. of New York at Albany, 1978.

BRADLEY, S.C. 42
Tolai women and development. PhD U. of London, University Coll. 1982.

BRADNEY, J. 43
The status of women among the southern Bantu. BSc U. of Oxford, 1950.

BRANDOW, S.K. 44
The role of women in a kibbutz. PhD Temple U. 1974.

BROWN, S.E. 45
Coping with poverty in the Dominican Republic: women and their mates. PhD U. of Michigan, 1972.

BROWN, J.C.K. 46
A cross-cultural study of female initiation rites. PhD Harvard U. 1962.

BROWN, P. 47
Language interaction and sex roles in a Mayan community: a study of politeness and the position of women. PhD U. of California, Berkeley, 1979.

BRUESKE, J.M. 48
The Petapa Zapotecs of the inland isthmus of Tehuantepec, Oaxaca, Mexico: an ethnographic description and an exploration into the status of women. PhD U. of California, Riverside, 1976.

BUCHMEIER, F.X. 49
The childbearing years, common residence with parents, and women's work in Korea. PhD U. of Hawaii, 1979.

BULLOUGH, C.H.W. 50
Traditional birth attendants in Malawi: the development of a training programme. MD U. of Glasgow, 1979.

BUTLER, L.M. 51
Bases of women's influence in the rural Malawian domestic group. PhD Washington State U. 1976.

BUZZARD, S.A. 52
Women's status and wage employment in Kisumu, Kenya. PhD American U. 1982.

BYBEE, D.A. 53
Muslim peasant women of the Middle East: their sources and uses of power. PhD Indiana U. 1978.

CALLIS, M.E. 54
Tradition and change in the status of Chinese women. PhD U. of Michigan, 1946.

CHAKI-SIRCAR, M. 55
Lai Harouba: the social position and ritual status of Meitei women of Manipur, India. PhD Columbia U. 1980.

CHANEY, E.M. 56
Women in Latin American politics: the case of Peru and Chile. PhD U. of Wisconsin, 1971.

CHANG, C.-H. 57
Female labor force participation in Taiwan. PhD Ohio State U. 1978.

CHARRAD, M. 58
Women and the state: a comparative study of politics, law and the family in Tunisia, Algeria and Morocco. PhD Harvard U. 1980.

CHAUDHARY, R.L. 59
The Hindu woman's limited estate with special reference to alienation and surrender. LLM U. of London, Sch. of Oriental and African Studies and King's Coll. 1959.

CHIANG, C.H. 60
Female labor force participation in socio-cultural perspective: Taiwan as a case. PhD U. of Chicago, 1981.

CHIPP, S.A. 61
The role of women elites in a modernizing country: the All Pakistan Women's Association. PhD Syracuse U. 1970.

CHO, H. 62
An ethnographic study of a female divers' village in Korea: focused on the sexual division of labor. PhD U. of California, Los Angeles, 1979.

COHEN, L.M. 63
Colombian professional women as innovators of culture change. PhD Catholic U. of America, 1966.

COLGATE, S.H. 64
Midwifery, mothering and behavioral assessments of African neonates. PhD U. of Illinois at the Medical Center, 1981.

CONTON, L. 65
Women's roles in a man's world: appearance and reality in a lowland New Guinea village. PhD U. of Oregon, 1977.

CORMACK, M.L. 66
Traditional patterns in the interiorization of the ideals of womanhood by Hindu girls. PhD Columbia U. 1951.

DANCZ, V.H. 67
Women's auxiliaries and party politics in western Malaysia. PhD Brandeis U. 1981.

DARWISH, M.A.R.M. 68
Factors affecting the education of women in the UAR (Egypt): a historical and comparative study of women's education below the university level. MA U. of London, Inst. of Educ. 1963.

DAVIN, D. 69
Women in China: policy developments from the 1930s to the 1950s. PhD U. of Leeds, 1974.

DAVIS, S.S. 70
Formal and nonformal roles of Moroccan village women. PhD U. of Michigan, 1978.

DE GRYS, M.S. 71
Women's role in a north coast fishing village in Peru: a study in male dominance and female subordination. PhD New Sch. for Social Research, 1973.

DE SAGASTI, H.E.E. 72
Social implications of adult literacy: a study among migrant women in Peru. PhD U. of Pennsylvania, 1972.

DESHON, S.K. 73
Women's position on a Yucatecan Henequen hacienda. PhD Yale U. 1959.

DEY, J.M. 74
Women and rice in the Gambia: the impact of irrigated rise development projects on the farming system. PhD U.of Reading, 1980.

DHINDSA, R.K. 75
Changing status of women in rural India. PhD U. of Illinois at Urbana–Champaign, 1968.

DINOVITZER-BASIS, D. 76
Transformations of the female labour force in the context of peripheral capitalism: the case of Chile. PhD U. of London, LSE, 1981.

DIRASSE, L. 77
The socioeconomic position of women in Addis Ababa: the case of prostitution. PhD Boston U. Grad. Sch. 1978.

DISSAROJANA, S. 78
The household context and women's labor force participation in Indonesia. PhD U. of Pennsylvania, 1982.

DOBERT, M. 79
Civil and political participation of women in French-speaking West Africa. PhD George Washington U. 1970.

DORSKY, S.J. 80
Women's lives in a North Yemeni highlands town. PhD Case Western Reserve U. 1981.

DOUGLAS, J.M. 81
Domestic servants in Kampala: anomaly or status symbol? MPhil U. of Edinburgh, 1979.

DURANT-GONZALEZ, V. *82*
Role and status of rural Jamaican women: higglering and mothering. PhD U. of California, Berkeley, 1976.

DURRANT, N.R. *83*
The changing social position of women in Tunisia since independence in 1956. BLitt U. of Oxford, 1975.

DWYER, D.H. *84*
Women's conflict behavior in a traditional Moroccan setting: an interactional analysis. PhD Yale U. 1973.

EADIE, F.A.W. *85*
The legal status of women in Latin America: an International Women's Year résumé. PhD U. of Miami, 1977.

EARLY, E.A. *86*
Baladi women of Cairo: sociability and therapeutic action. PhD U. of Chicago, 1980.

ECOMA E.E. *87*
Maternal and child care in a developing Nigerian community. MD U. of St Andrews, 1963.

EHLERS, T.B. *88*
La Sampedrana: women and development in a Guatemalan town. PhD U. of Colorado at Boulder, 1980.

EILAM, T. *89*
Women in relation to cattle among the Bahima of Uganda. PhD U. of Manchester, 1969.

EL-BUSTANI, A. *90*
Problems facing a selected group of Iraqi women. PhD Columbia U. 1956.

EL-JUNI, A.M. *91*
Determinants of female labor force participation: the case of Libya. PhD Oklahoma State U. 1978.

ELLOVICH, R.S. *92*
Adaptations to the urban setting: Dioula women in Gagnoa, Ivory Coast. PhD Indiana U. 1979.

ELTON, C. *93*
The economic determinants of female migration in Latin America. MA U. of Sussex, 1970.

ENGWALL, M.S. *94*
The status of women in a matrilineal society. PhD Hartford Seminary Foundation, 1941.

ESSIEN, R.A. *95*
Perceptions of Nigerian college students towards the role of women in Nigerian development. EdD U. of Southern California, 1981.

ESTEB, N. *96*
Sex and labor force participation in Brazil. PhD U. of Washington, 1979.

EVERETT, J.G.M. *97*
The Indian women's movement in comparative perspective. PhD U. of Michigan, 1976.

FARNOODYMEHER, N.S. *98*
Psychosocial survey of attitudes towards equal rights for women (Iran). PhD United States International U. 1975.

FARRAG, A.A.M. *99*
Mechanisms of social control amongst the Mzabite women of Beni-Isguen. MA U. of London, LSE, 1969.

FATTAH, Y.M. *100*
The role of rural women in family decision-making in Iraq. PhD U. of Tennessee, 1981.

FERNANDEZ, M.P. *101*
'Chavalas de Maquiladora': a study of the female labor force in Ciudad Juarez' offshore production plants. PhD Rutgers U. 1980.

FINLINSON, H.A. *102*
Women, work and reproduction: a study of female status in a lowland Guatemalan community. PhD U. of California, Davis, 1978.

FISCHER, A. *103*
The role of the Trukese mother and its effect on child training. PhD Radcliffe Coll. 1957.

FONG, M.S. *104*
Social and economic correlates of female labor force participation in West Malaysia. PhD U. of Hawaii, 1974.

FRUZZETTI, L.M. *105*
Conch-shells bangles, iron bangles: an analysis of women, marriage and ritual in Bengali society. PhD U. of Minnesota, 1975.

GAGNÉ, E. *106*
Stratégies et développement en éducation proposées par l'Unesco pour le Bangladesh – recherche des implications pour l'éducation de la femme bengalie. PhD U. of Ottowa, 1977.

GAILEY, C.W. *107*
'Our history is written . . . in our mats': state formation and the status of women in Tonga. PhD New Sch. for Social Research, 1981.

GATELEY, I.M. *108*
The formal education of African women and girls in Uganda: some social factors and social changes involved in its acceptance. PhD U. of London (External), 1971.

GERHOLD, C.R. *109*
Factors relating to educational opportunity for women residents of the Malay Peninsula. PhD Cornell U. 1971.

GHOLIZADEH-SARABI, A. *110*
The status of women in an Azarbayjáni village, Iran, with special reference to carpet manufacture. PhD U. of Edinburgh, 1982.

GILAD, L.M. *111*
Yemeni Jewish women: the changing family in an Israeli new town. PhD U. of Cambridge, 1983.

GILLISON, G. 112
'There is no other sweet life': perceptions of the female role in a New Guinea society. PhD City U. of New York, 1978.

GILPIN, S.M. 113
Female wage-earners in Kinshasa. BLitt U. of Oxford, 1971.

GINAT, J. 114
A rural Arab community in Israel: marriage patterns and woman's status. PhD U. of Utah, 1975.

GIORGIS, B.W. 115
Maternal and child health services in Tanzania: the role of women and its implications on maternal and child health. PhD Howard U. 1979.

GLYNN, A.L. 116
A view of women in Latin America with a focus on emerging feminism in Peru. EdD Fairleigh Dickinson U. 1978.

GOODALE, J.C. 117
The Tiwi women of Melville Island, Australia. PhD U. of Pennsylvania, 1959.

GOULD, T.F. 118
The educated woman in a developing country: professional Zaïrian women in Lubumbashi. PhD Union Grad. Sch. 1976.

GOULD-MARTIN, K. 119
Women asking women: an ethnography of health care in rural Taiwan. PhD Rutgers U. 1976.

GOUVEIA, A.J. 120
Student-teachers in Brazil: a study of young women's career choices. PhD U. of Chicago, 1962.

GREEN, I.J. 121
Women leaders of the Philippines: social backgrounds and political attitudes. PhD Syracuse U. 1970.

GRIFFITHS, J.F.S. 122
Girls' initiation ceremony among the Amapondo. DipAnthrop* U. of Cambridge, 1931.

GUERRERO, S.H. 123
Marital and family satisfaction among women migrants in Brasilia. PhD U. of Wisconsin, 1972.

HAGAMAN, B.L. 124
Beer and matriliny: the power of women in a West African society. PhD Northeastern U. 1977.

HALL, M.J. 125
The position of women in Egypt and Sudan as reflected in feminist writings since 1900. PhD U. of London, Sch. of Oriental and African Studies, 1978.

HALLAWANI, E.A.-R. 126
Working women in Saudi Arabia: problems and solutions. Phd, Claremont Grad. Sch.

HAMMAM, M. 127
Women workers and the practice of freedom as education: the Egyptian experience. PhD U. of Kansas, 1977.

HAMMOND, J.D. 128
'Tifaifai' of eastern Polynesia: meaning and communications in a women's reintegrated art form. PhD U. of Illinois at Urbana–Champaign, 1981.

HAMMOUD, H.R. 129
Personal, family and societal factors associated with Lebanese youth's attitudes toward the roles of women. PhD Case Western Reserve U. 1981.

HARVEY, Y.K. 130
Korean Mudang: socialization experiences of six female Shamans. PhD U. of Hawaii, 1976.

HEIN, C.R. 131
Industrialisation in Mauritius and the female labour force. PhD U. of Birmingham, 1982.

HENDERSON, H.K. 132
Ritual roles of women in Onitsha Ibo society. PhD U. of California, Berkeley, 1969.

HENDREY, R.J. 133
Ideal and practice: some aspects of family life in Central Mexico. BLitt U. of Oxford, 1975.

HEYMAN, B.N. 134
Urbanization and the status of women in Peru. PhD U. of Wisconsin, 1974.

HIGDON, J.M. 135
Ghanian schoolgirls: a study of opportunism as a social norm in a changing society. MA U. of Newcastle upon Tyne, 1978.

HO, T.J. 136
The labor market for married women in the rural Philippines. PhD Stanford U. 1980.

HOFFER, C.P. 137
Acquisition and exercise of political power by a woman paramount chief of the Sherbro people. PhD Bryn Mawr Coll. 1971.

HOLLANDER, N.C. 138
Women in the political economy of Argentina. PhD U. of California, Los Angeles, 1974.

HOLLANDER, R.B. 139
Out of tradition: the position of women in Kenya and Tanzania during the pre-colonial, colonial and post-independence eras. PhD American U. 1979.

HOLMES, B.E. 140
Women and Yucatec kinship. PhD Tulane U. 1978.

HONIG, E. 141
Women cotton mill workers in Shanghai, 1919–1949. PhD Stanford U. 1982.

HUBBELL, L.J.M. 142
The network of kinship, friendship, and 'compad-

razgo' among the middle-class women of Uruapan, Michoacan, Mexico. PhD U. of California, Berkeley, 1972.

HUNTER, P.A. *143*
The status of Chinese women in southeast Asia. MA U. of London, LSE, 1965.

IBRAHIM, B.L. *144*
Social change and the industrial experience: women as production workers in the urban Egypt. PhD Indiana U. 1980.

IZADPARAST, A.A. *145*
Position of women in Muslim Arab societies. PhD U. of Utah, 1974.

JABBRA, N.W. *146*
The role of women in a Lebanese community. PhD Catholic U. of America, 1975.

JACKAL, P.S. *147*
Development of policy for Yenan women, 1937–1947. PhD U. of Pennsylvania, 1979.

JOHNSON, A.G. *148*
Modernization and social change: attitudes toward women's roles in Mexico City. PhD U. of Michigan, 1972.

JOHNSON, C.J. *149*
Nigerian women and British colonialism: the Yoruba example with selected biographies. PhD Northwestern U. 1978.

JOHNSON, K.A. *150*
The politics of women's rights and family reform in China. PhD U. of Wisconsin–Madison, 1976.

JOHNSON, M.A. *151*
Black gold: goldsmiths, jewelry and women in Senegal. PhD Stanford U. 1980.

JONES, S.K. *152*
Domestic organization and the importance of female labor among the Limbu of Eastern Nepal. PhD State U. of New York at Stony Brook, 1977.

JOPLING, C.F. *153*
Women weavers of Yalálag: their art and its process. PhD U. of Massachusetts, 1973.

KANCHANASINITH, K. *154*
A comparative study of midwifery knowledge, attitudes, and practices of trained and untrained traditional birth attendants in Lampang Province, Thailand. DrPH Tulane U. Sch. of Public Health and Tropical Medicine, 1978.

KAPUR, V. *155*
Social character of women in the changing Indian society. PhD Catholic U. of America, 1973.

KARANJA, D. *156*
Perception of marriage, and family in Nigeria: a study of Lagos market women. DPhil U. of Oxford, 1980.

KASHKOULI, H.N. *157*
Comparison of familial roles among American and Qashqai women. PhD United States International U. 1981.

KATZIR, Y. *158*
The effects of resettlement on the status and role of Yemeni Jewish women: the case of Ramat Oranim, Israel. PhD U. of California, Berkeley, 1976.

KEINO, E.R.C. *159*
The contribution of *harambee* (self-help) to the development of post-primary education in Kenya: the case of Sogiot girls' high school, 1969–1978. EdD Harvard U. 1980.

KELLY, E.A. *160*
Women's chance of power in two Sudanese nomadic tribes. MPhil U. of London, Sch. of Oriental and African Studies, 1972.

KENDALL, K.W. *161*
Personality development in an Iranian village: an analysis of socialization practices and the development of the woman's role. PhD U. of Washington, 1968.

KENDALL, L.M. *162*
Restless spirits: shaman and housewife in Korean ritual life. PhD Columbia U. 1979.

KERNS, V.B. *163*
Daughters bring in: ceremonial and social organization of the Black Carib of Belize. PhD U. of Illinois at Urbana–Champaign, 1977.

KHAN, I. *164*
Women's education in India. MA U. of London, Inst. of Educ. 1947.

KHUTHAILA, H.M. *165*
Developing a plan for Saudi Arabian women's higher education. PhD Syracuse U. 1981.

KIM, S. *166*
Social origins, educational attainment and family formation among Korean women. PhD Utah State U. 1979.

KLEIN, L.F. *167*
Tlingit women and town politics. PhD New York U. 1975.

KNOTTS, M.A. *168*
The social and economic factors associated with the rural-urban migration of Kenyan women. PhD Johns Hopkins U. 1977.

KOKUHIRWA, H.N. *169*
Village women and nonformal education in Tanzania: factors affecting participation. EdD U. of Massachusetts, 1982.

KOMANYI, M.I. *170*
The real and ideal participation in decision-making of Iban women: a study of a longhouse

community in Sarawak, East Malaysia. PhD New York U. 1973.

KOO, J. *171*
Korean women in widowhood. PhD U. of Missouri–Columbia, 1982.

KRAUSE, M.L. *172*
Indian professional women: factors in vocational achievement. PhD Arizona State U. 1982.

KULAHCI, S.G. *173*
Factors influencing attitudes toward issues of women in development with special reference to Turkey. PhD Pennsylvania State U. 1981.

KUNG, L. *174*
Factory work, women, and the family in Taiwan. PhD Yale U. 1978.

LADERMAN, C.C. *175*
Conceptions and preconceptions: childbirth and nutrition in rural Malaysia. PhD Columbia U. 1979.

LAI, A.E. *176*
Peasants, proletarians and prostitutes: a preliminary investigation into the work of women of Chinese origin in peninsular Malaysia. MPhil U. of Sussex, 1981.

LAPCHAREUN, P. *177*
Adult education programmes for women in rural Thailand, with special reference to the Ministry of Education, the Ministry of the Interior, and the National Council of Women. PhD U. of Hull, 1980.

LEIS, N.B. *178*
Economic independence and Ijaw women: a comparative study of two communities in the Niger delta. PhD Northwestern U. 1964.

LEITINGER, I.A. *179*
The changing role of women in Latin America: a descriptive and theoretical analysis of six countries, 1950 to 1970. PhD U. of Denver, 1981.

LERCH, P.J.B. *180*
Warriors of justice: a study of women's roles in Umbanda in Porto Alegre, Brazil. PhD Ohio State U. 1978.

LEVINE, N.E. *181*
The Nyinba population and social structure in a polyandrous society. PhD U. of Rochester, 1977.

LEWANDO-HUNDT, G.A. *182*
Women's power and settlement: the effects of settlement on the position of Negev Bedouin women. MPhil U. of Edinburgh, 1978.

LEWIS, M.A. *183*
Female entrepreneurial styles: an examination of coastal Fante businesswomen. PhD U. of Washington, 1977.

LIBBY, D. *184*
Girls' puberty observances among northern Athabascans. PhD U. of California, Berkeley, 1952.

LITZLER, B.N. *185*
Women of San Blas Atempa: an analysis of the economic role of Isthmus Zapotec women in relation to family and community. PhD U. of California, Los Angeles, 1968.

LUCAS, D.W. *186*
The participication of women in the Nigerian labor force since the 1950s with particular reference to Lagos. PhD U. of London (External), 1976.

LUSCHINSKY, M.S. *187*
The life of women in a village of north India: a study of role and status. PhD Cornell U. 1962.

MCCABE, J. *188*
The status of aging women in the Middle East: the process of change in the life cycle of rural Lebanese women. PhD Duke U. 1979.

MCCALL, D.F. *189*
The effect on family structure of changing economic activities of women in a Gold Coast town. PhD Columbia U. 1956.

MCGUIRE, J.S. *190*
Seasonal changes in energy expenditure and work patterns of rural Guatemalan women. PhD Massachusetts Inst. of Technology, 1979.

MACLAY, S.R. *191*
Women's organizations in India: voluntary associations in a developing society. PhD U. of Virginia, 1969.

MCSWEENEY, B.G. *192*
The negative impact of development on women reconsidered: a study of the women's education project in Upper Volta. PhD Tufts U., Fletcher Sch. of Law and Diplomacy, 1979.

MADJHUB, M.E. *193*
The education of females in modern Egypt. PhD U. of Manchester, 1954.

MAHER, V.A. *194*
Social stratification and the role of women in the middle Atlas of Morocco. PhD U. of Cambridge, 1973.

MALDONADO, M.R. *195*
Education and the labor force participation of Peruvian women. PhD State U. of New York at Buffalo, 1981.

MALIWA, E.N. *196*
The legal status of women in Malawi: precolonial period to 1964. PhD U. of London (External), 1971.

MARCH, K.S. *197*
The intermediacy of women: female gender symbolism and the social position of women among Tamangs and Sherpas of highland Nepal. PhD Cornell U. 1979.

MAREI, W.A.-N. 198
Female emancipation and changing political leadership: a study of five Arab countries. PhD Rutgers U. 1978.

MARGLIN, F.A. 199
Wives of the god-king: the rituals of Hindu temple courtesans. PhD Brandeis U. 1980.

MARSHALL, G.A. 200
Women, trade and the Yoruba family. PhD Columbia U. 1964.

MARSHALL, S.E. 201
The power of the veil: the politics of female status in North Africa. PhD U. of Massachusetts, 1980.

MARTIN, C.M. 202
Women job seekers in Bauchi State, Nigeria: policy options for employment and training. EdD U. of Massachusetts, 1981.

MARUM, M.E. 203
Rural women at work in Bangladesh. [Foreign aid funding.] DSW U. of California, Berkeley, 1982.

MASSELL, G.J. 204
The strategy of social change and the role of women in Soviet Central Asia: a case study in modernization and control. PhD Harvard U. 1966.

MATHEWSON, M.A. 205
Southern Ghanaian women: urban residence and migrational cycles. PhD U. of Rochester, 1973.

MAYER, U.P. 206
Bridewealth among the Abugusii. BSc U. of Oxford, 1951.

MAYNARD, E.A. 207
The women of Palin: a comparative study of Indian and Latino women in a Guatemalan village. PhD Cornell U. 1963.

MAYOU, L.E. 208
Women's work and economic power in the family: a study of two villages in West Bengal. PhD U. of Cambridge, 1983.

MEYERHOFF, E.L. 209
The socio-economic and ritual roles of Pokot women. PhD U. of Cambridge, 1982.

MILLMAN, S.R. 210
Breast feeding in Taiwan: a study of change. PhD U. of Michigan, 1982.

MIRANDA G.V. 211
Education and other determinant factors of female labor force participation in Brazil. PhD Stanford U. 1979.

MIZZI, S.O. 212
Women in Senglea: the changing role of urban, working-class women in Malta. PhD State U. of New York at Stony Brook, 1981.

MOLNAR, A.M. 213
Flexibility and option: a study of the dynamics of women's participation among the Kham Magar of Nepal. PhD U. of Wisconsin, 1980.

MOON, U.C. 214
Married women and urban employment in Korea: class differentiation in income-opportunities. PhD U. of Hawaii, 1982.

MOORE, B.E.A. 215
Some working women in Mexico: traditionalists and modernists. PhD Washington U. 1970.

MULHARE, E.M. 216
Women, work and change in rural-industrial puebla, Mexico. PhD U. of Pittsburgh, 1981.

MULLICK, I.R. 217
The education of women in India: a consideration of urgent contemporary problems. MLitt, U. of Dublin, Trinity Coll. 1960.

MUSA, A.Z. 218
Assessment of societal perceptions and attitudes toward marriage and educated Hausa women in the northern states of Nigeria. PhD Ohio U. 1981.

MUSALLAM, B.F. 219
Sex and society in Islam: the sanction and medieval techniques of birth control. PhD Harvard U. 1973.

NELSON, M.C.N. 220
Dependence and interdependence: female household heads in Mathare valley; a squatter community in Nairobi, Kenya. PhD U. of London, Sch. of Oriental and African Studies, 1978.

NJUKI, C.W. 221
Problems of access to women's education in Kenya. PhD U. of Pittsburgh, 1982.

O'CONNOR, G.A. 222
The status and roles of West African women: a study in cultural change. PhD New York U. 1964.

ODONGA, B. 223
The rights of women in property and succession in Africa, with special reference to Zambia. LLM U. Coll. Cardiff, 1982.

ODU, D.B. 224
A conceptual programme planning model for adult education programmes for women in rural areas of Nigeria through extension home economics. PhD U. of Nebraska–Lincoln, 1978.

OKONJO, I.K. 225
The role of women in social change among the Igbo of southeastern Nigeria living west of the River Niger. PhD Boston U. Grad. Sch. 1976.

OUBOUZAR, S.O. 226
Dzair: Kabyle mothers, daughters, and granddaughters in the urban environment of Algiers. PhD U. of Kansas, 1974.

OXBY C.H. 227
Sexual division and slavery in a Tuareg community: a study of dependence. PhD U. of

London, Sch. of Oriental and African Studies, 1978.

PARK, K.-N.C. *228*
Labor force participation of professional women in Korea. EdD Boston U. Sch. of Educ. 1979.

PASTNER, C.M. *229*
Dichotomization in society and culture: the women of Panjgur, Baluchistan. PhD Brandeis U. 1971.

PATEL, T.N. *230*
The social status of Indian women during the last fifty years (1900–1950). PhD U. of London, Bedford Coll. 1954.

PATNAIK, B.M. *231*
Evolution of the proprietary status of women under the common law of the Hindus with special reference to the quantum of interest in immovable property acquired by way of inheritance and partition. LLM U. of London, LSE, 1948.

PELLOW, D. *232*
Women of Accra: a study in options. PhD Northwestern U. 1974.

PER-LEE, D.A. *233*
Employment, ingenuity and family life: Rajasthani women in Delhi, India. PhD American U. 1981.

PITTIN, R.I. *234*
Marriage and alternative strategies: career patterns of Hausa women in Katsina city. PhD U. of London, Sch. of Oriental and African Studies, 1980.

POWERS, M.M.N. *235*
Oglala women in myth, ritual and reality. PhD Rutgers U. 1982.

PRACHUABMOH, C. *236*
The role of women in maintaining ethnic identity and boundaries: a case of Thai–Muslims (the Malay-speaking group) in southern Thailand. PhD U. of Hawaii, 1980.

PRASERTSRI, R. *237*
Women in the parliament of Thailand: their characteristics and attitudes. PhD U. of Mississippi, 1982.

RAHMAN, S.A. *238*
Education of women for modern Indian society: a historical study with a critique of contemporary educational thought. PhD Ohio State U. 1963.

RANDERI, K.J. *239*
The relevance of liberal arts education in terms of the role of the educated Indian woman as perceived by students, parents, alumnae and administrators. PhD U. of Southern Illinois at Carbondale, 1974.

RAO, V.N.P. *240*
Role conflict of employed mothers in Hyderabad, India. PhD Mississippi State U. 1971.

REGE, P.W. *241*
The law of *stridhana*, the Hindu woman's separate estate, with special reference to acquisition, powers of disposition and intestate succession. PhD U. of London, Sch. of Oriental and African Studies, 1960.

RIVERA, M.C. *242*
Labor force participation and day-care utilization by low-income mothers in Bogota, Colombia. PhD Brandeis U, 1979.

ROBERTSON, C.C. *243*
Social and economic change in twentieth-century Accra: Ga women. PhD U. of Wisconsin–Madison, 1974.

ROBINSON, B.S. *244*
The Ramakrishna Sarada Math: a study of a women's movement in Bengal. PhD Columbia U. 1978.

ROY, M. *245*
Ideal and compensatory roles in the life cycle of upper-class Bengali women. PhD U. of California, San Diego, 1972.

RUNTY, C.T. *246*
The political role and status of women in the Muslim world. PhD U. of Nebraska–Lincoln, 1981.

SAGEMAN, P. *247*
An examination into the present educational opportunities of Egyptian girls in Egypt. MA U. of London, King's Coll. 1937.

SALLAM, A.M.A. *248*
The return to the veil among undergraduate females at Minya University, Egypt. PhD Purdue U. 1980.

SANASARIAN, E. *249*
The women's movement as a social movement in Iran. PhD State U. of New York at Buffalo, 1980.

SANKAR, A.P. *250*
The evolution of the sisterhood in traditional Chinese society from village girls' houses to Chai T'angs in Hong Kong. PhD U. of Michigan, 1978.

SARKAR, P. *251*
The development of education among girls and women in modern India. PhD U. of London, Inst. of Educ. 1962.

SARPONG, P. *252*
Girls' nubility rites in Ashanti. BLitt U. of Oxford, 1965.

SCHOTT, A.P. *253*
The role of the traditional birth attendant during the childbearing process of rural Iranian women. PhD U. of Utah, 1978.

SCHUSTER, I.M.G. *254*
Lusaka's young women: adaptation to change. DPhil U. of Sussex, 1976.

SCOTT, J.L. *255*
Action and meaning: women's participation in the mutual aid committees, Kowloon. PhD Cornell U. 1980.

SEARIGHT, S. *256*
The use and function of tattooing on Moroccan women. MPhil U. of Edinburgh, 1979.

SEDGHI, H. *257*
Women and class in Iran, 1900–1970. PhD City U. of New York, 1982.

SEIN, S. *258*
The position of women in Hinayana Buddhist countries (Burma, Ceylon and Thailand). MA U. of London, LSE, 1959.

SELBY, R.L. *259*
Women, industrialization and change in Queretaro, Mexico. PhD U. of Utah, 1979.

SELTZER, J.P. *260*
Huasteca widows. PhD U. of Texas at Austin, 1980.

SEMERGIEFF, K.B. *261*
The changing roles of women in the People's Republic of China, 1949–1967: with a case study of Ting Ling. PhD St John's U. 1981.

SEMLER, V.J. *262*
A study of third-world family planners' views toward women's role in society: a communication perspective. PhD Indiana U. 1977.

SEN GUPTA, A. *263*
The role of women in Indian public life in modern times. PhD American U. 1958.

SHAHSHAHANI, S.M. *264*
The four seasons of the sun: an ethnography of women of Oyun, a sedentarized village of the Mamasani pastoral nomads of Iran. PhD New Sch. for Social Research, 1981.

SHILLI, M.O. *265*
Maternal employment and androgyny: a study of sex role perception of Libyan female undergraduates in the Faculty of Education. EdD U. of New Mexico, 1980.

SHRIVASTAVA, V.A. *266*
Nonformal education programmes for women in Indian villages: a study of social change and leadership patterns. EdD U. of Toronto, 1980.

SIASSI, S.F. *267*
Self and role perception among young employed Iranian women of lower-class origin. PhD U. of Pittsburgh, 1976.

SIMMONDS, M.M. *268*
Factors involved in effective dissemination of new [infant] feeding practices in rural India. MPhil U. of Reading, 1979.

SINGH, J.A. *269*
Modern draped sari replaces traditional costumes of educated Indian women and the relation of this change to the development of education and communication in India. PhD Pennsylvania State U. 1966.

SMITH, M.L. *270*
Institutionalized servitude: the female domestic servant in Lima, Peru. PhD Indiana U. 1971.

SMITH, P.S.N. *271*
Caridad y superación: women's voluntary associations in a small Colombian town. PhD U. of Oregon, 1979.

SOFFAN, L.U. *272*
The role and status of women in contemporary U.A.E. society. PhD Johns Hopkins U. 1979.

SPIRO, H.M. *273*
The role of women in farming and trading in Oyo State, Nigeria: a case study in the Fifth World. PhD U. of Manchester, 1979.

STACEY, J. *274*
Toward a theory of women, the family and revolution: an historical and theoretical analysis of the Chinese case. PhD Brandeis U. 1979.

STANDING, G.M. *275*
Labour force participation in underdeveloped countries with special reference to female economic activities. PhD U. of Cambridge, 1978.

STAUDT, K.A. *276*
Agricultural policy, political power, and women farmers in western Kenya. PhD U. of Wisconsin–Madison, 1976.

STEADY, F.C. *277*
The social position of women: selected West African countries. BLitt U. of Oxford, 1970.

STRANGE, H. *278*
The weavers of Rusila: working women in a Malay village. PhD New York U. 1971.

STRATHERN, A.M. *279*
Women's status in the Mount Hagon area: a study of marital and court disputes among the Malpa-speaking people, New Guinea. PhD U. of Cambridge, 1968.

STROBEL, M.A. *280*
Muslim women in Mombasa, Kenya, 1890–1973. PhD U. of California, Los Angeles, 1975.

STUART, M.F. *281*
Developing labor resources in the Arab world: labor activity effects from school attendance and socioeconomic background among women in the East Jordan valley. PhD U. of Southern California, 1981.

SWAIN, M.B. *282*
Ailigandi women: continuity and change in Cuna female identity. PhD U. of Washington, 1978.

SYLVAIN, M.G. 283
Haiti et ses femmes: une étude d'évolution culturelle. PhD Bryn Mawr Coll. 1941.

TAHIR, M.I. 284
The progress and development of the education of women in India. MEd, U. of Leeds, 1928.

TAPLIN, R. 285
Muslim Arab women's status in the industrialising Middle East. MA, U. of Keele, 1979.

TAPPER, N.S.S. 286
The role of women in selected pastoral Islamic societies. MPhil U. of London, Sch. of Oriental and African Studies, 1969.

TEW, M.M. 287
A comparative study of bridewealth in Africa with special reference to kinship structure and tribal organization. BSc U. of Oxford, 1948.

THADANI, V.N. 288
The forgotten factor in social change: the case of women in Nairobi, Kenya. PhD Bryn Mawr Coll. 1976.

THOMAS, S.C. 289
The women of Chile and education for a contemporary society: a study of Chilean women, their history and present status and the new demands of a society in transition. PhD Saint Louis U. 1973.

THOMSON, M.E. 290
Nonformal education for rural development: the women's training center in Senegal. PhD U. of Illinois at Urbana–Champaign, 1981.

TONGUDAI, P. 291
Women migration and employment: a study of migrant workers in Bangkok. PhD New York U. 1982.

TRULY, M.E. 292
The Baptist educational program for girls in Nigeria. PhD Southwestern Baptist Theological Seminary, 1961.

TSUNG, S.-K.F. 293
Moms, nuns and hookers: extrafamilial alternatives for village women in Taiwan. PhD U. of California, San Diego, 1978.

TURNER, J. 294
Continuity and change: a social-psychological study of sex roles and fertility among mothers and daughters in a Latin American city. PhD York U. 1977.

UCHENDU, P.K. 295
The changing cultural role of Igbo women in Nigeria, 1914–1975. PhD New York U. 1981.

ULIN, P.R. 296
Utilization of maternal and child health resources in rural Botswana. PhD U. of Massachusetts, 1976.

VAN WATERS, M. 297
The adolescent girl among primitive peoples. PhD Clark U. 1913.

VEXLER, M.J. 298
Chachahuantla, a blouse-making village in Mexico: a study of the socio-economic roles of women. PhD U. of California, Los Angeles, 1981.

WAGNER, F.E. 299
Female employment in emerging societies. PhD Syracuse U. 1967.

WAHAIB, A.A. 300
Education and status of women in the Middle East with special reference to Egypt, Tunisia and Iraq. PhD Southern Illinois U. 1970.

WALTERS, L.M. 301
An assessment of the educative and training needs of American women who work in developing countries. DPA U. of Southern California, 1982.

WATSON, V.D. 302
Agarabi female roles and family structure: a study in sociocultural change. PhD U. of Chicago, 1966.

WEINER, A.B. 303
Women of value: the main road of exchange in Kiriwinda, Trobriand Islands. PhD Bryn Mawr Coll. 1974.

WHITE, E.H. 304
Women's status in an Islamic society: the problem of Purdah. PhD U. of Denver, 1975.

WILLIAMSON, M.H. 305
Kwoma society: women and disorder. PhD U. of Cambridge, 1975.

WITKE, R.H. 306
Transformation of attitudes towards women during the May Fourth era of modern China. PhD U. of California, Berkeley, 1970.

WOORTMANN, K.A.A.W. 307
Marginal men and dominant women: kinship and sex-roles among the Bahian poor. PhD Harvard U. 1975.

WU, D.T.L. 308
Beyond the bamboo door: a psychosocial study of women and organizations in metropolitan China, 1978–1979. PhD Wright Inst. 1980.

YEOH, S.-P. 309
Informal sector participation and women's economic position in West Malaysia. PhD Duke U. 1982.

ZALATIMO, Y.N. 310
Curriculum design for a developing society: a vocational business and office education program for women in Saudi Arabia. PhD Southern Illinois U. at Carbondale, 1981.

ZIMMERMAN, C.B. 311
The meaning of the role of women in a transition from a civilization to a Fellaheen social order: a study of continuity and change in the Maya culture. PhD Saint Louis U. 1960.

Checklist of Bibliographical and Reference Sources

Women's Studies

Bibliographies and guides

General guides to bibliographies on women are:

Ballou, P.K. 'Bibliographies for research on women' *Signs 3* (2) (1977) 436–50

——*Women: a bibliography of bibliographies* (Boston: G.K. Hall, 1980)

Ritchie, M. *Women's studies: a checklist of bibliographies* (London: Mansell, 1980)

Stafford, B. 'Getting started in women's studies: a comparative review of some basic bibliographies' *Reference service review* 8 (1980) 61–67

In recent years there has been a flow of women's studies bibliographies. The following is a representative selection:

Alauudin, T.K. *Status of women and socio-economic development: a selective and annotative bibliography* (Pakistan Institute of Development Economics, 1977)

Borenstein, A. *Older women in twentieth-century America: a selected annotated bibliography* (New York: Garland, 1982)

British Film Institute *Women and film resources handbook* (Catalogue of films by women, about women and of interest to women)

Brown, D.L. *A bibliography on women's issues* (Chicago: American College of Hospital Administrators, 1981)

Caplan, A.P. 'Indian women: model and reality: a review of recent books, 1975–1979' *Women's studies international quarterly* 2, 461–79

Chaff, Sandra et al. eds *Women in medicine: an annotated bibliography of the literature on women physicians* (Metuchen, NJ: Scarecrow Press, 1978)

Dworaczek, M. *Women at work: a bibliography of bibliographies* (Monticelle, Ill: Vance Bibliographies, 1984) (One of a series of short concise bibliographies of which several have recently been devoted to women's studies)

Farley, J. *Academic women and employment discrimination: a critical annotated bibliography* (New York: State School of Industrial and Labor Relations, 1982)

Feminist Book Fair Group, *259: an introduction to women's world of books* (Official catalogue to the First International Feminist Book Fair held at Jubilee Hall, Covent Garden, London WC2 7–9 June 1984)

Fox-Genouese, E. 'Placing women in history' *New Left review* 133 (May–June 1982) (A bibliographical survey citing over 500 books, articles and theses)

Frank, G. *Women at work and in society: a selective bibliography, 1970–1975* (Geneva: International Institute for Labor Studies, 1975)

Frey, L. et al. *Women in Western European history: a select chronological, geographical and topical bibliography from antiquity to the French Revolution* (Westport, Conn.: Greenwood Press, 1982)

Harrison, C.E. *Women's movement media: a source guide* (New York and London: Bowker, 1975)

Harrison, C. *Women in American History: a bibliography* Santa Barbara, Calif. American Bibliographic Center; Oxford, Clio Press, 1979. (One of the Clio Bibliographical series based on *America: History and Life*)

Huff, C.A. 'In their own images: a study of nineteenth-century British women's manuscript diaries' PhD University of Iowa, 1984 (A descriptive bibliography of 59 manuscript diaries)

Kanner, Barbara ed. *The women of England from Anglo-Saxon times to the present: interpretative bibliographical essays* (London: Mansell, 1980)

Koih, H.C. *Korean and Japanese women: an analytic bibliographic guide* (Westport, Conn.: Greenwood Press, 1982)

Leavitt, J.A. *Women in management: an annotated bibliography and source list* (Phoenix, Az.: Oryx Press, 1982)

McKee, K.B. *Women's studies: a guide to reference sources* (University of Connecticut Library, 1977)

Megedessian, S.R. *Status of the Arab women: a selected bibliography* (Westport, Conn.: Greenwood Press, 1980)

Rushing, A.D. 'Annotated bibliography of images

of black women in black literature' *CLA Journal* *25* (1981) 234–62

Sakala, C. *Women of South Asia: a guide to resources* (Millwood, NY: Kraus, 1980)

Simmons, D.V. and Yee, S.J. *Women: a bibliography* (Suva: University of the South Pacific Library, 1982) (Women in Oceania)

Stineman, E. and Loeb, C. *Women's studies: a recommended core bibliography* (Littleton, Colo.: Libraries Unlimited, 1979)

Terris, V.R. *Women in America: a guide to information sources* (Detroit, Mich.: Gale Research Co., 1980)

UNESCO *Bibliographic guide to studies on the status of women: development and population* (New York and London: Bowker, 1983)

Wilson, C.F. *Violence against women: an annotated bibliography* (Boston, Mass.: G.K. Hall, 1980)

Women and society: a critical review of the literature with a selected bibliography (Vol. 1 compiled by Marie B. Rosenberg and Len V. Bergstrom (Beverly Hills, Cal.: Sage, 1975); Vol. 2 compiled by Jane Debes Een and Marie B. Rosenberg-Dishman (1978)

Women and work: an inventory of research (Ottawa: Canadian Research Institute for the Advancement of Women, 1978)

Women's studies: a bibliography (London: Goldsmith College Library, 1977)

Abstracting and indexing services

Abstracting

Women's Studies Abstracts (Rush Publishing Co., Rush, New York) 1972–. Quarterly. Abstracts of a high standard for approximately 200 journal articles, special issues and pamphlets in each issue also listing several hundred more items. Ephemeral publications included.

Studies on Women Abstracts (Carfax Publishing Co., Abingdon, Oxon.) March 1983–. Quarterly. 100 to 200 abstracts for journal articles, books and pamphlets. Book reviews also indexed.

Indexing

Annotated Guide to women's periodicals in the United States and Canada (Richmond, Indiana) Twice yearly. *Feminist periodicals* (University of Wisconsin, Madison, Memorial Library) Quarterly.

Bibliofem: a joint library catalogue and continuing bibliography of women Jointly sponsored by Fawcett Library, City of London Polytechnic and Equal Opportunities Commission Library, Manchester) 1978–. Monthly. Cumulated microfiche alphabetical author/title, classified and subject indexes.

On-line searching

Falk, J.D. 'The new technology for research in European women's history: "on-line" bibliographies' *Signs* 9 (1) (1983) 120–133. Surveys the problems of on-line data searching in women's studies: very useful.

English-language journals

Atlantis: a women's studies journal (Mount Saint Vincent University, Halifax, Nova Scotia) 1975–. Twice yearly. Text in English and French. Book reviews.

Canadian woman studies (formerly *Canadian women's studies*) (York University, Centennial College published by Inanna Publications, Downsview, Ontario). 1978–. Quarterly. Book reviews.

Feminist issues (Transaction Periodicals Consortium, Rutgers University, New Brunswick).

Feminist review (Feminist review Collective) 1979–. Three times a year. Book reviews.

Feminist studies (Women's Studies Program, University of Maryland) 1972–. Three times a year. Book reviews.

Hecate: women's interdisciplinary journal (English Dept., University of Queensland). Book reviews.

International Council of Women. Newsletter (I.C.W., Paris) 1972–. Three times a year. Text in English and French. Book reviews.

International journal of women's studies (Eden Press Women's Publications, Montreal) 1978–. Four times a year. Book reviews and abstracts.

M/F: a feminist journal 1978–. Twice yearly. Book reviews.

MS: the new magazine for women (MS Magazine Corp.) 1972–. Monthly. Book reviews.

Plexus (Feminist Publicity Alliance, Oakland, Cal.) 1974–. Monthly. Book, play and film reviews.

Psychology of women quarterly (Human Sciences Press) 1976–. Book reviews.

Quest (Washington): a feminist quarterly. (PO Box 8843, Washington DC2) 1974–. Book and film reviews.

Resources for feminist research (Ontario Institute for Studies on Education, Toronto) 1972–. Quarterly notes on research, bibliographies, etc.

Sage: a scholarly journal on black women (Sage Women's Educational Press, Atlanta, Georgia) 1984–. Twice yearly. Book, film and play reviews.

Second wave: feminist journal of literature and radical politics (Second wave, PO Box 344, Cambridge, Mass.) 1971–. Quarterly. Book reviews.

Sex roles (Plenum Press) 1974–. Quarterly. Book reviews.

Signs: journal of women in culture and society (University of Chicago Press) 1975–. Quarterly. Focus on social sciences and humanities. Book reviews, surveys of ongoing research, notices on archives, review essays.

Spare rib (27 Clerkenwell Close, London EC1) 1972–. Monthly. Book reviews.

Trouble and strife (PO Box MT16 Leeds LS17 5PY) 1985–. Quarterly.

Women: a journal of liberation (3028 Greenmount Ave., Baltimore) 1969–. Quarterly. Book and film reviews.

Women and health: journal of women's health care (Haworth Press, New York) 1978–. Quarterly. Book reviews.

Women and history (Haworth Press, New York) 1982–. Quarterly. Book reviews; abstracts; bibliography.

Women and literature: a journal of women writers and the literary treatment of women (Holmes & Meier, New York). Annual. Includes an annual bibliography.

Women and politics (Haworth Press, New York) 1980–. Quarterly. Book reviews.

Women's review (20 Micheldever Road, London SE12 8LX). September 1985–. Book reviews.

Women's studies (Gordon & Breach) 1972–. 3 times a year. Book reviews.

Women's studies international forum (formerly Quarterly) (Pergamon Press) 1978–. Bimonthly. Multi-disciplinary journal for the rapid publication of research communications and review articles in women's studies. Each issue has a news and views supplement, *Feminist forum*.

Women and therapy: a feminist quarterly of research and opinion (Haworth Press, New York) 1982–. Quarterly. Book reviews.

Journals on microfilm include the Harvester Press collections *Rare political and reforming journals for and by women* (period 1870–1928) and *Sexual politics in Britain* (including runs of *Spare rib, Sappho* and *Women's struggle*).

Biographical directories

The Biographical dictionary of British feminists, compiled by Olive Banks (Brighton: Wheatsheaf Press, 1985–). With the projected publication of vol. 1: 1820–1930 later in 1985 this promises to be an important bibliographical sourcebook.

A directory of British and American women writers, 1660–1800 edited by Janet Todd (London, Methuen, 1985)

Encyclopaedia of women in India, edited by B.K. Vashista (New Delhi: Praveen Encyclopaedia Publications, 1976) (Pt 3: Biographies).

The Europa biographical directory of British women edited by Anne Crawford et al. (London: Europa, 1983)

The Macmillan dictionary of women's biography: compiled and edited by Jennifer S. Uglow and Frances Hinton. (London: Macmillan, 1982) (with excellent clear introduction to sources).

Notable American Women, 1607–1950: a biographical directory edited by Edward T. Jones et al. (Cambridge, Mass.: Belknap Press of Harvard University 3 vols.)

The world Who's Who of Women 8th edn. (Soham, Ely: International Biographical Centre, 1985) 5000 entries.

Statistical handbooks

Handbook of international data on women compiled by Elisec Boulding et al. (Beverley Hills, Cal.: Sage 1976)

Principal specialist libraries and collections

United Kingdom

Feminist Library and Information Centre (formerly Women's Research & Resources Centre) Hungerford House, Victoria Embankment, London WC2N 6PA. Founded in 1975 as 'major agency for the collection and distribution of feminist research material in the United Kingdom'. 4000 books and pamphlets, 700 runs of periodicals, 600 unpublished papers and reports; a large collection of ephemera from the Women's Liberation Movement. Compiles an index to feminist research in United Kingdom and abroad. Distributes a Newsletter every two months with information on women's studies courses and classes.

A Woman's Place Women's Liberation Information Service housed on the ground floor of Hungerford House, below the Feminist Library.

Fawcett Library Until 1977 this was managed by the Fawcett Society, direct descendant of Britain's first women's suffrage society. It is now housed in the Library of the City of London Polytechnic at Calcutta House. 45,000 books and pamphlets, 700 periodicals, papers of many women's organizations, ephemera covering the period 1852 to 1940. Special collections include *Cavendish Bentinck Collection* (antiquarian collection including much suffrage material and progressive literature of late nineteenth and early twentieth centuries); Library of the *Josephine Butler Society* – covering prostitution, psychiatry of sex, government reports and society archives; and *Sadd Brown* collection concerning Commonwealth women.

Equal Opportunities Commission Information Centre Based in Manchester, established in 1977. 14,000 books and pamphlets, 250 periodicals, press-cuttings collection, government reports, statistical material, ephemeral material (badges, posters and AV material). Compiles reading lists of un-sexist children's literature; subject bibliographies; register of research in progress. *Document bulletin* published fortnightly – record of all Women Studies courses and conferences. Produced *Equal opportunities international* since 1983.

Feminist Archive Founded in 1978 and housed in the University of Bath Library as a regional reference library and museum of women's work, and a repository of books, research papers, manuscripts and ephemera – leaflets, posters, photographs.

Gertrude Tuckwell Collection Housed in the Trades Union Congress Library – important for the study of trade union and women's movements in the period 1890–1920. Microfilm copy available.

A full survey of library collections and archival sources in the United Kingdom is to be found in *Women: 1870–1928: a select guide to printed and archival sources in the United Kingdom* by Margaret Barrow (London: Mansell, 1981).

North America

Arthur and Elizabeth Schlesinger Library on the History of Women in America Radcliffe College, Cambridge, Mass. Formerly known as The Women's Archives. 12,000 vols. with emphasis on women in the USA, women's rights and suffrage. Catalogue has been published by G.K. Hall.

Women's History Research Center Berkeley, Calif. Microfilm form of the collection of University of Wyoming Archive of Contemporary History, collection of women's periodicals at Northwestern University Library.

Northwestern University Library, Women's Collection International coverage of Women's Liberation Movement from early 1960s to the present.

Gerritsen Collection 'La Femme et al Feminisme' Now in Kenneth Spencer Research Library, University of Kansas, Lawrence, Kansas. Formerly housed at John Crerar Library. Especially strong in late nineteenth and early twentieth century European women's periodicals and newspapers. Published catalogue exists.

Sophia Smith Collection, Women's History Archive Smith College, Northampton, Mass.

Business and Professional Women's Foundation Library Washington, DC. 3500 vols – including manuscripts, audiotapes and microfilm collection.

Ella Strong Denison Library Claremont Colleges, Claremont, Calif. Emphasis on women in Westward movement. 2000 vols.

Wollman Library, Barnard College Columbia University, New York. 2300 vols. – especially collection of nearly 2000 rare editions of books by American women.

Herstory: microfilm collection of documents on women in history (Collections from Berkeley, and Chicago).

Two excellent guides to American collections are *Biblioteca femina: a herstory of book collections concerning women* by Maryann Turner (Warrensburg, New York: Author, 1978), and *Women in special collections* edited by Suzanne Hildenbrand and Lee Ash (New York: Haworth Press, 1984).

2 Dissertations

General guides

Borchard, D.H. and Thawlry, J.D. *Guide to the availability of theses* (London: Saur, 1981)

Davinson, D. *Theses and dissertations as information sources* (London: Bingley, 1977)

Reynolds, M.M. *A guide to theses and dissertations* (Detroit, Mich.: Gale, 1975; 2nd revised edn. in preparation)

Britain and Ireland

Three recent publications have greatly eased retrospective searching: *Retrospective index to theses of Great Britain and Ireland, 1710–1950*, Vol. 1: *Social sciences and humanities*, edited by R.R. Bilboul and F.L. Kent (Oxford: Clio Press, 1975); *History theses, 1901–1970: historical research for higher degrees in the universities of the United Kingdom*, compiled by P.M. Jacobs (London: Institute of Historical Research, 1976); and *History theses 1971–1980*, compiled by Joyce M. Horn (1984).

Since 1951 the standard checklist has been *Index to theses accepted for higher degrees by the universities of Great Britain and Ireland* published by ASLIB. The use of this index has been hampered by the lack of a detailed subject index. However, since volume 27 such a detailed index has been provided, and the appearance of *Abstracts of theses* since volume 26 has greatly helped to define the subject area of theses. Regrettably, there is not yet a complete coverage of all theses by this microfiche abstract service.

Added to the ASLIB index is *Historical research for university degrees in the United Kingdom. Part I: theses completed*, published annually by the Institute of Historical Research, University of London. This is very useful with its detailed subject index and more rapid and regular publication. However, it does have the failing of not always being reliable in the citation of titles. It is restricted to the field of historical research.

Subject bibliographies relating to the British Isles and Ireland include:

Bell, S. Peter *Dissertations on British history, 1815–1914: an index to British and American theses* (Metuchen, NJ: Scarecrow Press, 1974)

Gilbert, V.F. *Labour and social history theses: American, British and Irish university theses and dissertations in the field of British and Irish labour history, presented between 1900 and 1978* (London: Mansell, 1982) (with annual supplements in the Autumn issue of the *Bulletin of the Society for the Study of Labour History*)

Lawler, Unity R.E. *North West theses and dissertations, 1950–1978: a bibliography* (Lancaster: Centre for North West Regional Studies, University of Lancaster, 1981) (Supplement for 1979–1984 in preparation)

Wyke, Terry *Checklist of theses on the history of Lancashire* (Manchester: Manchester Polytechnic, 1979)

North America

A long-established full abstracting service has greatly eased access to American dissertations. The *Comprehensive dissertations index, 1861–1972* published in 37 volumes by Xerox University Microfilms in 1973 gave a keyword index to 417,000 theses. *Dissertations Abstracts International* has given an abstracting access to American dissertations since 1938. First known as *Microfilm Abstracts*, later *Dissertation Abstracts* it was divided into A and B series in 1969, A series covering the social sciences and humanities. Since 1969 it has become International with series C including a partial coverage of European universities from 1977. Searching Dissertation Abstracts International is greatly helped by the *Dissertation Abstracts On-Line* (formerly Comprehensive Dissertations Index) data base through the Dialog host. This data base corresponds to the coverage in *Dissertations Abstracts International, American Doctoral Dissertations, Masters Abstracts* and *Comprehensive Dissertation Index*. DAI is complemented by *Index to American doctoral dissertations* giving a complete institutional coverage. Other guides to American dissertations include: *Dissertations in history: an index to dissertations completed in history departments of United States and Canadian universities* compiled by W.F. Kuehl. Vol. 1: 1875–1960 (1965) and vol. 2: 1961–1970 (1972). Its detailed subject index makes this an invaluable guide. Canadian theses can also be traced in the Canadian national bibliography *Canadiana*, in the Canadian National Library's *Canadian theses on microfiche*, and in *Canadian graduate theses, 1919–1967 (covering economics, business and industrial relations*) by W.D. Wood, L.A. Kelly and P. Kumar (Kingston, Ontario: Industrial Relations Research Center, Queen's University, 1970).

Subject and regional bibliographies

Several bibliographies of dissertations covering specific subjects and regions have been published in recent years.

Africa

Theses on Africa accepted by universities in the United Kingdom and Ireland (Cambridge: Heffer for SCOLMA, 1964), covering the period 1920–1962

McIwaine, J.S. St. J. *Theses on Africa, 1963–1975 accepted by universities in the United Kingdom and Ireland*. (London: Mansell, 1978)

Asia

Bloomfield, B.C. *Theses on Asia accepted by universities in the United Kingdom and Ireland, 1887–1964* (London: Cass, 1967) (with annual supplements in the *Bulletin of British Orientalists* for the period 1965–1969)

Case, M.H. *South Asian history, 1750–1950: a guide to periodicals, dissertations and newspapers*. (Princeton: Princeton University Press, 1968) (includes American, British, Indian and Australasian theses)

Gopal, K. *Theses on the Indian sub-continent, 1877–1971: an annotated bibliography of dissertations in social sciences and humanities accepted by the universities of Australia, Canada, Great Britain and Ireland and United States of America*; compiled by Krishnan Gopal; edited by Dhanpat Rai. (Delhi: Hindustan Publishing Co., 1977)

Gordon, L.M.D. and Shulman, F.L. *Doctoral dissertations on China: a bibliography of studies in western languages, 1945–1970*. (Seattle: University of Washington Press for the Association of Asian Studies, 1972)

Jackson, J.C. *Recent higher degree theses on social, political and economic aspects of South East Asia presented in the universities of the United Kingdom and the Universities of Malaya and Singapore*. (Hull: University of Hull, Dept. of Geography, 1966)

Sardesai, D.R. and Sardessai, B.D. *Theses and dissertations on South East Asia: an international bibliography in social sciences, education and fine arts*. (Zug: Inter Documentation, 1970) (includes British, American and Australasian theses)

Shulman, F.J. *Japan and Korea: an annotated bibliography of doctoral dissertation in Western languages, 1877–1969*. (London: Cass, 1970)

——*Doctoral dissertations on Japan and Korea, 1969–1979: an annotated bibliography of studies in Western languages*. (Seattle: University of Washington Press, 1982)

——*Doctoral dissertations on South Asia, 1966–1970: an annotated bibliography covering North America, Europe and Australia*. (Ann Arbor: Centre for South and South East Asian Studies, University of Michigan, 1971)

Latin America and the Caribbean

Zubatsky, D.S. *Doctoral dissertations in history and the social sciences in Latin America and the Caribbean accepted by universities in the United Kingdom, 1920–1972*. (London: Institute of Latin American Studies, University of London, 1973)

——*Theses in Latin American studies at British universities in progress and completed* (published annually since 1966 by the Institute of Latin American Studies, University of London)

Middle East

Shulman, F.J. *American and British doctoral dissertations on Israel and Palestine in modern times.* (Ann Arbor: Xerox University Microfilms, 1973)

Sluglett, P. *Theses on Islam, the Middle East and North-West Africa, 1880–1978 accepted by universities in the United Kingdom and Ireland.* (London: Mansell, 1983)

USSR

Dossick, J.J. *Doctoral research on Russia and the Soviet Union.* (New York: New York University Press, 1960) (1900–1959)

——*Doctoral research on Russia and the Soviet Union,* 1960–1975. (New York: Garland, 1976) (covers American, Canadian and British theses) (annual listings in *Slavic Review* of American, Canadian and British university theses)

Education

Theses and dissertations in the history of education presented at British and Irish universities, 1900–1976, compiled by Victor F. Gilbert and Colin Holmes. (Lancaster: History of Education Society, 1979)

Register of theses on educational topics in universities in Ireland, compiled by John Coolahan (et al). (Galway: Officina Typographica for the Educational Studies Association of Ireland, 1980) (with annual supplements)

Research in the history of education (History of Education Society) (annual indexes to British and Irish University theses and dissertations)

Women's education – a world review: annotated bibliography of doctoral dissertations, compiled and edited by Franklin Parker and Betty June Parker. (Westport: Greenwood Press, 1977)

Immigrants and race relations

Immigrants, minorities and race relations: a bibliography of theses and dissertations presented at British and Irish universities, 1900–1981, compiled by Victor F. Gilbert and Darshan Singh Tatla with an introductory essay by Colin Holmes. (London: Mansell, 1984)

American ethnic groups: the European heritage: a bibliography of doctoral dissertations completed at American universities by Francesco Cordasco and David M. Alloway. (Metuchen, NJ: Scarecrow Press, 1981)

Literature

Altick, R.D. and Matthews, W.R. *Guide to doctoral dissertation in Victorian literature, 1886–1958* (Urbana: University of Illinois Press 1960)

Billick, D.J. 'Women in Hispanic literature: a checklist of doctoral dissertations and masters' theses, 1965–1975' *Women Studies Abstracts* 6 (2) (1977) 1–11.

McNamee, L.F. *Dissertations in English and American literature: theses accepted by American, British and German universities, 1865–1964.* New York; London: Bowker, 1968 (with supplements for 1964–1968 (1969) and 1969–1973 (1974)

Index

abolitionist movements (slavery) **9**: 384, 441, 558, 614
aboriginal women **21**: 134
abortion **3**: 61 **19**: 4, 11, 15, 16, 22–3, 25, 28, 31, 33, 36, 39, 41, 47, 51–2, 56–8, 61, 64, 70, 73, 81–2, 85–9, 91–2, 97, 103, 106, 118, 123, 131, 292, 430
  adolescents **19**: 75, 80
  Catholic students **19**: 21
  counselling **19**: 53, 105, 107
  health education **19**: 44
  law
    England **9**:125 **19**:32
    Europe, Eastern **3**: 68
    USA **19**: 48, 99, 102, 109, 117, 120
  moral & ethical aspects, **19**: 6, 17, 18, 35, 43, 54–5, 59, 69, 96, 100, 116
  opposition movements **19**: 60, 74, 127
  press coverage **19**: 13
  psychological aspects **19**: 2, 14, 18, 24, 29, 45, 49, 50, 62, 72, 75, 77, 80, 83–4, 98, 111–12, 114, 121
  students **19**: 68
  women's magazines **13**: 21
absenteeism **5**: 250, 272
accountants **5**: 509
achievement and under-achievement **17**: 12, 16, 21, 29, 32
Ackermann, Louise **12**: 2984
Acton, Eugenia de **12**: 1824
actresses **1**: 3, 10, 11, 16, 24, 30, 83–5, 91, 93–7, 100, 102–3, 107–8, 119, 121–33, 126, 129, 131–2, 139–42, 144, 147, 149–51, 154, 157–8, 160, 162, 168, 174–6, 182, 184, 187–90, 192–3 **9**: 610 **12**: 441
Adams, Abigail **9**: 475
Adams, Louisa Catherine Johnson **9**: 418
Adams, Marian Hoops (Clover) **9**: 526
Addams, Jane **9**: 461, 657, 719
administrators **4**: 723 **5**: 161, 503, 507, 526
adolescent girls (*see also*) juvenile delinquents **21**: 140 **23**: 298
  abortion **19**: 23, 75, 80
  anorexia nervosa **8**: 311, 316, 326
(adolescent girls *cont.*)
  assertiveness training **4**: 1138 **17**: 132
  attitudes to
    family life **6**: 102
    home making **21**: 2
    parents **6**: 107
  behaviour modification **17**: 45, 119
  body image **8**: 308, 316 **19**: 171, 224, 230
  Catholic religion **18**: 134
  child rearing influences **6**: 47
  clothing **21**: 88–9, 92
  contraception **19**: 10, 37–8, 40, 46, 63, 65, 93, 95, 104, 113, 122, 125 **20**: 15, 37
  critical illness **8**: 392
  drug-addiction **8**: 78
  family behaviour **6**: 809
  food habits **8**: 305
  group homes **21**: 298
  language **10**: 7
  leisure **21**: 185, 188
  literary portrayal **12**: 323, 465, 2855
  maternal employment **6**: 58
  menstruation **19**: 171, 224, 230
  obesity **8**: 338–9, 344, 360, 362, 371
  Pakistanis in London **21**: 154
  parental death **6**: 62
  parental role identification **6**: 105
  physical fitness & activity **15**: 94 **22**: 6, 31
  physiology **15**: 142
  pre-parental guidance **4**: 1085
  pregnancy **15**: 37, 171, 224, 230 **19**: 495–570 **20**: 1
  psychiatric treatment **8**: 177
  psychology **4**: 1065, 1100, 1304 **17**:
  sexuality **20**: 1, 15, 22, 34, 37, 82, 132, 136
  television **13**: 11
  weight control **8**: 305
adolescent mothers **6**: 309, 430, 497–8, 506, 529, 545, 741, 760
  contraception **19**: 104
  family planning services **19**: 20
  fertility **3**: 58
  health care **8**: 90
  high school education **4**: 1052
adoption **6**: 371, 537
adult education *see* continuing education
(adult education *cont.*)
adult literacy (Peru) **23**: 72
adulterous wives in literature **12**: 1473
advertisements
  health **21**: 45
  sportswomen **22**: 63
  women's magazines **13**: 23, 29
AFDC mothers
  employment **5**: 137, 198, 202 **6**: 256 **21**: 304
  family planning services **19**: 115
Africa (*see also* individual countries) **23**: 34, 43, 64, 79, 124, 201, 222, 223, 227, 288
Afro-Americans **9**: 494 **21**: 120
  abortion **19**: 47
  administrators **5**: 503
  adolescent delinquents **2**: 93 **6**: 751
  adolescent mothers **6**: 498, 529
  adolescent pregnancy **6**: 529 **19**: 519, 543, 555, 566
  adolescents:
    academic achievement **6**: 11
  adoption **6**: 537
  alcoholism **8**: 6, 23
  anti-lynching **9**: 694
  athletes **22**: 1
  autobiography **4**: 564 **12**: 209, 305, 457
  blues-singers **1**: 60
  business **4**: 1171
  career choices **4**: 1438, 1445, 1474, 1529, 1523, 1592, 1633, 1636
  career counselling **4**: 161
  career prospects **5**: 327
  child health **8**: 16
  child-rearing **6**: 288, 669, 744, 912
  children's sex role attitudes **17**: 857
  clothes **9**: 706 **21**: 64
  clubs **9**: 444 **21**: 26
  community colleges **4**: 315
  community workers **21**: 279
  composers **1**: 48
  dancers **1**: 104
  day care centres **21**: 258
  depression **8**: 215
  desegregation **21**: 107, 150, 178
  diabetes **8**: 398
  domestic workers **5**: 298
  drug addicts **8**: 66

(Afro-Americans *cont.*)
education **4**: 89, 124, 1281, 1419 **21**: 106
higher **4**: 231, 284, 298, 604, 697 **6**: 198
entrance **4**: 242
Roman Catholic **4**: 356
Secondary **4**: 196
educational administration
higher education **4**: 635, 651, 672, 702, 783, 810, 848, 852
schools **4**: 634, 685, 750, 762, 798, 814, 857
elderly **8**: 101, 116 **17**: 736, 737, 743, 749, 758–9
elocutionists **10**: 19
family **6**: 1, 2, 27, 751 **19**: 30
family size preferences **6**: 5
father-daughter relationships **16**: 81
feminist & traditional women **7**: 85
fertility **3**: 56
films **1**: 5
folk-tales **12**: 425
food habits **8**: 305
foster-mothers **6**: 522
girls **21**: 147
graduates **4**: 225
grandmothers **6**: 814
Harlem Renaissance **12**: 221, 338
high school girls **4**: 1102
hockey **22**: 126
ideal black woman **17**: 856
identity patterns **21**: 112
illegitimacy **19**: 298
job-training **5**: 73, 511
law **11**: 5
lawyers **4**: 1632
literary portrayal **12**: 216, 221, 309, 454, 456
literature **4**: 185
managers **5**: 326, 385, 543
marital & family relations **6**: 20
marriage **3**: 126
maternal health **8**: 117
mathematics **4**: 1223
media portrayal **13**: 20
menopause **19**: 239
mental health **8**: 128, 136
militancy **7**: 122 **17**: 0792
mother-child relations **6**: 316, 520, 560, 717, 783
communication **6**: 762, 769
retarded **6**: 752
education **6**: 722
mother-daughter relations **6**: 25, 118
mother's teaching **6**: 513
nursing students **8**: 403, 559
obesity **8**: 339, 377–8
occupational aspirations **5**: 548
office-workers: colleges **4**: 864
organizations **9**: 493
political activity **16**: 1, 72
power **21**: 113
pre-natal care **19**: 450
professions **5**: 437, 442, 450,

(Afro-Americans *cont.*)
488, 613, 623
psychology **19**: 283
psychotherapy **8**: 204
relations with whites **17**: 817, 821
rural culture **21**: 119
sexuality **20**: 130
singers **1**: 43, 45
single parent families **6**: 482, 512, 551, 688
slavery **9**: 711
students **4**: 317, 1225, 1301 **17**: 122, 524, 536, 539, 570–1, 593, 608, 610, 614, 652, 671, 675
suffrage movements **9**: 426, 693
suicide **21**: 181
teachers' views of **4**: 996
television **13**: 34
theology, feminist **7**: 14
unwed mothers **6**: 381, 771
vocational education **4**: 1059, 1300
voluntary service **21**: 250
wages **5**: 15, 169
welfare **21**: 299
widows **6**: 245, 272
wives of industrial workers **21**: 175
women's liberation movement **7**: 58, 138
women's rights **7**: 23
workers **5**: 20, 24, 103, 108, 258–9, 406, 602
working mothers **6**: 912
writers **12**: 27, 128, 219, 263, 272, 330, 338, 345, 367, 398, 406, 434, 442, 444, 446, 451, 456, 460, 517–20, 789, 811a–14, 821–2, 1000, 1223
Agoult, Marie de **12**: 2944, 2985–6
agricultural education **4**: 220, 1009, 1655
agricultural workers **5**: 196, 275, 300, 344 **21**: 189
in England **9**: 113, 188
in the Gambia **23**: 73
in Kenya **23**: 276
in Malaysia **23**: 176
in Nigeria **23**: 273
in the USA: Wisconsin media **13**: 40
Aguilar, Grace **18**: 315
Aichinger, Ilse **12**: 3358
air-line workers **4**: 1642 **5**: 254
Alabama, USA **4**: 1129, 1261, 1329, 1386 **19**: 406, 562
Alaska, USA **4**: 109, 1572
alcoholism (*see also* temperance movement) **8**: 1–61 **20**: 98
juvenile delinquents **2**: 168
lesbians **8**: 61 **20**: 196, 198
pregnancy **19**: 444
Alcott, Louisa May **12**: 481–6
Alderman Cogan's Girls' School **4**: 7
Aldrich, Bess Streeter **12**: 487
Algeria **23**: 58, 226
alienation **4**: 1196 **8**: 394 **12**:

(alienation *cont.*)
120, 3469, 3638
All-American Girls' Baseball League **22**: 177
Allart, Hortense **12**: 2944
Alrotts, Vittoria Raphaela **1**: 38
Allen, Viola **1**: 157
Amenhofpe III **9**: 35
American College for Girls, Cairo **4**: 312
American College for Girls, Istanbul **4**: 152
American Indians **9**: 652
acculturation **21**: 176
adolescents **6**: 59
Alaskan local politics **21**: 139A **23**: 167
boarding school **4**: 1191
Catholic missionary sisters **18**: 225
child-rearing **6**: 341
crafts **21**: 177
culture change **21**: 168
diabetes **8**: 309
fertility **3**: 44, 114
fictional portrayal **12**: 256, 346
food habits **8**: 309
girl's puberty rites: Canada **21**: 142a
industries **21**: 177
menopause **19**: 249
obesity **8**: 378
pregnancy **19**: 340, 365 **23**: 172
professional women **21**: 139b
urbanization **21**: 104
village life (Guatemala) **23**: 207
women in myth **21**: 127
women's role **21**: 136, 158, 165
Anat (Canaanite goddess) **18**: 4
Anderson, Margaret **13**: 8
Anderson, Mary **1**: 168 **9**: 435
androgyny **20**: 138–53
adolescents **20**: 150
art **12**: 135
assertiveness training **17**: 78
athletes **22**: 7, 13, 85
career/occupational choices **4**: 1675 **20**: 138, 142
business education **4**: 1286
Catholic sisters **18**: 157
dramatic portrayal **12**: 28
father-daughter relationship **6**: 92
feminism **14**: 16 **20**: 152
literary portrayal **12**: 102, 135, 277, 2776, 2826, 2857
maternal employment **23**: 265
maternal role **19**: 409
middle-aged **20**: 151
professional women **17**: 46
psychotherapists **20**: 151
re-training programme **17**: 85
sexuality **20**: 24
students **17**: 78 **20**: 138, 145, 147
Anglia, Margaret **1**: 124
Anglican Church **4**: 17 **18**: 77
in USA **18**: 94, 245, 248, 252, 258
Anna Comnena **9**: 13

Anne, St **18**: 66
Anne, Queen **9**: 197
Anne of Denmark **1**: 88
anorexia nervosa **8**: 311, 315–16, 319–21, 323–4, 326–7
Anthony, Susan B. **9**: 490
Aphrodite **12**: 1298
apprenticeship training **5**: 422
Arab countries (*see also* Middle East, Near East and individual countries) **4**: 248, 969, 1151, 1153 **23**: 6, 114, 145, 198
Arbus, Diane **1**: 256 **12**: 995
archery **22**: 125
architects **5**: 287
Arden, Jane **12**: 2511
Arendt, Hannah **14**: 19, 20, 23, 32 **16**: 19, 36, 47
Argentina **23**: 138
Ariadne **18**: 6
Arizona, US **4**: 616, 787, 1490
Arkansas, US **4**: 959 **5**: 99
Arnim, Bettina von **12**: 3359–60
Arnim, Elizabeth von **12**: 2540
Arnow, Harriette **12**: 401, 489
art and artists **1**: 203, 210, 236, 241, 245, 252, 255
  African **23**: 41
  American **1**: 205, 208, 213, 216, 223, 225–6, 229, 230, 240, 253–4 **9**: 645
  androgyny **12**: 135
  Brazilian **1**: 228
  children **1**: 233
  criticism **1**: 206, 220
  Dutch **1**: 218, 249
  education **4**: 25, 139, 930
  English **1**: 198, 215, 217, 237–8, 244, 257
  feminism **1**: 219, 221, 247 **12**: 106
  fictional portrayal **12**: 24, 92, 211, 2276, 2297, 2524, 2537, 2614–15, 2618, 2746, 2767, 2792, 2794, 2805
  Flemish **1**: 197
  French **12**: 2842, 2979, 2982
  literary portrayal **12**: 1731, 2700, 2705, 2724, 2746, 2789–90, 3445
  medieval **1**: 211, 231, 239, 242, 246, 250
  philosophy **14**: 1, 2, 10
  Polynesian **23**: 128
  Spanish **1**: 244
  students **1**: 204 **4**: 1108, 1669
Asia (*see also* individual countries) **23**: 143
Asian Americans (*see also* Chinese, Americans and Japanese Americans) **12**: 476
Asian immigrants in England **21**: 129, 174
assertiveness groups and training **17**: 48, 52–4, 56, 82, 87, 90–1, 94, 99, 101, 112, 117–18, 120–1, 127, 131, 133, 135, 141, 144, 146, 148, 155, 159, 168, 170–1
(assertiveness groups *cont.*)
  adolescents **4**: 1138 **17**: 132, 165
  girls **17**: 178
  immigrants (USA) **21**: 146
  married women **17**: 103, 138
  professional women **17**: 46, 163
  Puerto Ricans (USA) **21**: 170
  sex role changes **17**: 66
  single women **17**: 106
  students **17**: 50, 78, 81, 92, 108, 125, 145, 154, 162, 173
  working-class **21**: 253
Association for Inter-Collegiate Athletics for Women **22**: 112, 124
Association for Cinematography Television and Allied Technicans (ACTT) **5**: 223
Association of Southern Women for the Prevention of Lynching **9**: 452, 492, 694
Astell, Mary **12**: 1603
Aston, Louise **12**: 3295, 3361
Astor, Nancy (Viscountess) **9**:117
astronomy and astronomers **9**: 501
Atherton, Gertrude **12**: 213, 336, 490
athletes **5**: 519 **9**: 535, 555 **19**: 153 **22**: 1–5, 7–8, 10–11, 13–14, 16, 22, 24, 27–30, 32, 35, 37–9, 41, 48–50, 52, 55–8, 64–6, 70–1, 73–7, 79, 83–5, 89–92, 95, 97, 99, 101, 104, 106–7, 109, 113–14, 118–19, 121, 123, 147
athletics **4**: 560
  administration **4**: 478, 817 **22**: 71, 80, 82, 86–7, 93–4, 96, 100, 102–3, 108, 111–12, 117, 120, 124
  coaches **4**: 449 **22**: 73, 81, 98, 115, 122
attitude changes (Latin American women) **17**: 68
attitudes towards women **4**: 1279 **17**: 15, 58, 63, 86, 95, 116, 134, 142, 829–83 **23**: 307
Atwood, Margaret **12**: 22, 46, 1276
Audubon, Lucy Bakewell **9**: 442
Augustini, Delmita **12**: 3453, 3459–61
Aulnoy, Mme de **12**: 2987–91
Austen, Jane **1**: 111 **12**: 58, 87, 1682, 1720, 1727, 1729, 1742, 1773, 1782, 1796, 1806a, 1817, 1819, 1823, 1825–1949
Austin, Mary Hunter **12**: 491–6
Australia **3**: 57 **19**: 490 **21**: 134 **23**: 117
Austria **9**: 281, 285, 291
autobiographies (*see also* diaries; letters)
  Afro-American **4**: 564 **12**: 209, 305, 457
  American **12**: 54, 105, 337, 366 **18**: 149
  Asian Americans **12**: 476
  elderly women **17**: 742
  English **12**; 105, 1453, 1491, 2579
(autobiographies *cont.*)
  French **12**: 3008–9 **18**: 149
  German **12**: 3295
  Japanese **12**: 1262
  Spanish **18**: 149
autonomous learning groups **17**: 109
Avellaneda, Gertrudis de **12**: 3462–3
Avery, Martha Moore **9**: 414
Avison, Margaret **12**: 1280
Axmatova, Anna **12**: 3508, 3511, 3516

badminton **22**: 129, 164, 167, 186, 191–2
Baganda women **6**: 528
Bacon, Denise **1**: 74
Bagnold, Enid **12**: 2511
Baillie, Joanna **12**: 1950
Baldwin, Lillian **1**: 62
ballet and ballerinas **1**: 86
Bancroft, Marie **1**: 93
Bangladesh **3**: 111 **23**: 5, 106, 203
bank staff **5**: 287, 553
Bantu women **23**: 44
Baptists
  in USA (Texas) **18**: 106
  lay leaders **18**: 95
  missionary education **4**: 281 **23**: 293
  speaking by women **78**: 125
  women's liberation movement **18**: 101
Baraka, Imamu Amiri **12**: 27
Barbados **3**: 98, 117
Barbauld, Anna Laetitia **12**: 1604
Barnard College (physical education) **4**: 432
Barry, Elizabeth **1**: 121
baseball **22**: 177
basketball **15**: 13 **22**: 132–3, 136–7, 139–44, 148–50, 152, 162, 171, 175, 182–3, 187
basket-making **5**: 258
Bateman, Ellen **1**: 85
Bateman, Kate **1**: 85
Bathori, Jane **1**: 41
battered women and wives **2**: 209, 173–214 **11**: 10
Bauer, Catherine **9**: 424
Bavaria **2**: 141
Beaufort, Margaret **9**: 89
beauty culture (education) **4**: 583
Beauvoir, Simone de **12**: 61, 79, 102, 2494–3012 **14**: 4, 22, 26, 28
bedouins **23**: 182
Beecher, Catherine **9**: 664 **18**: 102
Behn, Aphra **12**: 1520–33
Beirut College for Women **4**: 301
Belgium **4**: 21 **5**: 207 **16**: 18
Belize **23**: 163
Bell, Gertrude **9**: 173
Bellanca, Dorothy Jacobs **9**: 377
Bench, H.H.A. **1**: 207
Benedictine Sisters **4**: 351, 404 **18**: 236
Bennett, Gwendolyn **1**: 213

Berkshire, UK **9**: 105
Bernard, Catherine **12**: 3013
Bernard, Jessie **9**: 649
Bernhardt, Sarah **1**: 177, 187, 189–190
Bernstein, Alice **1**: 89
Berry, Mary **9**: 111
Bertin, Célia **12**: 2918
Besant, Annie **9**: 176
Bethune College **4**: 305
Bethune, Mary McLeod **9**: 600
Bhandari, Mannu **12**: 1257
biological education **4**: 175, 371, 1245, 1265, 1302
biological necessity: feminist critique **7**: 33
biological sciences: career choices **4**: 1573
Birch-Pfeiffer, Charlotte **12**: 3362
birth *see* childbirth
birth control *see* contraception; family planning
biscuit factory workers **5**: 308, 313
Bishop, Elizabeth **12**: 313, 497–507
Blackwell, Elizabeth **9**: 501
Black Sash movement (South Africa) **16**: 50
blacks in USA *see* Afro-Americans
Blais, Marie-Claire **12**: 1281–2
Bloor, Ella Reeve **9**: 655
'blue collar' skilled workers **4**: 1654 **5**: 379
blue-stockings **12**: 1644
Blyton, Enid **12**: 2541
Bodichon, Barbara Leigh Smith **9**: 145a
Bodkin, Maud **12**: 2542
body images and attitudes **5**: 342 **17**: 794, 838
  adolescents **8**: 308, 316 **19**: 170, 222, 228
  businesswomen **21**: 79
  dance & music **17**: 102
  delinquents **2**: 133
  feminist & non-feminist **21**: 82
  graduate students **20**: 16
  infertility **19**: 135
  mastectomy **8**: 457
  mother-daughter **6**: 117
  obese women **8**: 332, 334, 351
  pregnancy **19**: 319, 321, 346, 359, 442, 480–1, 494
  professional women **21**: 79
  schizophrenics **8**: 265
  students **17**: 591
  training programmes **17**: 110, 124
Bogan, Louise **12**: 244, 386, 508–9
Bohemia **2**: 13
Bombal, María Luisa **12**: 3464–6
Bonaparte, Marie **17**: 2
Bonfant, Maria **1**: 86
book-binding trade **9**: 156
Boothe Luce, Clare **16**: 46
Botswana **23**: 297
Boulanger, Nadia **1**: 72
Bowen, Elizabeth **12**: 79, 103, 2481, 2516, 2543–58
bowling **22**: 135, 153
Bowman, Louise Morey **12**: 1283
Boyle, Kay **12**: 510
Bracegirdle, Anne **1**: 121
Bladdon, Mary Elizabeth **12**: 1951
Bradstreet, Anne **12**: 512–16
Brady, Alice **1**: 132
Braun, Lily **12**: 3363
Brazil **1**: 228 **3**: 21 **9**: 343, 346 **18**: 263 **19**: 455 **23**: 38, 96, 120, 123, 180, 211, 308
Bread and Roses (Boston women's liberation movement, 1969–71) **9**: 618
breast feeding (*see also* infant feeding) **6**: 549 **19**: 276, 327, 344, 381, 469, 474 **23**: 210
  & employment **3**: 84
  & fertility **3**: 96
Breckinridge, Madeline McDowell **9**: 499
Bremer, Frederika **12**: 3530
bridewealth **23**: 206, 288
Bridgeman, Mother Mary Francis **9**: 123
British Honduras **6**: 689
Brontë, Anne **12**: 1952–2027 *passim*
Brontë, Charlotte **12**: 58, 83, 1561, 1692, 1704, 1727, 1740, 1742, 1781, 1782, 1796, 1806a, 1807, 1815, 1817, 1819, 1820a, 1823, 1952–2027 *passim*
Brontë, Emily **12**: 51, 1817, 1820a 1950–2027 *passim*
Brooke, Frances **12**: 1594
Brooks, Gwendolyn **12**: 27, 517–20
Brophy, Brigid **12**: 2559
Broughton, Rhoda **12**: 2028
Brown, Alice **12**: 440, 472, 521–2
Brown, Hallie Quinn **10**: 19
Browning, Elizabeth Barrett **12**: 2029–39
Brückner, Christina **12**: 73
Brunton, Mary **12**: 1888
Bryn Mawr College **4**: 213, 424, 432
Buddhism **3**: 106 **18**: 20–1 **23**: 258
bulimarexia **8**: 312–5, 317–8, 322, 325
Bullrich, Silvina **12**: 3467–8
Burdett-Coutts, Angela **9**: 161
Burgos, Julia de **12**: 3619
Burma **21**: 220 **23**: 258
Burnett, Frances Hodgson **12**: 522
Burney, Fanny **12**: 58, 1544, 1570, 1582, 1606–16
business **5**: 69, 89, 363, 380, 559
  administrators **4**: 626, 653 **5**: 161, 332
  in American colonies **9**: 354
  attitudes to women **5**: 53
  clothing **21**: 79
  executives **5**: 16, 361, 460, 538, 598
  fictional portrayal **12**: 385, 428
  in Ghana **23**: 183
  managers **5**: 361, 418, 530, 538
  professionals **5**: 479
  women's clubs **5**: 573
(business *cont.*)
  adult education **4**: 410
business education **4**: 250, 253, 278, 902, 941, 1106, 1286 **5**: 48–9 **23**: 311
  career choices **4**: 1494, 1594
  students **4**: 1023, 1120, 1171, 1234, 1333
  teachers **4**: 991
  women's rights **7**: 137
Byrnes, Roane Fleming **12**: 523

Caccini Francesca **1**: 66
California, USA **2**: 19, 41, 256, 261 **4**: 219, 221, 251, 266–7, 269, 314, 422, 452, 507, 528, 537, 585, 623, 629, 638, 665–6, 678, 711, 713, 719–20, 727, 738, 784, 801, 814, 834, 846, 873, 955, 1206, 1209, 1388 **5**: 117, 553 **8**: 296 **9**: 380, 598 **16**: 35 **17**: 631 **19**: 91, 312, 499, 569 **21**: 177, 210
  Los Angeles **4**: 226, 876 **9**: 564 **18**: 81 **21**: 2131
  San Francisco **1**: 248 **5**: 226 **9**: 560, 564, 669 **21**: 142
Calisher, Hortense **12**: 524
Callas, Maria **1**: 46
Cameroon **3**: 28
Canada (*see also* individual provinces) **3**: 91 **4**: 182 **5**: 56, 197, 603 **8**: 114 **9**: 365, 379, 421, 591, 686 **15**: 158 **16**: 4, 9 **17**: 462 **18**: 191 **21**: 59 **22**: 96
cancer **8**: 430, 452–4, 476
  breast **8**: 426–9, 431–51, 453, 455–63, 465–72, 475
  cervical **8**: 459, 464, 474
  cytotests **8**: 473
  pastoral care **18**: 274
cannery workers (California) **5**: 322
capitalism **21**: 212, 219, 277
cardiac diseases **8**: 393, 416, 421–2
Cardinal, Marie **12**: 73
career change **4**: 1583 **6**: 891
career choices and aspirations **4**: 1016, 1068, 1078, 1104, 1175, 1185, 1235, 1281, 1436, 1439, 1441, 1487, 1489, 1499, 1510, 1520, 1524, 1532, 1536, 1539, 1544, 1549, 1570–1, 1587, 1593, 1607, 1628, 1668, 1674 **6**: 882, 903, 913
  tests **17**: 14, 17, 19, 20, 26, 30–1
  schools **4**: 1250, 1438, 1443–7, 1449, 1453–4, 1458, 1467, 1470–5, 1477, 1484–5, 1493, 1508–9, 1522, 1527, 1529, 1531, 1534–5, 1548, 1557, 1560, 1574, 1581, 1585, 1589, 1591, 1596–7, 1601, 1603–6, 1612, 1615, 1625, 1635, 1641, 1657, 1657, 1685
  universities & colleges **4**: 97–8, 1500–2, 1505, 1507, 1511–12, 1514–19, 1521, 1523, 1526, 1532, 1537–8, 1540, 1542, 1545–7,

(career choices and aspirations *cont.*)
1549–56, 1559, 1562, 1565, 1567, 1573, 1575–6, 1579, 1581, 1588, 1592, 1595, 1597–8, 1600–2, 1608–10, 1613–14, 1617, 1621, 1629–31, 1634, 1636, 1639–40, 1643, 1645–6, 1648, 1650, 1652, 1656, 1659, 1661–4, 1666–7, 1670, 1673, 1679, 1681–3, 1685 **17**: 543, 601, 616, 646
Catholic women **4**: 345
divorced mothers **6**: 229
mature women **4**: 1376, 1379
career counselling **4**: 1053, 1433, 1437, 1472–3, 1476, 1492, 1504, 1506, 1510, 1528, 1549, 1558, 1564, 1599, 1618, 1642, 1649, 1651, 1653, 1658, 1660, 1665, 1671–2 **5**: 468, 492, 539 **21**: 268, 272, 283, 303
schools **4**: 1483, 1561, 1580, 1583, 1586, 1590, 1623, 1646, 1654, 1675, 1677
universities & colleges **4**: 1133, 1435, 1471, 1481, 1541, 1543, 1563, 1566, 1611, 1616, 1624, 1676
sex-bias & discrimination **4**: 1483, 1573, 1626
career development and patterns **3**: 31 **4**: 1524, 1530, 1571, 1578, 1582, 1602, 1627–8, 1638, 1647, 1680 **5**: 9, 1391 **23**: 234
chemists **4**: 925
doctors **8**: 488
educational administrators **4**: 664, 763
higher education **4**: 678, 686, 688, 728, 756, 761, 774, 856, 862, 871, 879
marriage & its effects **6**: 858, 880, 914, 932 **9**: 581
mothers **6**: 818, 827, 877, 921, 937
nurses **8**: 522
physical education **4**: 483
principals (school) **4**: 771
school superintendents **4**: 753, 758, 873
teachers **4**: 100, 597, 607, 654, 725, 894, 1007, 1554, 1579
women university presidents **4**: 1176, 1294
Carlotta Joaquina, queen **9**: 341
Caroline of Anspach, queen **9**: 167
carpet industry and trade
Iran **23**: 110
USA **9**: 559
Carson, Rachel **12**: 525
Carter, Elizabeth **12**: 1544, 1617, 1644
Carter, Leslie **1**: 116
Castellaros, Rosario **12**: 3469–74
Cassatt, Marug **1**: 233
Cassidy, Claudia **1**: 183
Castillo, Madre **12**: 3475
Castro, Rosalia de **12**: 3547, 3620–27
Cather, Willa **12**: 232, 307, 319, 334, 336, 376, 526–83
Catherine II of Russia (the Great) **9**: 306, 322, 324
Catherine of Alexandria **18**: 26
Catherine of Siena **18**: 51
Catherwood, Mary Hartwell **12**: 584
Catholic worker movement **18**: 133, 139, 152
Catholic Worker, The **18**: 133, 139, 152
Catt, Carrie Chapman **9**: 528
cattle-keeping (Finland) **9**: 314
Cavendish, Margaret **12**: 1534
Cecilia, St **12**: 1363, 1366
Centlivre, Susanna **12**: 1618–22
Ceylon **4**: 1139 **23**: 258
Chandler, Elizabeth Margaret **12**: 585
Chapone, Hester **12**: 1623
Charlton, Margaret **18**: 126
Charrière, Mme de **12**: 2914, 3015–18
Chartism **9**: 174
Chase, Mary Ellen **12**: 586
Chauhan, Vijay **12**: 1257
chemistry (education) **4**: 1181
chemists **4**: 925 **5**: 307 **9**: 501
Chestnut, Mary Boykin **12**: 587
Child, Lydia Maria **12**: 588
child abuse **2**: 21, 27 **6**: 698, 784–806
child-bearing age **3**: 24, 37
child-care **3**: 36 **5**: 271, 432, 462 **6**: 637, 716
in Nigeria **23**: 87
housework **21**: 28
working mothers **5**: 179, 206 **9**: 665
child health *see* health and health services: children
child-rearing **6**: 86, 692–4, 768
adolescents **6**: 47
Afro-Americans **6**: 744, 912
American Indians: New Mexico **6**: 700
Caribs: British Honduras **6**: 689
Chinese Americans **6**: 554
Creoles: British Honduras **6**: 689
drug-addicts **8**: 70
effect on college women students **17**: 627
Iraqui **6**: 531
Italian Americans **6**: 360
Jewish **6**: 360
lesbian mothers **6**: 719
Malaysian **22**: 175
student mothers **6**: 757
Trukese (Micronesia) **23**: 103
child welfare (USA) **9**: 719
childbirth **19**: 261, 269–70, 311, 321–2, 339, 362, 387, 390, 393–4, 398, 402–3, 411, 417, 422, 424, 426–8, 438, 443, 465, 467–8, 470, 492
in England **9**: 108
Malawi **23**: 51
Malaysia **23**: 175
(childbirth *cont.*)
Caesarean section **19**: 266, 434
husband's presence **19**: 308, 341
post-natal **19**: 274, 277–8, 280, 310, 326
preparation classes **19**: 341, 383, 404, 476, 480
women's magazines **13**: 33
children's
books (women characters in) **4**: 199 **21**: 226, 231
play **4**: 1293
sex roles (teachers' attitudes) **7**: 112
toy preferences (stereotypes) **4**: 988
Children's Theatre Association of Baltimore **1**: 130
Childress, Alice **12**: 219
Chile **3**: 50 **23**: 56, 76, 290
China **3**: 15 **5**: 269 **9**: 45, 46, 47, 49, 50, 58, 64 **18**: 266, 268 **23**: 54, 69, 141, 150, 261, 274, 307, 309
Chinese Americans
acculturation **21**: 111
child rearing **6**: 554
divorce & marital satisfaction **6**: 159
high school girls **21**: 180
mother-child relations **6**: 540
Chinese minorities
Malaysia **23**: 176
South East Asia **23**: 143
cholecystectomy **8**: 391
Chopin, Kate **12**: 79, 268, 319, 326, 336, 377, 410, 590–605
Chorpenning, Charlotte B. **1**: 90, 165
Christian Science **18**: 82, 85, 88, 90, 119
Christian Socialists: USA: feminism **9**: 510
Christianity and the Christian Church (*see also* individual churches and sects)
consecration: medieval **18**: 65
early Church **18**: 29, 30, 33, 38, 40, 43
girls' clubs **21**: 256
Gnosticism **18**: 22a
mother-goddess: feminine principle **17**: 8
New Testament teaching & portrayal **18**: 22–5, 27–31, 36, 41–2, 44, 46–7, 49, 246–7, 255
ordination of women **18**: 242–61
pastoral care **18**: 269–84
patristic writers **18**: 37, 39, 48, 246
theological & religious thought **18**: 76, 100, 109, 112, 118, 121, 127–8, 130, 218
worship **18**: 130
Christine de Pisan **12**: 9, 3019–26
Chugtai, Ismat **12**: 1257
Church of Jesus Christ of Latter Day Saints **18**: 96, 123
Churchill, Sarah (Duchess of

(Churchill, Sarah *cont.*)
Marlborough) **12**: 1545
cinema **1**: 1–30 **12**: 3058, 3060 **13**: 37, 44
Cistercian nuns **18**: 55, 70
Civil Rights movement **7**: 30
Clairmont, Claire **12**: 2040
Clany, Laura **7**: 41
Clark, Frances Elliott **1**: 73
Clarke, Charlotte Cibber **1**: 102
Clarke, Shirley **1**: 18
class
in Denmark **21**: 228
Iran **23**: 257 **4**: 1016
Korea **23**: 214
USA **9**: 712
clothing **21**: 89, 101
family & feminism **7**: 2
housewives **21**: 22
mother-child relations **6**: 290
sex **7**: 92 **9**: 608
women students **4**: 1270
clerical workers (*see also* office workers, white collar workers) **5**: 12, 21, 82, 385, 393, 420, 522, 615 **9**: 129, 376, 438, 627, 641
career choices **4**: 1674
food habits **8**: 297, 301
married women **6**: 889
Clive Kitty **1**: 103
clothes **21**: 57–102
in Egypt (ancient) **9**: 5
England (Anglo-Saxon) **9**: 72
France (medieval) **9**: 234
India **23**: 269
USA **9**: 524
attitudes
Chinese & American **21**: 58
Canadian **21**: 59
single women **21**: 48
clothing industry and trade (*see also* seamstresses and tailoring) **5**:247, 257, 264, 289, 303, 305 **23**: 297
absenteeism **5**: 272
strikes: USA **9**: 571
clubs and associations
in England (Portsmouth) **5**: 573
Honduras **21**: 257
USA **4**: 410, 421 **9**: 393, 444, 642 **21**: 245, 261
girls' clubs **21**: 251, 256
Co. Durham, UK **4**: 130
Coalition for Women in State Service **5**: 229
Coalition of Labor Union Women **5**: 222
coal-mining industry **5**: 383 **9**: 159
Coit, Dorothy **1**: 164
Coleridge, Mary **12**: 2041
Coleridge, Sara **12**: 2042
Colette, Sidonie Gabrielle **12**: 3027–36
Colombia **3**: 12 **9**: 345 **19**:9, 34 **23**: 63, 242, 271
Colonna, Vittoria **12**: 3101
Colorado **4**: 41, 51, 643, 669, 685,
(Colarado *cont.*)
953, 1383 **5**: 237 **8**: 451 **11**: 2 **19**: 31, 107 **21**: 243
Colum, Mary **12**: 606
Columbia DC, USA **9**: 494
Washington **4**: 375 **8**: 305, 1405 **9**: 385, 592 **16**: 53
Colyer, Mary Mitchele **12**: 1624
Commonwealth, the British **9**: 194
communism (*see also* Marxism; socialism)
in China **9**: 49–50
England **9**: 126
Germany **9**: 283, 293a, 643
Italy **9**: 319
USA **9**: 408, 446, 605, 607, 621
women's position **21**: 212, 218
community colleges **4**: 226, 269, 315, 419, 422, 427, 590, 627, 629, 632, 687, 692, 713, 742, 786, 801, 858, 861, 1023, 1104, 1107, 1134, 1264, 1323, 1328, 1330, 1342, 1347, 1363, 1365–6, 1376, 1411, 1414, 1418, 1423, 1476, 1486, 1490, 1494–5, 1504, 1601, 1609, 1644, 1660 **5**: 37 **8**: 64 **21**: 305 **22**: 4 **17**: 523, 542, 545, 601, 615, 639, 664
teachers **4**: 590, 692
women's studies **4**: 573, 582
community homes **2**: 76
Compton-Burnett, Ivy **12**: 89, 2481
Conan, Laure **12**: 1284
confectionery industry **5**: 308
Connecticut, USA **4**: 339, 442, 618, 850, 892 **6**: 1 **9**: 617 **18**: 97 **19**: 459
consciousness-raising groups **4**: 1308, 1631 **7**: 12, 97, 106, 136 **8**. 242, 541 **17**: 13, 49, 51, 62, 97, 100, 107, 111, 120, 149, 156, 158, 167
consumer behaviour **21**: 42–5, 48, 50–3, 56
consumer credit **4**: 1420 **21**: 46, 49, 54
consumer education **4**: 1420 **21**: 51
Consumers' League of Ohio **9**: 497
Contagious Diseases Act **9**: 205, 703
continuing education **2**: 275 **4**: 405–31, 723, 1153, 1178, 1285, 1328, 1330, 1349–50, 1352–3, 1357–60, 1366, 1368–9, 1374, 1402, 1415, 1417–20, 1426–8 **21**: 114, 171, 237 **23**: 177, 224, 291
administration **4**: 609, 765 **9**
nutrition **8**: 300
contraception (*see also* family planning) **19**: 3, 5, 8, 33–4, 36, 42, 57, 67, 76, 78–9, 90, 94, 115, 119, 124, 129–30, 257
in Japan **19**: 16
Taiwan **19**: 58
Thailand **19**: 126
adolescents **19**: 10, 37–8, 40, 46,
(contraception, *cont.*)
63, 65, 93, 95, 104, 113, 122, 125 **20**: 15, 37
Afro-Americans **19**: 12, 30
college students **19**: 66, 70, 128
Islam **23**: 219
psychological aspects **19**: 26, 122, 132
Cooke, Anne Sybil **5**: 274
Cooke family **9**: 82
Cooke, Rose Terry **12**: 440, 607
Cooney, Joan Ganz **13**: 9
Cooper, Susan Fenimore **12**: 608
Corelli, Marie **12**: 2043–4
Cornelia, mother of the Gracchi **8**: 31
Cornell, Katharine **1**: 151
Costa Rica **3**: 99
costume design **1**: 12, 101, 136, 159 **9**: 539
costume jewellery industry and trade **21**: 80
Cottin, Mme **12**: 2914, 3037–8
cotton industry
managers **5**: 308
supervisors **5**: 308
workers **5**: 246, 269, 286 **9**: 146, 601 **23**: 141
Coulthard, Jean **1**: 67
Courasche **12**: 3282
Court of Chancery: 16thC **9**: 71
courtesans **12**: 1424, 2916 **23**: 199
courtship **9**: 541 **12**: 1869
Cowles, Betsey Mix **9**: 441
Crabtree, Lotta **1**: 98
crafts **1**: 210 **21**: 177
Craik, Dinah Mollock **12**: 1739, 2045
Crapsey, Adelaide **12**: 609
Crawford, Isabella **12**: 1285
Crenne, Hélisenne de **12**: 3039–43
creoles
in British Honduras **6**: 689
Sierra Leone **9**: 8
crime and criminals (*see also* juvenile delinquents; prisons) **2**: 1, 6, 8, 26, 47, 60, 75, 77, 83, 92, 97, 105, 108–110a, 115, 119, 125, 146–8, 152
in England **2**: 61, 144
Sri Lanka **2**: 61
USA **2**: 74
Massachusetts **2**: 6 **9**: 357
Philadelphia **2**: 1
drug addicts **8**: 67, 69
feminism **2**: 63
literature **12**: 14, 55
Marxism **2**: 35
parole & release **2**: 46, 52, 54–5, 69
recidivism **2**: 11, 25, 45–6, 67–8
rehabilitation **2**: 150
criminal justice
in California **2**: 19
Massachusetts **2**: 6
sentencing policies **2**: 23, 31
Crothers, Rachel **12**: 267, 610–11
Cruz, Sor Juana Ines de la **12**: 3476
Cuba **6**: 735 **21**: 212

Cuban Americans (adolescents' attitudes to working mothers) **6**: 893
curriculum (education) (*see also* specific subjects) **4**: 77, 138, 173, 177, 185, 201, 229, 236, 240, 265, 296, 318, 323, 335, 1175, 1177, 1282, 1494
Cuetaeva, Marina **12**: 3512, 3513, 3515, 3526, 3528
Cushman, Charlotte **1**: 189
Czechoslovakia **9**: 326

Dacre, Charlotte **12**: 1888
Daily Times (Nigeria) **13**: 1
Daly, Mary **18**: 128
dame schools **4**: 68
dance and dancing (*see also* ballet and ballerinas) **1**: 104, 115, 120, 170, 180 **21**: 181
  education **1**: 114 **4**: 475 **22**: 178
  Indian: sculpture **1**: 212
  novels **1**: 111
  physical fitness **15**: 13, 27, 44, 50
  self-esteem **17**: 47
D'Arusmont, Frances Wright **9**: 609
Darwinian theories **9**: 211
Dashkova, Princess **12**: 3520
daughters (*see also* father-daughter relationships; mother-daughter relationships)
  academic choices **4**: 1144
  alcoholic parents **8**: 3
  care of parents **6**: 31
  family communication **6**: 8
  father absence, influences **6**: 41, 48,57, 67–8, 104
  female roles **6**: 24, 55, 60–1, 94
  feminism **6**: 116
  friendships **6**: 29
  maternal employment **6**: 57
  parental death **6**: 62, 66, 74, 111
  perception of parents **6**: 59
  sexual values **6**: 91
Davenport, Fanny **1**: 192
Davis, Angela **11**: 5 **16**: 31
Davis, Katherine K. **1**: 34
Davis, Rebecca Harding **12**: 408, 613
Day, Doris **1**: 3
Day, Dorothy **18**: 133, 139, 152
day-care centres and nurseries **5**: 136, 170, 180 **6**: 347, 572, 637, 668, 937, 947 **21**: 258, 282 **23**: 242
deaconesses, Lutheran Church (USA) **18**: 250, 252, 260
Delaney, Shelagh **12**: 2511
Denen, Maya **1**: 18
Denis, Marie Louise **12**: 3044
Denmark **3**: 119 **9**: 336 **18**: 251 **19**: 121 **21**: 202, 228
Denny, Frances Ann **1**: 184
dental education **4**: 222, 273, 1274, 1277
dentists **5**: 310 **8**: 486, 490
Denver Opportunity School **4**: 51
depression (psychiatric) **8**: 209–42
  Afro-Americans **8**: 215
  bulimics **8**: 325
  college-aged mothers **6**: 604
  counselling **8**: 235, 237
  elderly **8**: 240
  married women **8**: 212, 222, 225, 245
  middle-aged women **8**: 211, 244
  Mormons **8**: 241
  mothers **6**: 306, 568, 724
  post-natal **19**: 251, 255, 286, 423, 457
  Puerto Ricans **8**: 217
  sex-role **8**: 221, 224, 229, 244
  single-parents **6**: 398
  students **8**: 239 **17**: 531, 537, 585
  young women **8**: 216
Derbyshire, UK **2**: 78
dermatitis **8**: 419
Deshoulières, Mme **12**: 3045
Deune, Sophie **1**: 101
Deutsch, Helen **17**: 2
development education: Bangladesh **23**: 5
development policies and programmes
  in Guatemala **23**: 42, 88
  Iran **23**: 21
  Nigeria **23**: 95
  Philippines **23**: 2
  Senegal **23**: 29
  Tolai **23**: 43
  Turkey **23**: 173
  Venezuela **23**: 24
Dhuoda **9**: 227
diabetes **8**: 395, 413 **19**: 453
Dial, The **9**: 635, 722
Diana **12**: 1503
diaries and diarists (*see also* autobiographies)
  American **9**: 398, 501
  English **9**: 74, 182 **12**: 2466, 2542
  Japanese **12**: 1263
Dickinson, Anna Elizabeth **9**: 621, 720
Dickinson, Emily **1**: 42, 81 **12**: 51, 52, 99, 313, 615–705
Dietrich, Marlene **1**: 3, 30
Dinesen, Isak **12**: 150, 3534, 3537
disabled (career mobility) **5**: 448
Disciples of Christ (sect) **18**: 75
divorce and marital separation **3**: 38 **6**: 202–4, 206–30, 259 **9**: 203 **18**: 284
  English literature **12**: 1691
  Jewish law **11**: 18
  pastoral care **18**: 284
Dix, Dorothea Lynde **9**: 579, 672
doctoral students and doctorates **4**: 235, 241, 278–9, 288, 322, 418, 604, 667, 1025, 1069, 1119, 1129–30, 1213, 1261, 1288 **5**: 307 **6**: 196, 198 **17**: 621, 623, 654, 668
doctors **5**: 310, 519 **8**: 483, 487–9, 492
(doctors *cont.*)
  in USA **9**: 449, 501, 673
  maternal employment **6**: 933
  sex roles **8**: 480–1
  women patients' relationships **8**: 412
doctors' wives **6**: 171, 175
Dodge, Grace Hoadley **9**: 529
Dolittle, Hilda **12**: 244, 313, 706–16
domestic servants **5**: 143, 259–60, 263, 298 **9**: 208, 249, 346, 549 **23**: 81, 270
  in drama & fiction **9**: 539 **12**: 1445
Domin, Hilde **12**: 3364
Dominican order **4**: 116, 330 **18**: 172
Dominican Republic **23**: 45
Doubler, Margaret H. **1**: 114
Douglas, Mary **18**: 138
dowry
  ancient Greece **9**: 14
  women religions **18**: 198
Drabble, Margaret **12**: 88, 2527, 2561–2
Dressler, Marie **1**: 158
dress-making **5**: 247
Drewitz, Ingeborg **12**: 73
Droste-Hülshoff, Annette von **12**: 3365–70, 52, 99
drug addiction **8**: 62–83 **19**: 433
Du Deffand, Mme **12**: 2959, 3046
Du Guillet, Pernette **12**: 3047–8
Duff, Mary Ann **1**: 131
Duffy, Maureen **12**: 2511
Dulac, Germaine **1**: 8–9
Dulles, Eleanor Lansing **16**: 34
Dunbar, Alice **12**: 717–18
Duncan, Sara Jeannette **12**: 1286–7
Duniway, Abigail Scott **9**: 597
Durand, Marguerite **9**: 236
Duras, Marguerite **12**: 2918, 3050–64

Eberhardt, Isabelle **12**: 3065
Ebner-Eschenbach Marie von **12**: 3295, 3371–3
education (*see also* art education, biological education, business education, careers, community colleges, continuing education, curriculum, dame schools, dance, dental education, doctoral candidates, educational administration, counselling, psychology and technology, English teaching, geography teaching, higher education, history teaching, home economics, industrial education, intermediate education, Latin, legal education, liberal arts colleges, mathematics, mature students, medical education, music, physical education, primary education, reading, re-entry students, religious education,

(education *cont.*)
Roman Catholic Church, scientific education, secondary schools/high schools; speech education, teacher-training, teachers, technical education, text-books, universities and colleges, vocational education)
in Alaska **4**: 109
Arabia **23**: 6
Bangladesh **23**: 5, 106
Brazil **23**: 211
Canada **4**: 182
Chile **23**: 290
Egypt **23**: 68, 173a, 193, 247, 301
England
Anglo-Saxon **4**: 91
medieval **9**: 62, 79 **18**: 68
16thC **4**: 105 **9**: 88
17th–18thC **4**: 15, 24, 80, 108, 146 **12**: 1552
18th–19thC **4**: 8, 21, 27, 49, 52, 62, 110, 142, 159 **9**: 116, 136
19th–20thC **4**: 38, 61, 78, 93, 122 **12**: 1704, 1855, 1883, 2048, 2294, 2341, 2430
Europe (Renaissance) **4**: 26
France **4**: 45, 50, 155, 161 **18**: 132
Germany **4**: 79, 141
Ghana **23**: 135, 192
India **3**: 8 **9**: 44, 48, 52–3, 59, 60 **23**: 13, 164, 217, 239, 251, 266, 285
Indonesia **3**: 2
Iran **4**: 1024 **23**: 21
Iraq **23**: 301
Ireland **4**: 82, 95
Jamaica **3**: 127
Japan **4**: 260
Kenya **23**: 211
Korea **23**: 166
Middle East **23**: 301
Nigeria **9**: 3 **18**: 262 **23**: 25, 293
Peru **23**: 195
Roman Empire **9**: 39
Senegal **23**: 291
Sri Lanka **3**: 59
Tanzania **23**: 169
Togo **23**: 36
Tunisia **23**: 301
USSR **4**: 85, 112, 134
USA **4**: 154, 160, 344, 376, 1024 **9**: 635, 648, 664, 716
Boston **4**: 81, 358
Connecticut **4**: 30
Florida **21**: 237
Indiana **4**: 340
Missouri **4**: 151
New Orleans **4**: 123
New York **4**: 357
North Carolina **4**: 4
Wales **4**: 120
alcoholism **8**: 25
Anglican Church **4**: 17
employment **4**: 136 **5**: 95,

(education *cont.*)
173 **9**: 648, 716 **23**: 195, 211
feminism **4**: 8 **7**: 48, 61, 65
fertility **3**: 2, 8, 31, 59
literature **4**: 52, 60, 159 **12**: 1552, 1704, 1855, 1883, 2048, 2294, 2341, 2430
magazines, women **4**: 153 **9**: 477
misogyny **4**: 1219
prisons **2**: 58
United Nations **16**: 32, 54
women's rights **7**: 23
working class mothers' attitudes **6**: 378
educational administration and administrators **4**: 9, 613, 622, 626, 631–2, 636, 642–3, 669, 678, 683, 692, 706, 714, 717, 730, 738, 740, 767, 776, 778, 782, 784, 785, 789–90, 794–5, 797–8, 803, 818, 831, 836, 840, 845, 849, 854, 857, 860, 865–6 **5**: 284, 460, 598
schools **4**: 369, 591–3, 598–600, 605, 607, 610–11, 633–4, 638, 644, 649, 670, 685, 701, 709–10, 724, 727, 729, 747, 750, 755, 759, 761, 763, 769, 777, 779, 781, 793, 806–9, 813–14, 821, 823, 825, 832, 1587
principals & vice-principals **4**: 369, 589, 595, 606, 619, 628, 630, 645, 647, 666, 671, 673, 675, 700, 705, 707, 719, 760, 764, 771, 787, 800, 815, 822, 833, 838, 999
superintendents **4**: 9, 641, 646, 650, 656, 663, 667, 711, 722, 729, 751, 753, 758, 770, 773, 805, 812, 824, 827, 841, 873 **17**: 831
school board members **4**: 676, 699, 737, 745, 780
higher education **4**: 620, 635, 651, 653, 657–8, 661, 664–5, 667, 672, 682, 686, 688, 690, 696, 698, 708, 712, 728, 731, 733–4, 743, 755–6, 761, 766, 768, 772, 774–5, 781, 783, 788, 810, 819, 830, 846–8, 856, 862, 874, 877, 879 **6**: 943
community colleges **4**: 591, 627, 629, 632, 687, 692, 713, 742, 801, 859, 861
liberal arts colleges **4**: 694, 837
student personnel administration **4**: 867, 870
trustees **4**: 689, 695
universities & colleges **4**: 478, 502, 594, 635, 639, 651, 678, 680–1, 689, 695, 702, 708, 739, 752, 799, 826, 828–9, 842, 844, 852, 871, 875
continuing education **4**: 609, 621, 765
physical education **4**: 489, 502
vocational education **4**: 652, 748
educational counselling **4**: 384,

(educational counselling *cont.*)
888, 1506, 1594
schools **4**: 1139, 1237, 1266, 1307–8, 1316–7, 1319, 1321, 1329, 1331, 1334, 1337–40
universities & colleges **4**: 1064, 1305–6, 1309–15, 1320, 1322–4, 1330, 1332, 1335–6, 1339, 1341–8
students **4**: 1279
educational psychology **4**: 400, 1012–1303
educational technology: administration **4**: 743
Eddy, Mary Baker **18**: 85, 88, 119
Edgeworth, Maria **12**: 1570, 2047–60
Edwards, Mrs E.H. **18**: 268
Egerton, George **12**: 1740, 2061
Egypt, Ancient **9**: 30, 32, 35, 40
Egypt **3**: 85 **4**: 173, 257, 312, 1092, 1227, 1265, 1302 **5**: 286 **9**: 1, 2, 5, 6 **23**: 18, 68, 86, 125, 127, 144, 193, 247, 248, 301
elderly women
Afro-Americans **8**: 101 **17**: 737
arthritis **21**: 66
body measurements **15**: 116
clothing **21**: 66, 93, 97
depression **8**: 244
diabetes **8**: 395
diet **8**: 303, 307, 311 **15**: 151
exercise **15**: 28, 129
health **8**: 97, 101 **17**: 737, 751, 756
health education **8**: 97
health visiting **8**: 108
housing **17**: 760
Lebanese **23**: 188
literary portrayal **12**: 23
mental health **8**: 131
Mexican American **21**: 169
physical **15**: 20
psychology **17**: 735–760
residential homes **17**: 738, 744, 752
Eleanor of Aquitaine **12**: 1444
Eleanor of Provence **9**: 93
electronics industry **5**: 213
Eliot, George **1**: 111 **12**: 57, 58, 60, 66, 72, 87, 93, 131, 1682, 1696, 1704, 1720, 1727, 1729, 1740, 1742, 1752, 1773, 1781, 1815, 1823, 2062–2315
Elizabeth I, queen **1**: 118, 171, 238 **19**: 70, 100 **12**: 1460, 1478, 1495, 1515
Elizabeth de Burgh, Lady of Clare **9**: 98
Elliott, Sarah Barnwell **12**: 719–20
Elmira College **4**: 432
elocutionists **10**: 19
Elstob, Elizabeth **12**: 1625
Emerson, Ellen Tucker **9**: 412
Emerson, Lilian Jackson **9**: 412
Emma, queen **9**: 94
employment (*see also* individual trades and industries; hours of work; industrial workers;

(employment *cont.*)
labour laws; trade unions; wages and salaries) **3**: 5, 9, 12, 30, 43, 53, 86, 105, 108, 112 **5**: 3, 9, 10, 22, 26–9, 33–4, 36, 38, 42, 55, 65, 68, 72, 74, 77, 81, 83, 87, 90, 97, 107, 113, 120–1, 225 **9**: 432 **21**: 235
in Bangladesh **23**: 203
Barbados **3**: 117
Brazil **3**: 21 **23**: 96, 211
Canada **3**: 91 **5**: 56, 197
Cameroon **3**: 28
Chile **23**: 76
China **3**: 50
Colombia **23**: 242
Denmark **3**: 119 **21**: 202, 228
Egypt **23**: 18, 127, 144
England
Coventry **5**: 11
Cray Valley **5**: 142
Lancashire **21**: 224
Yorkshire **9**: 121
Europe: medieval **9**: 220
Great Britain **5**: 11, 49, 51, 141, 152 **9**: 149–50, 164, 204, 216
Ghana **23**: 189
Greece **5**: 52
Guatemala **23**: 190
India **23**: 233
Indonesia **23**: 78
Iran **23**: 267
Ireland: Belfast **4**: 171
Japan **5**: 7, 64, 119, 158
Jordan **23**: 281
Kenya **23**: 53
Korea **3**: 60 **23**: 62
Latin America **3**: 46
Libya **23**:91
Malta **23**: 212
Malawi **9**: 7
Malaysia **23**: 104, 225a, 278
Chinese **23**: 176
Mauritius **23**: 131
Mexico **3**: 100 **23**: 101, 215–16, 299
New Zealand **5**: 85
Nigeria **23**: 202
Peru **23**: 195
Philippines **3**: 20, 25, 33, 72 **23**: 136
South Africa **5**: 62
Sri Lanka **3**: 59
Taiwan **23**: 58, 61, 174
Thailand **3**: 18, 25 **23**: 292
Turkey **5**: 104
USA **5**: 2, 19, 24, 40, 45, 47, 63, 66–7, 75, 105, 108, 140, 190, 501 **9**: 443, 486–7, 648, 653, 661
Arkansas **5**: 99
California **5**: 117
Durham, NC **9**: 518a
Georgia **5**: 376
Indiana **21**: 304
Los Angeles **9**: 564
Lowell, Mass. **9**: 450
Madison **5**: 348
Michigan **5**: 198

(employment *cont.*)
Philadelphia **5**: 163 **9**: 537
Pittsburgh **9**: 538
San Francisco **9**: 560, 564
South Dakota **5**: 114
Washington **5**: 609
Venezuela **23**: 17
Zaire: Kinshasa **23**: 113
adolescents **5**: 46, 608
birth control **3**: 83
developing countries **23**: 4, 275, 300
education **4**: 136 **5**: 95, 173 **9**: 648
family **6**: 3 **23**: 233
feminism **5**: 98 **7**: 34, 119
fertility **3**: 4, 5, 9, 12, 18–20, 25, 27–30, 32, 36, 39–41, 46–8, 50, 59, 60, 66, 69, 70, 72, 74, 87–8, 91, 103, 112, 117, 120, 123
graduates **4**: 11, 43, 1619 **5**: 35, 37, 48, 71, 105, 109, 159
high school girls **4**: 1622
higher education **4**: 208
immigrants **9**: 443
interviews **5**: 396 **17**: 798
literary portrayal **12**: 293, 432–3, 2302
married women **5**: 122–206 **21**: 9, 15, 23, 26, 32 **21**: 128
Marxism **5**: 98
menopause **19**: 237
menstruation **19**: 199, 214
mothers **5**: 134, 136–7, 149, 151, 163, 165, 168, 170, 175, 178–81, 186, 188, 195, 198, 202–3, 206 **6**: 36, 57–8, 624, 642 **21**: 17, 304
part-time **5**: 11, 184
re-entry students **5**: 49, 1362
sex-role
school counsellors **4**: 1329
attitudes **4**: 1069, 1333
suicide **5**: 364, 589
World War
1914–1918 **9**: 164
1939–1945 **9**: 204, 560
engineering **5**: 315
in London **9**: 148
absenteeism (manual workers) **5**: 250
career choices **4**: 1078, 1484, 1535, 1551, 1661, 1682
education (USA) **4**: 157, 1287
sex equality **5**: 273
English teachers and teaching **4**: 48, 995
entrepreneurs **5**: 17, 387, 524, 535
epilepsy **8**: 410
Épinay, Mme de **12**: 3066–7
Epstein, Marie **1**: 9
Equal Employment Opportunities Commission **5**: 216
equality of women **7**: 6
in Iran **23**: 98
international law **11**: 4
liberalism & Marxism **7**: 75
Erinyes **12**: 1326
Essex **2**: 212

Ethiopia **3**: 78 **4**: 1149 **23**: 77
Eugénie, Empress of France **9**: 225
Euphrasia, Mother **18**: 215
Europe **3**: 68 **6**: 708 **9**: 220–2 **16**: 76
European Economic Community **5**: 240, 241
Evangelical Covenant Church of America **18**: 86, 111
literature **12**: 1713, 1752, 1977, 2161, 2264, 2304
Eve in literature **12**: 1427, 1466, 1487, 1512–13
Evelyn College for Women, Princeton NJ **4**: 66
Ewing, Horatia **12**: 2316–17
executives *see* managers and executives
executives' wives **6**: 156, 164
existentialism: women's role **14**: 23

families and family life (*see also* daughters; household organization; marriage; single-parent families)
in Algeria **23**: 59
Brazil **23**: 123
China **23**: 150, 274
Egypt **9**: 6, 30
Germany **9**: 288
Ghana **6**: 1 **23**: 189
India **23**: 208, 233
Iraq **23**: 100
Israel **23**: 111
Jamaica **6**: 1
Japan **6**: 29
Kenya **23**: 220
Korea **23**: 166
Malawi **23**: 52
Mexico **9**: 342 **23**: 133
Morocco **23**: 59
Nigeria **23**: 156, 200
Portugal **6**: 19
Spain: Seville **6**: 15
Tunisia **23**: 59
USA **6**: 1, 13, 23, 615, 635 **9**: 373, 434
adolescent girls **6**: 809
Afro-American **6**: 2, 12, 20, 25, 27, 512
aggressive behaviour **6**: 4
class structure: feminism **7**: 2
communication **6**: 8, 11, 17
consumption behaviour **21**: 44
'disadvantaged' **6**: 201
employment **5**: 164, 166, 169, 204 **6**: 3, 816–958 **23**: 233
female achievement **6**: 12
female head of family **3**: 67 **23**: 220
feminine roles **6**: 9, 16, 17, 19, 23–4
feminism **9**: 389
incomes **6**: 14, 192, 825, 858, 896 **23**: 27
law **23**: 59
literary portrayal **12**: 445, 1842, 2082, 2250, 2287

(families and family life *cont.*)
Marxism **6**: 6
maternal behaviour **6**: 782
maternal illness **8**: 415
Mexican Americans **5**: 322
prisoners **6**: 135
professional sportsmen **6**: 144
psychoanalysis **6**: 6
study-course **4**: 1194
family planning **3**: 73, 83, 92 **7**: 109 **19**: 20, 483
in Barbados **3**: 98
China **3**: 15
developing countries **3**: 94, 107
France: politics **16**: 73
Great Britain **9**: 152
Iran **3**: 62
Mexico **3**: 95
Middle East **3**: 14
Nigeria **3**: 115
Philippines **3**: 51
Puerto Rico **3**: 149
Taiwan **3**: 82
Thailand **3**: 106
USA **9**: 401, 472, 533, 593 **19**: 56
family size **3**: 21–2
Afro-American preferences **6**: 5
women's employment: Lancashire **21**: 224
farm workers *see* agricultural workers
farmers' wives **4**: 1375 **5**: 555 **21**: 4
Farr, Florence **12**: 2563
fashion **1**: 159 **4**: 1553 **9**: 524, 563, 603
father-daughter relationships **4**: 1516 **6**: 28, 41–3, 46, 48–9, 53, 75–7, 80–2, 87–9, 92, 95, 97, 106, 111–2, 124–5
in English drama & fiction **12**: 1441, 1501, 1551, 1681, 1737
incest **2**: 215–28
Fauset, Jessie **12**: 398
Felician Sisters **4**: 357
Felix, Elizabeth Rachael **1**: 126
Female Chartist Associations **9**: 174
female circumcision (Kikuyu) **18**: 265
female infanticide (India) **9**: 56
Female Spectator, The **9**: 507
Female Tatler, The **12**: 1602a
feminine principle **7**: 110 **17**: 5
femininity **2**: 169 **4**: 1243 **9**: 211, 508 **17**: 6–7, 11, 27–8 **19**: 300 **20**: 123, 131, 137
feminism and feminists (*see also* assertiveness groups and training; consciousness-raising groups; lesbian-feminism; women's liberation movement; women's movement; women's rights) **7**: 10, 10a, 22, 27, 52, 72, 94, 103, 114 **9**: 378
in China **9**: 147
Czechoslovakia **9**: 293
Denmark **9**: 336

(feminism and feminists *cont.*)
Egypt **9**: 1 **23**: 125
England **9**: 103, 112, 116, 126, 141, 145a, 199, 207, 216 **12**: 1554, 1601, 1770, 2286, 2288, 2375, 2391, 2500, 2505, 2650, 2687, 2756, 2776, 2823
France **1**: 48 **4**: 913 **9**: 226, 228, 236, 239, 248, 251–2, 256, 261, 264 **12**: 2843, 2919, 2942, 2948–50, 2958, 2996, 3157, 3164, 3244, 3250, 3255–6
Japan **9**: 55
Peru **23**: 116
Spain **7**: 113 **12**: 3560, 3569, 3628, 3647, 3663, 3673
Sudan **23**: 125
USSR **9**: 312, 313, 316
USA **7**: 16, 20, 36, 55, 69, 79, 104 **9**: 382, 390, 403, 436, 445, 448, 473, 508, 510, 533, 551, 618–20, 632, 662, 671, 673, 684, 691
Afro-Americans **7**: 85
androgyny **20**: 152
anorexia nervosa **8**: 324
anti-feminism **7**: 37, 50, 68, 74, 102, 117 **12**: 3553, 3605
art **1**: 219, 221, 247 **12**: 106
attitudes to **7**: 15, 111, 114–15
authenticity theory **14**: 26
birth control **7**: 109
clothing & body image **21**: 82
counsellors **8**: 196
crime **2**: 63
development of women **7**: 141
education **4**: 8, 287, 1635 **7**: 48, 61, 65
employment **5**: 98, 582 **7**: 34, 119
family **7**: 2, 20 **9**: 389
films **1**: 7, 20 **12**: 106
health **7**: 57 **8**: 112, 540
home economics **4**: 1218
ideology **7**: 11, 25, 38, 64, 109
intelligence **9**: 691
law **11**: 17, 23
liberalism (J.S. Mill) **7**: 125
literary criticism **12**: 106, 110–11, 113, 117–19, 122, 125, 129, 136, 138, 140–1, 143
literature **9**: 256 **12**: 66, 83, 108–9, 121, 134, 137–8, 146, 303, 417, 1276, 1283, 1554, 1601, 1770, 1795, 1813, 1959, 2031, 2286, 2288, 2375, 2391, 2500, 2505, 2518, 2525, 2555, 2587, 2650, 2687, 2701, 2756, 2776, 2782, 2801, 2823, 2900, 3315–6, 3326, 3471, 3473, 3517, 3560, 3569, 3628, 3647, 3663, 3673
marriage **6**: 194 **7**: 93
medicine **9**: 449
mental health centres **8**: 156–7
morality **7**: 116
motherhood **6**: 116, 517 **7**: 109
patriarchy **7**: 33
philosophy **14**: 16, 17, 20
politics **7**: 69, 77 **9**: 126

(feminism and feminists *cont.*)
press **7**: 79 **9**: 165 **13**: 31
psychology of women **8**: 168
psychotherapy **8**: 168, 170, 176, 182, 185, 191, 206
rape **2**: 286
religion **18**: 89, 240
rhetoric **7**: 83, 134–5, 139
role-conflict **7**: 13
sex-roles **6**: 365, 517 **4**: 1635 **9**: 378 **17**: 842
sexuality **7**: 109, 128 **20**: 66, 99
social theory **7**: 60, 101
Socialism **9**: 403, 618, 684
songs **7**: 134
superintendents **4**: 751
teachers (France) **4**: 913
theatre **1**: 48, 84, 135 **12**: 384
theology **7**: 14 **18**: 241, 288
theory **7**: 1, 72a
therapy **17**: 53
universities **7**: 31, 88 **17**: 877
witchcraft **12**: 144
fencing **22**: 170
Fenwick, Eliza **12**: 1554
Ferber, Edna **12**: 721
Ferrier, Susan **12**: 2318–20
fertility **3**: 52, 73, 80–1, 123
in Australia **3**: 57
Bangladesh **3**: 111
Barbados **3**: 117
Cameroon **3**: 28
Canada **3**: 91
Chile **3**: 50
Columbia **3**: 12
Costa Rica **3**: 99
Denmark **3**: 119
Eastern Europe **3**: 68
Egypt **3**: 85
Ethiopia **3**: 78
Gambia **3**: 79, 113
India **3**: 8, 11
Indonesia **3**: 2, 84
Iran **3**: 96
Jamaica **3**: 97, 127
Korea **3**: 60
Latin America **3**: 47 **23**: 295
Mexico **3**: 100
Middle East **3**: 14
Nigeria **3**: 6
Pakistan **3**: 54, 76
Philippines **3**: 16, 20, 33, 72
Poland **3**: 104
Sri Lanka **3**: 59, 89, 111
Sweden **3**: 57, 125
Tanzania **3**: 75
Thailand **3**: 3, 18, 25
Turkey **3**: 42
USSR **3**: 43
USA **3**: 10, 26, 30, 43–5, 53, 55, 56, 63–4, 71, 74, 77, 86, 90, 93, 105, 112, 118
education **3**: 2, 8, 59, 127
employment **3**: 4, 5, 9, 12, 18–20, 27–30, 32, 36, 39–41, 43, 46, 48, 50, 53, 59, 60, 66, 69, 70, 72, 74, 86–8, 91–2, 100, 103, 105, 112, 117–20, 123
literature **12**: 1405

(fertility *cont.*)
marital separation **3**: 124
women's rights **3**: 129
Fielding, Sarah **12**: 1594, 1626–9
Fields, Mrs James T. **12**: 397
filicide **8**: 139
Filipino women **6**: 602 **10**: 2
film **1**: 4, 8–9, 14, 18, 22, 28 **12**: 106
Finland **2**: 495 **9**: 333a
Fisher, Dorothy Canfield **12**: 722
fisherwomen **5**: 248
Fiske, Minnie Maddern **1**: 106, 147, 154
Fitzgerald, Zelda Sayre **12**: 723–4
Flanagan, Hallie **1**: 146, 163, 185
Flanders **1**: 197
Flore, Jeanne **12**: 3068
Florence **1**: 227
Florida, USA **4**: 313, 293, 634, 667, 844, 1010, 1109, 1351, 1446, 1513, 1553, 1637 **9**: 522, 699 **16**: 45 **19**: 512 **21**: 105, 244 **22**: 119
Flynn, Elizabeth Gurley **9**: 408, 607, 655
folk-lore: pregnancy **19**: 464
Follett, Mary Parker **9**: 423, 430
food
advertising **13**: 23
Italian Americans **21**: 172
leisure **21**: 186
forestry workers **5**: 261
Fort, Gertrud von le **12**: 3396–3401
Foster, Abby Kelley **9**: 614
fostering **6**: 466, 491, 501, 523, 608, 612, 619, 674, 716, 728, 750
foundlings **9**: 256
France **1**: 257 **4**: 2, 45, 128, 155, 184 **9**: 120, 165, 223–73 **10**: 1 **16**: 4, 44, 74 **18**: 149
Paris **4**: 184 **9**: 230, 233, 255, 271 **21**: 108
Francis, Marianne **12**: 2321
Franciscan Sisters (Uganda) **18**: 264
Freeman, Mary E. Wilkins **12**: 200, 257, 376, 440, 725–30
Freeze, Mary Ann Burnham **18**: 113
French, Alice **12**: 731
French Revolution **9**: 230, 233, 244
French, Virginia **12**: 732
Friedan, Betty **7**: 59
friendship **17**: 765, 776, 779, 787, 789, 80
Fritz, Jean **12**: 733
Fuller, Loie **1**: 180
Fuller, Margaret **9**: 382, 582 **12**: 336, 734–42
fur trade (Canada) (*see also* clothing industry) **9**: 365
Fullerton, Georgina **12**: 2322
Fusae, Chikawa **9**: 55

Gage, Matilda Joslyn **9**: 702
Gambario, Griselda **12**: 3480–1
Gambia, the **3**: 79 **23**: 74
Gándara, Carmen **12**: 3482
Garro, Elena **12**: 3483
Gaskell, Elizabeth Cleghorn **12**: 1696, 1704, 1773, 1774, 1823, 2323–74
Gellhorn, Martha **12**: 743
gender/sex role **17**: 801
abortion **19**: 97
adolescents **6**: 58, 60 **8**: 129 **13**: 11 **17**: 176, 853, 856, 875 **20**: 37
alcoholics **8**: 2, 7, 21
American men & women **17**: 883
androgyny **20**: 143–5
athletes **22**: 7, 9, 21, 36
battered women **2**: 195, 200
breast feeding **19**: 237
business education **4**: 1014, 1021
career choices **4**: 1068, 1444, 1453–4, 1459, 1474–5, 1485, 1502–3, 1508, 1520–1, 1536, 1541–2, 1544–5, 1556, 1575–6, 1582, 1595, 1606, 1612, 1621, 1635, 1637, 1653, 1657, 1665
children **2**: 195, 200
family influences **6**: 393, 486, 494, 609, 703, 735, 891, 913
reading-books **21**: 226
teacher's attitudes **7**: 112
TV **13**: 41
women's careers **4**: 1282
clothing **21**: 96
counselling **4**: 1308, 1317 **8**: 160, 186–192, 203
counsellors **4**: 1338 **8**: 166, 187, 198–9, 202
criminals & delinquents **2**: 59, 70, 119, 135, 146 **20**: 169
daughters **6**: 40, 50, 52, 55, 61, 63, 68, 101, 127–8, 130 **23**: 295
doctors, medicine, & nursing **4**: 1620 **6**: 933 **8**: 477, 480–1, 553, 556
education (Iraq) **23**: 8
educational administrators **4**: 643, 651, 659, 667, 700, 706, 762, 786
family **6**: 9, 16, 17, 19, 23–4
feminism & anti-feminists **6**:365, 517 **7**: 108, 117–18 **9**: 378 **17**: 842
girls **4**: 1077 **17**: 187
higher education **4**: 1017, 1119
housework **21**: 1, 3, 4, 25, 30, 32, 37
illness **8**: 420
kindergarten teachers **4**: 988
liberals **17**: 840
literature **12**: 102, 1142
married women **6**: 139, 143, 184, 186 **17**: 114
menstruation **19**: 146, 148, 167, 171, 191, 202
mental health **8**: 137, 152, 221, 224, 229, 244
mothers **6**: 40, 50, 52, 63, 68, 101, 127–8, 130, 296, 336, 703, 735 **23**: 275
occupations **4**: 1491, 1659 **5**:
(gender/sex role *cont.*)
344, 352, 358, 360, 363, 365, 381–2, 392, 403, 413, 429, 435, 465–6, 469–70, 480, 482, 500, 559, 580, 595, 597, 619, 623
pastoral care **18**: 282
politicians **16**: 63
poor in Bahia **23**: 308
pregnancy **19**: 481–2, 494
psychology students **4**: 1156
psychotherapy **8**: 176
Puerto Ricans in New York **21**: 157, 167
re-entry students **4**: 1378
rural women **4**: 1415
schools & schoolchildren **4**: 1015, 1036, 1089, 1100, 1117, 1147, 1241, 1251, 1338 **17**: 880
separated women **6**: 221
sexuality **20**: 46, 55, 60, 87, 114, 118
single parents **6**: 202, 364
speech (Mayan society) **23**: 49
student nurses **8**: 553
student teachers **4**: 1008
students **4**: 1020, 1137 **17**: 527, 539, 559, 564, 566, 570, 573, 576, 578–9, 581–2, 585, 587–8, 595, 603, 605, 608–9, 611, 619–20, 624–6, 632, 636, 638, 650, 658, 665, 667 **23**: 265
teachers **4**: 597, 916, 940, 1000, 1021
training groups **17**: 70, 73, 76, 86, 95, 103, 114, 140, 151, 174
wives **4**: 1375 **6**: 133, 138, 139, 141, 143, 145, 183, 184, 186 **9**: 902, 925 **17**: 114
women's attitudes **17**: 876
women's studies courses **4**: 565, 567, 574
writers' creativity **12**: 118
young women **4**: 1068
youth: Lebanon **23**: 129
Genlis, Mme de **12**: 3069–70
geography teaching **4**: 193
George Peabody College for Teachers **4**: 322
Georgia **4**: 494, 655, 1183, 1230, 1292 **5**: 257, 297 **9**: 642, 712
Germany **4**: 2, 79, 121, 465 **6**: 656 **9**: 274, 276–80, 284, 287–90, 294–302 **18**: 73 **21**: 231
Ghana **6**: 1 **23**: 22, 135, 205, 232, 243, 252
Gilbert, Mrs G. **1**: 83
Gilder, Rosamond **1**: 105
Gilman, Charlotte Perkins **9**: 448, 619, 620
Gilzburg, Natalia **12**: 79, 3436–7
girl guides **8**: 175 **9**: 530 **21**: 254, 260, 264
girls (*see also* adolescents; daughters)
clothing **21**: 101
development psychology **17**: 175–188
family life **6**: 4

girls' camps **17**: 778 **8**: 181
girls' clubs **21**: 251, 256
Girls' Public Day School Trust **4**: 189
Glasgow, Ellen **12**: 79, 82, 213, 232, 288, 307, 376, 377, 462, 744–78
Glaspell, Susan **12**: 267, 779–80
Glenorchy, Lady **18**: 86
goddesses
  Canaanite **18**: 4
  Egyptian **18**: 8
  Greek **12**: 1298 **18**: 3
  Indian **18**: 287
  Mesopotamian **18**: 17
  mother-goddesses **17**: 8 **18**: 287
  Roman **12**: 1313, 1386, 1500 **18**: 2
  theosophy **17**: 5
Godey's Lady's Book **9**: 458, 723 **12**: 402a
Godwin, Gail **12**: 272
Gold Coast **23**: 189
golf **22**: 131, 134, 146, 165, 185, 189
Gordimer, Nadine **12**: 156, 159–62
Gordon, Carolina **12**: 781–4
Gottsched, Luise **12**: 3374
Goucher College **4**: 432
Gould, Lois **12**: 46
Gournay, Mlle de **12**: 3071–2
government administrators **5**: 460 **16**: 27–8
government workers **5**: 229, 251, 265, 278, 284, 290, 302, 316, 330, 439, 485 **9**: 705
governess in literature **12**: 1767
Grable, Bette **1**: 10
Grace, Patricia **12**: 1269
Graham, Martha **1**: 120, 178
grandmothers **6**: 35, 359, 373, 714, 814 **9**: 525
Gray, Shirley Ann **12**: 377, 785
Great Western Railway (clerical workers) **9**: 129
Greece, Ancient **9**: 9, 12, 14, 16, 18, 25, 26, 29, 36
Greece **2**: 44 **5**: 50, 52, 54
Green, Edith **16**: 60
Gregory, Lady **12**: 2564–72
Greiffenberg, Catharina Regina von **12**: 3375
Grier School **4**: 183
Griffith, Elizabeth **12**: 1594, 1630
Grimke, Angelica Wilde **9**: 558 **12**: 786
Grimké, Sarah **9**: 382, 558
Guam **21**: 132, 151
Guatemala **23**: 41, 88, 102, 190, 207
Guérin, Eugénie de **12**: 3074
Guggenheim, Peggy **1**: 223
Guido, Beatriz **12**: 3444, 3484
Guiney, Louise Imogen **12**: 787–8
Gulf-Coast Bible College **6**: 141
Gulf Park College for Women **4**: 48
Guyana **8**: 305
gymnastics **4**: 476 **22**: 72, 78, 88, 105, 110, 115

Habley, Faith **1**: 21
Hagen, Uta **1**: 182
Haiti **23**: 283
Hale, Sara Josepha **9**: 458, 723
Hall, Radclyffe **2**: 2573
Hamilton, Alice **9**: 666, 718
Hampshire, UK **5**: 573
Hansberry, Lorraine **12**: 219, 267, 789
Hansen, Julia Butler **16**: 61
Harand, Irene **9**: 282
Harris, Bernice Kelly **12**: 790
Harris, Margaret **1**: 101
Harrison, Maxwell S. **12**: 791
Hart, Nancy **9**: 350
Hausa women **23**: 218, 234 **12**: 155
Hawaii **4**: 611 **8**: 103 **21**: 264
Hayden, Magdalen **18**: 112
Hayes, Lucy Webb **9**: 474
Hays, Mary **12**: 1554, 2375
Hayward, Eliza **12**: 1631–4
Head, Edith **1**: 12
health and health services
  in Canada **8**: 114
    France **9**: 272
    Great Britain **9**: 214
    Israel **21**: 16
    Poland **3**: 104
    Puerto Rico **3**: 49 **8**: 107
    Taiwan **23**: 119
    Tanzania **23**: 115
    USA **9**: 518, 588
  advertisements **21**: 45
  ante-natal **19**: 252, 311–12, 334, 365, 396, 401, 463, 483
  breast-feeding **6**: 549
  children **8**: 117 **11**: 12 **19**: 314 **23**: 115
  cotton workers **5**: 286
  elderly **8**: 97, 101, 108 **17**: 737, 751, 756
  family planning (Nigeria) **3**: 115
  field workers **8**: 94
  Italian Americans **21**: 152
  magazine articles **13**: 28
  middle-aged **8**: 95
  middle-class **9**: 214
  mother & infant **6**: 766 **8**: 90, 97, 100, 117, 120 **19**: 305, 477–8
  physical activities **22**: 31
  preventive medicine **8**: 116, 118
  women's health movement **8**: 96, 100, 115
health education
  career counselling **4**: 1437
  pregnancy **19**: 463
  teachers **4**: 304, 443, 462
health visitors **8**: 92, 108 **9**: 135
Heathcote, Dorothy **1**: 195
Hébert, Anne **12**: 1288–92
Hecuba **12**: 1319
Hedda Gabler **1**: 152
Helen of Troy **12**: 15, 1297, 1300–1, 1306–7, 1318, 1321
Hellman, Lillian **12**: 54, 267, 792–806
Helvétius, Mme **12**: 3075

Hemans, Felicia **12**: 2376–9
Henrietta Maria, queen **9**: 67
Henry, Alice **9**: 536
Henry Street Visiting Nurses Service **9**: 436, 632
Hera (goddess) **18**: 3
Herbert, Mary (Countess of Pembroke) **12**: 1535–9
Herbst, Josephine **12**: 807–8
Herford, Beatrice **1**: 138
Hernandez, Luisa Josefina **12**: 3485
Heron, Matilda **1**: 122
herpes **8**: 423
Hickey, Mary A. **9**: 406
high schools *see* secondary schools
higher education (*see also* community colleges; liberal arts colleges; universities) **4**: 42, 148, 208, 224, 287, 332, 1044 **9**: 419 **18**: 154
  in Beirut **4**: 301
    Canada: Ontario **4**: 150
    Egypt **4**: 257
    England **4**: 14, 23, 88, 125, 130, 163
    India **4**: 206, 209, 223, 305, 309
    Ireland: Dublin **4**: 20, 116
    Japan **4**: 239
    Korea **4**: 261
    Saudi Arabia **23**: 165
    USSR **4**: 44
    USA **4**: 40, 63, 75, 102, 205, 218, 223, 234, 262, 296, 326, 338, 349, 394, 1017 **21**: 110
  women executives **5**: 598
  women's attitudes **4**: 1269
Higuchi Ichiyo **12**: 1264
Hildegard of Bingen **12**: 3376
Hillhouse, Mrs David **9**: 350
Hinduism
  educated women **23**: 155
  education **9**: 48
  girls' ideals of womanhood **23**: 66
  inheritance rights **11**: 22, 231
  law of *stridhana* **23**: 241
  mother-goddesses **17**: 8
  property rights **23**: 60, 231, 241
  rituals **18**: 289, 295
  temple courtesans **23**: 199
  theology **18**: 297
  widowhood **9**: 63
  women's position **18**: 285–6, 289, 291–4, 297
Hinkson, Katherine Tynan **12**: 2575
Hispanic Americans **21**: 164
  avoidance of academic success **21**: 162
  child health **19**: 467
  continuing education **21**: 114
  garment workers: New York **5**: 305
  high school girls: counselling **4**: 1321
  literary portrayal **12**: 346
  mathematics **4**: 1223
  mother-child relations **6**: 584

(Hispanic Americans *cont.*)
pregnancy **19**: 415, 467
historians **5**: 411 **9**: 119
history teaching **4**: 192, 1146
Hobhouse, Emily **9**: 160
hockey **22**: 126, 128, 130, 144, 151, 184
Hofland, Barbara **12**: 2379
Holland **1**: 218, 249
Holley, Marietta **12**: 359, 809–10
Hollis, Florence **17**: 9
Holy Child Sisters (Nigerian education) **18**: 262
Holyoke College **4**: 432
home economics **4**: 217, 232, 238, 245, 283, 311, 336, 1206, 1218
administration **4**: 709, 813
career choices **4**: 1565
continuing education **23**: 224
foreign students' wives **21**: 166
student values **21**: 1152
teacher training **4**: 890, 912
teachers **4**: 95
home workers **5**: 303 **9**: 231 **21**: 29
homosexual husbands **6**: 152
homosexuals (attitudes of female nursing students) **8**: 495
Honduras **21**: 257
Hong Kong **23**: 250, 255
Horney, Karen **12**: 2799 **17**: 2
horsemanship **22**: 160
Hospital Sisters of the Third Order of St Francis **9**: 428
hospitalization **8**: 414
hospitals: domestic workers **5**: 260
Hoult, Norah **12**: 2574
hours of work **5**: 126, 135, 232 **9**: 521, 561
household work
in Canada: Manitoba **21**: 20
Denmark **21**: 4
England **21**: 29, 98
Great Britain **21**: 6
India: Nepal **23**: 152
Tunisia **23**: 23
USA **9**: 712 **21**: 15,38, 40
adolescent girls' attitudes **21**: 2
capitalism **9**: 498
child care **21**: 28
college graduates' attitudes **21**: 5
division of labour **21**: 1, 3, 15–17, 25, 30, 37
farm-household **21**: 4
economic aspects **21**: 1, 7, 8, 11, 18, 38
education **9**: 709
household appliances **21**: 23, 33
kitchen: women's attitudes **21**: 4
physical disability **21**: 36
time spent on **21**: 16
housewives **21**: 35, 36
in Japan **21**: 13
USA **21**: 40
activities **21**: 24
American Jewish **21**: 121
class **21**: 22
consumption behaviour **21**:
(housewives *cont.*)
43–4, 53, 56
orientation **21**: 19
role attitudes **21**: 56
social attitudes **21**: 34, 39
travel **21**: 7
work attitudes **21**: 27
working wives **6**: 830, 842–3, 868, 870, 874, 878, 887, 918, 936
housing **17**: 760 **21**: 271, 278
housing movement **9**: 392, 424
Houssaye, Sidonie de la **12**: 614
Houston, Margaret Lea **9**: 656
Howe, Julia Ward **9**: 483
Howe, Mary Carlisle **1**: 82
Howitt, Mary **12**: 2380
Howland, Emily **9**: 398
Hoyers, Anna Owena **12**: 3377
Hrotsvitha **12**: 3378
Hsiao Hung **12**: 1250
Huch, Ricarda **12**: 3379–82
Huillet, Daniele **1**: 4
human service agencies **5**: 542
humanities (career choices) **4**: 1573
humourists and wits **12**: 234, 248, 359
Humberside **2**: 7
Hunt, Harriot **9**: 501
Huntingdon, Anna Hyatt **1**: 207
Hurst, Fannie **12**: 811
Hurston, Zora Neale **12**: 232, 367, 398, 812–14
Hutchinson, Anne **12**: 278
Huxley, Elspeth **12**: 149, 150
Hyder, Qurratul-Ain **12**: 1257
hyperthyroidism **8**: 401
hysterectomy **8**: 391, 408
hysteria **17**: 10

Ibarruri, Dolores **9**: 340
Iceland **9**: 334–5
iconography **1**: 197, 211, 214, 224, 227, 235, 239, 254
Idaho, US **4**: 1572
identity status **17**: 22
ikostomics **8**: 398
illegitimacy **19**: 430
Afro-American **19**: 298
Australia **3**: 57
Sweden **3**: 57
Illinois, USA **4**: 214, 247, 272, 291, 431, 432, 460, 479, 492, 686, 692, 742, 772, 858, 950, 1118, 1156, 1260 **6**: 268 **9**: 646 **17**: 713 **19**: 87
immigrants and immigration (*see also* individual ethnic groups) **9**: 443, 460, 557, 634 **21**: 146
Inanna (goddess) **18**: 17
incest **2**: 215–28 **12**: 236
Inchbald, Elizabeth **12**: 1636–8
India **1**: 212 **3**: 8 **4**: 206, 209, 223, 309, 365, 374, 510, 1002, 1147 **8**: 478 **9**: 42–4, 51, 53–4, 59–62, 65 **18**: 285–97 **19**: 164 **21**: 73 **23**: 13, 75, 97, 105, 155, 164, 172, 187, 191, 208,
(India *cont.*)
217, 230, 233, 238–40, 244–5, 251, 263, 266, 268–9, 285
Indiana, USA **4**: 244, 270, 340, 352, 482, 699, 780, 782, 853, 883, 1084, 1179, 1288 **9**: 667 **17**: 654 **21**: 245, 304 **22**: 160
Indonesia **3**: 2, 84 **23**: 78
Indonesian immigrants (Netherlands) **21**: 179
industrial education **4**: 169, 211, 221 **9**: 404
industrial health and medicine: USA **9**: 666, 718
industrial safety **5**: 277
industrial workers **5**: 12, 31, 54, 112, 279, 417, 419, 513–14, 517, 540, 574
in Egypt **23**: 144
England **9**: 120, 124, 166, 181, 189
France **9**: 120
Germany **9**: 279
India **9**: 43
Malaysia **23**: 3, 225a
Mauritius **23**: 131
Taiwan **23**: 174
USA **9**: 120, 569, 676, 712
food habits **8**: 301
managers & executives **5**: 16, 538
physique **9**: 218
workers' education **4**: 424
infant and child mortality **3**: 85 **9**: 585 **19**: 334
infant care **19**: 267, 412, 487
infant feeding (*see also* breast feeding) **6**: 531 **19**: 288, 475 **23**: 268
infertility **3**: 23, 102 **18**: 313 **19**: 133–41
inheritance rights **11**: 22 **23**: 231
initiation rites **23**: 48, 122, 252
inn-keepers **9**: 359
Institute for Coloured Youth **4**: 124
Institutes of technology **4**: 227
intelligence **4**: 180 **9**: 691
International Ladies' Garment Workers' Union **1**: 176 **9**: 391
international law **11**: 4
International Women's Year **23**: 85
interviews **5**: 396 **21**: 69
Iowa, USA **3**: 55 **4**: 450, 460, 730, 1061 **6**: 822 **9**: 470 **21**: 49, 101
Iran **3**: 62, 96 **4**: 781, 1016, 1024 **21**: 239 **23**: 21, 30, 98, 110, 161, 249, 253, 257, 264, 267, 284
Iranians in USA **21**: 124, 134a **23**: 157
Iraq **4**: 981, 1014 **6**: 531 **23**: 7, 8, 90, 100, 301
Ireland **4**: 20, 82, 96, 115–16, 195 **18**: 52
Irene, empress of Constantinope **9**: 10

Isabella, queen **9**: 75
Isis (goddess) **18**: 9, 19
Islam
  biographies of women **12**: 3426
  birth control **23**: 219
  continuing education **4**: 1153
  family planning **3**: 106
  inheritance rights **11**: 22
  Koran & courtly love **18**: 299
  minority in Thailand **23**: 236
  missionary activities **18**: 298
  purdah **23**: 305
  saints **18**: 301
  social conditions of women **12**: 3425
  status of women **18**: 302 **23**: 54, 145, 286–7, 305
  women in Mombassa, Kenya **23**: 280
Israel **17**: 578 **19**: 236 **21**: 161 **23**: 44, 111, 114, 158, 182
Italy **1**: 197 **2**: 164 **9**: 303–5 **18**: 55 **19**: 28 **21**: 198, 209
Italian Americans
  Catholic religion **18**: 150
  child-rearing **6**: 360
  city life **21**: 144
  dress **21**: 68
  food & work **21**: 172
  garment workers **5**: 264
  health & ritual **21**: 152
  leisure **21**: 155
Ivanovna, Anna **9**: 319
Ivory Coast **23**: 92
Izumi Shikibu **12**: 1263

Jackson, Helen Hunt **12**: 815–16
Jackson, Laura Riding **12**: 817–20
Jackson, Shirley **12**: 101, 821–2
Jacquemard, Simone **12**: 3076
Jahan, Rastid **12**: 1257
Jamaica **3**: 97, 127 **6**: 1, 830 **8**: 464 **19**: 478, 501 **23**: 82
James, Jessie Daniel **9**: 492
Janauscher, Fanny **1**: 100
Japan **4**: 239, 254, 260, 277, 1252 **5**: 7, 64, 119, 158, 231 **6**: 121 **9**: 55–6 **16**: 58 **18**: 153 **19**: 16, 85 **21**: 13, 211, 220, 223, 230
Japanese Americans **21**: 135, 137–8, 149
Jelinck, Elfriede **12**: 3315
Jellicoe, Ann **12**: 2511
Jennings, Elizabeth **12**: 2521, 2576
Jennings, May Maria **9**: 699
Jewett, Sarah Orne **12**: 200, 326, 334, 376, 397, 472, 823–9
Jews and Judaism
  in England **18**: 314
    Germany **9**: 284
    Palestine: law **18**: 302
    USA **18**: 303, 308
      elderly **17**: 747
      high school: sex role **4**: 1089
      housewives **21**: 121
      mother-daughter **6**: 122
      students: sexuality **20**: 109
      urban life **21**: 122
(Jews and Judaism *cont.*)
      writers **12**: 249
  Hasidic communities **23**: 33
  illness behaviour **8**: 418
  infertility **18**: 313
  law: wives & divorce **11**: 18
  married women: career choices **4**: 1672
  mothers: child-rearing **6**: 360
  prostitution: Hebrew Bible **18**: 306
  Rabbinical teaching **18**: 311
  widows **18**: 305
Joan of Arc **9**: 229, 246 **12**: 31, 76, 96, 1750 **16**: 44
Johnson, Adelaide **1**: 216
Johnson, Josephine W. **12**: 830
Johnson, Lady Bird **16**: 25
Johnson, Uwe **12**: 3314
Johnston, Mary **12**: 831
Jones, Margo **1**: 133, 166, 194
Jones, Mary Harris **9**: 655
Jones, Sissicretta **1**: 43
Jordan **4**: 1283 **23**: 281
journalism and journalists **13**: 7, 24
  France **9**: 258
  Great Britain **9**: 143
  USA **9**: 355a, 385, 502, 514, 577, 605, 621, 696 **13**: 15, 35 **18**: 110
judges **5**: 309
Judische Frauenbund **9**: 284
Julia Domna **9**: 33, 41
Julian of Norwich **12**: 1336, 1392 **18**: 64, 74
juvenile courts **2**: 157, 170
juvenile delinquents **2**: 18, 76, 78–82, 84–91, 93–96, 98, 100, 103–4, 106–7, 110–15, 117–18, 120–4, 126–43, 149, 153–69, 171–2
  adolescent pregnancy **19**: 508
  lesbians **2**: 122, 130 **20**: 169
  mother's attitudes of **2**: 99, 116 **6**: 354
  recidivism **2**: 103, 145, 151

Kahlman, Kathryn **18**: 99
Kansas, US **4**: 541, 977 **5**: 265 **9**: 576 **18**: 173
Kaschnitz, Marie Luise **12**: 3291, 3383
Kauffman, Angelica **1**: 253
Keene, Laura **1**: 188
Kelley, Edith Summess **12**: 401
Kellor, Frances **9**: 583
Kemble, Fanny **1**: 108
Kempe, Margery **12**: 1391, 1392
Kent, UK **5**: 142
Kentucky, US **2**: 17 **4**: 652 **5**: 2 **6**: 814 **18**: 125 **22**: 103
Kenya **18**: 265 **23**: 1, 52, 139, 159, 168, 220–1, 276, 280, 289
Kenyan College **4**: 1126
Key, Ellen **9**: 332
Kibbutzim **23**: 47
Kikuyu women **18**: 265 **23**: 1
King, Edith **1**: 164
King, Grace Elizabeth **12**: 268, 410, 832
Kinniard College, Lahore **4**: 276
Kirchwey, Freda **13**: 2
Kirkland, Carolina M. **12**: 833
Kollontai, Alexandra Mikhailovna **9**: 308, 315, 323
Korea **3**: 60 **4**: 261, 271, 1239 **6**: 352 **19**: 461 **21**: 78 **23**: 49, 62, 130, 162, 166, 171, 214, 228
Korean Americans **21**: 139
Krasner, Lee **1**: 224
Krudener, Mme de **12**: 2914, 3077
Kulisciaff, Anna **9**: 318
Kumin, Maxine **12**: 386
Kummer, Clare **12**: 834
Kurahaship Yumiko **12**: 1264
Kuskova, E.D. **9**: 321
Kuwait **23**: 11

La Follette, Belle Case **7**: 79
Labé, Louise **12**: 3078–82
labour legislation and policies **5**: 208, 211
  in EEC **5**: 240–1
    Great Britain **5**: 235 **9**: 179 **11**: 3
    Iraq **23**: 7
    Japan **5**: 231
    Sweden **5**: 235
    USA **5**: 209, 210, 237 **9**: 521, 553, 561, 644
  equal opportunities policies
    Great Britain **5**: 219, 227
    USA **5**: 215–17, 220–1, 227, 230, 238–9, 242
  equal pay **5**: 230, 236, 238–40 **9**: 56
  hours of work **5**: 232 **9**: 521, 561
  'sweated' trades **9**: 179
labour movement
  England **9**: 177
  USA **9**: 654, 655, 658
Labour Party (Great Britain): women's suffrage **9**: 154
'Labour Stage' **1**: 177
labour unions *see* trade unions
lacross **22**: 163
Ladies' Home Journal **9**: 511, 679
Ladies' Sanitary Association **9**: 135
Lafayette, Mme de **12**: 3083–92
Laforet **12**: 3561, 3628
Lake Erie College for Women **4**: 1217
Lamb, Mary **9**: 139a
Lancashire, UK **4**: 92–3 **9**: 146, 159 **21**: 224
Langer, Susanne K. **1**: 77 **14**: 1, 2, 10, 13
Langgässer, Elizabeth **12**: 3384–7
Langham Place Circle **9**: 219
Larsen, Nella **12**: 232, 367, 398
Lasker-Schüler, Else **12**: 3388–94
Latin **4**: 202
Latin America (*see also* individual countries) **3**: 47 **17**: 562 **23**: 85, 93, 116, 179, 295
Latin American immigrants

(Latin American immigrants *cont.*)
(USA) **21**: 107, 116, 126, 142
Laurence, Margaret **12**: 149, 1272, 1276, 1293
Lavant, Christine **12**: 3395
Lavin, Mary **12**: 2577–8
law (*see also* labour legislation; legal position of women)
in Canada **11**: 6, 22
France **9**: 269
Great Britain **11**: 3, 16
Middle East **11**: 11
USA **9**: 527, 704 **11**: 2, 20
abortion **19**: 32, 48, 99, 102, 109, 117, 120
battered wives **11**: 11
child health **11**: 12
courts of law **11**: 5, 12, 14
employment (Great Britain) **11**: 3
equality (international law) **11**: 4
feminism **11**: 17, 23
inheritance rights **11**: 22
Jewish law **11**: 18
maintenance of wives **11**: 9
married women (USA) **9**: 704
maternity service (USA) **11**: 12
nurses **8**: 539
professions (France) **9**: 269
prostitution **11**: 19, 21
rape **11**: 1, 13
secondary education **11**: 7
secondary wives (Middle East) **11**: 11
sex discrimination **9**: 527 **11**: 20
social security
Great Britain **11**: 16
USA **11**: 15
lawyers **4**: 1554, 1632 **5**: 287, 309–10, 420, 459, 519
Lawless, Emily **12**: 2381–2
Lawrence, Frieda **12**: 2579
Lazarus, Emma **12**: 835
LDS Relief Society **4**: 1360
Le Gallienne, Eva **1**: 166, 169, 189
le Guin, Ursula **12**: 836–7, 2505
Leadership Conference of Women Religions (USA) **18**: 216
leadership training **17**: 60, 93, 104
League of Women Voters **9**: 200, 617, 657a **16**: 6, 10, 39, 43, 63 **21**: 103
learning methods and style **17**: 36–8
Lebanon **2**: 301 **23**: 129, 146, 188
Lecouvreur, Adrienne **1**: 162
Leduc, Violette **12**: 2918, 3093
Lee, Ann **18**: 115, 119
Lee, Harriet **12**: 1594
LeFranc, Marie **12**: 1294
legal education **4**: 273
legal status of women
in ancient world **9**: 19
England **9**: 71, 87, 191 **11**: 16
Germany **9**: 294
India **18**: 286
Latin America **23**: 85
Malawi **23**: 196
(legal status of women *cont.*)
Nigeria **23**: 14
Palestine **18**: 302
Roman Empire **9**: 34
USA **9**: 429, 470, 479, 550, 611, 612 **11**: 17
Lehmann, Rosamond **12**: 2500, 2516, 2580
Leicestershire, UK **21**: 129
leisure **4**: 1450 **5**: 583 **21**: 182
adolescents (Manchester) **21**: 185, 188
farm workers **21**: 189
food **21**: 186
girls (Italian Americans) **21**: 155
graduates **21**: 184
students **21**: 183, 187
women's attitudes **17**: 843
Lenclos, Ninon de **12**: 3094
Leneru, Marie **12**: 3095
Lennox, Charlotte **12**: 1544, 1582, 1594, 1639–41
Leopoldina, Empress of Brazil **9**: 343
Le prince de Beaumont, Marie-Jeanne **12**: 3096
lesbians and lesbianism **7**: 10 **20**: 154–98
alcoholics **8**: 61 **20**: 196, 198
delinquent adolescents **2**: 122, 130 **20**: 169
feminism **7**: 4, 9–10, 21, 42, 53, 140 **20**: 183
French literature **12**: 2869
liberation of women **7**: 17
mother **6**: 452, 479, 486, 662, 719, 725 **20**: 172
Roman literature **12**: 1305
prisons **2**: 48 **20**: 181
sex-roles **20**: 87
Lessing, Doris **12**: 22, 66, 83, 88, 93, 101, 102, 131, 164–94, 2500, 2505, 2511, 2516, 2530
letters (*see also* autobiographies; diaries)
American **9**: 398, 475, 634
English **9**: 69, 74, 78 **12**: 1617, 2042, 2067, 2138, 2399, 2446–7
French **12**: 3214–5, 3218, 3245–6
Irish **12**: 2566, 2668
Russian **12**: 3525
Levertov, Denise **12**: 261, 313, 386, 553, 838–9
Levison, Jan **1**: 21
Lewald, Fanny **12**: 3295
Lewis, Janet **12**: 82
liberal arts colleges **4**: 268, 272, 290, 333, 346, 355, 374, 382, 392, 398, 410, 902, 1166, 1178, 1194, 1205, 1312–13, 1326, 1463, 1592
administration **4**: 694, 837
physical education **4**: 519, 526
speaking activities **10**: 24
students' dress **21**: 100
liberalism
equal rights **7**: 74
feminism (J.S. Mill) **7**: 125
women's liberation **7**: 126
(liberalism *cont.*)
women's movement **7**: 18
Libya **23**: 9, 37, 91, 265
librarians and libraries **5**: 249, 262, 271, 274, 280, 296 **9**: 471, 570, 598
Linden Hall (girls' boarding school, USA) **4**: 64
literary censorship **12**: 2573
literary patronage
England **9**: 89 **12**: 1475, 1519
France **9**: 245, 257a **12**: 2943
USA **9**: 645
Lincoln, Mary Todd **1**: 109
Lindbergh, Anne Morrow **12**: 370
Lindsay, Vachel **12**: 265
Linton, Eliza Lynn **9**: 115 **12**: 2383
Lira, Carmen **12**: 3487
literature
education **4**: 930
erotic responses **12**: 197
feminist criticism **12**: 106, 110–1, 113, 117–19, 122, 125, 129, 136, 138, 140–1, 143
higher education **4**: 257
school curriculum **4**: 185, 191, 194
women's studies courses **4**: 563, 566, 569, 1161
Little Review **13**: 8
Littlewood, Joan **1**: 113, 166
Loftus, Cissie **1**: 138
Logan, Deborah Norris **12**: 840
Logan, Olive **1**: 193
Loi Camille Sée **9**: 269
Lokhuitskaia, Mirra **12**: 3509
London, UK **4**: 184, 186, 1271 **6**: 310 **9**: 148, 172, 180, 202, 209, 539
Louise of Savoy **9**: 245
Louisiana, USA **4**: 124, 273, 857, 897 **5**: 530 **8**: 508, 515 **9**: 547, 562 **19**: 553 **21**: 120, 175
Lowell, Amy **12**: 389, 841–2
Loy, Mina **12**: 843
Luhan, Mabel Dodge **9**: 645
Lupino, Ida **1**: 22
Lussan, Marguerite de **12**: 3097
Luxemburg, Rosa **9**: 292, 293
Lydia E. Pinkham Medicine Co. **8**: 117
Lynch, Marta **12**: 3444, 3488–90
lynching **9**: 452, 492, 514, 694

MacAulay, Catherine **9**: 119
Macaulay, Rose **12**: 2581–5
McCullers, Carson **12**: 197, 201, 262, 288, 290, 320, 353, 377, 388, 435, 844–68
McDowell, Catherine **12**: 869
McPherson, Aimee Semple **18**: 119
Madison, Kitty **1**: 117
Magdeburg, Mechthild von **12**: 3289, 3402
Maintenon Madame de **4**: 10, 11, 34, 117
Major, Clare Tree **1**: 112

Malawi **9**: 7 **23**: 50–1, 196
Malaysia **23**: 3, 67, 104, 109, 170, 175–6, 310
Mallet-Joris, Françoise **12**: 13, 2918, 3098–9
Malta **23**: 212
managers and executives **5**: 4, 16, 41, 48–60, 84, 89, 95, 118, 220, 251, 267, 283, 318, 324, 326, 330, 334–6, 345, 352, 355–7, 361, 377, 385, 398, 401, 410, 418, 428, 430, 436, 443, 451, 460, 472, 481, 483, 485, 498, 512, 515–16, 527, 530, 532, 534, 538, 543, 545, 562, 567–8, 591, 604, 612, 626 **13**: 18
Manchester, UK **9**: 127, 166 **21**: 185
Manitoba, Canada **18**: 199 **21**: 20
Manley, Mary de la Rivière **12**: 1409, 1642–3
Manpower Services Commission **5**: 49
Mansfield, Katherine **12**: 2513, 2586–601
Margaret of Anjou **12**: 1444
Margaret of Austria **9**: 275
Margaret of Cortona **1**: 235
Margaret, of Scotland, Queen **9**: 66
Marguerite d'Angoulême **9**: 245
Marguerite de France **9**: 257 **12**: 2943
Marguerite de Navarre **9**: 237 **12**: 3100–23
Maria Christina of Austria **9**: 338
Maria Theresa, Empress **4**: 13 **9**: 285
Marie Antoinette **9**: 244
Marie de France **12**: 3124–39
Marie de Guise **9**: 242, 254
Marie de Lorraine **9**: 104, 109
Mariology **18**: 35, 198
  art **1**: 252
  iconography **1**: 211, 230
  literature **12**: 14, 1338, 1341, 1348, 1355, 1368, 1370, 1372, 1376–7, 1395, 1397–8, 1419, 2872, 2970, 2973, 3550, 3554, 3564
Markandaya, Kamala **12**: 1256, 1258
market-work **3**: 41 **6**: 944
  in Ghana **23**: 183
    Nigeria **23**: 156
    Peru **23**: 26
Marlowe, Julia **1**: 149, 179
Marquets, Anne de **12**: 3142
marriage (*see also* divorce; families; married women; wives)
  in Gambia **3**: 113
    India: Bengali **23**: 105
    Israel: Arabs **23**: 114
    Liberia **23**: 40
    Nigeria **23**: 156, 218, 234
  Afro-American **3**: 126 **6**: 20
  alcoholism **8**: 7, 31, 34, 40
  American drama & literature **12**: 301, 402, 445, 479
(marriage *cont.*)
  aristocracy **9**: 186
  army: England **9**: 212
  classical literature **9**: 15
  communication **6**: 160, 163, 180
  conflicts **6**: 167
  counselling **6**: 178
  doctorates **6**: 196, 198
  Dutch art **1**: 249
  educated women **6**: 132 **23**: 218
  English literature **12**: 1405, 1691, 1820, 1877, 1901, 2151, 2265, 2518
  equality **6**: 134
  female assertiveness **6**: 197
  female power **6**: 173
  feminism **7**: 93
  German literature **12**: 3302, 3324, 3373
  Kpelle society **23**: 40
  loneliness **6**: 177
  marriage-age: Taiwan **3**: 13
  Mexican-American **21**: 163
  psychological abuse **6**: 191
  serial: fertility **3**: 77
  sexual discrimination **6**: 131
  Spanish literature **12**: 3560
  women's magazines **13**: 14
married women (*see also* wives)
  assertiveness training **17**: 138
  careers **4**: 1578, 1683, 1686
  continuing education **4**: 1357
  counselling **6**: 178–9
  depression **8**: 212, 222, 228, 245
  feminism **6**: 194
  law: Quebec **11**: 6
  marital satisfaction **6**: 185
  mental health **6**: 139
  in Nigeria **23**: 14
  professions **4**: 1554
  relations with other women **6**: 165
  social drinking **6**: 184
  students **4**: 1042, 1088, 1134, 1296 **6**: 199
  voluntary service **21**: 259
  workers **5**: 122–206, 529 **9**: 146, 653 **21**: 1, 10, 15, 17, 26, 32, 136
  changing attitudes **17**: 832, 841
  children's fiction portrayal **12**: 81
  class and income **23**: 214
  consumer behaviour **21**: 44, 50
  health services **8**: 105
  home life: effects **9**: 146 **23**: 174
  nurses **8**: 496
  shopping **21**: 41
  teachers **4**: 887, 910, 998, 1003, 1005 **21**: 10
  work attitudes **5**: 374
Marriot, Emil **12**: 3403
Marshall, Paule **12**: 345, 367
Martin, Anne **9**: 372, 668
Martineau, Harriet **12**: 2384–91
Marxism (*see also* communism; socialism)
  in Germany **9**: 288, 292
(Marxism *cont.*)
    Soviet Union: feminism **9**: 317, 330
    spain **9**: 340
  feminism **9**: 317, 330
  sexuality **9**: 288
  women and crime **2**: 36
  women and family **6**: 6
  women's equality **7**: 74
  women's role **14**: 22
  women's work **5**: 98
Mary, mother of Christ (*see also* Mariology) **1**: 211, 229, 252 **12**: 1338, 1341, 1348, 1355, 1368, 1370, 1377, 1395, 1397, 1398, 2872, 3550, 3554, 3564 **18**: 34, 35, 45, 69, 198
Mary II, Queen **9**: 106
Mary Hardin Baylor College **4**: 1135
Mary Magdalene **1**: 214, 225, 239 **12**: 1340, 1350, 1362, 1364, 1367, 1431, 2911, 3544
Mary Stuart **1**: 88, 128 **9**: 76, 80, 107 **12**: 64, 1809
Maryknoll sisters **4**: 343 **18**: 197, 266
Maryland, USA **1**: 130 **4**: 432, 901 **6**: 176, 831 **9**: 574, 623
Mason, Marianne **4**: 38
Massachusetts, USA **1**: 226 **2**: 6 **4**: 31, 81, 142, 303, 358, 419, 432, 1112 **5**: 210, 247, 294 **9**: 357, 366, 396, 450, 532, 587, 626, 721 **17**: 517 **19**: 109, 363 **21**: 250
mastectomy **8**: 426, 429, 431, 433–6, 441, 443, 450, 455, 457, 463, 466–7, 470, 472
masturbation **20**: 18, 48, 62, 67, 70, 75, 107
maternal mortality **9**: 187
maternity health service **8**: 117 **9**: 187 **19**: 257, 314, 325, 379, 385, 388, 407, 412, 420, 445, 450–1, 456, 473, 485, 487
  in Botswana **23**
    Korea **19**: 461
    Nigeria **23**: 87
    Tanzania **23**: 115
    USA **11**: 12 **21**: 109
Mathematics and mathematical education **4**: 200, 995, 1000, 1046, 1051, 1055, 1070, 1081, 1095, 1103, 1121, 1125, 1160, 1199, 1201, 1212, 1223, 1244, 1247, 1257, 1273, 1319 **17**: 67
Matilde, Countess of Tuscany **1**: 246
matrilineal societies **23**: 35, 94, 124
mature students (*see also* re-entry students, continuing education) **3**: 121 **4**: 406, 418, 426, 429–30, 920–1, 1297, 1327, 1350–2, 1365, 1368, 1372, 1379–80, 1391–3, 1405–6, 1408, 1410, 1412–3, 1416, 1418, 1422–4, 1427, 1429 **17**: 662

Matute, Ana Maria **12**: 3561, 3629–40
Mauritius **23**: 131
Meden **12**: 3356
medical education **4**: 265, 273 **8**: 533
medical students **4**: 1246 **8**: 479, 484–5
  in India **8**: 478
  career patterns **4**: 1554
  professional roles **4**: 1620
  sex-roles **4**: 1167, 1620
  specialty choice **4**: 1512, 1568
medicine (*see also* doctors; health; nurses)
  feminism **9**: 449
  medieval **12**: 1354
  sex-role **8**: 477
Meireles, Cecilia **12**: 3491
Melville, Elizabeth Shaw **9**: 622 **12**: 870
Mendelssohn, Fanny **1**: 64, 70
Mennonite Church **6**: 175
menopause **19**: 164, 235–50
menstruation **15**: 7 **19**: 94, 142–234
mental health **8**: 122–152
  childbirth **19**: 468
  education **8**: 138, 145
  elderly **8**: 131
  hospitals **8**: 122, 140, 149–50
  married women **6**: 139
  Mexican-Americans **8**: 159
  mothers **8**: 142, 145
  nursing **8**: 498
  professional workers **8**: 133
  reform: USA **9**: 579, 672
  schools: child-aides **8**: 144
  sex life **8**: 148
mental retardation **8**: 274–93 **9**: 397
Merry, Anne Brunton **1**: 107
metaphysics and religious thought **14**: 6, 11, 12, 14, 18, 21, 24
Methodist Church **18**: 78, 83, 92, 114
Methodist Episcopal Church **18**: 105
Mexico **3**: 95, 100 **9**: 342, 347–9 **18**: 143 **21**: 212 **23**: 12, 19, 46, 73, 133, 140, 142, 148, 215–16, 259, 299
Mexican-Americans
  academic and professional attainments **5**: 339
  acculturation **21**: 115, 163
  battered women **2**:191
  cannery workers **5**: 322
  child health **19**: 314
  child-rearing **6**: 303
  continuing education **4**: 171, 409
  cultural attitudes **21**: 145
  drug addiction **8**: 66
  educational administration **4**: 669
  elderly women **21**: 169
  ethnic identity **21**: 133
  family planning **19**: 90
(Mexican-Americans *cont.*)
  fertility **3**: 116
  food habits **21**: 125
  girls: absence of fathers **6**: 41
  health **8**: 104
  maternal care **19**: 314
  mother-daughter relationship **21**: 153
  nursing students **8**: 549
  post-operative convalescence **8**: 425
  psychological counselling **8**: 159
  urbanization **21**: 118
  writers **12**: 263
middle-aged women (*see also* menopause)
  androgyny **20**: 151
  clothing **21**: 85–7, 93
  depression **8**: 211, 244
  health care **8**: 95
  health, diet and exercise **8**: 306
  literature **12**: 2499
  physical features **15**: 20, 50, 156
  psychology **17**: 679–734
Meynell, Alice **12**: 2602–8
Meysenbug, Malwida von **12**: 3295
Michigan, USA **2**: 121 **3**: 121 **4**: 33, 349, 543, 591, 621, 750, 759, 874, 971, 1075, 1134, 1285, 1358, 1366, 1643 **5**: 198 **6**: 13, 551, 820 **9**: 596 **17**: 854 **19**: 499 **21**: 56 **22**: 98
middle-class
  in England **9**: 144 **12**: 2518
    France **9**: 262
    Germany **9**: 276
    Mexico **23**: 142
    Peru: Lima **23**: 15
    USA: 19thC **9**: 613
  alcoholism **8**: 9
  dramatic portrayal **12**: 3267
  fictional portrayal **12**: 39
  mothers **6**: 714
  obesity **8**: 377, 382
  pastoral care **18**: 273
  working mothers **6**: 884
  working wives **6**: 879, 918
Middle East **3**: 14 **4**: 1151 **23**: 53, 286, 301
midwives and birth attendants **5**: 271 **8**: 529, 555 **19**: 407
  in Africa **23**: 64
    England **9**: 102, 134
    Iran **23**: 253
    Malawi **23**: 51
    Scotland **8**: 534
    Thailand **23**: 154
    USA **9**: 447, 506 **19**: 417
Miegel, Agnes **12**: 3404
migrants and migration **21**: 156
  Brazil **23**: 72
  Kenya **23**: 168
  Latin America **23**: 93
  Peru **23**: 72
  Thailand **23**: 292
  USA **5**: 528
Milburga, St **18**: 59
Miles, Emma Bell **12**: 871
Miles, Josephine **12**: 872
military wives **6**: 148–50, 153, 158, 169 **9**: 212
Mill, John Stuart **7**: 125 **14**: 30
Millay, Edna St Vincent **12**: 873–6
Millet, Kate **12**: 54
Millin, Sarah **12**: 156
millinery trade **5**: 294
Mills College **4**: 432
ministers' wives **6**: 133, 141, 145, 175, 183, 187–8, 200 **9**: 147 **18**: 277, 281
Mink, Patsy Takemoto **16**: 62
Minnesota, USA **4**: 466, 491, 605, 673, 776, 855, 880, 1019 **8**: 24 **15**: 148 **17**: 841 **19**: 87, 532 **21**: 284 **22**: 180
minoresses **18**: 54
missions and missionaries
  in Brazil **18**: 263
    China **18**: 266, 268
    India **9**: 52
    Kenya **18**: 265
    Nigeria **18**: 262, 293
    Uganda **18**: 264
    USA **18**: 91, 105, 225
  Baptists: education **4**: 281
  Islam **8**: 298
Mississippi, USA **4**: 295, 321, 578, 721, 926, 1006, 1142, 1157, 1180–1, 1190, 1234, 1262, 1301, 1563 **6**: 5
Missouri, USA **1**: 229 **4**: 151, 381, 405, 487, 501, 725, 916, 944, 977 **5**: 282 **9**: 404 **19**: 337 **21**: 295
Mistral, Gabriella **12**: 3453, 3492–4
Mitchell, Margaret **12**: 998
Mitchell, Maria **9**: 501
Mitchison, Naomi **12**: 2609
Mitford, Mary Russell **12**: 1743, 1774, 2351, 2392–3
mixed marriages (Korean-Americans) **21**: 139
Molette, Barbara **12**: 219
Monica, mother of St Augustine **18**: 39
Monroe, Harriet **12**: 389, 877
Monroe, Marilyn **1**: 24
Montau, Dorothea von **12**: 1391
Montagu, Elizabeth **1**: 101 **12**: 1644–5
Montagu, Lily H. **18**: 314
Montagu, Lady Mary Wortley **9**: 131 **12**: 1647–9
Montana, USA **4**: 1676 **9**: 615 **17**: 854
Montessori, Maria **4**: 5, 16, 58, 164
Montgomerie, Margaret **12**: 1557
Montgomery, Elizabeth **1**: 101
Monticello Female Seminary **4**: 167
Moore, Marianne **12**: 313, 878–95
Moragne, Mary Elizabeth **12**: 896
Moravian education **4**: 4, 64
More, Hannah **4**: 12, 37, 110 **12**: 1544
Moredet **11**: 18
Morlachhi, Giuseppina **1**: 86

Mormon women **4**: 1360 **8**: 241
Morocco **23**: 58, 70, 84, 194, 256
Morrison, Toni **12**: 272, 348
Mortimer, Penelope **12**: 2527
mother-child relationships **6**: 10, 35, 277–796
alcoholism **8**: 26
baby/infant **19**: 228, 259, 281, 284, 290–1, 301–2, 315, 330, 333, 338, 345, 347, 353–8, 364, 367–8, 377, 382–3, 386, 393, 421, 431, 434, 436–7, 439, 441, 462, 486, 491, 493
child abuse **2**: 21, 27, 206 **6**: 698, 784–806
delinquent children **2**: 99, 116 **6**: 354
drug addicts **8**: 63
grief and mourning **6**: 573, 582, 750 **19**: 273
Latin American immigrants **21**: 142
literary portrayal **12**: 222
prisoners **2**: 9, 22, 40, 43, 65
psychological theories:
Britain **6**: 670
schizophrenic **8**: 268
sex-role **6**: 703, 735
speech communication **6**: 312, 332, 336–7, 339, 366–9, 382, 384, 388, 400, 402, 411–12, 416, 455, 468, 480, 490, 511, 526, 533–4, 539, 543, 566, 607, 630, 635, 641, 658, 664, 671–3, 694, 701, 731, 739–40, 758, 762, 765, 769, 772, 777–9 **10**: 18
story-tellers **6**: 547
student-mothers **6**: 757
touch communication **6**: 358
TV **13**: 10, 16
welfare **21**: 290
where child is handicapped or ill:
allergies **6**: 279, 483, 524
asthma **6**: 376, 457, 515, 588–9, 621, 654, 775
autistism **6**: 580, 678
cancer **6**: 707
cardiac conditions **6**: 383, 410
cerebral palsy **6**: 291, 314, 467, 552, 557, 600
cleft palate **6**: 652
colic **6**: 331, 542
Down's syndrome **6**: 400, 421, 468, 524, 576, 658, 682
emotional disturbance **6**: 435
haemophilia **6**: 770
handicap **6**: 338, 388, 581, 606, 633, 639, 653, 690, 721 **19**: 364
hearing-impairment **6**: 402, 557, 738
hospitalization **6**: 759
hyperactivity **6**: 727
leukemia **6**: 397, 447
psychiatry **6**: 299
reading disability **6**: 685, 687, 743
retardation **6**: 305, 311, 320, 324, 372, 385, 409, 415, 417, 424, 456, 485, 493, 525, 629,

(mother and child relationships *cont.*)
675, 736–7, 752
schizophrenia **6**: 695, 711–12, 780
visual handicap **6**: 680
where mother is working **6**: 816, 822, 828, 837–8, 840–1, 846–7, 849–51, 853, 856–7, 859, 861, 875, 882, 886, 890, 892–3, 895, 899, 900, 903, 905, 907, 909, 912–13, 915, 917, 919–20, 922–3, 926, 929, 945–55 **23**: 240
mother-daughter relationships **6**: 25, 30, 33, 36–7, 39, 42, 44–5, 50–1, 69, 70, 72–3, 78–9, 83–5, 93, 96, 98, 100–1, 103–4, 108–9, 113–15, 118, 120, 122–3, 126, 129 **19**: 323
in Algiers **23**: 226
France **9**: 255
Japan **21**: 223
body image **6**: 117
career-choice **6**: 32, 109, 882, 903, 913, 1444, 1539, 1547, 1557, 1605
courtship **6**: 38
daughter's pregnancy **19**: 289, 498
education **6**: 114 **17**: 627
food habits **8**: 304
juvenile delinquents **2**: 133, 168
literary portrayal **12**: 3532
menstruation **19**: 233
Mexican-American **21**:
schizophrenic **8**: 273
sex education **20**: 9
sex-role **6**: 40, 50, 52, 63, 68, 101, 127–8, 130
working mothers **6**: 821, 867, 913
mother-teacher relationship **6**: 377
mothers **6**: 529, 708 **18**: 16, 18, 287 **17**: 8 **23**: 22
African **23**: 64
children in foster-care **6**: 612
children's fiction **12**: 81
children's periodicals **12**: 317
depression **6**: 305, 368, 604, 724
employment **5**: 134, 136–7, 149, 151, 163, 165, 168, 171, 175, 178–81, 186, 188, 195, 202–3, 206, 518 **6**: 36, 624, 642, 816, 818–9, 821–3, 826–8, 831–53, 856–7, 859–64, 866, 869, 872, 874–5, 881–4, 890, 892–5, 899–901, 903, 905, 907–10, 915, 917–28, 931, 937, 939, 941–3, 944–50, 953
feminism **21**: 17, 21, 28
health knowledge **7**: 109 **8**: 120
Korean **23**: 50
literary portrayals **12**: 86, 231, 1273, 1482, 1689, 1729, 1797, 2323, 2484, 3269, 3310, 3330, 3354–5, 3531–2, 3583, 3595, 3618
mental health **8**: 141
education **8**: 145

(mothers *cont.*)
middle-class:
women's movement **7**: 87
position in society **6**: 733
prisoners **2**: 9, 22, 40, 43, 65
psychiatric unit **8**: 183
schizophrenia **8**: 261, 264, 268–9, 273
Mothers' Aid movement: USA **9**: 491, 708
mothers-in-law **6**: 811, 815
'Motley' (costume design team) **1**: 101
Mount College **4**: 432
Mowatt, Anna Cora **12**: 897
mulatto woman in fiction **12**: 330
multi-national companies **5**: 443
munitions workers **9**: 157, 163, 209
Munro, Alice **12**: 1276
murder and murderesses **2**: 30 **12**: 79
Murdoch, Iris **12**: 63, 1820a, 2529, 2530, 2610–36
Murray Judith Sargent **4**: 43
Musgrave, Thea **1**: 61
music **1**: 31–82
in Brazil **1**: 228
Germany **1**: 65, 70
USA **1**: 64
Wales **1**: 56
choral **1**: 31, 33, 37, 49, 51, 78
composers **1**: 34–5, 38, 40, 47–8, 61, 65, 67–8, 72, 75, 82
education **1**: 62, 65, 73–4 **4**: 39
feminist songs **7**: 134
lament-song **1**: 54
opera **1**: 36, 39, 57, 79
philosphy **1**: 71, 77
singers and singing **1**: 32, 41, 43, 45–6, 53, 55, 58–60, 69

Naidu, Mrs Sarojini **12**: 1261
The nation **9**: 369 **13**: 2
National Association of Colored Women **9**: 493
National Association of Deans of Women **4**: 140
National Association of Local Government Officers (NALGO) **5**: 223
National Association of Teachers in Further and Higher Education (NATFHE) **5**: 223
National Association of Women Deans, Administrators and Counsellors **4**: 625, 637
National Council of Jewish Women **18**: 308
National Council of Women of Canada **9**: 686
National Council of Women of Thailand **23**: 177
National Labor Union: women's rights movement **9**: 546
National Organization for Public Health Nursing **8**: 513
National Organization of Women (USA) [NOW] **5**: 217

National Socialism
  girls' youth organizations **9**: 301
  women in Nazi propaganda **12**: 3
  women's position **21**: 218
National Society of the Daughters of the Revolution **9**: 548
National Union of Women's Suffrage Societies **9**: 151, 155
National Welfare Rights Organization **21**: 307
National Woman's Party **9**: 386, 394, 599
National Women's Political Caucus **16**: 48
nationalism and women
  China **9**: 45
  India **9**: 42, 65
Nazimova, Alla **1**: 139
Near East **4**: 248 **9**: 131, 173 **11**: 11 **18**: 309
Nebraska, USA **4**: 590, 644 **5**: 41 **8**: 510 **9**: 429, 431, 469, 634
Nepal **3**: 111 **23**: 16, 32, 152, 197, 213
Nebit, Edith **12**: 2637–8
Netherlands **21**: 179
Nevada, USA **5**: 507 **9**: 668
New England, USA **4**: 126, 1241, 1348, 1580 **9**: 352–3, 358–9, 364, 549, 570, 635 **17**: 288 **18**: 80
New Guinea **23**: 65, 112, 304
New Jersey, USA **2**: 50, 82 **4**: 66, 306, 370, 515, 596, 737, 741, 777, 935, 1030, 1059, 1173, 1412, 1480 **5**: 284 **6**: 722 **8**: 176 **9**: 480 **17**: 632
New Mexico, USA **4**: 669 **6**: 700
New Nigeria **13**: 1
New York, USA **2**: 67 **4**: 17, 215–16, 357, 389, 432, 443, 620, 828, 867, 908, 919, 939, 959, 1316 **5**: 209, 310, 537, 581 **7**: 98 **8**: 119 **9**: 383, 434, 455, 505, 627, 676 **11**: 17, 22 **16**: 3 **18**: 215 **19**: 48, 123, 425 **22**: 148
  New York City **2**: 12, 34, 157 **3**: 61 **4**: 216, 263, 287, 407, 414, 432, 806, 1550 **5**: 305 **6**: 433 **7**: 78 **8**: 484 **9**: 453, 539, 557, 595, 671, 677, 707 **13**: 13 **19**: 118 **21**: 17, 109, 123, 126, 157, 281
New York Times (abortion) **19**: 13
New Yorker **13**: 30
newspapers **9**: 381
  abortion **19**: 13
  American Labour
    attitudes to women **9**: 654
    comic strips (marriage) **13**: 41
    editors (feminism) **7**: 78
    Nigerian **13**: 1
    suffrage **9**: 196a, 534, 651, 680
    women's pages (advertisements) **13**: 38
New Zealand **5**: 85 **6**: 859 **21**: 237
Newfoundland, Canada **5**: 248 **10**: 10 **19**: 235
Nigeria **3**: 115 **4**: 1185, 1401 **8**: 427 **9**: 3 **13**: 1 **18**: 262 **23**: 14, 25, 87, 95, 149, 156, 178, 186, 202, 218, 224, 225, 234, 273, 293, 296
Nightingale, Florence **9**: 190
Nijo, Lady **12**: 1262
Nin, Anaïs **12**: 82, 93, 435, 898–908
Noailles, Mme de **12**: 3143–5
Noel, Marie **12**: 3140–1
nomadic tribes
  Iran **23**: 264
  Israel **23**: 182
  Sudan **23**: 160
North Carolina, USA **4**: 4, 19, 75, 292, 304, 675, 687, 804, 843, 1015, 1107, 1655 **8**: 309 **9**: 519, 644 **16**: 38, 69 **19**: 412, 517 **21**: 252
North Dakota, USA **17**: 865
North of England Council for Promoting the Higher Education of Women **4**: 88, 163
Northern Ireland **2**: 95, 171
Northumberland, UK **2**: 130
Norway **9**: 333 **16**: 49
Nova Scotia, Canada **9**: 640
nuns and nunneries (*see also* individual orders) **8**: 11 **18**: 52, 55, 57–8, 63, 67–8, 70–1, 151, 162, 184, 186, 188, 216, 223, 227–8 **23**: 294
  Buddhist **18**: 20
nursery nurses **5**: 253
nursery schools, playgroups and kindergartens **4**: 1235 **6**: 303, 406, 605, 776
nursing and nurses **8**: 493–556
  in Commonwealth **9**: 194
  England
    19thC **9**: 123, 141a, 171, 190, 416, 478
    20thC **8**: 512
  USA **8**: 507, 508, 513, 595 **9**: 428, 436, 632
    19th–20thC **9**: 416, 629
    Civil War **9**: 579
    military **9**: 660, 670
    veterans **9**: 406
  aides **8**: 494
  career choices **4**: 1554
  career patterns **4**: 522
  childbirth **19**: 422
  community mental health **8**: 498
  district nurses **8**: 521
  feminism **8**: 508
  health of nurses **8**: 505–6
  law **8**: 539
  managers **5**: 418
  married nurses **8**: 496
  military nurses **8**: 557
  physiology **15**: 40
  professional attitudes **8**: 499, 502, 528, 536, 546
(nursing and nurses *cont.*)
  Red Cross **8**: 121
  sex role **8**: 555
  smoking attitudes **8**: 85
  trade unions **8**: 493, 508, 513
  wages **8**: 493
  work attitudes **8**: 509, 553
nursing education **8**: 532, 550–1, 556 **9**: 419, 422 **18**: 173
  students **8**: 495, 503, 517, 519–20, 523–7, 530, 534, 538, 541, 545, 548, 552, 558 **19**: 118
nutrition **8**: 294–310
Nwapa, Flora **12**: 195

OASDI **6**: 256
Oates, Joyce Carol **12**: 393, 909–23
obesity and overweight **8**: 328–90 **15**: 16
O'Brien, Edna **12**: 2527
O'Connor, Flannery **1**: 172, 256 **12**: 67, 197, 262, 290, 320, 353, 388, 393, 925–97
Octavia, sister of Augustus **9**: 37
occupational psychology **5**: 323–626
occupational therapists **8**: 482, 491
occupations and careers **4**: 1376, 1449, 1503, 1524, 1537, 1539, 1545, 1624, 1634, 1657, 1664, 1673, 1681, 1684 **5**: 91, 337, 340, 342, 372, 379, 383–5, 388, 399, 433–4, 441, 446, 491–2, 494, 498, 510, 531, 537, 556, 578, 590, 594, 616, 620, 622–3 **6**: 954
office administration: education **4**: 1643
office education **4**: 1023, 1027, 1049, 1078, 1234, 1643, 1677
  career choices **4**: 1609
office work and workers (*see also* clerical workers; 'white collar' workers) **5**: 101, 109–10, 127, 347, 427, 621 **9**: 133, 627
  attitudes of high school students **4**: 1082
  literary portrayal **12**: 428
  managers **5**: 89
  typists **9**: 133
  universities **4**: 864
  word-processors **5**: 306
Ohio, US **4**: 3, 63, 285, 394, 500, 524, 769, 805, 815, 998, 1126, 1210–1, 1327 **8**: 552 **9**: 525, 541 **19**: 52, 538 **21**: 33 **22**: 15, 95, 121, 149
O'Keefe, Georgia **1**: 202, 208
Oklahoma, USA **3**: 11 **4**: 89, 279, 1041, 1115, 1126, 1155, 1286 **5**: 109 **6**: 500 **8**: 378 **15**: 153 **18**: 186 **19**: 450 **21**: 261
Oliphant, Margaret **12**: 1729, 2394–6
Olsen, Tillie **12**: 401
Olympic Games **9**: 555 **22**: 1, 56, 67, 69, 166
  Oneida community **9**: 434
O'Neil, Eliza **1**: 97

Ontario, Canada **4**: 150 **5**: 180, 439 **16**: 13 **19**: 522
Opie, Amelia **12**: 1888, 2397–8
Oregon, USA **4**: 454, 1060, 1267, 1363, 1486, 1572 **5**: 215 **8**: 106 **9**: 478, 521, 534, 564, 597, 665 **19**: 56
Orzeszkowa, Eliza **12**: 3517
Out-el-Kouloub **12**: 163
Ouyang Tzu **12**: 1251
Owenite communities and socialism **9**: 207, 434, 542
Oxfordshire, UK **2**: 112

pacifism and pacifists **9**: 441, 461, 495, 528, 681
pageants and pageantry **1**: 88, 171, 186
Paget, Violet **12**: 2639
Pakistan **3**: 54, 76, 109 **4**: 276 **21**: 91 **23**: 61, 229
Palestine **18**: 302
Pankhurst, Helen Huss **1**: 71
Panova, Vera **12**: 3523
Pappenheim, Bertha **21**: 270
paranoia **8**: 124, 130, 146, 255
Pardo Bazán, Emila **12**: 3547, 3642–67
Parra, Teresa de la **23**: 24
patriarchy
  criminalization of women **2**: 35
  dependency of women **21**: 277
  feminist critique **7**: 33
Peabody family **9**: 635
Penfield, Sarah Flynn **9**: 525
Pennsylvania, USA **4**: 183, 213, 424, 432, 670, 689, 703, 741, 838, 970, 1379 **5**: 251 **6**: 288 **9**: 399, 545, 611 **17**: 639 **19**: 79, 115
  Philadelphia **2**: 1, 230, 265 **4**: 1413, 1430 **5**: 163, 294 **9**: 360, 411, 491, 537, 544
  Pittsburgh **4**: 129, 1031, 1427 **9**: 538
pensions **5**: 106, 147
periodicals and magazines
  American **9**: 369, 400, 454, 458, 509, 512, 515, 570, 680, 722–3 **12**: 317, 327, 402a **13**: 2–3, 8, 14, 30
  English **9**: 507 **12**: 1499, 1514, 2252, 2345, 2356
  abortion **13**: 21
  childbirth **13**: 33
  childhood **13**: 6
  education **4**: 153, 477, 937 **13**: 26
  food advertisements **13**: 23, 29
  health articles **13**: 28
  suffrage movement **9**: 466, 680 **13**: 25, 32
Perkerson, Medora Field **12**: 998
Perkins, Frances **9**: 371
Perovskaya, Sofia Lvovna **9**: 310
Peru **23**: 15, 26, 56, 71, 72, 116, 134, 195, 270
Peterkin, Julia **12**: 999
Petre, Maud **18**: 137
Petry, Ann Lane **12**: 367, 398, 1000
pharmacists **5**: 276, 477, 570
Phelps, Elizabeth Stuart **12**: 1001–3
Philippines **3**: 16, 20, 33, 51, 72 **4**: 640, 890, 1140, 1203, 1268 **5**: 536 **6**: 602 **23**: 2, 121, 136
Philips, Katherine **12**: 1540–1
phobias **8**: 246–53
photography **1**: 199, 256 **12**: 995
physical education and activities **4**: 348, 446, 457, 465, 467, 471, 495, 503, 510, 513–14, 516, 547, 549 **22**: 60
  schools **4**: 437, 440, 445, 448, 468, 508, 544, 550, 554, 558
  universities and colleges **4**: 432–4, 438, 441–2, 444, 447, 450–3, 455–6, 458, 461, 463–4, 473–5, 477, 479–81, 484, 488, 493–4, 496, 498, 501, 504, 506, 509, 511, 515, 517, 519–20, 522, 526–7, 531–40, 542–3, 545, 548, 551, 555 **22**: 42, 54, 72
  teacher-training **4**: 436, 439, 460, 462, 469–70, 472, 485–7, 499, 507, 523, 525, 528–30, 541, 546, 552, 556 **22**: 16
  teachers **4**: 435, 438, 443, 459, 482, 487, 490–2, 497, 500, 512, 518, 524, 541, 545, 553, 557, 561–2, 1555 **22**: 177
    heads of dept **4**: 505, 521, 561
    careers **4**: 483
  administration **4**: 489, 502
Piatt, Sarah Morgan **12**: 1004
picara (female rogue) in literature **12**: 38, 597, 3601–2
Ping Asin **12**: 1246
pioneer women (USA) **9**: 615, 625 **12**: 274, 314, 318, 339, 350
Piozzi, Hester Lynch **12**: 2321
Pitter, Ruth **12**: 2531
Plantier, Thérêse **12**: 2895
Plath, Sylvia **12**: 46, 217, 261, 313, 404, 1005–14
Poland **3**: 104 **9**: 139 **10**: 21
  Polish **10**: 20
Poldowski, Lady Dean Paul **1**: 35
police
  attitudes to rape **2**: 248, 269, 284
  attitudes to wife-abuse **2**: 209
  suffragettes (England) **9**: 202
policewomen **5**: 281, 293, 297, 370, 453, 506, 520 **17**: 848
political participation and attitudes **16**: 20, 40, 52, 56–7, 60, 63, 74
  in Africa, North **23**: 201
    Africa, West **23**: 79
    Algeria **23**: 59
    Argentina **23**: 138
    Belgium **16**: 18
    Brazil **23**: 29
    Burma **21**: 220
    Canada **16**: 4, 9, 13
    Chile **23**: 57
    France **16**: 4, 73
(political participation and attitudes *cont.*)
    Great Britain **16**: 51
    Islamic countries **23**: 246
    Japan **16**: 58 **21**: 220
    Kenya **23**: 276
    Malaysia **23**: 67
    Morocco **23**: 59
    Norway **167**: 49
    Peru **23**: 57
    Philippines **23**: 121
    Scotland **16**: 2
    South Africa **16**: 50
    Tunisia **23**: 59
    USSR **16**: 11, 70, 75
    USA **16**: 1, 3, 4, 6, 7, 10, 14, 16, 23, 33, 35, 38, 42, 48, 53, 64–6, 68
  adolescents **16**: 17
    voluntary associations **21**: 263
    working class: local organizations **21**: 253
political thought and thinkers **14**: 9, 19 **16**: 40, 55
  ancient Greek **9**: 9, 25
  American **16**: 19, 29, 36, 47
  English **9**: 128, 167, 176, 183–4
politicians (women)
  in England **4**: 18, 21 **9**: 117, 119 **16**: 12, 21, 69
    Germany **9**: 278
    Korea **16**: 37
    Sierra Leone **23**: 137
    Thailand **23**: 237
    USA **4**: 9 **9**: 355, 367, 371–2, 386, 495, 531, 594, 628, 690, 705 **16**: 14–16, 22–4, 27, 29, 37, 46, 61–2
politicians' wives
  in England **9**: 201
    USA **9**: 418, 474–5, 523, 526, 656 **16**: 8, 15, 25–6, 34
polyandrous societies **23**: 181
polygyny **3**: 75
Polynesia **23**: 128
Pompadour, Madame de **1**: 125
Poor Law
  administration **9**: 195
  schools **4**: 38
Popora, Nicola **1**: 49
Porter, Anna Maria **12**: 1888
Porter, Jane **12**: 1888
Porter, Katharine Anne **12**: 1015–35
Portugal **6**: 20
Portuguese immigrants
  Paris **21**: 108
  USA **21**: 110
Proctor, Anne Benson **12**: 2399
postal workers
  France **9**: 224
  Great Britain **9**: 129
potters and pottery **1**: 222
pottery industry workers **9**: 219
preachers and evangelists
  England **9**: 110 **18**: 103
  USA **18**: 99, 113, 115, 119, 121
pregnancy **19**: 253, 256, 258,

(pregnancy *cont.*)
260–5, 268, 271, 275, 279, 282, 285, 287, 292–9, 303–4, 306, 309, 311, 313, 316–22, 324, 329, 331–2, 339–40, 343, 346, 349–52, 359–61, 363, 365–6, 369–70, 372–6, 378, 380, 385, 389, 391–2, 399, 400, 402, 404, 408, 410, 414–16, 418–19, 424–5, 432, 435, 440, 442–4, 446, 449, 452–6, 459–60, 463–7, 471–2, 477–9, 481–2, 484, 489–90, 493–4
adolescent pregnancy **19**: 495–570
Presbyterian Church **18**: 87, 107–8, 122, 126
Presentation convents (Kerry diocese) **4**: 82
Presentation Sisters (South Dakota) **18**: 222
priestesses
Ghana **18**: 5
Korea: Shamanism **23**: 130, 162
primary/elementary education **4**: 98, 343
in Bohemia **4**: 12
England **4**: 13
Ethiopia **4**: 1149
Ireland **4**: 96
athletics **22**: 102
psychology **4**: 1035, 1039, 1074, 1077, 1149, 1235, 1278
printing workers **5**: 252 **9**: 155, 355a, 502
prisons and prisoners **2**: 2, 5, 7, 9, 10, 16, 33–4, 36–9, 49, 51, 53, 56–7, 59, 62, 64
in Greece **2**: 44
USA **2**: 12, 17,28, 34, 41, 50, 66, 72, 73 **9**: 464, 467
clothing interests **21**: 61
communications **2**: 20
counselling **2**: 67, 102
drug-addicts **8**: 66, 74–6, 82–3
education **2**: 58
escape-attempts **2**: 13
lesbianism **2**: 48 **20**: 181
mothers as prisoners **2**: 9, 22, 40, 43, 65
ricividists **2**: 11, 25, 45–6, 67–8
recreation **2**: 73
release **2**: 52
sex-role **2**: 59, 70
tatooing **2**: 15
treatment **2**: 42–3
work **2**: 71
prison-officers **2**: 32 **5**: 288, 292, 478, 628
prisoners' wives **6**: 135, 189
Prix Femina **12**: 2844
problem-solving **17**: 32, 39, 43
professions and professional women **4**: 1450 **5**: 13, 17, 69, 86, 92, 160, 245, 266–7, 325, 339, 350, 358, 364, 372, 380, 390, 408, 415, 437, 442, 447, 450, 457, 463, 470, 473, 479, 495, 523, 526, 536, 542, 544, 547, 565, 569, 572, 577, 581,

(professions and professional women *cont.*)
584–5, 599, 601, 618–20, 623–4 **9**: 181, 354, 375, 488, 501, 513, 592, 603 **17**: 845 **21**: 139b **23**: 63, 118, 172, 228
alcoholism **8**: 46
assertiveness training **17**: 46, 163
career choices **4**: 1555, 1559
career patterns **4**: 1530
clothing **21**: 62, 79, 90
clubs **4**: 407 **5**: 573
continuing education **4**: 407
executives **5**: 16
leadership **5**: 389
marriage and career **4**: 1554–5, 1559 **6**: 817, 873, 916
mother-child relations **6**: 593
motherhood **6**: 326, 833, 842, 854, 885–6, 899, 930, 954
suicide **5**: 386
property rights
England **9**: 203
Greece (ancient) **9**: 12, 36
India **23**: 60, 231, 241
Scotland **9**: 140
USA **9**: 362, 383, 550
Zambia **23**: 223
prostitution and prostitutes **2**: 118 **9**: 142 **21**: 213–14
in England **9**: 161, 180, 205, 703
Ethiopia **23**: 77
France **9**: 253, 271
Italy **9**: 303
Malayasia: Chinese **23**: 176
Taiwan **23**: 294
USA **9**: 380, 411, 590, 638, 701, 707 **11**: 19 **21**: 203, 217
English literature **12**: 1385, 1440, 1455, 1486, 1555, 1708, 1814, 2080
German literature **12**: 3316
legal aspects **11**: 19, 21
psychological aspects **17**:83, 150, 784, 814
Provençal dialect **10**: 1
psychoanalysis
children and education **4**: 46
feminine development **17**: 2
women and family **6**: 6
psychological counselling **8**: 153, 159–60, 162–7, 178–81, 186–7, 190, 198–9, 207–8
education **8**: 153, 160–1, 184, 186, 194, 196, 200, 203, 208
feminists **8**: 196
women's studies **8**: 200
psychological theories
feminine and femininity **9**: 211 **17**: 4, 6, 7, 11
mother and child **6**: 670
woman's psychology **17**: 24
Roman Catholic **18**: 154
feminism **8**: 168
psychologists **17**: 3, 844
psychology (education) **4**: 1464, 1186 **8**: 200
psychotherapy **8**: 153–8, 168–72,

(psychotherapy *cont.*)
188–9, 195, 197, 199, 201, 204–5
androgyny **20**: 153
feminism **8**: 168, 170, 176, 182, 185, 191, 206
women's studies **8**: 200
Public School Teachers' Association of Baltimore **4**: 901
publishing **5**: 256
feminism **9**: 165
USA (suffrage) **9**: 580
Puerto Rico **2**: 51 **3**: 49 **4**: 223, 974 **6**: 620, 924 **18**: 227
Puerto Ricans in USA
abortion **19**: 47
acculteration **21**: 130, 173
assertiveness training **21**: 143, 170
bilingualism **21**: 160
depression **8**: 217
educational dropout **4**: 1228
family life **21**: 130
health and modern medicine **8**: 107
housework **21**: 15
maternity care: New York **21**: 109
mental illness: attitudes **8**: 125
mother-child relations **6**: 620, 762, 783
mother-son relations **21**: 159
politics **21**: 130
prison-life **2**: 51
roles **21**: 148, 157, 167
spiritualism **21**: 123
teachers: New York **4**: 919
weight attitudes **8**: 359
women's liberation movement New York **7**: 77
Puritans (New England) **18**: 80

Queens, empresses and royalty
Abomey, West Africa **23**: 31
Austria **9**: 275, 285, 388
Brazil **9**: 343
Byzantium **9**: 10
Egypt **9**: 35
England
medieval **9**: 93–4
16thC **9**: 70, 100 **12**: 1478, 1495, 1515, 1809
17thC **9**: 67, 106
18thC **9**: 96, 197
France **9**: 225, 237, 242, 254, 270
Portugal **9**: 341
Russia **9**: 306, 320, 323, 325, 328
Scotland **9**: 66, 76, 80, 104, 109
Spain **12**: 3556
Queen's College **6**: 277 **7**: 129
Quebec, Canada **11**: 22 **21**: 246
Quiroga, Elena **12**: 3561, 3668

racism **4**: 1572 **9**: 281, 374
Radcliffe, Ann **9**: 111 **12**: 1561, 1564, 1570, 1650–63
Radcliffe, Mary Ann **12**: 1561, 1582
Radcliffe College **4**: 142, 432
radio **13**: 12

railway workers (clerical) **9**: 129
Raine, Kathleen **12**: 2640–1
Rainey, Ma **1**: 60
Ramakrishna Sarada Math **23**: 244
Rankin, Jeannette **9**: 395, 495
Rankin, Melinda **18**: 112
rape **2**: 229–99
judicial aspects **2**: 231–2, 243, 246, 252, 258–60, 265, 268, 270, 276, 290, 293–8
legal aspects **11**: 1, 13
literature **12**: 1602
police attitudes **2**: 248, 269, 284
Rathbone, Eleanor **16**: 69
reading **4**: 174, 187, 203 **13**: 19 **21**: 190–1
reasoning and thought **17**: 33, 35, 39
Red Cross nursing **8**: 121
re-entry students (*see also* continuing education; mature students) **4**: 408, 410, 415, 417, 419, 422–3, 427–8, 1264, 1352, 1354–6, 1359, 1361–4, 1367, 1370–1, 1373, 1376, 1381, 1389–90, 1394, 1403–4, 1407, 1409, 1411–12, 1414, 1421–2, 1425, 1430, 1471, 1553, 1536, 1663 **6**: 829, 879, 888, 932
Reese, Lizette Woodward **12**: 1036
Reeve, Clara **12**: 1594, 1664–6
reform schools and reformatories (*see also* residential treatment centres; community homes) **2**: 78–9, 85, 94–5, 120, 123–4, 127, 132, 161, 172 **9**: 161, 396, 399, 404
Rehon, Ada **1**: 83
religion (*see also* Buddhism; Christianity; Hinduism; Islam; Jews and Judaism)
abortion **19**: 96
Australia (aborigines) **18**: 9
Ghanaian **18**: 5
Egyptian **18**: 8, 19
Greek **18**: 3, 6, 8, 11, 12, 19
Indian **18**: 285–97
Mexican **18**: 143
Near Eastern **18**: 1, 12, 15, 17
Roman **18**: 2, 7, 8, 11
women's rights **9**: 388
religious education **4**: 254, 366, 1158 **12**: 1345 **18**: 68, 94, 153
religious mystics
England **12**: 1333, 1335, 1337, 1391–2 **18**: 64, 74
French **18**: 69
Germany **12**: 328–9, 3403
Italy **18**: 51
religious orders (*see also* individual orders) **18**: 52–5, 57–8, 63, 67–8, 70–1, 73, 151, 156, 239
religious tract societies **12**: 1821
Rémy, Caroline **9**: 258
Renée de France **9**: 270
residential treatment centres **2**: 117, 137, 159–60
retirement **5**: 13, 23, 86, 147, 367, 380, 579 **18**: 192, 204, 216, 231
(retirement *cont.*)
education for **5**: 25, 298 **18**: 204, 231
Rennselar, Mariana Griswold van **1**: 206, 220
Repplier, Agnes **12**: 1037–8
Reuter, Gabriele **12**: 3405
revolutionaries
Europe **9**: 232
China **23**: 274
France **9**: 233, 243
Germany **9**: 292, 293A, 643
Mexico **9**: 347–9
Spain **9**: 340
USSR **9**: 308, 310, 316, 318–19, 324, 329–30
USA **9**: 607
rhetoric **10**: 21
birth control movement **9**: 472, 593
Dorothy Day **18**: 133
Anna Elizabeth Dickinson **7**: 96
Communists (USA) **9**: 607
feminism **7**: 82
feminist songs **7**: 134
Liberal Arts colleges **10**: 24
missions **18**: 91
nuns **18**: 223
politicians **16**: 12, 21, 30, 46
radical feminism **7**: 135
social reformers **9**: 700
suffrage movement **7**: 35 **9**: 128a, 415, 425, 463, 577
Ellen G. White and SDA Church **18**: 116
women speakers: USA **9**: 584, 604, 606, 717
women's liberation movement **7**: 107 **9**: 463, 485
women's movement: USA **7**: 35, 66
WSPU **9**: 128A, 415
WSTU **9**: 433
rheumatic diseases **8**: 402–3, 408
Rhode Island, USA **3**: 10, 74 **19**: 317
Rhys, Jean **12**: 22, 2642–6
Riccoboni, Mme de **12**: 2914, 3146–9
Rich, Adrienne **12**: 217, 244, 261, 386, 404, 1039–47
Richards, Ellen Swallow **9**: 501
Richards, Laura E. **12**: 1048
Richardson, Dorothy **1**: 25 **12**: 61, 2500, 2516, 2533, 2647–53
Richardson, Henry Handel **12**: 2400
Richmond, Mary **9**: 623
Riley, Bridget **1**: 215
Rinser, Luise **12**: 3406
ritual roles
Hindu women **18**: 289, 295
Ibo women, Nigeria **23**: 132
Korean shaman **23**: 162
Oglala women **23**: 235
Pokot women **23**: 235
Roberts, Elizabeth Madox **12**: 1049–52
Roberts, Michele **12**: 2505
Robins, Elizabeth **1**: 96 **12**: 1053
Robins, Margaret Dreier **5**: 228
Robinson, Mary **1**: 129 **12**: 1667
Roche, Regina **12**: 1561, 2401
Rochefort, Christiane **12**: 3150
Rogers, Elizabeth **1**: 68
Rogers, mary Josephine **18**: 197
Roland, Mme **12**: 3151–2
Roman Catholic Church (*see also* nuns; religious orders; saints)
in England **18**: 137
France **18**: 151
Japan **18**: 153
Mexico **18**: 143
USA **18**: 133, 135–6, 139, 140–1, 146, 150, 152, 155
abortion **19**: 21
alcoholism **8**: 11, 35
adolescents **18**: 134, 149
education **4**: 35, 82, 92–3, 96, 111, 116, 324–404, 680–1, 694, 766 **18**: 153–4
fertility **3**: 10
girl guides **9**: 530
literature **12**: 3300, 3378, 3475
missions: to American Indians **18**: 225
to Nigeria **18**: 262
to Uganda **18**: 264
nursing education **8**: 557, 559
Papacy **21**: 201
ritual **18**: 138
spirituality **18**: 112
students **18**: 141, 144
teacher-training **4**: 436
university ministry **18**: 142
women's role and psychology **18**: 154 **21**: 201
working-class **18**: 133, 139, 152
Rome, Ancient **9**: 17, 19–24, 27, 28, 34, 39
Romieu, Marie de **12**: 3153
Roosevelt, Anna Eleanor **9**: 367, 531 **16**: 8, 15, 29
Ross, Violet Martin **12**: 2668–9
Rossetti, Christina **12**: 2402–28
Rossner, Judith **12**: 272
Rouzade, Léonie **9**: 263
Rowlandson, Mary **12**: 1054–5
Rowson, Susanna Haswell **9**: 610 **12**: 1056–8
Roy, Gabrielle **12**: 1272, 1295
Rukeyser, Muriel **12**: 1059–60
Rumbold, Zoe Akins **12**: 1061
Russell, Lucy (Countess of Bedford) **12**: 1475, 1509
Russell, Lady Elizabeth **9**: 78
Russia (*see also* USSR) **2**: 44, 85, 112 **9**: 306–7, 311–14, 316–21, 327, 330–1

Sablé, Mme de **12**: 3154
Sachs, Nelly **12**: 3291
Sackville West, Victoria **12**: 2655–6
St Denis, Ruth **1**: 170
St Joseph College, West Hartford, Conn. **4**: 339
saints **12**: 2860, 1344, 1363, 1366, 1385, 3365, 3669–71 **18**: 50, 51,

(saints *cont.*)
59, 61, 66, 72, 133a, 139a **18**: 301
salons
French society **12**: 2849, 3154
German society **12**: 3359
Salvador, El **23**: 27
samplers **1**: 209
Sanchez, Sonia **12**: 219
Sand, George **12**: 57, 2942, 2944, 3155–84
Sands, Dorothy **1**: 138
Sandoz, Mari **12**: 1062–4
Sangali, Rita **1**: 86
Sanger, Margaret **9**: 472, 533, 593
sans-jupon **9**: 233
Sappho **12**: 3356
Saudi Arabia **23**: 10, 126, 165, 311
Sarraute, Nathalie **12**: 35, 36, 63, 70, 81, 89, 3185–205
Sarton, May **12**: 46, 244, 370, 1065–6
Sata Ineko **12**: 1264
Saumoneau, Louise **9**: 263
Sayers, Dorothy L. **12**: 2657–60
Scarborough, Dorothy **12**: 1068
Schaffner, Caroline **1**: 137
schizophrenia **8**: 254–79
Schneiderman, Rose **9**: 457, 655
Schreiner, Olive **12**: 156, 196, 1740
Schroeder, Margot **12**: 3315
Schwarz, Sibylle **12**: 3408
science
careers **4**: 1078, 1265, 1484, 1615, 1653 **5**: 245
education **4**: 175–6, 189, 226 265, 995, 1063, 1090, 1097, 1116, 1228, 1248
counselling **4**: 1319
university **4**: 210
Englishwomen (16th–17thC) **9**: 92
girls' interests **4**: 1116, 1265 **17**: 184
girls' view of women scientists **4**: 1615
Scotland **2**: 137 **8**: 534 **9**: 66, 77, 140, 186 **16**: 2 **17**: 856
Scott, Sarah **12**: 1668–9
Scudéry, Mlle de **12**: 3206–9
sculpture
American **1**: 207
Aztec-Mexican **1**: 200
French **1**: 248
Indian **1**: 212
seamstresses **9**: 139a, 468 **23**: 12
Sears, Zelda **12**: 1069
secondary schools/high schools **4**: 191
in Belgium **4**: 2
Canada **4**: 183
Egypt **4**: 173, 1092, 1227, 1265, 1302
England **4**: 65, 130, 184, 186, 1026, 1276 **21**: 154
France **4**: 2, 184
Germany **4**: 2
Great Britain **4**: 55, 122, 168, 170, 172–4, 177–8, 187, 198, 202
(secondary schools/high schools *cont.*)
Iran **4**: 1016 **23**: 284
Iraq **4**: 1015 **23**: 7–8
Ireland **4**: 115, 181, 195
Kenya **23**: 159
Malaysia **23**: 108
Sri Lanka **4**: 1139
Thailand **4**: 1240
Uganda **23**: 109
USA **4**: 180, 183, 192, 194, 196, 200, 324, 352, 354, 370, 375, 380, 385, 397, 400, 404, 1075, 1209, 1234 **6**: 5
Zambia **4**: 190
absenteeism **4**: 1083
adolescent mothers **4**: 1052
feminism **4**: 138
law **11**: 7
psychology **4**: 1018, 1037, 1040, 1054, 1058, 1063, 1067, 1071, 1074–5, 1080, 1096, 1113–14, 1122, 1228, 1132, 1150, 1162, 1168, 1170, 1172, 1182, 1189, 1191, 1197, 1204, 1207, 1216–17, 1228, 1231, 1240–2, 1261, 1272, 1275, 1278, 1290–1, 1295
students (sex role attitudes) **4**: 1036, 1080, 1089, 1100, 1117, 1241, 1251, 1338 **17**: 788
sport **22**: 3, 10, 17, 19, 30, 38, 41, 57, 90–1, 108, 117, 132, 139, 187
women's studies **4**: 570, 583
secretaries **4**: 723, 2674 **5**: 291, 317 **6**: 898
Sedgwick, Anne Douglas **12**: 1070
Sedgwick, Catharine Mario **12**: 1071–2
Seegar, Ruth Crawford **1**: 47
Seghers, Anna **12**: 3409–12
Ségur, Comtesse de **12**: 3210
Seidel, Ina **12**: 3413–14
Seiwa Women's College (religious education) **4**: 254
self-defence training **17**: 72
self-employed **5**: 412, 600
Selina, Countess of Huntingdon **18**: 83, 93
Senegal **23**: 29, 151, 291
service-women **4**: 411 **5**: 25, 279, 285, 301, 314, 319, 329, 366, 431, 474–5, 594, 622 **8**: 99 **9**: 456
settlement house movement (USA) **9**: 461–2, 657, 659
Seventh Day Adventists **18**: 76, 79, 100, 109–10, 116, 118, 121, 124, 127, 129
'Séverine, Mme' **9**: 258
Sévigné, Mme de **12**: 2959, 3211, 3220
Sewall, May Wright **9**: 682
Seward, Frances Adeline (Fanny) **9**: 523
Sewell, Elizabeth Missing **12**: 2429–30
sex and class **9**: 608
sex-discrimination and bias **17**:
(sex discrimination and bias *cont.*)
875
in USA **21**: 235
career counselling **4**: 1483
children's reading books **21**: 231
colleges **17**: 882
educational administration **4**: 854
law
battered women **11**: 10
USA **9**: 527
marriage **6**: 131
professions (France) **9**: 269
women teachers **4**: 936
sex guilt **8**: 39 **20**: 4, 25, 27, 53, 59, 76, 84, 98
sex role *see* gender role
sex stereotypes
athletes **22**: 36, 39
careers **4**: 1482, 1522, 1641, 1673, 1676, 1679
children's literature **9**: 53
children's toys **4**: 988
community colleges **8**: 64
counsellors **8**: 165
curriculum (schools) **4**: 1175 **17**: 772
drama **12**: 279
fiction **12**: 139, 437
literature **12**: 3333
Mexican village women **23**: 19
occupations **4**: 1047, 1091, 1375
Owenite communities **9**: 542
programme to combat **4**: 1084
psychiatric patients **8**: 127
single women (literature) **12**: 241
television **12**: 4–5
text-books **4**: 197, 1126
vocational education **4**: 1513, 1586, 1637
Sexton, Anne **12**: 217, 261, 404, 1073–7
sexual harassment
government **16**: 45
universities **14**: 1200, 1208
workplace **6**: 940
sexuality **20**: 1–137
American theories **9**: 602
feminism **7**: 109, 128
literature **12**: 1691
Marxism (Germany) **9**: 288
Shaginian, Marietta **12**: 3518
Shamans (Korea) **23**: 130
Shange, Ntozake **12**: 219
Shaw, Anna Howard **9**: 673
Shaw, Mary **1**: 123
Shelley, Mary **12**: 131, 1561, 2431–9
Sheridan, Frances **12**: 1670–1
ship-yard workers (Portland, Oregon) **9**: 665
shoe purchase **21**: 83
shop-keepers **9**: 359
shop-workers **5**: 484 **9**: 578
shopping **21**: 41, 55
Shose, Jane **12**: 1406, 1439

Shorter, Dora Sigerson **12**: 2440
Sicily **5**: 31
Siddons, Sarah **1**: 140–1, 160
Sierra Leone **4**: 1189 **9**: 8 **23**: 40
silk industry workers (France) **9**: 265
Sinclair, May **12**: 2441–4, 2500, 2516
single-parent families **6**: 202, 204, 206–9, 213–14, 217, 220, 225–6, 229, 302, 398, 419, 429, 452, 476, 482, 486, 495–6, 499, 512, 551, 557, 577, 588, 638, 662, 666, 688, 761, 763 **21**: 7
single women
  in USA **3**: 128
    alcoholism **8**: 38
    behaviour modification **17**: 106
    contraception **19**: 26
    literary portrayal **12**: 41, 241
    spending on clothes **21**: 48
sisters (family relationships) **6**: 808, 810, 812
Sisters of Charity of Nazareth **4**: 348
Sisters of Mercy **12**: 220
  education **4**: 96, 376, 381 **8**: 557
  nursing: Crimean War **9**: 123, 141a, 478
Sisters of Notre Dame de Namur **4**: 92–3, 376 **18**: 229
Sisters of Our Lady of Charity of the Good Shepherd **18**: 175, 215
Sisters of Saint Francis **4**: 340
Sisters of Saint Joseph **18**: 173
Sisters of the Holy Cross **4**: 363
Sisters of the Sacred Heart **4**: 118, 344
Sitwell, Edith **12**: 105, 2661–7
skiing **22**: 166
Skram, Amalie **12**: 3537a
slave-women and girls
  Abbāsids **9**: 4
  Tuareg society **23**: 227
  USA (Southern States) **9**: 711
  West Indies **9**: 344
Smedley, Agnes **12**: 401
Smith, Charlotte **12**: 1570, 1582, 1594, 1672–4
Smith, Elizabeth Oakes **9**: 631 **12**: 1079–80
Smith, Lillian **9**: 400
Smith, Margaret Chase **16**: 30
Smith College **4**: 432
smoking **8**: 84–9 **19**: 254, 313, 380 **21**: 78–9
soap operas **12**: 75
social reform and reformers
  in Great Britain **9**: 160
    Sweden **9**: 332
    USA **9**: 398, 414, 423, 429–30, 436, 461–2, 465, 497, 499, 505, 529, 583, 604, 614, 630, 646, 657, 659, 664, 685, 699, 700, 719 **18**: 103–4 **21**: 291
social scientists **5**: 295
  in USA
    social reform **9**: 430, 465
    view of women **9**: 639
social secutiy *see* welfare
social studies
  teachers **4**: 995
  text books: sex stereotyping **4**: 1226
social work, social and community workers **5**: 385, 420 **9**: 215, 300, 413, 423, 430, 623 **18**: 179, 183 **21**: 270, 275, 279–80, 288, 293, 296–7
  attitudes to women at work **17**: 832
  psychosocial case work **17**: 9
Socialism and Socialists (*see also* Communism, Marxism, Labour movements)
  in England (literature) **12**: 2652
    France **9**: 222, 228, 241
    Germany **9**: 283, 289, 298 **12**: 3363, 3409, 3411
    Italy **9**: 319
    USA **7**: 30 **9**: 403, 414 **12**: 296
  family and sexuality (Germany) **9**: 288
  feminism **9**: 170, 618, 684
    France **9**: 228
    Germany **9**: 283, 298
    USA **9**: 403 **12**: 296
  literature **12**: 296, 2652, 3363, 3409, 3411
  textile workers (France) **9**: 241
  'woman question'
    England **9**: 167a, 565
    France **9**: 222
  women's liberation movement **7**: 30, 132
  women's movement
    France **9**: 222
    Germany **9**: 289
  women's position **21**: 219
Society for Promoting the Employment of Women **9**: 216
Society of Friends **18**: 84, 117
sociological thought: feminism **7**: 101
sociologists: USA **9**: 649
softball **22**: 137, 140, 159, 168, 188
Sosiot Girl's High School, Kenya **23**: 159
Somerset, UK **2**: 12
Somerville, Edith **12**: 2668–9
Sontag, Susan **12**: 140
Soule, Elizabeth Sterling **8**: 530
South Africa **5**: 62 **16**: 50
South Carolina, USA **4**: 793 **5**: 258 **9**: 558 **13**: 34 **16**: 1 **17**: 826
South Dakota, USA **5**: 114
South Today **9**: 400
Southcott, Joanna **18**: 92, 120, 131
Southern School for Women Workers **4**: 413
Southern Women's Educational Alliance **4**: 57
Southey, Caroline Anne **12**: 2445
Southworth, Mrs E.D.E.N. **12**: 1081–2
Souza, Mme de **12**: 2914, 3221
Spain **6**: 15 **7**: 113 **9**: 337–9 **18**: 149
Spark, Muriel **12**: 2529, 2530, 2670–8
speech (*see also* elocution, rhetoric; mother-child relationships; speech communication) **10**: 10, 12, 16 **17**: 770
  college women **10**: 14, 22, 23
  girls **10**: 5
  male aggression **10**: 9
  Mayan society **23**: 49
  mother-daughter **6**: 129
  mothers **10**: 18
  women **10**: 17
    Newfoundland **10**: 10
    USA **10**: 12
speech education **4**: 6
speech therapists **10**: 8
Spencer, Anne **12**: 1083
Spofford, Harriet Prescott **12**: 1084
sport (*see also* athletes; physical education; individual sports) **22**: 18, 23, 26, 40, 44–5, 47, 59
  in England (literature) **12**: 1779
    Great Britain **22**: 62
    USSR **22**: 62
    USA **9**: 459, 675, 697 **22**: 15, 17, 19, 56, 68–9
  administration **22**: 34
  advertising **22**: 63
  coaches **22**: 12, 21, 33, 134, 142–3, 147, 149, 153–4, 183
  high school **22**: 17, 19
  menstruation **19**: 206
  sex role **22**: 9, 36
  teacher-training colleges **22**: 46
  universities **22**: 15, 25, 42–3, 51, 61, 67, 156
Sri Lanka **2**: 61 **3**: 59, 89, 111
Staël, Mme de **12**: 2942, 3222–48
Stafford, Jean **12**: 1085
Staffordshire, UK **9**: 218
Stampa, Gaspara **12**: 34, 38
Stanton, Elizabeth Cady **9**: 489, 700 **12**: 54
statutes (Roman) **9**: 27
Stead, Christina **12**: 101, 1268
Stefan, Verena **12**: 3315
Stein, Edith **12**: 12 **18**: 208
Stein, Gertrude **1**: 134, 153, 167, 231, 234 **12**: 54, 105, 311, 1086–110
Stephens, Ann **12**: 359
Stephens, Kate **12**: 111
stepmothers **6**: 279
sterilization of women **3**: 49 **19**: 1, 7, 110
Stern, Daniel *see* Agoult, Marie de
Stewart, Mary **12**: 2680
Stoddard, Elizabeth Barstow **12**: 1112
Stokes, Rose Pastor **9**: 655, 658
Stopes, Marie **9**: 152
Storni, Alfonsina **12**: 3453, 3495
Stowe, Harriet Beecher **12**: 72, 257, 278, 397, 408, 1113–19

stress and anxiety therapy **17**: 71, 75, 79, 88, 121, 136, 148, 153
Stretton, Hesba **12**: 1821
Strickland, Caroline **12**: 1120
Strickland family **12**: 1685
Strickland, Lily **1**: 50
Strong, Anna Louise **9**: 605, 621
Stuart, Ruth McEnery **12**: 268, 1121
Suckow, Ruth **12**: 334, 1122
Sudan **2**: 188, 220 **23**: 125, 160
Suffolk, UK **2**: 61
suffrage movements and suffragists
 in Canada **9**: 379
  England **9**: 122, 128a, 132, 141, 151, 154, 154a, 162, 177, 194a, 196, 196a, 202, 213, 415, 420, 511, 637 **12**: 2493
   opposition **9**: 192
   Socialism **9**: 170
    Manchester **9**: 128
  Japan **9**: 54
  USA **9**: 177, 213, 386, 391, 395, 405, 420, 426, 445, 451, 476, 482, 489–90, 495, 528, 543, 566–7, 673
   Afro-Americans **9**: 426, 493
   literature **12**: 2493
   magazines: humour **9**: 466
   newspapers **9**: 690
   opposition **9**: 407, 516
   publishing **9**: 580, 690
   rhetoric **7**: 35 **9**: 425, 463
   theatre **1**: 84, 123
    Florida **9**: 522
    Illinois **9**: 402, 480
    Indiana **9**: 667
    Kentucky **9**: 499
    Massachusetts **9**: 532, 587
    Nebraska **9**: 431, 469
    Nevada **9**: 668
    New York **9**: 481, 557
    Oregon **9**: 534, 597
    Pennsylvania **9**: 545
    Tennessee **9**: 689
    Wisconsin **9**: 483
suicide
 Afro-American **21**: 181
 alcoholism **8**: 33
 employment **5**: 364, 589
 literary portrayal **12**: 79
 professional women **5**: 386
supermarket shopping **21**: 41
supervisors **5**: 308, 461
supplementary benefits: Great Britain **11**: 16
Supreme Court (USA) **11**: 20 **19**: 100
Sussex, UK **9**: 113 **19**: 252
Sutherland, Joan **1**: 47
suttee [*sati*] **9**: 63
'sweated trades' **9**: 179
Sweden **3**: 57, 125 **5**: 235 **6**: 865
swimming **15**: 13 **22**: 127, 169, 173
Swiss-German immigrants (USA) **9**: 634
Switzerland **9**: 167b **21**: 236
syphilis **9**: 554 **19**: 452
tailoresses **5**: 255 **9**: 145
Tainter, Mabel **1**: 92
Taiwan **3**: 13, 82 **6**: 146 **19**: 58 **23**: 28, 57, 60, 119, 174, 210, 294
Tanzania **3**: 75 **23**: 115, 139, 169
Tarbell, Ida M. **9**: 696 **13**: 15, 35
Tarn, Pauline **12**: 3256
Tatler, The **12**: 1499
tattooing: Moroccan women **23**: 256
teacher-training **4**: 28, 35, 162, 215, 270, 288, 347, 350–1, 355, 363, 370, 383, 386, 392, 395, 401–2, 890, 894–5, 904, 908, 910, 912, 918, 921, 928, 943, 945, 1043, 1236, 1244, 1248, 1261, 1263, 1268, 1284, 1295 **8**: 520 **18**: 176
 career choice and commitment of students **4**: 1038, 1105, 1220, 1253, 1267, 1487, 1650, 1661 **23**: 120
 married women students **4**: 270
 residential halls **4**: 215, 247
 student-teachers **4**: 885, 1124, 1256
 tutors **4**: 768, 791, 839
teachers (*see also* individual subjects) **4**: 99, 100, 113, 126, 129, 165, 599, 714, 820, 886, 888, 906, 919, 924, 933–4, 944, 989, 1000, 1006 **9**: 266, 441, 490
 kindergarten **4**: 884, 931, 988
 primary **4**: 97, 128, 589, 887, 896, 900, 905, 913, 917, 921, 923, 932, 935, 938, 942, 946, 990, 997, 1000, 1004–5, 1007
 secondary **4**: 106, 402, 591, 596, 893, 916, 942, 992, 995, 1000–1, 1005
 community college **4**: 590, 692
 university (*see also* universities and colleges: faculty)
  attitudes to women's liberation movement **7**: 56, 112
  career patterns **4**: 100, 597, 607, 654, 725, 894, 1007, 1554, 1579
  feminism **4**: 913 **9**: 247
  leisure-reading **21**: 190–1
  literary portrayal **12**: 1760
  magazine portrayal **4**: 937
  married women teachers **4**: 887, 910, 998, 1003, 1005 **21**: 10
  professional attitudes **4**: 911, 986
  relationships with mothers **6**: 377
  salaries **4**: 99, 927
  sex-role **4**: 942, 1000
  sister-teachers **4**: 82, 92–3, 97, 116, 118, 325–6, 331, 338, 340, 342–4, 347–8, 350, 352, 358, 361–3, 365, 367–9, 373, 376, 378, 380–1, 386, 395, 399, 401–2
  standards and cost of living **4**: 892, 939
(teachers *cont.*)
  stereotypes by children **4**: 886
  teacher-aids **4**: 922, 1589 **21**: 300
  trade unions and associations **4**: 99, 901
technical education **4**: 184, 249, 265, 269, 1072, 1127, 1153
 career choices **4**: 1490
technicians **5**: 282
technology: skilled workers **5**: 115
television **13**: 17, 22
 Afro-Americans **13**: 34
 children **13**: 9
 home-maker programmes **13**: 36
 management **13**: 18
 mother and child **13**: 10
 portrayal of women **13**: 44
 soap operas **13**: 37
 women newscasters **13**: 13
 women's roles in situation comedies **13**: 27
temperance movement (USA) **9**: 433, 440, 445, 474, 476, 490, 588, 636, 673, 698, 710
Tencin, Mme de **12**: 3249
Tennessee, USA **4**: 114, 332, 550, 651, 701, 822 **5**: 410 **8**: 304 **9**: 689 **15**: 113 **21**: 67, 118
tennis **22**: 145–7, 157, 161, 172, 174, 179, 186, 190
Tennyson, Lady Emily **12**: 2446
Teresa of Avila, St **12**: 3669–71 **18**: 50, 61
Teresa de Jesús **18**: 72
Terhune, Mary Virginia **12**: 1123
Terry, Ellen **1**: 175
Terry, Megan **12**: 1124
Texas, USA **2**: 72 **4**: 205, 606, 632, 636, 648, 668, 710, 726, 745, 832, 869, 904, 943, 1123, 1274, 1145, 1317, 1468 **5**: 298 **8**: 102 **9**: 516, 550, 656 **18**: 105, 131 **19**: 362, 417, 443, 502, 547 **21**: 238, 251
text-books
 female image: science **4**: 1097
 sexism: Indian text-books **4**: 1147
 sex-stereotyping **4**: 197, 1226
 women's history: high school sex-role attitudes **4**: 1251
textile industry workers (*see also* cotton industry; silk industry) **5**: 268–9, 272
 in Egypt **23**: 18
  England **9**: 73
  France **9**: 241
  Great Britain **9**: 153
 hearing loss **5**: 311
Thackeray, Anne **12**: 2447–9
Thailand **3**: 3, 18, 25, 106 **4**: 1240 **19**: 126 **23**: 154, 177, 236–7, 258, 292
Thanet, Octave **12**: 1125
Thatcher, Margaret **16**: 12, 21
Thaxter, Celia **12**: 397, 472, 1125

theatre (*see also* actresses; costume designers)
in England **1**: 93, 97, 128, 145 **9**: 539
France **1**: 125
Ireland **12**: 2564
Norway **1**: 144
Peru **1**: 94
USA **1**: 83–4, 91, 95, 128, 146–7, 150, 152, 156, 161, 163 **9**: 539
children's theatre **1**: 90, 112, 130, 164–5
criticism **1**: 183
designers **1**: 89
domestic servants **9**: 539
musical comedy **1**: 98, 127
producers and directors **1**: 106, 124, 133, 151, 173, 178–9, 181, 185, 193–4, 196
Readers' theatre **1**: 172
repertory theatres **1**: 99, 113, 137, 166, 169
vaudeville **1**: 104, 117
theft **2**: 19
theological education **18**: 242
theology
black feminism **7**: 14
feminism **18**: 241
women's liberation movement **7**: 133
Thompson, Lydia **1**: 150
Tietjens, Eunice **12**: 1127
Times, The (of London) **9**: 197
Ting Ling **12**: 1246–7
Todd, Mabel Loomis **12**: 1129
Togo **23**: 36
Tonga **23**: 107
Toomer, Jean **12**: 311
Trade Boards Act, 1909 **9**: 179
trade unions (*see also* individual unions) **5**: 212, 218, 233
in Austria **9**: 291
Belgium **5**: 207
France **9**: 243
Great Britain **5**: 214, 223–4, 234 **9**: 157, 210, 213, 217, 219
USA **5**: 207, 213–14, 222, 226, 229 **9**: 157, 213, 217, 377, 391, 408, 435, 455, 457, 536, 546, 559, 654, 658
nurses **8**: 493, 508, 813
teachers **4**: 99, 901 **9**: 243
traders
in Ghana **23**: 183
Nigeria **23**: 156, 200, 273
Peru **23**: 26
Sierra Leone **9**: 8
training **5**: 73
Belfast **4**: 171
community colleges **4**: 1369
Nigeria **23**: 202
transsexuals **20**: 87, 97
travel and travellers
America to Frontier **9**: 368 **12**: 199
British **2**: 111, 131, 173, 175a, 238, 286, 361, 363
French: American women **9**: 439
Treadwell, Sophie **12**: 1130
Trevino, Elizabeth Borton de **12**: 3495–6
Trinidad **8**: 393
Triolet, Elsa **12**: 3250
Tristan, Flora **12**: 2942, 2944
Trollope, Frances **12**: 2450–1
Trotter, Catherine **12**: 1409
Troubetsky, Amelie Rives **12**: 1131
Tsretaera, Ivanovna **12**: 3507
tuberculosis **8**: 411
Tunisia **23**: 20, 23, 58, 83, 301
Turkey **2**: 152 **3**: 42 **5**: 104 **21**: 197 **23**: 173
Turner, Clorinda, Matteo de **12**: 3497
Tyler, Anne **12**: 1132

Uganda **6**: 528 **18**: 264 **23**: 81, 89, 108
Ullman, Regina **12**: 3415
Underhill, Evelyn **18**: 130
Undset, Sigrid **12**: 3539
unemployment **5**: 10, 122 **21**: 267, 288a, 294a
in Great Britain **5**: 1, 58 **9**: 172
USA **5**: 58
Unitarianism (Mrs Gaskell) **12**: 2072
United Arab Republic **23**: 68, 272
United Nations Development Decade **16**: 32, 54
United States Army Nurse Corps **9**: 660
United States Coast Guard Academy **4**: 246 **7**: 108
United States Navy Women's Reserve **9**: 456
United States Sanitary Commission **9**: 416
United States Veterans' Administration
hospitals and nursing **8**: 99
universities and colleges (*see also* community colleges; higher education; liberal arts colleges; mature students; re-entry students) **4**: 207
in Egypt **4**: 312 **23**: 248
Germany **4**: 121
Ghana **23**: 22
Great Britain **4**: 14, 122, 987
Ireland: Belfast **4**: 95
Japan **4**: 254, 277, 1133, 1252 **18**: 153
Korea **4**: 271
Libya **23**: 265
New Zealand **21**: 237
Pakistan **4**: 276
Philippines **4**: 640, 890, 1140, 1268
South East Asia **4**: 991
Sudan **4**: 220
United States **4**: 119, 210, 233, 235, 274, 286, 308, 327, 329, 387–8, 391, 1110
Alabama **4**: 1129, 1261; Bryn Manor **4**: 213; Buffalo **5**: 310; California **4**: 266, 528, 1163
(universities and colleges *cont.*)
(Santa Barbara **21**: 269; Stanford **4**: 267, 314, 537; UCLA **4**: 219, 452, 1206 **17**: 631) Chicago (Loyola) **4**: 273; Colorado **4**: 41; Columbia **4**: 288; Coffey College **9**: 631; Duke **4**: 19; Florida **4**: 293, 313, 744, 844, 1109, 1351, 1553 **21**: 105, 119; George Washington **4**: 1405; Georgia **4**: 1183, 1212, 1230; Harvard **4**: 303; Houston **4**: 726; Illinois **4**: 214, 247; Indiana **4**: 244, 1084, 1179, 1285 **17**: 654 **22**: 160; Iowa **4**: 450, 1061; Kansas **5**: 265; Kentucky **22**: 103; Louisiana **4**: 897–8, 1196; Louisville **6**: 814; Marillace College **18**: 211; Marquette **4**: 1048; Michigan **4**: 33, 543, 1211, 1285, 1643 **6**: 820 **22**: 98; Milwaukee **4**: 87 Minnesota **4**: 466, 1019 **22**: 180; Mississippi **4**: 295, 321, 578, 926, 1142, 1157, 1180, 1190, 1262, 1301; Montana **4**: 1676; Monticello **4**: 167; New York **4**: 215–6, 267, 389, 1550; North Carolina **4**: 292, 304, 1014; Northwestern **4**: 272, 291, 1156; Ohio **4**: 3, 285, 524, 1115, 1210, 1216, 1327 **21**: 33 **22**: 15, 95, 121; Oklahoma **3**: 11 **4**: 1041, 1287; Oregon **4**: 1060, 1267 **8**: 106; Pennsylvania **4**: 689, 1379; Pittsburgh **4**: 1031, 1457; Portland **4**: 454; Princeton **4**: 166, 1480; Radcliffe College, Boston **4**: 142; Rutgers **17**: 632; San José **4**: 251; Southern Illinois **4**: 431; Southern States **4**: 323; Syracuse **4**: 307, 867, 898; Temple **4**: 1413, 1430; Tennessee **4**: 114 **22**: 67, 118; Texas **4**: 648, 668 **18**: 131 **22**: 294; Texas Woman's Union **4**: 904, 943, 1277, 1468 **22**: 170; Tulane **4**: 273; Tuskegee Institute **22**: 118; Utah **4**: 1, 204, 282, 319; Vassar **4**: 67; Virginia **4**: 889, 1188; Washington **4**: 1225 **5**: 551, 609 **8**: 530; West Virginia **4**: 601; Western Reserve **4**: 63; Wyoming **4**: 1435
administration **4**: 594, 635, 639, 648, 651, 678, 680–1, 689, 695, 702, 708, 739, 744, 752, 799, 826, 828–9, 842, 844, 852, 871, 875, 1010
affirmative action **4**: 741, 927
deans of women **4**: 140, 608, 625, 637, 640, 668, 691, 704, 716, 718, 726, 732, 736, 749,

(universities and colleges *cont.*)
752, 796, 839, 1336
employees **4**: 601, 864 **5**: 609
faculty **4**: 32, 119, 140, 143, 277, 490, 521–4, 602, 604, 739, 889, 897–9, 907, 909, 925, 927, 929, 936, 940–1, 947, 987, 991, 994, 1010–11 **8**: 532 **12**: 422
health education **8**: 106, 1032–3, 1041, 1073, 1079, 1179
residential halls **4**: 215, 247, 612, 615, 660, 662, 684, 715, 721, 735, 743, 1325 **7**: 825, 1210, 1230, 1258, 1301
sports **22**: 5, 8, 11, 15, 16, 21, 25, 28–9, 33–4, 41–3, 48, 51, 53, 55, 61, 64, 66–7, 71, 73, 76, 80, 82–5, 91–4, 98, 100, 103, 106, 109, 116, 118–22, 124–5, 127, 129, 133–6, 139, 143–4, 146–7, 152–3, 156, 158, 160, 164, 167, 169–70, 172, 178–80, 182–4, 186, 191–2
trustees **4**: 689, 695
women presidents **4**: 293, 752, 802, 851, 1176, 1229, 1294
women's centres **4**: 811, 1214 **21**: 269, 290
women's liberation movement **7**: 127, 131 **23**: 22
women's movement **7**: 129
women's studies **4**: 563–69, 571–82, 584–8
university and college students **4**: 754
androgyny **17**: 78, 581 **20**: 138, 145, 147
assertiveness training **17**: 78, 81, 92, 145, 148, 154, 162, 173
careers **5**: 554
clothing **21**: 58–9, 61, 63, 70, 78, 81, 84, 93, 100
diet **8**: 294, 296, 299, 320
drug addiction **8**: 81
health **4**: 1173 **8**: 106, 109–11
housing **4**: 1255, 1270, 1296
Islam (Egypt) **23**: 248
leisure **21**: 183, 187
obesity and over-eating **8**: 324, 329–30, 332–3, 342, 371, 383
physiology and physical fitness **15**: 1, 2, 4, 5, 9, 11, 13, 15, 18, 19, 21, 23–4, 26–7, 32–3, 35, 37–8, 44, 47, 51–4, 62–3, 66–7, 69–70, 73, 79, 80–2, 85, 87, 89, 90, 92, 95–7, 101, 105, 113, 115, 117, 119–22, 130, 132–3, 136, 153–5, 157, 160–2, 164, 168–9 **17**: 522
psychological studies **4**: 1012–4, 1019–20, 1022–3, 1029–34, 1041, 1045, 1048, 1050, 1057, 1060–1, 1073, 1076, 1079, 1086–7, 1093–4, 1101, 1103, 1106–8, 1112, 1115, 1117–19, 1123, 1126, 1131, 1135–7, 1141–2, 1145, 1151–2, 1154–5, 1158–9, 1164, 1169, 1178, 1180–1, 1183–4, 1186–8, 1190, 1193, 1195–6,

(university and college students *cont.*)
1198, 1211, 1213, 1221–2, 1232–3, 1238, 1249, 1252–3, 1259–60, 1263, 1268, 1272, 1286, 1289, 1292, 1303 **17**: 521–678, 762, 765, 767, 774, 793, 813, 825, 872
psychotherapy **8**: 189
self-concept and esteem **17**: 143, 147, 527–8, 560, 564, 572, 578, 589, 600, 615, 640–1, 648, 675, 677
sex-role attitudes **4**: 1020, 1137 **17**: 527, 539, 559, 564, 566, 570, 573, 576, 578–9, 581–2, 585, 587–8, 595, 603, 605, 608–9, 611, 619–20, 624–6, 632, 636, 638, 650, 658, 665, 667 **23**: 265
sexual attitudes and behaviour **20**: 10, 13, 23, 25, 28, 45, 47–8, 63, 69, 71, 109, 113 **17**: 635
sexual harassment **4**: 1200, 1208
smoking **8**: 84, 87
stress and anxiety therapy **4**: 1046 **17**: 71, 79, 88, 136, 148, 153
weight control **8**: 384
women's issues **7**: 76
women's liberation **7**: 71 **17**: 582
women's rights **7**: 81
unwed mothers **2**: 80 **6**: 297, 307, 313, 316, 370–1, 375, 381, 500, 514, 518, 597, 601, 613, 642, 646, 655, 753, 771 **12**: 3355 **19**: 298, 307 **20**: 89 **21**: 278
Upper Volta **23**: 192
Urania Cottage (refuge for prostitutes) **9**: 161
Ursuline College **4**: 394
USSR (*see also* Russia) **3**: 43 **16**: 11, 71 **19**: 385 **21**: 212 **22**: 62, 105
Utah, USA **3**: 22 **4**: 1, 169, 204, 282, 319, 708, 724, 1657 **8**: 15, 142 **19**: 496

Vada, Usha Proiyan **12**: 1257
vagrancy **21**: 281
Varda, Agnes **1**: 9
Vassas College **4**: 432
Venezuela **23**: 17, 24
Venus **12**: 1386, 1433
Vesta and vestal virgins **18**: 12
Vestris, Madame **1**: 95
veterinary surgeons **5**: 266
Victoria, Queen **1**: 191
Viebig, Clara **12**: 3416–17
Vieira, Nellie **12**: 265
Vietnamese refugees in USA **21**: 128
Villedieu, Mme de **9**: 261 **12**: 3255
Villegas, Micaela **1**: 94
Virginia, USA **4**: 218, 437, 837, 889, 999, 1188, 1347, 1504 **5**: 523, 535 **9**: 552 **19**: 497

virginity
literature **12**: 17, 1315, 1405 **18**: 56
theology **18**: 56
Vivien, Renée **12**: 3256
vocational education **4**: 249, 1059, 1111
administration **4**: 603, 748
sex discrimination **16**: 59
sex stereotyping **4**: 1637
students **4**: 1028, 1072, 1300
teachers **4**: 603, 916
working mothers **6**: 937
vocational guidance *see* careers counselling
volleyball **22**: 142, 154–5, 158, 176, 180
voluntary service **5**: 341 **21**: 241–3, 247, 250, 252, 259, 276
voting patterns : USA **9**: 687

Waddell, Helen **12**: 2681
wages and salaries **5**: 15, 32, 39, 43, 70, 83, 102, 111, 135, 139, 268
in EEC **5**: 240
Great Britain **5**: 152 **9**: 121
USA **5**: 18, 61, 93, 221, 230, 236 **9**: 561
equal wages policies **5**: 230, 238–40
inequalities **5**: 5, 14, 45, 50, 71, 106, 242, 449
married women **5**: 184
minimum wages policy **5**: 225, 230
nurses **8**: 493
teachers **4**: 99, 927
young women **5**: 6, 30, 96
Wald, Lillian D. **9**: 436, 630
Wales **4**: 28, 158, 212, 544
Walker, Alice **12**: 272, 345
Walter, Hilda Saenger **12**: 1133
Ward, Mrs Humphrey **12**: 1134, 2452–62
Warren, Mercy Otis **9**: 370 **12**: 1135
Washington, DC *see* District of Columbia
Washington State, USA **3**: 71 **4**: 433, 550, 820, 1225, 1644 **5**: 609 **6**: 631 **8**: 530 **9**: 373 **18**: 303
weavers **23**: 153, 278
Webb, Beatrice **9**: 183, 184
Webb, Margot **1**: 104
Webb, Mary **12**: 2682–5
Webster, Margaret **1**: 173, 181, 196
Wedgwood, Fanny **12**: 2385
Weil, Simone **12**: 3257–63 **14**: 6, 7, 8, 11, 14, 25 **18**: 290
welfare/social security (*see also* AFDC mothers; supplementary benefits; unemployment insurance) **5**: 239 **11**: 15 **21**: 302, 306–7
in Denmark **21**: 228
Afro-Americans **21**: 299
education **21**: 292, 308

(welfare/social security *cont.*)
employment **21**: 304
family support **5**: 181 **21**: 285, 287, 294
mothers **21**: 274, 284, 286, 289, 294, 300
unemployment **21**: 294a
Wellesley College **4**: 32, 432
Wells College **4**: 300, 432
Wells-Barnett, Ida B. **9**: 513, 694
Welty, Eudora **12**: 46, 103, 197, 201, 262, 290, 320, 353, 388, 1136–7
Wertmuller, Lisa **1**: 28
Wesleyan movement **12**: 2021
West, Jane **12**: 1594
West, Rebecca **12**: 2686
West Indies (*see also* individual islands) **9**: 344
West Midlands, UK **5**: 11 **9**: 164
Wharton, Edith **12**: 40, 46, 62, 70, 79, 213, 288, 307, 309, 326, 376, 462, 1175–222
Wheatley, Phillis **12**: 1223
Whitcher, Frances **12**: 359
White, Ellen Gould **18**: 76, 79, 100, 109, 110, 116, 118, 121, 127, 129
White, Katharine S. **13**: 30
white collar workers (*see also* clerical workers; office-workers) **5**: 82, 234, 304
trade unions **5**: 234
work attitudes **5**: 374
white slave traffic **9**: 589, 688
Whitman, Sarah Helen **12**: 1224
widows and widowhood **6**: 224, 230–76 **9**: 105 **17**: 751
in France **9**: 267
India **9**: 63
Korea **23**: 171
Mexico **23**: 260
English literature **12**: 1449, 1469, 1749, 2578
pastoral care **18**: 270–1, 279–80, 284
Wied, Martina **12**: 3418
Wieland, Joyce **1**: 18
Wilder, Laura Ingalls **12**: 1225–6
Wilkinson, Ellen **16**: 69
Wilkinson, Jemima **18**: 119
Willard, Frances Elizabeth **9**: 445 **18**: 106
Williams, Helen Maria **9**: 111
Williams, Maria Jane **1**: 56
Wilson, Augusta Evans **12**: 1227
Wilson, Florence **12**: 2463
Winslow, Thyra Saunter **12**: 1228
Wisconsin, USA **2**: 28, 127 **4**: 87, 283, 460, 553, 649, 868, 1048 **5**: 290, 348 **9**: 483 **13**: 40
witches and witchcraft **18**: 10
in England **9**: 90, 99, 110
Germany **9**: 287, 299
USA **9**: 86, 357a, 366 **12**: 226, 470 **18**: 13
feminism **12**: 144
Wittig, Monique **12**: 3264–5
wives (*see also* married women)
of Afro American industrial workers **21**: 175
of alcoholic husbands **6**: 170, 176, 193
battered **2**: 173–214
of college presidents **6**: 137
communication with husbands **6**: 160, 163, 180
company wives **6**: 146
dependency on husbands **6**: 190
'disadvantaged' families **6**: 201
of doctors **6**: 171, 174
of executives **6**: 156, 164
family moves **6**: 161, 181
financial management **5**: 133
of homosexuals **6**: 152
of husbands with heart attack **6**: 142
of husbands in mental hospital **6**: 195
literary portrayal **12**: 3531
maintenance **11**: 9
of military personnel **6**: 148–50, 153, 158–9
of ministers **6**: 133, 141, 145, 175, 183, 187–8, 200
of overseas students (USA) **21**: 105, 117, 141, 166
of politicians **9**: 201, 418, 474–5, 523, 526, 656 **16**: 8, 15, 25–6, 34
of prisoners **6**: 135, 189
of professional athletes **6**: 144
of professional men **6**: 151
professional women **6**: 138
role: New England **9**: 364
satisfaction with husband's job **6**: 166
secondary (Middle East) **11**: 11
social mobility **6**: 147, 162
superintendent's (school) **4**: 792
working-class **6**: 138
Wohmann, Gabrielle **12**: 3420
Wolrott, Marion Post **1**: 199
Wolf, Christa **12**: 3421–2, 48, 61, 102
Wollstonecraft, Mary **9**: 111 **12**: 68, 1554, 1594, 1675–6 **14**: 3
'woman question'
in Austria **9**: 291
England **9**: 138, 169, 170, 565
Italy **9**: 304
USA **9**: 384
dramatic treatment: German and Scandinavian **12**: 3267
fictional treatment **12**: 1726, 2496
poetry **12**: 1751
Women's Art movement **1**: 205
Women's Athletic Association (USA) **9**: 435
Women's Bureau **5**: 236
women's centres **4**: 811, 1214 **21**: 269, 290
Women's Christian Temperance Union **9**: 433, 588, 673, 698, 710
women's economic role and position **16**: 71
in Argentina **23**: 138
Cuba **21**: 212
El Salvador **23**: 27
Ethiopia **23**: 77
Finland **9**: 314
Ghana **23**: 189, 243
Great Britain **9**: 101, 139
Guatemala **23**: 42
India: Bengal **23**: 208
Italy **9**: 305 **21**: 198
Kenya **23**: 209
Malaysia **23**: 310
Mexico **21**: 212
Nigeria **23**: 178
Poland **9**: 139
USA **9**: 552, 654, 721 **21**: 210, 212, 216
capitalism **21**: 212, 219
Communism **21**: 212, 218
graduates **21**: 232
industrialization **9**: 575 **21**: 193, 234
National Socialism **21**: 218
Socialism **21**: 219
Women's Educational and Industrial Union **9**: 520
women's health movement **8**: 96, 100, 114–15
Women's Institutes **4**: 212
Women's Jobs Corps **5**: 458 **8**: 102
Women's Learning Institute **4**: 571
women's liberation movement (*see also* assertiveness groups; consciousness raising groups; feminism; women's movement; women's rights) **7**: 5, 9, 39, 43, 47, 49, 59, 63, 82, 99, 105, 121 **9**: 463
in Arab countries **23**: 198
Egypt **9**: 2
Ghana **23**: 22
India **9**: 60
Latin America **7**: 83
USA **7**: 35 **9**: 500, 618
Afro-Americans **7**: 58, 138
attitudes to w.l.m. **7**: 90, 95
of Afro-American women **7**: 58
Liberals **7**: 126
men **7**: 34
school teachers **7**: 56
universities **7**: 87, 127 **23**: 22
university students **7**: 71
Baptists **18**: 101
Civil Rights movement **7**: 30
ideology **7**: 45
lesbians and heterosexuals **7**: 18
marital relations **17**: 805
marriage equality **6**: 134
policies **7**: 40
rhetoric **7**: 12, 107, 138 **9**: 485
sex relations **7**: 124
Socialism **7**: 30, 132
theology **7**: 133
theory **7**: 67
universities **7**: 131

women's movement **7**: 3, 8, 24, 26, 51, 100 **9**: 496
- in Austria **9**: 281
- China **9**: 45, 64
- England **9**: 216
- France **9**: 233
- Germany **9**: 315
- India **23**: 97, 244
- Iran **23**: 249
- USA **7**: 54, 66, 79, 80, 86 **9**: 361, 417, 445, 503, 556, 562, 624
- academic life **7**: 19
- journals **13**: 32
- language **10**: 6
- law courts **11**: 14
- liberalism: representation **7**: 17
- marketing **7**: 130
- middle-class mothers **7**: 91
- racism **9**: 734
- social consciousness **7**: 123
- socialization **7**: 120

Women's National Indian Association **9**: 65

women's organizations **21**: 249, 253, 255, 262
- in Canada **9**: 591 **21**: 246
- China **23**: 309
- Colombia **23**: 27
- England **9**: 199
- Hong Kong **23**: 250, 255
- India **9**: 65 **23**: 16, 191
- USA **9**: 416, 642, 695 **21**: 244, 246

women's rights
- in Africa **23**: 34
- China **23**: 150
- Germany **12**: 3325
- Iran **23**: 95
- USA **7**: 41, 70 **9**: 586, 674 **12**: 114
  - equal rights amendment **7**: 44, 46, 92 **9**: 402, 470
- Afro-Americans and education **7**: 23
- business education **7**: 137
- college students' support **7**: 81
- fertility **3**: 129
- National Labor Union **9**: 546
- nursing education **9**: 422
- religion **9**: 388
- sexism in language **10**: 15

women's Social and Political Union (WSPU) **9**: 128a, 194a

women's status, position and role in society **21**: 204, 206–7
- in Africa, North **23**: 201
- Africa, West **23**: 124, 222, 277
- Arab countries **4**: 1153 **23**: 6, 145, 272
- Asia, South East **23**: 143
- Brazil **23**: 180
- Burma **23**: 258
- Chile **23**: 290
- China **9**: 46, 58 **23**: 55, 69, 261, 307
- Egypt **23**: 125, 301 **9**: 6
  - ancient **9**: 30, 32, 40
- England
  - Anglo-Saxon **9**: 94

(women's status, position and role in society *cont.*)
  - medieval **9**: 79
  - 16thC **9**: 69, 82, 84–5, 95, 97
  - 17thC **9**: 69, 81, 83, 91, 101
  - 19thC **9**: 118, 130, 168, 203 **12**: 1725, 1789–90, 1820, 2119, 2286, 2301, 2317, 2393
  - 20thC **9**: 191, 2522
- Europe (medieval) **9**: 221
- Europe (Eastern) **16**: 75
- France **9**: 223, 230, 236, 250, 260, 268
- Germany **9**: 274, 297
- Ghana: Accra **23**: 232, 243
- Greece: ancient **9**: 16, 1316
- Guatemala **23**: 42
- Haiti **23**: 283
- Iceland **9**: 334–5
- India **9**: 42, 48, 51, 61 **12**: 1260 **18**: 285 **23**: 32, 56, 75, 105, 155, 187, 197, 213, 229–30
- Iran **21**: 239 **23**: 110, 161, 305
- Iraq **23**: 301
- Islam **4**: 1153 **12**: 3425 **23**: 246, 2867
- Israel (ancient) **18**: 307, 317–18
- Israel (modern) **23**: 158
  - Arabs **23**: 114
- Italy **12**: 3432 **21**: 209
- Jamaica **23**: 82
- Japan **21**: 230, 233
- Kenya **23**: 53, 139, 209, 289
- Kuwait **23**: 11
- Latin America **23**: 179
- Lebanon **23**: 146, 188
- Libya **23**: 37
- Mayan society **23**: 49, 312
- Mexico **9**: 342, 347 **23**: 46, 73, 148, 259
- Middle East **23**: 286, 301
- Morocco **23**: 70, 84, 194
- New Guinea **23**: 65, 112, 279
- Nigeria **23**: 225, 296
- Norway **9**: 333
- Peru **23**: 15, 71, 134
- Portugal **12**: 3606
- Roman Empire **9**: 17, 19–24, 28, 34 **12**: 1304
- Saudi Arabia **23**: 10
- Scotland **9**: 77
- Senegal **23**: 29, 151
- Sierra Leone **23**: 137
- South Africa **23**: 44
- Spain **9**: 337, 339 **12**: 3614
- Sri Lanka **23**: 258
- Sudan **23**: 125, 166
- Sweden **21**: 225
- Taiwan **23**: 28
- Tanzania **23**: 139
- Thailand **23**: 258
- Tonga **23**: 107
- Troriand Island **23**: 304
- Tunisia **23**: 20, 23, 83, 301
- Turkey **9**: 309 **12**: 3548 **21**: 197
- Uganda **23**: 89
- USSR **9**: 321
  - Central Asia **23**: 204

(women's status, position and role in society *cont.*)
- United Arab Emirates (UAE) **23**: 272
- USA **9**: 351, 356, 373, 409–10, 427, 512, 519, 568, 572, 633, 713, 716 **21**: 196, 225, 229, 240
  - Baltimore **9**: 574
  - Louisiana **9**: 547
  - Massachusetts **9**: 626
  - New England **9**: 352–3, 358
  - New York **9**: 453
  - St Louis **21**: 295
  - Southern states **9**: 647
  - Texas **21**: 238
- Venezuela **23**: 24
- Yemen **23**: 80
- developing countries: planners **23**: 262
- Hasidic communities **23**: 33
- Indo-European **21**: 215
- industrialization **21**: 193, 234 **23**: 259
- Papal thought **21**: 201
- political thought **16**: 58
- Roman Catholic viewpoint **18**: 154
- World War, 1939–45 **9**: 14

women's studies (curriculum and courses) **4**: 563–88, 1109, 1161 **8**: 200 **9**: 631

Women's Suffrage Association **9**: 673

Women's Trade Union League **5**: 214, 228 **9**: 158, 216, 455, 457, 536

Wood, Edith Elmer **9**: 392

Wood, Mrs Henry **12**: 2464

Wood, Peggy **1**: 174

Woodhull, Victoria C. **9**: 277

Woodhull and Claflin's Weekly **9**: 678

Woolf, Virginia **12**: 35, 36, 46, 48, 62, 66, 70, 81, 82, 83, 88, 93, 131, 2481, 2500, 2513, 2533, 2687–835

Woolson, Constance Fenimore **12**: 1229–34

Worboise, Emma Jane **12**: 1821

Wordsworth, Dorothy **12**: 51, 2465–7

work attitudes and values **5**: 338, 346, 369, 592 **17**: 166, 843
- business education graduate students **4**: 1333
- career choices **4**: 1547, 1588, 1667
- clerical and manual workers **5**: 374 **6**: 889
- counselling graduate students **4**: 1333
- disadvantaged women **5**: 349
- housewives **21**: 7
- married women workers **5**: 331, 374 **6**: 889
- young women **3**: 103 **6**: 889

workers' education **4**: 413, 424

working class
- in Belgium **16**: 18
- England

(working class *cont.*)
household **21**: 12
Labour movement: 19thC **9**: 177
politics **9**: 206
youth culture **21**: 277
France **9**: 259
Germany **9**: 302
Jamaica **6**: 830
Malta **23**: 212
Mexico **23**: 215
USSR **9**: 307, 312
USA
Catholic Church **18**: 133, 139, 152
drama **1**: 156
New York **9**: 677 **21**: 15
suffrage **9**: 557
Pittsburgh: industrialization **9**: 538
assertiveness groups **21**: 253
emotional support systems **17**: 796
employment: marital

(working class *cont.*)
adjustment **6**: 871
feminism: employment **7**: 34
industrialization **9**: 120, 538
mothers: attitudes to education **6**: 378
sex-role **13**: 16
voluntary service **21**: 276
world fairs: USA **9**: 437
World War I, 1914–18
in England **9**: 156, 163, 164, 209
France **9**: 250
Germany **9**: 276
USA **9**: 486
literature **12**: 2487
World War II, 1938–45
in England **9**: 114, 204
Germany **9**: 295
USA **9**: 295, 373, 410, 432, 487, 605, 683
cinema **1**: 1, 19
employment **5**: 56
literature **12**: 2487
magazines and women **9**: 509

Wright, Frances **9**: 382 **12**: 1235
Wylie, Elinor **12**: 1236–44
Wyoming, USA **4**: 1345 **5**: 539

Yemen **23**: 80
Yezierska, Anzia **12**: 1245
Yonge, Charlotte **12**: 1739, 2468–70
Yorkshire, UK **4**: 65, 69 **5**: 255 **9**: 121, 145, 200 **21**: 174
Young Women's Christian Association (YMCA) **8**: 90 **21**: 266
Yourcenar, Marguerite **12**: 3266
Youth Movement for Girls (National Socialism) **9**: 301
Yugoslavia **9**: 325

Zaïre **23**: 113, 118
Zasulich, Vera Ivanovna **9**: 328
Zaünemann, Sidonia Hedwig **12**: 3423
Zayas, Maria de **12**: 3672–9
Zambia **2**: 190 **23**: 223, 254
Zetkin, Clara **9**: 283